THE ROUTLEDGE COMPANION TO GLOBAL INDIGENOUS HISTORY

The Routledge Companion to Global Indigenous History presents exciting new innovations in the dynamic field of Indigenous global history while also outlining ethical, political, and practical research.

Indigenous histories are not merely concerned with the past but have resonances for the politics of the present and future, ranging across vast geographical distances and deep time periods. The volume starts with an introduction that explores definitions of Indigenous peoples, followed by six thematic sections which each have a global spread: European uses of history and the positioning of Indigenous people as history's outsiders; their migrations and mobilities; colonial encounters; removals and diasporas; memory, identities, and narratives; deep histories and pathways towards future Indigenous histories that challenge the nature of the history discipline itself. This book illustrates the important role of Indigenous history and Indigenous knowledges for contemporary concerns, including climate change, spirituality and religious movements, gender negotiations, modernity and mobility, and the meaning of 'nation' and the 'global'. Reflecting the state of the art in Indigenous global history, the contributors suggest exciting new directions in the field, examine its many research challenges and show its resonances for a global politics of the present and future.

This book is invaluable reading for students in both undergraduate and postgraduate Indigenous history courses.

Ann McGrath is the WK Hancock Distinguished Professor of History at the Australian National University, an ARC Laureate Fellow and Director of the Research Centre for Deep History.

Lynette Russell is an ARC Kathleen Fitzpatrick Laureate Fellow at Monash University's Indigenous Studies Centre and Deputy Director of the ARC's Centre of Excellence for Australian Biodiversity and Heritage.

THE ROUTLEDGE COMPANION TO GLOBAL INDIGENOUS HISTORY

Edited by
Ann McGrath and Lynette Russell

LONDON AND NEW YORK

First published 2022
by Routledge
2 Park Square, Milton Park, Abingdon, Oxon OX14 4RN

and by Routledge
605 Third Avenue, New York, NY 10158

Routledge is an imprint of the Taylor & Francis Group, an informa business

© 2022 selection and editorial matter, Ann McGrath and Lynette Russell; individual chapters, the contributors

The right of Ann McGrath and Lynette Russell to be identified as the authors of the editorial material, and of the authors for their individual chapters, has been asserted in accordance with sections 77 and 78 of the Copyright, Designs and Patents Act 1988.

All rights reserved. No part of this book may be reprinted or reproduced or utilised in any form or by any electronic, mechanical, or other means, now known or hereafter invented, including photocopying and recording, or in any information storage or retrieval system, without permission in writing from the publishers.

Trademark notice: Product or corporate names may be trademarks or registered trademarks, and are used only for identification and explanation without intent to infringe.

British Library Cataloguing-in-Publication Data
A catalogue record for this book is available from the British Library

Library of Congress Cataloging-in-Publication Data
A catalog record has been requested for this book

ISBN: 978-1-138-74310-6 (hbk)
ISBN: 978-1-032-07740-6 (pbk)
ISBN: 978-1-315-18192-9 (ebk)

DOI: 10.4324/9781315181929

Typeset in Bembo
by codeMantra

CONTENTS

Acknowledgements ix
Author statements x
List of contributors xi

1 History's outsiders? Global Indigenous Histories 1
  Ann McGrath and Lynette Russell

PART I
A global perspective **31**

2 European uses of history 33
  Henning Trüper

3 Theoretical frontiers 56
  Ben Silverstein

4 Indigenous peoples in Asia: a long history 86
  Robert Cribb

5 World conservation and genocidal frontiers: global environmentalism, settler colonialism, and Indigenous humanity in the early twentieth century 111
  Fiona Paisley

PART II
Migrations and mobilities 137

6 Indigenous global histories and modern human origins 139
  Martin Porr

7 Singing to ancestors: respecting and re-telling stories woven through ancient ancestral lands 165
  Paulette Steeves

8 The case for continuity of human occupation and rock art production in the Kimberley, Australia 194
  Peter Veth, Sam Harper, Kane Ditchfield, Sven Ouzman, and Balanggarra Aboriginal Corporation

9 Voyagers from the Havai'i diaspora: Polynesian mobility, 1760s–1850s 221
  Kate Fullagar

10 Walking the Indigenous city: colonial encounters at the heart of empire 241
   Coll Thrush

PART III
Colonial encounters 257

11 Treatied space: North American Indigenous treaties in a global context 259
   Joy Porter

12 Sámi indigeneity in nineteenth-century Swedish and British intellectual debates 279
   Linda Andersson Burnett

13 Language, translation, and transformation in Indigenous histories 302
   Laura Rademaker

14 'The case of Polly Indian': enslavement, Native ancestry, and the law in the British Caribbean 325
   Brooke N. Newman

Contents

15 Rethinking the colonial encounter in the Age of Trauma   345
    Taylor Spence

PART IV
Removals and diasporas   363

16 Sexual removals: Indigenous genders and
    sexualities as territory   365
    Manuela L. Picq

17 Reimagining home: Indian removal, Native storytelling,
    and the search for belonging   379
    Gregory D. Smithers

18 'Because of her, we can': gender and diaspora in
    Australian exemption policies   399
    *Lucinda Aberdeen, Katherine Ellinghaus, Kella Robinson,
    and Judi Wickes*

19 Damage and dispossession: Indigenous people and
    nuclear weapons on Bikini Atoll and the Pitjantjatjara
    lands, 1946 to 1988   419
    Heather Goodall

20 The bones of our mother: Adivasi dispossession in an Indian state   443
    Devleena Ghosh

PART V
Memory, identities, and narratives   465

21 Indigenous narratives, separations, denials, and memories:
    moving beyond loss   467
    Lynette Russell

22 Remembering removal: Indigenous narratives of colonial
    collecting practices in the Gulf of Papua (Papua New Guinea)   481
    Chris Urwin

23 Indigenous history and identity in the Caribbean   500
    B.W. Higman

24 Subttsasa Biehtsevuomátjistema: recalling the memories and
    stories from our little pine forest   524
    May-Britt Öhman Tuoeha Rim

25 Assisting Indigenous resistance through secularism: legal
    limits to Christianisation in Canada (1867–1939)   550
    Claude Gélinas

PART VI
Pathways towards future Indigenous histories   **569**

26 Transmission's end? Cataclysm and chronology in
    Indigenous oral tradition   571
    Chris Ballard

27 Archaeology, hybrid knowledge, and community
    engagement in Africa: thoughts on decolonising practice   603
    Paul Lane

28 Indigenous photography as subject and method for global history   629
    Oliver Haag

29 African literature as Indigenous history in South Africa's
    'decolonise the curriculum' movement   651
    Ashleigh Harris

30 Haptic history in Southeast Asia – archiving the past in
    bodies and landscapes   669
    Emilie Wellfelt

31 The uses of history in Greenland   690
    Claire McLisky and Kirstine Eiby Møller

32 Yuraki – an Australian Aboriginal perspective on deep history   722
    John Maynard

33 Deep history's digital footprints   736
    Ann McGrath

Index   759

ACKNOWLEDGEMENTS

We would like to introduce ourselves as editors and to acknowledge the unceded sovereignty of the Indigenous peoples upon whose lands we live and work. The two editors are both specialists in Indigenous history, particularly Australian and North American histories. Both editors work collaboratively with the traditional owners of the lands upon which we live and work and we appreciate their generosity as hosts and as supporters of our historical enterprises. In addition, we would like to thank all the contributors for their generosity and diligence. David Haworth, Hannah Cartmel, and Jennifer Bird acted as assistants on this project and we acknowledge their hard work. We benefited from the support of the Australian Research Council FL170100121, Rediscovering the Deep Human Past: Global Networks, Future Opportunities, and LP100100427 'Deepening Histories of Place', the Centre of Excellence in Australian Biodiversity and Heritage, and FL 190100161 'Global Encounters and First Nation's Peoples'.

AUTHOR STATEMENTS

Ann McGrath is of Irish, Scottish, and English descent, descended from people who migrated from the Northern Hemisphere to Australia at various times – 1789 on the second English convict fleet, and then into the late nineteenth and early twentieth centuries. She was raised in Meanjin/Brisbane, the lands of the Turrbal people, and she now works and lives on Ngunnawal lands, location of the Australian capital city, Canberra. Ann McGrath's interest in the field came out of a desire to learn more about the history of racism, as well as gender. Her work has focused on a variety of regions and cultural history topics in Australia and North America. She is interested in incorporating non-text-based storytelling into historical research, including oral history and film as delivery formats.

Both editors recognise the relevance of applying historical knowledge to the public sphere, to land rights, human rights, and overall the many struggles towards gaining recognition of Indigenous sovereignty. Committed to the history discipline due to its revelatory, truth-telling power, over the span of our careers, we have worked energetically to translate academic insights into social justice and educational initiatives. We see that as integral to our academic practice.

Lynette Russell descends from both Indigenous and settler communities. Her Aboriginal ancestors come from Western Victoria, and on her settler side she counts convicts and free settlers from southern England. Born, raised, and residing on Naarm (known as Melbourne), the traditional lands of the Kulin Nation, she strongly identifies with both her ancestors' lands and the lands and people of her home country. Originally trained in archaeology and anthropology, 30 years ago, she moved into Indigenous history. Over this period, she has worked closely with archaeologists and anthropologists, and has a strong commitment to interdisciplinary work. Her passion is to work with and for Indigenous peoples, repatriating knowledge and archival materials wherever possible.

CONTRIBUTORS

Lucinda Aberdeen is Adjunct Senior Research Fellow, School of Humanities and Social Sciences at La Trobe University Shepparton campus. She is of Irish and Scottish descent and grew up on Noongar country in the south-west of Western Australia. Her PhD in Sociology from La Trobe University examined racism and the role of the Australian state in country New South Wales. She has taught Australian Indigenous studies at the University of the Sunshine Coast and La Trobe University. Her research interests include ageing, anti-racist pedagogy, human rights, policy evaluation, racism and the settler colonial and contemporary state in Australia and youth transitions.

Linda Andersson Burnett is a Wallenberg Academy Fellow and Senior Researcher at the Department of History of Science and Ideas at Uppsala University in Sweden. Her research focuses on the exchange of scientific and cultural thought between Britain and Scandinavia in the long eighteenth century, and the importance of colonial and nation-building encounters with Indigenous peoples in the development of these exchanges. In her previous position, at the Linnaeus University, she convened an interdisciplinary research group on Nordic Colonialism. She is the author of a number of articles on Sámi history, ethnographic thought, scientific networks, and travel writing. She has co-edited two special issues of History of the Human Sciences (2019) and Scandinavian Studies (2019) and is currently writing a monograph on colonial ethnography during the Enlightenment.

The Balanggarra Aboriginal Corporation (registered native title body corporate) administers land on behalf of the Balanggarra people. Balanggarra (combined) recognises the Balanggarra people's native title rights and interest over approximately 26,025 square kilometres of land and sea in the northern Kimberley region of Western Australia, inclusive of the lands and sites in this paper. Balanggarra native title holders, the Board, IPA Rangers and additionally senior Kwini Traditional

Owners, foremost Ambrose Mungala Chalarimeri, contributed to the content of this paper.

Chris Ballard is Associate Professor in Pacific History at the Australian National University's College of Asia and the Pacific. His current research interests – in Indigenous historicities, cultural transmission, living heritage, and trans-disciplinary approaches to the genesis of cultural diversity – draw on and reflect long-term collaborative engagement with communities in Papua New Guinea, West Papua, and Vanuatu. His books and edited collections include *Confronting the Naturalness of Disaster in the Pacific* (2020), *'Rough Justice': Punitive Expeditions in Oceania* (2017), *Foreign Bodies: Oceania and the Science of Race, 1750–1940* (2008), *The Sweet Potato in Oceania* (2005), *Race to the Snow: Photography and the Exploration of Dutch New Guinea, 1907–1936* (2001); and *Fluid Ontologies: Myth, Ritual and Philosophy in the Highlands of Papua New Guinea* (1998).

Robert Cribb is Professor of Asian History at the Australian National University. His research focuses mainly on Indonesia and on issues of national identify, mass violence, historical geography, and environmental history. He is author of the *Historical Atlas of Indonesia* (2000), *Wild man from Borneo: a Cultural History of the Orangutan* (2014, with Helen Gilbert and Helen Tiffin), and *Japanese War Criminals: The Politics of Justice after the Second World War* (2017, with Sandra Wilson, Beatrice Trefalt and Dean Aszkielowicz).

Kane Ditchfield is an archaeologist at the University of Western Australia. He specialises in stone artefact analysis, method and theory, coastal archaeology, hunter-gatherer archaeology, Australian Pleistocene archaeology, chronological analyses, and geologically sourcing artefacts using petrographic and geochemical techniques. Kane has applied these specialisations in both Australia and Polynesia, most recently focusing on coastal and inland north-western Australia. He works in both the academic and consulting/industrial sectors of archaeology.

Katherine Ellinghaus is Associate Professor of History in the School of Archaeology and History at La Trobe University. She is of Irish, Scottish, and German descent and has researched and written extensively on Indigenous assimilation policies in Australia and the United States. In 2014 she was awarded an Australian Research Council Discovery Project grant to write a history of Aboriginal exemption policies in Australia.

Kate Fullagar is Professor of history at the Institute for Humanities and Social Sciences, Australian Catholic University. She is also honorary professor of history at Macquarie University and currently co-editor of the Australian Historical Association's journal, *History Australia*. Kate specialises in the history of the eighteenth-century world, particularly the British Empire and the many Indigenous societies it encountered. She is the author of the award-winning *The Warrior, the Voyager, and the Artist: Three Lives in an Age of Empire* (New Haven, 2020) and

The Savage Visit (Berkeley, 2012); the editor of The Atlantic World in the Antipodes: Effects and Transformations since the Eighteenth Century (Newcastle, 2012); and co-editor with Michael McDonnell of *Facing Empire: Indigenous Experiences in a Revolutionary Age* (Baltimore, 2018). She is Lead Chief Investigator of an ARC Linkage project with the National Portrait Gallery called *Facing New Worlds*.

Claude Gélinas (PhD Montreal, 1998) is an anthropologist and a full Professor at the Department of Philosophy and Applied Ethics of the University of Sherbrooke, Quebec, Canada. His teaching and research activities touch on the history and cosmologies of Indigenous peoples in Canada, as well as Canada's State policy regarding First Nations. His current research project focuses on Indigenous religious rights in Canada, both from a historical and contemporary perspective.

Devleena Ghosh was a Professor of Social and Political Sciences at the Faculty of Arts and Social Sciences at the University of Technology Sydney where she now holds an honorary position. She is the author of *Beyond the Coal Rush: A Turning Point for Global Energy and Climate Policy?* (with Goodman et al Cambridge University Press, 2020), *Teacher for Justice: Lucy Woodcock's Transnational Life* (with Goodall et al., ANU Press, 2019), *Colonialism and Modernity* (with Paul Gillen, UNSW Press, 2007) and editor of *Women in Asia: Shadowlines* (Cambridge Scholars Press, 2012), *Water, Sovereignty and Borders in Asia and Oceania* (with Heather Goodall and Stephanie Hemelryk Donald, Routledge, 2009), and *The Cultures of Trade: Indian Ocean Exchanges* (with Stephen Muecke, Cambridge Scholars Press, 2007). She has published widely in the areas of environmental, gender, and postcolonial studies in South Asia.

Heather Goodall is Professor Emerita, History, at the University of Technology Sydney. Her projects include those on Indigenous histories and environmental history in Australia, on twentieth-century decolonisation in India and Australia and on maritime history in the eastern Indian Ocean. Her publications include *From Invasion to Embassy: Land in Aboriginal Politics in NSW, 1770–1970* (Allen and Unwin, 1996); *Isabel Flick: The Many Lives of an Extraordinary Aboriginal Woman* (co-authored with Isabel Flick, Allen and Unwin, 2004); *Rivers and Resilience* (co-authored with Allison Cadzow, UNSW Press, 2009); *Making Change Happen: Black & White Activists Talk to Kevin Cook about Aboriginal, Union & Liberation Politics* (co-authored with Kevin Cook, Aboriginal History and ANU Press, 2013); *Beyond Borders: Indians, Australians and the Indonesian Revolution, 1939–1950* (Amsterdam University Press, 2018); and co-authored with Helen Randerson and Devleena Ghosh: *Teacher for Justice: Lucy Woodcock's Transnational Life* (ANU Press, 2019).

Oliver Haag (PhD, University of Edinburgh; MA, University of Vienna) is Senior Research Fellow at the Austrian Centre for Transcultural Studies, Vienna, and Visiting Professorial Fellow at Queen Mary's College/Madras University. His research interests are in the areas of European reception of Indigenous New Zealand and Australian literatures, the history of publishing and critical race and whiteness theory. Oliver has authored numerous articles in journals such as *Continuum*, *National Identities* and *Antipodes*. He is co-editor of *Ngapartji Ngapartji* (Australian National University Press, 2014) and the bilingual *Australian Studies Journal-Zeitschrift für Australianstudien*. His latest publication is *The Persistence of Race from the Wilhelmine Empire to National Socialism* (Berghahn, 2017).

Sam Harper is an archaeologist and rock art specialist based at the Centre for Rock Art Research + Management, University of Western Australia. Her research interests are style, identity, material culture, seascapes, arid-zones, recording methodologies, large-scale data management, and two-way knowledge exchange with Aboriginal communities. Sam works across the northwest of Australia, particularly the coastal Pilbara and Kimberley.

Ashleigh Harris is Professor in English at Uppsala University. She is the principle investigator on a research project entitled 'African Street Literature and the Futures of Literary Form', which is funded by the Swedish Research Council (2017–2020). She is also a participant in the research programme, 'Cosmopolitan and Vernacular Dynamics in World Literature', funded by the Bank of Sweden's Tercentenary Fund (2016–2021). Recent publications include *Afropolitanism and the Novel: De-Realizing Africa* (Routledge, 2019), 'Afropolitan style and unusable global spaces' in Bruce Robbins and Paulo Horta (eds.) *Cosmopolitanisms* (New York University Press), and 'Hot Reads, Pirate Copies, and the Unsustainability of the Book in Africa's Literary Future' (*Postcolonial Text*).

B.W. Higman is Emeritus Professor of History at the Australian National University and Emeritus Professor of The University of the West Indies. He is the author of ten books on Caribbean history, archaeology, and geography, including *Slave Population and Economy in Jamaica, 1807–1834* (1976, awarded the Bancroft Prize), *Plantation Jamaica 1750–1850: Capital and Control in a Colonial Economy* (2005), *Jamaican Food: History, Biology, Culture* (2008), and *A Concise History of the Caribbean* (2011). His most recent book is *Flatness* (2017).

Paul Lane has worked widely in African archaeology for over 35 years. He is the Jennifer Ward Oppenheimer Professor of the Deep History and Archaeology of Africa and Mandela Magdalene Memorial Fellow at the University of Cambridge, and formerly Professor of Global Archaeology at Uppsala University. He served as Director of the British Institute in Eastern Africa between 1998 and 2006, and as President of the Society of Africanist Archaeologists 2008–2010. He specialises in the landscape historical ecology and archaeology of eastern Africa over the last c. 5,000 years, with emphasis on the transitions to food production, landscape domestication, the trade in elephant ivory, settlement dynamics, maritime heritage, and the archaeology of enslavement and abolition.

John Maynard is a Worimi Aboriginal man from the Port Stephens region of New South Wales. He is currently Chair of Aboriginal History at the University of

Newcastle. He has held several major positions and served on numerous prominent organisations and committees, including Deputy Chairperson of the Australian Institute of Aboriginal and Torres Strait Islander Studies (AIATSIS), Executive Committee of the Australian Historical Association, and the New South Wales History Council. He has worked with and within many Aboriginal communities, urban, rural, and remote. Professor Maynard's publications have concentrated on the intersections of Aboriginal political and social history, and the history of Australian race relations. He is the author of a dozen books, including a finalist for the Walkley Awards in 2011 *The Aboriginal Soccer Tribe*, Dymocks Readers' Choice 2013 *Aborigines and the Sport of Kings* and finalist for the Victorian Premiers History Prize *Fight for Liberty and Freedom*.

Ann McGrath is the WK Hancock Distinguished Professor of History at the Australian National University and, through books, articles, films, and exhibitions, she has been a leading figure in ensuring that the hidden histories of Aboriginal people become more widely known. She is the Director of the Research Centre for Deep History and holds the Kathleen Fitzpatrick Laureate Fellowship of the Australian Research Council 2017–2022. She is both a Fellow of the Australian Academy of Humanities and the Australian Academy of Social Sciences. In recognition of her work, she has been awarded the Medal of the Order of Australia.

Claire McLisky is a historian of colonial Christian missions, their legacies, and lawful relations in post-colonial and settler societies, in particular in Australia, Denmark, and Greenland. She is an adjunct lecturer at Southern Cross University in the areas of cultural competence and Australian studies, and is a senior researcher on the ARC project 'Lawful Relations', based at Deakin University. She lives and works on Bundjalung country on the north coast of New South Wales, Australia.

Kirstine Eiby Møller is a PhD fellow at the Greenland National Museum and Archives with joint enrolment at Memorial University of Newfoundland and Labrador and Ilisimatusarfik – the University of Greenland. She is an Indigenous Arctic archaeologist whose research interests include identity narratives, entangled histories, cultural encounters and colonialism in the Arctic, and decolonisation practices. Her PhD project 'Colonial Encounters' (2019–2023) is funded by the Greenlandic Research Council.

Brooke N. Newman is an associate professor of history at Virginia Commonwealth University whose research specialties include gender and sexuality, race, and slavery in early modern Britain and the British Atlantic world. She is the author of *A Dark Inheritance: Blood, Race, and Sex in Colonial Jamaica* and co-editor of *Native Diasporas: Indigenous Identities and Settler Colonialism in the Americas*. A number of distinguished institutions on both sides of the Atlantic have supported her research, including, most recently, the Library Company of Philadelphia, the Eccles Centre for American Studies at the British Library, and the Omohundro Institute and Georgian Papers Programme for research in the Royal Archives at

Windsor Castle. Her current book project chronicles the evolving policies and attitudes of the British Crown and prominent members of the royal family towards imperial rule, slavery, and the transatlantic trade in enslaved Africans, and abolition and emancipation between 1660 and 1860.

May-Britt Öhman is Associate Professor in Environmental History, PhD in History of Technology, 2007, and Lule/Forest Sámi from Lule River/Julevädno, with ancestry also from the Torne river valley on the settler colonial border between Sweden and Finland. She leads the research group 'Dálkke: Indigenous Climate Change Studies' at the Centre for Multidisciplinary Studies on Racism, CEMFOR, Uppsala University, and is guest senior lecturer at the Division of History, Luleå University of Technology, LTU.

Sven Ouzman is an archaeologist and heritage specialist at the University of Western Australia's Discipline of Archaeology and Centre for Rock Art Research + Management. He works in northern Australia and southern Africa. He has expertise in academic, museum, government, and public sectors. He specialises in archaeological theory – notably notions of 'origin' and understandings of time – gatherer-hunter archaeology, rock art, symbolic behaviour, heritage theory and management, creolisation and contact, pedagogy, graffiti, homelessness, landscape, fakes, intellectual property issues, Indigenous archaeology, and the uses and abuses of archaeology in Australia, South Africa, Israel, and Palestine.

Fiona Paisley is Professor Emeritus of History at Griffith University. She studies progressive debates concerning the reform of settler colonialism in the first half of the twentieth century. Her recent books include *The Lone Protestor: AM Fernando in Australia and Europe* (2012), *Glamour in the Pacific: Cultural Internationalism and Race Politics in the Women's Pan-Pacific* (2009), and (with Pamela Scully) *Writing Transnational History* (2019). Currently she is researching internationalism, education, and 'race' in the 1930s; and British anti-slavery discourse in interwar Australia.

Manuela L. Picq is Professor of International Relations at Universidad San Francisco de Quito (Ecuador), and Loewenstein Fellow in the Departments of Sexuality, Women's and Gender Studies and Political Science at Amherst College (USA). She has held research positions at Freie Universität (2015), the Institute for Advanced Study (2013), and the Woodrow Wilson Center (2005). Her approach to international relations focuses on Indigenous rights, gender and sexuality in Latin America, and the politics of nature and extractivism. She is the author of *Vernacular Sovereignties: Indigenous Women Challenging World Politics* (University of Arizona Press 2018), and co-editor of *Sexuality and Translation in World Politics* (with Caroline Cottet, E-IR 2019), *Queering Narratives of Modernity* (with Maria Amelia Viteri, Peter Lang 2016) and *Sexualities in World Politics* (with Markus Thiel, Routledge 2015). Her publications appeared in peer-reviewed journals like *Latin American Politics and Society*, *Cahiers du Genre*, and *International Political Science Review*. She contributes to international media outlets and collaborates with Indigenous organisations in Ecuador and

Guatemala. Her work at the intersection of scholarship, journalism, and activism led her to be expelled from Ecuador in 2015 and to be nominated among a New Generation of Public Intellectuals in 2018.

Martin Porr is Associate Professor of Archaeology and a member of the Centre for Rock Art Research + Management at the University of Western Australia. He has published widely on European Palaeolithic art and archaeology, the Aboriginal art and rock art of Northwest Australia, the relevance of postcolonial approaches to archaeological practice, and critical and social theoretical aspects of archaeological and rock art research. He has conducted fieldwork in Germany, Thailand, Australia, India, and the Philippines. Most recently, he published the co-edited volume *Interrogating Human Origins. Decolonisation and the Deep Human Past* (Routledge, 2020).

Joy Porter is a scholar from Derry in the North of Ireland and a Professor of Indigenous History in relation to the environment, war, modernity, literature, politics, and culture at the University of Hull, U.K. She is currently a Leverhulme Major Research Fellow working on a new book on the environmental record of President Nixon and the Republican Party. From 2021, she is Principal Investigator of the AHRC Standard Research Grant, 'Brightening the Covenant Chain: Revealing Cultures of Diplomacy between the Crown and the Iroquois Confederacy' (931.032k). She is also Co-PI of the University Cluster Treatied Spaces: Environment & Peoples in America, 1607–1890 and PI Host for British Academy Global Professor Gregory D. Smithers, 2020–2024, who is working on the project 'Native Ecologies: Traditional Ecological Knowledge and Climate Change'.

Laura Rademaker is Postdoctoral Research Associate at the Australian National University and Deputy Director of the Research Centre for Deep History. Her research interests span histories of Indigeneity, gender, and religion as well as questions of deep history and Indigenous knowledges. Her first book, *Found in Translation: Many Meanings on a North Australian Mission* (2018), received the Australian Historical Association's Hancock Prize. She was awarded her doctorate from the Australian National University in 2015. Her thesis about language and the Angurugu mission also received numerous prizes: the J.G. Crawford Prize; John Moloney Prize; and Australian Historical Association's Serle Award.

Kella Robinson BEd, GCertCultHeritage, MA (Deakin) is a Wemba Wemba woman born in Hillston in central New South Wales. Her Ngiyampaa-speaking grandfather taught her the culture of her country. She has worked as a state schoolteacher, storyteller, and cultural interpreter. Since 2003, Kella has been the cultural adviser assisting the magistrate at the Victorian Koorie Court at Shepparton, and since 2012 she has been involved with the Dungala-Kaiela Writing Awards.

Lynette Russell is an award-winning historian and Indigenous studies scholar. Over the past two decades she has published numerous books and essays. Her work on Aboriginal whalers resulted in the acclaimed *Roving Mariners*. All her work is interdisciplinary, blending history, archaeology, and material culture studies. One of her most recent books in 2019 was the award winning *The First Naturalists*, with zoologist Penny Olsen. In 2020 she began an Australian Research Council's Laureate Fellowship to examine Global Encounters and First Nations People: 1000 Years of Australian History.

Ben Silverstein is a Postdoctoral Research Fellow at the Australian National University, working on the ARC Laureate Fellowship program titled 'Rediscovering the Deep Human Past', which seeks to engage with the long duration of Indigenous history in Australia. He has researched in colonial and Indigenous histories, engaging questions of race and settler colonialism, as well as contests over sovereignties and colonial government. He is the editor of *Conflict, Adaptation, Transformation: Richard Broome and the Practice of Aboriginal History* (Aboriginal Studies Press, 2018), and the author of *Governing Natives: Indirect Rule and Settler Colonialism in Australia's North* (Manchester University Press, 2019).

Gregory D. Smithers is professor of history at Virginia Commonwealth University and a British Academy Global Professor, based with the Treatied Spaces Research Cluster at the University of Hull, England. He has written widely on Indigenous history, and the intersecting histories of race, gender, and sexuality. His most recent books include *Native Southerners: Indigenous History from Origins to Removal* (2019) and *The Cherokee Diaspora: An Indigenous History of Migration, Resettlement, and Identity* (2015). His next book, *Reclaiming Two-Spirits: Sexuality, Spiritual Renewal, & Sovereignty in Native America*, is forthcoming from Beacon Press.

Taylor Spence writes histories and makes art about the history and legacies of U.S. colonialism in North America. He holds an MFA in Painting from the School of Visual Arts and a PhD in American History from Yale University. He lives in Albuquerque and Brooklyn, and is currently a Postdoctoral Fellow at the University of New Mexico. Blog and more about his work at https://www.taylorwyoming.com/the-cowboy-flaneur-a-culture-blog.

Paulette Steeves PhD – (Cree- Metis) was born in Whitehorse Yukon Territories and grew up in Lillooet, British Columbia, Canada. She is an Associate Professor in Sociology at Algoma University in Sault Ste. Marie, ON, and a Canada Research Chair Tier II in Healing and Reconciliation. She holds an adjunct faculty position at Mount Allison University in Sackville, NB. Her research focus is on the Pleistocene history of the Western Hemisphere (the Americas), reclaiming and rewriting Indigenous histories and healing and reconciliation. In her research she argues that Indigenous peoples were present in the Western Hemisphere as early as 100,000 years ago, and possibly much earlier. Dr. Steeves argues that counter stories to Western narratives of Indigenous histories address issues that remain critical to Indigenous people; sovereignty, self-determination, healing, and reconciliation. Dr. Steeves has stated that rewriting and un-erasing Indigenous histories should become a part of healing and reconciliation, transforming public consciousness, and confronting and challenging racism. Long-standing academic denial of the deep Indigenous past fosters racism and discrimination among the general or Settler population. Re-writing Indigenous histories, framed through Indigenous knowledge, will create discussions that counter racism and discrimination. Her first book, *The Indigenous Paleolithic of the Americas*, will be published on 1 July 2021.

Coll Thrush is Professor of history and faculty associate in critical Indigenous studies at the University of British Columbia in Vancouver, on unceded Musqueam territory. He is author of *Native Seattle: Histories from the Crossing-Over Place* (2007/2017), co-editor of *Phantom Past, Indigenous Presence: Native Ghosts in North American Culture and History* (2011), and author of *Indigenous London: Native Travelers at the Heart of Empire* (2016). He is also the international collaborator on the Arts & Humanities Research Council-funded project *Beyond the Spectacle: Native North American Presence in Britain*, and is currently working on a critical cultural and environmental history of shipwrecks on the northwest coast of North America, entitled *Wrecked: Ecologies of Failure in the Graveyard of the Pacific*.

Henning Trüper (PhD, European University Institute, Florence; 'habilitation' degree in modern history, University of Zurich) is a permanent research scholar at Leibniz Center for Literary and Cultural Studies, Berlin. He is the author of *Topography of a Method: François Louis Ganshof and the Writing of History* (2014), *Orientalism, Philology and the Illegibility of the Modern World* (2020), and co-editor, with Dipesh Chakrabarty and Sanjay Subrahmanyam, of *Historical Teleologies in the Modern World* (2015).

Chris Urwin is a postdoctoral research fellow at Monash University and the Australian Research Council's Centre of Excellence for Australian Biodiversity and Heritage. For his PhD research he worked with village communities in the Gulf of Papua (Papua New Guinea), using ethnoarchaeological methods to understand how people build and remember their ancestral places through time. Urwin previously worked as the senior curator for the remarkable First Peoples archaeology collection at Museums Victoria (Melbourne Museum). His latest research project examines narratives of Indigenous voyaging and American collecting through the social histories of Pacific canoes acquired by the Smithsonian Institution.

Peter Veth is based in the Archaeology discipline at the University of Western Australia and works in archaeology, heritage and the study of deserts and maritime societies. He has specialised in the occupational records and symbolic behaviours of the First Australians from the Western Desert, coastal Pilbara and Kimberley and the peoples of eastern Indonesia and East Timor. He is currently researching how settlers adapted rapidly to the large deserts of North West Australia, from the southern Kimberley and tropical coastlines to the most remote parts of the Sandy Deserts.

Emilie Wellfelt is an interdisciplinary researcher and teacher based at the Department of History, Stockholm University, Sweden. Her research focuses on maritime

Southeast Asia in local and global context and she is the author of a number of articles pertaining to history, culture, and religion of this region. She has run ethnographic projects in collaboration with the Museum of World Culture in Gothenburg, Sweden, worked for the University of Cologne, Germany, (2013–2016) in a worldwide documentation programme for endangered languages (DOBES) and received a PhD in History at Linnaeus University, Sweden, in 2017.

Her current research draws on a postdoctoral project at Stockholm University (2017–2019) and concerns the impact of global trade with exotic birds in the early modern period.

Judi Wickes BSocWk UQ, BA (Hons) MA Sunshine Coast, is a Kalkadoon and Wakka Wakka woman with Irish and English heritage born in Brisbane, Queensland. She is a respected community Elder, social worker, historian, and educator who writes and presents nationally and internationally on the Stolen Generations and Certificates of Exemption and their impacts on Aboriginal and Torres Strait Islander peoples. She lectures as a guest speaker on these topics at various universities. She is the first Indigenous Australian scholar to undertake a comprehensive study of Aboriginal exemption and has published widely on the subject.

1
HISTORY'S OUTSIDERS?
Global Indigenous Histories

Ann McGrath and Lynette Russell

Introduction

If we wish to draw lessons from the human past, the global scale and scope of Indigenous history is an illuminating place to start. The study of global history will be greatly enhanced, too, if it can meet the challenge of Indigenous history.[1] Over aeons, Indigenous peoples[2] have developed a vision of a world shared by humans and non-humans as not only mutually interdependent but intimately interconnected. On a planet where waterways, seas, and lands are being exploited ever more destructively, Indigenous people's respect for the environment as a living entity offers inspiring insights for future generations. Indigenous people's long custodianship and management of forests, rivers, and seas offer pathways to a more sustainable future. In the crises that the world faces today, in particular the mounting climate emergency, Indigenous people's knowledge is more important than ever.

The aim of this introduction is to canvas some of the wider questions important to Indigenous history. We discuss why Indigenous peoples have rarely featured in mainstream accounts of global history. We reflect upon the complexities around definitions of Indigenous people, noting common historical experiences and diversity. We then consider the multiple meanings of the term 'Indigenous history' and consider future approaches and directions for the history discipline. We contend that a collaborative, community-centred approach to scholarship will allow fresh interdisciplinary and Indigenous-focussed methodologies and approaches. The practice and purpose of history itself, and its associated disciplines, might be reconceptualised. So much can be learnt from Indigenous peoples.

First, however, we need to recognise that Indigenous peoples *have a history* – and a global history at that. It is a dynamic story that covers the full expanse of the human past. Indigenous histories encompass epic migrations, dramatic and slow changes over time, patterns of continuity, sustainability, adaptability, resilience, and survival. The history of Indigenous people took place on various scales –

at familial, community, and national levels – and in specific sites within wider regional land and waterscapes. Indigenous people have formed self-governing Indigenous Nations in the past and present, although today they often live under the umbrella of acquisitive, more powerful nations. Despite protracted historical negotiations, including treaty processes, Indigenous peoples have rarely elected to voluntarily relinquish their lands, their sovereignty, or their autonomy.[3]

For Indigenous Nations, the past several centuries have brought dramatic ruptures, primarily through imperialism, colonialism, and various forms of global expansionism and local land takeovers. What unites so many Indigenous peoples today are their common historical experiences under external impositions. This includes their long struggles to regain sovereignty over ancestral lands – estates that, in many cases, have been stolen by rapacious intruders. Indigenous identity is rightly connected with histories of struggle, often involving forced removal and exile to distant reserves and reservations. However, their histories also demonstrate displays of strength and creative reinvention – resistance, resilience, survival, and creativity, including the development of new economies and thriving diasporas of cultural transformation and renewal.[4] The long political struggles of Indigenous people for basic rights have created powerful global connections between groups. They have mobilised in trans-national and global movements to gain redress and to advance towards a better future for their communities.[5]

Indigenous peoples are by no means homogenous in their recent, modern, or deep-time experiences of history, or in their aspirations for the future.[6] This diversity – of residence, region, culture, and political arrangements – is clearly evident throughout this Companion. Some groups live on autonomously held lands, on tribal reservations, upon state-run reserves, in remote and rural areas. Many Indigenous peoples live in cities and towns, of varying sizes and composition. Even on the same continents, Indigenous peoples have contrasting historical experiences. Their lives are shaped by specific and ever-changing economies, climates, and ecosystems. Generally speaking, Indigenous people are proud of their collective ethos, but their individual stories also offer important histories that need to be told. Contributors to this Companion tell stories of outstanding leaders, the quiet achievers and the famed. As with all histories, each person has a unique experience, varying according to age, gender, sexuality, class, belief, politics, education, work, health, family, life stories, landed associations, rights, behaviours, talents, tendencies, and the myriad historical factors that nuance human lives.

Whether an individual is Indigenous is commonly a matter of self-identification, contingent upon recognition and acceptance by the relevant Indigenous organisation or community, who may require specific evidence criteria. The people around the world who identify as Indigenous belong to tribal nations and other entities, by which they are known. These include many different groups that share certain things in common but also have many differences. They have divergent cultures and economies, contrasting physical appearances or phenotypes, with distinctive hair and skin colouring that varies from light to dark and everything in between. Historical factors that ruptured their ties with land, combined with ethnic and cross-colonial intermixing, have led to serious obstacles to recognition and inclusion. When individuals could not enjoy cultural and community belonging, they often suffered anxiety and intergenerational trauma. Losing connections to land, and even community links, however, did not mean that Indigenous people permanently lost their identity or rights. Many fought hard to assert their Indigenous sovereignty, to forge new kinds of landed and community-oriented associations and systems of governance.

It is important that we do not view history exclusively through the lens of imperial chronologies and histories, which is the prevailing perspective of many written histories. In this volume, we were keen to foreground Indigenous perspectives and responses, but we did not overlook the significant colonising policies and actions that led to the impoverished and disadvantaged situation of many Indigenous people today. Over the last several hundred years, imperial strategies for eroding Indigenous autonomy and economies followed peremptory declarations of sovereignty by more powerful entities. These were generally argued according to the Law of Nations, an established mechanism of the European powers, on the basis of discovery or conquest.

Here, we summarise some of the violent patterns that emerged. Well-armed invaders arrived on Indigenous lands; they implemented takeovers by means of large-scale military operations and warfare. Various colonial states routinely condoned murders and acts of violence by frontiersmen and women, the ordinary civilians. From the sixteenth century, on their expeditions to South America, both Spanish conquistadors and French colonisers used gruesome means to kill and degrade gender-non-conforming men.[7] In some colonising nations, tens of thousands of Indigenous peoples – women and children included – were targeted and killed in cold blood. Women were raped, tortured, and subjected to ongoing sexual exploitation. Massacres were carried out and frequently covered up. Large-scale warfare, guerrilla warfare, poisonings, murders, state-endorsed executions, starvation, and disease led to shocking death tolls. Coloniser states also sought to exploit rivalries and to turn Indigenous Nations against each other; indigenous police forces were deployed against other Indigenous groups.[8] Indigenous people fought back, waging both short and sustained campaigns, and although there were many wins, the larger European populations and forces eventually gained control. Overall, these imperial and colonial takeovers constituted a reign of terror.

Even in regions where there was less violence, the uninvited arrival of outsider populations jeopardised or totally destroyed Indigenous hunting, herding, agricultural, and trading economies. Malnutrition, combined with exposure to introduced diseases such as smallpox, measles, rubella, chickenpox, and influenza, depleted Indigenous populations, facilitating the land resumptions that would permanently remove their sustenance and lifeways. In various settler-coloniser states, state authorities forcibly removed whole Indigenous communities from their traditional lands, and implemented numerous other forms of cultural genocide, including forced assimilation.[9]

Throughout the nineteenth and twentieth centuries, state authorities in several nations attacked the cohesion and autonomy of Indigenous families, splitting them on the basis of colour. They imposed contemporary Western-style gender roles on Indigenous families and regulated sexual and marital relations in ways alien to them. Government-sanctioned policies removed Indigenous children from their families, often violently, then raised them as if they were orphans in distant state-run institutions. In Canada, the United States, and Australia, Indigenous people suffered their lands being stolen and consequent poverty; in Greenland, too, the Inuit lost babies and the children that they dearly loved. Child-removal created lasting cross-generational trauma.[10]

After Europeans took over Indigenous lands, the prior occupants were routinely moved off to poorer lands. Colonial state authorities prevented them from residing and running viable economies on their lands and from ruling themselves. They prohibited Indigenous peoples from implementing their own systems of law, speaking their own languages, conducting key ceremonies, practising their own spirituality, and nurturing and raising their children according to their values and customs. Sacred sites, including places of deep storied significance, were destroyed by the intruders, their spiritual significance ignored. In Australia, in a particularly devastating move, in June 2020, the mining giant Rio Tinto destroyed two Juukan Gorge caves, sacred caves described as being of 'the highest archaeological significance', which contained artefacts dating back 46,000 years.[11]

Even the memory of their ancestors, and other fundamental ways that Indigenous peoples honoured their own pasts were subject to assault. Burials and human remains were routinely stolen, then resold to collectors. Thousands of Indigenous remains were shipped to distant European museums, and despite repatriation efforts many are still held there to this day.[12] This continues to be justified in the name of Western science. Yet, while Indigenous knowledge of navigation, hydrology, trackways, food resources, and ecologies were eagerly exploited for the purpose of European expansionism, such expertise was not recognised, let alone admitted into the pantheon of mainstream science. From an Indigenous perspective, the hypocrisy and immorality of the colonisers must have been unfathomable.

The forces of imperialism and colonialism disempowered Indigenous people around the globe, but it is important to avoid oversimplifying this as a binary of coloniser/colonised. The colonised were by no means unified, with sharply competing interests.[13] And Indigenous history, too, is extremely complicated, with factions, fusions, cross-overs, and conflicting survival strategies. Across the globe, Indigenous peoples mixed outside their communities with other peoples, Indigenous and non-Indigenous, exchanging ideas, teaching them, learning from them, and getting to know them as fellow humans. More often than not, their lives and their histories became entangled in the most intimate ways with people of other ethnicities, many of whom were at odds with each other – whether over religion, politics, or economic goals. Family, residency, everyday labour, working relationships, and marriages played roles in bringing peoples together.[14]

On Spanish, Portuguese, French, and English colonising frontiers, in a range of diverse collisions, collusions, and other relationships, Indigenous lives became enmeshed with the invaders, traders, and settler-colonisers. Rape and sexual assault were common forms of colonising violence, and led to children of mixed descent being born and accepted by Indigenous families. On plantations in the Caribbean, the local Indigenous people became enmeshed with people who arrived as slaves from the African continent, with the case of Polly Indian of Tobago, as explored in Brooke Newman's chapter, demonstrating the fluidity of the so-called 'race' categories.[15] Individuals across colonising boundaries intermingled sexually, and many consensual short- and longer-term love unions took place. On some frontiers, including Australian and North American, this forged a 'marital middle ground' where intermixed families created diplomatic and economic possibilities that allowed for community survival.[16] In Canada, fur traders mixed with and married local Indigenous women, although these were often temporary arrangements before they returned to France, Scotland, and their European homes. These unions led to the people formally recognised now as the Méti.[17] Mixed unions frequently led to transgenerational complications of identity and status. However, numerous people of mixed descent were raised to take great pride in their Indigenous identity, several becoming prominent leaders who campaigned for the recognition of their people's sovereignty.

Predating imperial invasions and colonisations, it is important to keep in mind that Indigenous peoples have much longer histories too. Although rarely recorded within the parameters of European-based archives and histories, these histories go far back in time. Indigenous people were the great global travellers who traversed the world's land bridges, who witnessed new rivers and bays being formed, and who lived through times when their lands were being inundated by seas.[18] They survived climatic and ecological changes; they adapted to new environments, invented new technologies, and sustained functional societies over aeons. They have epic stories. For example, for at least 65,000 years BP (Before the Present), Aboriginal Australians have lived on the Greater Australian continent that was joined to today's Papua New Guinea and is now known as Sahul.[19] In contrast, the neighbouring Māori, who have rich accounts of their journey across the Pacific and their earlier history in Polynesia, have occupied Aotearoa or New Zealand since CE 1300.

Who are the Indigenous?

The term 'Indigenous people' is particularly useful when reflecting upon broad global developments. The term Indigenous, however, is not straightforward to define and common dictionary definitions seem inadequate. Until recently, publishing style guides prohibited the use of the capital 'I' for Indigenous, because lexicographers classed it as an adjective rather than a proper name. Not all dictionaries recognise it as a term for a category of people. The *Cambridge Dictionary* defines Indigenous as 'existing naturally or having always lived in a place; native'. The *Collins English Dictionary* explains: 'Indigenous people or things belong to the country in which they are found, rather than coming there or being brought there from another country.' With definitions generally referring to original or earlier occupants, it is implied that a later group later became dominant. Today, the term is generally used to denote people who have been associated with a discrete area of land in a particular locality, and it also implies acts of dispossession or sublimation.

Indigenous peoples have their own group descriptors, often in their own languages. Depending on context, most Indigenous peoples identify first according to their particular tribe, band or sub-group, clan, Nation, language group, or community corporation. Many run their Nations as self-governing political entities. Indigenous people identify under the category of their Indigenous Tribe or Nation, as well as according to wider, even pancontinental descriptors such as Native Americans or American Indians. Some Australian Aboriginal people refer to their groups as tribes or Nations, which generally accord with a distinctive language. The Māori of New Zealand have a common language, but discrete tribal or *iwi* identities associated with one's *whanau* (family), and specific marae – or Māori meeting places – are fundamental to personal identity.[20] The Sámi of Scandinavia appoint representatives to sit on the Sámi Parliament, which includes people who reside in what are now several Scandinavian nations. They represent a diverse group with identities based upon regional origins and lifestyles, including not only the well-known reindeer herders but people with fishing and forest traditions.[21] Forced to move to regions beyond their traditional lands, many Indigenous people now occupy diasporic communities, and practise different economic enterprises, although this does not make their tribal or national Indigenous identity any less significant to them.[22]

One of the reasons that the term 'Indigenous' has been taken up more widely in recent decades is that it has become associated with international struggles for justice.[23] Its adoption by the United Nations (UN) has given the term empowering potential, with the UN acknowledging that Indigenous people have experienced great inequalities around the world, and recognising the urgent need to respect and promote their inherent rights. Naming oneself as Indigenous can be empowering, not only as a proud heritage, but to serve as a reminder that sovereignty was not ceded and that the struggle to gain rights continues.[24]

Indigenous-led deliberations resulted in the Declaration on the Rights of Indigenous Peoples (UNDRIP), ratified by the UN in 2007. Aimed at recognising and redressing their historical suffering and ongoing injustice on a global scale, it represented the culmination of meetings of over 700 Indigenous representatives, the participants hailing from many diverse environments and regions. As their report put it: 'from the forests of Amazonia to the north of Alaska and Greenland; from the Sámi people in Northern Russia to the Masai in Kenya to Australia's aborigines'.[25] By 2007, 144 countries voted to ratify the Declaration.[26] Several countries abstained, but the settler-coloniser nations of the United States, New Zealand, Canada, and Australia – all products of British imperial takeovers of Indigenous lands – opposed it outright. Although eventually agreeing to sign, they had been anxious that the Declaration would impinge on their exclusive rights to national sovereignty. Perhaps they had a cause for concern for the status quo, since the UNDRIP stated that 'Settler colonialism' was not a matter of past history but an 'ongoing process that the Declaration aims to circumvent'.[27] Effectively, it recognised that Indigenous rights had not been freely surrendered, and that the right to self-determination should be upheld.

The UNDRIP recognised Indigenous people as entitled to a special category of rights. Some participants were concerned that use of the term 'Indigenous peoples' would privilege collective over individual rights; however, most agreed that collective rights were a core value of Indigeneity.[28] The UN Committee understood that Indigenous people shared common bonds for positive and sustaining reasons, too, including the strength of their links to certain land and seascapes that derived from prior historical entitlements. They encapsulated these as 'their political, economic and social structures and ... their cultures, spiritual traditions, histories and philosophies, especially their rights to their lands, territories and resources'.[29]

However, the UNDRIP didn't offer any set definition of 'Indigenous peoples'. Representatives considered that 'a universal definition would prevent indigenous groups from defining themselves according to their own value systems and would, as such, constrain the right to self-determination'.[30] Similarly, in 2004, the UN's International Labour Organisation (ILO) declined to provide a definition. However, for readers seeking more clarity as to who came under special Indigenous protections, it may be helpful to share the ILO's 'statement of coverage' for the Indigenous and Tribal Peoples Convention (ILO Convention No. 169):

> Article 1
> (1) This Convention applies to:
> (a) tribal peoples in independent countries whose social, cultural and economic conditions distinguish them from other sections of the national community and whose status is regulated wholly or partially by their own customs or traditions or by special laws or regulations;
> (b) peoples in independent countries who are regarded as indigenous on account of their descent from the populations which inhabited the country, or a geographical region to which the country belongs, at the time of conquest or colonisation or the establishment of present state boundaries and who, irrespective of their legal status, retain some or all of their own social, economic, cultural and political institutions.[31]

The 2007 UNDRIP recognised the traumatic history that Indigenous peoples suffered under imperial, colonial, and national governments, and sought to improve their future. Aiming to put a stop to oppression, Article 7.2 states:

> Indigenous peoples have the collective right to live in freedom, peace and security as distinct peoples and shall not be subjected to any act of genocide or any other act of violence, including forcibly removing children of the group to another group.

Article 8 protects them against dispossession and 'forced assimilation or destruction of their culture',[32] and it proposes redress.[33] Articles 11 and 12 lay out Indigenous peoples' rights to protect their cultural, spiritual, and historical heritages.[34]

In certain regions of the world, there is ongoing controversy about Indigenous status within nation states. In a valuable overview chapter, historian Robert Cribb explains the political complexity and diversity around the history of Indigeneity in Asia. In Africa, whether people, and which groups of people, wish to identify as Indigenous is not straightforward. Nomadic and tribal people such as the Masai in Kenya are counted as indigenous, despite not necessarily occupying long-held estates. Minorities in China and Myanmar count themselves indigenous, as do the Mapuche of Chile. Other identities are contested, as in the status of the Travellers or Romani of Europe. Stateless in a sense, their landlessness has excluded them from being classed as Indigenous, so they are generally viewed as an ethnic minority rather than an Indigenous group. Many of the Irish and Welsh of the United Kingdom see themselves as Indigenous to the land – with cultures and languages that, against their wishes, were largely subsumed under English imperialism. In recent times, the Irish, many of whom migrated to the New World, have become proud of their links with Indigenous peoples.[35]

Various coloniser states defined Indigenous identities based on 'blood quantum' or racial ideas, and applied state and national policies accordingly. In Australia, state and federal governments used ugly terms that borrowed from the Indian caste system, including 'half-caste, quadroon and octoroon'. In the United States, recognised tribal status requires written proof of enrolment with a particular Indian nation by a certain date.[36] Depending on race and colonial policies, the percentage of Indigenous ancestry determined how individuals would fare; if they had European ancestry, some got paid higher wages; others were subjected to greater suspicion, scrutiny, and enjoyed fewer rights.

On the question of identity, in order to protect their families, many Indigenous people around the world were motivated to suppress their identity and sometimes to invent substitute identities considered of higher status. As explained in Lynette Russell's chapter, oppressive state policies and the stigma associated with Indigeneity led many people to keep their ancestry secret.[37] This is hardly surprising, as colonising regimes subjected Indigenous people to discriminatory laws, not to mention humiliating derogatory representations and stereotypes. Sadly, such submergence could reinforce the cultural loss that people already faced.[38] Other families had no choice but to be identified as Indigenous and to suffer accordingly. Such oppression and racist slurs led to transgenerational trauma and associated ill-health.[39] In North America, changing state policies, allotment and assimilation policies served to divide members of Indigenous Nations, splintering tribal identity and leading to conflicts over annuity and treaty entitlements. Yet, there are also positive signs. In the past decades, in New Zealand, for example, more people of Māori descent are proudly identifying as such. In Australia, pride in Indigenous identity is epitomised by the aphorism 'Always Was, Always Will Be', the slogan for 2020's National Aboriginal and Islanders Day Observance Committee (NAIDOC) celebrations, known as NAIDOC Week.[40]

Over the last few decades, some governments have attempted to address Indigenous disadvantage, leading to resentment by groups of people who are threatened by the possibilities of changes to the primacy of their longstanding entitlements as white colonisers. In some instances, positive discrimination policies have attracted imposters. Overall, where such strategies exist, they have led to promising results, especially in the sphere of educational opportunities. The most prominent plea from Indigenous people, however, continues to be for self-determination.[41]

★ ★ ★

Although it was not possible in this Companion to cover the history of every Indigenous people of the world, we have achieved as representative an overview as possible within the timeframe and subject to the availability of authors. Despite our best intentions, this volume will inevitably reflect some of the strongest fields of research enquiry, and of course the fields of those scholars who generously agreed to participate in this project. Much scholarship on the dispossession of Indigenous people has focussed on the British Empire. The strongest areas of published research, so much of which is in English, echo the skewed global distribution of scholarly and financial resources. The European powers of Portugal, Spain, Italy, the Netherlands, and France devastated the pre-existing worlds of the original occupants of so many lands around the world; European nations both competed and colluded to ensure their dominance. More recently, southeast Asian nations have enacted colonial dispossession, with the Indigenous people of Papua suffering under extreme relocation policies of the Indonesian government, and the Ainu in Japan continuing to be marginalised, despite their belated recognition.

Our coverage reaches beyond the Anglosphere towards a global story of settler colonialism, including its ongoing legacies and its continuing practices up until the present. We have actively sought out representative historical perspectives from regions where the prominent field of 'settler colonial studies' does not always readily match up – such as in Europe, Africa, Southeast Asia, the Indian subcontinent, and South America. As various contributors to this volume demonstrate, Indigenous peoples have been subjected to sustained imperial and economic, often capitalist, oppression in Southeast and North Asian nations, in the Caribbean, Africa, South America, and elsewhere. In some cases, for example the Caribbean and Asia, we requested chapters that would provide expansive surveys of these regions so that readers could be introduced to the particular political circumstances and complexities of their multiple Indigenous histories. The historical experiences of Indigenous peoples in independent and decolonised nations warrant further scholarly attention in the future.[42]

We cannot emphasise enough that Indigenous peoples of the world are diverse. Their specialised knowledge of their environments has developed over the *longue durée*, while in more recent centuries, their lives have been influenced by varied historical experiences. The Inuit of Alaska, for example, created societies in one of the coldest climates on the planet, and the Indigenous peoples of Ecuador, Indonesia, and African nations did so in some of the hottest environments on the planet. Moreover, over millennia, Indigenous peoples adapted to dramatically changing climates, ecologies, and to the frequently drastic impacts of intruders. Hunters became herders and herders became traders and agriculturalists.

Nor were Indigenous peoples fixed in place. Before and after the imperial era, they travelled locally, continentally, and across the seas; they were mobile people too. In Africa, continental migrations and mobilities across the Atlantic and other oceans make for entangled histories, giving rise to questions of definition around nomadism, landedness, and Indigeneity. The Pacific Islanders, the Polynesian and Melanesian peoples, were great navigators, skilled in diplomacy and confident in asserting their own social hierarchies in the courts of Europe. In this volume, we learn how the Tahitian man Ahutoru travelled aboard Captain Bougainville's triple-masted *Étoile*,⁴³ and about his people's mastery and knowledge of the Pacific Ocean, which long preceded the technologies of the European navigators. When Hawaiian, Indian, and other Indigenous men visited England in the late eighteenth and early nineteenth centuries, the royal courts of Europe feted them as high-status visitors from afar. In later times, for European audiences, Indigenous people became more like subjects of curiosity, featuring in human exhibitions and in the fair-ground entertainments known as human zoos.⁴⁴ By the same token, the Indigenous performers were keenly observing the novel Europeans that they encountered too. The Indigenous gaze and the story of indigenous agency are still missing from many history texts.

This volume is concerned not only with the long-term impacts of history and its interpretations, but also about how various Indigenous people engage in their own historical practices. As Paul Lane's chapter reveals, African history methodologies raise debates around decolonising approaches to historical evidence, effectively challenging scholarly presumptions about the parameters of 'history' and of historical evidence.

Indigenous people shared their knowledge of their Deep History with future generations through performative practices. Clues to ancient histories are embedded in Indigenous languages, dance, and song. Indigenous languages reveal knowledge of the natural world, its sustaining resources and medicines. Oral stories, songs, dances, art, and ritual contain both historical interpretations and encyclopaedic sets of scientific knowledge – botanical, hydraulic, ecological, and astronomical. Other traditions clearly demonstrate ways of remembering and interpreting natural events, including the eruption of volcanoes and island formation. As Chris Ballard's chapter outlines, these narratives recount the past that took place centuries ago, or over 10,000 years ago, and some pertain to the Creation Time. They provide insights into Indigenous sciences, theories about the earth's origins and other geographical features.⁴⁵ Their storytelling across many genres informed Indigenous systems of law and social organisation and interconnected them with neighbouring and distant groups. These narratives should rightly be described as modes of historical practice – as forms of historicity.⁴⁶

In order to work with these interpretative riches, plus a diverse array of other non-text-based evidence, researchers interested in Indigenous history need to expand their skill base. First, academic scholarship needs to develop a better understanding of Indigenous historical practices, but in order to consider Indigenous history in its full range of possibility, the academic history discipline needs to develop additional skills. These might include how insights might be gained from ancient memory narratives transmitted over multiple generations, and from the impressive array of rock art and its contemporary Indigenous interpretations. And it would involve research teams in such fields as archaeology, geomorphology, geography, museology, linguistics, and genomics. Such approaches, including the study of Indigenous histories through deep time, can only be developed in collaboration with Indigenous knowledge holders. In co-designed projects, Indigenous and non-Indigenous scholars and community members will need to ensure ethical protocols are followed at all times.

Ahistorical peoples?

So, readers might wonder why this volume is the first major compendium of global Indigenous history of this scope.[47] For one thing, as discussed in more detail in the First Section of this Companion, History with a capital 'H' has tended to be reserved for the imperial winners. Moreover, even today, Indigenous people may be acknowledged as having 'culture' but not necessarily as having history. Why is this so? In this volume, Henning Trüper examines how the evolution of the history discipline in German and other European institutions served to preclude them from scholarly history writing. Relevant factors include the kinds of text-based evidence and philological interpretative practices upon which the academic discipline grew. Additionally, history writing in the Western world has tended to pivot around rulers, with Kings and Queens defining historical time periods. Chinese historical traditions, too, were arranged around the imperial ruler of the time, the Emperor, with historical accounts divided into their major dynasties. History's metanarratives, including the ambitious new projects of Big History, still tend to pivot around ideas of evolutionary progress and to focus on stories of change, with an implicit plotline that marches through the European enlightenment towards a story of increasing technological complexity. Although some may be wary of the biologically oriented approach to Deep History as elucidated by Andrew Shryock and Daniel Lord Smail, their approach does allow for a plotline of human continuity and commonality.[48]

Overall, most written histories represented Indigenous people's lives as taking place outside the imagined march to progress, and hence outside history. Such hegemonic historical accounts have portrayed Indigenous people's societies as simple, as lacking imagination, innovation, and brilliant inventions. Furthermore, in nineteenth-century Europe, Indigenous peoples were relegated to the lower rungs of a ladder of ascendant human evolution upon which the dominant white elites placed themselves at the pinnacle. European museums promoted imperial agendas, presenting Indigenous people as primitive specimens, with their art also belonging to ethnographic exhibitions rather than high art.[49] This thinking continued through much of the twentieth century. It is as if Indigenous peoples were stuck in a static, primitive pastness that existed outside time – at least the time of history, or historical time. In such narrow European-focussed periodisations, Indigenous history was indeed considered more biological than social. While this has radically changed over the past few decades, it is still often presumed that History with a capital 'H' could only commence after a European arrival.

Despite their relatively recent dates compared with that of Indigenous arrivals, the arrival stories of Europeans came to mark the beginning dates of New World histories. On the American and Australian continents, and across the Pacific, the arrival of Europeans on Indigenous lands became the starting point of the history books, reinforcing a Eurocentric narrative that presupposed the prior absence of 'History'. Triumphal imperial discovery narratives referred only to European discoverers, not to any prior Indigenous discoverers. Historical narratives relied on early written accounts by Europeans – the moments that preceded larger invasions, planned European occupations, and the colonisation of Indigenous lands. In other words, only Europeans made history, wrote history, and featured prominently in its telling. In such imperial mythologies, Europeans were the ones that actually brought 'History' to Indigenous lands. This thinking implied that Indigenous people had previously lacked history altogether, were 'historyless' or in a state of *historia nullius*.[50]

This move robbed Indigenous people of their agency, of staking a place in history where they were the protagonists, the actors in their own story, with the capacity to shape their own worlds and to design their own histories. Additionally, it served to justify the denial of Indigenous rights to authority over their lands, their lives, and that of their own communities. Such histories served to rationalise the unjust removal of Indigenous peoples from their lands, the dispersal of their nations, the decimation of their populations, and the attempted destruction of their cultures. Mainstream accounts portrayed them as children or as child-like, or a child race – inherently lacking and undeserving of control over their own destinies. Such stereotypes served to support contemporary imperial and colonising agendas, and later, to justify European and national entitlements. Indigenous people could not be the history makers.

Mainstream history writing quite explicitly served imperial, colonial, and national political agendas. American, New Zealand, South African, and Canadian history texts displayed parallel preoccupations, although there were differences too. In Australia, state authorities continue to largely ignore the history of frontier warfare. Unlike the museums of Aotearoa/New Zealand, the Australian War Memorial to this day refuses to include the wars that took place between Indigenous Australians and colonisers on Australian soil. Other nations paid attention to histories of conquest and colonising warfare – in Aotearoa to the Māori wars, and in the United States especially to the later frontier wars of the 'Wild West'. Nevertheless, where large-scale warfare was recognised, the mainstream accounts reinforced the story of successful coloniser conquest.[51]

In the late nineteenth and for much of the twentieth century, historians were concerned with the story of Empire and the building of modern nations. Unsurprisingly, national histories reflect ruling interests, and, in this case, the need to justify why they denied Indigenous people their sovereignty. The longer history of this pattern of triumphalism and denialism was epitomised by the great Columbian Exposition in Chicago of 1893, its very name celebrating the vaunted European 'discoverer' of Indigenous lands. It was here that the historian Frederick Jackson Turner delivered his influential lecture on the frontier thesis. Its plotline followed the American history that led to the 'closing of the frontier', an archetypal story of European takeover of vast Indigenous lands. Its finale was contingent upon the 'disappearance of the native' – which took place after Indigenous people finally lost control over their domains in America's West. Turner's frontier thesis provided a compelling narrative about settler-coloniser ascendancy that became a model for history writing elsewhere.[52]

Reflecting such scholarly trends, school history texts patronised or sidelined the Indigenous peoples of their lands as largely irrelevant to the history of their modern nations, and by implication, to their futures. In the case of settler-coloniser nations, the few mentions of Indigenous people generally portrayed them as primitive and undeserving. If warriors, they were 'hostile natives'; such texts reinforced coloniser perspectives, particularly their entitlement to supposedly 'unoccupied' or underused lands. A search of any textbook of national or world history published in the first half of the twentieth century will reveal that accounts of Indigenous history are skewed in such false directions.

As school textbooks functioned as state propaganda justifying coloniser takeover and the suppression of their people, it is troubling to think of the psychological impact on the young Indigenous school children who had to study them.[53] For example, in 1917, 16 years after the Australian colonies federated, Walter Murdoch, a Professor of English in Western Australia, wrote a school textbook about the history of Australia. Echoing the powerful trope of 'undiscovered lands', he entitled his first chapter 'The Unknown Continent'. This was located in a larger section entitled 'The Finders'. By featuring European arrivals as indelibly marking the beginning of history on the Australian continent, he erased the possibility of an Indigenous Australian history or of an Indigenous future. There was nothing subtle about his stance, for he argued that Australian Aboriginal people 'have nothing that can be called a history'. As the stuff of history was change and progress, Aboriginal people must be excluded because 'these blacks knew no change and made no progress'. So 'the historian is not concerned with them. He [sic] is concerned with Australia only as the dwelling-place of white men and women, settlers from overseas.' Only scientists, not historians, he noted, would take an interest because of their 'strange customs'.[54]

Antiquarian interest in Indigenous peoples was overtaken by the increasingly sophisticated discipline of archaeology, which started to specialise in the study of not only the Middle Eastern civilisations but also Indigenous cultures around the globe. Archaeologists focussed on the remaining evidence of Indigenous material culture, particularly on technologies such as stone tools and other durable artefacts. Mid-twentieth-century developments in carbon dating opened up sophisticated dating methods, with more to follow. Although fascinated by technological change over time, scientific analyses often reinforced ideas of human evolution that placed Indigenous people low on the scale and gave pre-eminence to male occupations, overlooking women's manufactures and economic roles.[55]

In the first half of the twentieth century, anthropologists and ethnographers recorded aspects of Indigenous contemporary culture in retrieval projects that anticipated their final demise. Their research aimed to record the 'authentic' cultures, fixed in time, before 'degradation' by colonisers and by various corrupting elements and modernising social changes. It was as if their purpose was to preserve Indigenous cultures in aspic. Stereotypes of the 'authentic native' were already a touchstone in the popular imagination. Having virtually disappeared from the history books, it was envisaged that Indigenous people would soon disappear from the coloniser nation's future. Doomed race predictions even allowed colonisers to express sentimental views. As if in a glorious lament, colonial literature safely romanticised the surviving Indigenous people as 'remnants' or as the 'last of', and as noble savages.[56]

Such imaginings led to the view that to claim Indigeneity, these people had to exhibit features akin to the customs of their society when first recorded by Europeans. Indigenous dress, place of residency, profession, and modes of transport were presumed to be fixed in time. Philip Deloria's *Indians in Unexpected Places* adeptly critiques these views, its cover a commentary in itself, with 'Indians' travelling in a car across the plains. If colonial or any European peoples embraced technological change and adopted modern lifestyles, this was considered normal, essentially Western, and part of the historical 'march of progress' towards new forms of modernity.[57] Yet, when Indigenous people adopted new practices, including cultural and economic adaptations imperative to their survival, they frequently met with disapproval from mainstream society, including accusations of inauthenticity. Urbanised people or those whose families had intermixed were rejected as not fitting into the category.[58] Yet, Indigenous peoples, like all people, often eagerly embraced new technologies, more readily accessible foods, clothing fabrics, and styles. They also embraced new economic opportunities, including fur-trading with European traders, and exercised discernment in seeking out various efficiencies, including more rapid forms of transportation. Where possible, they took up advantageous marital unions.

Over the past four or five decades, the long overdue development of the academic field of Indigenous history has revealed to wider audiences the dynamic, adaptive history of Indigenous peoples, as well as their terrible oppression. New research has started to overturn the self-affirming imperial and coloniser propaganda, its omissions and denials. By the 1980s, a new social-justice-oriented, anti-racist historiography rejected the authority of the earlier, standardised interpretations.[59] These shifts were in part prompted by independence movements and other decolonising events taking place around the world. Although Indigenous protest movements had a much longer history,[60] as Fiona Paisley's chapter shows, the civil rights movements of the 1960s were an energising wake-up call to the world.

The flowering of research in the field of Indigenous history has produced one of the richest, most interdisciplinary fields of historical studies today. Historical truth-telling is having a growing impact on the national psyche of various settler-coloniser states, as they come to grapple with how their nations were founded and progressed. In the past few decades, academic historians have refuted the well-honed myth that benign colonisers and benevolent Empires had rescued, saved, or 'civilised the native'. Indeed, these new histories challenged national narratives to such an extent that in the United States and Australia, the strength of the backlashes that took place in the 1980s and 1990s were labelled the history wars and the culture wars.[61]

Despite the increasing profile of such retellings, this fraught history is not necessarily to the forefront of many national histories or their historical consciousness. Understandably, in the United States and the Caribbean, for example, the horrors of slavery, with its highly visible legacies, tend to dominate the discussion. In the Pacific, it is often the history of blackbirding and coercive labour and associated internecine violence and histories of emigration. In North America, the Indian reserves are usually in relatively remote locations away from the main population centres, and being out of the general purview, they are overlooked. Indigenous dispossession was fundamental to the formation of many nation states, enabling colonisers to gain the lands and resources upon which Indigenous Nations had relied. It continues to create the wealth and sustenance of settler-coloniser nations that reap the benefits. Indeed, Indigenous dispossession was the 'original sin' of many coloniser states.

Academic history is now at another kind of turning point, as new generations of talented Indigenous scholars enter the field, overturning well-worn approaches and enriching understandings. Recent work on the American frontier by Ojibwe historian Jean O'Brien served to underline the prevailing coloniser historical mythologies in which Europeans glorified 'firsting' or first European sightings of Indigenous lands, at the same time lamenting the 'last' Indigene like some accidental disappearance that needed to be closed off in a final chapter. Abenaki historian Lisa Brooks has mapped the politics and liveliness of ongoing, often thriving Indigenous worlds, including the power of kinship networks during periods of coloniser intrusion. Susan Sleeper-Smith and others have demonstrated how Native American women conducted far more successful agricultural and trading enterprises than the early colonists, until thwarted by state-backed gendered violence and suppression.[62]

Historical scholarship may be on the cusp of a new era that starts to articulate the primacy of Indigenous knowledge, often described as 'decolonising the academy'. Although the task, the underpinnings of which Ben Silverstein discusses in his chapter, is challenging, and a comprehensive 'decolonisation' of imperial institutions may be out of reach, the old order is being questioned powerfully and effectively. Indigenous historical traditions are being practised in fresh, inventive ways. As discussed in Ann McGrath's chapter, community knowledge websites, storytelling, cultural mapping, animation, interactive exhibitions, and other Indigenous-led digital projects are thriving. Some of this is changing academic practice. In recent decades, more Indigenous people are joining the academy as senior scholars, senior University executives, and in a new generation of students. Indigenous scholars and community members are writing their own histories, using approaches that draw upon standpoint theory, which does not shy away from foregrounding Indigenous subjectivities.[63] Indigenous curators and practitioners are working in the arts, in museums and public institutions; they are directing art gallery and museum exhibitions, music, dance, and other public performances that present Indigenous histories and that critique dominant histories. Paul Lane's chapter demonstrates how African scholars are likely to revolutionise approaches to archaeology. Indigenous practices of historical narration and interpretation have the potential to expand and deepen historical scholarship within the Western academy.

Greater insights into Indigenous history, and the prospect and possibilities of a Global Indigenous History, are urgently needed. As the UNDRIP recognised, the oppression of Indigenous peoples is historically based, but it continues in the present. In recent decades, Indigenous people are still being subjected to repeated dispossessions and attacks that impact their ability to practise their economic activities and cultural values and to live without interference. Despite their ongoing protests, they often lack the power to block the destruction of sacred places. As seen in the Amazon and parts of India, and for the residents of the Standing Rock Sioux Reservation near the Dakota pipeline development in North America, Indigenous peoples have little recourse, with state authorities prioritising capitalist enterprises and extractive industries over cherished Indigenous beliefs and aspirations. In the case of the British atomic testing at Maralinga in Central Australia in the 1950s and 1960s, as Heather Goodall's chapter explains, the Pitjantjatjara people were not even consulted. As previously mentioned, in June 2020, the mining company Rio Tinto destroyed important caves in Western Australia. Company executives had known that they were considered sacred by their traditional owners and an archaeologist had assessed them as of the highest archaeological significance, with rare items such as crafted human hair.[64] As Devleena Ghosh's chapter outlines, the lands of the Adivasi people of India are under continuous threat from mining. Clearly, it remains in the interest of certain companies and nations to overlook Indigenous values, and to portray Indigenous people as resisting modernity – as belonging to a static past rather than to an adaptive history or a productive future.

What is Indigenous history?

In discussing the relevance of greater knowledge of Indigenous history, it is worth noting that the term 'Indigenous history' can be variously interpreted. It can be defined as a practice that gives prominence to Indigenous experiences; that is, it focusses on Indigenous people as the main subjects or actors. It can also refer to histories that are compiled and written by Indigenous authors. Additionally, it can refer to Indigenous historical traditions that take place outside the academy – those previously classed as myth and legend, but which, as we previously argued, should be appreciated as Indigenous modes of historical practice.[65] This volume presents all three kinds of Indigenous history, and, in order to do so, the authors showcase a variety of writing styles and techniques.

The value of the multifaceted term 'Indigenous history' is that it signals that the author is emphasising Indigeneity or the Indigenous experience as the focus of their subject matter. People working in the field continue to fill yawning knowledge gaps, addressing serious shortcomings in the literature and in common understandings. As discussed, such perspectives are increasingly being integrated into mainstream historical accounts. At the same time, however, discrete Indigenous spaces such as specialist publishing enterprises and journals that present specialised Indigenous knowledges, along with dedicated Centres, research and teaching departments, remain necessary and beneficial.

As indicated, the contents of this Companion do not overlook the fact that Indigenous groups have strong, enduring traditions by which they narrate their own histories and communicate these to wider audiences. As chapters by Paul Lane, Gregory Smithers, May-Britt Öhman, and others attest, they do so within the lifespan scale of biographies and autobiographies, and within the longer span of cross-generational accounts and beyond, into deep time. In the early nineteenth century, the Cherokees, for example, developed a range of strategies for showcasing their long history in the southeastern United States, in particular the Smoky Mountains region. In a project, they designed in the 1830s to counter exclusively European-focussed histories and to provide proof of their enduring sovereignty, Chief John Ross of the Cherokee Nation engaged the popular American author and actor, John Howard Payne, to put together a written history of the Cherokee Nation. It was to be based upon a collection of the oral histories of the most knowledgeable Chiefs and elders. Authorities in the state of Georgia clearly saw this work as a political threat, as they arrested and imprisoned both Ross and Payne and temporarily confiscated the papers upon which they were working. Despite many reminders, Payne, who is best known for writing the lyrics of 'Home Sweet Home', never completed the task of writing the historical account for which Ross had engaged him.[66] However, he amassed a large collection of data, and the rich contents of the original archive are available at the Newberry library in Chicago and in a multi-volume publication.[67] Perhaps Payne was distracted, or perhaps he simply did not know how to turn this collection of Indigenous knowledge into something akin to a written history. After their move to Oklahoma, the Cherokees continued to develop a national archive that contained key records such as details of their Council meetings and other formal records of state, thereby enabling scholars to access curated sets of text-based evidence that lend themselves to Western-style history writing.

Although rarely acknowledged as authors or editors, Indigenous people around the world have generously agreed to record their histories for amateur collectors, ethnographers, and linguists, which has created an important global archive. In one unusual case in the 1920s, David Unaipon, a Ngarrindjeri man from South Australia, was engaged by a leading publisher and paid to record, translate, and prepare numerous Indigenous narratives for a publication. Acknowledging that these were commonly known as 'legends', he explained in the book's introduction that for his people they were 'histories'. In a scandal only made public in 2001, the publisher had attributed authorship to a European with the credentials of medical officer, coroner, and amateur anthropologist.[68] In recent decades, there has been an increasing demand for direct historical accounts by Indigenous authors and various mainstream and specialist Indigenous publishers have assisted in bringing these to light.

Debates over whether ancient Indigenous memories should be understood as myth or history continue. Climate scientist Patrick Nunn has argued that some accounts can be traced back more than 10,000 years before the present. Various scholars have argued against the credibility of Indigenous oral histories, while others are seeking to prove their veracity by matching them with Western scientific data.[69] In this volume, Chris Ballard helps us through this controversy, demonstrating how people of Papua New Guinea and the Pacific Islands developed complex accounts of historical events such as the eruption of volcanoes.

Inside and outside the academy, historical practices fulfil a range of functions, deploying various strategies and techniques. Using examples from India, Dipesh Chakrabarty discussed how the explanatory frameworks implicit in historical causation differed according to cultural beliefs.[70] As Peter Nabokov demonstrated in a *Forest of Time*, there are a great range of performative techniques by which

Native American histories are interpreted and presented.[71] In the 1990s, Jimmy Mangarrayi, an esteemed historian of the Gurindji in the Northern Territory of Australia, taught Japanese scholar Minoru Hokari how Gurindji historical accounts involved journeys across the landscape, following a moral direction from east to west.[72] In this volume, we learn of how the displaced Miami woman Elizabeth Lindsay Palmer used Indigenous storytelling to transmit a continuing identity which enhanced kinship and communal bonds.[73] Donald Fixico (Shawnee, Sac and Fox, Muscogee Creek, and Seminole) argued that history was 'medicine' that could achieve healing of the body and mind.[74]

Despite suppression and intrusions, on and off reserves, many Indigenous people adapted new techniques to ensure that they could continue to sustain their communities and modes of history telling. Indigenous storytelling and history telling through art, pottery, clothing, body painting, and craft skills have inspired wider artistic movements and Indigenous art exchanges around the world. Epic Indigenous narratives, songs, music, dance, art, and other traditions constitute distinctive cultural forms of historicity. Today, these long traditions of history telling are showcased in language revival programmes, in brilliant Indigenous-directed films, award-winning television series, podcasts, digital products, and innovative museum exhibitions.

Our approach

In aiming to achieve a global spread, we attempted to obtain coverage of the key continental and geographical areas of the planet: Oceania, the Americas, and Europe. While we were fully cognisant that there would be gaps, we were pleased to obtain chapters that discussed Greater Asia, the Southeast Asian region, Australia, the Pacific Islands, Papua New Guinea, Africa, the Americas, and the Caribbean. We included chapters set in Greenland and Sweden concerning the Inuit and Sámi people of northern Europe. No one chapter contains a complete global perspective as such, but through juxtaposing regional studies and tackling discrete themes, we hoped to escape the constraints of national framings and to piece together a much larger picture.

Practitioners of Indigenous history sometimes emphasise that Indigenous histories are inherently local and should be studied that way. By their nature, Indigenous histories certainly emphasise intimate connections with an animated, living landscape. Their storytelling modes are often prompted and told in special places of Indigenous connection. Yet, as Indigenous history is also a topic of significance across the planet, we seek to think about it as global too. We define a global approach as one that attempts a reach beyond the tribal and the national. As we believe in the value of rich, intimate, local studies, we did not ask every contributor to provide a comprehensive 'global approach' in tackling their subject matter. Some chapters emphasise the author's focus area and specialisation; others offer a more comprehensive introduction to a larger theme or geographic region. Overall, however, we encouraged authors to think of their key topics in both a local and a global context. In Fiona Paisley's chapter, for example, you will learn of

AM Fernando of Australia, who, through exposing the oppression of Aboriginal Australians on the European stage, attempted to influence the First World Conservation Conference in Bern, Switzerland towards a new internationalism.

We asked leading Indigenous and non-Indigenous historians and other experts to prepare chapters that contained a synthesis of major themes for a larger, non-specialist audience, but that also included original material and fresh analyses from their very latest research. Although, as indicated, we requested some overview and survey chapters, we balanced these with chapters that featured emblematic case studies. Contributors were encouraged to balance the micro and macro, zooming in and out between the specific and the larger picture. Richly told stories of individuals elucidate how various Indigenous peoples responded to local historical circumstances.

We encouraged people to write in ways that they considered most appropriate for what drives their practice and was best suited to their subject matter. We urged them to write in ways that would aptly reflect their own voice and subjectivity. Consequently, you will notice a diversity of voices and different approaches to writing. For example, Sámi scholar May-Britt Öhman shares a personal story about the Lule River Valley, which showcases the beautiful storytelling tradition of *subttsasa biehtsevuomátjistema* which means 'stories from our little pine forest'. Historian John Maynard, a Worimi man, writes from an Aboriginal Australian perspective, but his animal-human kinship stories of affinity with the dolphin and dingo evoke common themes applicable to many Indigenous people globally. In her moving chapter, Lynette Russell takes an autoethnographic approach to her family's history.

We see this volume as making some tentative steps towards enhancing a global perspective on Indigenous history. Several themes of global significance are tackled in individual chapters. While no Companion volume can be comprehensive, it can highlight the latest thinking and new developments on a range of themes and in a variety of contexts. Through the juxtaposition of studies conducted for various places and along various scales, we can glean insights about many of the differences and similarities in historical experiences and impacts. Embracing decolonising approaches, the contributors paid careful attention to collaborative and ethical approaches to their subject matter.

Introducing the sections

The Companion is organised into thematic sections. First, in **A global perspective,** the chapters reflect upon why Indigenous peoples have been excluded from mainstream histories. Henning Trüper discusses the European evolution of the history discipline and its uses, while Ben Silverstein summarises some of the theoretical frontiers and approaches of the new Indigenous histories. Robert Cribb then explores the long history of Indigenous peoples of Asia, which are often overlooked in studies of colonialism and imperialism. Fiona Paisley introduces the story of an Indigenous activist who was very much an outsider, but whose courageous international exposure of the atrocities committed against Indigenous people and their lands aimed to influence sectors of the global environmental movement.

The second section, **Migrations and mobilities**, starts with two well-informed accounts of the early human migrations across the globe and to North America – one by archaeologist and expert in early hominids, Martin Porr, another by Indigenous archaeologist Paulette Steeves. Peter Veth and team then explore the astonishing time-span over which the rock art practices of Western Australia were created. Kate Fullagar then takes us aboard ocean voyages that demonstrate the acumen of Polynesian voyagers from the Havai'i diaspora. Coll Thrush's chapter takes us on a unique walking tour of London, via the places visited by early Indigenous visitors from various parts of the globe to the imperial metropole. The third section, **Colonial encounters**, considers another kind of interactive place, with Joy Porter's analysis of treatied spaces. Linda Andersson Burnett's chapter focusses on the Sámi of Scandinavia and the British and Swedish scientists who were interested in studying them during the nineteenth century. Laura Rademaker's chapter explores the significance of language, translation, and transformation in Indigenous mission contexts. Brooke Newman enables readers to learn of the complexities of slavery, intermixing, and native ancestry in the Caribbean. Embracing the trauma of colonial encounter, Taylor Spence's chapter provides a deeply personal historical reflection that considers the emotional challenge of exploring historical and lived encounters.

Section four, **Removals and diasporas**, opens with Manuela Picq examining the impact of imperial gender modelling in the Americas, which was to the detriment of more fluid models of gender. Greg Smithers demonstrates how, after forced removal to the west, the Miami and other tribes remembered their traditional homes through native storytelling practices. Lucinda Aberdeen, Katherine Ellinghaus, Kella Robinson, and Judi Wickes reflect upon the power of Indigenous women in keeping Indigenous communities strong, even when away from their Country or homelands. Heather Goodall then exposes how British nuclear tests in Central Australia disregarded Indigenous health and well-being, with tragic after-effects. In 'The Bones of Our Mother', Devleena Ghosh follows with a study of how mining has devastated and continues to dispossess the Adivasi people of India.

Memory, identities, and narratives, the theme of section five, starts with Lynette Russell's story of researching and writing about the Indigenous secrets of her family's history, which saw the publication of the influential book *A Little Bird Told Me*. Archaeologist Chris Urwin then takes us to Papua New Guinea, where people narrate their memories of objects removed by colonisers. Barry Higman's chapter probes whether newly available scientific evidence, particularly DNA techniques, verifies common understandings of Indigenous identity in the Caribbean. May-Britt Öhman recalls childhood trips to her little pine forest and what that means for her Sámi identity, followed by Claude Gélinas considering secularism, Christianity, and the law in Canada.

The last section, **Pathways towards future Indigenous histories**, reflects upon the value of Indigenous strategies and methodologies that enrich and expand the discipline of history. Such pathways will enable researchers to develop collaborative approaches to researching, analysing, and presenting the global history of Indigenous peoples. Using Pacific and Oceanic examples, Chris Ballard provides a masterful overview of debates around ancient Indigenous memory narratives, carefully scrutinising their potential value for history telling. Focussing on Africa, Paul Lane considers academic archaeology in relation to community knowledge and develops the possibilities of 'hybrid knowledge'. Oliver Haag considers German attitudes to Indigenous people from the colonial era through to the Nazi era, analysing Indigenous photography as both subject and method. Ashleigh Harris's chapter explains how African literature is an important form of Indigenous history. Reintroducing the idea of Indigenous people as 'a people without history', and examining how traditional historiography over-emphasises the text and underplays the senses, Emilie Wellfelt provides a microstudy of the people of Alor – an island in the Indonesian archipelago – who, she argues, have archived the past in bodies and landscapes. As Claire McLisky and Kirstine Eiby Møller explain, although outsiders wrote numerous histories of Greenland, the Greenlanders themselves have produced innovative written and other histories that showcase their perspectives.

Moving to Australia, with its exceptionally long Indigenous history, two chapters reflect on the need to expand history's chronologies beyond the eras of imperialism and colonialism. John Maynard discusses anthropological portrayals of the Indigenous legends, of the dreaming concept, and provides his own take on animal-human narratives and engagements. Ann McGrath's chapter starts with the dinosaur footprints of Broome, to reflect upon present-day Indigenous and non-Indigenous engagements with histories that go back to the Pleistocene, including with individuals who lived in Western New South Wales at least 40,000 years ago, and places in the far north where Indigenous communities lived 65,000 years ago. She considers the future of Indigenous histories using digital projects.

In this Companion, we bring together the histories of many Indigenous people around the globe, on that tiny planet whose home is the Milky Way. Like other populations of the world, we make the case that should not need to be made, yet still does: that Indigenous people *have* a history. Their long histories have shaped their particular ways of looking at the world, both in the deep past that may span over 65,000 years, such as in the case of Indigenous Australians, or according to the arrival stories that took place hundreds of years ago for Māori people of Aotearoa.

As demonstrated in this volume, Indigenous people have histories in common, and histories that are quite distinctive from those of other Indigenous peoples. They share stories of curiosity, invention, intellectual work, of pain and resilience. As well as having such lived histories, they also had their own historicities, or ways of exploring, interpreting, and narrating their pasts. They practise rich traditions of storytelling in diverse languages and mediums. They have grand narratives that are genres of history too. Indigenous elders and scholars have led the way in sharing their histories with the wider public, arguably cultivating an Indigenous renaissance. For example, the National Museum of the American Indian, prominently located on the National Mall, Washington DC, which opened in 2004, represented community-curated exhibitions of Indigenous Nations across the Americas, taking in the continent from its far north to the tip of South America. The UN Year of Indigenous Peoples in 1993 and the UN Year of Indigenous Languages in 2019 saw major celebrations of cultural survival and new initiatives to record and revive Indigenous languages around the globe.

Being Indigenous should not be thought of in terms of deficit, of victimisation or defeat. Yes, there has been deep loss, but Indigenous ways of looking at the world offer insights into ways of living that touch the earth lightly. Their artistic and historical traditions are profound and inspiring, holding important clues and pathways towards a healthier global future. As suggested in the opening of this introduction, appreciating the wealth of indigenous culture and history holds lessons that could lead the way to a sustainable world and potentially towards more satisfying lives for individuals and communities.

Moreover, Indigenous people's stories constantly remind us of the beauties of sky, sea, and earth, and of the riches of historical imaginations. The vibrations of feet dancing can mean many things when you have knowledge of so many layers of a sacred environment that most city-dwellers would not even notice. All the elements are deeply important to many different Indigenous peoples, as is a close relationship with and knowledge of plants, rocks, ochres, animals and insects, clouds, winds, tides, mountains, plains, deserts, lakes, rivers, and sea. Indigenous peoples have a sense of being in place, of knowing the land – land that embraced them as kin, that enabled them to know a sense of well-being, strength, and belonging. They reject the idea that to be Indigenous is to be pre-modern, to be primitive, and to have to remain in a stasis defined by a Western gaze.

Understanding Indigenous history better will enable people to get out of this static ahistorical mind-set. As you will read in this Companion, Indigenous peoples travelled the globe in the most significant human migrations of deep time and through the imperial period.[75] Indigenous peoples were dynamic, rapidly transforming their societies for purposes of survival and revival, but also holding onto the values and aspirations that they held dear. Choosing to change aspects of their past practices, they do not over-romanticise the difficulties, regimes, and restrictions of their earlier lifestyles.

Everyone can learn from such histories, of how Indigenous Nations and individuals changed and how their societies evolved, despite adversity. By prompting reflection upon human resilience, and upon experiences that took place outside modernity, including in deep time, Indigenous histories can potentially unite humanity.

In order to expand their horizons, however, Indigenous and non-Indigenous scholars will need to experiment with and integrate relatively unfamiliar strategies for researching, writing, and otherwise presenting history. As is explored in the final thematic section of this Companion, both Indigenous and non-Indigenous historians could benefit by developing digital methodologies for representing and critiquing Indigenous storytelling, methodologies for analysing photography as a method for global history, and methods to incorporate relevant DNA, geological, and other scientific evidence relevant to Indigenous history not only in the modern and ancient times, but as far back as the Pleistocene period.

Indigenous histories remind us of human cruelty and the dominance of the powerful. Indigenous rituals and stories remind us of the principles and values behind building a strong community and encouraging peaceable relations with outsiders.[76] Stars guided Indigenous people in navigation, morality, and appropriate behaviour. Stories of the Seven Sisters are told by various Indigenous peoples around the world, and so too there are stories of sacred, all-powerful serpents.

Dynamically told, Indigenous histories will allow us to look beyond the pre-modern, the so-called medieval and the several thousand years usually called ancient history set in the Middle East and North Africa; we will journey further afield and into human history beyond the Anthropocene and the Holocene. Indigenous histories take us outside the temporal and spatial circuitry intrinsic to the histories and mythologies of European civilisations. Escaping these parameters will lead to enriching and vital new perspectives that will inform global history in general.

Notes

1 Numerous global histories have been published and global history is a field in itself. For example, see Jurgen Osterhammel, *The Transformation of the World: A Global History of the Nineteenth Century* (Princeton, NJ: Princeton University Press, 2014); Dipesh Chakrabarty, *The Crises of Civilization: Exploring Global and Planetary Histories* (New Delhi: Oxford University Press, 2018).
2 According to the United Nations Permanent Forum on Indigenous Issues, Indigenous people are defined as having (among other things) 'historical continuity with pre-colonial and/or pre-settler societies, and strong link to territories and surrounding natural resources'. The World Health Organization specifies, 'Indigenous populations are communities that live within, or are attached to, geographically distinct traditional habitats or ancestral territories, and who identify themselves as being part of a distinct cultural group, descended from groups present in the area before modern states were created and current borders defined.' There are currently over 370 million Indigenous people spread in 70 countries worldwide, from the Pacific Ocean in the South to the Arctic in the North. https://www.un.org/development/desa/indigenouspeoples/about-us.html, https://www.who.int/topics/health_services_indigenous/en/
3 Vine Deloria Jr, 'Self-Determination and the Concept of Sovereignty,' in *Native American Sovereignty*, ed. J.R. Wunder (New York and London: Garland, 1999), 107–114.
4 Gregory D. Smithers and Brooke N. Newman, eds., *Native Diasporas: Indigenous Identities and Settler Colonialism in the Americas* (Lincoln: University of Nebraska Press, 2014).
5 John Maynard, *Fight for Liberty and Freedom: The Origins of Australian Aboriginal Activism* (Canberra: Aboriginal Studies Press, 2007). See Paisley chapter.
6 Ann McGrath and Mary Anne Jebb, eds., *Long History Deep Time* (Canberra: ANU Press, 2015).
7 See Picq chapter.
8 Heather Burke, Bryce Barker, Noelene Cole, Lynley A. Wallis, Elizabeth Hatte, Iain Davidson, and Kelsey Lowe, 'The Queensland Native Police and Strategies of Recruitment on the Queensland Frontier, 1849–1901,' *Journal of Australian Studies* 42, no. 3 (2018): 297–313. See also Pekka Hämäläinen, *The Comanche Empire* (New Haven, CT: Yale University Press, 2008).
9 See Aberdeen, Ellinghaus, Robinson, and Wickes chapter; Ann McGrath, *Illicit Love: Interracial Sex and Marriage in the United States and Australia* (Lincoln: University of Nebraska Press, 2015); Ann McGrath, ed., *Contested Ground: Australian Aborigines Under the British Crown* (Sydney: Allen & Unwin, 1995); Jane Lydon, *Remembering the Myall Creek Massacre*, ed. Lyndall Ryan (Sydney: University of New South Wales Press, 2018). Philip G. Dwyer and Lyndall Ryan, eds., *Theatres of Violence: Massacre, Mass Killing and Atrocity Throughout History* (New York: Berghahn Books, Incorporated, 2012).
10 Margaret Jacobs, *White Mother to a Dark Race: Settler Colonialism, Maternalism, and the Removal of Indigenous Children in the American West and Australia, 1880–1940* (Lincoln: University of Nebraska Press, 2011); Margaret D. Jacobs, *A Generation Removed: The Fostering and Adoption of Indigenous Children in the Postwar World* (Lincoln: University of Nebraska Press, 2014). See also Aberdeen, Ellinghaus, Robinson, and Wickes chapter.

11. Jacinta Koolmatrie, 'Destruction of Juukan Gorge,' *The Conversation*, 2 June 2020; Ann McGrath, 'Monumental Discovery Narratives and Deep History,' *Humanities Australia* 11 (2020): 69–80.
12. Ian McNiven and Lynette Russell, *Appropriated Pasts: Indigenous Peoples and the Colonial Culture of Archaeology* (Lanham. MD: AltaMira Press, 2005).
13. A.L. Stoler, 'Tense and Tender Ties: The Politics of Comparison in North American History and (Post)Colonial Studies,' *The Journal of American History* 88, no. 3 (2001): 829–865; Tony Ballantyne and Antoinette Burton, *Empires and the Reach of the Global, 1870–1945* (Cambridge, MA: Belknap Press, 2012).
14. Stoler, 'Tense and Tender Ties.'
15. See Higman and Newman chapters; Claudio Saunt, *Black, White, and Indian: Race and the Unmaking of an American Family* (New York: Oxford University Press, 2006); Theda Perdue, *Mixed Blood Indians: Racial Construction in the Early South* (Athens: University of Georgia Press, 2003).
16. McGrath, *Illicit Love*; Richard White, *The Middle Ground: Indians, Empires, and Republics in the Great Lakes Region, 1650–1815* (Cambridge and New York: Cambridge University Press, 1991); Lynette Russell, *Roving Mariners: Australian Aboriginal Whalers and Sealers in the Southern Oceans, 1790–1870* (New York: SUNY Press, 2012).
17. Sylvia van Kirk, *Many Tender Ties: Women in Fur-Trade Society, 1670–1870* (Norman: University of Oklahoma Press, 1983).
18. See Maynard, Porr, and Steeves chapters.
19. Rhys Jones, 'Introduction,' in *Sunda and Sahul: Prehistoric Studies in Southeast Asia, Melanesia and Australia*, ed. Jim Allen, Jack Golson, and Rhys Jones (London: Academic Press, 1977), 2.
20. See Fullager, McClisky and Møller, and Rademaker chapters; Tony Ballantyne, *Webs of Empire: Locating New Zealand's Colonial Past* (Vancouver: UBC Press, 2010).
21. See Öhman chapter.
22. See Smithers chapter.
23. Elvira Pulitano, ed., *Indigenous Rights in the Age of the UN Declaration* (Cambridge: Cambridge University Press, 2012).
24. Pulitano, ed., *Indigenous Rights*.
25. Cited in Dominic O'Sullivan, *We Are All Here to Stay: Sovereignty, Citizenship and the UN Declaration on the Rights of Indigenous Peoples* (Canberra: ANU Press, 2020).
26. O'Sullivan, *We Are All Here to Stay*, 1; see also 'United Nations Declaration on the Rights of Indigenous Peoples,' 13 September 2007, https://www.un.org/development/desa/indigenouspeoples/declaration-on-the-rights-of-indigenous-peoples.html.
27. O'Sullivan, *We Are All Here to Stay*; see also Dominic O'Sullivan, *Indigeneity: A Politics of Potential: Australia, Fiji and New Zealand* (Bristol: Policy Press, 2017). Legal historian Dominic O'Sullivan has argued that a distinctive liberal theory of Indigeneity that embodies liberal concepts of sovereignty, citizenship, and democracy has been applied: 'A liberal theory of indigeneity is not a theory of egalitarian justice; nor is it a theory concerned with the rights of poor people.' Indeed, its claims went beyond property and the domain of material things, encompassing rights to a distinctive political voice, and rights to language and culture: 'These rights embody a special moral significance because they are rights that colonialism has usurped.' O'Sullivan, *We Are All Here to Stay*, 2–4; 13. See also Patrick Wolfe, 'Structure and Event: Settler Colonialism, Time, and the Question of Genocide,' in *Empire, Colony, Genocide: Conquest, Occupation, and Subaltern Resistance in World History*, ed. A. Dirk Moses (New York: Berghahn Books, 2008), 102–132; J. Kēhaulani Kauanui, '"A Structure, Not an Event": Settler Colonialism and Enduring Indigeneity,' *Lateral* 5, no. 1 (2016).
28. Megan Davis, 'The United Nations Declaration on the Rights of Indigenous Peoples,' *Indigenous Law Bulletin* 6, no. 30 (2007).
29. UNDRIP, 13 September 2007, https://www.un.org/development/desa/indigenous-peoples/wp-content/uploads/sites/19/2018/11/UNDRIP_E_web.pdf.

30 O'Sullivan, *We Are All Here to Stay*, 6.
31 'C169 - Indigenous and Tribal Peoples Convention, 1989,' Jakarta, International Labour Office, 25 June 2007, https://www.ilo.org/jakarta/whatwedo/publications/WCMS_124013/lang--en/index.htm.
32 UNDRIP, 9–10; see also Aberdeen, Ellinghaus, Robinson, and Wickes chapter.
33 National Inquiry into the Separation of Aboriginal and Torres Strait Islander Children from Their Families (Australia), *Bringing Them Home: Report of the National Inquiry into the Separation of Aboriginal and Torres Strait Islander Children from Their Families* (Sydney: Human Rights and Equal Opportunities Commission, 1997); Trish Luker, 'Reading the Evidentiary Void: The Body at the Scene of Writing,' *Griffith Law Review* 18, no. 2 (2009): 298–313.
34 UNDRIP, 11–12.
35 Ann McGrath, 'Shamrock Aborigines: The Irish, the Aboriginal Australians and Their Children,' *Aboriginal History* 34 (2010): 55–84.
36 See Aberdeen, Ellinghaus, Robinson, and Wickes, and Smithers chapters ; Katherine Ellinghaus, *Blood Will Tell: Native Americans and Assimilation Policy* (Lincoln: University of Nebraska Press, 2017).
37 See Russell chapter; Lynette Russell, *A Little Bird Told Me: Family Secrets, Necessary Lies* (St Leonards: Allen and Unwin, 2002).
38 See Russell chapter; Lynette Russell, 'What the Little Bird Didn't Tell Me,' *Victorian Historical Journal* 91, no. 1 (Jun 2020): 5–15; Sally Morgan, *My Place* (Fremantle: Fremantle Arts Centre, 1987); Jacobs, *White Mother to a Dark Race*.
39 Jackie Huggins, *Aunty Rita* (Canberra: Aboriginal Studies Press, 1994).
40 See Aberdeen, Ellinghaus, Robinson, and Wickes chapter; Anna Haebich, *Broken Circles: Fragmenting Indigenous Families 1800–2000* (Fremantle: Fremantle Arts Centre Press, 2000); Anna Haebich, *Spinning the Dream: Assimilation in Australia 1950–1970* (Fremantle: Fremantle Arts Centre Press, 2008); Bain Attwood, *Telling the Truth about Aboriginal History.* (St Leonards, Allen & Unwin, 2005).
41 Marcia Langton, Lisa Palmer, Maureen Tehan, and Kathryn Shain, eds., *Honour Among Nations? Treaties and Agreements with Indigenous People* (Carlton: Melbourne University Press, 2004); Marcia Langton, Odette Mazel, Lisa Palmer, Kathryn Shain, and Maureen Tehan, eds., *Settling with Indigenous People: Modern Treaty and Agreement-Making* (Annandale: Federation Press, 2006). Günter Minnerup and Pia Solberg, eds., *First World, First Nations: Internal Colonialism and Indigenous Self-Determination in Northern Europe and Australia* (Brighton: Sussex Academic Press, 2011); Laura Rademaker and Tim Rowse, eds., *Indigenous Self-Determination in Australia* (Canberra: ANU Press, 2020).
42 Pratik Chakrabarti, 'Gondwana and the Politics of Deep Past,' *Past & Present* 242, no. 1 (2019): 119–153.
43 See Fullagar chapter; Kate Fullagar and Michael A. McDonnell, eds., *Facing Empire: Indigenous Experiences in a Revolutionary Age* (Baltimore, MD: John Hopkins University Press, 2018).
44 See Andersson Burnett chapter; Roslyn Poignant, *Professional Savages: Captive Lives and Western Spectacle* (Sydney: University of New South Wales Press, 2004).
45 See Ballard, Lane, and Smithers chapters.
46 McGrath and Jebb, eds., *Long History Deep Time*.
47 See Kenneth Coates, *A Global History of Indigenous Peoples: Struggle and Survival* (Basingstoke and New York: Palgrave Macmillan, 2004).
48 Daniel Lord Smail, *On Deep History and the Brain* (Berkeley: University of California Press, 2008); Andrew Shryock and Daniel Lord Smail, *Deep History: The Architecture of Past and Present* (Berkeley: University of California Press, 2011); David Christian, *Maps of Time: An Introduction to Big History* (Berkeley: University of California Press, 2004); David Armitage, 'What's the Big Idea? Intellectual History and the *Longue Durée*,' *History of European Ideas* 38, no. 4 (2012): 493–507.

49 McNiven and Russell, *Appropriated Pasts*; Lynette Russell, *Savage Imaginings: Historical and Contemporary Constructions of Australian Aboriginalities* (Melbourne: Australian Scholarly Publishing, 2001); Lynette Russell, 'Remembering Places Never Visited: Connections and Context in Imagined and Imaginary Landscapes,' *International Journal of Historical Archaeology* 16, no. 2 (2012): 401–417; Wendy Shaw, *Possessors and Possessed: Museums, Archaeology, and the Visualization of History in the Late Ottoman Empire* (Berkeley: University of California Press, 2003); Bonnie Effros and Guolong Lai, eds., *Unmasking Ideology in Imperial and Colonial Archaeology: Vocabulary and Symbols* (Los Angeles: Cotsen Institute of Archaeology Press, 2018).

50 See Silverstein chapter; Patrick Wolfe, *Settler Colonialism and the Transformation of Anthropology: The Politics and Poetics of an Ethnographic Event* (London: Cassell, 1999).

51 See Chris Healy, *From the Ruins of Colonialism: History as Social Memory* (New York: Cambridge University Press, 1997).

52 Frederick Jackson Turner, *The Frontier in American History* (New York: Henry Holt, 1920).

53 Ann McGrath, 'Is History Good Medicine?' *Journal of Australian Studies* 38, no. 4 (2014): 396–414.

54 Walter Murdoch, *The Making of Australia* (Melbourne: Whitcombe and Tombs, 1917), 10; McGrath, 'Monumental Discovery Narratives and Deep History'; Robert J. Miller, Jacinta Ruru, Larissa Behrendt, and Tracey Lindberg, *Discovering Indigenous Lands: The Doctrine of Discovery in the English Colonies* (Oxford: Oxford University Press, 2010).

55 McNiven and Russell, *Appropriated Pasts*.

56 For an excellent overview of the dying race discourse from a North American perspective, see Robert F. Heizer and Theodora Kroeber, eds.,. *Ishi the Last Yahi: A Documentary History* (Berkeley: University of California Press, 1979).

57 Phil Deloria, *Indians in Unexpected Places* (Lawrence: University Press of Kansas, 2004).

58 Anita Heiss, *Am I Black Enough for You?* (Sydney: Bantam, 2012).

59 For an important interrogation of the role of feminism and 'white women' in the ongoing colonial project, see Aileen Moreton-Robinson, *Talkin' Up to the White Woman: Indigenous Women and Feminism* (St Lucia: University of Queensland Press, 2000).

60 Denise E. Bates, *The Other Movement: Indian Rights and Civil Rights in the Deep South* (Tuscaloosa: University of Alabama Press, 2012); Bain Attwood and Andrew Markus, eds., *The Struggle for Aboriginal Rights: A Documentary History* (Sydney: Allen & Unwin, 1998); John Chesterman, *Civil Rights: How Indigenous Australians Won Formal Equality* (St Lucia: University of Queensland Press, 2005); Russell McGregor, *Indifferent Inclusion: Aboriginal People and the Australian Nation* (Canberra: Aboriginal Studies Press, 2011); Gary Foley, Andrew Schaap, and Adwina Howell, eds., *The Aboriginal Tent Embassy: Sovereignty, Black Power, Land Rights and the State* (Abingdon: Routledge, 2013).

61 Edward Linenthal and Tom Engelhardt, *History Wars: The Enola Gay and Other Battles for the American Past* (New York: Metropolitan Books, 1996); Anna Clark and Stuart Macintyre, *The History Wars* (Carlton: Melbourne University Press, 2003).

62 Susan Sleeper-Smith, *Indian Women and French Men: Rethinking Cultural Encounter in the Western Great Lakes* (Amherst: University of Massachusetts Press, 2001); Susan Sleeper-Smith, *Indigenous Prosperity and American Conquest: Indian Women of the Ohio River Valley, 1690–1792* (Chapel Hill: Omohundro Institute of Early American History and Culture and the University of North Carolina Press, 2018); Lisa Brooks, *The Common Pot: The Recovery of Native Space in the Northeast* (Minneapolis: University of Minnesota Press, 2008). For African examples see Gloria Emeagwali and George J. Sefa Dei, *African Indigenous Knowledge and the Disciplines* (Rotterdam: SensePublishers, 2014).

63 See Silverstein chapter.

64 For pertinent critique of the processes that can lead to the destruction of such sites, see Goodall and Ghosh chapters.

65 Claudio Saunt, 'Telling Stories: The Political Uses of Myth and History in the Cherokee and Creek Nations,' *Journal of American History* 93, no. 1 (2006): 673–697; Minoru

Hokari, *Gurindji Journey: A Japanese Historian in the Outback* (Sydney: University of New South Wales Press, 2014); Peter Nabokov, *A Forest of Time: American Indian Ways of History* (New York: Cambridge University Press, 2002); Donald L. Fixico, *Call for Change: The Medicine Way of American Indian History, Ethos, and Reality* (Lincoln: University of Nebraska Press, 2013).

66 William L. Anderson, Jane L. Brown, and Anne F. Rogers, *The Payne-Butrick Papers*, vols 1–3 (Lincoln: University of Nebraska, 2010); Saunt, 'Telling Stories'; McGrath, *Illicit Love*, 196–197, 367.
67 Anderson, Brown, and Rogers, *The Payne-Butrick Papers*.
68 David Unaipon, *Legendary Tales of the Australian Aborigines* (Carlton: Miegunyah Press, 2011), xii.
69 See Ballard chapter. See also Sian Jones and Lynette Russell, 'Archaeology, Memory and Oral Tradition: An Introduction,' *International Journal of Historical Archaeology* 16, no. 2 (2012): 267–283.
70 Dipesh Chakrabarty, *Provincializing Europe: Postcolonial Thought and Historical Difference* (Princeton, NJ: Princeton University Press, 2007).
71 Nabokov, *A Forest of Time*.
72 Hokari, *Gurindji Journey*.
73 See Smithers chapter.
74 Fixico, *Call for Change*.
75 See Steeves chapter.
76 Ann McGrath, 'Deep Histories in Time, or Crossing the Great Divide?' in *Long History, Deep Time*, eds. Ann McGrath and Mary Anne Jebb (Canberra: ANU Press, 2015), 1–32; Sebouh Aslanian, Joyce E. Chaplin, Kristin Mann and Ann McGrath, 'AHR Conversation – How Size Matters: The Question of Scale in History,' *American Historical Review* 118, no. 5 (2013): 1431–1472.

Bibliography

Anderson, William L., Jane L. Brown, and Anne F. Rogers. *The Payne-Butrick Papers*, vols 1–3. Lincoln: University of Nebraska, 2010.
Armitage, David. 'What's the Big Idea? Intellectual History and the Longue Durée.' *History of European Ideas* 38, no. 4 (2012): 493–507.
Aslanian, Sebouh, Joyce E. Chaplin, Kristin Mann, and Ann McGrath. 'AHR Conversation – How Size Matters: The Question of Scale in History.' *American Historical Review* 118, no. 5 (2013): 1431–1472.
Attwood, Bain. *Telling the Truth about Aboriginal History*. St Leonards: Allen & Unwin, 2005.
Attwood, Bain, and Andrew Markus, eds. *The Struggle for Aboriginal Rights: A Documentary History*. Sydney: Allen & Unwin, 1998.
Ballantyne, Tony. *Webs of Empire: Locating New Zealand's Colonial Past*. Vancouver: UBC Press, 2010.
Ballantyne, Tony, and Antoinette Burton. *Empires and the Reach of the Global, 1870–1945*. Cambridge, MA: Belknap Press, 2012.
Bates, Denise E. *The Other Movement: Indian Rights and Civil Rights in the Deep South*. Tuscaloosa: University of Alabama Press, 2012.
Brooks, Lisa. *The Common Pot: The Recovery of Native Space in the Northeast*. Minneapolis: University of Minnesota Press, 2008.
Burke, Heather, Bryce Barker, Noelene Cole, Lynley A. Wallis, Elizabeth Hatte, Iain Davidson, and Kelsey Lowe. 'The Queensland Native Police and Strategies of Recruitment on the Queensland Frontier, 1849–1901.' *Journal of Australian Studies* 42, no. 3 (2018): 297–313.
'C169- Indigenous and Tribal Peoples Convention, 1989.' Jakarta, International Labour Office, 25 June 2007. https://www.ilo.org/jakarta/whatwedo/publications/WCMS_124013/lang--en/index.htm.

Chakrabarti, Pratik. 'Gondwana and the Politics of Deep Past.' *Past & Present* 242, no. 1 (2019): 119–153.
Chakrabarty, Dipesh. *The Crises of Civilization: Exploring Global and Planetary Histories.* New Delhi: Oxford University Press, 2018.
Chakrabarty, Dipesh. *Provincializing Europe: Postcolonial Thought and Historical Difference.* Princeton, NJ: Princeton University Press, 2007.
Chesterman, John. *Civil Rights: How Indigenous Australians Won Formal Equality.* St Lucia: University of Queensland Press, 2005.
Christian, David. *Maps of Time: An Introduction to Big History.* Berkeley: University of California Press, 2004.
Clark, Anna, and Stuart Macintyre. *The History Wars.* Carlton: Melbourne University Press, 2003.
Coates, Kenneth. *A Global History of Indigenous Peoples: Struggle and Survival.* Basingstoke and New York: Palgrave Macmillan, 2004.
Davis, Megan. 'The United Nations Declaration on the Rights of Indigenous Peoples.' *Indigenous Law Bulletin* 6, no. 30 (2007).
Deloria Vine Jr. 'Self-Determination and the Concept of Sovereignty.' In Native American Sovereignty, edited by J.R. Wunder, 107–114. New York and London: Garland, 1999.
Deloria, Phil. Indians in Unexpected Places. Lawrence: University Press of Kansas, 2004.
Dwyer, Philip G., and Lyndall Ryan, eds. *Theatres of Violence: Massacre, Mass Killing and Atrocity Throughout History.* New York: Berghahn Books, Incorporated, 2012.
Effros, Bonnie, and Guolong Lai, eds. *Unmasking Ideology in Imperial and Colonial Archaeology: Vocabulary and Symbols.* Los Angeles, CA: Cotsen Institute of Archaeology Press, 2018.
Ellinghaus, Katherine. *Blood Will Tell: Native Americans and Assimilation Policy.* Lincoln: University of Nebraska Press, 2017.
Emeagwali, Gloria, and George J. Sefa Dei. *African Indigenous Knowledge and the Disciplines.* Rotterdam: SensePublishers, 2014.
Fixico, Donald L. *Call for Change: The Medicine Way of American Indian History, Ethos, and Reality.* Lincoln: University of Nebraska Press, 2013.
Foley, Gary, Andrew Schaap, and Adwina Howell, eds. *The Aboriginal Tent Embassy: Sovereignty, Black Power, Land Rights and the State.* Abingdon: Routledge, 2013.
Fullagar, Kate, and Michael A. McDonnell, eds. *Facing Empire: Indigenous Experiences in a Revolutionary Age.* Baltimore, MD: John Hopkins University Press, 2018.
Haebich, Anna. *Broken Circles: Fragmenting Indigenous Families 1800–2000.* Fremantle: Fremantle Arts Centre Press, 2000.
Haebich, Anna. *Spinning the Dream: Assimilation in Australia 1950–1970.* Fremantle: Fremantle Arts Centre Press, 2008.
Hämäläinen, Pekka. *The Comanche Empire.* New Haven, CT: Yale University Press, 2008.
Healy, Chris. *From the Ruins of Colonialism: History as Social Memory.* New York: Cambridge University Press, 1997.
Heiss, Anita. *Am I Black Enough for You?* Sydney: Bantam, 2012.
Heizer, Robert F., and Theodora Kroeber, eds. *Ishi the Last Yahi: A Documentary History.* Berkeley: University of California Press, 1979.
Hokari, Minoru. *Gurindji Journey: A Japanese Historian in the Outback.* Sydney: University of New South Wales Press, 2014.
Huggins, Jackie. *Aunty Rita.* Canberra: Aboriginal Studies Press, 1994.
Jacobs, Margaret D. *White Mother to a Dark Race: Settler Colonialism, Maternalism, and the Removal of Indigenous Children in the American West and Australia, 1880–1940.* Lincoln: University of Nebraska Press, 2011.
Jacobs, Margaret D. *A Generation Removed: The Fostering and Adoption of Indigenous Children in the Postwar World.* Lincoln: University of Nebraska Press, 2014.
Jones, Rhys. 'Introduction.' In *Sunda and Sahul: Prehistoric Studies in Southeast Asia, Melanesia and Australia*, edited by Jim Allen, Jack Golson, and Rhys Jones, 2. London: Academic Press, 1977.

Jones, Sian, and Lynette Russell. 'Archaeology, Memory and Oral Tradition: An Introduction.' *International Journal of Historical Archaeology* 16, no. 2 (2012): 267–283.

Kauanui, J. Kēhaulani. '"A Structure, Not an Event": Settler Colonialism and Enduring Indigeneity.' *Lateral* 5, no. 1 (2016).

Koolmatrie, Jacinta. 'Destruction of Juukan Gorge.' *The Conversation*, 2 June 2020.

Langton, Marcia, Odette Mazel, Lisa Palmer, Kathryn Shain, and Maureen Tehan, eds. *Settling with Indigenous People: Modern Treaty and Agreement-Making*. Annandale: Federation Press, 2006.

Langton, Marcia, Lisa Palmer, Maureen Tehan, and Kathryn Shain, eds. *Honour Among Nations? Treaties and Agreements with Indigenous People*. Carlton: Melbourne University Press, 2004.

Linenthal, Edward, and Tom Engelhardt. *History Wars: The Enola Gay and Other Battles for the American Past*. New York: Metropolitan Books, 1996.

Luker, Trish. 'Reading the Evidentiary Void: The Body at the Scene of Writing.' *Griffith Law Review* 18, no. 2 (2009): 298–313.

Lydon, Jane. *Remembering the Myall Creek Massacre*, ed. Lyndall Ryan. Sydney: University of New South Wales Press, 2018.

Maynard, John. *Fight for Liberty and Freedom: The Origins of Australian Aboriginal Activism*. Canberra: Aboriginal Studies Press, 2007.

McGrath, Ann, ed. *Contested Ground: Australian Aborigines Under the British Crown*. Sydney: Allen & Unwin, 1995.

McGrath, Ann. 'Shamrock Aborigines: The Irish, the Aboriginal Australians and Their Children.' *Aboriginal History* 34 (2010): 55–84.

McGrath, Ann. 'Is History Good Medicine?' *Journal of Australian Studies* 38, no. 4 (2014): 396–414.

McGrath, Ann. 'Deep Histories in Time, or Crossing the Great Divide?' In *Long History, Deep Time*, edited by Ann McGrath and Mary Anne Jebb, 1–32. Canberra: ANU Press, 2015.

McGrath, Ann. *Illicit Love: Interracial Sex and Marriage in the United States and Australia*. Lincoln: University of Nebraska Press, 2015.

McGrath, Ann. 'Monumental Discovery Narratives and Deep History.' *Humanities Australia* 11 (2020): 69–80.

McGrath, Ann, and Mary Anne Jebb, eds. *Long History Deep Time*. Canberra: ANU Press, 2015.

McGregor, Russell. *Indifferent Inclusion: Aboriginal People and the Australian Nation*. Canberra: Aboriginal Studies Press, 2011.

McNiven, Ian, and Lynette Russell. *Appropriated Pasts: Indigenous Peoples and the Colonial Culture of Archaeology*. Lanham, MD: AltaMira Press, 2005.

Miller, Robert J., Jacinta Ruru, Larissa Behrendt, and Tracey Lindberg. *Discovering Indigenous Lands: The Doctrine of Discovery in the English Colonies*. Oxford: Oxford University Press, 2010.

Minnerup, Günter, and Pia Solberg, eds. *First World, First Nations: Internal Colonialism and Indigenous Self-Determination in Northern Europe and Australia*. Brighton: Sussex Academic Press, 2011.

Moreton-Robinson, Aileen. *Talkin' Up to the White Woman: Indigenous Women and Feminism*. St Lucia: University of Queensland Press, 2000.

Morgan, Sally. *My Place*. Fremantle: Fremantle Arts Centre, 1987.

Murdoch, Walter. *The Making of Australia*. Melbourne: Whitcombe and Tombs, 1917.

Nabokov, Peter. *A Forest of Time: American Indian Ways of History*. New York: Cambridge University Press, 2002.

National Inquiry into the Separation of Aboriginal and Torres Strait Islander Children from Their Families (Australia). *Bringing Them Home: Report of the National Inquiry into the Separation of Aboriginal and Torres Strait Islander Children from Their Families*. Sydney: Human Rights and Equal Opportunities Commission, 1997.

O'Sullivan, Dominic. *Indigeneity: A Politics of Potential: Australia, Fiji and New Zealand*. Bristol: Policy Press, 2017.

O'Sullivan, Dominic. *We Are All Here to Stay: Sovereignty, Citizenship and the UN Declaration on the Rights of Indigenous Peoples*. Canberra: ANU Press, 2020.

Osterhammel, Jurgen. *The Transformation of the World: A Global History of the Nineteenth Century*. Princeton, NJ: Princeton University Press, 2014.

Perdue, Theda. *Mixed Blood Indians: Racial Construction in the Early South*. Athens: University of Georgia Press, 2003.

Poignant, Roslyn. *Professional Savages: Captive Lives and Western Spectacle*. Sydney: University of New South Wales Press, 2004.

Pulitano, Elvira ed. *Indigenous Rights in the Age of the UN Declaration*. Cambridge: Cambridge University Press, 2012.

Rademaker, Laura, and Tim Rowse, eds. *Indigenous Self-Determination in Australia*. Canberra: ANU Press, 2020.

Russell, Lynette. *Savage Imaginings: Historical and Contemporary Constructions of Australian Aboriginalities*. Melbourne: Australian Scholarly Publishing, 2001.

Russell, Lynette. *A Little Bird Told Me: Family Secrets, Necessary Lies*. St Leonards: Allen and Unwin, 2002.

Russell, Lynette. 'Remembering Places Never Visited: Connections and Context in Imagined and Imaginary Landscapes.' *International Journal of Historical Archaeology* 16, no. 2 (2012): 401–417.

Russell, Lynette. *Roving Mariners: Australian Aboriginal Whalers and Sealers in the Southern Oceans, 1790–1870*. New York: SUNY Press, 2012.

Russell, Lynette. 'What the Little Bird Didn't Tell Me.' *Victorian Historical Journal* 91, no. 1 (Jun 2020): 5–15.

Saunt, Claudio. *Black, White, and Indian: Race and the Unmaking of an American Family*. New York: Oxford University Press, 2006.

Saunt, Claudio. 'Telling Stories: The Political Uses of Myth and History in the Cherokee and Creek Nations.' *Journal of American History* 93, no. 1 (2006): 673–697.

Shaw, Wendy. *Possessors and Possessed: Museums, Archaeology, and the Visualization of History in the Late Ottoman Empire*. Berkeley: University of California Press, 2003.

Shryock, Andrew, and Daniel Lord Smail. *Deep History: The Architecture of Past and Present*. Berkeley: University of California Press, 2011.

Sleeper-Smith, Susan. *Indian Women and French Men: Rethinking Cultural Encounter in the Western Great Lakes*. Amherst: University of Massachusetts Press, 2001.

Sleeper-Smith, Susan. *Indigenous Prosperity and American Conquest: Indian Women of the Ohio River Valley, 1690–1792*. Chapel Hill: Omohundro Institute of Early American History and Culture and the University of North Carolina Press, 2018.

Smail, Daniel Lord. *On Deep History and the Brain*. Berkeley: University of California Press, 2008.

Smithers, Gregory D., and Brooke N. Newman, eds. *Native Diasporas: Indigenous Identities and Settler Colonialism in the Americas*. Lincoln: University of Nebraska Press, 2014.

Stoler, A.L. 'Tense and Tender Ties: The Politics of Comparison in North American History and (Post)Colonial Studies.' *The Journal of American History* 88, no. 3 (2001): 829–865.

Turner, Frederick Jackson. *The Frontier in American History*. New York: Henry Holt, 1920.

Unaipon, David. *Legendary Tales of the Australian Aborigines*. Carlton: Miegunyah Press, 2011.

'United Nations Declaration on the Rights of Indigenous Peoples.' 13 September 2007, https://www.un.org/development/desa/indigenouspeoples/declaration-on-the-rights-of-indigenous-peoples.html.

van Kirk, Sylvia. *Many Tender Ties: Women in Fur-Trade Society, 1670–1870*. Norman: University of Oklahoma Press, 1983.

White, Richard. *The Middle Ground: Indians, Empires, and Republics in the Great Lakes Region, 1650–1815*. Cambridge and New York: Cambridge University Press, 1991.

Wolfe, Patrick. *Settler Colonialism and the Transformation of Anthropology: The Politics and Poetics of an Ethnographic Event*. London: Cassell, 1999.

Wolfe, Patrick. 'Structure and Event: Settler Colonialism, Time, and the Question of Genocide.' In *Empire, Colony, Genocide: Conquest, Occupation, and Subaltern Resistance in World History*, ed. A. Dirk Moses, 102–132. New York: Berghahn Books, 2008.

PART I
A global perspective

2
EUROPEAN USES OF HISTORY

Henning Trüper

The writing of history

Past forms of the pursuit of history in Europe are extremely varied, and a similarly varied literature has been devoted to their study. The common denominator of these forms appears to be the impact of cultures of writing on history.[1] Few cultural records of the past persist in Europe that have remained untouched by the diverse techniques of the writing of names, numbers, lists, and texts. Even those cultural practices that have produced historical meanings in media other than text usually display traces of interference with writing: visual documents rely on inscriptions to explicate their meanings, and, for many centuries, the production of most technical artefacts has presupposed writing. The interlacing of history with writing is so ubiquitous and subtle that it has often remained unacknowledged in a field that has 'writing' – Ancient Greek *graphe* – in its actual name, 'historiography', or 'history of historical writing'.[2]

Much more has been made of the etymology of the other component of the term, *historia*, as derived from the verb *historein*, to enquire, to research.[3] Interpretations of history as enquiry form a line of definition that has been dominant in academic discussions over the last three centuries. From this vantage point, history is above all a pursuit of knowledge about the past; that it requires various forms of writing is secondary. Historical writing appears as a primarily 'epistemological' project in the philosopher Gaston Bachelard's sense of a pursuit of scientific knowledge that aggressively seeks both to widen and to break with commonly held notions, in order to attain superior explanatory force.

Still, the explication of history as enquiry has its disadvantages. Not only is the concept of knowledge hardly clear in and of itself. One might also ask whether other uses of history – such as in political ideologies, for the commemoration of the dead, for the glorification of genealogies, or in religious contexts – are not illicitly relegated to second rank by a definition that overly privileges the pursuit of knowledge. Nonetheless, the epistemological type of definition remains dominant. Influential works in historiography tend to synthesise the development of the field in terms of shifts in methodology.[4] Much philosophical work in recent decades has also been invested in establishing the essentially explanatory character of historical writing.[5] The dominance of epistemological definitions has remained firmly in place since at least the mid-nineteenth century,[6] when the metaphor of 'source' and the institution of the state archive gained hold over the writing of history within the world of European universities. This peculiar social, institutional, and intellectual environment, however, provides the setting for only part of the history of historical writing even in nineteenth- and twentieth-century Europe, let alone over the course of European histories at large.

The phrase 'knowledge of the past' also does not sufficiently demarcate its range of objects, since 'history', whatever it is, is not identical with the past more generally; an additional determination of the difference between 'history' and 'the past' is needed. Therefore, any explication of 'history' in terms of mere processes (or changes, causal connections, bare facts) also falls short, since it fails to explain why some processes (etc.) are included (e.g. the French Revolution) and others are not (e.g. continental drift, or that headache last Friday). There are always upper and lower thresholds of inclusion into and exclusion from history that pertain to types of occurrence (e.g. in the schema that marks European historical writing since the nineteenth century: high politics v. the quotidian v. geological change), types of people (e.g. rulers v. subalterns, men v. women, colonisers v. colonised), and types of structures (e.g. society v. nature, humans v. deities). 'Historicity', the property of being historical (and narrower than just 'true of the past'), is assigned to kinds and instances of objects (in a wide sense) over the course of an open-ended process of making things historical, of 'historicisation'.[7]

In the last decades, debate has sought to promote a more pluralist sense of the overall landscape of uses of the past. A particular role in this regard has been played by discussion about the opposition of history and (social, collective) 'memory'. Early contributions focused in particular on a dualist confrontation of scholarly scientific knowledge with other representations of the past, whereas later ones have stressed the multitude of uses of the past.[8]

Arguably, however, this debate has ended up downplaying the specificity and cultural impact of the knowledge claims vested in scholarly historical writing. A more sustained focus on the varieties of writing that underpin and shape history will help achieving a more differentiated notion of how diverse uses of the past interact and of what is the specific situation of 'history' among them. An approach of this kind also opens the possibility of contrasting such 'regimes of historicity'[9] (the standards that govern what is regarded as historical) that are based on writing culture with those that are not. To be sure, in its dependence on writing, the European history of history is hardly unique; its particularities rather abound in the finer grain. On an abstract level, other textual traditions of historical writing, e.g. the Chinese or the Islamic, display similar traits.[10] Prominent among these traits is the constitution of historicity against such types of historical self-understanding as encountered in illiterate cultures. The 'lack' of writing is one of the indispensable components that historically went into the formation of the concept of indigeneity. The very idea of Indigenous history therefore challenges the foundations of writing-based cultures of history; European historical writing, in particular, has constituted itself by contrasting to, and by contributing to the regimentation of, 'Others' on its outside, the outside of writing culture. Surveying the multifarious uses of historical writing in European history, one returns to this point at crucial junctures.

Before 1500

In what is commonly recognised as 'the' European tradition, historical writing starts out in Ancient Greece. This origin story targets in particular the writings of fifth-century BCE scholars Herodotus and Thucydides. Herodotus, a traveller, assembled information on far-flung places, which he inserted into a broad, chronological account of the conflicts between the Greeks and the Persians in the sixth and fifth centuries BCE. Thucydides was the first to give a detailed written analysis of a single political event to which he had been a contemporary eyewitness, the Peloponnesian War between Sparta and Athens. The Greek genre of history was from the start bifurcated, and its tendency towards differentiation arguably hinged on the very nature of writing, forever the producer of novel patterns.

The comprehensive, seemingly boundless curiosity of Herodotus – who states as an aim that his work is to preserve in memory the great deeds not merely of the 'Greeks', but also of the 'barbarians' (the non-Greeks) – indicates a peculiar role for the practice of writing in the underlying conflict: it is a sign of the difference between Greeks and barbarians that the former also preserve the memory of the latter, whereas the latter, if literate, at most preserve their own. In terms of recurrent themes, Herodotus paid particular attention to differences of social order as regards constitutions, gender relations, the processing of the dead, and the relations with the divine. Providing a written account of such differences supposedly aimed to provide a 'mirror' that made visible one's own particularity, and superiority.[11] Thucydides, by contrast, according to his own account an exiled Athenian military leader, used a historical analysis for an exploration of political prudence and imprudence. His account was driven by a certain educational ambition, in line with the Athenian rhetorical tradition of addressing popular assemblies that would take political decisions. In this context, historical writing served to teach eternal truths about human nature, war, and politics. Establishing a heightened sense of the distinctness of past and present was not a target.[12] By contrast, establishing a sharp distinction between myth and history, so that the latter excluded divine affairs from the sphere of the human, was a chief goal.[13]

For centuries, Herodotus, Thucydides, and later the Roman Cicero – whose works provide the origin of the metaphor of 'source' and the handiest formula for the didactic character of the genre: *historia magistra vitae* ('history, the teacher of life') – along with Roman historians Livy, Sallust, Tacitus, and Suetonius, figured as progenitors of a purportedly unified European tradition of historical writing.[14]

Still, since the genre was split already at the time of its emergence, it is clear that its subsequent history was hardly unified, as recent research also consistently emphasises.[15]

A broader account also needs to include the tradition of Hebrew Scripture and the Greek New Testament appended to it, as equally powerful sources of a framework of purported facts of the course of world history, and of textual schemas in which to grasp these facts. Genealogies, chronicles of events, prophecies, laws and customs, and plain narratives of salient episodes (e.g. in Genesis) come to mind as biblical forms in which the past is accounted for in writing. Prophetism, as long lines of theological commentators of Christian as well as Jewish backgrounds noted, made a particularly significant addition. It tied the understanding of historicity to a notion of the future to come that was pervaded by divine agency and therefore was unpredictable without the intervention of revelation.[16] If the future was unique, so was the entire course of history. The cycles of eternal repetition that were prevalent in Greek and Roman thoughts about historical change – for instance, manifest in the sequences of necessarily unstable forms of government that Aristotle or the Latinate historian Polybius posited – were abandoned. By tendency, historicity became incompatible with the idea of repetition. Increasingly, in the first century CE, historicity also opened up in unprecedented fashion to the notion of its finality. Apocalypticism, as a tradition of thought in both the Jewish and Christian contexts (and in the plethora of doctrines between and around them, on the southeastern fringe of the Roman Empire), charged the understanding of the extension of worldly reality in time with notions of a final judgement and salvation of the faithful. A subtler charge emerged in the very word of 'scripture': for divine revelation to count, in those religious contexts that sought to project themselves into a distant future, it had to be written. The very writtenness of history therefore bore theological meaning.

A third ancient lineage of historical writing exists in the form of inscriptions, a technique of writing in stone that was shared around the Mediterranean, Egypt, and Mesopotamia and pervaded deep into Africa and Asia. Inscriptions cover a variety of contents: they occur sometimes as fleeting graffiti that often lack obvious projection into a historical future, but they also cross over into this terrain as funerary inscriptions, as genealogical assertions (which often occur in Middle Eastern records), as rulers' names and likenesses on coinage, or as elaborate monuments to the glories of rulers. Inscriptions of the monumental kind were clearly informed by the understanding that there needed to be a threshold of political-military dignity that granted access to the status of being historical, and to being preserved, in the most durable medium known, for an admiring future. It is also worth noting that in other genres of historical writing, inscriptions were acknowledged as a significant historical record. In the Book of Job, the prophet famously exclaims: 'Oh that my words were written! Oh that they were inscribed in a book! That with an iron stylus and lead they were engraved in the rock forever!'[17] In this context, however, the inscription is transformed from a record of glories into one of sufferings. Such versatility belonged to the 'European' or perhaps rather the Mediterranean regime of historicity already in antiquity.

A fourth type of ancient writing that can be categorised as engaging with historicity was the philological criticism of textual traditions. Already the Hellenist period, *c.* second century BCE, saw the emergence of a critical discussion and establishment of definitive versions of the older Greek textual heritage, especially the Homeric epics. Biblical text, but also, in sixth-century CE Byzantium, the corpus of Roman Law, was later subjected to similar treatment. Poetic, religious, and legal writing all comprised textual corpora that were marked as representing a historical past. Mediated by the work of textual scholarship, by methods of discerning authenticity, distinguishing archaic from current language, and past from present values and standards, historicity became a source of authority. As such, it could be useful to political power, or against it. Yet, the orientation towards the truth of original text did not entail a modern realist understanding of the plausibility of the contents of historical narrative. Scholarship did not consistently differentiate, e.g. the historical from the mythical, forbid the narration of prodigies, or the rendering of direct discourse (one of the prime markers that sets apart modern European historical writing from ancient forbears such as Thucydides).[18]

In the European Middle Ages, ancient forms of historical writing underwent further development.[19] For centuries, writing and book learning were monopolised by the Christian clergy; yet, political power was not. The ambiguous, legitimising and delegitimising, relationship between the authority of historicity and holders of political power became manifest across various waves of the rediscovery of ancient, pre-Christian heritages (such 'renaissances' marked the eighth, ninth, twelfth, and fifteenth centuries in particular). As far as historical writing is concerned, the Middle Ages were above all characterised by the spread of two already-established genres – annals and chronicles – both of which were records of events in chronological order (where the first gave particular prominence to the organising principle of the calendar year, and typically to a rhetoric of emphatic brevity).[20] Initially prompted by the problem of the movable date of Easter, scholars also developed an increasingly sophisticated tradition of chronological calculation that intersected with historical writing. Since scripture provided ample information on events and the number of years passed since the creation of the world, chronology also included the calculation of the age of the world as such. Annals and chronicles frequently sought to fill out the entire space of mundane history until the present. Their informational value, however, often changes fundamentally when events temporally and spatially proximate to the writer(s) are described. The flexibility of the genres was such that they allowed for the integration of the histories of rulers' *res gestae* (deeds, accomplishments), or the fortunes of principalities, ethnic groups, or institutions, into a world historical frame that was in itself inserted within the divine eternity beyond creation and salvation.

This manner of nesting worldly time into the divine also marked the writing of such texts that preserved the ancient genre name of 'histories'. The oeuvres of Gregory of Tours (sixth century) and the Venerable Bede (eighth century), since they are connected to a variety of genres of historical writing, are particularly instructive for understanding the array of textual forms available. Their works pay particular attention to church and ethnic histories, and they devote independent oeuvres to the lives of saints. In general, accounting for martyrs became a chief function of medieval historicity. Both the historian and the martyr were witnesses and gave testimony about, respectively, mundane and divine historical events. The position of the witness mediated between the sacred and the profane, but also between the high and low in social status. When put into writing, the reach of this mediation expanded. The privileging of testimony expressed a sense of participation in historicity. This became a broader feature of medieval historical culture. Participatory practices informed a rich culture of commemoration that also generated or redefined various forms of writing, e.g. the return of funerary inscriptions in imitation of older Roman customs, or the name lists of confraternities, in which subscribers paid clerical institutions to pray for the well-being of their souls 'in eternity'. This cultural practice integrated non-written forms of culture with sophisticated forms of writing; such was the prominence of 'memory' that medieval philosophy generated extensive normative and theoretical literature on the topic.[21] Arguably, it was also the needs of commemoration, both in scholarly and in popular culture, that informed the medieval invention of purgatory. Since the dead would be judged only on Doomsday, scholarship and popular belief relied on an elaborate fiction to account for the sojourn of souls that were already disembodied but neither damned nor saved.[22]

All things considered, the culture of commemoration ensured that historicity pertained to the individual, and that access to it could be mediated by money, so that the property of being historical became a matter of purchasable prestige. Acquiring higher status went along with acquiring historicity. This dynamism has not faded since in European history. No project of the emancipation of the oppressed is conceivable that does not also stake a claim to inclusion into historicity. In this manner, as a purveyor of status, historicity also became a component of the major languages of political thought in Europe.

Another major consequence of the manner in which history was built on the theological framework of mundane time and eternity, was the emergence of a political theology of monarchy that was both universal and apocalyptic. Based on sources in scripture, from the twelfth century onwards, speculative theologians such as Joachim of Fiore or Otto of Freising began to postulate different sequences of world historical 'ages' as connected with historical political entities, 'realms', or 'empires'. These theologies of history usually regarded the contemporary state of politics as the last world order before the Second Coming of Christ and the end of the world as laid out in the New Testament Book of Revelations. This also required that one monarchy – usually but not always the entity known as 'the Empire', nominally a continuation of the Roman one – held a status of supremacy over other states; it was to be regarded as the universal monarchy that was a placeholder for the divine government to come. Such notions pervaded political thought well into the seventeenth century.[23] The nexus between universal monarchy and apocalypticism remained a major framework for historical writing.[24]

Nonetheless, the symbolism around monarchical rulers continued to include varied forms of historical writing, such as the pervasive genealogies that related medieval noble families to ancient myth, or indeed the chronicling of events around specific courts. The manner in which, well into the twentieth century, the proximity of the historian to the monarchical centre was treated as a methodological advantage indicates that the very position of witness to history was shaped by norms about the acquisition of knowledge that privileged high socio-political status. Political ideas designed to challenge monarchical authority and hereditary rule, which emerged in the late Middle Ages, were forced to compete with this model within the framework of historicity. The dominant dissident political idiom, republicanism, included elaborate references to the pre-imperial ancient Roman system of government.[25] These references served to render republics competitive with monarchy and consequently copied the structural features that shaped historicity in courtly culture.

1500–1800

Given that its ambitions were informed by the broadest then conceivable 'rediscovery' of neglected and forgotten portions of ancient heritage, it is hardly surprising that the best-known Renaissance, that of the fifteenth and sixteenth centuries, also reshaped historical writing. Instead of merely emulating antiquity, however, the broader system of the production of knowledge edged away from earlier forms. The hold of scholastic theology over scholarship faded. The array of languages shifted. Under the influence of refugees from the Byzantine Empire, whose conquest by the Ottomans was concluded with the invasion of Constantinople in 1453, knowledge of Ancient Greek became more widespread in Western Europe. The successive displacements of Jewish populations from southern and western to northern and eastern Europe, from the fourteenth into the sixteenth centuries, led to novel contacts with Jewish learning and the first emergence of Hebraist scholarship in western Christianity, whereas earlier interrelations with the Arabophone Southern Mediterranean receded. Yet, it was a change in media technology, the introduction of moveable letter types for the printing press, that effected the most profound change. Writing split into a differentiation of handwriting and printing, and before long a book culture emerged that was based on relatively effortless technical reproduction. This was the beginning of a centuries-long spread of writing knowledge into societies that remained predominately illiterate well into the nineteenth century.

In a simultaneous development within the culture of learning, philological interest also resurged powerfully in the fifteenth century. On the one hand, this interest pertained to the text of scripture, which in all contexts of religious reform was a primary target of historical critique and verification. On the other hand, it pertained to the classical heritage, which the Italian scholar Lorenzo Valla mobilised *c.* 1440 to demonstrate the inauthenticity of the so-called 'Donation of Constantine', the charter by which the Roman Emperor Constantine had purportedly granted the Roman church dominion over the empire, foundational for the theology of the papacy and of universal monarchy alike. The authority of historical criticism here dealt a blow of delegitimisation to powerful political actors. Ever since, philology was reconstructive as well as deconstructive.

A novelty in material culture was the acquisition of authority through appropriation of profane ancient objects in the form of antiquarianism, which became a common pursuit among noblemen as well as scholars. Antiquarianism meant the collection and connoisseurship of all material and textual traces of classical antiquity.[26] For this pursuit, authenticity played a major role. Ruins of ancient buildings shifted from being nuisances and repositories of building materials to monuments of peculiar historical-aesthetic value. The signs of historicity became indissolubly interlaced with aesthetic value. Specifically, the category of the sublime, another ancient heirloom, was brought to bear on the historical. Over a protracted process, culminating only in the eighteenth century, scholars formulated a novel aesthetic theory of the sublime, the impression of overwhelming and terrifying immensity, which in the case of the historical past was prompted both by the greatness of the ancients and by the sheer temporal distance that had turned their designs into ruins. The notion of the sublime connected historicity with the tradition, especially in the visual arts, of depicting the condition of melancholia. This tradition served the partly theological purpose of highlighting the vanity of all worldly matters. While in earlier phases, such vanity was decried in crude symbolic forms, by the eighteenth century, a soberer sense of historical distance, the quiet mourning of the loss of antiquity, prevailed.[27] Subsequent European historical writing never fully shed the heritage of subdued melancholia.

In line with European mercantile and military 'expansion' around the world since the fifteenth century, the aesthetics of ruins also provided a tool for integrating the vestiges of other, sometimes even previously unknown 'civilisations' of the past into the framework of historicity. The confrontation with the records of China, India, and when they became legible in the 1820s, Egypt, posed problems to the established chronological order of world time as according to scripture. Attempts at reconciliation of the divergent traditions were widespread and ceased only over the course of the nineteenth century. Similar efforts were undertaken around the different forms of religious learning encountered abroad by European clerics: as a consequence of growing acquaintance with other parts of the world, European Christian scholarship sought to explain wildly different religious forms as emanating from a single event of divine revelation. The harmonising work scholars undertook on findings around the globe went to exorbitant lengths. One surprisingly tenacious seventeenth-century theory held that the Indigenous populations of the Americas were the descendants of the lost tribes of Israel listed in the Pentateuch. The millenarian zeal of missionaries to spread Christianity to every newly accessed portion of the globe in order to facilitate the Second Coming was itself an adaptation of the religious concept of world historical time to the new situation.

The aesthetic of history also applied to relics encountered abroad, especially in Asia. In the seventeenth and eighteenth centuries, classicism – the scholarly and aesthetic emulation and re-imagination of classical antiquity – unfolded along with, and against, orientalism, its parallel and counterpart. Well into the twentieth century, most forms of orientalism were devoted to the study of distant pasts, of civilisational origins, and carried the self-congratulatory notion that Europe had overtaken other civilisations. Indeed, the very emergence of a concept of 'civilisation' whose diverse instances could be conceived of as insulated from, and in competition with, each other, even when they had developed at vastly different times, was an important achievement of enlightenment-era scholarship.

This concept also required a counter-concept of those altogether untouched by the historical dynamism of civilisation: the 'savage'.[28] Use of this concept arguably was particularly salient in eighteenth-century theorising when the Swiss-French philosopher Rousseau coupled it with a notion of natural 'nobility'. The resources informing the concept of the savage had been accumulated since the sixteenth century, not least with the emergence of a genre of – written, but un-scholarly – narrative in which the author professed to have spent time in the captivity of natives. This popular genre, widespread well into the nineteenth century, evidenced the savagery of the captors by references to cannibalism and also other signs of religious, moral, and intellectual incompetence.[29] Especially in the Americas, the 'savagery' of the 'savages' was not merely imagined and projected, but also actively and violently produced. For instance, most brutally in present-day Mexico, the previous indigenous writing culture was suppressed and denied, and the Spanish destroyed Aztec and Mayan documents on a grand scale. Denials of the records of indigenous cultures and the production of 'savagery' in this sense became a standard procedure of colonial rule and scholarship.

The reversal in values that the concept of the 'savage' underwent when it became 'noble' in the eighteenth century is nonetheless an interesting occurrence. It stood in a larger context during which the extensive travel literature of Europeans abroad developed more rigorous norms for the representation of the distant Other. As was generally constitutive of the writing practices of enlightenment scholarship, tall tales of prodigies and monsters were increasingly suppressed as the sober and respectful reliance on local informants was valorised. The universal equality of humans became a prominent feature when, slowly, the scientific view of the unity, and 'monogenesis', of humankind as a species became prevalent and triumphed over simultaneous attempts to establish the 'polygenesis' of humans as a set of different species. In a parallel development, the rise of the notion of equality eroded the legitimacy of European slavery. This process pitted part of the writing system, namely the print market for religious and political-moral edification, of European learned elites against their own economic system, a contradiction that was never entirely resolved. Hence, slavery – broadly understood as the use of unfree or coerced labour – returned in ever-novel guises, in colonies as well as during European wars or simply in economic settings, while Europe continued to think of itself as having conclusively overcome this atrocious heritage.

The reversal of the meaning of the savage also aligned with a novel valorisation of the assumed, cast-off cultural origins of Europeans, who had long expressed their differences through origin stories. Celtic, Germanic, and Slavonic revivals emerged since the eighteenth century in ever-novel waves and celebrated alleged ancient ancestors before they were, as one liked to think, corrupted by contact with the Roman and Byzantine Empires and Christianisation. Historical writing and antiquarianism, but also emerging vernacular philologies, were at the forefront of this development, which in the romantic period, at the very end of the eighteenth century, produced a transformation of cultural values. At this point, for roughly a century, classicism had been a dominant norm in the arts and a prominent component of scholarship, albeit in competition with the rapidly expanding natural sciences. In response, an anti-classicist counter-aesthetic emerged that relied on ever-changing models – non-classical European ancestors, pagan or medieval, 'Orientals' – all of which helped produce a sense of autonomous modernism: a 'new time' had arrived that would have to set its own norms. Subsequently, none of the anti-classicist models fully held sway, and for a century and more, further ones, such as the 'primitives' and the 'indigenous', were added to produce a veritable encyclopaedia of cultural appropriation, in the service of formulating the 'modern'.

Even a peculiar tradition of systematising world historical synthesis emerged alongside these forms, in the late eighteenth century, as one of the first conscious attempts to lay the foundations for a secure, specific, and comprehensive methodology of historical research. Enlightenment philosophies of history at various centres, such as Naples (Vico), Scotland (Hume, Smith, and others), France (Turgot, Voltaire, Condorcet), or Germany (Hegel), were often formulated in terms of civilisational stages of human development. This pattern translated into a rich literature of more empirically minded accounts that nonetheless preserved the ambition to see humankind as a unified subject and agent of history.

The historicisation of the world at large brought along novel institutions, such as public access museums and a market for the sale of artefacts of all kinds. Such institutions were not just sites of autonomous learning and curiosity, but deeply entwined with the representation as well as the critique of political power in Europe (they served to demonstrate the state's access to distant areas of space and time while they challenged notions of inequality constitutive of political order). The most prominent political context of any concern about historicity since the eighteenth century was the building of nation states, to be dominated less by the traditional aristocratic elites than by bourgeois merchant, industrialist, and academic classes. Subsequent to the French Revolution of 1789, European nation states were to have constitutions and be subject to the equal rule of law over all citizens. At the same time, many of these reforming nation states rapidly expanded their imperial hold over far-flung portions of the globe,[30] and as the late modern era would amply demonstrate, the nation state did little to pacify Europe internally.

The nation state emerged from many roots. Perhaps the most important of them was the ability of states to act as war machines capable of mobilising entire populations on the one hand, and to make peace conclusively on the other. In this context, an important challenge for historical writing had emerged as early as the mid-seventeenth century. Peace treaties, such as that of Westphalia in 1648 – often cited as the end-point of any notion of universal monarchy in Europe and the point of origin of an international order of sovereign nation states – included a solemn 'formula of amnesia', in which the parties to the treaty promised each other the forgetting of past injuries and transgressions. Therefore, knowledge about history was a potential enemy of peace. Historical writing has been used as a technology both for breaking the peace by subverting amnesia and for stabilising peace by rewriting the past so as to mitigate previous enmities, injuries, and offences. The nation state, with its potential both for pacification and for violence, was marked by this ambivalence.

Already early in the eighteenth century, this diplomatic entanglement of history gave rise to one of the diverse factors that produced the modernisation of historical writing, the critical study of documents and testimony about contemporary peace treaties. In this context, research-driven history began as an oblique self-interrogation of historical writing (i.e. as to its contribution to peace). This finding, that the self-critique of historical writing was essential, also holds for other types of early modern historical study, for instance, the critical review of the saints' records on the part of Catholic theologians from the seventeenth century onwards (*Acta Sanctorum, Société des Bollandistes*). The phrase 'theory of history', which formalised this self-interrogating streak of historical writing, was around since at least the mid-eighteenth century, when historical writing also still routinely had to answer to a deep philosophical scepticism ('Pyrrhonism') about the very possibility of reliable historical knowledge.

For decades, the history of modern historical writing has been preoccupied with nation-building as the political and industrialisation as the economic frameworks that have at times appeared to provide the very condition of possibility of modern pursuits of historical knowledge.[31] Yet, the reverse type of argument, in favour of the impact of the writing system of history on the idiom of politics, also has appeal. European political language imported an entire language of abstract terms about structures and events from historical writing, and it has consistently relied on the thresholds of historicity in order to mark what does and does not belong to the political domain. Since the emergence of nation-building movements with appending public spheres, the criteria for being political have mostly been the same as those for being historical.

Nonetheless, historical writing did not enjoy autonomy over the changes in meaning that pervaded its own idiom. Rather, in the eighteenth century, the language of history was profoundly influenced by what was then called physics or natural philosophy.[32] The notion, known as teleology, that goal-directedness was inherent in natural entities as well as mental states translated itself into the many readings of world history as a progressive, open-ended structure, directed towards a goal of improvement. The age of the beginnings of research-driven historical writing was also the period of the most intimate intersection of philosophies of history with the dominant philosophies of the day. Often, it has been argued that these progressive understandings of history presented merely secular variants of earlier apocalyptic salvation histories. While some convergence between theology and history is hard to deny, the significance of the history of science for this process is often underemphasised and the more plural and fractured meaning of 'progress' therefore misrepresented.[33] One of these meanings was the emergence of an optimistic and deeply future-oriented manner of historical writing that supplemented, but did not replace, the antiquarian, melancholic, and critical traditions.

After 1800

No single mode of historical writing, not even the much-maligned 'grand narrative', was decisive for the tremendous political deployment of historical writing in nation-building; rather, all of these modes converged. The supply of diversified uses is presumably one of the most decisive features that allowed European historical writing to gain such importance for late modern politics. The labour of functional diversification was carried out in the medium of print, and it required this medium as a supplier of stable textual models that served as discrete targets for polemical differentiation.

Since the eighteenth century, historical writing had become increasingly incorporated, as a discipline in its own right, into the European university. Novel forms of presentation emerged in which both singular events and the national frame became paramount, to the detriment of the earlier world historical research model. The newly reshaped German university, with a novel focus on individual and original research, was emulated, and in the process adapted to local needs, across Europe and North America. Institutions and methods were often seen as intertwined, so there was much talk of German dominance in historical method as well. 'Historical method' meant in particular the practice of archival research, the 'critical' evaluation of source documents with a view to authenticity and reliability, and the collection and edition of manuscript texts and inscriptions with a view to completeness and methodical identification of the oldest variants of text, closest to the original writer's intention. Many of the new procedures actually emerged in various countries simultaneously. Although these practices were in many regards continuations of shared antecedents,[34] nineteenth-century historians restated them in polemical rejection of late enlightenment opponents, namely world history and progressive philosophies of history. These older forms of scholarship were rejected as insufficiently evidence-based and too lost in generalities to produce new knowledge.

The most decisive change was the comprehensive turn towards archival documents and the piecemeal reversal of the hierarchy between documents and testimony. If, previously, eyewitness testimony had often been ascribed higher trustworthiness than the merely instrumental textual products of government, after 1800 this relation was turned on its head. Access to written sources became more authoritative than personal participation in events. The new research practice favoured the unpublished and hidden-away textual document. It relied on a complex political landscape of state archives only slowly becoming available for research (the French revolutionary government was supposedly the first to grant all citizens legal access to national document collections, though the practical history of access is far more intricate).[35] This research practice, however, aligned historical writing with the state, its structure and political acts, to such an extent that other historical concerns – as connected, say, with society and culture, let alone Indigenous peoples – became marginalised.

Source-based historical writing also required considerable changes in the manner in which historical texts were put together. To begin with, inclusion of evidentiary annotations became a methodological and rhetorical necessity.[36]

Historicisation had previously rested on two pillars: the given general thresholds of inclusion and exclusion that determined what matters from the past could in principle be regarded as (worthy of being called) historical, and an ad-hoc decision, during the writing process, about the inclusion into actual historical text of data that in principle qualified for being historical. The archive, since it pre-selected potential sources, came to provide another, external instance of historicisation. It also required another writing process, that of the philological analysis of the documents, which actually added another layer of ad-hoc historicisation decisions on the part of the researcher, as concerned the textual history of the source. The historian's authorship was therefore made more intricate. Heightened insistence on the part-epistemological, part-ethical virtues of precision and objectivity was also a response to these novel complications. As a result, however, historical writing severed as many ties as it could with the field of artistic literature.[37]

It has been argued that this pursuit of difference to the literary field was altogether futile since the plot models of fiction continued subtly to work on academic historical text.[38] Indeed, the rise of the novel, including the historical one as pioneered by Walter Scott, provided indispensable inspiration for the development of academic historical writing. Nonetheless, there was symbolic significance in establishing history as a genre of non-fiction. This allowed history to shed not only traditional rhetorical requirements of style but also concomitant ambitions of political instruction. By and large, late modern European historical knowledge has been based on the premise that one could not learn anything practical from it and that it was merely driven by curiosity.[39] Ironically, this insistence on its lack of utility permitted historical writing to monopolise historical culture at large and to gain the massive political influence it enjoyed, in the age of nations and empires, over large-scale national publics rather than small-scale circles of political decision-makers. It was the prestige of 'scientific' reliability that persuaded various social groups to subscribe to the knowledge produced by the academic field, and to jettison pre-existing modes of historicisation – as, for instance, often present in families, regional, or religious communities. The success with which, throughout the nineteenth century, historical and natural-historical education especially in Protestant Europe – in line with an aggressively historicising approach to the Bible[40] – managed to eradicate trust in the veracity of biblical history remains remarkable, even in comparison with cognate societies such as the U.S.

The metaphor of the 'source' itself, with its indications of purity and clarity, but also the subtle nexus with the mythological figure of the nymph and thereby a distribution of gendered values and tropes of male desire, provided one of the central images that helped mediate the 'dry as dust' practice of archive-based history with national fantasies.[41] Indeed, the prestige of the 'source' rose so high that the lack of availability of textual documents became a criterion for the absence of historicity. This position emerged both from complex philosophical arguments about the civilisational evolution of the use of symbols – as influentially laid out by the philosopher Hegel – and from a research practice that, finally liberated from the frameworks of biblical chronology, began to classify certain archaeological relics as 'prehistorical'. In the last third of the nineteenth century, under the growing influence of Darwin's concept of evolution, a line of anthropology emerged that ranked cultures in terms of stages of development, in accordance with their acquisition of certain technologies, such as script. Admittedly, predecessors of such stagist views of the history of humankind abounded, from ancient mythology to the Scottish enlightenment. Yet, Darwinian anthropology, originating mainly in Britain, went further than any predecessor in the cataloguing and classification of actual societies the world over, and it naturalised the violent destruction of societies and cultures as historically inevitable. In many such models, entry into the sequence of civilisational stages was granted precisely by the acquisition of literacy. Writing itself then became the entry ticket into history as an evolutionary process. In a way, since Europeans administered historicity overwhelmingly through writing, they absolutised their own dependence on this family of media techniques. Twentieth-century political notions about 'modernisation' and 'development' originated here, while the former 'savages' became re-categorised, at least in scholarship, as 'primitives'. As part of the same development, historical writing became fully aligned with theories about differences among human 'races', a widespread pursuit of Western scientists already since the eighteenth century.

European historical writing also effected a manipulation of the cultural regimentation of temporality. Universalised astronomical clock time – 'empty, linear, and homogenous',[42] on account of its suppression of the rhythms and gaps with which many cultures ordered time in terms of the intrusions and withdrawals of the divine – became a symbol of European supremacy.[43] Non-European populations the world over were denied 'coevalness' with Europe; they were of another time and obliged to 'catch up' or develop resistant temporal regimes,[44] quite regardless of what lines of autonomous development had been in place earlier.[45] Arguably, the European category of historicity was one of the decisive formative influences for the conceptual field around the twentieth-century category of 'indigeneity', and the formula of 'indigenous history' arose as a provocation to one of the blatant blind spots of the European history of historical writing: as the historicisation of the allegedly unhistoricisable.[46]

In the second half of the nineteenth century, scholars from neighbouring disciplines began to feel dissatisfied with the bias towards statehood that the discipline of history had accrued, and therefore integrated elements of historical writing into their own fields. This dissatisfaction partly arose from the highly dynamic changes European societies were undergoing beyond the scope of governmental administration. In economics, for instance – not by a long shot as thoroughly mathematised as today – economic activity became an object of historical study, as did social conflict, under the influence of the often difficult and violent emergence of an entirely new class, the industrial proletariat. Darwinism and the theory of evolution provided a highly attractive, iconoclastic idiom for getting a hold on these novel objects of study. Socialist movements, since the late nineteenth century mostly excluded from the academic milieu, formed their own traditions of historical writing. Among these, the Darwinist idea of societal 'evolution' was popular until Marxist 'historical materialism' – the sophisticated, if rigid, analysis of the development of human history through the confrontation of economically determined social classes – fully prevailed.

Yet, this 'discovery of the social' was hardly limited to a revolutionary political context. Rather, particularly in France and Germany, it was also an inner-academic project that drew on anthropology and other disciplines as much as on academic history. If, a century earlier, historical writing had taken its abstract vocabulary from physics, the distance to the mathematised natural sciences had meanwhile become unbridgeable. Yet, the same was not the case for the still-descriptive evolutionist life sciences, and the impact of Darwinism indicates a novel conduit of idiomatic transfer. Around 1900, innovative historical writing swarmed with anonymous, unintentional, and goalless evolutionary processes. Neither the history of great men and great decisions nor the progressive philosophy of history ever disappeared, but they lost much scholarly prestige.

As economic, social, and cultural history became stronger currents and novel subfields such as the history of science emerged, innovative proposals for extending the scope of historicity abounded. But they also occasioned a specific sense of crisis that pertained to the comprehensive historicisation and thereby relativisation of social and religious values and scientific truths. If nothing in the ambit of the human-made was exempt from historical change, what stable values and knowledge were there to be had? Respective debates became common since the reemergence of 'classical' economics, in search for law-like mathematical models, in the 1880s. It was here that the concept of 'historicism' was first coined to denounce the pervasive sense of relativism among those who did not believe that general models for economic activity were attainable. Piecemeal, especially on the German scene, 'historicism' became the term for an entire purported nineteenth-century 'ideology' of historicity that the critical social-scientific treatment of history somehow aspired to overcome.

It has often been argued that the emergence of social history amounted to a revolution of historical thinking in general, which opened up to emancipatory processes and developed a multitude of novel methods. It is hard to deny that history became a more politically critical discipline over the course of the twentieth century. Still, it also became many other things. The discovery of the social, and the subsequent emergence of a field of institutionally high-powered social sciences, engendered a social class of experts that informed not only emancipatory politics, but all kinds of 'social engineering', of applied politics that sought to actively alter the social order. Early on, such efforts emerged particularly in the context of colonial rule and racist regimes of segregation, both in Europe and abroad.[47] At the same time, this kind of knowledge production fed into the development of welfare state models of re-constituting industrial society in many European countries. It also shaped totalitarian projects of politically streamlined society, including the forced removals of ethnic and social groups, under both fascist and communist regimes.

While, especially after the First World War, critical history attacked the 'myths' of nationalism, on the whole it retained an orientation towards functionality within the state as an institutional system and part of the array of technologies of rule. One criticised the state in order to improve or revolutionise it, in the hope of inserting some of the language of historical writing into that of the political sphere. It has remained a task of historiography to question history's ongoing alliance with state power. In the logic of this task, historical writing has also come to claim a novel role in generating, rather than disrupting, peaceful relations among former parties to conflict, by supplying expertise to a politics of reparations, apologies, and the restitution of stolen artefacts and human remains. This field has only grown since the Second World War, recently especially in regard to relations between European states and their former colonies. It also provides one of the main frameworks in which non-European Indigenous histories are written nowadays as enmeshed with European and European settler histories.

The most consistent producer of methodological innovation in historical writing, in the period from the 1920s to the 1970s, was the French academic field, particularly the group of historians around the journal *Annales*. They produced novel models for a history of the lower classes, rural life, mentalities, long-duration economic systems, demographics and other matters accessible by statistical means, and cultural histories, for instance, of resistance to statal oppression, of religious beliefs, quotidian practices, or the history of the book trade.[48] The concomitant shift, in Western historiographies, towards cultural history in the 1980s and 1990s favoured the study of symbolic orders, linguistic patterns, practices, and the experiences and first-person viewpoints of historical agents. Also within this overall array, the writing of histories of previously excluded sectors of society became forceful pursuits, such as women's histories and the histories of racial, sexual, and ethnic minorities, including the small Indigenous populations of northern Europe. Cultural history moreover entailed a partial move away from the dominance of archival textual sources. Socially dominant groups were overrepresented in all types of writing. Historians that refused to reproduce this overrepresentation needed to find alternative sources and approaches.

An important development in this regard was recourse to interview-based oral history; another was the broader study of cultures of commemoration practices and other manifestations of collective memory. The latter theme gained particular importance in relation to the World Wars and the Holocaust, where seminal debates around asymmetries in the historical writing about victims and perpetrators unfolded. Through propagandist and expertise writing, historians had been implicated in the German genocide of the European Jews, as the most extreme project of systematic political violence in European history. Yet, the victims, too, sought to create historical records of their sufferings, literally burying them in the grounds of the sites of murder, in a desperate bid for future historical justice. The pattern that history served as a tool of violence as well as a (putative) forum of (residual) justice was already entrenched in European history; and yet the twentieth century saw the most extreme contrasts in this regard, and debate, more clearly than before, came to understand history also in terms of its proper uses and abuses. Non-European critiques of European patterns of thought, among which those of indigenous actors, broadened and further sharpened the moral vocabulary vested in historical discourse. 'Historical justice' has become an ever more familiar problem and cause of discussion. As a consequence, since the 1990s, in the form of an often-delayed reflection about colonialism, decolonisation, immigration to Europe, and geopolitical shifts, European historical writing has in particular striven to develop perspectives on the continent's past global interconnections. Where cultural history had heightened attention for the micro-level, global history often tends to favour the macro-level of large-scale economic and political-strategic histories. The moral texture of contemporary historical discourse is present in both.

Nonetheless, a constant has remained throughout all shifts in historical writing: the privileging of change as such. As the anthropologist Claude Lévi-Strauss noted, the appreciation of change is a variable among societal orders the world over.[49] In European history, historical writing has itself become increasingly the chief agency for administering this appreciation. The inbuilt bias favouring those societies that produce a high level of change over time appears hard to overcome, although some contributors have argued that the hypostatisation of change in European culture has of late reached such extremes that historical writing increasingly undermines its own foundations, the very relevance of knowledge about the historical past.[50] Moreover, partly in response to debates about climate change and the 'Anthropocene', which challenge the eighteenth- and nineteenth-century division of human and natural histories, but partly also in response to exigencies of 'prehistory' and indeed of Indigenous history, a perspective on 'deep time' and a history settled into material traces rather than in textual and other symbolic ones appears to be on the horizon.[51] The history of the change of historical writing seems far from over.

Notes

1 Foundational works on the written quality of history are those of Michel de Certeau, *The Writing of History* [1975] (New York: Columbia University Press, 1992) and Jack Goody, e.g. *The Domestication of the Savage Mind* (Cambridge: Cambridge University Press, 1977), who partly followed the work on literacy among the Toronto-based media theorists Harold Innis, Marshall McLuhan, Eric Havelock, and Walter Ong. The potential epistemological costs of writing have also been subject to a heated debate, from the philosopher Jacques Derrida to social anthropology; see James Clifford and George E. Marcus, eds. *Writing Culture: The Poetics and Politics of Ethnography* (Berkeley: University of California Press, 1986).
2 Daniel Woolf, ed. *The Oxford History of Historical Writing*, 5 vols. (Oxford: Oxford University Press, 2011).
3 The most explicit development of this theme is perhaps in Johann Gustav Droysen, *Outline of the Principles of History*, trans. E. Benjamin Andrews (Boston, MA: Ginn & Co., 1893).
4 E.g. Peter Novick, *That Noble Dream: The 'Objectivity Question' and the American Historical Profession* (Cambridge: Cambridge University Press, 1988); Georg G. Iggers, *Historiography in the Twentieth Century: From Scientific Objectivity to the Postmodern Challenge* (Hanover: Wesleyan University Press, 1997); Donald R. Kelley, *Fortunes of History: Historical Inquiry from Herder to Huizinga* (New Haven, CT: Yale University Press, 2003; middle part of a three-volume synthesis); Jörn Rüsen, *History: Narration, Interpretation, Orientation* (New York: Berghahn, 2005).
5 E.g. Arthur C. Danto, *Narration and Knowledge* (New York: Columbia University Press, 1985), and most recently, Jouni-Matti Kuukanen, *Postnarrativist Philosophy of Historiography* (Basingstoke: Palgrave, 2015); older debates are admirably summarised and analysed in Paul Ricoeur, *Time and Narrative*, 3 vols. (Chicago, IL: University of Chicago Press, 1984–1988) and in Hayden White, 'The Question of Narrative in Contemporary Historical Theory,' *History and Theory* 23, no. 1 (1984): 1–33.

6 The first handbooks provided foundational codifications of these tenets: Ernst Bernheim, *Lehrbuch der historischen Methode* [1889], 5th–6th ed. (Leipzig: Duncker & Humblot, 1908); Charles-Victor Langlois and Charles Seignobos, *Introduction to the Study of History* [1898], trans. G.G. Berry (New York: Holt, 1932).
7 See further Henning Trüper, 'The Flatness of Historicity,' *History and Theory* 58, no. 1 (2019): 23–49.
8 Going back to the work of Maurice Halbwachs, *On Collective Memory* [1925], trans. Lewis Coser (Chicago, IL: University of Chicago Press, 1992), highly influential contributions are Yosef Hayim Yerushalmi, *Zakhor: Jewish History and Jewish Memory* (Seattle: University of Washington Press, 1982); Pierre Nora, *Rethinking France: Les Lieux de Mémoire* [1984–1992], 4 vols. (Chicago, IL: University of Chicago Press, 1999–2010); and a more recent body of works that seeks to revise the strong opposition between history and memory: Jan Assmann, *Cultural Memory and Early Civilization: Writing, Remembrance, and Early Civilization* [1992] (Cambridge: Cambridge University Press, 2011); Aleida Assmann, *Cultural Memory and Western Civilization: Functions, Media, Archives* (Cambridge: Cambridge University Press, 2012); Marianne Hirsch, *The Generation of Postmemory: Writing and Visual Culture after the Holocaust* (New York: Columbia University Press, 2012).
9 François Hartog, *Regimes of Historicity: Presentism and Experiences of Time* [2003], trans. Saskia Brown (New York: Columbia University Press, 2015).
10 For perspectives that seek to transcend European boundaries, see Daniel Woolf, *A Global History of History* (Cambridge: Cambridge University Press, 2011); Georg G. Iggers, Q. Edward Wang, and Supriya Mukherjee, *A Global History of Modern Historiography*, 2nd ed. (London: Routledge, 2017).
11 François Hartog, *The Mirror of Herodotus: The Representation of the Other in the Writing of History* [1980] (Berkeley: University of California Press, 1988).
12 As Zachary Sayre Schiffman, in *The Birth of the Past* (Baltimore, MD: Johns Hopkins University Press, 2011), has argued in particular.
13 As has been stressed in particular by Marshall Sahlins, who compares Greek and Polynesian historical thoughts, see his *Apologies to Thucydides: Understanding History as Culture and Vice Versa* (Chicago, IL: University of Chicago Press, 2004).
14 See e.g. Anthony J. Woodman, *Rhetoric in Ancient Historiography: Four Studies* (London: Routledge, 2014).
15 See e.g. John Marincola, *Authority and Tradition in Ancient Historiography* (Cambridge: Cambridge University Press, 2004) and Jonas Grethlein, *Experience and Teleology in Ancient Historiography: 'Futures Past' from Herodotus to Augustine* (Cambridge: Cambridge University Press, 2013).
16 Karl Löwith, *Meaning in History* (Chicago, IL: University of Chicago Press, 1949).
17 Job 19:23–24, New American Standard Bible, 1977.
18 On the complex relations between myth and reason in ancient thought, see Greta Hawes, *Rationalizing Myth in Antiquity* (Oxford: Oxford University Press, 2014).
19 As a survey, see Deborah Mauskopf Deliyannis, *Historiography in the Middle Ages* (Leiden: Brill, 2003). On ancient–medieval continuities, see also Matthew Kempshall, *Rhetoric and the Writing of History 400–1500* (Manchester: Manchester University Press, 2011).
20 See Richard W. Burgess and Michael Kulikowski, *Mosaics of Time: The Latin Chronicle Traditions from the First Century BC to the Sixth Century AD* (Turnhout: Brepols, 2013).
21 Frances A. Yates, *The Art of Memory* (London: Routledge and Kegan Paul, 1966); Janet Coleman, *Ancient and Medieval Memories: Studies in the Reconstruction of the Past* (Cambridge: Cambridge University Press, 1992).
22 Jacques Le Goff, *The Birth of Purgatory* [1981], trans. Arthur Goldhammer (Chicago, IL: University of Chicago Press, 1984).
23 See in general David Armitage, ed. *Theories of Empire, 1450–1800* (Aldershot: Ashgate Variorum, 1998), for the later stages, see also Anthony Pagden, *Lords of All the World: Ideologies of Empire in Spain, Britain and France c. 1500 to c. 1800* (New Haven, CT: Yale University Press, 1995).

24 On the far-reaching implications of this framework for modern notions of historical time, see Constantin Fasolt, *The Limits of History* (Chicago, IL: University of Chicago Press, 2006).
25 See Quentin Skinner and Martin van Gelderen, eds. *Republicanism: A Shared European Heritage*, 2 vols. (Cambridge: Cambridge University Press, 2002).
26 Arnaldo Momigliano, 'Ancient History and the Antiquarian' [1950], in *Studies in Historiography* (London: Weidenfeld and Nicolson, 1966), 1–39; Peter N. Miller, *History and Its Objects: Antiquarianism and Material Culture since 1500* (Ithaca: Cornell University Press, 2017).
27 Following the classical discussion by Erwin Panofsky, 'Et in Arcadia Ego: Poussin and the Elegiac Tradition,' in *Philosophy and History: Essays Presented to Ernst Cassirer*, eds. R. Klibansky and H. J. Paton (Oxford: Clarendon Press, 1936), 223–254.
28 On the historical development of theories of pre-civilised others, see still Anthony Pagden, *The Fall of Natural Man: The American Indian and the Origins of Comparative Ethnology* (Cambridge: Cambridge University Press, 1983); moreover Han F. Vermeulen, *Before Boas: The Genesis of Ethnography and Ethnology in the German Enlightenment* (Lincoln: University of Nebraska Press, 2015); Michel-Rolph Trouillot, 'Anthropology and the Savage Slot: The Poetics and Politics of Otherness,' in *Global Transformations: Anthropology and the Modern World* (Basingstoke: Palgrave Macmillan, 2003), 7–28; and Jack Goody, *The Oriental, the Ancient, and the Primitive* (Cambridge: Cambridge University Press, 1990).
29 For one of the earliest instances, see Eve Duffy, *The Return of Hans Staden: A Go-Between in the Atlantic World* (Baltimore, MD: Johns Hopkins University Press, 2012). The genre was later transferred to North America and Australia; an alternative is the genre of Barbary captivity, which involved the enslavement of Europeans and thus reflected back on European slaveholding; see Lawrence Peskin, *Captives and Countrymen: Barbary Slavery and the American Public, 1785–1816* (Baltimore, MD: Johns Hopkins University Press, 2009).
30 Following Kenneth Pomeranz, *The Great Divergence* (Princeton, NJ: Princeton University Press, 2000).
31 See the impressive series *Writing the Nation*, eds. Stefan Berger et al., 7 vols. (Basingstoke: Palgrave Macmillan, 2008–2015).
32 Following Peter Hanns Reill, *The German Enlightenment and the Rise of Historicism* (Berkeley: University of California Press, 1975) and *Vitalizing Nature in the Enlightenment* (Berkeley: University of California Press, 2005).
33 See Henning Trüper, Dipesh Chakrabarty, and Sanjay Subrahmanyam, eds. *Historical Teleologies in the Modern World* (London: Bloomsbury, 2015).
34 See e.g. Anthony Grafton, *What was History? The Art of History in Early Modern Europe* (Cambridge: Cambridge University Press, 2007).
35 See the contributions in the theme issue *Archives and History*, eds. Filippo de Vivo, Maria Pia Donato, and Philipp Müller, *Storia della Storiografia* 68 (2015).
36 Anthony Grafton, *The Footnote: A Curious History* (London: Faber & Faber, 1997).
37 For the analysis of writing practice in modern history, see Henning Trüper, *Topography of a Method: François Louis Ganshof and the Writing of History* (Tübingen: Mohr, 2014).
38 Hayden White, *Metahistory: The Historical Imagination in Nineteenth-Century Europe* (Baltimore, MD: Johns Hopkins University Press, 1973); on narration in history, see also Paul Veyne, *Writing History: Essay on Epistemology* [1971], trans. M. Moore-Rinvolucri (Middletown, CT: Wesleyan University Press, 1984); Ricoeur, *Time and Narrative*.
39 For the implications, see still Reinhart Koselleck, 'Historia Magistra Vitae: The Dissolution of the Topos Into the Perspective of a Modernized Historical Process,' in *Futures Past: On the Semantics of Historical Time* [1979], trans. Keith Tribe (New York: Columbia University Press, 2004), ch. 2.
40 See especially Magne Sæbø, ed. *Hebrew Bible/Old Testament: The History of Its Interpretation*, vol. 3, no. 1–2 (Göttingen: Vandenhoeck & Ruprecht, 2013).

41 See Mario Wimmer, 'On Sources: Mythical and Historical Thinking in Fin-de-Siècle Vienna,' *Res: Anthropology and Aesthetics* 63/64 (2013): 108–124; also Bonnie Smith, 'Gender and the Practices of Scientific History: The Seminar and Archival Research in the Nineteenth Century,' *American Historical Review* 100, no. 4 (1995): 1150–1176.
42 Walter Benjamin, 'Theses on the Concept of History' [1940], in *Illuminations*, ed. Hannah Arendt. trans. H. Zohn (New York: Schocken, 1968), 253–264.
43 Vanessa Ogle, *The Global Transformation of Time 1870–1950* (Cambridge, MA: Harvard University Press, 2015).
44 Johannes Fabian, *Time and the Other: How Anthropology Makes Its Object* (New York: Columbia University Press, 1983); Dipesh Chakrabarty, *Provincializing Europe*, 2nd ed. (Princeton, NJ: Princeton University Press, 2007).
45 E.g. Velcheru Narayana Rao, David D. Shulman, and Sanjay Subrahmanyam, *Textures of Time: Writing History in South India, 1600–1800* (New Delhi: Permanent Black, 2001).
46 As, for instance, laid out by Eric Wolf, *Europe and the People without History* (Berkeley: University of California Press, 1982); see also Kenneth Coates, *A Global History of Indigenous Peoples: Struggle and Survival* (Basingstoke: Palgrave Macmillan, 2004); for the origins of the concept in the life sciences, and specifically botany, see Alix Cooper, *Inventing the Indigenous: Local Knowledge and Natural History in Early Modern Europe* (Cambridge: Cambridge University Press, 2007).
47 Andrew Zimmerman, *Alabama in Africa: Booker T. Washington, the German Empire, and the Globalization of the New South* (Princeton, NJ: Princeton University Press, 2010).
48 Peter Burke, *The French Historical Revolution: The Annales School, 1929–1989* (Cambridge: Polity Press, 1990).
49 Claude Lévi-Strauss, *The Savage Mind* [1962] (Chicago, IL: University of Chicago Press, 1966).
50 Especially Koselleck, *Futures Past*; Hartog, *Regimes*.
51 Daniel Lord Smail, *On Deep History and the Brain* (Berkeley: University of California Press, 2007).

Bibliography

Armitage, David, ed. *Theories of Empire, 1450–1800*. Aldershot: Ashgate Variorum, 1998.
Assmann, Aleida. *Cultural Memory and Western Civilization: Functions, Media, Archives*. Cambridge: Cambridge University Press, 2012.
Assmann, Jan. *Cultural Memory and Early Civilization: Writing, Remembrance, and Early Civilization* [1992]. Cambridge: Cambridge University Press, 2011.
Benjamin, Walter. 'Theses on the Concept of History' [1940]. In *Illuminations*, ed. Hannah Arendt, 253–264. Translated by H. Zohn. New York: Schocken, 1968.
Berger, Stefan, et al. eds. *Writing the Nation*, 7 vols. Basingstoke: Palgrave Macmillan, 2008–2015.
Bernheim, Ernst. *Lehrbuch der historischen Methode* [1889]. 5th–6th ed. Leipzig: Duncker & Humblot, 1908.
Burgess, Richard W., and Michael Kulikowski. *Mosaics of Time: The Latin Chronicle Traditions from the First Century BC to the Sixth Century AD*. Turnhout: Brepols, 2013.
Burke, Peter. *The French Historical Revolution: The Annales School, 1929–1989*. Cambridge: Polity Press, 1990.
Certeau, Michel de. *The Writing of History* [1975]. New York: Columbia University Press, 1992.
Chakrabarty, Dipesh. *Provincializing Europe*. 2nd ed. Princeton, NJ: Princeton University Press, 2007.
Clifford, James, and George E. Marcus, eds. *Writing Culture: The Poetics and Politics of Ethnography*. Berkeley: University of California Press, 1986.
Coates, Kenneth. *A Global History of Indigenous Peoples: Struggle and Survival*. Basingstoke: Palgrave Macmillan, 2004.

Coleman, Janet. *Ancient and Medieval Memories: Studies in the Reconstruction of the Past*. Cambridge: Cambridge University Press, 1992.
Cooper, Alix. *Inventing the Indigenous: Local Knowledge and Natural History in Early Modern Europe*. Cambridge: Cambridge University Press, 2007.
Danto, Arthur C. *Narration and Knowledge*. New York: Columbia University Press, 1985.
Droysen, Johann Gustav. *Outline of the Principles of History*. Translated by E. Benjamin Andrews. Boston, MA: Ginn & Co., 1893.
Duffy, Eve. *The Return of Hans Staden: A Go-Between in the Atlantic World*. Baltimore, MD: Johns Hopkins University Press, 2012.
Fabian, Johannes. *Time and the Other: How Anthropology Makes Its Object*. New York: Columbia University Press, 1983.
Fasolt, Constantin. *The Limits of History*. Chicago, IL: University of Chicago Press, 2006.
Goody, Jack. *The Domestication of the Savage Mind*. Cambridge: Cambridge University Press, 1977.
Goody, Jack. *The Oriental, the Ancient, and the Primitive*. Cambridge: Cambridge University Press, 1990.
Grafton, Anthony. *The Footnote: A Curious History*. London: Faber & Faber, 1997.
Grafton, Anthony. *What was History? The Art of History in Early Modern Europe*. Cambridge: Cambridge University Press, 2007.
Grethlein, Jonas. *Experience and Teleology in Ancient Historiography: 'Futures Past' from Herodotus to Augustine*. Cambridge: Cambridge University Press, 2013.
Halbwachs, Maurice. *On Collective Memory* [1925]. Translated by Lewis Coser. Chicago, IL: University of Chicago Press, 1992.
Hartog, François. *The Mirror of Herodotus: The Representation of the Other in the Writing of History* [1980]. Berkeley: University of California Press, 1988.
Hartog, François. *Regimes of Historicity: Presentism and Experiences of Time* [2003]. Translated by Saskia Brown. New York: Columbia University Press, 2015.
Hawes, Greta. *Rationalizing Myth in Antiquity*. Oxford: Oxford University Press, 2014.
Hirsch, Marianne. *The Generation of Postmemory: Writing and Visual Culture after the Holocaust*. New York: Columbia University Press, 2012.
Iggers, Georg G. *Historiography in the Twentieth Century: From Scientific Objectivity to the Postmodern Challenge*. Hanover: Wesleyan University Press, 1997.
Iggers, Georg G., Q. Edward Wang, and Supriya Mukherjee. *A Global History of Modern Historiography*. 2nd ed. London: Routledge, 2017.
Kelley, Donald R. *Fortunes of History: Historical Inquiry from Herder to Huizinga*. New Haven, CT: Yale University Press, 2003.
Kempshall, Matthew. *Rhetoric and the Writing of History 400–1500*. Manchester: Manchester University Press, 2011.
Koselleck, Reinhart, *Futures Past: On the Semantics of Historical Time* [1979]. Translated by Keith Tribe. New York: Columbia University Press, 2004.
Koselleck, Reinhart. 'Historia Magistra Vitae: The Dissolution of the Topos Into the Perspective of a Modernized Historical Process.' In *Futures Past: On the Semantics of Historical Time* [1979]. Translated by Keith Tribe. New York: Columbia University Press, 2004.
Kuukanen, Jouni-Matti. *Postnarrativist Philosophy of Historiography*. Basingstoke: Palgrave, 2015.
Langlois, Charles-Victor, and Charles Seignobos. *Introduction to the Study of History* [1898]. Translated by G.G. Berry. New York: Holt, 1932.
Le Goff, Jacques. *The Birth of Purgatory* [1981]. Translated by Arthur Goldhammer. Chicago: University of Chicago Press, 1984.
Lévi-Strauss, Claude. *The Savage Mind* [1962]. Chicago, IL: University of Chicago Press, 1966.
Löwith, Karl. *Meaning in History*. Chicago, IL: University of Chicago Press, 1949.
Marincola, John. *Authority and Tradition in Ancient Historiography*. Cambridge: Cambridge University Press, 2004.

Mauskopf Deliyannis, Deborah. *Historiography in the Middle Ages.* Leiden: Brill, 2003.
Miller, Peter N. *History and Its Objects: Antiquarianism and Material Culture since 1500.* Ithaca: Cornell University Press, 2017.
Momigliano, Arnaldo. 'Ancient History and the Antiquarian' [1950]. In *Studies in Historiography*, 1–39. London: Weidenfeld and Nicolson, 1966.
Nora, Pierre. *Rethinking France: Les Lieux de Mémoire* [1984–1992], 4 vols. Chicago, IL: University of Chicago Press, 1999–2010.
Novick, Peter. *That Noble Dream: The 'Objectivity Question' and the American Historical Profession.* Cambridge: Cambridge University Press, 1988.
Ogle, Vanessa. *The Global Transformation of Time 1870–1950.* Cambridge, MA: Harvard University Press, 2015.
Pagden, Anthony. *The Fall of Natural Man: The American Indian and the Origins of Comparative Ethnology.* Cambridge: Cambridge University Press, 1983.
Pagden, Anthony. *Lords of All the World: Ideologies of Empire in Spain, Britain and France c. 1500 to c. 1800.* New Haven, CT: Yale University Press, 1995.
Panofsky, Erwin. 'Et in Arcadia Ego: Poussin and the Elegiac Tradition.' In *Philosophy and History: Essays Presented to Ernst Cassirer*, edited by R. Klibansky and H. J. Paton, 223–254. Oxford: Clarendon Press, 1936.
Peskin, Lawrence. *Captives and Countrymen: Barbary Slavery and the American Public, 1785–1816.* Baltimore, MD: Johns Hopkins University Press, 2009.
Pomeranz, Kenneth. *The Great Divergence.* Princeton, NJ: Princeton University Press, 2000.
Rao, Velcheru Narayana, David D. Shulman, and Sanjay Subrahmanyam. *Textures of Time: Writing History in South India, 1600–1800.* New Delhi: Permanent Black, 2001.
Reill, Peter Hanns. *The German Enlightenment and the Rise of Historicism.* Berkeley: University of California Press, 1975.
Reill, Peter Hanns, *Vitalizing Nature in the Enlightenment.* Berkeley: University of California Press, 2005.
Ricoeur, Paul. *Time and Narrative*, 3 vols. Chicago, IL: University of Chicago Press, 1984–1988.
Rüsen, Jörn. *History: Narration, Interpretation, Orientation.* New York: Berghahn, 2005.
Sahlins, Marshall. *Apologies to Thucydides: Understanding History as Culture and Vice Versa.* Chicago, IL: University of Chicago Press, 2004.
Schiffman, Zachary Sayre. *The Birth of the Past.* Baltimore, MD: Johns Hopkins University Press, 2011.
Skinner, Quentin, and Martin van Gelderen, eds. *Republicanism: A Shared European Heritage*, 2 vols. Cambridge: Cambridge University Press, 2002.
Smail, Daniel Lord. *On Deep History and the Brain.* Berkeley: University of California Press, 2007.
Smith, Bonnie. 'Gender and the Practices of Scientific History: The Seminar and Archival Research in the Nineteenth Century.' *American Historical Review* 100, no. 4 (1995): 1150–1176.
Sæbø, Magne, ed. *Hebrew Bible/Old Testament: The History of Its Interpretation*, vol. 3, no. 1–2. Göttingen: Vandenhoeck & Ruprecht, 2013.
Trouillot, Michel-Rolph. 'Anthropology and the Savage Slot: The Poetics and Politics of Otherness.' In *Global Transformations: Anthropology and the Modern World*, 7–28. Basingstoke: Palgrave Macmillan, 2003.
Trüper, Henning. *Topography of a Method: François Louis Ganshof and the Writing of History.* Tübingen: Mohr, 2014.
Trüper, Henning. 'The Flatness of Historicity.' *History and Theory* 58, no.1 (2019): 23–49.
Trüper, Henning, Dipesh Chakrabarty, and Sanjay Subrahmanyam, eds. *Historical Teleologies in the Modern World.* London: Bloomsbury, 2015.
Vermeulen, Han F. *Before Boas: The Genesis of Ethnography and Ethnology in the German Enlightenment.* Lincoln: University of Nebraska Press, 2015.

Veyne, Paul. *Writing History: Essay on Epistemology* [1971]. Translated by M. Moore-Rinvolucri. Middletown: Wesleyan University Press, 1984.

Vivo, Filippo de, Maria Pia Donato, and Philipp Müller, eds. *Archives and History*, theme issue *Storia della Storiografia* 68 (2015).

White, Hayden. *Metahistory: The Historical Imagination in Nineteenth-Century Europe*. Baltimore: Johns Hopkins University Press, 1973.

White, Hayden. 'The Question of Narrative in Contemporary Historical Theory.' *History and Theory* 23, no. 1 (1984): 1–33.

Wimmer, Mario. 'On Sources: Mythical and Historical Thinking in Fin-de-Siècle Vienna.' *Res: Anthropology and Aesthetics* 63/64 (2013): 108–124.

Wolf, Eric. *Europe and the People without History*. Berkeley: University of California Press, 1982.

Woodman, Anthony J. *Rhetoric in Ancient Historiography: Four Studies*. London: Routledge, 2014.

Woolf, Daniel. *A Global History of History*. Cambridge: Cambridge University Press, 2011.

Woolf, Daniel, ed. *The Oxford History of Historical Writing*, 5 vols. Oxford: Oxford University Press, 2011.

Yates, Frances A. *The Art of Memory*. London: Routledge and Kegan Paul, 1966.

Yerushalmi, Yosef Hayim. *Zakhor: Jewish History and Jewish Memory*. Seattle: University of Washington Press, 1982.

Zimmerman, Andrew. *Alabama in Africa: Booker T. Washington, the German Empire, and the Globalization of the New South*. Princeton, NJ: Princeton University Press, 2010.

3
THEORETICAL FRONTIERS

Ben Silverstein

The frontier as settler colonial condition

Noting the increasing density of population in the decade following 1880, the United States Superintendent of the Census announced in 1892 that he would no longer find a place for the 'frontier line' in census reports. The frontier era, he declared, was over. The 'unsettled area' of the American West had been 'so broken into by isolated bodies of settlement' that the prior frontier had been replaced by a newly settled population.[1] This finding famously prompted Frederick Jackson Turner to explain and emphasise the significance of the frontier to American history, arguing that it had been the 'expansion westward with its new opportunities' for 'perennial rebirth' through contact with the 'simplicity of primitive society' that had 'furnish[ed] the forces dominating American character'.[2] Turner's frontier thesis was, some 60 years later, a key reference in Russel Ward's influential argument that it was the 'ethos' of white Australian 'pastoral workers' that 'came to have a quite disproportionate influence on that of the whole nation'.[3] For Ward, the 1891 New South Wales census told of an increasing urban population, a change that, in part, was responsible both for ending the conditions that produced the 'old up-country ethos' and for 'embalm[ing]' that ethos 'in a national myth', securing its influence.[4] In relying on fin-de-siècle census data that explicitly defined a settler population against Indigenous peoples, both Turner and Ward were telling stories of nations being made through relationships between non-Indigenous populations and national territories.[5]

The point here is not just that these texts are ethnocentric or exclusive (though they certainly are and have been generatively critiqued on these grounds).[6] It is that, by narrating the creation of a nation as a developing relationship between (non-Indigenous) people and the land, they recapitulate a trope of settler colonialism, the imagined articulation of a new society to the land itself. For Turner, the land on the North American frontier was not just 'free' but was also just the right kind of challenging. It was rugged and well-suited to farming on smallholdings, encouraging a kind of resilient, defiant, and self-governing individualism. By contrast, Ward was to argue, the land on the Australian frontier was conducive to a mode of pastoralism that produced a class distinction between big landholders and a large, semi-itinerant outback proletariat from which emerged a collectivist ethos.[7] These were materialist approaches to history that set aside the dispossession that was fundamental to the establishment of these differently classed societies, and disregarded the labour of Indigenous, enslaved, and coerced peoples.[8] The corollary of these narrowed narrations of the frontier is what Patrick Wolfe described as a 'negative articulation', a social relationship between people and land that is premised on the elimination of those native societies who otherwise stood in the way.[9]

It may seem unusual to begin an essay on Indigenous histories with historical accounts that explicitly erase Indigeneity from the nation and that consolidate the self of the nation by, in Gayatri Chakravorty Spivak's phrasing, 'obliging the native to cathect the space of the Other on his home ground'. In this sense, these frontier stories are the historiographical correlate of what Haunani-Kay Trask described as the Indigenous juridical experience of having 'their nationality *forcibly changed in their own homeland*'.[10] And, to the extent that Turner's and Ward's frontier narrations deliberately exclude Indigenous peoples and occlude processes of conquest or dispossession, they have been subject to thoroughgoing critique that has moved the historiography beyond their fundamental precepts and re-imagined the actors, their doings, and the space of the 'frontier' itself. The field of research has moved on. What was once described as a frontier is now often understood in different terms, allowing us access to stories other than those of white men making themselves at home on free land. We can now learn much from studies of the many ways Indigenous peoples navigated life on their own country, of women and enslaved people and precarious immigrants making lives amid constrained possibilities, of the violence of conquest on the land, of shapeshifting actors on borderlands and middle grounds, of hybridities and contact zones. But the earlier histories that took 'frontiers' as their subject have not been completely left behind. This chapter is a necessarily partial sketch of the transition from these frontier historiographies into a more recent tendency within studies of settler colonialism to centre Indigenous situations. In this chapter, I take the frontier historiography in the U.S. and Australia as usefully related and divergent, and trace some of the ways a stream of critical Indigenous histories has emerged from the study of frontiers in each site.[11]

In these critical histories, the frontier emerges once more as a constitutive space, albeit in different ways to those of earlier schools of frontier history. For adherents to the 'frontier thesis', frontiers were unsettled spaces denoted by the relatively low density of non-Indigenous populations, where national character was defined through a struggle to conquer and possess the land. This is the archetypal settler colonial story. Scholarship on settler colonialism reminds us that processes of enacting possession were and are contentious, and that practices of placing Indigenous people on the margins rather than the centre of the frontier story are an ideological manifestation of a settler position in those battles. We might usefully differentiate here between the frontier as a historical place or time, and the frontier as performative representation. Setting the truthfulness of historical representation – the correspondence between historiography and the past – to one side, in this chapter I focus on the social effects produced or licenced by those representations.

The chapter first examines frontier histories and the way they have been transformed, starting from the 1970s, by practices of writing violence and conquest into the story in order to include Indigenous peoples in the national narration of the frontier. Since this revisionist move, from the 1980s and 1990s, historians turned to exploring resistance and accommodation, middle grounds and borderlands, Aboriginal agency and Indigenous political formations. While these histories departed from histories of the frontier that sought to naturalise conquest and were conducive to projects of invasion, they tended to sever pasts of violence or possibility from a postcolonial present, representing moments now gone.[12] Departing from this historical sequestration, the chapter then turns to examine some of the ways histories of settler colonialism have returned, over the past two decades, to the frontier motif to understand continuing histories of contention. If we take the frontier more expansively to denote the site where settler sovereignty is fabricated, we might use the concept to explore the way this process was refracted through the relationships Henry Reynolds described as fundamental to a frontier: those between 'Aborigines, settlers and land'.[13] And this is what a number of historians over the past two decades have done, using insights from analyses of settler colonialism to write revisionist histories that operationalise the frontier concept to narrate the production of sovereignties through relationships between Indigenous people and settlers that are enmeshed in struggles for and about the land, struggles that can be located in institutions of coercion and the streets of growing cities as much as they can be found in the outback or the West. The spatial and temporal continuity of struggles over land and over sovereignty is a central insight of recent historiography on settler colonialism, providing a theoretical approach to understanding contact histories. In registering this struggle, however, too many of these histories have either refused or failed to attend to Indigenous actions or practices. The chapter closes by calling for a turn to Indigenous structures, articulated with but not necessarily dominated by those structures of invasion inaugurated on frontiers. Both Indigenous and settler colonial structures endure within the contemporary social formation, demanding histories that tend to both.

From frontiersmen to Aborigines, settlers and land

Turner's frontier thesis was first articulated in a paper read to the annual meeting of the American Historical Association in 1893. Here, he advanced the argument that it was the frontier that explained America: the 'existence of an area of free land, its continuous recession, and the advance of American settlement' were the crucial components of American nationhood and exceptionalism. The frontier was a place, the 'hither edge of free land' where one found the 'meeting point between savagery and civilisation'. And it was also a process, the 'line of most rapid and effective Americanization'. In Turner's story, Indian society disintegrated before the force of civilisation and the colonist, by mastering the wilderness, emerged as an American, as a democratic individualist, intolerant of administration and antipathetic to control. Through the frontier, these individuals were formed into a 'composite nationality', an America big enough for all kinds of men, so long as they were colonists.[14] The motor of Americanisation for Turner was the desire for and availability of 'free land', a concept that rendered Indigenous sovereignties or ownership moot. The consequent sense of evolving inevitability at the heart of the frontier thesis raised the distinction between Indian and non-Indian to national creation story, an opposition that both produced and naturalised settler sovereignty.[15]

Some Australian historians began explicitly to take up Turner's thesis in the mid-twentieth century, usually in order to differentiate Australian frontiers from those Turner had described in the American West and thereby explain the emergence of an Australian collectivism.[16] But it was not until Ward's history of the Australian national mystique that this idea received its full treatment. Where Turner had sought to explain America by looking west to the frontier, Ward set out to understand Australia through the folklore of the outback. In a similarly almost deterministic account of the relation between national subject and land, Ward described the emergence of a 'nomad tribe' of men who formed the pastoral proletariat, working the land as casual farmhands and developing an ethos that sprang from 'their struggle to assimilate themselves and their *mores* to the strange environment'. From this emerged a sense of what it meant to be Australian: a commitment to equality and mateship, to democracy and collectivism, and to practical rather than intellectual pursuits.[17] In so doing, Ward worked within a post-Federation Australian historiographical tradition that wrote Aboriginal people out of the nation, a tradition W.E.H. Stanner was to dub 'The Great Australian Silence'. One finds 'snippets' of racialised frontier violence in Ward's text, as Angela Woollacott has pointed out, but these were 'buried rather than highlighted', rendered apart from the main story.[18]

It was by elevating such suggestive 'snippets' from the margins into the centre of the story that, in the 1970s, Australian scholars of the then relatively new field of Aboriginal history were able to re-cast the story of the frontier as one of violence. The frontier was a central theme of these first scholarly histories of Aboriginal people. Often explicitly responding to Ward's omissions, and influenced by Charles Rowley's then recent and transformative account of Aboriginal historical experiences of violence, they wrote revisionist histories where accounting for both 'sides' of the frontier led the historian to foreground warfare, resistance, and conquest. Lynette Russell has argued that the resistance model, and its concern for Aboriginal agency and action, characterises the Australian school of frontier history led by Henry Reynolds.[19] This approach turned the national story 'not upside down, but inside out', to relocate the battles mounted by Indigenous peoples from the margins to the heart of the national story. In *The Other Side of the Frontier*, Reynolds re-read the settler archive to emphasise and detail the patterns and tactics of Black resistance on every 'fringe of European settlement'. The book's impact came not from his explanation of conflict (though he did insist that land was at the centre of a broader complex of causes) nor from his exploration of creative and complex responses to and ideas about invaders and invasion, but from its emphasis on Black resistance as the key feature of Australia's frontier history. Reynolds found national heroes on the frontier – not in Ward's nomad tribe of white pastoral labourers but in the Aboriginal people who encountered and resisted invasion.[20] This model of violence and resistance was to shape the formation of a field of Aboriginal history that centred frontier conflict and that emphasised resistance as the source of a present-day tradition of Aboriginal survival and autonomy. In that sense, it was through a reassessment of the frontier that historians wrote of Aboriginal politics and resistance.[21]

But while these Australian histories re-framed their subject, telling 'new stories of the frontier', American scholars of the New Western History instead insisted that in order to narrate such new stories it was necessary to reject the model of the frontier entirely.[22] In Patricia Limerick's *The Legacy of Conquest*, the central story was not one of white men moving onto free land but of settlers seeking to conquer a land already inhabited (though to conquer a land is not, one must note, to conquer peoples; just as on Turner's frontier, the key relationship was between Americans and the land). This frame opened possibilities for a less ethnocentric history, enabling her to write of white women alongside Indians, Mexican-Americans, Chinese people, Japanese people, and African-Americans navigating their way through a new world of property and force. To do so, she retained the conceptual value of 'the West' while turning away from the concept of the frontier, praising Turner's historical imagination but bemoaning the corralling influence of his frontier thesis. The frontier, she wrote, was a 'white American ... origin myth', an 'unsubtle concept in a subtle world' that historians should understand for its power in the lives of people being researched but not deploy themselves. For Limerick, unlike Reynolds, to 'take the Indian side' offered 'no escape from ethnocentricity'. The very notion of an 'Indian side to the story' itself entrenched the 'Euro-American angle of vision, by which Indian diversity flattens out into one, simple story'.[23] This homogenising effect, characteristic especially of Reynolds' early work on the frontier, was a cul-de-sac from which histories of the American West sought to escape.

For Richard White, the early history of fur trade economies in the American Great Lakes region was characterised not so much by conquest or European (quests for) domination but by the search for common meaning among multiple peoples who were unable, and perhaps unwilling, to dominate the other. The middle ground he narrated, with its assorted boundary-straddlers, *coureurs de bois*, and mixed marriages, was a joint Indian–white creation produced by processes of creative misunderstandings from which arose new and shared meanings and practices.[24] This disposed of the frontier concept in order to emphasise the power and capacity of Indigenous peoples, alongside others, to craft accommodations. For some historians, this task was best served by foregrounding women as cultural brokers and mediators. Sylvia van Kirk's earlier history of the fur trade emphasised the importance of Indian women's role in overlapping spheres of intimacy and labour in crafting an essential economic connection between Indian and European societies, and Peggy Pascoe turned to late nineteenth-century Protestant missionary women in the American West and the emergence of a morality discourse in part through their relationships with the Chinese, Indigenous, and Mormon women who were their clients.[25]

As American historians re-imagined this period through the concept of the middle ground, their Australian counterparts began to re-work the concept of the frontier to move away from Reynolds' initial emphasis on antagonism and violence and towards studies of accommodation and compromise. They sought out instances of Aboriginal agency, as in Ann McGrath's study of the north Australian cattle industry, which was entirely reliant on Aboriginal labour for its survival. Excluded from Ward's 'nomad tribe', Aboriginal men and women appear in her account as workers who made the Australian pastoral industries, who adapted cattle work to their own purposes, and who developed a range of strategic compromises with white managers and workers that constituted 'Aborigines themselves' as 'the boundary-riders of the frontier' with 'a firm footing on either side'.[26] And Reynolds too provided an account of Aboriginal collaboration with white explorers, police forces, administrators, clergymen, and so on, in order to narrate Aboriginal contributions to a new nation. This emphasis on agency, adaptation, and collaboration emerged within histories of the frontier; as Reynolds was to argue, there was 'no middle ground in Australia'.[27] By the early 1990s, the Australian frontier had been re-imagined as a place and time made by both whites and Aboriginal people, and best approached through a study of Aboriginal agency. For Richard Broome, for instance, histories of warfare or massacre 'diminished Aboriginal people of the past'. Frontiers, he argued, should be understood as complex fields of shifting interests and relationships; of violence perpetrated by a range of people and directed towards a range of other subjects; of changing terms of engagement, understanding, and misunderstanding. This was an argument for Aboriginal agency: frontiers were populated by 'culturally alive and complex humans', people who were 'active not passive and able to make choices' based on considerations rooted in 'their own cultural imperatives and individual desires'.[28]

In these Australian historians' search for Aboriginal agency, they re-made the frontier as shifting and negotiated, as a line over which Aboriginal people could move to avail themselves of opportunities in the society they chose. Rather than avoiding the concept, they operationalised the frontier as a zone of mediation and accommodation constituted by a permeable and constitutive border. Similarly, some historians of the Mexican–American border turned to think of 'borderlands' across and around the lines dividing nations.[29] The 'borderlands' concept had been introduced to American historiography by Turner's student, Herbert Eugene Bolton, in his argument that the West had been shaped as much by the northward movement of the Spanish as it had by the westward movement of Anglo-Americans. The Spanish Borderlands were a zone in which Native Americans played a crucial role; Bolton lauded Spanish colonisation but wrote Indigenous peoples into that celebratory history.[30] By the 1980s, the concept had been critiqued and expanded geographically, chronologically, and epistemologically, further emphasising Indigenous centrality both to the U.S. and Mexico and to the crafting of distinct and complex spaces across and in between nations.

If frontiers are spaces where the nation is made, borderlands by contrast are spaces of uncertainty where, as Pekka Hämäläinen and Samuel Truett argue, the end of the story remains undetermined. The dispersed perspectives of borderlands histories seek to avoid centring the nation and its fabrication in favour of local stories that can be made part of but are certainly not containable within national histories. These are stories that pull in different directions, often staged around Indigenous cores, involving a proliferating cast of actors with divergent interests and complex affiliations to and across spaces and peoples.³¹ Borderlands histories thus focus on incessant contingency and negotiability, but do not shirk the force that was critical to nineteenth-century colonial worlds. Ned Blackhawk has shown how coexistence in the American Great Basin was constituted through and riven by violence, foregrounding the Ute, Paiute, and Shoshone peoples and exploring their experience of pain and its distribution as they were drawn into economies of slavery. Tracing the spaces between European empires, Hämäläinen has narrated the emergence of a Comanche Empire in the eighteenth and nineteenth centuries. This empire was organised around horse raiding and trading, and it was horse-borne mobility that formed the basis of their 'kinetic empire'.³² Such Indigenous histories of what is now the southwest of the U.S. explore the conditions of living in the borderlands to move beyond the overdetermination of the frontier, presenting us with an expanded sense of possibility.

Each of these varied American turns to narrate Indigenous histories within histories of the West, the middle ground, or borderlands may have contextualised those histories and provided the basis for a new complexity, but they also segmented them from national histories. Writing Indian history into the West disturbed Turner's triumphant, and triumphantly popular, narrative of the frontier. But, for a long while, it failed to replace it with an equally compelling narrative. White worried in 1991 that New Western Historians had produced stories of tragedy and irony, neither of which could match the sweeping ambition and drama of older narratives. As a consequence, as Daniel Richter bemoaned in 1993, the New Indian History had then produced only a 'scant impact on larger areas of scholarship, on high school and college textbooks, and on the popular mind'. Pascoe similarly complained that American historians of that era were 'far less likely to challenge our conclusions than to ignore us altogether'.³³

By contrast, the Australian retention of the frontier concept placed Aboriginal history at the centre of the national frame, prompting a so-called 'history war' in which representations of frontier violence became central to national narrations.³⁴ But it did so, Gillian Cowlishaw argued, by confining a racist and violent history to the time of the frontier, immersing readers in the horrors of an 'awful past' but, through performances of empathy with Aboriginal victims and voyagers, distancing that past from ongoing contemporary cultures of colonialism.³⁵ Seeking to sidestep these often moralising debates over the nature of the nation, some Australian historians turned to explore that colonial continuity identified by so many of the Indigenous thinkers to whom we turn in the following section.

The return of the frontier

Histories of settler colonialism present one way of bridging these twin problems of marginalisation and segmentation. They centre the problem of continuity, return to the frontier but with a different temporality, and speak to the formation of nations and empires. There are several possible genealogies one might cite to trace the emergence of a settler colonial analytic. One could, as Dean Saranillio has recently done, emphasise the importance of Haunani-Kay Trask's work in 'offering ... new pedagogies for – different ways of knowing, being, and responding to – the living force of the colonial past in the present' in Hawai'i.[36] One might alternatively cite the circulation of the term in discussions of the Israeli occupation of Palestinian land and people, discussions that influenced Trask's work.[37] Here, I want to locate settler colonialism as a method of doing history as it emerged from Koori analyses of Australian frontier violence in the early 1990s. In 1993, the poet Lisa Bellear connected contemporary violence with the invasion that was both enacted and symbolised by the arrival of the First Fleet at Warrane/Sydney Cove. Tony Birch took up this theme of continuity in a series of pieces studying the Western District of Victoria, documenting an 'imperialist nostalgia' that reproduced and perpetuated over 200 years of colonial practices. Similarly, Gary Foley insisted that present contestations should be understood as the outcomes of a (settler) colonial structure that are best considered in the context of a longer history.[38]

These works emphasised continuity and refused any hard separation between the frontier and the present; 'Nothing Has Changed', Birch insisted. The closure of the frontier did not necessarily signify a rupture. And each of these writers and activists worked with and influenced Patrick Wolfe in the 1990s as he formulated an account of settler colonial continuity that returned conceptually to the frontier to understand the present. Wolfe expressed this continuity by reconfiguring invasion as a structure, not an event. The frontier was no longer to be considered the period of violence or the process of becoming American, for instance, but could be rethought as establishing a set of enduring relationships conducive to colonial extraction. Settler colonisation, in Wolfe's analysis, takes form as a project of dispossession whose primary object – as it relates to Indigenous people – was (is) the land itself rather than mixing native labour with it; it is distinguishable from other colonial formations on this ground, even if its many iterations articulate with and shade into other modes of generating surplus value. This was, then, a form of colonialism 'premised on displacing indigenes from (or *replacing* them on) the land'. This account helps us describe an ongoing 'logic of elimination' that characterises the relationship between settlers and Indigenous peoples, as the emergent settler nation works to fabricate a relationship with territory in place.[39]

The frontier is the 'primary paradigm' of this settler colonisation, a sign expressing a basic polarity between settlers and Indigenous people and connoting the historical reality of an invasion that works towards effecting a project of land theft. This polarity, brought into being by invasion, persists. While assimilationist positions mark the closure of the frontier by presuming the successful domestication of Indigeneity and the containment or erasure of Indigenous sovereignty, many

Indigenous analyses of historical continuity have noted differences between the violence of the frontier and that of more recent assimilation but have preferred to emphasise their linkage. This representation of invasion as an enduring structure is, as Shannon Speed has noted, 'the crucial insight of settler colonial theory'. It means that, in Wolfe's terms, invasion's 'history does not stop ... when it moves on from the era of frontier homicide'. The history of invasion rather involves charting the processes by which 'a logic that initially informed frontier killing transmutes into different modalities, discourses and institutional formations as it undergirds the historical development and complexification of settler society'.[40] As a way of doing history, then, settler colonialism offers us a perspective on frontiers that does not sever them from the contemporary situation, that does not render them past.

This turn marks a historiographical shift from responses to earlier frontier models. As discussed above, Limerick, for example, had sought to replace the frontier with a story of conquest. But hers was a conquest that had ended. In the insistence of so many New Western Historians on the continuity of the West as a place, they set aside the continuity of the frontier as a process. Stressing invasion rather than conquest, and structure rather than event, renders processes of dispossession as ongoing and the consequent relation between settler and native as persistent. Making this move opened up a space for historians to think through the temporality of the frontier concept and to operationalise it to recognise, after a century of assimilationist onslaught, an ongoing clash between Indigenous sovereignty and independent existence on the one hand and settler colonial attacks on that sovereignty and independence on the other.[41]

This is not to say that an analysis of settler colonialism adopts the frontier as truthful, or as the only way to present a history.[42] Rather, it turns our attention to the frontier as both a material and ideological effect of settler colonial expansion, the latter of which might be historicised and analysed as a performative representation.[43] The historical frontier is a way of expressing the coming together of societies that had previously been separate. It is not, as has been discussed above, the only way of describing this process. It is a way of framing that process historically in relation to national origins and we can dwell here, for a moment, on the way it works as a performative. The frontier, as Deborah Bird Rose has pointed out, is 'quite explicitly not the nation, but rather a site for the making of the nation'. The frontier as border appears as a line in time rather than space, a 'Rolling Year Zero' which predates and constitutes the nation. The frontier, then, is the space and time where settler sovereignty is produced. And in naming this a frontier, the resolution of conflict is overdetermined; it ends in the erasure of Aboriginal communities, in the constitution of the practice of Aboriginal sovereignties as anomalous and marginal. The frontier is thus purposeful, a space whose naming actively authorised an asymmetrical violence that produces settler sovereignty through prohibiting any opposing force.[44]

Its failure to describe historical situations accurately does not mean that we should, as historians, dispose of the frontier concept altogether; rather, we might historicise it, making it work.[45] The frontier marks the establishment of a structure of invasion, a structure that, for now, persists. And to the extent that settler society is driven both to remove Indigeneity and to establish a new, replacement society on an expropriated land base, it is an antagonistic structure in which Indigeneity 'continues to shape the colonial society that settlers construct', remaining 'an absent centre that structures settler discourse' and practice in all contexts.[46] This is one way of relating Indigenous and national histories, albeit one that foregrounds a colonial or imperial narrative.[47] Researching settler colonialism, then, emerges as a way of doing history that offers a sense of continuity, a return to the material that can (though it does not necessarily) centre Indigeneity, and a transnational, comparative, or imperial perspective that refuses national proclamations of exceptionality.

This approach – reading invasion into settler colonial situations across time and space – has come to influence a range of scholarship in both Australia and the U.S. In 2008, Frederick Hoxie called for scholars of American Indian history to think with settler colonial frameworks to narrate native struggles against colonial rule rather than stories of national incorporation. It was an idea whose time had come. Though the theoretical paradigm of settler colonialism has a longer genealogy in Australian, Hawaiian, and Palestinian histories, since 2008 it has spread through American historiography with 'stunning rapidity'. As Nancy Shoemaker proclaimed in 2015, with an ironic claim to possession, 'settler colonial theory has taken over my field, Native American studies'.[48]

Theorising the frontier as the site where the nation is made via attacks on Indigeneity has opened up a field that extends frontier histories beyond the earlier frontier paradigm. From this perspective, the passing of the frontier does not signal the birth of a new nation but rather a turn to assimilating practices of domestication. This is a turn in settler discourse and practice from considering and engaging Indigenous people as external to the nation to considering and seeking to render them surrounded and contained by it.[49] But the violence does not go away. Rather, the colonial formation inaugurated on the frontier persists, structuring relationships between peoples, resources, and sovereignties. Scholars of comparative histories have drawn on and extended these insights into spaces less frequently understood as frontiers, including cities and towns across the Pacific Rim, and to times long after the proclaimed closure of the frontier, including practices of child removal and institutionalisation performed under the rubric of assimilation or protection. This kind of analysis underpins, for instance, Penelope Edmonds' reading of the prosecution of Aboriginal women for prostitution as an instance of racialisation, as a way of marking the bounds of legitimate presence in urban space, and as a means of legitimising some forms of reproduction by casting others as illicit. These were, she suggests, settler techniques for clearing Indigenous women away to claim space for a settler town, and for clearing Indigeneity from a future to be inhabited by a settler population. Urban policing emerges as akin to a frontier action.[50] For others, studying settler colonialism offers a useful way of understanding frontiers outside but still in relation to the nation. It reinscribes the American West or the Australian outback as 'part[s] of the flow and webs within and between empires and effectively associates ... [them] with the world of empires'.[51] Thinking with this work can illuminate the distinct relationships Indigenous people crafted with differently racialised migrants to their territories.[52] It can provide a basis for comparative studies of race across and in the wake of settler colonial frontiers.[53] And it has prompted renewed attention to settler colonial narrative forms and to historical and popular representations of the so-called Indigenous 'disappearance'.[54]

Has this work been useful? We must, as Jodi Byrd notes, ask here whether thinking about the frontier enables Indigenous peoples 'to intervene in or theorize differently the violences of empire'. In her analysis, the answer depends upon whether a frontier or settler colonialism approach might further obscure the Indigenous sovereignties that slip 'amongst and through' the binarisms of civilised/savage or settler/native, respectively.[55] It is to this question, and to historians' concern with what is left unsaid and, perhaps, is obscured by the binarist frontier focus of histories informed by settler colonial studies, that I will turn in the final section of this essay.

Native agents

An argument for the utility of settler colonialism as an explanatory framework should not be confused with the claim that the framework will always and everywhere be of use, nor that it is all that we need to understand Indigenous or (settler) colonial history.[56] Settler colonialism as a way of looking at history can illuminate relationships between peoples. But it is not without its limitations.[57] Here, I want to address one recurrent critique, posed by a number of historians who have found little in theories of settler colonialism that helps them to describe Indigenous agency. In different ways, Lisa Ford and Shino Konishi have suggested that the structuralism of settler colonialism limits the space available for explicating the Indigenous agency they seek empirically to account for.[58] For Tim Rowse, this is a result of the supposition that the structure of invasion is governed by an enduring logic of elimination. Histories pursuing this approach, he argues, are trapped by the suspicion that any historical inscription of Indigeneity is a repressive move inscribing it within settler discourse. To describe Indigenous difference, that is, is to recapitulate settler colonialism in its post-frontier assimilationist mode. Rowse argues, then, that this reduces Indigenous people to 'minor characters' in their history and diminishes Indigenous agency either to a 'state-conceded' remnant or to a phenomenon of resistance that is 'beyond empirical specification, an unrepresented and unrepresentable thing'.[59]

These are not entirely novel criticisms. In reflecting on and critiquing his earlier work on *Settler Capitalism*, in 1995 Donald Denoon described as 'misleading' his scholarship based on research 'privileging the narratives of governments and resource-owners' that thereby 'denies people agency in their own destinies, except as an amorphous mass within larger contests between forms of economic and political organization'. Rather, he wrote of New Caledonia, the 'struggle was unequal but not one-sided. Every French advance was in some degree negotiated, even when it was also enforced by violence. Each combatant was affected by the values of the other, but their values could never converge. The Kanaks did not abandon hope or identity.'[60] Wolfe, too, was aware of the possibility that an emphasis on strategies of settler colonialism 'might seem to run the risk of negating Indigenous agency, representing domination as unidirectional and, accordingly, as total'. His explicit aim in describing settler colonialism was not to analyse the 'nature or practice of Aboriginality' but rather to map the 'settler-colonial will'.[61] But this task cannot be undertaken without engaging with Indigeneity. Invasion, as Manu Karuka has argued, is 'inherently reactive to Indigenous modes of relationship preceding it, persisting despite its violations'.[62] The settler colonial will is not complete prior to the encounter with Indigenous people and Indigeneity; it is constituted and transformed through such articulations. It is, then, incumbent on the historian to tend to the Indigenous alongside the settler colonial. As Kēhaulani Kauanui has insisted, in asserting Indigeneity as a 'category of analysis, the question of its substance always arises'. Similarly, Konishi writes, historians must seek to 'understand both the extra-colonial Indigenous histories which coincide with shared histories of colonisation, and the continuing modes of Indigenous resurgence which respond to colonial discourses' and, we might add, colonial dispossessions.[63]

To flesh out these histories, then, one needs to account for Indigeneities, for Indigenous cosmologies and philosophies of spatiality and temporality, for the many ways Indigenous peoples have articulated their societies with encroaching others, and for the ways Indigenous people have acted upon and towards those others: negotiating, refusing, resisting, accommodating, transforming, and so on. We can usefully frame this problematic in terms of what Glen Coulthard quotes Marx describing as 'modes of life', or 'interconnected social totalit[ies]' encompassing the 'economic, political, spiritual, and social'.[64] If we are to elaborate specific colonial or imperial sites as social formations, we might turn to examine them as comprising particular configurations of these modes of life, articulated together in unpredictable ways that can be reconstructed through careful historical research and analysis. Structures can be discerned through identifying their effects, working through relations of production, ideological conditions, discursive currencies, and forms of subjectivity and subjection. The settler colonial social formation, in other words, conjoins multiple modes that emerge in relation to each other; an account of social relations, for instance, then requires an understanding of the multiple structures that comprise the social formation, the terms of their articulation, their relations of domination and resistance, the conditions of social reproduction, and so on. These structures are articulated together but not collapsible, determining and being determined by each other.[65]

The structure of settler colonialism is, as described above, that of settler invasion, comprising practices of land dispossession, Indigenous elimination, the reproduction of a new replacement society, and so on. But a history of a place or a people cannot stop at that. It must also trace Indigenous and other emergent structures, rendering them in relation to each other. Some scholars working with theories of settler colonialism have taken up the task of historicising these structures and the ways they were constituted as parts of shared histories and negotiations, work for which Wolfe left room in his account but that he did not himself undertake.[66] Katherine Ellinghaus has shown some of the ways Indigenous people have performed in ways intended to manoeuvre within and between various policies of settler administrations in order to get 'the result[s] they wanted'. In her compelling account, reading the colonial archive through survivance can enable historians both to examine and to understand the words and actions of Indigenous people as they act against and in relation to settler colonialism. Thinking Indigenous histories through survivance, perhaps, offers one way of moving on from this critique, or, as Ellinghaus has suggested, 'rather to see it no longer as a critique but as a warning, an encouragement, and a guide for scholars who work on this material'.[67]

In her study of nineteenth-century Aboriginal engagements with maritime industries, Lynette Russell used the term 'attenuated agency' to connote the 'degree of personal autonomy and agency' that Aboriginal people engaged in when they 'acted and reacted', making 'unexpected choices' to move 'between their own native worlds and the world of nineteenth century European colonialism'. Here, I want to adopt this phrase but to attribute the attenuation of agency not to the colonial onslaught that compromised an otherwise unconstrained individual capacity to act freely and in a considered way, but rather to structural overdeterminations.[68] One might work to trace Indigenous structures through their emergence as modes of life which must also be read as productive, as making agentic subjects.

The question of what can be discerned of Indigenous modes of life is a historical and literary one, a question of listening and reading through gaps and silences, refusals and often incomplete accounts. To what extent is historical knowledge of Indigeneity available to those working in archives? Scholars have long debated the problems with using ethnographic sources; in his study of social anthropology, for instance, Wolfe argued that Indigenous discourses barely intrude on anthropological knowledge, which instead emerges as a 'kind of soliloquy – as Western discourse talking to itself'. Turning instead to Indigenous texts may not offer relief. Christopher Pexa describes the ways Dakhóta writers of the allotment and assimilation era tended to obscure the 'ethical and political heart of the people' in their English-language work, rendering their texts as strategically valuable translations but inevitably incomplete as historical sources, demanding a sophisticated reading practice that works well beyond the text itself.[69]

But while many historians may find it impossible to complete the work of reading Indigenous structures, this does not mean that desisting from the task is the only option. Perhaps we can begin to grasp towards Indigenous structures – and therefore to fill in our picture of the social formation as a whole – by rethinking the nature and evidence of agency. A theory of agency that describes independence and choice as the basis for individuals' actions has long been the subject of historical critique. Walter Johnson described that theory as supposing 'the universality of a liberal notion of selfhood' and smuggling the 'categories of nineteenth-century liberalism' into 'considerations of human-ness lived outside the conditions of liberal agency'. While Johnson pointed out that such agency was originally defined against the condition of slavery, one might similarly suggest that the so-called natural freedom of white men was in many instances defined against Indigenous peoples' supposed incapacity to act outside the strictures of their tribal societies.[70] To step outside this historical dichotomy, and to step therefore away from its basis in the historical diminution of Indigenous people, we might instead theorise agency as both enabled by and constituting structures, determined by outside considerations even while it makes and remakes them. Against mechanistic analyses that reduce human action to effects of a prior structure, and similarly against those accounts of agency resting on self-determining individualism, this is an approach that conceives both structure and agency as co-determinate. And structures are not isolates. Social formations comprise a multitude of overlapping and interlocking structures, whose uneven and contingent articulation is both constraining and productive.[71]

We might think, then, of tracing multiple articulations of settler colonialisms and Indigeneities, across time and space, in transformative relations with one another. Such an approach offers us a way to consider Indigeneity as an analytic, to frame projects of colonial enrichment through their material and discursive conditions, to trace the interactions of extractive projects with diverse ways of being Indigenous. And in recent years, a number of scholars have pursued such approaches, reading Indigenous structure from their effects. Crystal McKinnon has written of the ways that Koori musicians in late twentieth-century Melbourne created urban spaces of Aboriginal autonomy, spaces where they could both enact community and elaborate a critique of settler colonial projects of assimilation and enact community. Writing of the regular band nights organised by Melbourne-based Indigenous band The Stray Blacks, for instance, she describes spaces being manifested through two modes of resistance: one directed externally, while the other takes shape within and for a community. McKinnon emphasises this internally directed latter form, which creates a space for distinctive relationships and practices that constitute Indigenous relationality as a structure, but which is also only fully intelligible as resistance through a complementary analysis of settler colonial projects of assimilation.[72]

Departing from resistance, Audra Simpson has instead explored Mohawk refusals of North American settler colonialism. These refusals maintain and reproduce a social space in which they enact their ongoing political formation, their sovereignty, on and in relation to the Kahnawà:ke reserve. Mohawk people's insistence on identifying themselves as Mohawk Nationals and their continued practice of nationhood constitute a proliferating set of refusals that emerge as events in the articulation of two structures. And, turning to western New South Wales, Hannah Forsyth and Altin Gavranovic have identified a Barkindji social structure with a logic of survival – a structure in which the 'bush is there to nurture you'. This structure, whose history they trace from invasion in the mid-nineteenth century until today, has helped Barkindji sustainably endure transforming settler colonial domination. To trace these varied Indigenous histories, in other words, requires an appreciation of the relationships between Indigenous and settler colonial structures.[73]

Kēhaulani Kauanui has traced the many overlapping, complementary, and contradictory expressions of Kanaka Maoli independence and self-determination in Hawaiian sovereignty movements. Working through histories of American imperialism on the one hand, and Hawaiian engagements with colonial and global legal regimes on the other, she provides a history of Indigenous political movements whose relation to international law generates paradoxes that are an effect of ongoing settler colonialism, and that cannot be resolved without dealing with the questions this raises. Tracey Banivanua Mar similarly provides a history of decolonisation in the Pacific that charts a form of decolonisation that is ongoing and recurrent, detached from the nation-state, mobile, diasporic, and sovereign. This approach connects stateless forms of self-determination with territorial independence, tending closely to the ways Indigenous Pacific peoples have woven together experiences with different colonial formations to develop new ways of doing decolonisation that emerge as a 'process, rather than an event'.[74]

Examples could multiply, but these are the kinds of histories that are illuminated by an approach that tends to the articulations between structures of Indigeneity and settler colonialism.[75] They are locally specific yet related closely to broader national, transnational, and global processes. They theorise sovereignties in their varied manifestations rather than as epistemologically or historically unitary. And they elaborate transformations over time while establishing underlying continuities. They speak historically to today. The virtue of the frontier was its capacity to represent invasion; returning to that frontier but rethinking invasion's temporality helps to understand the settler colonial present.[76] But understanding invasion is insufficient to help us historicise Indigenous situations. We need, as I have suggested, to tend to both invasion and Indigeneity as articulated structures, as demanding close attention to the contingent and specific forms they take over time and space, and as persisting in antagonism. These are the kinds of histories that can help us make sense of the constraints that have, to this point, arrested moves towards settler decolonisation.

Acknowledgements

I am grateful to the editors for their many helpful comments and suggestions on this essay, and to Frank Bongiorno for his assistance and recommendations. I am especially thankful to Alex Trimble Young and Claire McLisky for their incisive readings of earlier drafts and suggestions of further texts to consider.

Notes

1 Robert P. Porter, *Compendium of The Eleventh Census: 1890* (Washington, DC: Department of the Interior, Census Office, 1892), Part I, xlviii.
2 Frederick Jackson Turner, 'The Significance of the Frontier in American History' (1893), in *The Frontier in American History* (New York: Henry Holt and Company, 1920), 1–3. Not coincidentally, 1890 was also marked by the massacre of Lakota people at Wounded Knee, representing for so many non-Indigenous Americans the end of any feasible Indian military struggle. Philip J. Deloria, *Indians in Unexpected Places* (Lawrence: University of Kansas Press, 2004), 16.
3 Russel Ward, *The Australian Legend*, 2nd ed. (Melbourne: Oxford University Press, 1966), 238.
4 Ward, *The Australian Legend*, 210–211. Ward cited Allan Martin's research here, which was based on the Statistician's Report on the 1891 Census; A.W. Martin, 'Political Groupings in New South Wales, 1872–1889: A Study in the Working of Responsible

Government' (PhD diss., The Australian National University, June 1955), 25; T.A. Coghlan, *General Report on the Eleventh Census of New South Wales* (Sydney: Statistician's Office, 1894), 127.

5 The population of the U.S. was measured 'exclusive of Indians and other persons in Indian territory, on Indian reservations, and in Alaska,' though those described as 'civilized Indians' were enumerated. Porter, *Compendium*, xxxv, 470, 474. The NSW census also counted Indigenous people but subtracted 'Aborigines and … natives of the Fijis … who cannot scientifically be regarded as Australasians'. Coghlan, *General Report*, 177. As is well known, the exclusion of 'aboriginal natives' from the population of the Commonwealth of Australia was entrenched in the Constitution of 1901 until amended by referendum in 1967.

6 From a field too large to include here; see, for example, Patricia Nelson Limerick, *The Legacy of Conquest: The Unbroken Past of the American West* (New York: W.W. Norton, 1987); Frank Bongiorno and David Andrew Roberts, eds., 'Russel Ward: Reflections on a Legend,' *Journal of Australian Colonial History* 10, no. 2 (2008): i–iv, 1–250; Marilyn Lake, 'The Politics of Respectability: Identifying the Masculinist Context,' *Historical Studies* 22, no. 86 (1986): 116–131.

7 Turner, 'The Significance of the Frontier,' 30; Ward, *The Australian Legend*, 242–245.

8 On dispossession, see Robert Nichols, 'Theft Is Property! The Recursive Logic of Dispossession,' *Political Theory* 46, no. 1 (2018): 14–15.

9 Patrick Wolfe, *Settler Colonialism and the Transformation of Anthropology: The Politics and Poetics of an Ethnographic Event* (London: Cassell, 1999), 2.

10 Gayatri Chakravorty Spivak, 'The Rani of Sirmur: An Essay in Reading the Archives,' *History and Theory* 24, no. 3 (1985): 253; Haunani-Kay Trask, *From a Native Daughter: Colonialism and Sovereignty in Hawai'i*, rev. ed. (Honolulu: University of Hawai'i Press, 1999), 30.

11 This essay does not present an exhaustive survey, and might be strengthened and rendered more complex by taking into account the historiographies of the frontier in other colonial sites, including Canada, Aotearoa/New Zealand, Hawai'i, Palestine, South Africa, and elsewhere. But a focus on Australia and the U.S. has a heuristic value, given the particular and related development of both frontier and Indigenous historiographies between those nations. I offer this essay in the hope that it resonates with some of these other contexts, with their own distinctive local, national, and imperial traditions of memorialising and historicising the frontier.

12 On the Australian postcolonial present, see Bill Ashcroft, Gareth Griffiths, and Helen Tiffin, *The Empire Writes Back: Theory and Practice in Post-Colonial Literatures* (London: Routledge, 2003), 2; Tony Hughes-d'Aeth, 'Cooper, Cather, Prichard, "Pioneer": The Chronotope of Settler Colonialism,' *Australian Literary Studies* 31, no. 3 (2016): 1, 3.

13 Henry Reynolds, *Frontier: Aborigines, Settlers and Land* (Sydney: Allen & Unwin, 1987).

14 Turner, 'The Significance of the Frontier,' 1, 3–4, 9, 22, 30, 32. And see Kerwin Lee Klein, *Frontiers of Historical Imagination: Narrating the European Conquest of Native America, 1890–1990* (Berkeley: University of California Press, 1997), 13–22.

15 Richard White, 'Frederick Jackson Turner and Buffalo Bill,' in *The Frontier in American Culture*, ed. James R. Grossman (Berkeley: University of California Press, 1994), 26; Philip J. Deloria, 'Historiography,' in *A Companion to American Indian History*, eds. Philip J. Deloria and Neal Salisbury (Malden, MA: Blackwell Publishers, 2002), 8.

16 See, e.g., W.K. Hancock, *Survey of British Commonwealth Affairs*, vol II, part I (London: Oxford University Press: 1940), 4–6; G.V. Portus, 'Americans and Australians,' *Australian Quarterly* 14, no. 2 (1942): 33–34; Fred Alexander, *Moving Frontiers: An American Theme and Its Application to Australian History* (Port Washington: Kennikat Press, 1969), 26, 35. Frank Bongiorno argues that it was most likely Harry Allen who introduced Ward to Turner's work while both were in Canberra, Ward working on his doctoral thesis at the Australian National University, and Allen researching a comparative study of American and Australian frontiers. See Frank Bongiorno, 'Russel Ward's *The Australian Legend*: A Reconsideration' (unpublished manuscript, 2012), 9.

17 Ward, *The Australian Legend*, 1, 10–11, 240. Graeme Davison famously argued that Ward's 'up-country ethos' was not so much transmitted to the cities in the 1890s as it was a projection of urban values, derived from writers' experiences of Sydney's 'sleazy urban frontier', onto the Bush. Graeme Davison, 'Sydney and the Bush,' *Historical Studies* 18, no. 71 (1978): 194.
18 Nineteenth-century historians of the Australian colonies tended to discuss Aboriginal dispossession and frontier violence extensively, before the field turned away from such subjects after Federation in 1901. W.E.H. Stanner, *After the Dreaming: Black and White Australians, an Anthropologist's View* (Sydney: Australian Broadcasting Commission, 1969), 18–29; Angela Woollacott, 'Russel Ward, Frontier Violence and Australian Historiography,' *Journal of Australian Colonial History* 10, no. 2 (2008): 24, 35–36. Henry Reynolds most evocatively charged Ward with obscuring both Aboriginal people and the violence perpetrated against them in his national history. See Henry Reynolds, 'Violence, the Aboriginals, and the Australian Historian,' *Meanjin Quarterly* 31, no. 4 (1972): 474; Henry Reynolds, *Why Weren't We Told? A Personal Search for the Truth about Our History* (Melbourne: Viking, 1999), 128–132. See also Ann McGrath, *Illicit Love: Interracial Sex and Marriage in the United States and Australia* (Lincoln: University of Nebraska Press, 2015), 23.
19 C.D. Rowley, *The Destruction of Aboriginal Society* (Canberra: ANU Press, 1970); Lynette Russell, 'Introduction,' in *Colonial Frontiers: Indigenous–European Encounters in Settler Societies*, ed. Lynette Russell (Manchester: Manchester University Press, 2001), 4. See also R.H.W. Reece, *Aborigines and Colonists: Aborigines and Colonial Society in New South Wales in the 1830s and 1840s* (Sydney: Sydney University Press, 1974). Under the rubric of race relations and as part of a history of white supremacy in Queensland, Raymond Evans had described a frontier characterised by European violence and Aboriginal resistance. His narration of a constant state of war set the tone for works to come. Raymond Evans, Kay Saunders, and Kathryn Cronin, *Exclusion, Exploitation and Extermination: Race Relations in Colonial Queensland* (Sydney: Australia and New Zealand Book Company, 1975), 25–145. See, e.g., Judith Wright, *The Cry for the Dead* (Melbourne: Oxford University Press, 1981).
20 Henry Reynolds, *The Other Side of the Frontier: Aboriginal Resistance to the European Invasion of Australia* (Melbourne: Penguin Books, 1982), 30–60, 61–62, 96–127, 199; Bain Attwood and Tom Griffiths, 'Frontier, Race, Nation,' in *Frontier, Race, Nation: Henry Reynolds and Australian History*, eds. Bain Attwood and Tom Griffiths (Melbourne: Australian Scholarly Publishing, 2009), 47. Reynolds followed this study first with an account of settler experiences of the frontier wars, entrenching resistance and warfare at the centre of Australian frontier histories, and then with a history of accommodation and cooperation between Aboriginal people and settlers. Reynolds, *Frontier*; Henry Reynolds, *With the White People* (Melbourne: Penguin, 1990).
21 M.F. Christie, *Aborigines in Colonial Victoria 1835–86* (Sydney: Sydney University Press, 1979), 55–56; Lyndall Ryan, *The Aboriginal Tasmanians* (Brisbane: University of Queensland Press, 1981); Noel Loos, *Invasion and Resistance: Aboriginal–European relations on the North Queensland frontier 1861–1897* (Canberra: ANU Press, 1982); Peter Read, *A Hundred Years War: The Wiradjuri People and the State* (Canberra: ANU Press, 1988). See Lorenzo Veracini, 'A Prehistory of Australia's History Wars: The Evolution of Aboriginal History during the 1970s and 1980s,' *Australian Journal of Politics and History* 52, no. 3 (2006): 445.
22 Reynolds, *Why Weren't We Told?*, 126. On the divergence in national historiographies, see Eric Altenbernd and Alex Trimble Young, 'Introduction: The Significance of the Frontier in an Age of Transnational History,' *Settler Colonial Studies* 4, no. 2 (2014): 131.
23 Limerick, *The Legacy of Conquest*, 25, 217, 322; Patricia Nelson Limerick, 'The Adventures of the Frontier in the Twentieth Century,' in *The Frontier in American Culture*, ed. James R. Grossman (Berkeley: University of California Press, 1994), 73. See also Donald Worster, *Rivers of Empire: Water, Aridity, and the Growth of the American West* (New

York: Pantheon Books, 1985), 11–12; Richard White, *'It's Your Misfortune and None of My Own': A History of the American West* (Norman: University of Oklahoma Press, 1991), 4.
24 Richard White, *The Middle Ground: Indians, Empires, and Republics in the Great Lakes Region, 1650–1815* (New York: Cambridge University Press, 1991). On the specificity and utility of White's 'middle ground', see Philip J. Deloria, 'What is the Middle Ground, Anyway?,' *William and Mary Quarterly* 63, no. 1 (2006): 15–22.
25 Sylvia van Kirk, *Many Tender Ties: Women in Fur-Trade Society, 1670–1870* (Norman: University of Oklahoma Press, 1980); Peggy Pascoe, *Relations of Rescue: The Search for Female Moral Authority in the American West, 1874–1939* (New York: Oxford University Press, 1990).
26 Ann McGrath, *'Born in the Cattle': Aborigines in Cattle Country* (Sydney: Allen & Unwin, 1987), 23.
27 Reynolds, *With the White People*; Henry Reynolds, *The Other Side of the Frontier: Aboriginal resistance to the European invasion of Australia*, rev. ed. (Sydney: UNSW Press, 2006), 7. Some, though, have found the concept of the 'middle ground' of value in historicising the early periods of colonisation in New South Wales. See, e.g., Grace Karskens, *The Colony: A History of Early Sydney* (Sydney: Allen & Unwin, 2009), 449, 456, 497; Paul Carter, *Meeting Place: The Human Encounter and the Challenge of Coexistence* (Minneapolis: University of Minnesota Press, 2013), 155–162; Shino Konishi, 'Bennelong and Gogy: Strategic Brokers in Colonial New South Wales,' in *Brokers and Boundaries: Colonial Exploration in Indigenous Territory*, eds. Tiffany Shellam, Maria Nugent, Shino Konishi, and Alison Cadzow (Canberra: ANU Press and Aboriginal History Monographs, 2016), 15–37.
28 Richard Broome, 'Aboriginal Victims and Voyagers: Confronting Frontier Myths,' *Journal of Australian Studies* 18, no. 42 (1994): 71–72, 77.
29 Limerick, *The Legacy of Conquest*, 253–254. Australian historians have made little use of the concept of borderlands. See Frank Bongiorno, '"The Men Who Made Australia Federated Long Ago": Australian Frontiers and Borderlands,' in *Borderlands in World History, 1700–1914*, eds. Paul Readman, Cynthia Radding, and Chad Bryant (Basingstoke: Palgrave Macmillan, 2014), 49–50. Cf. Tracey Banivanua Mar, *Violence and Colonial Dialogue: The Australia–Pacific Indentured Labour Trade* (Honolulu: University of Hawai'i Press, 2007), 70–100.
30 Herbert E. Bolton, *The Spanish Borderlands: A Chronicle of Old Florida and the Southwest* (New Haven: Yale University Press, 1921); Stephen Aron, 'Frontiers, Borderlands, Wests,' in *American History Now*, eds. Eric Foner and Lisa McGirr (Philadelphia: Temple University Press: 2011), 264–265.
31 Pekka Hämäläinen and Samuel Truett, 'On Borderlands,' *Journal of American History* 98, no. 2 (2011): 338, 352. Cf. Jeremy Adelman and Stephen Aron, 'From Borderlands to Borders: Empires, Nation-States, and Peoples in Between in North American History,' *American Historical Review* 104, no. 3 (1999). For a study of power and the constitution of borderlands subjectivities, see Gloria Anzaldúa, *Borderlands/La Frontera: The New Mestiza* (San Francisco: Aunt Lute Books, 1987). Louis Owens has described borderlands produced by the 'mixedbloods' who embody the frontier space. Frontier emerges in his work as a concept that, when examined 'from the "other" direction', describes a 'transcultural zone of contact' that is 'always unstable, multidirectional, hybridized, characterised by heteroglossia, and indeterminate'. Louis Owens, *Mixedblood Messages: Literature, Film, Family, Place* (Norman: University of Oklahoma Press, 1998), 26, 30.
32 Ned Blackhawk, *Violence over the Land: Indians and Empires in the Early American West* (Cambridge, MA: Harvard University Press, 2006); Pekka Hämäläinen, *The Comanche Empire* (New Haven, CT: Yale University Press, 2008); Pekka Hämäläinen, 'What's in a Concept? The Kinetic Empire of the Comanches,' *History and Theory* 52, no. 1 (2013): 85.
33 Richard White, 'Trashing the Trails,' in *Trails: Toward a New Western History*, eds. Patricia Nelson Limerick, Clyde A. Milner II, and Charles E. Rankin (Lawrence: University

Press of Kansas, 1991), 32–35; Daniel K. Richter, 'Whose Indian History?' *William and Mary Quarterly* 50, no. 2 (1993): 380; Peggy Pascoe, 'Western Women at the Cultural Crossroads,' in *Trails: Toward a New Western History*, eds. Patricia Nelson Limerick, Clyde A. Milner II, and Charles E. Rankin (Lawrence: University Press of Kansas, 1991), 43. Jean O'Brien has argued that this long-standing marginality has been a benefit, leading to transformative archives and methodologies that produce 'rich possibilities'. Jean M. O'Brien, 'Historical Sources and Methods in Indigenous Studies: Touching on the Past, Looking to the Future,' in *Sources and Methods in Indigenous Studies*, eds. Chris Andersen and Jean M. O'Brien (London: Routledge, 2017), 18.

34 Bain Attwood and S.G. Foster, eds., *Frontier Conflict: The Australian Experience* (Canberra: National Museum of Australia, 2003). This return to historical argument around frontier violence provoked historians to carry out new, and often more nuanced, research into frontier relations. See, e.g., Tony Roberts, *Frontier Justice: A History of the Gulf Country to 1900* (Brisbane: University of Queensland Press, 2005); Tiffany Shellam, *Shaking Hands on the Fringe: Negotiating the Aboriginal World at King George Sound* (Perth: University of Western Press, 2009); Karskens, *The Colony*; Darrell Lewis, *A Wild History: Life and Death on the Victoria River Frontier* (Melbourne: Monash University Press, 2012); Libby Connors, *Warrior: A Legendary Leader's Dramatic Life and Violent Death on the Colonial Frontier* (Sydney: Allen & Unwin, 2015); Kate Darian-Smith and Penelope Edmonds, eds., *Conciliation on Colonial Frontiers: Conflict, Performance, and Commemoration in Australia and the Pacific Rim* (New York: Routledge, 2015).

35 Gillian Cowlishaw, 'Studying Aborigines: Changing Canons in Anthropology and History,' in *Power, Knowledge and Aborigines*, eds. Bain Attwood and John Arnold (Melbourne: La Trobe University Press, 1992), 27.

36 Dean Saranillio, 'Haunani-Kay Trask and Settler Colonial and Relational Critique: Alternatives to Binary Analyses of Power,' *Verge: Studies in Global Asias* 4, no. 2 (2018): 36–37; Haunani-Kay Trask, 'Settlers of Color and "Immigrant" Hegemony: "Locals" in Hawai'i,' *Amerasia Journal* 26, no. 2 (2000): 1–24.

37 J. Kēhaulani Kauanui, '"A Structure, Not an Event": Settler Colonialism and Enduring Indigeneity,' Forum: Emergent Critical Analytics for Alternative Humanities Issue, *Lateral* 5, no. 1 (2016), citing Fayez Sayegh, *Zionist Colonialism in Palestine* (Beirut: Research Center, Palestine Liberation Organization, 1965); Maxime Rodinson, *Israel: A Colonial-Settler State?* (New York: Monad Press, 1973); Rosemary Sayigh, *Palestinians: From Peasants to Revolutionaries; A People's History* (London: Zed Books, 1979).

38 Lisa Bellear, 'Justice?' in *Dreaming in Urban Areas* (Brisbane: University of Queensland Press, 1996), 71; Tony Birch, '"Nothing Has Changed": The Making and Unmaking of Koori Culture,' *Meanjin* 51, no. 2 (1992): 234, 238; Tony Birch, 'A Mabo Blood Test?,' *The Australian Journal of Anthropology* 6, nos. 1 & 2 (1995): 33; Tony Birch, '"Come See the Giant Koala": Inscription and Landscape in Western Victoria,' *Meanjin* 58, no. 3 (1999): 66; Gary Foley, 'The Australian Labor Party and the *Native Title Act*,' in *Sovereign Subjects: Indigenous Sovereignty Matters*, ed. Aileen Moreton-Robinson (Sydney: Allen & Unwin, 2007), 139. See also Deloria, *Indians in Unexpected Places*, 103–104; Edward Cavanagh, 'History, Time and the Indigenous Critique,' *Arena* 37/38 (2012): 39.

39 The phrases 'invasion is a structure, not an event' and 'logic of elimination' have become axiomatic in settler colonial studies, perhaps over-cited to the detriment of more thorough analyses: Kauanui, '"A Structure, Not an Event",' citing an unpublished paper by Alyosha Goldstein. Wolfe first made this argument in Patrick Wolfe, 'Nation and MiscegeNation: Discursive Continuity in the Post-Mabo Era,' *Social Analysis* 36 (1994): 93, 96. See Wolfe, *Settler Colonialism and the Transformation of Anthropology*, 1–2, 163, 167. For related discussions of genocide and settler colonialism, see A. Dirk Moses, ed., *Genocide and Settler Society: Frontier Violence and Stolen Indigenous Children in Australian History* (New York: Berghahn Books, 2004); Mohamed Adhikari, ed., *Genocide on Settler Frontiers: When Hunter-Gatherers and Commercial Stock Farmers Clash* (New York:

Berghahn Books, 2015); 'A Roundtable of Responses to Gary Clayton Anderson,' *Western Historical Quarterly* 47, no. 4 (2016): 435–448.
40 Wolfe, *Settler Colonialism and the Transformation of Anthropology*, 163–165; Shannon Speed, 'Structures of Settler Capitalism in Abya Yala,' *American Quarterly* 69, no. 4 (2017): 789; Patrick Wolfe, 'Settler Colonialism and the Elimination of the Native,' *Journal of Genocide Research* 8, no. 4 (2006): 402. On the return to the frontier in settler colonial studies, see Alex Trimble Young, 'Settler Sovereignty and the Rhizomatic West, or, The Significance of the Frontier in Postwestern Studies,' *Western American Literature* 48, nos. 1 & 2 (2013): 116. See also Doug Kiel, 'Untaming the Mild Frontier: In Search of New Midwestern Histories,' *Middle West Review* 1, no. 1 (2014): 12, 18.
41 See Gregory D. Smithers, 'Renewing Sacred Fires: The Cherokee People and the Shifting Frontiers of Settler Colonialism,' *Journal of the West* 56, no. 4 (2017): 36–47.
42 Russell, 'Introduction,' 2.
43 Wolfe, *Settler Colonialism and the Transformation of Anthropology*, 165; Elizabeth Furniss, 'Imagining the Frontier: Comparative Perspectives from Canada and Australia,' in *Dislocating the Frontier: Essaying the Mystique of the Outback*, eds. Deborah Bird Rose and Richard Davis (Canberra: ANU Press, 2005), 23; Daniel K. Richter, *Facing East from Indian Country: A Native History of Early America* (Cambridge, MA: Harvard University Press, 2001), 108. For Mark Rifkin, the frontier emerges as a settler imaginary and sensation, a structure of feeling. Mark Rifkin, 'The Frontier as (Movable) Space of Exception,' *Settler Colonial Studies* 4, no. 2 (2014): 177.
44 Deborah Bird Rose, 'Hard Times: An Australian Study,' in *Quicksands: Foundational Histories in Australia and Aotearoa New Zealand*, eds. Klaus Neumann, Nicholas Thomas, and Hilary Ericksen (Sydney: UNSW Press, 1999), 6; Banivanua Mar, *Violence and Colonial Dialogue*, 20–42; Julie Evans, 'Where Lawlessness is Law: The Settler-Colonial Frontier as a Legal Space of Violence,' *Australian Feminist Law Review* 30 (2009): 3–22; Tracey Banivanua Mar, 'Frontier Space and the Reification of the Rule of Law: Colonial Negotiations in the Western Pacific, 1870–74,' *Australian Feminist Law Review*, 30 (2009): 23–39. Nancy Shoemaker traces rather the reverse process, whereby multivarious differences congealed into a new binary only in the eighteenth century. Polarity, in this account, emerges as an effect of the frontier. Nancy Shoemaker, *A Strange Likeness: Becoming Red and White in Eighteenth-Century North America* (New York: Oxford University Press, 2004).
45 Alex Trimble Young and Lorenzo Veracini, '"If I Am Native to Anything": Settler Colonial Studies and Western American Literature,' *Western American Literature* 52, no. 1 (2017): 4–5.
46 Patrick Wolfe, *Traces of History: Elementary Structures of Race* (London: Verso, 2016), 33; Patrick Wolfe, 'Introduction,' in *The Settler Complex: Recuperating Binarism in Colonial Studies*, ed. Patrick Wolfe (Los Angeles: UCLA American Indian Studies Center, 2016), 9; Mark Rifkin, *Settler Common Sense: Queerness and Everyday Colonialism in the American Renaissance* (Minneapolis: University of Minnesota Press, 2014). On the absent centre, see Ben Silverstein, 'Submerged Sovereignty: Native Title within a History of Incorporation' in *Sovereignty: Frontiers of Possibility*, eds. Julie Evans et al. (Honolulu: University of Hawai'i Press, 2013), 73–78.
47 Cf. Peter Read, 'Making Aboriginal History,' in *Australian History Now*, eds. Anna Clark and Paul Ashton (Sydney: NewSouth Publishing, 2013), 38.
48 See Lorenzo Veracini, '"Settler Colonialism": Career of a Concept,' *Journal of Imperial and Commonwealth History* 41, no. 2 (2013); Frederick Hoxie, 'Retrieving the Red Continent: Settler Colonialism and the History of American Indians in the U.S,' *Ethnic and Racial Studies* 31, no. 5 (2008); Jeffrey Ostler and Nancy Shoemaker, 'Settler Colonialism in Early American History: Introduction,' *William and Mary Quarterly* 76, no. 3 (2019): 364; Nancy Shoemaker, 'A Typology of Colonialism,' *Perspectives on History*, October 2015, https://www.historians.org/publications-and-directories/perspectives-on-history/october-2015/a-typology-of-colonialism; K. Tsianina Lomawaima,

'Indigenous Studies,' *American Quarterly* 68, no. 1 (2016): 150; Alyssa Mt. Pleasant, Caroline Wigginton, and Kelly Wisecup, 'Materials and Methods in Native American and Indigenous Studies: Completing the Turn,' *William and Mary Quarterly* 75, no. 2 (2018): 231–232.

49 On domestication, see Mark Rifkin, 'Indigenizing Agamben: Rethinking Sovereignty in Light of the "Peculiar" Status of Native Peoples,' *Cultural Critique* 73 (2009): 102, 106; Mark Rifkin, *Manifesting America: The Imperial Construction of U.S. National Space* (Oxford: Oxford University Press, 2009); Carole Pateman, 'The Settler Contract,' in *Contract and Domination*, Carole Pateman and Charles W. Mills (Cambridge: Polity, 2007), 59.

50 Penelope Edmonds, *Urbanizing Frontiers: Indigenous Peoples and Settlers in 19th-Century Pacific Rim Cities* (Vancouver: UBC Press, 2010), 6; Margaret Jacobs, *White Mother to a Dark Race: Settler Colonialism, Maternalism, and the Removal of Indigenous Children in the American West and Australia, 1880–1940* (Lincoln: University of Nebraska Press, 2009), 25.

51 Janne Lahti, 'What Is Settler Colonialism and What It Has to Do with the American West?' *Journal of the West* 56, no. 4 (2017): 9–10. See also Tracey Banivanua Mar and Penelope Edmonds, eds., *Making Settler Colonial Space: Perspectives on Race, Place and Identity* (Basingstoke: Palgrave Macmillan, 2010); Jane Carey and Jane Lydon, eds., *Indigenous Networks: Mobility, Connections, and Exchange* (New York: Routledge, 2014); Zoë Laidlaw and Alan Lester, eds., *Indigenous Communities and Settler Colonialism: Land Holding, Loss and Survival in an Interconnected World* (Basingstoke: Palgrave Macmillan, 2015); Kate Fullagar and Michael A. McDonnell, eds., *Facing Empire: Indigenous Experiences in a Revolutionary Age* (Baltimore, MD: Johns Hopkins University Press, 2018).

52 Candace Fujikane and Jonathan Y. Okamura, eds., *Asian Settler Colonialism: From Local Governance to the Habits of Everyday Life in Hawai'i* (Honolulu: University of Hawai'i Press, 2008); Jodi Byrd, *The Transit of Empire* (Minneapolis: University of Minnesota Press, 2011); Shona N. Jackson, *Creole Indigeneity: Between Myth and Nation in the Caribbean* (Minneapolis: University of Minnesota Press, 2012); Toula Nicolacopoulos and George Vassilacopoulos, *Indigenous Sovereignty and the Being of the Occupier: Manifesto for a White Australian Philosophy of Origins* (Melbourne: re.press, 2014); Iyko Day, *Alien Capital: Asian Racialization and the Logic of Settler Colonial Capitalism* (Durham: Duke University Press, 2016); Manu Vimalassery, Juliana Hu Pegues, and Alyosha Goldstein, 'On Colonial Unknowing,' *Theory & Event* 19, no. 4 (2016); Nadia Rhook, '"Annamese Coolies" at Australian ports: Charting Colonial Geographies of Emotion, and Settler Memory, from French Vietnam to New Caledonia via Interwar Australia,' *Australian Historical Studies* 48, no. 3 (2017).

53 See Gregory D. Smithers, *Science, Sexuality, and Race in the United States and Australia, 1780–1940*, rev. ed. (Lincoln: University of Nebraska Press, 2017); Marilyn Lake, *Progressive New World: How Settler Colonialism and Transpacific Exchange Shape American Reform* (Cambridge, MA: Harvard University Press, 2019).

54 Jean O'Brien, *Firsting and Lasting: Writing Indians Out of Existence in New England* (Minneapolis: University of Minnesota Press, 2010); Tracey Banivanua Mar, 'Settler-Colonial Landscapes and Narratives of Possession,' in *Stolen Lands, Broken Cultures: The Settler-Colonial Present*, eds. John Hinkson, Paul James, and Lorenzo Veracini (Melbourne: Arena Publications, 2012), 176–198. See also Philip Deloria, *Playing Indian* (New Haven, CT: Yale University Press, 1998).

55 Jodi Byrd, 'Follow the Typical Signs: Settler Sovereignty and Its Discontents,' *Settler Colonial Studies* 4, no. 2 (2014): 151.

56 Though Ghassan Hage has described what he terms the 'globalization of the settler-colonial ethos'. Relatedly, but with a contrasting temporality, David Lloyd and Patrick Wolfe have argued that settler colonialism is 'not some transitional phase that gives way to – or even provides a laboratory for – the emergent order. In both the originary and the continuing senses, it is foundational to that order'. Ghassan Hage, '*État de Siège*: A

Dying Domesticating Colonialism,' *American Ethnologist* 43, no. 1 (2016): 38–49; David Lloyd and Patrick Wolfe, 'Settler Colonial Logics and the Neoliberal Regime,' *Settler Colonial Studies* 6, no. 2 (2016): 113.

57 One key critique emerging from critical scholars working in Indigenous studies in North America has focused on the limitations of a binary approach in accounting fully for practices and processes of relationality between and among variously racialised peoples in complex imperial contexts. See debates in Byrd, *The Transit of Empire*, xix, xxxix, 53, 119; Iyko Day, 'Being or Nothingness: Indigeneity, Antiblackness, and Settler Colonial Critique,' *Journal of the Critical Ethnic Studies Association* 1, no. 2 (2015): 106–107; J. Kēhaulani Kauanui, 'Tracing Historical Specificity: Race and the Colonial Politics of (In)Capacity,' *American Quarterly*, 69, no. 2 (2017): 259–263.

58 Lisa Ford, 'Locating Indigenous Self-Determination in the Margins of Settler Sovereignty,' in *Between Indigenous and Settler Governance*, eds. Lisa Ford and Tim Rowse (Oxford: Routledge, 2012), 11; Shino Konishi, 'First Nations Scholars, Settler Colonial Studies, and Indigenous History,' *Australian Historical Studies* 50, no. 3 (2019): 293–295. See also Joanne Barker, 'Settled Contradictions, Necessary Boycotts: A Report from NAISA,' 21 May 2011, http://tequilasovereign.blogspot.com/2011/05/settled-contradictions-necessary.html.

59 Tim Rowse, 'Indigenous Heterogeneity,' *Australian Historical Studies* 45, no. 3 (2014): 300; Tim Rowse, 'Indigenous Incorporation as a Means to Empowerment,' in *Native Title from Mabo to Akiba: A Vehicle for Change and Empowerment?* eds. Sean Brennan et al. (Sydney: The Federation Press, 2015), 196. See also A. Dirk Moses, 'Official Apologies, Reconciliation, and Settler Colonialism: Australian Indigenous Alterity and Political Agency,' *Citizenship Studies* 15, no. 2 (2011): 158–159; Miranda Johnson, *The Land is our History: Indigeneity, Law, and the Settler State* (New York: Oxford University Press, 2016), 169. Cf. Jane Carey, 'On Hope and Resignation: Conflicting Visions of Settler Colonial Studies and its Future as a Field,' *Postcolonial Studies* 23, no. 1 (2020): 21–42.

60 Donald Denoon, 'Settler Capitalism Unsettled,' *New Zealand Journal of History* 29, no. 2 (1995): 132, 135; Donald Denoon, *Settler Capitalism: The Dynamics of Dependent Development in the Southern Hemisphere* (Oxford: Clarendon Press, 1983). See also Francesca Merlan, 'Reply to Patrick Wolfe,' *Social Analysis: The International Journal of Social and Cultural Practice* 41, no. 2 (1997): 16, 18.

61 Wolfe, *Settler Colonialism and the Transformation of Anthropology*, 167; Wolfe, *Traces of History*, 271.

62 Manu Karuka, *Empire's Tracks: Indigenous Nations, Chinese Workers, and the Transcontinental Railroad* (Oakland: University of California Press, 2019), 171.

63 J. Kēhaulani Kauanui, *Paradoxes of Hawaiian Sovereignty: Land, Sex, and the Colonial Politics of State Nationalism* (Durham, NC: Duke University Press, 2018), 33; Konishi, 'First Nations Scholars,' 304. See also Audra Simpson, 'Whither Settler Colonialism,' *Settler Colonial Studies* 6, no. 4 (2016): 440; Ben Silverstein, *Governing Natives: Indirect Rule and Settler Colonialism in Northern Australia* (Manchester: Manchester University Press, 2019).

64 Glen Sean Coulthard, *Red Skin, White Masks: Rejecting the Colonial Politics of Recognition* (Minneapolis: University of Minnesota Press, 2014), 65.

65 Louis Althusser and Etienne Balibar, *Reading Capital*, trans. Ben Brewster (London: NLB, 1970), 99, 188–189; Patrick Wolfe, 'History and Imperialism: A Century of Theory, from Marx to Postcolonialism,' *American Historical Review* 102, no. 2 (1997): 397.

66 For Wolfe, a settler colonial analytic prioritised 'the Natives' points of view' but did not seek to ventriloquise Indigenous voices; it foregrounded a structure of invasion less to achieve a 'reassertion of these voices' than it was intended to provide a 'condition of their audibility'. This was, to borrow the terms Kauanui used above, Indigeneity as analytic but not substance. Patrick Wolfe, 'Race and the Trace of History: For Henry Reynolds,' in *Studies in Settler Colonialism: Politics, Identity, Culture*, eds. Fiona Bateman and Lionel Pilkington (Basingstoke: Palgrave Macmillan, 2011), 289, 293nn.

67 Katherine Ellinghaus, 'George Newkirk Jr's Café, Competency, and Settler Colonialism,' *Journal of the West* 56, no. 4 (2017): 26, 32; Katherine Ellinghaus, '"You Are Not Really Free, You Are Just Turned Loose": Settler Colonialism, Survivance and Competency at the Osage Agency,' *Settler Colonial Studies* 8, no. 1 (2018): 19; Gerald Vizenor, *Manifest Manners: Postindian Warriors of Survivance* (Hanover: Wesleyan University Press, 1994).

68 Lynette Russell, *Roving Mariners: Australian Aboriginal Whalers and Sealers in the Southern Oceans, 1790–1870* (Albany: State University of New York Press, 2012), 6–7, 13. On overdetermination, see Louis Althusser, *For Marx*, trans. Ben Brewster (London: Allen Lane, 1969), 99–107.

69 Wolfe, *Settler Colonialism and the Transformation of Anthropology*, 4; Christopher Pexa, *Translated Nation: Rewriting the Dakhóta Oyáte* (Minneapolis: University of Minnesota Press, 2019). Working towards that reading practice turns our attention to the question of standpoint, and the possibility of being attuned to specific Indigenous ontologies that may not be legible to all. Aileen Moreton Robinson, 'Towards an Australian Indigenous Women's Standpoint Theory,' *Australian Feminist Studies* 28, no. 78 (2013): 340–344.

70 Walter Johnson, 'On Agency,' *Journal of Social History* 37, no. 1 (2003): 115; Kay Anderson and Colin Perrin, '"The Miserablest People in the World": Race, Humanism and the Australian Aborigine,' *The Australian Journal of Anthropology* 18, no. 1 (2007).

71 Stuart Hall, 'Pluralism, Race and Class in Caribbean Society,' in *Race and Class in Post-colonial Society*, ed. United Nations Educational Scientific and Cultural Organisation (Paris: UNESCO, 1977), 162, 179; William H. Sewell Jr, *Logics of History: Social Theory and Social Transformation* (Chicago, IL: University of Chicago Press, 2005), 204–209.

72 Crystal McKinnon, 'Indigenous Music as a Space of Resistance,' in *Making Settler Colonial Space: Perspectives on Race, Place and Identity*, eds. Tracey Banivanua Mar and Penelope Edmonds (Basingstoke: Palgrave Macmillan, 2010), 264.

73 Audra Simpson, *Mohawk Interruptus: Political Life across the Borders of Settler States* (Durham, NC: Duke University Press, 2014), 11–12; Hannah Forsyth and Altin Gavranovic, 'The Logic of Survival: Towards an Indigenous-Centred History of Capitalism in Wilcannia,' *Settler Colonial Studies* 8, no. 4 (2018): 482.

74 Kauanui, *Paradoxes of Hawaiian Sovereignty*; Tracey Banivanua Mar, *Decolonisation and the Pacific: Indigenous Globalisation and the Ends of Empire* (Cambridge: Cambridge University Press, 2016), 20, 185, 218, 225.

75 See also, for example, Michael Witgen, *An Infinity of Nations: How the Native New World Shaped Early North America* (Philadelphia: University of Pennsylvania Press, 2012); Lisa Brooks, *Our Beloved Kin: A New History of King Philip's War* (New Haven, CT: Yale University Press, 2018).

76 The phrase is borrowed from Lorenzo Veracini, *The Settler Colonial Present* (Basingstoke: Palgrave Macmillan, 2015).

Bibliography

'A Roundtable of Responses to Gary Clayton Anderson.' *Western Historical Quarterly* 47, no. 4 (2016): 435–448.

Adelman, Jeremy, and Stephen Aron. 'From Borderlands to Borders: Empires, Nation-States, and Peoples in between in North American History.' *American Historical Review* 104, no. 3 (1999): 814–841.

Adhikari, Mohamed, ed. *Genocide on Settler Frontiers: When Hunter-Gatherers and Commercial Stock Farmers Clash*. New York: Berghahn Books, 2015.

Alexander, Fred. *Moving Frontiers: An American Theme and Its Application to Australian History*. Port Washington: Kennikat Press, 1969.

Altenbernd, Eric, and Alex Trimble Young. 'Introduction: The Significance of the Frontier in an Age of Transnational History.' *Settler Colonial Studies* 4, no. 2 (2014): 127–150.
Althusser, Louis. *For Marx*. Translated by Ben Brewster. London: Allen Lane, 1969.
Althusser, Louis, and Etienne Balibar. *Reading Capital*. Translated by Ben Brewster. London: NLB, 1970.
Anderson, Kay, and Colin Perrin. '"The Miserablest People in the World": Race, Humanism and the Australian Aborigine.' *The Australian Journal of Anthropology* 18, no. 1 (2007): 18–39.
Anzaldúa, Gloria. *Borderlands/La Frontera: The New Mestiza*. San Francisco, CA: Aunt Lute Books, 1987.
Aron, Stephen. 'Frontiers, Borderlands, Wests.' In *American History Now*, edited by Eric Foner and Lisa McGirr, 261–284. Philadelphia, PA: Temple University Press: 2011.
Ashcroft, Bill, Gareth Griffiths, and Helen Tiffin. *The Empire Writes Back: Theory and Practice in Post-Colonial Literatures*. London: Routledge, 2003.
Attwood, Bain, and S.G. Foster, eds. *Frontier Conflict: The Australian Experience*. Canberra: National Museum of Australia, 2003.
Attwood, Bain, and Tom Griffiths. 'Frontier, Race, Nation.' In *Frontier, Race, Nation: Henry Reynolds and Australian History*, edited by Bain Attwood and Tom Griffiths, 3–52. Melbourne: Australian Scholarly Publishing, 2009.
Banivanua Mar, Tracey. *Violence and Colonial Dialogue: The Australia–Pacific Indentured Labour Trade*. Honolulu: University of Hawai'i Press, 2007.
Banivanua Mar, Tracey. 'Frontier Space and the Reification of the Rule of Law: Colonial Negotiations in the Western Pacific, 1870–74.' *Australian Feminist Law Review*, 30 (2009): 23–39.
Banivanua Mar, Tracey. 'Settler-Colonial Landscapes and Narratives of Possession.' In *Stolen Lands, Broken Cultures: The Settler-Colonial Present*, edited by John Hinkson, Paul James, and Lorenzo Veracini, 176–198. Melbourne: Arena Publications, 2012.
Banivanua Mar, Tracey. *Decolonisation and the Pacific: Indigenous Globalisation and the Ends of Empire*. Cambridge: Cambridge University Press, 2016.
Banivanua Mar, Tracey, and Penelope Edmonds, eds. *Making Settler Colonial Space: Perspectives on Race, Place and Identity*. Basingstoke: Palgrave Macmillan, 2010.
Barker, Joanne. 'Settled Contradictions, Necessary Boycotts: A Report from NAISA.' 21 May 2011. http://tequilasovereign.blogspot.com/2011/05/settled-contradictions-necessary.html.
Bellear, Lisa. *Dreaming in Urban Areas*. Brisbane: University of Queensland Press, 1996.
Birch, Tony. '"Nothing Has Changed": The Making and Unmaking of Koori Culture.' *Meanjin* 51, no. 2 (1992): 229–246.
Birch, Tony. 'A Mabo Blood Test?' *The Australian Journal of Anthropology* 6, nos. 1 & 2 (1995): 32–42.
Birch, Tony. '"Come See the Giant Koala": Inscription and Landscape in Western Victoria.' *Meanjin* 58, no. 3 (1999): 60–72.
Blackhawk, Ned. *Violence over the Land: Indians and Empires in the Early American West*. Cambridge, MA: Harvard University Press, 2006.
Bolton, Herbert E. *The Spanish Borderlands: A Chronicle of Old Florida and the Southwest*. New Haven, CT: Yale University Press, 1921.
Bongiorno, Frank. '"The Men Who Made Australia Federated Long Ago": Australian Frontiers and Borderlands.' In *Borderlands in World History, 1700–1914*, edited by Paul Readman, Cynthia Radding, and Chad Bryant, 46–62. Basingstoke: Palgrave Macmillan, 2014.
Bongiorno, Frank. 'Russel Ward's *The Australian Legend*: A Reconsideration.' Unpublished manuscript, 2012.
Bongiorno, Frank, and David Andrew Roberts, eds. 'Russel Ward: Reflections on a Legend.' *Journal of Australian Colonial History* 10, no. 2 (2008).
Brooks, Lisa. *Our Beloved Kin: A New History of King Philip's War*. New Haven, CT: Yale University Press, 2018.

Broome, Richard. 'Aboriginal Victims and Voyagers: Confronting Frontier Myths.' *Journal of Australian Studies* 18, no. 42 (1994): 70–77.

Byrd, Jodi. *The Transit of Empire*. Minneapolis: University of Minnesota Press, 2011.

Byrd, Jodi. 'Follow the Typical Signs: Settler Sovereignty and Its Discontents.' *Settler Colonial Studies* 4, no. 2 (2014): 151–154.

Carey, Jane. 'On Hope and Resignation: Conflicting Visions of Settler Colonial Studies and Its Future as a Field.' *Postcolonial Studies* 23, no. 1 (2020): 21–42.

Carey, Jane, and Jane Lydon, eds. *Indigenous Networks: Mobility, Connections, and Exchange*. New York: Routledge, 2014.

Carter, Paul. *Meeting Place: The Human Encounter and the Challenge of Coexistence*. Minneapolis: University of Minnesota Press, 2013.

Cavanagh, Edward. 'History, Time and the Indigenous Critique.' *Arena* 37/38 (2012): 16–39.

Christie, M.F. *Aborigines in Colonial Victoria 1835–86*. Sydney: Sydney University Press, 1979.

Coghlan, T.A. *General Report on the Eleventh Census of New South Wales*. Sydney: Statistician's Office, 1894.

Connors, Libby. *Warrior: A Legendary Leader's Dramatic Life and Violent Death on the Colonial Frontier*. Sydney: Allen & Unwin, 2015.

Coulthard, Glen Sean. *Red Skin, White Masks: Rejecting the Colonial Politics of Recognition*. Minneapolis: University of Minnesota Press, 2014.

Cowlishaw, Gillian. 'Studying Aborigines: Changing Canons in Anthropology and History.' In *Power, Knowledge and Aborigines*, edited by Bain Attwood and John Arnold, 20–31. Melbourne: La Trobe University Press, 1992.

Darian-Smith, Kate, and Penelope Edmonds, eds. *Conciliation on Colonial Frontiers: Conflict, Performance, and Commemoration in Australia and the Pacific Rim*. New York: Routledge, 2015.

Davison, Graeme. 'Sydney and the Bush.' *Historical Studies* 18, no. 71 (1978): 191–209.

Day, Iyko. 'Being or Nothingness: Indigeneity, Antiblackness, and Settler Colonial Critique.' *Journal of the Critical Ethnic Studies Association* 1, no. 2 (2015): 102–121.

Day, Iyko. *Alien Capital: Asian Racialization and the Logic of Settler Colonial Capitalism*. Durham, NC: Duke University Press, 2016.

Deloria, Philip J. *Playing Indian*. New Haven, CT: Yale University Press, 1998.

Deloria, Philip J. 'Historiography.' In *A Companion to American Indian History*, edited by Philip J. Deloria and Neal Salisbury, 6–24. Malden, MA: Blackwell Publishers, 2002.

Deloria, Philip J. *Indians in Unexpected Places*. Lawrence: University of Kansas Press, 2004.

Deloria, Philip J. 'What Is the Middle Ground, Anyway?' *William and Mary Quarterly* 63, no. 1 (2006): 15–22.

Denoon, Donald. *Settler Capitalism: The Dynamics of Dependent Development in the Southern Hemisphere*. Oxford: Clarendon Press, 1983.

Denoon, Donald. 'Settler Capitalism Unsettled.' *New Zealand Journal of History* 29, no. 2 (1995): 129–141.

Edmonds, Penelope. *Urbanizing Frontiers: Indigenous Peoples and Settlers in 19th-Century Pacific Rim Cities*. Vancouver: UBC Press, 2010.

Ellinghaus, Katherine. 'George Newkirk Jr's Café, Competency, and Settler Colonialism.' *Journal of the West* 56, no. 4 (2017): 25–35.

Ellinghaus, Katherine. '"You Are Not Really Free, You Are Just Turned Loose": Settler Colonialism, Survivance and Competency at the Osage Agency.' *Settler Colonial Studies* 8, no. 1 (2018): 16–29.

Evans, Julie. 'Where Lawlessness Is Law: The Settler-Colonial Frontier as a Legal Space of Violence.' *Australian Feminist Law Review* 30 (2009): 3–22.

Evans, Raymond, Kay Saunders, and Kathryn Cronin. *Exclusion, Exploitation and Extermination: Race Relations in Colonial Queensland*. Sydney: Australia and New Zealand Book Company, 1975.

Foley, Gary. 'The Australian Labor Party and the *Native Title Act*.' In *Sovereign Subjects: Indigenous Sovereignty Matters*, edited by Aileen Moreton-Robinson, 118–139. Sydney: Allen & Unwin, 2007.

Ford, Lisa. 'Locating Indigenous Self-Determination in the Margins of Settler Sovereignty.' In *Between Indigenous and Settler Governance*, edited by Lisa Ford and Tim Rowse, 1–11. Oxford: Routledge, 2012.

Forsyth, Hannah, and Altin Gavranovic. 'The Logic of Survival: Towards an Indigenous-Centred History of Capitalism in Wilcannia.' *Settler Colonial Studies* 8, no. 4 (2018): 464–488.

Fujikane, Candace, and Jonathan Y. Okamura, eds. *Asian Settler Colonialism: From Local Governance to the Habits of Everyday Life in Hawaiʻi*. Honolulu: University of Hawaiʻi Press, 2008.

Fullagar, Kate, and Michael A. McDonnell, eds. *Facing Empire: Indigenous Experiences in a Revolutionary Age*. Baltimore, MD: Johns Hopkins University Press, 2018.

Furniss, Elizabeth. 'Imagining the Frontier: Comparative Perspectives from Canada and Australia.' In *Dislocating the Frontier: Essaying the Mystique of the Outback*, edited by Deborah Bird Rose and Richard Davis, 23–46. Canberra: ANU Press, 2005.

Hage, Ghassan. '*État de Siege*: A Dying Domesticating Colonialism.' *American Ethnologist* 43, no. 1 (2016): 38–49.

Hall, Stuart. 'Pluralism, Race and Class in Caribbean Society.' In *Race and Class in Post-colonial Society*, edited by United Nations Educational Scientific and Cultural Organisation, 150–182. Paris: UNESCO, 1977.

Hämäläinen, Pekka. *The Comanche Empire*. New Haven, CT: Yale University Press, 2008.

Hämäläinen, Pekka. 'What's in a Concept? The Kinetic Empire of the Comanches.' *History and Theory* 52, no. 1 (2013): 81–90.

Hämäläinen, Pekka, and Samuel Truett. 'On Borderlands.' *Journal of American History* 98, no. 2 (2011): 38–61.

Hancock, W.K. *Survey of British Commonwealth Affairs*. London: Oxford University Press: 1940.

Hoxie, Frederick. 'Retrieving the Red Continent: Settler Colonialism and the History of American Indians in the U.S.' *Ethnic and Racial Studies* 31, no. 5 (2008): 1153–1167.

Hughes-d'Aeth, Tony. 'Cooper, Cather, Prichard, "Pioneer": The Chronotope of Settler Colonialism.' *Australian Literary Studies* 31, no. 3 (2016).

Jackson, Shona N. *Creole Indigeneity: Between Myth and Nation in the Caribbean*. Minneapolis: University of Minnesota Press, 2012.

Jacobs, Margaret. *White Mother to a Dark Race: Settler Colonialism, Maternalism, and the Removal of Indigenous Children in the American West and Australia, 1880–1940*. Lincoln: University of Nebraska Press, 2009.

Johnson, Miranda. *The Land is our History: Indigeneity, Law, and the Settler State*. New York: Oxford University Press, 2016.

Johnson, Walter. 'On Agency.' *Journal of Social History* 37, no. 1 (2003): 113–124.

Karskens, Grace. *The Colony: A History of Early Sydney*. Sydney: Allen & Unwin, 2009.

Karuka, Manu. *Empire's Tracks: Indigenous Nations, Chinese Workers, and the Transcontinental Railroad*. Oakland: University of California Press, 2019.

Kauanui, J. Kēhaulani. '"A Structure, Not an Event": Settler Colonialism and Enduring Indigeneity.' Forum: Emergent Critical Analytics for Alternative Humanities Issue, *Lateral* 5, no. 1 (2016).

Kauanui, J. Kēhaulani. 'Tracing Historical Specificity: Race and the Colonial Politics of (In)Capacity.' *American Quarterly*, 69, no. 2 (2017): 257–265.

Kauanui, J. Kēhaulani. *Paradoxes of Hawaiian Sovereignty: Land, Sex, and the Colonial Politics of State Nationalism*. Durham, NC: Duke University Press, 2018.

Kiel, Doug. 'Untaming the Mild Frontier: In Search of New Midwestern Histories.' *Middle West Review* 1, no. 1 (2014): 8–38.

Klein, Kerwin Lee. *Frontiers of Historical Imagination: Narrating the European Conquest of Native America, 1890–1990*. Berkeley: University of California Press, 1997.

Konishi, Shino. 'Bennelong and Gogy: Strategic Brokers in Colonial New South Wales.' In *Brokers and Boundaries: Colonial Exploration in Indigenous Territory*, edited by Tiffany Shellam, Maria Nugent, Shino Konishi, and Alison Cadzow, 15–37. Canberra: ANU Press and Aboriginal History Monographs, 2016.

Konishi, Shino. 'First Nations Scholars, Settler Colonial Studies, and Indigenous History.' *Australian Historical Studies* 50, no. 3 (2019): 285–304.

Lahti, Janne. 'What Is Settler Colonialism and What It Has to Do with the American West?' *Journal of the West* 56, no. 4 (2017): 8–12.

Laidlaw, Zoë, and Alan Lester, eds. *Indigenous Communities and Settler Colonialism: Land Holding, Loss and Survival in an Interconnected World*. Basingstoke: Palgrave Macmillan, 2015.

Lake, Marilyn. 'The Politics of Respectability: Identifying the Masculinist Context.' *Historical Studies* 22, no. 86 (1986): 116–131.

Lake, Marilyn. *Progressive New World: How Settler Colonialism and Transpacific Exchange Shape American Reform*. Cambridge, MA: Harvard University Press, 2019.

Lewis, Darrell. *A Wild History: Life and Death on the Victoria River Frontier*. Melbourne: Monash University Press, 2012.

Limerick, Patricia Nelson. *The Legacy of Conquest: The Unbroken Past of the American West*. New York: W.W. Norton, 1987.

Limerick, Patricia Nelson. 'The Adventures of the Frontier in the Twentieth Century.' In *The Frontier in American Culture*, edited by James R. Grossman, 67–102. Berkeley: University of California Press, 1994.

Lloyd, David, and Patrick Wolfe. 'Settler Colonial Logics and the Neoliberal Regime.' *Settler Colonial Studies* 6, no. 2 (2016): 109–118.

Lomawaima, K. Tsianina. 'Indigenous Studies.' *American Quarterly* 68, no. 1 (2016): 149–160.

Loos, Noel. *Invasion and Resistance: Aboriginal–European Relations on the North Queensland Frontier 1861–1897*. Canberra: ANU Press, 1982.

Martin, A.W. 'Political Groupings in New South Wales, 1872–1889: A Study in the Working of Responsible Government.' PhD diss., The Australian National University, June 1955.

McGrath, Ann. *'Born in the Cattle': Aborigines in Cattle Country*. Sydney: Allen & Unwin, 1987.

McGrath, Ann. *Illicit Love: Interracial Sex and Marriage in the United States and Australia*. Lincoln: University of Nebraska Press, 2015.

McKinnon, Crystal. 'Indigenous Music as a Space of Resistance.' In *Making Settler Colonial Space: Perspectives on Race, Place and Identity*, edited by Tracey Banivanua Mar and Penelope Edmonds, 255–272. Basingstoke: Palgrave Macmillan, 2010.

Merlan, Francesca. 'Reply to Patrick Wolfe.' *Social Analysis: The International Journal of Social and Cultural Practice* 41, no. 2 (1997): 10–19.

Moreton Robinson, Aileen. 'Towards an Australian Indigenous Women's Standpoint Theory.' *Australian Feminist Studies* 28, no. 78 (2013): 331–347.

Moses, A. Dirk, ed. *Genocide and Settler Society: Frontier Violence and Stolen Indigenous Children in Australian History*. New York: Berghahn Books, 2004.

Moses, A. Dirk. 'Official Apologies, Reconciliation, and Settler Colonialism: Australian Indigenous Alterity and Political Agency.' *Citizenship Studies* 15, no. 2 (2011): 145–159.

Mt. Pleasant, Alyssa, Caroline Wigginton, and Kelly Wisecup. 'Materials and Methods in Native American and Indigenous Studies: Completing the Turn.' *William and Mary Quarterly* 75, no. 2 (2018): 207–236.

Nichols, Robert. 'Theft Is Property! The Recursive Logic of Dispossession.' *Political Theory* 46, no. 1 (2018): 3–28.

Nicolacopoulos, Toula, and George Vassilacopoulos. *Indigenous Sovereignty and the Being of the Occupier: Manifesto for a White Australian Philosophy of Origins*. Melbourne: re.press, 2014.

O'Brien, Jean. *Firsting and Lasting: Writing Indians Out of Existence in New England*. Minneapolis: University of Minnesota Press, 2010.

O'Brien, Jean M. 'Historical Sources and Methods in Indigenous Studies: Touching on the Past, Looking to the Future.' In *Sources and Methods in Indigenous Studies*, edited by Chris Andersen and Jean M. O'Brien, 15–22. London: Routledge, 2017.
Ostler, Jeffrey, and Nancy Shoemaker. 'Settler Colonialism in Early American History: Introduction.' *William and Mary Quarterly* 76, no. 3 (2019): 361–368.
Owens, Louis. *Mixedblood Messages: Literature, Film, Family, Place*. Norman: University of Oklahoma Press, 1998.
Pascoe, Peggy. *Relations of Rescue: The Search for Female Moral Authority in the American West, 1874–1939*. New York: Oxford University Press, 1990.
Pascoe, Peggy. 'Western Women at the Cultural Crossroads.' In *Trails: Toward a New Western History*, edited by Patricia Nelson Limerick, Clyde A. Milner II, and Charles E. Rankin, 40–58. Lawrence: University Press of Kansas, 1991.
Pateman, Carol, and Charles W. Mills. *Contract and Domination*. Cambridge: Polity, 2007.
Pexa, Christopher. *Translated Nation: Rewriting the Dakhóta Oyáte*. Minneapolis: University of Minnesota Press, 2019.
Porter, Robert P. *Compendium of The Eleventh Census: 1890*. Washington, DC: Department of the Interior, Census Office, 1892.
Portus, G.V. 'Americans and Australians.' *Australian Quarterly* 14, no. 2 (1942): 30–41.
Read, Peter. *A Hundred Years War: The Wiradjuri People and the State*. Canberra: ANU Press, 1988.
Read, Peter. 'Making Aboriginal History.' In *Australian History Now*, edited by Anna Clark and Paul Ashton, 24–39. Sydney: NewSouth Publishing, 2013.
Reece, R.H.W. *Aborigines and Colonists: Aborigines and Colonial Society in New South Wales in the 1830s and 1840s*. Sydney: Sydney University Press, 1974.
Reynolds, Henry. 'Violence, the Aboriginals, and the Australian Historian.' *Meanjin Quarterly* 31, no. 4 (1972): 471–477.
Reynolds, Henry. *The Other Side of the Frontier: Aboriginal Resistance to the European Invasion of Australia*. Melbourne: Penguin Books, 1982.
Reynolds, Henry. *Frontier: Aborigines, Settlers and Land*. Sydney: Allen & Unwin, 1987.
Reynolds, Henry. *With the White People*. Melbourne: Penguin, 1990.
Reynolds, Henry. *Why Weren't We Told? A Personal Search for the Truth about Our History*. Melbourne: Viking, 1999.
Reynolds, Henry. *The Other Side of the Frontier: Aboriginal Resistance to the European Invasion of Australia*. Rev. ed. Sydney: UNSW Press, 2006.
Rhook, Nadia. '"Annamese Coolies" at Australian ports: Charting Colonial Geographies of Emotion, and Settler Memory, from French Vietnam to New Caledonia via Interwar Australia.' *Australian Historical Studies* 48, no. 3 (2017): 399–415.
Richter, Daniel K. 'Whose Indian History?' *William and Mary Quarterly* 50, no. 2 (1993): 379–393.
Richter, Daniel K. *Facing East from Indian Country: A Native History of Early America*. Cambridge, MA: Harvard University Press, 2001.
Rifkin, Mark. 'Indigenizing Agamben: Rethinking Sovereignty in Light of the "Peculiar" Status of Native Peoples.' *Cultural Critique* 73 (2009): 88–124.
Rifkin, Mark. *Manifesting America: The Imperial Construction of U.S. National Space*. Oxford: Oxford University Press, 2009.
Rifkin, Mark. 'The Frontier as (Movable) Space of Exception.' *Settler Colonial Studies* 4, no. 2 (2014): 176–180.
Rifkin, Mark. *Settler Common Sense: Queerness and Everyday Colonialism in the American Renaissance*. Minneapolis: University of Minnesota Press, 2014.
Roberts, Tony. *Frontier Justice: A History of the Gulf Country to 1900*. Brisbane: University of Queensland Press, 2005.
Rodinson, Maxime. *Israel: A Colonial-Settler State?* New York: Monad Press, 1973.
Rose, Deborah Bird. 'Hard Times: An Australian Study.' In *Quicksands: Foundational Histories in Australia and Aotearoa New Zealand*, edited by Klaus Neumann, Nicholas Thomas, and Hilary Ericksen, 2–19. Sydney: UNSW Press, 1999.

Rowley, C.D. *The Destruction of Aboriginal Society.* Canberra: ANU Press, 1970.
Rowse, Tim. 'Indigenous Heterogeneity.' *Australian Historical Studies* 45, no. 3 (2014): 297–310.
Rowse, Tim. 'Indigenous Incorporation as a Means to Empowerment.' In *Native Title from Mabo to Akiba: A Vehicle for Change and Empowerment?* edited by Sean Brennan et al., 184–198. Sydney: The Federation Press, 2015.
Russell, Lynette. 'Introduction.' In *Colonial Frontiers: Indigenous–European Encounters in Settler Societies*, edited by Lynette Russell, 1–15. Manchester: Manchester University Press, 2001.
Russell, Lynette. *Roving Mariners: Australian Aboriginal Whalers and Sealers in the Southern Oceans, 1790–1870.* Albany: State University of New York Press, 2012.
Ryan, Lyndall. *The Aboriginal Tasmanians.* Brisbane: University of Queensland Press, 1981.
Saranillio, Dean. 'Haunani-Kay Trask and Settler Colonial and Relational Critique: Alternatives to Binary Analyses of Power.' *Verge: Studies in Global Asias* 4, no. 2 (2018): 36–44.
Sayegh, Fayez. *Zionist Colonialism in Palestine.* Beirut: Research Center, Palestine Liberation Organization, 1965.
Sayigh, Rosemary. *Palestinians: From Peasants to Revolutionaries; A People's History.* London: Zed Books, 1979.
Sewell, William H., Jr. *Logics of History: Social Theory and Social Transformation.* Chicago, IL: University of Chicago Press, 2005.
Shellam, Tiffany. *Shaking Hands on the Fringe: Negotiating the Aboriginal World at King George Sound.* Perth: University of Western Press, 2009.
Shoemaker, Nancy. *A Strange Likeness: Becoming Red and White in Eighteenth-Century North America.* New York: Oxford University Press, 2004.
Shoemaker, Nancy. 'A Typology of Colonialism.' *Perspectives on History*, October 2015. https://www.historians.org/publications-and-directories/perspectives-on-history/october-2015/a-typology-of-colonialism.
Silverstein, Ben. 'Submerged Sovereignty: Native Title within a History of Incorporation.' In *Sovereignty: Frontiers of Possibility*, edited by Julie Evans et al., 60–85. Honolulu: University of Hawai'i Press, 2013.
Silverstein, Ben. *Governing Natives: Indirect Rule and Settler Colonialism in Northern Australia.* Manchester: Manchester University Press, 2019.
Simpson, Audra. *Mohawk Interruptus: Political Life across the Borders of Settler States.* Durham, NC: Duke University Press, 2014.
Simpson, Audra. 'Whither Settler Colonialism.' *Settler Colonial Studies* 6, no. 4 (2016): 438–445.
Smithers, Gregory D. 'Renewing Sacred Fires: The Cherokee People and the Shifting Frontiers of Settler Colonialism.' *Journal of the West* 56, no. 4 (2017): 36–47.
Smithers, Gregory D. *Science, Sexuality, and Race in the United States and Australia, 1780–1940.* Rev. ed. Lincoln: University of Nebraska Press, 2017.
Speed, Shannon. 'Structures of Settler Capitalism in Abya Yala.' *American Quarterly* 69, no. 4 (2017): 783–790.
Spivak, Gayatri Chakravorty. 'The Rani of Sirmur: An Essay in Reading the Archives.' *History and Theory* 24, no. 3 (1985): 247–272.
Stanner, W.E.H. *After the Dreaming: Black and White Australians, an Anthropologist's View.* Sydney: Australian Broadcasting Commission, 1969.
Trask, Haunani-Kay. *From a Native Daughter: Colonialism and Sovereignty in Hawai'i.* Rev. ed. Honolulu: University of Hawai'i Press, 1999.
Trask, Haunani-Kay. 'Settlers of Color and "Immigrant" Hegemony: "Locals" in Hawai'i.' *Amerasia Journal* 26, no. 2 (2000): 1–24.
Turner, Frederick Jackson. *The Frontier in American History.* New York: Henry Holt and Company, 1920.
van Kirk, Sylvia. *Many Tender Ties: Women in Fur-Trade Society, 1670–1870.* Norman: University of Oklahoma Press, 1980.

Veracini, Lorenzo. 'A Prehistory of Australia's History Wars: The Evolution of Aboriginal History during the 1970s and 1980s.' *Australian Journal of Politics and History* 52, no. 3 (2006): 439–454.
Veracini, Lorenzo. '"Settler Colonialism": Career of a Concept.' *Journal of Imperial and Commonwealth History* 41, no. 2 (2013): 313–333.
Veracini, Lorenzo. *The Settler Colonial Present*. Basingstoke: Palgrave Macmillan, 2015.
Vimalassery, Manu, Juliana Hu Pegues, and Alyosha Goldstein. 'On Colonial Unknowing.' *Theory & Event* 19, no. 4 (2016).
Vizenor, Gerald. *Manifest Manners: Postindian Warriors of Survivance*. Hanover: Wesleyan University Press, 1994.
Ward, Russel. *The Australian Legend*. 2nd ed. Melbourne: Oxford University Press, 1966.
White, Richard. *'It's Your Misfortune and None of My Own': A History of the American West*. Norman: University of Oklahoma Press, 1991.
White, Richard. *The Middle Ground: Indians, Empires, and Republics in the Great Lakes Region, 1650–1815*. New York: Cambridge University Press, 1991.
White, Richard. 'Trashing the Trails.' In *Trails: Toward a New Western History*, edited by Patricia Nelson Limerick, Clyde A. Milner II, and Charles E. Rankin, 26–39. Lawrence: University Press of Kansas, 1991.
White, Richard. 'Frederick Jackson Turner and Buffalo Bill.' In *The Frontier in American Culture*, edited by James R. Grossman, 6–65. Berkeley: University of California Press, 1994.
Witgen, Michael. *An Infinity of Nations: How the Native New World Shaped Early North America*. Philadelphia: University of Pennsylvania Press, 2012.
Wolfe, Patrick. 'Nation and MiscegeNation: Discursive Continuity in the Post-Mabo Era.' *Social Analysis* 36 (1994): 93–152.
Wolfe, Patrick. 'History and Imperialism: A Century of Theory, from Marx to Postcolonialism.' *American Historical Review* 102, no. 2 (1997): 388–420.
Wolfe, Patrick. *Settler Colonialism and the Transformation of Anthropology: The Politics and Poetics of an Ethnographic Event*. London: Cassell, 1999.
Wolfe, Patrick. 'Settler Colonialism and the Elimination of the Native.' *Journal of Genocide Research* 8, no. 4 (2006): 387–409.
Wolfe, Patrick. 'Race and the Trace of History: For Henry Reynolds.' In *Studies in Settler Colonialism: Politics, Identity, Culture*, edited by Fiona Bateman and Lionel Pilkington, 272–296. Basingstoke: Palgrave Macmillan, 2011.
Wolfe, Patrick. 'Introduction.' In *The Settler Complex: Recuperating Binarism in Colonial Studies*, edited by Patrick Wolfe, 1–24. Los Angeles, CA: UCLA American Indian Studies Center, 2016.
Wolfe, Patrick. *Traces of History: Elementary Structures of Race*. London: Verso, 2016.
Woollacott, Angela. 'Russel Ward, Frontier Violence and Australian Historiography.' *Journal of Australian Colonial History* 10, no. 2 (2008): 23–36.
Worster, Donald. *Rivers of Empire: Water, Aridity, and the Growth of the American West*. New York: Pantheon Books, 1985.
Wright, Judith. *The Cry for the Dead*. Melbourne: Oxford University Press, 1981.
Young, Alex Trimble. 'Settler Sovereignty and the Rhizomatic West, or, the Significance of the Frontier in Postwestern Studies.' *Western American Literature* 48, nos. 1 & 2 (2013): 115–140.
Young, Alex Trimble, and Lorenzo Veracini. '"If I Am Native to Anything": Settler Colonial Studies and Western American Literature.' *Western American Literature* 52, no. 1 (2017): 1–23.

4
INDIGENOUS PEOPLES IN ASIA
A long history

Robert Cribb

The modern concept of indigeneity was shaped principally by the experience of the long-standing inhabitants of North America and Australasia. Until the era of European colonial expansion, the first peoples in those regions had lived in relatively small communities. Their economies were often based on a mix of agriculture and hunting, with commodity production artisanal, rather than industrial. Their cultures were consequently especially attuned to the natural environment. Settlers from Europe, arriving at first in small numbers, characterised them as 'tribes' rather than nations, judged their technological achievements as 'primitive', and, above all, dismissed or ignored their title over the land. Settlers often brought diseases that devastated Indigenous communities and they possessed what soon proved to be overwhelming military advantage over the earlier inhabitants. As the number of European arrivals grew, the settler societies of North America and Australasia dispossessed Indigenous peoples, turning them into marginalised minorities in the lands they had once held. Especially in the nineteenth century and after, settler discourse about Indigenous peoples was marked by racialist attitudes that understood the social and intellectual character of Indigenous people to be genetically determined. Only after the Second World War did a political movement arise among Indigenous peoples and their allies in the settler communities to seek redress for historical wrongs, remedies for contemporary disadvantage, and recognition of the value of indigenous culture. In the emergence of this movement, the racialist distinction that the colonisers had made between themselves and Indigenous peoples was in some ways turned into an asset for the indigenous claim to separate status.

The experience of Indigenous peoples in Asia was different from that of first peoples in North America and Australasia in three important respects. First, rather than being the product of a sudden juxtaposition of societies from the sixteenth century, the incorporation of Asian first peoples into larger polities was a much older process, marked by much longer periods of prior contact during which first peoples themselves selectively adopted technology and culture from what were to become settler metropoles. Second, the destruction of first-people communities in Asia took place in the historical context of vast, destructive conflicts which enveloped all Asians, not just first peoples. And third, doctrines of Asian nationalism that confronted Western imperialism and colonialism from the late nineteenth century actively worked against acknowledging a separate identity for first peoples. Although discrimination and prejudice against first peoples were common in many Asian societies, for the most part nationalists refused to problematise the position of first peoples, often taking for granted that they were an undifferentiated part of the national community. This ideological disregard for first peoples was especially acute in Southeast Asia during the twentieth century, where colonialism had both enabled and been responsible for large-scale immigration by Chinese and Indian settlers. A campaign against this derivative settler colonialism was often close to the heart of the nationalist campaign against European colonialism, leading nationalists to have terms such as 'indigenous' and 'native' encompassing a much wider group than only first peoples.

Only in the late twentieth century did the rights of first peoples in Asia enter the political agenda, partly as a consequence of the increasingly acute pressures on surviving indigenous groups, partly because of a sophisticated international articulation of the plight of Indigenous peoples and measures that might relieve that plight.

First peoples in Asia and the expansion of pre-modern empires

Asia's long history has traditionally been written in terms of the emergence and growth of major civilisations. Five thousand years ago, people of the Indus Valley civilisation inhabited more than a thousand carefully planned cities, dwelling in baked-brick houses, and communicating with a complex script. Three and a half thousand years ago, complex states began to emerge on the North China plain, employing an early version of writing that included the distinctive characters now used to write Chinese. In India in the sixth century BCE, Siddhartha Gautama laid down basic principles of the religion we now call Buddhism, while, at almost the same time in China, Confucius set out basic principles of what became Confucianism. Over the next thousand years, the vast, fertile, and well-watered plains of North India and North China became the enduring heartlands of imperial Indian and Chinese civilisations. Other civilisations emerged in smaller fertile zones – on the Korean peninsula, in the Japanese archipelago, in what became Vietnam, Cambodia, and Burma, and on the fertile islands of Java, Sumatra, and Ceylon (Sri Lanka). Distinct complex civilisations with elaborate economic and administrative structures emerged in the valleys of the Himalayas and on the Tibetan and Mongolian Plateaux. All these civilisations drew upon some combination of Indian and Chinese cultures, blending outside forms with local traditions to create distinct identities.

In the familiar story of these civilisations, the experience of peoples who lived in the hills, the forests, the arid and frigid zones, the swamps, at sea and on smaller islands – that is, in regions on the margin of empire, or far beyond – has received little attention. These peoples, living in smaller communities with less complicated political and social structures, often without a written language, left few or no records of their own, and we can view them only imperfectly through the records left by larger civilisations and, in some cases, through reconstructions on the basis of archaeological, linguistic, and genetic investigation. Something of the flavour of records compiled by officials in settled civilisations can be seen in an extract from a Chinese geographical compendium called *Comprehensive Institutions*, which was completed in 801 CE but which drew on records going back several centuries. The short description refers to people living in northern Siberia. The description, like most such Chinese accounts, is brief and focusses on the characteristics of these people that most strongly distinguish their culture from that of Chinese people. It appears to interpret features of their usual costume as animalistic, referring to:

> the realm of Majing [Manao], whose people make a noise like wild geese or wild ducks. From the knees up to their heads their bodies are human, while from the knees down they are covered with fur and have horse shanks and hooves. They do not ride horses but can run faster than horses. They are brave and stout and daring in battle.[1]

Chinese texts commonly refer to non-Chinese peoples by terms translated today as 'barbarian', but it is probable that those terms did not have the derogatory force that they acquired in the nineteenth century, but instead simply meant 'foreigner'. Indian civilisations similarly used the word *mleccha* (originally meaning 'incomprehensible') as a collective term for the cultures of first peoples in regions surrounding the North Indian heartland.[2] Like Chinese writers, Indian observers were inclined to interpret first peoples as animalistic. The monkey tribes led by Hanuman who assisted Prince Rama in the Indian Ramayana epic are very likely a representation of first-people communities.[3]

Geography was the great protector of the smaller communities from their larger neighbours. From 300 BCE until the seventeenth century, the imperial polities based in fertile valleys of the Indus and Ganges in northern India and of the Huanghe and Yangtze in northern China were hampered in their territorial expansion by hills, seas, deserts, and swamps. Indian empires could never push far or long into the Himalayan mountains nor extend their control to the southern tip of the Indian subcontinent. Chinese empires were hemmed in by the Mongolian steppe, the Gobi and Taklamakan deserts and the rugged mountains of the south and southwest. Neither Indian nor Chinese empires could project enduring power across the seas.

Evolving technologies of warfare and communication, however, gradually diminished the topographical obstacles to imperial expansion at the expense of first peoples. In the first century CE, for instance, the Chinese kingdom of Wu launched a sustained campaign against 'barbarians' known as the Shanyue in the mountains of what is now the province of Anhui. Using a combination of military action, subsidies to Shanyue leaders, and sponsored settlement by Han Chinese from northern China,

Indigenous peoples in Asia

Figure 4.1 Representatives of the indigenous Emishi people in Japan paying homage to Prince Shotoku in about 1069
Source: Egami Namio, Umehara Takeshi, and Ueyama Shunpei, *Ainu to kodai Nippon: Shinpojūmu Hoppō Bunka o Kangaeru* (Tokyo: Shogakukan, 1982), 92.

the Wu authorities succeeded in subduing the Shanyue and assimilating them into mainstream Chinese culture.[4] Over the course of about six centuries from 400 to 1000 CE, the Emishi peoples of Japan's northern Honshu were gradually subdued and absorbed into the expanding Japanese state (Figure 4.1).[5]

Conquest, however, was not the only mechanism of imperial expansion. The empires and the surrounding communities of first peoples were enmeshed in complex economic relationships, sometimes predatory, sometimes mutually beneficial. Traders, especially those carrying high value goods, could breach geographical barriers more readily than large, cumbersome armies. Empires and small communities also regularly conducted raids to extort payments – these were called 'subsidies' when paid by empires to militant communities and 'tribute' when paid by communities to empires. The slave trade was also a massive burden on first-people communities. Both imperial polities and local rival communities conducted raids to seize Indigenous people as slaves. Sometimes lowland empires undertook raids to seize slaves; sometimes the leaders of these communities were slave traders themselves.

Culture, too, could penetrate where armies could not. The process of cultural transmission from civilisations to first-people communities was once seen as a form of cultural submission to cultural great powers, but more recent approaches have emphasised the selectivity of the recipient societies. Imperial powers were seldom interested in missionising to spread their religion, political doctrines, and cultural forms beyond their own limits. Instead, small communities borrowed opportunistically from what have been characterised as 'exemplary centres' – cultural powerhouses that generated a smorgasbord of political, cultural, and social forms, which other communities adopted selectively in the service of their own political, cultural, and social agendas.⁶ The effect of this process was to create a penumbra of partially acculturated smaller societies around each of the major empires – not just those of China and India but also of the smaller civilisations such as Java and Japan.

Once incorporated into a larger empire by military force, however, the common fate of first peoples was assimilation. Chinese authorities from the tenth century to the eighteenth routinely described first peoples within the borders of successive Chinese empires as 'raw' or 'cooked' barbarians, according to their degree of assimilation.⁷ The aim, of course, was that in due course, they would be fully assimilated to and indistinguishable from the Han Chinese majority. This aim was achievable because Chinese ethnic thinking at this time was without any significant idea of inherent or genetic difference among peoples: under the principle of *tianxia* ('all under Heaven') that was articulated by the first Chinese emperor Qin Shi Huang in the third century BCE, all peoples of the world would eventually be brought into the benevolence of Chinese civilisation.⁸ In India, by contrast, it appears that first peoples were often assimilated into Hindu society as distinct castes (*jati*), generally based upon occupation and kept socially distinct from other castes.⁹

Although the descriptions of first peoples recorded by settled empires can be unreliable, they point to the fact that few if any of the communities we might now call 'first peoples' were necessarily first in the lands they occupied. People moved; communities split and merged. Speakers of Austroasiatic languages (Mon, Cambodian, Vietnamese), for example, are believed to have migrated from what is now south-central China into mainland Southeast Asia and perhaps Sumatra around 10,000 years ago, but they were partly displaced and absorbed by later immigrants speaking languages related to Burmese and Thai. The former inhabitants of western Indonesia, probably related to today's Papuans, were displaced and absorbed by Austronesian-speaking settlers who arrived via the Philippines from Taiwan in about 500 BCE. The Baduy of western Java and the Orang Rimba (literally 'jungle people') of southern Sumatra are believed to have originated as settled farmers who withdrew from the strains of agriculture to take up a hunter-gather life in the forests. The mountain people of central Vietnam, collectively known as Montagnards, believed that they had fled to the mountains to escape the Vietnamese and Cambodians of the plains in the fourteenth and fifteenth centuries. Some scholars suggest that the Shanyue of Anhui were former lowland farmers who fled to the mountains to avoid oppressive tax regimes.¹⁰

The anthropologist James C. Scott has argued forcefully that the first peoples of a vast upland zone stretching from the Himalayas to the mountains of mainland Southeast Asia constitute a distinct region whose peoples fought to remain free of the vexatious rule of lowland empires.¹¹ Although Scott's arguments have been sharply criticised for their romanticism and weak empirical basis,¹² they offer a useful corrective to the assumption that incorporation in larger empires was only beneficial for once-isolated first peoples (Figure 4.2).

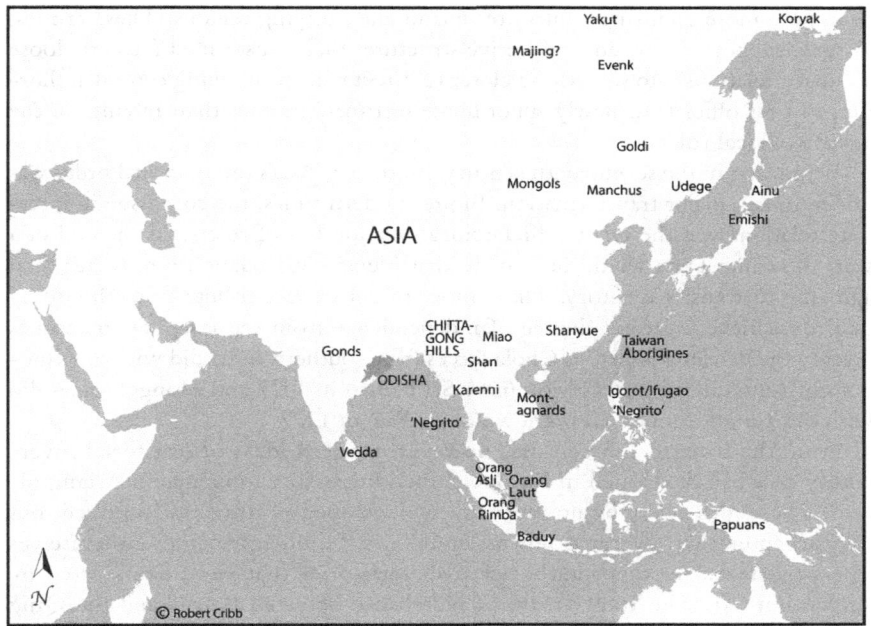

Figure 4.2 Asia, showing approximate location of Indigenous peoples mentioned in the text

First peoples in Asia in the early modern and colonial eras

From the sixteenth century, new empires of unprecedented power began to emerge in Asia. The reasons for this transformation are complex. They include the development of new military technologies (especially firearms), new administrative techniques, and the adoption of new food crops from the Americas, most notably maize. These crops facilitated settlement in ecologically marginal regions and supported denser populations, thereby giving the imperial centres still greater demographic advantage over first peoples. The Mughal empire in India, founded in 1526, extended its rule over nearly all the Indian subcontinent and subdued significant parts of the hill and mountain country abutting the Indian plains in the north. In China, Manchu rulers who came to power as the Qing dynasty in 1644 more than doubled the territorial extent of the empire ruled by the preceding Ming dynasty, incorporating Mongolia, Xinjiang, and Tibet into their domains. In Japan, the Tokugawa military authorities extended their authority in the northern island of Hokkaido. In Vietnam, on a smaller scale, the Nguyen lords extended their control over the Annamite cordillera as well as the Mekong delta. The Konbaung dynasty in Burma (founded 1752) established hegemony over the many peoples of the hills surrounding the Ayeyarwady valley. In what is now Thailand, the Bangkok dynasty began to fill out Thai hegemony over the hills around the Chao Phraya valley. These developments marked an intensification of the assimilationist processes of earlier centuries. Imperial armies now had the technology to impose more enduring control of upland and outlying regions. These armies, in turn, supported new administrative structures that transformed formerly loose tributary relations into something closer to direct rule by allowing central authorities to post officials to newly subordinate territories, rather than relying on the agency of local rulers.

Beginning in the seventeenth century, moreover, Asia's international order was undergoing a major transformation. In pre-modern times, the core issue in interstate relations was the relative hierarchical relationship of rulers. At the end of a war, the combatants would recalibrate that hierarchical relationship, rather than agreeing to transfer territory. The winner might extract tribute from the losing side, or achieve a greater degree of independence from the loser, or sometimes destroy the defeated polity, as Chola forces from southern India did with the kingdom of Anuradhapura in Ceylon (now Sri Lanka) in 1027 and Mongol forces did with the Tangut Empire (also known as Xi Xia) in 1227.

From the seventeenth century, however, modern ideas of territorial sovereignty that had developed in Europe gained increasing influence in Asian polities. These ideas were by no means fully developed or universally agreed, but they accepted that sovereign powers could and should agree among themselves to recognise each other's authority over territories that were demarcated by agreed borders. The 1689 Treaty of Nerchinsk between Russia and the Qing was a landmark in delimiting a fixed, though partial, border between the two empires in Northeast Asia.[13] The peoples who lived in these lands, however, were not Russian, Manchu, or Chinese, but rather first peoples such as Evenk and Goldi.

In the decades and centuries that followed, in a kind of geopolitical enclosure movement, the whole of the Asian landmass was divided, at least notionally, among states. Each state held sovereignty running unabated to its borders, where its authority stopped abruptly to give way to the sovereignty of the neighbouring state. In many cases, as in the Treaty of Nerchinsk, these new borders ran along mountain watersheds and rivers in lands that were occupied by first peoples. In other cases, they simply reflected a freezing of once-fluid zones of demarcation created by earlier military action. Britain's annexation of Burma in the nineteenth century, for instance, fixed borders around the territories that had been loosely subordinate to the preceding Konbaung dynasty. The lines of such borders paid little attention to the wishes of these peoples or even to the rough extent of their lands.

The most arbitrary of these borders were those drawn by Dutch, German, and British diplomats in partitioning the island of New Guinea in the late nineteenth century. The negotiators allocated the western half of the island to Dutch sovereignty and drew a line running north-south along the meridian 141°E, cutting arbitrarily through mountain, jungle, and the lands of local Papuan communities. The border was later shifted to run in part along the Fly River, but there was still no attention to the human geography of the island. Modern ideas of sovereignty thus worked alongside changes in imperial capacity to constrict the previous autonomy of first peoples.

Within the framework created by these borders, the experience of first peoples varied greatly. In some regions, annexation was followed by the rise of a frontier economy, in which outsiders collaborated with local people to extract valuable commodities. Furs such as sable, hunted by the first peoples of Siberia, were much in demand.[14] In the seventeenth century, outside collectors made repeated incursions into first-people lands in Manchuria to obtain ginseng.[15] In Taiwan, which was inhabited until the seventeenth century by first peoples related to today's Filipinos, traders struck advantageous deals with local people for the supply of deer skins.[16] In parts of New Guinea, European hunters worked with local men to locate and capture birds-of-paradise for the international feather trade in the late nineteenth century[17]; in Sumatra and other Indonesian islands, entrepreneurs relentlessly extracted gutta-percha trees in the second half of the nineteenth century for their latex, which was used to seal underwater telegraph cables.[18] In all of these cases, sudden intense contact with global markets led to social disruption. This disruption involved alcohol, sexually transmitted diseases, and violence ensuing from the competition over valuable resources and the monetisation of social relationships. When the various periods of resource extraction were over, the first peoples were left with ravaged societies and ravaged ecologies.

Except in Siberia, Europeans did not settle in Asia in numbers that were sufficient to overwhelm local peoples, as was the case in North America and Australasia. Nonetheless, the quickening of trade and communication that accompanied the arrival of Western imperial power in Asia stimulated an era of Asian settler colonialism. Following the establishment of a Dutch trading settlement in Taiwan (then known as Formosa) in the early seventeenth century, Chinese settlers began to arrive on the island, soon displacing its first peoples from the fertile lowland plains and leading eventually to the incorporation of the island into the Qing empire.[19] In the late eighteenth century, Chinese people who had arrived in western Borneo to mine gold set up a number of independent republics as a political framework for long-term settlement.[20] In the second half of the nineteenth century, Koreans left harsh conditions at home and settled in large numbers in what had become the Russian territories of eastern Siberia.[21] In other parts of Siberia, Russian settlers predominated: the city of Vladivostok grew on lands that had once belonged to the Udege first people; other settlers cleared arable land along the Amur River to create new communities that soon outnumbered those of first peoples such as the Goldi.[22]

In the same era, Chinese settlers entered Manchuria in large numbers, shifting the demographic balance away from the region's first peoples.[23] Qing authorities encouraged this settlement in order to create a new demographic reality in the north as a barrier to continued Russian territorial expansion in the region. In southern China, rebellion and civil war, especially in the nineteenth century, displaced millions of Chinese people, some of whom fled for safety into mountain regions that were previously dominated by first-people communities. In the eighteenth and nineteenth centuries, Japanese authorities promoted settlement in the former lands of the Ainu in Hokkaido in order to forestall the risk of Russian settlement. In the Netherlands Indies, Dutch authorities sponsored the settlement of Javanese in parts of Sumatra, partly to relieve poverty in Java, partly as a way of promoting development in other regions in the early twentieth century.[24] In all these settlement processes, first peoples were pushed from their lands. In China's southwestern provinces of Yunnan and Guizhou, formerly dominated by first peoples, a steady inflow of Chinese settlers changed the balance of political and economic power. With more sophisticated financial tools and with the backing of Chinese officials, these settlers appropriated Indigenous lands commercially and legally, forcing first peoples to retreat to less fertile mountain regions.[25] In India and Ceylon, settlers moved into the lands of first peoples in much the same way.[26] Dispossessed of their lands and marginalised in a growing economy, many first peoples sank into poverty.

The colonial plantation sector also became an important cause of demographic change at the expense of first peoples in the nineteenth century. While the earliest colonial plantations had mainly appropriated agricultural land and labour in the settled lowlands for the cultivation of annual or semi-annual crops such as sugar and the dye-plant indigo, the subsequent growth of tree-crop plantations – tea, coffee, rubber – led to the clearing of forest, the displacement of first peoples who had lived there and the importation of labourers from densely populated regions. In this way, the uplands of Vietnam, Sumatra, the Malay Peninsula, and Assam were transformed ecologically and socially.[27]

First peoples who resisted expropriation and assimilation for the most part experienced a grim fate. In the early eighteenth century, Cossack forces operating under the loose authority of the Russian tsar carried out brutal campaigns of extermination against the Koryak people who lived north of Kamchatka, killing thousands and reducing their population by around 60%.[28] First peoples collectively known as Miao in the Chinese province of Guizhou revolted repeatedly against Qing imperial authorities; the suppression of each rebellion was marked by mass killings in which hundreds of thousands of people died.[29] In both Siberia and China from the seventeenth century to the nineteenth, dozens of smaller military operations against resistant first peoples, sometimes ordered by central governments, sometimes carried out on the initiative of local settlers, cut a terrible swathe.

Especially in China, the scale of violence against first peoples has been overshadowed historiographically by the violence among non-first-people Chinese people. The Taiping Rebellion of 1850–1864 was one of the most destructive wars of all time, claiming an estimated 20 million deaths.[30] The Panthay Rebellion (1856–1873) and the Dungan Revolt (1862–1877) each cost millions of lives. Only a small proportion of the casualties in these conflicts were first peoples, but for small first-people communities the social destruction wrought by warfare was enormous. In India, political disorder accompanying the disintegration of the Mughal empire in the eighteenth century also enveloped many first peoples. The British colonial administration in India classified a number of first peoples as 'criminal tribes', on the basis of their reputation for attacking outsiders who entered or passed through their territory.[31] These 'tribes' were then subject to punitive raids that forced them to allow outsiders into their lands. Once formally brought under colonial rule, they quickly lost control of their lands but repeatedly sought to recover autonomy in actions that the British authorities then characterised as 'revolt'. As in China, the importance of uprisings by non-first-peoples has tended to overshadow the specific element of suppression and expropriation that was imposed on Indian first peoples.[32]

Defining indigeneity in colonial Asia

Western colonial authorities were the first to develop a system of ethno-political classification that recognised first peoples. This system grew initially out of practicality and was subsequently reinforced by symbolic utility. In governing their Asian territories, British, Dutch, and French authorities employed both direct and indirect rule. Direct rule enabled relatively close supervision of society in the interests of colonial exploitation. Directly ruled territories were therefore for the most part the densely populated heartlands where control of land and mobilisation of Asian labour was central to colonial economic interests. Indirect rule relied on traditional authorities to act as agents for colonial powers. It was useful for colonial powers where their interests were smaller or less complicated. In some colonies – the Netherlands Indies, French Indochina, British Malaya – first peoples were left under the authority of lowland monarchs who had little interest in them. In other colonies – British India, British Burma, the U.S. colony of the Philippines, and the Japanese colony of Taiwan – first-people lands had something of the character of the 'native' reservations of North America and Australasia. First peoples were largely left to their own devices as long as they refrained from causing trouble for the colonial power and as long as colonial authorities did not want their lands for some other purpose. The common designation of first peoples as 'hill tribes' was a mark of the fact that they were allocated to remote upland regions that had no special value to the colonial powers.[33]

For colonial powers, however, recognition of first peoples also had a symbolic value. Conscious of the huge historical significance of Western migration to and settlement of the Americas and Australasia, European historians and philosophers interpreted the earlier history of their colonial territories in similar terms. In India, they adopted a narrative that stressed the arrival in around 1300 BCE of people they called 'Aryans', pale-skinned relatives of the peoples who also settled Europe. These people were said to have conquered and destroyed the Indus Valley civilisation but, possessing the vigour of barbarians fresh from the steppe, to have laid the foundations for a newer and greater civilisation in north India.[34] The Sinhala people were said to have conquered and marginalised the original Vedda inhabitants of Ceylon. Subsequent invasions of India by Muslim peoples from central Asia and the long history of pre-Mongol and Mongol invasions of China were also incorporated into this dialectical model of invigorating barbarian conquest. The same discourse stressed successive waves of Thai and Burmese intrusion and occupation in mainland Southeast Asia. Island Southeast Asia was said to have been settled by successive waves of 'Proto-Malays' and 'Deutero-Malays'. In the context of nineteenth-century colonialism, this discourse normalised takeover and settlement, treating Western rule as simply the latest episode of invigorating conquest.

The place of first peoples in this discourse was both marginal and instructive. On the one hand, they were seen as having been left behind by history; on the other hand, they were believed to have preserved the way of life of earlier times. Understanding the nature of 'primitive man' was crucial to understanding the effects, good and bad, of modern civilisation on humankind.[35] Symbolic acts of barbarism such as cannibalism and head-hunting were routinely attributed to first peoples, but at the same time close observers admired their peaceful engagement with the natural world.[36] Colonial authorities thus approached first peoples with varied degrees of contempt, condescension, curiosity, and paternalist concern, all manifest in special systems of first-people classification.[37]

As Asian nationalist movements emerged to challenge colonial rule, official recognition of first peoples became a means to refute the claim of Asian majorities to sovereignty in their own lands. By pointing to tiny minorities as the truly original inhabitants, colonial powers could portray majority communities as immigrants whose title to the land was no stronger than that of the more recent conquerors. Japan, a late-comer to Western-style colonialism in Asia, pointed to the Austronesian-speaking first peoples of its Taiwan colony and to the long-standing Mongol and Manchu inhabitants of its quasi-colony in Manchuria to refute the claim that the Chinese majority in both territories, descended from relatively recent settlers, had rendered them part of China.[38] White settlers in South Africa used similar arguments to resist the claim of black Africans to Indigenous rights, emphasising the Khoi and San peoples as the 'true' Indigenous peoples of the region, in contrast with the immigrant Bantu.[39]

First peoples also became the objects of self-serving colonial solicitude. In the decades immediately before the Second World War, Western colonial powers increasingly deployed the argument that colonial rule was necessary to keep order between naturally antagonistic social and ethnic groups and to protect the weak from their stronger neighbours. In this discourse, protecting first peoples against their neighbours became part of the colonial agenda. In the 1930s, colonial authorities in the Netherlands Indies considered establishing a conservation reserve in Dutch New Guinea which would preserve both the natural environment and the 'primitive humans' who lived there (Figure 4.3).[40]

The first peoples selected to be granted 'aboriginal' status were relatively few in number and the basis for their classification varied from colony to colony. Remote, black-skinned communities in Southeast Asia, collectively characterised as 'Negritos', were widely identified as descendants of original Melanesian inhabitants of the region. In British Malaya, anthropologists identified the Orang Asli (literally 'original people'), speaking Austroasiatic languages, as the descendants of a more recent, but still pre-Malay, population.[41] The 'Montagnards' in French Indo-China and the Ifugao (Igorot) of Luzon were identified as preserving customs and beliefs that had been extinguished by the imposition of Vietnamese and Spanish civilisations, respectively, in the lowlands. All these classifications brought together communities that had previously had little in common but whose common identity was decided mainly by outside anthropologists and bureaucrats.[42] By far, the most elaborate system of recognition was in British India, where dozens of 'scheduled

Figure 4.3 Indigenous man of Negros Island, before 1900, described as 'Negrito'
Source: Frederic H. Sawyer, *The Inhabitants of the Philippines* (London: S. Low, Marston and Co, 1900), facing 207.

districts' identified with individual 'scheduled tribes' were established across the colony, most notably in the 1935 Government of India Act.[43] Some 300,000 square kilometres, inhabited by around 11 million people, were demarcated in this way (Figure 4.4).[44]

Neither Qing China nor Tsarist Russia, by contrast, offered any formal recognition to first peoples. Asian nationalist movements, too, were for the most part hostile, or at least unsympathetic, to the idea of identifying first peoples as a distinct political category. They feared that recognition of first-nationhood was an extension of colonial-era policies of stressing division within Asian societies and that it might lead to the removal of first-nation regions from the national territory. These fears were not entirely unfounded: Dutch concern for the fate of 'primitive' Papuans in an independent Indonesia was a core public justification for attempts to detach West New Guinea as a continuing Dutch colony after international recognition of Indonesian independence in 1949.[45] The first constitution of the Union of Burma created constituent states for the Shan and Karenni peoples and gave those states the right to secede from after ten years, if they chose.[46]

At the core of nationalist ideology in most Asian countries, moreover, was an aspiration for modernity. The aspects of first-nation culture that most strongly warranted separate status – adherence to traditional beliefs and a way of life closely entwined with the natural environment – were precisely those out of which the nationalist governments wished to lift their people. India's first prime minister Jawaharlal Nehru contemptuously dismissed the scheduled district system as an 'anthropological zoo'.[47] Although China had not been comprehensively colonised, the Chinese Republic that replaced the Qing dynasty after the nationalist revolution of

Figure 4.4 Gondi, Indigenous people of Central India
Source: El Mundo en la mano: Viaje Pintoresco a las Cinco Partes del Mundo por los Más Célebres Viajeros, Tomo 3 (Barcelona: Montaner y Simón, 1878), 229.

1911 took a similar integrationist approach towards first peoples, asserting that the entire population of China shared a common ethnic Chinese ancestry and therefore could be reassimilated to Han Chinese culture.[48]

The 1917 Bolshevik revolution led to civil war in Siberia that cost many lives among first peoples, but the nationality policy of the Soviet Union at first offered them ambiguous hope. Unlike the Chinese Republic, the Soviet Union formally recognised not just ethnic diversity but far-reaching rights of self-government for distinct ethnic communities.[49] The new Soviet state was dominated by Russians, but nested within it at different levels were formally autonomous territorial units identified with specific ethnic groups. In 1922, for instance, an autonomous republic was constituted in eastern Siberia for the Yakut first people. Soviet policy within this republic, however, was determinedly focussed on modernisation. Although there were measures to preserve traditional language and artistic forms, Soviet policies sought to force the Yakut people from their traditional nomadic ways into farming collectives and to participate in Soviet modernity.[50] The Chinese

Communist Party followed a similar policy after it came to power in 1949, recognising 56 distinct ethnic groups (*shaoshu minzu*), each with its own designated territory whose place in the territorial hierarchy corresponded to its size and economic strength. As in the Soviet Union, however, the state for the most part forced on the minorities modernisation in Chinese terms, so that many of them have now largely ceased to exist as distinct cultural communities.[51]

In Burma, Malaya (later Malaysia), and Indonesia, the dominant nationalist movements had defined their goals not just in opposition to European colonialism but also in opposition to the derivative settler colonialism of Indian and Chinese migrants. In Burma, Indians dominated the capital, Rangoon (now Yangon); in Malaya, Chinese dominated the largest city, Singapore, and comprised around half the population of the entire colony. Chinese settlers in Indonesia were a much smaller part of the population, but Chinese business-owners dominated the retail commerce and money-lending. Nationalist movements sought to varying degrees in all three countries to diminish the legitimacy of the settlers by contrasting their foreign origins with the allegedly local credentials of the nationalists. The Indonesian term *pribumi* ('first on the land') and its Malaysian equivalent, *bumiputera* ('son of the land') became common means of asserting the indigeneity of all those whose ancestry lay mainly in the Indonesian archipelago, even though a significant proportion of the 'Malay' population of Malaya/Malaysia had its origins in the Indonesian islands of Sumatra, Java, and Sulawesi. In the aftermath of decolonisation, thus, the meagre protections for first peoples in Southeast Asia largely disappeared.

A further difficulty for first-nation communities in the post-colonial period was the spread of Cold War armed conflicts to what had previously been isolated mountain and jungle areas. During the Malayan Emergency (1948–60), when British forces fought Chinese communist guerrillas in the Malayan jungle, the Orang Asli were drawn willy-nilly into the conflict, though they were sometimes able to negotiate advantages by virtue of their expert knowledge.[52] The first peoples of the Indo-China uplands were catastrophically drawn into the Second Indo-China War (1955–75). Organised in an armed movement called FULRO (United Front for the Liberation of Oppressed Races), they fought with and against both the communist and anti-communist sides in the conflict, but never achieved their aim of greater autonomy.[53] During the Cold War, Thailand withheld citizenship from first-people communities in some mountain regions on the grounds that they were aliens who had migrated into what had become Thailand's territory within the last three centuries.[54] From the early 1980s, first peoples in central India were increasingly involved in a widespread rural Maoist insurgency, prompted above all by threats to their control of forest land.[55]

The experience of first peoples in independent India has been perhaps the most complex. Despite Nehru's misgivings, the Indian Constitution preserved the category of 'scheduled tribes', and more than 600 such groups, now generally known as Adivasi ('original inhabitants'), have been formally recognised across the country. However, immediately after Indian independence in 1946, many of the laws and regulations that restricted the access of outsiders to Adivasi lands were dismantled, with the result that Adivasi communities close to areas of dense population often quickly lost control of their lands. Unlike in China and the Soviet Union, however, there was no general policy of forcing modernisation on first-people communities, with the result that many communities remained intact. The newly independent Indian government, moreover, implemented a far-reaching programme of affirmative action for individuals of first-people descent by means of a well-developed system of privileged access to education and government jobs. This programme was designed primarily to address the depressed position of low-status castes, but was fully available to first-nation people as well. These measures were significant in facilitating the participation of first-nation persons in the modern economy and society, but they did little to help preserve the cultural integrity of first-nation communities.[56] In recent times, Indian government authorities have insisted that the term 'Adivasi' cannot be translated as indigenous (thereby implying ancestral rights to land), but simply as 'tribal', implying that their future is one of full integration into modern India (Figure 4.5).

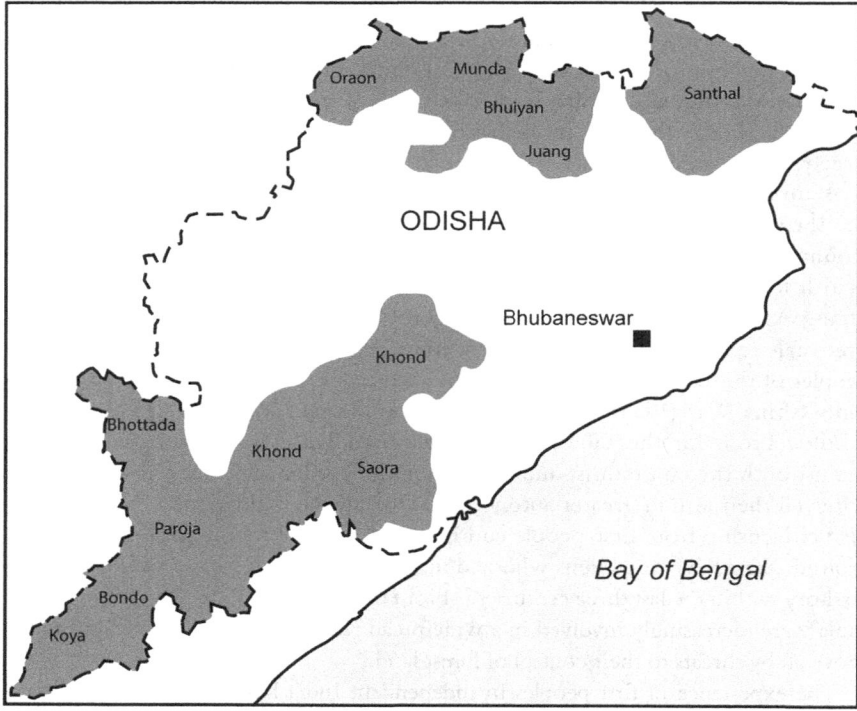

Figure 4.5 Map 2: The Indian state of Odisha (formerly Orissa), showing Scheduled Districts and the principal first peoples who inhabit them

Source: Based on Kundan Kumar and Pranab Ranjan Choudhary, *A Socio-Economic and Legal Study of Scheduled Tribes' Land in Orissa* (World Bank Report, Bhubaneswar, 2005), http://citeseerx.ist.psu.edu/viewdoc/download?doi=10.1.1.631.7926&rep=rep1&type=pdf

Legal recognition and the modern Indigenous movement in Asia

In the second half of the twentieth century, a global movement for Indigenous rights began to develop, spearheaded initially by the International Labour Organization (ILO). The ILO's interest in first peoples had grown initially out of its concern that they were subject to modern slavery.[57] The ILO approach aligned broadly with the modernising, assimilating principles adopted by many independent Asian governments, while attempting to identify and halt breaches of those principles. In 1957, the ILO sponsored the Indigenous and Tribal Populations Convention, an international treaty that was intended principally to ensure that Indigenous peoples would gain equitable access to the benefits of modernisation. The convention endorsed the policy of assimilation, while requiring that it be implemented with care.[58] India and Pakistan were the only Asian countries to ratify the 1957 Convention.

In the late 1960s, the scope of international concern for the position of Indigenous peoples began to broaden, encompassing the question of land rights and the issue of cultural integrity. The International Work Group for Indigenous Affairs (IWGIA), a non-governmental organisation founded in Copenhagen in 1968, played a leading role in this reorientation, though its focus was initially only on the condition of Indigenous peoples in Latin America.[59] In 1974, Indigenous peoples themselves began to play a global advocacy role, initially through the World Council of Indigenous Peoples. Asian first peoples, however, played relatively little role in this early mobilisation, largely because the indigeneity discourse focussed on the consequences for Indigenous peoples of European and Europe-derived settlement in first-people lands. There was no concerted challenge to the standard nationalist assertion in Asian countries that all their citizens were indigenous.[60]

In the 1970s, the growing pace of economic development in non-communist Asia began to place increasing pressure on surviving first-people communities. Legal frameworks derived from the colonial era generally failed to give first peoples secure title to their traditional land, and the rush for development often overwhelmed the meagre rights that they did possess. Logging and mining in once-remote regions, as well as the construction of roads, facilitated settlement by outsiders. First peoples lost land to dam construction projects. In 1969, the Indonesian government revived the Dutch policy of sponsoring settlement from Java and Bali to other islands. The programme peaked between 1979 and 1984 but continued until 2015. Although precise figures are difficult to obtain – partly because the Indonesian government also encouraged so-called 'spontaneous transmigrants' who moved without direct official support – it is likely that the number of settlers exceeded seven million. They often took over territory that had formerly been inhabited by first peoples.[61]

In these circumstances, first-nation activists in Asia and their supporters came to play a more prominent role in the global campaign. Indigenous activism in Asia began in the 1980s, initially in countries – India, Bangladesh, the Philippines – where independent governments had inherited an administrative framework that gave some recognition to first peoples. The IWGIA undertook an international campaign in support of Indigenous peoples in the Chittagong Hill Tracts, part of Bangladesh, who had been displaced by dam construction.[62] It also worked with Indigenous groups from the mountain regions of Luzon in the Philippines.

In 1989, the ILO sponsored a new Indigenous and Tribal Peoples Convention, which largely abandoned the principle of assimilation in favour of an absolute right of Indigenous peoples to preserve their traditional cultures and ways of life and to control their own land.[63] Nepal, however, is the only Asian country to have ratified the new Convention. The 1989 Convention was a forerunner to the 2007 United Nations Declaration on the Rights of Indigenous Peoples, drafting of which had begun in 1994.[64] Although the tone of the Declaration embodies a ringing endorsement of Indigenous rights, the actual wording gives governments a great deal of freedom in interpreting just how the provisions might be applied and does not clearly define who might be considered as indigenous.

Nonetheless, since the late twentieth century, there has been a gradual, but far from uniform, recognition of Indigenous peoples as a legal category in Asian countries. Following the disintegration of the Soviet Union, the Russian Federation adopted legislation that recognises as Indigenous communities smaller than 50,000 who continue to follow a traditional way of life. Some 41 communities have been recognised, but a 2001 Law on the Territories of Traditional Nature Use has not been implemented. Consequently, many Indigenous communities have been unable to prevent the loss of land to mining, industrial, and forestry projects. Various Indigenous organisations have also emerged, but in many cases they have faced harsh restrictions. In 2012, the Russian government suspended activities of the country's main Indigenous activist group, the Russian Association of Indigenous Peoples of the North.[65] In 1997, following a long campaign by the Coalition for Indigenous People's Rights and Ancestral Domains (CIPRAD), the Philippines passed the Indigenous People's Rights Act which recognised extensive rights to ancestral lands on the part of first peoples.[66] In 1999, Indigenous peoples in Indonesia created the Traditional Communities Alliance of the Archipelago (Aliansi Masyarakat Adat Nusantara, AMAN); the term *masyarakat adat*, although commonly translated as 'indigenous peoples', avoids official sensitivities by emphasising cultural orientation, rather than first-people status.[67] Thailand formally recognises nine 'mountain tribes', but on the grounds of their distinctive cultures and special vulnerability, rather than as first peoples; some of them indeed arrived in what is now Thailand within the last three centuries.[68] In 2008, the Japanese parliament passed a non-binding resolution calling on the government to recognise the Ainu as indigenous and to acknowledge the injustices done to them in the past. A bill formally providing recognition was passed in 2019.[69] In Taiwan from early in the twenty-first century, government authorities seeking to strengthen the island's claim to a separate existence from mainland China began to celebrate the heritage of the first peoples who had been largely marginalised in Taiwan society until then. Formal recognition of indigeneity as a political status, however, has not yet been achieved.[70] China, Vietnam, and Laos have continued to employ the framework of minority-defined administrative districts, which has largely failed to protect first peoples from incursions by outsiders.[71]

Conclusion

It has been estimated that 70% of the world's 250 million Indigenous people live in Asia.[72] Their experiences have been overshadowed in research on indigenous issues by the attention given to the stark and relatively well-documented injustices experienced by Indigenous peoples in the Americas and Australasia. Over many centuries, the encounter of Asian Indigenous peoples with settler societies was as violent as the encounter in the Americas and Australasia. It was marked by slaughter, dispossession, epidemic disease, and socio-economic disruption and marginalisation which led directly and indirectly to the deaths of millions of people and the loss of countless cultural expressions.

The violent encounter between Asian first peoples and Asian settler societies, however, followed a much longer period of cultural, economic, and political contact that somewhat blurred the distinction between the two groups. The sharp racialisation of the distinction between Indigenous peoples and settlers that was widespread in the Americas and Australasia was largely missing in Asia: instead, both the cultural self-assurance of older civilisations and the inclusive modernising discourse of the later nationalists naturalised the discourse of assimilation and contributed to a myth of peaceful absorption. The assimilationist discourse was strengthened by the specific politics of race in colonial societies, which in effect set the interests of first peoples in conflict with those of majority communities. For more than three centuries, moreover, this Asian encounter took place in the context of both Western imperial expansion in Asia and appallingly destructive conflict among Asian peoples. The death toll and the scale of cultural destruction experienced by Asian societies at the hands of both Westerners and other Asians vastly exceeded that of Asian first peoples in absolute terms, even if not in proportion to community size.

Notes

1 Marc S. Abramson, *Ethnic Identity in Tang China* (Philadelphia: University of Pennsylvania Press, 2008), 112.
2 Romila Thapar, 'The Image of the Barbarian in Early India,' *Comparative Studies in Society and History* 13, no. 4 (1971), 409–410; Aloka Parasher, *Mlecchas in Early India: A Study in Attitudes toward Outsiders up to AD 600* (New Delhi: Munshiram Manoharlal, 1991).
3 Shruti Chakraborty, 'Hanuman: Myths, Legends and Lore,' Sahapedia, 11 December 2018, accessed 13 January 2020, https://www.sahapedia.org/hanuman-myths-legends-and-lore.
4 Rafe de Crespigny, *Generals of the South: The Foundation and Early History of the Three Kingdoms State of Wu* (Canberra: Faculty of Asian Studies, Australian National University, 1990), 253–265.
5 William H. McCullough, 'The Heian Court, 794–1070,' in *The Cambridge History of Japan, Volume 2: Heian Japan*, eds. Donald H. Shively and William H. McCullough (Cambridge: Cambridge University Press, 1999), 29–32.
6 The term 'exemplary center' was coined by Clifford Geertz, *Negara: The Theatre State in Nineteenth-Century Bali* (Princeton, NJ: Princeton University Press, 1980), but has been widely used to characterise what might be called the 'soft power' of early empires.

7 Magnus Fiskesjö, 'On the "Raw" and the "Cooked" Barbarians of Imperial China,' *Inner Asia* 1, no. 2 (1999), 139–168.
8 Chun Shan, *Major Aspects of Chinese Religion and Philosophy: Dao of Inner Saint and Outer King* (Berlin: Springer, 2012), 203–212.
9 Michael Bamshad, Alexander E. Fraley, Michael H. Crawford, Rebecca L. Cann, Baskara R. Busi, J.M. Naidu, and Lynn B. Jorde, 'mtDNA Variation in Caste Populations of Andhra Pradesh, India,' *Human Biology* 68, no. 1 (February 1996): 1–28.
10 Wing-hoi Chan, 'Ethnic Labels in a Mountainous Region: The Case of She "Bandits",' in *Empire at the Margins: Culture, Ethnicity, and Frontier in Early Modern China*, eds. Pamela Kyle Crossley, Helen F. Siu, and Donald S. Sutton (Berkeley: University of California Press, 2006), 258.
11 James C. Scott, *The Art of Not Being Governed: An Anarchist History of Upland Southeast Asia* (New Haven, CT: Yale University Press, 2009).
12 See, for instance, Tom Brass, 'Scott's "Zomia," or a Populist Post-modern History of Nowhere,' *Journal of Contemporary Asia* 42, no. 1 (2011): 123–133.
13 Li Narangoa and Robert Cribb, *Historical Atlas of Northeast Asia, 1590–2010: Korea, Manchuria, Mongolia, Eastern Siberia* (New York: Columbia University Press, 2014), 55–56.
14 Alexander Etkind, *Internal Colonization: Russia's Imperial Experience* (Cambridge: Polity Press, 2011), 78.
15 Seonmin Kim, 'Ginseng and Border Trespassing between Qing China and Chosŏn Korea,' *Late Imperial China* 28, no. 1 (2007): 33–61.
16 John E. Wills, 'The Seventeenth-Century Transformation: Taiwan under the Dutch and the Cheng Regime,' in *Taiwan: A New History*, ed. Murray A. Rubinstein (Armonk: M.E. Sharpe, 2007), 87–88.
17 Robert Cribb, 'Birds of Paradise and Environmental Politics in Colonial Indonesia, 1890–1931,' in *Paper Landscapes: Explorations in the Environmental History of Indonesia*, eds. Peter Boomgaard, Freek Columbijn, and David Henley (Leiden: KITLV Press, 1997), 379–408.
18 John Tully, 'A Victorian Ecological Disaster: Imperialism, the Telegraph, and Gutta-Percha,' *Journal of World History* 20, no. 4 (2009): 559–579.
19 John R. Shepherd, 'The Island Frontier of the Ch'ing, 1684–1740,' in Rubinstein, *Taiwan*, 107–132.
20 Mary Somers Heidhues, *Golddiggers, Farmers, and Traders in the 'Chinese Districts' of West Kalimantan, Indonesia* (Ithaca: Cornell University, Southeast Asia Program Publications, 2003), 33–35.
21 Jon K. Chang, *Burnt by the Sun: the Koreans of the Russian Far East* (Honolulu: University of Hawai'i Press, 2016), 9–16.
22 Ernst Georg Ravenstein, *The Russians on the Amur: Its Discovery, Conquest, and Colonization, with a Description of the Country, Its Inhabitants, Productions, and Commercial Capabilities* (London: Trübner, 1861).
23 Thomas R. Gottschang and Diana Lary, *Swallows and Settlers: The Great Migration from North China to Manchuria* (Ann Arbor: Center for Chinese Studies, 2000).
24 Herman Th. Verstappen, *Zwerftocht door een Wereld in Beweging* (Assen: Van Gorcum, 2006), 60–62.
25 C.P. Fitzgerald, *The Southern Expansion of the Chinese People: 'Southern Fields and Southern Ocean'* (Canberra: Australian National University Press, 1972), 66–67.
26 Govind Sadashiv Ghurye, *The Scheduled Tribes of India* (Bombay: Popular Book Depot, 1959), 77.
27 There is a vast literature on the labour system in colonial-era plantations; see, for instance, Nitin Varma, *Coolies of Capitalism: Assam Tea and the Making of Coolie Labour* (Berlin: De Gruyter Oldenbourg, 2017). This literature, however, pays relatively little attention to the consequences of the establishment of plantations for earlier inhabitants.
28 Igor V. Naumov, *The History of Siberia* (London: Routledge, 2006), 88.

29 Robert D. Jenks, *Insurgency and Social Disorder in Guizhou: The 'Miao' Rebellion, 1854–1873* (Honolulu: University of Hawai'i Press, 1994).
30 Jen Yu-wen, *The Taiping Revolutionary Movement* (New Haven, CT: Yale University Press, 1973).
31 Bhawani Shanker Bhargava, *The Criminal Tribes: A Social and Economic Study of the Principal Criminal Tribes and Castes in Northern India* (Lucknow: Ethnographic and Folk Culture Society, United Provinces, 1949).
32 The classic analysis of anti-colonial revolt is Ranajit Guha, *Elementary Aspects of Peasant Insurgency in Colonial India* (Durham, NC: Duke University Press, 1999).
33 Pratik Chakrabarti, 'Gondwana and the Politics of Deep Past,' *Past & Present* 242, no. 1 (2019): 119–153.
34 On the controversies surrounding this theory, see Edwin Bryant and Laurie L. Patton, eds., *The Indo-Aryan Controversy: Evidence and Inference in Indian History* (New York: Routledge, 2005).
35 Chakrabarti, 'Gondwana and the Politics of Deep Past,' 119–153.
36 See, for instance, Samuel E. Kane, *Life or Death in Luzon: Thirty Years of Adventure with the Philippine Highlanders* (Indianapolis: Bobbs-Merrill, 1933), 330–331.
37 The discussion in this paragraph draws out a line of European thinking concerning first peoples that ultimately led to their being identified as a distinct historical-cultural category. It does not do justice to the enormous variety of ideas about history, race, and culture that were propounded by scientists and philosophers in the eighteenth and nineteenth centuries, nor to the extent that those ideas, even when propounded dogmatically, were intended as hypotheses to be investigated further. For an account that places in its intellectual context the idea that there was an aboriginal substrate in Indian society, see Crispin Bates, 'Race, Caste and Tribe in Central India: The Early Origins of Indian Anthropometry,' in *The Concept of Race in South Asia*, ed. Peter Robb (New Delhi: Oxford University Press, 1995), 219–259.
38 Li Narangoa, 'The Power of Imagination: Whose Northeast and Whose Manchuria?' *Inner Asia* 4, no. 1 (2002): 3–25.
39 See also F.M. Brookfield, *Waitangi and Indigenous Rights: Revolution, Law and Legitimation* (Auckland: Auckland University Press, 1999).
40 Robert Cribb, 'Nature Conservation and Cultural Preservation in Convergence: Orang Pendek and Papuans in Colonial Indonesia,' in *A Sea for Encounters: Essays towards a Postcolonial Commonwealth*, ed. Stella Borg Barthet (Amsterdam and New York: Rodopi: 2009), 223–242.
41 Sandra Khor Manickam, *Taming the Wild: Aborigines and Racial Knowledge in Colonial Malaya* (Singapore: NUS Press, 2015).
42 On the construction of the 'Igorot' by United States colonial policy, see Gerard A. Finin, *The Making of the Igorot: Contours of Cordillera Consciousness* (Manila: Ateneo de Manila University Press, 2005); on the colonial construction of the Montagnards, see Oscar Salemink, *The Ethnography of Vietnam's Central Highlanders: A Historical Contextualization, 1850–1990* (Honolulu: University of Hawai'i Press 2003), 40–99.
43 Christoph von Fürer-Haimendorf, *Tribes of India: The Struggle for Survival* (Berkeley: University of California Press, 1982), 39.
44 'The Scheduled and Tribal Areas,' *Indian Journal of Public Administration* 23, no. 3 (1977): 821.
45 Pieter Drooglever, *An Act of Free Choice: Decolonization and the Right to Self-determination in West Papua* (Oxford: Oneworld, 2009).
46 U Maung Maung, *Burma's Constitution* (The Hague: Martinus Nijhoff, 1959), 193–194.
47 Crispin Bates, 'Congress and the Tribals,' in *The Indian National Congress and the Political Economy of India 1985–1995*, eds. Mike Shepperdson and Colin Simmons (Aldershot: Avebury, 1988), 231.
48 Thomas S. Mullaney, *Coming to Terms with the Nation: Ethnic Classification in Modern China* (Berkeley: University of California Press, 2011), 28.

49 For an introduction to the complexities of Soviet nationality policy, see Jeremy Smith, 'Was There a Soviet Nationality Policy?' *Europe-Asia Studies* 71, no. 6 (2019): 972–993.
50 John Tichotsky, *Russia's Diamond Colony: The Republic of Sakha* (London: Routledge, 2000), 80.
51 Mullaney, *Coming to Terms with the Nation*, 28; Juha Janhunen, *Manchuria: An Ethnic History* (Helsinki: Finno-Ugrian Society, 1996), 93–128.
52 John Leary, *Violence and the Dream People: The Orang Asli in the Malayan Emergency, 1948–1960* (Athens: Ohio University Center for International Studies, 1995).
53 Salemink, *Ethnography of Vietnam's Central Highlanders*, 262.
54 See Chayan Vaddhanaphuti, 'The Thai State and Ethnic Minorities: From Assimilation to Selective Integration,' in *Ethnic Conflicts in Southeast Asia*, eds. Kusuma Snitwongse and W. Scott Thompson (Singapore: Institute of Southeast Asian Studies, 2005), 161.
55 Jonathan Kennedy and Lawrence King, 'Adivasis, Maoists and Insurgency in the Central Indian Tribal Belt,' *European Journal of Sociology* 54, no. 1 (2013): 1–32.
56 Fürer-Haimendorf, *Tribes of India*.
57 *Indigenous Peoples: Living and Working Conditions of Aboriginal Populations in Independent Countries* (Geneva: International Labour Organisation, 1953).
58 C107 – Indigenous and Tribal Populations Convention, 1957 (No. 107), https://www.ilo.org/dyn/normlex/en/f?p=NORMLEXPUB:12100:0::NO::P12100_ILO_CODE:C107
59 Jens Dahl, *IWGIA: A History* (Copenhagen: IWGIA, 2009).
60 Christian Erni, 'The Concept of Indigenous Peoples in Asia,' in *The Concept of Indigenous Peoples in Asia: A Resource Book*, ed. Christian Erni (Copenhagen: International Work Group for Indigenous Affairs; Chiang Mai: Asia Indigenous Peoples Pact Foundation, 2008), 13–25.
61 Robin Osborne, *Transmigration in Indonesia* (Canberra: Australian Council for Overseas Aid, 1985); Riwanto Tirtosudarmo, *The Politics of Migration in Indonesia and Beyond* (Singapore: Springer Nature, 2018), 3–28.
62 Chittagong Hill Tracts Commission, *'Life is Not Ours': Land and Human Rights in the Chittagong Hill Tracts, Bangladesh* (Copenhagen: IWGIA, International Workgroup for Indigenous Affairs, 2000).
63 C169 – Indigenous and Tribal Peoples Convention, 1989 (No. 169), https://www.ilo.org/dyn/normlex/en/f?p=NORMLEXPUB:12100:0::NO::P12100_ILO_CODE:C169. The definition makes no mention of seas, thereby missing what has come to be recognised as an important element in indigenous identity and rights, most notably for the Orang Laut ('Sea People') of Indonesia and Malaysia, who live on boats.
64 'United Nations Declaration on the Rights of Indigenous Peoples,' United Nations, 2008, accessed 5 June 2020, https://www.un.org/esa/socdev/unpfii/documents/DRIPS_en.pdf.
65 'Who Are the Indigenous Peoples of Russia?,' *Cultural Survival*, 19 February 2014, accessed 5 October 2019, https://www.culturalsurvival.org/news/who-are-indigenous-peoples-russia.
66 June Prill-Brett, 'Contested Domains: The Indigenous Peoples Rights Act (IPRA) and Legal Pluralism in the Northern Philippines,' *Journal of Legal Pluralism and Unofficial Law* 39, no. 55 (2007): 11–36.
67 Arianto Sangaji, 'The Masyarakat Adat Movement in Indonesia: A Critical Insider's View,' in *The Revival of Tradition in Indonesian Politics: The Deployment of Adat from Colonialism to Indigenism*, Jamie Davidson and David Henley (Abingdon: Routledge, 2007), 319–336; Brigitta Hauser-Schäublin, ed., *Adat and Indigeneity in Indonesia: Culture and Entitlements between Heteronomy and Self-Ascription* (Göttingen: Göttingen University Press, 2013).
68 Abigaël Pesses, 'Highland Birth and Citizenship Registration in Thailand: Final Report on Karen Focus Group Discussions in Chiang Mai Province' (UNESCO; UNESCO Highland Birth and Citizenship Registration Promotion Project Funded by the United Kingdom Sustainable Development Programme, 2007), https://hal.archives-ouvertes.fr/hal-01736494/document.

69 Isabella Steger, 'Who are the Indigenous Ainu People of Japan?' *Quartz*, 18 February 2019, accessed 5 October 2019, https://qz.com/1551496/who-are-the-indigenous-ainu-people-of-japan/.
70 Mark Munsterhjelm, 'The First Nations of Taiwan: A Special Report on Taiwan's Indigenous Peoples,' *Cultural Survival*, June 2002, accessed 5 October 2019, https://www.culturalsurvival.org/publications/cultural-survival-quarterly/first-nations-taiwan-special-report-taiwans-indigenous.
71 Jean Michaud, 'Handling Mountain Minorities in China, Vietnam and Laos: From History to Current Concerns,' *Asian Ethnicity* 10, no. 1 (2009): 25–49.
72 Dev Nathan and Govind Kelkar, 'Introduction,' in *Globalization and Indigenous Peoples in Asia: Changing the Local–Global Interface*, eds. Dev Nathan, Govind Kelkar, and Pierre Walter (New Delhi: Sage, 2004), 16.

Bibliography

Abramson, Marc S. *Ethnic Identity in Tang China*. Philadelphia: University of Pennsylvania Press, 2008.
Bamshad, Michael, Alexander E. Fraley, Michael H. Crawford, Rebecca L. Cann, Baskara R. Busi, J.M. Naidu, and Lynn B. Jorde. 'mtDNA Variation in Caste Populations of Andhra Pradesh, India.' *Human Biology* 68, no. 1 (February 1996): 1–28.
Bates, Crispin. 'Congress and the Tribals.' In *The Indian National Congress and the Political Economy of India 1985–1995*, edited by Mike Shepperdson and Colin Simmons, 231–252. Aldershot: Avebury, 1988.
Bates, Crispin. 'Race, Caste and Tribe in Central India: The Early Origins of Indian Anthropometry.' In *The Concept of Race in South Asia*, edited by Peter Robb, 219–259. Delhi: Oxford University Press, 1995.
Bhargava, Bhawani Shanker. *The Criminal Tribes: A Social and Economic Study of the Principal Criminal Tribes and Castes in Northern India*. Lucknow: Ethnographic and Folk Culture Society, United Provinces, 1949.
Brass, Tom. 'Scott's "Zomia," or a Populist Post-modern History of Nowhere.' *Journal of Contemporary Asia* 42, no. 1 (2011): 123–133.
Brookfield, F.M. *Waitangi and Indigenous Rights: Revolution, Law and Legitimation*. Auckland: Auckland University Press, 1999.
Bryant, Edwin, and Laurie L. Patton, eds. *The Indo-Aryan Controversy: Evidence and Inference in Indian History*. New York: Routledge, 2005.
C107 – Indigenous and Tribal Populations Convention, 1957 (No. 107), https://www.ilo.org/dyn/normlex/en/f?p=NORMLEXPUB:12100:0::NO::P12100_ILO_CODE:C107
C169 – Indigenous and Tribal Peoples Convention, 1989 (No. 169), https://www.ilo.org/dyn/normlex/en/f?p=NORMLEXPUB:12100:0::NO::P12100_ILO_CODE:C169.
Chakrabarti, Pratik. 'Gondwana and the Politics of Deep Past.' *Past & Present* 242, no. 1 (2019): 119–153.
Chakraborty, Shruti. 'Hanuman: Myths, Legends and Lore.' Sahapedia, 11 December 2018. Accessed 13 January 2020. https://www.sahapedia.org/hanuman-myths-legends-and-lore.
Chan, Wing-hoi. 'Ethnic Labels in a Mountainous Region: The Case of She "Bandits".' In *Empire at the Margins: Culture, Ethnicity, and Frontier in Early Modern China*, edited by Pamela Kyle Crossley, Helen F. Siu, and Donald S. Sutton, 255–284. Berkeley: University of California Press, 2006.
Chang, Jon K. *Burnt by the Sun: the Koreans of the Russian Far East*. Honolulu: University of Hawai'i Press, 2016.
Chittagong Hill Tracts Commission. *'Life is Not Ours': Land and Human Rights in the Chittagong Hill Tracts, Bangladesh*. Copenhagen: IWGIA, International Workgroup for Indigenous Affairs, 2000.
Crespigny, Rafe de. *Generals of the South: The Foundation and Early History of the Three Kingdoms State of Wu*. Canberra: Faculty of Asian Studies, Australian National University, 1990.

Cribb, Robert. 'Birds of Paradise and Environmental Politics in Colonial Indonesia, 1890–1931.' In *Paper Landscapes: Explorations in the Environmental History of Indonesia*, edited by Peter Boomgaard, Freek Columbijn, and David Henley, 379–408. Leiden: KITLV Press, 1997.

Cribb, Robert. 'Nature Conservation and Cultural Preservation in Convergence: Orang Pendek and Papuans in Colonial Indonesia.' In *A Sea for Encounters: Essays towards a Postcolonial Commonwealth*, edited by Stella Borg Barthet, 223–242. Amsterdam and New York: Rodopi: 2009.

Dahl, Jens. *IWGIA: A History*. Copenhagen: IWGIA, 2009.

Drooglever, Pieter. *An Act of Free Choice: Decolonization and the Right to Self-Determination in West Papua*. Oxford: Oneworld, 2009.

Erni, Christian. 'The Concept of Indigenous Peoples in Asia.' In *The Concept of Indigenous Peoples in Asia: A Resource Book*, edited by Christian Erni, 13–25. Copenhagen: International Work Group for Indigenous Affairs; Chiang Mai: Asia Indigenous Peoples Pact Foundation, 2008.

Etkind, Alexander. *Internal Colonization: Russia's Imperial Experience*. Cambridge: Polity Press, 2011.

Fiskesjö, Magnus. 'On the "Raw" and the "Cooked" Barbarians of Imperial China.' *Inner Asia* 1, no. 2 (1999): 139–168.

Finin, Gerard A. *The Making of the Igorot: Contours of Cordillera Consciousness*. Manila: Ateneo de Manila University Press, 2005.

Fitzgerald, C.P. *The Southern Expansion of the Chinese People: 'Southern Fields and Southern Ocean'*. Canberra: Australian National University Press, 1972.

Fürer-Haimendorf, Christoph von. *Tribes of India: The Struggle for Survival*. Berkeley: University of California Press, 1982.

Geertz, Clifford. *Negara: The Theatre State in Nineteenth-Century Bali*. Princeton, NJ: Princeton University Press, 1980.

Ghurye, Govind Sadashiv. *The Scheduled Tribes of India*. Bombay: Popular Book Depot, 1959.

Gottschang, Thomas R., and Diana Lary. *Swallows and Settlers: The Great Migration from North China to Manchuria*. Ann Arbor: Center for Chinese Studies, 2000.

Guha, Ranajit. *Elementary Aspects of Peasant Insurgency in Colonial India*. Durham, NC: Duke University Press, 1999.

Hauser-Schäublin, Brigitta, ed. *Adat and Indigeneity in Indonesia: Culture and Entitlements between Heteronomy and Self-Ascription*. Göttingen: Göttingen University Press, 2013.

Heidhues, Mary Somers. *Golddiggers, Farmers, and Traders in the 'Chinese Districts' of West Kalimantan, Indonesia*. Ithaca: Cornell Southeast Asia Program, 2003.

Indigenous Peoples: Living and Working Conditions of Aboriginal Populations in Independent Countries. Geneva: International Labour Organisation, 1953.

Janhunen, Juha. *Manchuria: An Ethnic History*. Helsinki: Finno-Ugrian Society, 1996.

Jen Yu-wen. *The Taiping Revolutionary Movement*. New Haven, CT: Yale University Press, 1973.

Jenks, Robert D. *Insurgency and Social Disorder in Guizhou: The 'Miao' Rebellion, 1854–1873*. Honolulu: University of Hawai'i Press, 1994.

Kane, Samuel E. *Life or Death in Luzon: Thirty Years of Adventure with the Philippine Highlanders*. Indianapolis: Bobbs-Merrill, 1933.

Kennedy, Jonathan, and Lawrence King. 'Adivasis, Maoists and Insurgency in the Central Indian Tribal Belt.' *European Journal of Sociology* 54, no. 1 (2013): 1–32.

Kim, Seonmin. 'Ginseng and Border Trespassing Between Qing China and Chosŏn Korea.' *Late Imperial China* 28, no. 1 (2007): 33–61.

Leary, John. *Violence and the Dream People: The Orang Asli in the Malayan Emergency, 1948–1960*. Athens: Ohio University Center for International Studies, 1995.

Manickam, Sandra Khor. *Taming the Wild: Aborigines and Racial Knowledge in Colonial Malaya*. Singapore: NUS Press, 2015.

Maung, U Maung. *Burma's Constitution*. The Hague: Martinus Nijhoff, 1959.

McCullough, William H. 'The Heian Court, 794–1070.' In *The Cambridge History of Japan, volume 2: Heian Japan*, edited by Donald H. Shively and William H. McCullough, 20–96. Cambridge: Cambridge University Press, 1999.
Michaud, Jean. 'Handling Mountain Minorities in China, Vietnam and Laos: From History to Current Concerns.' *Asian Ethnicity* 10, no. 1 (2009): 25–49.
Mullaney, Thomas S. *Coming to Terms with the Nation: Ethnic Classification in Modern China*. Berkeley: University of California Press, 2011.
Munsterhjelm, Mark. 'The First Nations of Taiwan: A Special Report on Taiwan's Indigenous Peoples.' *Cultural Survival*, June 2002. Accessed 5 October 2019. https://www.culturalsurvival.org/publications/cultural-survival-quarterly/first-nations-taiwan-special-report-taiwans-indigenous.
Narangoa, Li. 'The Power of Imagination: Whose Northeast and Whose Manchuria?' *Inner Asia* 4, no. 1 (2002): 3–25.
Narangoa, Li, and Robert Cribb. *Historical Atlas of Northeast Asia, 1590–2010: Korea, Manchuria, Mongolia, Eastern Siberia*. New York: Columbia University Press, 2014.
Nathan, Dev, and Govind Kelkar. 'Introduction.' In *Globalization and Indigenous Peoples in Asia: Changing the Local–Global Interface*, edited by Dev Nathan, Govind Kelkar, and Pierre Walter, 6–36. New Delhi: Sage, 2004.
Naumov, Igor V. *The History of Siberia*. London: Routledge, 2006.
Osborne, Robin. *Transmigration in Indonesia*. Canberra: Australian Council for Overseas Aid, 1985.
Parasher, Aloka. *Mlecchas in Early India: A Study in Attitudes toward Outsiders up to AD 600*. New Delhi: Munshiram Manoharlal, 1991.
Pesses, Abigaël. 'Highland Birth and Citizenship Registration in Thailand: Final Report on Karen Focus Group Discussions in Chiang Mai Province.' UNESCO; UNESCO Highland Birth and Citizenship Registration Promotion Project Funded by the United Kingdom Sustainable Development Programme, 2007. https://hal.archives-ouvertes.fr/hal-01736494/document.
Prill-Brett, June. 'Contested Domains: The Indigenous Peoples Rights Act (IPRA) and Legal Pluralism in the Northern Philippines.' *Journal of Legal Pluralism and Unofficial Law* 39, no. 55 (2007): 11–36.
Ravenstein, Ernst Georg. *The Russians on the Amur: Its Discovery, Conquest, and Colonization, with a Description of the Country, Its Inhabitants, Productions, and Commercial Capabilities*. London: Trübner, 1861.
Salemink, Oscar. *The Ethnography of Vietnam's Central Highlanders: A Historical Contextualization, 1850–1990*. Honolulu: University of Hawai'i Press 2003.
Sangaji, Arianto. 'The Masyarakat Adat Movement in Indonesia: A Critical Insider's View.' In *The Revival of Tradition in Indonesian Politics: The Deployment of Adat from Colonialism to Indigenism*, Jamie Davidson and David Henley, 319–336. Abingdon: Routledge, 2007.
Scott, James C. *The Art of Not Being Governed: An Anarchist History of Upland Southeast Asia*. New Haven: Yale University Press, 2009.
'The Scheduled and Tribal Areas.' *Indian Journal of Public Administration* 23, no. 3 (1977): 821–836.
Shan, Chun. *Major Aspects of Chinese Religion and Philosophy: Dao of Inner Saint and Outer King*. Berlin: Springer, 2012.
Shepherd, John R. 'The Island Frontier of the Ch'ing, 1684–1740.' In *Taiwan: A New History*, edited by Murray A. Rubinstein, 107–132. Armonk: M.E. Sharpe, 2007.
Smith, Jeremy. 'Was There a Soviet Nationality Policy?' *Europe-Asia Studies* 71, no. 6 (2019): 972–993.
Steger, Isabella. 'Who Are the Indigenous Ainu People of Japan?' *Quartz*, 18 February 2019. Accessed 5 October 2019. https://qz.com/1551496/who-are-the-indigenous-ainu-people-of-japan/.
Thapar, Romila. 'The Image of the Barbarian in Early India.' *Comparative Studies in Society and History* 13, no. 4 (1971): 408–436.

Tichotsky, John. *Russia's Diamond Colony: The Republic of Sakha*. London: Routledge, 2000.

Tirtosudarmo, Riwanto. *The Politics of Migration in Indonesia and Beyond*. Singapore: Springer Nature, 2018.

Tully, John. 'A Victorian Ecological Disaster: Imperialism, the Telegraph, and Gutta-Percha.' *Journal of World History* 20, no. 4 (2009): 559–579.

'United Nations Declaration on the Rights of Indigenous Peoples.' United Nations, 2008. Accessed 5 June 2020. https://www.un.org/esa/socdev/unpfii/documents/DRIPS_en.pdf.

Vaddhanaphuti, Chayan. 'The Thai State and Ethnic Minorities: From Assimilation to Selective Integration.' In *Ethnic Conflicts in Southeast Asia*, edited by Kusuma Snitwongse and W. Scott Thompson, 151–166. Singapore: Institute of Southeast Asian Studies, 2005.

Varma, Nitin. *Coolies of Capitalism: Assam Tea and the Making of Coolie Labour*. Berlin: De Gruyter Oldenbourg, 2017.

Verstappen, Herman Th. *Zwerftocht door een Wereld in Beweging*. Assen: Van Gorcum, 2006.

'Who Are the Indigenous Peoples of Russia?' *Cultural Survival*, 19 February 2014. Accessed 5 October 2019. https://www.culturalsurvival.org/news/who-are-indigenous-peoples-russia.

Wills, John E. 'The Seventeenth-Century Transformation: Taiwan under the Dutch and the Cheng Regime.' In *Taiwan: A New History*, edited by Murray A. Rubinstein, 84–106. Armonk: M.E. Sharpe, 2007.

5
WORLD CONSERVATION AND GENOCIDAL FRONTIERS
Global environmentalism, settler colonialism, and Indigenous humanity in the early twentieth century

Fiona Paisley[1]

During his keynote at the Eighth International Zoological Congress held in Graz, Switzerland in 1903, renowned anthropologist and zoologist Paul Sarasin called for the 'Global Protection of Nature'. As a member of the British Zoological Society and founder of the Swiss League for Nature Protection, he invited the gathered scholars and officials present to agitate for endangered 'living nature': the 'merciless industrial speculation' of the current world economy was reaping 'temporary profit' while 'sacrific[ing] the beauties of mother Earth to the vanity of man'.[2] Urgent action had to be taken. Ten years later, at the invitation of the Swiss government, Sarasin convened the First World Conservation Conference in Bern. Before an audience of official representatives from 20 nations, he argued not only against the predatory exploitation of natural resources but for the just treatment of 'native' peoples in the colonial world. Combining conservation through the sustainable management of economic resources with the preservation of wildlife and the so-called primitive peoples, Sarasin's vision of conservation offered a global perspective that predicted dire consequences without action.[3] The Indigenous peoples of Australia would be his case in point.

With its focus on Sarasin's critique of the imperial world order in 1913, this chapter sets out to contribute to recent scholarship on the imperial contexts of conservation[4] by bringing the field into closer dialogue with histories of humanitarianism and protectionism.[5] It seeks to think across these domains in ways that reanimate the agencies of the 'colonised' otherwise represented as a cause for intervention, or as a way to moderate Western regimes based on occupation, extraction, profit, and development.[6] It reads these concerns alongside progressive thinking about the fragility of animal and natural ecologies as well as that animated by the pragmatism of preserving (human, animal, and natural) resources for ongoing exploitation. As will be shown, Sarasin's dysgenic vision of interlinked systems at tipping point failed to engage with competing worldviews articulated by Indigenous activists that emphasised land, community, education, labour rights, and membership in the nation as well as a distinct First Peoples status. His vision of an authentic, endangered 'primitive' other also elided the myriad contact histories, for example in Australia, that are illustrative of dynamism, resilience, and resistance. As Lynette Russell has argued, Indigenous Australian societies and cultures have always been 'utterly modern', 'dynamic', and 'adaptive'.[7] Sarasin's internationalist worldview worked to occlude from sight the vibrancy of Indigenous modernities and internationalisms articulating their own claims for self-rule, land, and community as First Peoples in these and future decades.[8]

In the second half of this chapter, Sarasin's account of a genocidal frontier in northern Australia is contrasted with that made by Aboriginal commentator and protestor AM Fernando. He was in Bern in the early 1920s at around the same time as Sarasin was lobbying the League of Nations. In a remarkable turn of events, the published proceedings of the 1913 conference was to provide a reference point for the editors of a newspaper approached by Fernando, making him perhaps the first Aboriginal person to take the Aboriginal cause directly to the European press. As a middle-aged man, before he left Australia nearly 20 years earlier Fernando had himself protested the genocidal conditions of the northern frontier, later claiming that he had been forced to leave Australia forever after accusing police of murdering Aboriginal people in outback Western Australia in 1903. Although, as will be argued, he too mobilised the spectre of imminent extinction as a result of a genocidal British Australia, Fernando rejected any notion of Aboriginal proximity to animal life, asserting instead their intelligence and his agency as an international commentator on world affairs.[9]

The discussion of a 'genocidal frontier' in the following pertains, therefore, to its contested mobilisations within and between competing world visions. It concerns the term's circulations among experts as extinction narratives, and compares these to actual places and peoples onto which they were projected. Earlier in the century, settler/colonial governments had become increasingly aware that, rather than 'dying out', the ongoing presence of native peoples would require sustained management. They sought to find ways of doing this that would finally resolve the 'problem' of settler colonialism while distancing their own efforts from those of previous regimes.[10] Asserting Western authority in promoting the ethical management of resources, including those of 'primitive' life, spoke eloquently of white concerns about the very direction of progress itself.[11] Yet, progressivism also assumed the effectiveness of public campaigns. Contemporary enthusiasm for the national and international regulation of labour, evident in new agendas for women's rights, anti-vivisection, anti-animal cruelty, and domestic animal welfare movements,[12] reminds us that the progressive era in which Sarasin's conference took place assumed that, once informed of wrongs, the power of science, the will of governments, and the conscience of publics would act towards their correction.[13] The concluding sections of this chapter point to the fragility of such assumptions.

As will be discussed in the following, Sarasin's analysis of colonial rule went well beyond a rehearsal of past wrongs. The injustices of Aboriginal Australia occurring at the time would be central to his analysis that industrial greed combined with cruelty to threaten humanity. It underlined his understanding of a just and sustainable world where progress should lead to betterment for all and not at the expense of those he considered most vulnerable.[14] Recent technological advances, Sarasin warned, predicted new levels of resource and labour extraction that echoed the horrors of nineteenth-century colonisation but would exceed them in scale and brutality.[15] Australia offered no more chilling an example of the propensity for wanton destruction that Sarasin declared fundamental to Caucasians.

The dreadful prediction Sarasin saw in Australia reflected the worsening impacts of a second phase of settlement across its central and northern regions.[16] From the 1890s, what James Belich has called a 'settler revolution' fuelled the emergence of an 'Anglo World'.[17] Northern and central Australia were indicative of that revolution. More broadly throughout the colonised world, new technologies of extraction, mobility, and oppression created devastation on the ground and led to greater competition between the European imperial powers over access to territory that, in turn, led to a global war.[18] As he witnessed the rise of imperial nationalism over this same period, Sarasin foresaw an apocalyptic end point leading humanity further away from the Edenic beginnings he considered still evident in the ways of life among remaining primitive peoples.[19] Conserving these would be vital to humankind's knowledge of its own past, while the just treatment of Indigenous peoples would offer some indication of a new era in world affairs.

As new international histories have pointed out, conservation was one of the progressive world visions of the early twentieth century.[20] Non-government and expert networks informed international reform agendas, anthropologists and zoologists like Sarasin among them.[21] A few studies of the early history of conservation in Europe have referred to the 1913 conference in passing, as context for (what would be) Sarasin's unsuccessful campaign in the early 1920s to have conservation brought under the League of Nations.[22] Only one, however, comments that 'unusually for the time' Sarasin made a case for Indigenous rights.[23] One of the reasons for this relative lack of commentary is that, following the First World War, native status and conditions in the former German colonies had been brought under the League of Nations' mandates scheme and responsibility for 'natives' in the colonies more broadly became a sacred duty of the 'advanced nations'. Thus, when he made his case at the League, Sarasin no longer included Indigenous peoples in his account of world conservation.[24]

Another reason for this absence is that critical environmental and colonial histories have tended to study resource management and colonisation separately. Yet, the two were intimately interpolated, not least in the mandates system, based as it was on the idea of indirect rule. This concept was outlined by Lord Lugard in his influential book *The Dual Mandate in British Tropical Africa* (1922) in which he proposed the dual aims of a humane and sustainable development in the tropics for the benefit of the world as well as for the 'natives' living in those territories.[25] Not only Indigenous peoples, but forests and wildlife would be integral to the reformed colonial rule promoted as progressive and humane via the League during the interwar decades.[26] It was agreed by member nations that the former German colonies be placed under the guardianship of mandated powers like Australia, while the conditions of Indigenous peoples in the settler colonies should remain the domestic concern of their governments.[27] Nevertheless, Indigenous conditions in the settler colonies were debated internationally throughout these years, by the London-based Anti-Slavery and Aborigines Protection Society (ASAPS), for example, that was active in Geneva and that included Aboriginal status and conditions in Australia among the modern slaveries it considered active across the world.[28] Sarasin's mobilisation of 'the Aborigines of Australia' in 1913 underlines the point that a great deal was at stake for Indigenous peoples as 'humanitarian imperialism'[29] took shape in the years that followed.

Moreover, by directing his critique towards Australia, Sarasin drew attention to one of the new white settler nations of the British Commonwealth, proclaimed by its advocates as leading the world in the reform of colonial relations.[30] Modern forms of racial management involving 'reserves' modelled in South Africa, the U.S., and Kenya were being discussed by the ASAPS in its widely read journal,[31] at the same time as anthropological knowledges were being applied by settler governments towards better 'understanding' their Indigenous subjects.[32] Sarasin would mobilise his own claim to anthropological expertise in the name of Aboriginal Australian suffering. By declaring white rule rapacious and destructive, he cast Indigenous people as the collective victims of a universal structure, and in comparing their exploitation to that of the animal and natural world, he lent his voice to calls for their protective administration in segregated reserves not unlike those sought for threatened animal species.

The asserted proximity of 'primitive peoples' to nature was hardly controversial in Australia – for example, at federation in 1901, responsibility for Aboriginal people had been incorporated into departments of Fisheries and Wildlife.[33] The longevity of aligning Indigenous peoples with 'nature' and thus as subject likewise to the forces of progress is illustrated by the worldview of early colonists in the Pacific. Marvelling at the diversity of human, animal, and plant lives, they proclaimed a desire to conserve both nature and primitive society from the barbarities and voracities of modern man. Faced with the evident contradictions between the civilising project of colonisation in which they were engaged and the destruction wrought in its wake, according to Richard Grove, the relegation of 'primitive man' to the realm of nature meant that his fate was rendered as inevitable alongside that of his environment.[34]

Transnational histories tracing the emergence of national parks and wildlife reserves around the Anglo World in the nineteenth century point to the proximities between environmentalism and nationalist, imperialist visions of progress. Along with animal rights, anti-cruelty, and the control of hunting, the future of manly empire and the status of the white nations was played out in conservation.[35] From the late 1890s, national parks were established at home and wildlife and game preserves in British and Portuguese African colonies.[36] Claire Brennan has written of the history of safari in Australia.[37] Ella Shohat has argued that the preservation of animal life contributed to the legitimacy of modern colonial rule over this period.[38] The preservation of 'wild animal' life for the purposes of hunting became part of colonial authority in British Africa.[39] An international 'Conference on African Wild Life' convened in 1900 by the British Foreign Office first linked the international control of hunting and environmental management, and in 1909 the Society for the Preservation of Fauna in the Empire (founded in 1903 and led by Charles Rothschild), joined with the Boone and Crockett Club, part of U.S. President Roosevelt's manliness movement, to hold an international conference on wildlife at the Hague. By the turn of the century, however, new technologies of killing raised questions about the morality of the heroic struggle of (imperial) man over beast. When Roosevelt toured Europe in 1910, he was well received by conservationists who agreed with his contrast of the ennobling struggle of man over beast and the debasing inhumanity of modern mass killing technologies.[40] The 1910s and 1920s witnessed the rise in popularity of 'hunting with the camera' undertaken by expedition filmmakers, who returned from the 'wild' with sensational images of the world's endangered animal species and its supposedly last remaining authentic 'natives'.[41]

If wildlife hunting was coming into question, then scandals emerging of the treatment of native peoples seemed to confirm the continuing propensity of white man for cruelty and violence of a sort evidenced by slavery and colonisation in the previous century.[42] During his conference, Sarasin noted conditions in rubber plantations in Putumayo, Portuguese West Africa, which had been the subject of a damning report by Roger Casement in 1911. As Kevin Grant has shown, reports of the Belgian Congo in 1903 also involving the Anti-Slavery Society in London had met with similar international condemnation.[43] But rather than Africa, Sarasin chose to feature settler colonialism in his 1913 keynote, referring to shootings in Australia without any apparent need of elaboration. Indeed, over the previous century a series of 'dispersals' involving police and vigilantes in the Australian colonies had received international attention.[44] Such reports also informed early anticolonial movements: in his widely read book *Nationalism* (1917), the leading Indian commentator Rabindranath Tagore wrote that everyone knew that in 'America and Australia, Europe has simplified her problem by almost exterminating the original population', and that these efforts continued into the present.[45]

In Sarasin's argument, further significance adhered to the Aboriginal Australian case because they supposedly provided a living link between animal and human life. Like many of his contemporaries, Sarasin was informed by an evolutionary worldview that readily combined zoology, archaeology, palaeontology, and ethnography. With his younger cousin, Fritz, he had undertaken fieldwork in Sri Lanka to study its rare animals and 'Stone Age' men, the Veddas. Drawing on theories developed by evolutionists like Herman Klaatsch, who had also influenced Australian anthropology,[46] and informed by previous fieldwork in central and northern Australia, the Sarasins hoped to identify the Indo-German ancestors of modern man by mapping migration flows between Sri Lanka, Australia, and Samoa.[47] They considered the Australian 'Aborigines' one of the last living links between the higher apes and early European man.

In Australia, Indigenous peoples had long been represented as subhuman by laymen advocating their 'disappearance'. For example, in an 1884 editorial excoriating the 'sentiment' of humanitarians concerned for the treatment of Aboriginal people, The *Northern Territory Times* referred to the latter as unfeeling and treacherous like 'Siberian wolves'.[48] While two years later, one of those ridiculed humanitarians, a missionary who was a Protector of the Aborigines for the New South Wales government, wrote with some irony in a local newspaper that if the Aboriginal people were indeed 'brutes' – as was so often declared – then they should be protected under prevention of cruelty to animal legislation.[49] In their recent account of the imperial worlds of animal-human life, Antoinette Burton and Renisa Mawani point out that historically 'the lines that divided human from animal [have been] ... the result of contingencies of time and place that shaped the limits and possibilities of imperial power on the ground and, equally, in the metropolitan imagination'.[50] One such international moment in this contingent, politicised process of demarcation occurred during a debate at the League in 1928 at which Lord Lugard called upon the Mandates Commission to help protect gorillas and chimpanzees in the African mandated territories. According to newspaper reports, although:

> [a]dmitting that the apemen were near extinction, the commissioners were undecided whether the gorillas should be considered defenceless members of the homo sapien family entitled to protection as "indigenous natives" or as a "natural resource" which can be administered in accordance with the wishes of the authorities in the territories.[51]

Indigenous peoples in the settler colonies were of the former, but under international agreement relegated to the latter.

As discussed below, something of this dual status is evident in the pre-circulated pamphlet of the lecture that Sarasin presented in Bern. In its pages, he reproduced an already notorious photograph of a group of Australian Aboriginal men shown in neck chains while in police custody in northwestern Australia. The German anthropologist Herman Klaatsch had taken the image while on fieldwork in the early 1900s.[52] Sarasin used this visual evidence to condemn the contemporary government in Australia. In actuality, ten years earlier a highly critical royal commission into Aboriginal conditions in Western Australia had recommended the 'more' humane policy of chaining hands and feet, while its Commissioner Walter Roth had condemned more broadly the behaviour of police and magistrates.[53] The practice continued nonetheless over following decades, as will be returned to at the end of the chapter.

★★★

In November 1913, a group of delegates representing countries, including Germany, the U.S., Argentina, Austria, Australia, Hungary, Belgium, Denmark, Spain, France, Britain, Italy, Norway, Portugal, Sweden, and Switzerland gathered in Bern to discuss world conservation. Concerned by impending extinctions across the globe, Sarasin opened by pointing out that statistics gathered since the late 1800s had revealed various land and sea animals important to science and the 'worldwide economy' to be increasingly under threat. Just as the 1892 Bering agreement between the U.S. and Britain had halted whaling and sealing in the Antarctic region for several years,[54] so international agreement should protect the Spitzbergen Peninsula, home to Arctic polar bears, walruses, seals, and birds. The age of exploration was over: with the age of exploitation in full swing, the greed of trappers, traders, and importers was feeding an ever-expanding market. Without immediate action, whole species of life would be wiped out forever.[55] Sarasin saw in these mass resource economies clear evidence of a global struggle between grossly unequal forces, and he applied this same narrative to the treatment of the native peoples of the world.

Because such struggles had previously taken place largely out of sight, Sarasin continued, it had been difficult to raise public opinion. But now less accessible places were feeling the brunt of Western man and formerly 'undisturbed' regions were becoming subject to a 'threatening evil'. The global trade in natural resources and animal life that had relied on colonial rule was founded on the cruelty and barbarism perpetrated by 'Caucasians' everywhere. Establishing 'inviolable free regions' might yet 'restore mutilated nature' and international agreements 'create protective regions in the colonies' to ensure the survival of native peoples. That primitive peoples were the victims of murder, economic exploitation, and the destruction of their native habitat was a crime against their humanity.

Even though depicting Indigenous peoples as defenceless against the brutalities of modern life, Sarasin simultaneously alluded to and veiled Indigenous agency. Thus, he condemned the endangerment of the bison in late nineteenth-century North America where once-thriving herds managed by the Native Americans had been drastically reduced by the building of railways through their territory. The presence of Indigenous peoples was implicit in his case: Sarasin had most likely been influenced by an evocative report published that same year, attracting headlines around the English-speaking world. In its pages, the lawyer, artist, and traveller George Catlin had described the devastating impact on local people as well as their herds in a destructive frontier economy. He regretted what he considered to have been its devastating effects on their culture and way of life and hoped that any future reserve for the bison would include Native Americans where he considered that they could earn a living by performing for tourists.[56]

In contrast, Sarasin tended to mobilise biblical images of Indigenous peoples. They were the 'most noble of all free living creations of nature' who had once lived in a pre-colonial Eden. They had been subjected to the murderous white frontiersman who 'destroyed just as he also has in the animal world by slaughtering entire tribes in murderous greed, dripping in blood'. Continuing in this vein, Sarasin asserted that world history revealed a pathological capacity for extreme violence against Indigenous peoples. Its continuation into the present confirmed that modern (white) man had inherited a propensity for the wanton destruction of innocent animals and Indigenous humans. According to Sarasin, the extinction of the

Tasmanians in the previous century offered graphic evidence of this propensity: their demise was both 'tragic for science' and a 'human sacrifice' to the 'banality of average European culture'.[57] Moreover, Christianity's claim to civilise the world had facilitated a lack of conscience in Europe, as once 'the act of destruction [was] done, the church bells of the so-called religious stock-farmers – their murderers – can ring to take the last survivors to their graves as well'. Sarasin offered a grim summation of the extent of the problem: 'Yes, the white man is the ruin of creation, is the devastator of the paradise of our planet and his steps into this paradise are marked by epidemics, poison, fire, blood, and tears.'

To underline this point, he set two chilling images side by side on one page in the published version of his lecture. One showed the mechanised harpooning of seals, and the other a row of Aboriginal men in neck chains. When viewed together, they evoked innocent vulnerability in the face of modern brutality. As noted at the outset, the use of neck chaining had been highlighted by Roth royal commission report in 1905 leading to questions in the press about 'British justice' in relation to Aboriginal people.[58] In similar vein, Sarasin chose to caption the photograph 'Mistreatment of Indigenous Australians through Mock Justice'.

The next section draws from the proceedings of the conference to consider the responses of the two delegates sent by Australian state and federal governments.[59] Each was an expert in resources dominating world markets at that time such as timber, whaling and sealing, feather down, and fur. As the first to speak following Sarasin's dramatic keynote, Peter McBride, the Agent General for Victoria in London, set about emphasising the protection of nature in Victoria since the late previous century.[60] According to Tim Bonyhady, although the natural world was important to colonial and later national discourse in Australia, governments mostly failed to translate sentiment into legislation.[61] Heather Goodall points out that, by the early twentieth century, 'the Aborigines' – along with wattle, koala, and kangaroo – had become elements in a heroic narrative of progressive nationhood favoured by those celebrating White Australia's separateness from the Old Country.[62] In this vein, Aboriginal reserves were visited by tourists eager to witness the performance of primitive culture alongside the supposedly civilising effects of Christianity.[63]

On the treatment of Indigenous Australians, however, McBride rejected Sarasin's accusations. He declared the image of Aboriginal men in chains to be out of date, and that Victoria was in any case distant from the northern frontier the picture purported to represent. He spoke rather of a system of reserves, perhaps referring to Coranderrk Mission in Victoria, to which he ascribed forms of humane care that paid attention to (what he described as) the 'mentality' and interests of inmates, such as hunting. McBride omitted thereby the long and powerful history of Aboriginal political agitation through missions such as Coranderrk to hold governments to account.[64] In the 1930s, one of the leading figures from Coranderrk, William Cooper, would write to the ASAPS calling for international intervention into the conditions of his people.[65]

Eager to represent the Australian nation as worldly and progressive, the Australian Agent General to Switzerland, Ernst Carroll, asserted in his presentation that – if a young nation – Australia was not 'behind in thinking about the important questions which agitate the great spirits of the civilized world' and asserted that it was the intention of the Commonwealth of Australia to join in pursuing the global regulation of commerce. Regarding the treatment of its Indigenous people, Carroll admitted that in the early days of colonisation, 'Australia [had] sinned'. But he blamed early colonisers (presumably referring here to the convict era widely blamed for early brutalities) for bringing to the Antipodes a habit of 'kill[ing] for the pleasure of killing and devastating nature'.[66]

What of the damning image of Australian settler rule circulated by Sarasin? As a footnote in his published paper indicated, the photograph had been taken in northern Australia in 1904. In fact, it had been published a few years after that date in an ethnographic paper by the German anthropologist Herman Klaatsch. Sensational comments in this publication and in a speech given by Klaatsch at the Australian Science Congress held in Adelaide, South Australia, in January 1907, regarding what he stated was the increasing endangerment of Indigenous Australians in the north, were reported in the Australian press, and in *The Times* (London) where they appeared under the headline 'Alleged Ill-Treatment of Australian Natives'.[67] These claims circulated also through the pages of the ASAPS' *The Reporter*, and by these various means contributed to larger debate about the veracity of the findings of the Roth Royal Commission, whose conclusions Klaatsch sought to confirm.[68] In the published version of his paper, Klaatsch stated that during his trip, he had found 'the relations between whites and blacks comparable only with the terrible state of affairs which existed in Tasmania from 1820s to 1830s, which resulted in extinction …', a conclusion he had reached while watching 'the arrival of [a group of] native prisoners at Wyndham which had travelled from 300 to 400 miles chained by the neck'.[69]

Like Sarasin, Klaatsch considered the Aboriginal people pivotal to understanding human evolution.[70] He hoped to gather evidence in Australia confirming his theory that 'the Aborigines' were a living link between the higher apes and early man.[71] And so, while disavowing their treatment, Klaatsch declared that by 'bringing in' such men, the local police had provided him with valuable 'material'.[72] Because other Indigenous Australians he encountered were terrified of white men and ran away, those in custody afforded him vital opportunity to take measurements and make ethnographic photographs. Seemingly unselfconscious about the contradiction between anticipating each 'fresh transport' and the 'fate' of these 'poor sons of the wilderness', Klaatsch concluded that: 'The outrageous wrong that Christianity and our culture was doing to these poor creatures at least had a positive scientific effect. The material that I gained from it was unique.'[73] Furthermore, he would openly describe removing the head and other body parts of a recently deceased Aboriginal man from the Broome hospital.[74] As a result of their sustained campaigning, it was only in May 2017 that a Berlin museum finally returned remains taken by Klaatsch from Queensland during this same period to their descendants.[75]

Following the First World War, in 1921 Sarasin hoped to have his vision for world conservation brought under the auspices of the League of Nations. But despite some support from some of the top officials like Inazō Nitobe (an Undersecretary

General of the League) and the co-lobbying of animal welfare organisations, it was concluded that other issues like reconstruction were more pressing.[76] It is remarkable, therefore, that in the same year the proceedings of the 1913 conference would become essential reading for a group of Swiss newspaper men seeking confirmation for the views of an Aboriginal protestor who had arrived in person in their offices in central Berlin. Despite the fact that the Indigenous peoples of the Dominions had been excluded from League oversight, Indigenous rights activists in Australia, as elsewhere in the world, hoped that international pressure might renew impetus for reform in their own country.[77] The promise of minority rights and a new approach to colonisation asserted by the League attracted Chief Deskaheh from Canada to Geneva in the early 1920s, for example. Having failed to gain support from British authorities, he aimed to persuade the General Assembly to endorse the Iroquois' claim for self-rule via the adjudication of an International Court. He was unsuccessful.[78] In 1938, the year of a national Aboriginal protest in Sydney during the sesquicentenary of Australia's 'founding', Pearl Gibbs wrote to the League on behalf of the Aborigines Progressive Association (in which William Cooper was another leading figure) for its intervention in the conditions of Aboriginal people in the Northern Territory.[79] Cooper was at this time involved in national and international debates about how to 'develop' the north of Australia in ways that Sarah Irving has argued expressed disagreement on how to 'govern nature' as much as it did on the parameters of White Australia.[80]

Rejecting the League as the British League of Nations, AM Fernando decided instead to make his argument for international intervention directly through the pages of the Swiss progressive newspaper, *Der Bund*. After an initial meeting in June 1921, the editors asked Fernando to write down his claims and shortly afterwards published his 'letter to the Swiss people'. As his conversations with them and his letter indicate, Fernando aimed to counter the very kinds of conservation discourse built upon notions of Indigenous incapacity that had been mobilised by Sarasin eight years earlier.

Opening his letter by asserting his humanity and that of the Aboriginal people, Fernando declared himself and them among the most advanced of 'primitive native people' in the world. Yet despite this 'intellectual characteristic', they faced what he described as a lethal mix of murder, poisoning, and the abuse of women by which means they were being 'expelled from the face of this earth'. Occupation, exploitation, and extraction dominated, rather than Christianise or uplift, as British settlers used Indigenous labour to 'clear the virgin forest' and 'amass British riches under the cruellest of conditions ...'. In a marked departure from Sarasin, however, Fernando argued that this process of resource and human destruction was enabled by efforts to limit the capacity of Indigenous Australians to represent themselves. It had relied upon denying them access to an education by which Aboriginal people could mobilise the value of their own labour in real terms.[81] 'Is that Christian?' he asked, 'Is that the much-praised civilization?'[82] And then, more in step with Sarasin's focus on the devastation wrought by technology, Fernando advised that the rapid extension of settlement inland from the coast was an immediate and catastrophic threat, stating unequivocally that 'where the train gets to, that means the end for us ...'.[83]

In a follow-up conversation, Fernando returned to the distinction between nature and Aboriginal life. He told the editors that while the 'lion, the tiger' might be brought under the will of the white man, this would never be possible with the Aboriginal people who even 'the British say ... cannot be tamed'.[84] In their account of this exchange published in their paper, the editors quote Fernando as saying that the Aboriginal people of Australia 'too are created after the image of god, we are not animals but human beings with souls and emotions ...'.[85] Nevertheless in their expression of support for him, they resorted to the terms of Sarasin's 1913 call for preservation of a primitive race, writing that even though the 'primitive human being is called the noblest of wild living creatures settlers still continued to shoot the natives like wild animals, or relegated them to a slow but nonetheless sure death through slavery'. Despite being '[a]ccording to natural justice ... the first owners of the land', the birthright of the 'indigenous inhabitants' was being 'snatched from them'.[86] The recent world war had revealed that white people could be 'worse than savages', and so it was urgent for the world community to 'not only to preserve scientifically interesting races, but particularly to prevent white people from actions any conscience would be ashamed of'.[87]

Conclusion

The connections drawn by Sarasin in 1913 Switzerland between conservation, humanitarianism, and colonialism make explicit, if fleetingly, the intersecting genealogies of these more usually separately treated fields of study. Their drawing together in his progressive account of empire and settler/colonisation offers a hitherto overlooked case study of more recent postcolonial critiques of 'green imperialism' in contemporary world politics.[88] It underlines the usefulness of examining settler colonisation in order to understand the ways in which the histories of protection, conservation, and preservation have overlapped. Scientific knowledge, Christian progressivism, and humanitarian concern combined in Bern early last century and politicised conditions in the Australian north in ways that would soon be occluded by member states of the League of Nations, including by Australia itself. Furthermore, Sarasin's argument for a world perspective that included 'primitives' points to the proximities of animal and human life in progressive imperial worldviews.[89] Sarasin recommended that 'world conservation' be concerned with what he considered to be the remaining Indigenous cultures and peoples as a matter of justice but also because of their intrinsic value to the 'world', a response that echoed progressive imperial views on wild animal and environmental preservation but also pointed to the blurred edges between that which was declared to be of value in its own right, and that which was worth saving for future exploitation.

Regarding scale and perspective in global history, this chapter has pointed to the ways in which progress in world affairs in the first half of the last century was framed as in imperial and colonial terms. The two were sometimes sufficiently distinct to allow for spaces of critique and protest. Settler societies were highlighted in some quarters as among the greatest challenges facing the modern world, the northern frontiers of Australia providing graphic evidence of the capacity of the white race for barbarity and injustice that was anachronistic and harmful to both its victims and its perpetrators. In making his humanitarian call for action, Sarasin effectively erased a parallel history of Indigenous modernity, resistance, and agency, whether in local exchanges or internationally. In his efforts to promote the Aboriginal cause, Sarasin reprised an image that proposed an Indigenous people innocent of any wrong who were, therefore, like animal life, defenceless in the face of modernity at its worst. But what of resistance – or even defiance – in the picture taken by Klaatsch? Numbers of Aboriginal men brought in to face 'British justice' in this fashion bravely gave evidence against police or white settlers.[90] By considering the production of the visual evidence circulated by Sarasin, this chapter has pointed to the possibility of Aboriginal agency even under the extreme conditions it purported to document, conditions moreover that were indicative of larger histories of massacre, police abuse, body theft, and cultural, social, and ecological traumas. And it has offered graphic evidence of this agency in the reporting of AM Fernando in Europe, an Aboriginal man who had left Australia (he asserted) in fear of his life after having protested white inhumanity.

In many ways, Sarasin's claims were prescient. Over the following years, multiple cases of abuse and murder involving police and the courts in central and northern parts of Australia were to reach national and international attention, often amplified via the ASAPS. Australian governments continued to defend their administrations against accusations of cruelty evoked by images of neck chaining, and evidenced by forced labour, the abuse of women, the taking of children, killings, and injustice in the courts.[91] The Roth Royal Commission recommendations against the use of neck chains in the early 1900s were not carried out; in 1930, a complaint from the ASAPS would force the Minister for Home affairs to call once again for them to be outlawed.[92] However in 1947, during his own condemnation of Aboriginal conditions he had witnessed in the north, the Australian anthropologist Donald Thomson noted that neck chains were still in use.[93]

Finally, a postscript. In a recent contemplation of the future of environmental history, John MacKenzie looked forward to greater engagement with 'the interconnections and interrelationships of the perceptions and uses of nature by indigenous peoples on the one hand and imperial people, the white settlers, on the other ...' as well as the vast differences between them.[94] In the 1990s, Australian environmental historian Tom Griffiths had hoped that Australia might offer an example of such engagement.[95] Recently anthropologists working closely with local communities, such as Deborah Bird Rose in her book *Nourishing Terrains*, helped to convey the complexity of Indigenous cosmologies to both government authorities and non-Indigenous audiences.[96] And yet in 2020, the year in which I began writing this chapter, developmentalism was shown to still outweigh cultural recognition with devastating consequences. In December, anthropologists Jon Altman and Dan Tout published an essay titled 'Again and Again', in which they denounced the recent destruction by a mining company of 46,000-year-old inhabitation sites of the Puutu, Kunti, Kurrama, and Pinikura peoples in Western Australia, declaring it indicative of the resilience of 'settler-colonial extractivism' in Australia despite assertions of 'never again', government protocols for Aboriginal heritage, and Australia's international role as a signatory of the UN Declaration on the Rights of Indigenous Peoples.[97]

Notes

1. I wish to acknowledge and pay my respects to the Traditional Custodians of the Land and to Elders past and present, particularly of the Yugarabul, Yuggera, Jagera, and Turrbal Peoples where I work and live in Southeast Queensland, Australia.
2. Paul Sarasin, *The Global Protection of Nature* (Basel: Emil Birkhaüser, 1911). My thanks to Amelia Rosel and Veronika Folkmanova for their research assistance and translations. On the longer history of extinction in evolutionary anthropology, see George Stocking Jr, *Victorian Anthropology* (New York: The Free Press, 1987).
3. Garland E. Allen, '"Culling the Herd": Eugenics and the Conservation Movement in the United States, 1900–1940,' *Journal of the History of Biology* 46 (2013): 31–72. Previous international conferences had met to discuss Africa, but none claimed a whole 'world' perspective. Corey Ross, *Ecology and Power in the Age of Empire: Europe and the Transformation of the Tropical World* (Oxford: Oxford University Press, 2017), 255ff. See also Alison Bashford, 'Nation, Empire, Globe: The Spaces of Population in the Interwar Years,' *Studies in Society and History* 49, no. 1 (2007): 170–201. See also Nancy J. Christie, 'Environment and Race: Geography's Search for a Darwinian Synthesis,' in *Darwin's Laboratory: Evolutionary Theory and Natural History in the Pacific*, ed. R. MacLeod and Philip F. Rehbock (Honolulu: University of Hawai'i Press, 1994), 42–73.
4. For example, John M. MacKenzie, ed., *Imperialism and the Natural World; The Problem of Nature* (Manchester: Manchester University Press, 1996); Tom Griffiths and Libby Robin, eds., *Ecology and Empire: Environmental History of Settler Societies* (Melbourne: Melbourne University Press, 1997); Alfred W. Crosby, *Ecological Imperialism: The Biological Expansion of Europe 900–1900* (Cambridge: Cambridge University Press, 2004); and William Beinart and Lottie Hughes, eds., *Environment and Empire* (Oxford: Oxford University Press, 2007). See also Arturo Escobar, 'The Problem of Nature Revisited: History and Anthropology,' *Current Anthropology* 39, no. 3 (1998): 385–386.
5. Amanda Nettelbeck, *Indigenous Rights and Colonial Subjecthood: Protection and Reform in the 19th Century British Empire* (Cambridge: Cambridge University Press, 2019).
6. For example, Antoinette Burton, *The Trouble with Empire: Challenges to Modern Imperialism* (Oxford: Oxford University Press, 2015).
7. Lynette Russell, 'Indigenous Knowledge and Archives: Accessing Hidden History and Understandings,' *Australian Academic and Research Libraries* 36, no. 2 (2005): 162. See for Australian examples Ann McGrath, *Illicit Love: Interracial Sex and Marriage in the United States and Australia* (Lincoln: University of Nebraska Press, 2015); Tiffany Shellam, *Meeting the Waylo: Aboriginal Encounters in the Archipelago* (Crawley, WA: UWA Press, 2020); Penny Olsen and Lynette Russell, *Australia's First Naturalists: Indigenous Peoples' Contribution to Early Zoology* (Canberra: NLA Publishing, 2019); and Cassandra Pybus, *Truganini: Journey through the Apocalypse* (Sydney: Allen and Unwin, 2020).
8. Ben Silverstein argues that, in comparison to contemporaneous humanitarian and government reform agendas, Aboriginal visions of a just future were counterhegemonic. See Silverstein, *Governing Natives: Indirect Rule and Settler Colonialism in Australia's North* (Manchester: Manchester University Press, 2019), 126. See also Tim Rowse, 'Indigenous Heterogeneity,' *Australian Historical Studies* 45, no. 3 (2014): 297–310; Jane Carey and Jane Lydon, eds., *Indigenous Networks: Mobility, Connections and Exchange* (London: Routledge, 2014); Rachel Standfield, ed., *Indigenous Mobilities: Across and Beyond the Antipodes* (Canberra: ANU Press, 2018); and Marilyn Lake, 'Indigenous Progressivism Calls Settler Colonialism to Account,' in *Progressive New World: How Settler Colonialism and Transpacific Exchange Shaped American Reform*, ed. Marilyn Lake (Cambridge, MA: Harvard University Press, 2019), 224–249. And more broadly, see Fiona Paisley and Kirsty Reid, eds., *Critical Perspectives on Colonialism: Writing the Empire from Below* (London: Routledge, 2014); and Ann Curthoys and Marilyn Lake, 'Introduction,' in *Connected Worlds: History in Transnational Perspective*, ed. Curthoys and Lake (Canberra: ANU Press, 2005), 5–20.

9 Fiona Paisley, *The Lone Protestor: AM Fernando in Australia and Europe* (Canberra: Aboriginal Studies Press, 2012).
10 On the popularisation of tragic narratives of extinction, see Patrick Brantlinger, *Dark Vanishings: Discourse on the Primitive Races, 1800–1930* (Ithaca: Cornell University Press, 2003), ch 6. In her work on embodied, environmental, and ecological zones of contact in early Sydney, Grace Karskens distinguishes 'the history of massacres' from 'the convenient narrative device' of 'massacre *history*' that '"clears" the stage' for white history to begin. See Karskens, *The People of the River: Lost Worlds of Early Australia* (Sydney: Allen and Unwin, 2020), 125. For a discussion of the 'ecological turn' in genocide studies, see Martin Crook and Damien Short, 'Developmentalism and the Genocide-Ecocide Nexus,' *Journal of Genocide Research* 23, no. 2 (Dec 2020): 162–188.
11 Fiona Paisley, 'Applied Anthropology and Interwar Internationalism: Felix and Marie Keesing and the (White) Future of the 'Native' Pan-Pacific,' *Journal of Pacific History* 50, no. 3 (2015): 304–321. For anthropology and eugenics, see Philippa Levine, 'Anthropology, Colonialism and Eugenics,' in *The Oxford Handbook of the History of Eugenics*, ed. Alison Bashford and Philippa Levine (Oxford: Oxford University Press, 2010), 43–61. For eugenics and conservation, see Allen, '"Culling the Herd"'; Alison Bashford, 'Internationalism, Cosmopolitanism, and Eugenics,' in *The History of Eugenics*, ed. Bashford and Levine (Oxford: Oxford University Press, 2010), 167; and Jonathan Peter Spiro, *Defending the Master Race: Conservation, Eugenics, and the Legacy of Madison Grant* (Lebanon: University of Vermont Press, 2008).
12 Lake, *Progressive New World*.
13 Allen, '"Culling the Herd".'
14 Jeanne Morefield, *Covenants without Swords: Idealist Liberalism and the Spirit of Empire* (Princeton, NJ: Princeton University Press, 2005), 98ff. See also Paul B. Rich, *Race and Empire in British Politics* (Cambridge: Cambridge University Press 1986, 1990); and Christine Twomey, 'Protecting Slaves and Aborigines: The Legacies of European Colonialism in the British Empire,' *Pacific Historical Review* 87, no. 1 (2018): 10–29.
15 Michael Adas, *Machines as the Measure of Men: Science, Technology, and Ideologies of Western Dominance* (Ithaca: Cornell University Press, 1989), 210ff. The use of modern warfare against colonised peoples offered one such indication; for example, on the mandates system and the 1922 Bondelswarts rebellion, see Neta C. Crawford, *Argument and Change in World Politics: Ethics, Decolonization and Humanitarian Intervention* (Cambridge: Cambridge University Press, 2004), 276–281. And in relation to Australian humanitarianism, see Fiona Paisley, 'The Italo-Abyssinian Crisis and Australia Settler Colonialism in 1935,' *History Compass: Special Issue on Anti-Slavery and Settler Colonialism in World History* 15, no. 5 (2017).
16 Tim Rowse, *Indigenous and Other Australians since 1901* (Sydney: New South, 2017); and Russell McGregor, *Imagined Destinies: Aboriginal Australians and the Doomed Race Theory, 1880–1939* (Melbourne: Melbourne University Press, 1997).
17 James Belich, *Replenishing the Earth: The Settler Revolution and the Rise of the Anglo-World 1793–1939* (Oxford: Oxford University Press, 2009); and Antoinette Burton and Tony Ballantyne, 'Remaking the World,' in *A World Connecting: 1870–1945*, ed. Emily Rosenberg (Cambridge, MA: Harvard University Press, 2012), 348–390.
18 John M. MacKenzie, *The Partition of Africa 1880–1900 and European Imperialism in the Nineteenth Century* (London: Routledge, 1983).
19 Allen, '"Culling the Herd",' 37.
20 Ross, *Ecology and Power*, 263. See also Sebastian Conrad and Dominic Sachsenmaier *Competing Visions of World Order: Global Moments and Movements 1880s to 1930s* (New York: Palgrave Macmillan, 2007).
21 See Glenda Sluga and Patricia Clavin, eds., *Internationalisms: A Twentieth-Century History* (Cambridge: Cambridge University Press, 2017). And on imperial networks of expertise, see Joseph M. Hodge, 'Colonial Experts, Developmental and Environmental Doctrines, and the Legacies of Late British Colonialism,' in *Cultivating the Colonies:*

Colonial States and their Environmental Legacies, ed. Christina Folke Ax et al. (Athens: Ohio University Press, 2011), 315–341.
22 Anna Katharina Wöbse, 'Oil on Troubled Waters?: Environmental Diplomacy in the League of Nations,' *Diplomatic History* 32, no. 4 (2008): 521–522; Ian Tyrrell, 'America's National Parks: The Transnational Creation of National Space in the Progressive Era,' *Journal of American Studies* 46, no. 1 (2012): 7; and Paul Jepson and Robert J. Whittaker, 'Histories of Protected Areas: Internationalisation of Conservationist Values and their Adoption in the Netherlands Indies (Indonesia),' *Environment and History* 8, no. 2 (2002): 138.
23 Ross, *Ecology and Power*, 263–264. In fact, Sarasin had rehearsed these ideas before 1913, through the World Conservation committee he established in 1910, and later took to the League of Nations hoping for accreditation under its auspices. The first meeting included a representative from South Australia. In a pamphlet on the first meeting in September that year, Sarasin based his argument for Indigenous peoples on the (supposed) extinction of the Tasmanian Aborigines. Sarasin, *Weltnaturschutz* (Basel: Emil Birkhaüser, 1911), 22–23.
24 Sarasin chose a whale for his logo. But as a recent essay on 'the whale' indicates, his selection points to the ways in which Indigenous peoples and knowledges are marginalised by the kinds of imagery associated more commonly with 'animal' rights. See Jonathan Goldberg-Hiller, 'W is for Whale,' in *An Anti-Imperial Bestiary for our Times*, ed. Antoinette Burton and Renisa Mawani (Durham, NC: Duke University Press, 2020), 198–202.
25 For an analysis of the uses of concept in the Australian reform context, see Silverstein, *Governing Natives*, ch 2.
26 On forest management, see Lugard, *The Dual Mandate*, 109, quoted in Tobias J. Lanz, 'The Origins, Development and Legacy of Scientific Forestry in Cameroon,' *Environment and History* 6, no. 1 (2000): 99–120. And on the interpolation of wildlife, nature, and resource management in German Africa, see Bernard Gissibli, 'German Colonialism and the Beginnings of International Wildlife Preservation in Africa,' *GHI Bulletin Supplement* 3 (2006): 121–143.
27 Susan Pedersen, 'Settler Colonialism at the Bar of the League of Nations,' in *Settler Colonialism in the Twentieth Century*, ed. Caroline Elkins and Susan Pedersen (New York: Routledge, 2005), 113–134; and Amanda Behm, *Imperial History and the Global Politics of Exclusion: Britain, 1880–1940* (London: Palgrave Macmillan, 2018).
28 James Heartfield, *The British and Foreign Anti-Slavery Society, 1838–1956: A History* (London: Hurst and Company, 2016); and Kevin Grant, *A Civilized Savagery: Britain and the New Slaveries in Africa, 1884–1926* (London: Routledge, 2004). See also Fiona Paisley, 'Introduction,' *History Compass: Special Issue on Anti-Slavery and Settler Colonialism in World History* 15, no. 5 (2017) https://doi.org/10.1111/hic3.12336.
29 Amalia Ribi Forclaz, *Humanitarian Imperialism: The Politics of Anti-Slavery Activism, 1880–1940* (Oxford: Oxford University Press, 2015).
30 Mrinalini Sinha, 'Whatever Happened to the Third British Empire? Empire, Nation, Redux,' in *Writing Imperial Histories*, ed. Andrew S. Thompson (Manchester: Manchester University Press, 2013), 168–187; Behm, *Imperial History*, ch7; and Marilyn Lake and Henry Reynolds, *Drawing the Global Colour Line: White Men's Countries and the Question of Racial Equality* (Melbourne: Melbourne University Press, 2008).
31 Heartfield, *The British and Foreign*.
32 Paisley, 'Applied Anthropology'.
33 Fiona Paisley, 'Federalising the Aborigines? Constitutional Reform in the late 1920s,' *Australian Historical Studies* 29, no. 111 (1998): 248–266.
34 Richard Grove, *Green Imperialism: Colonial Expansion, Tropical Island Edens and the Origins of Environmentalism, 1600–1860* (Cambridge: Cambridge University Press, 1995). See also William Cronin, *Changes in the Land: Indians, Colonists, and the Ecology of New England* (New York: Hill and Wang, 1983/1992); and Richard White, *The Middle Ground: Indians, Empires, and Republics in the Great Lakes Region, 1650–1815* (Cambridge: Cambridge University Press, 1994, first published 1991).

35 On early conservation as hunting culture, see Marc Cioc, *The Game of Conservation: International Treaties to Protect the World's Migratory Animals* (Athens: Ohio University Press, 2009); and John M. MacKenzie, *The Empire of Nature: Hunting, Conservation and British Imperialism* (Manchester: Manchester University Press, 1988).
36 Jepson and Whittaker, 'Histories of Protected Areas'; MacKenzie ed., *Imperialism and the Natural World*.
37 Claire Brennan, '"An Africa on Your Front Doorstep": The Development of an Australian Safari,' *Journal of Australian Studies* 39, no. 3 (2015): 396–410. And on 'nature' in imperial youth cultures see Kristine Alexander, *Guiding Modern Girls: Girlhood, Empire, and Internationalism in the 1920s and 1930s* (Vancouver: UBC Press, 2017), ch. 4; Fiona Paisley, 'Childhood and Race: Growing up in the Empire,' in *Gender and Empire*, ed. Philippa Levine (Oxford; Oxford University Press, 2004), 240–259; and J.A. Mangan and James Walvin, eds., *Manliness and Morality: Middle-class Masculinity in Britain and America, 1800–1940* (Manchester: Manchester University Press, 1987).
38 Ella Shohat, 'Imagining Terra Incognita: The Disciplinary Gaze of Empire,' *Public Culture* 3, no. 2 (1991): 41–70; MacKenzie, 'The Persistence of Empire in Metropolitan Culture' in *The New Imperial Histories Reader*, ed. S. Howe (London: Routledge, 2010), 273–283; and William Beinart and Peter Coates, *Environment and History: The Taming of Nature in the USA and South Africa* (London: Routledge, 1995), for example, 80–81.
39 Bill Schwarz, *The White Man's World* (Oxford: Oxford University Press, 2011), ch 4; and David K. Prendergast and William M. Adams, 'Colonial Wildlife Conservation and the Origins of the Society for the Preservation of the Wild Fauna of the Empire (1903–1914),' *Oryx* 37, no. 2 (2003): 251–260.
40 Griffiths, *Ecology and Empire*; and David Pepper, *Modern Environmentalism: An Introduction* (London: Routledge, 1996).
41 Prue Ahrens, Lamont Lindstrom and Fiona Paisley, *Across the World with the Johnsons: Visual Culture and American Empire in the Twentieth Century* (Burlington: Ashgate, 2013).
42 Tim Bonyhady, *The Colonial Earth* (Melbourne: The Miegunyah Press, 2000), 144. And see Geoffrey Bolton, *Spoils and Spoilers: A History of Australians Shaping their Environment* (Sydney: Allen and Unwin, 1981/1992).
43 Grant, *A Civilised Savagery*, chs 3 and 4.
44 For example, Jane Lydon 'The Bloody Skirt of Settlement: Arthur Vogan and Anti-Slavery in 1890s Australia', *Australian Historical Studies* 45, no. 1 (2014): 46–70.
45 Rabindranath Tagore, *Nationalism* (London: Macmillan and Co., 1917), 89. On the cross-national anti-imperial politics to which Tagore contributed, see Elleke Boehmer, *Empire, The National, and the Postcolonial 1890–1920: Resistance in Interaction* (Oxford: Oxford University Press, 2002). And on anticolonialism more broadly see Priyamvada Gopal, *Insurgent Empire: Anticolonial Resistance and British Dissent* (London: Verso, 2019); and Adom Getachew, *Worldmaking After Empire: The Rise and Fall of Self-Determination* (Princeton, NJ: Princeton University Press, 2019).
46 Ian Harmstorf, *Basedow, Herbert (1881–1933), Australian Dictionary of Biography*, vol. 7 (Melbourne: Melbourne University Press, 1979), 202–203.
47 Fritz Sarasin, *About a Happy Life* (Basel: AG Frobenius, 1941), and 'Obituary for Paul Sarasin', Newspaper Clipping, State Archive of Switzerland, Schaffhausen.
48 'Outrages by the Blacks', *The Northern Territory Times*, 4 October 1884, 2.
49 Quoted in Martin Thomas, *The Many Worlds of RH Mathews: In Search of an Australian Anthropologist* (Sydney: Allen and Unwin, 2012), 227–228.
50 Antoinette Burton and Renisa Mawani, 'Introduction: Animals, Disruptive Imperial Histories, and the Bestiary Form,' in *Animalia*, ed. Burton and Mawani, 9. See also Ruth Mayer, 'Of Ape-Men and Man-Apes,' in *Artificial Africas: Colonial Images in the Times of Globalization* (Hanover: University Press of New England, 2002), 48–75; and C. Philo and C. Wilbert, eds., *Animal Spaces, Beastly Places: New Geographies of Human-Animal Relations* (London: Routledge, 2000).

51 'British Member Asks League to Save Gorillas,' 13 November 1928; and 'Darwin at Geneva,' 20 November 1928. Newsclippings. 6A/9246/9246, Problems in Connection with Conservation of a Mandate. Mandates: General. R2346 Registry Files 1929–1932, Series 5196. League of Nations Archives, Geneva.
52 Matthew Fitzpatrick, 'Indigenous Australians and German Anthropology in the Era of "Decolonisation",' *The Historical Journal* 63, no. 3 (2020): 686–709; and Andrew Zimmerman, 'Adventures in the Skin Trade: German Anthropology and Colonial Corporeality,' in *Worldly Provincialism: German Anthropology in the Age of Empire*, ed. H. Glenn Penny and Matti Bunzl (Ann Arbor: The University of Michigan Press, 2003), 156–177. On living exhibits in museums and zoos, worlds fairs and sideshows, including Indigenous Australians, see, for example, Rosalind Poignant, *Professional Savages: Captive Lives and Western Spectacle* (New Haven, CT: Yale University Press, 2014). And on the importance of visual evidence to the creation of sentiment in humanitarian campaigns, see Jane Lydon, *Photography, Humanitarianism, Empire* (London: Bloomsbury, 2016).
53 Roth's findings echoed public outcry over previous decades. See Amanda Nettelbeck, '"Keeping the Magistrates Straight": Magistrates and Aboriginal "Management" on Australia's North-West Frontiers, 1883–1905,' *Aboriginal History* 38 (2014): 19–37.
54 Margaret Beattie Bogue, 'To Save the Fish: Canada, the United States, the Great Lakes, and the Joint Commission of 1892,' *The Journal of American History* 79, no. 4 (1993): 1429–1454; Forest L. Grieves, 'Leviathan, the International Whaling Commission and Conservation as Environmental Aspects of International Law,' *The Western Political Quarterly* 25, no. 4 (1972), 711–725; and Charles S. Campbell, Jr, 'The Anglo-American Crisis in the Bering Sea, 1890–1891,' *The Mississippi Valley Historical Review* 48, no. 3 (1961): 393–414.
55 Paul Sarasin, *About the Tasks of World Conservation. Exposé Read at the Conference of All Delegates of International Conservation, Bern, 18 November 1913* (Basel: Emil Birkhaüser, 1913), 1–32. Swiss Archives, Berne. In the following references to this document, quotations are taken from throughout its 32 pages, particularly 28–32, and are not individually indicated.
56 William Cronin, *Nature's Metropolis: Chicago and the Great West* (New York: W.W. Norton and Co., 1991), 217–218.
57 Ann Curthoys, 'Genocide in Tasmania: The History of an Idea,' in *Empire, Colony, Genocide: Conquest, Occupation, and Subaltern Resistance in World History*, ed. A. Dirk Moses (New York: Berghahn Books, 2010), 229–252.
58 'Dr Roth's Investigations: Prosecution of Aboriginals,' *West Australian*, 14 February 1905, 2–3, quoted in Nettelbeck, '"Keeping the Magistrates Straight"', 33.
59 Proceedings of the Berne Conference for the International Protection of Nature, 19 November 1913, Document No 9, Political Dept, 24 e 7, Swiss Archives, Berne; and 'Explanatory Memo: Accompanying the Invitation of the Swiss Federal Council to the Conference on the 17 November 1913,' Political Dept, 24 e 7, Swiss Archives, Berne.
60 Andrew Spaull, 'McBride, Sir Peter (1967–1923), *Australian Dictionary of Biography*, vol. 10 (Melbourne: Melbourne University Press, 1986), 205–206. Bolton, *Spoils and Spoilers*, 97–107; Libby Robin, 'Nature Conservation as a National Concern: The Role of the Australian Academy of Science,' *Historical Records of Australian Science* 10, no. 1 (1994): 1–24; Derek Whitelock, *Conquest to Conservation: History of Human Impact on the South Australian Environment* (Adelaide: Wakefield Press, 1985); Sarah Mirams, '"For their Moral Health": James Barrett, Urban Progressive Ideas and National Park Reservation in Victoria,' *Australian Historical Studies* 33, no. 120 (2002): 249–266; Libby Robin, 'Nationalising Nature: Wattle Days in Australia,' *Journal of Australian Studies* 73 (2002): 13–26.
61 Bonyhady, *The Colonial Earth*, 1–13.
62 Heather Goodall, *Invasion to Embassy: Land in Aboriginal Politics in New South Wales, 1770–1972* (St Leonards: Allen and Unwin, 1996), 157; see also John Maynard, 'Vision,

Voice and Influence: The Rise of the Australian Aboriginal Progressive Association,' *Australian Historical Studies* 34, no. 121 (2003): 91–105.
63. Jane Lydon, *Eye Contact: Photographing Indigenous Australians*, (Durham, NC: Duke University Press, 2005), ch 3. Lydon examines Aboriginal agency in such exchanges.
64. See, for example, Penny Van Toorn, *Writing Never Arrives Naked: Early Aboriginal Cultures of Writing in Australia* (Canberra: Aboriginal Studies Press, 2006).
65. Bain Attwood and Andrew Markus, *Thinking Black: William Cooper and the Australian Aborigines' League* (Canberra: Aboriginal Studies Press, 2004); Bain Attwood, *Rights for Aborigines* (Sydney: Allen and Unwin, 2003), ch 3; and McGregor, *Imagined Destinies*, 249ff.
66. 'Proceedings of the Berne Conference.' See also P.N. Hutton, 'The Importance of Being Ernst: The Forgotten First Australian Official Overseas Representative Outside the British Empire,' MS 9523, National Library of Australia, Canberra.
67. 'Alleged Ill-Treatment of Australian Natives,' *The Times*, 11 January 1907, 3.
68. Lydon, *Photography, Humanitarianism, Empire*, 98. Klaatsch commented also in support of the findings of his 'friend', the 1904 Royal Commissioner Walter Roth. See Fitzpatrick, 'Indigenous Australians', 695.
69. Herman Klaatsch, 'Some Notes on Scientific Travel Amongst the Black Population of Tropical Australia in 1904, 1905, 1906.' Paper read at the Adelaide Meeting of the Australasian Association for the Advancement of Science, held January 1907', National Library of Australia. The English-language version of his paper was quoted in *The Times*, but only the German version contained the photograph reproduced by Sarasin. Herman Klaatsch, 'Schlussbericht uber meine Reise nach Australian in den Jahren 1904–1907,' *Zeitschrift fur Ethnologie* 39 (1907): 634–690.
70. 'The Aborigines of Australia' were central to late nineteenth-century debates about human evolution that featured in transnational networks. See Thomas, *The Many Worlds*, 243–244.
71. Herman Klaatsch, *The Evolution and Progress of Mankind* (London: T. Fisher Unwin Ltd, 1913). His findings were destined to be widely criticised in anthropological circles: McGregor, *Imagined Destinies*, 42–43.
72. Klaatsch also spoke of police routinely bringing in Aboriginal women as supposed witnesses when their real use was well-known. 'Dr Klaatsch on the Blacks,' *The Daily News* (Perth), 11 January 1907, 5.
73. Klaatsch, 'Schlussbericht uber meiner Reise,' 665.
74. Klaatsch, *The Evolution and Progress of Mankind*, 145. Brigitte Stehik, 'Herman Klaatsch and the Tiwi, 1906,' *Aboriginal History* 10, no. 1 (1986): 59–77.
75. 'Indigenous Ancestor Remains Returned to Queensland,' *ABC News*, 2 May 2017. https://www.abc.net.au/news/2017-05-02/indigenous-ancestor-remains-returned-to-queensland/8479888.
76. Ross, *Ecology and Power*, 263–264.
77. Ravi de Costa, *A Higher Authority: Indigenous Transnationalism and Australia* (Sydney: UNSW Press, 2006); and Timothy Rowse, 'Indigenous Redemption of Liberal Universalism,' *Modern Intellectual History* 12, no. 3 (2015): 579–603.
78. 'Complaint of the Six Nations Indians against the Government of Canada,' R612, 28075/1923, League of Nations Archives, Geneva.
79. Pearl Gibbs, General Secretary, Aborigines Progressive Association to President, League of Nations, 4 July 1938, 'Situation of Aborigines in Australia', Political Division, 1/34895/1 34895, League of Nations Archives, Geneva. See also Rachel Standfield, Ray Peckham, and John Nolan, 'Aunty Pearl Gibbs: Leading for Aboriginal Rights,' in *Diversity in Leadership: Australian Women, Past and Present*, ed. Joy Damousi et al. (Canberra: ANU Press, 2014), 53–68.
80. Sarah Irving, 'Governing Nature: The Problem of Northern Australia', *Australian Historical Studies* 45, no. 3 (2014): 388–406.

81 'Call for Help from Australia,' *Der Bund*, 30 June 1921. Transcript, 3. Buser Papers. HI.BW-N5656.5a. Australian Institute of Aboriginal and Torres Strait Islander Studies, Canberra. Thanks to Christine Winter for the translation.
82 *Der Bund*, 30 June 1921, Transcript, 4.
83 *Der Bund*, 30 June 1921, Transcript, 1. See also Fiona Paisley, *Loving Protection? Australian Feminism and Aboriginal Women's Rights, 1919–1939* (Melbourne: Melbourne University Press, 2000), ch 4.
84 Paisley, *The Lone Protestor*, 59.
85 *Der Bund*, 30 June 1921, Transcript, 2.
86 *Der Bund*, 30 June 1921, Transcript, 1 and 5.
87 *Der Bunde* 1 July 1921, Transcript, 7–8. In Australia, the concept of preservation by segregation continued to dominate in the 1930s. McGregor, *Imagined Destinies*, ch 6.
88 For example, Yohan Ariffin, 'On the Scope and Limits of Green Imperialism,' *Peace Review* 22, no. 4 (2010): 373–381.
89 Burton, 'Animals, Disruptive Imperial Histories,' 1–19.
90 Fiona Paisley, 'Race Hysteria, Darwin 1938' *Australian Feminist Studies* 16, no. 34 (2001): 43–60; and Mark Finnane and Fiona Paisley, 'Policing on a Colonial Frontier: the "Borroloola Case" and the Limits of Rule of Law in 1930s Australia,' *Law and History* 28, no. 1 (2010): 141–171.
91 Fiona Paisley, 'An Echo of Black Slavery: Emancipation, Forced Labour and Australia in 1933,' *Australian Historical Studies* 45, no. 1 (2014): 103–125.
92 Markus, *Governing Savages* (Sydney: Allen and Unwin, 1990), insert opposite page 135.
93 Geoffrey Gray, *A Cautious Silence: The Politics of Australian Anthropology* (Canberra: Aboriginal Studies Press, 2007), ch. 10.
94 John M. MacKenzie, 'A Meditation on Environmental History,' in *The Nature of Empires and the Empires of Nature: Indigenous Peoples and the Great Lakes Environment*, ed. Karl S. Hele (Waterloo, Can.: Wilfred Laurier University Press, 2013), 8.
95 Tom Griffiths, 'Introduction: Ecology and Empire, Towards an Australian History of the World,' in *Ecology and Empire*, ed. Griffiths and Robin, 1–16.
96 Deborah Bird Rose, *Nourishing Terrains: Aboriginal Australian Views of Landscape and Wilderness* (Canberra: Australian Heritage Commission, 1996).
97 Jon Altman and Dan Tout, 'Again and Again: Settler-Colonial Extractivism and the Juukan Gorge Inquiry's Interim Report,' *Arena Online*, 17 December 2020, https://arena.org.au/again-and-again/.

Bibliography

Adas, Michael. *Machines as the Measure of Men: Science, Technology, and Ideologies of Western Dominance*. Ithaca, NY: Cornell University Press, 1989.
Ahrens, Prue, Lamont Lindstrom, and Fiona Paisley. *Across the World with the Johnsons: Visual Culture and American Empire in the Twentieth Century*. Burlington: Ashgate, 2013.
Alexander, Kristine. *Guiding Modern Girls: Girlhood, Empire, and Internationalism in the 1920s and 1930s*. Vancouver: UBC Press, 2017.
'Alleged Ill-Treatment of Australian Natives.' *The Times*, 11 January 1907.
Allen, Garland E. '"Culling the Herd": Eugenics and the Conservation Movement in the United States, 1900–1940.' *Journal of the History of Biology* 46 (2013): 31–72.
Altman, Jon, and Dan Tout. 'Again and Again: Settler-Colonial Extractivism and the Juukan Gorge Inquiry's Interim Report.' *Arena Online*, 17 December 2020. https://arena.org.au/again-and-again/.
Ariffin, Yohan. 'On the Scope and Limits of Green Imperialism.' *Peace Review* 22, no. 4 (2010): 373–381.
Attwood, Bain. *Rights for Aborigines*. Sydney: Allen and Unwin, 2003.

Attwood, Bain, and Andrew Markus. *Thinking Black: William Cooper and the Australian Aborigines' League*. Canberra: Aboriginal Studies Press, 2004.

Bashford, Alison. 'Nation, Empire, Globe: The Spaces of Population in the Interwar Years.' *Studies in Society and History* 49, no. 1 (2007): 170–201.

Bashford, Alison. 'Internationalism, Cosmopolitanism, and Eugenics.' In *The History of Eugenics*, edited by Alison Bashford and Philippa Levine, 154–172. Oxford: Oxford University Press, 2010.

Behm, Amanda. *Imperial History and the Global Politics of Exclusion: Britain, 1880–1940*. London: Palgrave Macmillan, 2018.

Beinart, William, and Peter Coates. *Environment and History: The Taming of Nature in the USA and South Africa*. London: Routledge, 1995.

Beinart, William, and Lottie Hughes, eds. *Environment and Empire*. Oxford: Oxford University Press, 2007.

Belich, James. *Replenishing the Earth: The Settler Revolution and the Rise of the Anglo-World 1793–1939*. Oxford: Oxford University Press, 2009.

Boehmer, Elleke. *Empire, The National, and the Postcolonial 1890–1920: Resistance in Interaction*. Oxford: Oxford University Press, 2002.

Bogue, Margaret Beattie. 'To Save the Fish: Canada, the United States, the Great Lakes, and the Joint Commission of 1892.' *The Journal of American History* 79, no. 4 (1993): 1429–1454.

Bolton, Geoffrey. *Spoils and Spoilers: A History of Australians Shaping their Environment*. Sydney: Allen and Unwin, 1981/1992.

Bonyhady, Tim. *The Colonial Earth*. Melbourne: The Miegunyah Press, 2000.

Brantlinger, Patrick. *Dark Vanishings: Discourse on the Primitive Races, 1800–1930*. Ithaca, NY: Cornell University Press, 2003.

Brennan, Claire. '"An Africa on Your Front Doorstep": The Development of an Australian Safari.' *Journal of Australian Studies* 39, no. 3 (2015): 396–410.

'British Member Asks League to Save Gorillas.' 13 November 1928. Newsclippings. 6A/9246/9246, Problems in Connection with Conservation of a Mandate. Mandates: General. R2346 Registry Files 1929–1932, Series 5196. League of Nations Archives, Geneva.

Burton, Antoinette. *The Trouble with Empire: Challenges to Modern Imperialism*. Oxford: Oxford University Press, 2015.

Burton, Antoinette, and Tony Ballantyne. 'Remaking the World.' In *A World Connecting: 1870–1945*, edited by Emily Rosenberg, 348–390. Cambridge, Mass.: Harvard University Press, 2012.

Burton, Antoinette, and Renisa Mawani. 'Introduction: Animals, Disruptive Imperial Histories, and the Bestiary Form.' In *Animalia*, edited by Antoinette Burton and Renisa Mawani, 1–19. Durham: Duke University Press, 2020.

'Call for Help from Australia.' *Der Bund*, 30 June 1921. Transcript, 3. Buser Papers. HI.BW-N5656.5a. Australian Institute of Aboriginal and Torres Strait Islander Studies, Canberra.

Campbell, Charles S., Jr. 'The Ango-American Crisis in the Bering Sea, 1890–1891.' *The Mississippi Valley Historical Review* 48, no. 3 (1961): 393–414.

Carey, Jane, and Jane Lydon, eds. *Indigenous Networks: Mobility, Connections and Exchange*. London: Routledge, 2014.

Christie, Nancy J. 'Environment and Race: Geography's Search for a Darwinian Synthesis.' In *Darwin's Laboratory: Evolutionary Theory and Natural History in the Pacific*, edited by R. MacLeod and Philip F. Rehbock, 42–73. Honolulu: University of Hawai'i Press, 1994.

Cioc, Marc. *The Game of Conservation: International Treaties to Protect the World's Migratory Animals*. Athens: Ohio University Press, 2009.

'Complaint of the Six Nations Indians against the Government of Canada' R612, 28075/1923, League of Nations Archives, Geneva.

Conrad, Sebastian, and Dominic Sachsenmaier. *Competing Visions of World Order: Global Moments and Movements 1880s to 1930s*. New York: Palgrave Macmillan, 2007.

Crawford, Neta C. *Argument and Change in World Politics: Ethics, Decolonization and Humanitarian Intervention.* Cambridge: Cambridge University Press, 2004.
Cronin, William. *Changes in the Land: Indians, Colonists, and the Ecology of New England.* New York: Hill and Wang, 1983/1992.
Cronin, William. *Nature's Metropolis: Chicago and the Great West.* New York: W.W. Norton and Co., 1991.
Crook, Martin, and Damien Short. 'Developmentalism and the Genocide-Ecocide Nexus.' *Journal of Genocide Research.* December 23, no. 2 (Dec 2020): 162–188.
Crosby, Alfred W. *Ecological Imperialism: The Biological Expansion of Europe 900–1900.* Cambridge: Cambridge University Press, 2004.
Curthoys, Ann. 'Genocide in Tasmania: The History of an Idea.' In *Empire, Colony, Genocide: Conquest, Occupation, and Subaltern Resistance in World History,* edited by A. Dirk Moses, 229–252. New York: Berghahn Books, 2010.
Curthoys, Ann, and Marilyn Lake. 'Introduction.' In *Connected Worlds: History in Transnational Perspective,* edited by Ann Curthoys and Marilyn Lake, 5–20. Canberra: ANU Press, 2005.
'Darwin at Geneva.' 20 November 1928. Newsclippings. 6A/9246/9246, Problems in Connection with Conservation of a Mandate. Mandates: General. R2346 Registry Files 1929–1932, Series 5196. League of Nations Archives, Geneva.
de Costa, Ravi. *A Higher Authority: Indigenous Transnationalism and Australia.* Sydney: UNSW Press, 2006.
'Dr Klaatsch on the Blacks.' *The Daily News* (Perth), 11 January 1907.
'Dr Roth's Investigations: Prosecution of Aboriginals.' *West Australian,* 14 February 1905.
Escobar, Arturo. 'The Problem of Nature Revisited: History and Anthropology.' *Current Anthropology* 39, no. 3 (1998): 385–386.
'Explanatory Memo: Accompanying the Invitation of the Swiss Federal Council to the Conference on the 17 November 1913.' Political Dept, 24 e 7, Swiss Archives, Berne.
Finnane, Mark, and Fiona Paisley. 'Policing on a Colonial Frontier: the "Borroloola Case" and the Limits of Rule of Law in 1930s Australia.' *Law and History* 28, no. 1 (2010): 141–171.
Fitzpatrick, Matthew. 'Indigenous Australians and German Anthropology in the Era of "Decolonisation".' *The Historical Journal* 63, no. 3 (2020): 686–709.
Forclaz, Amalia Ribi. *Humanitarian Imperialism: The Politics of Anti-Slavery Activism, 1880–1940.* Oxford: Oxford University Press, 2015.
Getachew, Adom. *Worldmaking After Empire: The Rise and Fall of Self-Determination.* Princeton: Princeton University Press, 2019.
Gibbs, Pearl. General Secretary, Aborigines Progressive Association to President, League of Nations, 4 July 1938. 'Situation of Aborigines in Australia.' Political Division, 1/34895/1 34895, League of Nations Archives, Geneva.
Gissibli, Bernard. 'German Colonialism and the Beginnings of International Wildlife Preservation in Africa.' *GHI Bulletin Supplement* 3 (2006): 121–143.
Goldberg-Hiller, Jonathan. 'W is for Whale.' In *An Anti-Imperial Bestiary for our Times,* edited by Antoinette Burton and Renisa Mawani, 198–202. Durham: Duke University Press, 2020.
Goodall, Heather. *Invasion to Embassy: Land in Aboriginal Politics in New South Wales, 1770–1972.* St Leonards: Allen and Unwin, 1996.
Gopal, Priyamvada. *Insurgent Empire: Anticolonial Resistance and British Dissent.* London: Verso, 2019.
Grant, Kevin. *A Civilized Savagery: Britain and the New Slaveries in Africa, 1884–1926.* London: Routledge, 2004.
Gray, Geoffrey. *A Cautious Silence: The Politics of Australian Anthropology.* Canberra: Aboriginal Studies Press, 2007.
Grieves, Forest L. 'Leviathan, the International Whaling Commission and Conservation as Environmental Aspects of International Law.' *The Western Political Quarterly* 25, no. 4 (1972): 711–725.

Griffiths, Tom. 'Introduction: Ecology and Empire, Towards an Australian History of the World.' In *Ecology and Empire: Environmental History of Settler Societies*, edited by Griffiths and Robin, 1–16. Melbourne, Melbourne University Press, 1997.

Griffiths, Tom, and Libby Robin eds. *Ecology and Empire: Environmental History of Settler Societies*. Melbourne: Melbourne University Press, 1997.

Grove, Richard. *Green Imperialism: Colonial Expansion, Tropical Island Edens and the Origins of Environmentalism, 1600–1860*. Cambridge: Cambridge University Press, 1995.

Harmstorf, Ian. 'Basedow, Herbert (1881–1933).' In *Australian Dictionary of Biography* Vol. 7, 202–203. Melbourne: Melbourne University Press, 1979.

Heartfield, James. *The British and Foreign Anti-Slavery Society, 1838–1956: A History*. London: Hurst and Company, 2016.

Hodge, Joseph M. 'Colonial Experts, Developmental and Environmental Doctrines, and the Legacies of Late British Colonialism.' In *Cultivating the Colonies: Colonial States and their Environmental Legacies*, edited by Christina Folke Ax et al., 315–341. Athens: Ohio University Press, 2011.

Hutton, P.N. 'The Importance of Being Ernst: The Forgotten First Australian Official Overseas Representative Outside the British Empire.' MS 9523, National Library of Australia, Canberra.

'Indigenous Ancestor Remains Returned to Queensland.' *ABC News*, 2 May 2017. https://www.abc.net.au/news/2017-05-02/indigenous-ancestor-remains-returned-to-queensland/8479888.

Irving, Sarah, 'Governing Nature: The Problem of Northern Australia', *Australian Historical Studies* 45, no. 3 (2014): 388–406.

Jepson, Paul, and Robert J Whittaker. 'Histories of Protected Areas: Internationalisation of Conservationist Values and their Adoption in the Netherlands Indies (Indonesia).' *Environment and History* 8, no. 2 (2002): 129–172.

Karskens, Grace. *The People of the River: Lost Worlds of Early Australia*. Sydney: Allen and Unwin, 2020.

Klaatsch, Herman. 'Schlussbericht uber meine Reise nach Australien in den Jahren 1904–1907.' *Zeitschrift fur Ethnologie* 39 (1907): 634–690.

Klaatsch, Herman. 'Some Notes on Scientific Travel Amongst the Black Population of Tropical Australia in 1904, 1905, 1906.' Paper read at the Adelaide Meeting of the Australasian Association for the Advancement of Science, held January 1907, National Library of Australia.

Klaatsch, Herman. *The Evolution and Progress of Mankind*. London: T. Fisher Unwin Ltd, 1913.

Lake, Marilyn. 'Indigenous Progressivism Calls Settler Colonialism to Account.' In *Progressive New World: How Settler Colonialism and Transpacific Exchange Shaped American Reform*, edited by Marilyn Lake, 224–249. Cambridge, Mass.: Harvard University Press, 2019.

Lake, Marilyn, and Henry Reynolds. *Drawing the Global Colour Line: White Men's Countries and the Question of Racial Equality*. Melbourne: Melbourne University Press, 2008.

Lanz, Tobias J. 'The Origins, Development and Legacy of Scientific Forestry in Cameroon.' *Environment and History* 6, no. 1 (2000): 99–120.

Levine, Philippa. 'Anthropology, Colonialism and Eugenics.' In *The Oxford Handbook of the History of Eugenics*, edited by Alison Bashford and Philippa Levine, 43–61. Oxford: Oxford University Press, 2010.

Lydon, Jane. *Eye Contact: Photographing Indigenous Australians*. Durham, Duke University Press, 2005.

Lydon, Jane. *Photography, Humanitarianism, Empire*. London: Bloomsbury, 2016.

Lydon, Jane. 'The Bloody Skirt of Settlement: Arthur Vogan and Anti-Slavery in 1890s Australia', *Australian Historical Studies* 45, no. 1 (2014): 46–70.

MacKenzie, John M. *The Partition of Africa 1880–1900 and European Imperialism in the Nineteenth Century*. London: Routledge, 1983.

MacKenzie, John M. *The Empire of Nature: Hunting, Conservation and British Imperialism.* Manchester: Manchester University Press, 1988.
MacKenzie, John M., ed. *Imperialism and the Natural World.* Manchester: Manchester University Press, 1990.
MacKenzie, John M. 'The Persistence of Empire in Metropolitan Culture.' In *The New Imperial Histories Reader*, edited by S. Howe, 273–283. London: Routledge, 2010.
MacKenzie, John M. 'A Meditation on Environmental History.' In *The Nature of Empires and the Empires of Nature: Indigenous Peoples and the Great Lakes Environment*, edited by Karl S. Hele, 1–21. Waterloo, ON: Wilfred Laurier University Press, 2013.
Mangan, J.A., and James Walvin, eds. *Manliness and Morality: Middle-class Masculinity in Britain and America, 1800–1940.* Manchester: Manchester University Press, 1987.
Markus, Andrew. *Governing Savages.* Sydney: Allen and Unwin, 1990.
Mayer, Ruth. 'Of Ape-Men and Man-Apes.' In *Artificial Africas: Colonial Images in the Times of Globalization*, 48–75. Hanover: University Press of New England, 2002.
Maynard, John. 'Vision, Voice and Influence: The Rise of the Australian Aboriginal Progressive Association.' *Australian Historical Studies* 34, no. 121 (2003): 91–105.
McGrath, Ann. *Illicit Love: Interracial Sex and Marriage in the United States and Australia.* Lincoln: University of Nebraska Press, 2015.
McGregor, Russell. *Imagined Destinies: Aboriginal Australians and the Doomed Race Theory, 1880–1939.* Melbourne: Melbourne University Press, 1997.
Mirams, Sarah. '"For their Moral Health": James Barrett, Urban Progressive Ideas and National Park Reservation in Victoria.' *Australian Historical Studies* 33, no. 120 (2002): 249–266.
Morefield, Jeanne. *Covenants without Swords: Idealist Liberalism and the Spirit of Empire.* Princeton, NJ: Princeton University Press, 2005.
Nettelbeck, Amanda. *Indigenous Rights and Colonial Subjecthood: Protection and Reform in the 19th Century British Empire.* Cambridge: Cambridge University Press, 2019.
Nettelbeck, Amanda. '"Keeping the Magistrates Straight": Magistrates and Aboriginal "Management" on Australia's North-West Frontiers, 1883–1905.' *Aboriginal History* 38 (2014): 19–37.
'Obituary for Paul Sarasin.' Newspaper Clipping, State Archive of Switzerland, Schaffhausen.
Olsen, Penny, and Lynette Russell. *Australia's First Naturalists: Indigenous Peoples' Contribution to Early Zoology.* Canberra: NLA Publishing, 2019.
Paisley, Fiona. 'An Echo of Black Slavery: Emancipation, Forced Labour and Australia in 1933.' *Australian Historical Studies* 45, no. 1 (2014): 103–125.
Paisley, Fiona. 'Applied Anthropology and Interwar Internationalism: Felix and Marie Keesing and the (White) Future of the "Native" Pan-Pacific.' *Journal of Pacific History* 50, no. 3 (2015): 304–321.
Paisley, Fiona. 'Childhood and Race: Growing up in the Empire.' In *Gender and Empire*, edited by Philippa Levine, 240–259. Oxford: Oxford University Press, 2004.
Paisley, Fiona. 'Federalising the Aborigines? Constitutional Reform in the late 1920s.' *Australian Historical Studies* 29, no. 111 (1998): 248–266.
Paisley, Fiona. 'Introduction.' *History Compass: Special Issue on Anti-Slavery and Settler Colonialism in World History* 15, no. 5 (2017).
Paisley, Fiona. *Loving Protection? Australian Feminism and Aboriginal Women's Rights, 1919–1939.* Melbourne: Melbourne University Press, 2000.
Paisley, Fiona. 'Race Hysteria, Darwin 1938.' *Australian Feminist Studies* 16, no. 34 (2001): 43–60.
Paisley, Fiona. 'The Italo-Abyssinian Crisis and Australia Settler Colonialism in 1935.' *History Compass: Special Issue on Anti-Slavery and Settler Colonialism in World History* 15, no. 5 (2017).
Paisley, Fiona. *The Lone Protestor: AM Fernando in Australia and Europe.* Canberra: Aboriginal Studies Press, 2012.

Paisley, Fiona, and Kirsty Reid, eds. *Critical Perspectives on Colonialism: Writing the Empire from Below*. London: Routledge, 2014.
Pedersen, Susan. 'Settler Colonialism at the Bar of the League of Nations.' In *Settler Colonialism in the Twentieth Century*, edited by Caroline Elkins and Susan Pedersen, 113–134. New York: Routledge, 2005.
Pepper, David. *Modern Environmentalism: An Introduction*. London: Routledge, 1996.
Philo, C., and C. Wilbert, eds. *Animal Spaces, Beastly Places: New Geographies of Human-Animal Relations*. London: Routledge, 2000.
Poignant, Rosalind. *Professional Savages: Captive Lives and Western Spectacle*. New Haven, CT: Yale University Press, 2014.
Prendergast, David K., and William M. Adams. 'Colonial Wildlife Conservation and the Origins of the Society for the Preservation of the Wild Fauna of the Empire (1903–1914).' *Oryx* 37, no. 2 (2003): 251–260.
Proceedings of the Berne Conference for the International Protection of Nature, 19 November 1913, Document No 9, Political Dept, 24 e 7, Swiss Archives, Berne.
Pybus, Cassandra. *Truganini: Journey through the Apocalypse*. Sydney: Allen and Unwin, 2020.
Rich, Paul B. *Race and Empire in British Politics*. Cambridge: Cambridge University Press 1986, 1990.
Robin, Libby. 'Nature Conservation as a National Concern: The Role of the Australian Academy of Science.' *Historical Records of Australian Science* 10, no. 1 (1994): 1–24.
Robin, Libby. 'Nationalising Nature: Wattle Days in Australia.' *Journal of Australian Studies* 73 (2002): 13–26.
Rose, Deborah Bird. *Nourishing Terrains: Aboriginal Australian Views of Landscape and Wilderness*. Canberra: Australian Heritage Commission, 1996.
Ross, Corey. *Ecology and Power in the Age of Empire: Europe and the Transformation of the Tropical World*. Oxford: Oxford University Press, 2017.
Rowse, Tim. *Indigenous and Other Australians since 1901*. Sydney: New South, 2017.
Rowse, Tim. 'Indigenous Heterogeneity.' *Australian Historical Studies* 45, no. 3 (2014): 297–310.
Rowse, Tim. 'Indigenous Redemption of Liberal Universalism.' *Modern Intellectual History* 12, no. 3 (2015): 579–603.
Russell, Lynette. 'Indigenous Knowledge and Archives: Accessing Hidden History and Understandings.' *Australian Academic and Research Libraries* 36, no. 2 (2005): 161–171.
Sarasin, Fritz. *About a Happy Life*. Basel: A.G. Frobenius, 1941.
Sarasin, Paul. *About the Tasks of World Conservation. Exposé read at the conference of all delegates of international conservation, Bern, 18 November 1913*. Basel: Emil Birkhaüser, 1913.
Sarasin, Paul. *Weltnaturschutz*. Basel: Emil Birkhaüser, 1911.
Schwarz, Bill. *The White Man's World*. Oxford: Oxford University Press, 2011.
Shellam, Tiffany. *Meeting the Waylo: Aboriginal Encounters in the Archipelago*. Crawley: UWA Press, 2020.
Shohat, Ella. 'Imagining Terra Incognita: The Disciplinary Gaze of Empire.' *Public Culture* 3, no. 2 (1991): 41–70.
Silverstein, Ben. *Governing Natives: Indirect Rule and Settler Colonialism in Australia's North*. Manchester: Manchester University Press, 2019.
Sinha, Mrinalini. 'Whatever Happened to the Third British Empire? Empire, Nation, Redux.' In *Writing Imperial Histories*, edited by Andrew S. Thompson, 168–187. Manchester: Manchester University Press, 2013.
Sluga, Glenda, and Patricia Clavin, eds. *Internationalisms: A Twentieth-Century History*. Cambridge: Cambridge University Press, 2017.
Spaull, Andrew. 'McBride, Sir Peter (1967–1923).' In *Australian Dictionary of Biography*, Vol. 10, 205–206. Melbourne: Melbourne University Press, 1986.
Spiro, Jonathan Peter. *Defending the Master Race: Conservation, Eugenics, and the Legacy of Madison Grant*. Lebanon: University of Vermont Press, 2008.

Standfield, Rachel, ed. *Indigenous Mobilities: Across and Beyond the Antipodes*. Canberra: ANU Press, 2018.

Standfield, Rachel, Ray Peckham, and John Nolan. 'Aunty Pearl Gibbs: Leading for Aboriginal Rights.' In *Diversity in Leadership: Australian Women, Past and Present*, edited by Joy Damousi et al., 53–68. Canberra: ANU Press, 2014.

Stehik, Brigitte. 'Herman Klaatsch and the Tiwi, 1906.' *Aboriginal History* 10, no. 1 (1986): 59–77.

Stocking, George, Jr. *Victorian Anthropology*. New York: The Free Press, 1987.

Tagore, Rabindranath. *Nationalism*. London: Macmillan and Co., 1917.

Thomas, Martin. *The Many Worlds of RH Mathews: In Search of an Australian Anthropologist*. Sydney: Allen and Unwin, 2012.

Toorn, Penny Van. *Writing Never Arrives Naked: Early Aboriginal Cultures of Writing in Australia*. Canberra: Aboriginal Studies Press, 2006.

Twomey, Christine. 'Protecting Slaves and Aborigines: The Legacies of European Colonialism in the British Empire.' *Pacific Historical Review* 87, no. 1 (2018): 10–29.

Tyrrell, Ian. 'America's National Parks: The Transnational Creation of National Space in the Progressive Era.' *Journal of American Studies* 46, no. 1 (2012): 1–21.

White, Richard. *The Middle Ground: Indians, Empires, and Republics in the Great Lakes Region, 1650–1815*. Cambridge: Cambridge University Press, 1994, first published 1991.

Whitelock, Derek. *Conquest to Conservation: History of Human Impact on the South Australian Environment*. Adelaide: Wakefield Press, 1985.

Wöbse, Anna Katharina. 'Oil on Troubled Waters?: Environmental Diplomacy in the League of Nations.' *Diplomatic History* 32, no. 4 (2008): 519–537.

Zimmerman, Andrew. 'Adventures in the Skin Trade: German Anthropology and Colonial Corporeality.' In *Worldly Provincialism: German Anthropology in the Age of Empire*, edited by H. Glenn Penny and Matti Bunzl, 156–177. Ann Arbor: The University of Michigan Press, 2003.

PART II

Migrations and mobilities

6
INDIGENOUS GLOBAL HISTORIES AND MODERN HUMAN ORIGINS

Martin Porr

With reference to a review of current knowledge about recent human evolution and history in Asia and Australasia, I want to explore in this chapter how an Indigenous-histories perspective can enhance our understanding of human origins. This endeavour seemingly brings together two fields that are divided by a range of deep and crucial differences. The modern study of human origins is the product of the development of archaeology as a global academic subject. It is deeply intertwined with the dramatic intellectual and socio-economic changes that affected the world from the eighteenth century onwards and gave rise to the modern globalised world.[1] An important part of these changes was the successive recognition of the enormous antiquity of the world and the human species. Human origins studies are the domain of Palaeolithic archaeology and palaeoanthropology, which study the oldest traces of human presence on the planet. They have historical and methodological affiliations with geology and with (human) biology for comparative purposes. The fields are firmly linked to the establishment of biological evolution in the nineteenth century and the recognition of deep connections between human beings and other organisms, especially the great apes.[2] Human origins studies have developed into a truly global field of archaeological research that is to a large extent aimed at elucidating grand narratives of the deep human past. Key areas of investigation are, for example, the origins of the hominin lineage, the origins of the genus *Homo*, the discovery of the first artefacts, the establishment of the time and mechanism of the first human movements out of Africa (Out-of-Africa I), the origin of *Homo sapiens*, and understanding the timing and mechanisms of the dispersal of *Homo sapiens* outside of Africa (Out-of-Africa II). Perhaps more than other fields within archaeology, Palaeolithic archaeology and palaeoanthropology make extensive use of a large number of highly specialised scientific methods from geology, geomorphology, microscopic trace analysis, a wide range of physical dating techniques, and so on. The field of human origins studies reflects the modernist

DOI: 10.4324/9781315181929-8

foundations of archaeology possibly more than other fields in archaeology. It has also remained largely unaffected by more recent critical developments in archaeology that emerged from the so-called processual/post-processual debates from the 1980s onwards.[3]

How can an Indigenous-histories perspective be framed and how can it be productively related to the field of human origins studies? In my understanding, the former can be approached in three interrelated ways. First, an Indigenous-histories perspective can refer to the historical processes that have affected Indigenous people in the past and have contributed to the formation of today's Indigenous groups and identities. In academic terms, such a subject would be addressed by historical and historical-anthropological research approaches. Archaeological methods have also been successfully employed in such circumstances, which all hold much potential for collaborative methodologies and interpretations. Academic approaches to Indigenous histories will most likely also include oral testimonies and discussions. This draws attention to questions of authority and the weighting of different types of sources that participate in the generation of a group's past and its identity. These questions have been discussed within social anthropology extensively. They lead to the second way in which an Indigenous-histories perspective can be understood. Indigenous people everywhere possess their own histories and narratives. Identities are created through stories that refer to recent or more distant pasts. Engagement with these histories continues to be controversial. Anthropological, archaeological, and historical research has often attempted to establish the authenticity of Indigenous narratives based on a Western understanding of history. In some cases, impressive findings have been made along these lines and oral traditions have proved to preserve memories of past events for an astonishingly long time.[4] However, more often, it must be acknowledged that Indigenous historical understanding expresses variable notions of time and temporality. These latter aspects directly relate to the crucial importance of different types of stories in Indigenous worldviews and ontologies.[5] The recognition of the significance of narratives as expressions of ontological difference leads to the third way of approaching an Indigenous-histories perspective. In recent years, many academic fields have undergone significant shifts towards greater reflexivity and an awareness of the dependencies of scientific knowledge production. At least some of these developments are driven by an engagement with Indigenous voices and authors, and ways of knowledge production and communication as well as postcolonial critique.[6] A key element of these critiques is a deep engagement with the political, ontological, and epistemological foundations of scientific knowledge.

In a later section of this paper, I want to elaborate foremost the latter two ways of understanding an Indigenous-histories perspective in relation to the notion of modern human origins. I hope that these explorations will allow for reflection on the ontology and epistemology of human origins research from new and different angles. One key dimension to consider will be the impact of essentialist elements in reconstructions of human origins. The definition and ontology of modern humanity is equally affected by such an orientation as well as the understanding of time and temporal processes. The entanglement of the latter aspects with deep historical legacies of Western modernity draws attention to the influences of processes that can be described with the notions of chronopolitics and political ontology.[7] Explanations of modern human origins and the notions of time, history, and causality are not natural or self-evident. They are products of narratives that are intertwined with ontological orientations and socio-economic interests. Archaeological evidence and its significance are created by situated and active agents with reference to material objects and their respective intellectual circumstances. I would firmly argue that the adoption of such a perspective does not undermine the value and significance of scientific reasoning. It rather strengthens it and supports responsible and reflective decision-making in the present and for the future.

African modern human origins and the Asian and Australasian evidence

The theme of human origins can be approached from many different angles. As outlined by Marks,[8] dealing with human evolution and origins is not a taxonomic exercise like others in biology. It concerns human beings and their identity directly and is entangled in numerous social decision-making processes and value judgements. The boundary between humanity and animality is a complex negotiation between material evidence, interpretative frameworks, political interests, and historical dependencies. Hence, it continues to be located at different times and different locations. Below, I want to review the current most widely accepted understanding of the origins of our own species, *Homo sapiens*, in relation to the current evidence from Asia and Australasia.

Currently, most researchers agree that the deep roots of the human lineage are located in Sub-Saharan Africa. This situation is foremost a product of post-WWII developments and the well-known discoveries of fossil hominin and hominid remains in Southern and Eastern Africa from the 1950s onwards.[9] It can be argued that the most widely accepted view of human origins has since then been foremost structured along a centre-and-periphery narrative in which Africa is understood as the centre and the rest of the world as periphery.[10] However, this has not always been the case. During the nineteenth century and the establishment of modern evolutionary thinking, Asia was seen as a similarly likely place for the origins of humanity. Because of the absence of fossil finds, the assessment was based on the known geographical distribution of the Great Ape species, foremost the chimpanzee in Africa and the Orangutan in Southeast Asia.[11] Before the outbreak of WWII, the most significant fossil discoveries were made in Asia. The latter included the famous *Homo erectus* finds in Southeast Asia and China.[12] This evidence also formed the core for the early formulation of a multiregional understanding of human origins put forward by Franz Weidenreich.[13] He proposed a model of human evolution that largely avoided evolutionary centres of origin. He rather envisaged the pathway to today's human populations as a network of interconnected populations and slow shifts in morphology across the whole Old World. Weidenreich's understanding implied that *Homo sapiens* had an extensive temporal depth and also fuzzy boundaries. It also suggested regional continuity with the so-called archaic populations in different parts of the world, for example Neanderthals in Europe and *Homo erectus* in East and Southeast Asia.[14] Such implied continuities were regularly interpreted for the Asian and Australasian evidence in racist and derogatory terms. N.W.G. Macintosh infamously asserted for Aboriginal Australians that 'the mark of Ancient Java is on all of them'.[15] For a very long time, East and Southeast Asia were seen within an Orientalist framework that was most prominently established by Hallam Movius[16] in an influential paper that was published shortly after WWII. In this paper, he stated that:

> as early as Lower Palaeolithic times, southern and eastern Asia was a region of cultural retardation [...] it seems very unlikely that this vast area could ever have played a vital and dynamic role in early human evolution [...] Very primitive forms of Early Man apparently persisted there long after types at a comparable stage of physical evolution had become extinct elsewhere.[17]

Although Movius' view was based on surprisingly little evidence, until very recently, Western narratives about the East and Southeast Asian deep past continued to be dominated by motives of slow development and stagnation, an understanding that was almost exclusively based on the alleged absence of bifacial tools in Lower and Middle Pleistocene archaeological contexts.[18] More recently, the latter assertion has been demonstrated to be untrue.[19] There is also a stronger recognition of the specific trajectories that need to be considered in the vast and complex regions of East Asia and Australasia, which remain not very well studied in terms of their deep human occupational histories, which are now established to stretch back to more than two million years.[20]

The debates surrounding the origins of *Homo sapiens* have recently undergone a significant shift under the influence of molecular genetic evidence and new fossil and archaeological finds. During the decades after WWII, Sub-Saharan Africa has increasingly been recognised as the origin region not only for the deep roots of the hominin lineage but also for *Homo sapiens* more specifically. Apart from fossil finds in Eastern and Southern Africa, this assessment was deeply influenced by the early mitochondrial DNA analyses that located the origins of all living human populations in Africa.[21] The idea of a 'Mitochondrial Eve' supposedly meant the end of multiregional models of modern human origins. The genetic evidence pointed to a single origin of all modern humans and subsequent replacement processes of archaic populations by modern invasive populations outside of Africa. Since the 1980s, bitter disputes between the respective camps have been fought with mutual accusations of racism and misunderstanding of biological and evolutionary mechanisms.[22] It is, therefore, slightly ironic that it has also been the rapidly expanding evidence from human molecular genetics or evolutionary genomics that has more recently contributed to a critical reassessment of the dichotomous understanding of earlier models of modern human origins and global dispersal. It is now clear that the ancestors of all contemporary non-African populations encountered and admixed with Neanderthals.[23] Furthermore, particular populations in East and Southeast Asia and Australasia also carry nuclear gene sequences that are linked to a morphologically unknown population of hominins that has so far only been detected genetically and through skeletal fragments in Siberia and the Himalayans. These so-called Denisovans – named after the first find location in Siberia – appear to be a sister species of Neanderthals and supposedly represent the eastern portion of archaic hominins in Eurasia before the arrival of modern humans from Africa.[24] While the character, morphology, and distribution of the Denisovans in Eastern and South-eastern Eurasia remain unresolved, current models of human evolutionary history present such an intertwined understanding between the different population strands (or species or sub-species) that they appear to resemble aspects of multiregional thinking.[25]

In the case of the African evidence, a multiregional interpretation has recently gained much more prominence because of the redating and reanalysis of the Jebel Irhoud fossils in Morocco in 2017. Human fossils from this site were known since the 1960s. They were believed to be around 40,000 years old but presented a palaeoanthropological puzzle because of their supposedly archaic features. The remains were interpreted as remnant population that was ultimately swept away by anatomically modern humans, who originated in Eastern Africa around 200,000 years ago.[26] The latter interpretation was based on palaeoanthropological as well as genetic evidence, which pointed to the origins of the *Homo sapiens* lineage in Sub-Saharan Africa within this broad timeframe.[27] The Jebel Irhoud fossils have now been redated to between 280,000 and 350,000 years ago. This result caused a reinterpretation of the processes of modern human origins and a movement away from a single-origin narrative within Africa. The new findings have initiated a crucial reassessment of the African evidence and the interpretation of the processes and causalities of modern human origins on this continent. Current views seem to gravitate towards an understanding that assumes the deep existence of morphologically diverse populations throughout Africa that were linked to each other in variable ways and degrees over time. This complexity is also reflected in the genetic evidence and it is proposed that the genetic complexities of today's populations have to be extended into deep time as well.[28] The understanding of the African biological evidence (morphological, genetic) is also reflected in the interpretation of the archaeological evidence. A most recent continent-wide review suggests that models that propose developments that encompassed the whole of Africa are not supported. Rather, 'continent-wide, directional, and unilinear models of cultural change' should be abandoned in favour of 'more highly contextualised, temporally variable, and historically contingent trajectories in different regions, encapsulated in the concept of complex landscapes of cultural evolution'.[29] The full consequences of recent interpretative shifts will certainly be debated for some time. They point to a much more localised view of past processes of human anatomical and cultural development that do not only refer to general evolutionary mechanisms. Explanations also have to consider historical conditions and contingencies. They, consequently, include cultural trajectories as independent causal factors that cannot be reduced to processes of biological adaptation.[30]

Overall, most recent proposals appear to move beyond earlier models of modern human origins that either favoured a gradual long-term or a late revolutionary understanding. The latter was a product of the influence of molecular genetic studies as mentioned above but also a consequence of a focus on the European evidence as an analogue to interpret the African evidence. According to this understanding, modern humans originated as a result of a genetic mutation less than 80,000 years ago.[31] McBrearty and Brooks have subsequently rejected a revolutionary scenario.[32] Following a comprehensive review of the African archaeological and fossil evidence, they proposed a gradual and cumulative view of modern human origins that featured a slow accumulation of defining traits over the last 500,000 years.

On a conceptual as well as empirical level, the understanding of the African archaeological and fossil record continues to have a significant impact on the reading of the evidence in Asia and Australasia.[33] Similarly, findings in these parts of the world also have complex consequences for the interpretation of the African and European evidence. Intertwined with the issues of the timing and processes of human origins and historical or evolutionary trajectories in Africa is the question of the presence of modern human beings outside of Africa and how this presence needs to be understood. As outlined above, this theme has been formulated since the 1980s (and the widespread rejection of Old World multiregionalism) largely in terms of the timing and the character of the movement of modern humans out of Africa.

The earliest evidence for hominin presence in Asia is currently dated to around two million years ago. Key findings are the hominin remains from Dmanisi in Georgia, stone tools in Chinese sites, and human fossil finds on the island of Java.[34] It will not be possible to discuss these findings from the Lower and Middle Pleistocene and their implications in greater detail here. However, it needs to be stressed that any Out-of-Africa scenario for the spread of modern humans must consider the presence of ancestral hominins across Eurasia and the possibility of a range of scenarios of cultural and biological interactions, avoidance, competition, and so on across this vast geographical space and over vast time periods.[35] Insights into those aspects can come from geochronological, archaeological, palaeoanthropological, and genetic evidence.

Out-of-Africa II: the fossil and genetic evidence in East Asia and Australasia

For a considerable amount of time, researchers have favoured a single Late Pleistocene dispersal event to explain the presence of modern humans in Eurasia. In this model, modern humans left the African continent around 60,000 years ago.[36] Earlier fossils of modern humans outside of Africa, such as the famous finds from Skhul and Qafzeh in Israel that are dated between 120,000 and 90,000 years ago, were regarded as evolutionary dead ends.[37] The model is still broadly supported by current genetic evidence. However, insecurities about the calibration of the genetic clock (e.g. related to variable mutation rates) allow for considerably earlier dispersal scenarios sometime during the Late Pleistocene.[38] A range of fossil finds from East Asia seem to support the view that *Homo sapiens* groups were present in this region up to 130,000 years ago. This would imply, of course, an even earlier dispersal out of Africa in the Late Middle Pleistocene, possibly evidenced by the recent modern human fossil finds at Misliya Cave in Israel that have been dated between 177,000 and 194,000 years ago.[39] The fossil finds from China are generally not well preserved, morphologically ambiguous, and often not precisely dated. They have consequently been disputed to be of relevance for assessing the early dispersal of *Homo sapiens* in Eurasia.[40] However, more recent evidence from Fuyan Cave in Southern China provides clear evidence that modern humans were in the region at least 80,000 and up to 120,000 years ago.[41] The fossil finds here comprise 47 teeth that can be unequivocally assigned to *Homo sapiens*. The metrics and cusp morphology also show overlap with living populations, which seems to suggest that they cannot be linked to ancestral *Homo erectus* populations in the same region. Hence, these human remains appear to be the result of a dispersal event that has distant links to the African continent. Teeth with a clear modern morphology are also the only human remains in the Lidar Ajer Cave on Sumatra that have recently been dated to an age between 63,000 and 73,000 years ago.[42] A similar argument has been put forward for a human premolar from the site of Punung on Java, Indonesia, that has also been dated to more than 118,000 years ago.[43]

Because of its generally fragmentary character, it needs to be stressed that a lot of the early evidence remains disputed for different reasons.[44] It is clear, however, that ca. 50,000 years ago, the fossil record in East and Southeast Asia becomes much clearer and more extensive.[45] The so-called 'Deep Skull' from Niah Cave on Borneo was already recovered in 1958 and together with associated postcranial remains it constituted the oldest modern human fossil remains outside of Africa at this time.[46] The skull is dated to between 39,000 and 45,000 years ago, and its identification as *Homo sapiens* is undisputed. The 'Deep Skull' is broadly contemporary to comparable evidence from the Tabon Caves on Palawan, Philippines, and Tam Pa Ling Cave in Laos.[47] In each case, the finds are highly fragmented but generally accepted as representative of modern *Homo sapiens*. A growing number of finds from China can be described in a similar way, such as the remains from Tianyuan Cave and Zhoukoudian Upper Cave.[48]

In recent years, the hominin fossil record of Southeast Asia has produced some unexpected surprises, which have contributed to an appreciation of the complexity of the human evolutionary histories in the region. Certainly, the most significant find has been the discovery of *Homo floresiensis* at Liang Bua Cave on the island of Flores, Indonesia.[49] Initially dated to an age of only ca. 18,000 years ago, the dating of the skeletal remains has now been revised to between ca. 60,000 and 100,000 years ago.[50] *Homo floresiensis* appears to be the product of the process of island dwarfism and it is most likely that this species' ancestral population did accidentally arrive on the island. Archaeological evidence from other sites on Flores points to the presence of hominins from about one million years ago.[51] Most recently, a very similar scenario has been evoked by new findings on Luzon, Philippines. In 2010, the first fragmented skeletal remains from a small-bodied hominin were published and dated to ca. 67,000 years ago.[52] Subsequent work has extended human presence on Luzon to almost 800,000 years ago[53] and new finds at Callao Cave have been interpreted to belong to a new human species, *Homo luzonensis*.[54] In the case of the latter, it has been argued that the curved morphology of a metatarsal bone points towards an adaptation for climbing, which would link *Homo luzonensis* to Australopithecines in Africa more than two million years ago. The fragmented and limited skeletal evidence, however, makes it difficult to draw such clear conclusions and only with further finds it might become possible to assess these aspects with greater accuracy. In any case, the relationships between these local populations and dispersing *Homo sapiens* groups remain unknown at this stage.

In recent years, the impact of molecular genetic research on human evolutionary studies has grown exponentially through the study of both ancient and recent human DNA. Among other significant discoveries, Asia has been the place for possibly some of the most unexpected results connected to the so-called Denisovans.[55] DNA sequencing of a finger bone that had been excavated from Denisova Cave in the Altai Mountains in Southern Siberia pointed towards a so far unknown human species.[56] Until today, the Denisovans remain morphologically elusive and are defined foremost through genetic sequences that are statistically different from both Neanderthals and modern humans. Skeletal remains that have been ascribed to Denisovan individuals are so far only known from Denisova Cave and the Baishiya Karst Cave on the Tibetan Plateau.[57] As briefly mentioned above, based on genetic analyses alone, Denisovans are currently seen as a sister species of Neanderthals. The relationship between these species or populations is currently unknown, a picture that is further complicated by the observation that Denisova Cave itself contained Neanderthal bones.[58] It has long been known that recent populations outside of Africa carry a small percentage of Neanderthal DNA.[59] Denisovan genetic material, however, has also been found in many non-African populations. Although the absolute amount is very small, its occurrence is most pronounced in Australasia, particularly New Guinea and Australia. Researchers have consequently suggested that genetic admixture between Denisovans and the ancestors of today's Indigenous people in Australia and New Guinea must have taken place during the first movements of modern humans out of Africa, most likely in Southeast Asia itself.[60,61] No evidence exists that could suggest that Denisovans or any other non-modern human groups succeeded in colonising the Pleistocene continent of Sahul. The oldest human remains in Australia are from the Lake Mungo burials and are dated to around 40,000 years ago. Their morphology is fully modern, which also applies to all other Pleistocene skeletal remains from Australia.[62]

Out-of-Africa II: the archaeological evidence in East Asia and Australasia

The detection of the movement of modern humans out of Africa from the Late Middle Pleistocene onwards has not only been approached through human fossils or skeletal remains. Various models have been put forward to track modern human dispersals through Asia and Australasia based on artefact types or favourable environmental conditions.[63] The traditional late dispersal model along a southern coastal route that rests on Upper Palaeolithic or Late Stone Age lithics (e.g. microliths) is finding less and less support.[64] The main hurdle for any archaeological models is the observation that the artefact record within the relevant regions is highly complex and cannot be unequivocally linked to different human species or populations. This is, for example, evidenced through the widely known situation in the Levant in the Early Late Pleistocene. Neanderthals and modern humans have shared this part of the world from almost 200,000 years ago and have also alternately occupied similar sites. However, until the development of the earliest Upper Palaeolithic technologies ca. 45,000 years ago, both populations used Middle Stone Age/Middle Palaeolithic tools, and behavioural differences were generally marginal.[65] This general pattern seems to be replicated across most of Asia.[66] Artefacts and technologies during the Pleistocene appear to be mostly influenced by local conditions and environments. Standardised forms are relatively rare. It also appears that the available evidence is heavily impacted by negative taphonomic factors.[67] The maritime and tropical adaptation strategies in South, East, and Southeast Asia do not favour the development and preservation of artefact categories that have previously been used to identify modern human behaviours in Europe and Africa. This situation makes it particularly difficult to trace any dispersal movements along a coastal route through the Indian Ocean from Africa towards Southeast Asia and, eventually, Australia.[68] Environmental modelling gives some indication of possible dispersal routes at different times during the Late Pleistocene.[69] However, it appears that even the Toba volcanic super-eruption 74,000 years ago did not fundamentally interrupt the continual presence of human populations in South Asia, which suggests a great resilience and flexibility in dealing with a wide range of environmental conditions.[70]

Researchers working in Australia and Asia have not only drawn attention to the fact that the study of this part of the world requires different methods to understand the Pleistocene archaeological record. They have also made the case for a re-evaluation of the categories that have traditionally been used to distinguish modern from archaic or pre-modern behaviours. The critique was directed against the use of European Upper Palaeolithic artefact categories as general indicators of cognitive or behavioural complexity.[71] Among other aspects, common elements included lithic blade and micro blade technologies, the extensive use of organic raw materials, the occurrence of beads and ornaments, long-distance movements of raw materials, and figurative art.[72] While some of these elements have now also been demonstrated to have an equally deep antiquity in the relevant region, such as figurative parietal art,[73] authors have argued that these categories need to be fundamentally questioned. Cosgrove and Pike-Tay[74] have argued that the Pleistocene archaeological record of Tasmania provides a significant challenge to established thinking. Under comparable environmental and climatic conditions, fully modern humans thrived in the absence of many Upper Palaeolithic artefacts and items. It, therefore, becomes difficult to deny Middle Palaeolithic populations the ability for fully modern behaviour elsewhere, including Neanderthals. Habgood and Franklin[75] have used an extensive review of the Pleistocene evidence from Sahul to argue against the idea that modern humans carried with them a package of characteristic behaviours and material culture items that ultimately originated somewhere else, either in Africa or in Europe. Although, for example, seemingly non-functional and symbolic behaviours are present already in the earliest sites in

Australia,[76] other elements only make their appearance much later and are consequently rather a product of historical contingencies and demographic patterns. It has also been argued that the sea crossing to Sahul itself has to be seen as evidence for modern human behaviour, because it required cognitive, communicative, and social abilities that were not in the repertoire of earlier hominins.[77] These elements support the assessment that the specific conditions of Southeast Asia and Australasia also produced expressions of modern behaviours that did not follow African or European trajectories.[78]

What does it mean to be 'modern'?

Palaeoanthropology and Palaeolithic archaeology gain a large amount of their significance and public interest from their concern with human origins. They are in a fascinating and challenging position to enhance our understanding of the events and processes that produced humanity as we know it today. As such, scientific concern with the deep human past must engage – in one form or another – with the boundary between nature and culture, between humanity and animality, and between the natural and the social sciences. These boundaries remain difficult spaces to navigate, although they are rarely addressed specifically. The aim of the study of human origins is often claimed to be the investigation of how 'we' became who 'we' are today. This aim is equally often related to a humanistic and ethical project that should demonstrate that and how all living humans are similar and united by a common heritage. Proctor[79] has demonstrated how the current situation is a relatively recent phenomenon and to a large extent a product of the post-WWII rejection of racist ideologies and methodologies. There can be little doubt that the demise of racism represents one of the most important developments in the human sciences in the twentieth century.[80] However, as Ingold[81] has argued, this rejection also created significant theoretical challenges and contradictions that are foremost the products of the attempt to preserve the idea of universal human exceptionalism within a framework of Darwinian evolutionary thinking. Therefore, current researchers implicitly tend to reproduce the eighteenth-century Enlightenment paradigm of humanity's past and present. This means that it is assumed that modern humanity is united by similar moral and intellectual faculties, by a universal and fixed human nature that distinguishes humanity from all animals. This human nature came into existence as the product of natural biological evolution, but it transformed humans in such a way that they could transcend nature and develop along a unique evolutionary/historical pathway. In this way, Ingold has concluded, the current discourse about human origins perpetuates the key twin Western ontological dichotomies of nature/culture and evolution/history and 'the longstanding imperialist conceits of a western science that has written the essence of humanity in its own image'.[82]

However, who is the 'we' in these narratives or origin stories? The answer to this question is usually presented along the lines of 'people like us' or 'people living today' or '*Homo sapiens*' or 'people within the variability of living, historically and ethnographically known hunter-gatherers'. While a biological or morphological definition of anatomically modern humans was rejected after WWII, current models of humanity's becoming tend to stress that the defining characteristics of modern humans must be in behavioural or cognitive abilities, which are usually related to human's unique ability to use symbolic communication or language.[83] One might expect that this orientation leads to an intense concern with cultural variabilities and notions of alterity that have been discussed in social anthropology and the social sciences for some time. However, this is generally not the case.

Since the establishment of discourses about a behavioural modernity within archaeology in the late 1980s,[84] discussions have operated within a materialist framework that ultimately relates cultural variability to processes of adaptation and the optimisations of resource use and extraction. These aspects are still present in more recent attempts to frame the characteristics of modern human behaviour in terms of behavioural flexibility, plasticity, or 'generalist specialist niche construction'.[85] Explanations in this context generally exhibit a very fuzzy boundary between biological/evolutionary and economic arguments. It is not possible here to delve deeper into the respective paradoxes and contradictions of this situation.[86] However, it is important to note that explanations in human evolutionary studies or Palaeolithic archaeology often recreate key elements that can be found in certain areas of economic theory. The latter particularly applies to the understanding of actors and their fundamental motivations and characteristics. It is often the case that explanations are constructed based on assumptions that show some similarity with classical or neoclassical economic thinking.[87] In each case, the most important entity is the human individual, who is foremost or completely guided by self-interest and rational decision-making.

Sahlins has argued that the modern understanding of 'economic man' and the modern cosmology have a long history that can be related to a Christian worldview.[88] The Christian idea of human beings as creatures of lack and need was ultimately 'bourgeoisified', and free will was cast into rational choice: 'the same scarcity-driven creature of need survived long enough to become the main protagonist of all of human sciences'.[89] This understanding is connected to a view of human-nature relationships that locates agency purely on the side of human beings. Therefore, the Western ontology or cosmology consists of a combination of an ingrained individualism and a naturalistic materialism. The individualised human actor is opposed to a radically different world of things, resources, and products. The latter were conceptualised to belong to a mute and impersonal nature 'that human beings strove to interpret more or less plausibly and from which they endeavoured to profit, with varying degrees of success'.[90]

The assessment of 'success' in this context refers not only to an individual's success but is also applied to populations, species, and so on. It easily becomes a moral exercise that oscillates between economic and biological causalities and vastly different temporal scales. Wagner recognised the underlying relationships in his seminal book *The Invention of Culture* more than 40 years ago.[91] He argued that within the Western tradition, 'human' is equally equated with a 'natural' and biological phenomenon as well as a set of moral assumptions. Each human being is consequently assumed to be born with certain capacities and its 'humanity' is assessed against the degree to which it lives up to those capacities. The result is a mirroring of the process of human evolution and individual human growth:

> Thus 'becoming human' in our tradition is a moral task for the individual as well as an evolutionary one for the species, and the resolution to treat these two aspects as the same thing has given our study of man's origins its teleological and moralistic overtones.[92]

The structure of these arguments allows the establishment of assessments, justifications, and value judgements across vastly different time scales. To give one example from Australia, in the famous essay 'From Three Cheers to the Black Armband', the prominent Australian historian Geoffrey Blainey included the following assessment of the Aboriginal Australian hunting and gathering way of life: 'The world's history has depended heavily on the eclipse of this old and wasteful economic way of life – wasteful in terms of human potential.'[93] This statement portrays the processes of history as universal and inevitable and caused by a connection between human potential and nature itself, which is realised in economic terms or in the appropriate use and exploitation of the environment. The colonisation was consequently a product of a merciless temporality that will eventually sweep away lesser cultures and life forms. This understanding ultimately removes the elements of agency and contingency from historical analysis. It also has ethical and moral implications. It is no accident that Blainey argued against the Native Title Act[94] in the early 1990s, because the Aboriginal 'way of life was bound to be overthrown eventually because it supported so few people on so much land'. The Native Title bill would be 'introducing a form of ownership and an attitude to the land that served the world well in the Stone Age but will be self-defeating in the twenty-first century'.[95] Again, the inevitability that is driving human history is connected to the proper economic exploitation of the land and its resources.

Conclusion – human evolution and Indigenous histories

I want to argue here that the current understanding of modern human origins still largely reflects a universalist understanding of humanity and history. It frames the origin story of humanity as one global narrative. The imposition of temporal regimes was and continues to be a mechanism to exert power and domination in social and economic interactions as well as the generation of scientific narratives.[96] Within these structures, it is certainly naïve to view Indigenous and Western knowledge systems and histories as equivalent and on an equal level. This understanding underestimates the dramatic power differences in which they operate.[97] It is quite significant that in virtually all discussions about human origins and the deep human past, Indigenous voices and histories tend to be completely absent.[98] The reason for this reluctance appears to be the deep entanglement of the project of archaeology with the modern worldview and its related linear understanding of time.[99] In addition, human evolutionary studies are generally regarded as subfields of biology with respective natural science-focused theoretical frameworks and methodologies. These elements tend to replicate the twin ideas of a unified human global history and a universal vision of the human being. Both reflect modern Western values and the modern Western idea of the individual and its defining characteristics and motivations. Implicitly or explicitly, they create a teleological narrative of human evolution with modern Western society as benchmark and endpoint.[100] This vision seemingly leaves little room for an integration of human evolution narratives and Indigenous histories.

However, while the dominant explanatory frameworks in palaeoanthropology and Palaeolithic archaeology often appear to be very monolithic, their foundations are, in fact, far from equivocal and undisputed. The respective contributions allow spaces for constructive explorations beyond the boundaries between nature and culture. In a recent paper on the limitations of biological explanations in human evolution, McManus has argued along these lines and has suggested that biology must avoid epistemologies of exclusion and replacement.[101] Rather, it should aim for more reflexivity and inclusiveness in terms of different perspectives and voices. Similarly, Ingold has for several decades argued for a truly anthropological approach in the study of human evolution, which dissolves the boundaries between social and biological anthropologies.[102] Therefore, I want to suggest that the exploration of the relationships between human evolution and Indigenous histories provides an opportunity to critically assess and negotiate the historical dependencies, limitations, and potentials of different knowledge systems. Such a process should involve the identification of ontological and epistemological similarities and differences as well as contradictions and areas of overlap. Most importantly, these mutual assessments have to equally involve Western scientific as well as Indigenous interpretative frameworks and methodologies.[103]

In this spirit, it is possible to gain some inspiration from the recent collaborative work of researchers, curators, and Indigenous communities in the context of archaeological and ethnographic museums. They are also facing the challenge of navigating issues related to dominant Western knowledge systems and their relationships with Indigenous philosophies, epistemologies, ontologies, and value systems.[104] Often notions of history and time play a key role here as well. The solutions that are reached are often well-intentioned and are agreed upon by all parties involved, such as the parallel presentation of Western and Indigenous interpretations and terminologies to make sure that both views and perspectives are represented and communicated.[105] However, crucial challenges remain. The museum itself, as a manifestation of Western knowledge and ontology, remains the framework of institutional power relationships in which solutions must be negotiated.[106] For Indigenous communities, this is rarely a level playing field. In this sense, the museum context provides a valuable analogue to archaeological research into the deep human past and human evolution and related issues of epistemology, power structures, interpretation, and communication. Comparable processes can be observed in the context of many archaeological sites, particularly in settler colonial settings outside of Europe. While scientific interpretations are often presented in a hegemonic fashion, the establishment of the meaning and significance of every archaeological find or site always involves a range of different frames of reference and temporal scales. For example, the famous sites and human fossils of Olduvai Gorge in East Africa are interpreted with reference to the global palaeoanthropological record by the international scientific community.[107] However, at the same time, relationships between the local Indigenous Maasai people and researchers have not been without conflicts. The Maasai community members have their own worldviews, systems of knowledge production and negotiation, and their own stories to tell, which rarely receive a similar amount of attention.[108] Similarly, conflicts around the famous Willandra Lakes human remains from New South Wales, Australia, can be understood as conflicts about different frames of reference and different ontologies that require the negotiation between local and global frames of references and temporalities.[109] These are rarely straightforward processes that need to consider the intersection between political power relationships and ontological orientations.[110]

The examples above demonstrate that a concern with Indigenous histories and human evolution is not purely an academic exercise. It directly affects the processes of the creation of heritage through and with archaeological and palaeoanthropological evidence in the present. Because of its antiquity, human evolutionary evidence is often assumed to have little relevance for today's Indigenous communities. However, apart from ethical issues of archaeological research, an engagement with Indigenous histories shows that such an assessment depends on the processes of the construction of history itself as well as notions of time and causality. Indigenous histories demonstrate the temporal diversity and complexity of human existence, and related challenges of the writing of historical narratives. It is no accident that an intriguing juxtaposition can be discerned with postcolonial literature and research, which is dealing with very similar issues.[111] Unfortunately, no easy answers can be expected. According to Chakrabarty, it is necessary to:

> view the human simultaneously on contradictory registers: as a geophysical force and as a political agent, as a bearer of rights and as author of actions; subject to both the stochastic forces of nature (…) and open to the contingency of individual human experience; belonging at once to differently scaled histories of the planet, of life and species, and of human societies.[112]

Chakrabarty made these comments in relation to the challenges of understanding humanity and human history in the face of global climate change. But they are equally applicable to the challenges of integrating human evolution and Indigenous-histories narratives. Archaeological research and writing must take seriously its own position in the complex histories of the world and must consider its ethical and moral implications. The past and the future of humanity are simultaneously local and global histories.

Notes

1 Julian Thomas, *Archaeology and Modernity* (New York: Routledge, 2004).
2 Raymond Corbey and Wil Roebroeks, eds., *Studying Human Origins: Disciplinary History and Epistemology* (Amsterdam: Amsterdam University Press, 2001); Raymond Corbey and Annette Lanjouw, eds., *The Politics of Species: Reshaping our Relationships with other Animals* (Cambridge: Cambridge University Press, 2013).

3 Martin Porr and Jacqueline Maree Matthews, 'Post-colonialism, Human Origins and the Paradox of Modernity,' *Antiquity* 91, no. 358 (2017): 1058–1068.
4 Patrick D. Nunn, *The Edge of Memory: Ancient Stories, Oral Tradition and the Post-Glacial World* (London: Bloomsbury Sigma, 2018).
5 Martin Porr and Jacqueline Maree Matthews, 'Thinking Through Story,' *Hunter Gatherer Research* 2, no. 3 (2016): 249–274.
6 M.M. Bruchac, S.M. Hart, and H. Martin Wobst, eds., *Indigenous Archaeologies: A Reader in Decolonization* (Walnut Creek: Left Coast Press, 2010); M. Liebmann and Uzma Z. Rizvi, eds., *Archaeology and the Postcolonial Critique* (Lanham, MD: AltaMira Press, 2008).
7 Christopher Witmore, 'Chronopolitics and Archaeology,' in *The Encyclopedia of Global Archaeology*, ed. Claire Smith (New York: Springer, 2014), 1471–1476; Mario Blaser, 'Ontology and Indigeneity: On the Political Ontology of Heterogeneous Assemblages,' *Cultural Geographies* 21, no. 1 (2014): 49–58.
8 Jonathan Marks, *Tales of the Ex-Apes: How We Think About Human Evolution* (Oakland: University of California Press, 2015).
9 See overview in Clive S. Gamble, *Settling the Earth. The Archaeology of Deep Human History* (Cambridge: Cambridge University Press, 2014); Bernard Wood, 'Reconstructing Human Evolution: Achievements, Challenges, and Opportunities,' *Proceedings of the National Academy of Sciences* 107, supplement 2 (2010): 8902–8909; Richard Potts, 'Evolution and Environmental Change in Early Human Prehistory,' *Annual Review of Anthropology* 41 (2012): 151–167.
10 Robin Dennell, 'From Sangiran to Olduvai, 1937–1960: The Quest for "Centres" of Hominid Origins in Asia and Africa,' in *Studying Human Origins: Disciplinary History and Epistemology*, eds. Raymond Corbey and Wil Roebroeks (Amsterdam: Amsterdam University Press, 2001), 45–66.
11 Jeffery H. Schwartz, *The Red Ape: Orangutans and Human Origins* (Cambridge, MA: Westview Press, 2005).
12 Robin Dennell, *The Palaeolithic Settlement of Asia* (Cambridge: Cambridge University Press, 2009).
13 Franz Weidenreich, *Apes, Giants and Man* (Chicago, IL: The University of Chicago Press, 1946).
14 Rachel Caspari and Milford H. Wolpoff, 'Weidenreich, Coon, and Multiregional Evolution,' *Human Evolution* 11, no. 3–4 (1994): 261–268.
15 N.W.G. Macintosh, 'The Physical Aspect of Man in Australia,' in *Aboriginal Man in Australia: Essays in Honour of Emeritus Professor A.P. Elkin*, eds. R.M. Berndt and C.M. Berndt (Sydney: Angus & Robertson, 1965), 59.
16 Hallam L. Movius Jr, 'The Lower Palaeolithic Cultures of Southern and Eastern Asia,' *Transactions of the American Philosophical Society* 38, no. 4 (1948): 329–420.
17 Movius, 'Lower Palaeolithic Cultures,' 411.
18 Robin Dennell, 'Life without the Movius Line: The Structure of the East and Southeast Asian Early Palaeolithic,' *Quaternary International* 400 (2015): 14–22; Stephen J. Lycett and Christopher J. Bae, 'The Movius Line Controversy: The State of the Debate,' *World Archaeology* 42, no. 4 (2010): 521–544.
19 Adam Brumm and Mark W. Moore, 'Biface Distributions and the Movius Line: A Southeast Asian Perspective,' *Australian Archaeology* 74 (2012): 32–46; Michael D. Petraglia and Ceri Shipton, 'Large Cutting Tool Variation West and East of the Movius Line,' *Journal of Human Evolution* 55 (2008): 962–966.
20 Dennell, *The Palaeolithic Settlement of Asia*; Zhaoyu Zhu et al., 'Hominin Occupation of the Chinese Loess Plateau Since About 2.1 Million Years Ago,' *Nature* 559 (2018): 608–612; Robin Dennell and Martin Porr, eds., *Southern Asia, Australia and the Search for Human Origins* (Cambridge: Cambridge University Press, 2014).
21 R.L. Cann, Mark Stoneking, and A.C. Wilson, 'Mitochondrial DNA and Human Evolution,' *Nature* 325 (1987): 31–36.

22 Rachel Caspari and Milford H. Wolpoff, 'The Process of Modern Human Origins: The Evolutionary and Demographic Changes Giving Rise to Modern Humans,' in *The Origins of Modern Humans: Biology Reconsidered*, eds. Fred H. Smith and James C.M. Ahern (New York: John Wiley & Sons, 2013), 355–391; Milford H. Wolpoff and Rachel Caspari, *Race and Evolution* (New York: Simon & Schuster, 1997); Chris Stringer, *The Origin of Our Species* (London: Allen Lane, 2011); Paul Mellars and Chris Stringer, eds. *The Human Revolution: Behavioural and Biological Perspectives in the Origins of Modern Humans* (Edinburgh: Edinburgh University Press, 1989).

23 Svante Pääbo, *Neanderthal Man: In Search of Lost Genomes* (New York: Basic Books, 2014).

24 David Reich et al. 'Genetic History of an Archaic Hominin Group from Denisova Cave in Siberia,' *Nature* 468 (2010): 1053–1060.

25 Overview in Rasmus Nielsen et al., 'Tracing the Peopling of the World through Genomics,' *Nature* 541 (2017): 302–310.

26 T.D. White et al. 'Pleistocene *Homo sapiens* from Middle Awash, Ethiopia,' *Nature* 423 (2003): 742–747; Ian McDougall, Francis H. Brown, and John G. Fleagle, 'Stratigraphic Placement and Age of Modern Humans from Kibish, Ethiopia,' *Nature* 433 (2005): 733–736.

27 Chris Stringer, 'The Origin and Evolution of *Homo sapiens*,' *Philosophical Transactions of the Royal Society B* 371 (2016): 20150237.

28 See especially Eleanor Scerri et al., 'Did Our Species Evolve in Subdivided Populations across Africa, and Why Does It Matter?' *Trends in Ecology & Evolution* 33, no. 8 (2018): 582–594.

29 Manuel Will, Nicholas J. Conard, and Christian A. Tryon, 'Timing and Trajectory of Cultural Evolution on the African Continent 200,000–30,000 Years Ago,' in *Modern Human Origins and Dispersal*, eds. Yonatan Sahle, Hugo Reyes-Centeno, and Christian Bentz (Tübingen: Kerns Verlag, 2019), 25.

30 Andrew Kandel et al., 'Increasing Behavioral Flexibility? An Integrative Macro-Scale Approach to Understanding the Middle Stone Age of Southern Africa,' *Journal of Archaeological Method and Theory* 23, no. 2 (2016): 623–668.

31 See e.g. Richard Klein and Blake Edgar, *The Dawn of Human Culture: A Bold New Theory on What Sparked the 'Big Bang' of Human Consciousness* (New York: John Wiley & Sons, 2002); Mellars and Stringer, *The Human Revolution*.

32 Sally McBrearty and Alison S. Brooks, 'The Revolution That Wasn't: A New Interpretation of the Origin of Modern Human Behavior,' *Journal of Human Evolution* 39 (2000): 453–563.

33 Dennell and Porr, *Southern Asia, Australia and the Search for Human Origins*.

34 Zhu et al., 'Hominin Occupation of the Chinese Loess Plateau'; overview in Dennell, *The Palaeolithic Settlement of Asia*.

35 Yousuke Kaifu, 'Archaic Hominin Populations in Asia before the Arrival of Modern Humans: Their Phylogeny and Implications for the "Southern Denisovans",' *Current Anthropology* 58, supplement 17 (2017): S418–S434.

36 See e.g. Paul Mellars, 'Why Did Modern Human Populations Disperse from Africa ca. 60,000 Years Ago? A New Model,' *Proceedings of the National Academy of Sciences* 103, no. 25 (2006): 9381–9386.

37 John Shea and Ofer Bar-Yosef, 'Who Were the Skhul/Qafzeh People? An Archaeological Perspective on Eurasia's Oldest Modern Humans,' *Journal of the Israel Prehistoric Society* 35 (2005): 451–468.

38 Scerri et al., 'Did Our Species Evolve in Subdivided Populations?'

39 Israel Hershkovitz et al. 'The Earliest Modern Humans Outside Africa,' *Science* 359, no. 6374 (2018): 456–459.

40 For a summary, see e.g. Christopher J. Bae, Katerina Douka, and Michael D. Petraglia, 'On the Origin of Modern Humans: Asian Perspectives,' *Science* 358, no. 6368 (2017): 1–7; overview in Robin Dennell, *From Arabia to the Pacific: How Our Species Colonised Asia* (New York: Routledge, 2020).

41 Robin Dennell, 'Palaeoanthropology: *Homo sapiens* in China 80,000 Years Ago,' *Nature* 526 (2015): 647–648; Wu Liu et al., 'The Earliest Unequivocally Modern Humans in Southern China,' *Nature* 526 (2015): 696–699.
42 Kiera E. Westaway et al., 'An Early Modern Human Presence in Sumatra 73,000–63,000 Years Ago,' *Nature* 548 (2017): 322–325.
43 Paul Storm et al., 'Late Pleistocene *Homo sapiens* in a Tropical Rainforest Fauna in East Java,' *Journal of Human Evolution* 49, no. 4 (2005): 536–545.
44 See e.g. James O'Connell et al., 'When Did *Homo sapiens* First Reach Southeast Asia and Sahul?' *Proceedings of the National Academy of Sciences* 115, no. 34 (2018): 8482–8490.
45 Robin Dennell, 'Smoke and Mirrors: The Fossil Record for *Homo sapiens* between Arabia and Australia,' in Dennell and Porr, *Southern Asia, Australia and the Search for Human Origins*, 33–50.
46 Graeme Barker et al., 'The "Human Revolution" in Lowland Tropical Southeast Asia: The Antiquity and Behavior of Anatomically Modern Humans at Niah Cave (Sarawak, Borneo),' *Journal of Human Evolution* 52 (2007): 243–261.
47 Fabrice Demeter et al., 'Early Modern Humans and Morphological Variation in Southeast Asia: Fossil Evidence from Tam Pa Ling, Laos,' *PLoS ONE* 10, no. 4 (2015): 1–17; Florent Détroit et al., 'Upper Pleistocene *Homo sapiens* from Tabon Cave (Palawan, the Philippines): Description and Dating of New Discoveries,' *C.R. Palevol* 3 (2004): 705–712.
48 Jane Qui, 'The Forgotten Continent,' *Nature* 535 (2016): 22–25; Hong Shang et al., 'An Early Modern Human from Tianyuan Cave, Zhoukoudian, China,' *Proceedings of the National Academy of Sciences* 104, no. 16 (2007): 6573–6578.
49 P. Brown et al., 'A New Small-Bodied Hominin from the Late Pleistocene of Flores, Indonesia.' *Nature* 431 (2004): 1055–1061.
50 Thomas Sutikna et al., 'Revised stratigraphy and chronology for *Homo floresiensis* at Liang Bua in Indonesia,' *Nature* 532 (2016): 366.
51 Adam Brumm et al., 'Hominins on Flores, Indonesia, by One Million Years Ago,' *Nature* 464 (2010): 748–752.
52 Armand Salvador Mijares et al., 'New Evidence for a 67,000-Year-Old Human Presence at Callao Cave, Luzon, Philippines,' *Journal of Human Evolution* 59, no. 1 (2010): 123–132.
53 Thomas Ingicco et al., 'Earliest Known Hominin Activity in the Philippines by 709 Thousand Years Ago,' *Nature* 557 (2018): 233–237.
54 Florent Détroit et al., 'A New Species of *Homo* from the Late Pleistocene of the Philippines,' *Nature* 568 (2019): 181–186.
55 Martin Sikora, 'A Genomic View of the Pleistocene Population Bistory of Asia,' *Current Anthropology* 58, supplement 17 (2017): S397–S405.
56 Reich et al., 'Genetic History of an Archaic Hominin Group.'
57 Fahu Chen et al., 'A Late Middle Pleistocene Denisovan Mandible from the Tibetan Plateau,' *Nature* 569 (2019): 409–412.
58 Kay Prüfer et al., 'The Complete Genome Sequence of a Neanderthal from the Altai Mountains,' *Nature* 505 (2013): 43–49.
59 Pääbo, *Neanderthal Man*.
60 This view is, of course, not accepted by all Indigenous Australians.
61 David Reich et al., 'Denisova Admixture and the First Modern Human Dispersals into Southeast Asia and Oceania,' *American Journal of Human Genetics* 89, no. 4 (2011): 516–528; Anna-Sapfo Malaspinas et al., 'A Genomic History of Aboriginal Australia,' *Nature* 538 (2016): 207–214; A. Cooper and Chris Stringer, 'Did the Denisovans Cross Wallace's Line?' *Science* 342 (2013): 321–323.
62 James M. Bowler et al., 'New Ages for Human Occupation and Climatic Change at Lake Mungo, Australia,' *Nature* 421 (2003): 837–840; Sandra Bowdler, '"Rattling the Bones": The Changing Contribution of the Australian Archaeological Record to Ideas about Human Evolution,' in Dennell and Porr, *Southern Asia, Australia and the Search for*

Human Origins, 21–32; Colin Pardoe, 'Becoming Australian: Evolutionary Processes and Biological Variation from Ancient to Modern Times,' *Before Farming* 1 (2006): 1–21; Helen Lawrence, ed., *Mungo over Millennia: The Willandra Landscape and Its People* (Rosny Park: Maygog Publishing, 2006); Jim Bowler and Alan Thorne, 'Human Remains from Lake Mungo: Discovery and Excavation of Lake Mungo III,' in *The Origin of the Australians*, eds. R.L. Kirk and Alan Thorne (Canberra: Australian Institute for Aboriginal Studies, 1976), 127–138.

63 Paul Mellars et al., *Rethinking the Human Revolution: New Behavioural and Biological Perspectives on the Origin and Dispersal of Modern Humans* (Cambridge: McDonald Institute for Archaeological Research, 2007); Mellars and Stringer, *The Human Revolution*.

64 Mellars, 'Why Did Modern Human Populations Disperse from Africa?'

65 John J. Shea, 'Neandertals and Early Modern *Homo sapiens* in the Near East,' in *South-Eastern Mediterranean Peoples between 130,00–10,000 Years Ago*, ed. Elena Garcea (Oxford: Oxford University Press, 2010), 126–143.

66 Dennell and Porr, *Southern Asia, Australia and the Search for Human Origins*; Yousuke Kaifu et al. eds., *Emergence and Diversity of Modern Human Behavior in Paleolithic Asia* (College Station: Texas A&M University Press, 2015).

67 Michelle C. Langley, Christopher Clarkson, and Sean Ulm, 'From Small Holes to Grand Narratives: The Impact of Taphonomy and Sample Size on the Modernity Debate in Australia and New Guinea,' *Journal of Human Evolution* 61 (2011): 197–208.

68 Stephen Oppenheimer, 'The Great Arc of Dispersal of Modern Humans: Africa to Australia,' *Quaternary International* 202, no. 1–2 (2009): 2–13.

69 Robin Dennell and Wil Roebroeks, 'An Asian Perspective on Early Human Dispersal from Africa,' *Nature* 438 (2005): 1099–1104; Julie S. Field and Marta Mirazon Lahr, 'Assessment of the Southern Dispersal: GIS-Based Analyses of Potential Routes of Oxygen Isotopic Stage 4,' *Journal of World Prehistory* 19, no. 1 (2006): 1–45.

70 Michael D. Petraglia et al., 'The Toba Volcanic Super-Eruption, Environmental Change, and Hominin Occupation History in India over the Last 140,000 Years,' *Quaternary International* 258 (2012): 119–134.

71 Martin Porr, 'Identifying Behavioural Modernity: Lessons from Sahul,' *Bulletin of the Indo-Pacific Prehistory Association* 30 (2010): 28–34.

72 See e.g. McBrearty and Brooks, 'The Revolution That Wasn't,' 492.

73 M. Aubert et al., 'Pleistocene Cave Art from Sulawesi, Indonesia,' *Nature* 514 (2014): 223–227.

74 Richard Cosgrove and Anne Pike-Tay, 'The Middle Palaeolithic and Late Pleistocene Tasmania Hunting Behaviour: A Reconsideration of the Attributes of Modern Behaviour,' *International Journal of Osteoarchaeology* 14 (2004): 321–332.

75 Philip J. Habgood and Natalie Franklin, 'The Revolution That Didn't Arrive: A Review of Pleistocene Sahul,' *Journal of Human Evolution* 55 (2008): 187–222.

76 Christopher Clarkson et al., 'Human Occupation of Northern Australia by 65,000 Years Ago,' *Nature* 547 (2017): 306–310.

77 Iain Davidson, 'The Colonization of Australia and Its Adjacent Islands and the Evolution of Modern Cognition,' *Current Anthropology* 51 (2010): S177–S189; Iain Davidson and William Noble, 'Why the First Colonisation of the Australian Region Is the Earliest Evidence of Modern Human Behaviour,' *Archaeology in Oceania* 27 (1992): 135–142.

78 Miriam Haidle and Alfred Pawlik, 'Pleistocene Modernity: An Exclusively Afro-European Issue?' *Bulletin of the Indo-Pacific Prehistory Association* 30 (2010): 3–8; Kaifu et al., *Emergence and Diversity*; Barker et al. 'The "Human Revolution" in Lowland Tropical Southeast Asia.'

79 Robert N. Proctor, 'Three Roots of Human Recency: Molecular Anthropology, the Refigured Acheulean, and the UNESCO Response to Auschwitz,' *Current Anthropology* 44, no. 2 (2003): 213–239.

80 Jonathan Marks, 'Race: Past, Present, and Future,' in *Revisiting Race in a Genomic Age*, eds. Barbara A. Koenig, Sandra Soo-Jin Lee, and Sarah S. Richardson (New Brunswick:

Rutgers University Press, 2008), 21–38; Jonathan Marks, *Is Science Racist?* (Cambridge: Polity, 2017).
81 Tim Ingold, 'Beyond Biology and Culture: The Meaning of Evolution in a Relational World,' *Social Anthropology* 12, no. 2 (2004): 209–221.
82 Ingold, 'Beyond Biology and Culture,' 220.
83 April Nowell, 'Defining Behavioral Modernity in the Context of Neandertal and Anatomically Modern Human Populations,' *Annual Review of Anthropology* 39, no. 1 (2010): 437–452; Stringer, 'The Origin and Evolution of *Homo sapiens*.'
84 Mellars and Stringer, *The Human Revolution*; William Noble and Ian Davidson, 'The Evolutionary Emergence of Modern Human Behaviour: Language and Its Archaeology,' *Man (N.S.)* 26, no. 2 (1991): 223–253; Davidson and Noble, 'Why the First Colonisation of the Australian Region Is the Earliest Evidence of Modern Human Behaviour.'
85 Patrick Roberts and Brian A. Stewart, 'Defining the "Generalist Specialist" Niche for Pleistocene *Homo sapiens*,' *Nature Human Behaviour* 2, no. 8 (2018): 542–550; Martin Porr, 'One Step Forward, Two Steps Back: The Issue of "Behavioral Modernity" Again: A Comment on Shea,' *Current Anthropology* 52, no. 4 (2011): 581–582; John J. Shea, '*Homo sapiens* Is as *Homo sapiens* Was,' *Current Anthropology* 52, no. 1 (2011): 1–35.
86 Tim Ingold, *The Perception of the Environment: Essays in Livelihood, Dwelling and Skill* (London: Routledge, 2000).
87 J. K. Galbraith, *A History of Economics: The Past as the Present* (London: Penguin, 1989); A. Roncaglia, *The Wealth of Ideas: A History of Economic Thought* (Cambridge: Cambridge University Press, 2005).
88 Marshall Sahlins, 'The Sadness of Sweetness: The Native Anthropology of Western Cosmology,' *Current Anthropology* 37, no. 3 (1996): 395–428.
89 Sahlins, 'The Sadness of Sweetness,' 397.
90 Marshall Sahlins, in Philippe Descola, *Beyond Nature and Culture* (Chicago, IL: Chicago University Press, 2013).
91 Roy Wagner, *The Invention of Culture*, 2nd ed. (Chicago, IL: Chicago University Press, 2016).
92 Wagner, *The Invention of Culture*, 133.
93 Geoffrey Blainey, 'From Three Cheers to the Black Armband,' in *The Words That Made Australia: How a Nation Came to Know Itself*, eds. Robert Manne and Chris Feik (Collingwood: Black Inc. Agenda, 2012), 201.
94 Native Title legislation was introduced in Australia in 1993 after the High Court determined in the case of *Mabo and Others v. The State of Queensland* in 1992 that the people of the Murray Islands retained native title despite European colonisation. It ended the doctrine of *terra nullius* and paved the way for many subsequent court cases to determine Indigenous land rights; see R. Bartlett, *Native Title in Australia* (Sydney: Butterworths, 2004); David Ritter, *Contesting Native Title: From Controversy to Consensus in the Struggle over Indigenous Land Rights* (Crows Nest: Allen & Unwin, 2009); Sandy Toussaint, ed., *Crossing Boundaries: Cultural, Legal, Historical and Practical Issues in Native Title* (Melbourne: Melbourne University Press, 2004).
95 Quoted in Shayne Breen, 'Human Agency, Historical Inevitability and Moral Culpability: Rewriting Black-White History in the Wake of Native Title,' *Aboriginal History* 20 (1996): 126.
96 Witmore, 'Chronopolitics and Archaeology.'
97 Mario Blaser, 'Ontological Conflicts and the Stories of Peoples in Spite of Europe,' *Current Anthropology* 54, no. 4 (2013): 547–568.
98 Martin Porr and Jacqueline Maree Matthews, eds., *Interrogating Human Origins: Decolonisation and the Deep Human Past* (Archaeological Orientations) (London: Routledge, 2020).
99 Thomas, *Archaeology and Modernity*.

100 Martin Porr, 'The Temporality of Humanity and the Colonial Landscape of the Deep Human Past,' in Porr and Matthews, *Interrogating Human Origins*, 184–207; Martin Porr, 'Essential Questions: "Modern Humans" and the Capacity for Modernity,' in Dennell and Porr, *Southern Asia, Australia and the Search for Human Origins*, 257–264.
101 Siobhan McManus, 'Biological Explanations and Their Limits: Paleoanthropology among the Sciences,' in *Rethinking Human Evolution*, ed. Jeffery H. Schwartz (Cambridge, MA: The MIT Press), 31–52.
102 See for e.g. Tim Ingold, 'From Complementarity to Obviation: On Dissolving the Boundaries between Social and Biological Anthropology, Archaeology and Psychology,' *Zeitschrift für Ethnologie* 123 (1998): 21–52; Tim Ingold, *Being Alive: Essays on Movement, Knowledge and Description* (London: Routledge, 2011); Tim Ingold and Gisli Palsson, eds., *Biosocial Becomings. Integrating Social and Biological Anthropology* (Cambridge: Cambridge University Press, 2013).
103 Martin Porr, 'Lives and Lines: Integrating Molecular Genetics, the "Origins of Modern Humans" and Indigenous Knowledge,' in *Long History, Deep Time: Deepening Histories of Place*, eds. Ann McGrath and Mary Anne Jebb (Canberra: ANU Press, 2015), 203–219.
104 Bryony Onciul, *Museums, Heritage and Indigenous Voice: Decolonising Engagement* (London: Routledge, 2015); Howard Morphy, *Museums, Infinity and the Culture of Protocols* (New York: Routledge, 2020).
105 Alison Brown and Laura Peers, eds., *Museums and Source Communities: A Routledge Reader* (London: Routledge, 2003).
106 Tony Bennett, *Museums, Power, Knowledge: Selected Essays* (London: Routledge, 2018).
107 Dennell, 'From Sangiran to Olduvai.'
108 Asmeret G. Mehari and Kokeli Ryano, 'Maasai People and Oldupai (Olduvai) Gorge: Looking for Sustainable People-Centred Approaches and Practices,' in *Community Archaeology and Heritage in Africa*, eds. Peter R. Schmidt and Innocent Pikirayi (New York: Routledge, 2016), 21–45.
109 Nicola Stern, 'The Archaeology of the Willandra,' in McGrath and Jebb, *Long History, Deep Time*, 221–240; Malcolm Allbrock and Ann McGrath, 'Collaborative Histories of the Willandra Lakes,' in McGrath and Jebb, *Long History, Deep Time*, 241–252.
110 Blaser, 'Ontological Conflicts.'
111 Porr and Matthews, *Interrogating Human Origins*.
112 Dipesh Chakrabarty, 'Postcolonial Studies and the Challenge of Climate Change,' in *The Crises of Civilisation: Exploring Global and Planetary Histories*, ed. Dipesh Chakrabarty (New Delhi: Oxford University Press), 242.

Bibliography

Allbrock, Malcolm, and Ann McGrath. 'Collaborative Histories of the Willandra Lakes.' In *Long History, Deep Time: Deepening Histories of Place*, edited by Ann McGrath and Mary Anne Jebb, 241–252. Canberra: ANU Press, 2015.
Aubert, M., A. Brumm, M. Ramli, T. Sutikna, E.W. Saptomo, B. Hakim, M.J. Morwood, G D. van den Bergh, L. Kinsley, and A. Dosseto. 'Pleistocene Cave Art from Sulawesi, Indonesia.' *Nature* 514 (2014): 223–227.
Bae, Christopher J., Katerina Douka, and Michael D. Petraglia. 'On the Origin of Modern Humans: Asian Perspectives.' *Science* 358, no. 6368 (2017): 1–7.
Barker, Graeme, Huw Barton, Michael I. Bird, Patrick Daly, Ipoi Datan, Alan Dykes, Lucy Farr, David Gilbertson, Barbara Harrisson, Chris Hunt, et al. 'The "Human Revolution" in Lowland Tropical Southeast Asia: The Antiquity and Behavior of Anatomically Modern Humans at Niah Cave (Sarawak, Borneo).' *Journal of Human Evolution* 52 (2007): 243–261.
Bartlett, R. *Native Title in Australia*. Sydney: Butterworths, 2004.

Bennett, Tony. *Museums, Power, Knowledge: Selected Essays*. London: Routledge, 2018.
Blainey, Geoffrey. 'From Three Cheers to the Black Armband.' In *The Words That Made Australia: How a Nation Came to Know Itself*, edited by Robert Manne and Chris Feik, 193–203. Collingwood: Black Inc. Agenda, 2012.
Blaser, Mario. 'Ontological Conflicts and the Stories of Peoples in Spite of Europe.' *Current Anthropology* 54, no. 4 (2013): 547–568.
Blaser, Mario. 'Ontology and Indigeneity: On the Political Ontology of Heterogeneous Assemblages.' *Cultural Geographies* 21, no. 1 (2014): 49–58.
Bowdler, Sandra. '"Rattling the Bones": The Changing Contribution of the Australian Archaeological Record to Ideas about Human Evolution.' In *Southern Asia, Australia and the Search for Human Origins*, edited by Robin Dennell and Martin Porr, 21–32. Cambridge: Cambridge University Press, 2014.
Bowler, James M., Harvey Johnston, Jon M. Olley, John R. Prescott, Richard G. Roberts, Wilfred Shawcross, and Nigel A. Spooner. 'New Ages for Human Occupation and Climatic Change at Lake Mungo, Australia.' *Nature* 421 (2003): 837–840.
Bowler, Jim, and Alan Thorne. 'Human Remains from Lake Mungo: Discovery and Excavation of Lake Mungo III.' In *The Origin of the Australians*, edited by R.L. Kirk and Alan Thorne, 127–138. Canberra: Australian Institute for Aboriginal Studies, 1976.
Breen, Shayne. 'Human Agency, Historical Inevitability and Moral Culpability: Rewriting Black-White History in the Wake of Native Title.' *Aboriginal History* 20 (1996): 108–132.
Brown, Alison, and Laura Peers, eds. *Museums and Source Communities: A Routledge Reader*. London: Routledge, 2003.
Brown, P., Thomas Sutikna, M.J. Morwood, R.P. Soejono, Jatmiko, E.W. Saptomo, and Rokhus Awe Due. 'A New Small-Bodied Hominin from the Late Pleistocene of Flores, Indonesia.' *Nature* 431 (2004): 1055–1061.
Bruchac, M.M., S.M. Hart, and H. Martin Wobst, eds. *Indigenous Archaeologies: A Reader in Decolonization*. Walnut Creek: Left Coast Press, 2010.
Brumm, Adam, Gitte M. Jensen, Gert D. van den Bergh, Michael J. Morwood, Iwan Kurniawan, Fachroel Aziz, and Michael Storey. 'Hominins on Flores, Indonesia, by One Million Years Ago.' *Nature* 464 (2010): 748–752.
Brumm, Adam, and Mark W. Moore. 'Biface Distributions and the Movius Line: A Southeast Asian Perspective.' *Australian Archaeology* 74 (2012): 32–46.
Cann, R.L., Mark Stoneking, and A.C. Wilson. 'Mitochondrial DNA and Human Evolution.' *Nature* 325 (1987): 31–36.
Caspari, Rachel, and Milford H. Wolpoff. 'Weidenreich, Coon, and Multiregional Evolution.' *Human Evolution* 11, no. 3–4 (1994): 261–268.
Caspari, Rachel, and Milford H. Wolpoff. 'The Process of Modern Human Origins: The Evolutionary and Demographic Changes Giving Rise to Modern Humans.' In *The Origins of Modern Humans: Biology Reconsidered*, edited by Fred H. Smith and James C.M. Ahern, 355–391. New York: John Wiley & Sons, 2013.
Chakrabarty, Dipesh. 'Postcolonial Studies and the Challenge of Climate Change.' In *The Crises of Civilisation: Exploring Global and Planetary Histories*, edited by Dipesh Chakrabarty, 223–243. New Delhi: Oxford University Press, 2018.
Chen, Fahu, Frido Welker, Chuan-Chou Shen, Shara E. Bailey, Inga Bergmann, Simon Davis, Huan Xia, Hui Wang, Roman Fischer, Sarah E. Freidline, et al. 'A Late Middle Pleistocene Denisovan Mandible from the Tibetan Plateau.' *Nature* 569 (2019): 409–412.
Clarkson, Chris, Zenobia Jacobs, Ben Marwick, Richard Fullagar, Lynley Wallis, Mike Smith, Richard G. Roberts, Elspeth Hayes, Kelsey Lowe, Xavier Carah, et al. 'Human Occupation of Northern Australia by 65,000 Years Ago.' *Nature* 547 (2017): 306–310.
Cooper, A., and Chris Stringer. 'Did the Denisovans Cross Wallace's Line?' *Science* 342 (2013): 321–323.
Corbey, Raymond, and Annette Lanjouw, eds. *The Politics of Species: Reshaping our Relationships with other Animals*. Cambridge: Cambridge University Press, 2013.

Corbey, Raymond, and Wil Roebroeks, eds. *Studying Human Origins: Disciplinary History and Epistemology*. Amsterdam: Amsterdam University Press, 2001.

Cosgrove, Richard, and Anne Pike-Tay. 'The Middle Palaeolithic and Late Pleistocene Tasmania Hunting Behaviour: A Reconsideration of the Attributes of Modern Behaviour.' *International Journal of Osteoarchaeology* 14 (2004): 321–332.

Davidson, Iain. 'The Colonization of Australia and Its Adjacent Islands and the Evolution of Modern Cognition.' *Current Anthropology* 51 (2010): S177–S189.

Davidson, Iain, and William Noble. 'Why the First Colonisation of the Australian Region Is the Earliest Evidence of Modern Human Behaviour.' *Archaeology in Oceania* 27 (1992): 135–142.

Demeter, Fabrice, Laura Shackelford, Kira Westaway, Philippe Duringer, Anne-Marie Bacon, Jean-Luc Ponche, Xiujie Wu, Thongsa Sayavongkhamdy, Jian-Xin Zhao, Lani Barnes, et al. 'Early Modern Humans and Morphological Variation in Southeast Asia: Fossil Evidence from Tam Pa Ling, Laos.' *PLoS ONE* 10, no. 4 (2015): 1–17.

Dennell, Robin. 'From Sangiran to Olduvai, 1937–1960: The Quest for "Centres" of Hominid Origins in Asia and Africa.' In *Studying Human Origins: Disciplinary History and Epistemology*, edited by Raymond Corbey and Wil Roebroeks, 45–66. Amsterdam: Amsterdam University Press, 2001.

Dennell, Robin. *The Palaeolithic Settlement of Asia*. Cambridge: Cambridge University Press, 2009.

Dennell, Robin. 'Smoke and Mirrors: The Fossil Record for *Homo sapiens* between Arabia and Australia.' In *Southern Asia, Australia and the Search for Human Origins*, edited by Robin Dennell and Martin Porr, 33–50. Cambridge: Cambridge University Press, 2014.

Dennell, Robin. 'Life without the Movius Line: The Structure of the East and Southeast Asian Early Palaeolithic.' *Quaternary International* 400 (2015): 14–22.

Dennell, Robin. 'Palaeoanthropology: *Homo sapiens* in China 80,000 Years Ago.' *Nature* 526 (2015): 647–648.

Dennell, Robin. *From Arabia to the Pacific: How Our Species Colonised Asia*. New York: Routledge, 2020.

Dennell, Robin, and Martin Porr, eds. *Southern Asia, Australia and the Search for Human Origins*. Cambridge: Cambridge University Press, 2014.

Dennell, Robin, and Wil Roebroeks. 'An Asian Perspective on Early Human Dispersal from Africa.' *Nature* 438 (2005): 1099–1104.

Descola, Philippe. *Beyond Nature and Culture*. Chicago, IL: Chicago University Press, 2013.

Détroit, Florent, Eusebio Dizon, Hameau Falgueres, Sebastien, Wilfredo Ronquillo, and Francois Semah. 'Upper Pleistocene *Homo sapiens* from Tabon Cave (Palawan, the Philippines): Description and Dating of New Discoveries.' *C.R. Palevol* 3 (2004): 705–712.

Détroit, Florent, Armand Salvador Mijares, Julien Corny, Guillaume Daver, Clément Zanolli, Eusebio Dizon, Emil Robles, Rainer Grün, and Philip J. Piper. 'A New Species of *Homo* from the Late Pleistocene of the Philippines.' *Nature* 568 (2019): 181–186.

Field, Julie S., and Marta Mirazon Lahr. 'Assessment of the Southern Dispersal: GIS-Based Analyses of Potential Routes of Oxygen Isotopic Stage 4.' *Journal of World Prehistory* 19, no. 1 (2006): 1–45.

Galbraith, J.K. *A History of Economics: The Past as the Present*. London: Penguin, 1989.

Gamble, Clive S. *Settling the Earth: The Archaeology of Deep Human History*. Cambridge: Cambridge University Press, 2014.

Habgood, Philip J., and Natalie Franklin. 'The Revolution That Didn't Arrive: A Review of Pleistocene Sahul.' *Journal of Human Evolution* 55 (2008): 187–222.

Haidle, Miriam, and Alfred Pawlik. 'Pleistocene Modernity: An Exclusively Afro-European Issue?' *Bulletin of the Indo-Pacific Prehistory Association* 30 (2010): 3–8.

Hershkovitz, Israel, Gerhard W. Weber, Rolf Quam, Mathieu Duval, Rainer Grün, Leslie Kinsley, Avner Ayalon, Miryam Bar-Matthews, Helene Valladas, Norbert Mercier, et al. 'The Earliest Modern Humans Outside Africa.' *Science* 359, no. 6374 (2018): 456–459.

Ingicco, T., G.D. van den Bergh, C. Jago-on, J.J. Bahain, M.G. Chacón, N. Amano, H. Forestier, C. King, K. Manalo, S. Nomade, et al. 'Earliest Known Hominin Activity in the Philippines by 709 Thousand Years Ago.' *Nature* 557 (2018): 233–237.
Ingold, Tim. 'From Complementarity to Obviation: On Dissolving the Boundaries between Social and Biological Anthropology, Archaeology and Psychology.' *Zeitschrift für Ethnologie* 123 (1998): 21–52.
Ingold, Tim. *The Perception of the Environment: Essays in Livelihood, Dwelling and Skill.* London: Routledge, 2000.
Ingold, Tim. 'Beyond Biology and Culture: The Meaning of Evolution in a Relational World.' *Social Anthropology* 12, no. 2 (2004): 209–221.
Ingold, Tim. *Being Alive: Essays on Movement, Knowledge and Description.* London: Routledge, 2011.
Ingold, Tim, and Gisli Palsson, eds. *Biosocial Becomings: Integrating Social and Biological Anthropology.* Cambridge: Cambridge University Press, 2013.
Kaifu, Yousuke. 'Archaic Hominin Populations in Asia before the Arrival of Modern Humans: Their Phylogeny and Implications for the "Southern Denisovans".' *Current Anthropology* 58, supplement 17 (2017): S418–S434.
Kaifu, Yousuke, Masami Izuho, Ted Goebel, Hiroyuki Sato, and Akira Ono, eds. *Emergence and Diversity of Modern Human Behavior in Paleolithic Asia.* College Station: Texas A&M University Press, 2015.
Kandel, Andrew W., Michael Bolus, Knut Bretzke, Angela A. Bruch, Miriam N. Haidle, Christine Hertler, and Michael Märker. 'Increasing Behavioral Flexibility? An Integrative Macro-Scale Approach to Understanding the Middle Stone Age of Southern Africa.' *Journal of Archaeological Method and Theory* 23, no. 2 (2016): 623–668.
Klein, Richard G., and Blake Edgar. *The Dawn of Human Culture: A Bold New Theory on What Sparked the 'Big Bang' of Human Consciousness.* New York: John Wiley & Sons, 2002.
Langley, Michelle C., Christopher Clarkson, and Sean Ulm. 'From Small Holes to Grand Narratives: The Impact of Taphonomy and Sample Size on the Modernity Debate in Australia and New Guinea.' *Journal of Human Evolution* 61 (2011): 197–208.
Lawrence, Helen, ed. *Mungo over Millennia: The Willandra Landscape and its People.* Rosny Park: Maygog Publishing, 2006.
Liebmann, M., and Uzma Z. Rizvi, eds. *Archaeology and the Postcolonial Critique.* Lanham: AltaMira Press, 2008.
Liu, Wu, Maria Martinon-Torres, Yan-jun Cai, Song Xing, Hao-wen Tong, Shu-wen Pei, Mark Jan Sier, Xiao-hong Wu, R. Lawrence Edwards, Hai Cheng, et al. 'The Earliest Unequivocally Modern Humans in Southern China.' *Nature* 526 (2015): 696–699.
Lycett, Stephen J., and Christopher J. Bae. 'The Movius Line Controversy: The State of the Debate.' *World Archaeology* 42, no. 4 (2010): 521–544.
Macintosh, N.W.G. 'The Physical Aspect of Man in Australia.' In *Aboriginal Man in Australia: Essays in Honour of Emeritus Professor A.P. Elkin*, edited by R.M. Berndt and C.M. Berndt, 29–70. Sydney: Angus & Robertson, 1965.
Malaspinas, Anna-Sapfo, Michael C. Westaway, Craig Muller, Vitor C. Sousa, Oscar Lao, Isabel Alves, Anders Bergström, Georgios Athanasiadis, Jade Y. Cheng, Jacob E. Crawford, et al. 'A Genomic History of Aboriginal Australia.' *Nature* 538 (2016): 207–214.
Marks, Jonathan. 'Race: Past, Present, and Future.' In *Revisiting Race in a Genomic Age*, edited by Barbara A. Koenig, Sandra Soo-Jin Lee, and Sarah S. Richardson, 21–38. New Brunswick: Rutgers University Press, 2008.
Marks, Jonathan. *Tales of the Ex-Apes. How We Think About Human Evolution.* Oakland: University of California Press, 2015.
Marks, Jonathan. *Is Science Racist?* Cambridge: Polity, 2017.
McBrearty, Sally, and Alison S. Brooks. 'The Revolution That Wasn't: A New Interpretation of the Origin of Modern Human Behavior.' *Journal of Human Evolution* 39 (2000): 453–563.

McDougall, Ian, Francis H. Brown, and John G. Fleagle. 'Stratigraphic Placement and Age of Modern Humans from Kibish, Ethiopia.' *Nature* 433 (2005): 733–736.
McManus, Siobhan. 'Biological Explanations and Their Limits: Paleoanthropology among the Sciences.' In *Rethinking Human Evolution*, edited by Jeffery H. Schwartz, 31–52. Cambridge, MA: The MIT Press, 2017.
Mehari, Asmeret G., and Kokeli Ryano. 'Maasai People and Oldupai (Olduvai) Gorge: Looking for Sustainable People-Centred Approaches and Practices.' In *Community Archaeology and Heritage in Africa*, edited by Peter R. Schmidt and Innocent Pikirayi, 21–45. New York: Routledge, 2016.
Mellars, Paul. 'Why Did Modern Human Populations Disperse from Africa ca. 60,000 Years Ago? A New Model.' *Proceedings of the National Academy of Sciences* 103, no. 25 (2006): 9381–9386.
Mellars, Paul, K. Boyle, Ofer Bar-Yosef, and Chris Stringer, eds. *Rethinking the Human Revolution: New Behavioural and Biological Perspectives on the Origin and Dispersal of Modern Humans*. Cambridge: McDonald Institute for Archaeological Research, 2007.
Mellars, Paul, and Chris Stringer, eds. *The Human Revolution. Behavioural and Biological Perspectives in the Origins of Modern Humans*. Edinburgh: Edinburgh University Press, 1989.
Mijares, Armand Salvador, Florent Détroit, P.J. Piper, Rainer Gruen, Peter Bellwood, Maxime Aubert, Guillaume Champion, Nida Cuevas, Alexandra De Leon, and Eusebio Dizon. 'New Evidence for a 67,000-Year-Old Human Presence at Callao Cave, Luzon, Philippines.' *Journal of Human Evolution* 59, no. 1 (2010): 123–132.
Morphy, Howard. *Museums, Infinity and the Culture of Protocols*. New York: Routledge, 2020.
Movius, Hallam L., Jr. 'The Lower Palaeolithic Cultures of Southern and Eastern Asia.' *Transactions of the American Philosophical Society* 38, no. 4 (1948): 329–420.
Nielsen, Rasmus, Joshua M. Akey, Mattias Jakobsson, Jonathan K. Pritchard, Sarah Tishkoff, and Eske Willerslev. 'Tracing the Peopling of the World through Genomics.' *Nature* 541 (2017): 302–310.
Noble, William, and Ian Davidson. 'The Evolutionary Emergence of Modern Human Behaviour: Language and Its Archaeology.' *Man (N.S.)* 26, no. 2 (1991): 223–253.
Nowell, April. 'Defining Behavioral Modernity in the Context of Neandertal and Anatomically Modern Human Populations.' *Annual Review of Anthropology* 39, no. 1 (2010): 437–452.
Nunn, Patrick D. *The Edge of Memory: Ancient Stories, Oral Tradition and the Post-Glacial World*. London: Bloomsbury Sigma, 2018.
O'Connell, James F., Jim Allen, Martin A.J. Williams, Alan N. Williams, Chris S.M. Turney, Nigel A. Spooner, Johan Kamminga, Graham Brown, and Alan Cooper. 'When Did *Homo sapiens* First Reach Southeast Asia and Sahul?' *Proceedings of the National Academy of Sciences* 115, no. 34 (2018): 8482–8490.
Onciul, Bryony. *Museums, Heritage and Indigenous Voice: Decolonising Engagement*. London: Routledge, 2015.
Oppenheimer, Stephen. 'The Great Arc of Dispersal of Modern Humans: Africa to Australia.' *Quaternary International* 202, no. 1–2 (2009): 2–13.
Pääbo, Svante. *Neanderthal Man: In Search of Lost Genomes*. New York: Basic Books, 2014.
Pardoe, Colin. 'Becoming Australian: Evolutionary Processes and Biological Variation from Ancient to Modern Times.' *Before Farming* 1 (2006): 1–21.
Petraglia, Michael D., Peter Ditchfield, Sacha Jones, Ravi Korisettar, and J.N. Pal. 'The Toba Volcanic Super-Eruption, Environmental Change, and Hominin Occupation History in India over the Last 140,000 Years.' *Quaternary International* 258 (2012): 119–134.
Petraglia, Michael D., and Ceri Shipton. 'Large Cutting Tool Variation West and East of the Movius Line.' *Journal of Human Evolution* 55 (2008): 962–966.
Porr, Martin. 'Identifying Behavioural Modernity: Lessons from Sahul.' *Bulletin of the Indo-Pacific Prehistory Association* 30 (2010): 28–34.
Porr, Martin. 'One Step Forward, Two Steps Back: The Issue of "Behavioral Modernity" Again: A Comment on Shea.' *Current Anthropology* 52, no. 4 (2011): 581–582.

Porr, Martin. 'Essential Questions: "Modern Humans" and the Capacity for Modernity.' In *Southern Asia, Australia and the Search for Human Origins*, edited by Robin Dennell and Martin Porr, 257–264. Cambridge: Cambridge University Press, 2014.

Porr, Martin. 'Lives and Lines: Integrating Molecular Genetics, the "Origins of Modern Humans" and Indigenous Knowledge.' In *Long History, Deep Time: Deepening Histories of Place*, edited by Ann McGrath and Mary Anne Jebb, 203–219. Canberra: ANU Press, 2015.

Porr, Martin. 'The Temporality of Humanity and the Colonial Landscape of the Deep Human Past.' In *Interrogating Human Origins: Decolonisation and the Deep Human Past*, edited by Martin Porr and Jacqueline Maree Matthews, 184–207. London: Routledge, 2020.

Porr, Martin, and Jacqueline Maree Matthews. 'Thinking Through Story.' *Hunter Gatherer Research* 2, no. 3 (2016): 249–274.

Porr, Martin, and Jacqueline Maree Matthews. 'Post-colonialism, Human Origins and the Paradox of Modernity.' *Antiquity* 91, no. 358 (2017): 1058–1068.

Porr, Martin, and Jacqueline Maree Matthews, eds., *Interrogating Human Origins: Decolonisation and the Deep Human Past* (Archaeological Orientations). London: Routledge, 2020.

Potts, Richard. 'Evolution and Environmental Change in Early Human Prehistory.' *Annual Review of Anthropology* 41 (2012): 151–167.

Proctor, Robert N. 'Three Roots of Human Recency: Molecular Anthropology, the Refigured Acheulean, and the UNESCO Response to Auschwitz.' *Current Anthropology* 44, no. 2 (2003): 213–239.

Prüfer, Kay, Fernando Racimo, Nick Patterson, Flora Jay, Sriram Sankararaman, Susanna Sawyer, Anja Heinze, Gabriel Renaud, Peter H. Sudmant, Cesare de Filippo, et al. 'The Complete Genome Sequence of a Neanderthal from the Altai Mountains.' *Nature* 505 (2013): 43–49.

Qui, Jane. 'The Forgotten Continent.' *Nature* 535 (2016): 22–25.

Reich, David, Richard E. Green, Martin Kircher, Johannes Krause, Nick Patterson, and Eric Y. Durand. 'Genetic History of an Archaic Hominin Group from Denisova Cave in Siberia.' *Nature* 468 (2010): 1053–1060.

Reich, David, Nick Patterson, Martin Kircher, Frederick Delfin, M.R. Nandineni, Irina Pugach, Albert Min-Shan Ko, Ying-Chin Ko, Timothy A. Jinam, Maude E. Phipps, et al. 'Denisova Admixture and the First Modern Human Dispersals into Southeast Asia and Oceania.' *American Journal of Human Genetics* 89, no. 4 (2011): 516–528.

Ritter, David. *Contesting Native Title. From Controversy to Consensus in the Struggle over Indigenous Land Rights*. Crows Nest: Allen & Unwin, 2009.

Roberts, Patrick, and Brian A. Stewart. 'Defining the "Generalist Specialist" Niche for Pleistocene *Homo sapiens*.' *Nature Human Behaviour* 2, no. 8 (2018): 542–550.

Roncaglia, A. *The Wealth of Ideas: A History of Economic Thought*. Cambridge: Cambridge University Press, 2005.

Sahlins, Marshall. 'The Sadness of Sweetness: The Native Anthropology of Western Cosmology.' *Current Anthropology* 37, no. 3 (1996): 395–428.

Scerri, Eleanor M.L., Mark G. Thomas, Andrea Manica, Philipp Gunz, Jay T. Stock, Chris Stringer, Matt Grove, Huw S. Groucutt, Axel Timmermann, G. Philip Rightmire, et al. 'Did Our Species Evolve in Subdivided Populations across Africa, and Why Does It Matter?' *Trends in Ecology & Evolution* 33, no. 8 (2018): 582–594.

Schwartz, Jeffery H. *The Red Ape. Orangutans and Human Origins*. Cambridge, MA: Westview Press, 2005.

Shang, Hong, Haowen Tong, Shuangquan Zhang, Fuyou Chen, and Erik Trinkaus. 'An Early Modern Human from Tianyuan Cave, Zhoukoudian, China.' *Proceedings of the National Academy of Sciences* 104, no. 16 (2007): 6573–6578.

Shea, John J. 'Neandertals and Early Modern *Homo sapiens* in the Near East.' In *South-Eastern Mediterranean Peoples between 130,00–10,000 Years Ago*, edited by Elena Garcea, 126–143. Oxford: Oxford University Press, 2010.

Shea, John J. '*Homo sapiens* Is as *Homo sapiens* Was.' *Current Anthropology* 52, no. 1 (2011): 1–35.

Shea, John J., and Ofer Bar-Yosef. 'Who Were the Skhul/Qafzeh People? An Archaeological Perspective on Eurasia's Oldest Modern Humans.' *Journal of the Israel Prehistoric Society* 35 (2005): 451–468.

Sikora, Martin. 'A Genomic View of the Pleistocene Population History of Asia.' *Current Anthropology* 58, supplement 17 (2017): S397–S405.

Stern, Nicola. 'The Archaeology of the Willandra.' In *Long History, Deep Time: Deepening Histories of Place*, edited by Ann McGrath and Mary Anne Jebb, 221–240. Canberra: ANU Press, 2015.

Storm, Paul, Fachroel Aziz, Jan de Vos, Dikdik Kosasih, Sinung Baskoro, Ngaliman, and Lars van den Hoek Ostende. 'Late Pleistocene *Homo sapiens* in a Tropical Rainforest Fauna in East Java.' *Journal of Human Evolution* 49, no. 4 (2005): 536–545.

Stringer, Chris. *The Origin of Our Species*. London: Allen Lane, 2011.

Stringer, Chris. 'The Origin and Evolution of *Homo sapiens*.' *Philosophical Transactions of the Royal Society B* 371 (2016): 20150237.

Sutikna, Thomas, Matthew W. Tocheri, Michael J. Morwood, E. Wahyu Saptomo, Jatmiko, Rokus Due Awe, Sri Wasisto, Kira E. Westaway, Maxime Aubert, Bo Li, et al. 'Revised stratigraphy and chronology for *Homo floresiensis* at Liang Bua in Indonesia.' *Nature* 532 (2016): 366–369.

Thomas, Julian. *Archaeology and Modernity*. New York: Routledge, 2004.

Toussaint, Sandy, ed. *Crossing Boundaries: Cultural, Legal, Historical and Practical Issues in Native Title*. Melbourne: Melbourne University Press, 2004.

Wagner, Roy. *The Invention of Culture*. 2nd ed. Chicago, IL: Chicago University Press, 2016.

Weidenreich, Franz. *Apes, Giants and Man*. Chicago, IL: The University of Chicago Press, 1946.

Westaway, K.E., J. Louys, R. Due Awe, M.J. Morwood, G.J. Price, J. x Zhao, M. Aubert, R. Joannes-Boyau, T.M. Smith, M.M. Skinner, et al. 'An Early Modern Human Presence in Sumatra 73,000–63,000 Years Ago.' *Nature* 548 (2017): 322–325.

White, T.D., B. Asfaw, D. DeGusta, H. Gilbert, G.C. Richards, G. Suwa, and F.C. Howell. 'Pleistocene *Homo sapiens* from Middle Awash, Ethiopia.' *Nature* 423 (2003): 742–747.

Will, Manuel, Nicholas J. Conard, and Christian A. Tryon. 'Timing and Trajectory of Cultural Evolution on the African Continent 200,000–30,000 Years Ago.' In *Modern Human Origins and Dispersal*, edited by Yonatan Sahle, Hugo Reyes-Centeno, and Christian Bentz, 25–72. Tübingen: Kerns Verlag, 2019.

Witmore, Christopher. 'Chronopolitics and Archaeology.' In *The Encyclopedia of Global Archaeology*, edited by Claire Smith, 1471–1476. New York: Springer, 2014.

Wolpoff, Milford H., and Rachel Caspari. *Race and Evolution*. New York: Simon & Schuster, 1997.

Wood, Bernard. 'Reconstructing Human Evolution: Achievements, Challenges, and Opportunities.' *Proceedings of the National Academy of Sciences* 107, supplement 2 (2010): 8902–8909.

Zhu, Zhaoyu, Robin Dennell, Weiwen Huang, Yi Wu, Shifan Qiu, Shixia Yang, Zhiguo Rao, Yamei Hou, Jiubing Xie, Jiangwei Han, and Tingping Ouyang. 'Hominin Occupation of the Chinese Loess Plateau Since About 2.1 Million Years Ago.' *Nature* 559 (2018): 608–612.

7
SINGING TO ANCESTORS
Respecting and re-telling stories woven through ancient ancestral lands

Paulette Steeves[1]

Tansi (Hello), my name is Paulette Steeves, I am Cree-Metis and European. I was born in Whitehorse, Yukon Territories, and grew up in British Columbia. As an Indigenous academic, I work to weave Indigenous practices of respect, relationality, and reciprocity into all that I do. In introducing myself and acknowledging my ancestors, I clarify my position as an Indigenous academic and researcher. I intentionally locate myself as an Indigenous person first and a researcher second – this presents the ways of being, knowing, and doing that my research is based in. In providing this background and these details, 'I am also identifying, defining, and describing the elements of Indigenist research.'[2]

Research that is framed in Indigenous ways of knowing, being, and doing is based on respect, relationality, and reciprocity; it is praxis that weaves through institutional and public spaces to create social change. Such social change addresses the past real-world consequences of colonial archaeology in the present.[3] For Indigenous scholars, research is ceremony.[4] Reclaiming Indigenous histories and links to the land weaves ancestors' voices throughout the universe, in songs and practices of respect.

Ceremonies of reclaiming, re-telling, and respect

Respect is woven through Indigenous research in many ways. However, in most Western scholars' discussions of Indigenous people, this is an often-missing aspect of research and discussions. In my research, I discuss the entire area of the Western Hemisphere. This is a land area that includes thousands of diverse Indigenous communities. What do you call a land that is known to Indigenous people by many different names? The Iroquois and Mohawks share creation stories of their homelands, Turtle Island, the area we know today as North America. In present-day Mesoamerica, Indigenous people's oral histories hold knowledge of their homeland, known as the Land Between the Waters. The diversity of Indigenous people of the Western Hemisphere, the areas known today as North and South America, is immense. More than half of the world's language families are found in the Western Hemisphere,[5] attesting to an incredible diversity of Indigenous cultures and people across time.

> The unmistakable testimony of the linguistic evidence is that the New World had been inhabited nearly as long as Australia or New Guinea, perhaps some 35,000 years.[6]

The diversity of language families in the Western Hemisphere provides evidence of numerous distinct cultural groups. On a global scale, there are roughly 6,000 languages that fall into approximately 300 separate families.[7] The Western Hemisphere's language families account for minimally 150–180 of the 300 currently known language families in the world, that is, over half of the linguistic diversity of the world.[8] The Indigenous languages of the Western Hemisphere emerged during the time of Indigenous people within the region.

Western knowledge production of Indigenous histories has a way of erasing many things: humanity, diversity, languages, knowledge, rights, and land. Colonisation has never ended for Indigenous people; it continues in insidious ways to erase, deny, and dehumanise, fuelling racism and ongoing normalisation of violence against Indigenous people. Indigenous homelands in the Western Hemisphere buckle beneath the heavy weight of colonial words and enforced identities such as *terra nullius, savage, infantile, New World*. Indigenous people's names for places on the land, and their oral histories, rock art, and petroglyphs are most often ignored by Western academics. However, Indigenous histories tell of thousands of years of living on the land in the areas we know today as the Americas. So, referring back to my question: what do you respectfully call a land that is known to diverse communities of Indigenous people by many different names? The land that is known today as the Americas I call The Indigenous Homelands of the Western Hemisphere. In this chapter, I highlight Indigenous histories in the Western Hemisphere, prior to the violence of Western-imposed histories of a wild, uncivilised, *terra nullius*. Western academic literature regarding Indigenous histories of the Western Hemisphere is most often framed by archaeologists' discussions and archaeological site reports.

Archaeologists study to earn their degrees in Western Universities; they learn to apply Western theories and research methods to all the work that they do. Very few Western Universities require students in anthropology or archaeology programmes to take courses on Indigenous histories, literature, or languages. Some Western Universities offer courses focused on Indigenous history as an elective course for a degree in anthropology. In a 2019 review of hundreds of archaeological programmes on a global scale, I found that none required a course on Indigenous people of the particular region the programmes were located in. There may be archaeology programmes that require regional studies to earn an archaeology degree, but my research team and I found none requiring a course on Indigenous history.

Unless scholars and writers know the literature of the peoples that they are studying or writing about they cannot provide what their students and readers are seeking and deserving of. There is, fortunately, enough literature, both oral and written, available for scholarly study, but it has for the most part been neglected. Myths, legends, and songs have not been regenerated and set in modern terms to earn immortalization in poetry, dramatization in plays, or romanticization in novels. What has prevented the acceptance of Indian literature as a serious and legitimate expression of native thought and experience has been indifferent and inferior translation, a lack of understanding and interest in the culture and a notion that it has little of importance to offer to the larger white culture.[9]

All communities have creation stories. Archaeologists, palaeontologists, geologists, and other researchers also share stories of their understanding of human and mammalian evolution. However, Western scholars most often view the world half-blind, generally uninformed of the worldviews and languages of the people whose histories they most often invent. Indigenous histories and Indigenous knowledge of the past are found in many forms, oral histories, rock art, petroglyphs, songs, dances, and ceremonies, all in a language not accessible to anyone outside of a particular Indigenous community. Though a few scholars have dedicated space in courses and programmes to sharing Indigenous knowledges and voices, most have not attempted to teach or to learn history from an Indigenous perspective.

> Every human society maintains its sense of identity with a set of stories that explain, at least to its satisfaction, how things came to be. A good many societies begin at creation and carry forward a tenuous link of events, which they consider to be historical which is to say actual experiences of that group that often serve as precedents for determining present and future actions.[10]

Many Western discussions of the Indigenous past of the Western Hemisphere are not based in facts, but in Eurocentric conjecture. Such discussions create perceptions of Indigenous people that are framed more by what people are *not* taught than what they *are* taught. Based on my own experience and research in Western academies, students are not often, if ever, provided books or articles authored by Indigenous communities and scholars. However, there are many stories of the past, many voices to draw on, in teaching history. Stories travel around and through perceptions of people and place in the past, weaving through the present. Indigenous histories held in oral traditions, rock art, and petroglyphs are often not known to Western scholars or archaeologists, and are ignored in Western-centred discussions of the Indigenous past and present. As Vine Deloria Jr explains:

> The Indian explanation is always cast aside as superstition, precluding Indians from having an acceptable status as human beings, and reducing them in the eyes of educated people to a prehuman level of ignorance. Indians must simply take whatever status they have been granted by scientists at the point at which they become acceptable to science.[11]

A few self-informed Western scholars have worked to provide factual stories of the deep Indigenous past through archaeology.[12] However, they have often faced ridicule and extreme criticism for their honesty. The archaeological evidence for an earlier than 11,000–12,000-year human habitation of the Western Hemisphere (the Americas), published by a few archaeologists, pushed back against the normalised violence of erasure of Indigenous links to the land in academic circles. As I have argued elsewhere:

> The Indigenous past of the Western Hemisphere (the Americas) has been fabricated to fit into neoliberal timeframes of imagined 'New Worlds'. The deep past of the Indigenous people of the Western Hemisphere has traditionally been and in many ways remains a tool of dis-empowerment and dehumanizing oppression, created by American archaeologists to keep Indigenous civilizations as 'infantile' on a global scale.[13]

Weaving the past through Indigenous oral traditions links people to places, to all beings as relations, through stories, songs, dances, and memories held in the land. People have been in the Western Hemisphere since creation, since time immemorial. Indigenous oral traditions carry the past through intricate metaphors and languages that are beyond Western academic conceptions. Indigenous histories spoken and sung in Indigenous languages have been carefully beaded through the fabric of life and land with respect and reciprocity for all beings.

Archaeological sites

In studies of archaeological sites, pieces of Indigenous histories emerge from the land where ancestral people left their stories. From stone tools found at many sites in the Western Hemisphere, American archaeologists created stories about the so-called Clovis People, a fictional pan-hemispheric cultural group that archaeologists claimed were the first people to enter the Western Hemisphere 11,000–12,000 years ago. However, there are hundreds of archaeological sites in the Western Hemisphere that date to earlier than these Clovis timeframes. The oldest sites are concentrated in the southwest coastal area of North America and central Mexico.[14]

American archaeologists have long denied that Indigenous communities were present in the Western Hemisphere (the Americas) prior to 11,000–12,000 years ago. Many people who have published articles on archaeological sites older than this, or older than the so-called Clovis horizon, have experienced academic bullying and censure for their honesty.[15] Overly aggressive critiques of earlier-than-12,000-year-old archaeological sites have created a dangerous academic field of study, where archaeologists are attacked for discussing evidence that goes against a colonial status quo of recent time for the initial peopling of the Western Hemisphere. Deloria, a prominent Sioux scholar, discussed the dehumanisation and erasure of Indigenous people and histories. He has critiqued the history presented by archaeologists as recent on a world scale and the hypothesis of the Bering Land Bridge theory of initial recent migrations into the Americas as absurd.[16] Holm and Reid remind us that Western discussions of the past are not supported by a solid body of evidence, and that other stories and first-hand accounts of the history are valid:

> In the world today, there is a common held belief that thousands of years ago, as the world counts time, Mongolian nomads crossed a land bridge to enter the Western Hemisphere, and became the people known as the American Indians. There is, it can be said, some scanty evidence to support the myth of the land bridge. But there is enormous wealth of proof that the other truths are all valid.[17]

Material evidence of a human presence from archaeological sites throughout the world is similar; Pleistocene age artefacts are mainly stone and bone. Many archaeological sites contain stone tools and artefacts, evidence of the human use of fire, and animal butchering. In understanding the evidence of a killing or butchering site, researchers have conducted controlled replication experiments to understand the difference between human and animal marks on bone.[18] From archaeological evidence and research into bone breakage patterns, it is clear that on a global scale early humans used animal bone to fashion tools, and in some areas for structures and for marrow as a source of food.

Some archaeological sites have excellent preservation of materials and provide numerous forms of evidence. Monte Verde in Chile is one site where preservation was excellent. The evidence included wood tent remains, hearths, a lance, medicinal and edible plants, animal bones, hide and soft tissue, human foot prints, pebble tools, and biface fragments.[19] The upper level at Monte Verde dated to 14,600 cal yr BP.[20] In another area of the site, at a deeper level, man-made artefacts and burned areas were found. Dates returned from this evidence suggest that people were in the Americas as early as 30,000 years ago.[21] Dillehay et al. found evidence of marine plant species at Monte Verde, which is located 90 km inland from the coast of Chile:

> Remains of nine species of marine algae were recovered from hearths and other features at Monte Verde II, an upper occupational layer, and were directly dated between 14,220 and 13,980 calendar years before the present (~12,310 and 12,290 carbon-14 years ago). These findings support the archaeological interpretation of the site and indicate that the site's inhabitants used seaweed from distant beaches and estuarine environments for food and medicine.[22]

What techniques were used to gain this information?

Knowledge related to plants, food medicine, seasons, astronomy, and ceremonies are recorded in oral histories, rock art, and petroglyphs. To understand the linkages between archaeological sites (stories held in the land) oral traditions, rock art, and petroglyphs, we are required to listen to Indigenous knowledge held in many forms. Evidence of Indigenous people's knowledge and their recording of events and the environment have been ignored and disputed by academic scholars in the Americas for centuries. Academic scholars have reported on evidence of Indigenous people documenting flora and fauna, celestial events, and ceremonies. For example, research on a carving of a mammoth, on bone, that was found in Florida has been dated to the late Pleistocene, providing recorded evidence of human experiences with a species known to be extinct for over 10,000 years.

> In 1916, Dr E.H. Sellards, the State Geologist of Florida, announced the discovery of human skeletal remains in apparent association with numerous species of extinct late Ice Age animals from the main canal at Vero Beach, Florida. His claim has been disputed for 95 years, even though it is now well known that people were in the Western Hemisphere and hunted those animals during the Terminal Pleistocene. The results of the testing done in this work of the recently discovered fragmented fossil bone bearing the unmistakable engraving of an ancient proboscidean recovered from the same area of the canal as the human and animal fossils reported in 1916 appear to support E.H. Sellards argument that the Vero site provided evidence of a Pleistocene human presence in North America.[23]

Purdy et al. studied the carving, applying rare earth element analysis showing that the fossil was from Vero Beach, and optical and electron microscopy that supported the argument that mineralisation on the bottom of the carving matched the surrounding bone, and that the carving was a legitimate Pleistocene-age artefact.[24]

Not all archaeological sites hold ancient art or human remains, or provide such an extensive view of the human past as the Monte Verde site. However, even one small piece of bone can challenge embedded theories of the human past and completely change what we know about our own evolution. This is clear from recent genetic studies of Hominin (the group consisting of modern humans and extinct human species, including Ardipithecus, Australopithecus, Paranthropus, and all modern human immediate ancestors) remains found in the Eastern Hemisphere that provided evidence for a previously unknown Hominin species.[25] Researchers are now re-evaluating the claims that all modern humans descended from one small group that came out of Africa and replaced all other hominins. This re-evaluation is due to the discovery of evidence for new hominins, namely Denisovans, known from fragmented fossil remains found in current-day Siberia, Russia, and genetic evidence showing that some modern humans carry genetic materials of Neanderthals, Denisovans, and another yet-unknown ancestor.[26] Recent challenges to simple linear theories of modern human evolution are a strong reminder that there is often a lot we do not know, and thus an acknowledgement of our own ignorance is an important starting point in research and in decolonising knowledge production.[27]

Some archaeological sites in North America have been linked to Indigenous communities' oral traditions of the area, and discuss interactions of extinct Pleistocene species. The Kimmswick archaeological site in Missouri[28] and the La Sena archaeological site[29] in southwest Nebraska, to name just two. Weaving Indigenous histories and knowledge together with archaeological stories from the land creates a much more informed and richer understanding of the past. To understand people's movements across time and space in the Western Hemisphere, it is pivotal to create a hemisphere-wide view of known archaeological sites, rock art sites, and oral traditions of genesis stories and histories linking people to places across time. This is an enormous undertaking, one that will take years, and will constantly be a work in progress as new sites and oral histories come to be known.

Mapping the locations of archaeological sites on a continental scale provides a way to visualise human movements across time. Though mapping archaeological sites does not provide a comprehensive view of the human past, but a selective view of what we may know to date – we will never know all there is to know about the human past, and new archaeological sites are discovered every year. The following map shows a selection of Pleistocene archaeological sites in both the Eastern and Western Hemispheres, during the Pleistocene when the Eastern and Western Hemispheres were connected by a land mass area 57 miles across. Early humans left stories on the land (archaeological sites) everywhere in the world. The map is selective, not a representation of all Pleistocene archaeological sites. The time given of the archaeological sites on the map is prior to the height of the Last Glacial Maximum. There were many glacial and interglacial periods during the Pleistocene, times when the Eastern and Western Hemispheres were virtually ice free and areas in the Northern and Southern Hemispheres were covered in forest and grasslands (Figure 7.1; Table 7.1).

From the maps, we can see that early humans travelled across areas we know today as Asia and the Middle East before two million years ago. The land in the northern Eastern and Western Hemispheres was during interglacial times of the

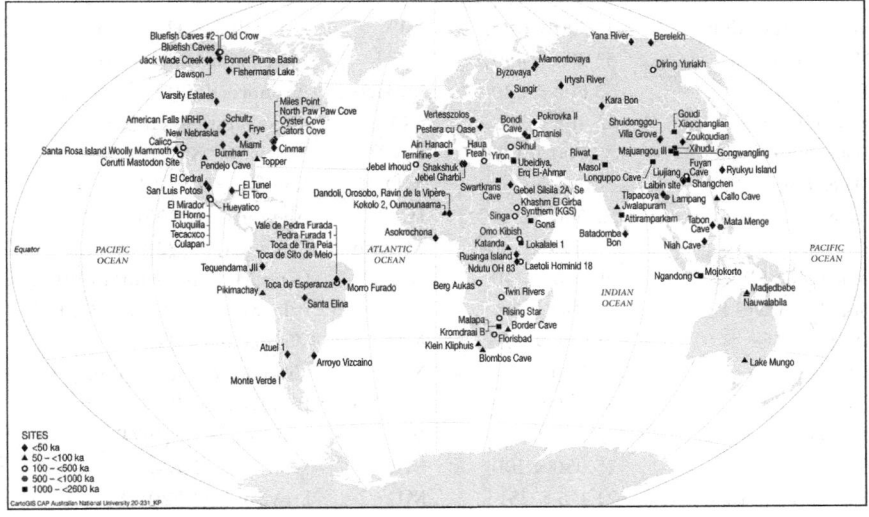

Figure 7.1 Map of selected Pleistocene archaeological sites.

171

Table 7.1 List of selected Pleistocene archaeological sites

North America archaeological sites list

Site name	^{14}C BP Noted	Area unless otherwise	References
El Horno	280,000 230 Th	Mexico	Malde et al. (2011)
Hueyatlaco-Valsequillo	245,000	Mexico	Steen-McIntire et al. (1981)
El Mirador-Valsequillo	200,000	Mexico	Steen-McIntyre et al. (1981)
Texacaxco-Valsequillo	200,000	Mexico	Camacho (1978)
Calico	200,000	CA	Leakey et al. (1968)
Cerutti Site	135,000 Th/U	CA	Holen et al. (2017)
Pendejo Cave	55,000	NM	MacNeish and Liddy (2003)
Topper	54,700	SC	Adovasio and Peddler (2017)
Old Crow	12,000–120,000	YK	Bryan (1986)
Schultz	39,350 ± 770	SD	Holen and Holen (2017)
Toluquilla	38,000 ± 8570	Mexico	Gonzalez et al. (2006)
Santa Rosa Island Wooly Mammoth	40,000	CA	Cressman (1977)
Burnham	40,900 ± 1600	OK	Wycoff (1990)
El Cedral	33,300 ± 2700	Mexico	Lorenzo and Mirambell (1986)
Malakoff	Geological 26 ft deep	TX	Sellards (1941)
Bonnet Plume	36,000 ± 300	YT	Hughes (1981)
Frye	35,000–40,000	IL	Munson and Frye (1965)
Miami Mastodon	41,700 ± 6100	MO	Dunnell and Hamilton (1995)
New Nebraska	33,590 ± 450	NE	Holen and Holen (2014)
Tlapacoya	33,500 ± 3200	Mexico	Agenbroad (2005)
Villa Grove	33,405 ± 340	CO	Holen and Holen (2014)
Fisherman's Lake	32,700 ± 1900	NWT	Miller (1968)
Miles Point	32,562 ± 290	MD	Lowery et al. (2010)
American Falls	31,300 ± 2300	ID	Agenbroad (2005)
San Luis Potosi	30,000–25,000	Mexico	Perez-Crespo (2011)
Jack Wade Creek	29,700 ± 240	AK	Cinq Mars and Morlan (1982)
Bluefish Caves I	24,820 ± 115	YT	Adovasio and Peddler (2017)
Oyster Cove	25,800 ± 120	MD	Wah et al. (2014)
Bluefish Caves II	23,500	YT	Cinq-Mars and Morlan (1999)
Dawson	23,900 ± 470	AK/YT	Bonnichsen (1979)
Cinmar (Not in Situ)	22,760 ± 90	VA	Stanford et al. (1974)
Cators Cave	25,050 ± 100	MD	Wah et al. (2014)
North Paw Paw Cove	21,116 ± 251	MD	Lowery et al. (2010)
Wakula springs	18,000 ± 4500	FL	Rink et al. (2012)

North America archaeological sites list

Site name	¹⁴C BP Noted	Area unless otherwise	References
Shaffert	15,600 ± 60	NE	Holen and May (2002)
Varsity Estates	21,000	Mexico	Gruhn and Bryan (2007)
El Tunel	21,000–11,000	Mexico	Gonzalez et al. (2006)
El Toro	21,000–11,000	Mexico	Gonzalez et al. (2006)
Cooperton	20400 ± 450	OK	Anderson (1975)
Cualapan	22,000 ± 2000	Mexico	Sazbo et al. (1969)
Cooper	10,800–10,200	OK	Bement (1997)
Lovewell	20,430 ± 300	KS	Holen and Holen (2012)
La Sena	18,860 ± 360	NE	Holen and May (2002)
Los Rayez La Paz	14,770 ± 280	Mexico	Cook (1975)
Saltville	14,510 ± 80	VA	McDonald (2000)
Petronilla Creek	18,560 ± 280	TX	Lewis (2009)
Arroyo Arenillas	18,000	Mexico	Arroyo-Cabrales et al. (2006)
Page Ladson	12,570 ± 100	FL	Collins et al. (2013)
False Cougar cave	14,590 ± 300	MT	Bonnichsen et al. (1986)
Enoch Fork Rock Shelter	10,960 ± 240	KT	Lepper (1999)
Lubbock Lake	12,650 ± 250	TX	Holliday et al. (1983)
Crane Point	18,000–12,700	MD	Lowery et al. (2010)
Hamburger	16,480 ± 60	KS	Holen and Holen (2012)
Sand Creek	16500	TX	Pertulla (2004)
Selby	16,530 ± 320	CO	Holen and Holen (2012)
Dutton	16,330 ± 320	CO	Holen and Holen (2012)
Rimrock Draw Rockshelter	15,800	OR	Henderson (2016)
Hebior 2017	12,590 ± 50	WI	Adovasio and Peddler (2017)
Prospect Shelter	16,272 ± 85	WY	Chorn et al. (1988)
Coopers Ferry	16,560–15,280	ID	Wade (2019)
Trail Creek Caves	13,070 ± 280	AK	Hamilton and Goebel (2005)
Santa Isabel Iztapan	16,000	Mexico	Hester (1960)
Debra Friedkin Site	15,500–13,200	TX	Jennings and Waters (2014)
Big Eddy	12,950 ± 120	MO	Haynes (2015)
Dry Creek	23,930 ± 9,300	AK	Powers and Hoffecker (1989)
Cactus Hill	16,670 ± 730	VA	Adovasio and Pedler (2017)
Akmak	11,000–10,000	AK	Hamilton and Goebel (2005)
Jensen	14,830 ± 230	NB	Holen and Holen (2012)
Levi Site	13,750 ± 410	TX	Alexander (1982)
Bonfire Shelter	12,430 ± 490	TX	Adovasio and Pedler (2017)
Meadowcroft Rockshelter	21,070 ± 475	PA	Adovasio and Pedler (2017)
Wilson Butte Cave	15,000 ± 800	ID	Plew et al. (1982)

(*Continued*)

North America archaeological sites list

Site name	^{14}C BP Noted	Area unless otherwise	References
Gault Site	18,500 ± 1,500	TX	Williams et al. (2018)
Las Palmas	14,500–11,000	Mexico	Gonzales et al (2008)
Sloth Hole	11,050 ± 50	FL	Waters et al. (2007)
Lucy	14,300 ± 650	NM	Agenbroad (2005)
Smith Creek Cave	14,220 ± 650	NV	Goebel et al. (2007)
Paisley Caves	12,400 ± 60	OR	Adovasio and Pedler (2017)
Heiltsuk Nation territory	14,000	BC	Jodry et al. (2017)
Vero Beach	12,130 ± 70	FL	Agenbroad (2005)
Manis	12,000 ± 310	WA	Dixon (1999)
Dust Cave	12,450	AL	Sherwood et al. (2004)
Nogabahara	11,815 ± 70	AK	Holmes et al. (2008)
Rodgers Shelter	10,530 ± 650	MO	Haynes (1991)
Perry Mastodon	11,700 ± 60	IL	Neïburger (2011)
Warm Mineral Springs	10,960 ± 40	FL	Cockrell (1987)
Mud Lake	13,530 ± 50	WI	Neff (2015)
Eve of Naharon	11,670 ± 60	Mexico	González et al. (2008)
Schaefer	12,570 ± 45	WI	Adovasio and Pedler (2017)
Fenske	13,510 ± 50	WI	Neff (2015)
MacHaffie Site	10,390 ± 40	MT	Davis et al. (2002)
Pangunguin Creek	13,500	TX	Hamilton and Goebel (2005)
Little Salt Springs	13,450 ± 190	FL	Clausen et al. (1979)
Chesrow	10,000–12,000	WI	Overstreet (1993)
Owl Ridge	11,340 ± 930	AK	Hamilton and Goebel (2005)
Wasden- Owl Cave	12,850 ± 150	ID	Plew et al. (1982)
Fort Rock Cave	13,200	OR	Bedwell (1973)
Lamb Springs	13,140 ± 1,000	CO	Stanford et al. (1981)
Paleo Crossing	13,100 ± 100	OH	Brose (1994)
Tule Springs	28,000	NV	Harrington and Simpson (1961)
McMinnville	12,890 ± 70	OR	Stenger (2012)
Shriver	12,855 ± 1,500	MO	Reagan et al. (1978)
Pleasant Lake	12,845 ± 165	MI	Shipman et al. (1984)
Bonneville Estates	12,300–10,900	NV	Goebel (2007)
Dutchess Quarry Cave	12,580 ± 370	NY	Funk and Steadman (1994)
Shoop	12,750	PA	Adovasio and Pedler (2017)
Johnson	12,660 ± 970	TN	Barker et al. (1996)
Moose Creek	11,730 ± 250	AK	Powers and Hoffecker (1989)
Cloudsplitter Rockshelter	12,360 ± 400	KT	Cowan et al. (1981)
Puckett	12,330	TN	Norton et al. (1993)
Eppley Rock Shelter	12,185 ± 130	OH	Steele (2010)

North America archaeological sites list

Site name	^{14}C BP Noted	Area unless otherwise	References
Swan Point	12,290 ± 40	AK	Adovasio and Pedler (2017)
Coats Hines NRHP	12,869 ± 60 OCR	TN	Deter-Wolf et al. (2011)
Kanorado	12,670 ± 35	KS	Holen and Holen (2012)
Lindsay Site	12,330 ± 50	MT	Agenbroad (2005)
Debert	10,600 ± 47	NS	McDonald (1985)
Ayer Pond Orcas Island	11,760 ± 70	WA	Kenady et al. (2010)
Smith Mountain	10,150 ± 70	VA	Childress & Blanton (1997)
Brown Valley Man	12,000	MN	Dixon (1999)
Cougar Mountain Cave II	11,950 ± 350	OR	Bedwell (1973)
Agate Basin	11,840 ± 130	WY	Agenbroad (2005)
Dry Creek	11,100	AK	Hamilton & Goebel (2005)
Firelands Ground Sloth	11,740 ± 35	OH	Redmond et al. (2012)
Broken Mammoth	15,830 ± 70	AK	Hamilton & Goebel (2005)
Mesa	11,700	AK	Kunz & Reanier (1995)
Putu Site	11,470 ± 500	AK	Hamilton & Goebel (2005)
Blackwater Draw	12,400 ± 350	NM	Agenbroad (2005)
Burning Tree	12,620 ± 90	OH	Haynes (2015)
Aubrey	11,565	TX	Haynes (2015)
Union Pacific Mammoth Site	11,560 ± 60	WY	Haynes et al. (2013)
Mill Iron	11,570 ± 170	MT	Agenbroad (2005)
Jaguar Cave	11,580 ± 250	ID	Plew et al. (1982)
Danger Cave	11,453 ± 600	UT	Jennings (1957)
Arlington Springs	10,960 ± 80	CA	Johnson et al. (2002)
Domebo	11,480 ± 450	OK	Agenbroad (2005)
Lehner	12,000 ± 450	AZ	Adovasio & Peddler (2017)
Healy Lake Village	11,410–11,090	AK	Hamilton & Gobel (2005)
Miami Site	11,415 ± 125	TX	Holiday at al. (1994)
State Road Ripple	11,385 ± 140	PA	Goreczny (2017)
La Villa de Guadalupe	11,320	Mexico	Arroyo-Cabrales et al. (2006)
Ventana Cave	11,300 ± 1,200	AZ	Haury (1950)
Marmes Rock Shelter	10,500	WA	Sheppard et al. (1987)
Charlie Lake Cave	10,500	BC	Driver & Guerrero (2015)
Whally Beach	11,350 ± 80	AB	Kooyman et al. (2001)
Lamb Site	11,400 ± 100	NY	Gramly (1999)
Fishbone Cave	11,200 ± 250	NV	Broecker et al. (1956)

(Continued)

South America archaeological sites

Site name	^{14}C BP Noted	Area unless otherwise	References
Toca da Esperanza	295,000 ± 780 (geological)	Brazil	Beltrao et al. (1987)
Pikimachay	50,000–20,200 ± 1,050	Peru	MacNeish et al. (1970)
	44,800 ± 1,400	Brazil	Guidon & Delibrias (1986)
Monte Verde I	33,370 ± 530	Chile	Dillehay (2000)
Vale da Pedra Furada	36,400 ± 3,600 OSL	Brazil	Boëda et al. (2014)
Arroyo Vizcaino	29,150 ± 290	Uruguay	Fariña et al. (2014)
Tequendama	28,890 ± 840	Colombia	Urrego & Van der Hammen (1977)
Santa Elina	27,000 ± 2,000	Brazil	Vialou et al. (2017)
Toca de Sitio do Meio	25,170 ± 140	Brazil	Boëda et al. (2016)
Atuel	23,490	Argentina	MacNeish (1978)
Toca de Tira Peia	22,000 ± 1,500 OSL	Brazil	Lahaye et al. (2013)
Morro Furado	21,090 ± 420	Brazil	Kipnis (1998)
Pubenza	17,790 ± 120	Colombia	Dillehay (2000)
Caldeirao de Rodriguez	18,600 ± 600	Brazil	Kipnis (1998)
Monte Verde II	18,500–14,500 cal BP	Chile	Dillehay et al. (2015)
Muaco	16,375 ± 400	Venezuela	Gnecco & Aceituno (2006)
Alice Böer	14,200 ± 1,150	Brazil	Beltrao et al. (1983)
Haunta	14,150	Peru	MacNeish et al. (1970)
Rancho Peludo	13,915 ± 200	Venezuela	Gnecco & Aceituno (2006)
LT Ji-Paraná-Rolim de Moura	13,720 ± 160	Brazil	Meggers & Miller (2003)
LT Brazil	13,560	Venezuela	Meggers & Miller (2003)
Quebrada El Membrillo	13,500 ± 65	Chile	Jackson et al. (2004)
Huargo Cave	13,460 ± 700	Peru	Cardich et al. (1999)
Lauricocha Cave	13,460 ± 700	Peru	Cardich (1978)
Cueva Cacao	13,300	Argentina	Aschero et al. (2013)
Cuva de la Indes	13,280	Argentina	Aschero et al. (2013)
El Inga	13,166	Ecuador	Mayer-Oakes (1986)
Atuel II	13,100	Argentina	MacNeish (1978)
Huaca Prieta	14,200 cal BP	Peru	Dillehay et al. (2017)
Sueva	13,000–10,000	Colombia	Dillehay (2000)
El Jordán	12,910 ± 60	Colombia	Salgado (1998)
El Puesto	12,890 ± 90	Argentina	Miotti & Rabassa (2000)

South America archaeological sites

Site name	^{14} C BP Noted	Area unless otherwise	References
Taima-Taima	12,890	Venezuela	Ochsenius & Gruhn (1979)
Piedra Museo	12,980 ± 90	Argentina	Miotti et al. (2003)
Complejo Paijan	12,845 ± 280	Peru	Dillehay (2000)
Rio Uruguay Basin	12,750	Uruguay	Weber (1981)
Quirihuac	12,400 ± 750	Peru	Ossa (1978)
Arroio dos Fosseis	12,770 ± 220	Brazil	Borrero (1996)
RS 1 50	12,770 ± 220	Brazil	Borrero (1996)
Santana do Riacho	12,760 ± 70	Brazil	Prous (1986)
RS Q-2	12,690 ± 100	Brazil	Miller (1987)
El Ceibo	12,600 ± 600	Uruguay	Nami (2007)
Los Toldos	12,600 ± 600	Argentina	Borrero (1996)
Guitarrero Cave	12,560 ± 360	Peru	Dillehay (2000)
Chinchihuapi	12,420 ± 130	Chile	Dillehay (2015)
El Abra	12,400 ± 160	Colombia	Dillehay (2000)
Cueva del Medio	12,390 ± 180	Chile	Borrero (1996)
La Cumbre	12,360 ± 700	Peru	Ossa (1978)
La Moderna	12,330 ± 370	Argentina	Borrero (1996)
Abrigo de Sol	12,300 ± 95	Brazil	Borrero (1996)
Garrincho	12,210 ± 40	Brazil	Guidon et al. (2000)
Lapa do Boquete	12,070 ± 170	Brazil	Prous (1996)
Telarmachay	12,040 ± 120	Peru	Lavallee et al. (1995)
Quereo 1	12,000 ± 195	Chile, Argentina	Borrero (1996)
Cerro Chivateros	12,000	Peru	Borrero (1996)
Lapa Mortuaria	11,990 ± 50	Brazil	Neves & Hubbe (2005)
Ana Riacho	11,960 ± 250	Brazil	Borrero (1996)
Largo Santa	11,950	Brazil	Neves et al. (2005)
Tres Arroyos	11,880 ± 250	Argentina	Massone et al. (1998)
Pachamachay	11,800 ± 930	Peru	Borrero (1996)
Arroyo Seco Sitio 2	14,064 cal BP	Argentina	Politis et al. (2016)
Tibito	11,740 ± 110	Colombia	Dillehay (2000)
Urupez II	11,690 ± 80	Uruguay	Nami (2008)
Lapa Vermelha	11,680 ± 500	Brazil	Guidon & Delibrias (1985)
El Palto	11,650	Peru	Dillehay (1992)
Cuevo Sofia 1	11,570 ± 60	South Andes	Nunez (1983)

(*Continued*)

South America archaeological sites

Site name	¹⁴ C BP Noted	Area unless otherwise	References
Cerro Tres Tetas	11,560 ± 140	Argentina	Paunero (2003)
RS-I-68	11,555 ± 230	Brazil	Miller (1987)
Tagua Tagua II	11,380 ± 320	Chile	Nunez (1994)
El Tigre	11,355 ± 30	Uruguay	Suárez et al. (2018)
San Jose	11,248	Ecuador	Dillehay (2000)
Talara	11,200 ± 115	Peru	Borrero (1996)

Eastern Hemisphere archaeological sites

Date	Site name	Area	References
2.6 Ma	Masol	India	Sao et al. (2016)
2.4 Ma	Yiron	Israel	Ronen (2016)
2.12-1.26 Ma	Shangchan	China	Zhu et al. (2018)
2.0–1.7 Ma	Olduvai Gorge	Tanzania	Leakey et al. (1964)
2.0–1.7 Ma	Erq El- Ahmar	Israel	Ron &Levi (2001)
2.1-1.9 Ma	Riwat	Pakistan	Dennell et al. (1988)
2.33 Ma	Kadar	Ethiopia	Kimbel et al. (1996)
2.3-1.9 Ma	Koobi Fora	Kenya	Leakey (1976)
1.95-1.77 Ma	Ain Hanech	Algeria	Sahnouni et al. (2002)
1.96-1.78 Ma	Longuppo Cave	China	Hou & Zhao (2010)
1.85-1.78 Ma	Dmanisi	Georgia	Ferring et al. (2011)
1.63 Ma	Gongwangling	China	Zhu et al. (2015)
1.66-1.36 Ma	Goudi	China	Gao et al. (2005)
1.49 Ma	Mojokorto	Indonesia	Morwood et al. (2003)
1.5 Ma	Attiramparkam	India	Pappu et al. (2011)
1.4-1.0 Ma	Ubeidiya	Israel	Gaudzinski (2004)
1.66-1.3 Ma	Majuangou III	China	Liu et al. (2014)
1.34 Ma	Xiaochangliang	China	Shen & Chen (2003)
1.27 Ma	Xihoudu	China	Bar-Yosef &Wang (2012)
1.22 Ma	Sima del Elefante	Spain	Carbonell et al. (2008)
1.4 Ma	Barranco Leon	Spain	Toro-Moyano et al. (2013)
950 ka	Lampang	Thailand	Pope et al. (1986)
780 ka	Gran Dolina	Spain	Falgueres et al. (1999)
900-800 ka	Mata Menge	Indonesia	Morwood et al. (1999)
380-240 ka	Vallparadis	Spain	Martinez et al. (2014)
380 ka	Terra Amata	France	De Lumley (1969)
500-350 ka	Vertesszölös	Hungary	Kretzoi & Dobosi (1990)
100–27 ka	Ngandong	Java	Balzeau et al. (2003)
370 ka	Sima de los Huesos	Spain	Arsuaga et al. (1997)

Eastern Hemisphere archaeological sites

Date	Site name	Area	References
160 ka	Diring Yuriakh	Siberia	Waters et al. (1999)
154 ka	Herto	Ethiopia	Clark et al. (2003)
123–50 ka	Crete	Greece	Strasser et al. (2011)
125 ka	Jebel Faya	UAE	Armitage et al. (2011)
120–80 ka	The Fuyan Cave	China	Liu et al. (2015)
139-111 ka	Liujiang	China	Shen et al. (2002)
130-100 ka	Skhul	Israel	Grün et al. (2005)
43 ka uncal. BP	Kara-Bom	Siberia	Zwyns et al. (2012)
74 ka	Jwalapuram	India	Petraglia et al. (2007)
66.7 ka	Callao Cave	Philippines	Mijares et al. (2010)
47 ka	Tabon Cave	Malaysia	Detroit et al. (2004)
50-40 ka	Lake Mungo	Australia	Bowler et al. (2003)
46-34 ka	Niah Cave	Malaysia	Barker et al. (2007)
45 ka	Irtysh River	Siberia	Fu et al. (2009)
39 ka	Bondi Cave	Georgia	Tushabramishvili et al. (2012)
36-34 ka	Pestera cu Oase	Romania	Trinkaus et al. (2003)
29-24 ka	Shuidonggou	Siberia	Madsen et al. (2001)
36-35 ka	Mamontovaya Kurya	Russia	Pavlov & Svendsen (2001)
44-38 ka	Laibin	China	Shen et al. (2007)
30-27 ka	Batadomba	Sri Lanka	Perera et al. (2011)
26 ka	Paviland	Wales	Aldhouse-Green (1998)
33-31 ka	Ryukyu Island	Japan	Ono et al. (2002)
32 ka	Chauvet Cave	France	Valladas et al. (2001)
28.6 ka	Byzovaya	Russia	Heggen et al. (2010)
27 ka	Berelekh	Siberia	Pitulko et al. (2004)
34-29 ka	Zoukoudian	China	Wu et al. (1995)
28 ka	Gorham's Cave	Gibraltar	Finlayson et al. (2006)
28 ka	Yana River Valley	Siberia	Basilyan et al. (2011)
28.6–27 ka	Krems Wachtberg	Austria	Einwögerer et al. (2009)
27.2	Dolni Vestonice	Czech Republic	Trinkaus & Svoboda (2006)
26.4 ka	Sunghir 3	Russia	Kuzmin et al. (2004)
27.7 ka	Pokrovka 2	Russia	Akimova et al. (2010)
18.25 ka	Minatogawa	Japan	Baba & Narasakei

Pleistocene – a viable environment for supporting humans and all their relations, the winged, finned, four-legged, rooted, and crawlers.

A few Western archaeologists have argued that the evidence of a human presence in the lands we know today as North and South America was much older than commonly accepted.[30] Recently, a few American archaeologists have conceded that initial migrations to the Western Hemisphere were likely earlier than 13,000–12,000 years ago.[31]

Indigenous history written on the land

Rock art

The Western Hemisphere has thousands of rock art and petroglyph sites. Thousands of stories, ceremonies, and histories recorded on the land. Thousands of records of people's interactions with their four-legged, winged, crawling, rooting, swimming relations. Each area where rock art or petroglyphs are located is an archaeological site (a story in or on the land), that may not yet have been fully researched or recorded. Discussing Coast Salish rock art – specifically Tsleil-Waututh First Nation who are a Halkomelem-speaking Coast Salish group in southern British Columbia – Arnett and Morin cited Galloway, regarding the term for rock art:

> In Hunq'imnum, all rock art, including petroglyphs (carvings) and pictographs (paintings), are designated by the sake descriptive term – *xela:ls* or 'writing', an 'action-oriented naming' closer in meaning to 'the act of writing'.[32]

Arnett and Morin stated that the term *xela:ls* is not limited to rock art but also describes marking and designs on artefacts, clothing, and bodies (Figure 7.2).[33]

One area where both archaeological sites and rock art have been researched for decades is Pedra Furada in Brazil. The Pedra Furada archaeological site is located in Serra da Capivara National Park located in the state of Piaui, northeastern Brazil. Serra da Capivara National Park is a UNESCO heritage site.

> Over 300 archaeological sites have been found within the park, the majority consisting of rock and wall paintings dating from 50,000–30,000 years Before Present. Many of the numerous rock shelters in the Serra da Capivara National Park are decorated with rock paintings, some more than 25,000 years old. The analysis and dating of the evidence and artifacts found in Serra da Capivara National Park serve to confirm the millennial presence of human beings on the American continent, and the importance of the heritage.[34]

Figure 7.2 Pedra Furada rock art, Brazil
Source: Photo by Diego Rego Monteiro, used under a Creative Commons licence (CC BY-SA 4.0)

Archaeological sites that date to the Pleistocene, near and within the park, include Pedra Furada, Vale da Pedra Furada, Toca da Tira Peia, Toca da Pena, Baixão da Esperança, and Sítio do Meio. In a 2008 paper, Kinoshita et al. stated that:

> On the overall the region, that was declared a Human Heritage site by UNESCO, has up to the present 940 archeological sites registered by the National Institute for the Historical and Artistic Heritage (Instituto do Patrimônio Histórico e Artístico Nacional – IPHAN). Among those sites, 45 were already excavated and the data collected show a continuous human occupation since at least 100,000 yr BP.[35]

Some of the rock art in the area of Pedra Furada depicts hunting and trapping practices, dancing, even somersaults, clearly a documentation of history written on the land.

Rock art sites (pictographs and petroglyphs) have been documented throughout North and South America. In southern Alberta along the Milk River, Writing-on-Stone Provincial Park, or Aísínai'pi, was created around one of the largest collections of rock art in the Great Plains. Aísínai'pi means 'it is pictured' or 'it is written' in the Blackfoot language. Aísínai'pi is in the heart of Blackfoot traditional homelands and holds great spiritual significance to the people. There are over 1,000 stories carved and painted in stone on the sandstone cliffs along the Milk River. One story with over 250 figures, depicted below, is clearly a written story of a battle.

The stories on the land at Aisinai'pi are discussed as being from the 1800s to as early as 5,000 years ago. The rock art sites at Writing-on-Stone vary greatly in size, ranging from single isolated glyphs to large concentrations of panels with thousands of individual glyphs.[36]

In Nevada, petroglyphs at Lake Winnemucca have been dated and are discussed as possibly being as old as 14,800 years ago.[37] This rock art site pre-dates the so-called Clovis first theory of initial colonisation that argues humans were not present in the Western Hemisphere prior to 11,000–12,000 years ago.

Figure 7.3 Lake Winnemucca petroglyphs in Nevada

Source: U.S. Photo by Larry V. Benson, Geological Survey, Department of the Interior/USGS U.S. Geological Survey

Figure 7.4 Nine Mile Canyon, Utah. The famous *Cottonwood Panel*, also called *The Great Hunt*, May 2006

Source: Photo by Scott Catron, used under a Creative Commons licence (CC BY 2.5)

The Lake Winnemucca petroglyphs have provided the oldest dates currently known for rock art in North America. The carvings are not of anthropomorphic (human-like) figures that are found at many other rock art sites in the Americas. Patterns and lines similar to leaves are deeply carved into the rock; geometric designs cover the rock faces, their meaning held in the land. From a distance, one entire rock face (Figure 7.3) includes a boulder that resembles the shape of a fish with a design similar to fish scales.

With an estimated 10,000 ancient rock art sites, the Nine Mile Canyon rock art site in Utah is called the longest art gallery in the world (Figure 7.4).

> For the Ute people these pictures on the wall, 'rock art', are not just a history of their people but a 'sacred memorial to the canyon.' Hopi, Northern Cheyenne, Ute, and various Pueblo communities have all banded together to show the world that this place is sacred and that we should all revere the place for its unrivaled glimpse into native art and culture, as well as its stunning natural beauty.[38]

The Nine Mile Canyon site area has the largest concentration of rock art in North America and it is listed on the United States National Register of Historic Places. The stories on the land were written by the Freemont and Ute communities. The history written on the land includes many everyday scenes of hunting, and interacting with mammals such as big horn sheep, horses, buffalo, reptiles, birds, and many other animals.

There has never been a comprehensive accounting of all of the rock art (pictography and petroglyph) sites in either North or South America. The rock art sites in North and South America often have thousands of figures at one site. This is unlike some European rock art sites where a single panel was created. When I discuss rock art sites with students, I ask them what are famous sites that contain rock art they are aware of and where the sites are located. Students have always answered the rock art sites in France. No one seems to have learned about the thousands of rock art sites in North and South America. This reflects how knowledge of Indigenous peoples of the Western Hemisphere (North and South America) written histories and links to the land have often been excluded from educational curriculum and general social discussions in the Americas.

Oral traditions

Many oral traditions of Indigenous people speak to their community's genesis,[39] telling in vivid details how their people have been here forever.[40] Oral traditions tell stories of how the people came to be through ceremony and rituals, finding and naming their places on the land.[41] In consideration of a group of first people whose distinct identities, culture, and traditions grew from their relationship to their homelands, it could be said that they have been here forever.[42] For Indigenous people, 'forever' may mean from their physical creation, or from the beginning of their cultural identities in a specific place, 'an emergence into a precise cultural identity'.[43]

Roger Echo-Hawk defined two major subdivisions of North American oral literature: oral history defined as verbal first-hand memories, and oral traditions defined as first-hand observations passed down to others.[44] Margaret Kovach, a Cree scholar, discussed oral traditions as having both mythical elements and personal narratives of place.[45]

Attention to detail is an essential feature of oral traditions; stories are consistent across time as storytellers strive to remember details.[46] There are many oral traditions that tell of Pleistocene weather patterns, movements of sea ice, solar events, sea level changes, volcanic eruptions, Pleistocene species, and glacial lakes.[47] Echo-Hawk stated that oral traditions that contain historical information can reach back across 40,000 years.[48]

Colin Elder argued that the oral traditions of the Anishinabek accurately explain early Holocene environmental processes that created the Great Lakes and St Mary's River.[49] The Great Lakes – Lake Erie, Lake Superior, Lake Michigan, and Lake Huron – are located around the border of the northern United States and Ontario in Canada. Elder stated that Anishinabek oral traditions:

> ... speak of ecocultural changes to the natural baseline and the effects of climate change on the St Mary's River during the early Holocene period. The origin story and early histories of the Anishinabek world in particular, highlight the fundamental importance of water, its role in the birth of the Anishinabek, and the maternal connection which the Anishinabek feel towards the Great Lakes. The way in which the Anishinabek link their own history to the creation of the Great Lakes (and the attendant development of Holocene ecology) further illuminates the value of these early histories. Accordingly, by exploring the geo-philosophical tracks of Indigenous oral tradition, we gain important insight into the geographical landscape of the Pleistocene and the ethno-genesis of the Anishinabek within a new Great Lakes world as well as a sense of how Anishinabek populations adapted to the dramatic changes that marked the epoch.[50]

Oral traditions and intergenerational memories are not exclusive to any one population; they have sustained human survival throughout time.[51] Knowledge of seasonal resource procurement, material sources, celestial bodies, and species habitats have been critical for human survival.[52] Dorris stated that the oral-literary tradition is a cornerstone of every tribal society. It is the vehicle through which wisdom is passed from one generation to the next.[53] Oral traditions and myths have been used by societies on a global scale to make sense of everyday realities, catastrophic events, environmental changes, and relationships.[54]

> Archaeologists frequently say that the sites they excavate and the artifacts they recover can speak to us across the centuries … In oral traditions, we can hear the echoes of the actual voices of the people who made those artifacts and who were the original owners of the skeletons. As researchers explore the contribution to the history of oral traditions in Africa, Australia, and the Americas, it has become increasingly difficult to ignore arguments that historical information has been preserved through verbal means for great lengths of time.[55]

A few Western scholars have recently begun to pay attention to oral traditions and linkages to historic environmental events. Darby Stapp stated:

> The idea of archaeologists using oral histories as evidence about the past is slowly gaining acceptance … it is intriguing that Native Americans were talking about a great flood in the Columbia Basin even before the geologists started talking about it.[56]

In reading oral traditions written in the English language, scholars must be mindful of pitfalls in translations. English words, which have been used to interpret oral traditions, often do not exist in Indigenous languages, that is to say, key words in Indigenous languages often have no straightforward translation into the English language. 'Nature' is an example of one of those words – in the Cree language, there is no word that corresponds to nature.[57] In Cree, there is a word for life, *pimaatisiiwin*, which includes animal persons and humans.

> The Eastern Cree were traditionally working under the premise that all persons, including human, animal, spirit are part of an inter-relational network involving direct personal communication and response through action. As hunters, the Cree saw themselves not as dominant over animals, but as ethical and moral participants in a form of community between themselves, the animals, the environment, and the spirit persons who were responsible for the animals.[58]

Creation histories

Thousands of distinct Indigenous communities have been documented across the continents we know today as North and South America. Many oral histories have been documented and published by non-Indigenous academics. The translation of history from Indigenous languages into French, English, Portuguese, and other languages has not always been correct. For my Master's degree, I was required to translate historical information from a language other than English. I found French recordings of 'Indian' stories that were collected along the Mississippi River in the 1700s. The written versions of the stories were taken back to France, stored in a library and digitised in the early twenty-first century. The story I translated was about a father teaching his three daughters lessons about respectful behaviour. It was clear that a lot was lost in translation as the French explorers had no understanding of the Indigenous language or the rich metaphors in the telling. It was amazing to me that the stories travelled so far and came back to Turtle Island hundreds of years later. It was noted in the translations that the French explorers had wanted to collect the stories as they were afraid that all the Indians would be killed and their stories lost forever.

In Diné oral history, there are five worlds that the Navajo travel through before they settle in their homelands.

> Diné history begins with the creation story in the First World where the Insect People move through the four lower worlds to the Fifth World. In the First World, there was no sun, moon, or stars – only an ocean to the east, south, west, and north. A flood came and the Insect People were pushed into the Second World, which was only bare ground. The Third World was a place inhibited by grasshoppers with a river in the east. In the Fourth World, the Insect People found a land of snow-covered mountains and Pueblo people. The Fourth World was Dinétah where the Mirage People laid 'two ears of white corn and two ears of yellow corn on the ground and covered them with buckskin' subsequently creating First Man and First Woman. Frightened by a flash flood, First Man and First Woman came up through reeds in the center of a lake rising onto the surface of the earth into the Fifth World. The Fifth World was where the four sacred mountains are today creating Diné Bikéyah.[59]

Diné history is a testimony to people's connections to the land, to specific places. The four sacred Diné mountains are Tsisnaajinni (Blanca Peak) to the east, Tsoodzil (Mount Taylor) to the south, Diné Ntsaa (Mount Hesperus in the La Plata Mountains) to the north, and Dook'o'oosłííd (San Francisco Peaks) to the west – the four sacred mountains, the place of genesis, where the Diné were created from corn.[60]

The Anishnaabe creation history, told by Basil Johnston, shares the story of Kitchi-Manitou who created the earth, sky, sun, and waters, and all creatures seen and unseen, that inhabit the earth.[61] There was a flood that destroyed the earth creation, and only the water beings, the Manitous, survived. During the time of the flood, Geezhigo-Quae (Sky-Woman), who lived in the heavens, became pregnant with twins. The creatures of the seas invited Sky-Woman to come down to earth; they asked the turtle to provide his back as a place for her to rest. Sky-Woman joined the earth creatures and asked them for soil to spread on Turtle's Back. Many creatures dove deep into the seas but none were able to reach the bottom to bring back soil. Finally, one small muskrat was successful in bringing up a very small fistful of soil, and Sky-Woman spread it out on Turtle's Back, creating an island.[62]

> Geezhigo-Quae gave birth to twins who begot the tribe called the Anishinaubaeg. Millenia later the tribe dreamed Nanabush into being. Nanabush represented themselves and what they understood of human nature. One day his world too was flooded. Like Geezhigo-Quae, Nanabush recreated his world from a morsel of soil retrieved from the depths of the sea. As a factual account of the origin of the world and of being, the story has no more basis than the biblical story of creation and the flood. But the story represents a belief in God, the creator, a Kitchi-Manitou, the Great Mystery. It also represents a belief that Kitchi-Manitou sought within himself, his own being, a vision. Or perhaps it came from within his being and that Kitchi-Manitou created what was beheld and set it into motion. Even the lesser manitous, such as Geezhigo-Quae and Nanabush, must seek a morsel of soil with which to create and recreate their world, their spheres. So, men and women must seek within themselves the talent or the potential and afterward create their own worlds and their own spheres and a purpose to give meaning to their lives. The people begotten by Geezhigo-Quae on that mythological island called them- selves Anishinaubaeg, the good beings who meant well and were human beings, therefore fundamentally good.[63]

Many Indigenous communities share a similar genesis history of Sky-Woman, telling of the earth covered in water (histories of great floods), of the respect and reciprocity between all relations, (how birds save Sky-Woman from her long fall), of *wiingaashk*, sweetgrass, the first plant to grow after the land is created by Sky-Woman on Turtle's Back.[64] Indigenous oral histories are woven throughout the land, in ways that link mnemonic memories to place, scents, sounds, and relations.

> Our stories say that of all the plants, *wiingaashk*, or sweetgrass, was the very first to grown on the earth, its fragrance a sweet memory of Sky-Woman's hand. Accordingly, it is honored as one of the four sacred plants of my people. Breathe in its scent and you start to remember things you didn't know you'd forgotten. Our elders say that ceremonies are the way we 'remember to remember'.[65]

The creation of the earth, and people's place on it, is linked to the land, woven through Indigenous oral histories since time immemorial. The earth is discussed as a place of emergence of the first people who then moved throughout the land, waters, and sky. In consideration of a group of first people whose distinct identities, culture, and traditions grew from their relationship to their homelands, it could be said that they have been here forever.

> The most important qualities of our culture are our language and our stories. In oral traditions such as ours, telling stories is how we pass on the history and

the teachings of our ancestors. Without these stories, we would have to rely on other people for guidance and information about our past. Teachings in the form of stories are an integral part of our identity as a people and as a nation. If we lose these stories, we will do a disservice to our ancestors – those who gave us the responsibility to keep our culture alive.[66]

In many creation histories, there are discussions of major environmental catastrophes, times when the earth is covered in water, when people are forced to relocate. In oral traditions, we find evidence of people's interactions with extinct species, ceremonies, seasons, astronomy, migrations, and an intimate knowledge of the environment. Stories of the stars and planets and all relations two legged, four-legged, crawlers, finned, and winged beings are found in rock art and carvings on bone. Rock art is found throughout both North and South America, thousands of places of recorded histories about relations, events, ceremonies, and people. All of these bodies of knowledge add to the stories that archaeological sites (histories held in the land) have to tell.

Conclusion

The past as it has been created by Western scholars has been used in the present as a weapon of erasure, creating acceptable social memories that dehumanise Indigenous communities, fuel racism, and create a present that is not safe for Indigenous people in their own lands. Western scholars' denial and erasure of deep Indigenous histories creates ruptures and cleaves Indigenous links to their homelands across time and space. The Indigenous past of the Western Hemisphere (the Americas) has been fabricated to fit into neoliberal timeframes of imagined 'New Worlds', a tool of dis-empowerment and dehumanising oppression, created by American archaeologists to keep Indigenous civilisations as 'infantile' on a global scale.[67]

Although Indigenous oral traditions have not been considered facts or histories by Western academics, the academy is slowly changing as scholars realise that there are many ways to express histories and experiences. 'This creates possibilities of new paradigms through which the experience of non-western peoples can be explored.'[68] Recently discovered as well as re-examined archaeological sites in the Western Hemisphere with older than 12,000 years before present dates are now being discussed in academic publications.[69] It is reassuring to see that a few American archaeologists are now willing to step outside the colonial box and publish on older Pleistocene archaeological sites in the Western Hemisphere. That said, I have been informed of a strong fear within the field of American archaeology to researching and publishing on Pleistocene archaeological sites in the Western Hemisphere dating to earlier than 14,000–15,000 years ago.

What we know about the human past is not a finality, our knowledge of the human past has never been static, and we should not expect it be. Our understanding of history is always changing and evolving as research is carried out and new scientific technologies open windows into the past. Oral traditions and rock art provide evidence of people's interactions with the land and with non-human species across thousands of years. People have been in the Western Hemisphere since time immemorial; this is where they are from. The archaeological record of the Western Hemisphere (North and South America) provides evidence for people being in the Western Hemisphere for over 130,000 years. Archaeological evidence places people in the Eastern Hemisphere in the area we know today as Asia over two million years ago. Mammals, including camels, horses, saber-toothed cats, elk, bison, mammoths, mastodon, and others, have been migrating from the Western Hemisphere to the Eastern Hemisphere across a dry land mass in both directions for millions of years.[70] Though the acceptance of earlier than 11,000- to 12,000-year-old Pleistocene archaeological sites in the Western Hemisphere has recently begun to change, colonialist discourses within archaeology and academia remain a factor in the maintenance of discrimination, racism, and reproduction of colonialism.[71] To argue that people were not in the Western Hemisphere until 12,000 years ago is an anomaly and does not fit with the known global record of human migrations. To learn about the human past, it is pivotal to open our eyes, hearts, and minds, and learn to listen to other ways of knowing, being, and telling.

Notes

1 Some information and discussions in this book chapter are extracted from an upcoming book publication: Paulette Steeves, *The Indigenous Paleolithic of the Western Hemisphere* (Lincoln: University of Nebraska Press, 2021).
2 Lester-Irabinna Rigney, 'Internationalism of an Aboriginal or Torres Strait Islander Anti-colonial Cultural Critique of Research Methodologies, a Guide to Indigenist Research Methodology and Its Principles,' in *Research and Development in Higher Education, Advancing International Perspectives* (Higher Education Research and Development Society of Australia, Annual International conference proceedings, 1997), 629–636; Karen Martin and Booran Mirraboopa, 'Ways of Knowing, Being and Doing: A Theoretical Framework and Methods for Indigenous Indigenist Research,' *Journal of Australian Studies* 27 (2003): 203–214.
3 P.F. Steeves, 'Decolonizing Indigenous Histories, Pleistocene Archaeology Sites of the Western Hemisphere' (PhD diss., State University of New York at Binghamton, 2015).
4 S. Wilson, *Research is Ceremony: Indigenous Research Methods* (Black Point: Fernwood Publishing, 2008).
5 Johanna Nichols, 'Linguistic Diversity and the First Settlement of the New World,' *Language* 66, no. 3 (1990): 475–521.
6 Nichols, 'Linguistic Diversity,' 475.
7 Johanna Nichols, 'The First American Languages,' in *The First Americans*, ed. N.G. Jablonski (San Francisco, CA: Alan Press, 2002), 273.
8 Nichols, 'First American Languages.'
9 Basil H. Johnston, 'Is That All There Is? Tribal Literature,' *Canadian Literature* 128 (1991): 56.
10 Vine Deloria Jr, *Red Earth, White Lies: Native Americans and the Myth of Scientific Fact* (Golden: Fulcrum Publishing, 1997), 23.
11 Deloria, *Red Earth, White Lies*, 7.
12 J.M. Adovasio et al., 'Two Decades of Debate on Meadowcroft Rock Shelter,' *North American Archaeologist* 19, no. 4 (1998): 317–341; A.L. Bryan and R. Gruhn, 'Some Difficulties in Modeling the Original Peopling of the Americas,' *Quaternary International* 109–110 (2003): 175–179; Thomas D. Dillehay, *The Settlement of the Americas: A New Prehistory* (New York: Basic Books, 2000); Steven R. Holen et al., 'A 130,000-Year-Old

Archaeological Site in Southern California, USA,' *Nature* 544, no. 7651 (2017): 479–483; Richard MacNeish, 'A New Look at Early Peopling of the New World as of 1976,' *Journal of Anthropological Research* 34, no. 4 (1978): 475–496; N. Guidon and B. Arnaud, 'The Chronology of the New World: Two Faces of One Reality,' *World Archaeology* 23, no. 2 (1991): 167–178.
13 P.F. Steeves, 'Unpacking Neoliberal Archaeological Control of Ancient Indigenous Heritage,' *Archaeologies* 13, no. 1 (2017): 48–65.
14 Steeves, 'Decolonizing Indigenous Histories.'
15 J.M. Adovasio and J. Page, *The First Americans: In Pursuit of Archaeology's Greatest Mystery* (New York: Random House, 2002); Deloria, *Red Earth, White Lies*; Dillehay, *The Settlement of the Americas*.
16 Deloria, *Red Earth, White Lies*.
17 B. Holm and B. Reid, *Indian Art of the Northwest Coast* (Seattle: University of Washington Press, 1976), 7.
18 Pat Shipman, 'Applications of Scanning Electron Microscopy to Taphonomic Problems,' *Annals of the New York Academy of Sciences* 376, no. 1 (1981): 357–385; David R. Braun, Michael Pante, and William Archer, 'Cut Marks on Bone Surfaces: Influences on Variation in the Form of Traces of Ancient Behaviour,' *Interface Focus* 6, no. 3 (2016): 20160006.
19 Thomas Dillehay et al., 'Monte Verde: Seaweed, Food, Medicine, and the Peopling of South America,' *Science* 320, no. 5877 (2008): 784–786.
20 Dillehay et al., 'Monte Verde.'
21 Dillehay, *The Settlement of the Americas*.
22 Dillehay et al., 'Monte Verde,' 784.
23 Barbara A. Purdy et al., 'Earliest Art in the Americas: Incised Image of a Proboscidean on a Mineralized Extinct Animal Bone from Vero Beach, Florida,' *Journal of Archaeological Science* 38, no. 11 (2011): 2908–2913.
24 Purdy et al., 'Earliest Art in the Americas.'
25 Svante Pääbo, 'The Diverse Origins of the Human Gene Pool,' *Nature Reviews Genetics* 16, no. 6 (2015): 313–314.
26 Pääbo, 'Diverse Origins of the Human Gene Pool.'
27 Steeves, 'Decolonizing Indigenous Histories.'
28 Ashley Montagu, *The Direction of Human Development: Biological and Social Bases* (New York: Harper, 1955); Adrienne Mayor, *Fossil Legends of the First Americans* (Princeton, NJ: Princeton University Press, 2005); Steeves, 'Decolonizing Indigenous Histories.'
29 Steeves, 'Decolonizing Indigenous Histories.'
30 Among others: Adovasio and Page, *The First Americans*; Bryan and Gruhn, 'Some Difficulties'; Jacques Cinq-Mars and Richard E. Morlan, 'Bluefish Caves and Old Crow Basin: A New Rapport,' in *Ice Age Peoples of North America: Environments, Origins, and Adaptations of the First Americans*, eds. Robson Bonnichsen and Karen L. Turnmire (Corvallis: Oregon State University Press for the Center for the Study of the First Americans, 1999), 200–212; Dillehay, *The Settlement of the Americas*; Niède Guidon and Georgette Delibrias, 'Inventory of South-American Archaeological Sites More Than 12,000 Years Old' [Inventaire des Sites Sud-Americains Anterieurs a 12000 Ans'], *L'Anthropologie* 89, no. 3 (1985): 385–408; Holen et al., 'A 130,000-Year-Old Archaeological Site'; Richard S. MacNeish, 'Early Man in the New World: A Survey of the Archaeological Evidence Suggests That a Number of Specialized Tool Complexes Were Widely Distributed in the Americas before 12,000 Years Ago,' *American Scientist* 64, no. 3 (1976): 316–327.
31 Ted Goebel and Sergei B. Slobodin, 'The Colonization of Western Beringia: Technology, Ecology, and Adaptations,' in *Ice Age Peoples of North America*, eds. Bonnichsen and Turnmire, 104–155; Nicholas Toth, 'The Material Record,' in *The First Americans: Search and Research*, eds. Tom Dillehay and David Meltzer (Boca Raton, FL: CRC Press, 1991), 53–76; Nicole M. Waguespack, 'Why We're Still Arguing about the Pleistocene Occupation of the Americas,' *Evolutionary Anthropology* 16, no. 2 (2007): 63–74.

32 Chris Arnett and Jesse Morin, 'The Rock Painting/Xela:ls of the Tsleil-Waututh: A Historicized Coast Salish Practice,' *Ethnohistory* 65, no. 1 (2018): 101–127, citing Brent D. Galloway, *Dictionary of Upriver Halkomelem* (Berkeley: University of California Press, 2009), 1668.
33 Arnett and Morin, 'The Rock Painting/Xela:ls of the Tsleil-Waututh.'
34 'Serra da Capivara National Park,' UNESCO, accessed 27 October 2020, https://whc.unesco.org/en/list/606/.
35 Angela Kinoshita et al., 'Electron Spin Resonance Dating of Human Teeth from Toca da Santa Shelter of São Raimundo Nonato, Piauí, Brazil,' *Nuclear Instruments and Methods in Physics Research Section B: Beam Interactions with Materials and Atoms* 266, no. 4 (2008): 636.
36 James D. Keyser, 'Writing-On-Stone: Rock Art on the Northwestern Plains,' *Canadian Journal of Archaeology/Journal Canadien d'Archéologie* 1 (1977): 15–80.
37 Larry V. Benson et al. 'Dating North America's Oldest Petroglyphs, Winnemucca Lake Sub-Basin, Nevada,' *Journal of Archaeological Science* 40, no. 12 (2013): 4466–4476.
38 Raylon Silberman, 'Nine Mile Canyon,' Indigenous Religious Traditions website, accessed 27 October 2020, https://sites.coloradocollege.edu/indigenoustraditions/sacred-lands/nine-mile-canyon/ (citing The Pluralism Project, https://pluralism.org, and the Sacred Land Film Project, https://sacredland.org/nine-mile-canyon-united-states/).
39 George Bird Grinnell, 'Pawnee Mythology,' *Journal of American Folklore* 6, no. 21 (1893): 113–130; Anna Secco, 'The Search for Origins through Storytelling in Native American Literature: Momaday, Silko, Erdrich,' *RSA Journal* 3 (1993): 59–71.
40 Colin G. Calloway, *First Peoples: A Documentary Survey of American Indian History* (Boston, MA: Bedford/St Martin's, 2008).
41 Calloway, *First Peoples*; Vine Deloria Jr and Clifford Lytle. *The Nations Within: The Past and Future of American Indian Sovereignty* (New York: Pantheon Books, 1984).
42 Steeves, 'Decolonizing Indigenous Histories.'
43 Leslie Marmon Silko, 'Landscape, History, and the Pueblo Imagination,' in *The Ecocriticism Reader: Landmarks in Literary Ecology*, eds. Cheryll Glotfelty and Harold Fromm (Athens: University of Georgia Press, 1996), 264–275.
44 Roger C. Echo-Hawk, 'Ancient History in the New World: Integrating Oral Traditions and the Archaeological Record in Deep Time,' *American Antiquity* 65, no. 2 (2000): 267–290.
45 Margaret Kovach, *Indigenous Methodologies: Characteristics, Conversations, and Contexts* (Toronto, ON: University of Toronto Press, 2009).
46 Mayor (2005).
47 Echo-Hawk, 'Ancient History.'
48 Echo-Hawk, 'Ancient History.'
49 Colin Elder, 'A River Worshipped, A River Wronged: The History of the St. Mary's River, and Its People, from its Formation to Industrialization (15,000 ybp–present)' (PhD diss., University of Kent, 2019).
50 Elder, 'A River Worshipped.'
51 Cynthia J. Wiley, 'Collective Memory of the Prehistoric Past and the Archaeological Landscape,' *Nebraska Anthropologist* 23 (2008): 81.
52 Wiley, 'Collective Memory.'
53 Michael Dorris, 'Native American Literature in an Ethnohistorical Context,' *College English* 41, no. 2 (1979): 157.
54 Peter M. Whiteley, 'Archaeology and Oral Traditions: The Scientific Importance of Dialogue,' *American Antiquity* 67, no. 3 (2002): 405–415.
55 Echo-Hawk, 'Ancient History,' 285
56 Darby Stapp, 'In Search of the Mid-Columbia's First People,' *The Pleistocene Post: Quarterly Newsletter of the Ice Age Floods Institute* 1, no. 4 (2004): 3.
57 Susan M. Preston, 'Meaning and Representation: Landscape in the Oral Traditions of the Eastern James Bay Cree' (PhD diss., University of Guelph, 1999).

58 Preston, 'Meaning and Representation,' 38.
59 H.J. Todacheene, 'She Saves Us from Monsters: The Navajo Creation Story and Modern Tribal Justice,' *Tribal Law Journal* 15 (2015): 32, citing M. Weisiger and W. Cronon, *Dreaming of Sheep in Navajo Country* (Seattle: University of Washington Press, 2009).
60 Todacheene, 'She Saves Us.'
61 Johnston, 'Is That All There Is?'
62 Johnston, 'Is That All There Is?'
63 Johnston, 'Is That All There Is?,' 58.
64 Robin Wall Kimmerer, *Braiding Sweetgrass: Indigenous Wisdom, Scientific Knowledge and the Teachings of Plants* (Minneapolis: Milkweed Editions, 2013).
65 Kimmerer, *Braiding Sweetgrass*.
66 Darwin Hannah and Mamie Henry, eds., *Our Tellings: Interior Salish Stories of the Nlha7kápmx People* (Vancouver: UBC Press, 1995), 210.
67 Steeves, 'Unpacking Neoliberal Archaeological Control.'
68 John C. Mohawk, 'A View From Turtle Island: Chapters in Iroquois Mythology, History and Culture' (PhD diss., State University of New York at Buffalo, 1994), iv.
69 Holen et al., 'A 130,000-Year-Old Archaeological Site'; Lauriane Bourgeon, Ariane Burke, and Thomas Higham, 'Earliest Human Presence in North America Dated to the Last Glacial Maximum: New Radiocarbon Dates from Bluefish Caves, Canada,' *PloS ONE* 12, no. 1 (2017).
70 Steeves, 'Decolonizing Indigenous Histories.'
71 Jodi A. Byrd, *The Transit of Empire: Indigenous Critiques of Colonialism* (Minneapolis: University of Minnesota Press, 2011).

Bibliography

Adovasio, J.M. and J. Page. *The First Americans: In Pursuit of Archaeology's Greatest Mystery*. New York: Random House, 2002.

Adovasio, J.M., R. Pedler, J. Donahue, and R. Stuckenrath. 'Two Decades of Debate on Meadowcroft Rock Shelter.' *North American Archaeologist* 19, no. 4 (1998): 317–341.

Arnett, Chris, and Jesse Morin. 'The Rock Painting/Xela:ls of the Tsleil-Waututh: A Historicized Coast Salish Practice.' *Ethnohistory* 65, no. 1 (2018): 101–127.

Braun, David R., Michael Pante, and William Archer. 'Cut Marks on Bone Surfaces: Influences on Variation in the Form of Traces of Ancient Behaviour.' *Interface Focus* 6, no. 3 (2016): 20160006.

Benson, Larry V., Eugene M. Hattori, John R. Southon, and B. Aleck. 'Dating North America's Oldest Petroglyphs, Winnemucca Lake Sub-Basin, Nevada.' *Journal of Archaeological Science* 40, no. 12 (2013): 4466–4476.

Bourgeon, Lauriane, Ariane Burke, and Thomas Higham. 'Earliest Human Presence in North America Dated to the Last Glacial Maximum: New Radiocarbon Dates from Bluefish Caves, Canada.' *PloS ONE* 12, no. 1 (2017).

Bryan, A.L., and R. Gruhn. 'Some Difficulties in Modeling the Original Peopling of the Americas.' *Quaternary International* 109–110 (2003): 175–179.

Byrd, Jodi A. *The Transit of Empire: Indigenous Critiques of Colonialism*. Minneapolis: University of Minnesota Press, 2011.

Calloway, Colin G. *First Peoples: A Documentary Survey of American Indian History*. Boston, MA: Bedford/St Martin's, 2008.

Cinq-Mars, Jacques, and Richard E. Morlan. 'Bluefish Caves and Old Crow Basin: A New Rapport.' In *Ice Age Peoples of North America: Environments, Origins, and Adaptations of the First Americans*, edited by Robson Bonnichsen and Karen L. Turnmire, 200–212. Corvallis: Oregon State University Press for the Center for the Study of the First Americans, 1999.

Deloria, Vine, Jr. *Red Earth, White Lies: Native Americans and the Myth of Scientific Fact*. Golden: Fulcrum Publishing, 1997.

Deloria, Vine, Jr, and Clifford Lytle. *The Nations Within: The Past and Future of American Indian Sovereignty.* New York: Pantheon Books, 1984.

Dillehay, Thomas D. *The Settlement of the Americas: A New Prehistory.* New York: Basic Books, 2000.

Dillehay, Thomas D., C. Ramírez, M. Pino, M.B. Collins, J. Rossen, and J.D. Pino-Navarro. 'Monte Verde: Seaweed, Food, Medicine, and the Peopling of South America.' *Science* 320, no. 5877 (2008): 784–786.

Dorris, Michael. 'Native American Literature in an Ethnohistorical Context.' *College English* 41, no. 2 (1979): 147–162.

Echo-Hawk, Roger C. 'Ancient History in the New World: Integrating Oral Traditions and the Archaeological Record in Deep Time.' *American Antiquity* 65, no. 2 (2000): 267–290.

Elder, Colin. 'A River Worshipped, A River Wronged: The History of the St. Mary's River, and its People, from Its Formation to Industrialization (15,000 ybp.–present).' PhD diss., University of Kent, 2019.

Galloway, Brent D. *Dictionary of Upriver Halkomelem.* Berkeley: University of California Press, 2009.

Goebel, Ted, and Sergei B. Slobodin. 'The Colonization of Western Beringia: Technology, Ecology, and Adaptations.' In *Ice Age Peoples of North America: Environments, Origins, and Adaptations of the First Americans,* edited by Robson Bonnichsen and Karen L. Turnmire, 104–155. Corvallis: Oregon State University Press for the Center for the Study of the First Americans, 1999.

Grinnell, George Bird. 'Pawnee Mythology.' *Journal of American Folklore* 6, no. 21 (1893): 113–130.

Guidon, Niède, and B. Arnaud. 'The Chronology of the New World: Two Faces of One Reality.' *World Archaeology* 23, no. 2 (1991): 167–178.

Guidon, Niède, and Georgette Delibrias. 'Inventory of South-American Archaeological Sites More Than 12,000 Years Old' [Inventaire des Sites Sud-Americains Anteriers a 12000 Ans']. *L'Anthropologie* 89, no. 3 (1985): 385–408.

Hannah, Darwin, and Mamie Henry, eds. *Our Tellings: Interior Salish Stories of the Nlha7kápmx People.* Vancouver: UBC Press, 1995.

Holen, Steven R., Thomas A. Deméré, Daniel C. Fisher, Richard Fullagar, James B. Paces, George T. Jefferson, Jared M. Beeton, et al. 'A 130,000-Year-Old Archaeological Site in Southern California, USA.' *Nature* 544, no. 7651 (2017): 479–483.

Holm, B., and B. Reid. *Indian Art of the Northwest Coast.* Seattle: University of Washington Press, 1976.

Johnston, Basil H. 'Is That All There Is?: Tribal Literature.' *Canadian Literature* 128 (1991): 54–62.

Keyser, James D. 'Writing-On-Stone: Rock Art on the Northwestern Plains.' *Canadian Journal of Archaeology/Journal Canadien d'Archéologie* 1 (1977): 15–80.

Kimmerer, Robin Wall. *Braiding Sweetgrass: Indigenous Wisdom, Scientific Knowledge and the Teachings of Plants.* Minneapolis: Milkweed Editions, 2013.

Kinoshita, Angela, Ana Maria G. Figueiredo, Gisèle Daltrini Felice, Maria Conceição Soares Meneses Lage, Niède Guidon, and Oswaldo Baffa. 'Electron Spin Resonance Dating of Human Teeth from Toca da Santa Shelter of São Raimundo Nonato, Piauí, Brazil.' *Nuclear Instruments and Methods in Physics Research Section B: Beam Interactions with Materials and Atoms* 266, no. 4 (2008): 635–639.

Kovach, Margaret. *Indigenous Methodologies: Characteristics, Conversations, and Contexts.* Toronto, ON: University of Toronto Press, 2009.

MacNeish, Richard S. 'Early Man in the New World: A Survey of the Archaeological Evidence Suggests That a Number of Specialized Tool Complexes Were Widely Distributed in the Americas before 12,000 Years Ago.' *American Scientist* 64, no. 3 (1976): 316–327.

MacNeish, Richard. 'A New Look at Early Peopling of the New World as of 1976.' *Journal of Anthropological Research* 34, no. 4 (1978): 475–496.

Marmon Silko, Leslie. 'Landscape, History, and the Pueblo Imagination.' In *The Ecocriticism Reader: Landmarks in Literary Ecology,* edited by Cheryll Glotfelty and Harold Fromm, 264–275. Athens: University of Georgia Press, 1996.

Martin, Karen, and Booran Mirraboopa, 'Ways of Knowing, Being and Doing: A Theoretical Framework and Methods for Indigenous Indigenist Research,' *Journal of Australian Studies* 27 (2003): 203–214.

Mayor, Adrienne. *Fossil Legends of the First Americans*. Princeton: Princeton University Press, 2005.

Mohawk, John C. 'A View From Turtle Island: Chapters in Iroquois Mythology, History and Culture.' PhD diss., State University of New York at Buffalo, 1994.

Montagu, Ashley. *The Direction of Human Development: Biological and Social Bases*. New York: Harper, 1955.

Nichols, Johanna. 'Linguistic Diversity and the First Settlement of the New World.' *Language* 66, no. 3 (1990): 475–521.

Nichols, Johanna. 'The First American Languages.' In *The First Americans*, edited by N.G. Jablonski, 273–293. San Francisco, CA: Alan Press, 2002.

Pääbo, Svante. 'The Diverse Origins of the Human Gene Pool.' *Nature Reviews Genetics* 16, no. 6 (2015): 313–314.

Preston, Susan M. 'Meaning and Representation: Landscape in the Oral Traditions of the Eastern James Bay Cree.' PhD diss., University of Guelph, 1999.

Purdy, Barbara A., Kevin S. Jones, John J. Mecholsky, Gerald Bourne, Richard C. Hulbert Jr., Bruce J. MacFadden, Krista L. Church, et al. 'Earliest Art in the Americas: Incised Image of a Proboscidean on a Mineralized Extinct Animal Bone from Vero Beach, Florida.' *Journal of Archaeological Science* 38, no. 11 (2011): 2908–2913.

Rigney, Lester-Irabinna. 'Internationalism of an Aboriginal or Torres Strait Islander Anti-colonial Cultural Critique of Research Methodologies, a Guide to Indigenist Research Methodology and Its Principles.' In *Research and Development in Higher Education, Advancing International Perspectives*, Higher Education Research and Development Society of Australia, Annual International Conference Proceedings, 1997.

Secco, Anna. 'The Search for Origins through Storytelling in Native American Literature: Momaday, Silko, Erdrich.' *RSA Journal* 3 (1993): 59–71.

Shipman, Pat. 'Applications of Scanning Electron Microscopy to Taphonomic Problems.' *Annals of the New York Academy of Sciences* 376, no. 1 (1981): 357–385.

Silberman, Raylon. 'Nine Mile Canyon.' Indigenous Religious Traditions website. Accessed 27 October 2020. https://sites.coloradocollege.edu/indigenoustraditions/sacred-lands/nine-mile-canyon.

Stapp, Darby. 'In Search of the Mid-Columbia's First People.' *The Pleistocene Post: Quarterly Newsletter of the Ice Age Floods Institute* 1, no. 4 (2004): 3.

Steeves, P.F. 'Decolonizing Indigenous Histories, Pleistocene Archaeology Sites of the Western Hemisphere.' PhD diss., State University of New York at Binghamton, 2015.

Steeves, P.F. 'Unpacking Neoliberal Archaeological Control of Ancient Indigenous Heritage.' *Archaeologies* 13, no. 1 (2017): 48–65.

Todacheene, H.J. 'She Saves Us from Monsters: The Navajo Creation Story and Modern Tribal Justice.' *Tribal Law Journal* 15 (2015): 30–66.

Toth, Nicholas. 'The Material Record.' In *The First Americans: Search and Research*, edited by Tom Dillehay and David Meltzer, 53–76. Boca Raton, FL: CRC Press, 1991.

UNESCO. 'Serra da Capivara National Park.' Accessed 27 October 2020. https://whc.unesco.org/en/list/606/.

Waguespack, Nicole M. 'Why We're Still Arguing about the Pleistocene Occupation of the Americas.' *Evolutionary Anthropology* 16, no. 2 (2007): 63–74.

Whiteley, Peter M. 'Archaeology and Oral Traditions: The Scientific Importance of Dialogue.' *American Antiquity* 67, no. 3 (2002): 405–415.

Wiley, Cynthia J. 'Collective Memory of the Prehistoric Past and the Archaeological Landscape.' *Nebraska Anthropologist* 23 (2008): 405–415.

Wilson, S. *Research Is Ceremony: Indigenous Research Methods*. Black Point: Fernwood Publishing, 2008.

8
THE CASE FOR CONTINUITY OF HUMAN OCCUPATION AND ROCK ART PRODUCTION IN THE KIMBERLEY, AUSTRALIA

Peter Veth, Sam Harper, Kane Ditchfield, Sven Ouzman, and Balanggarra Aboriginal Corporation

Glossary

Epistemology: The theory of knowledge, as it relates to a particular group of people

Heterogeneity: Culturally or stylistically different

Holocene: < 11.7 ka–present, the current epoch, subsequent to the Last Glacial Maximum

Homogeneity: Culturally or stylistically similar

LGM (Last Glacial Maximum): 26–19 ka, the most recent period of global glaciation, which in Australia dramatically decreases sea level and sees large areas of increased aridity

Palaeoclimate and Palaeoenvironment: Climate and environment from the past, as opposed to current climatic and environmental systems

Pleistocene: 2.6 million years ago (M) to ~11.7,000 years ago (ka), the first epoch of the Quaternary Period, marked by numerous glacial periods or 'ice ages'

Rock art: Intentional human made marks on stone (parietal), these can be additive (e.g. painted, drawn, stencil, direct print, beeswax) or subtractive (engraved, scratched), figurative (recognisable form e.g. kangaroo) or non-figurative (e.g. geometric)

Introduction

The Kimberley: landscape, people, and rock art over the last 50,000 years

The Kimberley (Figure 8.1) is today a vast landscape of ~423,000 km² with a similar area submerged by ocean level rise over the last 20,000 years. Archaeological evidence establishes human occupation for at least 50,000 years,[1,2,3,4] which an Aboriginal epistemological perspective recasts as people having been on country forever.[5] Within these temporalities, Aboriginal people made rock art and produced material culture at tens of thousands of locations, leaving a rich and varied source of evidence through which to understand past and present lifeways. We provide a broad outline for the major style phases in the region's rock art and characterise occupation trends over the *longue durée* of 50,000 years.

Using archaeological knowledge, we can locate extensive human occupation and activity in the Kimberley through both time and space. While we are aware that the term 'continuous occupation' is seldom fully comprehended, recent work has, for example, shown that the dry, cold conditions of the Last Glacial Maximum (LGM) may not have been as severe in the Kimberley, where human activity is still very much in evidence and has been recovered archaeologically[6] (see Table 8.1). Rather than a simple archaeological narrative focusing on the 'oldest' known occupation sites, we consider the entire temporal range until the present, paying attention to the varying

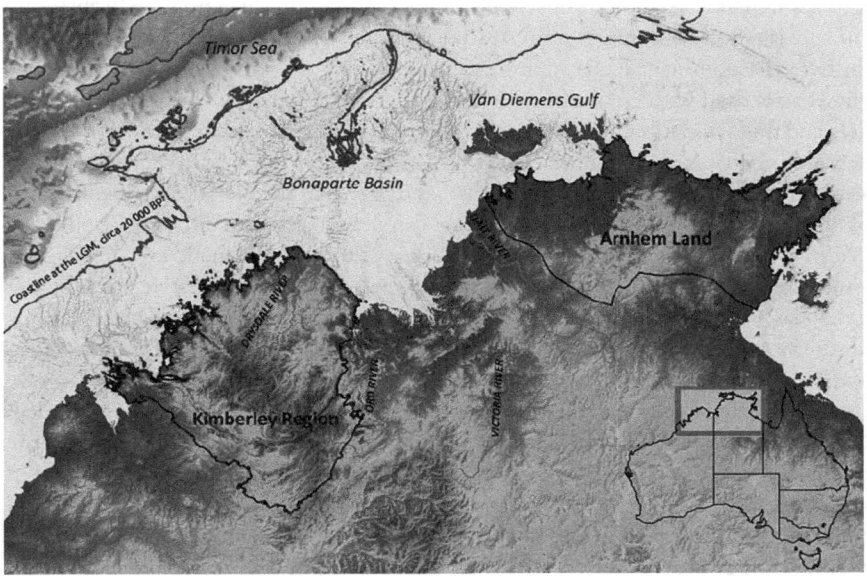

Figure 8.1 Map of Australia's Kimberley and Bonaparte Gulf area showing current coastline as well as the expanded coastal shelf that would have been exposed as land during the Last Glacial Maximum (LGM) at circa 20 ka

Source: Figure by Jillian Barteaux, UWA.

Table 8.1 Selected onset of occupation age ranges from both optically stimulated luminescence (OSL) and accelerator mass spectrometry (AMS) samples from Kimberley Visions Project, north-east Kimberley (Veth et al. 'Minjiwarra'). These occupations persist through the LGM and when combined with all occupation dates for the Kimberley (Figure 10) show persistence through time with an expected exponential increase in the Holocene likely due to issues of preservation, visibility, and researcher focus.

Site name	Age range	Lab number
Minjiwarra SU D	51.4–47.1 ka	Shfd17121 OSL
Minjiwarra SU C	32.7–30.0 ka	Shfd17120 OSL
Minjiwarra SU B	18.7–20.5 ka	Shfd17119 OSL
Minjiwarra SU A	8.0–7.4 ka	Shfd17118 OSL
DRY104 Rockshelter 35 cm	5,299–5,038 cal. BP	(Wk48208) IntCal13
DRY007 Borologa Rockshelter	3,390–3,230 cal. BP	(Wk47580) SHCal13
KGR037 Oomarri open site	2,710–12,570 cal. BP	(Wk44319) IntCal13
DRY025 Rockshelter	1,710–1,560 cal. BP	(Wk47582) SHCal13
KGR128 Open Site	1,120–980 cal. BP	(Wk47579) SHCal13
FOR001 Camera Pool	730–670 cal. BP	(Wk44396) IntCal13
KGR010 Rockshelter	490–320 cal. BP	(Wk47574) SHCal13

intensity and type of occupation as well as activity through time; we seek to unfurl the symbolic kernels of a Deep History of the Kimberley.

This dynamic relationship between human behaviour, changing landscapes, and climate[7] is reflected in studies from Australia's north and north-west, which show clear shifts in the dominant fauna, flora, and material culture portrayed in rock art style phases associated with environmental changes.[8,9] In order to best characterise and understand this association, we use contextualised iconographic or 'stylistic' analysis, understanding that 'style' is often a poorly understood and badly applied concept in rock art research.[10] We use the term 'style phase' as reported in the literature to identify a set of motifs with shared core conventions that can nonetheless also display variability.[11,12] We are aware that phase-based dating of rock art can be problematic by, for example, assuming that a succeeding style phase wholly replaces the previous style phase or that style phases cannot overlap, co-exist, or re-occur at different times and places. While northern Australia does seem – based on superimpositioning and landscape-level recording of sites and motifs – broadly to follow known style phases, new style phases are constantly being identified[13] and our understanding of existing style phases expanded. Using Information Exchange Theory (IET),[14] future research will investigate more closely the variation within and between style phases in order to better understand key themes such as human identity and social boundary formation, maintenance and evolution. We here present the style phases in their current, simplified form for the purposes of our heuristic.

We contextualise changing Kimberley rock art style phases using three data sets: new rock art dates, data recovered from archaeological excavation, and palaeoclimatic modelling. Superimposition sequences suggest that figurative rock art traditions likely occurred as 'proliferation' events.[15,16,17] LGM (26–19 ka) and Holocene-era ages are suggested for surviving figurative art in rock shelter contexts,[18] which are separate from the earliest proposed 'marking' of landscape in the form of cupules and grass prints. The earliest figurative art is likely of terminal Pleistocene age (~20–30 ka), with a gap in dated charcoal and pigment parietal art between c. 50 ka[19] and <30 ka.[20] In order to best explore changes in art style phases, social organisation, and landscapes at time scales measured in thousands and tens of thousands of years, we use a parallel deployment of Group Boundary Formation (GBF) Theory and IET.[21,22,23] We then describe known Kimberley rock art style phases before more closely analysing their chronology, and then argue for a persistence and continuity of Aboriginal occupation of the Kimberley. We frame continuity as also being continually responsive to changes in the natural and social worlds.

Theoretical approach

Group Boundary Formation Theory

Central to our linking of known art style phases to Quaternary records is GBF Theory,[24,25] which we articulate with climate and biome changes that likely influenced hunter-gatherer mobility[26] and changing information exchange networks.[27,28,29] Cultural practices such as the repeated use of places and continued depiction of attributes such as headdresses and waist decorations on anthropomorphic figures across rock art style phases are acknowledged.[30,31,32] We find Mirazón Lahr's[33] argument compelling that, following the global dispersal of modern peoples by 50,000 years ago (Marine Isotope Stages S 3–2), inter-group diversity increased and symbolic behaviours became more sensitive to complex group dynamics. No Kimberley rock art *per se* has yet been dated to this period, but rock art from nearby Sulawesi and Borneo has been,[34,35] making rock art of this antiquity in Arnhem Land and the Kimberley very likely. Northern Australia already preserves symbolic behaviour, manifest in haematitic and micaceous ochre and ochre-sprayed limestone plaques that date as far back as 41 ka from stratified archaeological contexts.[36,37] Indeed, our definition of 'rock art' may be too skewed towards a figurative 'end product', masking the cognitive capabilities required to source, mix, apply, and maintain pigment in a variety of non-figurative ways.

In examining the evolution and diversity of cultures through time, Foley and Mirazón Lahr[38] argue that the *rate* of change in culture is linked to social forces and that the 'fissioning' of groups will typically be due to reconfiguration of resources, demography, and territorial competition.[39] A model of this process is provided in Figures 8.2 and 8.3, showing a continuum of human responses to modelled social and environmental changes. At one end of the continuum, groups have equal access to resources and GBF is predicted to be low.[40] Conversely, as competition increases (e.g. patchy resources and/or increase in demographic pressure), GBF is predicted to become significantly higher. GBF is also increased when two or more populations are involved in a competitive rather than co-operative scenario. The net result of two human populations with potential asymmetry coming into contact is an increase in group boundaries, resulting in geographic differentiation and, potentially, the material marking of such boundaries and territories.

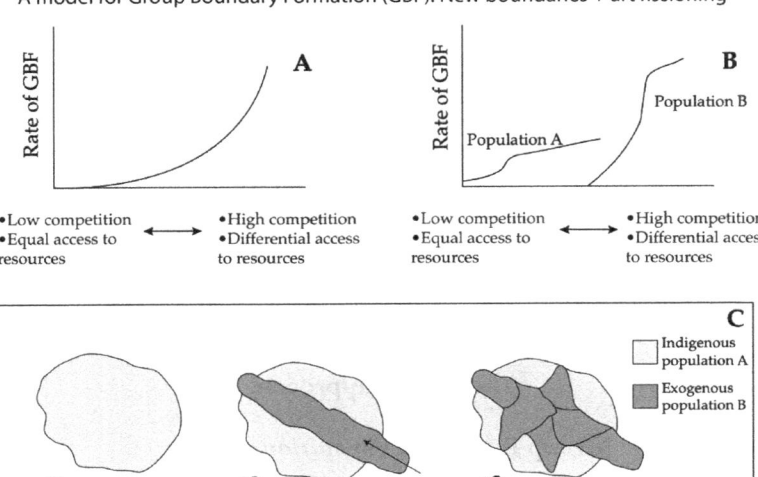

Figure 8.2 A model for GBF with fissioning and increasing heterogeneity in rock art
Source: After Foley, 'The Evolutionary Ecology of Linguistic Diversity': Figure 5.5

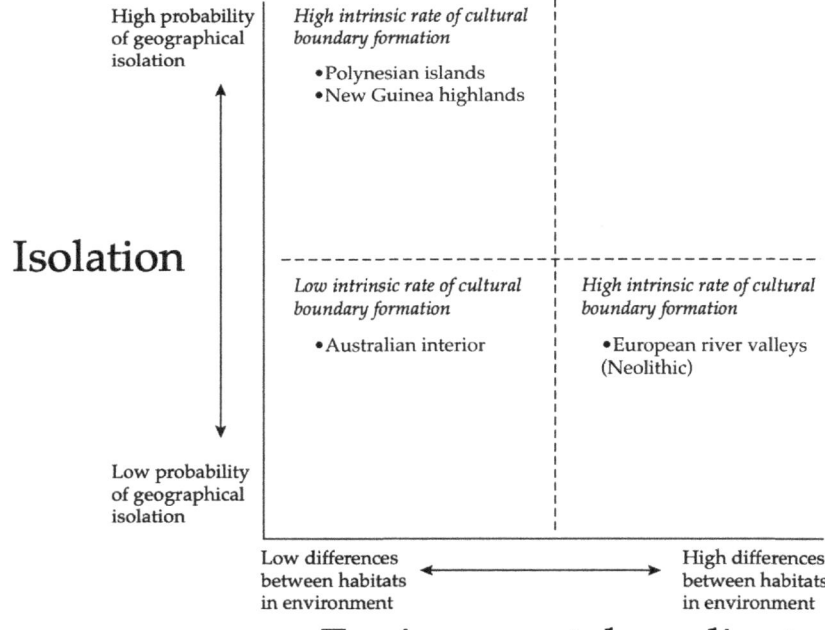

Figure 8.3 Boundary formation as a product of environmental gradient and isolation
Source: Foley, 'The Evolutionary Ecology of Linguistic Diversity': Figure 5.4

It is the capacity of socially transmitted behaviours, and specifically the ability to retain intra-group homogeneity and inter-group differences, that informs the links between biological and cultural differentiations.[41] Humans bring the particular cognitive ability of a high rate of socially transmitted behaviours across a whole realm of activities such as language, performance, body modification, production of distinctive material culture, and place-making and marking. We here focus on rock art production and changing temporal distributions of motifs at the local and regional scales as marking and making group boundaries across the Kimberley.[42,43,44,45,46]

Information Exchange Theory

GBF pairs very well with IET when using style phases as a vehicle for social identity and information exchange. Wobst's pioneering work[47] posited that the more visible an artefact, the more likely style would be used to convey information about social group affiliation. Rock art has the advantage of being especially visible as well as theoretically informed. Where it can be shown that a social group is actively using style in rock art to convey information, questions around the function of the art can be explored. In addition, Weissner's analysis of style[48] questioned how to assess whether style was being used actively or passively, and in what contexts this kind of functionality was expected. For example, she proposed that if the function of style is for boundary maintenance, as suggested here for the Kimberley, and applied under GBF, active iconological style would be present. Relying on both IET and GBF, we can use Kimberley rock art style phases, and their territorial extents to assess how identity-marking changes through time in this place.

Kimberley rock art style phases

Rock art, *sensu lato*, has been argued to be part of the colonising repertoire of the First Australians.[49] Indeed, the ~50–41 ka dates for rock art in adjacent Borneo and Sulawesi provide empirical support for this.[50,51,52] This position is consistent with widespread evidence for early symbolic behaviour in other First Australians' material cultures such as ochre and its distribution, the production and trade of shell beads, complex tools such as the edge-ground axe, and funerary rites, including cremation.[53,54,55] The earliest surviving Kimberley rock art likely comprises cupules (semi-spherical hollows ground into vertical and horizontal rock surfaces and rock shelters) and other rock markings (abraded grooves, incisions, and similar) that suggest an early marking or genuflection where people transform existing natural landscape shapes and forms into cultural artefacts.[56] These rock markings likely also overlap with early animal-dominated figurative rock art, which is numerous and widespread, covering extensive areas of the Kimberley and Northern Territory. This figurative art is thought to display increasing regionalism in concert with changing stone tool organisational strategies and other economic behaviours.[57] Currently, six different macro-style phases of Kimberley rock art have been identified, some of which have further divisions. Figure 8.4a

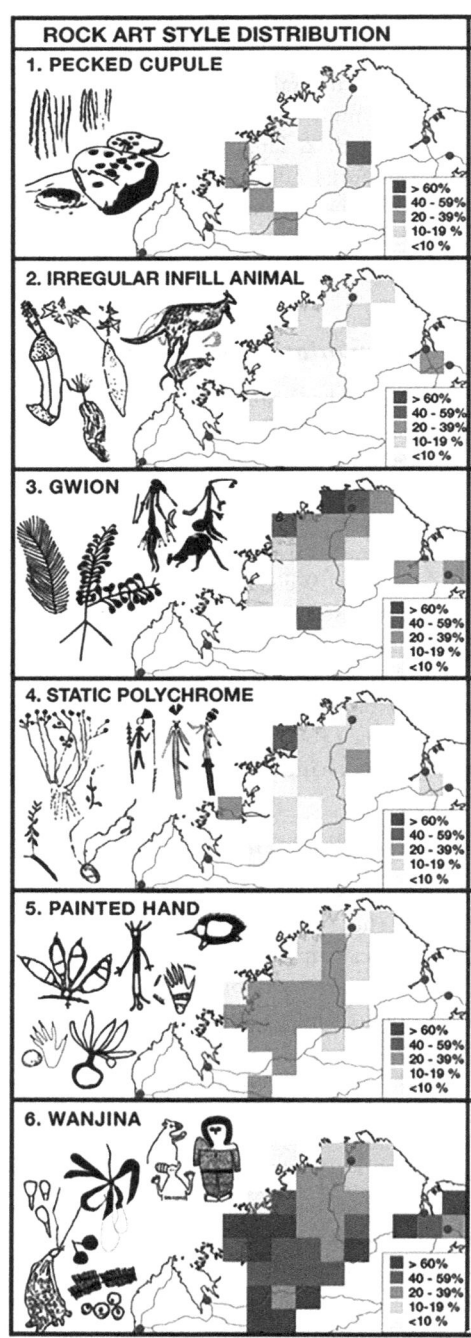

Figure 8.4a Proposed style phases and distributions for the Kimberley
Source: From Veth et al. 'Plants Before Farming'; figure by Pauline Heaney

The case for continuity

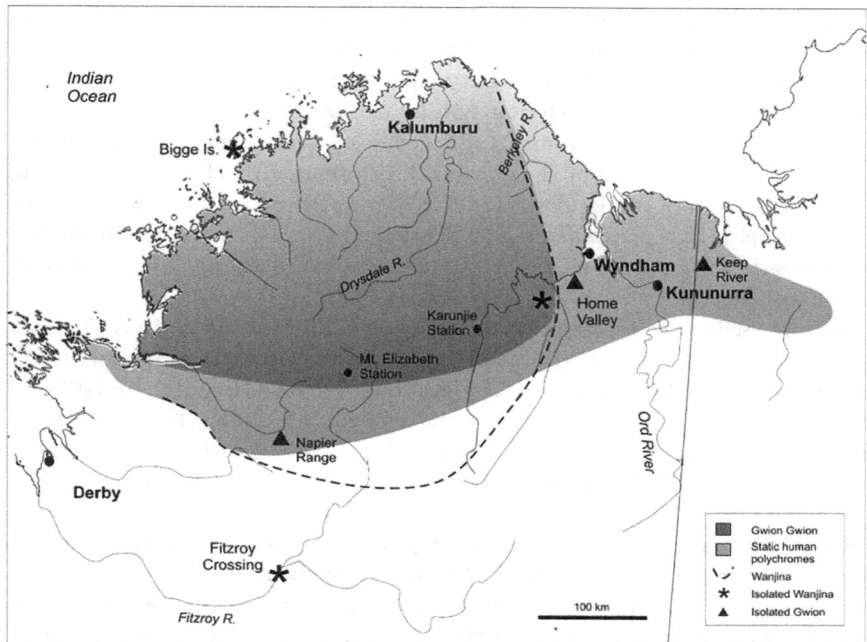

Figure 8.4b Approximate distributions of three major art traditions across the Kimberley and into the Keep River region. All three traditions have different spatial patterning from Gwion Gwion on the Kimberley Plateau and some islands (reflecting lower sea stand level), bichrome and polychrome human figures and material culture depictions south and east through to the Keep River, and finally Wandjina imagery approximating the current Worrorran language boundary. Boundaries will change with more survey and changing definitions

recasts this sequence as a socially and environmentally contextualised style phase sequence and temporality, which focuses on representative human and plant motifs from 3,750 sites recorded from across the Kimberley.[58,59] Figure 8.4b illustrates the spatial extents of these style phases.[60] Plant motifs form a significant component of Kimberley rock art (occurring in up to 25% of image clusters) and are found across the six styles. Anthropomorphised plant forms are argued to reflect their central and ongoing importance in the economic, settlement, and totemic realms. Current dating programmes grouped within Phases 2 (Irregular Infill Animal; IIA), 3 (Gwion Gwion), and 4 (Static Polychrome; see also Figure 8.4a) indicate that the figurative traditions may date to between the terminal Pleistocene (~30 ka) and the early Holocene (~7 ka).[61,62,63,64,65]

A discussion of possible age ranges for Kimberley rock art

In the Kimberley, the earliest pigment style phase (IIA) is thought to be large, figurative motifs with irregular or peripheral infill and often of animals and plants with some human figures.[66,67,68] This phase is followed by highly variable assemblages of

Gwion Gwion human figures, often with emblematic headdresses and accoutrements. These human figures transition from monochrome to bi- and polychrome human figures with complex weaponry and material culture in the Static Polychrome style phase. This switch from non-human animals to an extended focus on humans and their material cultures is also seen in adjacent Arnhem Land,[69] where it is proposed to have begun by the terminal Pleistocene–early Holocene transition. Previous analyses of similarities and differences in shared attributes between anthropomorphic style phases and regions[70,71] suggest processes that are more gradual and complex than a phase sequence assumes, and that there may also be reversals in the sequence.[72,73]

Our revised modelling also considers changes in the intensity of the Australian–Indonesian summer monsoon, rainfall, temperature, and sea levels. Against this are inferred Aboriginal settlement and aggregation behaviours according to GBF and IET, which we present as a heuristic device for further testing. In this spirit, we use climatic and environmental data from a 35,000-year record for the Tropics[74,75] together with regional data for the Kimberley[76,77,78] to create a mutually enabling and constraining data set. Using GBF and IET, different settlement and mobility patterns are modelled potentially to be in *phase* with – and not determined by – different environmental settings.[79,80] We argue that changes in a group's boundary maintenance and information exchange behaviours are often expressed and managed most visibly via rock art style phases. Style phases are a specific coding of a group's self-image and subsistence as groups respond to environmental and cultural drivers.[81] For example, during higher precipitation regimes, more 'closed' information systems tend to occur with greater emblematic group-identifying behaviour and higher stylistic heterogeneity. In contrast, arid phases tend to result in more 'open' information systems where more stylistically homogeneous schemes occur across permeable group boundaries and over larger landscapes.

A recent rock art dating project from the north-west Kimberley[82,83] has used three dating techniques – optically stimulated luminescence (OSL), accelerator mass spectrometry (AMS) radiocarbon, and uranium-series – to produce 13 minimum age estimates for rock art motifs. Nine of these age estimates were derived using OSL on fossilised mud-wasp nests overlying a range of rock art style phases. The other four minimum ages were obtained with AMS^{14}C. While the results indicate a terminal Pleistocene antiquity for some art, the superimposition sequence for these phases was found to be complex and overlapping, and even suggests hitherto unrecognised style phases. For example, one 'yam-like' motif, not attributable to a specific art style phase, returned an OSL minimum age estimate of 16 ± 1 ka.[84] This age overlaps the previous OSL age estimate from a mud-wasp nest (KERC4) lying partially over, and arguably associated with, a Gwion Gwion Phase anthropomorphic figure with a minimum age estimate of 16,400 ± 1,800 ka.[85,86]

Prior to the work of Ross and colleagues, the oldest date for the most recent known style phase was from a Wandjina (also 'Wanjina') motif made from beeswax pellets with an AMS date of 3,780 ± 60 cal. BP. Ross et al.'s minimum OSL age of 5.1 ± 0.2 ka for a mud-wasp nest overlying a Wandjina style macropod clearly pushes this style phase back to the mid-Holocene.[87] Ross et al. conclude that:

... the results have identified at least one case of the co-occurrence of recent Kimberley rock art stylistic phases previously considered sequential, thus signalling that the relationships between styles may not necessarily be temporally separated.[88]

What Ross et al.'s research suggests is the importance of unpacking stylistic phases such that their temporal linearity can be questioned.

The Kimberley Rock Art Dating Project has begun to produce dates on key rock art styles and, contra to Ross et al., provides evidence for linear stylistic development from IIA motifs to Gwion.[88] Finch and team have provided 24 AMS dates from mud-wasp nest stubs both above and below motifs that fall within the classic Gwion style phase, which (with one outlier) suggest that this particular style, at least for the NE Kimberley, was produced over a short period of time around 12,000 cal. BP. The outlier reported is an overlying nest (minimum age) dated to 16.3–17.0 cal. BP and suggests an earlier adoption of this style, followed by a proliferation or regionally wide uptake of the Gwion style. Finch has noted that preliminary dates from AMS dates on organics within mud-wasp nests for IIA style art from the same region, depicting predominantly naturalistic animals with partial infill, are older than these Gwion dates ranging from 17 to 13 ka, and do not appear to overlap.[89]

While the co-occurrence of multiple styles observed by Ross et al. may seem to contradict IET and GBF frameworks, we argue that these are by nature broad brushstrokes, and that detailed on-the-ground work will expose invaluable variability and variance at the site and motif levels. Style phases still mark group identity, and their potential temporal overlap has functional implications between styles. Importantly, we begin to recognise transitional rather than abrupt changes between styles. Ross and Travers[90] and colleagues have made a detailed case for the different styles sharing many core attributes (e.g. headdress and waist attributes) through time. The Correspondence Analysis carried out by Travers[91] shows the styles have cladal relationships to each other, with similar graphic elements co-occurring in human forms across style phases. An interpretation of the analysis and dating programmes is that the style boundaries are permeable and do not sit conformably with a unidirectional phase model (including the Finch et al.[92] outlier date). There is greater sharing, reactivation of older styles, and 'noise' than simple staged approaches have allowed for.

Proposed age ranges – Kimberley rock art style phases

Taking these new dates and caveats into consideration, we provide a broad outline for the major Kimberley style phases[93,94] (Figures 8.4a and 8.4b). We acknowledge that there are likely overlapping boundaries between style phases, consistent with 'proliferation events', and that recursive images may be made through time. Proposed age ranges are therefore approximate but useful in understanding the rock art corpus *sensu stricto*, to better connect rock art data to parallel palaeoenvironmental, landscape, and even ethnographic data sets. We now characterise each style phase in terms of character and temporality.

Cupule and rock marking style phase (c. 50 ka and ongoing)

The earliest proposed 'settlement repertoire' consists of rock 'markings',[95,96] which comprise cupules (Figure 8.5), grooves, incised, abraded, and flaked rock surfaces. While these rock markings were also made at other, more recent times, including ethnographically recorded instances such as the re-engraving of cupules,[97] their first emergence is suggested to be at settlement, where the continent was experiencing a pluvial phase marked by full lake conditions.[98] Visual and contextual evidence of some cupules' antiquity includes case hardening, covering by thick mineral crusts, fossil mud-wasp nests overlying these crusts, and cupules sometimes extending into archaeological deposit (Figure 8.5). Together, this suggests a Pleistocene antiquity. Cupules are subject to ongoing dating efforts.[99]

Irregular infill animal style phase (c. 20–14 ka)

This phase is modelled to begin with sea levels as low as −130 m with a near-doubling of the Kimberley land mass (see Figure 8.1; note extended coastline), and is followed by sea level rise and generally cooler, drier conditions.[100,101,102,103] The IIA style phase is characterised by aquatic species such as fish and long-necked tortoises as well as birds, echidnas, snakes, possums, macropods (Figure 8.6), plants, and rare human figures. This early style phase is characterised by the parsimonious use of dark ochre in short stroke and dot infill, with some complete infill of peripherals such as head, tails, and feet. Visually and in terms of 'style', the IIA style phase correlates with early phase Large Naturalistic Figures from Arnhem Land.[104] It has also been suggested that IIA images may be as old as visually similar figures from Island Southeast Asia, recently dated to over 35 ka.[105,106]

Figure 8.5 Cupule-covered rock walls in a rock shelter along the Drysdale River, NE Kimberley. Excavation shows cupules extending 15 cm below present surface level

Source: Balanggarra Aboriginal Corporation and UWA Centre for Rock Art Research + Management

The case for continuity

Figure 8.6 IIA macropod from Drysdale River, NE Kimberley. Image is approximately 120 cm long.
Source: Balanggarra Aboriginal Corporation and UWA Centre for Rock Art Research + Management

Gwion Gwion and elegant action figure style phases (c. 14–10 ka)

This period seems to be marked initially by an arid phase and then the re-establishment of the summer monsoon overlapping with the most rapid rise in sea level during the deglacial period.[107] Gwion Gwion figures occur in red/mulberry hues (Figure 8.7), and include visually animated figures referred to as 'Elegant Action Figures',[108] which have marked similarities to the 'Dynamic Figures' of Arnhem Land.[109,110,111,112,113] Finch et al. have confirmed this terminal Pleistocene window in the NE Kimberley,[114] indicating that Gwion Gwion (and variant) distributions almost certainly continued to the east across the Bonaparte Depression under what are now the Timor and Arafura Seas, connecting to Arnhem Land.[115] This apparently similar style phase coincides with an extended arid phase after the LGM, and possibly as late as 12,000 BP.[116,117] De Deckker et al., using offshore cores on Australia's North West Shelf, note that before 13 ka rainfall, river discharge into the ocean was low.[118] It was only after 13 ka that the entire system moved away from glacial period conditions, and more likely closer to 14 ka in the Kimberley. This is consistent with recent data from pollen cores in the north Kimberley.[119] It seems that the Gwion Gwion style phase did not end abruptly at the Pleistocene–Holocene boundary, but transformed into the next style phase – human Static Polychrome Phase bichrome and polychrome figures. This research has immediate relevance in its power to empirically debunk a persistent discontinuity myth – that 'Bradshaws' (as Gwion Gwions were then called) were not of Aboriginal authorship but represented an earlier, non-Aboriginal group of people. Not only is there no empirical evidence of any non-Aboriginal people at this time, both dating and stylistic analysis show that this is one of multiple Aboriginal rock art styles, with demonstrable continuities to other rock art style phases, notably Static Polychrome (and bichrome) figures. What is interesting is the switch to a

Figure 8.7 Superimposed Gwion Gwion figures from King George River, NE Kimberley. Largest human figure 140 cm tall

Source: Balanggarra Aboriginal Corporation and UWA Centre for Rock Art Research + Management

focus on human figures and material culture from the earlier IIA emphasis on animals. Here, we may be seeing a more formal art, indicating highly regulated modes of conduct that people have by this stage developed with what may have been an especially dynamic and changing landscape.

Static Polychrome style phase (10–6 ka)

Static Polychromes (formerly 'Clothes Peg Figures'; Figure 8.8) generally comprise bichrome and occasional polychrome human figures with detailed material cultures, such as armatures and bags, and detailed headdresses. They have been recorded consistently superimposed over Gwion Gwion figures with which they

The case for continuity

Figure 8.8 Static Polychrome human figures at either end of a painted cluster or 'panel' from the Drysdale River, NE Kimberley
Source: Balanggarra Aboriginal Corporation and UWA Centre for Rock Art Research + Management

share common core attributes such as headdresses and accoutrements.[120] Static Polychromes have also been argued to share some attributes with the 'Hooked Stick' Figures of Arnhem Land,[121] some of which have been dated to 9,540 cal. BP to 9,260 cal. BP[122] – an antiquity that accords with the relative position of Static Polychromes within the Kimberley rock art style phase sequence. This is a period with an increasingly active summer monsoon, producing warmer and wetter conditions,[123] causing increasing loss of lands as sea levels rose. Applying GBF and IET, we would expect these conditions to encourage accelerated symbolic boundary-making behaviour and increased stylistic heterogeneity in the art.

Painted Hand and Wandjina style phases (mid/late Holocene–present)

In reality two iconographically very distinct style phases, both Painted Hand (previously 'Clawed Hand') and Wandjina (also 'Wanjina'; Figure 8.9) seem to occur within the last ~5,800 years and may be coeval, at least for some time.[124] Wandjina art has been recorded ethnographically and is still made and renewed today.[125] The introduction of bifacial stone point technology by 5 ka is seen by Maloney[126] to be part of a risk-reduction strategy whereby groups mitigated more variable climate and less predictable resource structuring in the Kimberley. Symbolic practices likely accompanied these changes in lithic organisational strategies in the form of increased emblematic marking of clan estates and boundaries. A strengthening in the summer monsoon in the last 1,000 years[127] may have contributed to an increase in stylistic heterogeneity and boundary-making behaviour. While clearly bound by rules and conventions, Painted Hand and Wandjina are perhaps the most heterogeneous of all the style phases. This heterogeneous period would facilitate the production of multiple types of rock art and place marking, and it is likely several style phases co-existed.

Figure 8.9 Wandjina paintings from the Drysdale River, NE Kimberley
Source: Balanggarra Aboriginal Corporation and UWA Centre for Rock Art Research + Management

Chronological analysis

These style phases are best understood when modelled as part of a continuously occupied Kimberley landscape. While the style phases suggest different periods of rock art production, they do not suggest periods of landscape occupation lacunae. In contrast, Walsh envisioned Kimberley cultural sequences as discontinuous with three separate 'epochs' of art production.[128] This schema relied on a devolutionary narrative and has been (re)activated from time to time. It is part of an historical practice that Ian McNiven has described as a 'dissociative archaeology'.[129] This discontinuity trope selectively interprets key sites as providing geological and cultural support for occupational lacunae and by implication cultural replacement.[130] A basic examination of available occupation dates refutes the discontinuity scenario. We build on the AustArch database[131] for the Kimberley. Dates with missing information (e.g. specimen type that determines calibration curve, date range) were removed and arranged chronologically in 2,500 year blocs or 'bins' (0–2,500 cal. BP, 2,501–5,000 cal. BP, 5,001–7,500 cal. BP, and so on – until 50,000 cal. BP), at which point one final chronological bin is used, >50,000 cal. BP (Figure 8.10). The dates are assigned to bins based upon their median age. While the error ranges for some dates may span two chronological bins, given the chronological size of each (2,500 years), this effect is minimal. This simple approach also allows us to examine dates independent of issues commonly associated with probability density plots.[132]

The results suggest that the Kimberley was continuously occupied, from 50,000 cal. BP onwards, with a predictable increase of dated archaeological evidence for occupation in the mid–late Holocene, which is most likely due to preservation, taphonomy, and research agendas. We do not suggest that the Holocene increase in dates represents an increase in population or occupational intensity. This spread of dates simply shows that the Kimberley remains occupied throughout the late

The case for continuity

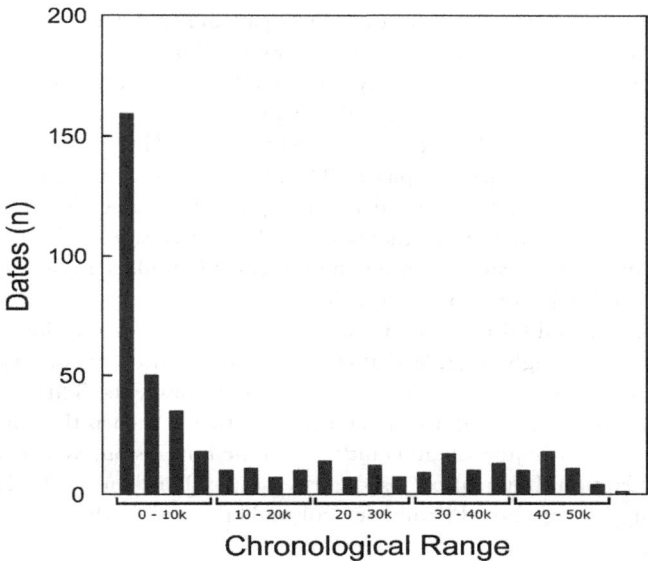

Figure 8.10 Radiocarbon, OSL and thermoluminescence (TL) dates associated with archaeological evidence for occupation in the Kimberley region, arranged by chronological bins. The youngest (0–2,500 cal. BP) occur on the left-end horizontal axis and increasing age range progresses to >50,000 cal. BP on the right-end of the horizontal axis. All dates are in cal. BP

Pleistocene and Holocene. While some individual archaeological records may contain evidence for site-scale occupational discontinuities, at a landscape scale, there is no evidence that the Kimberley region was ever unoccupied. Indeed, there are good records of persistence across times of major climate and environmental changes, at Riwi[133] and Carpenter's Gap 1[134] during the LGM and then on the edge of the desert.

Conclusion

The currently published c. 50,000-year occupation history of the Kimberley[135,136,137] and evidence for it being a refuge during environmentally challenging times,[138] coupled with the widespread presence of early symbolic behaviours,[139,140] make us conclude that Kimberley rock art will have a long chronology, marked by periods of proliferation. Indeed, rock art production is likely rhythmed, increasing and decreasing in intensity and distribution as the drivers for its production are activated or stopped over time. Cupules and rock markings are modelled to occur from 50 ka, while the first recognisable surviving style phase – Irregular Infill Animal – likely dates from the LGM or earlier. The complex multi-phase Gwion Gwion anthropomorphic traditions are modelled to date from the end of an extended arid phase, which was punctuated by short episodes of higher rainfall. This art repertoire is thought to be located within cultural landscapes with relatively open social boundaries. Shared traditions may imply past and contemporary information exchange but do not necessarily assume migration. Long-term contact across to what is today Arnhem Land is strongly suggested by iconographically similar rock arts, notably Elegant Action Figures and Dynamic Figures, and Static Polychrome Figures and Hooked Stick Figures. The current dates for Holocene-era art include Painted Hand and Wandjina style phases. The former is as yet enigmatic and under-researched, while the latter could date from pre-5 ka but seems most strongly marked in the last millennium. Increasing stylistic diversity in the Holocene is most likely linked to estate formation and increased boundary marking as groups exercise cultural trajectories over ecological ones.

Applying IET and GBF to the six major Kimberley styles and their territorial distribution[141,142] strongly suggests that changing distributions of core styles reflect changing social symbolic practices to dynamic environments. This includes the movement of particular religious and cultural practices – such as the ethnographically documented Wanjina-Ungud cult[143] – and the impacts on associated rock art and its proliferation. Boundaries observed are fluid rather than rigid (Figures 8.4a and 8.4b), suggesting a broad Kimberley cultural bloc with both regional and clan differentiations.

Previously, some writers have cast the Kimberley as too environmentally variable to permit continuous human occupation. Human agency was under-valued and archaeological and palaeo-environmental data points were few. Today, we have much more information at our disposal and are able to reverse models of discontinuity by acknowledging the full capabilities of the many Aboriginal cultures, which have lived on this landscape for the past 50,000 or more years. A review of available scientific dating proves that there are no 'gaps' of any size in the occupation record. The scale of our analysis is broad, and we acknowledge that at a micro level there would have been localised lineage extinctions, forced movements of people as sea levels changed, and even displacement through conflict, ritual, or similar. But these localised events do not constitute widespread 'abandonment' or 'collapse'.[144] Moreover, there is almost certainly a vast record of sites now submerged, due to post-LGM sea level rise, further refuting a discontinuity narrative. It is also important to qualify this occupation as more than 'survival', as this privileges an environmental determinist discourse. There is evidence of multiple, strongly functioning groups – in the exceptional rock art record, long distance trade of goods and time spent on 'non-utilitarian' activities such as making beads. Rock art is not simply a record or reflection of these lives; it is integral to it – focusing people's thoughts and crystallising identity in particular places using distinctive iconographies, but also allowing for linkage with other people and places.

We have set out explicitly to connect symbolic practices, the archaeology of rock art and Quaternary records in testable and culturally informed ways to consider the nature of Aboriginal lifeways in the Kimberley. By adopting the lens of GBF and IET and building on the seminal work of Lewis,[145] changes in rock art styles can be coupled to changes in ecology and climate of significance to hunter-gatherers. This interpretive framework provides a clear and empirical basis for predicting different group identity and territorial signalling practices through time. These practices and their archaeological signatures are evident throughout the Kimberley, proving continuous human action that nonetheless displays considerable variability as people mould themselves to the world around them and vice versa.

Acknowledgements

This paper is based on a version presented by Peter Veth at Alta, Norway for the ACRA III conference 'Perspectives on Differences in Rock Art', held in September 2015. Research has been conducted in partnership with Balanggarra Aboriginal Corporation under a research agreement brokered by the Kimberley Land Council. Content regarding published rock art dates has been updated and the phase model revised. We thank Tristen Jones (ANU), Bruno David (Monash University), Andy Gleadow, Helen Green, and Damien Finch (University of Melbourne), and Darrell Lewis (UNE) for providing access to unpublished materials and advices, though we accept responsibility for the views expressed here. Rock art recording from a total of >1,200 sites in the Australian Research Council *Kimberley Visions Project: rock art style provinces in northern Australia* (LP150100490) and the Takarakka database administered by Pauline Heaney have been relied on for further observations on the superimposition sequences. We thank Jillian Barteaux and Pauline Heaney for preparing Figures 8.1 and 8.4a, respectively. *Kimberley Visions* is led by CI Sven Ouzman, with CIs Peter Veth, Bruno David, Andy Gleadow, Martin Porr, PI Leslie Zubieta, and RAs Jean-Jacques Delannoy, Pauline Heaney, Cecilia Myers, Jean-Michel Geneste and Emilie Chalmin. Partners include Balanggarra Aboriginal Corporation, Balanggarra Rangers, Balanggarra Traditional Owners, University of Melbourne, Monash University, Université de Savoie (France), Western Australian Department of Biodiversity, Conservation and Attractions, Dunkeld Pastoral Pty. Ltd. and the Kimberley Foundation Australia.

Notes

1 Tim Maloney et al. 'Carpenters Gap 1: A 47,000 Year Old Record of Indigenous Adaption and Innovation,' *Quaternary Science Reviews* 191 (2018): 204.
2 Dorcas Vannieuwennhuyse, Sue O'Connor, and Jane Balme 'Settling in Sahul: Investigating Environmental and Human History Interactions through Micromorphological Analyses in Tropical Semi-arid North-West Australia,' *Journal of Archaeological Science* 77 (2017): 172–173.
3 Rachel Wood et al. 'Towards an Accurate and Precise Chronology for the Colonization of Australia: The Example of Riwi, Kimberley, Western Australia,' *PLoS ONE* 11, no. 9 (2016): 1–26.
4 Peter Veth et al. 'Minjiwarra: Archaeological Evidence of Human Occupation of Australia's Northern Kimberley by 50,000 BP.' *Australian Archaeology* 85, no. 2 (2019): 115–125.
5 Valda Blundell et al. *Barddabardda Wodjenangorddee: We're Telling All of You* (Fremantle: Fremantle Press, 2017), 1–5.
6 Vannieuwennhuyse, O'Connor, and Balme, 'Settling in Sahul.'
7 Peter Veth, Sue O'Connor, and Lynley Wallis, 'Perspectives on Ecological Approaches in Australian Archaeology,' *Australian Archaeology* 50 (2000): 54–60.

8 Jo McDonald, 'I Must Go Down to the Seas Again: Or, What Happens When the Sea Comes to You? Murujuga Rock Art as an Environmental Indicator for Australia's North-West,' *Quaternary International* 385 (2015): 124–135.
9 Paul Taçon et al., 'Changing Ecological Concerns in Rock-Art Subject Matter of North Australia's Keep River Region,' *Before Farming* 3, no. 4 (2003): 1–14.
10 Ines Domingo Sanz and D. Fiore, 'Style: Its Role in the Archaeology of Art,' in *Encyclopedia of Global Archaeology*, ed. Clare Smith (New York: Springer, 2014), 7104–7111.
11 A. d'Alleva, 'Captivation, Representation, and the Limits of Cognition: Interpreting Metaphor and Metonymy in Tahitian Tamau,' in *Beyond Aesthetics: Art and the Technologies of Enchantment*, ed. C. Pinney and N. Thomas (Oxford: Berg, 2001), 79–96.
12 Robert Gunn, Leigh Douglas, and R.L. Whear, 'The "Ngar-Mimi" Motif from the Arnhem Land Plateau,' *Rock Art Research* 30, no. 2 (2013): 217–234.
13 Robert Gunn et al., "Kimberley Stout Figures": A New Motif Type in Kimberley Rock Art, North-Western Australia,' *Australian Archaeology* 85, no. 2 (2019): 85:2, 151–169.
14 H. Martin Wobst 'Stylistic Behaviour and Information Exchange,' in *For the Director: Research Essays in Honor of James B. Griffin*, ed. C.E. Cleland (Michigan: Ann Arbor Press, 1977), 317–344.
15 Peter Hiscock, *Archaeology of Ancient Australia* (London: Routledge, 2008), 110–115.
16 Tristen Jones, 'Disentangling the Styles, Sequences and Antiquity of the Early Rock Art of Western Arnhem Land' (PhD diss., Australian National University, 2017).
17 Sally May et al., 'Early Australian Anthropomorphs: Jabiluka's Dynamic Figure Rock Paintings,' *Cambridge Archaeological Journal* 28, no. 1 (2018): 67–83.
18 Peter Veth et al., 'Plants before Farming: The Deep History of Plant-Use and Representation in the Rock Art of Australia's Kimberley Region,' *Quaternary International* 489 (2018): 26–45.
19 Maxime Aubert et al., 'Pleistocene cave art from Sulawesi, Indonesia,' *Nature* 514, no. 7521 (2014): 223–227.
20 Bruno David et al., 'How Old Are Australia's Pictographs: A Review of Rock Art Dating,' *Journal of Archaeological Science* 40, no. 1 (2013): 3–10.
21 R. Foley and M. Mirazón Lahr, 'The Evolution of the Diversity of Cultures,' *Philosophical Transactions of the Royal Society B: Biological Sciences* 366, no. 1567 (2011): 1080–1089.
22 Darrell Lewis, 'Bradshaws: The View from Arnhem Land,' *Australian Archaeology* 44 (1997): 1–16.
23 Jo McDonald and Peter Veth, *A Companion to Rock Art* (Oxford: Wiley-Blackwell, 2012).
24 R. Foley 'The Evolutionary Ecology of Linguistic Diversity in Human Populations,' in *Traces of Ancestry: Studies in Honour of Colin Renfrew*, ed. M Jones (Oakville: David Brown Book Company, 2004), 61–71.
25 Foley and Mirazón Lahr, 'The Evolution of the Diversity of Cultures.'
26 Steve Kuhn, D. Raichlen, and A. Clark, 'What Moves Us? How Mobility and Movement Are at the Center of Human Evolution,' *Evolutionary Anthropology* 25, no. 3 (2016): 86–97.
27 Lewis, 'Bradshaws.'
28 Jo McDonald and Peter Veth, 'Rock Art in Arid Landscapes: Pilbara and Western Desert Petroglyphs,' *Australian Archaeology* 77 (2013): 66–81.
29 Wobst, 'Stylistic Behaviour.'
30 Jo McDonald and Peter Veth, 'The Archaeology of Memory: The Recursive Relationship of Martu Rock Art and Place,' *Anthropological Forum* 23, no. 4 (2013): 367–386.
31 Meg Travers, 'Continuity and Change: Exploring Stylistic Transitions in the Anthropomorphic Figures of the Northwest Kimberley Rock Art Assemblage and the Varying Contexts of Rock Art Production' (PhD diss., University of New England, 2015).
32 Meg Travers and June Ross, 'Continuity and Change in the Anthropomorphic Figures of Australia's Northwest Kimberley,' *Australian Archaeology* 82, no. 2 (2016): 148–167.

33 M. Mirazón Lahr, 'The Shaping of Human Diversity: Filters, Boundaries and Transitions,' *Philosophical Transactions of the Royal Society B: Biological Sciences* 371, no. 1698 (2016).
34 Aubert et al., 'Pleistocene Cave Art from Sulawesi.'
35 Maxime Aubert et al., 'Palaeolithic Cave Art in Borneo,' *Nature* 564, no. 7735 (2018): 254.
36 Chris Clarkson et al., 'Human Occupation of Northern Australia by 65,000 Years Ago,' *Nature* 547, no. 7663 (2017): 306–310.
37 Sue O'Connor and B. Fankhauser, 'Art at 40,000 BP? One Step Closer: An Ochre Covered Rock from Carpenter's Gap Shelter 1, Kimberley Region, Western Australia,' in *Histories of Old Ages: Essays in Honour of Rhys Jones*, eds. Atholl Anderson, Ian Lilley, and Sue O'Connor (Canberra: Pandanus Books, 2001), 287–300.
38 Foley and Mirazón Lahr, 'The Evolution of the Diversity of Cultures.'
39 S. Ambrose and K. Lorenz, 'Social and Ecological Models of the Middle Stone Age in Southern Africa,' in *The Emergence of Modern Humans*, ed. P Mellars (Edinburgh: Edinburgh University Press, 1990), 3–33.
40 Foley, 'The Evolutionary Ecology of Linguistic Diversity.'
41 Foley and Mirazón Lahr, 'The Evolution of the Diversity of Cultures', 1087.
42 Hiscock, *Archaeology of Ancient Australia*, 246–248.
43 McDonald and Veth, 'The Archaeology of Memory.'
44 Veth et al., 'Plants before Farming.'
45 Veth et al. 'Minjiwarra.'
46 Polly Wiessner, 'Is There a Unity to Style?' in *New Directions in Archaeology*, eds. Meg Conkey and Christine Hastorf (Cambridge: Cambridge University Press, 1990), 105–112.
47 Wobst, 'Stylistic Behaviour.'
48 Wiessner, 'Is There a Unity to Style?'
49 Jane Balme et al., 'Symbolic Behaviour and the Peopling of the Southern Arc Route to Australia,' *Quaternary International* 202, no. 1–2 (2009): 59–68.
50 Maxime Aubert, 'A Review of Rock Art Dating in the Kimberley, Western Australia,' *Journal of Archaeological Science* 39, no. 3 (2002): 573–577.
51 Aubert et al., 'Pleistocene Cave Art from Sulawesi.'
52 Aubert et al., 'Palaeolithic Cave Art in Borneo.'
53 Clarkson et al., 'Human Occupation of Northern Australia.'
54 Michelle Langley, Chris Clarkson and Sean Ulm, 'From Small Holes to Grand Narratives: The Impact of Taphonomy and Sample Size on the Modernity Debate in Australia and New Guinea,' *Journal of Human Evolution* 61, no. 2 (2011): 197–208.
55 Peter Veth et al., 'The Role of Information Exchange in the Colonisation of Sahul,' in *The Role of Information in Hunter-Gatherer Band Adaptations*, eds. R. Whallon, W.A. Lovis and R.K. Hitchcock (Los Angeles: Cotsen Institute of Archaeology Press of UCLA, 2011), 203–220.
56 Sven Ouzman et al., 'Cupule Engravings from Jinmium-Granilpi (Northern Australia) and Beyond: Exploration of a Widespread and Enigmatic Class of Rock Markings,' *Antiquity* 71 (1997): 942–965.
57 Hiscock, *Archaeology of Ancient Australia*, 110–115.
58 Sven Ouzman et al., 'Plants before Animals? Aboriginal Rock Art as Evidence of Ecoscaping in Australia's Kimberley,' in *The Oxford Handbook of the Archaeology and Anthropology of Rock Art,* eds. Bruno David and Ian J. McNiven (New York: Oxford University Press, 2018).
59 Veth et al., 'Plants before Farming.'
60 Grahame Walsh, *Bradshaws: Ancient Rock Paintings of North-West Australia* (Geneva: Limiteé, 1994).
61 Bruno David et al., *The Archaeology of Rock Art in Western Arnhem Land, Australia* (Canberra: Department of Archaeology and Natural History, The Australian National University, 2017).

62 Bruno David et al., 'Determining the Age of Paintings at JSARN–113/23, Jawoyn Country, Central-Western Arnhem Land Plateau,' in *The Archaeology of Rock Art in Western Arnhem Land, Australia,* eds. Bruno David et al. (Canberra: Department of Archaeology and Natural History, The Australian National University, 2017), 371–422.
63 Helen Green et al., 'Mineral Deposition Systems at Rock Art Sites, Kimberley, Northern Australia – Field Observations,' *Journal of Archaeological Science: Reports* 14 (2017): 340–352.
64 June Ross et al., 'Into the Past: A Step towards a Robust Kimberley Rock Art Chronology,' *PLoS ONE* 11, no. 8 (2016): 1–33.
65 Travers and Ross, 'Continuity and Change in the Anthropomorphic Figures of Australia's Northwest Kimberley.'
66 Ouzman et al., 'Plants before Animals?'
67 Veth et al., 'Plants before Farming.'
68 Chris Chippindale and Paul Taçon, *The Archaeology of Rock-Art* (Cambridge: Cambridge University Press, 1998).
69 May et al., 'Early Australian Anthropomorphs.'
70 Travers, 'Continuity and Change: Exploring Stylistic Transitions.'
71 Travers and Ross, 'Continuity and Change in the Anthropomorphic Figures of Australia's Northwest Kimberley.'
72 McDonald and Veth, 'The Archaeology of Memory.'
73 Ross et al., 'Into the Past.'
74 J. Reeves et al., 'Climate Variability over the Last 35,000 Years Recorded in Marine and Terrestrial Archives in the Australian Region: An OZ-INTIMATE Compilation,' *Quaternary Science Reviews* 74 (2013): 21–34.
75 J. Reeves et al., 'Palaeo Environmental Change in Tropical Australasia over the Last 30,000 Years – a Synthesis by the OZ-INTIMATE Group,' *Quaternary Science Reviews* 74 (2013): 97–114.
76 R. Denniston et al., 'A Stalagmite Record of Holocene Indonesian–Australian Summer Monsoon Variability from the Australian Tropics,' *Quaternary Science Reviews* 78 (2013): 155–168.
77 Emily Field et al., 'A Late Quaternary Record of Monsoon Variability in the Northwest Kimberley, Australia,' *Quaternary International* 449 (2017): 119–135.
78 Kasih Norman et al., 'An Early Colonisation Pathway into Northwest Australia 70–60,000 Years Ago,' *Quaternary Science Reviews* 180 (2018): 229–239.
79 Veth, O'Connor, and Wallis, 'Perspectives on Ecological Approaches.'
80 R. Whallon, 'Social Networks and Information: Non-"Utilitarian" Mobility among Hunter-Gatherers,' *Journal of Anthropological Archaeology* 25, no. 2 (2006): 259–270.
81 McDonald and Veth, 'Rock Art in Arid Landscapes.'
82 Ross et al., 'Into the Past.'
83 Travers and Ross, 'Continuity and Change in the Anthropomorphic Figures of Australia's Northwest Kimberley.'
84 Ross et al., 'Into the Past.'
85 R. Roberts et al., 'Luminescence Dating of Rock Art and Past Environments Using Mud-Wasp Nests in Northern Australia,' *Nature* 387, no. 6634 (1997): 696–699.
86 Aubert, 'Review of Rock Art Dating.'
87 Ross et al., 'Into the Past': 42.
88 D. Finch et al., '12,000-Year-Old Aboriginal Rock Art from the Kimberley Region, Western Australia,' *Science Advances* 6 (2020): eaay3922.
89 Damien Finch, et al. "Ages for Australia's oldest rock paintings." *Nature human behaviour* 5, no. 3 (2021): 310–318.
90 Travers and Ross, 'Continuity and Change in the Anthropomorphic Figures of Australia's Northwest Kimberley.'
91 Travers, 'Continuity and Change: Exploring Stylistic Transitions.'
92 Finch et al., '12,000-Year-Old Aboriginal Rock Art from the Kimberley Region.'

93 Veth et al., 'Plants before Farming.'
94 Ouzman et al., 'Plants before Animals?'
95 Andrée Rosenfeld, 'Rock Art and Rock Markings,' *Australian Archaeology* 49 (1999): 28–33.
96 Paul Taçon and Sven Ouzman, 'Worlds within Stone: The Inner and Outer Rock-Art Landscapes of Northern Australia and Southern Africa,' in *The Figured Landscapes of Rock-Art: Looking at Pictures in Place*, eds. Chris Chippindale and Grahame Nash (Cambridge: Cambridge University Press, 2004), 39–68.
97 Ouzman et al., 'Cupule engravings from Jinmium-Granilpi.'
98 Peter Veth et al., 'Excavations at Parnkupirti, Lake Gregory, Great Sandy Desert: OSL Ages for Occupation before the Last Glacial Maximum,' *Australian Archaeology* 69 (2009): 1–10.
99 Helen Green et al., 'Mineral Deposition Systems at Rock Art Sites.'
100 M. Burrows et al., 'A New Late Quaternary Palaeohydrological Record from the Humid Tropics of Northeastern Australia,' *Palaeogeography, Palaeoclimatology, Palaeoecology* 451 (2016): 164–182.
101 Denniston et al., 'A Stalagmite Record.'
102 Reeves et al., 'Climate Variability over the Last 35,000 Years.'
103 Reeves et al., 'Palaeoenvironmental Change in Tropical Australasia.'
104 Jones, 'Disentangling the Styles.'
105 Aubert et al., 'Pleistocene Cave Art from Sulawesi.'
106 Aubert et al., 'Palaeolithic Cave Art in Borneo.'
107 Field et al., 'A Late Quaternary Record of Monsoon Variability.'
108 As labelled in Walsh, *Bradshaws: Ancient Rock Paintings* and Grahame Walsh, *Bradshaw Art of the Kimberley* (Toowong: Takarakka Nowan Kas Publications, 2000).
109 Darrell Lewis, *The Rock Paintings of Arnhem Land, Australia* (London: British Archaeological Reports, BAR International Series 415, 1998).
110 Lewis, 'Bradshaws.'
111 Michael Rainsbury, 'Mimi and Gwion: An Investigation into the Links between Dynamic Figures of Arnhem Land and Bradshaw Figures of the Kimberley, Northern Australia' (MA diss., University of Durham, 2002).
112 Paul Taçon et al., '"Bradshaws" – an Eastern Province?' *Rock Art Research* 16, no. 2 (1999): 127–128.
113 Taçon et al., 'Changing Ecological Concerns.'
114 Finch et al., '12,000-Year-Old Aboriginal Rock Art from the Kimberley Region.'
115 Lewis, 'Bradshaws': Figure 1.
116 Burrows et al. 'A New Late Quaternary Palaeohydrological Record.'
117 Field et al., 'A Late Quaternary Record of Monsoon Variability.'
118 Patrick De Deckker, T.T. Barrows, and J. Rogers, 'Land-Sea Correlations in the Australian Region: Post-Glacial Onset of the Monsoon in Northwestern Western Australia,' *Quaternary Science Reviews* 105 (2014): 181–194.
119 Field et al., 'A Late Quaternary Record of Monsoon Variability.'
120 Travers and Ross, 'Continuity and Change in the Anthropomorphic Figures of Australia's Northwest Kimberley.'
121 Lewis, 'Bradshaws.'
122 David et al., 'Determining the Age of Paintings at JSARN–113/23.'
123 Denniston et al., 'A Stalagmite Record.'
124 Ross et al., 'Into the Past.'
125 Blundell et al., *Barddabardda Wodjenangorddee*.
126 Tim Maloney, 'Technological Organisation and Points in the Southern Kimberley' (PhD diss., Australian National University, 2015).
127 Field et al., 'A Late Quaternary Record of Monsoon Variability.'
128 Walsh, *Bradshaw Art of the Kimberley*.

129 Ian McNiven, 'The Bradshaw Debate: Lessons Learned from Critiquing Colonialist Interpretations of Gwion Gwion Rock Paintings of the Kimberley, Western Australia,' *Australian Archaeology* 72 (2011): 35–44.
130 Veth et al. 'Minjiwarra.'
131 Alan Williams et al., 'AustArch: A Database of 14C and Non-14C Ages from Archaeological Sites in Australia – Composition, Compilation and Review (Data Paper),' *Internet Archaeology* 36 (2014).
132 Douglas B. Bamforth and Brigid Grund, 'Radiocarbon Calibration Curves, Summed Probability Distributions, and Early Paleoindian Population Trends in North America,' *Journal of Archaeological Science* 39 (2012): 1768–1774.
133 Wood et al., 'Towards an Accurate and Precise Chronology.'
134 Maloney et al., 'Carpenters Gap 1.'
135 Maloney et al., 'Carpenters Gap 1.'
136 Wood et al., 'Towards an Accurate and Precise Chronology.'
137 Veth et al. 'Minjiwarra.'
138 Alan Williams et al., 'Human Refugia in Australia during the Last Glacial Maximum and Terminal Pleistocene: A Geospatial Analysis of the 25–12 ka Australian Archaeological Record,' *Journal of Archaeological Science* 40, no. 12 (2013): 4612–4625.
139 Balme et al., 'Symbolic Behaviour.'
140 Langley, Clarkson, and Ulm, 'From Small Holes to Grand Narratives.'
141 Veth et al., 'Plants before Farming.'
142 Ouzman et al., 'Plants before Animals?'
143 Blundell et al., *Barddabardda Wodjenangorddee*.
144 Emma Gause, 'A Critique: Jared Diamond's Collapse Put in Perspective,' *Papers from the Institute of Archaeology* 24, vol. 1 (2014): 16.
145 Lewis, 'Bradshaws.'

Bibliography

Ambrose, S.H., and K.G. Lorenz. 'Social and Ecological Models of the Middle Stone Age in Southern Africa.' In *The Emergence of Modern Humans*, edited by P. Mellars, 3–33. Edinburgh: Edinburgh University Press, 1990.

Aubert, M. 'A Review of Rock Art Dating in the Kimberley, Western Australia.' *Journal of Archaeological Science* 39, no. 3 (2012): 573–577.

Aubert, M., A. Brumm, M. Ramli, T. Sutikna, E.W. Saptomo, B. Hakim, M.J. Morwood, G.D. Van Den Bergh, L. Kinsley, and A. Dosseto. 'Pleistocene Cave Art from Sulawesi, Indonesia.' *Nature* 514, no. 7521 (2014): 223–227.

Aubert, M., P. Setiawan, A.A. Oktaviana, A. Brumm, P.H. Sulistyarto, E.W. Saptomo, B. Istiawan, T.A. Ma'rifat, V.N. Wahyuono, F.T. Atmoko, J.-X. Zhao, J. Huntley, P.S.C. Taçon, D.L. Howard, and H.E.A. Brand. 'Palaeolithic Cave Art in Borneo.' *Nature* 564, no. 7735 (2018): 254–257.

Balme, J., I. Davidson, J. McDonald, N. Stern, and P. Veth. 'Symbolic Behaviour and the Peopling of the Southern Arc Route to Australia.' *Quaternary International* 202, no. 1–2 (2009): 59–68.

Bamforth, D.B., and B. Grund. 'Radiocarbon Calibration Curves, Summed Probability Distributions, and Early Paleoindian Population Trends in North America.' *Journal of Archaeological Science* 39 (2012): 1768–1774.

Blundell, V., K. Doohan, D. Vachon, M. Allbrook, M.A. Jebb, and J. Bornman. *Barddabardda Wodjenangorddee: We're Telling All of You*. Fremantle: Fremantle Press, 2017.

Burrows, M.A., H. Heijnis, P. Gadd, and S.G. Haberle. 'A New Late Quaternary Palaeohydrological Record from the Humid Tropics of Northeastern Australia.' *Palaeogeography, Palaeoclimatology, Palaeoecology* 451 (2016): 164–182.

Chippindale, C., and P.S.C. Taçon. *The Archaeology of Rock-Art*. Cambridge: Cambridge University Press, 1998.

Clarkson, C., Z. Jacobs, B. Marwick, R. Fullagar, L. Wallis, M. Smith, R.G. Roberts, M. Smith, E. Hayes, K. Lowe, X. Carah, A.S. Florin, J. McNeil, D. Cox, L.J. Arnold, Q. Hua, J. Huntley, H.E.A. Brand, T. Manne, A. Fairbairn, J. Shulmeister, L. Lyle, M. Salinas, M. Page, K. Connell, G. Park, K. Norman, T. Murphy, and C. Pardoe. 'Human Occupation of Northern Australia by 65,000 Years Ago.' *Nature* 547, no. 7663 (2017): 306–310.

d'Alleva, A. 'Captivation, Representation, and the Limits of Cognition: Interpreting Metaphor and Metonymy in Tahitian Tamau.' In *Beyond Aesthetics: Art and the Technologies of Enchantment*, edited by C. Pinney and N. Thomas, 79–96. Oxford: Berg, 2001.

David, B., J.-M. Geneste, F. Petchey, J.-J. Delannoy, B. Barker, and M. Eccleston. 'How Old Are Australia's Pictographs: A Review of Rock Art Dating.' *Journal of Archaeological Science* 40, no.1 (2013): 3–10.

David, B., P.S.C. Taçon, J.-J. Delannoy, and J.-M. Geneste. *The Archaeology of Rock Art in Western Arnhem Land, Australia*. Terra Australis 47. Canberra: Department of Archaeology and Natural History, The Australian National University, 2017.

David, B., J.-J. Delannoy, R. Gunn, L. Drady, F. Petchey, J. Mialanes, E. Chalmin, J.-M. Geneste, I. Moffat, K. Aplin, and M. Katherine. 'Determining the Age of Paintings at JSARN–113/23, Jawoyn Country, Central-Western Arnhem Land Plateau.' In *The Archaeology of Rock Art in Western Arnhem Land, Australia*, edited by B. David, P.S.C. Taçon, J.-J. Delannoy, and J.-M. Geneste. Terra Australis 47, 371–422. Canberra: Department of Archaeology and Natural History, The Australian National University, 2017.

De Deckker, P., T.T. Barrows, and J. Rogers. 'Land-Sea Correlations in the Australian Region: Post-Glacial Onset of the Monsoon in Northwestern Western Australia.' *Quaternary Science Reviews* 105 (2014): 181–194.

Denniston, R., K-H. Wyrwoll, V.J. Polyak, J.R. Brown, Y. Asmerom, A.D. Wanamaker, Z. LaPointe, R. Ellerbroek, M. Barthelmes, D. Cleary, J. Cugley, D. Woods and W.F. Humphreys. 'A Stalagmite Record of Holocene Indonesian–Australian Summer Monsoon Variability from the Australian Tropics.' *Quaternary Science Reviews* 78 (2013): 155–168.

Field, E., H.A. McGowan, P.T. Moss, and S.K. Marx. 'A Late Quaternary Record of Monsoon Variability in the Northwest Kimberley, Australia.' *Quaternary International* 449 (2017): 119–135.

Finch, D., A. Gleadow, J. Hergt, P. Heaney, H. Green, C. Myers, P. Veth, S. Harper, S. Ouzman, and V.A. Levchenko. 'Ages for Australia's oldest rock paintings.' *Nature Human Behaviour* 5, no. 3 (2021): 310–318.

Finch, D., A. Gleadow, J. Hergt, V.A. Levchenko, P. Heaney, P. Veth, S. Harper, S. Ouzman, C. Myers, and H. Green. '12,000-Year-Old Aboriginal Rock Art from the Kimberley Region, Western Australia.' *Science Advances* 6 (2020): eaay3922.

Foley, R.A. 'The Evolutionary Ecology of Linguistic Diversity in Human Populations.' In *Traces of Ancestry: Studies in Honour of Colin Renfrew* edited by M. Jones, 61–71. Oakville: David Brown Book Company, 2004.

Foley, R.A., and M. Mirazón Lahr. 'The Evolution of the Diversity of Cultures.' *Philosophical Transactions of the Royal Society B: Biological Sciences* 366, no. 1567 (2011): 1080–1089.

Gause, E. 'A Critique: Jared Diamond's Collapse Put in Perspective.' *Papers from the Institute of Archaeology* 24, no. 1 (2014): 16.

Gunn, R.G, B. David, L.C. Douglas, J.-J. Delannoy, S. Harper, P. Heaney, S. Ouzman, and P. Veth. '"Kimberley Stout Figures": A New Motif Type in Kimberley Rock Art, North-Western Australia.' *Australian Archaeology* 85, no. 2 (2019): 151–169.

Gunn, R.G., L.C. Douglas, and R.L. Whear. 'The "Ngar-Mimi" Motif from the Arnhem Land Plateau.' *Rock Art Research* 30, no. 2 (2013): 217–234.

Green, H., A. Gleadow, D. Finch, J. Hergt, and S. Ouzman. 'Mineral Deposition Systems at Rock Art Sites, Kimberley, Northern Australia – Field Observations.' *Journal of Archaeological Science: Reports* 14 (2017): 340–352.

Hiscock, P. *Archaeology of Ancient Australia*. London: Routledge, 2008.

Jones, T. 'Disentangling the Styles, Sequences and Antiquity of the Early Rock Art of Western Arnhem Land.' PhD diss., Australian National University, 2017.
Kuhn, S., D. Raichlen, and A. Clark. 'What Moves Us? How Mobility and Movement Are at the Center of Human Evolution.' *Evolutionary Anthropology* 25, no. 3 (2016): 86–97.
Langley, M.C., C. Clarkson, and S. Ulm. 'From Small Holes to Grand Narratives: The Impact of Taphonomy and Sample Size on the Modernity Debate in Australia and New Guinea.' *Journal of Human Evolution* 61, no. 2 (2011): 197–208.
Lewis, D. *The Rock Paintings of Arnhem Land, Australia*. London: British Archaeological Reports, BAR International Series 415 (1988).
Lewis, D. 'Bradshaws: The View from Arnhem Land,' *Australian Archaeology* 44 (1997): 1–16.
Maloney, T.R. 'Technological Organisation and Points in the Southern Kimberley.' PhD diss., Australian National University, 2015.
Maloney, T.R., S. O'Connor, W. Rachel, A. Ken, and J. Balme. 'Carpenters Gap 1: A 47,000 Year Old Record of Indigenous Adaption and Innovation.' *Quaternary Science Reviews* 191 (2018): 204.
May, S.K., I.G. Johnston, P.S.C. Taçon, I. Domingo Sanz, and J. Goldhahn. 'Early Australian Anthropomorphs: Jabiluka's Dynamic Figure Rock Paintings.' *Cambridge Archaeological Journal* 28, no. 1 (2018): 67–83.
McDonald, J. 'I Must Go Down to the Seas Again: Or, What Happens When the Sea Comes to You? Murujuga Rock Art as an Environmental Indicator for Australia's North-West.' *Quaternary International* 385 (2015): 124–135.
McDonald, J. and P. Veth. *A Companion to Rock Art*. Oxford: Wiley-Blackwell, 2012.
McDonald, J. and P. Veth. 'The Archaeology of Memory: The Recursive Relationship of Martu Rock Art and Place.' *Anthropological Forum* 23, no. 4 (2013): 367–386.
McDonald, J. and P. Veth. 'Rock Art in Arid Landscapes: Pilbara and Western Desert Petroglyphs.' *Australian Archaeology* 77 (2013): 66–81.
McNiven, I. 'The Bradshaw Debate: Lessons Learned from Critiquing Colonialist Interpretations of Gwion Gwion Rock Paintings of the Kimberley, Western Australia.' *Australian Archaeology* 72 (2011): 35–44.
Mirazón Lahr, M. 'The Shaping of Human Diversity: Filters, Boundaries and Transitions,' *Philosophical Transactions of the Royal Society B: Biological Sciences* 371, no. 1698 (2016): 1–12.
Norman, K., J. Inglis, C. Clarkson, J.T. Tyler, J. Faith, J. Shulmeister, and D. Harris. 'An Early Colonisation Pathway into Northwest Australia 70–60,000 Years Ago,' *Quaternary Science Reviews* 180 (2018): 229–239.
O'Connor, S. and B. Fankhauser. 'Art at 40,000 BP? One Step Closer: An Ochre Covered Rock from Carpenter's Gap Shelter 1, Kimberley Region, Western Australia.' In *Histories of Old Ages: Essays in Honour of Rhys Jones*, edited by A. Anderson, I. Lilley and S. O'Connor, 287–300. Canberra: Pandanus Books, The Australian National University, 2001.
Ouzman, S., P. Taçon, K. Mulvaney, and R. Fullagar. 'Cupule Engravings from Jinmium-Granilpi (Northern Australia) and Beyond: Exploration of a Widespread and Enigmatic Class of Rock Markings.' *Antiquity* 71 (1997): 942–965.
Ouzman, S., P. Veth, C. Myers, P. Heaney, and K. Kenneally. 'Plants before Animals? Aboriginal Rock Art as Evidence of Ecoscaping in Australia's Kimberley.' In *The Oxford Handbook of the Archaeology and Anthropology of Rock Art*, edited by Bruno David and Ian J. McNiven, 469–480. New York: Oxford University Press, 2018.
Rainsbury, M. 'Mimi and Gwion: An Investigation into the Links between Dynamic Figures of Arnhem Land and Bradshaw Figures of the Kimberley, Northern Australia.' MA diss., University of Durham, 2002.
Reeves, J.M., T.T. Barrows, T.J. Cohen, A.S. Kiem, H.C. Bostock, K.E. Fitzsimmons, J.D. Jansen, J. Kemp, C. Krause, L. Petherick, and S.J. Phipps. 'Climate Variability over the Last 35,000 Years Recorded in Marine and Terrestrial Archives in the Australian Region: An OZ-INTIMATE Compilation.' *Quaternary Science Reviews* 74 (2013): 21–34.

Reeves, J.M., H.C. Bostock, L.K. Ayliffe, T.T. Barrows, P. De Deckker, L.S. Devriendt, G.B. Dunbar, R.N. Drysdale, K.E. Fitzsimmons, and M.K. Gagan. 'Palaeoenvironmental Change in Tropical Australasia over the Last 30,000 Years – a Synthesis by the OZ-INTIMATE Group.' *Quaternary Science Reviews* 74 (2013): 97–114.
Roberts, R., Walsh, G., Murray, A., Olley, J. Jones, R., Morwood, M., Tuniz, C., Lawson, E., Macphail, M., Bowdery, D. and I. Naumann. 'Luminescence Dating of Rock Art and Past Environments Using Mud-Wasp Nests in Northern Australia.' *Nature* 387, no. 6634 (1997): 696–699.
Rosenfeld, A. 'Rock Art and Rock Markings.' *Australian Archaeology* 49 (1999): 28–33.
Ross, J., Westaway, K., Travers, M., Morwood, M.J., and J. Hayward. 'Into the Past: A Step towards a Robust Kimberley Rock Art Chronology.' *PLoS ONE* 11, no. 8 (2016): 1–33.
Sanz, I.D. and D. Fiore. 'Style: Its Role in the Archaeology of Art.' In *Encyclopedia of Global Archaeology*, edited by Clare Smith, 7104–7111. New York: Springer, 2014.
Taçon, P.S.C., K. Mulvaney, R. Fullagar, and L. Head. '"Bradshaws" – an Eastern Province?' *Rock Art Research* 16, no. 2 (1999): 127–129.
Taçon, P.S.C., K. Mulvaney, S. Ouzman, R. Fullagar, L. Head, and P. Carlton. 'Changing Ecological Concerns in Rock-Art Subject Matter of North Australia's Keep River Region.' *Before Farming* 3, no. 4 (2003): 1–14.
Taçon, P.S.C. and S. Ouzman. 'Worlds within Stone: The Inner and Outer Rock-Art Landscapes of Northern Australia and Southern Africa.' In *The Figured Landscapes of Rock-Art: Looking at Pictures in Place*, edited by Chris Chippindale and Grahame Nash, 39–68. Cambridge: Cambridge University Press, 2004.
Travers, M. 'Continuity and Change: Exploring Stylistic Transitions in the Anthropomorphic Figures of the Northwest Kimberley Rock Art Assemblage and the Varying Contexts of Rock Art Production.' PhD diss., University of New England, 2015.
Travers, M., and J. Ross. 'Continuity and Change in the Anthropomorphic Figures of _Australia's Northwest Kimberley.' *Australian Archaeology* 82, no. 2 (2016): 148–167.
Vannieuwennhuyse, D., S. O'Connor, and J. Balme. 'Settling in Sahul: Investigating Environmental and Human History Interactions through Micromorphological Analyses in Tropical Semi-arid North-West Australia.' *Journal of Archaeological Science* 77 (2017): 172–173.
Veth, P., K. Ditchfield, M. Bateman, S. Ouzman, M. Benoit, A.P. Motta, D. Lewis, Harper, S., and Balanggarra Aboriginal Corporation. 'Minjiwarra: Archaeological Evidence of Human Occupation of Australia's Northern Kimberley by 50,000 BP.' *Australian Archaeology* 85, no. 2 (2019): 115–125.
Veth, P., C. Myers, P. Heaney, and S. Ouzman. 'Plants Before Farming: The Deep History of Plant-Use and Representation in the Rock Art of Australia's Kimberley Region.' *Quaternary International* 489 (2018): 26–45.
Veth, P., S. O'Connor, and L. Wallis. 'Perspectives on Ecological Approaches in Australian Archaeology.' *Australian Archaeology* 50, no. 1 (2000): 54–66.
Veth, P., M. Smith, J. Bowler, K. Fitzsimmons, A. Williams, and P. Hiscock. 'Excavations at Parnkupirti, Lake Gregory, Great Sandy Desert: OSL Ages for Occupation before the Last Glacial Maximum.' *Australian Archaeology* 69 (2009): 1–10.
Veth, P., N. Stern, J. McDonald, J. Balme, and I. Davidson. 'The Role of Information Exchange in the Colonisation of Sahul.' In *The Role of Information in Hunter-Gatherer Band Adaptations*, edited by R. Whallon, W.A. Lovis and R.K. Hitchcock, 203–220. Los Angeles, CA: Cotsen Institute of Archaeology Press of UCLA, 2011.
Walsh, G.L. *Bradshaws: Ancient Rock Paintings of North-West Australia.* Geneva: Limiteé, 1994.
Walsh, G.L. *Bradshaw Art of the Kimberley.* Toowong: Takarakka Nowan Kas Publications, 2000.
Welch, D. *Aboriginal Paintings of Drysdale River National Park, Kimberley, Western Australia.* Australian Aboriginal Culture Series, Issue 10. Darwin: David M. Welch, 2015.
Whallon, R. 'Social Networks and Information: Non-"Utilitarian" Mobility among Hunter-Gatherers.' *Journal of Anthropological Archaeology* 25, no. 2 (2006): 259–270.

Wiessner, P. 'Is There a Unity to Style?' In *New Directions in Archaeology*, edited by Meg Conkey and Christine Hastorf, 105–112. Cambridge: Cambridge University Press, 1990.

Williams, A.N., S. Ulm, A.R. Cook, M.C. Langley, and M. Collard. 'Human Refugia in Australia during the Last Glacial Maximum and Terminal Pleistocene: A Geospatial Analysis of the 25–12 ka Australian Archaeological Record.' *Journal of Archaeological Science* 40, no. 12 (2013): 4612–4625.

Williams, A.N., S. Ulm, M. Smith, and J. Reid. 'AustArch: A Database of 14C and Non-14C Ages from Archaeological Sites in Australia – Composition, Compilation and Review (Data Paper).' *Internet Archaeology* 36 (2014).

Wobst, H. Martin. 'Stylistic Behaviour and Information Exchange.' In *For the Director: Research Essays in Honor of James B. Griffin*, edited by C.E. Cleland, 317–344. Michigan: Ann Arbor Press, 1977.

Wood, R., Z. Jacobs, D. Vannieuwenhuyse, J. Balme, S. O'Connor, and R. Whitau. 'Towards an Accurate and Precise Chronology for the Colonization of Australia: The Example of Riwi, Kimberley, Western Australia,' *PLoS ONE* 11, no. 9 (2016): 1–26.

9
VOYAGERS FROM THE HAVAI'I DIASPORA
Polynesian mobility, 1760s–1850s

Kate Fullagar[1]

Climbing aboard Captain Bougainville's triple-masted *Étoile*, Tahitian man Ahutoru was not 'in the least uneasy'.[2] Why would he be? Ocean-going vessels were part of his everyday landscape. They also stood at the centre of his historical understanding: Ahutoru knew that he was part of a diaspora forged, linked, and defined by ambitious voyaging. The French sailors who welcomed Ahutoru onto their ship in 1768 were surprised by the frank transparency of his determination, but nothing could have been likelier.[3] Louis-Antoine de Bougainville's *Étoile* was not even the first European-style vessel that Ahutoru had encountered. The Tahitian had experienced the arrival of Samuel Wallis' *Dolphin* further north in Matavai Bay nine months earlier. He'd seen the unusual weapons that pale-skinned sailors carried, or at least heard tales about them.[4] Ahutoru's desire to join this second lot of European sailors was driven by a wish either to go to a nearby island, or to see about acquiring some of the visitors' *mana*, or special powers. He had no reason to feel anxious about joining these wide-eyed newcomers: they seemed to want to learn a lot from him.

Growing up on the island of Tahiti in the 1740s, Ahutoru would have learned from his elders that he was a part of the Havai'i diaspora. By the eighteenth century, the sacred island of Havai'i was more commonly called Ra'iātea, and Ahutoru knew that this place was only a short journey away to the west. He'd learned that the god Ta'aroa had entered the world at Ra'iātea and from there had created all the other gods and islands as well as the first people.[5] From Ra'iātea, Ahutoru's ancestors had set out on voyages to settle their oceanic domain. Islanders and archaeologists confirm that humans first arrived in the archipelago surrounding Ra'iātea (also known as the Society Islands) around 600–1000 CE. They note that very similar peoples arrived in Mokupuni o Hawai'i (the Hawaiian archipelago) to the north between 800 and 1000 CE and in Aotearoa (today also called New Zealand) to the south by 1200–1300 CE. Today, there is some debate about whether the settlement of Hawaii stemmed from Ra'iātea or from a simultaneous wave from further west, but certainly the present-day Indigenous peoples of all three island groups (Society, Hawaiian, and Aotearoa) feel part of the one historical identity. That identity is also often called Polynesian.[6]

The sense of belonging to the Havai'i diaspora among Society, Hawaiian, and Aotearoa Islanders consolidated during the near-century following Europe's re-engagement with the eastern Pacific. Between the 1760s and the 1850s, Islanders in all three archipelagos shared common experiences of contact that went on to bind their identity tighter together in the modern era. They all suffered from the deadly pathogens brought by Europeans; later, they all had to negotiate Europe's theologies to a greater or lesser extent, and eventually they all had to face varying degrees of economic and political threats. Less often acknowledged, all three island groups also shared a common reinvigoration of their ancient voyaging practices. European ships brought opportunities to extend established Polynesian sailing customs. Society, Hawaiian, and Aotearoa Islanders took up these opportunities, on the whole, with gusto. Most Islander voyagers on European ships in this period were self-motivated, designed to further an Indigenous-centred goal in an Indigenous-centred world. Some were forced, but even these voyagers usually managed to reclaim some Indigenous agency over their circumstances. Voyagers from the Havai'i diaspora between the late eighteenth century and the late nineteenth century not only redefined their ocean-faring heritage; they also often used their travels to overcome some of the harsher effects of European intrusion.

Few scholars have linked the surge in Polynesian world-voyaging from the 1700s with the earlier voyages of the Havai'i-descended people. The only historian to do so in a comprehensive fashion is David Chappell. His study, *Double Ghosts* (1997), traced the voyages made by peoples from across all Oceania during the age of European empire and likened them to the originary voyages of the whole Pacific world.[7] Indeed, he called these voyages a 'second diaspora'.[8] The present chapter focuses on travellers from the three main points of the second Havai'i diaspora – those from the Society Islands around Ra'iātea itself (known by locals as Tōtaiete mā), those from the Hawaiian archipelago, and those from Aotearoa. It sketches aspects of the travels via a few biographies per archipelago. Biography is the best means of glimpsing the Indigenous perspective on this phenomenon when primary sources are overwhelmingly European.[9]

In his study of the second great Pacific diasporic movement, Chappell also tried to calculate the total numbers involved. Of his conservative estimate of 30,000 voyagers for the century after European contact, around two-thirds were probably from the Society, Hawaiian, and Aotearoa Islands.[10] Chappell organised travellers into three categories: those who stayed within the inner Pacific, those who ventured to the Pacific Rim, and those who went even further afield. Since voyaging within Oceania carried on to some degree without interruption from the era of the first diaspora, my chapter will focus only on the voyagers of the second Havai'i diaspora who travelled outside of the inner Pacific (to Asia, America, or Europe).[11] By Chappell's restrained account, this amounts to around 15,000 persons.[12]

Comparison as well as biography defines my methodology. Where biography enables a way to foreground Indigenous perspectives against a strong European bias in the sources, comparison encourages us to reach beyond simplistic accounts of Indigenous motivation. The desire to emphasise Indigenous agency now dominates scholarship about historical Polynesian interactions with Europeans, but too often this work reduces Indigenous agency to either mere curiosity or individualist power plays.[13] By comparing the whole lives of certain exemplars, however, the theme of collectivist political motivation comes more readily to the fore. Ahutoru is an illustrative instance. Most historians frame his agency as a form of inquisitiveness, possibly concealing a darker grab for personal prestige. Such an assumption is understandable since this was the motivation that drove Bougainville himself to take on Ahutoru – historians have assumed a similar inclination on the part of Ahutoru.[14] However, when considered alongside other voyagers like Mai from Huahine, Hongi Hika from the Ngāpuhi, or Liholiho from Hilo – each of whom emerges as activists for larger collectives like families, *iwi*, or kingdoms – Ahutoru starts to appear as a more complex agent. His mournful gazing at the island of Ra'iātea as Bougainville's ship passed it, for example, hints in this context at deeper and further-reaching bonds than first assumed.[15] It prompts a closer investigation into Ahutoru's biographical background, which soon reveals links to a bigger network of local interests than otherwise imagined.

The voyagers of the second Havai'i diaspora were in many ways historical hinges between the old and the new: they re-fashioned their core voyaging heritage into a means of accessing – and shaping – the modernising world. Like their ancestors, and unlike their European counterparts, they mostly did so as communal agents.[16]

Tōtaiete mā

Ahutoru was the son of a Tahitian chief and an exiled Raiatean woman. Bougainville guessed him to be in his thirties in 1768, which backdates his birth to the mid-1730s.[17] In this decade, Ra'iātea standing as the pre-eminent sacred isle of the eastern Pacific world – the island of ancient Havai'i – was strong. Only a decade or so before, the Raiateans had sent out missionaries of their then-dominant god, 'Oro, to convert surrounding Islanders to this newly ascendant deity. The mission had been remarkably successful in Tahiti, just over 100 miles to the east of Ra'iātea. During Ahutoru's youth, most Tahitians were 'Oro worshippers, so it's possible that Ahutoru's mother had been an associate of one of the Raiatean missionaries.

The Rāiatean 'Oro-worshipping elite had also recently converted the inhabitants of another isle in the archipelago – Bora Bora to its northwest. This effort had been in some ways *too* successful. By the late 1750s, zealous Bora Boran 'Oro worshippers had their eyes on a takeover of the motherland, Ra'iātea, on the grounds that it was now insufficiently pious. The guerrilla raids began, by canoe, in 1760. Raiateans fled in their hundreds to still-friendly Tahiti. By 1763, the Bora Boran offensive was complete and Raiateans were *persona non grata* on their own island.[18]

The French officers who befriended Ahutoru did not relate whether his mother was still alive in 1768. If she were alive, she would have found herself in permanent exile – a refugee dependent on the goodwill of her host island, regardless of the honour of being from the diasporic heartland. If she were dead, Ahutoru would still have shared much of this anguished subjectivity. Even Tahitians of unmixed heritage were not as free as they had been in their relations with Ra'iātea: the Bora Borans had a reputation throughout Tōtaiete mā as 'incorrigible blockheads'.[19] Few could imagine standing up to their violent rule.

An understanding of Ahutoru's mixed heritage challenges any easy guesses at his motivation in joining Bougainville. His French friends assumed that he wanted to travel for 'adventure' and for 'women'.[20] This might be a more accurate summary of the desires of the average European seaman. Historians have tended to trust in the opinions expressed in primary sources – this includes even the great scholar Anne Salmond, who, however, recognised that when Ahutoru tried desperately to make Bougainville turn his vessel to an island called 'Oumaitia' and appeared distraught when the captain refused, he was indicating Ra'iātea.[21] Keeping in mind Ahutoru's background, Ahutoru probably wanted the French ship to visit his mother's homeland. Perhaps he thought that French guns might strike a blow against the Bora Boran ascendancy? When thwarted in this wish, he may have thought that a journey all the way to France itself would deliver better, if more circuitously acquired, aid.

In the end, it was not to be. Ahutoru was denied a visit to Ra'iātea, and died on his return leg from France.[22] By delving into Ahutoru's backstory, it is possible to discern a reasoning for his voyage that goes further than just curiosity or personal gratification. Taking into account his attachments to precious Ra'iātea gives weight to Ahutoru as a political and ancestrally aware actor.

Similar conclusions may be drawn for the voyager Mai. Born around 20 years after Ahutoru, Mai was of full Raiatean ancestry. He was born on the sacred island, living through the Bora Boran onslaught when still a small boy. During the final battle for Raiatean sovereignty in 1763, Mai's father was killed, and his surviving family fled to Tahiti. Mai spent his teen years as a privileged yet dispossessed refugee in the northern Tahitian district around Matavai Bay. He was definitely present when Wallis *Dolphin* anchored there in 1767. He reported later to a British friend that he had been hit by a stray bullet during the major altercation between Tahitians and Britons – his scar remained visible on his torso until the end of his days.[23]

Mai also claimed to see and meet with various officers of James Cook's *Endeavour* voyage in 1769, one year after Bougainville's arrival.[24] By the time Cook came to the archipelago again – the fourth such tall-masted ship to arrive at Tahiti in six years – Mai had decided on a clear and bold plan. He would befriend the crew of this expedition and sail with them back to their homeland. There, he would acquire European guns, and possibly European manpower, in order to wrest familial rights from the Bora Borans. Mai had every reason to believe that he could return to the islands from Europe since ships from Europe seemed by now to arrive with almost yearly regularity.

Many histories of Mai still defer to the major British shipboard sources when explaining his motivations for voyaging with Cook. The naturalist on board, Georg Forster, commented that he seemed 'intelligent' and 'lively', which for a scientist completely explained why a person would leap into an unknown world.[25] Fellow officer James Burney agreed that Mai appeared 'a fellow of quick parts' – the Islander's sociable nature seemed reason enough to him to go journeying.[26] Cook himself was not as impressed with Mai, calling him a 'downright blackguard'.[27] This did not cause him, however, to wonder deeply at all about Mai's determination to travel. Since Britons only seemed interested in Mai as a curiosity, they assumed that he was correspondingly interested in them. Few scholars have questioned this assumption so far. If they do consider political motives, historians usually couch them in the language of individualism. Mai is thus seen as a 'callow' man, strategising solely for his own benefit, to become an undeserved big man on Ra'iātea.[28]

Evidence for Mai's more collectivist thinking, however, exists in less obvious sources. The housekeeper of Mai's patron when in Britain, Mrs Hawley, reported that Mai 'says he wants to return with men & guns in a Ship' and that this was due to a passion to redeem familial 'property'.[29] His patron's sister, Sarah Banks, likewise claimed to hear Mai talk about a broad-based, whole-of-island programme of redemption.[30] The little-known sailor, James King, noted too that Mai's mission was about 'freeing his [whole] Native Island'.[31] Far from being a selfish operative, Mai's own utterances – if indirectly received – suggest a more noble purpose. True to these utterances, when Mai did manage to return to Tōtaiete mā in 1777, he worked hard to assemble large parties of supporters for his aims among other displaced Raiateans. He did this despite the rather paltry legacies, in the end, of his British reconnaissance.[32] That Mai ultimately failed in his quest does not diminish the sincerity of his hopes for his wider community.

Unbeknownst to Mai when he encountered Cook on an island in between Ra'iātea and Tahiti, a Spanish expedition had arrived in the eastern part of Tahiti a few months earlier. If he had realised, Mai would probably have chosen these Europeans over the British – he had no particular preference between bearers of Western weaponry. As it was, the *Águila* from Peru, commissioned by the Viceroy at this Spanish colony, sailed into intense local fighting among Tahitians in 1772.

At that time, two different blocs of high chiefs were arguing over who might win precedence on the isle. Tahitians were followers of 'Oro, and indeed were devotees of all things Raiatean, but this did not mean that they ceded local matters to their neighbours. Just as Ra'iātea had been, the island of Tahiti was organised into pie-shaped districts, each with their own order of high chiefs. There had not been a central, all-powerful chief of the whole island in living memory. However, around about the time of Europe's re-engagement with Tahiti, the prospect of a supreme ruler arose (largely unrelated to the European visits). The best contenders were the leaders of the southern Papara district, Amo and his wife Purea, and an emergent leader, a young man called Tu from the northern district around Matavai Bay.[33]

In late 1772, the *Águila* landed in a far eastern bay which seemed to be aligned mostly with the young Tu. At this bay, the Spanish agreed to pick up four young Tahitians, who seemed at first too young or too lowly to have much political nous at all. Later events, however, suggest that they were volunteered by Tu's supporters to go to the Spaniards' lands in order to obtain reinforcements, favour, or simply foreign *mana* for the anticipated local battle ahead. The four men were recorded by the Spanish as Pautu, Tipitipia, Heiao, and Tetuanui.[34]

Sadly, Tipitipia died en route to South America and Heiao died while there. But both Pautu and Tetuanui survived their journeys – the 17 months in Lima as well as the return leg home. Their inner thoughts are almost completely lost to us now, but their joyous meeting with Tu upon their return to Tahiti suggests that at least they viewed their missions as political.[35] Combined with other evidence, it also indicates that they were uninterested in Spanish culture. When Pautu regaled Tu with stories of Lima, the chief thought them so silly that he wondered if his minion was insane.[36] When Cook's officers encountered Pautu in 1777, they noted that he mocked Spain's 'self-denying' religion.[37] Once again, like Ahutoru and Mai, these Islanders probably embarked on their super-voyaging with local aims firmly in mind.

By the time that William Bligh agreed to take on board a Tahitian Islander in 1792 – 20 years later – Tu's rise was almost assured. He had secured much of his final advantage by forging relationships with the mutineers of Bligh's earlier voyage back in 1790. These mutineers had thrown their weight behind Tu's ambitions, and thus the northern ruler had acquired what Ahutoru, Mai, and probably Pautu and Tetuanui had tried so hard to get – third-party assistance in a domestic war.[38]

In 1792, eager to shore up his ascendant rule, Tu asked Bligh if he could send with him to Britain one of his servants – presumably to bring back *mana* of various kinds. Bligh, in fact, recorded that Tu himself wanted to go, but it seems likelier that such an important figure would stay put, while he sent out others to scout for extra ballast.[39] In order to persuade Bligh to agree, Tu reminded the captain of all that Tahitians had done for George III thus far, and how much he had done personally to help the British government track down Bligh's own accursed mutineers. 'So I complied to his request,' reported Bligh. The servant was called Maititi, aged around 22. Bligh asserted that a young menial worker was a better candidate for super-voyaging since he would be 'more eligible for the purpose of learning than a chief ... who might be led into idleness and dissipation, as was the case with Omai [Mai]'. His remark showed how little he understood either of the huge ambitions of Tu or of the valiant history of Mai.

As Bligh pulled away from Tahiti, bound for Jamaica, he discovered that he carried not just Maititi but also another Tahitian, stowed away under deck. This man he called 'Jackets', or Bobbo. Bligh guessed that Bobbo had been moved to join his expedition because he was just naturally adventuresome, or at best because he exhibited a special interest in the botanists aboard the vessel. Unfortunately, Bobbo's agency is almost totally obscured in the sources, but it is not unreasonable to suspect that he had rather also been motivated to go aboard, like Maititi, to serve Tu's greater goals.

Both Maititi and Bobbo became ill while in Jamaica. Bobbo stayed there and died six months later. Maititi sailed on to London, but also succumbed to foreign germs, and was buried in a Christian churchyard in Deptford.[40] Tu's plans for Bligh's intercession had come to nought.

This was not the end of Tu using European voyagers to his own bloc's political ends, however. In 1797, a British whaling ship arrived in Tahiti. Years later, a missionary recorded that during its layover, Tu 'enquired who of his people were desirous to go to England?'[41] A man called Tapioi stepped forward, but whether he was doing so voluntarily or was pushed is unclear. Either way, few of the British travellers – whalers or missionaries – questioned his motives much at all. Tapioi had a more than usually complicated voyage experience. He journeyed to Tonga, Sydney, Aotearoa, and then Tonga again, where he met another travelling Tahitian, Tomma, and decided to disembark and try to get home. He had a two-year wait in Tonga before joining another British ship – a trading vessel – that took him to Britain rather than his desired Tahiti. In Britain, he met, incredibly, Tomma, who had also tried his luck with a passing European ship. Tomma disappears from the written sources at this point. Tapioi managed to get back at least as far as Sydney. He died there in 1812 awaiting a chance to make it home to Tu.[42]

Into the 1800s, as Tu – now called Pomare – and his descendants secured power throughout Tōtaiete mā, voyaging beyond the Pacific became less about formal politics and more about the power of trade and religion. This was not as related to the shift in type of European visitor from imperial explorer to entrepreneur and missionary as it was to the neutralising effect of the Pomare dynasty's takeover. Local Indigenous politics became literally less intriguing with a stable victor in place. That said, the shift in European visitor type did influence Islanders, especially those who joined the pork traders and mobile protestants from the 1820s onwards. These Islanders travelled now mostly in order to expand a community's wealth or to further its spiritual conversion. Notably, these were still collective rather than individualist motivations. Numbers are hard to calculate, but they surely account for many hundreds before the middle of the century.[43] A hundred years on from Wallis' first arrival, Islanders from Tōtaiete mā had more than reinvigorated their central ancestral practice. They had expanded their worldly horizons, but kept a local perspective.

Mokupuni o Hawai'i

The Hawaiian chapter of the history of the second Havai'i diaspora currently boasts the richest scholarship. Recent works by Indigenous scholars David Chang and Kealani Cook have delved, respectively, into Hawaiian understandings of the wider world through the nineteenth century and into Hawaiian connections to other Oceanians in the same period. Both Chang and Cook have been at pains to point out that this history should not be understood solely as an outcome of renewed European voyaging in the region; rather that European voyaging amplified an existing drive. Hawaiians had kept memories of Havai'i alive in their culture from the beginning of settlement, despite the apparent 300–400-year hiatus in their voyaging from around 1400. They more often called it Kahiki.[44] When opportunities came again in the shape of European scouts, Hawaiian voyagers jumped at the chance to reconnect with old histories and to help forge new ones.

A key early Hawaiian voyager of this second-diaspora era was, unusually, a woman. Remembered in the archives as Winee, her real name is, as Chang explains, now lost: Winee was the British approximation of Wahine, meaning woman. Chang prefers to call her Ka Wahine, The Woman, in an effort to return her some dignity.⁴⁵ In the spring of 1787, Ka Wahine was among scores of locals who pulled up in a canoe with exchangeable goods beside the British trading vessel *Imperial Eagle*. This ship would not have been exceptional to her; it was the eighth such vessel to arrive in the archipelago in nine years.⁴⁶ Perhaps Ka Wahine had hatched her plan during earlier arrivals. Her precise motivations remain opaque in the written sources, but we know that she quickly became the personal servant to the captain's wife, Frances Barkley. She was unlikely, then, in this context to have been a sex worker, which some have assumed. She was instead probably looking for ways to extend her already-established trading practice. Chappell's wider research into just how often Islanders asked to join European ships suggests that Ka Whine's request was not at all unusual.⁴⁷ It was unusual that the Barkleys relented, this time, and allowed her to join them.⁴⁸

Ka Wahine travelled first to Nootka Island with the crew, and then reached Chinese Macao by November. To underscore just how dynamic the Hawaiian part of the Havai'i diaspora was already, it's worth noting that Ka Wahine befriended no less than three other Hawaiians already living in the cosmopolitan entrepot.⁴⁹ Hawaiians had started their practice of joining European trading vessels from the 1780s. All three of the Hawaiians at Macao would join Ka Wahine on her proposed leg home.

The diary of Frances Barkley records that Ka Wahine chose to leave the *Imperial Eagle* at Macao and find a ride back to Mokupuni o Hawai'i. We know that she had acquired many foreign goods by this time, so perhaps her trading ambitions were now sated. Or perhaps meeting her compatriots after six months away had made her want to go home with them. However, the account of Ka Wahine's later escort suggests a darker reason: Ka Wahine had become extremely ill at Macao, so Barkley may have no longer had any use for her servant.⁵⁰

Sadly, like so many of her predecessors, Ka Wahine succumbed to the unfamiliar pathogens met in voyaging and died during a layover in the Philippines. Attending her shipboard deathbed was one of the Hawaiians she had met in Macao. This was Ka'iana, a significantly more aristocratic personage than any voyager of the second Havai'i diaspora thus far. Ka'iana had left his home three months after his compatriot, but because his ship had gone straight to China he had arrived one month earlier.

Unlike the two other men who met Ka Wahine at Macao, Ka'iana had definitely *not* joined his voyage as a labourer. He had been the honoured guest of the captain, John Meares, on board the British trading vessel *Nootka*. Meares had instantly recognised Ka'iana's high status at Kaua'i, recognising him as the brother of the person he assumed to be that island's sovereign.⁵¹ Some scholars have suggested that Ka'iana and Meares were also *aikāne*, or 'romantic same-sex friends'.⁵² Nonetheless, Chang argues that Ka'iana's main motivation was intellectual: he was already a learned man, and through the opportunity extended by Meares, 'he wanted to learn more'.⁵³ Chang emphasises the way this motivation establishes Europeans as the vehicles for educational continuation rather than as the instigators of revelation: 'Kanaka Maoli [Hawaiians] did not begin their intellectual lives or their exploration of the world with the arrival of the Haole [Europeans] any more than Ka'iana boarded Meares's ship as a naïve and untutored child.'[54]

All the same, a third motivation was probably also at play for Ka'iana. In addition to the opportunities for friendship and intellectual extension, Ka'iana no doubt wished to use his observations of other societies for the furtherance of more effective modes of governance in his region. Upon his return to the archipelago in late 1788, after also visiting Nootka, Ka'iana chose to disembark on the island of Hawai'i rather than his home island of Kaua'i. On this influential and rapidly changing island, he engaged with an emergent and charismatic chief, Kamehameha. This chief had risen rather unexpectedly to be the ruler of several different districts on Hawai'i. His power was unexpected both in that he was technically second in status to his own cousin in his particular birth-district, and – as in Tahiti– there was no historical reason to presume that district leaders would vie to take over nearby districts. But Kamehameha was driven by an ambition – some said a prophecy – to rule not only over all Hawai'i but also over other islands too – possibly as far as all the long-lost corners of the Havai'i diaspora.[55] He did so by maximising Hawai'i's rich resources, deploying modern military tactics, and exercising conciliation as much as coercion on subdued populations.[56]

In 1788, Ka'iana saw a bold man with good ideas and decided to throw his considerable learning, and now worldly experiences, behind him. He went on to serve as a key advisor to Kamehameha for the next six years, enjoying with him the expansion of their Hawai'i-centred power to nearby Maui, Moloka'i, and Lana'i. Scholars have recently argued over the extent to which European goods aided Kamehameha's rise; some cite Ka'iana as a chief conduit for these goods.[57] Paul D'Arcy, though, argues convincingly that these foreign goods were less critical than Kamehameha's new style of managing resources, offensives, and conquered peoples.[58] Furthermore, it seems that Ka'iana arrived with less weaponry from his travels than often claimed. What Ka'iana mostly brought, rather, were fresh, or at least reassuring, ideas; these were ideas sharpened by Ka'iana's observations of Chinese and American ports – not to mention his experiences in the micro-societies of ships. Voyaging for Ka'iana had consolidated his mental brilliance, and he now lent his honed mind to Kamehameha's policies and ongoing quest for expansion.[59]

Kamahameha went on to conquer all of Mokupuni o Hawai'i by 1810. Upon his death in 1819, his first-born son Liholiho became Kamehameha II. He was raised mostly by one of his stepmothers, the powerful Ka'ahumanu, who in fact reigned in partnership with Liholiho throughout his brief ascendancy. Liholiho is most famous for dismantling, at his stepmother's urging, the *kapu* system of ancient Mokupuni o Hawai'i. This involved loosening the grip of religious conventions on the exercise of earthly power – a kind of secularisation. Ka'ahumanu saw in the wake of her husband's death the potential of all of Kamehameha's recently subdued chiefs to reclaim their lands and *mana* through appeals to tradition.[60] Liholiho consented to her argument, not entirely happily.

Surprisingly, though, on another occasion, Liholiho chose to defy his stepmother's wishes in order to preserve his father's legacy. This instance concerned the Hawaiian relationship with Britain. During the last 20 years of his life, Kamehameha

I had found British traders to be useful in the consolidation of his kingdom; British sandalwood trade had been a significant part of his empire-building. He had made overtures towards formally sealing the relationship twice, though had never received confirmation back from George IV.[61] Liholiho took it upon himself to get that official sanction. In 1823, he commissioned a passing British whaler to give up its original target and take him instead to London. His elders were doubtlessly opposed to his plan because they knew that Europeans had not awarded Kamehameha his power in the first place; these outsiders had been useful but never essential. Despite their shared voyaging heritage, the elders evidently thought it more prudent for newly installed leaders to keep close to home.

Liholiho nonetheless left, carried by the agreeable Captain Valentine Starbuck. He took his wife and seven other Hawaiians in entourage. As they departed in ceremony from Honolulu harbour, the party must have reminded onlookers of the legendary seafarers of the past.[62]

Liholiho's party arrived in Portsmouth in mid-May 1824. It experienced several weeks of crowd-gawking in London, as well as an audience with George IV. Unfortunately, illness also stymied this visit: both Liholiho and his wife died from measles while in London. After lying in state for some days, their bodies were transported back to Mokupuni o Hawai'i in lead coffins. In late 1825, his loyal subjects received the remains as testaments to the continued achievements of a cosmopolitan people.[63]

In the reign of Kamehameha III, Liholiho's brother, the whaler became the most common example of Hawaiian super-voyaging. Whalers represent by far the greatest proportion of the roughly 15,000 Polynesian voyagers travelling in the century after 1768. Hawaiian whalers were mostly voluntary labourers on European or Euro-American ships – some scholars estimate that up to 20% of the entire American whaling fleet were Hawaiian.[64] Most Hawaiians that turned to whaling did so as a consequence of both the rapid globalisation of the Hawaiian economy and the increasingly straitened circumstances of the Hawaiian population. Many felt pressure to acquire through whaling the only kind of wealth now recognised for a community: foreign currency. By mid-century, for the first time in the history of the second Havai'i diaspora, many of these voyagers chose to migrate permanently as a consequence of their travels. This augured the start of a different kind of diaspora altogether.

Aotearoa

The Aotearoa chapter of the story of the second Havai'i diaspora had an unpromising start. The first known traveller on a European ship was Ranginui, a Māori man from the far northern tip of the northern island. He had been kidnapped by French explorer J.F.M. de Surville in late 1769, supposedly as punishment for theft. De Surville was en route to South America. Ranginui died from shipboard conditions – and possibly despair – a few months later.[65]

The second documented example of Māori voyagers into a new world was hardly an improvement. Tuki Tahua and Huru Kokoti were captured by British explorers on orders of the crown in early 1793. Bureaucrats in London thought that they could transport Māori men from Aotearoa over to their colony in New South Wales and make them teach colonists how to harvest native flax. Tuki and Huru survived their trip but resolutely refused to help the British in any way. Sydney's Governor, Phillip Gidley King, had to admit an error in judgement and carried them home within the year.[66]

This grim tale of forced travel had begun to change by 1800. As for Tōtaiete mā in the same period, trade and religion dominated the Aotearoa chapter of nineteenth-century voyaging. These themes were established by one of the most important voyagers of the era, the Ngāpuhi headman Te Pahi – though he in fact never went further than the Neo-Europe of New South Wales. Te Pahi knew of the British interest (however mismanaged) in Māori skills. In 1805, he set off on a reconnaissance mission to Sydney, with a sizeable entourage in tow. Governor King and Te Pahi recognised mutual needs and status in each other: both were strong leaders, around the same age, with economic expansion on their minds. During the nearly full year that Te Pahi stayed in Sydney, the two carved out a plan for a productive trade, mostly of housing manufactures in exchange for timber and potatoes. While in Sydney, Te Pahi also met the charismatic protestant chaplain, Samuel Marsden. The two turned out to have much in common and debated theology with enthusiasm via translators.[67]

The first Māori person to venture completely out of the Pacific region was Moehanga, who was also Ngāpuhi and intrigued by the potential of British trade for his people. In late 1805, Te Pahi had not yet made it home, so Moehanga seems to have volunteered to start his own attempt at an alliance by joining the British naval vessel *Ferret*. This ship took him all the way to Britain by early 1806. Moehanga's escort was a naval surgeon called John Savage, who penned an account of his observations of Moehanga. Although warmly disposed towards Moehanga, Savage continued the by now established trope of casting Polynesian voyagers as wide-eyed naïfs. Just as Ahutoru, Mai, Ka'iana, and countless others were portrayed, Moehanga appears in Savage's book in a constant state of wonder over European ways. He is perpetually delighted and laughing.[68] Savage also assumed that Moehanga had volunteered for the journey in order to become rich and popular.[69] Since Savage's account is the most immediately available, it has sent coloured ideas about the place of Moehanga in diasporic history through the centuries. Few scholars have figured him instead as part of a tradition in search of collective advantage. Placing him alongside Tu, Liholiho, and the others, however – and especially alongside Te Pahi – we see that Moehanga was more likely than not acting on behalf of something larger than his own reputation.

Moehanga arrived home in 1807, and lived for at least another 20 years – long enough to meet Marsden, too, and to see the fortunes of the British-Māori alliance fluctuate in less than ideal ways.[70] At first, the alliance had seemed to be in good health. Te Pahi's triumphant return in 1806 produced great optimism among at least the Ngāpuhi. The chief sent one of his sons, Matara, to London via a whaling vessel in 1807 in order to meet the monarch and cement agreements.[71] It appeared that he did have an interview with George IV and, more importantly, with the influential advisor to the Board of Trade, Sir Joseph Banks.[72] It was Banks who arranged for Matara's leg to Sydney the following year, though the Māori man was not to see Aotearoa again until 1809. The captain who transported him home, Alexander Berry, was unusually insightful about Matara's personal reflections. Instead of undiluted wonder at all that Europe presented, Matara in Berry's eyes seemed rather 'indefatigable' during the final crossing to 'regain a knowledge' of his own culture.[73] Matara had served his father well, but now wanted only re-immersion into his society.

The story of Te Pahi's daughter, however, symbolises the downsides of the fledgling alliance. In 1806, Te Pahi had married off his daughter Atahoe to British settler George Bruce in order to aid relations between the two peoples. A year later, Bruce and Atahoe were kidnapped by a British trading ship bound for Malaysia, one evidently unaware of the sensitive negotiations going on between the Ngāpuhi and the British. At the Malaccas, Bruce and Atahoe were dramatically separated, and the ruthless British trader sold Atahoe into slavery at Penang. Bruce managed to find her again, though, and the two then caught vessels all the way to India. There, they appealed to British obligations towards their Māori partners, and were returned as far at Sydney. Atahoe tragically died of dysentery in Sydney, three years after being taken from her home. The British-Māori relations so desired and fostered by Atahoe's father had some dire effects for individuals, too.[74]

After Te Pahi died in 1810, the trade aspect of the alliance faltered for a good decade – Governor King's sacking from his post in Sydney and various Indigenous-imperial altercations in Aotearoa overrode much of the original good will. Unexpectedly, though, the religious connection that had ignited between Te Pahi and Marsden flourished. Scores of Māori people made the trip to Marsden's Sydney parish during the 1810s to learn more about the kind of Christianity practised there. One of these travellers was a young man called Tuai, a member of the Ngare Raumati, who were rivals to the Ngāpuhi and thus an example of how Christianity had spread out from the Bay of Islands. Tuai found himself in Marsden's Parramatta locality in 1814 and then again in 1815, learning more about the Church of England as well as teaching the missionaries the basics of Māori language and customs.[75] During his second stay, he met up with another Māori man called Tītere, who was from the Ngāpuhi. That they together requested a voyage to the mission's heartland, and then travelled happily with each other for the next two years, speaks of the greater bonds (for the moment at least) of their religious ambitions than of their political rivalries. Tuai and Tītere spent all of 1818 in Britain, mainly with church members in the provinces. They arrived back in Aotearoa in 1820.

It is notable that, as far as Tuai and Tītere have made it into history books (which is not very far), they mostly exist as examples of connection between Māori and British. Indeed, that is the function they serve in this chapter. However, what happened next to these two men impacts how we assess the meaning of that connection. Tītere lived for another 20 years after returning from Britain, yet in that time had very little to do with Europeans in his homeland at all.[76] Tuai remained engaged with British interlopers for the four brief remaining years of his life, but generally not with missionaries: his interest in Christianity diminished once he disembarked in the Bay of Islands.[77] Such biographical postscripts do not take away from the men's initial interest in expanding trading and religious horizons via voyaging with outsiders, but they do remind us that these expansions were most often about improving Indigenous lives at home, rather than about achieving personal ambitions elsewhere. When these specific interests failed, people like Tuai and Tītere – if lucky enough to survive – reintegrated into communities relatively seamlessly. If their voyaging had been about individualist ideas, they would probably not have given up their connections so readily, or would have been more broken when their ambitions were not realised. The full lives of voyagers yet again give us deeper insight into the meaning of their travel than would an analysis of the voyage itself.

The last example here of a nineteenth-century Māori voyager is probably the most famous of all – Hongi Hika of the Ngāpuhi people. A generation younger than Te Pahi, Hongi was a military rather than political leader. He had risen to prominence during the early years of Te Pahi's contact with Britain – chiefly through winning local inter-Indigenous battles.[78] His interest in Te Pahi's trading and religious aspirations was always minimal. He did, however, see how they might turn out to be useful for his people's military causes. Like Tuai, Hongi visited Sydney during the mid-1810s. There, he acquired weaponry and an acquaintance with Marsden, but unlike Te Pahi he was never overly concerned with developing either a market for the weapons or an attachment to Christianity. His interests remained martial and Indigenous.

In 1814, Hongi invited Marsden to establish a mission station on Ngāpuhi land, which he further extended in 1819. He himself never converted, later pronouncing Christianity a religion unfit for warriors and more suited to slaves.[79] However, the mission provided a permanent base from which he could grow his relationship with Sydney. By 1818, Hongi had acquired enough muskets to gain a decisive victory over rival *iwi* around the Bay of Plenty.

A year later, Hongi decided to voyage all the way to Britain in order to secure a steadier line of these power-enhancing implements. As the historian Vincent O'Malley remarks, the warrior 'hardly needed to travel halfway round the world to buy guns – these were readily available in Sydney'.[80] Rather, Hongi went to guarantee the flow, to secure the deal with the head of the British people – George IV himself – and to show to anyone observing that he was on an equal footing with European kings. The meeting was productive: George IV gave him many gifts, including a suit of armour, and authorised the sale of muskets galore when he stopped back in Sydney on his way home. Trading a combined package of his royal gifts plus some Ngāpuhi land, Hongi acquired several hundred guns.[81] They would contribute to his exceptional success in local battles between 1821 and 1827.

The role of European weaponry in what were later called the Musket Wars has long been debated. Certainly, these wars resulted in a devastating loss of life – as much as a quarter of the entire population of Aotearoa.[82] But, as Angela Ballara has pointed out, muskets should not be centred as the key determinant here. The wars were part of ongoing disputes, and followed Indigenous conventions for battle. Muskets made conflicts more deadly but they did not start them.[83] Hongi's success, in other words, stemmed more from his command over the musket flow – his access to it, his control of it – than from his discovery or even actual use of it.

Importantly, Hongi did not take advantage of European voyagers in quite the same way as Tu and Kamehameha had done one and two generations earlier. Hongi had no real aspirations for complete archipelagic rule. After noting his lack of interest in governing the various *iwi* he defeated in battle, many historians now suggest that Hongi's military aims were coded more by Māori understandings of the warrior, masculinity, and tribal obligation. Placing Hongi Hika's travels in a wider Indigenous context prompts us to recognise, too, that his other life achievements were similarly Indigenous-centred.

★ ★ ★

Recently, Indigenous scholar Kealani Cook has warned against the continued emphasis on studying Pacific peoples in relation to European imperialists. Doing so, he insists, has 'naturalised empire' and, furthermore, 'makes it very difficult to truly envision an [Indigenous] future without empire'. Even when done to celebrate Indigenous resistance, such work can 'still reify both the normality of those relationships and the political borders created by such relationships'.[84] Cook's message is timely, and a critical challenge to all historians of the Pacific eighteenth and nineteenth centuries. When the trappings of European empire are so central to a segment of Pacific history – such as the history of the second Havai'i diaspora – one way to address Cook's critique is to attempt new approaches. Biographical and comparative analysis can work to go beyond accounts of Indigenous resistance, which more often than not are reduced to stories of individual opportunism. It can instead de-dramatise the means of the voyage – the European role – and re-centre the deeper Indigenous background to it.

Polynesian voyagers between the 1760s and the 1850s mostly travelled to further broad aims for their home community, be they familial, village-based, district-based, or archipelagic. They did not always succeed; sometimes, when they did triumph, it hurt other Indigenous players. Either way, and more significantly, they constitute a history of super-voyaging that kept the idea of ancient Havai'i always at its core.

Notes

1 I would like to acknowledge from the start my position as a non-Pasifika historian undertaking research into Pasifika history: this chapter owes incalculably to preceding work done by Indigenous archivists, memory-holders, and scholars.
2 J.R. Forster, ed., *Voyage around the World by Lewis de Bougainville 1766–9* (London: Nourse & Davies, 1772), 106.
3 Forster, *Voyage by Bougainville*, 128.
4 For an account of Wallis' arrival, see Anne Salmond, *Aphrodite's Island: The European Discovery of Tahiti* (Berkeley: University of California Press, 2009), 45–86.
5 Salmond, *Aphrodite's Island*, 22–25.
6 Salmond, *Aphrodite's Island*, 24. See also Patrick Vinton Kirch, *On the Roads of the Winds: An Archaeological History of the Pacific Islands before European Contact* (Berkeley:

University of California Press, 2000), 230–301. Kirch had earlier been a leading exponent of the theory that Ra'iātea was the initial centre of east Pacific migrations; he now suggests that it might have involved three separate migrations from the west. The debates are ongoing. See also Kirch and R.C. Green, *Hawaiki, Ancestral Polynesia: An Essay in Historical Anthropology* (Cambridge: Cambridge University Press, 2001); Deryck Scarr, *The History of the Pacific Islands: Kingdoms of the Reefs* (Melbourne: Macmillan, 1990), 26–30; and Kealani Cook, *Return to Kahiki: Native Hawaiians in Oceania* (New York: Cambridge University Press, 2018), 1–3. Note that 'Polynesia' also includes Rapa Nui, the Marquesas, Tonga, Samoa, and several other groupings: this chapter will only focus on the three island groups here stated.

7 David Chappell, *Double Ghosts: Oceanian Voyagers on EuroAmerican Ships* (Armonk: Sharpe, 1997). Nicholas Thomas also traced these journeys in a patchwork way in *Islanders: The Pacific in the Age of Empire* (New Haven, CT: Yale University Press, 2010). Recently, Hawaiian scholars David Chang and Kealani Cook have examined the parallels for Hawai'i: David A. Chang, *The World and All the Things upon It: Native Hawaiian Geographies of Exploration* (Minneapolis: University of Minnesota Press, 2016), and Cook, *Return to Kahiki*.

8 Chappell, *Double Ghosts*, 4.

9 For an extended elaboration of biography's role in explicating Indigenous perspectives, see Kate Fullagar, 'Envoys of Interest,' in *Facing Empire: Indigenous Experiences in a Revolutionary Age*, ed. K. Fullagar and M.A. McDonnell (Baltimore, MD: Johns Hopkins University Press, 2018), 241.

10 Chappell, *Double Ghosts,* 4, 179–180.

11 On the general continuity of Oceanian voyaging throughout history, see Paul D'Arcy, 'Connected by the Sea: Towards a Regional History of the Western Caroline Islands,' *Journal of Pacific History* 36, no. (2001): 163–165. On the brief Hawaiian hiatus in this history, see Chang, *The World and All the Things upon It,* 4–5.

12 Chappell, *Double Ghosts*, 160.

13 See Eric McCormick, *Omai: Pacific Envoy* (Auckland: Auckland University Press, 1977), vii, 132; Paul D'Arcy, *The People of the Sea: Environment, Identity, and History in Oceania* (Honolulu: University of Hawai'i Press, 2006), 137; Coll Thrush, *Indigenous London: Native Travellers at the Heart of the Empire* (New Haven, CT: Yale University Press, 2016), 142, 147, 152. Vincent O'Malley lists a range of motivations for Māori travellers: 'They travelled for a variety of reasons – out of curiosity or a sense of adventure, to facilitate trade and commerce, to enhance their own standing by returning with stories of all they had seen or done, to perform in concerts or exhibitions, to work on whaling ships or to meet the [monarch]. Some went with an explicitly political mission. Others had no choice in the matter, being kidnapped or transported as prisoners of the Crown. Together they were part of an international movement.' *Haerenga: Early Maori Journeys Across the Globe* (Wellington: Bridget Williams Books, 2015), 64.

14 See, for instance, John Dunmore, *Storms and Dreams: Louis de Bougainville* (Sydney: ABC Books, 2005), and Véronique Dorbe-Larcade, 'La disparition d'Ahutoru, Perspectives sur le séjour à l'île de France de Poutaveri/Aoutourou (Ahutoru), l'Indien de Bougainville (23 Octobre 1770–18 Octobre 1771),' *Revue Historique de l'Océan Indien* 5 (2009): 156–173.

15 Forster, *Voyage by Bougainville*, 132–133.

16 For recent cognate arguments in different fields, see also Victoria Stead and Jon Altman, eds., *Labour Lines and Colonial Power: Indigenous and Pacific Islander Labour Mobility in Australia* (Canberra: Aboriginal History Press, 2019), and R. Standfield, ed., *Indigenous Mobilities: Across and Beyond the Antipodes* (Canberra: ANU Press, 2018).

17 Forster, *Voyage by Bougainville*, 122, 264.

18 See K.R. Howe, *Where the Waves Fall: A New South Seas Island History from First Settlement to Colonial Rule* (Honolulu: University of Hawai'i Press, 1984), 127–128, and see Salmond, *Aphrodite's Island*, 28–37.

19. Daniel Solander reporting Raiatean views to Joseph Banks in *The Journals of Captain James Cook on his Voyages of Discovery*, ed. J.C. Beaglehole (Cambridge: Cambridge University Press, 1955–1974), 2: 953. In eighteenth-century England, Solander would have understood *blockhead* to mean a thick or stupid person. See, for translations of similar disparagements, James Magra, *A Journal of a Voyage Round the World in HMS Endeavour* (London: Becket & De Hondt, 1771), 62.
20. Forster, *Voyage by Bougainville*, 118. See also Salmond, *Aphrodite's Island*, 111.
21. Forster, *Voyage by Bougainville*, 132–133, and see Salmond, *Aphrodite's Island*, 111.
22. For a good narrative of Ahutoru's time in France, see Neil Rennie, *Far-Fetched Facts: The Literature of Travel and the Idea of the South Seas* (Oxford: Oxford University Press, 1995), 109–125. For a work that similarly ponders the little-recognised motivations of Indigenous people for connection, see Tiffany Shellam, *Shaking Hands on the Fringe: Negotiating the Aboriginal World at King George's Sound* (Crawley: University of Western Australia Press, 2009).
23. Solander in Beaglehole, *The Journals*, ii, 949. For a narrative of Mai's childhood, see Kate Fullagar, *The Warrior, the Voyager, and the Artist: Three Lives in an Age of Empire* (New Haven, CT: Yale University Press, 2020), 134–142.
24. See Solander in Beaglehole, *The Journals*, 2: 949.
25. Georg Forster, cited in Salmond, *Aphrodite's Island*, 284.
26. James Burney in B. Hooper, ed., *With Captain James Cook in the Antarctic and Pacific* (Canberra: National Library of Australia, 1975), 70.
27. See Cook in Beaglehole, *The Journals*, 2: 428.
28. Glyn Williams, 'Tupaia: Polynesian Warrior,' in *The Global Eighteenth Century*, ed. F. Nussbaum (Baltimore, MD: Johns Hopkins University Press, 2003), 41. See also Frank McLynn, *Captain Cook: Master of the Seas* (New Haven, CT: Yale University Press, 2011), 330–331, and Dan O'Sullivan, *In Search of Captain Cook* (London: I.B. Tauris, 2008), 154–157.
29. Mrs Hawley cited in Sarah S. Banks, [unpublished] Memorandums, August–November 1774, Papers of Sir Joseph Banks, National Library of Australia, MS9.
30. Sarah Sophia Banks, Memorandums, in Papers of Sir Joseph Banks, MS9. Eric McCormick traces Sarah Banks's information chiefly from a Dr Mills in Exeter, who got it from a Mr Desalis, who got it from Mr Bates, the secretary to Lord Sandwich: Eric McCormick, *Omai: Pacific Envoy* (Auckland: Auckland University Press, 1977), 95.
31. King in Beaglehole, *The Journals*, 3: 187.
32. See Fullagar, *The Warrior, the Voyager, and the Artist*, 232–233.
33. Salmond, *Aphrodite's Island*, 249–254. Tu later renamed himself Pomare.
34. Salmond, *Aphrodite's Island*, 253.
35. Salmond, *Aphrodite's Island*, 347, 366.
36. Salmond, Aphrodite's Island, 366.
37. David Samwell in Beaglehole, *The Journals*, 3: 1053.
38. See Howe, *Where the Waves Fall*, 131–133.
39. Ida Lee, ed., *Captain Bligh's Second Voyage to the South Sea* (London: Longmans, 1920), http://gutenberg.net.au/ebooks12/1204361h.html.
40. Lee, *Captain Bligh's Second Voyage*.
41. Joseph Fox, *An Appeal to the Members of the London Missionary Society against a Resolution of the Directors of That Society Dated March 26, 1810* (London, 1810). See also Rhys Richards, 'Indigenous Beachcombers: The Case of Tapeooe,' *The Great Circle* 12, no.1 (1990): 2.
42. See Sujit Sivasundaram, *Nature and the Godly Empire: Science and Evangelical Mission in the Pacific, 1795–1850* (Cambridge: Cambridge University Press, 2005), 110–111. See also Thomas, *Islanders*, 49–52, and Richards, 'Indigenous Beachcombers,' 1–14.
43. See Chappell, *Double Ghosts*, 160, and Sivasundaram, *Nature and the Godly Empire*, 110–111.

44 See Chang, *The World and All the Things upon It*, vii–viii, and Cook, *Return to Kahiki*, 3–4.
45 Chang, *The World and All the Things upon It*, 33.
46 James Cook had been the first European to visit in 1778. He came again, fatefully, in 1779. Chang records five more arrivals before the *Imperial Eagle*: *The World and All the Things upon It*, 33.
47 Chappell, *Double Ghosts*, 11–16.
48 See Beth Hill and Cathy Converse, *The Remarkable World of Frances Barkley* (Surrey, BC: Touch Wood Editions, 2003), 40.
49 See Chang, *The World and All the Things upon It*, 36.
50 Hill and Converse, The Remarkable World, 70. See also Chang, *The World and All the Things upon It*, 36.
51 John Meares, *Voyages Made in the Years 1788 and 1789* (London: Walter, 1790), xxxix.
52 Samuel Manaiākalani Kamakau, 'Ka Moolelo o Hawaii Nei,' *Ka Nupepa Kuokoa* 14 (1865), and Chang, *The World and All the Things upon It*, 44–45.
53 Chang, *The World and All the Things upon It*, 40–42.
54 Chang, *The World and All the Things upon It*, 42.
55 See S.L. Desha, *Kamehameha and His Warrior Kekūhaupi'o* (Honolulu: Kamehameha Schools Press, 2000), chapters 1 & 6, and Paul D'Arcy, *Transforming Hawai'i: Balancing Coercion and Consent in Eighteenth-Century Kānaka Maoli Statecraft* (Canberra: ANU Press, 2018), 10.
56 See the developing arguments on this topic in Marshall Sahlins, *Historical Metaphors and Mythical Realities: Structure in the Early History of the Sandwich Islands Kingdom* (Ann Arbor: University of Michigan Press, 1981) and D'Arcy, *Transforming Hawai'i*.
57 Samuel Manaiākalani Kamakau, *Ruling Chiefs of Hawaii* (Honolulu: Kamehameha Schools Press, 1961), 153.
58 D'Arcy, *Transforming Hawai'i*, 5, 9, 19, 25, 28, 40.
59 The alliance did not last forever. Kamehameha had fallen out with Ka'iana by 1795; Ka'iana sensed this and defected to the losing chiefs of Oahu by the end of that year. He died in battle soon after. See D.G. Miller, 'Ka'iana, the Once Famous "Prince of Kaua'i",' *The Hawaiian Journal of History* 22 (1988): 1–21.
60 S.S. Levin, 'The Overthrow of the Kapu System,' *Journal of the Polynesian Society* 77, no.4 (1968): 402–430.
61 R.E.A. Hackler, 'Alliance or Cession? Missing Letter from Kamehameha I to King George III of England Casts Light on 1794 Agreement,' *The Hawaiian Journal of History* 20 (1986): 1–14. On the sandalwood trade see Howe, *Where the Waves Fall*, 160–162.
62 John Dunmore, *Who's Who in Pacific Navigation* (Honolulu: University of Hawai'i, 1991), 238. Dunmore notes the displeasure that Starbuck's employers showed when Starbuck changed his ship's mission.
63 See J.S. Corley, 'The British Press Greets the King of the Sandwich Islands: Kamehameha II in London, 1824,' *The Hawaiian Journal of History* 42 (2008), and Coll Thrush, *Indigenous London*, 146–151. See also an account of the grand return in Hiram Bingham, *A Residence of Twenty-One Years in the Sandwich Islands* (Hartford: H. Huntington, 1847).
64 Chappell, *Double Ghosts*, 163. Note that the voluntary aspect of the Hawaiian kanaka experience differs dramatically to the experience of most Micronesian and Melanesian kanaks.
65 See O'Malley, *Haerenga*, 103.
66 For an excellent overview of Māori history in Sydney, see Jo Kamira, 'Māori,' Dictionary of Sydney, 2012, https://dictionaryofsydney.org/entry/maori. See also Kate Fullagar, 'Facing New Worlds,' *SL Magazine* (Autumn 2019): 20–23. Note that both Te Weherua and Koa travelled on board James Cook's third Pacific expedition from Aotearoa to Tahiti in 1777, after Ranginui – however, we might count that as inner-Pacific travel.

67 See Fullagar, 'Facing New Worlds,' 21–23. Note also that after Te Pahi the next Māori to venture to Sydney was Teina, presumably also to investigate Sydney's interest in the labouring and possibly trade potential of his people. Still very much a youth, and not an official leading spokesman, Teina had less effect and chose to continue his scouting after Sydney. He went on further whaling expeditions around the Pacific: see O'Malley, *Haerenga*, 9–11.
68 John Savage, *Some Account of New Zealand* (London: Murray, 1807), 99–110.
69 Savage, *Some Account*, 38–39.
70 See O'Malley, *Haerenga*, 15–20, and Anne Salmond, *Between Worlds: Early Exchanges between Maori and Europeans 1773–1815* (Penguin NZ, [1997] 2018), 343–348.
71 Christopher Spencer to Joseph Banks, 11 May 1807, National Library of Australia MS9/139, cited in Salmond, *between Worlds*, 360.
72 See Alexander Berry in Hugh Murray, *Adventures of British Seamen* (Edinburgh: Constable & Co., 1827), 333. Note that O'Malley is sceptical about Berry's information regarding the royal visit: O'Malley, *Haerenga*, 20.
73 See O'Malley, *Haerenga*, 20.
74 O'Malley, *Haerenga*, 20–23, and Salmond, *between Worlds*, 356–366.
75 A. Jones and K.K. Jenkins, *Tuai: A Traveller in Two Worlds* (Wellington: BWB, 2017), 33–44.
76 Jones and Jenkins, *Tuai*, 194–195.
77 Jones and Jenkins, *Tuai*, 195.
78 For an overview, see D.U. Cloher, *Hongi Hika: Warrior Chief* (Auckland: Penguin, 2003).
79 See Christina A. Thompson, 'A Dangerous People Whose Only Occupation Is War: Maori and Pakeha in 19th-Century New Zealand,' *Journal of Pacific History* 32, no.1 (1997): 116.
80 O'Malley, *Haerenga*, 31.
81 O'Malley, *Haerenga*, 33. Note that Hongi travelled with fellow Ngāpuhi warrior Waikato.
82 James Belich, *Making Peoples: A History of the New Zealanders From Polynesian Settlement to the End of the Nineteenth Century* (Auckland: Penguin, 1996), 157.
83 Angela Ballara, *Taua: 'Musket Wars', 'Land Wars' or Tikanga? Warfare in Maori Society in the Early Nineteenth Century* (Auckland: Penguin, 2003). See also Paul D'Arcy, 'Maori and Muskets from a Pan-Polynesian Perspective,' *New Zealand Journal of History* 34, no. 1 (2000): 117–132.
84 Cook, *Return to Kahiki*, 19.

Bibliography

Ballara, Angela. *Taua: 'Musket Wars', 'Land Wars' or Tikanga? Warfare in Maori Society in the Early Nineteenth Century*. Auckland: Penguin, 2003.
Banks, J. MS9, Papers of Sir Joseph Banks, National Library of Australia.
Beaglehole, J.C., ed. *The Journals of Captain James Cook on his Voyages of Discovery*. Cambridge: Cambridge University Press, 1955–1974.
Belich, James. *Making Peoples: A History of the New Zealanders from Polynesian Settlement to the End of the Nineteenth Century*. Auckland: Penguin, 1996.
Bingham, Hiram. *A Residence of Twenty-One Years in the Sandwich Islands*. Hartford: H. Huntington, 1847.
Chang, David. *The World and All the Things upon It: Native Hawaiian Geographies of Exploration*. Minneapolis: University of Minnesota Press, 2016.
Chappell, David. *Double Ghosts: Oceanian Voyagers on Euro American Ships*. Armonk: Sharpe, 1997.
Cloher, D.U. *Hongi Hika: Warrior Chief*. Auckland: Penguin, 2003.

Cook, Kealani. *Return to Kahiki: Native Hawaiians in Oceania*. New York: Cambridge University Press, 2018.
Corley, J.S. 'The British Press Greets the King of the Sandwich Islands: Kamehameha II in London, 1824.' *The Hawaiian Journal of History* 42 (2008): 69–103.
D'Arcy, Paul. 'Maori and Muskets from a Pan-Polynesian Perspective.' *New Zealand Journal of History* 34, no. 1 (2000): 117–132.
D'Arcy, Paul. 'Connected by the Sea: Towards a Regional History of the Western Caroline Islands.' *Journal of Pacific History* 36, no. 2 (2001): 163–182.
D'Arcy, Paul. *The People of the Sea: Environment, Identity, and History in Oceania*. Honolulu: University of Hawai'i Press, 2006.
D'Arcy, Paul. *Transforming Hawai'i: Balancing Coercion and Consent in Eighteenth-Century Kānaka Maoli Statecraft*. Canberra: ANU Press, 2018.
Desha, S.L. *Kamehameha and His Warrior Kekūhaupi'o*. Honolulu: Kamehameha Schools Press, 2000.
Dorbe-Larcade, V. 'La disparition d'Ahutoru, Perspectives sur le séjour à l'île de France de Poutaveri/Aoutourou (Ahutoru), l'Indien de Bougainville (23 Octobre 1770–18 Octobre 1771).' *Revue Historique de l'Océan Indien* 5 (2009): 156–173.
Dunmore, John. *Who's Who in Pacific Navigation*. Honolulu: University of Hawai'i Press, 1991.
Dunmore, John. *Storms and Dreams: Louis de Bougainville*. Sydney: ABC Books, 2005.
Forster, J.R., ed. *Voyage Around the World by Lewis de Bougainville 1766–9*. London: Nourse & Davies, 1772.
Fox, James. *An Appeal to the Members of the London Missionary Society*. London, 1810.
Fullagar, Kate. 'Envoys of Interest.' in *Facing Empire: Indigenous Experiences in a Revolutionary Age*, edited by K. Fullagar and M.A. McDonnell, 239–255. Baltimore: Johns Hopkins University Press, 2018.
Fullagar, Kate. 'Facing New Worlds.' *SL Magazine* (Autumn 2019), 20–23.
Fullagar, Kate. *The Warrior, the Voyager, and the Artist: Three Lives in an Age of Empire*. New Haven, CT: Yale University Press, 2020.
Hackler, R.E.A. 'Alliance or Cession? Missing Letter from Kamehameha I to King George III of England Casts Light on 1794 Agreement.' *The Hawaiian Journal of History* 20 (1986): 1–14.
Hill, Beth, and Cathy Converse. *The Remarkable World of Frances Barkley*. Surrey, BC: TouchWood Editions, 2003.
Hooper, B., ed. *With Captain James Cook in the Antarctic and Pacific*. Canberra: National Library of Australia, 1975.
Howe, K.R. *Where the Waves Fall: A New South Seas Island History from First Settlement to Colonial Rule*. Honolulu: University of Hawai'i Press, 1984.
Jones, Alison, and K.K. Jenkins. *Tuai: A Traveller in Two Worlds*. Wellington: B.W.B., 2017.
Kamakau, Samuel Manaiākalani. 'Ka Moolelo o Hawaii Nei.' *Ka Nupepa Kuokoa* 4 (1865): 1–2.
Kamakau, Samuel Manaiākalani. *Ruling Chiefs of Hawaii*. Honolulu: Kamehameha Schools Press, 1961.
Kamira, Jo. 'Māori.' Dictionary of Sydney, 2012, https://dictionaryofsydney.org/entry/maori.
Kirch, P.V., and R.C. Green. *Hawaiki, Ancestral Polynesia: An Essay in Historical Anthropology*. Cambridge: Cambridge University Press, 2001.
Kirch, P.V. *On the Roads of the Winds: An Archaeological History of the Pacific Islands before European Contact*. Berkeley: University of California Press, 2000.
Lee, Ida, ed. *Captain Bligh's Second Voyage to the South Sea*. London: Longmans, 1920.
Levin, S.S. 'The Overthrow of the Kapu System.' *Journal of the Polynesian Society* 77, no. 4 (1968): 402–430.
Magra, James. *A Journal of a Voyage Round the World in HMS Endeavour*. London: Becket & De Hondt, 1771.
McCormick, Eric. *Omai: Pacific Envoy*. Auckland: Auckland University Press, 1977.

McLynn, Frank. *Captain Cook: Master of the Seas*. New Haven, CT: Yale University Press, 2011.
Meares, John. *Voyages Made in the Years 1788 and 1789*. London: Walter, 1790.
Miller, D.G. 'Ka'iana, the Once Famous "Prince of Kaua'i".' *The Hawaiian Journal of History* 22 (1988): 1–21.
Murray, Hugh. *Adventures of British Seamen*. Edinburgh: Constable & Co., 1827.
O'Malley, Vincent. *Haerenga: Early Maori Journeys across the Globe*. Wellington: Bridget Williams Books, 2015.
O'Sullivan, Dan. *In Search of Captain Cook*. London: I.B. Tauris, 2008.
Rennie, Neil. *Far-Fetched Facts: The Literature of Travel and the Idea of the South Seas*. Oxford: Oxford University Press, 1995.
Richards, Rhys. 'Indigenous Beachcombers: The Case of Tapeooe.' *The Great Circle* 12, no.1 (1990): 1–14.
Sahlins, Marshall. *Historical Metaphors and Mythical Realities: Structure in the Early History of the Sandwich Islands Kingdom*. Ann Arbor: University of Michigan Press, 1981.
Salmond, Anne. *Aphrodite's Island: The European Discovery of Tahiti*. Berkeley: University of California Press, 2009.
Salmond, Anne. *Between Worlds: Early Exchanges between Maori and Europeans 1773–1815*. Auckland: Penguin NZ, [1997] 2018.
Savage, John. *Some Account of New Zealand*. London: Murray, 1807.
Scarr, D. *The History of the Pacific Islands: Kingdoms of the Reefs*. Melbourne: Macmillan, 1990.
Shellam, Tiffany. *Shaking Hands on the Fringe: Negotiating the Aboriginal World at King George's Sound*. Crawley: University of Western Australia Press, 2009.
Sivasundaram, Sujit. *Nature and the Godly Empire: Science and Evangelical Mission in the Pacific, 1795–1850*. Cambridge: Cambridge University Press, 2005.
Standfield, R., ed. *Indigenous Mobilities: Across and Beyond the Antipodes*. Canberra: ANU Press, 2018.
Stead, Victoria, and Jon Altman, eds. *Labour Lines and Colonial Power: Indigenous and Pacific Islander Labour Mobility in Australia*. Canberra: Aboriginal History Press, 2019.
Thomas, Nicholas. *Islanders: The Pacific in the Age of Empire*. New Haven, CT: Yale University Press, 2010.
Thompson, C.A. 'A Dangerous People Whose Only Occupation Is War: Maori and Pakeha in 19th-century New Zealand.' *Journal of Pacific History* 32, no. 1 (1997): 109–119.
Thrush, Coll. *Indigenous London: Native Travellers at the Heart of the Empire*. New Haven, CT: Yale University Press, 2016.
Williams, G. 'Tupaia: Polynesian Warrior.' In *The Global Eighteenth Century*, edited by F. Nussbaum, 38–51. Baltimore, MD: Johns Hopkins University Press, 2003.

10
WALKING THE INDIGENOUS CITY
Colonial encounters at the heart of empire

Coll Thrush

When we think of colonial encounter, we tend to think of it happening in locations that are coded as Other: a beach in the Marquesas Islands, a treaty tree in Pennsylvania, a river junction in the Amazon. These are Indigenous spaces, to be sure, each with their own distinct histories, but because of the ways in which the broad sweep of empire has usually been narrated, they are typically understood as peripheral – literally – to the places where 'real' history happens. The colonial, therefore, is all too often estranged from the metropolitan, which is to that say that, for example, the Indigenous is all too often estranged from the urban. Models of core and periphery that have so influenced the shape of global historiography are remarkably persistent, and one task of scholars working in global Indigenous history should be to challenge such models, showing instead how the spaces of 'metropole' and 'frontier' are deeply imbricated and entangled with each other. Doing so has the potential to place Indigenous peoples and places at the heart of the story of globalisation, and to show the ways in which the 'centre' has been transformed by the 'edge'. A place such as London is but one location where this sort of work can be done. This essay explores the colonial history of London through the experiences of Indigenous men, women, and children who travelled there, willingly or otherwise, from places that became Canada, the United States, and Australia. In doing so, it builds on a growing body of scholarly work that centres Indigenous people as cosmopolitan co-creators of the modern world, with their own histories of exploration and discovery, while simultaneously provincialising London, to use Dipesh Chakrabarty's well-known framing.[1]

This is a long history. Indigenous people have been coming to London since the very beginning of the sixteenth century, and their diverse panoply of experiences confound easy categorisation or clear narrative structure. That being the case, this essay tracks only some of the journeys made by Indigenous visitors, and it does so through a particularly London-ish genre: the walking tour. Taking the reader on a meandering path from Covent Garden to Westminster, it offers but one subset of Indigenous encounters with the city while drawing on walking as a kind of embodied historical praxis. The goal of this essay, then, is to disorient the reader by imagining an Indigenous London that has largely been forgotten by the city's inhabitants (but, in many cases, remembered by descendant Indigenous communities). More importantly, though, it takes cues from Linda Tuhiwai Smith's canonical *Decolonizing Methodologies* by arguing for an Indigenisation of the spaces of an imperial city – 'a centring of the landscapes, images, languages, themes, metaphors and stories in the indigenous world', to use Smith's phrasing – as well as a re-reading of London, illuminating what Smith calls 'a different sort of origin story, the origins of imperial policies and practices, the origins of the imperial visions, the origins of ideas and values'.[2]

We begin our walk through Indigenous London by emerging from the crowded lifts at the Covent Garden Tube Station and turning right, into the throngs of tourists and shoppers and buskers. It was in this neighbourhood in 1710 that four Indigenous men – three of them Mohawk, the fourth Mahican – made their mark. Their names were Tejonihokarawa, Sagayenkwaraton, Onioheriago, and Etowaucum, but they were more often referred to by the British as the 'Four Kings'. Together, they instantly captured the city's attention, having arrived from a place that anyone who kept abreast of world affairs would have heard of: Canada. They were members of the Iroquois Confederacy, or the Haudenosaunee as its citizens called (and call) it, which dominated the vast, abundant territory between the English colonies and New France. They managed diplomacy with European newcomers and other Indigenous nations through the Covenant Chain, a religious metaphor and set of diplomatic rituals that linked the Haudenosaunee to other peoples in keeping with the Gayanashagowa, the Great Law of Peace.[3]

Immediately upon their arrival, the Four Kings embarked on a gruelling social calendar that would be typical of many Indigenous delegations, recorded in detail in the press. For example, during a single three-day stretch at the end of April, they waited for hours outside a special meeting of the Society for the Propagation of the Gospel, which was considering their request for missionaries and the construction of a chapel; they took a meal with William Penn at the Devil Tavern in Fleet Street; and they heard a sermon by the Bishop of London before spending the evening socialising at the extravagant Bloomsbury home of the Duke of Montague. Over the course of the spring of 1710, the Four Kings found themselves at the centres of British power. They dined with the illustrious military leader James Butler, Duke of Ormonde; were entertained by the Archbishop of Canterbury; and met with the trade commissioners who oversaw British interests from New York to Virginia, Jamaica, and beyond. They toured the Guildhall, seat of London's powerful mercantile community; Gresham College, where the city's leading minds taught law, geometry, and divinity; and the Royal Exchange, venue for the deals that drove Britain's growing empire. They experienced rituals of British sovereignty in the Banqueting House at Whitehall, on the Queen's private yacht, and at the parading of the Life Guards in Hyde Park. They saw first-hand British maritime power and its human consequences, visiting both the dockyards at Woolwich and the naval hospital at Greenwich. They were also the first Indigenous people known to have surveyed the entirety of the city from the top of St Paul's Cathedral. And perhaps most importantly, they met with Queen Anne, presenting a written statement intended to build political, economic, religious, and military alliances, which was reproduced in print and distributed throughout the city to a fascinated public.

The Four Kings did not, however, only interact with London's elite. Their lodgings were at a Covent Garden inn called The Crown and Two Cushions, situated among the noisy theatres and crowded closes. They met the city's poor and middling classes in places like Leadenhall Market, where Londoners of all sorts sold and bought meat; the bear-baiting venues at Hockley-in-the-Hole in Clerkenwell; and even Bedlam Hospital. It was an itinerary that would deplete any visitor, and yet they appear to have taken it in stride: 'they are generally affable to all that come to see them', wrote one observer. If the foreigners, with their dark skin, tattoos, and limited English, were exotic and strange to many observers, they were clearly intensely popular; the editor of *The Spectator* wrote that, 'when the four Indian Kings were in this Country ... I often mix'd with the Rabble and followed them a whole Day together.'[4]

Tejonihokarawa and his colleagues returned to their homelands in 1710, but they remained in the imagination of Londoners. In March of 1712, the pamphleteer and essayist Jonathan Swift wrote in his diary, 'Here is nothing talked about but men that goes in partys about the street and cuts people with swords or knives, and they call themselves by som hard name that I can nethere speak nor spell.' That name was 'Mohocks'. Swift continued over the next few days to describe numerous assaults in the streets around Covent Garden. On 14 March, he wrote that the Mohocks 'put an old woman into a hogshead, and rolled her down a hill, they cut some nosis, others hands, and several barbarass tricks'. Identifying them as young men of the upper classes, Swift noted that the 'Grubstreet Papers about them fly like Lightning'. Meanwhile, the dramatist John Gay penned a play entitled *The Mohocks* in which a character asked, 'Who has not trembled at the *Mohock's* Name?' and in which the gang's members sang a refrain of unfettered urban violence:

> Then a Mohock, a Mohock I'll be,
> No Laws shall restrain, our Libertine reign,
> We'll riot, drink, and be free.

Later observers have questioned whether the Mohocks even existed, or if they were a literary device to critique certain elements of London society or a titillating urban legend to thrill Gay and Swift's audiences. Either way, in Covent Garden, as during other visitations, Indigenous people were opportunities for Londoners to talk about themselves and even fashion new urban identities.[5]

Over the decades and centuries to come, the theatres and markets of Covent Garden would become a standard element of many Indigenous journeys to London. In 1793, for example, two Eora men named Bennelong and Yemmerrawanie were brought to the city from lands that would eventually become Sydney, and during their visit they enjoyed a performance of *Doctor Faustus* at a Covent

Garden theatre.⁶ Thirty years later, the king and queen of Hawai'i, Liholiho and Kamāmalu, also attended performances at the area's venues, drawing both attention and admiration from the higher classes of society.⁷ Covent Garden, then, was an important node in the networks of encounter that criss-crossed the city, a place where Indigeneity and urbanity encountered each other.

Leaving Covent Garden via King Street, we pass posh shops and restaurants that obscure the rather more nefarious reputation of the neighbourhood in earlier eras. High above on the right, a blue plaque is affixed to one of the buildings, commemorating the eighteenth-century composer Thomas Arne. But the plaque, at least obliquely, also references London's Indigenous history. As noted before, the Four Kings had resided in Covent Garden. The crowds thronging around the inn must have been an enormous burden on the householder's wife, who was nursing a small infant. That baby, named Thomas, grew up to create stridently rousing music that accompanied some of the most assertive lyrics in the English language. There are no Mohawk or Mahican characters in the song. Instead, it is flush with other symbols: shouting angels crowding a commanding heaven, native oaks and foreign tyrants, generous flames and shining cities of commerce. First heard in 1745 in London, the song's influence expanded, along with Britain's, as part of what Winston Churchill would famously refer to as the 'first world war'. The composer Thomas Arne had no doubt grown up with family stories of Tejonihokarawa and his compatriots. And surely, he must have had 'Indians', and the question of empire's 'Others' more broadly, in mind when he set these words to music: 'Rule, Britannia! Britannia rule the waves / Britons never will be slaves.'

Crossing Bedford Street into New Row, one gets the sense of the crowded nature of the Georgian city as the lanes narrow and become primarily pedestrian thoroughfares. But today's city is not the London of the past: compared to the eighteenth-century metropolis, the twenty-first-century urban landscape is clean, quiet, and relatively orderly. Its earlier and more chaotic incarnations, so well documented by observers such as William Hogarth, did not escape critique from Indigenous travellers. One such critic was a Mohegan minister from Connecticut named Samson Occom, who arrived in London in 1766 to embark on a tour to raise money for a school of Indigenous boys (and to lodge complaints about settler encroachments on his people's territory). His journals – the earliest known firsthand written accounts of London by an Indigenous person – reveal a man horrified by what he found in a city that claimed to be civilised:

> Saw Such Confusion as I never Dreamt of – there was Some at Churches, Singing & Preaching, in the Streets some Cursing Swaring & Damning one another, others was hollowing, Whestling, talking gigling, & Laughing, & Coaches and footmen passing and repassing, Crossing and Cross-Crossing, and the poor Begars Praying, Crying, and Beging upon their knees.⁸

For Occom, who had never encountered anything like London despite being well-travelled in America, the city compared unfavourably to his beloved, imagined Jerusalem. And the 'confusion' he described was in fact a moral state, represented especially by disparities between the wealthy and the impoverished. In this, Occom was like many of his Indigenous peers, who – when we have records of their opinions – often viewed the city as a place of horror, and perhaps more importantly, as evidence of imperial hypocrisy. Around the turn of the twentieth century, for example, the Mohawk poet and performer Tekahionwake, also known as E. Pauline Johnson, wrote that, 'with slums like this in the heart of London, they'll *dare* to send missionaries to our Indians in Canada!'[9] This sort of critique is an important through-line in London's Indigenous history, and speaks to particularly salient issues of inequality that persist into the present and to the ways in which the urban landscape itself interacted with Indigenous values and worldviews.

Next, we turn left into St Martin's Lane and make our way to Trafalgar Square, an iconically imperial space and, as it turns out, an important Indigenous one as well. Indeed, three of the four sides of the square hold important Indigenous histories. First, on the east side of the square, sits Christopher Wren's St Martin in the Fields, one of the most celebrated churches in the city. It was here in 1823 that Liholiho and Kamāmalu lay in state after their tragic deaths from measles. First in a room at Osborn's Hotel, and later in the crypt of St Martin's, the king and queen reposed in scenes that were both imposing and heartbreaking: two lead coffins, covered with red velvet, surrounded by red and yellow 'ahuʻula (feather cloaks) and tall kāhili (feather-topped poles), the floor strewn with red rose petals, and the whole scene lit with candles. One observer described it as 'a kind of decoration of death which so pleased the Eriis [aliʻi, a term referring to the monarchs' elite retinue]', but it obviously attracted others, as well: guards had to run off several men who attempted to break into the crypt and steal the royal bodies. As they had been in life, the king and queen were recognised by many Londoners as true royalty, and their funerals proved this. As the *Times* reported, 'the whole was conducted with a simplicity, regularity, and solemnity, consistent with the most rational taste.' Public opinion seemed to find deep empathy with the Hawaiians, and newspapers reported that much of London society was 'inconsolable' to learn that they had both died.[10]

Meanwhile, the north side of Trafalgar Square is dominated by the imposing National Gallery. Its massive columns, which once were part of a grand home in nearby Pall Mall, speak to a different history altogether: that of Thayendanagea or Joseph Brant, a Mohawk military leader and intellectual who made two trips to London in the late eighteenth century. Born in 1743, he was a member of the Wolf Clan and kin to Tejonihokawara, one of the Four Kings; as a young boy, Thayendanagea must have heard stories about the 1710 delegation's trip to London. But Thayendanagea was also connected to Samson Occom: both had attended the same school for Indigenous boys. By the 1770s, Thayendanagea was a well-known military leader among both his own people and the British, which led him to make journeys to London in 1776 and 1785. There he conducted archival research, was interviewed by James Boswell for the *London Magazine*, attended masked balls, and even became a Freemason – all in addition to lobbying for the Crown's support of his people against settler land encroachment and violence. He was also a close associate of the Prince of Wales (later George IV, whose statue stands in

Trafalgar Square), who entertained him at Carlton House on Pall Mall. When the house was demolished in 1826, its portico and columns were incorporated into the new National Gallery. We might imagine Thayendanagea having passed between them – a faint echo of Haudenosaunee history and sovereignty only metres away from Nelson's Column and Landseer's famous lions.[11]

Lastly, on the west side of the square sits Canada House, home to the High Commission, and as such a locus of Indigenous diplomacy, activism, and resistance. In 2013, for example, First Nations leaders from across Canada held a ceremony there to observe the 250th anniversary of the Proclamation of 1763, a foundational element of colonial law in the settler nation, even as Commission leaders prevented the travellers from meeting with representatives of the Crown as they had intended. Organised by the Federation of Indian Nations of Saskatchewan, the delegation had a full schedule that included a reception at the Canadian High Commission, a pipe ceremony at Guards Chapel in honour of Indigenous veterans who had taken up arms in defence of the Crown, and a viewing of archival documents associated with the Proclamation at the British Library. They also met up with representatives of Idle No More London, an activist group that expressed solidarity with the Indigenous grassroots movement of the same name then sweeping Canada. The Proclamation of 1763 commemoration journey also allowed its members to connect with their Indigenous predecessors through a walking tour on which this essay is based. As one of the delegation members noted, learning about these earlier travellers linked the 2013 delegation to a broader Indigenous history. 'They're like our ancestors,' she told me.

From St Martin in the Fields, turn left into Duncannon Street. Ahead of you, you will see the Victorian memorial cross that honours Eleanor of Castile (d. 1290). This is Charing Cross, perhaps not an obvious place to consider Indigenous history. But in the 1570s, English explorer Martin Frobisher layered this name on to a point of land in what is currently known as the Canadian arctic, in doing so entangling this ancient place with both colonial and Indigenous geographies. The area around Charing Cross, meanwhile, was known in the early seventeenth century as the Bermudas, in part because of the prevalence of tobacco houses here – another exchange of places between the 'old' and 'new' worlds.[12]

Carry on, crossing the Strand into Villiers Street, the pedestrianised thoroughfare going down the hill to the left of Charing Cross train station. At John Adam Street, turn left and walk to the corner of Durham House Street. Sir Walter Raleigh's palace of Durham House is long gone, but its name remains, along with those of other great houses that once stood along the Strand. This is where, in the late sixteenth century, the polymath Thomas Harriot attempted to describe his experiences in a land across the Atlantic that he called Virginia, but whose residents knew it as Ossomocomuck. But Harriot's *A briefe and true report of Virginia* was not authored solely by the English scholar; it was informed by the knowledge and labour of at least two Roanoke men, Manteo and Wanchese, and perhaps a third, Towaye, all of whom were brought to London in the 1580s both as witnesses to English 'superiority' and to serve as helpmates to colonisation. Perhaps the most poignant remnant of this exchange of knowledge is a single sheet of parchment on which Harriot inscribed an experimental orthography for the Roanoke language and which, at the bottom, bears a line of text that reads 'King Manteo did this' – the earliest known example of Indigenous alphabetic literacy north of Mexico. The entanglements of colonial knowledge production with Indigenous ways of knowing produced an artefact that is both English and Roanoke. Here, in a now-vanished palace, Indigenous presence helped London learn to be colonial.[13]

Retrace your steps to Villiers Street and turn left. Partway down the hill, enter the Arches shopping arcade and walk through the arcade until you emerge into Craven Street. In 1761, an unnamed 11-year-old Odawa boy was held captive in the Craven Street home of Major General George Townshend, who had acquired him as spoil of war after the Battle of Ticonderoga, in which Townshend's brother Roger was killed. The boy was used as entertainment for Townshend's guests. One of those guests was the poet Thomas Gray, who in a letter described the boy's captor presenting a box of human scalps, which the child recognised as being from his own people. Meanwhile, another guest, Scottish designer Robert Adam, pencilled a sketch of the boy that was used in the creation of twin statues that serve as a monument to Roger Townshend that still stands in Westminster Abbey. The boy's fate, like his name, is unknown, and speaks to the brutal realities of colonial violence in which Londoners played no small part.[14]

Follow Craven Street to the left towards Northumberland Avenue. Cross the avenue and enter Whitehall Gardens, continuing until Horse Guards Avenue, where you should turn right. Walking up this hill, it is impossible to miss the fact that you are passing through a landscape of raw power; for centuries, Whitehall has been the centre of British sovereignty. No. 10 Downing Street is just up ahead, and the edifices around you now are simply the latest in a long series of buildings that have housed the machinations of empire. From here until the end of the tour, you are at the true heart of English and British colonialism. Next, cross Whitehall and pass through the Horse Guards archway into the parade ground. To your right, you can see the masts and rigging of the Admiralty. This is the institution that oversaw the explorations of Captain James Cook (indeed, a monumental statue of him can be seen by going around the corner to the front of the building). From this place emanated scientific discovery, imperial competition, and doctrines such as *terra nullius*, which denied Indigenous presence on and title to the land. At the same time, Cook's experiences on his voyages were just as diverse as the people he encountered, ranging from diffidence to threat to peaceful trade to all-out violence, including Cook's violent death at Kealakekua Bay in 1778.

But it is St James's Park, straight ahead, that is our goal for the moment. Here, in 1615, a Dutch soldier painted a watercolour picture of an Indigenous man among a menagerie of animals. The soldier's subject was likely Eiakintomino, a citizen of the Powhatan Confederacy, whose homeland of Tsenacomoco was also part of the area known as Virginia by the English. Eiakintomino was only one of many Powhatan visitors to London in the early seventeenth century; some came as captives or servants, while others, like the famous Powhatan noblewoman Pocahontas, travelled to the city as diplomats and explorers in their own right. Of Eiakintomino specifically, very little is known. Aside from the soldier's illustration, the only record of his existence is a Virginia Company lottery circular from the same year, where he appears alongside his countryman Matahan. Likely read out in public places such as Smithfield or St Paul's Churchyard, the circular included a powerful message attributed to the two men:

> Once, in one State, as of one Stem
> Meere Strangers from IERVSALEM,
> As Wee, were Yee; till Others Pittie
> ought, and brought You to That Cittie.
> Deere Britaines, now, be You as Kinde;
> Bring Light, and Sight, to Vs yet blinde:
> Leade Vs, by Doctrine and Behauiour,
> Into one Sion, to one SAVIOVR.[15]

Aggressive evangelisation was a core element of the Virginia Company's mission in America, and here Eiakintomino and his kinsman are deployed to that end. Meanwhile, the picture of Eiakintomino in St James Park, alongside a goose, a crane, and a ram, reminds us of the very real fascination Londoners held for the exotic, even as the Powhatan man's regalia – a deerskin mantle, three necklaces and an armband made of beads or pearls, and a beaded or painted purse – suggest a person of status who likely had his own agenda, even if it is overshadowed in the archive by English colonial aspirations and expectations.[16]

Go left along Horse Guards Road until you reach Great George Street, where you will turn left and continue into Parliament Square. Westminster Abbey towers over the square, and perhaps unsurprisingly, is another important node in London's Indigenous geography. During a visit to Westminster Abbey in 1823, for example, the Hawaiian monarchs Liholiho and Kamāmalu were, according to one observer, 'much pleased'. But their reactions were more complicated than simple pleasure. They were also 'impressed with great veneration for the place where they knew the remains of so many great men were deposited ... hearing that the ancient kings of England were buried there, they said it was too sacred, and no argument could prevail upon the king to enter it'. For two leaders from society where even talking too much about one's progenitors was deeply frowned upon – mai kaulaʻi wale i ka iwi o na kūpuna ('do not dry out the bones of the ancestors') goes the proverb – entering someone else's ancestral burial ground was beyond the pale.[17]

Then, a few decades later in 1906, a delegation of four Indigenous men from the Canadian province of British Columbia came to London in search of protection for their unceded lands, their goal a meeting with the reigning Edward VII. They included Ispaymilt from the Cowichan Nation, whose territories rest on the eastern coast of Vancouver Island, and Basil David, a Secwepmc from the Bonaparte Reserve in British Columbia's interior. The party also included Simon Pierre, a translator from the Katzie reserve of the Stó:lō people along the Fraser River. But the man who would become the most famous member of the group was S7aplek, a leader from the Squamish Nation, whose territory ranges from what is now the city of Vancouver north into the mountains. S7aplek carried the ancestral name Capilano – given to him by Squamish elders specifically for the journey – which linked him to a leader who had greeted the first Europeans to arrive in Squamish territory in the late eighteenth century.

Immediately after their arrival, the foursome was taken to their lodgings in officers' barracks at Buckingham Gate. From there, they explored the city. They saw the London Zoo, where a stranger asked if he might clip some of S7aplek's hair for his pillatory collection. To a Squamish man, for whom hair, like any body part, was a source of personal spiritual power, such a request caused deep offence. 'He make too free and ask too much,' was the response. Indeed, the noise and hectic pace of the city could easily overwhelm the visitors; Basil David seems to have suffered, thrashing and crying out in his sleep from nightmares involving motorcars and traffic. Most important, of course, was their time with the king. 'We talk with the King,' S7aplek described, 'and at the end he shake my right hand hard and with his left hand pat my left shoulder three times ... and say "Chief we see this matter righted but it may take a long time, five years perhaps".' Lastly, during their visit to Westminster Abbey, they encountered the Stone of Scone and the shrine of Edward the Confessor.

As historian Keith Carlson has argued, for the four visitors, for whom stones could be ancestors and sources of spiritual and political authority and for whom ancestral names could carry power across the generations, such sights would have been legible according to Indigenous ways of knowing. The stone under the Coronation Chair would have made immediate sense, while the space between Edward the Confessor and Edward VII was likely, in their minds, small indeed. But this moment of encounter also tells us something about the city: at the height of its imperial modernity, an ancient block of sandstone and a set of 900-year-old bones still emanated power that served as the basis of sacred political authority. Perhaps this was a city that was not entirely modern after all.[18]

In the end, though, perhaps the most poignant and pointed clues to Indigenous history at Westminster Abbey are the paired statues based on the young, unnamed Odawa captive, tucked among all the other monuments in the church's south aisle. The twin figures serve as atlantes, holding up a frieze of Townshend's death scene on the battlefield of Ticonderoga; as such, they also support a narrative of colonial sacrifice and redemption that links the boy's life to the broader sweep of empire.

Finally, we come to Westminster Hall, just nearby. The last remnant of the medieval Westminster Palace, it is a site of tremendous cultural and political power, and in 1501 or 1502, something quite unprecedented took place there:

> This yere also were browgth unto the kyng iij men takyn In the Newe ffound Ile land, that beffore I spak of In wylliam purchas tyme beyng mayer, These were clothid In bestys skynnys and ete Rawe fflesh and spak such speech that noo man cowde undyrstand theym, and In theyr demeanure lyke to bruyt bestis whom the kyng kept a tyme afftyr, Of the whych upon (ij) yeris passis (afftir) I sawe ij of theym apparalyd afftyr Inglysh men In westmynstyr paleys, which at that tyme I cowde not discern ffrom Inglysh men tyll I was lernyd what men they were, But as ffor spech I hard noon of them uttyr oon word.
>
> This year also were brought unto the king three men taken in the new found island, that before I spoke of in William Purchas's time being mayor.

> These were clothed in beasts' skins and ate raw flesh and spoke such speech that no man could understand them, and in their demeanour like to brute beasts, whom the king kept a time after. Of the which upon two years passed after I saw two of them apparelled after Englishmen in Westminster Palace, which at that time I could not discern from Englishmen until I was learned what men they were, but as for speech I heard none of them utter one word.[19]

The only evidence of a visitation by strangers seemingly from another world, this lone archival fragment tells us very little, but also offers hints as to the identity of these foreigners. The reference to raw flesh suggests that the visitors were Inuit, people for whom uncooked meat was the sole source of crucial vitamins in their far northern homeland. But beyond that, their presence is a mystery. How did they get there? Did they come willingly, or as captives? And what happened to them? The archive of Indigenous London, like that of early modern London more generally, is often fragmentary at best. But the presence of these three men at Westminster shows that London's Indigenous history in fact predates its colonial North American history, rather than the other way around. After all, these three strangers appeared in the palace only a decade after Columbus 'discovered' the 'new' world. Since the dawn of the sixteenth century, then, London has been entangled with Indigenous worlds and lives.

These are just some of the many spaces of Indigenous history and colonial encounter in London. From Southwark Cathedral to Sadler's Wells, Greenwich to Earl's Court, St Paul's Cathedral to Buckingham Palace, the city is replete with sites associated with Indigenous migration, whether willing or otherwise. The point here is more than anecdote; rather, it is to assert that Indigenous history in London is diverse, deep, and vital – even if much of it has been forgotten by Londoners. Indeed, the larger processes of empire are simultaneously ever-present and oft-muted. Most histories of twentieth-century London, for example, have virtually nothing to say about the relationship between the empire and its metropolis during the twentieth century, focusing instead primarily on narrower, if still crucial, civic issues such as municipal governance, environmental management, or social unrest. At the same time, though, the urban landscape remains littered with the detritus of empire. As historian John M. MacKenzie has eloquently written:

> It may be that those who hurry down Whitehall seldom reflect on the extraordinary imperial façade of the Foreign Office with its busts of heroes; that passers-by in Kensington Gore scarcely notice the statues of Livingstone and Shackleton that project from the walls of the Royal Geographical Society; and that visitors to the Victoria and Albert Museum are only dimly aware of the imperial origins of some of its collections. Moreover, even if familiar and overlooked, statues and war memorials everywhere speak of an imperial past.[20]

But while London might have for the time being forgotten its Indigenous past, that past is often held tightly by descendant Indigenous communities: in stories of the Four Kings and Thayendanagea among the Mohawk; in accounts of the monarchs retold during discussions of Hawaiian sovereignty; in remembrances of men like Bennelong and women like E. Pauline Johnson. And as more and more Indigenous communities seek repatriation of ancestral remains and cultural belongings from the British Museum and other institutions, they will no doubt also reassert their historical presence in the city. Indigenous London remains.

One final place to visit, then. From Westminster, take the Circle or District Line to Embankment, then change for the Bakerloo Line to Oxford Circus. There, emerge into a hub for late capitalism: Uniqlo, McDonald's, Urban Outfitters, Apple, H&M. Walk west along Oxford Street to numbers 105 to 109, and look up. There, atop an ornate Victorian building, stand some very strange gargoyles: beavers. This is Henry Heath's late nineteenth-century factory, which produced some of the city's finest beaver-skin top hats, which means that it is also a site of Indigenous history. If we were to imagine those top hats disassembling themselves and transforming back into pelts, then the pelts getting back on a ship in the Thames and crossing the Atlantic before returning up the St Lawrence to Ojibwe, Cree, Métis, and Dene territories, we would understand that the wealth that made the hat factory possible existed only because of the knowledge and labour of Indigenous people, and in particular Indigenous women. Thus, this site in Oxford Street is in fact an extension of Indigenous territory, and London not necessarily the centre of empire but a place at the margins of several Indigenous worlds.[21]

These are the sorts of narratives that are possible if we take seriously the history of Indigenous engagement with London. To return to Linda Tuhiwai Smith, the articulation of histories such as these, embodied literally in the palimpsestic urban landscape, is perhaps one way of decolonising the centre of empire, creating space for narratives that overturn our expectations of where and when Indigenous histories belong. Those narratives have meaning: they speak not just to the history of settler colonialism, empire, and Indigenous survivance in the past, but to the ways in which all of these things continue to resonate into the present and the future.

Notes

1 For three key examples of this approach to Indigenous history, see Jace Weaver, *The Red Atlantic: American Indigenes and the Making of the Modern World, 1000–1927* (Chapel Hill: University of North Carolina Press, 2015); David Chang, *The World and All the Things upon It: Native Hawaiian Geographies of Exploration* (Minneapolis: University of Minnesota Press, 2016); and Nancy E. van Deusen, *Global Indios: The Indigenous Struggle for Justice in Sixteenth-Century Spain* (Durham, NC: Duke University Press, 2014). For provincialising, see Dipesh Chakrabarty, *Provincializing Europe: Postcolonial Thought and Historical Difference* (Princeton, NJ: Princeton University Press, 2007).

2 Linda Tuhiwai Smith, *Decolonizing Methodologies: Research and Indigenous Peoples* (New York: Zed, 1999), 146, 149.

3 For the most comprehensive accounts of the journey, see Richmond P. Bond, *Queen Anne's American Kings* (Oxford: Oxford University Press, 1952); and Eric Hinderaker, 'The "Four Indian Kings" and the Imaginative Construction of the British Empire,' *William & Mary Quarterly* 53, no. 3 (July 1996): 487–526. For the political context of their voyage, see Matthew Dennis, *Cultivating a Landscape of Peace: Iroquois-European Encounters in Seventeenth-Century America* (Ithaca: Cornell University Press, 1993).

4 *The Spectator*, 27 April 1711.

5 Lady Strafford, 'The Mohock Club,' *The Wentworth Papers 1705–1739*, ed. Thomas Wentworth (1883), quoted in Jon E. Lewis, *London: The Autobiography* (London: Robinson, 2009), 199–200; and John Fuller, ed., *John Gay: Dramatic Works*, vol. 1 (Oxford: Clarendon Press, 1983), 3–5, 81, 98–99. For discussions of the Mohocks, see Daniel Statt, 'The Case of the Mohocks: Rake Violence in Augustan London,' *Social History* 20, no. 2 (May 1995): 179–199; and John Timbs, *Clubs and Club Life in London* (London: Chatto & Windus, 1872), 33–37.

6 Accounts of Bennelong and Yemmerrawannie's time in England can be found in Jack Brook, 'The Forlorn Hope: Bennelong and Yemmerrawannie Go to England,' *Australian Aboriginal Studies* 1 (2001): 36–47; Kate Fullagar, 'Bennelong in Britain,' *Aboriginal History* 33 (2009): 31–51; and John Turnbull, *A Voyage around the World, in the Years 1800, 1801, 1802, 1803, and 1804; in Which the Author Visited the Principal Islands in the Pacific Ocean, and the English Settlements of Port Jackson and Norfolk* (Philadelphia, PA: Benjamin and Thomas Kite, 1810), 42–44. See also the website findingbennelong.com.

7 For the story of the Hawaiian monarchs' journey, see Coll Thrush, *Indigenous London: Native Travelers at the Heart of Empire* (New Haven, CT: Yale University Press, 2016), 145–151.

8 Leon Burr Richardson, *An Indian Preacher in England: Being Letters and Diaries Relating to the Mission of the Reverend Samson Occom and the Reverend Nathaniel Whitaker* (Hanover: Dartmouth College Publications, 1933), 82–83. For an overview of Occom's life and a comprehensive collection of his works, see Joanna Brooks, ed., *The Collected Writings of Samson Occom, Mohegan: Leadership and Literature in Eighteenth-Century Native America* (Oxford: Oxford University Press, 2006).

9 Quoted in Charlotte Gray, *Flint and Feather: The Life and Times of E. Pauline Johnson, Tekahionwake* (Toronto, ON: Phyllis Bruce Books Perennial, 2003), 329.

10 Lord Byron, *Voyage of the H.M.S. Blonde to the Sandwich Islands, in the Years 1824–1825: Captain the Right Hon. Lord Byron, Commander* (London: John Murray, 1826), 71; *The Times*, 15 July 1824, 2.

11 For one comprehensive biography of Thayendanagea, see Isabel Thompson Kelsay, *Joseph Brant, 1743–1807: Man of Two Worlds* (Syracuse: Syracuse University Press, 1986).

12 For Frobisher's explorations, see James McDermott, *Martin Frobisher: Elizabethan Privateer* (New Haven, CT: Yale University Press, 2001). For a map including the place Frobisher renamed Charing Cross, see George Best, *A True Discourse of the Late Voyages of Discovery* (London: Henry Bynneman, 1578).

13 John W. Shirley's *Thomas Harriot: A Biography* (Oxford: Clarendon Press, 1983) remains the most comprehensive biography of Harriot. For the intellectual context of his life, especially in terms of his mathematical work and relationship with colonisation, see Robert Fox, *Thomas Harriot and His World: Mathematics, Exploration, and Natural Philosophy in Early Modern England* (Farnham: Ashgate, 2012). The actual inscription on the orthography manuscript is MATEOROIDN, literally 'Manteo roi done', in keeping with the highly idiosyncratic and partial spelling and grammar seen, for example, in the Lord's Prayer at the top of the document. The original is held in the archives of the Westminster School in London. For discussions of the orthography, see Shirley, *Thomas Harriot*, 108–112; Miriam Rukeyser, *Traces of Thomas Hariot* (New York: Random House, 1971), 164–167; and Vivian Salmon, 'Thomas Harriot and the English Origins of Algonkian Linguistics,' Durham Thomas Harriot Seminar Occasional Paper No. 8 (Durham, NC: University of Durham, 1993). The only other known use of the orthography is on a seventeenth-century property map from Ireland; see Eric Klingelhoffer and James Lyttleton, 'Molana Abbey and Its New World Master,' *Archaeology Ireland* 24, no. 4 (Winter 2010): 32–35.

14 For references to the boy, discussion of Townshend's relationship with the Odawa, and the history of the Townshend monument in Westminster Abbey, see John Fleming, 'Robert Adam, Luc-François Breton, and the Townshend Monument in Westminster Abbey,' *Connoisseur* 150, no. 165 (July 1962): 162–171; Thomas Gray, *Correspondence of*

Thomas Gray, ed. Paget Toynbee and Leonard Whibley, vol. 2, letter 308, to Thomas Wharton, 23 January 1760 (Oxford: Oxford University Press, 1935), 367; Hugh Honour, *The New Golden Land: European Images of America from the Discoveries to the Present Time* (London: Allen Lane, 1975), 128; Alan McNairn, *Behold the Hero: General Wolfe at the Arts in the Eighteenth Century* (Liverpool: Liverpool University Press, 1997), 168; and Stephanie Pratt, *American Indians in British Art, 1700–1840* (Norman: University of Oklahoma Press, 2005), 45–48.
15 Thrush, *Indigenous London*, 49–51.
16 For the most detailed discussion of the watercolour, see June Schlueter, *The Album Amicorum & the London of Shakespeare's Time* (London: The British Library, 2011), 134–136.
17 Byron, *Voyage of the H.M.S. Blonde*, 62; and Mary Kawena Pukui, *'Olelo No'eau: Hawaiian Proverbs and Poetical Sayings* (Honolulu: Bishop Museum, 1997), 225.
18 See Keith Thor Carlson, 'Rethinking Dialogue and History: The King's Promise and the 1906 Aboriginal Delegation to London,' *Native Studies Review* 16, no. 2 (2005) and Keith Thor Carlson, 'The Indians and the Crown: Aboriginal Memories of the Royal Promises in Pacific Canada,' in *Majesty in Canada: Essays on the Role of Royalty*, ed. Colin Coates (Toronto, ON: Dundurn Press, 2006), 68–95.
19 *The Great Chronicle of London* (1580), ed. A. H. Thomas and I. D. Thornley (London: George W. Jones, 1939), 288, discussed and quoted in James A. Williamson, *The Cabot Voyages and Bristol Discovery under Henry VII* (Cambridge: Cambridge University Press, 1962), 128 and 220.
20 John M. MacKenzie, general editor's introduction, *British Culture and the End of Empire*, ed. Stuart Ward (Manchester: Manchester University Press, 2001), vi.
21 For a general overview of the trade in beaver pelts in the late nineteenth century, see Arthur J. Ray, *The Canadian Fur Trade in the Industrial Age* (Toronto, ON: University of Toronto Press, 1990). For Heath's factory specifically, see 'Ye Felt Hatterie in the Exhibition of 1884,' number 5874 in the British Library's Evanion collection and the back page of Charles Dickens's *London, 1879: An Unconventional Handbook* (London: Charles Dickens, 1879).

Bibliography

Best, George. *A True Discourse of the Late Voyages of Discovery*. London: Henry Bynneman, 1578.

Bond, Richmond P. *Queen Anne's American Kings*. Oxford: Oxford University Press, 1952.

Brook, Jack. 'The Forlorn Hope: Bennelong and Yemmerrawannie Go to England.' *Australian Aboriginal Studies* 1 (2001): 36–47.

Brooks, Joanna, ed. *The Collected Writings of Samson Occom, Mohegan: Leadership and Literature in Eighteenth-Century Native America*. Oxford: Oxford University Press, 2006.

Byron, George Gordon (Lord). *Voyage of the H.M.S. Blonde to the Sandwich Islands, in the Years 1824–1825: Captain the Right Hon. Lord Byron, Commander*. London: John Murray, 1826.

Carlson, Keith Thor. 'Rethinking Dialogue and History: The King's Promise and the 1906 Aboriginal Delegation to London.' *Native Studies Review* 16, no. 2 (2005): 1–38.

Carlson, Keith Thor. 'The Indians and the Crown: Aboriginal Memories of the Royal Promises in Pacific Canada.' In *Majesty in Canada: Essays on the Role of Royalty*, edited by Colin Coates, 68–95. Toronto, ON: Dundurn Press, 2006.

Chakrabarty, Dipesh. *Provincializing Europe: Postcolonial Thought and Historical Difference*. Princeton, NJ: Princeton University Press, 2007.

Chang, David. *The World and All the Things upon It: Native Hawaiian Geographies of Exploration*. Minneapolis: University of Minnesota Press, 2016.

Dennis, Matthew. *Cultivating a Landscape of Peace: Iroquois-European Encounters in Seventeenth-Century America*. Ithaca: Cornell University Press, 1993.

Dickens, Charles. *London, 1879: An Unconventional Handbook*. London: Charles Dickens, 1879.

Fleming, John. 'Robert Adam, Luc-François Breton, and the Townshend Monument in Westminster Abbey.' *Connoisseur* 150, no. 165 (July 1962): 162–171.

Fox, Robert. *Thomas Harriot and His World: Mathematics, Exploration, and Natural Philosophy in Early Modern England*. Farnham: Ashgate, 2012.

Fullagar, Kate. 'Bennelong in Britain.' *Aboriginal History* 33 (2009): 31–51.

Fuller, John, ed. *John Gay: Dramatic Works*, vol. 1. Oxford: Clarendon Press, 1983.

Gray, Charlotte. *Flint and Feather: The Life and Times of E. Pauline Johnson, Tekahionwake*. Toronto, ON: Phyllis Bruce Books Perennial, 2003.

Gray, Thomas. *Correspondence of Thomas Gray*, edited by Paget Toynbee and Leonard Whibley, vol. 2. Oxford: Oxford University Press, 1935.

Hinderaker, Eric. 'The "Four Indian Kings" and the Imaginative Construction of the British Empire,' *William & Mary Quarterly* 53, no. 3 (July 1996): 487–526.

Honour, Hugh. *The New Golden Land: European Images of America from the Discoveries to the Present Time*. London: Allen Lane, 1975.

Kelsay, Isabel Thompson. *Joseph Brant, 1743–1807: Man of Two Worlds*. Syracuse: Syracuse University Press, 1986.

Klingelhoffer, Eric, and James Lyttleton. 'Molana Abbey and Its New World Master.' *Archaeology Ireland* 24, no. 4 (Winter 2010): 32–35.

Lewis, Jon E. *London: The Autobiography*. London: Robinson, 2009.

MacKenzie, John M. General editor's introduction, in *British Culture and the End of Empire*, ed. Stuart Ward. Manchester: Manchester University Press, 2001.

McDermott, James. *Martin Frobisher: Elizabethan Privateer*. New Haven, CT: Yale University Press, 2001.

McNairn, Alan. *Behold the Hero: General Wolfe at the Arts in the Eighteenth Century*. Liverpool: Liverpool University Press, 1997.

Pratt, Stephanie. *American Indians in British Art, 1700–1840*. Norman: University of Oklahoma Press, 2005.

Pukui, Mary Kawena. *'Olelo No'eau: Hawaiian Proverbs and Poetical Sayings*. Honolulu: Bishop Museum, 1997.

Ray, Arthur J. *The Canadian Fur Trade in the Industrial Age*. Toronto, ON: University of Toronto Press, 1990.

Richardson, Leon Burr. *An Indian Preacher in England: Being Letters and Diaries Relating to the Mission of the Reverend Samson Occom and the Reverend Nathaniel Whitaker*. Hanover: Dartmouth College Publications, 1933.

Rukeyser, Miriam. *Traces of Thomas Hariot*. New York: Random House, 1971.

Salmon, Vivian. 'Thomas Harriot and the English Origins of Algonkian Linguistics,' Durham Thomas Harriot Seminar Occasional Paper No. 8. Durham, NC: University of Durham, 1993.

Schlueter, June. *The Album Amicorum & the London of Shakespeare's Time*. London: The British Library, 2011.

Shirley, John W. *Thomas Harriot: A Biography*. Oxford: Clarendon Press, 1983.

Smith, Linda Tuhiwai. *Decolonizing Methodologies: Research and Indigenous Peoples*. New York: Zed, 1999.

Spectator, The. 27 April 1711.

Statt, Daniel. 'The Case of the Mohocks: Rake Violence in Augustan London.' *Social History* 20, no. 2 (May 1995): 179–199.

Thomas, A. H., and I. D. Thornley, eds. *The Great Chronicle of London* (1580). London: George W. Jones, 1939.

Thrush, Coll. *Indigenous London: Native Travelers at the Heart of Empire*. New Haven, CT: Yale University Press, 2016.

Timbs, John. *Clubs and Club Life in London*. London: Chatto & Windus, 1872.

Times, The. 15 July 1824.

Turnbull, John. *A Voyage around the World, in the Years 1800, 1801, 1802, 1803, and 1804; in Which the Author Visited the Principal Islands in the Pacific Ocean, and the English Settlements of Port Jackson and Norfolk*. Philadelphia: Benjamin and Thomas Kite, 1810.

Van Deusen, Nancy E. *Global Indios: The Indigenous Struggle for Justice in Sixteenth-Century Spain*. Durham, NC: Duke University Press, 2014.

Weaver, Jace. *The Red Atlantic: American Indigenes and the Making of the Modern World, 1000–1927*. Chapel Hill: University of North Carolina Press, 2015.

Williamson, James A. *The Cabot Voyages and Bristol Discovery under Henry VII*. Cambridge: Cambridge University Press, 1962.

PART III

Colonial encounters

11
TREATIED SPACE
North American Indigenous treaties in a global context

Joy Porter

The case for re-examination of North American Indian treaty history

There is currently a movement to better comprehend the Indigenous agency inherent within treaties across time, to transcend existing approaches to them, understand more about their diverse nature, and enhance their intellectual and intersocial valency. In 1928, the librarian and scholar Lawrence C. Wroth wrote how he wished he had been poured 'the strong wine' of Indian treaties as a student, instead of the 'invincible mediocrity' of the duller literature on the colonial period. This chapter is part of a more liberal pouring of just such 'strong wine' at a point in intellectual life when indigenous North American treaty texts and what surrounds them are beginning to take on a more appropriately central place within debates on literature, history, law, political science, and Indigenous studies.

Wroth's emphasis on the literary, aesthetic, and dramatic aspects of treaties worked to shift focus away from their primary intercultural, contractual, and political significance, but he made an important point nonetheless. He identified treaties as the archetypal American literature and recognised them for what they were – some of the most deeply significant foundational records of intercultural dialogue on American soil. However, to Wroth, treaties were an embodiment of the great tragedies of the pre-revolutionary period and he was therefore unsurprised to find a strong private publishing market for them in the eighteenth century. He knew that they were collaborative documents, but being a product of his time, he thought that Indian peoples were fated for doom. For Wroth, Indigenous peoples may have played off one interest against another to their own benefit in the short term, but this was simply evidence that it was 'possible to hold the balance of power and be at the same time the corn between the millstones' of great European interests.[1] Wroth saw treaties as artefacts of ultimate Indigenous powerlessness, but today they are again taking centre stage as models of intercultural practice and as a means for rekindling reciprocally positive interrelationship.

Frustration with the limited ability of 'rights talk' to effect practical, on-the-ground change has prompted reflection backwards, in particular to the late seventeenth and eighteenth centuries, on occasions when tribes, bands, and communities engaged to their specific advantage as sovereign entities in bilateral governmental relations, exercised pervasive control over their land and resources, and maintained discreet and coherent internal self-government. Paying attention to the history of the treaties made in such contexts has the potential to focus attention and develop understanding of *Indigenous* visions of law, justice, reciprocal relationships, and peace. Early American Indian treaties provide a window into the ways agreements struck between Indigenous and settler communities transcended narrow legal/political entitlements or 'rights' and instead encompassed dynamic interdependencies between community health and well-being, access to resources, spiritual life, cultures, and the environment. There is increasing awareness of treaties as they were understood in Indigenous contexts – as 'living' documents that were process-orientated, required renewal, often invoked a sacred dimension, and drew upon textured traditions surrounding alliance and trade that were well-established prior to contact with Europeans.

Analysing previous treaty and diplomatic texts as well as the conditions of their formulation may now prove especially helpful as Indigenous peoples respond to calls by contemporary activists and thinkers such as those of the Kahnawá:ke Mohawk leader Taiaiake Alfred, that Native peoples 'start remembering the qualities of our ancestors, and act on those remembrances' and 'reject the colonists' control and authority, their definition of who we are and what our rights are, their definition of what is worthwhile and how one should live, their hypocritical pacifying moralities'. Alfred argues that this kind of spiritual revolution is what will ensure indigenous survival. In a broadly comparable fashion, Michif (Métis) scholar Chris Andersen has called for critical attention to shift towards the 'density' of indigenous existence and its epistemological complexity. In so doing, he echoes an earlier call made by the African-American scholar Robin Kelley that density be taken seriously as a means towards emancipation.[2]

These are responses to an overarching drive to find ways to build Indigenous-authored futures, a desire articulated in 2011 by Michi Saagiig Nishnaabeg scholar Leanne Betasamosake Simpson in *Dancing on Our Turtle's Back*. Resolutely setting to one side Audre Lorde's advice that the master's tools will never dismantle the master's house, Simpson instead orientated indigenous thinking inwards and backwards, stating: 'I am not so concerned with how we dismantle the master's house, … but I am very concerned with how we (re)build our own house, or our own houses.'[3]

The debate over whether Indigenous peoples should engage with the dominant states and in what form, and whether Indigenous energies should be reserved exclusively for internal development, continues to grow. According to the Anishinaabe scholar Dale Turner, author of *This Is Not a Peace Pipe*, what is needed is more, rather than less, careful involvement with the state. A practical example is his involvement with the development of the Chi-Naaknigewin Constitution of the Anishinabek Nation, proclaimed on 6 June 2012. The Constitution is based upon a ritual or declamatory preamble, Ngo Dwe Waangizid Anishinaabe, that invokes 'the Inherent, Traditional, Treaty, and Unceded Lands of [Anishinaabe] Territories'. In its assertion and re-iteration of the fact that Anishinaabe people, land, and language are all constitutive of Anishinaabe nationhood, the Constitution serves at a minimum two functions: it communicates aspects of Anishinaabe interests and values externally, and reinforces aspects of Anishinaabe values and interests internally. Such a focus upon the renewal of existing relationships between Indigenous peoples and settler communities may not be where authors such as Glen Coulthard suggest that Indigenous energies should best be placed, but it is nonetheless a type of considered engagement with dominant powers with a long and significant indigenous pedigree.[4]

In the U.S. context, the fundamental significance of treaties to Indigenous history within the United States remains under-researched, despite interesting recent quantitative work by the Harvard political scientist Arthur Spirling, various North American and tribe-specific studies since the late 1970s, and significant work by Frances Paul Prucha, Vine Deloria Jr and Raymond J. DeMallie, and David E. Wilkins.[5] This is partly as a result of conceptual and social changes in the 1960s and 1970s that brought into sharp relief successive historical failures to uphold treatied relationships. Since then, issues linked to representation, identity, and culture have achieved much greater prominence in comparison to the messy, inherently political, diplomatic intricacies of how treaties came into being and how they impact materially and culturally upon the present. As a result, too few of us are aware that over 600 treaty documents were signed in the United States between the revolutionary war and the onset of the twentieth century, and that today only 367 U.S.-Indian treaties have undisputed status. Be that as it may, treaties remain the fundamental diplomatic entities that have codified and articulated relationships between settlers and Indigenous peoples over time.

All communities and individuals living on American land are, in this sense, 'treaty people' and attention to treaty history is vital if we are to successfully re-vision cross-cultural relationships and norms at the onset of the twenty-first century, which heralds profound cultural, technological, and environmental changes. Treaties matter because they are an exceptional avenue of intercultural diplomacy, a means whereby different cultures can arrive at shared norms and a shared language, however articulated. They offer the potential for 'overlapping consensus', the aspiration at the core of the political liberalism described by John Rawls and the social unity within democracy that the liberal democratic ideal espouses.[6] This is not to suggest that attention to treaty history will necessarily yield easily applicable models from the past or that entirely new frameworks should be ruled out as Indigenous and settler communities develop agreements in the future.

What seems certain, however, is that some form of fundamental reckoning must be achieved between Indigenous and settler laws, which, in turn, is linked to fundamental long-standing unresolved tensions between concepts of international law and state sovereignty.[7] The early colonial period of the seventeenth and eighteenth centuries made for regional balances of power that at specific times and places fostered relationships of parity between Indigenous and settler nations, but particularly from the nineteenth century, a process occurred whereby Indigenous nations were progressively removed from the international legal sphere.[8] The dream of justice for minorities enshrined and respected at an international level, with laws and arbitration operating within an international system, had its genesis during the first half of the twentieth century in the decades following the lowest ebb for Native American peoples – 1890, when Native numbers within the U.S. boundaries reached a nadir of 248,000 and the frontier was deemed by historical authorities to have 'closed'. The question of the status of Indigenous nations as global entities remains unresolved and this fundamental question is at the heart of the perceived failures of the contemporary 'rights' agenda.

Prominent legal scholars have tended to relate changes in how treaties operated primarily to how Anglophone governments developed and conceived of their own sovereignty, despite a growing body of historical scholarship emphasising Indigenous agency in relation to treaties, and in the North American context, Indigenous peoples having had regional military and political supremacy up until and across most of the eighteenth century. Thus, seminal studies such as Paul McHugh's 2004 *Aboriginal Societies and the Common Law* explain the strong self-governance exercised by sovereign tribes in the seventeenth and early eighteenth centuries as being acceptable to Anglo-colonial states at that time because sovereignty then was generally understood as a personal relationship between the ruler and the ruled. In the late eighteenth and nineteenth centuries, non-Indigenous conceptualisations altered so that sovereignty came to be thought of as a unitary power within a defined geographic area. This made Indigenous sovereignty – what Charles F. Wilkinson identified as 'measured separatism' within U.S. law, because tribes often negotiated treaties that entailed protection, provisions, or support – seem legally anomalous. This, in turn, helped to fuel disastrous drives to enforce indigenous assimilation to national norms. These persisted in policy terms until President Nixon's reversal of American Indian tribal termination and the enshrining of American Indian self-determination within federal law in 1970.[9]

Re-examination of treaties today is particularly valuable as movements for decolonisation continue with treatied obligations relating to trade, land, and resource use at their core. Moreover, Indigenous treaties continue to be central to efforts across the globe to protect natural environments for the benefit of all. This has been the case, for example, in relation to legal conflict in 2019 over the TransCanada Keystone XL Pipeline, described as being in specific violation of two treaties struck by the U.S. federal government: the 1855 Lame Bull Treaty with the Blackfoot Confederacy or Niitsitapi, and the 1868 Treaty of Fort Laramie with bands of the Lakota.[10] The Canadian government's purchase of the Canadian Trans Mountain portion of the pipeline – from the Texas multinational Kinder Morgan on 29 May 2018 for C$4.5 billion – has done little to assuage the fears of Indigenous peoples and affiliated groups about the impact of tanker-traffic on fragile coastal ecosystems, the potential for a major bitumen spill, and the likely impingement of Indigenous treatied rights as a result of pipeline activities. The approximately

712-mile Canadian section of pipeline would bring oil from Edmonton, Alberta to the west coast, with profound implications for the Canadian economy, which is geared around resource extraction.

Despite Indigenous peoples being at the forefront of resistance to the pipeline, indigenous responses to it and to its relationship to specific treaties have not been uniform. For example, inter-tribal treaties are being employed to protect the environment, including the Treaty Alliance Against Tar Sands Expansion, within which 'allied signatory Indigenous Nations aim to prevent a pipeline/train/tanker spill from poisoning their water and to stop the Tar Sands from increasing its output and becoming an even bigger obstacle to solving the climate crisis'.[11] On the other side, a number of Indigenous nations, including some Secwepemc Nations, have officially signed up for Trans Mountain, despite the fact that many feel that the pipeline will pose a severe threat to unceded Secwepemc'ecw territory overall.[12] For example, Chief Nathan Matthew, a leader of the Simpcw First Nation community, made clear in 2018 that the Simpcw agreed to the conditions they had negotiated with the Trans Mountain parent company. These included both direct financial and other economic benefits accruing from employment contracts. As Chief Matthew put it, 'If the project doesn't go, there would be quite a number of contracts … and people wouldn't have the opportunity to work or contract to all of the different pieces of the construction.'[13]

Aside from the importance of Indigenous treaties to the protection of the environment, the fact that indigenous treaty-making, both inter-tribally and with other sovereign nations, is not confined to the past is yet another reason for thinking further about treaties in interdisciplinary contexts. The history of modern treaty-making in Canada, which continues to develop alongside existing treaty commitments, is especially instructive in this regard. Despite a 1969 Canadian federal White Paper that echoed the thinking of then Prime Minister Pierre Trudeau and then Minister for Indian Affairs Jean Chétien that having treaties between nations within Canada was 'anomalous', in the same year the Nisga'a people of the Nass River Valley, British Columbia began pursuit of their inherent treaty rights within the British Columbia Supreme Court. These proved productive and by 1976, negotiations had begun with the Canadian Crown that ultimately resulted in a 1996 treaty guaranteeing Nisga'a self-government and control of around 2000 sq km of Nisga'a land.

The 1975 James Bay and Northern Québec agreement is another point of departure marking a beginning for modern treaty-making in Canada. Here, Cree and Inuit peoples used the media and asserted their unceded rights in court at a critical juncture as Canada sought to benefit from the hydroelectric power inherent in the rivers in the eastern section of James Bay. The resulting 1975 James Bay Treaty provided a model and pathway for a variety of subsequent nation-to-nation agreements where Indigenous communities set up municipal and corporate frameworks and engaged as shareholders and stakeholders in the use of natural resources.[14] In the wake of Section 35(1) of the *Constitution Act, 1982*, all existing treaty rights of the aboriginal peoples of Canada were explicitly recognised and affirmed within the constitutional fabric of Canada.

Additionally, outside of the treaty context, First Nations and the government of Canada established various means of generating permanent bilateral agreements, including memorandums of understanding and partnership committees. The province of British Columbia established its own alternative Treaty Commission in 1992, which stands in tension with the 'whole of government approach' to implementing modern treaties that was subsequently enshrined within Canadian government in 2015. The B.C. Treaty Commission holds that the treaty context in B.C. is distinct because when it joined the Canadian confederation in 1871, only 14 treaties on Vancouver Island (Douglas Treaties) had been signed, and aboriginal title to the rest of the province was 'unresolved'. Although Section 35 of the *Constitution Act 1982* affirmed that aboriginal title and rights in Canada exist whether or not a treaty is in existence, B.C. holds that modern treaties are nevertheless necessary because Section 35 does not define those rights. As Canada's fifth largest province and a region extremely rich in valuable natural resources, the stakes are unprecedentedly high in B.C., and the modern treaty-making process there is one of the most complex ever entered into in the world.

Modern treaty-making

Overall, the positive gloss placed upon modern-day treaties in Canada is that they give all concerned a vested interest in making the agreements negotiated work, they establish effective multilateral arrangements between Indigenous, federal, provincial, territorial, and municipal levels of government, they make Indigenous governance systems transparent and accountable, and they are likely to lead in time to fuller Indigenous self-determination and self-sufficiency.[15] Yet, modern treaty-making remains extremely controversial and the cultural incomprehension and bad faith rooted in asymmetries of power that were characteristic of certain historic treaties are not confined to the past. It is worth considering in this regard the armed stand made in 1995 by the Defenders of the Shuswap/Secwepemc Nation at Ts'peten (Gustafsen Lake). The group protested non-Native occupation of Shuswap Nation lands in the absence of treaties and voiced profound concern about the legitimacy of the modern treaty process per se. The Defenders of the Shuswap are part of ongoing Indigenous critique of the way modern treaty-making contrasts with the model of historic treaty negotiations. In the Canadian context, in contrast to a number of respected treaties made in the past, modern treaties typically minimise the role of Indigenous protocols and ceremony, take years to complete, and result in large quantities of densely argued, inaccessible legal prose. The overarching question of how such modern treaties relate to Canada's ongoing financial responsibilities to its Indigenous peoples is not resolved.

Further concerns surround the use of a language of extinguishment of Indigenous rights within modern treaties, and the fact that they are perceived as working to replace broad, undefined traditional rights with smaller, closely articulated subsets of those rights. Furthermore, the B.C. Treaty Commission has come under specific scrutiny in relation to how the treaty-making process is funded. B.C. has provided grants of 20% of costs to First Nations to engage in treaty negotiations, but the remaining 80% of costs is provided as a loan to be repaid. Arguably, this encourages short-term First Nations engagement in treaty-making, but discourages the prolonged levels of negotiation that may well be necessary so to establish lasting, balanced agreements.[16]

Yet, further profound disquiet has been expressed over perceived conflicts of interest in relation to the Indigenous individuals chosen to work on changing modern First Nation treaty policies at a federal level. An example is the Canadian Liberal government's repeated choice since 2016 of Kim Baird – former chief of the approximately 358-member Tsawwassen First Nation – to be involved in ongoing federal-level talks with First Nations over modern treaties, despite her having prior links to Trans Mountain. Positive rulings and decisions in relation to the enormous unceded territories of B.C., as well as significant areas of Quebec, Atlantic Canada, and elsewhere, nevertheless offer hope for responsible land use in the future under First Nations stewardship.[17]

Although there are serious limitations and significant scope for improvement, the contemporary Canadian federal commitment to treaties as vehicles for dynamic negotiation of Indigenous relationships stands out as progressive in an international context. To give just one contrast, for the Sámi peoples of Sápmi – whose lands span sections of northern Norway, Sweden, Finland, and the Kola Peninsula of Russia – no historic treaties are agreed to exist, although Sámi representatives cite the Lapp Kodicill, an annex to a 1751 agreement between Norway and Sweden that describes Sámi rights. Indeed, despite the fact that a long external intervention from the sixteenth to eighteenth century led to the Nordic countries gaining possession of Sámi territories, the whole question of whether the Sámi experienced colonisation is still disputed.[18] One example of Sámi conflict with the Norwegian government suggests that disputes are likely to continue as pressures over land use sharpen. Leaders and community members protested in 2018 against Norwegian government demands to cull reindeer herds to combat 'overgrazing', and highlighted the absence of treatied environmental and property rights for Sámi peoples as well as Norwegian resistance to formal recognition of their Indigenous status. Herder Jovsset Ánte Sara, whose herd faced reduction, brought his complaints to the Norwegian Supreme Court, to no avail. His sister, artist Maret Anne Sara, publicised the forced slaughter by bringing her artwork, involving reindeer heads topped by the Norwegian flag, to court events. Given the pressures to expand extractive mining on Sámi lands, the Norwegian government has been accused of practising eco-colonialism, or as Maret Anne Sara put it in 2019, of acting as 'the invisible monster of new colonialism, with politics and laws allowing stately abuse upon lands, animals, culture and rights'.[19]

In contrast to Canada, where First Nations' rights to be consulted have developed as a result of domestic case law, any rights possessed by the Indigenous peoples in Finland, Norway, and Sweden to be consulted over land and resource use have been achieved primarily via international negotiations and agreements. Around 90% of Finnish Sámi land belongs to the government, and, like Sweden, Finland has not ratified the 1989 Indigenous and Tribal Peoples Convention of the International Labour Organization No. 169, which protects Indigenous land rights. Norway has ratified the convention, but has interpreted it in ways considered inappropriate to its spirit and that place limits upon Sámi influence. In 2005,

Sámi peoples did, however, obtain land and water rights under the Finnmark Act. Sámi parliaments were set up in Finland in 1973, Norway in 1989, and Sweden in 1993, being tasked with advising each respective national government.

While Canada can be described as forging new pathways in relation to Indigenous treatied space, it is important to recognise that the Government of Canada sees the agreements being struck with Indigenous peoples in the modern era as *sui generis* in terms of international law, that is, as not being international treaties in the same way as conventional treaties struck between other sovereign nations.[20] This is part of a centuries-long process of domestication of Indigenous nations' sovereign legal personalities in terms of their global context.

The government of New Zealand extends a similar sense of indigenous treaty-making being legally unique backwards into time and treats the 1840 Treaty of Waitangi, which was originally negotiated with the British Crown and which affirmed Māori rights over tribal fisheries and rights of self-determination, as enforceable only to the extent that the New Zealand parliament legislates it to be so. This remains the case, even though Indigenous peoples in New Zealand had the capacity to strike a treaty that was valid internationally under natural law in 1840. Today, claims related to the Treaty are investigated under the auspices of the Waitangi Tribunal set up in 1975, but profound and fundamental tensions and differences persist in relation to the meaning of the Treaty from aboriginal and non-aboriginal perspectives. Many maintain that there were two treaties, an English version and te Tiriti, the Māori version. The English translation of the agreement says that Māori leaders gave the Queen sovereignty over their land, a word with no direct translation in Māori. In contrast, the Māori text references 'kawanatanga' or 'governance', reflecting a Māori belief that they ceded to the Queen only a right of governance in return for protection, all the while retaining the Chiefs' right to authority over their own territories. Until te reo Māori attains status as a language within New Zealand law, this conflict will persist.[21]

The limitations of 'rights talk'

Modern treaties are evidence of how, across the globe, international efforts to retain or develop sustainable relationships on Indigenous homelands and/or to re-assert Indigenous nationhood are gaining pace. As this happens, prior examples of Indigenous-settler interrelationship and of indigenous forms of diplomacy take on new significance.

It is a shift spurred by dissatisfaction with the rights discourse generated in the wake of the 2007 United Nations Declaration on the Rights of Indigenous Peoples, as well as by complaints about what has been termed the *illusion of indigenous inclusion* within global forums such as the UN Permanent Forum on Indigenous Issues, established in 2000. For commentators such as Cherokee political scientist Jeff Corntassel, one of the central problems is that

> the framing of rights as political/legal entitlements has deemphasised the cultural responsibilities and relationships that indigenous peoples have with their

families and the natural world (homelands, plant life, animal life, etc.) that are critical for their well-being and the well-being of future generations.[22]

Paul McHugh echoed similar thinking in his magisterial 2016 discussion, *Aboriginal Title*, stating that 'the possession of legal rights has not made tribes worse off, but equally it is less clear whether it has significantly – or even marginally – improved their general lot'. He pointed out that in Australia, all the social indicators suggest that after 20 years of native title, aboriginal peoples are in fact generally in a worse position.[23]

Whether the rights agenda has improved the lot of Indigenous peoples in the United States has also been up for debate. The 2010 Census recorded that America's over 5.2 million American Indian or Alaska Natives experienced a poverty rate 136% larger than Whites. Commentators point out, however, that such a poverty rate is comparable to that of U.S. Black and Hispanic people.[24] Given this fact, and because levels of social inequality within developed nations continue to grow, increasing pressure is being placed on existing justifications for parsing Indigenous disadvantage separately from that of other numerical minorities. As a result, the assertion of Indigenous rights now regularly gets subsumed within what are perceived as wider, encompassing discussions of the world's biggest and most pressing problems, including climate change, poverty, food and water security, health, and nuclear and technological changes. Despite widespread international endorsement, it is worth noting that the UN Declaration on the Rights of Indigenous Peoples, like the Universal Declaration on Human Rights, is non-binding and unenforceable.

To many, recent efforts to bring about positive change within indigenous life have been too limited in scope. Resistance by settler-colonial nations such as the United States, Canada, New Zealand, and Australia to the idea of *collective* Indigenous rights in relation to the Declaration on the Rights of Indigenous Peoples is thought to have fundamentally limited what could be achieved, even though the United States acknowledged the existence of such rights in 2010. Overall, human rights discourse since 1989 has been applied in an increasingly individualistic way that denies Indigenous self-determination, supports the primacy of state sovereignty, and places limits upon cultural rights. Indigenous people have a right to culture, but Indigenous peoples as a collective do not. Just one of several examples is the case of the Maliseet Indian woman known as Sandra Lovelace, who complained against Canada because she lost her status as an Indian under Canada's Indian Act after marrying a non-Indian. The Human Rights Committee used Article 27 to find for Lovelace on the basis of her right as an individual to her culture. Article 46 (1) of the UNDRIP, however, makes clear that the right to culture 'does not prejudice the sovereignty and territorial integrity of a State party'.[25]

For prominent writers within critical whiteness literature, such as Goenpul scholar Aileen Moreton-Robinson, profound limits upon what could be achieved were in fact solidly in place from the outset. She has described how, even as the Declaration was formulated, settler nations labelled Indigenous groups as seeking to promote 'disharmony' while at the same time continued to busily signal their own virtue. 'With missionary zeal', she notes, 'these states have already determined what is best for "their" Indigenous peoples by defining what Indigenous rights are acceptable. In this way they stake a possessive claim to us.'[26] The high-profile impetus towards reconciliation and recognition within Anglophone countries has also been further critiqued as being epiphenomenal to wider issues held to be truly determinant. Dene political scientist Glen Coulthard argues that such issues are structural and linked fundamentally to land and underlying economic systems geared towards the accumulation of capital. The last 40 years, he points out, have seen Indigenous peoples participating in Canadian legal and political practices that have simply reproduced the very racist, sexist, economic, and political configurations of power that many of them engaged with the dominant state to challenge in the first place. Instead, he desires an indigenous future that transcends this and brings about 'a resurgent politics of recognition that seeks to practice decolonial, gender-emancipatory, and economically nonexploitative alternative structures of law and sovereign authority grounded on a critical refashioning of the best of Indigenous legal and political traditions'.[27] Such calls have been either welcomed as visionary and inspirational, or relegated and dismissed as utopian and destined to forever remain aspirational. However, the emphasis placed upon settler colonialism as a structurally embedded ongoing process remains intellectually reverberative.

Looking to the past to inform the future

In sum, this is an apposite moment for scholars across disciplines to help in the process of recontextualising treaty history. Modern treaty-making is pursuing its own contested course, particularly in Canada, but historic treaties and our collective understanding of the conditions of their making will remain vital to Indigenous-settler relationships in legal, cultural, and social terms in the future. Significant demographic change is also a factor helping to return American Indian treaties to centrality. Since the early 1970s, tribes across the United States have developed a growing capability to litigate. A Native American Indian legal and professional class is now poised to invoke treaty provisions and to advance Indian interests and rights internationally. A leading example in this regard today is the Fond du Lac Ojibwe scholar Maggie Blackhawk, who has made a recent prominent call for American constitutional law to be reconceived to include federal Indian law. Doing so would entail reformulation of the general principles of American public law, which rest upon judgements related to Jim Crow and segregation. It would shed a whole new light on how government power is best constituted, distributed, and limited and would foreground localism and the bestowal of powers rather than rights, via Congress and the executive, as an optimal means of ensuring minorities thrive.[28]

American Indian peoples have also continued to develop how they engage with the national political process. Record numbers ran for political office in 2018, over 80 Indian candidates at every level, and unprecedented numbers of these were female. Such candidates have a growing base who identify as Indigenous and who are on average significantly younger than the American population overall. Around 5.2 million Americans identified as American Indian or Alaska Native alone or in combination with other races in the 2010 census and about 32% of these are aged under 18, compared to 24% of the American population overall. A key political issue in Indian Country, as it is nationwide, is healthcare. Its provision is a clause within specific treaties and is enshrined federally, but Native Americans have a life expectancy 5.5 years less than the national average and the National Congress of American Indians is currently demanding a $36 billion increase in Indian Health Service funding.[29]

The importance of inter-generational or 'longue durée' thinking: American Indigenous voices on law and treaty reform

Modern Indigenous thinkers arguing forcefully that treaty reform holds the key to Indian resurgence has a long history. In 1972, cross-tribal protesters attempted to deliver to the Nixon administration a reassertion of treatied power and demands for treaty reform within a Twenty Point Position Paper. On several levels, the intellectual status across disciplines of American Indian treaties has yet to recover from this event and its ramifications. The Position Paper and its significance was soon accessibly contextualised by the best-selling author, Standing Rock Hunkpapa Lakota lawyer Vine Deloria Jr, in the collectively authored volume *Behind the Trail of Broken Treaties* (1974). The text stands as part of serious, sustained multi-volume effort by Deloria and various co-authors to reform and develop legal and treatied relationships between Indian communities and the federal government. Published as the Wounded Knee occupation came to an end, it attracted withering criticism. Yet though described as simplistic, illogical, confused, and as simply proposing the substitution of one federal court for another, the publication nevertheless imagined something that at that time seemed largely unimaginable – a future in which American Indian nations took their place as sovereign nations within international forums and enjoyed 'a status of quasi-international independence with the United States acting as their protector'. Controversially, the book pointed out that a number of Indian nations in 1974 had more land than other sovereign countries such as Israel, a UN member since 1949, and had populations comparable to other small countries.

Above all, *Behind the Trail of Broken Treaties* urged that the United States' 1871 prohibition against treaty-making with Indians be rescinded and that treaties once again become the agreed mechanism for the assertion of American Indian tribal rights. Although regularly accused of the opposite, the book displayed a firm sense of political pragmatism. It recognised, for example, that treaties were 'meant to be broken', were 'nothing more than a construct to describe the relationship of political entities', but yet could nonetheless again become a basis for the assertion of Indigenous sovereignty, a concept that in itself was recognised as 'not static or absolute'. Perhaps most significantly, the book was future-oriented and concerned itself with the potential for change across the longue durée, as was the case within a number of Deloria's other publications. Deloria's collection asked penetratingly unsettling questions of a non-Indigenous readership habituated to concentrating on immediate problems and to thinking in the short term. These included:

> Can one view the re-creation of the state of Israel after two thousand years of exile and seriously maintain that the Oglala Sioux will never again ride their beloved plains as rulers of everything they see? Or that the might of the Iroquois will not once again dominate the eastern forests?[30]

Underpinning these questions was a confident, extremely long-term, intergenerational, and in that sense, patient, commitment to the process of bringing about restitution and change.

Versions of *Behind the Trail of Broken Treaties*' key ideas have continued to resurface in a variety of contexts, with some of the most prominent Indigenous voices today being even more ambitious in relation to the scale of change they envision. They are bent upon on altering the existing international order both morally and structurally. For example, scholars such as Sheryl Lightfoot of the Anishinaabe nation spell out that implementing Indigenous rights 'will mean that patterns of exploitation, conquest, extraction, and inequality must give way to entirely different, more just, and sustainable forms of global political and economic relations'. All of this is to occur at the same time as the international world order negotiates 'new plural, over-lapping, and multiple types of sovereignties – state and indigenous – within and across state borders, including sovereignties that may or may not be tied to exclusive authority over territories'.[31] This is a Herculean aim, but not a priori an impossible one.

Ideas expressed since the mid-1990s by the non-Indigenous Canadian political philosopher James Tully have mapped potential pathways to achieving this aim, with Indigenous diplomacy and treaty-making at their core. Tully argues that an 'intercultural middle ground' can be arrived at based upon principles common to Europeans and Indigenous Americans, in doing so he echoes a concept of beneficent if asymmetrical communion beloved of liberal thinkers across disciplines within his generation.[32] His 1995 book, *Strange Multiplicity*, argued for non-uniform and mutable overlapping sorts of constitutional association between Indigenous and settler polities, whereby the idea of a political constitution is reconceived as 'an activity, an intercultural dialogue in which the culturally diverse citizens of contemporary societies negotiate agreements on their ways of association over time in accordance with the three conventions of mutual recognition, consent and cultural continuity'. Tully argues that the shared norms inherent in the successful diplomacy and treaties struck between the British and indigenous North Americans and later between the British and the French in Canada after the British gained control of New France provide an invaluable template for just such a pluralistic vision for the future. At the root of Tully's vision is an insight drawn from Wittgenstein in *Philosophical Investigations* about the situational nature of knowledge and communication – in essence, an awareness that the general terms used within any political interaction cannot be fully understood outside of the norms of their cultural context. As Tully points out, to understand a general term, and so know your way around its maze of uses, it is always necessary to enter into dialogue with further descriptions and come to recognise the aspects of the phenomenon in question that they bring to light, aspects which go unnoticed from one's own familiar set of examples.[33]

John Borrows, a Chippewa of the Nawash First Nation of Southern Ontario and Canada Research Chair in Indigenous Law at the University of Victoria, has been at the forefront of recent efforts to apply aspects of such an awareness to contemporary legal and treaty contexts in Canada. Borrows emphasises a constitutional narrative that centralises the spirit of the Royal Proclamation of 1763 and the Treaty of Niagara of 1764, political crossroads at the creation of Canada as a nation state, when Indigenous sovereignty was respected. To a significant number of Indigenous peoples and others, especially in Canada's prairies, the treaties struck with the Crown at this time were sacred covenants, agreed via mutual respect. This, it is argued, is the consensual tradition that now needs to be restored, or to use an indigenous diplomatic metaphor, 'brightened' or 'polished'. Such a 'brightening' would dispense with the originalism that has characterised many Supreme Court dealings with Indigenous peoples in Canada to date and required that they demonstrate forms of cultural and intellectual life that are frozen in time. In its place, Borrows recommends that any notion of a single, essential Indigenous identity is dispensed with in legal, social, and political terms and is replaced by greater understanding of inherent indigenous diversity.[34] Analysis of treaties, including those struck between the British and Indigenous groups from 1763 to 1768 in what is now the United States, provides clear evidence of such diversity. Any nuanced comprehension of indigenous diplomacy and legal tradition in relation to foundational treaties such as Niagara, however, will also involve engaging with indigenous metaphor, with spheres of understanding within which humans are not the only parties capable of reasoned political engagement and into the specifics of place-based oral cultures with discrete approaches to gender, kinship, ritual, and material texts such as wampum. This process, whereby the non-Indigenous world begins to comprehend the spiritual, moral, tactical, and technical contours of Indigenous law, is only just the beginning.[35]

Concluding thoughts: the stone in the midst of all

Treaties today stand at a point of constitutional inflection within post-colonial societies, or societies attempting to become so. Yet without change at international and domestic levels, Indigenous peoples will remain with the set of sub-optimal choices James Tully set out:

> They can accept the authoritative language and institutions, in which case their claims are rejected by conservatives, or comprehended by progressives within the very language and institutions whose sovereignty and impartiality they question. Or they can refuse to play the game, in which case they become marginal and reluctant conscripts, or they take up arms.[36]

Figure 11.1 William Penn's Treaty with the Indians, 1775

As discussed in the introduction to this chapter, for Lawrence Wroth, writing in 1928, indigenous Americans were the corn between the millstones of great European powers, inevitably to be ground down and perhaps blown away by the wind. This has not happened. To the contrary, Indigenous peoples are working to exercise interpretative sovereignty in relation to both key treaties of the past and the treaties of today. Perhaps, then, a better metaphor is to think of Indigenous treaties as the 'stone in the midst of all', centred in the living stream of history, evidence of intercultural relationship that makes it impossible to forget the actions of ancestors past (Figure 11.1).[37]

Acknowledgements

The author extends her thanks and appreciation to the Anishinaabe scholar Dale Turner (University of Toronto, Scarborough) for his conviviality and the sharing of his wisdom on treaty history and its modern significance. The research within this chapter benefitted from support from The British Academy, the Leverhulme Trust and the UKRI SRG: AH/T006099/1.

Notes

1 Lawrence C. Wroth, 'The Indian Treaty as Literature,' *Yale Review* 17 (1928): 327–766.
2 Taiaiake, Alfred, *Wasáse: Indigenous Pathways of Action and Freedom* (Toronto, ON: University of Toronto Press, 2005), 598; Chris Andersen, 'Critical Indigenous Studies:

From Difference to Density,' *Cultural Studies Review* 15, no. 2 (2011): 80–100; Robin Kelley, 'On the Density of Black Being,' in *Scratch*, ed. Christine Kim (New York: Studio Museum of Harlem, 2005), 10.

3 Wider study of Lorde's oeuvre suggests that her ideas and those of Simpson are in a number of ways in violent agreement. See Alexis De Veaux, *Warrior Poet: A Biography of Audre Lorde* (New York: Norton, 2006); Stella Bolaki and Sabine Broeck, *Audre Lorde's Transnational Legacies* (Amherst: University of Massachusetts Press, 2015); Leanne Betasamosake Simpson, *Dancing On Our Turtle's Back: Stories of Nishnaabeg Re-Creation, Resurgence, and a New Emergence* (Winnipeg: Arbeiter Ring, 2011), 93.

4 Dale Turner, *This Is Not a Peace Pipe: Towards a Critical Indigenous Philosophy* (Toronto, ON: University of Toronto Press, 2006); Grand Council Resolution 2012–21, *Anishinaabe Chi-Naaknigewin Anishinabek Nation Constitution*, 2012, amended 1 May 2018, accessed 27 January 2020, http://www.anishinabek.ca/wp-content/uploads/2019/03/Anishinaabe-Chi-Naaknigewin-Amended-May-1st-2018-FINAL.pdf.

5 Arthur Spirling, 'U.S. Treaty Making with American Indians: Institutional Change and Relative Power, 1784–1911,' *American Journal of Political Science* 56, no.1 (January 2012): 84–97; Frances Paul Prucha, *American Indian Treaties: The History of a Political Anomaly* (Berkeley and Los Angeles: University of California Press,1994); Vine Deloria Jr and Raymond J. DeMallie, *Documents of American Indian Diplomacy: Treaties, Agreements, and Conventions, 1775–1979* (Norman: University of Oklahoma Press, 1999); David E. Wilkins, *American Indian Politics and the American Political System*, 2nd ed. (Lanham, MD: Rowman and Littlefield Publishers, 2007). On the transnational history of treaty-making, see M.F. Lindley, *The Acquisition and Government of Backward Territory in International Law: Being a Treatise on the Law and Practice Relating to Colonial Expansion* (London: Longman, Green, 1926); Saliha Belmessous's exemplary edited collection *Empire By Treaty: Negotiating European Expansion, 1600–1900* (New York: Oxford University Press, 2015); Stuart Banner, *Possessing the Pacific: Land, Settlers and Indigenous People from Australia to Alaska* (Cambridge, MA: Harvard University Press, 2007). On North America, see Alexandra Harmon, ed., *The Power of Promises: Rethinking Indian Treaties in the Pacific Northwest* (Seattle: University of Washington Press, 2008); Robert A. Williams, *Linking Arms Together: American Indian Treaty Visions of Law and Peace, 1600–1800* (New York: Oxford University Press, 1997); Stuart Banner, *How the Indians Lost Their Land: Land, and Power on the Frontier* (Cambridge, MA: Harvard University Press, 2007); William Campbell, *Speculators in Empire: Iroquoia and the 1768 Treaty of Fort Stanwix* (Norman: University of Oklahoma Press, 2012); Cynthia J. Van Zandt, *Brothers Among Nations: The Pursuit of Intercultural Alliances in Early America 1580–1660* (New York: Oxford University Press, 2008); Tom Arne Midtrød, *The Memory of All Ancient Customs: Native American Diplomacy in the Colonial Hudson Valley* (Ithaca: Cornell University Press, 2012); Dorothy V. Jones, *License for Empire: Colonialism by Treaty in Early America* (Chicago, IL: University of Chicago Press, 1983); Colin Calloway, *Pen & Ink Witchcraft: Treaties and Treaty Making in American Indian History* (New York: Oxford University Press, 2013).

6 See John Rawls, 'The Idea of an Overlapping Consensus,' *Oxford Journal of Legal Studies* 7, no.1 (Spring 1987): 1–25.

7 For more, see Dorothy V. Jones, *Toward a Just World: The Critical Years in the Search for International Justice* (Chicago, IL: The University of Chicago Press, 2002).

8 A landmark case in the Canadian context in this regard was *Simon v. The Queen* in 1985. The court ruled in favour of the appellant – a 'resident Micmac Indian' prosecuted for having a rifle and cartridges so as to hunt – citing the Treaty of 1752, but also stipulated that 'the principles of international treaty law were not determinative … because an Indian treaty is unique and sui generis'. *Simon v. The Queen*, 2 S.C.R. 387 (1985).

9 P.G. McHugh, *Aboriginal Societies and the Common Law: A History of Sovereignty, Status and Self-Determination* (Oxford: Oxford University Press, 2004); Charles F. Wilkinson,

American Indians, Time and the Law (New Haven, CT and London: Yale University Press, 1987), 14, 53–54.
10 See Rosebud Sioux Tribe & Fort Belknap Indian Community v. Donald J. Trump, case 4:18-cv-00118-BMM, filed 23 April 19 in the United States District Court for the District of Montana Great Falls Division.
11 'Treaty Alliance Against Tar Sands Expansion,' December 2016, accessed 27 January 2020, http://www.treatyalliance.org/wp-content/uploads/2016/12/TreatyandAdditionalInformation-20161216-OL.pdf.
12 The numbers of indigenous nations signing up to the pipeline are being monitored by the Tracking Trans Mountain database. See '#TrackingTransMountain' on Twitter, accessed 27 January 2019, https://twitter.com/hashtag/trackingtransmountain.
13 Chief Nathan Matthew in Simon Little, '"We've Made Our Decision": B.C. First Nation Speaks Up for Trans Mountain Pipeline,' *Global News*, 24 April 2019, accessed 27 January 2020, https://globalnews.ca/news/4165979/first-nation-support-transmountain-pipeline/.
14 Refer, for example, to the Inuvialuit Treaty, 1984; the Nunavut Land Claims Agreement, 1993; the Final Agreements arrived at with the Canadian government from 1993 to 2005 with the 11 First Nations of the Yukon; the 2003 Tlicho Land Claims and Self Government Agreement and the 2014 Supreme Court of Canada granting of title to the Tsilhqot'in over 1,700 sq km in British Columbia.
15 See Kim Baird, Clint Davis and Jason Madden, 'Modern Day Treaties Fundamentally Reshaping Canada for the Better,' *CBC News*, 13 February 2016, accessed 27 January 2020, https://www.cbc.ca/news/indigenous/modern-day-treaties-reshaping-canada-1.3440267.
16 The British Columbia Treaty Commission, *Socio-economic Benefits of Modern Treaties in BC*, Deloitte Touche Tohmatsu Ltd, October 2016, accessed 27 January 2020, http://www.bctreaty.ca/sites/default/files/Deloitte-BCTC-FinalReport.pdf 18.
17 An example is the landmark Supreme Court of Canada *William* decision of 2014, recognising the title of 1,750 sq km of Tsilhqot'in land in central B.C. *Tsilhqot'in Nation v. British Columbia*, S.C.C. 44 (2014).
18 See Veli-Pekka Lehtola, 'Sámi Histories, Colonialism, and Finland,' *Artic Anthropology* 52, no.2 (2015): 22–36.
19 Instagram post @maretannesara, October 2019.
20 See Government of Canada, Expert Seminar on Treaties, Agreements and Other Constructive Arrangements between States and Indigenous Peoples, Organized by the Office of the United Nations High Commissioner for Human Rights, *Perspectives on Treaties, Agreements and Other Constructive Arrangements between States and Indigenous Peoples*, UN Document: Geneva, 15–17 December 2003, 14, accessed 27 January 2020, HR/GENEVA/TSIP/SEM/2003/BP.17, 14
21 See Alan Ward, 'Interpreting the Treaty of Waitangi: The Maori Resurgence and Race Relations in New Zealand,' *The Contemporary Pacific* 3, no. 1 (Spring 1991): 85–113.
22 Jeff Corntassel, 'Toward Sustainable Self-Determination: Rethinking the Contemporary Indigenous-Rights Discourse,' *Alternatives* 33, no.1 (2008): 107.
23 See P. G. McHugh, *Aboriginal Title: The Modern Jurisprudence of Tribal Land Rights* (Oxford: Oxford University Press, 2011), x.
24 See Jens Manuel Krogstad, 'One-in-four Native Americans and Alaska Natives are Living in Poverty,' *Pew Research Center*, 13 June 2014, accessed 27 January 2020, https://www.pewresearch.org/fact-tank/2014/06/13/1-in-4-native-americans-and-alaska-natives-are-living-in-poverty/.
25 Sandra Lovelace v. Canada, Communication No. 24/1977, Views of the Human Rights Committee adopted on 30 July 1980, UN Doc. No. CCPR/C/13/D/24/1977, at para. 15; UN Human Rights Committee, CCPR General Comment No. 23: The Rights of Minorities (Art. 27), at para. 3.2, UN doc. CCPR/C/21/Rev.1/Add.5. 1994. See

Karen Engle, 'On Fragile Architecture: The UN Declaration on the Rights of Indigenous Peoples in the Context of Human Rights,' *European Journal of International Law* 22, no.1 (2011): 141–163.

26 Aileen Moreton-Robinson, *The White Possessive: Property, Power and Indigenous Sovereignty* (Minneapolis: University of Minnesota Press, 2015), 184.
27 Glen Sean Coulthard, *Red Skin, White Masks: Rejecting the Colonial Politics of Recognition* (Minneapolis: University of Minnesota Press, 2014), 179.
28 Maggie Blackhawk, 'Federal Indian Law as Paradigm within Public Law,' *Harvard Law Review* 132, no.7 (May 2019): 1787–1876.
29 'Demographics,' National Congress of the American Indian, accessed 19 May 2019, http://www.ncai.org/about-tribes/demographics.
30 Vine Deloria Jr, *Behind the Trail of Broken Treaties*, 2nd ed. (Austin: University of Texas Press, 1985), 161, 262, 108, 83, 110. For a strongly negative review, see Robert A. Fairbanks, 'Review of *Behind the Trail of Broken Treaties* by Vine Deloria Jr,' *American Indian Law Review* 2, no. 2 (Winter 1974): 169–172. Deloria's other contributions on the reform of treaties include: Deloria, ed., *Of Utmost Good Faith* (San Francisco, CA: Straight Arrow Books, 1971); Deloria and Raymond J. DeMallie, *Proceedings of the Great Peace Commission of 1867–1868* (Washington, DC: Institute for the Development of Indian Law, 1975); Deloria and Clifford M. Lytle, *American Indians, American Justice* (Austin: University of Texas Press, 1983); Deloria, *The Nations Within: The Past and Future of American Indian Sovereignty* (Austin: University of Texas Press, 1984); Deloria and DeMallie, *Documents of American Indian Diplomacy*; Deloria and David E. Wilkins, *Tribes, Treaties and Constitutional Tribulations* (Austin: University of Texas Press, 1999).
31 The idea that the larger Native American Indian Nations should have a seat at the United Nations, with smaller nations being represented there via confederacies reappeared in Anthony Bothwell, 'We Live on Their Land: Implications of Long-Ago Takings of Native American Indian Property,' *Annual Survey of International and Comparative Law* 6, no.1, article 9 (2000): 175–209; Sheryl Lightfoot, *Global Indigenous Politics: A Subtle Revolution* (New York: Routledge, 2016), 206.
32 Perhaps the best-known example in this regard within Native American Indian Studies is Richard White's *The Middle Ground: Indians, Empires, and Republics in the Great Lakes Region, 1650–1815* (Cambridge: Cambridge University Press, 1991). For a more extensive critique of the attractions of 'middleness' as an idea, see the chapter 'On Middle Way Thinking' in Joy Porter, *Native American Environmentalism: Land, Spirit and the Idea of Wilderness* (Lincoln: University of Nebraska Press 2014), 21–39.
33 James Tully, *Strange Multiplicity: Constitutionalism in an Age of Diversity*, The John Robert Seeley Lectures, 1994 (Cambridge: Cambridge University Press, 1995), 184, 110. See also Tully, *Public Philosophy in a New Key*, vols. 1 & 2 (Cambridge: Cambridge University Press, 2008); Tully, 'Aboriginal Property and Western Theory: Recovering a Middle Ground,' in *Property Rights and Eminent Domain*, eds. Ellen Frankel Paul et al. (Cambridge: Cambridge University Press, 1994), 153–80; Tully, 'Consent, Hegemony, and Dissent in Treaty Negotiations,' in *Between Consenting Peoples*, eds. Jeremy Webber and Colin M. Macleod (Vancouver: UBC Press, 2010), 233–256.
34 See John Borrows, *Freedom and Indigenous Constitutionalism* (Toronto, ON: University of Toronto Press, 2016), 103–105, and Borrows and Michael Coyle, eds. *The Right Relationship: Reimagining the Implementation of Historical Treaties* (Toronto, ON: University of Toronto Press, 2016).
35 See, for example, Brian P. Owensby and Richard J. Ross, *Justice in a New World: Negotiating Legal Intelligibility in British, Iberian and Indigenous America* (New York: New York University Press, 2018).
36 Tully, *Strange Multiplicity: Constitutionalism in an Age of Diversity*, 56.
37 The phrase is inspired by W.B. Yeats' poem 'Easter, 1916,' in *Michael Robartes and the Dancer* (Dublin: The Cuala Press, 1920).

Bibliography

Alfred, Taiaiake. *Wasáse: Indigenous Pathways of Action and Freedom*. Toronto, ON: University of Toronto Press, 2005.
Andersen, Chris. 'Critical Indigenous Studies: From Difference to Density.' *Cultural Studies Review* 15, no. 2 (2011): 80–100.
Baird, Kim, Clint Davis, and Jason Madden. 'Modern Day Treaties Fundamentally Reshaping Canada for the Better.' *CBC News*, 13 February 2016. https://www.cbc.ca/news/indigenous/modern-day-treaties-reshaping-canada-1.3440267.
Banner, Stuart. *How the Indians Lost Their Land: Land, and Power on the Frontier*. Cambridge, MA: Harvard University Press, 2007.
Banner, Stuart. *Possessing the Pacific: Land, Settlers and Indigenous People from Australia to Alaska*. Cambridge, MA: Harvard University Press, 2007.
Belmessous, Saliha. *Empire By Treaty: Negotiating European Expansion, 1600–1900*. New York: Oxford University Press, 2015.
Blackhawk, Maggie. 'Federal Indian Law as Paradigm Within Public Law.' *Harvard Law Review* 132, no.7 (May 2019): 1787–1876.
Bolaki, Stella and Sabine Broeck. *Audre Lorde's Transnational Legacies*. Amherst: University of Massachusetts Press, 2015.
Borrows, John. *Freedom and Indigenous Constitutionalism*. Toronto, ON: University of Toronto Press, 2016.
Borrows, John, and Michael Coyle, eds. *The Right Relationship: Reimagining the Implementation of Historical Treaties*. Toronto, ON: University of Toronto Press, 2016.
Bothwell, Anthony. 'We Live on Their Land: Implications of Long-Ago Takings of Native American Indian Property.' *Annual Survey of International and Comparative Law* 6, no. 1, article 9 (2000): 175–209.
British Columbia Treaty Commission, The. *Socio-economic Benefits of Modern Treaties in BC*. Deloitte Touche Tohmatsu Ltd, October 2016. http://www.bctreaty.ca/sites/default/files/Deloitte-BCTC-FinalReport.pdf
Calloway, Colin. *Pen & Ink Witchcraft: Treaties and Treaty Making in American Indian History*. New York: Oxford University Press, 2013.
Campbell, William. *Speculators in Empire: Iroquoia and the 1768 Treaty of Fort Stanwix*. Norman: University of Oklahoma Press, 2012.
Corntassel, Jeff. 'Toward Sustainable Self-Determination: Rethinking the Contemporary Indigenous-Rights Discourse.' *Alternatives* 33, no. 1 (2008): 107.
Coulthard, Glen Sean. *Red Skin, White Masks: Rejecting the Colonial Politics of Recognition*. Minneapolis: University of Minnesota Press, 2014.
De Veaux, Alexis. *Warrior Poet: A Biography of Audre Lorde*. New York: Norton, 2006.
Deloria, Vine, Jr, ed. *Of Utmost Good Faith*. San Francisco, CA: Straight Arrow Books, 1971.
Deloria, Vine, Jr. *The Nations Within: The Past and Future of American Indian Sovereignty*. Austin: University of Texas Press, 1984.
Deloria, Vine, Jr. *Behind the Trail of Broken Treaties*. 2nd ed. Austin: University of Texas Press, 1985.
Deloria, Vine, Jr, and Raymond J. DeMallie. *Proceedings of the Great Peace Commission of 1867–1868*. Washington: Institute for the Development of Indian Law, 1975.
Deloria, Vine, Jr, and Raymond J. DeMallie. *Documents of American Indian Diplomacy: Treaties, Agreements, and Conventions, 1775–1979*. Norman: University of Oklahoma Press, 1999.
Deloria, Vine, Jr, and Clifford M. Lytle. *American Indians, American Justice*. Austin: University of Texas Press, 1983.
Deloria, Vine, Jr, and David E. Wilkins. *Tribes, Treaties and Constitutional Tribulations*. Austin: University of Texas Press, 1999.
'Demographics.' National Congress of the American Indian. Accessed 19 May 2019. http://www.ncai.org/about-tribes/demographics.

Engle, Karen. 'On Fragile Architecture: The UN Declaration on the Rights of Indigenous Peoples in the Context of Human Rights.' *European Journal of International Law* 22, no.1 (2011): 141–163.

Fairbanks, Robert A. 'Review of *Behind the Trail of Broken Treaties* by Vine Deloria, Jr.' *American Indian Law Review* 2, no. 2 (Winter 1974): 169–172.

Grand Council Resolution 2012–21. *Anishinaabe Chi-Naaknigewin Anishinabek Nation Constitution.* 2012, amended 1 May 2018. http://www.anishinabek.ca/wp-content/uploads/2019/03/Anishinaabe-Chi-Naaknigewin-Amended-May-1st-2018-FINAL.pdf.

Harmon, Alexandra, ed. *The Power of Promises: Rethinking Indian Treaties in the Pacific Northwest.* Seattle: University of Washington Press, 2008.

Jones, Dorothy V. *License for Empire: Colonialism by Treaty in Early America.* Chicago, IL: University of Chicago Press, 1983.

Jones, Dorothy V. *Toward a Just World: The Critical Years in the Search for International Justice.* Chicago, IL: The University of Chicago Press, 2002.

Kelley, Robin. 'On the Density of Black Being.' In *Scratch*, edited by Christine Kim, 9–10. New York: Studio Museum of Harlem, 2005.

Krogstad, Jens Manuel. 'One-in-four Native Americans and Alaska Natives are Living in Poverty.' *Pew Research Center*, 13 June 2014. https://www.pewresearch.org/fact-tank/2014/06/13/1-in-4-native-americans-and-alaska-natives-are-living-in-poverty/.

Lehtola, Veli-Pekka. 'Sámi Histories, Colonialism, and Finland.' *Artic Anthropology* 52, no. 2 (2015): 22–36.

Lightfoot, Sheryl. *Global Indigenous Politics: A Subtle Revolution.* New York: Routledge, 2016.

Lindley, M.F. *The Acquisition and Government of Backward Territory in International Law: Being a Treatise on the Law and Practice Relating to Colonial Expansion.* London: Longman, Green, 1926.

Little, Simon. '"We've Made Our Decision": B.C. First Nation Speaks Up for Trans Mountain Pipeline.' *Global News*, 24 April 2019. https://globalnews.ca/news/4165979/first-nation-support-trans-mountain-pipeline/.

McHugh, P.G. *Aboriginal Societies and the Common Law: A History of Sovereignty, Status and Self-Determination.* Oxford: Oxford University Press, 2004.

McHugh, P.G. *Aboriginal Title: The Modern Jurisprudence of Tribal Land Rights.* Oxford: Oxford University Press, 2011.

Midtrød, Tom Arne. *The Memory of All Ancient Customs: Native American Diplomacy in the Colonial Hudson Valley.* Ithaca: Cornell University Press, 2012.

Moreton-Robinson, Aileen. *The White Possessive: Property, Power and Indigenous Sovereignty.* Minneapolis: University of Minnesota Press, 2015.

Owensby, Brian P and Richard J. Ross. *Justice in a New World: Negotiating Legal Intelligibility in British, Iberian and Indigenous America.* New York: New York University Press, 2018.

Porter, Joy. *Native American Environmentalism: Land, Spirit and the Idea of Wilderness.* Lincoln: University of Nebraska Press, 2014.

Prucha, Frances Paul. *American Indian Treaties: The History of a Political Anomaly.* Berkeley and Los Angeles: University of California Press, 1994.

Rawls, John. 'The Idea of an Overlapping Consensus.' *Oxford Journal of Legal Studies* 7, no.1 (Spring 1987): 1–25.

Simpson, Leanne Betasamosake. *Dancing On Our Turtle's Back: Stories of Nishnaabeg Re-Creation, Resurgence, and a New Emergence.* Winnipeg: Arbeiter Ring, 2011.

Spirling, Arthur. 'U.S. Treaty Making with American Indians: Institutional Change and Relative Power, 1784–1911.' *American Journal of Political Science* 56, no.1 (January 2012): 84–97.

Tully, James. 'Aboriginal Property and Western Theory: Recovering a Middle Ground.' In *Property Rights and Eminent Domain*, edited by Ellen Frankel Paul et al., 153–180. Cambridge: Cambridge University Press, 1994.

Tully, James. *Strange Multiplicity: Constitutionalism in an Age of Diversity.* The John Robert Seeley Lectures, 1994. Cambridge: Cambridge University Press, 1995.

Tully, James. *Public Philosophy in a New Key*. Volumes 1 & 2. Cambridge: Cambridge University Press, 2008.
Tully, James. 'Consent, Hegemony, and Dissent in Treaty Negotiations.' In *Between Consenting Peoples*, edited by Jeremy Webber and Colin M. Macleod, 233–256. Vancouver: UBC Press, 2010.
Turner, Dale. *This Is Not a Peace Pipe: Towards a Critical Indigenous Philosophy*. Toronto, ON: University of Toronto Press, 2006.
'Treaty Alliance Against Tar Sands Expansion.' December 2016. http://www.treatyalliance.org/wp-content/uploads/2016/12/TreatyandAdditionalInformation-20161216-OL.pdf.
Van Zandt, Cynthia J. *Brothers Among Nations: The Pursuit of Intercultural Alliances in Early America 1580–1660*. New York: Oxford University Press, 2008.
Ward, Alan. 'Interpreting the Treaty of Waitangi: The Maori Resurgence and Race Relations in New Zealand.' *The Contemporary Pacific* 3, no. 1 (Spring 1991): 85–113.
White, Richard. *The Middle Ground: Indians, Empires, and Republics in the Great Lakes Region, 1650–1815*. Cambridge: Cambridge University Press, 1991.
Wilkins, David E. *American Indian Politics and the American Political System*. 2nd ed. Lanham, MD: Rowman and Littlefield Publishers, 2007.
Wilkinson, Charles F. *American Indians, Time and the Law*. New Haven, CT and London: Yale University Press, 1987.
Williams, Robert A. *Linking Arms Together: American Indian Treaty Visions of Law and Peace, 1600–1800*. New York: Oxford University Press, 1997.
Wroth, Lawrence C. 'The Indian Treaty as Literature.' *Yale Review* 17 (1928): 327–766.
Yeats, W.B. 'Easter, 1916.' In *Michael Robartes and the Dancer*. Dublin: The Cuala Press, 1920.

12
SÁMI INDIGENEITY IN NINETEENTH-CENTURY SWEDISH AND BRITISH INTELLECTUAL DEBATES

Linda Andersson Burnett

ALEXANDRA PALACE. Arrival of a large and representative GROUP OF LAPPS (from Finmarken, Norway), one of the few surviving Aboriginal Races in Europe, a branch of the wide-spread Finno-Tataric family. The Lapps bring with them their Reindeer, Dogs, Tents, and Sledges, and thus give for the first time in England a true picture of a Lapp Encampment, as they live in their Artic homes.[1]

On 19 April 1885, the British newspaper *The Globe* announced to its readers that a 'large and representative group' of Sámi people had arrived at the popular entertainment venue Alexandra Palace in Muswell Hill, London. Amid a plethora of restaurants, minstrel shows, a boating lake, a monkey house, orchestras, an Indian pavilion, and horse races, the public could – according to the newspaper – study and encounter 'one of the few surviving Aboriginal races in Europe'.[2] The people held up to represent Europe's Aboriginal race was a troupe consisting of seven Sámi from Karasjok in Norwegian Finnmark: Ole Nilsen Ravna, Amund Johansen Anti, Elen Johansen Lindi, Johannes Larsen Anti, Anders Amundsen Anti, Johannes Amundsen Anti, and Anne Johannesdatter Guttorm.[3] Human exhibitions such as this one grew in popularity in the nineteenth century, with large numbers of customers paying to see the performances of foreign peoples such as Zulus, Australian Aborigines, San, Inuit, and the Indigenous Sámi of Scandinavia and Russia. This was a lucrative market – or to use Roslyn Poignant's term, an 'economy of exploitation' – in which considerable profits could be made from transporting human beings who were often members of Indigenous and colonised peoples to the Victorian metropolis.[4] At various venues, British audiences could view these 'exotic' specimens of humanity in comfort. The shows were marketed both as entertainment and as educational and scientific opportunities for studying human variety.[5] The Physician John Connelly noted in 1855, to the Ethnological

Society of London, that 'scarcely a year [passed] in which, among the miscellaneous attractions of a London season' one could not observe 'some exhibition illustrative of the varieties of mankind'.[6] These exhibitions remained popular until the end of the nineteenth century, with British university anthropologists such as A.H. Keane and W.L.H. Duckworth visiting them.[7]

Human exhibitions utilised and traded on racial narratives and stereotypes, thereby providing a powerful lens through which to study the debates and discussions taking place on human variety at that time. By examining the archival materials associated with the Sámi exhibition of 1885 in London, including newspaper articles, adverts, archaeological, and anthropological reports, this chapter will examine how Sámi featured alongside other Indigenous and colonised peoples in nineteenth-century British and Scandinavian debates on indigeneity, prehistory, and colonisation. By focusing on the Swedish polymath Sven Nilsson and his social and intellectual network, it will pay close attention to the co-production of the loaded concepts of 'Aborigines' and 'prehistory' by British and Scandinavian commentators in this period. European travelling natural historians, anthropologists, archaeologists, anatomists, and large numbers of the exhibition-going public imagined Indigenous peoples as static subjects trapped in the past and who were doomed to become extinct.[8] Prehistory and Aboriginality became the conceptual means by which they did so. These were potent concepts applied to both justify and underpin colonisation of Indigenous peoples within Scandinavia and in the British colonies.

The Scandinavian countries are often imagined, internally and externally, as not having 'colonial histories'. Yet, they possessed overseas colonies and slave forts in North America, India, Africa, and the Caribbean and had ongoing colonial relations with Greenland and Sápmi within the Nordic region.[9] Scandinavian travellers, missionaries, and scientists moreover 'hitch-hiked', to use a term applied to Nordic colonial actors, on other countries' colonies. In so doing, they contributed to intellectual discourses that depicted and classified Indigenous and colonised peoples as inferior[10] – narratives that carried great material force.

The Scandinavian states did not colonise the Sámi with soldiers but with words – written laws functioned alongside intellectual discourses on prehistory and Aboriginality to depict the Sámi as primitive, unable to manage their own land and natural resources, and unequipped for education. These narratives were shaped partly by national agendas and discourses, but they were also co-produced transnationally between Swedish and other European writers. Archaeologists, anthropologists, exhibition managers, and anatomists were important actors in this web of colonial exchange.

Prehistoric colonialism

Scandinavian authors were at the forefront of developing the three-stage chronological development model in which societies progressed through the Stone, Bronze, and Iron Ages. Christian Jürgensen Thomsen, curator at the newly founded National Museum of Denmark in the 1820s, organised objects according to the material of the artefacts. Other Scandinavian scholars interested in these issues were J.J.A. Worsaae, Oscar Montelius, Bror Emil Hildebrand, and Sven Nilsson (whose writing on the Sámi was widely circulated in Britain as this chapter will illustrate); they were followed by Paul Tournal in France, Sir Daniel Wilson in Scotland, and Sir John Lubbock in England.[11] Following an age of the classification of plants and animals (including humans), artefacts were now also to be classified. This new sequence was applied to determine the age of artefacts that were dug out from the ground. Those that were deepest in the soil were believed to belong to the most distant past, the Stone Age, and those closest to the top were from the Iron Age, the latter being regarded as the final and ultimate epoch.

Sven Nilsson, professor of Zoology at Lund University, added to Thomson's system a chronology in which mankind progressed through four economic stages.[12] These stages were hunting and fishing, pastoral, agricultural, and, finally, commercial. They were identical to those used in Scottish stadial theory developed in the 1760s by intellectuals such as Adam Smith, William Robertson, Lord Kames, and Adam Ferguson. Charting humanity's development from savagery to civilisation, Scottish philosophers had argued in the eighteenth century that contemporary 'savages' provided, to quote Ferguson, a 'mirrour' on the past.[13] Nilsson likewise adhered to and developed this comparative ethnography. He regarded the Stone Age to be the equivalent to the 'savage state' and argued that stone artefacts that contemporary 'primitive' people produced were compatible with stone artefacts used in prehistory during the Stone Age.[14] Unlike written sources, which were believed to require a certain advanced degree of civilisation before they could be composed, archaeology was presented as providing a long lens to the deep history of mankind. While the study of fossils had provided scholars of natural history with a longer view of the history of animals, archaeology and the study of contemporary primitive artefacts were believed to provide the same telescope to the remote human past.[15]

In *Skandinavisk Fauna* in 1835, Nilsson had discussed prehistoric hunters and fishers (*Utkast till jagtens och fiskets historia*) and he extended this work in his four-part *Skandinaviska Nordens Urinvånare* between 1838 and 1843. He was one of the first scientists in Europe to articulate and develop the concept of prehistory (Swedish term, *förhistorisk*), as research by Peter Rowley-Conwy has demonstrated.[16] Although Christian Molbech in Denmark (*forhistorisk*) and Paul Tournal in France (*anté-historique*) had used equivalent terms a few years earlier, Nilsson and the physiologist Daniel Eschricht (in 1837) were the first to apply the concept in its modern meaning in their publications.[17] In the foreword to the 1838 edition of *Skandinaviska Nordens Urinvånare*, Nilsson wrote:

> By the original inhabitants of Scandinavia I mean not just the first people who immigrated or were originally present in the country, but all those who lived here throughout the time that went before history; I thus mean the prehistoric people of Scandinavia, of one or several tribes.[18]

He also discussed the term in a number of articles published in the 1840s.[19]

Nilsson subscribed to the progressive notion in stadial theory by noting that objects were 'fragments of a progressive series of civilisation' and 'that the human race has always been, and still is, steadily advancing in civilisation'.[20] Progress was, he argued, inevitable for humanity:

Nations spring into existence, and in their turn, decline and fall, but civilisation and humanity are steadily progressing ... (the) human race, notwithstanding apparent or partial retrogression, constantly undergoing a gradual and progressive development. Of this even history convinces us, by showing that nations originally rude and barbarous have by degrees progressed to a higher civilisation and more *true* humanity.[21]

People labelled as savages were, in Nilsson's view, less human or not fully human. He was part of a growing number of European intellectuals who produced works that dehumanised Indigenous and colonised peoples. These intellectuals used Indigenous people to illustrate European ontologies, rendering such people as static objects who provided insights into the emergence of 'developed' European societies such as Sweden or Britain. They conflated, as historian Dipesh Chakrabarty has argued, European development with universal development.[22]

The pertinent question of whether all people were capable of progress had existed already in some eighteenth-century stadial writing.[23] For example, William Robertson, in his *History of America* (1777), portrayed Native Americans as ignoble savages who were almost chained to their base existence.[24] Lord Kames, likewise, dwelt on the alleged stagnation of the Sámi people, arguing that the Sámi could not progress because of cold weather, which prevented the growth of corn.[25] A few decades later, G.W.F. Hegel argued in his *Lectures on the Philosophy of World History* (1822–1828) that non-European peoples did not possess the same humanity as Europeans since they were not capable of historical movement. In his discussion of progress, he focused on African peoples but also included the Sámi in a discussion of how climate halted intellectual growth:

> The frost which grips the inhabitants of Lapland and the fiery heat of Africa are forces of too powerful a nature for man to resist, or for the spirit to achieve free movement and to reach that degree of richness which is the precondition and source of a fully developed mastery of reality.[26]

Hegel placed these people outside of the theatre of history and also believed that colonisation was justified. Nilsson likewise presented colonisation as natural and as an engine of progress. Colonial and cross-ethnic encounters, he argued, were permeated by hatred and a 'universal' desire to exterminate people deemed to be inferior and in a different stage of development:

> [P]eople in the same phase of civilization are in their natural disposition very much alike; that the savage hates the colonist, and amongst the rude races themselves, those more favoured by nature pursue and endeavour to extirpate those who are, in a physical and intellectual point of view, their inferiors. This appears to be a universal law of nature.[27]

Nilsson's emphasis on hatred leading to an alleged natural elimination of weaker peoples can also be detected in a later passage in his book in which he argued that it was in the very 'code of creation' that 'everything meaner, when it has fulfilled its mission here on earth, shall perish and make room for something better'.[28] Nilsson's examples of hatred between groups included contemporary examples of colonial clashes and uneven encounters in places such as North America, supposed ethnic hatred between Copper Indians and Inuit as depicted in Samuel Hearne's account of the Coppermine massacre in Hudson Bay, and examples from the historic settlement and colonisation of Scandinavia.[29] By naturalising hatred and murder, Nilsson provided narratives that justified and legitimised the colonisation and attempted erasure of Indigenous peoples.

In addition to popularising Thomson's three-age system and the concept of prehistory in Britain, Nilsson was instrumental in shaping British scientific and lay thinking on the Sámi in the Victorian period. He argued that the original inhabitants of Scandinavia, and large parts of northern Europe, were a dwarfish Polar race related to the Sámi, whom the invading 'dolichocephalic race' had killed or pushed to the northern parts of the Scandinavian peninsula.[30] This Polar race had been indigenous not only to Scandinavia but also to northern and western Europe, including Germany and Britain. Nilsson drew comparisons to contemporary Sámi and argued that there was a continuing colonial hatred between them and 'Gothic' Scandinavians:

> The Lapland race is considered inferior to, and is despised by, the Goths living in their neighbourhood. In consequence of this hereditary hatred between the tribes, a Swede or a Norwegian rarely marries a Lapland woman. Mr P. Laestadius, although a great friend of the Laplanders, says: 'The races appear to be so distinctly divided from each other, that it seems to be repugnant even to physical nature to unite them.'[31]

Nilsson's argument was partly based on stories about the Norsemen's hatred of dwarfs in the Sagas, who he referred to as a 'degraded race'. He made the associations between the dwarfs in the Sagas and Sámi, since both were, in his opinion, 'ugly and short'.[32] Other 'evidence' included clothing, being 'cunning and deceitful', collecting metals, being skilled in sorcery, being despised by Gothic neighbours, and not marrying outside their race.[33] Although Nilsson made case for archaeology as a distinct discipline, it is clear that this was a period in which there were no strict boundaries between folklore, literature, archaeology, and physical anthropology.

Nilsson also utilised cranial measurements of skulls classified as Sámi since they were deemed to be 'short-headed' or brachycephalic. These, he argued, resembled those of Stone-Age skulls and thus racially linked contemporary Sámi to prehistoric ones.[34] Nilsson was a friend of the Swedish craniologist Anders Retzius, whose cranial index and collection he used to classify the skulls. Nilsson also had access to human crania in Sweden's Naturhistoriska riksmuseet (natural history museum), of which he was the director from 1828 to 1831. However, the sample he had of both crania and 'primitive' ethnographic artefacts was relatively small and in 1836, two years before the publication of *Skandinaviska Nordens Urinvånare*, he carried out an influential European tour during which he visited museum collections in Denmark, Germany, Britain, and France.[35] In the introduction written for the translated *The Primitive Inhabitants of*

Scandinavia (discussed later in this chapter), he emphasised the importance of the trips to these museums and how it developed his evolutionary thinking:

> I found that it would be necessary to visit those foreign museums in which were preserved a great number of such implements and weapons as are still used at the present time by people who live in so low a degree of civilisation that they are even yet ignorant of the use of metals, but have for implements and weapons only stone, bone, and other hard substances, suitable for the purpose.[36]

The visits to Britain and France in particular had a significant impact on Nilsson's thought. In London, he visited the city's museums and private collections, which were crammed with colonial artefacts from across the globe. He spent hours studying the artefacts in the British museum and his notebooks are full of notes and drawings of artefacts such as an axe from Tierra del Fuego, a stone knife from New Zealand, and Inuit artefacts from Labrador and Greenland.[37] It was while in London that Nilsson noted 'all savage people … have tools made out of stone or bone'.[38] Some of the people constructed as savages were the Maori, Polynesians, Inuit, Native Americans, and Australian Aborigines (Figure 12.1).

In London, Nilsson saw the skeleton of the so-called Irish Giant Charles O'Brien whose body had been preserved, despite his explicit instructions that it be left alone, by the Scottish anatomist and surgeon John Hunter.[39] Although

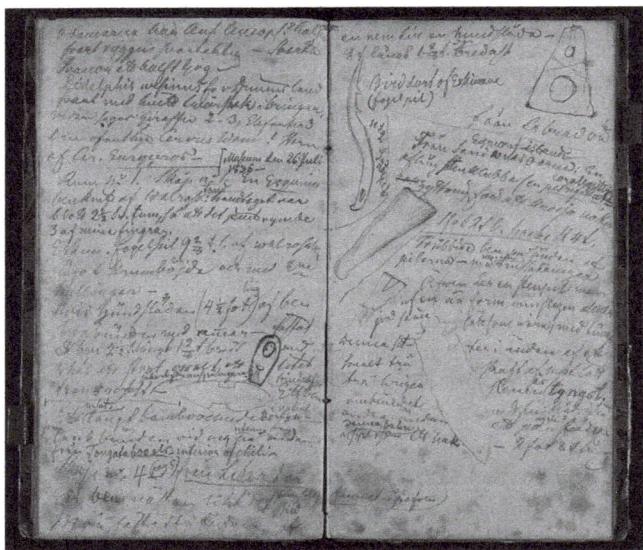

Figure 12.1 Artefacts in the British Museum in Sven Nilsson's Notebook, Lund University Library, Samling Nilsson, C14

Sámi indigeneity

British institutions contained collections of human remains, and although Nilsson spent time in London with scientists, such as Robert Brown, who had participated in anatomical study and collecting during their expeditions, it was primarily in France that Nilsson accessed and studied human remains.[40] There he studied under Georges Cuvier and had access to the huge collection of skulls in the Muséum national d'histoire naturelle. It was in this collection that he made the association between 'Mongolian Skulls' (Kalmuck) and those that he had labelled as Sámi (Figure 12.2).[41]

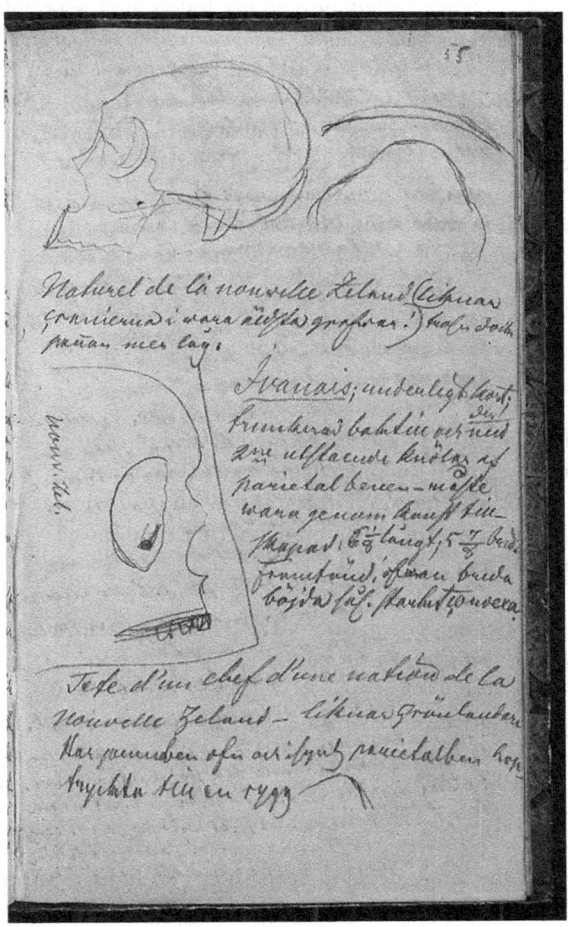

Figure 12.2 Drawings by Sven Nilsson of human crania in the Muséum national d'histoire naturelle, Paris. Sven Nilsson's Notebook, Lund University Library, Samling Nilsson, C16

He was also shown the skeleton of Sarah Baartman, a Khoikhoi woman who was displayed with the stage-name 'The Hottentot Venus' in London and later Paris and whom Cuvier had dissected following her death. Nilsson recorded that they had discussed her resemblance to an ape.[42]

Nilsson made a number of trips in Europe during his career, visiting England in 1847, 1860, 1864, and 1868. In 1860, he studied J.F. Blumenbach's collection of crania in Göttingen.[43] During his travels, he presented his work at conferences and met with prominent scholars interested in primitive or prehistoric cultures such as Charles Lyell, Thomas Henry Huxley, Edward Burnett Taylor, and Francis Trevelyan Buckland, and colonial travellers, including John Franklin and David Livingstone.[44] Nilsson's fame gained momentum following the popular translation of his book into English (as *The Primitive Inhabitants of Scandinavia*) in 1868 by Sir John Lubbock. This was not only a translation but a new edition for the British market and it contained a new introduction by Nilsson. Lubbock was a politician and polymath scientist with interests in natural selection, ethnographic studies, and archaeology. He had travelled with his wife in Denmark, Sweden, and Norway in 1863 and met Nilsson at a conference in Stockholm.[45] Lubbock, who expressed that he was interested in translating Nilsson's work to English, was an early supporter of the three-age system in archaeology and likewise applied a comparative approach to artefacts in his *Pre-historic Times*.[46] Lubbock, working with preconceived views of savages and evolution, cherry picked depictions of non-European and Indigenous people from travelogues, including Jean-François Regnard's pejorative account of the Sámi from 1731:

> Travellers and naturalists have varied a good deal in opinion as to the race of savages which is entitled the unenviable reputation of being the lowest in scale of civilization. Cook, Darwin, Fitzroy and Wallis were decidedly in favor, if I may so say, of the Fuegian ... one French writer even insinuates that monkeys are more human than Laplanders.[47]

Lubbock adhered to Nilsson's depiction of the Sámi as a dwarf race who were the original inhabitants of Northern Europe:

> Carrying our imagination back into the past, we see before us on the low shores of the Danish Archipelago a race of small men, with heavy overhanging brows, round heads, and faces probably much like those of the present Laplanders.[48]

Lubbock adhered to the same 'development' theory of human history as Nilsson in that all societies had originally been savage and that humanity culminated in an advance to industrial and commercial civilisation.

Lubbock was primarily interested in Nilsson's work on the Stone Age. While they initially planned to also publish Nilsson's writing on the Bronze Age, it was only the section on the Stone Age that was printed and gained traction in Britain.[49] This occurred at the very time that Nilsson's construction of the Sámi as the original and 'savage' inhabitants of Scandinavia was losing popularity in Sweden. Nilsson was strongly criticised by Gustav von Düben for presenting such savage people, which he believed the Sámi to be, as the Indigenous people of Scandinavia.[50] In Britain, however, Nilsson's work was receiving good reviews and was starting to circulate more widely. The *Supplement to John Bull* expressed its delight that Nilsson's work was finally available in English.[51] The English edition notified its readers that the work contained valuable illustrations of 'stone implements' and 'crania'. In a period of deep interest in Vikings and Norse legends, several reviewers focused on those aspects in Nilsson's writing. *Literature* highlighted Nilsson's depiction of the 'superstitions, traditions and Sagas of Scandinavia', and *The Literary Examiner* singled out Nilsson's portrayal of the 'kinship' between Sámi and the dwarfs of old literature as particularly interesting: 'in the dwarfs, giants, and goblins whom [the stories] describe Professor Nilsson sees reminiscences of the older people whom the Gothic races displaced, and either exterminated or drove into distant quarters'.[52] The idea of encounters between alleged Goths and 'Laplanders' pushing the Sámi further north within Scandinavia was also picked up by *Literature*, which noted that the Sámi had been 'more diffused in the North of Europe in former times than now'.[53]

Presenting and constructing the 'Aborigines of Europe'

The advertisement for the London exhibition of 1885 at Alexandra Palace, which was published in a range of newspapers, emphasised that this exhibition provided the first 'true picture of a Lapp encampment'. While this might have been the first British exhibition that consisted of an outdoor encampment, there had been in fact a number of exhibitions of Sámi people that had promised an 'authentic' Lapland experience in Britain in the nineteenth century. These included, for example, the popular display of Jens and Karina Holm, their child and reindeer in 1822, and the exhibition of Christina Larsdotter in 1851 who was displayed both because she was Sámi and because of her tallness, measuring approximately 210 cm. In 1775, at the Royal Aquarium in London, the American-Canadian impresario Guillermo Antonio Farini put four young Sámi – named in the press as Nils, Eln, Siri, and Joseph – from Kautokeino on display.[54] The seven individuals who participated in the 1885 show numbered thus among a large number of Sámi exhibited in the metropolitan centres of Britain, Germany, and North America during the eighteenth and early nineteenth centuries.

The large troupe of 1885 had been brought to Britain by Zacharias Øwre, the sheriff in Karasjok, and by Hans Lien Brækstad, a Norwegian resident in England. The latter was an influential writer, journalist, and political activist who campaigned for Norwegian independence from Sweden. He was also a patron for Scandinavian literature and music, and supported the translations of Henrik Ibsen and Hans Christian Andersen into English.[55] Now he had turned his attention to mediating and profiting from another aspect of Norway – its Indigenous Sámi culture. Recruited by Øwre, the Sámi arrived in England at the port of Hull on the steamship liner *Hero* together with dogs, tents, and sledges, and were exhibited in

London between late April and June. Six reindeer had arrived a few weeks earlier.[56] Brækstad paid the Sámi a salary and travel costs. The participants reportedly also received a share of the ticket sales.[57] According to an article in *The Standard*, from May 1885, the audience was informed that the Sámi were poor.[58] The financial reward was therefore probably a strong motivating factor for the members of the troupe to agree to leave home and to become 'show people'.[59]

There are unfortunately no reports of what the different members of the troupe made of their time in London. It is likewise difficult to hear their voices in the published British material about the exhibition; they remain anonymous in most primary sources. There are, for example, no references to their names in adverts or reviews of the exhibition. The members of the troupe are instead referred to by their biological sex and whether they were adults or children. However, an anthropological report by Professor Augustus Henry Keane from University College London does name and describe them:

1   Ole Nilsen Plavna, 'a Mountain Lapp, 40 years old'.
2   Amund Johannesen Anti, 'formerly nomad, but since his father's death a River Lapp, 30 years old'.
3   Ellen Johannesen Lindi, 'Amund's wife, 29 years old'.
4   Johannes Larsen Anti, 'Amund's cousin, 20 years old'.
5   Anders Amundsen Anti, 'son of Amund, 3 years old'.
6   Johannes Amundsen Anti, 'son of Amund, 9 months old'.
7   Anna Johannesdatter Guttorm 'maid-servant, 21 years old'.[60]

It was probably Brækstad who provided Keane with this information. In the press, the Sámi were presented as silent objects who existed to be studied and whose lives and thoughts were determined completely by their racial identities. The journalist in *The Era* stated, for instance, that they were 'worth a thorough inspection'.[61] Ethnographic exhibitions were permeated by this kind of ocularcentrism, which venerated and encouraged the gaze of the audience. Human exhibitions, as the work of Barbara Kirshenblatt-Gimblett has demonstrated, tended to produce objectified and essentialised representations of culture rather than presenting individuals with different lives.[62]

This does not mean that the Sámi in the show lacked agency. Interaction, which was impossible to control, would have taken place between them and their audience, whether oral or through body language. One of the participants, Ole Nilsen Ravna (Bikkan Ovlla in Sámi) – who later participated in expeditions to Greenland with Fridtjof Nansen and Knud Rasmussen – is recorded to have understood English.[63] The Sámi were also connected to other exhibited people in London since ethnographic exhibitions provided, as Danika Medak-Saltzman has argued, the possibility of encounters between exhibited peoples.[64] Alexandra Palace placed Indigenous people next to other peoples whose cultures interested the British. The grounds contained, for instance, a 'Japanese village'. While there don't seem to be any recorded encounters between the Sámi and the Japanese people, the fact that the Sámi engaged with fellow performers in principle was noted in the press. For instance, *The Era* recorded the Sámi 'wondering greatly at the feats of "Chevalier" Blondin on a tight-rope stretched high in the air'.[65] Chevalier Blondin, born Jean François Gravelet in France, was a famous tightrope artist who had crossed Niagara Falls 17 times – crossing it, for example, blindfolded, pushing a wheelbarrow, and carrying a stove in order to stop half way across to cook an omelette.[66] He had toured Britain and was now billed alongside the Sámi. The troupe's members therefore also took the opportunity to admire the strange feats and wonders at display in London.

There was a colonial ambivalence, as described by Robert Young, in which the press expressed concurrent attraction and revulsion towards the Sámi.[67] *The Daily News* told its readers that the exhibition was a 'picturesque' display of 'uncivilised' life:

> The tents – one of which is of a woollen material and the other of a thinner fabric – are filled with skins, rugs, knives, pots and various other articles of domestic utility, including an eccentrically shaped cradle. In the centre of the tent a fire was smouldering yesterday, and in the surrounding ground were grouped sledges, skins drying in the sun, logs of wood, and other picturesque accessories of uncivilised habitations.[68]

While the encampment was presented as providing a 'novel' experience and a 'pleasant afternoon's holiday', its attendant 'savagery' was simultaneously frowned upon. Although the Sámi were not particularly geographically distant from the spectators – unlike many other Indigenous peoples who participated in human exhibitions – they were constructed as being temporally remote by being living representations of 'savagery'. While these narratives on savagery debased the Sámi, they elevated the alleged superiority of the British.

Savagery was, moreover, read into the physiognomy of the Sámi who were described in pejorative terms as dirty and unkempt.[69] This reflected a climate of increasingly pejorative and racialised narratives about Indigenous peoples in the second half of the nineteenth century. The women and children were, for example, described as being as 'grotesque as anything in Ally Sloper's perennial *Half Holiday*'.[70] This early British comic strip magazine also published a short note on the exhibition in which they questioned and ridiculed the display of the Sámi troupe:

> The Lapps now at the Alexandra Palace only wash once a week, and seldom have their hair cut. It seems superfluous to fetch persons from such a great distance to illustrate the virtue of unseemliness. We have abundant instances of a praiseworthy dislike of soap in the metropolis; and any interprising [sic] agent might supply the Alexandra Palace with any number of parties ....[71]

This comment illustrates the anxiety over cleanliness in Victorian Britain. The targets were, as can be seen, not only to non-European or Indigenous subjects but also to poor people within Britain.[72]

Not all reviews were this negative and one of the children, probably Anders, received some praise. It is worth noting that the child's light hair was singled out for admiration, such hair being regarded as unusual for the Sámi who tended to be depicted as swarthy with black hair. *The Daily News* wrote, for instance, that 'ladies' visiting the exhibition were charmed by the little boy 'whose open frank face and light flaxen hair gained for him quite a collection of toys and coppers'.[73] The adults, however, were portrayed by *The Standard* as having 'very dark hair' and were compared to animals by being described as having hair, 'almost as coarse as the tail of a horse'. Their physiognomy was depicted as 'square and squat'.[74]

Nineteenth-century ethnographic exhibitions were viewed as providing not only lay education and entertainment to the spectators but also anthropological research opportunities for scientists.[75] These scientists gave lectures to the public in conjunction with the exhibitions. In 1885, Keane gave several public lectures on the Sámi, speaking about their 'Origin, Affinities, Physical Type, Habits, and Customs'. He also delivered a paper for a more select crowd at the Anthropological Institute of Great Britain and Ireland on 9 June. Keane, sounding like an exhibition impresario, drummed up excitement at the prospect of observing the Sámi:

> To the members of this Institute, devoted as they are to the special study of mankind, an intellectual treat of no ordinary interest is now afforded by the enterprising management of the Alexandra Palace which, without inconvenience to ourselves, offers the rare opportunity of observing on the living subject the physical qualities, social usages, and domestic life of perhaps the most interesting group of aborigines still surviving in Europe.[76]

He continued dramatically, 'A section ... of the Arctic region of Lapland has been brought to our very doors ... They are here in our very midst.'[77] The focus was on three inter-related aspects of the Sámi: their alleged racial characteristics as a 'Mongol race', that they inhabited an Arctic landscape, and that that they were Aborigines of Europe.

Talking about the Sámi 'race' at the same meeting was also Dr J.G. Garson, a council member of the Royal Anthropological Institute. Garson had studied medicine at the University of Edinburgh and now provided lectures on comparative anatomy for the Charing Cross Hospital. Together with Keane, he examined the bodies of the troupe members. He provided a table containing their names, and then individual entries for height, shape of head, nasal index, hair, and span of arms, among other features.[78]

A third presentation was the display of a large collection of photographs of Sámi by Prince Roland Bonaparte who was the grandson of one of Napoleon Bonaparte's brothers. In 1884, he spent three months in Scandinavia together with the photographer G. Roche. Bonaparte informed his audience that 'each Lapp was photographed in full face and in profile, the two positions being rigorously exact'.[79] Trained by the anatomist and anthropologist Paul Broca, Bonaparte created photographic portfolios of Omaha Indians, Hindus, Kalmyks, Khoikhoi, Somalis, Acehnese, and Surinamese. In addition to his travels in Sápmi and North America, he also utilised human exhibitions and colonial expositions in places such as Paris and Amsterdam to photograph people.[80] His activities – and the same applies to

Keane and Garson – were driven by biological determinism or, as Stephen J. Gould has labelled it, the 'mismeasure of man'.[81]

The Sámi's Aboriginality was a key feature in both press reports and advertisements, and in Keane's report. Keane presented them as being 'true aborigines' who had lived in Scandinavia 'from prehistoric times' where they had become 'secluded' and 'differentiated physically and intellectually from all the surrounding peoples'.[82] This was not the first group of displayed Indigenous peoples that Keane had taken the opportunity to study. Keane had also examined a group of Krenak in 1883 and Botocudos from Brazil in 1884.[83] Now, he was studying and constructing Europe's indigenes who he imbued with temporal difference from other Europeans. The Sámi were, Keane argued, 'rude' and 'unprogressive nomads' incapable of progress, and he compared them unfavourably to their allegedly dynamic and progressive neighbours who had settled Scandinavia after the Sámi:

> But while the Norsemen soon emerged from the savage state, passing rapidly through the stone, bronze, and iron ages, their sluggish northern neighbours have remained almost stationary to the present day.[84]

Keane's inclusion of the three-stage chronological development model from archaeology reflects the growing influence of archaeology on racial discourses in the second half of the nineteenth century. He also narrated, in a similar vein to Sven Nilsson, colonial encounters between these peoples, with the invading 'Teutonic Scandinavians' being presented as having historically pressed the 'sluggish' Sámi further north within Scandinavia.[85] As Andrew Wawn's work has illustrated, the Norsemen were, unlike the Sámi, a people that Britons associated themselves with racially and culturally, and Britons drew colonial comparisons between themselves and Norsemen or 'Vikings'.[86]

European and non-European Aborigines

In an 1885 presentation in London, Keane proclaimed that the Sámi were the 'shortest people not only in Europe but in the whole of the eastern hemisphere'.[87] The Sámi's alleged shortness fascinated and preoccupied a number of British scientists who linked short stature to primeval indigeneity. The polymath and traveller John Francis Campbell of Islay, for example, was an early promoter of the so-called Scottish 'pygmy theory' which argued that a swarthy, dwarfish, and Aboriginal people consisting of 'Lapps' had once inhabited Scotland before being pushed aside by invading Celts and Scandinavian Teutons and that their historical presence was remembered in Scottish folktales about fairies.[88] There were a number of influential British commentators adhering to this theory. They included the folklorist and antiquarian David MacRitchie, the anthropologist Alfred C. Haddon, the public servant and folklorist George Laurence Gomme, the folklorist John Stuart Stuart-Glennie, the president of the Anthropological Society of London John Beddoe and the anthropologist Edward Burnett Tylor. Tylor's *Primitive Culture* included a discussion of Indigenous people being connected to 'myths of giants and dwarf' which he argued had been 'settled beyond doubt by the evidence brought forward by Grimm, Nilsson, and Hanusch'.[89] This British fascination with the alleged shortness of the Sámi can be compared with British depictions of African peoples of short statue such as the BiAka (Aka) people who, after the 1870s, were likewise constructed as an Aboriginal dwarf species, whom some claimed were not even fully human but belonged to a species that predated *Homo sapiens*.

Although the Sámi inhabited Europe, they were never held up as representing nineteenth-century Europe. They were instead portrayed as a people who provided a mirror to a distant and savage past — an exotic and pre-modern race of people. A reviewer of S. Tromholt's *Under the Rays of the Aurora Borealis* (1885), a book Keane referred to in his presentation of the troupe, expressed such views in 1885 when he presented the Sámi as Asiatic people, whose 'presence in Europe' was 'an interesting relic of the time when all that makes Europe European had not yet so much as begun to be'.[90] The Sámi were one of the many Indigenous and colonised peoples in the nineteenth century who were frequently portrayed as people without a future. The cleric Frederic William Farrar described, for example, 'savage' peoples as having no 'past' and being 'without a future' since 'savage and civilised life *cannot* co-exist side by side'.[91] Farrar was, alongside Lubbock, one of the pallbearers at Charles Darwin's funeral in 1882. Lubbock was a close friend of Darwin and Nilsson also corresponded with the latter.[92] In a climate of Darwinian thinking, Nilsson had put forward an attractive narrative to Victorian Britons of a clash of civilisations between the Sámi and other Scandinavian Norsemen.

Keane presented the Sámi as an indolent people that were doomed to become extinct. This was something the press picked up on and the alleged dwindling of their numbers was compared to that of other Indigenous peoples such as the Maori.[93] Keane argued that primitive peoples 'lagged behind in the race' and would always become 'extinct or disappear' — a process that could happen by 'extermination, by slow decay, or by absorption'.[94] He held that the last of these three outcomes applied to the Sámi whose land, he argued, was 'encroached upon by surrounding populations' by the 'more numerous and progressive Scandinavian populations' and through Sámi adopting Scandinavian languages and culture when becoming farmers and merging with the 'more numerous and progressive Scandinavian population'.[95] This, he argued, could be seen in the features of the Sámi on display who were 'fair and flushed like that of most Norse and English people'.[96] At the Alexandra Palace, Keane helped drum up interest in the Sámi display by claiming that since the 'Lapps' would soon die out along with their reindeer — the animal being referred to as the 'associate' of the 'men of the stone age' — the present Sámi group was likely to be last one to *ever* visit England.[97] This was a colonial prediction that could only be good for business.

Colonising Indigenous people through concepts of time

The mediation of the 1885 exhibition of the Sámi troupe contained a rhetoric that propelled and justified colonialism by depicting Indigenous people as 'savage', 'primitive', 'prehistoric', and people without a future. It was a rhetoric that denied Indigenous peoples the possession of historical forward motion. They were constructed as remnants of the Stone Age, whom visitors were encouraged to observe – in order to get a glimpse of a primal past – before those remnants became extinct. The archaeological model of development was an intrinsically European yardstick, but was presented as a universal episteme. It elevated certain strands of European identity, the Teutonic or Aryan, and had northern Europe as its epicentre. Within this north, however, were people – the Sámi and the Inuit – who were associated with primeval savagery and who were therefore linked to and associated with other colonised and Indigenous peoples who were also located in prehistory.

While Sámi areas were presented as not containing any potential riches for Britain, in Scandinavia, the message was one of a prehistoric arcadia soon to be erased by the inevitable exploitation of great industrial opportunities.[98] A journalist in *The Globe* wrote that he had learned from Keane's lecture that there was 'but little chance of exploiting Lapland to any great advantage'.[99] In Sweden, by contrast, northern parts of the country – including Sámi territories – were imagined in the period around 1870–1920 as a land of endless natural resources that could provide wealth for all of Sweden through timber and ore extraction.[100] This was a period of industrialisation that coincided with a growing 'wilderness tourism' in which metropolitan travellers from both Scandinavia and Britain increasingly wanted to walk in Scandinavia's alleged last 'wilderness'.[101] For these 'time travellers', the impending threat to wilderness posed by industrialisation added to the exotification of northern Scandinavia and provided – as the ethnographic exhibitions had done – a marketable urgency to the act of travelling *now* since both the landscape and the Sámi people were believed to be the inevitable victims of industrial progress and the march of history.

The rhetoric of primitivism and extinction was a vehicle that brought destructive material and ideological change to the traditional society and culture of Sámi people during the nineteenth century – but in doing so it also awoke a popular resistance. Colonial policies at their most extreme attempted to simultaneously extirpate and preserve Sámi society amid the industrial advance. Land dispossession and racialist biological studies were accompanied by the denial of a regular education for the children of reindeer-herding Sámi.[102] The reindeer-herding communities were constructed and classified as the *true* Sámi by the Swedish state and specific boarding schools were set up designed to shield their children from 'civilisation'. The Sámi were therefore concurrently criticised for their primitivism and 'protected' from losing it. Vitalis Karnell, a vicar in Karesuando who was one of the men behind the segregated school system and who wanted the Sámi to be safeguarded from 'civilisation', wrote in 1906:

> Do favour the Lapps in their occupations, make them moral, sober, and sufficiently educated – but do not let them drink from the cup of civilisation … it has never been and will never be a blessing [for them]. A Lapp should be a Lapp.[103]

In response to colonial encroachment and social engineering from outside, there emerged from within Sápmi a modern Sámi nationalism. Nineteenth and early twentieth-century activists such as Elsa Laula Renberg, Johan Enok Nilsson, Torkel Tomasson, Daniel Mortensen, and Karin Stenberg voiced powerful challenges to how the Scandinavian states depicted the Sámi as savage people who could not look after their own land.[104] Stenberg, a teacher in Arvidsjaur, published together with the journalist Valdemar Lindholm the book *Dat läh mijen situd: En vädjan till svenska nationen från samefolket* (1920). In this book, she criticised how Swedish writers had constructed the Sámi and how their narratives were accepted as truths:

> [D]escriptions as well as reports have been carried out by people, who, although they may have been physically close to and have spent a year or so with us, spiritually have been so infinitely remote, that our voice has reached them only as a distant, opaque murmur, difficult to determine, whether it emanates from the forest or from the great waters. [...] The many, both knowledgeable and well-meaning men and women, who otherwise have portrayed Sami life, have in general, even when the purpose has been benevolence, portrayed it only from the Swedish point of view, made main issues into sideshows and vice versa. *The Sami people* have not been portrayed, *but Swedish life as tourists in an exotic land* with a population, interesting enough, but which has grown in interest the more different from other human beings and the closer to the position of animals that one could present them. Swedes, who travel through the Lappmarks with horse-carts of conserved food and their heads full of their own grandeur, without knowing our language, without being able to follow us on our migrations, in our work, but allow themselves to be carted as luggage through the countryside, they write, supported by the state and by individuals, books about us and our life, hallmarked as 'the truth about the Lapp'.[105]

A growth in Sámi activism manifested in a fight for rights to land and education, as can be seen in the formation of the Sámi organisation in Stockholm in 1904 and in the national Sámi assembly in Trondheim in 1917 that consisted of Sámi from both Sweden and Norway. Rather than becoming extinct, as British and Scandinavian scientists, entrepreneurs, and journalists had predicted throughout the nineteenth century, the Sámi responded to their precarious position with a demand for modernisation on their own terms.

Acknowledgement

This research has been supported by the research grant "Collecting Mankind: Prehistory, Race and Instructions for 'Scientific Travelers', circa 1750–1850," Swedish Research Council (2019-03358), 2020–24.

Notes

1 *The Globe*, 19 April 1885, 8.
2 *The Globe*, 19 April 1885, 8

3 The exhibition has been discussed briefly by Gunnar Broberg, 'Lappkaravaner på villovägar: Antropologin och synen på samerna fram mot sekelskiftet 1900,' *Lynchnos* (1981/1982): 33, and Cathrine Baglo, 'På ville veger? Levande utstillinger av samer i Europa og America' (PhD. diss., University of Tromsø, 2011), 85–87.
4 Roslyn Poignant, *Professional Savages: Captive Lives and Western Spectacle* (New Haven, CT and London: Yale University Press, 2004), 6.
5 Sadiah Qureshi, *Peoples on Parade: Exhibitions, Empire, and Anthropology in Nineteenth-Century Britain* (Chicago, IL: The University of Chicago Press, 2011), 185; Linda Andersson Burnett, 'Selling the Sami: Nordic Stereotypes and Participatory Media in Georgian Britain,' in *Communicating the North: Media Structures and Images in the Making of the Nordic Region*, eds. Jonas Harvard and Peter Stadius (Farnham: Ashgate, 2013), 175–180, 185–187.
6 Quoted in Qureshi, *Peoples on Parade*, 185.
7 Qureshi, *Peoples on Parade*, 259.
8 Vital new work is renewing historiographic attention to the construction of Indigenous peoples as hunter gatherers or as prehistoric. See, for example, Bruce Pascoe, *Dark Emu: Aboriginal Australia and the Birth of Agriculture* (Broome: Magabala Books, 2014/2018). Historians of science and archaeology are also developing new analyses of the construction of this concept in authoritative texts and museum collections drawn from colonial field studies in India, Scandinavia, or the United States in the nineteenth century; Pratik Chakrabarti, 'Gondwana and the Politics of Deep Past,' *Past and Present* 241, no. 1 (2019): 119–153; Samuel J. Redman, *Bonerooms: From Scientific Racism to Prehistory in Museums* (Cambridge, MA: Harvard University Press, 2016); Påvel Nicklasson, 'Sven Nilsson och Den Skandinaviska Nordens Urinvånare,' *Fornvännen: Journal of Swedish Antiquarian Research* 106 (2011): 161–78.
9 For literature on Scandinavian colonialism, see, for example, Magdalena Naum and Jonas M. Nordin, eds., *Scandinavian Colonialism and the Rise of Modernity: Small Time Agents in a Global Arena* (New York: Springer, 2013); Linda Andersson Burnett and Johan Höglund, eds., 'Exploring Nordic Colonialisms,' *Scandinavian Studies* 91, nos. 1 and 2 (2019).
10 Miles Macallister, 'The Scandinavians "Hitchhiked" Their Way to the Boons of Empire,' *Aeon*, 31 January 2018, https://aeon.co/ideas/the-hitchhiking-scandinavian-way-to-the-imperial-riches.
11 Peter Rowley-Conwy, *From Genesis to Prehistory: The Archaeological Three Age System and Its Contested Reception in Denmark, Britain, and Ireland* (Oxford: Oxford University Press, 2007).
12 Sven Nilsson, *The Primitive Inhabitants of Scandinavia*, 3rd ed., ed. Sir John Lubbock (London: Longmans, 1868), lxiv.
13 Adam Ferguson, *An Essay on the History of Civil Society* (Edinburgh: Printed for A. Kincaid & J. Bell, 1767), 122; Ronald. L. Meek, *Social Science and the Ignoble Savage* (Cambridge: Cambridge University Press, 1976); Silvia Sebastiani, *The Scottish Enlightenment: Race, Gender and the Limits of Progress* (Basingstoke: Palgrave, 2013).
14 Påvel Nicklasson, 'Sven Nilssons resa 1836,' *Fornvännen: Journal of Swedish Antiquarian Research* 108 (2013): 37.
15 Nilsson, *Primitive Inhabitants*, lx; Rowley-Conwy, *Genesis to Prehistory*, 5. For the influence of Cuvier and fossils on Nilsson, see Johan Hegardt, 'Sven Nilsson and the Invention of Modern Man,' *Current Swedish Archaeology* 4 (1996): 51–67; Påvel Nicklasson, 'Johan Haquin Wallman, Sven Nilsson och den moderna arkeologins genombrott,' *Fornvännen: Journal of Swedish Antiquarian Research* 103 (2008): 108–109.
16 Peter Rowley-Conwy, 'The Concept of Prehistory and the Invention of the Terms "Prehistoric" and "Prehistorian": The Scandinavian Origin, 1833–1850,' *European Journal of Archaeology* 9, no. 1 (2006): 103–130.
17 The English term was later developed by the Scotsman Daniel Wilson who probably picked it up from the Norwegian Peter Andreas Munch. Rowley-Conwy, 'The Concept of Prehistory.'

18 Quoted in Rowley-Conwy, 'The Concept of Prehistory,' 111.
19 Rowley-Conwy, 'The Concept of Prehistory,' 112.
20 Nilsson, *Primitive Inhabitants*, lviii.
21 Nilsson, *Primitive Inhabitants*, lviii–lix.
22 Dipesh Chakrabarty, *Provincialising Europe: Postcolonial Thought and Historical Difference* (Princeton, NJ: Princeton University Press, 2000), 7–8.
23 Roxann Wheeler, *The Complexion of Race: Categories of Difference in Eighteenth-Century Britain* (Philadelphia: University of Pennsylvania Press, 2000), 184.
24 Sebastiani, *Scottish Enlightenment*, 94.
25 Lord Kames, *Sketches of the History of Man*, vol. I (Edinburgh: W. Creech, 1774), 101–10.
26 G.W.F. Hegel quoted in Robert Bernasconi, 'Hegel at the Court of the Ashanti,' in *Hegel after Derrida*, ed. Stuart Barnett (London: Routledge, 2001), 52.
27 Nilsson, *Primitive Inhabitants*, 1.
28 Nilsson, *Primitive Inhabitants*, 190.
29 Nilsson, *Primitive Inhabitants*, 176–189; Nicklasson, 'Sven Nilssons resa,' 43.
30 Nilsson, *Primitive Inhabitants*, 1, 256.
31 Nilsson, *Primitive Inhabitants*, 225.
32 Nilsson, *Primitive Inhabitants*, 222–224.
33 Nilsson, *Primitive Inhabitants*, 223–226.
34 Nilsson, *Primitive Inhabitants*, 121.
35 For earlier discussions of Nilsson's travels, see Berta Stjernquist, 'Sven Nilsson som banbrytare i svensk arkeologi,' in *Sven Nilsson: En lärd i 1800-talets Lund*, ed. Gerhard Regnéll (Lund: Kungl. Fysiografiska Sällskapet i Lund, 1983), 191–202, and Nicklasson, 'Sven Nilssons resa.'
36 Nilsson, *Primitive Inhabitants*, xlviii.
37 Sven Nilsson, Notebook, Lund University Library (LUB), Samling Nilsson C14 (no pagination).
38 Sven Nilsson, Notebook, Lund University Library (LUB), Samling Nilsson C15.
39 Sven Nilsson, Notebook, Lund University Library (LUB), Samling Nilsson C15, 17.
40 For an account of Brown's participation in anatomical collecting, see Bruce Buchan and Linda Andersson Burnett, 'Knowing Savagery: Australia and the Anatomy of Race,' *History of the Human Sciences* 32, no. 4 (2019).
41 Nicklasson, 'Sven Nilssons resa,' 41–43; Nilsson, Notebooks, C 16, 54–55, 59; Nilsson, *Primitive Inhabitants*, xlviii, 106.
42 Nilsson, Notebook, c16, 66.
43 Sternquist, 'Nilsson som banbrytare,' 194.
44 Nilsson, Notebooks, C14, C15, C16, C17, C18a, C34; Stjernquist, 'Nilsson som banbrytare,' 197–198; and Nicklasson, 'Sven Nilssons Resa,' 35.
45 Mark Patton, *Science, Politics, and the Business in the Works of Sir John Lubbock: A Man of Universal Mind* (Aldershot: Ashgate, 2007), 62.
46 John Lubbock, *Pre-historic Times, as Illustrated by Ancient Remains, and the Manners and Customs of Savages* (London: Williams and Norgate, 1865); Sternquist, 'Nilsson som banbrytare,' 182.
47 Lubbock, *Pre-historic Times*, 445–446.
48 Lubbock, *Pre-historic Times*, 116–117, 188–189.
49 Stjernquist, 'Nilsson som banbrytare,' 182.
50 Nilsson himself acknowledged the criticism, in *Primitive inhabitants*, xlix. See also Jacob Christensson, 'Sven Nilsson och Skandinaviens urinvånare,' in *Kulturanatomiska studier: tillägnade Anja Edén och Sten Kindlundh*, ed. Gunnar Broberg (Lund: Avd. för idé- och lärdomshistoria, Lunds universitet, 2001), 46.
51 *Supplement to John Bull*, 31 October 1868, 751.
52 *Literature*, 29 February 1868; *The Literary Examiner*, 14 March 1868.
53 *Literature*, 29 February 1868.

54 For literature on these Sami exhibitions, see Broberg, 'Lappkaravaner'; Baglo, 'På ville veger'; Andersson Burnett, *Selling the Sami*, and '"The Lapland Giantess" in Britain: Reading Concurrences in a Victorian Ethnographic Exhibition,' in *Concurrent Imaginaries, Postcolonial Worlds: Towards Revised Histories*, eds. Diana Brydon, Gunlög Fur, and Peter Forsgren (Brill: Leiden, 2017), 123–143.
55 Kathryn Walches, *Gamle Norge and Nineteenth-Century British Women Travellers in Norway* (London: Anthem Studies in Travel, 2014), 14; Baglo, 'På ville veger,' 85–86.
56 *Lincolnshire Chronicle*, 1 May 1885.
57 Baglo, 'På ville veger,' 86.
58 *The Standard*, 14 May 1885.
59 This is a term that Roslyn Poignant uses for Indigenous peoples who participated in human exhibitions. Poignant, *Professional Savages*, 4.
60 Augustus H. Keane, 'The Lapps: Their Origin, Ethnical Affinities, Physical and Mental Characteristics, Usages, Present Status, and Future Prospects,' *The Journal of the Anthropological Institute of Great Britain and Ireland* 15 (1886): 214–215.
61 *The Era*, 23 May 1885.
62 Barbara Kirshenblatt-Gimblett, *Destination Culture: Tourism, Museums, and Heritage* (Berkeley: University of California Press, 1998), 55.
63 Baglo, 'På ville veger,' 224.
64 Danika Medak-Saltzman, 'Transnational Indigenous Exchange: Rethinking Global Interactions of Indigenous Peoples at the 1904 St. Louis Exposition,' *American Quarterly* 62, no 3 (2010): 591–615.
65 *The Era*, 23 May 1885.
66 'The Blondin Memorial Trust,' accessed 22 June 2020, https://www.blondinmemorialtrust.com/.
67 Robert Young, *Colonial Desire: Hybridity in Theory, Culture and Race* (London: Routledge, 1995), 161
68 *The Daily News*, 5 May 1885.
69 See, for example, *The Sportsman*, 16 May 1885, 3; see also *The Daily News*, 5 May 1885.
70 *The Sportsman*, 16 May 1885, 3.
71 *Ally Sloper's Half-Holiday*, 16 May 1885, 158.
72 See, for example, Ann McClintock's book *Imperial Leather: Race, Gender, and Sexuality in the Colonial Contest* (Routledge: New York, 1995). For depictions of the urban poor as savages, see the writings of Henry Mayhew such as *London Labour and the London Poor*, 4 vols. (London: George Woodfall and Son; Griffin, Bohn, and Company, 1851–1862), and Rachel Ginnis Fuchs, *Gender and Poverty in Nineteenth-Century Europe* (Cambridge: Cambridge University Press, 2005).
73 *The Daily News*, 5 May 1885.
74 *The Standard*, 14 May 1885, 2.
75 Qureshi, *Peoples on Parade*, 259.
76 Keane, 'The Lapps,' 213.
77 Keane, 'The Lapps,' 213.
78 J.G. Garson, 'On the Physical Characteristics of the Lapps,' *The Journal of the Anthropological Institute of Great Britain and Ireland* 15 (1886): 238.
79 Roland Bonaparte, 'Note on the Lapps of Finmark (in Norway), Illustrated by Photographs,' *The Journal of the Anthropological Institute of Great Britain and Ireland* 15 (1886): 210–213.
80 Anne Maxwell, *Colonial Photography and Exhibitions: Representations of the Native and the Making of European Identities* (London: Leicester University Press, 1999), 44–46. See also Elizabeth Edwards, *Anthropology and Photography, 1860–1920* (New Haven, CT and London: Yale University Press, 1992) and Jane Lydon, *Photography, Humanitarianism, Empire* (London: Bloomsbury Academic, 2016).

81 Stephen J. Gould, *The Mismeasure of Man* (New York: W.W. Norton & Norton, 1981); Poignant, *Professional Savages*, 6–7.
82 Keane, 'The Lapps,' 216–217.
83 Qureshi, *Peoples on Parade*, 259, 348.
84 Keane, 'The Lapps,' 222–223.
85 Keane, 'The Lapps,' 222.
86 Andrew Wawn, *The Vikings and the Victorians: Inventing the Old North in Nineteenth Century Britain* (Cambridge, MA: Brewer, 2000).
87 Keane, 'The Lapps,' 218.
88 John Francis Campbell, *Popular Tales of the West Highlands: Orally Collected*, vol. 1 (Edinburgh: Edmonston and Douglas, 1860), cvii.
89 Edward Burnett Taylor, *Primitive Culture: Researches into the Development of Mythology*, vol. 1 (London: John Murray, 1871), 348.
90 *The Pall Mall Gazette*, 22 May 1885; see also *St. James's Gazette*, 19 May 1885, 7.
91 Frederic William Farrar, 'Aptitudes of Races,' *Transactions of the Ethnological Society of London* 5 (1867): 120–122.
92 See, for example, letter from Nilsson to Darwin, 31 December 1868. Darwin Correspondence Project, 'Letter no. 6517,' accessed 22 June 2020, https://www.darwinproject.ac.uk/letter/DCP-LETT-6517.xml.
93 *The Standard*, 14 May 1885; *The Morning Post*, 14 May 1885.
94 Keane, 'The Lapps,' 233.
95 Keane, 'The Lapps,' 233–234.
96 Keane, 'The Lapps,' 219.
97 *The Morning Post*, 14 May 1885.
98 Pratik Chakrabarti discusses this symbiotic relationship between primitivism and colonisation in India in his article 'Gondwana and the Politics of Deep Past'.
99 *The Globe*, 15 May 1885.
100 Sörlin, 'Framtidslandet: debatten om Norrland och Naturresurserna under det industriella genombrottet' (PhD diss., Umeå University, 1988).
101 Gunlög Fur, 'Always Already Cosmopolitan: Indigenous Peoples and Swedish Modernity,' in *European Cosmopolitanism: Colonial Histories and Postcolonial Societies*, eds. Gurminder K. Bhambra and John Narayan (London: Routledge, 2017), 65–81.
102 Lennart Lundmark, *Stulet land: Svensk makt på samisk mark* (Stockholm: Ordfront, 2008).
103 Quoted in Lundmark, *Stulet land*, 155. My translation.
104 Fur, 'Always Already Cosmopolitan,' 65–81; Patrik Lantoo and Ulf Mörkenstam, 'Sami Rights and Sami Challenges: The Modernization Process and the Swedish Sami Movement, 1886–2006,' *Scandinavian Journal of History* 33, no. 1 (2008): 26–51.
105 Lindholm was the official author but Stenberg stated in the foreword that the book was her initiative and that she was responsible for the views in it. The quote is cited in Fur, 'Always Already Cosmopolitan,' 77.

References

Manuscripts in Lund University Library (LUB)

Sven Nilsson, Samling Nilsson, Notebooks: C14, C15, C16, C17, C18a, C34

Published sources

Andersson Burnett, Linda. 'Selling the Sami: Nordic Stereotypes and Participatory Media in Georgian Britain.' In *Communicating the North: Media Structures and Images in the Making of the Nordic Region*, edited by Jonas Harvard and Peter Stadius, 171–196. Farnham: Ashgate, 2013.

Andersson Burnett, Linda. '"The Lapland Giantess" in Britain: Reading Concurrences in a Victorian ethnographic exhibition.' In *Concurrent Imaginaries, Postcolonial Worlds: Towards Revised Histories*, edited by Diana Brydon, Gunlög Fur, and Peter Forsgren, 123–143. Leiden: Brill, 2017.

Andersson Burnett, Linda, and Johan Höglund, eds. 'Exploring Nordic Colonialisms.' *Scandinavian Studies* 91, nos. 1 and 2 (2019): 1–12.

Baglo, Cathrine. 'På ville veger? Levande utstillinger av samer i Europa og America.' PhD diss., University of Tromsø, 2011.

Bernasconi, Robert. 'Hegel at the Court of the Ashanti.' In *Hegel after Derrida*, edited by Stuart Barnett, 41–63. London: Routledge, 2001.

Bonaparte, Roland. 'Note on the Lapps of Finmark (in Norway), Illustrated by Photographs.' *The Journal of the Anthropological Institute of Great Britain and Ireland* 15 (1886): 210–213.

Broberg, Gunnar. 'Lappkaravaner på villovägar: Antropologin och synen på samerna fram mot sekelskiftet 1900.' *Lychnos* (1981/1982): 27–86.

Buchan, Bruce, and Linda Andersson Burnett. 'Knowing Savagery: Australia and the Anatomy of Race.' *History of the Human Sciences* 32, no. 4 (2019).

Campbell, John Francis. *Popular Tales of the West Highlands: Orally Collected*, 4 vols. Edinburgh: Edmonston and Douglas, 1860–1862.

Chakrabarti, Pratik. 'Gondwana and the Politics of Deep Past.' *Past and Present* 241, no. 1 (2019): 119–153.

Chakrabarty, Dipesh. *Provincialising Europe: Postcolonial Thought and Historical Difference*. Princeton, NJ: Princeton University Press, 2000.

Christensson, Jacob. 'Sven Nilsson och Skandinaviens urinvånare.' In *Kulturanatomiska studier: tillägnade Anja Edén och Sten Kindlundh*, edited by Gunnar Broberg, 29–52. Lund: Avd. för idé- och lärdomshistoria, Lunds universitet, 2001.

Edwards, Elizabeth. *Anthropology and Photography, 1860–1920*. New Haven, CT and London: Yale University Press, 1992.

Farrar, Frederic William. 'Aptitudes of Races.' *Transactions of the Ethnological Society of London* 5 (1867): 115–126.

Ferguson, Adam. *An Essay on the History of Civil Society*. Edinburgh: Printed for A. Kincaid & J. Bell, 1767.

Fuchs, Rachel Ginnis. *Gender and Poverty in Nineteenth-Century Europe*. Cambridge: Cambridge University Press, 2005.

Fur, Gunlög. 'Always Already Cosmopolitan: Indigenous Peoples and Swedish Modernity.' In *European Cosmopolitanism: Colonial Histories and Postcolonial Societies*, edited by Gurminder K. Bhambra and John Narayan, 65–81. London: Routledge, 2017.

Garson, J.G. 'On the Physical Characteristics of the Lapps.' *The Journal of the Anthropological Institute of Great Britain and Ireland* 15 (1886): 235–238.

Gould, Stephen J. *The Mismeasure of Man*. New York: W.W. Norton & Norton, 1981.

Hegardt, Johan. 'Sven Nilsson and the Invention of Modern Man.' *Current Swedish Archaeology* 4 (1996): 51–67.

Kames, Henry Home, Lord. *Sketches of the History of Man*. Edinburgh: W. Creech, 1774.

Keane, Augustus Henry. 'The Lapps: Their Origin, Ethnical Affinities, Physical and Mental Characteristics, Usages, Present Status, and Future Prospects.' *The Journal of the Anthropological Institute of Great Britain and Ireland* 15 (1886): 213–235.

Kirshenblatt-Gimblett, Barbara. *Destination Culture: Tourism, Museums, and Heritage*. Berkeley: University of California Press, 1998.

Lantoo, Patrik, and Ulf Mörkenstam. 'Sami Rights and Sami Challenges: The Modernization Process and the Swedish Sami Movement, 1886–2006.' *Scandinavian Journal of History* 33, no. 1 (2008): 26–51.

Lubbock, John. *Pre-historic Times, as Illustrated by Ancient Remains, and the Manners and Customs of Savages*. London: Williams and Norgate, 1865.

Lundmark, Lennart. *Stulet land: Svensk makt på samisk mark*. Stockholm: Ordfront, 2008.

Lydon, Jane. *Photography, Humanitarianism, Empire*. London: Bloomsbury Academic, 2016.
Macallister, Miles. 'The Scandinavians "Hitchhiked" Their Way to the Boons of Empire.' *Aeon* (31 January 2018). https://aeon.co/ideas/the-hitchhiking-scandinavian-way-to-the-imperial-riches.
Maxwell, Anne. *Colonial Photography and Exhibitions: Representations of the Native and the Making of European Identities*. London: Leicester University Press, 1999.
Mayhew, Henry. *London Labour and the London Poor*. 4 vols. London: George Woodfall and Son; Griffin, Bohn, and Company, 1851–1862.
McClintock, Ann. *Imperial Leather: Race, Gender, and Sexuality in the Colonial Contest*. Routledge: New York, 1995.
Medak-Saltzman, Danika. 'Transnational Indigenous Exchange: Rethinking Global Interactions of Indigenous Peoples at the 1904 St. Louis Exposition.' *American Quarterly* 62, no. 3 (2010): 591–615.
Meek, Ronald L. *Social Science and the Ignoble Savage*. Cambridge: Cambridge University Press, 1976.
Naum, Magdalena, and Jonas M. Nordin, eds. *Scandinavian Colonialism and the Rise of Modernity: Small Time Agents in a Global Arena*. New York: Springer, 2013.
Nicklasson, Påvel. 'Johan Haquin Wallman, Sven Nilsson och den moderna arkeologins genombrott.' *Fornvännen: Journal of Swedish Antiquarian Research* 103 (2008): 102–110.
Nicklasson, Påvel. 'Sven Nilsson och Den Skandinaviska Nordens Urinvånare.' *Fornvännen: Journal of Swedish Antiquarian Research* 106 (2011): 161–178.
Nicklasson, Påvel. 'Sven Nilssons resa 1836.' *Fornvännen: Journal of Swedish Antiquarian Research* 108 (2013): 33–48.
Nilsson, Sven. *The Primitive Inhabitants of Scandinavia*, 3rd ed., edited by Sir John Lubbock. London: Longmans, 1868.
Pascoe, Bruce. *Dark Emu: Aboriginal Australia and the Birth of Agriculture*. Broome: Magabala Books, 2014/2018.
Patton, Mark. *Science, Politics, and the Business in the Works of Sir John Lubbock: A Man of Universal Mind*. Aldershot: Ashgate, 2007.
Poignant, Roslyn. *Professional Savages: Captive Lives and Western Spectacle*. New Haven, CT and London: Yale University Press, 2004.
Qureshi, Sadiah. *Peoples on Parade: Exhibitions, Empire, and Anthropology in Nineteenth-Century Britain*. Chicago, IL: The University of Chicago Press, 2011.
Redman, Samuel J. *Bonerooms: From Scientific Racism to Prehistory in Museums*. Cambridge, MA: Harvard University Press, 2016.
Rowley-Conwy, Peter. 'The Concept of Prehistory and the Invention of the Terms "Prehistoric" and "Prehistorian": The Scandinavian Origin, 1833–1850.' *European Journal of Archaeology* 9, no. 1 (2006): 103–130.
Rowley-Conwy, Peter. *From Genesis to Prehistory: The Archaeological Three Age System and Its Contested Reception in Denmark, Britain, and Ireland*. Oxford: Oxford University Press, 2007.
Sebastiani, Silvia. *The Scottish Enlightenment: Race, Gender and the Limits of Progress*. Basingstoke: Palgrave, 2013.
Stjernquist, Berta. 'Sven Nilsson som banbrytare i svensk arkeologi.' In *Sven Nilsson: En lärd i 1800-talets Lund*, edited by Gerhard Regnéll, 157–212. Lund: Kungl. Fysiografiska Sällskapet i Lund, 1983.
Sörlin, Sverker. 'Framtidslandet: debatten om Norrland och Naturresurserna under det industriella genombrottet.' PhD diss., Umeå University, 1988.
Tylor, Edward Burnett. *Primitive Culture: Researches into the Development of Mythology*, 2 vols. London: John Murray, 1871.
Young, Robert. *Colonial Desire: Hybridity in Theory, Culture and Race*. London: Routledge, 1995.
Walches, Kathryn. *Gamle Norge and Nineteenth-Century British Women Travellers in Norway*. London: Anthem Studies in Travel, 2014.

Wawn, Andrew. *The Vikings and the Victorians: Inventing the Old North in Nineteenth Century Britain*. Cambridge, MA: Brewer, 2000.

Wheeler, Roxann. *The Complexion of Race: Categories of Difference in Eighteenth-Century Britain*. Philadelphia: University of Pennsylvania Press, 2000.

Newspapers

Ally Sloper's Half-Holiday, 16 May 1885.
The Daily News, 5 May 1885.
The Era, 23 May 1885.
The Globe, 19 April 1885.
The Globe, 15 May 1885.
Lincolnshire Chronicle, 1 May 1885.
Literature, 29 February 1868.
The Literary Examiner, 14 March 1868.
The Morning Post, 14 May 1885.
The Pall Mall Gazette, 22 May 1885.
The Sportsman, 16 May 1885.
St. James's Gazette, 19 May 1885.
The Standard, 14 May 1885.
Supplement to John Bull, 31 October 1868.

Other

Letter from Nilsson to Darwin, 31 December 1868. Darwin Correspondence Project. 'Letter no. 6517.' https://www.darwinproject.ac.uk/letter/DCP-LETT-6517.xml.

13
LANGUAGE, TRANSLATION, AND TRANSFORMATION IN INDIGENOUS HISTORIES

Laura Rademaker

As the International Year of Indigenous Languages, 2019 brought the vitality of Indigenous languages (and the urgency of upholding them) to the world's attention. Along with the cosmologies, philosophies, and ways of life of their ancestors, many Indigenous peoples are claiming their language as integral to their intellectual sovereignty.[1] And Indigenous languages are a matter of sovereignty. This is not only because of languages' intellectual, aesthetic, and cultural value, but for the way they link Indigenous peoples to their land. Indigenous languages name places and features of the landscape. For many Indigenous peoples, these languages were spoken or sung by the beings who brought the landscape and its peoples into formation. In Australian Aboriginal traditions, language indicates how one is related to the land.[2] Each language is connected to a particular country because it is the language of the Creative Beings who shaped that place. Language is embedded in the earth. By recognising the language of the country, therefore, one also recognises the speakers of the language as owning and belonging to the land – that is, as sovereigns.

Given the primacy of language to Indigenous systems of belonging and landownership, the struggle for sovereignty has also involved a struggle for the survival and legitimacy of Indigenous languages.[3] The invasion by colonisers of Indigenous lands in many places presented an existential threat to the survival of Indigenous languages. This being true, it is also true that in many places, colonisers took up Indigenous languages as tools in the colonial process. Colonisers considered Indigenous languages the key to understanding, and so manipulating, the 'native mind'. Yet, as we shall see, these moves also meant that Indigenous people could and did use their linguistic expertise and translation to thwart or transform the designs of colonisers.

This chapter explores the ways Indigenous people engaged with, evaded, and undermined colonisers' efforts through language and translation. It can be said that 'translation' is present in all cross-cultural encounters, as the signs and signifiers of others' worlds take on new meanings across cultures. In this chapter, I focus on translation of language, although insights around language can be applied to translation of symbols, ideas, practices, and traditions. I focus, in particular, on Indigenous encounters with missionary translation and linguistic projects because these were often the sites of most intensive engagement with Indigenous languages in colonial contexts. Of course, Indigenous peoples have long had their own traditions of translation in cross-cultural contexts, quite apart from their experiences of colonisation. Indeed, Indigenous people drew on these traditions in their engagement with colonisers. But here I am interested in colonial contexts because they reveal the ways translation was wielded both against and by Indigenous peoples. I argue that Indigenous people have had their own varied reasons for embracing, resisting, or redirecting missionary attempts at translation. Indigenous people created new meanings and opportunities for themselves through translation. As Anna Brickhouse puts it, 'Indigenous epistemologies both appropriate and transform rather than simply resist their colonial counterparts.'[4] Through the ambiguities and opportunities of language and text in translation, Indigenous peoples pushed and pulled missionaries and other colonial authorities into or away from their own worlds.

Interpreters and mediators

When European missionaries arrived in Indigenous lands, they were compelled to depend on interpreters. Sometimes, other Europeans could fill this role. The missionaries on the *Duff* in Tahiti in the late eighteenth century used European beachcombers already living among Tahitians.[5] But otherwise, missionaries' presence opened opportunities for linguistically gifted Indigenous people to create roles for themselves as mediators of the spoken word for the newcomers and various local peoples. For example, the Society for the Propagation of the Gospel sent Philip Quaque to the Cape Coast in the late eighteenth century. Quaque was African himself but, having grown up in England, spoke no African languages, so Frederick Adoy, a local, became his interpreter. For Adoy, this was an opportunity. Sometimes, he made Quaque cut short his sermon, then he began demanding a salary; Quaque was at the mercy of the local interpreter.[6] Often, the mediators like Adoy were men, but in some places, they were women. Around the Western Great Lakes Region, for instance, Native women found that cooperating with Jesuit missionaries as their interpreters became a means to grow their prominence and authority in their own community.[7] These privileges were not only in a missionary context. In colonial French West Africa in the late nineteenth century, local African intermediaries could rise to positions of considerable authority in the colonial bureaucracy due to the need for interpretation. Being multilingual meant the ability to cultivate, exploit, or evade relationships with European officials.[8] One French commander complained that he was surrounded by a 'circle of iron', that is, he was trapped by deceptions and 'mistranslations' that the local interpreter and chief used to limit his influence.[9] Yet as colonial power became more entrenched, these opportunities for subversion through language increasingly evaporated.

Where missionaries failed to win converts or to establish themselves in a community, they often blamed interpreters. Missionary James Pucky claimed that the 'sole cause' of missionaries leaving Tahiti in 1798 was that their beachcomber interpreters misrepresented what they were trying to tell Tahitians.[10] Missionaries believed that interpreters simplified their message.[11] Sometimes, there must have been a kind of 'Chinese whispers'. George Brown in New Ireland, for instance, addressed villagers in 'pigeon English'. His interpreter translated to a neighbouring language and another man then translated to the local language. Any subtlety in Brown's message was surely lost.[12] So missionaries fretted about their message being distorted, underexplained, or simplified. They often concluded that while interpreters were sufficient for day-to-day talk, they were inadequate to convey spiritual matters.[13]

One way for missionaries to do away with the dependence on Indigenous mediators was to silence Indigenous languages altogether. In Australia, for instance, missionaries (along with other settlers) mostly gave little attention to Aboriginal languages until the second half of the twentieth century. Although missionaries had been in operation in Australia since the 1830s, Protestant missionary linguists' great ambition, the translation of the entire Bible, was only accomplished in any Aboriginal language as recently as 2007. The widespread disregard for Indigenous languages was due largely to missionary enthusiasm for assimilatory policies, according to which there could be no future for Aboriginal languages. Aboriginal languages were hushed through mission schools, dormitories, and mission confines, where English was dominant. Few missionaries learned languages or translated scripture; missions such as Hermannsburg and Ernabella, which used the vernacular, were the exception. For most missionaries, English was the language in which they could most comfortably assert their authority, intelligence, and knowledge. English also did away with the need to depend on Indigenous translators and mediators.

In New Zealand, however, missionaries took the opposite approach. The Church Missionary Society (CMS) in New Zealand in the nineteenth century avoided English, and missionaries did not teach Māori people to read, speak, or understand it. Instead, they deliberately restricted all written material available to te reo Māori. Teaching English, missionaries worried, would enable Māori to bond with traders and seamen or other 'undesirables'. It would give access to secular literature.[14] The Māori exclusion from English also functioned to establish missionaries as sole representatives of Māori. Tejaswini Niranjana argues that translation used in this way is an instrument of containment because colonised people can be represented in a way that justifies their domination.[15] In this case, missionaries used writing to represent Māori as vulnerable, in need of protecting. Māori people's exclusion from English, as Tony Ballantyne argues, meant that they could not shape representations of themselves to Europeans in the Colonial Office. Māori depended on missionaries to translate and promote their writing for their claims to be heard in the settlers' world.[16] For this reason, as Torres Strait Islander Martin Nakata points out, Indigenous people have often demanded schooling in English; their demands have been about 'working out what the language of "white" people and their institutions do that keeps us at a disadvantage, that keeps us as the less "knowers" in situations'.[17]

Missionary translation projects and reducing language to writing

In many places, however, missionaries turned to translation as their primary tool for converting and 'civilising' native peoples. This, of course, was consistent with the missionary belief that all languages could be vehicles of God's truth, and that all cultures were destined to receive the Gospel. Although missionaries often treated local cultures with contempt, these theological commitments often led them to take a greater interest in Indigenous cultures (for better or worse) than other colonisers. In the Philippines, for instance, such was the importance of communicating the Gospel in the local language that, in 1582, the Manila Ecclesiastical Junta made translation the official policy and, in 1603, the Spanish king decreed that every missionary must know 'the language of the *indios*'.[18] The study of Indigenous languages was also a project of seeking to know and control Indigenous people. As Joseph Errington puts it, colonial agents 'made alien ways of speaking into objects of knowledge, so that their speakers could be made subjects of colonial power'.[19] Missionaries studied Indigenous language and culture to seek to know (and change) the 'native mind'.[20] Anthropologists Jean and John Comaroff describe missionaries' project as the 'colonisation of consciousness'.[21] For them, colonisation entails a struggle over meaning, over the ways people perceive themselves and their place in the world.[22] The Comaroffs call the project of developing an orthography and translating the Bible 'colonisation of language', because missionaries used Indigenous people's own symbols and language to penetrate their culture and to re-make it from inside in their own image.[23]

'Reducing' Indigenous languages to writing was central to this project. It would, colonisers hoped, do away with the uncertainty introduced when interpreters used the spoken word. Writing enabled the presentation of Indigenous languages in a standardised code, known to colonisers. Errington, therefore, calls colonial linguists' work to 'reduce' oral languages to writing an 'act of symbolic violence'.[24] Imperial historian Jane Sampson calls it 'linguistic colonialism'.[25] 'Reducing' languages in the Renaissance sense meant ordering and, supposedly, purifying them to an ideal form.[26] By 'reducing' the languages, later linguists claimed to capture the empirical reality of languages in European letters and symbols without reference to language as embodied talk.[27] Missionaries therefore controlled the representation of this aspect of Indigenous culture, presenting it as an unchanging objective fact on a page – a grammar and a dictionary – removing it from the mouths of Indigenous speakers and cementing it in writing.

Through developing orthographies, missionaries recreated Indigenous languages in the likeness of European languages. Many were forced uncomfortably into Latin letters, reading left to right. In his history of nineteenth-century missions in China, Eric Rainders finds that some missionaries considered the Chinese language a 'curse' upon the Chinese, blaming illiteracy on a supposedly 'impossible' orthography.[28] At African missions, the dream of a uniform orthography was an aspect of the dream of the 'unification of languages… and ultimately unification of Africa under Christianity'.[29] Reducing and standardising Indigenous languages, therefore, was part of an attempt to recast and recreate these languages in Christian terms – in print – for Christian purposes.

In some places, therefore, Indigenous people resisted the 'reduction' of their language. To many, their language is an oral language, and outsiders have no right to put it in print. In her conversations with Nakoda people, for instance, Mindy Morgan found deep resistance to their language in written form. Their concerns were not simply about writing but questions of cultural authority, authenticity, knowledge, and, ultimately, sovereignty.[30]

In other contexts, dissatisfied with the Western orthographies imposed on their language, Indigenous people created their own writing systems, often drawing on their own traditions to do so. Sequoyah of the Cherokee nation famously invented a Cherokee writing system. His work was to the great frustration of colonisers who sought a uniform orthography for Native American peoples. But the Cherokee resisted this project, preferring their laws, scriptures, and newspapers to be represented in their own alphabet.[31] The bilingual *Cherokee Phoenix* (the first Indigenous newspaper in the world) used the Cherokee script. By moving across both English and Cherokee literacies, the Cherokee used writing to demonstrate their unity and sophistication.[32] Ho-Chunk (Winnebago) people, similarly, adopted a syllabic script for their language in the 1880s.[33] Mi'kmaq people and French Catholic missionaries together developed the pre-existing Mi'kmaq hieroglyphic script into a script that could communicate Catholic prayers in the late seventeenth century (Figure 13.1).[34]

Once introduced by missionaries to writing, this means of communication often became very attractive to Indigenous people. Despite their initial scepticism about the missionaries' message, Tahitians found their writing particularly valuable. A 'literate revolution' rolled through the Pacific as Indigenous peoples demanded more access to texts. Although exactly why is debated, as Pacific people had diverse reasons for wanting translated Bibles, it is likely that they associated script with European power and prestige. Becoming literate meant new opportunities for gaining powerful spiritual knowledge, so the translated Bible was of great interest.[35] According to missionaries, Tahitians were obsessed with reading, day and night.[36] While the missionaries had a reason to exaggerate this enthusiasm, the quantity of literature produced to cater for their needs reflects an enormous Pacific appetite for texts. In 1877, for instance, the British and Foreign Bible Society claimed to have circulated 81,000 Māori New Testaments and 20,000 full Bibles in Samoan.[37] The Māori New Testament printed in runs of 20,000 in 1841, 1843, and 1845. That is, two New Testaments for every three Māori every two years.[38] Māori people themselves taught each other to read, often without European intervention, encouragement, or even their knowledge.[39]

Nevertheless, missionaries presumed that they had authority over writing in Indigenous languages. Such was this presumption that in New Zealand, missionary translator Robert Maunsell set himself the task of using the second edition of the Bible to make the language more 'convenient'. He explained his method:

> The Māori Bible is much larger than English Bible. This is an inconvenience to [the] Māori, who is almost always moving. It is a wordy language …

Language, translation, and transformation

Figure 13.1 Sequoyah
Source: Library of Congress, Washington, DC (Digital file no. cph 3g02566)

[including] particles and adjuncts which have no meaning. We have agreed to cut off adjuncts (ornamental, as in *kote miatanga mai; o Te tino whakatikanguaki o*), though a Māori would use them. There was no written language when we came. We are now making one, and compelling, as it were, the colloquial language to reduce its dimensions.[40]

Maunsell literally went to work 'reducing' the language, clearing it of inefficiencies according to his preferences. Presuming that missionaries owned the language by writing it down, he claimed authority to reshape it. The Māori did not appreciate his work and the second edition failed to sell. When the first full Bibles came in 1868, they attracted little interest compared to the boom of the 1840s.[41] 'We got our Christ from you, now we return it back', a Māori leader told the Bishop of Waiapu.[42]

It was impossible for missionaries to ever 'standardise' languages. Syntax, grammars, and orthographies were always unstable because Indigenous people used their language and various systems of writing in different ways and for different purposes. As Historian Derek Peterson argues, standard Gikuyu, for instance, was never 'standard'. In the 1930s, it had three orthographies, and a fourth developed among Gikuyu politicians and converts for their journals and correspondence. In the 1980s, postcolonial Gikuyu writers created a fifth.[43]

Moreover, the representation of Indigenous languages in print, even as the vessel for communicating 'holy scripture', was also an inadvertent recognition of the prestige and value of Indigenous languages according to European norms.[44] Religious studies scholar Lamin Sanneh describes missionary use of vernacular languages as a 'tacit surrender to indigenous primacy'.[45] Whenever a Bible was completed in an Indigenous language, it became a tangible record of that language in a medium the colonisers recognised as valuable. It now conveyed the Word of God – albeit in the materiality of the written text. Indigenous languages were, perhaps inadvertently, put on the same level as English. Recognising this may have motivated some Indigenous people to have their language in print and to translate the Bible. The Massachusett *Indian Grammar* (1666) revealed that this language could be described according to a set of rules, just like the classical languages so esteemed by Europeans.[46] Historian Anna Johnston similarly finds that nineteenth-century missionaries' realisation that Polynesian languages were in fact complex and sophisticated brought a 'crisis in European self-confidence'. As these languages were complex, subtle, and expressive *like English*, they challenged missionary distinctions between themselves and 'heathen' societies.[47]

Indigenous co-translators as authors

Colonial translators depended on dialogue with native linguists who taught (Figure 13.2), advised, and interpreted for them. John Eliot's Massachusett Bible of 1663, for instance, was not his own work – he did not have the linguistic competency – it was produced by two Native translators, James Printer and Job Nesuton.[48] Though missionary linguists may have sought to 'mitigate or manage' the presence of native speakers in their translations, they could never erase their influence.[49] Peterson sees missionary linguists' dictionaries – the 'reduction' of Indigenous languages to writing – as implements of colonisation. Nonetheless, he finds Indigenous voices embedded in these texts.[50] Missionary discourses were 'inflected with multiple and often contradictory meanings as they were translated' and therefore 'inherently hybrid'.[51] Rachael Gilmour suggests that language has been used to assert control but missionaries' attempts to evangelise by translation could be subverted by their Indigenous co-translators; translation was not imposed on passive populations but occurred through partnership with Indigenous people who always had their own ideas.[52] By remaking Christian texts in their own languages, Indigenous translators imbued these texts with new meanings.[53] There is evidence that Indigenous translators consciously understood themselves as authors. That is, they knew their contribution was more than simply transfer of a message from

Language, translation, and transformation

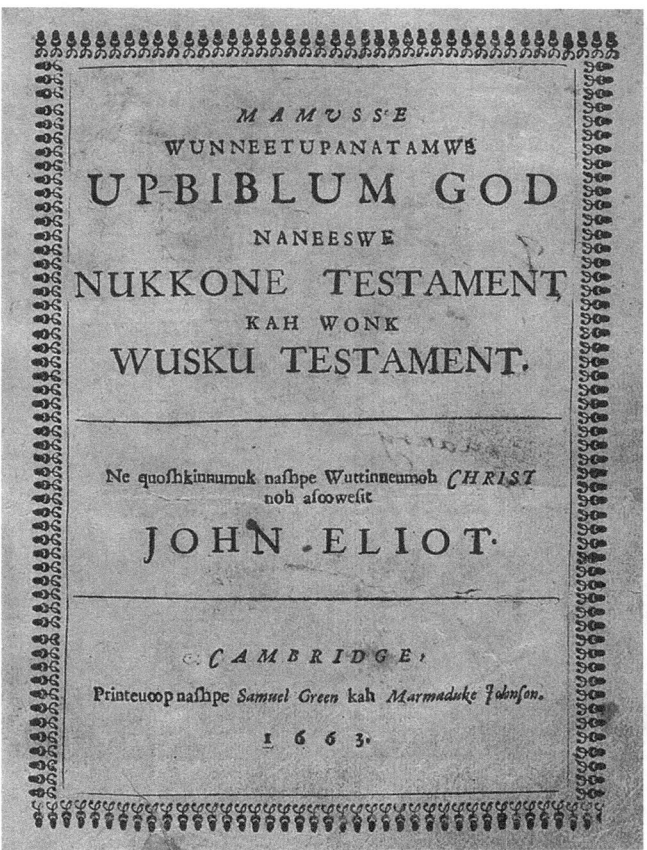

Figure 13.2 The Massachusett Bible, 1663

one language to another; they were authors. The Gospel of Mark was published in Mohawk in 1774 through the work of Thayendanegea (Joseph Brant), the Haudenosaunee leader. Where the English text ended, the Mohawk version continued with a statement of authorship and date. Thayendanegea did not use the Mohawk word for 'translate' here; he stated in Mohawk that he *wrote* it (Figure 13.3).[54]

Missionaries were rightly concerned that their message might take on unintended meanings in translation. It might even be corrupted by its association with Indigenous concepts or simply through the use of Indigenous words. For example, the most difficult, but the most important translation for missionaries, was finding a word for the divine, for 'God', in a 'heathen' language. Missionaries took care not to 'take the name of the Lord thy God in vain'. In some contexts, missionaries hoped to demonstrate that Indigenous peoples had a concept of the divine. For example, in Central Australia, missionary Carl Strehlow and anthropologist Baldwin Spencer clashed over the translation of the Western Arrernte word *altyerre*. Strehlow translated it 'God'; Spencer called it 'the dream times'.[55] Yet using vernacular words

Figure 13.3 'Portrait of the Mohawk Chieftain Thayendanegea, known as Joseph Brant (1742–1807)' Gilbert Stuart 1786

to describe the spiritual realm risked confusing Christian doctrine with pagan ideas. The Jesuits in the sixteenth-century China used '*Shangti*' for God. This identified the Christian God with the Confucian Most-High (*Shangti*), offending non-Christian Chinese intellectuals.[56] Most missionaries, therefore, preferred to import a loan-word, rather than risk the identification of the Christian God with a foreign deity. The 1663 Massachusett Bible used the word 'God', as missionaries claimed no Massachusett word was 'sufficient to convey knowledge of Divine things'.[57] But this also carried some risk. Unfortunate Jesuit missionaries in Japan in the sixteenth century unwittingly alliterated the Latin *Deus* to the Japanese *Daiusu*, but this was heard as 'Great Lie' (*dai usō*) by the Japanese.[58]

Ultimately, Indigenous people themselves controlled whether translations would be acceptable. Sanneh finds that Zulu converts rejected both the Anglican missionaries' *uDio* (imported from Latin *Deus*) and the Methodists' *uJehova* and began using their own word, *uNkulunkulu*. Eventually, missionaries from all denominations were compelled to adopt the Zulu word, even though it meant revising all their translations.[59] In Kenya, irresolvable translation disputes had to be put to a vote, so 1913 Africa Inland Mission linguists and Gikuyu converts voted on how to translate key terms.⁶⁰ In colonial New South Wales in the 1920s, missionary Lancelot Threlkeld searched for a word in Awabakal for the Christian deity. His Awabakal co-translator Biraban suggested *Koun*, the name of the Eaglehawk Creative Spirit and law-giver. Threlkeld thought this inappropriate and introduced a word from the Hebrew: *Eloi*. Regardless, Biraban persisted in his honour of *Koun*, finding that his own traditions resonated with his new learning about the Christian deity.⁶¹ On Groote Eylandt, the CMS introduced the word 'god' into Anindilyakwa. Yet, the decision was overturned by Indigenous converts. In the 1970s, Anindilyakwa speakers began referring to *Neningikarrawara* which means 'Him belonging to above'.⁶² Their law-giver, Nambirrirrma, also came from above, suggesting an association with the Christian God. Indigenous people fitted their own concepts to Christian doctrines and missionary linguists had to re-write their translations accordingly.

Setting the message loose in translation

Just as translated texts were inevitably inflected with Indigenous meanings, Indigenous evangelists preached a transformed message. The missionary expansion across the Pacific was rapid, but it was Pacific Islanders themselves who spread Christianity. In many areas, Europeans had little to do with it; before missionaries arrived in Samoa in 1835, Tongan families had already introduced Christianity there.⁶³ The faith spread along existing trade networks and complemented Indigenous relationships of reciprocity that dictated trading patterns. In New Zealand, Māori people spread Christianity and Māori language literacy (they went together). Evangelism presented Māori – especially those with chiefly status – with an opportunity for greater honour and authority.⁶⁴

Missionaries could not control Indigenous Christianities. They sprang up too quickly for missionaries to have any hope of regulating them. The expansion of local, hybrid Indigenous Christianities was accelerated by the missionary practice of sending 'native evangelists' ahead. In the Pacific, for instance, Indigenous preachers prepared the way for missionaries to come in later. This was because missionary societies needed to harness the networks and the cultural and linguistic knowledge of Indigenous converts; they could not go alone. Polynesians instructed by the London Missionary Society went all the way to the Cook Islands, New Hebrides, and New Guinea. The first missionaries in New Guinea were Melanesians in the 1870s, followed by Polynesians in the 1880s. Europeans only came in substantial numbers in the 1890s.⁶⁵ In New Zealand, Māori chiefs Matene Te Whiwhi and Tamihana Te Rauparaha were the first Anglican missionaries in the southernmost parts of the South Island.⁶⁶ 'Native evangelists' were, in historian Matt Matsuda's words, the 'advanced guard', preparing the way for European missionaries.⁶⁷

This was not only a Pacific phenomenon. In the Atlantic context, Native American missionaries had many advantages over Europeans, due to Natives' linguistic and cultural knowledge.⁶⁸ Native missionaries could not only translate languages; they could translate concepts, so were vital to missions' evangelistic success.⁶⁹ Of course, many Native people chose not to cooperate with Europeans, sometimes mocking their efforts or even giving misinformation.[70] Native preachers were both an opportunity and a challenge for the European missionaries – the Native message could not be controlled.[71] Even where Europeans understood the Indigenous language, they might not grasp the hidden meaning of a message, veiled in cultural allusions or inuendo.[72] Historian Elizabeth Elbourne argues, therefore, that African converts 'took up Christianity and transformed it from within', sometimes even using Christianity to 'combat colonialism'.[73] Though missionaries envisaged their faith as a 'coherent, rationalising, globalising system that taught one universal truth', in reality, 'Christianity was out of control, unorthodox and an available subject for reinterpretation according to the needs of its interlocutors.'[74]

Literacy was especially valuable for Indigenous people in creating space to redirect the missionary message towards Indigenous ends. This is because texts and stories – especially when translated – have the capacity to be constantly reinterpreted. Vicente Rafael describes the 'uneasy relationship between translation and conversion' in the Spanish colonisation of the Philippines. He finds that the translation of religious texts simultaneously instituted and subverted colonial rule, consolidating colonisers' hierarchies and authorities while also validating local reinterpretations of the text.[75] This was the case in New Zealand. Māori people were also able to use texts in translation to create new identities and political alliances. Yet, the Treaty of Waitangi, in translation, was famously a betrayal of the Māori, with continuing ramifications today.

While missionaries tried to harness this linguistic revolution, again, they had no hope of controlling it. Māori developed their own scriptural hermeneutic and debated Biblical interpretation at length. As an early Pākehā observer commented, 'they will often sit for hours together criticising the meaning of a phrase in their books.'[76] The result was a hybridised tradition, drawing on Christian and Biblical elements as well as their own traditions. Some Māori found, within the missionaries' book itself, a way to express their rejection of missionaries. They discovered the Jews. Samuel Marsden was first to speculate that Māori might be lost descendants of Israel in 1819.[77] To suggest that Indigenous people are not, in fact indigenous is a common strategy of settler-colonialism as it works to negate Indigenous people's claim to their land.[78] Māori people, however, co-opted this discourse and made it a form of religious dissent. Perplexing the missionaries, in the 1830s and 1840s, some Māori began calling themselves 'unbelievers' and 'Tiu' ('Jews') to express their defiance of missionary Christianity.[79]

It took until 1858 for the publication of the Old Testament in the Māori language because the Anglican Bishop opposed its gradual publication in pamphlet form, fearing that Māori would develop strange reinterpretations if given such free access.[80] To Māori, therefore, it held special esoteric, restricted knowledge like that of their *whare wanaga* (secret law).[81] When the Old Testament finally came, Māori liked it better than the New. Its production coincided with a time of Māori disillusionment with missionaries, given the failure of the Treaty of Waitangi to secure their interests. For them, the Old Testament told them that they were Israel and their land the Promised Land. Its narrative of slavery, liberation, and imperial domination resonated with their own lives.[82] They found commonalities between God as revealed in the Old Testament and their own *atua*. The God of the New Testament, one commented, was 'too quiet, too lazy and not so good for the Māori'.[83]

From the 1860s, therefore, a new generation of Māori called themselves 'Tui'. Doing so, they were embracing the parts of the Bible most relevant to them without accepting the missionaries' message. Māori even assimilated Noah and Shem into their *whakapapa* (genealogies), grounding Māori identity in the Genesis narratives.[84] They began calling their land *Kanana*, that is, Canan, the Promised Land, God's inheritance to them.[85] Of course, to missionaries, these were misinterpretations. Missionaries ridiculed the idea that Māori were Israelites and that their land was holy.[86] Yet, Māori mapped Biblical themes into their geographies, translating them into their world in ways which asserted their rights to their land in the face of settler-colonial challenges to it.[87]

For other Māori, embracing Christian identities did not necessarily mean embracing Pākehā institutions or authority. Many Māori converts, including teacher, missionary, and lay reader Henare Wiremu Taratoa, fought and died in battles against the British.[88] Christianity became another resource for some Māori prophets to use against the colonisers. CMS missionary at Otaki, Octavius Hadfield reported in 1860 that the Māori 'had carefully examined the New Testament' and concluded that 'either the English nation ... was not Christian ... or Christianity was not true'.[89] Māori used the Bible – their 'weapon' – to critique settler violence, while retaining their Māori identities and separateness. As one Māori leader claimed:

> See! this [New Testament] is my weapon; the white man's book. You sent us this book, and it tell us not to fight: you have got other weapons – weapons of blood: use them not; fight not; or my heathen relations will fight too. Remember your book! Remember your book![90]

Yes, the Bible was his weapon, but he could always summon his 'heathen relations' if appeals to the Bible failed to correct the Pākehā. He used a Christian Māori identity as a double-edged sword against the colonists (Figure 13.4).

Indigenous writing cultures

Indigenous peoples developed their own writing cultures, what Phillip Round calls 'syncretic literacy practices'.[91] The introduction of literacy does not inevitably replace oral traditions, nor does it replace existing cultures of epistemology and interpretation.[92] The Mapuche people of Chile, for instance, developed shamanic literacies. Biographic books or 'Bibles' could serve as ritual objects and means of storing shamanic power in text.[93] George Augustus Robinson found an ochre-covered prayer book in Van Diemen's Land in 1831 in what similarly appeared to be a book transformed for a ritual purpose.[94]

As Ballantyne shows, in an environment of rapid changes, Māori people embraced writing as a tool for recasting Indigenous identity.[95] Michael Stevens

Figure 13.4 Henare Wiremu Taratoa, c.1860. 1/2–011005-F, Alexander Turnbull Library

describes a 'Māori modernity' that included English literacies as a modern resource for Indigenous people.[96] Writing in English had strategic, practical benefits in terms of negotiation with colonisers and books and newspapers also offered new types of entertainment and enjoyment. Writing in te reo Māori also created new ways of being Māori.[97] Writing is portable, so literacy brought Māori closer together. They began to write letters to each other. The ability to do so proved essential for Māori political organisation in later decades. Missionaries promoted the circulation of Māori language newspapers, which were pivotal to the development of a collective Māori consciousness that bridged tribal identities.[98] From the 1860s, some newspapers were owned and operated by Māori themselves. These worked to unify Māori thought on issues such as land, and educate Māori about their world and society.[99] Māori also used print to record their *whakapapa* (genealogies) in the front of family Bibles or in notebooks from the 1860s. This effectively democratised important, authoritative cultural knowledge about ancestors and identity.

Anyone who could read could now access this knowledge; it was no longer the preserve of learned individuals.[100] At the same time, writing also created new ways to display *mana* (prestige). Māori leaders took to letter-writing, newspapers, and displaying their knowledge of the Bible in writings and preaching to show their learnedness.[101] Māori took up literacy in ways that transformed traditional patterns of transmitting knowledge and conveying prestige.

In many places, Indigenous people turned their mission education to subversive ends. As Nakata writes, such education has enabled Indigenous people to 'cut better deals for ourselves and our traditional heritage in changing times'.[102] When mission-educated African preachers in colonial Natal established independent churches, teaching that the Bible said 'Ethiopians' would be freed from Europeans, F.R. Moor, the Minister for Native Affairs opposed 'native preachers' and recommended that all missionary work be limited to Europeans. Missionary education, he believed, was 'wasted' on Africans; missionaries should only teach trades.[103] Historian Norman Etherington suggests that the eventual forced closure of mission schools that refused to teach the government curriculum under the Bantu Education Act (1953) was a continuation of the uneasy relationship between missions and the colonial state over the subversive power of Indigenous education. 'It was no accident', he concludes, that many of the leaders of the African National Congress in 1912 had been educated at missions.[104] In Australia, mission-educated people used their education and, in particular, the power of writing to pursue Indigenous political interests. Yorta Yorta man William Cooper learned to write at Maloga mission. His 1937 petition to King George VI gained over 2,000 signatures, many obtained (likely surreptitiously) through circulation to other Aboriginal missions.[105] The 1963 Yolngu Bark Petition to the Australian Parliament claimed Yolngu rights to land. Written in Yolŋu Matha with English translation, it arose from Yolngu people's encounter with missionaries and writing at the Yirrkala mission. Even the typewriter that Wandjuk Marika (one of the signatories) used to make the Yolngu claim was purchased from a departing missionary.[106] Though the missions in Australia (and their educational programmes) were deeply entangled in colonising the agendas of the settler state, even these could become hotbeds of Indigenous dissent and spaces for the repurposing of writing towards Indigenous political ends.

Nevertheless, for other peoples, literacy was not an ideal. Penny Van Toorn argues that when Aboriginal people in colonial Australia first encountered writing, it came entangled in colonisers' ideologies of literacy and civilisation and that this context shaped Aboriginal peoples' varied engagement with writing.[107] On Groote Eylandt, many Aboriginal people never learned to read in English or their own language. Such was the association of writing with attempts to assimilate them into the colonisers' culture; they opted out of missionaries' literacies.[108] Morgan shows that for many Native American communities, English literacy and the institutional power of colonisers were likewise inextricably linked.[109] The use of documents as mechanisms of control in the context of unequal power relationships shaped how Indigenous people perceived the use and purpose of literacies. Writing could become laden with cultural meanings associated with colonisers and was not always readily reconciled with Indigenous identities.[110] Native Americans did use writing in various ways, but not all were eager to become writers themselves. In the 1760s, Onoongwandekha advised the Oneida against accepting missionaries and, specifically, against accepting their book. The Bible was 'a white people's book ... [that] was never made for Indians'. Instead, 'the Great Spirit [already] gave us a book' and 'he wrote it in our hands and in our minds'.[111] For him, their knowledge and spirituality could not be contained in writing.

Long traditions and translating for the future

Translation at missions became a vital way of preserving knowledge with a view to future generations. Indigenous linguists could use missions, paradoxically, as a means of preserving and defending their culture because missions created a space where Indigenous people's linguistic and cultural autonomy and knowledge of language could be retained, albeit channelled through Christianity.[112] Texts produced through the missionary encounter are, today, invaluable for Indigenous people who are reclaiming their linguistic and cultural sovereignty. As Sean Harvey and Sarah Rivett argue, this is possible due to 'incipient forms of linguistic sovereignty present in colonial indigenous language encounters all along'.[113] There was also an implicit concession to Indigenous knowledge and sovereignty where colonisers engaged with Indigenous languages.

Today's language revival projects are direct resistance to processes of settler-colonisation and its dominating language – English – but they also continue the work of Indigenous people who recorded their languages generations ago in a tradition of resistance. The Wompanoag Language Reclamation Project, for instance, depends on the vast array of words recorded in the Eliot Bible. Likewise, although Mohawk is still spoken (but endangered), mission sources continue to inform those studying the language because those translations were made by Mohawk people.[114] In Australia, language revival projects in Awabakal and Kaurna likewise depend primarily on mission sources. While, in the nineteenth century, Biraban was thought to be one of the last speakers of his Awabakal language, his translation work has meant that many more Awabakal are speaking their language today. As Hawai'ian scholars put it, generations today are reaping the benefits that their ancestors imagined from a distance:

> In the twenty-first century, we are who they foresaw: descendants whose primary language is now that of the colonizer, but who need and are benefiting from their efforts to write in Hawaiian.[115]

This means that the very projects that sought to undermine Indigenous sovereignty and undercut Indigenous cultural autonomy (as discussed in this chapter) have, in fact, turned out to be the foundations for new movements of cultural resurgence. In many cases, translation projects of centuries ago are ultimately working in the interests of Indigenous communities that continue to use them for their own purposes. Yet as the historical insights of this chapter reveal, these language resurgence and revival movements can, in many ways, be understood as continuing longstanding traditions of Indigenous people who have used language, translation, linguistics, and literacy to pursue the interests of their communities in the face of ongoing processes of colonisation. Of course, this occurred differently in different places, according to the cultures, politics, and power dynamics of the missionary and colonial encounters. Yet, language and translation have been, and continue to be, crucial weapons in Indigenous people's arsenal in resurgence movements, upholding, defending, and promoting their intellectual and cultural sovereignty.

Notes

1 Noenoe K. Silva and Ngugi Wa Thiong'o, *The Power of the Steel-Tipped Pen: Reconstructing Native Hawaiian Intellectual History* (Durham, NC: Duke University Press, 2017), 211.
2 Nicholas Evans, *Dying Words Endangered Languages and What They Have to Tell Us* (Oxford: Wiley-Blackwell, 2010), 6.
3 Laura Rademaker, *Found in Translation: Many Meanings on a North Australian Mission* (Honolulu: University of Hawai'i Press, 2018), 8.
4 Anna Brickhouse, *The Unsettlement of America: Translation, Interpretation, and the Story of Don Luis de Velasco, 1560–1945* (Oxford: Oxford University Press, 2014), 46.
5 Nicholas Thomas, *Islanders: The Pacific in the Age of Empire* (New Haven, CT: Yale University Press, 2010), 36.
6 Edward E. Andrews, 'Christian Missions and Colonial Empires Reconsidered: A Black Evangelist in West Africa, 1766–1816,' *Journal of Church and State* 51, no. 4 (2009): 680.
7 Susan Sleeper-Smith, *Indian Women and French Men: Rethinking Cultural Encounter in the Western Great Lakes* (Amherts: University of Massachusetts Press, 2001), 21.
8 Benjamin N. Lawrance, Emily Lynn Osborn, and Richard L. Roberts, *Intermediaries, Interpreters, and Clerks: African Employees in the Making of Colonial Africa* (Madison: University of Wisconsin Press, 2006), 12–13.
9 Emily Lynn Osborn, '"Circle of Iron": African Colonial Employees and the Interpretation of Colonial Rule in French West Africa,' *The Journal of African History* 44, no. 1 (2003): 29.
10 Niel Gunson, *Messengers of Grace: Evangelical Missionaries in the South Seas 1797–1860* (Oxford: Oxford University Press, 1978), 255.
11 William J. Samarin, 'Language in the Colonization of Central Africa, 1880–1900,' *Canadian Journal of African Studies/La Revue Canadienne des Études Africaines* 23, no. 2 (1989): 233.
12 Helen Bethea Gardner, *Gathering for God: George Brown in Oceania* (Dunedin: Otago University Press, 2006), 57.
13 Rachael Gilmour, *Grammars of Colonialism: Representing Languages in Colonial South Africa* (Basingstoke: Palgrave, 2006), 59.
14 Bronwyn Elsmore, *Like Them That Dream: The Maori and the Old Testament*, 2nd ed. (Auckland: Reed Books, 2000), 29.
15 Tejaswini Niranjana, *Siting Translation: History, Post-Structuralism, and the Colonial Context* (Berkeley: University of California Press, 1992), 3.
16 Tony Ballantyne, *Entanglements of Empire: Missionaries, Māori, and the Question of the Body* (Auckland: Auckland University Press, 2015), 257.
17 Martin Nakata, *Disciplining the Savages: Savaging the Disciplines* (Canberra: Aboriginal Studies Press, 2007), 161.
18 Vicente L. Rafael, *Contracting Colonialism: Translation and Christian Conversion in Tagalog Society Under Early Spanish Rule* (Ithaca: Cornell University Press, 1988), 19.
19 Joseph Errington, *Linguistics in a Colonial World: A Story of Language, Meaning, and Power* (Malden, MA: John Wiley & Sons, 2007), vii.

20 Gilmour, *Grammars of Colonialism*, 164.
21 Jean Comaroff and John Comaroff, *Of Revelation and Revolution, Volume 1: Christianity, Colonialism and Consciousness in South Africa* (Chicago, IL: University of Chicago Press, 1991), 252.
22 Comaroff and Comaroff, *Of Revelation and Revolution*, xi.
23 Comaroff and Comaroff, *Of Revelation and Revolution*, 215, 218.
24 Errington, *Linguistics in a Colonial World*, viii.
25 Jane Samson, 'Translation Teams: Missionaries, Islanders, and the Reduction of Language in the Pacific,' in *Missionaries, Indigenous Peoples and Cultural Exchange*, ed. Patricia Grimshaw and Andrew May (Eastbourne: Sussex Academic Press, 2010), 96.
26 Byron Ellsworth Hamann, 'How to Chronologize with a Hammer, Or, The Myth of Homogeneous, Empty Time,' *HAU: Journal of Ethnographic Theory* 6, no. 1 (2016): 267–268. See also William F. Hanks, *Converting Words: Maya in the Age of the Cross* (Berkeley: University of California Press, 2010), 4.
27 Errington, *Linguistics in a Colonial World*, 6.
28 Eric Reinders, *Borrowed Gods and Foreign Bodies: Christian Missionaries Imagine Chinese Religion* (Berkeley: University of California Press, 2004).
29 Gilmour, *Grammars of Colonialism*, 139.
30 Mindy Morgan, *The Bearer of This Letter: Language Ideologies, Literacy Practices, and the Fort Belknap Indian Community* (Lincoln: University of Nebraska Press, 2009), 4.
31 Sean P. Harvey and Sarah Rivett, 'Colonial-Indigenous Language Encounters in North America and the Intellectual History of the Atlantic World,' *Early American Studies: An Interdisciplinary Journal* 15, no. 3 (2017): 443.
32 Ann McGrath, *Illicit Love: Interracial Sex and Marriage in the United States and Australia* (Lincoln: University of Nebraska Press, 2015), 150, 183, 188.
33 Phillip H. Round, *Removable Type: Histories of the Book in Indian Country, 1663–1880* (Chapel Hill: University of North Carolina Press, 2010), 7.
34 Bruce Greenfield, 'The Mi'kmaq Hieroglyphic Prayer Book: Writing and Christianity in Maritime Canada, 1675–1921,' in *The Language Encounter in the Americas, 1492–1800: A Collection of Essays*, eds. Edward G. Gray and Norman Fiering (New York: Berghahn Books, 2000), 190.
35 Michael J. Stevens, 'Kāi Tahu Writing and Cross-Cultural Communication,' *Journal of New Zealand Literature* 28 (2010): 132–133; Gunson, *Messengers of Grace*, 266.
36 *Twenty-Fifth Report of the British and Foreign Bible Society* (London: British and Foreign Bible Society, 1829), xvii.
37 *Seventy-Third Report of the British and Foreign Bible Society* (1877), 309–311.
38 Tony Ballantyne, *Orientalism and Race: Aryanism in the British Empire* (New York: Palgrave, 2002), 152.
39 Raeburn Lange, 'Indigenous Agents of Religious Change in New Zealand, 1830–1860,' *Journal of Religious History* 24, no. 3 (2000): 280, 282.
40 'R. Maunsell to Secretary, 30 January 1885,' in *Bible & Society: A Sesquicentennial History of the Bible Society in New Zealand*, ed. Peter James Lineham (Wellington: Bible Society in New Zealand, 1996), 148. For a discussion of missionary work to 'improve' African languages see Johannes Fabian, 'Missions and the Colonization of African Languages: Developments in the Former Belgian Congo,' *Canadian Journal of African Studies/La Revue Canadienne des Études Africaines* 17, no. 2 (1983): 165–187.
41 Lineham, *Bible & Society*, 142.
42 'Press, 10 May 1865,' 2, in Lineham, *Bible & Society*, 142.
43 Derek R. Peterson, *Creative Writing: Translation, Bookkeeping, and the Work of Imagination in Colonial Kenya* (Portsmouth: Heinemann, 2004), 8.
44 William B. Hart, 'Mohawk Schoolmasters and Catechists in Mid-Eighteenth-Century Iroquoia: An Experiment in Fostering Literacy and Religious Change,' in Gray and Fiering, eds., *The Language Encounter in the Americas*, 233.

45 Lamin Sanneh, *Encountering the West: Christianity and the Global Cultural Process: The African Dimension* (Maryknoll: Orbis Books, 1993), 17.
46 Kathleen Bragdon, 'Native Languages as Spoken and Written: Views from Southern New England,' in Gray and Fiering, eds., *The Language Encounter in the Americas*, 176–177.
47 Anna Johnston, *Missionary Writing and Empire, 1800–1860* (Cambridge: Cambridge University Press, 2003), 130.
48 Harvey and Rivett, 'Colonial-Indigenous Language Encounters,' 443.
49 Gilmour, *Grammars of Colonialism*, 3.
50 Derek R. Peterson, 'Colonizing Language? Missionaries and Gikuyu Dictionaries, 1904 and 1914,' *History in Africa* 24 (1997): 257.
51 Derek R. Peterson, 'Translating the Word: Dialogism and Debate in Two Gikuyu Dictionaries,' *Journal of Religious History* 23, 1 (1999): 32.
52 Gilmour, *Grammars of Colonialism*, 167.
53 A. Zuercher Reichardt, 'Translation,' *Early American Studies: An Interdisciplinary Journal* 16, no. 4 (2018): 809. Helen Bethea Gardner, '"New Heaven and New Earth": Translation and Conversion on Aneityum,' *The Journal of Pacific History* 41, no. 3 (2006): 310–311.
54 Reichardt, 'Translation,' 806–7.
55 Diane Austin-Broos, 'Translating Christianity: Some Keywords, Events and Sites in Western Arrernte Conversion,' *The Australian Journal of Anthropology* 21, no. 1 (2010): 16.
56 Sangkeun Kim, *Strange Names of God: The Missionary Translation of the Divine Name and the Chinese Responses to Matteo Ricci's 'Shangti' in Late Ming China, 1583–1644* (New York: Peter Lang, 2004), 1.
57 Round, *Removable Type*, 29.
58 Kim, *Strange Names of God*, 85.
59 Lamin Sanneh, *Translating the Message: The Missionary Impact on Culture* (Maryknoll: Orbis Books, 1989), 171–172.
60 Peterson, *Creative Writing*, 2.
61 Anne Keary, 'Christianity, Colonialism, and Cross-Cultural Translation: Lancelot Threlkeld, Biraban, and the Awabakal,' *Aboriginal History* 33 (2009): 144.
62 Julie Waddy, 'How Does God Fit In? Developing Translations of *Logos* and Other Words in John's Gospel in Anindilyakwa' (unpublished manuscript).
63 Gardner, *Gathering for God*.
64 Lange, 'Indigenous Agents,' 280–84.
65 David Wetherell, *Reluctant Mission: The Anglican Church in Papua New Guinea, 1891–1942* (St Lucia: University of Queensland Press, 1977), 96.
66 Richard Boast, 'Vanquished Theocracies: Christianity, War and Politics in Colonial New Zealand 1830–80,' in *Between Indigenous and Settler Governance*, eds. Lisa Ford and Tim Rowse (London: Routledge, 2012), 72.
67 Matt Matsuda, *Pacific Worlds: A History of Seas, Peoples and Cultures* (Cambridge: Cambridge University Press, 2012), 144.
68 Edward E. Andrews, *Native Apostles* (Cambridge, MA: Harvard University Press, 2013), 7.
69 Andrews, *Native Apostles*, 147.
70 Harvey and Rivett, 'Colonial-Indigenous Language Encounters,' 455.
71 Andrews, *Native Apostles*, 123.
72 Noenoe K. Silva, *Aloha Betrayed: Native Hawaiian Resistance to American Colonialism* (Durham, NC: Duke University Press, 2004), 8.
73 Elizabeth Elbourne, 'Christian Soldiers, Christian Allies: Coercion and Conversion in Southern Africa and Northeastern America at the Turn of the Nineteenth Century,' in *Beyond Conversion & Syncretism: Indigenous Encounters with Missionary Christianity, 1800–2000*, ed. Miles Richardson (New York: Berghahn Books, 2012), 79.

74 Elizabeth Elbourne, 'Word Made Flesh: Christianity, Modernity, and Cultural Colonialism in the Work of Jean and John Comaroff,' *The American Historical Review* 108, no. 2 (2003): 435–459.
75 Rafael, *Contracting Colonialism*, xv.
76 Ernst Dieffenbach, *Travels in New Zealand* (London: Murray, 1843), quoted in Lange, 'Indigenous Agents,' 283.
77 Samuel Marsden, 'Journal, 9 November 1819,' in *The Letters and Journals of Samuel Marsden 1765–1838*, ed. J.R. Elder (Dunedin, 1932), 219, quoted in Ballantyne, *Orientalism and Race*, 59. Marsden was not the only person to speculate that Indigenous people may be the 'lost tribe'. Elias Boudinot IV of the American Bible Society, for instance, suggested that Native Americans were. See McGrath, *Illicit Love*, 180.
78 Lorenzo Veracini, *Settler Colonialism: A Theoretical Overview* (New York: Palgrave Macmillan, 2010), 36.
79 Ballantyne, *Orientalism and Race*, 165; Mary Huie-Jolly, 'Maori "Jews" and a Resistant Reading of John 5.10–47,' in *The Postcolonial Biblical Reader*, ed. R.S. Sugirtharajah (Malden, MA: Blackwell, 2008), 232.
80 Elsmore, *Like Them That Dream*, 74.
81 Elsmore, *Like Them That Dream*, 80.
82 Huie-Jolly, 'Maori "Jews,"' 230; Ballantyne, *Orientalism and Race*, 165.
83 Elsmore, *Like Them That Dream*, 72–73.
84 Ballantyne, *Orientalism and Race*, 191.
85 Elsmore, *Like Them That Dream*, 100.
86 Lineham, *Bible & Society*, 136.
87 Ballantyne, *Orientalism and Race*, 148.
88 Taratoa had worked as an Anglican missionary in various places in the Pacific before he died in 1864 at Tauranga, fighting the British. Boast, 'Vanquished Theocracies,' 76.
89 Jenny Murray, 'Moving South with the CMS,' in *Mission and Moko*, ed. Robert Glen (Christchurch, 1992), quoted in Boast, 'Vanquished Theocracies,' 75.
90 'BFBS 40th Report, 1844,' cxvi, in Lineham, *Bible & Society*, 21.
91 Round, *Removable Type*, 13.
92 Peterson, *Creative Writing*, 5; Stephanie Newell, *Literary Culture in Colonial Ghana: 'How to Play the Game of Life'* (Manchester: Manchester University Press, 2002), 3.
93 Ana Mariella Bacigalupo, 'The Potency of Indigenous "Bibles" and Biographies: Mapuche Shamanic Literacy and Historical Consciousness,' *American Ethnologist* 41, no. 4 (2014): 648.
94 Penny Van Toorn, *Writing Never Arrives Naked: Early Aboriginal Cultures of Writing in Australia* (Canberra: Aboriginal Studies Press, 2006), 98.
95 Ballantyne, *Orientalism and Race*, 146.
96 Stevens, 'Kāi Tahu Writing,' 130–131.
97 Tony Ballantyne, 'Paper, Pen, and Print: The Transformation of the Kai Tahu Knowledge Order,' *Comparative Studies in Society and History* 53, no. 2 (2011): 236.
98 Lachy Paterson, 'Print Culture and the Collective Māori Consciousness,' *Journal of New Zealand Literature* 28 (2010): 105–110.
99 Jenifer Curnow, 'A Brief History of Maori-Language Newspapers,' in *Rere atu, Taku Manu!: Discovering the History, Language and Politics in Maori-Language Newspapers*, eds. Jenifer Curnow, Ngapare Hopa, and Jane McRae (Auckland: Auckland University Press, 2002), 17
100 Ballantyne, 'Paper, Pen, and Print,' 251–252.
101 Ballantyne, *Orientalism and Race*, 148.
102 Nakata, *Disciplining the Savages*, 169.
103 Norman Etherington, 'When Settlers Went to War Against Christianity,' in *Between Indigenous and Settler Governance*, eds. Lisa Ford and Tim Rowse (London: Routledge, 2012), 88.
104 Etherington, 'When Settlers Went to War,' 94.

105 Andrew Markus, 'William Cooper and the 1937 Petition to the King,' *Aboriginal History* 7 (1983): 46–60.
106 Laura Rademaker, 'We Want a Good Mission Not Rubish Please,' *Aboriginal History* 40 (2016): 129.
107 Van Toorn, *Writing Never Arrives Naked*, 13.
108 Rademaker, *Found in Translation*, 107.
109 Morgan, *The Bearer of This Letter*, 5.
110 Morgan, *The Bearer of This Letter*, 11.
111 Round, *Removable Type*, 14.
112 Andrews, *Native Apostles*, 62.
113 Harvey and Rivett, 'Colonial-Indigenous Language Encounters,' 473.
114 Scott Manning Stevens, 'The Path of the King James Version of the Bible in Iroquoia,' *Prose Studies* 34, no. 1 (2012): 14.
115 Silva and Thiong'o, *The Power of the Steel-Tipped Pen*, 7.

Bibliography

Andrews, Edward E. 'Christian Missions and Colonial Empires Reconsidered: A Black Evangelist in West Africa, 1766–1816.' *Journal of Church and State* 51, no. 4 (2009): 663–691.
Andrews, Edward E. *Native Apostles*. Cambridge, MA: Harvard University Press, 2013.
Austin-Broos, Diane. 'Translating Christianity: Some Keywords, Events and Sites in Western Arrernte Conversion.' *The Australian Journal of Anthropology* 21, no. 1 (2010): 14–32.
Bacigalupo, Ana Mariella. 'The Potency of Indigenous "Bibles" and Biographies: Mapuche Shamanic Literacy and Historical Consciousness.' *American Ethnologist* 41, no. 4 (2014): 648–663.
Ballantyne, Tony. *Orientalism and Race: Aryanism in the British Empire*. New York: Palgrave, 2002.
Ballantyne, Tony. 'Paper, Pen, and Print: The Transformation of the Kai Tahu Knowledge Order.' *Comparative Studies in Society and History* 53, no. 2 (2011): 232–260.
Ballantyne, Tony. *Entanglements of Empire: Missionaries, Māori, and the Question of the Body*. Auckland: Auckland University Press, 2015.
Boast, Richard. 'Vanquished Theocracies: Christianity, War and Politics in Colonial New Zealand 1830–80.' In *Between Indigenous and Settler Governance*, edited by Lisa Ford and Tim Rowse, 70–82. New York: Routledge, 2012.
Bragdon, Kathleen. 'Native Languages as Spoken and Written: Views from Southern New England.' In *The Language Encounter in the Americas, 1492–1800*, edited by Edward G. Gray and Norman Fiering, 169–184. New York: Berghahn Books, 2000.
Brickhouse, Anna. *The Unsettlement of America: Translation, Interpretation, and the Story of Don Luis de Velasco, 1560–1945*. Oxford: Oxford University Press, 2014.
British and Foreign Bible Society. *Seventy-Third Report of the British and Foreign Bible Society*. London: British and Foreign Bible Society, 1877.
British and Foreign Bible Society. *Twenty-Fifth Report of the British and Foreign Bible Society*. London: British and Foreign Bible Society, 1829.
Comaroff, Jean, and John Comaroff. *Of Revelation and Revolution, Volume 1: Christianity, Colonialism and Consciousness in South Africa*. Chicago, IL: University of Chicago Press, 1991.
Curnow, Jenifer. 'A Brief History of Maori-Language Newspapers.' In *Rere atu, Taku Manu!: Discovering the History, Language and Politics in Maori-Language Newspapers*, edited by Jenifer Curnow, Ngapare Hopa, and Jane McRae, 16–41. Auckland: Auckland University Press, 2002.
Dieffenbach, Ernst. *Travels in New Zealand*. London: Murray, 1843.
Elbourne, Elizabeth. 'Word Made Flesh: Christianity, Modernity, and Cultural Colonialism in the Work of Jean and John Comaroff.' *American Historical Review* 108, no. 2 (2003): 435–459.

Elbourne, Elizabeth. 'Christian Soldiers, Christian Allies: Coercion and Conversion in Southern Africa and Northeastern America at the Turn of the Nineteenth Century.' In *Beyond Conversion & Syncretism: Indigenous Encounters with Missionary Christianity, 1800–2000*, edited by Miles Richardson, 79–114. New York: Berghahn Books, 2012.

Elsmore, Bronwyn. *Like Them That Dream: The Maori and the Old Testament*. 2nd ed. Auckland: Reed Books, 2000.

Errington, Joseph. *Linguistics in a Colonial World: A Story of Language, Meaning, and Power*. Malden, MA: John Wiley & Sons, 2007.

Etherington, Norman. 'When Settlers Went to War Against Christianity.' In *Between Indigenous and Settler Governance*, edited by Lisa Ford and Tim Rowse, 83–94. New York: Routledge, 2012.

Evans, Nicholas. *Dying Words Endangered Languages and What They Have to Tell Us*. Oxford: Wiley-Blackwell, 2010.

Fabian, Johannes. 'Missions and the Colonization of African Languages: Developments in the Former Belgian Congo.' *Canadian Journal of African Studies/La Revue Canadienne des Études Africaines* 17, no. 2 (1983): 165–187.

Gardner, Helen Bethea. *Gathering for God: George Brown in Oceania*. Dunedin: Otago University Press, 2006.

Gardner, Helen Bethea. '"New Heaven and New Earth": Translation and Conversion on Aneityum.' *The Journal of Pacific History* 41, no. 3 (2006): 293–311.

Gilmour, Rachael. *Grammars of Colonialism: Representing Languages in Colonial South Africa*. Basingstoke: Palgrave, 2006.

Greenfield, Bruce. 'The Mi'kmaq Hieroglyphic Prayer Book: Writing and Christianity in Maritime Canada, 1675–1921.' In *The Language Encounter in the Americas, 1492–1800*, edited by Edward G. Gray and Norman Fiering, 185–210. New York: Berghahn Books, 2000.

Gunson, Niel. *Messengers of Grace: Evangelical Missionaries in the South Seas 1797–1860*. Oxford: Oxford University Press, 1978.

Hamann, Byron Ellsworth. 'How to Chronologize with a Hammer, or, the Myth of Homogeneous, Empty Time.' *HAU: Journal of Ethnographic Theory* 6, no. 1 (2016): 261–292.

Hanks, William F. *Converting Words: Maya in the Age of the Cross*. Berkeley: University of California Press, 2010.

Hart, William. 'Mohawk Schoolmasters and Catechists in Mid-Eighteenth-Century Iroquoia: An Experiment in Fostering Literacy and Religious Change.' In *The Language Encounter in the Americas, 1492–1800*, edited by Edward G. Gray and Norman Fiering, 226–253. New York: Berghahn Books, 2000.

Harvey, Sean P., and Sarah Rivett. 'Colonial-Indigenous Language Encounters in North America and the Intellectual History of the Atlantic World.' *Early American Studies: An Interdisciplinary Journal* 15, no. 3 (2017): 442–473.

Huie-Jolly, Mary. 'Maori "Jews" and a Resistant Reading of John 5.10–47.' In *The Postcolonial Biblical Reader*, edited by R.S. Sugirtharajah, 224–237. Malden, MA: Blackwell, 2008.

Johnston, Anna. *Missionary Writing and Empire, 1800–1860*. Cambridge: Cambridge University Press, 2003.

Keary, Anne. 'Christianity, Colonialism, and Cross-Cultural Translation: Lancelot Threlkeld, Biraban, and the Awabakal.' *Aboriginal History* 33 (2009): 117–155.

Kim, Sangkeun. *Strange Names of God: The Missionary Translation of the Divine Name and the Chinese Responses to Matteo Ricci's 'Shangti' in Late Ming China, 1583–1644*. New York: Peter Lang, 2004.

Lange, Raeburn. 'Indigenous Agents of Religious Change in New Zealand, 1830–1860.' *Journal of Religious History* 24, no. 3 (2000): 279–295.

Lawrance, Benjamin, Emily Lynn Osborn, and Richard Roberts. *Intermediaries, Interpreters, and Clerks: African Employees in the Making of Colonial Africa*. Madison: University of Wisconsin Press, 2006.

Lineham, Peter James. *Bible & Society: A Sesquicentennial History of the Bible Society in New Zealand*. Wellington: Bible Society in New Zealand, 1996.

Markus, Andrew. 'William Cooper and the 1937 Petition to the King.' *Aboriginal History* 7 (1983): 46–60.
Marsden, Samuel. 'Journal, 9 November 1819.' In *The Letters and Journals of Samuel Marsden 1765–1838*, edited by J.R. Elder. Dunedin, 1932.
Manning Stevens, Scott. 'The Path of the King James Version of the Bible in Iroquoia.' *Prose Studies* 34, no. 1 (2012): 5–17.
Matsuda, Matt. *Pacific Worlds: A History of Seas, Peoples and Cultures*. Cambridge: Cambridge University Press, 2012.
McGrath, Ann. *Illicit Love: Interracial Sex and Marriage in the United States and Australia*. Lincoln: University of Nebraska Press, 2015.
Morgan, Mindy. *The Bearer of This Letter: Language Ideologies, Literacy Practices, and the Fort Belknap Indian Community*. Lincoln: University of Nebraska Press, 2009.
Murray, Jenny. 'Moving South with the CMS.' In *Mission and Moko*, edited by Robert Glen. Christchurch, 1992.
Nakata, Martin. *Disciplining the Savages: Savaging the Disciplines*. Canberra: Aboriginal Studies Press, 2007.
Newell, Stephanie. *Literary Culture in Colonial Ghana: 'How to Play the Game of Life.'* Manchester: Manchester University Press, 2002.
Niranjana, Tejaswini. *Siting Translation: History, Post-Structuralism, and the Colonial Context*. Berkeley: University of California Press, 1992.
Osborn, Emily Lynn. '"Circle of Iron": African Colonial Employees and the Interpretation of Colonial Rule in French West Africa.' *The Journal of African History* 44, no. 1 (2003): 29–50.
Paterson, Lachy. 'Print Culture and the Collective Māori Consciousness.' *Journal of New Zealand Literature* 28 (2010): 105–129.
Peterson, Derek R. 'Colonizing Language? Missionaries and Gikuyu Dictionaries, 1904 and 1914.' *History in Africa* 24 (1997): 257–272.
Peterson, Derek R. 'Translating the Word: Dialogism and Debate in Two Gikuyu Dictionaries.' *Journal of Religious History* 23, 1 (1999): 31–50.
Peterson, Derek R. *Creative Writing: Translation, Bookkeeping, and the Work of Imagination in Colonial Kenya*. Portsmouth: Heinemann, 2004.
Rademaker, Laura. '"We Want a Good Mission Not Rubish Please."' *Aboriginal History* 40 (2016): 119–143.
Rademaker, Laura. *Found in Translation: Many Meanings on a North Australian Mission*. Honolulu: University of Hawai'i Press, 2018.
Rafael, Vicente L. *Contracting Colonialism: Translation and Christian Conversion in Tagalog Society Under Early Spanish Rule*. Ithaca: Cornell University Press, 1988.
Reichardt, Zuercher. 'Translation.' *Early American Studies: An Interdisciplinary Journal* 16, no. 4 (2018): 801–811.
Reinders, Eric. *Borrowed Gods and Foreign Bodies: Christian Missionaries Imagine Chinese Religion*. Berkeley: University of California Press, 2004.
Round, Phillip. *Removable Type: Histories of the Book in Indian Country, 1663–1880*. Chapel Hill: University of North Carolina Press, 2010.
Samarin, William. 'Language in the Colonization of Central Africa, 1880–1900.' *Canadian Journal of African Studies/La Revue Canadienne des Études Africaines* 23, no. 2 (1989): 232–249.
Samson, Jane. 'Translation Teams: Missionaries, Islanders, and the Reduction of Language in the Pacific.' In *Missionaries, Indigenous Peoples and Cultural Exchange*, edited by Patricia Grimshaw and Andrew May, 96–109. Eastbourne: Sussex Academic Press, 2010.
Sanneh, Lamin. *Translating the Message: The Missionary Impact on Culture*. Maryknoll: Orbis Books, 1989.
Sanneh, Lamin. *Encountering the West: Christianity and the Global Cultural Process: The African Dimension*. Maryknoll: Orbis Books, 1993.
Silva, Noenoe K. *Aloha Betrayed: Native Hawaiian Resistance to American Colonialism*. Durham, NC: Duke University Press, 2004.

Silva, Noenoe K., and Ngugi Wa Thiong'o. *The Power of the Steel-Tipped Pen: Reconstructing Native Hawaiian Intellectual History.* Durham, NC: Duke University Press, 2017.

Sleeper-Smith, Susan. *Indian Women and French Men: Rethinking Cultural Encounter in the Western Great Lakes.* Amherst: University of Massachusetts Press, 2001.

Stevens, Michael J. 'Kāi Tahu Writing and Cross-Cultural Communication.' *Journal of New Zealand Literature* 28 (2010): 130–157.

Thomas, Nicholas. *Islanders: The Pacific in the Age of Empire.* New Haven, CT: Yale University Press, 2010.

Van Toorn, Penny. *Writing Never Arrives Naked: Early Aboriginal Cultures of Writing in Australia.* Canberra: Aboriginal Studies Press, 2006.

Veracini, Lorenzo. *Settler Colonialism: A Theoretical Overview.* New York: Palgrave Macmillan, 2010.

Waddy, Julie. 'How Does God Fit In? Developing Translations of *Logos* and Other Words in John's Gospel in Anindilyakwa.' Unpublished manuscript, no date.

Wetherell, David. *Reluctant Mission: The Anglican Church in Papua New Guinea, 1891–1942.* St Lucia: University of Queensland Press, 1977.

14
'THE CASE OF POLLY INDIAN'

Enslavement, Native ancestry, and the law in the British Caribbean

Brooke N. Newman

In February 1824, the commissioners of legal enquiry for the British Caribbean submitted a report to the Colonial Office explaining their decision respecting the case of an enslaved woman in Tobago named Polly, 'called Polly Indian', and her children.[1] Registered as the property of Elphinstone Piggott, Chief Justice of the Tobago Court of Common Pleas, though technically owned by his wife, Deborah Piggott (née Thornhill), Polly had claimed freedom for herself and her three daughters in 1822 on the basis of Indian maternal ancestry.[2] According to Polly's testimony, her mother, Sophy, had worked as an enslaved domestic for the Thornhill family in Barbados and bore three children who were also treated as slaves, although 'everyone who saw her [Sophy] knew she was an Indian, and not an African'.[3] In 1779, when Polly was approximately ten years old, the provost marshal seized her from the Thornhills, who were heavily indebted, and sold Polly at public auction to repay a creditor. Mary Clarke, Deborah Thornhill's widowed mother, purchased Polly on behalf of the family and moved her to Bell estate, from which she routinely rented Polly out to other plantations.[4] Two years later, in the aftermath of the great hurricane of 1780 that devastated Barbados, killing Mary Clarke and further indebting the family, the Thornhills sold Polly's mother and two siblings, Phillis and Chamont, to one Mr Forbes, who brought them to Tobago to labour on a sugar plantation.[5]

Sometime between 1786 and 1789, Sophy absconded from her master's premises and travelled to the island's capital, Scarborough, to complain to Count Dillon, Tobago's governor during the French occupation, of mistreatment at the hands of her British enslaver. Struck by her appearance, Governor Dillon freed Sophy 'as an Indian', along with her two children, Phillis and Chamont. Polly, meanwhile, remained enslaved in Barbados, unaware that her mother and siblings had escaped bondage. A decade later, Polly relocated to Tobago after her mistress, Deborah Thornhill, gifted Polly and her children to her 23-year-old daughter,

Miss Deborah Thornhill, upon her marriage to Elphinstone Piggott in December 1799.[6] In Tobago, Polly discovered that her mother had died a free woman and 'reputed Indian' in Scarborough; her sister, Phillis, had worked as a domestic servant and moved to Trinidad, where she later died; and her brother, Chamont, had accompanied a gentleman to France as his servant, severing ties with his enslaved past.[7] Polly's tenuous claim to freedom thus rested on a maternal connection to a long-deceased freed woman, who – as the commissioners saw it – may have been neither her mother nor of Indian descent.

In July 1822, after Polly first came forward to claim freedom for herself and her children, Governor Frederick Philipse Robinson examined several witnesses who had known Sophy, Polly's alleged Indian mother, and then forwarded the results of his investigation to the Crown for review. The personal involvement of the island's chief justice heightened the complexity and importance of Polly's case, which had generated 'great public interest' in Tobago. The following year, Henry Maddock and Fortunatus Dwarris, the commissioners charged with enquiring into the administration of criminal justice in Britain's Caribbean colonies, arrived in Tobago bearing Earl Bathurst's instructions to investigate 'whether Polly called Polly Indian and her issue are or are not slaves'. Bathurst, Secretary of State for War and the Colonies, sent Maddock and Dwarris to Tobago with explicit orders. If their enquiry demonstrated the legitimacy of Polly's claim, he expected Chief Justice Piggott to liberate Polly and her children immediately and place an official declaration of their free status in the island's record office. Conversely, if the commissioners determined that Polly and her children were rightfully enslaved, Bathurst instructed Governor Robinson to publicise the results of the investigation and clear Chief Justice Piggott of any wrongdoing in the eyes of the public.[8]

One of many municipal-level examinations conducted by the commissioners of legal enquiry during their comprehensive tour of the British Caribbean in the 1820s, the case of Polly Indian offered an opportunity for imperial lawyers to pry into colonial affairs and administer justice in the name of the Crown. The commissioners' review of colonial legal practices and disputes, as Lauren Benton and Lisa Ford have argued, 'belonged to a larger project of constitutional intervention', devised to bring order and the king's impartial justice to an empire characterised by widespread legal diversity.[9] Beginning in 1822, the British Crown dispatched London barristers with ties to the islands to visit Britain's Caribbean colonies and report on laws, courts, the treatment of enslaved labourers, and the administration of justice. Word of the commissioners' project led to an unprecedented number of petitions submitted by or on behalf of enslaved and free people of African, Native, and multiple ancestries throughout the British Caribbean, including in Dominica, Grenada, Jamaica, Antigua, Montserrat, St Kitts, St Vincent, St Lucia, Tobago, Trinidad, and Honduras.[10] According to Dwarris, a Jamaican-born, Oxford-educated barrister, upon arrival in each colony, the commissioners announced that their doors would remain 'widely open to receive complaints and representations of every kind; provided only they did relate, more or less intimately, to the administration of justice'.[11]

The unlawful enslavement of Indians was a reoccurring theme. The same year Polly brought her case forward to the governor of Tobago, dozens of enslaved men and women in British Honduras presented freedom petitions to the Superintendent of the colony on the basis of Native ancestry. The Superintendent submitted the petitions to the attorney general of Jamaica for review and appointed a local commission to investigate their claims. In the interim, he removed the enslaved people in question (approximately 90 men, women, and children) from their proprietors, placing them in the custody of the provost marshal. Cognisant of the importance of maintaining Britain's strategic alliance with the Indigenous people of Honduras, who had historical connections to the British Crown and English colonisers, Bathurst ordered Maddock and Dwarris to examine 'the claims of reputed Indians and their descendants at Honduras' and to render a judgement. Although Polly's case in Tobago and the freedom claims in Honduras hinged on questions of Native lineage and legal decisions dating back half a century, the commissioners arrived at two entirely different conclusions. Both cases underscored the British imperial government's willingness to mediate freedom suits directly rather than rely on local authorities to adjudicate. As with the ameliorative measures adopted by the House of Commons in 1823 to improve conditions for enslaved workers, and subsequently imposed upon colonial governors, investigating claims of unlawful enslavement extended the sphere of British imperial jurisdiction and signalled Crown support for a uniform set of slave laws.[12]

But as the commissioners attempted to bring systematic legal order to Britain's Atlantic colonies and release Indians from slavery, verifying Indian ancestry proved incredibly challenging. In the absence of legal documentation proving Indian descent, individual assertions of Native lineage centred on reputed maternal ties, physical appearance, and conformity to vague 'Indian' characteristics. Focused on the largely unverifiable claims of a single enslaved woman owned by a colonial official, Polly's case was never published in Britain and generated only local interest in Tobago. In contrast, the case of the enslaved Indians in Honduras resulted in a widely publicised Parliamentary debate and became bound up with other scandals of empire.[13] While the unlawful enslavement of many people of Native ancestry in Honduras offered evidence of the despotic ruling practices of colonial administrators in the Caribbean, thus necessitating calls for Crown intervention, the case of Polly Indian faded into obscurity.[14] Yet, as I argue here, Polly's singular freedom claim offers insight into the contested nature and meanings of Indian identity during an era of British imperial interventions aimed at transforming the Atlantic slave system (Figure 14.1).

Indian slavery and partus sequitur ventrem

Although Polly claimed freedom on behalf of herself and her children in Tobago, first in 1822 before the governor and council and then again in 1824 before the commissioners, the evidentiary basis for her appeal originated in biological connections forged in Barbados. Her surviving statements indicate Polly's awareness that her legal status and that of her descendants hinged on knowledge and evidence of

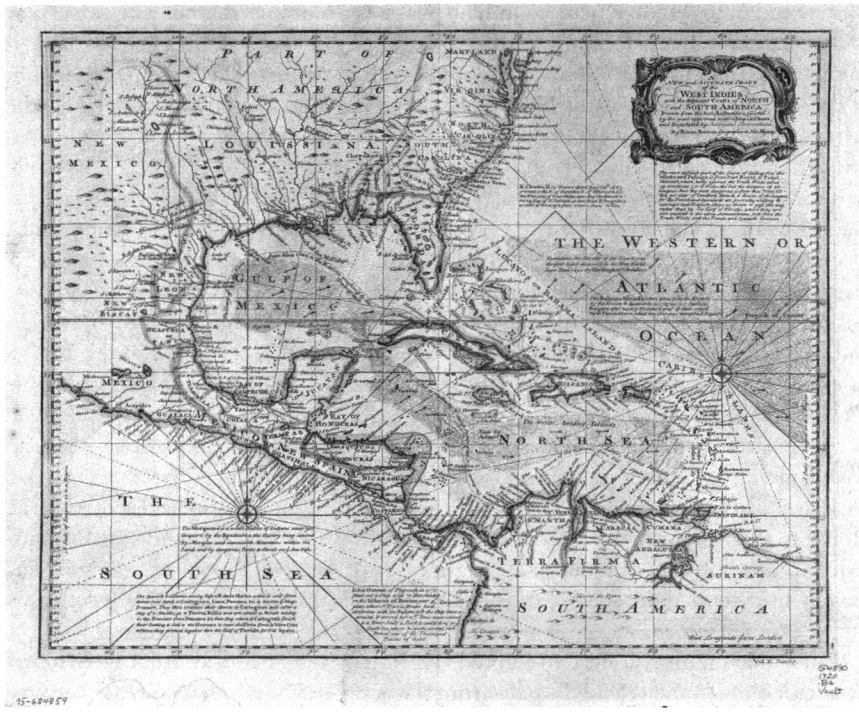

Figure 14.1 Emanuel Bowen, *A New and Accurate Chart of the West Indies with the Adjacent Coasts of North and South America*. London, 1720

Source: The Library of Congress, Geography and Map Division

parentage – specifically maternal lineage. In Barbados, and throughout the British Caribbean, the principle of *partus sequitur ventrem* ('offspring follows the womb') had long prevailed in assigning slave status.[15] As early as the mid-seventeenth century, and despite the absence of a statute law specifying or justifying enslaved matrilineality, slave status as a perpetual, hereditary condition transmitted through an enslaved mother had become a customary practice in Barbados. Unlike Virginia, the first colony in English America to adopt an explicit law of maternal descent that broke with the English common law rule that a child follows the father's condition (*partus sequitur partem*), Barbados did not construct a specific legal definition of slavery. Anglo-Barbadians privileged customary understandings because their notion of slave status, as Bernard Handler contends, 'derived from an Iberian ideology of African enslavement that was widespread in the Euro-Atlantic world and buttressed by English common law relating to property, particularly the ownership of domestic animals'.[16] In the seventeenth and eighteenth centuries, colonial authorities across the British Caribbean presumed that the descendants of enslaved women, whether of African, Indian, or multiple ancestries, had inherited slave status, unless a private act of manumission or positive law declared otherwise.[17] Throughout the early modern Americas, the adoption of the gendered legal principle of *partus sequitur ventrem* in perpetuating hereditary racial slavery urged both enslavers and enslaved people to pay careful attention to maternal lineage.[18]

After the British Parliament passed the Slave Trade Act in March 1807, abolishing the British slave trade, the customary legal practice of enslaved matrilineality assumed greater significance in the Caribbean colonies. The prohibition of slave trading limited the supply of African captives available for purchase, concentrating reformers and planters' attention on enhancing enslaved women's reproductive potential, precisely as abolitionists had intended.[19] At the same time, between 1807 and full emancipation in the 1830s (a period known as the amelioration era), acceptable categories of racialised groups enslaved on the basis of maternal ancestry narrowed. Although colonial legislators in Barbados and elsewhere in the British Caribbean had consigned the offspring of women of African, Indian, and multiple ancestries to hereditary slavery since the seventeenth century, during the amelioration era demonstrating 'Indian extraction' on the mother's side offered sufficient grounds for an enslaved person to challenge their legal status. By the early nineteenth century, as Indian slavery expanded in the American West, Southwest borderlands, and Mexico, spurred by the activities of Euro-American settlers and Native peoples, most prominently, Comanche raiders, British imperial authorities increasingly deemed the enslavement of Indians illegitimate.[20]

This shift took place gradually, primarily as a result of the perceived need to negotiate alliances with Native groups in imperial frontier zones. To protect British trading interests on the Mosquito Shore, the Jamaica assembly passed a law as early as 1741 to prevent Indian enslavement in the colony. The act was revised in 1776, and further bolstered by a proclamation issued by Sir Basil Keith, then governor of Jamaica. However, the last clause permitted colonists to retain in their possession or sell any enslaved Indians and their descendants already in bondage, allowing for the continuation of hereditary Native slavery in a colony dominated demographically by enslaved captives of African origin.[21] In 1808, when the former Dutch territories of Berbice, Demerara, and Essequibo were under British rule, the British colonial government republished a 1793 Dutch ordinance forbidding the enslavement of Indians or the offspring of Indian women.[22] Even in colonies such as Barbados and Tobago, where no statute law, special ordinance, or proclamation expressly prohibited hereditary Native slavery, imperial authorities investigated cases involving the enslavement of Indians. The legal protection of a handful of individuals of Indian ancestry lent a veneer of legitimacy to a centuries-old British Atlantic slave system decried by the public and reformers as immoral and fated to collapse.[23]

Indian slavery in Barbados

Seventeenth-century Barbados was a colony hungry for labourers. In the decades after the English colonised the island in the 1620s, planters acquired small numbers of enslaved Indian captives from the circum-Caribbean region, including Caribs and Arawaks from the Lesser Antilles and Guiana and Tapuyas from Brazil, in addition to enslaved Africans.[24] English expansion on the east coast of North

America led to intense periods of Indian resistance and Anglo-Indian warfare, resulting in a forced Native diaspora as New Englanders and Chesapeake colonists seized rebellious Indians and dispersed them to trading partners around the Atlantic. Barbados, due to its increased demand for labourers as a result of sugar cultivation and its isolated, easternmost Caribbean location, attracted a steady stream of Indian captives from North America.[25] New Englanders captured Pequots, Narragansetts, Hassanemesits, and Wampanoags and shipped them to Barbados as slaves, while Chesapeake colonists sold Algonquian war captives to English traders.[26] In June 1676, as word of King Philip's War and Native attacks on English settlements in the Chesapeake reached Barbados, the Barbados assembly passed an Act prohibiting the importation of 'Indian slaves and as well to send away... those already brought to this island from New England and adjacent colonies'. After suppressing an alleged colony-wide slave uprising the previous year, colonial authorities in Barbados feared hostile Indians would encourage the island's majority enslaved African population to rebel.[27] Indians from New England and surrounds, the Barbados Assembly asserted, were a people 'of too subtle, bloody, and dangerous nature and inclination to be and remain here'.[28] Bermuda, Barbados, and Jamaica all passed laws banning the importation of New England Indians in 1675 and 1676, 'not because of a wider moral prohibition against Indian slavery', Linford Fisher has noted, but rather as a precaution to prevent the contagion of insurrection from spreading to the islands.[29]

In 1688, the Barbados assembly reissued and expanded the 1676 ban on the importation of New England Indians, this time prohibiting the introduction, sale, or purchase of 'any Indians' into the colony. Nevertheless, the law did not require colonists to free Native peoples and their children already enslaved in Barbados. Nor was it rigorously enforced. Barbadians continued to buy and sell indigenous captives from North America and the circum-Caribbean surreptitiously, and enslaved Indians remained readily available well into the eighteenth century. On the southeast coast of North America, Anglo-Indian warfare and English slaving raids on Indian missions in Spanish Florida funnelled thousands of Native captives into Charles Town, South Carolina for export to sites across the British Atlantic. To obscure the presence of Indian slaves, Barbadians either applied the umbrella term 'Negro' to designate anyone enslaved or classified enslaved Indians in generic terms as 'other slaves'. During the entirety of the slave era, local statutes made repeated reference to 'Negroes and other slaves', obfuscating the presence of enslaved Indians in Barbados as well as guaranteeing the erasure of their distinct tribal identities and geographic origins.[30] Consequently, as the years passed, determining the ethnic composition of enslaved men and women of Native descent in Barbados proved increasingly difficult – if not impossible.[31]

After American Independence in 1783 and into the nineteenth century, Indian slavery had nearly disappeared on the east coast of North America and throughout the British Caribbean, replaced by the large-scale enslavement of West African captives and their descendants. For the minority of people of Native ancestry who remained enslaved, their Indian heritage was often hidden or discounted as a result of interethnic mixture with Africans and Europeans over multiple generations.

'When Americans spoke or wrote about slavery in the nineteenth century', Andrés Resendez has emphasised, 'they invariably meant African slavery'.[32] The same was true in the British Caribbean, even though most colonial slave laws, including Tobago's slave code of 1775 (renewed in 1794), continued to refer obliquely to 'Negroes and other slaves'.[33] In custom if not law, Indians were categorised as racially distinct from Africans, entitled to freedom and the protection of the British Crown. But the burden of proof rested on the enslaved. In lieu of documentary evidence proving Indian descent, to which enslaved individuals very rarely had access, challenging one's legal status on the basis of Native maternal ancestry demanded, at minimum, two separate forms of evidence: the testimony of free persons willing to swear under oath to the existence of kinship ties between the enslaved person and an Indian mother, and the body of an enslaved individual exhibiting physical evidence of Indian heritage. Both could prove deceptive. The former relied on potentially fallible oral sources and memory, the latter on subjective assessments of physical appearance and British notions of 'Indianness'. From a legal standpoint, Polly faced an uphill battle in demonstrating that Native maternal descent entitled her and her descendants to freedom.

Establishing Native maternal ancestry

When the commissioners interrogated Polly in January 1824, after gaining the consent of her master, Chief Justice Piggott, she freely admitted that she had lived in a state of slavery since birth. Polly did not dispute her master's claim that she came to him 'as the property of his wife' and 'had been always treated as a slave', as had her mother before her, until Sophy's liberation in Tobago by Governor Dillon.[34] Still, being raised in bondage did not make her enslavement legally valid, Polly argued. 'My claim is that I know my mother was an Indian and that I and my children should be free,' she told the commissioners. Indeed, her Indian heritage was common knowledge, though conveniently ignored by her enslavers. 'I was called Polly Indian ever since I was born. I was called so then, but was treated as a slave.'[35] Derived from oral traditions and enslaved local knowledge of kinship ties, Polly's testimony indicates an awareness of the legal significance of demonstrating lineal descent from a woman of Indian ancestry. Though her enslavers disregarded the familial connections of the people they owned, Polly sought to secure freedom for herself and her children on the basis of inherited Indigeneity.[36]

For Henry Maddock and Fortunatus Dwarris, the case of 'Polly Indian' turned on establishing proof of Native maternal lineage in accordance with 'the strict rules of law'. Dispensing the Crown's justice demanded verifiable facts, not hearsay, they insisted. 'To establish the right to freedom upon the principles and reasoning which must govern this case it is absolutely necessary to ascend to a mother, herself an Indian,' the commissioners outlined. 'For the train of reasoning is obviously this, "All Indians are free: Sophy was an Indian. Therefore, &c."' Simply resembling an Indian was insufficient. If Polly or any other enslaved claimant 'was born of an African mother – a slave – though by an Indian father, *partus sequitur ventrem*!' The rule of maternal inheritance alone proved determinative. To assess the validity of Polly's claim, the commissioners therefore sought answers to three central questions: '1. Whether Polly has the appearance of an Indian? 2. Whether she was the daughter of Sophy? 3. Whether Sophy was free because she was Indian, or on any other account?' Over a period of six days, Maddock and Dwarris examined a total of 14 witnesses in their attempt to ferret out the most plausible version of the truth with respect to Polly's maternal ancestry and appropriate legal status.[37]

The commissioners began their examinations by questioning Polly's master, Chief Justice Elphinstone Piggott, who had acquired a reputation in Tobago as an honourable and learned justice. In 1813, he ruled against a white servant who murdered an enslaved woman, arguing that enslaved individuals possessed as much right to protection against wrongful death as free colonists, irrespective of 'distinctions of colour or condition'.[38] Although known for his sympathy for the enslaved, Chief Justice Piggott disputed Polly's claim of unlawful enslavement as a fabrication. Reminding Maddock and Dwarris that 'slaves were real property in Tobago', he informed the commissioners that Polly and her children were 'the absolute property of Mrs Piggott, now in England, no settlement having been made on her marriage with him'.[39] In his deposition in September 1822, Chief Justice Piggott stated that his wife had received Polly as a gift from her mother, Deborah Thornhill, when she moved to Tobago in 1799. His wife's mother, in turn, had inherited Polly from her own mother, Mary Clarke, over 40 years ago in Barbados; and Mrs Clarke had originally purchased Polly at a provost marshal's sale. Chief Justice Piggott remarked that Polly had laboured for more than 20 years in his household and never once asserted her right to freedom owing to an Indian mother – until his most recent absence from the island to visit England.[40] Now, two years later, Maddock and Dwarris lacked the authority to rule on Polly's case due to the absence of Polly's rightful owner, Deborah Piggott, from Tobago. Confident in the justness of his position, Chief Justice Piggott granted the commissioners permission to act as arbitrators and render a binding decision regarding Polly's rightful legal status.

Maddock and Dwarris next summoned Polly and asked her a series of questions about her childhood, her family, and her treatment at the hands of her master. Chief Justice Piggott remained a silent, watchful presence throughout the commissioners' examinations, occasionally interjecting and posing questions to the witnesses. Exhibiting striking self-possession, Polly described herself as the daughter of Sophy, an Indian woman, and a 'mulatto' footman belonging to the Thornhills in Barbados. Her siblings, Phillis and Chamont, had a different father, she explained, an enslaved black footman named Small-hope; but all three children descended from the same Indian mother. Asked for the grounds on which she claimed her freedom, Polly said, 'I claim it because Sophy my mother was an Indian.' The commissioners pressed her to explain how she knew her mother descended from Indians. Everyone who saw Sophy could tell that she was Indian and not African, Polly asserted. 'The appearance is very different.' She recounted her experiences as an enslaved domestic rarely required to perform manual labour, except for one occasion when she angered her mistress and Mr Thornhill forced her to work in the field for six months. After moving with her mistress to Tobago, she cooked for the Piggott family and 'was treated as a slave', Polly said.[41]

The commissioners attempted to determine if Chief Justice Piggott treated Polly the same as his other slaves or if her supposed Indian ancestry garnered her special treatment. When asked if her master ever punished her as a slave, Polly responded: 'I was treated as a slave but never received any punishment at all.' Her master was not a cruel man, she stressed; he treated his enslaved workers kindly. But her master's behaviour was beside the point. Polly reiterated that she and her three surviving adult daughters, Sophy, Maria, and Harriett, who between them had seven children of their own, were lineally descended from an Indian woman and deserved their freedom accordingly. Why, then, did she wait until 1821 to claim her freedom, enquired the commissioners? Polly acknowledged that her master frequently absented himself from Tobago for long stretches to visit his estate in England. 'When Mr Pigott went home this last time, I claimed freedom for myself and my children. ... I thought as Mr Piggott had gone away from the island, I should be sold.' Maddock and Dwarris noted that the prospect of an impending sale, not ill treatment, prompted Polly to claim the freedom to which she believed that both she and her daughters were legally entitled as women of Indian descent.[42]

Enslavement and freedom in Tobago

There is nothing to suggest that the Piggotts intended to sell Polly in 1822. But if they had sold her, Polly's concerns would have been well justified. Tobago's total recorded enslaved population in 1819, the date of the island's first slave returns, was 15,457, and approximately 90 per cent of this population was concentrated on large plantations and engaged in sugar cultivation. Faced with an unusually low birth rate and the highest death rate in the British Caribbean among workers of both sexes and all age groups, Tobago's enslaved population was in decline and unable to maintain itself. Although mortality rates among the minority of slaves living in urban areas were lower due to the less arduous work regime, urban slaves also faced the prospect of being sold on the open market and separated from their families.[43] An enslaved cook based in the urban household of the island's chief justice, Polly occupied a relatively privileged position within Tobago's slave community. A decade earlier Sir William Young, governor of Tobago from 1807 to 1815, estimated that there were at most 700 enslaved domestics in Scarborough, or roughly 4.4 per cent of the island's total enslaved population of 15,822 (Figure 14.2).[44]

Polly must have known that her future survival and that of her children and grandchildren depended on avoiding the overwork, malnourishment, and brutal conditions associated with rural enslavement. As Randy Browne has observed, 'enslaved people were painfully aware of what historians have generally recognised only as a demographic fact: that the basic problem of Atlantic slavery was one of survival.'[45] According to Piggott's slave return, dated 1 January 1819, he owned 4 enslaved men and 14 enslaved women, including Polly – listed as a 50-year-old 'creole' cook of 'mulatto' complexion – and her 3 daughters: Sophy, age 32, a 'creole' washer of 'mulatto' complexion; Maria, age 23, a 'creole' seamstress of 'yellow' complexion; and Harriett, age 20, a 'creole' domestic of 'mulatto' complexion.

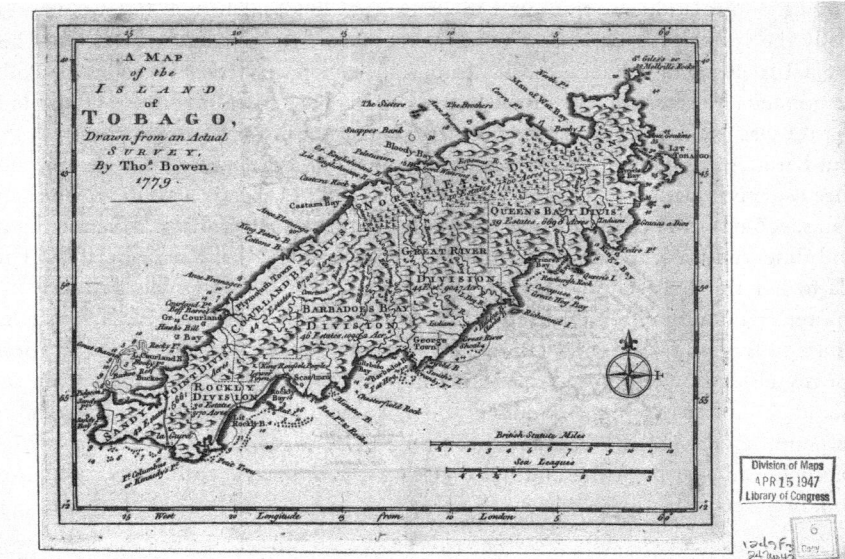

Figure 14.2 Thomas Bowen, *A Map of the Island of Tobago*. London, 1779
Source: The Library of Congress, Geography and Map Division

Nearly all of Piggott's enslaved workers performed household tasks, serving as washers, cooks, seamstresses, and domestics, rather than the harsh toil of the plantations.[46] For Polly, earning her freedom and avoiding future sale was a matter of life and death for herself and her family members.

In addition to the majority African enslaved population, Tobago possessed a small community of free people of African and multiple ancestries numbering in the hundreds. A tightknit group, free people clustered in and around the towns, particularly the island's capital, and members of this community typically knew one another by sight.[47] Hence the commissioners brought in four free people for examination, all of whom had previously given depositions related to Polly's case when questioned by the governor and council in 1822. According to Polly, these were the only free individuals still living who had known her mother, Sophy. Maddock and Dwarris asked the first witness, Jane Forbes, a 'free mulatto woman', if she remembered Sophy. They wanted to know if Sophy was in fact Polly's mother, and if Sophy had resembled an Indian. Forbes said that she had been acquainted with Sophy but had not known her well. 'She went by the name of Indian Sophy. I heard her so called. I do not know that she was an Indian and could not say from her appearance whether or not she was one.' 'I do not know much of Indians', Forbes clarified. 'She had straight hair, like mine, but I am not an Indian.' When pressed, Forbes refused to swear that Sophy was an Indian or the mother of Polly, only that she was 'said to be the mother of Polly' and 'called an Indian woman'. Maddock and Dwarris then produced a copy of Forbes's sworn deposition, dated 20 July 1822, in which she swore to both points. Forbes claimed she had signed her name to the paper 'immediately after it was written and before it was read over to me. It was not taken down rightly and I would not swear to it'.[48]

On the second day of examinations, the commissioners interrogated Louis Julien, a free man of multiple ancestry who had once played with Sophy's son, Chamont, in Scarborough when they were young children. He personally remembered Old Sophy as a 'fair working woman with straight hair' but did not know if she had a daughter named Polly. While delivering bread to the government house in his role as a baker's errand boy, Julien had heard that Governor Dillon freed Sophy because she was an Indian. Like Forbes, Julien disagreed with the sworn deposition he had signed before the governor in 1822, in which he stated 'positively that she was an Indian'. 'It was not so read to me for if it had been I should have directly found fault with it,' he argued; 'I do not read myself.' Julien said that he had always considered Sophy an Indian but could not swear positively. 'She was called so, and had always been considered as such, since I knew her. She looked like one.'[49] Confronted with an imperial commission of enquiry from Britain, free people laid bare the limitations of local and personal knowledge in the eyes of the law.

A third free person, Judy Graham, highlighted the potentially deceptive nature of Sophy's Indian appearance. Claiming to have seen many Indians in Grenada, Graham stated that it was impossible to say with certainty whether Sophy was an Indian, 'only that she looked like one'. Sophy had a 'yellow complexion like a mulatto', Graham elaborated, as well as 'long, straight hair like an Indian's' and a noticeable swing in her walk 'like an Indian's'. Graham, too, declined to confirm that Governor Dillon had freed Sophy 'as an Indian', despite a sworn deposition stating the same, and bearing her mark, from July 1822.[50] Both her knowledge of Sophy's alleged Indian ancestry and her release from slavery, Graham asserted, stemmed from nothing more than town rumours. Jane Maloney, the final free person of multiple heritage examined by Maddock and Dwarris, said she had known Sophy's daughter, Phillis, and heard her mention leaving behind unnamed family – 'I believe, sisters' – in Barbados. Maloney also offered additional details regarding the possible motivation underlying Count Dillon's decision to release Sophy and her children from bondage. 'I heard some white French people say she [Sophy] was an Indian, and that they were very angry with Mr Forbes for bringing her here, and trying to sell her as a slave, and said that the great French people freed her on that account.' That French colonists and royal officials such as Governor Dillon would oppose the enslavement of an Indian woman is unsurprising given the emergence of new laws banning Indian slavery in the French Atlantic after the 1760s.[51] Releasing individuals of Native descent wrongfully enslaved by the British would demonstrate French superiority. Yet while Governor Dillon may have been convinced of Sophy's Indian ancestry, Maloney refused to support unequivocally Polly's claim that Sophy was her mother, even if her previous deposition from 1822 stated otherwise.[52]

Determining 'Indian' identity

Henry Maddock and Fortunatus Dwarris expressed dismay at the varying, contradictory statements provided by the witnesses from the free community who claimed to have known Sophy prior to her death. They chalked up the irregularities to the ignorance of an 'unskillful' clerk of council posing leading questions to illiterate free people and assuming acquiescence based on their bodily movements or limited responses. For the remainder of the examinations, the commissioners questioned British colonists in Tobago and focused much of their attention on pinning down the supposed racial characteristics shared by all Indians. If the witnesses failed to help them establish whether Sophy was an Indian or the mother of Polly, Maddock and Dwarris would instead attempt to assess whether Polly herself resembled an Indian as imagined by British colonial residents in Tobago. During this portion of their investigation, which lasted two days, the commissioners paraded Polly before five white men and instructed them to inspect her body for evidence of Indian ancestry. Subjecting Polly to an intimate, public examination, Maddock and Dwarris posed the following questions to each witness: 'Have you seen many Indians? Is Polly like an Indian? What are the distinguishing marks of an Indian? From your knowledge of Indians should you pronounce Polly to be of Indian extraction?'[53] One by one the men scrutinised Polly's physical appearance while her master, Chief Justice Piggott, observed the proceedings. The visual examination failed to clarify Polly's heritage, however.

Samuel Spears, the assistant register, claimed that in Tobago he had seen several Indians, all of whom appeared stout and robust with skin the colour of copper, and dark, lank straight hair. Armed with this personal eyewitness knowledge, Spears assessed Polly for signs of Indian heritage when the commissioners presented her for comparison. 'Polly is yellow but has nothing like so deep a copper colour as an Indian,' Spears mused. 'Her hair is not the least like that of those Indians.' Failing to see a clear resemblance between Polly and the other Indians he had encountered, Spears speculated that Polly's yellow complexion might make sense if she were 'the descendant of a Mulatto and an Indian'.[54] Another witness, Mr Crook, declared that he had observed many Indians in Trinidad and was struck by Polly's likeness to them when he passed her in the streets of Scarborough years ago. 'On Polly, however, being produced for him at his examination', Maddock wrote to Bathurst, 'he said he did not think any person on seeing her would swear to her being of Indian extraction.'[55] Swearing Polly was of Indian descent under oath was a far cry from surmising a variety of ancestral possibilities for her based on superficial characteristics.

When the commissioners asked an elderly man named James Denoon if Polly resembled an Indian, he said: 'I should not hesitate for a moment to say so.' Maddock and Dwarris urged him to look more closely at Polly's body. Inspecting her hair, stature, and skin tone for signs of 'Indianness', Denoon noticed that Polly's features differed slightly from those of other Indians he had seen. 'Her hair curls a little, it is not quite straight,' Denoon acknowledged; 'it is black, but not exactly like an Indian's.' Maddock and Dwarris leapt on his admission of uncertainty, prompting the witness to confirm what they appear to have already suspected. 'Do you know any person here', they pressed Denoon, 'who from having seen Indians is capable of saying whether a person is an Indian or of Indian extraction?' 'I do not', Denoon confessed.[56]

When the commissioners queried five additional British colonists, including the deputy provost marshal, about Polly's appearance and probable lineage, they arrived at the same conclusion. None could definitively verify Polly's Indian heritage. While multiple witnesses agreed that she may have exhibited some of the supposed signs of 'Indian extraction' – including light, olive- or golden-coloured skin and dark, straight hair – Polly's features failed to conform fully to generalised British norms of Indian racial identity. The notion that Native peoples throughout the Americas fell under the same homogenous racial group and shared similar physical features had emerged in the late sixteenth century as result of Anglo-Indian encounters and persisted over the centuries.[57] Despite the durability of racialised assumptions about Indians across time and cultural contexts, British colonists in Tobago struggled to pin down 'Indianness' as a clear, easily recognisable racial category. 'Do you know an Indian when you see one?' Maddock and Dwarris asked a woman named Polly Wheeler, who claimed to have lived among Indians at Porto Toko in Trinidad. 'Yes, Indians are different than mulattoes,' Wheeler replied. 'I could not take an oath that Polly was one. I wouldn't take her word for it. The hair of Indians at Toko is long and straight and black as your jacket and reaches down to their feet.'[58] Thus, although Polly purported to be the descendant of an Indian mother, and many people in Scarborough knew her as 'Polly Indian', her claim to Native maternal lineage failed to withstand the commissioners' close scrutiny.

The commissioners' verdict

As lawyers tasked by the Crown to review and improve the administration of justice in the Caribbean colonies, Henry Maddock and Fortunatus Dwarris expressed serious misgivings about the case of 'Polly Indian'. Evidence demonstrating Polly's blood connection to Sophy did not exist, they asserted. Moreover, the commissioners doubted Sophy's local reputation as an Indian woman released by a French governor from wrongful enslavement by a British master. In their view, Count Dillon's decision to liberate a British subject's enslaved property on the mere presumption of Indian origin seemed, at best, overzealous and passionate, and at worst, tyrannical and arbitrary. The French had agreed to honour the British constitution and laws after the capitulation, therefore rendering Governor Dillon's act irregular and unlawful. 'The evidence of Sophy's being of Indian origin *at all* rested upon accounts of her personal appearance; upon hearsay and presumptions', Dwarris detailed in a letter to Bathurst justifying the commissioners' decision. 'It was thus left uncertain by the evidence whether Sophy was of Indian origin, of a mixed breed, or by what father or mother? It appeared that after complaining to Count Dillon she was free *de facto*, but it was certainly nowhere shewn that she was *de jure* free.' In other words, Governor Dillon subverted British colonial law when he declared Sophy free without any evidence of Indian ancestry. Polly's claim to freedom rested on the thinnest strand of a web of presumptions and assumptions.[59]

At the end of the six-day investigation, Maddock and Dwarris concluded that 'we find deciding according to the strict rules of law, with the exclusion of hearsay evidence, that the said Polly and her issue are slaves'.[60] The commissioners noted that they may have arrived at a different conclusion had the various, conflicting accounts regarding Sophy and Polly's alleged relationship and Native identity been clarified and substantiated. What is more, the supposed distinguishing racial characteristics shared by all Indians remained unclear. 'It was found extremely difficult, amid the most inconsistent accounts, to ascertain what *those* were but as far as they could be discovered she did not! Her complexion is that of a Mulatto; the Indian is a deep copper colour. *Their* hair is said to be long, straight, lank, and coal-black; hers was short, frizzy, and dark but not black.' Even with Polly's body available for assessment as physical evidence, 'the test of personal appearance proved much too uncertain to place any great reliance upon it'. The inability of the witnesses to agree on what a 'real Indian' looked like complicated the commissioners' task of determining whether Polly herself resembled an Indian. 'For these reasons', Dwarris summarised, 'I thought that Sophy was an Indian and free – not proved at all. That Polly was the daughter of Sophy – insufficiently proved: consequently that Polly was entitled to freedom – not established.'[61] Offering 'Polly Indian' the benefit of the doubt aligned with neither the commissioners' legal sensibilities nor the British imperial government's reforming agenda. In their final estimation, Polly was simply the enslaved property of one of the few colonial magistrates in the British Caribbean with an impeccable reputation.

Epilogue

The commissioners of legal enquiry did not include Polly's case in their official published report on the island of Tobago.[62] Surviving records indicate that Polly remained enslaved in the household of Elphinstone and Deborah Piggott in Scarborough until her sudden death on 8 April 1826. In January 1827, Chief Justice Piggott reported that Polly, a 'mulatto', had died of an 'apoplectic fit' the previous spring, reducing the total number of enslaved workers in his service to 5 males and 18 females.[63] One could scan Chief Justice Piggott's slave returns without having any inkling that Polly self-identified as a Native woman, or that she was commonly known as 'Polly Indian' in Tobago. If the records of her contested legal case had not survived, Polly's claim to Indigenous identity would have remained obscured – as her master and the commissioners intended. Erasing Polly's self-proclaimed Native identity and kinship connections enabled the Piggotts to exercise control over her labour for the entirety of her life and, critically, to retain her children and grandchildren in permanent, hereditary bondage.

Three years after Polly's death, her daughter, Sophy, gave birth to a 'creole' child named Polly on 22 October 1829. Deborah Piggott, now a widow following the death of her husband 2 years earlier, included Sophy and her infant, Polly, among the 8 men and 19 women she listed in her official slave return, dated 1 January 1830.[64] Deborah Piggott continued to benefit from the labour of Polly's descendants until the British Emancipation Act of 1833 compelled her to manumit her enslaved labourers following a temporary period of apprenticeship. Like other British West Indian slave owners, Piggott received financial compensation for the release of her enslaved property. In May 1836, the British government awarded Deborah Piggott £562.17s.5d in exchange for the emancipation of 25 enslaved persons in the town of Scarborough, Tobago.[65] Both Sophy and Polly, as well as Polly Indian's other children and grandchildren, were among those whom Deborah Piggott listed as lost property.

As particularly evident in the case of Polly Indian, although the British imperial government strove to resolve cases of wrongful enslavement in the Caribbean colonies in the 1820s, the enslavement of individuals of suspected Native origin remained permissible so long as their ancestry could not be proved legally. When enslaved men and women, who prioritised their own oral traditions and personal knowledge of kinship ties, challenged their legal standing on the basis of matrilineal Native descent, they found both colonial and imperial officials unwilling to take their claims seriously – unless they could provide documentary, physical, and oral evidence proving Indian extraction on the mother's side. In the absence of genealogical records or witnesses willing to swear positively that an enslaved person was an Indian or the child of an Indian mother, convincing local or imperial authorities of unambiguous Native origin required that a claimant's body conform to long-held British assumptions about the supposed distinguishing features of Indians. The result was the historical marginalisation and silencing of enslaved individuals such as Polly who failed to fit within homogenising imperialist racial constructions of Indian identity.

Notes

1 'The Case of the Slave Polly Belonging to Chief Justice Piggott,' The National Archives of the United Kingdom, Kew [hereafter TNA], Commissioners of Legal Enquiry, West Indies, 1822–1824, volume 1, CO 318/57, nf.

2 Beginning in Trinidad in 1812, slave registration acts or orders in council spread across the British Caribbean in response to abolitionists' calls to monitor the colonial enslaved population and track demographic changes resulting from births, deaths, sale, or manumission. In Tobago, the first slave registration was returned in 1819. See B.W. Higman, *Slave Populations of the British Caribbean, 1807–1834* (Mona: University of the West Indies Press, 1995), 6–8.

3 'Statement and examination of Polly Indian, taken with the consent of Mr Piggott,' TNA, CO 318/57, ff. 2–10.

4 Deborah Thornhill was the daughter of Mary Clarke and Gedney Clarke Senior, a wealthy merchant, planter, and customs collector for Bridgetown, who was born in Salem, Massachusetts in 1711 and moved to Barbados in 1733. In 1752, Clarke purchased the 500-acre Bell plantation in Barbados. See S.D. Smith, *Slavery, Family, and Gentry Capitalism in the British Atlantic: The World of the Lascelles, 1648–1834* (New York: Cambridge University Press, 2006), 127; Matthew Mulcahy, *Hubs of Empire: The Southeastern Lowcountry and British Caribbean* (Baltimore, MD: Johns Hopkins University Press, 2014), 177.

5 Sophy's owner, Mr Forbes, was likely either George Forbes or his brother and business partner, William Forbes, who co-owned three lots of land in St David Parish, which became part of Runnemede and Culloden estates, and three lots in St Mary Parish that formed the Morne d'Or estate. 'William Forbes,' Legacies of British Slave-ownership database, accessed 4 August 2019, http://wwwdepts-live.ucl.ac.uk/lbs/person/view/2146632378.

6 Henry and Deborah Thornhill had five children; Deborah was their only daughter. James C. Brandow, *Genealogies of Barbados Families: From Caribbeana and the Journal of the Barbados Museum and Historical Society* (1983; repr. Baltimore, MD: Clearfield Company, Inc., 2001), 521.

7 'Statement and examination of Polly Indian,' TNA, CO 318/57, ff. 2–10.
8 'Copy, Bathurst's Instructions to the Commissioners,' Henry Hill, nd, TNA, CO 318/57, nf.
9 Lauren Benton and Lisa Ford, *Rage for Order: The British Empire and the Origins of International Law, 1800–1850* (Cambridge, MA: Harvard University Press, 2016), 57. On legal divergence as the defining feature of the British Atlantic empire, see esp. Mary Sarah Bilder, *The Transatlantic Constitution: Colonial Legal Culture and the Empire* (Cambridge, MA: Harvard University Press, 2004).
10 Brooke N. Newman, *A Dark Inheritance: Blood, Race, and Sex in Colonial Jamaica* (New Haven, CT: Yale University Press, 2018), 1–3; A. Wood Renton, 'The Work of the West Indian Commissioners,' *Juridical Review: A Journal of Legal and Political Science* 2, no. 4 (1890): 357–365.
11 Fortunatus Dwarris, *Substance of the Three Reports of the Commissioners of Inquiry into the Administration of Civil and Criminal Justice in the West Indies* (London, 1827), 44.
12 *Substance of the Debate in the House of Commons, on the 15th May, 1823, On a Motion for the Mitigation and Gradual Abolition of Slavery Throughout the British Dominions* (London, 1823), xxix.
13 See James Epstein, *Scandal of Colonial Rule: Power and Subversion in the British Atlantic during the Age of Revolution* (New York: Cambridge University Press, 2012).
14 Lauren Benton, 'Just Despots: The Cultural Construction of Imperial Constitutionalism,' *Law, Culture and the Humanities* 9, no. 2 (2013): 213–226; Benton and Ford, *Rage for Order*, 28–55.
15 Newman, *Dark Inheritance*, 13, 81–82.
16 Jerome S. Handler, 'Custom and Law: The Status of Enslaved Africans in Seventeenth-Century Barbados,' *Slavery & Abolition* 37, no. 2 (2016): 248.
17 Melanie J. Newton, 'Returns to a Native Land: Indigeneity and Decolonization in the Anglophone Caribbean,' *Small Axe* 17, no. 2 (2013): 115–116.
18 Joseph C. Dorsey, 'Women without History: Slavery, Jurisprudence, and the International Politics of *Partus Sequitur Ventrem* in the Spanish Caribbean,' *Journal of Caribbean History* 28, no. 2 (1994): 165–207; Jennifer L. Morgan, '*Partus Sequitur Ventrem*: Law, Race, and Reproduction in Colonial Slavery,' *Small Axe* 22, no. 1 (2018): 1–17.
19 Sasha Turner, *Contested Bodies: Pregnancy, Childrearing, and Slavery in Jamaica* (Philadelphia: University of Pennsylvania Press, 2017), 20–21.
20 Andrés Reséndez, *The Other Slavery: The Uncovered Story of Indian Enslavement in the Americas* (Boston, MA: Houghton Mifflin Harcourt, 2016), 218–219; James F. Brooks, *Captives and Cousins: Slavery, Kinship, and Community in the Southwest Borderlands* (Chapel Hill: University of North Carolina Press, 2002), 364–365; Pekka Hämäläinen, *The Comanche Empire* (New Haven, CT: Yale University Press, 2008), 223–224.
21 'An act for Recovering and Extending the Trade with the Indian Settlements in America and Preventing for the Future some evil practices formerly committed in that Trade,' 8 May 1741, *The Laws of Jamaica* (Kingston, 1792), 291–292; Report of His Majesty's Council Concerning the Mosquito Shore, in Sir Basil Keith's of the 18th January 1776, Jamaica, Original Correspondence, TNA, CO 137/71, f. 55; 'Report of His Majesty's Commissioners of legal enquiry on the case of certain persons at Honduras who claimed to be entitled to their freedom on the grounds of Indian descent,' 1822, TNA, CO 318/67, Commissioners of Legal Enquiry, West Indies, 1827, volume 11, ff. 4–6.
22 Mary Noel Menezes, *The Amerindians in Guyana 1803–1873: A Documentary History* (1979; repr. New York: Routledge, 2019), 174.
23 On the role of notions of protection to the maintenance of empires, see Lauren Benton and Adam Clulow, 'Introduction: The Long, Strange History of Protection,' in *Protection and Empire: A Global History*, eds. Lauren Benton, Adam Clulow, and Bain Attwood (Cambridge: Cambridge University Press, 2018), 1–10.
24 Jerome S. Handler, 'The Amerindian Slave Population of Barbados in the Seventeenth and Eighteenth Centuries,' *Caribbean Studies* 8, no. 4 (1968): 38–64; Carolyn Arena,

'Indian Slaves from Guiana in Seventeenth-Century Barbados,' *Ethnohistory* 64, no. 1 (2017): 65–90. See also Carolyn Arena, 'Indian Slaves from Caribana: Trade and Labor in the Seventeenth-Century Caribbean' (PhD diss., Columbia University, 2017).

25 See esp. Jace Weaver, *The Red Atlantic: American Indigenes and the Making of the Modern World, 1000–1927* (Chapel Hill: University of North Carolina Press, 2014); Reséndez, *The Other Slavery*; Rebecca Ann Goetz, 'Indian Slavery: An Atlantic and Hemispheric Problem,' *The History Compass* 14, no. 2 (2016): 59–70.

26 New Englanders sold numerous Native Americans as slaves to colonists in seventeenth-century Barbados, particularly Indians convicted of crimes. See Margaret Ellen Newell, *Brethren by Nature: New England Indians, Colonists, and the Origins of American Slavery* (Ithaca: Cornell University Press, 2015), 115–116, 129–130; Alan Gallay, *The Indian Slave Trade: The Rise of the English Empire in the American South, 1670–1717* (New Haven, CT: Yale University Press, 2002), 300.

27 *A Continuation of the State of New-England: Being a Farther Account of the Indian Warr ... Together with an Account of the Intended Rebellion of the Negroes in the Barbadoes* (London: Printed by T.M. for Dorman Newman, 1676). See also Jerome Handler, 'Barbados Slave Conspiracies of 1675 and 1692,' *Journal of the Barbados Museum and Historical Society* 36, no. 4 (1982): 312–333; Elaine G. Breslaw, *Tituba, Reluctant Witch of Salem: Devilish Indians and Puritan Fantasies* (New York: New York University Press, 1996), 31–32; Newell, *Brethren by Nature*, 148.

28 The act is listed in William Rawlin, *The Laws of Barbados, Collected in One Volume* (London: Printed for William Rawlin, 1699), 122. For the broader context of the act, see Linford D. Fisher, '"Dangerous Designes": The 1676 Barbados Act to Prohibit New England Slave Importation,' *The William and Mary Quarterly* 71, no. 1 (2014): 99–124.

29 Linford D. Fisher, '"Why Shall Wee Have Peace to Bee Made Slaves": Indian Surrenderers During and After King Philip's War,' *Ethnohistory* 64, no. 1 (2017): 91–114.

30 Joyce E. Chaplin, 'Enslavement of Indians in Early America: Captivity without the Narrative,' in *The Creation of the British Atlantic World*, eds. Elizabeth Mancke and Carole Shammas (Baltimore, MD: Johns Hopkins University Press, 2005), 66.

31 Handler, 'Amerindian Slave Population,' 38–39.

32 Reséndez, *The Other Slavery*, 218.

33 'An Act for the Good Order and Government of Slaves,' 1775, *Acts of the Legislature of the Island of Tobago; from 1768, to 1775, inclusive* (London, 1776), 107–119.

34 Dwarris to Bathurst, Trinidad, 27 February 1824, TNA, CO 318/57, f. 3.

35 'The statement and examination of Polly Indian,' TNA, CO 318/57, f. 9.

36 Freedom suits based on Indian maternal ancestry proved successful in Virginia during the same period. See Peter Wallenstein, 'Indian Foremothers: Race, Sex, Slavery, and Freedom in Early Virginia,' in *The Devil's Lane: Sex and Race in the Early South*, eds. Catherine Clinton and Michele Gillespie (New York: Oxford University Press, 1997), 57–73.

37 Maddock to Bathurst, Trinidad, 20 March 1824, TNA, CO 318/57, nf.

38 K.O. Laurence, *Tobago in Wartime, 1793–1815* (Kingston: University Press of the West Indies, 1995), 123, 129.

39 'Examination of Mr Piggott,' TNA, CO 318/57, ff. 1–2.

40 'Statement of Elphinstone Piggott,' September 1822, TNA, CO 318/57, f. 17.

41 'Statement and examination of Polly Indian,' TNA, CO 318/57, ff. 2–9.

42 'Statement and examination of Polly Indian,' TNA, CO 318/57, ff. 9–10.

43 Laurence, *Tobago in Wartime*, 33–36; Higman, *Slave Populations of the British Caribbean*, 6.

44 Sir William Young, *An Historical, Statistical, and Descriptive Account of the Island of Tobago, Introductory to an Essay on the Commercial and Political Importance of the Possession to Great Britain* (London, 1812); Laurence, *Tobago in Wartime*, 37–38.

45 Randy Browne, *Surviving Slavery in the British Caribbean* (Philadelphia: University of Pennsylvania Press, 2017), 3.

46 'Original Return of Unattached Slaves belonging to the Honourable Elphinstone Piggott, of the Town of Scarborough, Tobago, January 1, 1819,' TNA, T 71/461, f. 226.

47 Laurence, *Tobago in Wartime*, 22.
48 'Examination of Jane Forbes,' and 'Deposition of Jane Forbes,' 20 July 1822, TNA, CO 318/57, ff. 11–15, 16.
49 'Examination of Louis Julien,' TNA, CO 318/57, ff. 17–27.
50 'Examination of Judy Graham,' TNA, CO 318/57, ff. 28–34.
51 Brett Rushforth, *Bonds of Alliance: Indigenous and Atlantic Slaveries in New France* (Chapel Hill: University of North Carolina Press, 2012), 379.
52 'Examination of Jane Maloney,' TNA, CO 318/57, ff. 37–45.
53 Dwarris to Bathurst, Trinidad, 27 February 1824, TNA, CO 318/57, ff. 5–6.
54 'Examination of Samuel Spears, Esq.,' TNA, CO 318/57, ff. 49–53.
55 'Examination of the Honorable J. Crook,' TNA, CO 318/57, ff. 63–67.
56 'Examination of Mr Denoon,' TNA, CO 318/57, ff. 53–60.
57 On early English constructions of Native identity, see esp. Karen Ordahl Kupperman, *Indians and English: Facing Off in Early America* (Ithaca: Cornell University Press, 2000); Joyce E. Chaplin, *Subject Matter: Technology, the Body, and Science on the Anglo-American Frontier, 1500–1676* (Cambridge, MA: Harvard University Press, 2001).
58 'Examination of Mr Collier, deputy provost marshal,' and 'Examination of Polly Wheeler,' TNA, CO 318/57, ff. 68–69, 77.
59 Dwarris to Bathurst, Trinidad, 27 February 1824, TNA, CO 318/57, f. 6.
60 Henry Hill, Secretary to the Commissioners, to Wilmott, Tobago, 17 January 1824, TNA, CO 318/57, nf.
61 Dwarris to Bathurst, Trinidad, 27 February 1824, TNA, CO 318/57, f. 8.
62 'First Report of the Commissioners of Enquiry into the Administration of Criminal and Civil Justice in the West Indies: Barbados, Tobago, Grenada,' *House of Commons Parliamentary Papers*, no. 157, XV (London, 1825).
63 'Office of Registry of Colonial Slaves and Slave Compensation Commission: Records, Tobago, 1827,' TNA, T 71/477, f. 135.
64 'Tobago: Annual Return of Unattached Slaves, Return of Deborah Piggott, executrix, to the estate of the late Elphinstone Piggott,' 1 January 1830, T 71/484, f. 242
65 'Deborah Piggott,' Legacies of British Slave-ownership database, accessed 9 August 2019, http://wwwdepts-live.ucl.ac.uk/lbs/person/view/2146632378.

Bibliography

Acts of the Legislature of the Island of Tobago; from 1768, to 1775, inclusive. London, 1776.
Arena, Carolyn. 'Indian Slaves from Caribana: Trade and Labor in the Seventeenth-Century Caribbean.' PhD diss., Columbia University, 2017.
Arena, Carolyn. 'Indian Slaves from Guiana in Seventeenth-Century Barbados.' *Ethnohistory* 64, no. 1 (2017): 65–90.
Benton, Lauren. 'Just Despots: The Cultural Construction of Imperial Constitutionalism,' *Law, Culture and the Humanities* 9, no. 2 (2013): 213–226.
Benton, Lauren, and Adam Clulow. 'Introduction: The Long, Strange History of Protection.' In *Protection and Empire: A Global History*, edited by Lauren Benton, Adam Clulow, and Bain Attwood, 1–10. Cambridge: Cambridge University Press, 2018.
Benton, Lauren, and Lisa Ford. *Rage for Order: The British Empire and the Origins of International Law, 1800–1850.* Cambridge, MA: Harvard University Press, 2016.
Bilder, Mary Sarah. *The Transatlantic Constitution: Colonial Legal Culture and the Empire.* Cambridge, MA: Harvard University Press, 2004.
Brandow, James C. *Genealogies of Barbados Families: From Caribbeana and the Journal of the Barbados Museum and Historical Society.* 1983; repr. Baltimore, MD: Clearfield Company, Inc., 2001.
Breslaw, Elaine G. *Tituba, Reluctant Witch of Salem: Devilish Indians and Puritan Fantasies.* New York: New York University Press, 1996.

Brooks, James F. *Captives and Cousins: Slavery, Kinship, and Community in the Southwest Borderlands*. Chapel Hill: University of North Carolina Press, 2002.

Browne, Randy. *Surviving Slavery in the British Caribbean*. Philadelphia: University of Pennsylvania Press, 2017.

Chaplin, Joyce E. 'Enslavement of Indians in Early America: Captivity without the Narrative.' In *The Creation of the British Atlantic World*, edited by Elizabeth Mancke and Carole Shammas, 45–70. Baltimore, MD: Johns Hopkins University Press, 2005.

Chaplin, Joyce E. *Subject Matter: Technology, the Body, and Science on the Anglo-American Frontier, 1500–1676*. Cambridge, MA: Harvard University Press, 2001.

A Continuation of the State of New-England: Being a Farther Account of the Indian Warr ... Together with an Account of the Intended Rebellion of the Negroes in the Barbadoes. London: Printed by T.M. for Dorman Newman, 1676.

The Defense of the Settlers of Honduras against the Unjust and Unfounded Representations of Colonel George Arthur, Late Superintendent of that Settlement. London, 1824.

Dorsey, Joseph C. 'Women without History: Slavery, Jurisprudence, and the International Politics of *Partus Sequitur Ventrem* in the Spanish Caribbean.' *Journal of Caribbean History* 28, no. 2 (1994): 165–207.

Dwarris, Fortunatus. *Substance of the Three Reports of the Commissioners of Inquiry into the Administration of Civil and Criminal Justice in the West Indies*. London, 1827.

Epstein, James. *Scandal of Colonial Rule: Power and Subversion in the British Atlantic during the Age of Revolution*. New York: Cambridge University Press, 2012.

'First Report of the Commissioners of Enquiry into the Administration of Criminal and Civil Justice in the West Indies: Barbados, Tobago, Grenada.' *House of Commons Parliamentary Papers*, no. 157, XV. London, 1825.

Fisher, Linford D. '"Dangerous Designes": The 1676 Barbados Act to Prohibit New England Slave Importation.' *The William and Mary Quarterly* 71, no. 1 (2014): 99–124.

Fisher, Linford D. '"Why Shall Wee Have Peace to Bee Made Slaves": Indian Surrenderers During and After King Philip's War.' *Ethnohistory* 64, no. 1 (2017): 91–114.

Gallay, Alan. *The Indian Slave Trade: The Rise of the English Empire in the American South, 1670–1717*. New Haven, CT: Yale University Press, 2002.

Goetz, Rebecca Ann. 'Indian Slavery: An Atlantic and Hemispheric Problem.' *The History Compass* 14, no. 2 (2016): 59–70.

Hämäläinen, Pekka. *The Comanche Empire*. New Haven, CT: Yale University Press, 2008.

Handler, Jerome S. 'The Amerindian Slave Population of Barbados in the Seventeenth and Eighteenth Centuries.' *Caribbean Studies* 8, no. 4 (1968): 38–64.

Handler, Jerome S. 'Barbados Slave Conspiracies of 1675 and 1692.' *Journal of the Barbados Museum and Historical Society* 36, no. 4 (1982): 312–333.

Handler, Jerome S. 'Custom and Law: The Status of Enslaved Africans in Seventeenth-Century Barbados.' *Slavery & Abolition* 37, no. 2 (2016): 233–255.

Higman, B. W. *Slave Populations of the British Caribbean, 1807–1834*. Mona: University of the West Indies Press, 1995.

Kupperman, Karen Ordahl. *Indians and English: Facing Off in Early America*. Ithaca: Cornell University Press, 2000.

Laurence, K.O. 'Tobago and British Imperial Authority, 1793–1802.' In *Trade, Government, and Society in Caribbean History, 1700–1920*, edited by B.W. Higman, 39–56. Kingston: Heinemann, 1983.

Laurence, K.O. *Tobago in Wartime, 1793–1815*. Kingston: University Press of the West Indies, 1995.

The Laws of Jamaica. Kingston, 1792.

Legacies of British Slave-Ownership Database. Accessed 9 August 2019. https://www.ucl.ac.uk/lbs/.

Menezes, Mary Noel. *The Amerindians in Guyana 1803–1873: A Documentary History*. 1979; repr. New York: Routledge, 2019.

Morgan, Jennifer L. '*Partus Sequitur Ventrem*: Law, Race, and Reproduction in Colonial Slavery.' *Small Axe* 22, no. 1 (2018): 1–17.
Mulcahy, Matthew. *Hubs of Empire. The Southeastern Lowcountry and British Caribbean*. Baltimore, MD: Johns Hopkins University Press, 2014.
Newell, Margaret Ellen. *Brethren by Nature: New England Indians, Colonists, and the Origins of American Slavery*. Ithaca: Cornell University Press, 2015.
Newman, Brooke N. *A Dark Inheritance: Blood, Race, and Sex in Colonial Jamaica*. New Haven, CT: Yale University Press, 2018.
Newton, Melanie J. 'Returns to a Native Land: Indigeneity and Decolonization in the Anglophone Caribbean.' *Small Axe* 17, no. 2 (2013): 108–122.
Rawlin, William. *The Laws of Barbados, Collected in One Volume*. London: Printed for William Rawlin, 1699.
Renton, A. Wood. 'The Work of the West Indian Commissioners.' *Juridical Review: A Journal of Legal and Political Science* 2, no. 4 (1890): 357–365.
Reséndez, Andrés. *The Other Slavery: The Uncovered Story of Indian Enslavement in the Americas*. Boston, MA: Houghton Mifflin Harcourt, 2016.
Rushforth, Brett. *Bonds of Alliance: Indigenous and Atlantic Slaveries in New France*. Chapel Hill: University of North Carolina Press, 2012.
Smith, S.D. *Slavery, Family, and Gentry Capitalism in the British Atlantic: The World of the Lascelles, 1648–1834*. New York: Cambridge University Press, 2006.
Substance of the Debate in the House of Commons, on the 15th May, 1823, On a Motion for the Mitigation and Gradual Abolition of Slavery throughout the British Dominions. London, 1823.
Turner, Sasha. *Contested Bodies: Pregnancy, Childrearing, and Slavery in Jamaica*. Philadelphia: University of Pennsylvania Press, 2017.
Wallenstein, Peter. 'Indian Foremothers: Race, Sex, Slavery, and Freedom in Early Virginia.' In *The Devil's Lane: Sex and Race in the Early South*, edited by Catherine Clinton and Michele Gillespie, 57–73. New York: Oxford University Press, 1997.
Weaver, Jace. *The Red Atlantic: American Indigenes and the Making of the Modern World, 1000–1927*. Chapel Hill: University of North Carolina Press, 2014.
Young, Sir William. *An Historical, Statistical, and Descriptive Account of the Island of Tobago, Introductory to an Essay on the Commercial and Political Importance of the Possession to Great Britain*. London, 1812.

Archival Sources

The National Archives of the United Kingdom, Kew CO 137/33, Colonial Office and Predecessors: Jamaica, Original Correspondence, 1762–1765.
CO 137/71, Colonial Office and Predecessors: Jamaica, Original Correspondence, 6 November 1775–29 October 1776.
CO 318/57, Commissioners of Legal Enquiry, West Indies, 1822–1824, volume 1.
CO 318/67, Commissioners of Legal Enquiry, West Indies, 1828, volume 11.
T 71/461, Office of Registry of Colonial Slaves and Slave Compensation Commission: Records, Slave Registers. Tobago: Unattached Slaves, 1819.
T 71/477, Office of Registry of Colonial Slaves and Slave Compensation Commission: Records, Slave Registers. Tobago: Unattached Slaves, 1827.

15
RETHINKING THE COLONIAL ENCOUNTER IN THE AGE OF TRAUMA

Taylor Spence

In the 'Age of Trauma', individual traumatic repetitions collect into an archive that signals the depredations of the settler-colonial past.[1] This represents a challenge to historical practice, which often serves political power by erasing or silencing traumatic histories. Trauma poses an un-ignorable question to the discipline of history: can the past tenses of traditional history-practice make sense to people for whom the past constantly and repeatedly intrudes into the present? Trauma represents a coming-home-to-roost of the histories of postcolonial nation-states, which are struggling to uphold exceptionalist façades. Multiple, divergent communities are arriving at the realisation that they live in an existential state of trauma, and this signposts the failure on the part of modern liberal nation-states to reckon with their pasts.[2] While political powers would like nothing more than to forget the past, the people they are governing are incapable of letting the past go. History must adapt to this postcolonial reality by developing methods that reflect the histories intrinsic to a traumatic inheritance.

All modern nation-states arose from imperialism and colonialism. Therefore, modern nation-states are trauma-states, where citizens (as well as those many populations without citizenship privilege) carry the burden of past traumas. These walking archives of trauma point to fruitful directions of historical enquiry, often representing historical erasure or suppression of past events deemed 'marginal' or 'unacceptable' to mainstream historical narratives. They carry stories within them, through which historians can investigate traumatic pasts. They force historians to rethink how to write about these histories, and for whom they are writing history. Trauma represents an opportunity for historians to deepen their relevance to contemporary society.

The opposite of a historical consciousness informed by trauma – that is, a repetitious and interlinked relationship between the present and the past – is the classic notion of the colonial encounter. Since Michel de Certeau first conceptualised these moments of discovery and contact between different cultures in imperialism as radical 'breaks' in the fabric of European historical consciousness, colonial historians have been imbuing them with a kind of mystical power.[3] De Certeau, who was nevertheless most concerned with how colonial encounters transformed European identity, became a canonical text for practitioners in the emerging field of ethnohistory – a field that melded 'historical and anthropological methodologies', according to Devon A. Mihesuah, '[like] for example, archival research and oral accounts', in order to arrive at a more objective view of the colonial past.[4] Perhaps the most impassioned and widely published defender of the ethnohistorical approach, James Axtell, understood the concept of encounter as the perfect metonym for a host of colonial-Indigenous relational experiences:

> Encounter has much to recommend it. Encounters are mutual, reciprocal-two-way rather than one-way streets. Encounters are generically capacious: there are encounters of people but also of ideas, institutions, habits, values, plants, animals, and micro-organisms. Encounters are temporally and spatially fluid: they can occur at any time in any place, before or after 1492, around the globe. And, although natives, critics, and activists may not approve the idea, encounters are morally neutral: the term does not prejudge the nature of the contact or its outcome. In sum, encounter is a spacious description that jettisons normative baggage to make room for disinterestedness and parity.[5]

However, as Axtell himself implies in this passage, critics, particularly Indigenous scholars, recognised in ethnohistory an attempt to create a sanitised (read depoliticised) historical imaginary, where settler colonials might be relieved of the burden of egregious violence and criminality. In colonial histories, there is a fine line between embodying multiple different historical viewpoints in service to a project of objectivity, and the eliding of historical inequities and injustices. As Vine Deloria Jr observes:

> There never has been an objective point of view regarding Indians and there never will be. Conflict between red and white has been the predominant characteristic of race relations for half a millennium and will continue to influence all efforts to bring about an interpretation of what the invasion of this continent has meant – to both Indians and non-Indians.[6]

Ethnohistory's encounters imply that history began when Europeans arrived. The concept of the colonial encounter allows scholars to continuously imagine that the so-called Discovery of the New World was actually a real, singular experience, rather than part of a historically traceable process, equal parts chance and intention. It enables them to consign Indigenous peoples to a static pre-Columbian timelessness, and ignore how Europeans were part of Indigenous histories both before and after Columbus. Indigenous peoples and invaders only rarely discovered each other without preconceptions and judgements. Indigenous nations already had extensive encounters with all kinds of 'others' (including Europeans) before European invasions in the fifteenth century, and, as one would expect, had developed social and political networks through trade and diplomacy.[7]

Moreover, in emphasising encounter, the violence of colonial history becomes ceaselessly episodic rather than structural. At the same time, ethnohistorians do not recognise their own roles in the structural inequalities of history. In seeking to see 'both sides' of unequal and contingent colonial interactions, encounter scholars are participating in an act of auto-rehabilitation. As the demographics of the academy change, many intellectuals are wondering if what they thought was objective ethnohistory may have in fact been what de Certeau called a 'hermeneutics of the other', where encounter research merely contributed to a closed loop of scholarship that reflected their own privileged worldviews.

In spite of these problems, the sometimes-heated debates about the 'colonial encounter' have been fruitful. They have forced historians to reckon with their own blind spots, and to widen their practice to include new approaches to evidence, analysis, and interpretation of the Early American past. Rayna Green opened a rich vein of study by demonstrating how settler-colonial views and interpretations of Indigenous peoples created a mirror reflecting coloniser ideologies.[8] Henry Nash Smith and Richard Slotkin documented the unfolding coloniser consciousness, by mapping, and using psychology to analyse, the settler nation's symbols.[9] Jill Lepore and others created an approach to American history that uses contemporary signs, images, and traditions as the means of tracing the historical lineages of settler belief systems.[10] Memory has created a way for some scholars, who might normally have been resistant to it, to make a place for oral history in their analyses, opening up a usable continuum between the Early American past and the present.[11]

The Age of Trauma and the interdisciplinary field of Trauma Studies offer historians another opportunity to build meaningful connections with the settler-colonial past. A trauma approach to history entails loosening the grip on the linear timeline and chronology. Trauma and its attendant psychological phenomenon known as post-traumatic stress disorder (PTSD) cause people to experience repetitious intrusions of the past into the present. Time, for a traumatised person, jumps back and leaps forward, creating a circular rather than linear timeline. Learning to master trauma entails becoming comfortable with simultaneity, what Walter Benjamin called "Messianic time," where "the past and future" flash in an "instantaneous present."[12] Flashbacks and *flashforwards* (or future disaster thinking) are not a choice for the traumatised. These simultaneous experiences of time make the linear, chronological timeline appear all the more like a fantasy. For Indigenous people, the tendency to silence the past's echoes into the present makes mainstream historical practice appear insensitive and disrespectful.

Awareness of trauma creates a new kind of archive for historians, one that imbues oral histories with a genetic component. Psychologists, social workers, and social geneticists argue that trauma can become intergenerational. This is something that Indigenous people and psychological practitioners have known for a long time. Trauma causes the traumatised to create trauma in others. Its effects, as well as the behaviours it engenders, can become cultural traditions as well.

Historians can trace trauma traditions back like a trail of toxic breadcrumbs into an originary past. But it appears that trauma imprints on the human genome as well as behaviour. Since the Holocaust, psychologists have been finding disturbing signs of inherited signs of trauma, even in groups not directly in touch with each other. Now, bio-geneticists are finding marks on genes that they say come from trauma. Oral history, long discounted by mainstream history, now has a potentially powerful ally in behavioural science. Diverse groups, including Indigenous people, sexual abuse survivors, and soldiers might actually represent an untapped archive of history.

Saving stories

As Walter Benjamin was climbing through the French Pyrenees in the autumn of 1940 with other Jewish refugees fleeing the Nazis, were memories of his childhood in Berlin flooding through his mind? Or was he focused on the future: on getting to Spain and then to New York? Earlier that year, while barely surviving in Paris, he wrote that 'memory ... flashes up at a moment of danger'.[13] Now, a half a year later, Benjamin was certainly in danger. The Wehrmacht had conquered France, and there was a warrant for the philosopher's arrest. A German Jew, Benjamin had spoken out as Hitler was grasping the reins of power in the 1930s. In January of 1940, he wrote 'Theses on the Philosophy of History', because he now understood that sometimes history kills. He was fleeing certain death, but he was also running from a violent and aggressive state with a version of history that he knew was not only inaccurate and racist, but also deadly. For Jews like Benjamin, the Nazi version of the German past was the end of all history. What remained were stories. Did Benjamin's memories flash at this moment of dire need, spurring him onwards?

Benjamin made it to Spain and crossed the border, but the Spanish police stopped him and told him that they would return him and the other Jews to the German authorities the next day. That night Benjamin chose death rather than return to death, but his writings lived, smuggled out of Vichy France, to remind us that we need our stories, our versions of the past, which may be, and in fact often are, the repudiation of a version of history that is death. I do not think Benjamin was against historians or the writing of history. Rather, I think he was trying to save us from a history bent on killing us. I think he was saying that every generation carries within itself the stories without which historians cannot helpfully make sense of the world. He was reminding us historians how important it is to remain sceptical of standard narratives but also to remain open to the stories our readers, students, and the public carry inside. They may possess greater wisdom than any history book we read or write; perhaps not wisdom based on archival facts, but a wisdom of intuitive knowledge, or of lived experience.

Benjamin's life and death exemplify the truism that sometimes history is pure falsehood, while memory, story, and intuition are truth. Indeed, another part of the passage I quoted goes as follows: 'In every era the attempt must be made anew to wrest tradition away from a conformism that is about to overpower it.'[14]

What I think Benjamin is saying tradition is not conformity. Tradition naturally emerges in societies; people carry tradition forward because it means something to them. Conformity is a by-product of politics, of people marshalling and deploying influence and power in society; people create conformity with an agenda. We should be sceptical of mainstream history. Tradition, or what we call oral history, is the unofficial story, which Benjamin was arguing might actually be the real story.

In our present age, Benjamin's story may resonate in a different way for those experiencing the ongoing and daily effects of past traumas or PTSD. In important ways, the experience of trauma is very similar to Benjamin's description of memories that 'flash' in moments of danger. Like memory, trauma is an inherently historical process, but one where painful stories reappear repetitively in the present. This can be a difficult way to live. Nevertheless, trauma may be trying to tell us something. If Benjamin were here today, he might say that the recollection inherent to PTSD is a form of personal truth-telling – a message from the past that ought to be heeded by those who receive it. Trauma may offer us valuable lessons, even life-saving lessons. They say that broken bones once healed are stronger than before. The other side of trauma is resilience.

The Age of Trauma

I do believe, as some have claimed, that the Age of Trauma is upon us. I like the idea because it encompasses the possibility that trauma is an actual, existential experience of today, while also accounting for trauma as a sociological phenomenon. The concept of trauma has always been, and continues to be, very controversial. Sigmund Freud first identified what he called 'traumatic neurosis' in his 1920 essay 'Beyond the Pleasure Principle', and psychologists and others have been arguing about its reality ever since. Freud was responding to soldiers' accounts of 'shell shock' from the trench warfare of the First World War. In this population, he noted two things that baffled him: first, soldiers suffered from 'peace neurosis' – hysteria after combat – as much or more than 'war neurosis'; second, if a soldier experienced a physical wound, they generally did not develop traumatic neurosis. Freud reported that as cuts to flesh and breaks of bone healed up, they instructed people on the processes of mending, scarring, and resilience. Other kinds of wounds – a tearing of one's sense of security, a surprise dislocation from one's culture, a fracturing of one's family or community, a witnessing of torture or suffering – appeared to recapitulate to an unlimited extent after the fact.[15]

It was not until the 1970s that the military began documenting the symptoms of PTSD, when returning soldiers from the Vietnam War were exhibiting them. Yet, in spite of all of the stories and documentation, the medical establishment resisted trauma until 2013, when the American Psychiatric Association included PTSD as a legitimate diagnosis in its *Diagnostic and Statistical Manual of Mental Disorders* (DSM-5), its official compendium of all psychological ailments.[16] Still, there continues to be much discussion and scepticism about trauma, both as a social-psychological phenomenon and as a way of labelling communities of experience.

In particular, some groups deemed 'marginalised' have wondered if 'trauma' is just a new package to an old set of deterministic beliefs, which informed earlier generations' assumptions about the so-called 'Indian Problem'. Athabascan scholar Dian Million argues that the Canadian nation-state frames Indigenous trauma as a set of 'medicalized' problems like 'poverty, drug addiction, alcoholism, and social dissolution', which pose a threat to 'future development . . . [and the] reconciliation of the [Canadian] nation', and not as the means of healing and self-determination.[17] Yet, when applied to how we historians research and write history, the concept of trauma may nonetheless have a salutary effect.

Generations of stories

Dakota historian Waziyatawin (also known as Angela Cavender Wilson) grew up with a story about her family fleeing from the Dakota homeland in western Minnesota after the beginning of the U.S.-Dakota War (or 'Great Sioux Uprising') in the late summer of 1862.[18] I include this oral history in my teaching of the American Civil War, but it was equally part of the history of Dakota resistance to dispossession. I share this story – one that Waziyatawin's grandmother told her and Waziyatawin, in turn, published – as an opening to define the concept of historical trauma, and think about its philosophical and methodological implications for history.

It was in 1862 that Abraham Lincoln threatened to emancipate some of the Confederacy's slaves if seceded states did not surrender and return to the Union. About a decade earlier, in 1851, the Dakota had negotiated a treaty with the U.S. that guaranteed them a homeland in western Minnesota, but since that time settlers had been squatting on their territories, taking lumber and hunting their game. The territorial governor openly encouraged such behaviour. Accepting a reservation boundary required the Dakota to begin to change the ways that they had fed themselves and organised their communities for generations. Corrupt traders and Indian agents used this forced transition as an opportunity to enrich themselves, charging exorbitant prices for second-rate food, livestock, seeds, and tools. The eruption of the Civil War and the exodus of young men to the east to enlist sparked hopes on the part of the Dakota that settlers might retreat permanently. They recalled the days before the settler invasion and longed for a return to the past. In 1862, they started seeking to enact this return through violence, attacking settler outposts and traders. Both President Lincoln and the state of Minnesota were swift to respond. Mounted militia and regular army swept into the region to round up every Dakota person they could find.[19]

After a hasty investigation and trial into the actions of the Dakota, President Lincoln signed the death warrants of 39 warriors. On 26 December 1862, 38 human beings dropped through a special gallows built for the occasion, in the largest public execution in U.S. history, a spectacle presided over by hundreds of Minnesotans gathered in Mankato's town square. How many children witnessed this mass execution? How many remembered what they saw for the rest of their lives?

Waziyatawin tells how in September 1862 her family – including her grandmother's grandmother, Maza Okiye Win, who was just ten years old at the time – had filled their wagon with their belongings and bumped out into the prairie to get away from the violence. They came to a bridge over a creek, and the oxen, who were pulling their cart, became restive, apparently thirsty for water. So, they stopped the wagon and the entire family got out while the animals drank. Maza Okiye Win was standing on the bridge with her mother and grandmother when a group of armed men (either U.S. soldiers or militia) galloped up, and began gesturing and yelling at them. Many Plains Indians – and especially women – could neither understand nor speak English, and their incomprehension appeared to frustrate the men. There was a scuffle, and one of the men pushed Maza Okiye Win's grandmother off the bridge. She tumbled down the embankment and into the water. Her daughter rushed down and helped her up and back onto the bridge, amid general shouting and crying. Then, inexplicably, one of the soldiers rushed at the elderly woman and stabbed her in the stomach with his sabre.

The old woman fell to the ground, crying in agony and clutching her stomach as blood gushed out. Her family tried to help her, but she pleaded with them to escape while they still could. 'Please daughter, go,' she said, 'I am done for anyway. If they kill you, the children will have no one.' Waziyatawin's family fled. They left their beloved kin alone on the bridge to bleed to death. They returned later in the dark and found dried blood on the wooden bridge, and in the grass a little away, a bloody blanket, but no sign of her body. Waziyatawin's grandmother remembers her grandmother saying, 'Up to today we don't even know where my grandmother's body is. If only they had given the body back to us we could have given her a decent funeral.'[20]

The first step to building an understanding of historical trauma, and how it functions in the past and the present, is to conceptualise how experiences like the murder of Maza Okiye Win's grandmother, or the execution of the Dakota 38 warriors, might resonate for those witnessing such incomprehensible violence. To begin with, we must acknowledge that for us, as for those witnesses in 1862, an unbridgeable divide exists between the wounded and the witness. We can never comprehend the physical suffering Waziyatawin's great-great-great-great-grandmother underwent. Indeed, the evidence indicates that her suffering was psychic rather than physical – she worried for her family rather than for herself. We can never comprehend her suffering, but we can embody the experience of being a witness to her suffering.

For individuals, the experience of trauma is an experience of *living the past in the present*. Psychologists call this bi-temporal state of being *transposition*. To become a witness, we transpose ourselves from the present to *the present of the past*, employing a technique I use with my students called 'body questioning'. We move through (on the page or in class) any sensory details of the moment we can render – air, sound, smell, temperature, and vision – and then we imagine and share verbally ('unpack') how witnessing this suffering might have affected us. 'A traumatic event', explains the DSM-5, 'such as a natural disaster, a serious accident, a terrorist act, war/combat, rape or other violent personal assault ... [causes some] people [to] have intense, disturbing thoughts and feelings related to their experience that last long after the traumatic event has ended'.[21] The word 'last' does not quite capture the intrusive quality of these flashbacks. They appear to be in control, manifesting at will. Sigmund Freud wrote that for the person suffering traumatic neurosis

> the dream life ... continually takes the patient back to the situation of his disaster, from which he awakens in renewed terror ... the obtrusion on the patient over and again, in his sleep, of the impression made by the traumatic experience is taken as merely a proof of its strength.[22]

Psychologists call this constant intrusion of the violence of the past into the present 'traumatic repetition'.

Dominic LaCapra calls an event that becomes the vector of traumatic repetition a 'limit experience'.[23] In the case of Waziyatawin's story, one persuasive piece of evidence that this experience was indeed a limit experience for those who witnessed it was that her grandmother had heard it, remembered it, and repeated it to her granddaughter. Generations decided that it should be passed down. Oral histories do not benefit from a professional framework to support their creation, production, and dissemination. There is a reason that stories such as this one last the generations; they contain a core truth. Waziyatawin's grandmother needed this story. She believed that her granddaughter needed this story. Oral history is the avenue through which the necessary stories from the past come to the light of day.

In a settler-colonial society, we would be foolish to expect the so-called 'legitimate' history to accurately document the past. History is most comfortable serving power, and in settler-colonial societies, its job is often to make excuses for injustice. A Native or African American person today might say that history is in fact traumatic repetition. Mainstream history is just as likely to erase and silence as it is to document and illuminate. 'Silences signify the making of archives', Haitian historian Michel-Rolph Trouillot reminds us.[24] In a parallel fashion, psychologists tell us that common symptoms of PTSD include psychic numbing and dissociation (checking out). Substance abuse and addiction can be the means of silencing traumatic repetition. Psychologist Wendy Maltz writes that after recovering from addiction, her patients often discover an unacknowledged trauma at the origin of their substance abuse.[25] What if archives themselves, like people, can manifest the symptoms of trauma? Archival silences may be the places where trauma resides.

I would argue that in settler-colonial societies, the repetition of oral histories from generation to generation is analogous to the repetition inherent to trauma. Trauma is the way that the past forces itself into the present to speak to us. For people who suffer from traumatic repetition, that intrusion is not welcome. Similarly, oral histories are often not welcome in professional history. Yet some of the most important interventions in history have come from persistent oral traditions that refused to remain silent. Indeed, the relationship between the two is what makes a living history.

The ever-elaborating creation of history is, on a meta level, always and continually the dialogic relationship between the anecdotal and the archival. It is the historian's job to weigh and assess the relative significance of the anecdotal in relationship to the archival. The problem with many historians is that they close their minds to the anecdotal. However, an awareness of trauma sensitises historians to be more open-minded to the anecdotal they encounter in the archive. If we, as historians, begin with that awareness, we might take the oddities, the inconsistencies, and the unexplained more seriously. These 'perturbations', as Ann Laura Stoler calls them – these slight ripples in the smooth homogenous grain of the sources with which historians create history – come forth with greater significance when we see them through the eyes of trauma.[26]

To return to our example, Waziyatawin's family story illuminates an aspect of the standard narrative of the so-called Great Sioux Uprising about which historians have written very little: the story of Indigenous non-combatants. The surprising and unlikely insertion of soldiers into this story creates a link between an event in Native American history and an event in U.S. history. Historians rarely if ever include the U.S.-Dakota War in broader narratives of the American Civil War. Waziyatawin's oral history draws that connection, and opens up new avenues for interpretation and analysis. But, more importantly, it also demonstrates the potential irrationality underlying those events. Why did the soldier attack an old lady? What possible purpose, either in putting down the rebellion or in winning the Civil War, could this action have achieved? There may be a rational explanation that we have yet to discover. But anyone who researches or writes history knows that the nonsensical comprises a much larger proportion of the archival record than most would care to admit. Trauma gives the lie to the teleological and rationalist assumptions of history. It also suggests that historians might look for the irrational as signs of trauma in the archive. Moments of irrationality and traumatic experiences are often one and the same thing. So, thinking historiographically, we might add repetitive irrationality to the theoretical tools historians have developed, such as Trouillot's silence and Stoler's perturbations.

Hauntings

There's a saying that if it's hysterical, it's historical. All trauma is historical, so on a certain level, the term 'historical trauma' is redundant. However, by this point I hope you can see that the term 'historical trauma' comes out of the experience of the colonised, where one's individual traumas most often find their origin points in the political history of colonialism. Maria Yellow Horse Brave Heart offers one example of a Lakota person driving through a piece of their lost homeland.

> When I was driving [here] ... I felt angry. I looked at the beauty of the land, of the Black Hills. I thought, "where are the Indians?" ... I had a dream the other day. It was kind of scary. I got up shaking [starting to cry]. I saw people carrying guns and shooting people [Indians] in the Black Hills again. It was a hard dream. That's what I saw.[27]

An empty landscape opens up, and the recollection of a dream gallops in. Anger sparked in the present, flashing the memory of a scary dream, which held within it the remembrance of an even older past trauma. This story demonstrates that historical trauma causes a chain of *individual* feelings about *communal* experiences that move along a fluid chronological continuum from the present to the past and back again.

However, as painful as this recollection may have been for Brave Heart, the manner with which they revealed their traumatic repetition might actually be a sign of healing. Eduardo and Bonnie Duran, psychologists who were early proponents of using culturally specific practices to treat traumatic repetition in Indigenous communities, developed the idea of 'trauma mastery'. In this practice, patients find relief from trauma by pinpointing the vector of their individual trauma to historical, structural, and systemic violence, racism, and colonisation. Therefore, the term 'historical trauma' itself signifies an important step by which the traumatised distance themselves from trauma by politicising it. Out of this insight have come specific subcategories of PTSD, such as American Indian historical trauma (AIHT) and post-traumatic slave syndrome (PTSS). Labelling can have healing power.[28]

Furthermore, the great irony of this insight is that the only people residing in the settler-colonial nation-state who do not appear interested in making this connection between the anecdotal and the archival, between the individual and the communal, are the white descendants of settler colonials. Trauma teaches us that perpetrators of and witnesses to violence can also be traumatised. Settler-colonial historical trauma may be best described as a *haunting*. Stoler writes that 'haunting occupies the space between what we cannot see and what we know'.[29] Have the past actions of settlers created intergenerational patterns in their descendants' ways of thinking? Have they left an inheritance of fear, paranoia, and anxiety that lurks on the edges of consciousness, seeping into worldviews, informing assumptions, and occasionally jumping out of dark corners to manifest unpleasantly in daily experience, just as ghosts hover on the edge of our vision?

Stoler's definition of haunting aptly describes how growing up in the American West felt to me. As a disabled, queer young man, I lived with a low-grade anxiety born from the disconnect between what I felt and saw, and what the adults in my life told me. This uneasiness with my as-told family history drove me to question the stories my family recounted around the kitchen table. One of these stories was about a Spence relative who was present at a well-documented occurrence of genocide – the 1864 Sand Creek Massacre. This particular relative suffered from consumption and, like many others, had come to Colorado for his health. He found work as a member of John M. Chivington's Third Colorado Cavalry, an unofficial territorial posse that instigated and perpetrated the murder of more than 200 unarmed Arapahoe and Cheyenne people, including elderly people, women, and children. According to his wife, my great-great-grandmother, Sarah Milner, who dictated her memories in a book called *Pioneer Epic*, what he witnessed at Sand Creek 'broke' him, and he died at a relatively young age.[30]

Her grandson, my grandfather, wrote a book too, one that began with he and his brother listening to their uncle telling 'thrilling' stories about their grandfather, including about Sand Creek. My grandfather recalls how his grandfather became a 'peace officer' in what his uncle called 'Chivington's Colorado Territorial Constabulary'. In this capacity, my great-great-grandfather executed those whom the community deemed criminal. He rode with a prisoner and two other men out into the prairie, and when his companions were out 'scouting', he shot the prisoner, claiming that he had tried to escape. 'He could not forget these cold-blooded killings,' according to my grandfather. Later, my great-great-grandfather joined in the bloody violence at Sand Creek. 'He could never forget the final clean-up,' my grandfather writes, 'the killing of the wounded, the women and children'. He could never forget. The memories flashed up unbidden, uncontrollable, and finally he told his son, who told my grandfather, who told my uncle, who told me.[31]

A key difference between the stories of the colonised and the coloniser is that this narrative inheritance includes justifications and explanations. Settler-colonial histories are histories of justification. Yet, the trauma just keeps on giving and giving. My great-great-grandfather had not wanted to murder people, the story went. He was ill; he had to have to work. The executioner's posse drew straws to decide who would do the killing. My great-great-grandfather had drawn 'the short straw'. Similarly, he had not instigated the killing at Sand Creek. He had only 'witnessed' the massacre, and became an active participant at the end, when he had only done his job of 'cleaning up' – his killing of women and children became more like acts of mercy, rather than murder.[32] By the time my uncle told me the story, my great-great-grandfather had become a secretary to Chivington, and therefore only a bystander, not a killer. What he saw, not what he had done, had destroyed him. The final step of the settler-colonial story-telling tradition transforms perpetrators into victims. It did not take very much research to discover that there were no secretaries at the Sand Creek Massacre. My great-great-grandfather met his future brother-in-law behind a Howitzer, positioned strategically on a bluff above the Indigenous encampment. Two settler-colonial families married in a collaborative work of genocide was the real pioneer epic.

The womb of mythologies I grew up within held a pattern, and 'that pattern', to adopt Patricia Nelson Limerick's insight about western history, was 'one of betrayal'.[33] In the expansion of North American settler states, 'good people' often found themselves doing some really bad things to their neighbours, Indigenous and other. Probably more commonly, they knew of bad things being done – their neighbours may have been the people doing those things. From that secret complicity, those who knew they were the beneficiaries of injustice began the work of carrying the burden of that knowledge. They formulated excuses and made justifications, but also left signs that they knew something that was not quite right. To my grandfather's credit, he admitted (more than once) that the stories he inherited did not 'accord with the historical record'. He also did not fail to include the important fact that the government granted my great-great-grandfather an honourable discharge, with an $8-per-month pension that grew to $75 per month by the time my great-great-grandmother died in 1938.[34]

Genetic archives

How trauma passes from individual to community, and indeed across generations, is the subject of current biological and sociological research. It does appear that trauma is contagious. A famous 1988 study of Israeli veterans of the 1982 war in Lebanon found that the descendants of Holocaust survivors experienced much higher rates of PTSD, as well as a wider range of symptoms, even three years after the conflict, than did soldiers without that traumatic heritage. This older study accords with a new, award-winning study of 167 babies conducted at Tulane University that demonstrated a definitive correlation between the functioning of a child's hypothalamic-pituitary-adrenal (HPA) axis – the body's system for regulating stress – and a mother's cumulative stress over the course of her lifetime. Mothers with abuse history, high prenatal-stress levels, and prenatal depression produce babies who responded sluggishly to surprising or scary stimuli, and then, once they responded, were much slower to return to normal than other babies. For the inheritors of trauma, it's as if the clutch of a car has become worn down. Gears can't smoothly shift. They grind, mash, and get stuck. Engines roar when they should be idling, or can't accelerate when they need to speed up. Trauma babies are like new cars born with old transmissions.[35]

Many Indigenous people are not surprised by studies purporting to document intergenerational trauma. Journalist and member of the Red Cliff Band of Ojibwe, Mary Annette Pember, writes that 'folks in Indian country wonder what took science so long to catch up with traditional Native knowledge?' In her reporting, she cites LeManuel 'Lee' Bitsoi, a PhD Research Associate in Genetics at Harvard University and a member of the Navajo Nation, who says, 'Native healers, medicine people and elders have always known this and it is common knowledge in Native oral traditions.'[36] Just as oral histories track through time, paralleling mainstream history, to burst forth in moments of danger to help us, so too then might intergenerational trauma be carrying messages from the past into the present that we need to hear.

If intergenerational trauma is not just a sociological phenomenon but also a biological one, then it may be the evidence of a kind of genetic archive that historians may be able to utilise to travel more productively into the past. They might do this by borrowing a method from anthropology known as 'upstreaming' and adapting it to traumatic histories. James Axtell describes upstreaming as the process by which researchers begin with 'cultural knowns of the present' and work backwards in order to make some informed hypotheses about the past. William N. Fenton writes that upstreaming

> rests on three assumptions: (1) that major patterns of culture remain stable over long periods, producing repeated uniformities; (2) that these patterns can best be seen by proceeding from the known ethnographical present to the unknown past, using recent sources first and then earlier ones; and

(3) that those sources that ring true at both ends of the time span merit confidence.[37]

Like upstreaming, which tries to use the present as the basis for constructing a vision of the past, 'trauma tracking' begins with contemporary symptoms of trauma to tease out the DNA of traumatic repetition. Using standard oral-history interview techniques, historians construct a lineage of stories leading into the past, and possibly to an originary traumatic event. In some cases, as with Waziyatawin or my family, generations have passed down a story of the originary event, which can frame this lineage of symptoms. In some cases, the originary event remains elusive, yet the symptoms become the sign of an event as yet unknown. The resulting 'contextual, three-dimensional, analytic narrative(s)' are a brand of microhistory 'in which', according to Richard D. Brown, 'actual people as well as abstract forces shape events'.[38] These deep trauma histories are both anecdotal and representative, grounded in individual familial experiences but ramified through the disparate and opposing constituents of the self-identified community of those who experience traumatic repetition.

Trauma threatens to explode the most cherished creation of the historical profession, the linear chronology. But in the aftermath of that destruction lies the promise of a healing history. When we research, write, and read colonial encounters as trauma histories, we can grow comfortable with traversing the ups and downs, the circling back and forth of a looping timeline, which is the hallmark of trauma. Seen in this light, though it is disturbing and disorienting, traumatic repetition might also represent an inheritance that, when understood and accepted, and when paired with history, might constitute a special kind of 'super power' that is capable of bringing us together. If we traumatised – the ancestors of both the victims and the perpetrators – can recognise the signs of our own traumas in each other's trauma histories, we might be able to master the settler-colonial past together, in collaboration rather than in conflict.

Walter Benjamin understood that, I think, even if he could not see his way forward to practise such a history. 'There is a painting by Klee called *Angelus Novus*,' he wrote (Figure 15.1).

> An angel is depicted there who looks as though he were about to distance himself from something which he is staring at. His eyes are opened wide, his mouth stands open and his wings are outstretched. The Angel of History must look just so. His face is turned towards the past. Where we see the appearance of a chain of events, he sees one single catastrophe, which unceasingly piles rubble on top of rubble and hurls it before his feet. He would like to pause for a moment so fair, to awaken the dead and to piece together what has been smashed. But a storm is blowing from Paradise, it has caught itself up in his wings and is so strong that the Angel can no longer close them. The storm drives him irresistibly into the future, to which his back is turned, while the rubble-heap before him grows sky-high. That which we call progress, is this storm.[39]

Figure 15.1 Paul Klee, *Angelus Novus*, 1920, oil transfer and watercolour on paper, Israel Museum

Notes

1 Jason Tougaw and Nancy K. Miller, eds., *Extremities: Trauma, Testimony, and Community* (Urbana: University of Illinois Press, 2002), 1.
2 Taylor Spence, 'The Trauma Consensus: History Method in the "Age of Trauma",' *Continuum: Journal of Media and Cultural Studies* 31, no. 5 (2017): 671–681.
3 Michel de Certeau, 'Ethno-Graphy: Speech, or the Space of the Other: Jean de Lery,' in *The Writing of History*, trans. Tom Conley (New York: Columbia University Press, 1988), 218–221.
4 Devon A. Mihesuah and Angela Cavender Wilson, *Indigenizing the Academy: Transforming Scholarship and Empowering Communities* (Lincoln: University of Nebraska Press, 2004), 146.
5 James Axtell, 'Columbian Encounters: Beyond 1992,' *The William and Mary Quarterly* 49, no. 2 (April 1992): 336.
6 Vine Deloria Jr, 'Comfortable Fictions and the Struggle for Turf: An Essay Review of *The Invented Indian: Cultural Fictions and Government Policies*,' in *Natives and Academics: Researching and Writing about American Indians*, ed. Devon A. Mihesuah (Lincoln: University of Nebraska Press, 1998), 66.
7 Rayna D. Green, 'A Tribe Called Wannabee: Playing Indian in America and Europe,' *Folklore* 99, no. 1 (1988): 33–35.
8 Rayna D. Green, 'The Pocahontas Perplex: The Image of Indian Women in American Culture,' *The Massachusetts Review* 16, no. 4 (Autumn 1975): 698–714; Green's ground-breaking work began with this essay, and continued in 'A Tribe Called Wannabee', cited earlier in

this chapter. See also: Jean M. O'Brien, *Firsting and Lasting: Writing Indians Out of Existence in New England* (Minneapolis: University of Minnesota Press, 2010).

9   Smith began (as far as I can tell) the discussion about American 'consciousness' as a historical development. Henry Nash Smith, *Virgin Land: The American West as Symbol and Myth* (Cambridge: Harvard University Press, 1950), 4; Richard Slotkin, *Regeneration Through Violence: The Mythology of the American Frontier, 1600–1860* (Norman: University of Oklahoma Press, 2000), 4–5, 550–567.

10 Jill Lepore, *The Name of War: King Philip's War and the Origins of American Identity* (New York: Vintage, 1999), 227–235; Ari Kelman, *A Misplaced Massacre: Struggling Over the Meaning of Sand Creek* (Cambridge, MA: Harvard University Press, 2013).

11 A notable example is the story of the first Decoration Day. David W. Blight, *Race and Reunion: The Civil War in American Memory* (Cambridge, MA: Belknap Press of Harvard University Press, 2001), 69.

12 Walter Benjamin quoted in Benedict Anderson, *Imagined Communities: Reflections on the Origin and Spread of Nationalism*, Revised Edition (New York, Verso, 2006) 24.

13 Walter Benjamin, 'Theses on the Philosophy of History,' in *Illuminations*, ed. Hannah Arendt, trans. Harry Zohn (New York: Schocken Books, 1968), 255.

14 Benjamin, 'Theses on the Philosophy of History,' 255.

15 Sigmund Freud, 'Beyond the Pleasure Principle' (1920), in *The Standard Edition of the Complete Psychological Works of Sigmund Freud*, trans. James Strachey, vol. XVIII (London: Hogarth Press, 1955), 10–11.

16 American Psychiatric Association (APA), 'Trauma and Stressor-Related Disorders,' in *Diagnostic and Statistical Manual of Mental Disorders: DSM-5* (Arlington: American Psychiatric Association, 2013).

17 Dian Million, *Therapeutic Nations: Healing in an Age of Indigenous Human Rights* (Critical Issues in Indigenous Studies; Tucson: University of Arizona Press, 2013), 19.

18 Angela Cavender Wilson (Waziyatawin), 'Grandmother to Granddaughter: Generations of Oral History in a Dakota Family,' *The American Indian Quarterly* 20, no. 1 (Winter 1996): 7–11.

19 David A. Nichols, 'The Other Civil War: Lincoln and the Indians,' *Minnesota History* 44, no. 1 (Spring 1974): 8.

20 Wilson, 'Grandmother to Granddaughter,' 11.

21 APA, 'Trauma and Stressor-Related Disorders,' *DSM-5*.

22 Freud, 'Beyond the Pleasure Principle,' 8.

23 Dominick LaCapra, 'Representing the Holocaust: Reflections on the Historians' Debate,' in *Probing the Limits of Representation: Nazism and the 'Final Solution,'* ed. Saul Freidlander (Cambridge, MA: Harvard University Press, 1992), 108–127.

24 Michel-Rolph Trouillot, *Silencing the Past: Power and the Production of History* (Boston, MA: Beacon Press, 1995).

25 Wendy Maltz, *The Sexual Healing Journey: A Guide for Survivors of Sexual Abuse*, rev. ed. (New York: William Morrow Paperbacks, 2012), 25.

26 Ann Laura Stoler, *Along the Archival Grain: Epistemic Anxieties and Colonial Common Sense* (Princeton, NJ: Princeton University Press, 2009), 19.

27 Maria Yellow Horse Brave Heart, 'Wakiksuyapi: Carrying the Historical Trauma of the Lakota,' *Tulane Studies in Social Welfare* 21–22 (2000): 257.

28 Eduardo Duran and Bonnie Duran, *Native American Postcolonial Psychology* (Albany: State University of New York Press, 1995); Joseph P. Gone, 'Reconsidering American Indian Historical Trauma: Lessons from an Early Gros Ventre War Narrative,' *Transcultural Psychiatry* 51, no. 3 (2014): 387–406; Joy DeGruy, *Post Traumatic Slave Syndrome: America's Legacy of Enduring Injury and Healing* (Milwaukie: Uptone Press, 2005).

29 Ann Laura Stoler, *Haunted by Empire: Geographies of Intimacy in North American History* (Durham, NC: Duke University Press, 2006), xiii.

30 Sarah Ann Milner Smith and Eugene Bradford Smith, *Pioneer Epic: The Life History of Sarah Ann (Milner) Smith* (Boulder, CO: Johnson Pub. Co, 1951), 47; Jeffrey Ostler,

The Plains Sioux and U.S. Colonialism from Lewis and Clark to Wounded Knee (New York: Cambridge University Press, 2004), 45.
31. Gerald M. Spence, *The Evolution of a Hillbilly Kid* (Riverton: Big Bend Press, 1989), 6–9.
32. Spence, *Evolution of a Hillbilly Kid*, 6–9.
33. Patricia Nelson Limerick, 'Making the Most of Words: Verbal Activity and Western America,' in *Under an Open Sky: Rethinking America's Western Past*, eds. William Cronon, George A. Miles, and Jay Gitlin (New York: W.W. Norton & Company, 1992), 168–169.
34. Spence, *Evolution of a Hillbilly Kid*, 7–8.
35. Zahava Solomon, Moshe Kotler, and Mario Mikulincer, 'Combat-Related Posttraumatic-Stress Disorder Among Second-Generation Holocaust Survivors: Preliminary Findings,' *American Journal of Psychiatry* 145, no. 7 (July 1988): 865–868; Stacy S. Drury et al., 'Thinking Across Generations: Unique Contributions of Maternal Early Life and Prenatal Stress to Infant Physiology,' *Journal of the American Academy of Child and Adolescent Psychiatry* 56, no. 11 (2017): 922–929.
36. Mary Annette Pember, 'Intergenerational Trauma: Understanding Natives' Inherited Pain,' *Indian Country Today* (2016), 3.
37. James Axtell, 'Ethnohistory: An Historian's Viewpoint,' *Ethnohistory* 26, no. 1 (Winter 1979): 1–13; William N. Fenton, *American Indian and White Relations to 1830: Needs and Opportunities for Study* (Chapel Hill: University of North Carolina Press, 1957), 21–22.
38. Richard D. Brown, 'Microhistory and the Post-Modern Challenge,' *Journal of the Early Republic* 23, no. 1 (2003): 18.
39. Benjamin, 'Theses on the Philosophy of History,' 257.

Bibliography

American Psychiatric Association. 'Trauma and Stressor-Related Disorders.' In *Diagnostic and Statistical Manual of Mental Disorders: DSM-5*. Arlington: American Psychiatric Association, 2013.

Axtell, James. 'Ethnohistory: An Historian's Viewpoint.' *Ethnohistory* 26, no. 1 (Winter 1979): 1–13.

Axtell, James. 'Columbian Encounters: Beyond 1992.' *The William and Mary Quarterly* 49, no. 2 (April 1992): 335–350.

Benjamin, Walter. 'Theses on the Philosophy of History.' In *Illuminations*, edited by Hannah Arendt, translated by Harry Zohn, 255–263. New York: Schocken Books, 1968.

Blight, David W. *Race and Reunion: The Civil War in American Memory*. Cambridge, MA: Belknap Press of Harvard University Press, 2001.

Brown, Richard D. 'Microhistory and the Post-Modern Challenge.' *Journal of the Early Republic* 23, no. 1 (2003): 1–20.

de Certeau, Michel. 'Ethno-Graphy: Speech, or the Space of the Other: Jean de Lery.' In *The Writing of History*, translated by Tom Conley, 209–243. New York: Columbia University Press, 1988.

DeGruy, Joy. *Post Traumatic Slave Syndrome: America's Legacy of Enduring Injury and Healing*. Milwaukie: Uptone Press, 2005.

Deloria, Vine, Jr. 'Comfortable Fictions and the Struggle for Turf: An Essay Review of *The Invented Indian: Cultural Fictions and Government Policies*.' In *Natives and Academics: Researching and Writing about American Indians*, edited by Devon A. Mihesuah, 65–83. Lincoln: University of Nebraska Press, 1998.

Drury, Stacy S., A.O. Gray, Christopher W. Jones, Katherine P. Theall, and Erin Glackin. 'Thinking Across Generations: Unique Contributions of Maternal Early Life and Prenatal Stress to Infant Physiology.' *Journal of the American Academy of Child and Adolescent Psychiatry* 56, no. 11 (2017): 922–929.

Duran, Eduardo, and Bonnie Duran. *Native American Postcolonial Psychology*. Albany: State University of New York Press, 1995.
Fenton, William N. *American Indian and White Relations to 1830: Needs and Opportunities for Study*. Chapel Hill: University of North Carolina Press, 1957.
Freud, Sigmund. 'Beyond the Pleasure Principle' (1920). In *The Standard Edition of the Complete Psychological Works of Sigmund Freud*, trans. James Strachey, vol. XVIII. London: Hogarth Press, 1955.
Gone, Joseph P. 'Reconsidering American Indian Historical Trauma: Lessons from an Early Gros Ventre War Narrative.' *Transcultural Psychiatry* 51, no. 3 (2014): 387–406.
Green, Rayna D. 'The Pocahontas Perplex: The Image of Indian Women in American Culture.' *The Massachusetts Review* 16, no. 4 (Autumn 1975): 698–714.
Green, Rayna D. 'A Tribe Called Wannabee: Playing Indian in America and Europe.' *Folklore* 99, no. 1 (1988): 33–55.
Kelman, Ari. *A Misplaced Massacre: Struggling Over the Meaning of Sand Creek*. Cambridge, MA: Harvard University Press, 2013.
LaCapra, Dominick. 'Representing the Holocaust: Reflections on the Historians' Debate.' In *Probing the Limits of Representation: Nazism and the 'Final Solution'*, edited by Saul Freidlander, 108–127. Cambridge, MA: Harvard University Press, 1992.
Lepore, Jill. *The Name of War: King Philip's War and the Origins of American Identity*. New York: Vintage, 1999.
Limerick, Patricia Nelson. 'Making the Most of Words: Verbal Activity and Western America.' In *Under an Open Sky: Rethinking America's Western Past*, edited by William Cronon, George A. Miles, and Jay Gitlin, 167–184. New York: W.W. Norton & Company, 1992.
Maltz, Wendy. *The Sexual Healing Journey: A Guide for Survivors of Sexual Abuse*. Rev. ed. New York: William Morrow Paperbacks, 2012.
Mihesuah, Devon A., and Angela Cavender Wilson. *Indigenizing the Academy: Transforming Scholarship and Empowering Communities*. Lincoln: University of Nebraska Press, 2004.
Million, Dian. *Therapeutic Nations: Healing in an Age of Indigenous Human Rights* (Critical Issues in Indigenous Studies). Tucson: University of Arizona Press, 2013.
Nichols, David A. 'The Other Civil War: Lincoln and the Indians.' *Minnesota History* 44, no. 1 (Spring 1974): 2–15.
O'Brien, Jean M. *Firsting and Lasting: Writing Indians Out of Existence in New England* Minneapolis: University of Minnesota Press, 2010.
Ostler, Jeffrey. *The Plains Sioux and U.S. Colonialism from Lewis and Clark to Wounded Knee*. New York: Cambridge University Press, 2004.
Pember, Mary Annette. 'Intergenerational Trauma: Understanding Natives' Inherited Pain.' *Indian Country Today* (2016). https://amber-ic.org/wp-content/uploads/2017/01/ICMN-All-About-Generations-Trauma.pdf.
Slotkin, Richard. *Regeneration through Violence: The Mythology of the American Frontier, 1600–1860*. Norman: University of Oklahoma Press, 2000.
Smith, Henry Nash. *Virgin Land: The American West as Symbol and Myth*. Cambridge, MA: Harvard University Press, 1950.
Smith, Sarah Ann Milner, and Eugene Bradford Smith. *Pioneer Epic: The Life History of Sarah Ann (Milner) Smith*. Boulder: Johnson Pub. Co, 1951.
Solomon, Zahava, Moshe Kotler, and Mario Mikulincer. 'Combat-Related Posttraumatic-Stress Disorder Among Second-Generation Holocaust Survivors: Preliminary Findings.' *American Journal of Psychiatry* 145, no. 7 (July 1988): 865–868.
Spence, Gerald M. *The Evolution of a Hillbilly Kid*. Riverton: Big Bend Press, 1989.
Spence, Taylor. 'The Trauma Consensus: History Method in the "Age of Trauma".' *Continuum: Journal of Media and Cultural Studies* 31, no. 5 (2017): 671–681.
Stoler, Ann Laura. *Haunted by Empire: Geographies of Intimacy in North American History*. Durham, NC: Duke University Press, 2006.

Stoler, Ann Laura. *Along the Archival Grain: Epistemic Anxieties and Colonial Common Sense.* Princeton, NJ: Princeton University Press, 2009.
Tougaw, Jason, and Nancy K. Miller, eds. *Extremities: Trauma, Testimony, and Community.* Urbana: University of Illinois Press, 2002.
Trouillot, Michel-Rolph. *Silencing the Past: Power and the Production of History.* Boston, MA: Beacon Press, 1995.
Wilson, Angela Cavender (Waziyatawin). 'Grandmother to Granddaughter: Generations of Oral History in a Dakota Family.' *The American Indian Quarterly* 20, no. 1 (Winter 1996): 7–11.
Yellow Horse Brave Heart, Maria. 'Wakiksuyapi: Carrying the Historical Trauma of the Lakota.' *Tulane Studies in Social Welfare* 21–22 (2000): 245–266.

PART IV

Removals and diasporas

16
SEXUAL REMOVALS
Indigenous genders and sexualities as territory

Manuela L. Picq[1]

Hawai'ians and Zapotecs see gender as a continuum. They recognise that some people are not simply female *or* male. In Hawai'i, *māhū* are the ones in the middle, those who embrace both feminine and masculine traits.[2] In Zapotec society, *muxes* are neither men nor women, but a third gender that refuses to be reduced to LGBT+ categorisation.[3] *Māhū* and *muxes* have long been respected as healers who transmit knowledge and valued as they embody Polynesian and Zapotec principles of spiritual duality, the female/male synthesis. But if such fluid understandings of gender defined indigenous worldviews for millennia, they were progressively criminalised, then replaced, by colonial processes of dispossession.

Indigenous genders and sexualities are untranslatable. They cannot be exported or replicated because they refer not to action but to worldviews. In ancient Zapotec, for instance, pronouns did not refer to gender but to beings. There was no 'he' or 'she', instead *la-ave* referred to people, *la-ame* to animals, and *la-ani* to inanimate beings like mountains.[4] This changed with the arrival of the Spaniards who introduced the feminine and masculine genders. The introduction of Spanish language brought a new way of organising gender and the gradual replacement of Zapotec language implied the erasure of a certain worldview, a new ontology on what it means to be human.

Indigenous sexualities were as diverse as the peoples who practise them, ranging from non-monogamous relations and non-conforming practices to homo-affective families. But Indigenous registries were largely erased in colonial processes of dispossession. Indigenous dispossession expanded beyond territory – the forced removal of peoples from their lands was accompanied by a systematic disruption of lifeways. Colonial violence destroyed indigenous authority, breaking social trust and undoing systems of accountability. It also regulated indigenous intimacies. Indigenous genders and family relations were one of the main targets of colonialism. Colonial rules dispossessed women of their political and economic power, turning them into property, and associated one-on-one, lifelong heterosexual marriage with private property.[5] Love and sex were at the heart of colonialism, and marriage was especially threatening to the colonial order of white supremacy.[6] The codification of sex was a key element in regulating gender and family to assert power.[7]

This chapter analyses the logic of sexual colonisation to show dispossession as a multifaceted phenomenon. The colonial regulation of gender and sexuality is directly related to territorial control and the doctrine of discovery. Sexuality was used as a tool to criminalise Native peoples, frame them as pervert, and validate European violence against non-Christian others labelled as savage, heretic, and sodomite. This research explores the role of sexual heteronormativity for disciplining Native peoples in colonial projects. Estevão Rafael Fernandes and Barbara M. Arisi suggest that Indigenous sexualities matter because of what we can learn *from* them.[8] Their value lies not in the diversity of grammars they offer, but in what they allow us to see about colonisation. Colonialism disrupted Indigenous political and intimate relations. That is why Native scholar Kim TallBear insists on the importance of recognising indigenous intimacies to escape settler sex and decolonise our ways of relating, such as the Dakota concept of extended family *tiospaye* or the Kichwa notion of *ayllu*.[9]

Indigenous experiences are valuable because they expand epistemes. This is why Native sexualities should not be discussed to increase sexual vocabularies or from anthropological standpoints that exoticise indigeneity. Rather, they contribute to post-colonial debates regarding colonial dispossession, the criminalisation of non-European sexualities, and the always incomplete control of colonised bodies, desires, and intimacies. This research hopes to shed light on the mechanisms of conquest, understanding how knowledge is lost. It contributes to ongoing efforts to decolonise queer studies and queer decolonial studies.[10]

Yet, this analysis is stuck in the impossibility of epistemological translation. First, the study of sexualities in the colonial past is vulnerable to anachronisms. Sodomy archives from colonial Latin America are inevitably embedded in certain preconceptions of sex and interpretations of the body. Second, to engage with Indigenous sexualities in the English language runs the permanent risk of anachronism and misrepresentation. The meanings of gender roles and sexual practices are cultural constructions that inevitably get lost when they are decontextualised in cultural (and linguistic) translation.[11] The idea that a person is homosexual, for instance, stems from contemporary assumptions of sexual identity and is only possible after the invention of the concept of homosexuality.[12] Heterosexual lenses are as inappropriate as the binary imagination to understand Indigenous worlds, which do not fit the confined Western registries of LGBT+ codification. Categories like 'female' and 'woman' are increasingly problematic; yet, I use them in this chapter to refer broadly to people assigned female at birth (and I'll use 'male' and 'man' similarly) because there is vast spectrum for naming gender identities, ever-evolving as this research argues, and it is not for me to ascertain individuals' specific gender identities.

The idea of indigeneity is also problematic because this notion refers to a multiplicity of peoples and has many variations – Indian, Native, First Nations,

Indigenous, and Originary peoples. There are different words to refer to Indigenous peoples because their experiences refer to different colonial processes of state-making. Indigeneity refers to a historical process, an identity relational to the state. In the sixteenth century, colonial governance started to conflate distinct peoples in this homogenising legal status; 'Indian' became an all-encompassing category referring to non-European peoples from the East and West Indies, a cluster of Europe's homogenous other.[13] Indigenous peoples are as diverse as the processes of colonisation they continue to endure; their identities are as fluid and contested as their political struggles. States continue to manipulate legislation and information on indigenous presence depending on their interest to erase, regulate, or displace them.[14] For Mohawk and Cherokee scholars Taiaiake Alfred and Jeff Corntassel, Indigenousness is an oppositional identity linked to the consciousness of struggle against (ongoing) dispossession by settler states that spread from Europe.[15]

This chapter focuses on Indigenous concepts of gender and sexuality to analyse colonial dispossession. A first section looks at the vast diversity of Indigenous genders and sexualities across time and borders, notably through language. A second section explains the regulation of indigenous intimacies through charges of sodomy, and the theological invention of 'crimes against nature'. A third section argues that sexual colonisation matters because it was an element of the doctrine of discovery, supplanting Native lifeways with Western codes associated with the Christian European order.

Sexual and gender diversity in Indigenous worlds

Non-heteronormative sexualities were celebrated across pre-colonial Indigenous societies. Moche pottery (15–800 CE), in contemporary Peru, depicted same-sex phallic acts that represented exchange of fluids between bodies as a form of connection and relation. Across the Pacific, Māori carvings celebrated same-sex and multiple relationships.[16] Andean peoples revered the queer figure *chuqui chinchay* and utilised this mountain deity to mediate political decisions until the late fifteenth century.[17] *Chuqui chinchay*, patron of dual-gendered peoples in Inka ceremonies, embodied a third creative force between the masculine and the feminine in Andean philosophy, performing rituals that involved same-sex erotic practices.

Colonial chronicles told of genders that Europeans could not comprehend (or accept). Will Roscoe, in his book *Changing Ones*, examines colonial archives reporting alternative genders in North America.[18] Reports from French expeditions in Florida described 'hermaphrodites' among the Timucua Indians in 1564, portraying them as warriors, hunters, and weavers. In the Mississippi Valley, they also reported a third gender called *ikoueta*, a word in Algonkian language that refers to males who adopted different gender roles. *Ikouetas* were holy, and nothing could be decided without their advice. In the same region, another French coloniser described males that did women's work and had sex with men among the Natchez in the eighteenth century. Spanish chronicles reported men who dressed and lived like women in what is today Texas. Russian traders reported gender diversity among Native communities in Alaska's sub-arctic region. Russia tried to suppress third genders, but the Chugach and Koniag considered the 'two persons in one' to be lucky.

Expansive understandings of gender abounded in the New World, with a linguistic index documenting more than two genders in over 150 languages in North America. Alternative genders existed among the Creek, Chickasaw, and Cherokee. In the Diné language, *nádleehí* means 'the changing one', while in the Osage, Omaha, Kansa, and Oto languages, the term *mixu'ga* literally means the 'moon-instructed' one, referring to the abilities conferred by the moon.[19] Often, alternative genders were associated with spiritual powers. The Potawatomi considered them extraordinary people. For the Lakota, *winkte* people had auspicious powers and could predict the future. In Cheyenne philosophy, the *he'emane'o* embodied the principles of balance and synthesis and were the ones to lead the victory-dance.[20] The Mohave *hwame* were considered to be powerful shamans gifted for curing disease.[21]

Although women engaged with same-sex practices and alternative genders, they are less visible in colonial archives. The disinterest in women is partly due to a colonial male gaze concerned with deviations from the masculine norms. Female homoerotic activity was also less scrutinised because the dominant idea of 'passive' women made it almost impossible to imagine such activity between women.[22] Evelyn Blackwood argues that the female cross-gender role in Native American contexts constituted an opportunity to assume male roles permanently and to marry women.[23] A trader for the American Fur Company that travelled up the Missouri River reported that Woman Chief, a Crow woman who led men into battle, had four wives, and was a respected authority who sat in Crow councils.[24] Roscoe's linguistic index shows wording referring specifically to women who undertook male roles in one third of native languages.

Gender was a complex, fluid affair unrelated to identity. Blackwood argues that Native American ideology among Western tribes dissociated sexual behaviour from concepts of male/female gender roles.[25] Gender roles did not restrict sexual partners – people's gender identity did not imply a sexual identity. Blackwood stresses the unimportance of biological sex for gender roles in Native worldviews for Western tribes. There was much overlapping between masculine and feminine, and people who were once married and had kids would later in life pursue same-sex relationships. Roscoe interprets this fluidity as a distinction between reproductive and non-reproductive sex rather than a distinction between heterosexual and same-sex sexualities.[26] Although a lot is lost in temporal and linguistic translations, what is certain is that Indigenous societies have long recognised and even revered alternative genders and sexualities.

Amazon Indigenous languages are testimony of that complexity. In Tikuna, an Amazon language with no common ancestry or demonstrable genealogy with any other known language, *Kaigüwecü* describes a man who has sex with another man and *Ngüe Tügümaêgüé*, a woman who has sex with another woman.[27] Fernandes and Arisi also indicate wording signifying plural sexualities in other Amazonian languages.[28] In Tupinambá, *tibira* is a man who has sex with men and *çacoaimbeguira* is a woman who has sex with women – the documentary *Tibira Is Gay* shows a variety of sexual identities in Indigenous communities.[29] Other languages have words for queer practices: *cudinhos* in Guaicurus, *guaxu* in Mbya, *cunin* in Krahò, *kudina* in Kadiwéu, *hawakyni* in Javaé. There are various accounts of anthropologists describing homo/bi-sexuality across Amazonia for a reason.[30]

Historical and linguistic archives defy translation – they refer to social fabrics that have been violently disrupted, repressed, and removed. Each language entails a singular understanding of gender that cannot be reduced to contemporary LGBT+ frames because alternative genders were constitutive of a whole. Native sexualities invoke complex social fabrics that are untranslatable in the limited framework of hetero/homosexuality. They embody epistemes beyond sexuality; they represent alternative worldviews that were destroyed by conquest. The arrival of Europeans marked the beginning of a process of profound removal, marked by a dispossession of territories and lifeways.

Regulating sex: crimes against nature

Colonisers framed native sexualities as immoral, perverse, and unnatural, and brutally repressed them. They described Natives as 'great sodomites' who 'engage in carnal acts with both men and women without shame'.[31] French colonisers reported that the *ikouetas* practised 'sodomy' and Loskiel accused the Delaware of 'unnatural crimes'.[32] Spaniards established that Andeans were 'all sodomites'.[33] Europeans saw non-binary sexualities as abject and called for their extermination. Indigenous sexualities were brutally disappeared.

European colonisers punished with death those they determined were sodomites. In 1513, Spanish conquistador Vasco Nuñez de Balboa massacred the brother of Chief Quaraca and 40 companions for being dressed as women.[34] The men were thrown to the dogs, a scene of brutal subjugation to Christian morals. In 1536, Frey Bartolomé de las Casas recorded the killing of three men because they dressed as women.[35] Spaniards decided that they were corrupted by the sin of sodomy and threw them to the dogs. In another macabre episode, French colonisers tied a gender non-conforming man to a cannon in northern Brazil. The French chased the man for being 'more man than a woman' and killed him 'to purify the land'.[36]

Colonialism regulated gender and bodies. The narrative of conquest emphasised European ideals of gender that depicted the invaders as masculine, rational, and powerful and Indigenous populations as feminine, irrational, and sinful.[37] The concept of sodomy was intertwined with Spanish perceptions of manliness, which organised power structures in colonial governance. Sodomy was mostly a crime of manliness, a disruption of established hierarchies, and colonisers used the crime of sodomy against native men. Women were rarely charged with crimes of sodomy, leading the Portuguese Inquisition to declare that sodomy among women was no longer part of its jurisdiction in 1646.[38]

But it was not clear what the crime of sodomy actually meant. It was an ambiguous concept filled with contradictions that referred less to a specific act than to any practice considered outside Catholic codes of conduct.[39] Mark D. Jordan traces the notion of sodomy to the eleventh century. He credits theologian Peter Damian for coining the word *sodomia* in analogy to blasphemy. In the Old Testament, 'sodomy' first referred to the explicit sin of denying God.[40] Divine punishment in the story of Sodom is for those who contest divine authority – it is about (dis)obedience, not (same) sex. It is a crime associated with heresy: the first sodomites were above all heretics.[41] Then in the thirteenth century, sodomy is associated with sins against nature by Thomas Aquinas, one of the moral teachers of Catholicism. His *Summa Theologiae* defined six sins of *luxuria*, carnal sins that manifest in the excess of pleasure.[42] Although Aquinas did not single it out nor associate it with homosexuality, sodomy evolved from blasphemy to become synonymous with 'unnatural acts'. It then set the limit between the order of nature (as defined by God) and the savage world of Indians. It defined the borders of Christian authority and became a powerful tool to justify European invasions across the so-called New World.

Confusion is thus foundational to the codification of sodomy – it has historically been used without accountability. Sodomy was everything and anything contravening Christian codes of authority. Colonisers invoked it to repress any practice contrary to their rule. This was clear during the 1550 Debate of Valladolid, as Spanish theologians debated whether Indians had a soul and could be enslaved. Juan Ginés de Sepúlveda argued that the Indigenous peoples of the Americas had no soul, and equated their moral status to that of women. Sepúlveda used the notion of sodomy to delegitimise Indigenous authority and suggested that Europeans should fulfil the role of the Lord, making it lawful to subject them to Spanish dominion: 'due to the sin of nefarious intercourse fell from heaven fire and brimstone and destroyed Sodom and Gomorrah'.[43] Framing Indians as sodomites deprived them of Christian morality, and therefore of political authority. What was at stake was not sexuality, but the appropriation of their lands. Sexual colonisation was but one more tool of conquest.

Laws on sodomy separating 'civilised' and 'savage' bodies spread across colonies and endured through the centuries. The legal uses of sodomy were particularly prevalent in the eighteenth century. In an unprecedented archival research of more than 300 documents relating to 'unnatural' sex cases from New Spain, Zeb Tortorici found over 170 from the eighteenth century and 80 from the first two decades of the nineteenth century – compared to just over 50 cases from the seventeenth century and only 13 from the sixteenth.[44] In the British Empire, Section 377 expanded across colonies and survived decolonial struggles.[45] Modelled on the Buggery Act of 1533 in England, it made sexual activities 'against the order of nature' illegal. It was introduced into the Indian Penal Code in 1861 during British rule – and was still law in India until 2018. Although crimes of sodomy spread across colonial regions, the reversal of sodomy laws was less homogenous and varies greatly across the post-colonial world. The French Revolution decriminalised homosexuality in France but not in Haiti, and most former colonies and protectorates of the British Empire, notably Uganda, maintained (or still maintain) sodomy laws and laws that further criminalised same-sex male practices. In the Americas, countries like Brazil and Guatemala annulled laws on 'crimes against nature' during the liberal reforms of the late nineteenth century, but Nicaragua maintained that legislation through the Sandinista revolution until the 2009 constitutional reform abolished it.

Sex and the doctrine of discovery

The removal of Indigenous expressions of gender and sexuality should not be analysed as mere evangelisation nor reduced to individual forms of violence; it served as a tool in a much broader project of dispossession. Framing Indigenous peoples as sodomites legitimised the unprecedented land-grab justified by the Christian doctrine of discovery. This doctrine was based on the notion of *terra nullius*, or no one's land, established in a papal bull that Pope Urban II issued in 1095 to legitimise Christian crusades into Palestine. It considered lands occupied by 'barbarous nations' as empty wastelands and encouraged Christian crusaders to invade these territories and dominate its people to bring them under Christian dominion.[46] Four centuries later, Pope Alexander VI designed four similar papal bulls establishing a Christian 'law of nations' that encouraged the invasion of the New World.[47] The *Inter Caetera* bulls issued in 1493 'granted' Spain and Portugal the right to conquer areas that were not under Christian dominion in the Americas, arguing that, like Palestine, the Americas could be 'justly' invaded if its inhabitants did not obey the Christian order. The notion of *terra nullius* established the Christian faith as the sole source of legitimate political authority, defining non-Christian territories as wastelands up for grabs. Indigenous peoples were framed as infidels, 'barbarians', or 'savages' to 'be brought to faith'. The colonial narratives that portrayed them as sodomites directly responded to the framing of the doctrine, identifying the local inhabitants with disobedience to the Christian God, either as infidels or savages, and therefore laying the framework for the dispossession across the New World. Scholars have discussed in depth how the doctrine's principle of Christian superior political authority shaped the foundations of international law.[48] These tropes of sodomy are constitutive of what Vine Deloria Jr has called 'conquest masqueraded as law'.[49]

Colonial chronicles told of sodomites because they provided European monarchs with justification to bring territories under Christian dominion. Chronicles that appeared to be about sex were in fact about territory. They were not intended to describe actual sexual practices, but to frame the latest 'just war' against sinners outside the Christian faith.[50] European invaders gained from reporting sodomites in the lands they conquered. Reports were marked by excesses and extrapolations, making abundant use of ambiguous terms like sodomy, unnatural crimes, and abominable sins.[51] Colonisers were framing their narratives within the context of the doctrine of discovery to 'legalise' the invasion. Sodomites were the rationale of conquest; they constituted the other on which to build a discourse of Empire.[52]

Colonial chronicles on sexuality simultaneously located Indigenous peoples outside the Christian faith and in its past. In 1690, John Locke articulated this notion of temporal difference: 'In the beginning, all the world was America.'[53] Indigenous peoples were framed in a permanent state of nature outside political modernity,[54] and were seen, in contrast to Europe, as peoples without history.[55] Non-Western people were placed outside of Europe's political present, inventing a subaltern temporality that is condemned to follow behind the Christian, modern coloniser. Indeed, a fundamental trait of colonial projects is to bring the uncivilised savages into the political (Christian) present. British rule over India was tied to British time because to civilise meant, among other things, to bring others into European present time.[56] This Western practice of temporalising difference continues to shape international politics, especially narratives of development that seek to export democracy as sexual modernity, locating non-Western peoples in a sexual past.[57]

From the early moments of conquest, to the nineteenth century, the sexual disciplining of Native peoples was one such modernising project. Fernandes and Arisi explain how the colonisation of native sexualities imposed a foreign configuration of family and intimate relations in Brazil. The state created bureaucratic structures to civilise the Indians. In the 1750s, the Directory of Indians established administrative control of intimacy and domesticity that restructured sex and gender in daily life. Bureaucratic interventions decried the 'incivility' of Indigenous homes where 'several families ... live as beasts not following the laws of honesty ... due to the diversity of the sexes'.[58] Indigenous households were subject to the monogamous 'laws of honesty' and Indigenous heterosexualisation initiated the process of civilisation. Mark Rifkin refers to a similar process of 'heterohomemaking' in Native North America.[59] Heteronormativity prohibited any other sexuality, gender, or form of family organising. All peoples were forced to translate themselves in terms consistent with the European Christian state and its jurisdiction. Sexuality was codified and became a referent to racial boundaries, creating a new grammar to access political and property rights.[60]

Sexual colonisation has had the same intent in a wide variety of contexts: it destroys to replace.[61] The various bureaucratic forms of erasure are nothing less than termination – the actions of colonial governments may change over time, but the intended result is always to erase Indigenous presence on the land. Leanne B. Simpson sees a direct connection between the dispossession of Nishnaabeg lifeways and the attack on territories through Canadian colonialism as the state continues to take 'legal' rights to Nishnaabeg lands for the extraction of natural resources:

> The removal and erasure of Michi Saagiig Nishnaabeg bodies from land make it easier for the state to acquire and maintain sovereignty over land because this not only removes physical resistance to dispossession, it also erases the political orders and relationships housed within Indigenous bodies that attach our bodies to our land.[62]

Colonialism destroys non-nuclear families to suppress connections as it steals land. In Māori contexts, for instance, land dispossession destroyed large communal kinship networks, and forced people to live in smaller, nuclear families. The result of territorial dispossession was the erosion of Māori forms of child-raising – by the early twentieth century, many Māori who had lost access to land were unable to maintain extended *wharau* life within a communal family home setting.[63] In the context of Hawai'i, Native scholar J. Kēhaulani Kauanui argues that it is imperative to reconsider Hawai'ian indigeneity as an epistemological resource for rethinking land, gender, sexuality, and the very concept of sovereignty.[64]

Ongoing violence forced Indigenous peoples to conform to Christian codes of sexuality and family to survive genocide and dispossession. In that sense, European tropes of sodomy did more than obfuscate complex Indigenous sexualities, they destroyed Indigenous lifeways, from the most immediate forms of governance to the deepest ontologies making sense of the cosmos.

Conclusion

Conceptualisations of gender and sexuality varied profoundly across Indigenous societies, but they were all criminalised in similar ways with European colonial invasions. Indigenous sexualities and the relations they sustained were brutally repressed through force, legality, then autocracy. Allegations of sodomy became a strategic signifier to reframe invasion as a just war under the Christian doctrine of discovery. To this day, the logic of sexual removal is deeply entangled in the many forms of dispossession that Indigenous peoples endure – removal seeks not only to dispossess territories, but also to destroy all the connections that hold peoples and their habitats together.

A close look at the colonial removal of Indigenous sexualities forces us to expand the analysis of dispossession to understand the broad destruction of lifeways. It denaturalises the gender binaries that continue to define monogamous heterosexual family codes; they were not always the norm, but remain central to colonial logics. This analysis sheds light on subtle, ongoing forms of dispossession. Sexual colonisation did not end with declarations of independence nor was it reverted by international human right law. It continues to shape intimacies and expectations in post-colonial contexts because desire itself was colonised. This is why Ngũgĩ wa Thiong'o insists on the decolonising of the mind and Silvia Rivera Cusicanqui calls us to the daily work of emancipating ourselves from internal colonialism.[65]

Indigenous lifeways resist, in loving and belonging, in silence, and in contestation. The challenge of contemporary struggles for self-determination is to reconnect what colonial violence separated: territorial self-determination with bodily emancipation. The challenge is to reconnect what conquest fragmented, because there can be no emancipated territories without emancipated bodies.

Notes

1 This chapter draws upon some previously published and co-authored work, particularly Josi Tikuna and Manuela L. Picq, 'Indigenous Sexualities: Resisting Conquest and Translation,' in *Sexuality and Translation in World Politics*, eds. Caroline Cottet and Manuela L. Picq (Bristol: E-International Relations, 2019) and Manuela L. Picq, 'Decolonizing Indigenous Sexualities: Between Erasure and Resurgence,' in *The Oxford Handbook of Global LGBT and Sexual Diversity Politics*, eds. Michael J. Bosia, Sandra M. McEvoy, and Momin Rahman (Oxford: Oxford University Press, 2020), 169–184.
2 Ty P. Kāwika Tengan, *Native Men Remade: Gender and Nation in Contemporary Hawai'i* (Durham, NC: Duke University Press, 2008), 152.
3 Alfredo Mirandé, *Behind the Mask: Gender Hybridity in a Zapotec Community* (Tucson: University of Arizona Press, 2017).
4 Ivan Olita, dir., *Third Gender: An Entrancing Look at Mexico's Muxes* (2017) National Geographic, Short Film Showcase, online video, 9:36, https://youtu.be/S1ZvDRxZlb0.

5. Kim TallBear, 'Making Love and Relations Beyond Settler Sex and Family,' in *Making Kin Not Population*, eds. Adele Clarke and Donna Haraway (Chicago, IL: Prickly Paradigm Press, 2018), 145–166.
6. Anne McClintock, *Imperial Leather: Race, Gender and Sexuality in the Colonial Conquest* (Abingdon: Routledge, 1995).
7. Holly J. McCammon and Allison R. McGrath, 'Litigating Change? Social Movements and the Court System,' *Sociology Compass* 9, no. 2 (2015): 128–139.
8. Estevão Rafael Fernandes and Barbara M. Arisi, *Gay Indians in Brazil: Untold Stories of the Colonization of Indigenous Sexualities* (Cham: Springer, 2017).
9. TallBear, 'Making Love and Relations,' 148.
10. See, for example, Qwo-Li Driskill, ed., *Queer Indigenous Studies: Critical Interventions in Theory, Politics, and Literature* (Tucson: University of Arizona Press, 2011).
11. Caroline Cottet and Manuela L. Picq, eds., *Sexuality and Translation in World Politics* (Bristol: E-International Relations, 2019).
12. Jonathan Ned Katz and Lisa Duggan, *The Invention of Heterosexuality* (Chicago, IL: University of Chicago Press, 2007). See also Mark Rifkin, *When Did Indians Become Straight? Kinship, the History of Sexuality, and Native Sovereignty* (New York: Oxford University Press, 2011).
13. Vanita Seth, *Europe's Indians: Producing Racial Difference, 1500–1900.* (Durham, NC: Duke University Press, 2010). See also Nancy Van Deusen, *Global Indios: The Indigenous Struggle for Justice in Sixteenth-Century Spain* (Durham, NC: Duke University Press, 2015).
14. J. Kēhaulani Kauanui, *Hawaiian Blood: Colonialism and the Politics of Sovereignty and Indigeneity* (Durham, NC: Duke University Press, 2008).
15. Taiaiake Alfred and Jeff Corntassel, 'Being Indigenous: Resurgences Against Contemporary Colonialism,' *Government and Opposition* 40, no. 4 (2005): 597–614.
16. Ngahuia Te Awekotuku, 'He Reka Ano: Same Sex Lust and Loving in the Ancient Maori World,' in *Outlines: Lesbian & Gay Histories of Aotearoa*, eds. Alison J. Laurie and Linda Evans (Wellington: Lesbian & Gay Archives of New Zealand, 2005), 6–9.
17. Michael J. Horswell, *Decolonizing the Sodomite: Queer Tropes of Sexuality in Colonial Andean Culture* (Austin: University of Texas Press, 2005).
18. Will Roscoe, *Changing Ones: Third and Fourth Genders in Native North America* (New York: Palgrave, 1998).
19. Roscoe, *Changing Ones*, 13.
20. Roscoe, *Changing Ones*, 14.
21. Evelyn Blackwood, 'Sexuality and Gender in Certain Native American Tribes: The Case of Cross Gender Females,' *Signs* 10, no. 1 (1984): 27–42.
22. Lilian Faderman, *Odd Girls and Twilight Lovers: A History of Lesbian Life in Twentieth Century America* (New York: Columbia University Press, 2011).
23. Blackwood, 'Sexuality and Gender in Certain Native American Tribes,' 31.
24. Roscoe, *Changing Ones*, 78.
25. Blackwood, 'Sexuality and Gender in Certain Native American Tribes,' 35.
26. Roscoe, *Changing Ones*, 10.
27. Tikuna and Picq, 'Indigenous Sexualities.'
28. Fernandes and Arisi, *Gay Indians in Brazil*.
29. Emilio Gallo, dir., *Tibira Is Gay* (*Tibira É Gay*), (Brazil, 2007), 35 mm film and digital video, 10:05.
30. See, for example, Claude Levi-Strauss, *The Story of Lynx*, trans. Catherine Tihanyi (Chicago, IL: University of Chicago Press, 1996).
31. Mirandé, *Behind the Mask*, 53.
32. Roscoe, *Changing Ones*, 13, 251.
33. Horswell, *Decolonizing the Sodomite*, 2.
34. Kenneth Hamilton, 'Colonial Legacies, Decolonized Spirits: Balboa, Ugandan Martyrs and AIDS Solidarity Today,' *Journal of Bisexuality* 10, no. 1–2 (2010): 121–136.

35 Isaac E. Carrillo Can, 'El Erotismo Andróginx en la Cosmovisión y Lenguaje Maya,' in *Andar Erótico Decolonial*, ed. Raúl Moarquech Ferrera-Balanquet (Buenos Aires: Ediciones del Signos, 2015): 73–81.
36 Fernandes and Arisi, *Gay Indians in Brazil*, 7.
37 Pete Sigal, *The Flower and the Scorpion: Sexuality and Ritual in Early Nahua Culture* (Durham, NC: Duke University Press, 2011).
38 Ronaldo Vainfas, *A Heresia Dos Indios: Catolicismo e Rebeldia no Brasil Colonial* (São Paulo: Companhia das Letras, 1995).
39 Horswell, *Decolonizing the Sodomite*.
40 Mark D. Jordan, *The Invention of Sodomy in Christian Theology* (Chicago, IL: University of Chicago Press, 1997), 29.
41 Jordan, *Invention of Sodomy*, 36.
42 Jordan, *Invention of Sodomy*, 144.
43 Philip Colin Hawkins, 'New World Sodom: Biblical Tales of Conquest and Acculturation,' *Electronic Journal of Human Sexuality* 15 (January 2012).
44 Zeb Tortorici, *Sins Against Nature: Sex & Archives in Colonial New Spain* (Durham, NC: Duke University Press, 2018).
45 Puri Jyoti, *Sexual States: Governance and the Struggle Over the Antisodomy Law in India* (Durham, NC: Duke University Press, 2016).
46 Steve Newcomb, *Pagans in the Promised Land: Decoding the Doctrine of Christian Discovery* (Golden: Fulcrum, 2008).
47 Robert J. Miller, 'The International Law of Colonialism: A Comparative Analysis,' *Lewis & Clark Law Review* 15, no. 4 (2011): 847.
48 See, for example, Antony Anghie, *Imperialism, Sovereignty and the Making of International Law* (Cambridge: Cambridge University Press, 2007).
49 Vine Deloria Jr, 'Conquest Masquerading as Law,' in *Unlearning the Language of Conquest: Scholars Expose Anti-Indianism in America*, ed. Four Arrows (Austin: University of Texas Press, 2006), 94–107.
50 Newcomb, *Pagans in the Promised Land*.
51 Tortorici, *Sins Against Nature*.
52 Federico Carvajal, *Butterflies Will Burn: Prosecuting Sodomites in Early Modern Spain and Mexico* (Austin: University of Texas Press, 2003).
53 John Locke, *Second Treatise of Government* (London: Awnsham Churchill, 1690).
54 Barry Hindess, 'The Past is Another Culture,' *International Political Sociology* 1, no. 4 (2007): 325–338.
55 Eric Wolf, *Europe and the People Without History* (Berkeley: University of California Press, 1982).
56 Vanessa Ogle, *The Global Transformation of Time: 1870–1950* (Cambridge, MA: Harvard University Press, 2015).
57 Jasbir Puar, *Terrorist Assemblages: Homonationalism in Queer Times* (Durham, NC: Duke University Press, 2007). See also Momin Rahman, *Homosexualities, Muslim Cultures and Modernity* (London: Palgrave Macmillan, 2014).
58 Fernandes and Arisi, *Gay Indians in Brazil*, 32.
59 Rifkin, *When Did Indians Become Straight?*, 9
60 McClintock, *Imperial Leather*. See also Kim TallBear, *Native American DNA: Tribal Belonging and the False Promise of Genetic Science* (Minneapolis: University of Minnesota Press, 2013).
61 Patrick Wolfe, 'Settler Colonialism and the Elimination of the Native,' *Journal of Genocide Research* 8, no. 4 (2006), 388. See also Kathleen A. Brown-Pérez, 'By Whatever Means Necessary: The U.S. Government's Ongoing Attempts to Remove Indigenous Peoples During an Era of Self-(De)termination,' *New Diversities* 19, no. 2 (2017), 7–23.
62 Leanne B. Simpson, *As We Have Always Done: Indigenous Freedom Through Radical Resistance* (Minneapolis: University of Minnesota Press, 2017), 42.

63 Helene Connor, 'Māori Mothering: Repression, Resistance and Renaissance,' in *Mothers of the Nations: Indigenous Mothering as Global Resistance, Reclaiming and Recovery*, eds. D. Memee Lavell-Harvard and Kim Anderson (Bradford: Demeter Press, 2014), 231–250.
64 Kēhaulani J. Kauanui, *Paradoxes of Hawaiian Sovereignty: Land, Sex, and the Colonial Politics of State Nationalism* (Durham, NC: Duke University Press, 2018), 21.
65 Ngũgĩ wa Thiong'o, *Decolonizing the Mind: The Politics of Language in African Literature* (London: James Currey, 1986); Silvia Rivera Cusicanqui, 'The Gaze: Visual Regimes and Colonialism' (seminar, Five Colleges Women Studies Research Center, 19 September 2019).

Bibliography

Alfred, Taiaiake, and Jeff Corntassel. 'Being Indigenous: Resurgences Against Contemporary Colonialism.' *Government and Opposition* 40, no. 4 (2005): 597–614.
Anghie, Antony. *Imperialism, Sovereignty and the Making of International Law*. Cambridge: Cambridge University Press, 2007.
Blackwood, Evelyn. 'Sexuality and Gender in Certain Native American Tribes: The Case of Cross Gender Females.' *Signs* 10, no. 1 (1984): 27–42.
Brown-Pérez, Kathleen A. 'By Whatever Means Necessary: The U.S. Government's Ongoing Attempts to Remove Indigenous Peoples During an Era of Self-(De)Termination.' *New Diversities* 19, no. 2 (2017): 7–23.
Carrillo Can, Isaac E. 'El Erotismo Andróginx en la Cosmovisión y Lenguaje Maya.' In *Andar Erótico Decolonial*, edited by Raúl Moarquech Ferrera-Balanquet, 73–81. Buenos Aires: Ediciones del Signos, 2015.
Carvajal, Federico. *Butterflies Will Burn: Prosecuting Sodomites in Early Modern Spain and Mexico*. Austin: University of Texas Press, 2003.
Connor, Helene. 'Māori Mothering: Repression, Resistance and Renaissance.' In *Mothers of the Nations: Indigenous Mothering as Global Resistance, Reclaiming and Recovery*, edited by D. Memee Lavell-Harvard and Kim Anderson, 231–250. Bradford: Demeter Press, 2014.
Cottet, Caroline, and Manuela L. Picq, eds. *Sexuality and Translation in World Politics*. Bristol: E-International Relations, 2019.
Cusicanqui, Silvia Rivera. 'The Gaze: Visual Regimes and Colonialism.' Seminar, Five Colleges Women Studies Research Center. 19 September 2019.
Deloria, Vine, Jr. 'Conquest Masquerading as Law.' In *Unlearning the Language of Conquest: Scholars Expose Anti-Indianism in America*, edited by Four Arrows, 94–107. Austin: University of Texas Press, 2006.
Driskill, Qwo-Li, ed. *Queer Indigenous Studies: Critical Interventions in Theory, Politics, and Literature*. Tucson: University of Arizona Press, 2011.
Faderman, Lilian. *Odd Girls and Twilight Lovers: A History of Lesbian Life in Twentieth Century America*. New York: Columbia University Press, 2011.
Fernandes, Estevão Rafael, and Barbara M. Arisi. *Gay Indians in Brazil: Untold Stories of the Colonization of Indigenous Sexualities*. Cham: Springer, 2017.
Gallo, Emilio, dir. *Tibira Is Gay (Tibira É Gay)*. 2007. 35 mm film and digital video, 10:05.
Hamilton, Kenneth. 'Colonial Legacies, Decolonized Spirits: Balboa, Ugandan Martyrs and AIDS Solidarity Today.' *Journal of Bisexuality* 10, no. 1–2 (2010): 121–136.
Hawkins, Philip Colin. 'New World Sodom: Biblical Tales of Conquest and Acculturation.' *Electronic Journal of Human Sexuality* 15 (2012).
Hindess, Barry. 'The Past Is Another Culture.' *International Political Sociology* 1, no. 4 (2007): 325–338.
Horswell, Michael J. *Decolonizing the Sodomite: Queer Tropes of Sexuality in Colonial Andean Culture*. Austin: University of Texas Press, 2005.

Jordan, Mark D. *The Invention of Sodomy in Christian Theology.* Chicago, IL: University of Chicago Press, 1997.
Jyoti, Puri. *Sexual States: Governance and the Struggle Over the Antisodomy Law in India.* Durham, NC: Duke University Press, 2016.
Katz, Jonathan Ned, and Lisa Duggan. *The Invention of Heterosexuality.* Chicago, IL: University of Chicago Press, 2007.
Kauanui, J. Kēhaulani. *Hawaiian Blood: Colonialism and the Politics of Sovereignty and Indigeneity.* Durham, NC: Duke University Press, 2008.
Kauanui, J. Kēhaulani. *Paradoxes of Hawaiian Sovereignty: Land, Sex, and the Colonial Politics of State Nationalism.* Durham, NC: Duke University Press, 2018.
Levi-Strauss, Claude. *The Story of Lynx.* Translated by Catherine Tihanyi (originally published 1991 as *Histoire de Lynx*). Chicago, IL: University of Chicago Press, 1996.
Locke, John. *Second Treatise of Government.* London: Awnsham Churchill, 1690.
McCammon, Holly J., and Allison R. McGrath. 'Litigating Change? Social Movements and the Court System.' *Sociology Compass* 9, no. 2 (2015): 128–139.
McClintock, Anne. *Imperial Leather: Race, Gender and Sexuality in the Colonial Conquest.* Abingdon: Routledge, 1995.
Miller, Robert J. 'The International Law of Colonialism: A Comparative Analysis.' *Lewis & Clark Law Review* 15, no. 4 (2011): 847–922.
Mirandé, Alfredo. *Behind the Mask: Gender Hybridity in a Zapotec Community.* Tucson: University of Arizona Press, 2017.
Newcomb, Steve. *Pagans in the Promised Land: Decoding the Doctrine of Christian Discovery.* Golden: Fulcrum, 2008.
Ngũgĩ wa Thiong'o. *Decolonizing the Mind: The Politics of Language in African Literature.* London: James Currey, 1986.
Ogle, Vanessa. *The Global Transformation of Time: 1870–1950.* Cambridge, MA: Harvard University Press, 2015.
Olita, Ivan, dir. *Third Gender: An Entrancing Look at Mexico's Muxes.* 2017. National Geographic, Short Film Showcase. Online video, 9:36. https://youtu.be/S1ZvDRxZlb0.
Picq, Manuela L. 'Decolonizing Indigenous Sexualities: Between Erasure and Resurgence.' In *The Oxford Handbook of Global LGBT and Sexual Diversity Politics,* edited by Michael J. Bosia, Sandra M. McEvoy, and Momin Rahman, 169–184. Oxford: Oxford University Press, 2020.
Puar, Jasbir. *Terrorist Assemblages: Homonationalism in Queer Times.* Durham, NC: Duke University Press, 2007.
Rahman, Momin. *Homosexualities, Muslim Cultures and Modernity.* London: Palgrave Macmillan, 2014.
Rifkin, Mark. *When Did Indians Become Straight? Kinship, the History of Sexuality, and Native Sovereignty.* New York: Oxford University Press, 2011.
Roscoe, Will. *Changing Ones: Third and Fourth Genders in Native North America.* New York: Palgrave, 1998.
Seth, Vanita. *Europe's Indians: Producing Racial Difference, 1500–1900.* Durham, NC: Duke University Press, 2010.
Sigal, Pete. *The Flower and the Scorpion: Sexuality and Ritual in Early Nahua Culture.* Durham, NC: Duke University Press, 2011.
Simpson, Leanne B. *As We Have Always Done: Indigenous Freedom Through Radical Resistance.* Minneapolis: University of Minnesota Press, 2017.
TallBear, Kim. *Native American DNA: Tribal Belonging and the False Promise of Genetic Science.* Minneapolis: University of Minnesota Press, 2013.
TallBear, Kim. 'Making Love and Relations beyond Settler Sex and Family.' In *Making Kin Not Population,* edited by Adele Clarke and Donna Haraway, 145–166. Chicago, IL: Prickly Paradigm Press, 2018.

Te Awekotuku, Ngahuia. 'He Reka Ano: Same Sex Lust and Loving in the Ancient Maori World.' In *Outlines: Lesbian & Gay Histories of Aotearoa*, edited by Alison J. Laurie and Linda Evans, 6–9. Wellington: Lesbian & Gay Archives of New Zealand, 2005.

Tengan, Ty P. Kāwika. *Native Men Remade: Gender and Nation in Contemporary Hawai'i.* Durham, NC: Duke University Press, 2008.

Tikuna, Josi, and Manuela L. Picq. 'Indigenous Sexualities: Resisting Conquest and Translation.' In *Sexuality and Translation in World Politics*, edited by Caroline Cottet and Manuela L. Picq. Bristol: E-International Relations, 2019.

Tortorici, Zeb. *Sins Against Nature: Sex & Archives in Colonial New Spain.* Durham, NC: Duke University Press, 2018.

Vainfas, Ronaldo. *A Heresia dos Indios: Catolicismo e Rebeldia no Brasil Colonial.* São Paulo: Companhia das Letras, 1995.

Van Deusen, Nancy. *Global Indios: The Indigenous Struggle for Justice in Sixteenth-Century Spain.* Durham, NC: Duke University Press, 2015.

Wolf, Eric. *Europe and the People without History.* Berkeley: University of California Press, 1982.

Wolfe, Patrick. 'Settler Colonialism and the Elimination of the Native.' *Journal of Genocide Research* 8, no. 4 (2006): 387–409.

17
REIMAGINING HOME
Indian removal, Native storytelling, and the search for belonging

Gregory D. Smithers

Elizabeth Lindsay Palmer was born at the Miami Mission in Kansas on 5 May 1860.[1] Palmer grew up in a foreign land made familiar by the stories, traditions, and ceremonies that Miamis carried with them from their traditional homelands in Indiana and Ohio. She entered the world on lands that the Pawnee, Iowa, and Sac and Fox peoples had called home for as long as anyone could remember. Palmer, her parents, and scores of Miamis, continued west and to Indian Territory, located in the eastern half of what is today Oklahoma. Here, Palmer and fellow Miamis rewove kinship, family, and communal bonds.

In diaspora, Elizabeth Palmer and her family nurtured new relationships with the land and with neighbouring Native communities, and to the Miami people's historical connection to settler colonialism. The 'collision' between Native and settler colonial sovereignties, the 'cacophony' of encounters – from the violent, to the transactional, and occasionally intimate – led both to the renewal of long-held traditions and to the incorporation of newer histories of human migration, relocation, and place.[2] But if settler colonialism catalysed the westward dispersal and resettlement of Palmer's Miami forebears, as it did for many other eastern Native Americans, pre-existing kinship and trade networks that connected eastern Indian communities, coupled with time-honoured narrative traditions, helped guide families like Palmer's as they navigated the uncertainties of a diasporic life.[3]

Palmer's memories of establishing a sense of home and connection to a kinship community overlapped with recollections of her childhood. Speaking to Nannie Lee Burns, an employee of the federal government's Indian-Pioneer Papers (IPP) project, Palmer narrated her personal history in April 1937. During the height of the Great Depression in the 1930s, federal employees conducted thousands of interviews with Native American people. These interviews, and subsequent decades of oral histories, provide unique and deeply personal insights into a constantly evolving historical consciousness in Native American communities. Personal narratives, when combined with the written records of American settler colonialism, reveal both the traumas caused by the federal government's removal policy and the ways in which Native Americans reconstituted a sense of home out of the tumult of removal.[4]

In this chapter, I want to focus on how Native Americans forced into diaspora as a result of United States removal policy nurtured meaningful concepts of home. This chapter focuses particularly on the decades between the Georgia Compact of 1802 and the removal of the Miami people from Indiana in 1846. During this period, the federal government used the treaty making process to coerce an estimated 70,000–100,000 Native people from their homelands in the eastern half of the United States.[5] Local and state authorities, with assistance from regional militias, provided an important supplement to federal power. In the Southeast as in the Old Northwest, local courts and politicians combined with vigilante violence to fragment Indian communities and ratchet up pressure on Native Americans that ultimately led to their territorial dispossession and relocation to the trans-Mississippi West. Building on this historical context, this chapter then moves to a consideration of how the storytelling traditions of eastern Native Americans grappled with the legacies of Indian removal throughout the nineteenth century and into the twentieth. In particular, how did Native storytelling integrate the removal era into a larger tradition of oral narration that explored the complexities of home and a sense of belonging to a kinship community?

Elizabeth Palmer did not experience the removal era directly. Nonetheless, stories about removal impacted her personal history, her kinship ties, and her understanding of home. Like thousands of other Native people, Palmer's connection to the history of Indian removal bound her to a particular Miami experience of exile while also shaping her pan-Indian appreciation for historical traumas experienced by other Indigenous people in a settler colonial setting. Palmer grew up hearing harrowing stories about her family's exodus towards Kansas along overland trails and the water routes that took unwilling migrants 'slowly down the river on large flat-boats'. These stories echoed the oral narratives of other Native people and framed a larger historical consciousness about the suffering, hardship, and death that eventually gave way to tales of renewal across Indian Territory in the wake of removal and the subsequent allotment and assimilation era of the late nineteenth and early twentieth centuries. Elders looked back on their forced migration and recalled how people slept, smoked, and held on to a sense of community as they 'gathered together solemnly talking with children gathered near and some of the women cooking and doing various tasks'. These stories built on older traditions about travel and the potential dangers lurking beyond the borderlands of one's home. Such narratives also re-created a sense of home that was as much about a physical place as it was a cultural and psychological connection to a deeper genealogy of identity.

★★★

Memories – kept alive in stories, songs, and a multitude of social and cultural expressions – proved vital to Native people as they reimagined 'home' during the nineteenth century. We can find Native American memories in oral narratives, art, and written archives. These diverse bodies of knowledge constitute a living repository rich in meaning and competing perspectives. These sources also add depth, texture, and specificity to the vast scholarship that charts the unrelenting territorial expansion of the United States.[6] For scores of Native communities throughout the eastern half of the United States, the western expansion of settler communities and removal policies of the early nineteenth century eventually separated tens of thousands of Indigenous people from their ancient homelands and opened a new chapter in their collective histories.

That newer history came to be defined by diaspora. Diaspora is a framework seldom associated with Indigenous histories. It nonetheless became the backdrop from which this reimagining of 'home' took shape for Native Americans.[7] Diaspora is a word derived from the ancient Greek term meaning to scatter, spread, disperse, or sow. It can involve both institutional structures and political processes that culminate in the coerced removal of a group of people. During the early nineteenth century, Native people became refugees as they were forced from the places they recently identified as their homeland and into exile in a foreign space.[8] In general terms, a sense of collective trauma often accompanies the diasporic community, be it trauma generated through the violence of coerced migrations or attempts to flee political persecution.[9]

Elements of both physical and political persecutions impacted Native American communities in the United States during the late eighteenth and early nineteenth centuries. That such persecution intensified as the nineteenth century unfolded should not surprise us. The settler state that became the United States of America in the 1780s did not include Native Americans in its body politic.[10] Instead, Indian policy – from 'civilization with honor' during George Washington's administration to the enactment of removal policy during the Andrew Jackson and Martin Van Buren presidencies – undermined Native political structures, fractured communities, and operated to eliminate American Indians from lands coveted by settlers. And the acquisition of new lands, most notably with president Thomas Jefferson's purchase of the Louisiana Territory in 1803, convinced growing numbers of local, state, and federal lawmakers that Native Americans in the eastern half of the country should be relocated to the 'empty' spaces of the trans-Mississippi West (Figure 17.1).[11]

Although removal was not inevitable, newspaper reports of frontier violence and American settler colonial policies set the stage for the unmooring of eastern Native Americans from the places they were not simply from, but *of*. As the nineteenth century began, Indigenous people entered a new and uncertain period in their long histories.[12]

In 1802, an example of how settler colonial politics and law combined during the nineteenth century to dispossess eastern Native Americans was signed into law. The Compact of Georgia declared that in return for the state of Georgia relinquishing its claims to land below Tennessee and between the Chattahoochee and Mississippi Rivers, the United States government agreed to pay the state $1,250,000 and vowed to remove all Native Americans from the states.[13] The western frontiers

Figure 17.1 Map of the Indian tribes of North America, about 1600 A.D. Along the Atlantic, & about 1800 A.D. Westwardly, by Albert Gallatin, ca. 1836
Source: Library of Congress Geography and Map Division, Washington, DC

of Georgia, what are today the states of Alabama and Mississippi, became federal territories as a result of the 1802 Compact. When president Thomas Jefferson purchased the Louisiana Territory from the French the following year, the United States government responded to growing calls for Indian removal by surveying an area of land that became 'Indian Territory'.[14] Political pressure for Indian removal – led by slaveholding interests in the South – grew louder over the ensuing decades.[15]

During the first two decades of the nineteenth century, pressure on Native communities to leave their eastern homelands intensified. Outbreaks of Indian-settler violence across the Old Northwest from the 1780s, in addition to newspaper coverage of the Red Stick War (1813–1814) and the outbreak of the First Seminole War in Florida in 1817, amplified calls for political representatives to make good on promises to remove Indians into the trans-Mississippi West.[16] American politicians weren't deaf to these calls. Beginning with major political figures like Thomas Jefferson, who urged Overhill Cherokees to leave their homelands in what is today Tennessee, the political will to craft an Indian removal policy hardened.[17]

Native leaders also recognised the turn that federal Indian policy was taking. Throughout eastern North America, tribal leaders worked to set out and defend their respective nation's political and territorial sovereignty. Such moves proved critical to protecting the spiritual attachment to place that shaped daily life and gave meaning to cultural norms throughout Indian Country. In response, American settler populations tested the sovereignty of Indigenous nations by questioning the validity of American citizens being tried in tribal courts for crimes committed on Native lands. Alternatively, state courts tested tribal sovereignty by trying tribal citizens in their courtrooms. The 1830 trial and conviction of George Corn Tassel, a member of the Cherokee Nation, in a Georgia court on a homicide charge provided a legal rationale for treating Native Americans as 'conquered subjects of the state'.[18]

The legal challenges to the sovereignty of Indian nations and their inherent rights in their tribal homelands accelerated during the 1830s. The Indian Removal Act, signed into law by president Andrew Jackson in 1830, set off a flurry of diplomatic activity as federally appointed Indian agents worked to persuade Native leaders to sign removal treaties and relocate to Indian Territory. Native people and their political and missionary allies resisted removal efforts, while the Seminole fought another war in defence of their homelands in Florida.[19] These resistance efforts meant that the coerced relocation of Native Americans from their eastern homes was far from inevitable following the passage of the Indian Removal Act. That removal eventually did dispossess scores of Indigenous communities during the remainder of the 1830s and into the 1840s. Removal tested the strength of both kinship communities and the sociocultural foundations of these bonds. Prominent Cherokee families with surnames like Ross and Boudinot used kin and non-kin connections in New England, the Mid-Atlantic, and throughout the American West to re-establish family and friend networks. Other Cherokees maintained an active epistolary culture or travelled between Indian Territory and their ancestral homelands in the American South to renew kinship bonds.[20]

★★★

A federal Indian policy that emphasised the removal of Native Americans east of the Mississippi River to reservation lands in the American West reminded Indigenous people of the importance of a connection to place. But recognising the importance of place and the location of a kinship group's sacred fire did not mean that movement and migration wasn't part of the narrative traditions of eastern Indians. Oral and visual traditions about migration were recounted in stories, ceremonies, and pictoglyphs. Storytelling, in other words, proved foundational to the retelling of origin narratives, stories about rebirth, and the framing of renewed understandings of place in the world. This proved true for Elizabeth Palmer's Miami forebears. Across lands that now encompass the states of Ohio and Illinois, Palmer's Miami ancestors told stories that anchored their communities to a sense of place. By the early nineteenth century, the stories they told were recounted amid growing colonial challenges and threats to Miami homelands.[21]

For Miamis – as for Pottawatomies, Wyandots, Delawares, Shawnees, and other Native communities from the Great Lakes to the Mid-Atlantic – travel, migration, and contact with non-kin outsiders weren't uncommon. Throughout the eighteenth century, trade and intermarriage with the French contributed to expanded kinship networks.[22] Prior to this, in the seventeenth century, the expansion of French trading posts into the Illinois country heightened pre-existing tensions among Chippewas, Ottawas, and Hurons, and incursions from Iroquois warriors from the east sparked migrations and resettlement patterns as the people we know today as the Miami sought refuge from the violence disrupting communal life. In the mid-seventeenth century, Jesuit missionaries reported palisaded Miami villages near the mouth of Green Bay and the headwaters of the Fox River. By the opening of the eighteenth century, the Miami established newer settlements near the sights of modern-day Chicago, Detroit, along the St. Joseph River, and near the Kalamazoo River.[23]

Working back in time, the Miami started to use strategies to renew connections to home. Migration and resettlement proved fundamental to the preservation of kinship and community, without which home meant little. Kinship, as historian Malinda Maynor Lowery has written of the Lumbee, constituted a flexible and inclusive social system that made it possible for Native people to renew connections to place and community.[24] This was true for the members of Native communities across eastern North America. Storytelling proved critical to tribal-centred conceptualisations of kinship and homelands. What Europeans condescendingly referred to as 'myths' were in actuality traditions that kept vast storehouses of medicinal, scientific, and religious knowledge alive. Stories helped Native people remember, and they taught children the importance of community, ceremony, and kinship.[25]

Oral traditions recorded by non-Native travellers and ethnologists after the eighteenth century suggest that European invasions impacted how Indigenous people narrated their place in the world. The Iroquois, who struck fear into the minds of Miami and other Native communities in the Great Lakes region during the seventeenth century, told stories about the dangers posed by non-kin travellers. These stories took a variety of forms, with some reiterating the importance of kinship and the safety of their homelands. In one of these oral traditions, a Stone Giant wandered over a frozen wasteland beyond the northwest borderlands of the Iroquois. *Ge-no'sqwa*, or the Stone Giant, purportedly lived a 'nomadic life' in these faraway lands, subsisting on 'raw meat and fish'. In time, the Stone Giant travelled into the borderlands of the Iroquois people and inched closer towards the centres of their communities. This alarmed the Iroquois because the Stone Giant had 'drifted into cannibalism, revelling in human flesh'. The story of *Ge-no'sqwa* provided Iroquois people with a narrative example of the dangers that lay beyond the safety of their homelands. As occurred in the oral traditions of other eastern Native communities, the trope of cannibalism highlighted these dangers.[26] But if the Stone Giant reminded the Iroquois people of the support and safety to be found in remaining connected to kin and homelands, other Native traditions in eastern North America used travel and migration to tell tales of finding new homelands.

The Seneca tale of 'The Powerful Boy' narrates a story about travel and conquest.[27] The Seneca, a member of the Iroquois, or Haudenosaunee, Confederacy, recounted versions of 'The Powerful Boy' that emphasised lessons about life and death, of human-animal and flora-human shape-shifting, and of connection and reconnection to the land. 'The Powerful Boy' centres on a 'man and his wife' who lived with their young son 'in an ugly-looking lodge in the woods', but tragically the woman died while giving birth to a second son. The infant child, no bigger than an adult's hand, appeared near death so the father lovingly wrapped the newborn and placed him in a tree hollow. Then one day, the older son heard crying coming from the tree. Finding his brother, the older boy prepared him a meal, and later the two boys chased mice around the hollow tree. As they laughed and played, the tree transformed into a man, capturing the tiny boy in its arms and insisting that the boy strike the tree with a club. The boy did this and the tree fell; in fact, everything the boy hit died. Despite being small in stature, the tiny boy possessed immense strength. The father, however, warned the boy not to test his powers and cautioned against travelling north. The boy ignored his father and convinced his older brother to accompany him on a journey north. The boys continued to ignore their father's warnings and embarked on other expeditions. On a journey west, the boys discovered a baby in a pine tree, but when they awoke it, the voices of Father and Mother Thunder boomed across the sky, prompting the tiny boy to crush their heads. The tiny boy then struck and killed the boy in the pine tree and made a tobacco pouch out of his remains. When the father discovered the tiny boy's deeds, he again admonished his sons. He implored the boys not to travel north to where 'Stone Coat' lived. Again, the powerful little boy ignored his father. The boy journeyed north and, jumping into a chestnut tree, found Stone Coat, then killed him and returned home with his dog. This angered the boy's father, who once again warned against further travel, this time into the southwest – the land of gambling. The father also warned the tiny boy not to go to the east, the land 'where they play ball'. The boy ignored all of these warnings. In the east, the tiny boy won the ball game and convinced his father to relocate to this new land and be chief.

'The Powerful Boy' is a tale of travel, external dangers, and resettlement. The tiny boy, small yet powerful, becomes the agent who quashes foreign threats to the Seneca. Used metaphorically, such stories helped to empower the Seneca to arrive at new insights into the significance of migration and resettlement. Most importantly, 'The Powerful Boy' narrates a tale of origins in which travel and reconnection to a new homeland embed the importance of the east (one of the cardinal directions) in the Seneca's sacred culture.[28]

For Native people throughout eastern North America, origin narratives contained important lessons that clarified the cultural significance of travel, migration, and connection to a homeland (or homelands). Some of these traditions may have incorporated elements of Western intellectual traditions, but their focus remained on distinguishing Native communities and their homelands from non-kin people. In contrast, Europeans have for centuries speculated about the foreign origins and migratory routes taken by Native Americans into North America. Theories have abounded, from speculation that Indigenous Americans were members of the 'Lost

Tribe of Israel' to tall tales about American Indians being descended from ancient Welsh migrants. Others have expressed indifference about Native American origins. For example, in 1833, the writer Caleb Atwater declared: 'When the red man first came into America, no one knows. Nor ever will know; indeed, I see no use to be derived from such a knowledge.'[29] At the height of the removal crisis, Atwater saw people without history, roots, or a home.

Colonial narratives about Native American origins and migration became part of a larger imperial knowledge system that operated to denigrate Indigenous culture and rationalise territorial dispossession.[30] Native people, however, remained active interpreters of their own traditions in the nineteenth century and beyond. The Catawba – a multi-ethnic kinship community whose nearest neighbours included the Cherokees – revised and renewed their origin narratives during the eighteenth and nineteenth centuries.[31] Some accounts of Catawba origins emphasise their northern Siouan-speaking ancestors.[32] Other narratives hint at the influence of Christianity and the incorporation of the story of Adam and Eve into Catawba oral traditions. One of the more famous Catawba stories focuses on the original woman – the mother of all Catawbas – who developed a desire to 'explore the wild country' that surrounded her valley home.[33] Drawn to the humming wings of a scarlet butterfly that 'invited her away', the woman followed the butterfly up 'a rocky ravine' and eventually arrived at 'a huge waterfall'. On reaching the top of the waterfall, the butterfly suddenly disappeared. Left alone in a foreign and potentially dangerous location, the woman felt fearful. In vain she tried to retrace her footsteps.

After a short time, a 'mysterious being' appeared and identified himself as 'a native of the far off sky'. He told the woman that he found her while travelling from the 'evening to the morning star'. Against the wishes of the Great Spirit, the mysterious being told the woman of his wish to spend the rest of his days with her. The couple eventually returned to the valley and began a family. Their life together had its challenges, but they persisted and 'these lone inhabitants of the earth' were soon rewarded for their hard work. Seeing that the couple had persevered through difficult times, the Great Spirit aided them by sending a wind that forced the mountains closer together. The valleys and rivers of the world the couple shared became even more beautiful and fertile. This is the world the Catawbas inherited from the original couple and must work hard to preserve.

The syncretism of this story blends Indigenous people's attachment to place with a familiar Biblical tale about an original couple. Throughout the Southeast, similar traditions were recorded by ethnologists during the nineteenth and twentieth centuries. These narratives recount stories that emphasise movement and migration as key aspects of belonging to a kinship community and being of a specific homeland. For example, the Hitchiti and Alabama peoples shared stories about their forebears 'crossing upon the ice' or migrating into the Southeast from the 'cold land of the Northwest'. Among the Muscogee, elders took a story that originated among the Coosa people and crafted a narrative about their ancestors arriving at a 'big water too wide to cross' before finally coming to the land they called home in the Southeast.

These narratives were, and remain, dynamic. They represent storytelling traditions that educated children and informed decision-making among elders. Importantly, they provided the members of kinship communities with a language to talk about their communal identities, attachment to place, and how best to respond to foreign threats.[34] This remained true as political calls for Indian removal intensified during the early nineteenth century. At the same time, narratives about travel and migration took on renewed meaning as the prospect of exile loomed.

In fact, once eastern Native communities were forced to confront the reality of exile in Indian Territory, older narratives about travel, kinship, and home took on renewed meaning. Drawing on such traditions empowered exiled Native communities to find the strength to reconstitute their kinship networks and renew their sacred fires by drawing on their cultural traditions and pre-removal diplomatic and trade networks. Far from experiencing a sense of 'anomie' – or feelings of rootlessness and social instability –eastern Native people in Indian Territory remained rooted to a sense of community and to neighbouring Indigenous nations by weaving together these cultural traditions while overlaying them with the historical experiences of removal.[35] This is not to say that divisions within, and between, Native communities didn't exist in Indian Territory during the 1830s, 1840s, and beyond; they did.[36] However, those divisions and difficult pioneering years served to highlight the urgency of rebuilding kinship communities and a renewed sense of home in diaspora.

Ed Sunday recalled those tough times in the 1930s. 'I am one of the few Cherokee Indians', Sunday explained to an interviewer from the IPP, 'who has witnessed the many changes that have taken place in this country, from the earliest days to the present time'. Sunday, who was born in Indian Territory in November 1856, recalled friends and relatives telling him that when 'the Cherokees came to Indian Territory, this was, literally speaking, a wilderness with no improvements of any kind'.[37] Indian Territory wasn't a wilderness for all Cherokees – a number of communities had migrated and resettled in the West during the opening decades of the nineteenth century – but the use of that word revealed both the intercultural influences and sense of rebirth that such narratives sought to convey.

The word 'wilderness' revealed feelings of anxiety caused by the separation of kinship communities from an ancestral homeland. Such stories echoed the moral dimensions of older narrative traditions that emphasised the dangers existing beyond the borderlands of a community's homeland. Additionally, the narrative use of 'wilderness' revealed the syncretic nature of Indigenous oral traditions and how Christian notions of 'wilderness' spaces as unsettled, uncivilised, and populated by heathenish people complemented Native oral traditions. Exposure to Christianity pre-dated the removal decades, but in the 1840s and 1850s, missionaries continued to proselytise as they accompanied eastern Native people into Indian Territory. Their goal was simple: continue efforts to win Indigenous converts. Christian educators also expressed a desire to press on with the work of educating Indian children. One Presbyterian educator reflected on her work among the Seminoles in Indian Territory, writing that they 'need to be showed [sic] how to study continually and kept at it or they will make but little progress'.[38] Not all Native communities welcomed the intrusions of Christian missionaries and educators in Indian Territory. The Sacs, for example, resisted missionary overtures to educate their children during the 1840s.[39]

The influence of Christianity in Native communities relocated to Indian Territory was not universal. However, for those kinship communities influenced by Christianity, weaving together language and concepts from Native American and Christian traditions became a feature of syncretic narrative expressions during the latter half of the nineteenth century and into the twentieth. Such narratives did not shy away from the violence that brought these traditions together. Jake Simmons, a Creek (Muskogee) man, provided an insight into this violence when he reflected on the sense of physical rootlessness and general sense of anxiety that shadowed his ancestors as they were forced into exile. Simmons recalled elders telling him about the 'many hardships' during the unwelcome migration into Indian Territory. The United States military forced the Creeks 'to go or die', Simmons remembered. And when Creek communities finally arrived in Indian Territory, they made for a 'weary, ragged, and tattered' caravan of migrants. These exhausted exiles had virtually no material possessions, save for the 'flint and steel with which to start a fire, a big eyed hoe, and ax, some corn and a few little articles together with a few little things that they had gathered together which they had back in the old Country [Alabama]' (Figure 17.2).[40]

Holding on to the physical remains of a previous life and drawing on memories to renew traditions – old and new – helped many eastern Native Americans navigate the experiences of exile and reconstitute kinship ties. Such traditions took on added importance during the late nineteenth and early twentieth centuries, decades in which the federal government worked to break up communal landholdings through allotment and the assimilation of individual Indians into 'mainstream' American society. As historian Rose Stremlau observes of the Cherokees,

Figure 17.2 A 1906 Portrait of Potawatimis who kept their hereditary kinship system alive
Source: Prints and Photographs Division, Library of Congress, Washington, DC

'communal land empowered social systems based on kinship'.[41] Federal government efforts to dissolve communal landholdings meant that kinship systems needed to be adaptive. In the case of the Cherokees, Stremlau argues that a bilateral system of kinship emerged. Cherokee households containing a Cherokee husband revolved around a patrilineal connection to Cherokee kinship, whereas a home in which the wife was Cherokee remained centred on more traditional understandings of matrilineal inheritance. In these ways, Native Southerners living in diaspora rearticulated the stories they told about themselves, remade kinship, and narrowed their definition of home in the context of the assimilation and allotment era.[42]

★ ★ ★

In a chapter of such brevity, it is not possible to do justice to the range of historical experiences associated with Indian removal, the rich diversity of kinship networks, and the re-establishment of communities in Indian Territory. That said, a deeper history of Native cultures and ceremonies has the potential to reveal a far more dynamic understanding of migration, communalism, and home. As Stremlau's analysis of the reworking Cherokee kinship networks reminds us, Native Southerners in diaspora adapted their sense of home and kinship connections to meet the challenges of settler colonialism.

At the same time, embedded in the oral and artistic traditions of eastern Native Americans living in diaspora was an inclusive system of kinship. Remaining conscious of this inclusiveness made it possible to accommodate change in kinship networks and rearticulate connections to both ancestral homelands in eastern North America and diasporic homelands in Indian Territory. Importantly, these late nineteenth- and early twentieth-century innovations expanded on early nineteenth-century kinship systems, trade networks, and storytelling traditions. In Indian Territory, renewed kinship networks and reconceptualised understandings of homelands emerged, even as the stresses of the allotment era sometimes divided communities and forced families into new residential patterns. However, durability of Native cultural traditions and social systems provided Native Southerners living in diaspora with the necessary insights to meet these challenges.[43]

Yes, place mattered to nineteenth-century Native people, and removal caused (and continues to cause) great pain, but the moving map of kinship, trade, and diplomatic relations that Native Americans nurtured meant that the adaptive and innovative strength of Native storytelling traditions and social structures made it possible to reimagine kinship networks and renewed a sense of home – now in the Indian Territory to the west, following the trauma of removal in the early nineteenth century.

Notes

1 Quotes attributed to Elizabeth Lindsay Palmer can be found at 'A Miami Indian Woman', interview with Nannie Lee Burns, 14 April 1937, Indian-Pioneer Papers [hereafter IPP], Western History Collections, University of Oklahoma, Norman; R. Douglas Hurt, *The Indian Frontier, 1763–1846* (Albuquerque: University of New Mexico Press, 2002), 186.

2 N. Scott Momaday, 'Native Attitudes to the Environment,' in *Seeing with a Native Eye: Essays on Native American Religion*, ed. W.H. Capps (New York: Harper and Row, 1976), 79–85; Leroy Little Bear, 'Jagged Worldviews Colliding,' in *Reclaiming Indigenous Voice and Vision*, ed. Marie Ann Battiste (Vancouver: University of British Columbia Press, 2000), 77–85; Jodi Byrd, *The Transit of Empire: Indigenous Critiques of Colonialism* (Minneapolis: University of Minnesota Press, 2011), 117; Keith H. Basso, *Wisdom Sits in Places: Landscape and Language among the Western Apache* (Albuquerque: University of New Mexico Press, 1996), 105.

3 Stewart Rafert, *The Miami Indians of Indiana: A Persistent People, 1654–1994* (Indianapolis: Indiana Historical Society, 1996), 290; Amy Lonetree, *Decolonizing Museums: Representing Native America in National and Tribal Museums* (Chapel Hill: University of North Carolina Press, 2012), 5, 125; On the risks associated with 'historical trauma' as a framework for redeeming the past for contemporary commemorative endeavours, see Andrew Denson, *Monuments to Absence: Cherokee Removal and the Contest over Southern Memory* (Chapel Hill: University of North Carolina Press, 2017), 194.

4 Bernard L. Fontana, 'American Indian Oral History: An Anthropologist's Note,' *History and Theory* 8, no. 3 (1969): 366–370; Theda Perdue, *Nations Remembered: An Oral History of the Five Civilized Tribes, 1865–1907* (Norman: University of Oklahoma Press, 1980); Devon A. Mihesuah, 'Commonalty of Difference: American Indian Women and History,' in *Natives and Academics: Researching and Writing about American Indians*, ed. Devon A. Mihesuah (Lincoln: University of Nebraska Press, 1998), 37–54; Paul Thompson with Joanna Bornat, *The Voice of the Past: Oral History*, 4th ed. (New York: Oxford University Press, 2017).

5 Claudio Saunt, 'The War the Slaveholders Won: Indian Removal and the State of Georgia,' *Southern Spaces*, 15 March 2016, https://southernspaces.org/2016/war-slaveholders-won-indian-removal-and-state-georgia.

6 See footnote 11 of this essay for a sampling of this historiography.

7 James T. Carson has cautioned that diaspora may have the unintended consequence of reifying racialised concepts of 'civility' and 'mobility' in historical understandings of Native America. See his 'Who Was First and When? The Diasporic Implications of Indigeneity,' in *Between Dispersion and Belonging: Global Approaches to Diaspora in Practice*, eds. Amitava Chowshury and Donald Harman Akenson (Montreal & Kingston: McGill-Queens University Press, 2016), 123.

8 On indigeneity, identity, and diaspora see Robin Delugan, 'Indigeneity Across Borders: Hemispheric Migrations and Cosmopolitan Encounters,' *American Ethnologist* 37, no. 1 (February 2010): 83–97; Paul Burke, 'Indigenous Diaspora and the Prospect of Cosmopolitan "Orbiting": The Warlpiri Case,' *Asia Pacific Journal of Anthropology* 14 (August 2013): 304–322; Gregory D. Smithers, '"What Is an Indian?" The Enduring Question of American Indian Identity,' in *Native Diasporas: Indigenous Identities and Settler Colonialism in the Americas*, eds. Gregory D. Smithers and Brooke N. Newman (Lincoln: University of Nebraska Press, 2014), 1–27; Sami Lakomäki, *Gathering Together: The Shawnee People through Diaspora and Nationhood, 1600–1870* (New Haven, CT: Yale University Press, 2014); Gregory D. Smithers, *The Cherokee Diaspora: An Indigenous History of Migration, Resettlement, and Identity* (New Haven, CT: Yale University Press, 2015); Mikaela M. Adams, *Who Belongs? Race, Resources, and Tribal Citizenship in the Native South* (New York: Oxford University Press, 2016); Kathryn Magee Labelle and Thomas Peace, 'Introduction,' in *From Huronia to Wendakes: Adversity, Migrations, and Resilience, 1650–1900* (Norman: University of Oklahoma Press, 2016), 3–16.

9 Robin Cohen, *Global Diasporas: An Introduction* (Seattle: University of Washington Press, 1997), 180–187; Martin Baumann, 'Exile,' in *Diasporas: Concepts, Intersections, Identities*, eds. Kim Knott and Seán McLoughlin (New York: Zed Books, 2013), 19–28; Bahar Baser, *Diasporas and Homeland Conflicts: A Comparative Perspective* (New York: Routledge, 2016).

10 Edward Countryman, 'Indians, the Colonial Order, and the Social Significance of the American Revolution,' *William and Mary Quarterly* 53, no. 2 (April 1996): 342–362; Frank Pommersheim, *Broken Landscape: Indians, Indian Tribes, and the Constitution* (New York: Oxford University Press, 2009); Kristopher Ray, '"The Indians of Every Denomination Were Free, and Independent of Us": Anglo-Virginian Explorations of Indigenous Slavery, Freedom, and Society, 1772–1830,' in *Indigenous Histories of the American South during the Long Nineteenth Century*, ed. Gregory D. Smithers (London and New York: Routledge, 2018), 11–31, espec. 19.

11 On 'civilization with honor', see George C. Herring, *From Colony to Superpower: U.S. Foreign Relations since 1776* (New York: Oxford University Press, 2008), 269–270; Lakomäki, *Gathering Together*, 134; Smithers, *Cherokee Diaspora*, 43–44. On Indian removal see Grant Foreman, *Indian Removal: The Emigration of the Five Civilized Tribes of Indians* (Norman: University of Oklahoma Press, 1972); Michael P. Rogin, *Fathers and Children: Andrew Jackson and the Subjugation of the American Indian* (New York: Alfred Knopf, Inc., 1975); Ronald Satz, *American Indian Policy in the Jacksonian Era* (Norman: University of Oklahoma Press, 1975); Anthony F.C. Wallace, *The Long, Bitter Trail: Andrew Jackson and the Indians* (New York: Hill and Wang, 1993); Tim Alan Garrison, *The Legal Ideology of Removal: The Southern Judiciary and the Sovereignty of Native American Nations* (Athens: University of Georgia Press, 2002); John P. Bowes, *The Trail of Tears: Removal in the South* (New York: Chelsea House Publishing, 2007); Theda Perdue and Michael D. Green, *The Cherokee Nation and the Trail of Tears* (New York: Viking, 2007); Amy H. Sturgis, *The Trail of Tears and Indian Removal* (Westport, CT: Greenwood Press, 2007); Gary Clayton Anderson, *Ethnic Cleansing and the Indian: The Crime that Should Haunt America* (Norman: University of Oklahoma Press, 2014). On the 'logic of elimination' and settler colonialism, see Patrick Wolfe, *Settler Colonialism and the Transformation of Anthropology: The Politics and Poetics of an Ethnographic Event* (London: Cassell, 1999), 25–29; Patrick Wolfe, 'Land, Labor, and Difference: Elementary Structures of Race,' *American Historical Review* 106, no. 3 (June 2001): 866–905; Patrick Wolfe, 'Settler Colonialism and the Elimination of the Native,' *Journal of Genocide Research* 8, no. 4 (2006): 387–409; Lorenzo Veracini, *Settler Colonialism: A Theoretical Overview* (New York: Palgrave Macmillan, 2010), 13; Patrick Wolfe, *Traces of History: Elementary Structures of Race* (London: Verso, 2016).

12 Frontier violence included the 1802 murders of prominent Cherokees and Creeks. See American State Papers, *Documents, Legislative and Executive, of the Congress of the United States, from the First Session of the First and Third Session of the Thirteenth Congress, Inclusive: Commencing March 3, 1789, and Ending March 3, 1813*, vol. 5 (Washington, DC: Gales and Seaton, 1832), xlviii; F.A. Michaux, *Travels to the West of the Alleghany Mountains, in the States of Ohio, Kentucky, and Tennessee, and Back to Charleston, by the Upper Carolines* (London: B. Crosby & Co., 1805), 263; William G. McLoughlin, *Cherokee Renascence in the New Republic* (Princeton: Princeton University Press, 1986), 51; Theda Perdue, *Cherokee Women: Gender and Culture Change, 1700–1835* (Lincoln: University of Nebraska Press, 1998), 142. On missionaries and their responses to frontier conflicts see *Memoirs of David Brainerd* (Philadelphia: American Sunday School Union, 1830), 28–29; William G. McLoughlin, *Champions of the Cherokees: Evan and John B. Jones* (Princeton, NJ: Princeton University Press, 1990); William G. McLoughlin, *Cherokees and Missionaries, 1789–1839* (Norman: University of Oklahoma Press, 1995); Emily Conroy-Krutz, *Christian Imperialism: Converting the World in the Early American Republic* (Ithaca: Cornell University Press, 2015).

13 William G. McLoughlin, 'Georgia's Role in Instigating Compulsory Indian Removal,' *Georgia Historical Quarterly* 70, no. 4 (Winter 1986): 605–632; Mary Young, 'The Exercise of Sovereignty in Cherokee Georgia,' *Journal of the Early Republic* 10, no. 1 (Spring 1990): 43–63; Garrison, *Legal Ideology of Removal*, 20. For the complete text of the Compact see 'Articles of Agreement … April 24, 1802,' in Clarence E. Carter and

John Porter Bloom, eds., *Territorial Papers of the United States*, vol. 5 (Washington, DC, 1934–1975), 142–146.

14 Laurence French, 'The Death of a Nation,' *American Indian Journal of the Institute for the Development of Indian Law* 4, no. 6 (June 1978): 2–9.

15 R.S. Cotterill, 'The National Land System in the South, 1803–1812,' *The Mississippi Valley Historical Review* 16, no. 4 (March 1930): 495–506; Jane Elsmere, 'The Notorious Yazoo Land Fraud Case,' *Georgia Historical Quarterly* 51 (Dec. 1967): 425–442.

16 Reginald Horsman, 'American Indian Policy in the Old Northwest, 1783–1812,' *William and Mary Quarterly* 18, no. 1 (January 1961): 35–53; Colin G. Calloway, *The Victory with No Name: The Native American Defeat of the First American Army* (New York: Oxford University Press, 2015); Garrison, *Legal Ideology of Removal*, 21–22.

17 Smithers, *Cherokee Diaspora*, 49; John P. Bowes, *Land Too Good for Indians: Northern Indian Removal* (Norman: University of Oklahoma Press, 2016), 11.

18 Garrison, *Legal Ideology of Removal*, 131; Lisa Ford, *Settler Sovereignty: Jurisdiction and Indigenous People in America and Australia, 1788–1836* (Cambridge, MA: Harvard University Press, 2010), 183, 195. See also Jonathan Gendzier, 'The Tennessee Supreme Court and Cherokee Sovereignty: *State v. Foreman* and Indian Removal,' *Journal of Southern Legal History* 25 (2018): 309–341.

19 Theodore Frelinghuysen to Jeremiah Evarts, 27 February 1830, MMC-2920, Jeremiah Evarts Collection, 1784–1851, Manuscript Division, Library of Congress, Washington, DC; William D. Smith to [illegible], 19 June 1833, box 3, reel 1, vol. 1, MF2 In25g,r.3, American Indian Correspondence [hereafter AIC], Presbyterian Historical Society, Philadelphia; William G. McLoughlin, 'An Alternative Missionary Style: Evan Jones and John B. Jones among the Cherokees,' in *Between Indian and White Worlds: The Cultural Broker*, ed. Margaret Connell Szasz (Norman: University of Oklahoma Press, 1994), 106; Alfred A. Cave, 'Abuse of Power: Andrew Jackson and the Indian Removal Act of 1830,' *The Historian* 65, no. 6 (Winter 2003): 1330–1353; Smithers, *Cherokee Diaspora*, 105; John P. Bowes, *Exiles and Pioneers: Eastern Indians in the Trans-Mississippi West* (New York: Cambridge University Press, 2007), 56–57; C.S. Monaco, *The Second Seminole War and the Limits of American Aggression* (Baltimore, MD: Johns Hopkins University Press, 2018).

20 On this point, see Rose Stremlau, *Sustaining the Cherokee Family: Kinship and the Allotment of an Indigenous Nation* (Chapel Hill: University of North Carolina Press, 2001); Ann McGrath, *Illicit Love: Interracial Sex and Marriage in the United States and Australia* (Lincoln: University of Nebraska Press, 2018); Smithers, *Cherokee Diaspora*.

21 Bruce P. Smith, 'Negotiating Law and Frontier: Responses to Cross-Cultural Homicide in Illinois, 1810–1825' in *The Boundaries between Us: Natives and Newcomers along the Frontiers of the Old Northwest Territory, 1750–1850*, ed. Daniel P. Barr (Kent: Kent State University Press, 2006), 161–177; Melissa Rinehard, 'Miami Resistance and Resilience during the Removal Era,' in *Contested Territories: Native Americans and Non-Natives in the Lower Great Lakes, 1700–1850*, eds. Charles Beatty-Medina and Melissa Rinehart (East Lansing: Michigan State University Press, 2012), 137–165. Also note that efforts to unite Native warriors in pan-Indian opposition to settler expansion coincided with these efforts. See R. Douglas Hurt, *The Ohio Frontier: Crucible of the Old Northwest, 1720–1830* (Bloomington: Indiana University Press, 1996); Gregory Evans Dowd, *A Spirited Resistance: The North American Indian Struggle for Unity, 1745–1815* (Baltimore, MD: Johns Hopkins University Press, 1993); Bethel Saler, *The Settlers' Empire: Colonialism and State Formation in America's Old Northwest* (Philadelphia: University of Pennsylvania Press, 2015), 58, 62, 255, 288.

22 Bert Ansom, *The Miami Indians* (Norman: University of Oklahoma Press, 1970), 55; Rob Harper, *Unsettling the West: Violence and State Building in the Ohio Valley* (Philadelphia: University of Pennsylvania Press, 2018), 6–7.

23 Alfred T. Goodman, *Journal of Captain William Trent from Logstown to Pickawillany, A.D. 1752* (Cincinnati, OH: Printed by Robert Clarke & Co., for William Dodge, 1871),

6–7, 14–15, 86–89; Emma Helen Blair, ed., *The Indian Tribes of the Upper Mississippi Valley and Region of the Great Lakes*, vol. 1 (Cleveland, OH: The Arthur H. Clark Company, 1911); Reuben Gold Thwaites, ed., *The Jesuit Relations and Allied Documents: Travels and Explorations of the Jesuit Missionaries in New France, 1610–1791*, vol. 50 (Cleveland, OH: The Burrows Brothers Company, Publishing, 1899), 17, 38, 63, 117, 263, 306–307, 316.

24 Malinda Maynor Lowery, *Lumbee Indians: An American Struggle* (Chapel Hill: University of North Carolina Press, 2018), 92.

25 Karl Kroeber, 'To the Reader,' in *Native American Storytelling: A Reader of Myths and Legends*, ed. Karl Kroeber (Malden, MA: Blackwell Publishing, Ltd., 1988), 1–2; Joseph Bruchac, *Our Stories Remember: American Indian History, Culture, and Values through Storytelling* (Golden: Fulcrum, 1999).

26 Gregory D. Smithers, 'Rituals of Consumption: Cannibalism and Native American Oral Traditions in Southeastern North America,' in *Cannibalism in the Early Modern Atlantic*, ed. Rachel Herrmann (Tuscaloosa: University of Alabama Press, 2019), 19–35.

27 The following account is based on the 1910 report of Jeremiah Curtin and J.N.B. Hewitt in Richard Erdoes and Alfonso Ortiz, *American Indian Myths and Legends* (New York: Pantheon Books, 1984), 20–24.

28 On the cultural significance of the four cardinal directions, see Arthur C. Parker, *Seneca Myths and Folk Tales* (Buffalo: Buffalo Historical Society, 1923), 7, 170.

29 Benjamin Smith Barton to Thomas Pennant, 12 September 1792, series I, Mss.B.B284d, Benjamin Smith Barton Papers, American Philosophical Society, Philadelphia; Caleb Atwater, *The Writings of Caleb Atwater* (Columbus: Published by the Author, 1833), 271.

30 On this point the biting critique of Vine Deloria Jr remains germane. See his *Custer Died for Your Sins: An Indian Manifesto* (New York: Scribner, 1969).

31 James Adair writes that among the more prominent ethnic groups to form kinship communities in what became Catawba Country were the 'Saraw or Cheraw, the Sugaree or Shocoree, the Catawba proper, the Wisack or Waxhaw, the Wateree, Congaree, Santee, Sewee, and Pedee …' James Adair, *The History of American Indians* (London: Edward and Charles Dilly, 1775). See also James H. Merrell, *The Indians' New World: Catawbas and Their Neighbors from European Contact through the Era of Removal* (New York: W.W. Norton and Company, 1991).

32 David G. Moore, *Catawba Valley Mississippian: Ceramics, Chronology, and Catawba Indians* (Tuscaloosa: University of Alabama Press, 2002), 37–38.

33 The following narration is derived from Charles Lanman, *Adventures in the Wilds of the United States and British American Provinces*, vol. 2 (Philadelphia, PA: John W. Moore, 1856), 410–412.

34 George E. Lankford, ed., *Native American Legends of the Southeast: Tales from the Natchez, Caddo, Biloxi, Chickasaw, and Other Nations* (Tuscaloosa: University of Alabama Press, 2011), 141–142.

35 Laurence A. French, 'Anomie and Violence among Native Americans,' *International Journal of Comparative and Applied Criminal Justice* 4, no. 1 (1980): 75–84; William G. McLoughlin, 'Cherokee Anomie, 1794–1910: New Roles for Red Men, Red Women, and Black Slaves' in *The Cherokee Ghost Dance: Essays on Southeastern Indians, 1789–1861*, ed. William G. McLoughlin (Macon: Mercer University Press, 1984), 3–37.

36 On this point, see David La Vere, *Contrary Neighbors: Southern Plains and Removed Indians in Indian Territory* (Norman: University of Oklahoma Press, 2000).

37 'Life History of a Cherokee Native,' 26 July 1937, IPP.

38 J.R. Ramsay to J.L. Wilson, 2 August 1858, box 6, vol. 1, reel 1 of 2, MF2 In25gr.6, AIC.

39 William Hamilton to Walter Lowrie, 4 July 1840, box 32, record group 224, AIC.

40 Jake Simmons Interview, 1937, IPP.

41 Stremlau, *Sustaining the Cherokee Family*, 75. See also 6–8, 43.

42 Another insightful analysis of this process, centred on the Choctaw people, is Donna L. Akers, 'Removing the Heart of the Choctaw People: Indian Removal from a Native Perspective,' *American Indian Culture and Research Journal* 23, no. 3 (1999): 63–76.

43 Alfred Pickens Seabolt Interview, 1 February 1938, IPP; John Thomas Estes, 15 July 1937, IPP; 'Lists of Intruders,' 1877, vol. 208, box 1, RG 75, Records of the Bureau of Indian Affairs, Land Division, Letters Received Relating to Cherokee Citizenship, 1875–89, National Archives and Records Administration [hereafter NARA], Washington, DC; 'Application for enrollment to Cherokee citizenship by Charles E. Daugherty et al. 20 September 1897,' Demurer & Answers of the Cherokee Nation, 1896–1897, RG 75, NARA, Fort Worth.

Bibliography

Adair, James. *The History of American Indians.* London: Edward and Charles Dilly, 1775.
Adams, Mikaela M. *Who Belongs? Race, Resources, and Tribal Citizenship in the Native South.* New York: Oxford University Press, 2016.
Akers, Donna L. 'Removing the Heart of the Choctaw People: Indian Removal from a Native Perspective.' *American Indian Culture and Research Journal* 23, no. 3 (1999): 63–76.
American State Papers. *Documents, Legislative and Executive, of the Congress of the United States, from the First Session of the First and Third Session of the Thirteenth Congress, Inclusive: Commencing March 3, 1789, and Ending March 3, 1813*, vol. 5. Washington, DC: Gales and Seaton, 1832.
Anderson, Gary Clayton. *Ethnic Cleansing and the Indian: The Crime that Should Haunt America.* Norman: University of Oklahoma Press, 2014.
Ansom, Bert. *The Miami Indians.* Norman: University of Oklahoma Press, 1970.
Atwater, Caleb. *The Writings of Caleb Atwater.* Columbus: Published by the Author, 1833.
Baser, Bahar. *Diasporas and Homeland Conflicts: A Comparative Perspective.* New York: Routledge, 2016.
Basso, Keith H. *Wisdom Sits in Places: Landscape and Language among the Western Apache.* Albuquerque: University of New Mexico Press, 1996.
Baumann, Martin. 'Exile.' In *Diasporas: Concepts, Intersections, Identities,* edited by Kim Knott and Seán McLoughlin, 19–28. New York: Zed Books, 2013.
Blair, Emma Helen, ed. *The Indian Tribes of the Upper Mississippi Valley and Region of the Great Lakes.* Cleveland, OH: The Arthur H. Clark Company, 1911–1912.
Bowes, John P. *The Trail of Tears: Removal in the South.* New York: Chelsea House Publishing, 2007.
Bowes, John P. *Exiles and Pioneers: Eastern Indians in the Trans-Mississippi West.* New York: Cambridge University Press, 2007.
Bowes, John P. *Land Too Good for Indians: Northern Indian Removal.* Norman: University of Oklahoma Press, 2016.
Brainerd, David. *Memoirs of David Brainerd.* Philadelphia, PA: American Sunday School Union, 1830.
Bruchac, Joseph. *Our Stories Remember: American Indian History, Culture, and Values through Storytelling.* Golden: Fulcrum, 1999.
Burke, Paul. 'Indigenous Diaspora and the Prospect of Cosmopolitan "Orbiting": The Warlpiri Case.' *Asia Pacific Journal of Anthropology* 14 (August 2013): 304–322.
Byrd, Jodi. *The Transit of Empire: Indigenous Critiques of Colonialism.* Minneapolis: University of Minnesota Press, 2011.
Calloway, Colin G. *The Victory with No Name: The Native American Defeat of the First American Army.* New York: Oxford University Press, 2015.
Carson, James T. 'Who Was First and When? The Diasporic Implications of Indigeneity.' In *Between Dispersion and Belonging: Global Approaches to Diaspora in Practice,* edited by Amitava Chowshury and Donald Harman Akenson, 107–124. Montreal & Kingston: McGill-Queens University Press, 2016.
Carter, Clarence E., and John Porter Bloom, eds., *Territorial Papers of the United States,* vol. 5. Washington, DC: Government Printing Office, 1934–1975.

Cave, Alfred A. 'Abuse of Power: Andrew Jackson and the Indian Removal Act of 1830.' *The Historian* 65, no. 6 (Winter 2003): 1330–1353.
Cohen, Robin. *Global Diasporas: An Introduction.* Seattle: University of Washington Press, 1997.
Conroy-Krutz, Emily. *Christian Imperialism: Converting the World in the Early American Republic.* Ithaca: Cornell University Press, 2015.
Cotterill, R.S. 'The National Land System in the South, 1803–1812.' *The Mississippi Valley Historical Review* 16, no. 4 (March 1930): 495–506.
Countryman, Edward. 'Indians, the Colonial Order, and the Social Significance of the American Revolution.' *William and Mary Quarterly* 53, no. 2 (April 1996): 342–362.
Deloria, Vine, Jr. *Custer Died for Your Sins: An Indian Manifesto.* New York: Scribner, 1969.
Delugan, Robin. 'Indigeneity across Borders: Hemispheric Migrations and Cosmopolitan Encounters.' *American Ethnologist* 37, no. 1 (February 2010): 83–97.
Denson, Andrew. *Monuments to Absence: Cherokee Removal and the Contest over Southern Memory.* Chapel Hill: University of North Carolina Press, 2017.
Dowd, Gregory Evans. *A Spirited Resistance: The North American Indian Struggle for Unity, 1745–1815.* Baltimore, MD: Johns Hopkins University Press, 1993.
Elsmere, Jane. 'The Notorious Yazoo Land Fraud Case.' *Georgia Historical Quarterly* 51 (Dec. 1967): 425–442.
Erdoes, Richard, and Alfonso Ortiz. *American Indian Myths and Legends.* New York: Pantheon Books, 1984.
Fontana, Bernard L. 'American Indian Oral History: An Anthropologist's Note.' *History and Theory* 8, no. 3 (1969): 366–370.
Ford, Lisa. *Settler Sovereignty: Jurisdiction and Indigenous People in America and Australia, 1788–1836.* Cambridge, MA: Harvard University Press, 2010.
Foreman, Grant. *Indian Removal: The Emigration of the Five Civilized Tribes of Indians.* Norman: University of Oklahoma Press, 1972.
French, Laurence. 'The Death of a Nation.' *American Indian Journal of the Institute for the Development of Indian Law* 4, no. 6 (June 1978): 2–9.
French, Laurence. 'Anomie and Violence among Native Americans.' *International Journal of Comparative and Applied Criminal Justice* 4, no. 1 (1980): 75–84.
Garrison, Tim Alan. *The Legal Ideology of Removal: The Southern Judiciary and the Sovereignty of Native American Nations.* Athens: University of Georgia Press, 2002.
Gendzier, Jonathan. 'The Tennessee Supreme Court and Cherokee Sovereignty: *State v. Foreman* and Indian Removal.' *Journal of Southern Legal History* 25 (2018): 309–341.
Goodman, Alfred T. *Journal of Captain William Trent from Logstown to Pickawillany, A.D. 1752.* Cincinnati, OH: Printed by Robert Clarke & Co., for William Dodge, 1871.
Harper, Rob. *Unsettling the West: Violence and State Building in the Ohio Valley.* Philadelphia: University of Pennsylvania Press, 2018.
Herring, George C. *From Colony to Superpower: U.S. Foreign Relations since 1776.* New York: Oxford University Press, 2008.
Horsman, Reginald. 'American Indian Policy in the Old Northwest, 1783–1812.' *William and Mary Quarterly* 18, no. 1 (January 1961): 35–53.
Hurt, R. Douglas. *The Indian Frontier, 1763–1846.* Albuquerque: University of New Mexico Press, 2002.
Hurt, R. Douglas. *The Ohio Frontier: Crucible of the Old Northwest, 1720–1830.* Bloomington: Indiana University Press, 1996.
Kroeber, Karl. *Native American Storytelling: A Reader of Myths and Legends.* Malden, MA: Blackwell Publishing, Ltd., 1988.
Labelle, Kathryn Magee, and Thomas Peace. *From Huronia to Wendakes: Adversity, Migrations, and Resilience, 1650–1900.* Norman: University of Oklahoma Press, 2016.
Lankford, George E., ed. *Native American Legends of the Southeast: Tales from the Natchez, Caddo, Biloxi, Chickasaw, and Other Nations.* Tuscaloosa: University of Alabama Press, 2011.

Lanman, Charles. *Adventures in the Wilds of the United States and British American Provinces*. Philadelphia, PA: John W. Moore, 1856.

Lakomäki, Sami. *Gathering Together: The Shawnee People through Diaspora and Nationhood, 1600–1870*. New Haven, CT: Yale University Press, 2014.

La Vere, David. *Contrary Neighbors: Southern Plains and Removed Indians in Indian Territory*. Norman: University of Oklahoma Press, 2000.

Little Bear, Leroy. 'Jagged Worldviews Colliding.' In *Reclaiming Indigenous Voice and Vision*, edited by Marie Ann Battiste, 77–85. Vancouver: University of British Columbia Press, 2000.

Lonetree, Amy. *Decolonizing Museums: Representing Native America in National and Tribal Museums*. Chapel Hill: University of North Carolina Press, 2012.

Lowery, Malinda Maynor. *Lumbee Indians: An American Struggle*. Chapel Hill: University of North Carolina Press, 2018.

McGrath, Ann. *Illicit Love: Interracial Sex and Marriage in the United States and Australia*. Lincoln: University of Nebraska Press, 2018.

McLoughlin, William G. *The Cherokee Ghost Dance: Essays on Southeastern Indians, 1789–1861*. Macon: Mercer University Press, 1984.

McLoughlin, William G. *Cherokee Renascence in the New Republic*. Princeton, NJ: Princeton University Press, 1986.

McLoughlin, William G. 'Georgia's Role in Instigating Compulsory Indian Removal.' *Georgia Historical Quarterly* 70, no. 4 (Winter 1986): 605–632.

McLoughlin, William G. *Champions of the Cherokees: Evan and John B. Jones*. Princeton, NJ: Princeton University Press, 1990.

McLoughlin, William G. 'An Alternative Missionary Style: Evan Jones and John B. Jones among the Cherokees.' In *Between Indian and White Worlds: The Cultural Broker*, edited by Margaret Connell Szasz, 98–121. Norman: University of Oklahoma Press, 1994.

McLoughlin, William G. *Cherokees and Missionaries, 1789–1839*. Norman: University of Oklahoma Press, 1995.

Merrell, James H. *The Indians' New World: Catawbas and Their Neighbors from European Contact through the Era of Removal*. New York: W.W. Norton and Company, 1991.

Michaux, F.A. *Travels to the West of the Alleghany Mountains, in the States of Ohio, Kentucky, and Tennessea, and Back to Charleston, by the Upper Carolines*. London: B. Crosby & Co., 1805.

Mihesuah, Devon A. *Natives and Academics: Researching and Writing about American Indians*. Lincoln: University of Nebraska Press, 1998.

Monaco, C.S. *The Second Seminole War and the Limits of American Aggression*. Baltimore, MD: Johns Hopkins University Press, 2018.

Moore, David G. *Catawba Valley Mississippian: Ceramics, Chronology, and Catawba Indians*. Tuscaloosa: University of Alabama Press, 2002.

Momaday, N. Scott. 'Native Attitudes to the Environment.' In *Seeing with a Native Eye: Essays on Native American Religion*, edited by W.H. Capps, 79–85. New York: Harper and Row, 1976.

Parker, Arthur C. *Seneca Myths and Folk Tales*. Buffalo: Buffalo Historical Society, 1923.

Perdue, Theda. *Nations Remembered: An Oral History of the Five Civilized Tribes, 1865–1907*. Norman: University of Oklahoma Press, 1980.

Perdue, Theda. *Cherokee Women: Gender and Culture Change, 1700–1835*. Lincoln: University of Nebraska Press, 1998.

Perdue, Theda, and Michael D. Green. *The Cherokee Nation and the Trail of Tears*. New York: Viking, 2007.

Pommersheim, Frank. *Broken Landscape: Indians, Indian Tribes, and the Constitution*. New York: Oxford University Press, 2009.

Ray, Kristopher. '"The Indians of Every Denomination Were Free, and Independent of Us": Anglo-Virginian Explorations of Indigenous Slavery, Freedom, and Society,

1772–1830.' In *Indigenous Histories of the American South during the Long Nineteenth Century*, edited by Gregory D. Smithers, 11–31. London and New York: Routledge, 2018.

Rinehard, Melissa. 'Miami Resistance and Resilience during the Removal Era.' In *Contested Territories: Native Americans and Non-Natives in the Lower Great Lakes, 1700–1850*, edited by Charles Beatty-Medina and Melissa Rinehart, 137–165. East Lansing: Michigan State University Press, 2012.

Rogin, Michael P. *Fathers and Children: Andrew Jackson and the Subjugation of the American Indian*. New York: Alfred Knopf, Inc., 1975.

Rafert, Stewart. *The Miami Indians of Indiana: A Persistent People, 1654–1994*. Indianapolis: Indiana Historical Society, 1996.

Saler, Bethel. *The Settlers' Empire: Colonialism and State Formation in America's Old Northwest*. Philadelphia: University of Pennsylvania Press, 2015.

Satz, Ronald. *American Indian Policy in the Jacksonian Era*. Norman: University of Oklahoma Press, 1975.

Saunt, Claudio. 'The War the Slaveholders Won: Indian Removal and the State of Georgia.' *Southern Spaces*. 15 March 2016. https://southernspaces.org/2016/war-slaveholders-won-indian-removal-and-state-georgia.

Smith, Bruce P. 'Negotiating Law and Frontier: Responses to Cross-Cultural Homicide in Illinois, 1810–1825.' In *The Boundaries between Us: Natives and Newcomers along the Frontiers of the Old Northwest Territory, 1750–1850*, edited by Daniel P. Barr, 161–177. Kent: Kent State University Press, 2006.

Smithers, Gregory D. '"What is an Indian?" The Enduring Question of American Indian Identity.' In *Native Diasporas: Indigenous Identities and Settler Colonialism in the Americas*, edited by Gregory D. Smithers and Brooke N. Newman, 1–27. Lincoln: University of Nebraska Press, 2014.

Smithers, Gregory D. *The Cherokee Diaspora: An Indigenous History of Migration, Resettlement, and Identity*. New Haven, CT: Yale University Press, 2015.

Smithers, Gregory D. 'Rituals of Consumption: Cannibalism and Native American Oral Traditions in Southeastern North America.' In *Cannibalism in the Early Modern Atlantic*, edited by Rachel Herrmann, 19–35. Tuscaloosa: University of Alabama Press, 2019.

Stremlau, Rose. *Sustaining the Cherokee Family: Kinship and the Allotment of an Indigenous Nation*. Chapel Hill: University of North Carolina Press, 2001.

Sturgis, Amy H. *The Trail of Tears and Indian Removal*. Westport, CT: Greenwood Press, 2007.

Thwaites, Reuben Gold, ed. *The Jesuit Relations and Allied Documents: Travels and Explorations of the Jesuit Missionaries in New France*. Cleveland, OH: The Burrows Brothers Company, Publishing, 1896–1901.

Thompson, Paul, with Joanna Bornat. *The Voice of the Past: Oral History*. 4th ed. New York: Oxford University Press, 2017.

Veracini, Lorenzo. *Settler Colonialism: A Theoretical Overview*. New York: Palgrave Macmillan, 2010.

Wallace, Anthony F.C. *The Long, Bitter Trail: Andrew Jackson and the Indians*. New York: Hill and Wang, 1993.

Wolfe, Patrick. *Settler Colonialism and the Transformation of Anthropology: The Politics and Poetics of an Ethnographic Event*. London: Cassell, 1999.

Wolfe, Patrick. 'Land, Labor, and Difference: Elementary Structures of Race.' *American Historical Review* 106, no. 3 (June 2001): 866–905.

Wolfe, Patrick. 'Settler Colonialism and the Elimination of the Native.' *Journal of Genocide Research* 8, no. 4 (2006): 387–409.

Wolfe, Patrick. *Traces of History: Elementary Structures of Race*. London: Verso, 2016.

Young, Mary. 'The Exercise of Sovereignty in Cherokee Georgia.' *Journal of the Early Republic* 10, no. 1 (Spring 1990): 43–63.

Archival sources

American Indian Correspondence: The Presbyterian Historical Society Collection of Missionaries' Letters. Presbyterian Historical Society, Philadelphia. https://www.history.pcusa.org/collections/research-tools/guides-archival-collections/rg-224.

Benjamin Smith Barton Papers. Mss.B.B284d. American Philosophical Society, Philadelphia. https://search.amphilsoc.org//collections/view?docId=ead/Mss.B.B284d-ead.xml#top.

Indian-Pioneer Papers. Western History Collections. University of Oklahoma, Norman. https://digital.libraries.ou.edu/whc/pioneer/.

Jeremiah Evarts Collection, 1784–1851. Manuscript Division, Library of Congress, Washington, DC. https://lccn.loc.gov/mm80020024.

Records of the Bureau of Indian Affairs. National Archives and Records Administration. https://www.archives.gov/research/guide-fed-records/groups/075.html.

18
'BECAUSE OF HER, WE CAN'
Gender and diaspora in Australian exemption policies

*Lucinda Aberdeen, Katherine Ellinghaus,
Kella Robinson, and Judi Wickes*

Displacement and disconnection are among the crucial dimensions of the dispossession of Aboriginal and Torres Strait Islander people. From the first moment of invasion into what became known as Australia, Europeans made a variety of determined and violent efforts to control the movement of Indigenous people, removing them from desirable tracts of land and forcing them to reside in places convenient to settlers, with little thought of their spiritual connection to Country.[1] During the late nineteenth and early twentieth centuries, various pieces of legislation, passed by colonies and later states, set up legal regimes that gave government administrators the power to disrupt Aboriginal and Torres Strait Islander families by forcibly moving people and determining where they lived, whom they married, and who looked after their children. These laws, which had many different titles but are now collectively known by historians as 'protectionist legislation', also set in place definitions of identity that then defined where and how governments expected people to live. They were in action roughly from 1869, when the first was passed in the state of Victoria, to 1967, when a federal referendum shifted the responsibility for Aboriginal Affairs from the states to the federal government.[2] Historians who have documented the creation of Indigenous diasporas through protectionist legislation in Australia have focused largely on the removal of children by government officials and welfare officers and the enforced movement of Indigenous groups onto missions and reserves under the guise of 'protection'.[3]

This chapter examines the history of one particular category of clause that appeared in the legislation of five states at different times in the twentieth century: clauses that allowed certain people to apply for 'exemption' from the protectionist legislation that applied to them. These policies of exemption created a diaspora of Indigenous families and individuals who lived away from reserves and communities. In Queensland (1897), Western Australia (1905), Northern Territory (1936), South Australia (1939), and New South Wales (1943), legislation stated that some

Aboriginal and Torres Strait Islander people could be granted certificates of 'exemption' technically freeing them from the various controls imposed on them 'under the Act'. The certificates presented Indigenous people with opportunities for employment, education, and freedom to marry and rear their own children. However, the freedom, mobility, and 'equality' offered by exemption were tempered by the requirement that exempted people cease contact with family, friends, and community who were not exempt. In this way, exemption was clearly a legislative expression of the urge to 'civilise' or 'assimilate' Aboriginal and Torres Strait Islander people into mainstream Australia. Even though the clauses themselves pre-dated the later post-war policies that stressed assimilation, they supported the ubiquitous view that Aboriginal and Torres Strait Islander people should be separated from their communities and absorbed into 'white' Australia.[4] In the post-war period, exemption in many places became intertwined even further with government efforts to force Aboriginal and Torres Strait Islander families to live a normative white lifestyle, and offered administrators – as Heather Goodall characterised it – a 'carrot-and-stick' tool of control and surveillance.[5]

Being exempt required people to live away from the reserves and missions where many Aboriginal and Torres Strait Islander people resided. Taking advantage of the ability to seek and work for an employer of their choice often also meant moving into cities and towns. This resulted in exemptees and their families experiencing varying levels of separation and dislocation from their communities. Exemption thus contributed to the creation of a diaspora of families who lived away from reserves and missions.[6] Exemption certificates could also be readily revoked by authorities. This meant that people were subject to the stress of continuing surveillance by Chief Protectors, Protection/Welfare Boards, and the police. In some places, government administrators imposed other restrictions such as night curfews and rules forbidding the use of Indigenous language in public places. Exemption could be used by government officials as a punishment – it was sometimes applied to people (especially those perceived of being of 'mixed descent') when they did not desire it, and it required the promise that they turn away from cultural activities and responsibilities.[7] For some people, exemption could offer advantages. Because they were no longer 'under the Act', people who gained exemption might (depending on their locality and the particularities of the law) receive better wages, become eligible for social welfare, and have less chance of having their children removed. They might also be allowed to own property, vote, move around the state unchecked, and enter hotels or shops. Nonetheless, exemption was for many a poisoned chalice that had significant and adverse impacts on Aboriginal families and communities.[8] The heart of this chapter is two first-hand accounts of how exemption impacted families. Because exemption policies varied across states and according to the whims and biases of government officials, it is important for readers to note that experiences with exemption were varied.[9]

We argue in this chapter that if we are to properly account for the diasporic history of exemption policies, we must pay attention to themes of gender and family and look beyond the generation of the original holder of a certificate. Exemption is often remembered and historicised only as a licence to drink alcohol, and thought about as a status that only impacted on single men. In many places, the 'dog tag' was synonymous with the ability to drink at hotel bars – a function of the fact that, as we will show, the freedom and rights promised by the policy were rarely fully experienced by recipients. In 1948, the *Sydney Morning Herald*, for example, noted that there was a new conception of citizenship operating west of Bourke in New South Wales, where an 'Aboriginal shearer' produced his exemption certificate and proclaimed 'There you are. I'm as much a citizen as you are. I can breast the bar and have a drink anywhere.'[10] Historians have noted that both government and applicants saw exemption as 'only a ticket to alcohol',[11] and have discussed how intertwined alcohol and citizenship were for Aboriginal men.[12] Western Arrernte artist Albert Namatjira, who was probably the most well-known recipient of the status of exemption, embodies the remembered connection between exemption and alcohol. In 1957, having been exempted by the federal government from the Northern Territory's *Welfare Ordinance 1953–1955*, Namatjira was infamously jailed for supplying alcohol to relatives.[13]

The skewed view of exemption as a mainly male experience leaves out the stories of Aboriginal and Torres Strait Islander women, who rarely drank in hotels and bars even if they were exempt.[14] The fact that exemption meant different things to men and women was noted at the time. As Francis Moy, then Director of Native Affairs in the Northern Territory, told a conference of 'experts' on the 'Native problem' in 1948: '"Exemption" means a licence to drink for men and permission to cohabitate with white men for women.'[15] This chapter aims to add the gendered impact of exemption to the historical record, by focusing not just on exemptees but also on their families. Two of the authors of this chapter, Judi Wickes and Kella Robinson, had grandfathers who were exemptees. Their family stories are windows into the diasporic movement undertaken by Aboriginal families in response or resistance to assimilation policies and the controls of protection legislation. Kella and Judi's stories both show that their lives and the lives of their parents and grandparents were shaped by various kinds of mobility. Exemption could enable movement towards a financially stable life, as Judi Wickes shows in the story of her grandparents using the status to move away from Purga Mission in Queensland and into the mainstream community. Exemption was also sometimes just a small part of a longer family history of mobility, undertaken, as Kella Robinson writes, to escape child removal or to take advantage of educational or employment opportunities. In 1942, amendments to the *Invalid and Old-age Pension Act 1908* (Commonwealth) finally opened up these schemes to Aboriginal and Torres Strait Islander people, and Kella's grandfather took advantage of this opportunity. Movement could also cause a loss of contact with family members. In Judi's experience, separation from relatives resulted from restrictions on exemptees associating with their people, whereas in Kella's experience, this was due to relatives being separated through geographic distance. In the final section, Lucinda Aberdeen shows the profound impact the diasporic effect of exemption had on Judi's mother and the silencing of history.

The clauses that created exemption policy in protection legislation did not discriminate on the basis of gender. Nevertheless, in some places, more men than women applied and were awarded exemption (in J.W. Bleakley's long reign as the Chief Protector in Queensland from 1914 to 1942, for example, exemptions were more heavily weighted towards men; in Western Australia between 1905 and 1943 of the 205 or so applications in the archives, only 36 were definitely from women).[16] This is not to say that women were not impacted on by the policy in great numbers. In some states (Western Australia from 1944 and New South Wales from 1943), wives and children were included on a man's certificate. Elsewhere, as Judi's story shows, the wives and daughters of exempted men could be affected by the policy just as if they held a certificate themselves. In 1951, Jack McGinness described how his daughters' marriage to a white man required her to apply for exemption in the Northern Territory. She:

> had two children before the authorities discovered she was an unexempted person. Under the Aboriginal Ordinance her husband is liable to arrest and prosecution for consorting with a female half-caste Aboriginal, so to avoid that, my son-in-law has to apply to the authorities for an exemption for his wife and two children.[17]

Being exempt or related to an exemptee often meant, in practice, that government officials expected Aboriginal and Torres Strait Islander women to conform to the Victorian model of middle-class white domesticity.[18] Historians Francesca Bartlett, Anna Cole, and Victoria Haskins have explored the impact of assimilation policies on Aboriginal women more broadly.[19] Heather Goodall has shown how assimilationists expected 'Aboriginal women to be, like Trojan horses, the bearers of white culture and lifestyle into the heart of Aboriginal family and community life, to change the cultural practices of the families which they re-entered'.[20] Similarly, in order to be exempt, women were expected to adopt the lifestyle and characteristics of Euro-American middle-class women, and government officials could use their failure to do so as a reason to penalise them or their families under the exemption system. In its official rhetoric, for example, New South Wales awarded certificates to 'advanced aborigines' or to someone they thought was 'a fit and proper person'.[21] The Board expected that a female exemptee should be thrifty, moral, clean, and drink only moderately, if at all. Welfare officers provided the Board with reports that described applicant's homes in detail. With this emphasis on the home as a marker of assimilation, Goodall has argued, in relation to New South Wales, that women 'came to bear a significant proportion of the increased surveillance generated by … "Assimilation" policy from 1943 onwards'.[22]

The archives left behind by exemption document, for the most part, only the application process. This does not show the ongoing impact of the policy on exemptees and their families. In addition, because (as discussed above) more men than women applied for exemption, only half of the history of the diasporas caused by exemption policies can be found in the records. However, Aboriginal and Torres Strait Islander women who may not have been exempt themselves but who lived with, or were descended from, exempted men, also bore the brunt of the policy. These women's stories can be found in the memories and knowledge of people (like Judi and Kella) who have experienced it as part of their family histories. We believe that the history of exemption is most clearly demonstrated when it is woven into the stories of families touched by the policy. By teasing out the gendered and transgenerational aspects of the theme of diaspora, we aim to get close to a true understanding of the widespread and damaging effects of exemption policies.

Journeys of the women in my family

Judi Wickes

My maternal grandmother, Daisy Power (Kalkadoon nation and Irish), was born in 1900 on Boomarra Station, in the north-west of Queensland. When the property owner (R. Hillcoat) sold Boomarra Station in 1914, Daisy and her young cousin Nancy moved down with them to Brisbane, first to the suburb of St Lucia and later to Teneriffe. It was from there in 1920 that Daisy (aged 19) and Nancy (aged 10) were removed by government officials and taken to Purga Aboriginal Mission, located near the town of Ipswich in the south-east corner of Queensland. Daisy and Nancy's government documents record that they were removed 'for their own protection'. The *Aboriginals Restriction and the Sale of Opium Act 1897*, with its 33 clauses, controlled and coerced Queensland's Indigenous population for around 70 years, which included the lives of Daisy, Nancy, and my grandfather, Roy.

It was while at Purga Mission that Daisy met Roy Smith (Wakka Wakka nation and Irish). In 1914, as a 13-year-old, Roy had been removed from Nanango, in the Burnett region of Queensland. Government document searches failed to reveal why he was removed. Only recently I discovered that Roy was removed with other members of his Aboriginal family.[23] I was shocked and surprised to find this information after so many years researching my family history. One of the impacts of the dislocations experienced by families like mine is the long journeys to find our histories, and the emotional difficulties of occasionally finding new pieces of information.

Daisy and Roy married in 1924 in the Salvation Army church on Purga. The following year, their first child was born. As an Aboriginal person living on the mission, Roy first applied in 1917 to the Chief Protector of Native Affairs (a government department) for his Certificate of Exemption. It is not clear how many times Roy applied, but he was finally successful and received his exemption on 25 March 1926. Gaining the exemption allowed Roy and his family to move into the wider community to live as other Australians did. As Roy was now classed as '*non-aboriginal*', it wasn't necessary for Daisy or his daughter to apply for their exemption.

When I think of Daisy Smith now, what a trailblazer she was! She was a wife and mother who raised four children, and she could be described as a worker, a community member, and a businesswoman. Daisy's cakes nearly always won top prizes at the local school and church fetes. Another thing she enjoyed doing was the crossword puzzle competitions in the *Courier Mail* newspaper. She frequently won cash prizes, which helped with the family finances. Daisy was a fine needle worker and she had a treadle Singer sewing machine. She used the machine to make dresses and clothes as well as household items. In addition, during the Second World War, Daisy showed her patriotism in many ways, working towards the war effort. For example, in her 1944 diary, she mentions that 'she swept the hall for the incoming troops when they were in town'.[24]

Daisy entertained in her own home by having morning and afternoon teas with family and friends, as well as attending their homes. One such family friend was Mr John Bleakley, ex Chief Protector of Aborigines. I can recall meeting Mr Bleakley's son on many occasions when my mother and I visited the large department store in Brisbane where he worked during the 1960s. Now, I wonder about that relationship, considering that Mr Bleakley was the Chief Protector when my grandfather applied for his certificate of exemption. When and how did they become friends?

During the 1940s and 1950s, Daisy kept six diaries that record and highlight the significance of citizenship and family activities.[25] Daisy's resilience and strength of character are revealed within their pages. Today, I can see those same traits in each generation of women in our family, which I believe bears testimony to Daisy's legacy. How fitting it was that the theme of the 2018 National Aborigines and Islanders Day of Observance Committee, acknowledging the contribution of Aboriginal and Torres Strait Islander women, 'Because of her, we can!'.

Aboriginal women who were married to exemptees were often seen as 'uptown' to others and yet to some non-Aboriginal women, they were deemed as 'not quite equal'. My family rarely mingled with other Aboriginal families because we were raised in accordance with the rules and regulations of exemption. A few years ago, I was introduced to an Aboriginal man who had lived in my own town for decades. When I asked my mother, 'Who is he?', I was told he was her cousin. This served as a powerful reminder of some of the tragic consequences of the exemption rules. Exemptees and their families were prohibited to speak to other Aboriginal people, and had to remain disassociated from them. I felt so sad that I had missed out on knowing anything about my mother's cousin and his family.

When I was a teenager in the 1960s, my mother and I were walking on the main street of our town when she saw an Aboriginal woman on the other side of the street. She asked me, 'Who is that darkie?'[26] She wanted me to go over and ask her name. I am sure my mother felt that if she did it herself, she would be breaking the law, and we could be sent back to Purga Mission. This incident highlights the ongoing power, control, and fear wielded by the government and internalised by individuals to discipline themselves: the phenomenon described by French social theorist Michel Foucault.[27]

Education was very important to my grandparents, especially to Daisy. She taught herself to read and write, because she was denied a state education at the time. Those important self-taught skills allowed Daisy to read newspapers and magazines as well as to write letters to family, friends, and even businesses. Daisy always said to her family, 'Education is the way.' Her own children attended state school, although my mother only achieved a grade six education before going out to work. Fortunately, several of Daisy's grandchildren and great-grandchildren have continued on with their education in order to ultimately gain university degrees and work as professionals in their chosen fields.

Daisy was a working woman, both within and outside the home. She worked to supplement the family income, and that is something that all the women in our family have done in one way or another through the generations. The 'good work ethic' set by Daisy all those years ago has been well adhered to by her descendants. In fact, it was part of the exemption rule 'to be steady in employment'. What I can say is that Daisy was a woman before her time. She was a role model showing strength of character throughout her life, while dealing with and adhering to the government's strict rules and regulations of exemption.

It was while I was at university doing post-graduate studies that I was given an opportunity to visit Boomarra Station and see for myself where my grandmother was born and raised. It was such a powerful experience; the sense of 'who I am' was overwhelming. In addition, I have been to Taabinga Station, which covers the land of my ancestors through my grandfather. And if you are wondering what happened to Nancy – she gained her certificate of exemption in 1934 and was able to leave Purga Mission to live in the community. Nancy and Daisy continued to have contact throughout their lives (Figure 18.1).

Figure 18.1 The Power women: Daisy Smith (née Power, left) and Nancy Mittabong (née Power) in the late 1940s. Permission from Judi Wickes

Journeys of the women in my family

Kella Robinson

My Indigenous heritage can be traced back to my maternal great-grandmother, Sarah Taylor (née Ingram). She belonged to the Wemba-Wemba nation whose country covers an area around the Loddon River in north-west Victoria and extends into south-western New South Wales. It is understood that the Wemba-Wemba people sought refuge from colonisation in the Werai Forest, until the 1870s when they moved to the banks of the Edwards River, situated 40 km north-west of Deniliquin in New South Wales. In 1911, a state school was established in this location, with an Aboriginal lead teacher,[28] but it wasn't until 1916 that the Moonahcullah Mission was formally established (Figure 18.2).

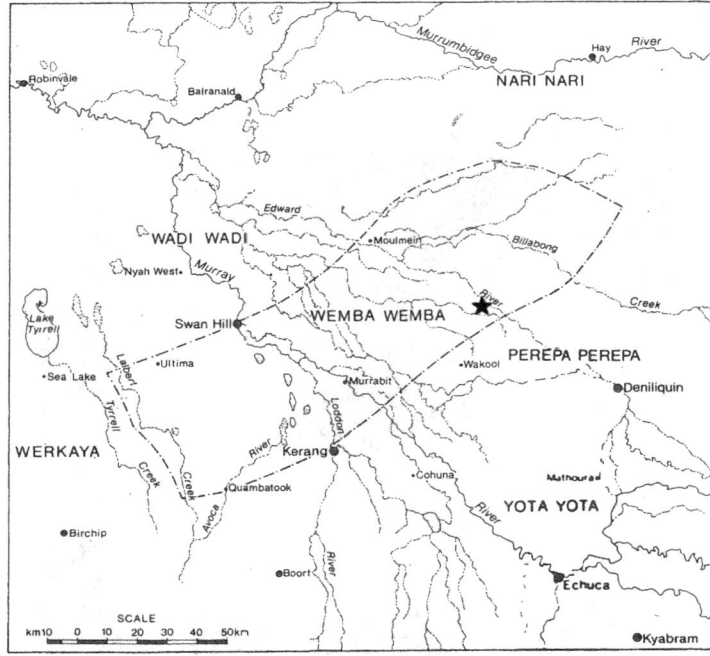

Figure 18.2 Map of Wemba-Wemba country with approximate location of Moonahcullah Mission shown by star. This illustration, 'Map of Wembawemba country and surrounding areas by V. Potezny', adapted from Luise Anna Hercus, *Wembawemba Dictionary* (Canberra: Australian Institute of Aboriginal and Torres Strait Island Studies, 1992). Reproduced with kind permission of copyright owner, Luise A. Hercus Estate

My grandmother, Nan Kelly (then Lala Campbell née Taylor), took her five children to live with her parents at Moonahcullah, following the sudden death of her husband in a horse-riding accident. She could safely leave her children in the care of her parents, Robert and Sarah Taylor, which allowed her to support her family by working as a maid on one of the local properties. For her three daughters, Evelyn, Alice (who later became my mother), and their younger sister Alma, going to school at Moonahcullah was a new experience as they had never attended school before. Mum Alice in particular enjoyed the encouragement that the missionary teachers gave them, and learning to read and write.[29] School holidays were spent roaming the bush, swimming, fishing for yabbies, and spending time with their mum and grandparents.

A few years later, in 1911, Lala married Alf Kelly, a widower with one child. Alf was born at Roto, a small town north of Hillston in central New South Wales. He was the son of a Wongaibon (Waangaypuwan) woman and an Irish father. As a boss, drover Alf's work took him away for weeks at time, leaving Nan Kelly at home to care for the children. Life settled down as her children got used to their stepfather coming and going and providing for them through his droving business. A particular worry for Nan Kelly, however, was the poor state of the roads at the mission during the winter months. Combined with dangerous high-water levels of the Edwards River, this restricted the whole community from accessing medical care.

During 1913, Alf Kelly Junior was born at Moonahcullah, and in 1915 Nan Kelly gave birth to another child, Mary Kelly, there. The following year, her 11-year-old niece, Ruth Taylor, was removed, along with family friend and later well-known activist Margaret Tucker and her younger sister. Despite the fight put up by Margaret's mother and Ruth's grandmother and aunts, the three girls were taken to Cootamundra Aboriginal Girls' Home by an officer of the Aboriginal Welfare Board, with the help of the local police.[30] According to Mum Alice, this removal, like others, was timed for when the fathers of the children chosen for removal were away at work. The family later found out that Ruth Taylor was taken because she was classified as an orphan, even though she had a father and loving grandparents and aunts.

Following this experience, the threat of child removals was forever in Nan Kelly's mind and the family decided to leave Moonahcullah Mission. Grandfather Alf used his knowledge of stock and station agents and droving mates to find a house for the family in the township of Deniliquin. Here Nan Kelly enjoyed the convenience of services, such as the doctors and grocers, being nearby. No longer did she have to walk to the nearest property to call a doctor. For Mum Alice and her sister, Alma, life in Deniliquin was another new experience. They began attending an all-white school, separated from their older sister Evelyn who chose to remain with her grandparents at Moonahcullah. Mum Alice's interest in education and learning continued and grew to a passion, leaving her with a lifelong belief in the power of education. On one occasion, Alice's teacher suggested that she might like to attend boarding school and become a teacher herself. Upon hearing this news, my grandparents were horrified by the possibility of their daughter being separated from her family, resulting in the loss of her cultural identity in the name of assimilation. Grandfather Alf went to the school, where he threatened to pull the headmaster over his desk if he continued to encourage Alice to leave her family.

Fearing the possibility that they could still lose their daughter, the Kelly family packed up and moved to Balranald. Here, Grandfather Alf continued his working relationship with the Naughton family, who were pastoralists. As was the norm, the Kelly family moved into one of the worker's cottages on the Naughton's property, Canally Station. Sadly for Mum Alice and her sister Alma, at that time Balranald State School refused to enrol Aboriginal students. Further, Nan Kelly refused to allow them to attend any school due to the fear of their removal. So the two sisters began working at Canally Station – Alice as a housemaid/laundress and Alma as a housemaid/waitress – under the management of the daughter of the station owner, Miss Patricia Naughton (Figure 18.3).

Nan Kelly's fear of child removal carried on down to all her younger children, who were not allowed to attend school until after their mother passed in 1929, aged 51. Nevertheless, Alice's ability to read and interpret newspapers for her parents, who had no formal education, provided benefits to the Kelly family. It meant that she could write away for mail order catalogues and place orders to buy clothing and, on one occasion, a sewing machine that allowed Nan Kelly to make clothing for her children. Alice's belief in the value of education was a powerful influence. For example, after Nan Kelly's death she convinced Grandfather to move the family away from Canally Station and build a house near Balranald Mission so that her siblings could attend school in the town. Then later Grandfather Kelly himself insisted that his grandchildren attend school to learn to read and write. After his retirement in 1945, he regularly transported them to school himself in his horse drawn cart, with anywhere up to eight children on board. Mum Alice's skills and belief in education also enabled and encouraged my own education. Early on, it meant that she was able to supervise my primary school lessons that I did by correspondence at home on North Woe sheep and cattle station in New South Wales.

Figure 18.3 First boss to Alice and Alma Kelly, daughter of the house, Miss Patricia Naughton, Canally Station, NSW (circa 1919). Permission from Kella Robinson

This made me feel proud as it meant that my mother was like the stations manager's wife who supervised her own children's correspondence lessons.

It was not until 1945 that my grandfather became acquainted with the exemption certificate because of his need to obtain an old age pension upon his retirement. As far as the family knows, Grandfather Alf was the only family member to obtain an exemption certificate. Interestingly, almost a decade later in 1953, his stepdaughter Mum Alice, aged 53 years, did not require an exemption certificate in order to receive a widow's pension. She and my father had been renting a property at Murrin Bridge Aboriginal Mission, and they were financially independent owing to his continuous employment. But after my father's unexpected death, Mum Alice's financial independence was as stake. She was not prepared, however, to come under the policies of the day that forbade any Aboriginal people in missions and reserves from receiving an old age or widow's pension. Therefore, my mother decided to leave Murrin Bridge and live with her sister, Mary, and her family in Hillston, where her financial independence could continue, as it did for the rest of her life.[31]

Shortly after the death of my husband in 2006, I was invited along with other Wemba-Wemba descendants to go on a day trip to visit Moonahcullah. As I had never had the opportunity to walk on in my mother's country, I gladly accepted. Arriving just on lunchtime with an esky (cooler box) full of food, we were invited by the people who lived in the first house we called into to use their outside kitchen. From them, we learnt that a few descendants like themselves had returned to build and live at Moonahcullah full-time, while others had decided to visit whenever they had the chance. After lunch, we were taken on a walk around the cemetery. I'm not really sure what I expected, but I was unable to locate any evidence of the graves of my great-grandparents, Robert and Sarah Taylor, nor of their grandchildren who had remained at Moonahcullah, Evelyn and Jeffery Campbell.

I am sure that my great-grandparents would have been proud of Nan Kelly and Mum Alice. Both were strong women. My grandmother Nan Kelly battled the environment, as well as the policies, to give her children a safe life. Mum Alice and her siblings were determined to give their children educational opportunities that they were denied. Their father showed similar determination, following his retirement, by transporting his grandchildren to school every morning. Through their struggles and achievements, successive generations of Kelly descendants have gained education to work in areas such as criminal justice, youth justice, education, health, housing, conservation, and public safety, to benefit the communities in which they live. The strong influence of the Kelly women means that 'because of her, we can!'.

The half-life of exemption

Lucinda Aberdeen

Technically, the various state policies regarding Aboriginal exemption in twentieth century Australia ended in the late 1960s, after the 1967 referendum saw the Commonwealth Government assume responsibilities for Aboriginal Affairs nationally. Those becoming acquainted for the first time with the injustices and hardships resulting from exemption policies may think that, as they ceased by law last century, they are safely in the past. However, this overlooks a well-known lesson of history, namely that the past remains in the present. Nowhere is this more evident than in the ongoing impact of Aboriginal exemption on identity. In early twentieth-century Queensland, a key component of exemption required exemptees to reconfigure their cultural identity and that of their offspring to conform to respectable and law-abiding norms of Anglo-Australian citizens and to not associate with Aboriginal people.[32] Failure to assimilate in this way could result in the removal of the entitlements of exemption and a forced return to live on missions and reserves under close supervision and tight restrictions. Thus, successive generations of exemptees in Queensland and their children were required to identify and behave as 'respectable' Anglo-Australians or risk loss of freedom from reserve life. As noted earlier, similar requirements operated to varying degrees in other Australian states that later adopted exemption policies. This raises the question: How can decades of internalised assimilation – and its associated cultural dislocation and family displacement – dissipate when government policies and practices of exemption no longer exist? Is it possible they continue to shape not only the lives of Aboriginal and Torres Strait Islander people but those of all Australians?

A meeting in Brisbane, Queensland between two women in their 80s in 2007 serves to illustrate the complexities of the matter. One of the women was Judi's mother, Gwen, a resident of suburban Brisbane. She was the first child born in 1925 to Roy and Daisy Smith, before they left Purga Mission as result of her father's exemption in 1926. The other woman was my mother, Kathleen, a resident of Perth, Western Australia. She was a fourth-generation Anglo-Australian born in 1921 to parents in the health professions, Kenneth and Dorothy Aberdeen, in regional Western Australia. Judi and I had by then known each other over a number of years, during which time Judi had successfully written an Honours thesis about Aboriginal exemption in Queensland with me as her supervisor. We arranged for our mothers to meet socially over afternoon tea while my mother was visiting Brisbane. During the meeting that followed, both our mothers reflected on their lived experiences as children, young women, mothers, wives, and grandmothers. In this way, they exchanged and shared memories over several hours, while Judi and I listened with much interest.

At no stage during this exchange did Gwen refer specifically to her own cultural heritage. Her appearance as a dignified, older, dark-skinned Aboriginal woman, nonetheless, was a point of interest to my mother for several reasons. Firstly, she knew that Judi identified as Aboriginal and worked as an Aboriginal worker in various government roles over many years. Secondly, in her early life Kathleen had understood her own father to be a champion of Aboriginal rights in his role as a government medical officer in regional Western Australia. Much later in her life, however, my mother had become critical of the racism towards Noongar people in the 1920s and 1930s in the town where she had grown up and what she believed to be her own complicity in this. Thirdly, through her interest in my teaching and research as an academic, Kathleen knew that injustices towards Aboriginal

Australians were not a matter in the past. Opportunities for her to socialise with Aboriginal and Torres Strait Islander people had been quite limited, however, like many non-Aboriginal Australians. Therefore, she was very much enjoying becoming acquainted with Gwen, and during a break in the conversation she quietly asked me about Gwen's cultural heritage.

Before I had begun to answer her question, my mother started to add, 'Is she Aboriginal?' This alarmed me. I knew from extensive discussions with Judi that Gwen did not identify as 'Aboriginal'. In accordance with the conditions of exemption in Queensland taught to her by her parents in the 1930s and 1940s, Gwen had rarely ever associated with Aboriginal people. She considered herself as 'just Australian' or an 'ordinary Australian' and in the 1950s and 1960s she had reared her seven children to see themselves in the same way.[33] Four decades later although the Queensland system of exemption had formally ceased and some of Gwen's adult children had received public recognition specifically for their contributions as Indigenous Queenslanders, her sense of cultural identity remained unchanged. All of this flashed through my mind and I felt compelled to interrupt my mother before she finished uttering the word 'Aboriginal'. In a voice raised to prevent Gwen hearing Kathleen, I answered my mother by telling her that Gwen was 'just Australian'. This intervention succeeded in that Kathleen politely enquired no more and the matter fell silent.

The fact that I had felt driven to shut down my mother's enquiry out of respect for Gwen is illustrative of the complex legacy of exemption. The exemption certificate granted to Gwen's father secured his family's freedom from the extreme hardships of reserve and mission life, but came at a very high cost. It required that Gwen, like her younger siblings, be reared and live her adult life in steadfast denial of her Aboriginal cultural heritage or risk losing the hard-won freedom offered by exemption. From a contemporary perspective, this constitutes an historic violation by the state of Gwen's right to culture as set out in Article 8 of the United Nations Declaration on the Rights of Indigenous Peoples. Thus, denying the Aboriginal Australian heritage of Gwen in order to respect her sense of an 'Australian' identity at an awkward conversational moment highlights the problematic and ongoing impact of cultural suppression required of her and others by the Queensland system of exemption last century.

Conclusion

In the stories told above, it is apparent that the exemption era has a cultural afterlife, a 'half-life', like radiation, that extends beyond the life of legislation that gave it a basis in law in all Australian states except Victoria and Tasmania. Kella's family were able to maintain connection to each other and their culture but did so by using mobility as a means to make the best of the various pressures placed up on them by colonial governments. Meanwhile, Judi had been told by her parents – when she enquired into her heritage in the 1950s – that she was 'Australian', which denied any recognition of her family's Indigenous heritage.[34] Over half a century later in a post-exemption era, Lucinda provided the same description of Gwen's cultural heritage to her own mother. She felt compelled to do so to avoid disregarding Gwen's deeply engrained experience as a law-abiding 'Australian' woman who worked hard to ensure security and stability for her own children during the height of assimilationist policies in Australia. In both instances, however, such a response powerfully serves not only to erase Indigenous cultural heritage but also to suppress knowledge about cultural dislocation and family displacement resulting from policies of exemption Australia-wide and the opportunity to confront them. As Judi's research into her family history has continued, she has had the distressing experience of discovering significant pieces of information about her family that had been lost due to dislocation. Judi recently found that Roy had other family members and that Daisy and Nancy, long thought to be sisters, were, in fact, cousins. The loss of these details is just one of the painful and ongoing impacts of exemption policies. Finding them again, and writing these family histories down, as Judi and Kella have done here and elsewhere, is an important contribution to healing the harm caused by government policies.

The accounts in this chapter also point to the ways in which family histories of exemption were intertwined with an emphasis on education as a means of empowerment. For both Kella's mother and Judi's grandmother, education was a priority, and they actively encouraged their children and grandchildren to learn and succeed in school and beyond. Exemption may have indirectly given these families the opportunity to gain a better education – though perhaps it is more accurate to say that exemption and education were adjacent strategies of survival.

While in both Judi and Kella's stories it was their grandfathers who became exempt, the policy had a profound effect on the women in their families as well. Judi and Kella's mothers (Gwen and Alice) and their grandmothers (Daisy and Lala) were women who looked after husbands, children, and other kin, maintained important social connections, engineered and endured various moves around the country, and did the best they could in difficult circumstances to hold their families together. It is fitting that we wrote this chapter in 2018, when the theme of NAIDOC (National Aborigines and Islanders Day of Observance Committee) week, 'Because of her, we can!', called upon us to recognise the important contribution of Aboriginal and Torres Strait Islander women to this nation.

Notes

1 The term 'Country', when used by Aboriginal and Torres Strait Islander people, encompasses more than the Australian English meaning of nation or a region outside urban areas. Instead, the word encompasses a custodianship and belonging to land expressed through law, culture, and tradition. See, for example, 'Share Mungo Culture – Aboriginal Country,' http://www.visitmungo.com.au/aboriginal-country, accessed 15 January 2020.
2 It should be noted that legislation that impacted Aboriginal and Torres Strait Islander people was passed in several colonies before 1869. For example, in Queensland the *Industrial and Reformatories Schools Act 1865* allowed Indigenous children to be sent to industrial schools or reformatories on the grounds of 'neglect'.

3 See John Chesterman and Brian Galligan, *Citizens without Rights: Aborigines and Australian Citizenship* (Melbourne: Cambridge University Press, 1997) for a general overview. A comprehensive list of the legislation passed by each state that impacted on Aboriginal and Torres Strait Islander people can be found on the AIATSIS website's 'To Remove and Protect,' accessed 25 January 2020, aiatsis.gov.au/collections/collections-online/digitised-collections/remove-and-protect. Detailed discussion of the varying impact of protection legislation in different states can be found in Anna Haebich, *For Their Own Good: Aborigines and Government in the Southwest of Western Australia* (Nedlands: University of Western Australia Press, 1992); Ben Silverstein, *Governing Natives: Indirect Rule and Settler Colonialism in Australia's North* (Manchester: Manchester University Press, 2018); Ros Kidd, *The Way We Civilise: Aboriginal Affairs – The Untold Story* (St Lucia: University of Queensland Press, 1997); Heather Goodall, *Invasion to Embassy: Land in Aboriginal Politics in New South Wales, 1770–1972* (St Leonards: Allen & Unwin in association with Black Books, 1996); Richard Broome, *Aboriginal Victorians: A History Since 1800* (St Leonards: Allen & Unwin, 2005); and Lyndall Ryan, *The Aboriginal Tasmanians* (St Leonards: Allen & Unwin, 1996).
4 See Anna Haebich, *Spinning the Dream: Assimilation in Australia 1950–1970* (Fremantle: Fremantle Press, 2008); Haebich, *Broken Circles: Fragmenting Indigenous Families, 1800–2000* (Fremantle: Fremantle Arts Centre Press, 2000); Haebich, 'Imagining Assimilation,' *Australian Historical Studies* 33, no. 118 (2002), 61–70; Russell McGregor, *Indifferent Inclusion: Aboriginal People and the Australian Nation* (Canberra: Aboriginal Studies Press, 2011); Tim Rowse, *White Flour, White Power: From Rations to Citizenship in Australia* (Cambridge: Cambridge University Press, 1998); Rowse, ed., *Contesting Assimilation* (Perth: API Network, 2005).
5 Goodall, *Invasion to Embassy*, 267.
6 Other diasporas of Aboriginal and Torres Strait Islander people living away from reserves and missions, often as fringe dwellers or 'border hoppers', were formed by those who left without exemption as a result of dissatisfaction or disagreement with the Reserve or Mission Manager, as happened with the 1939 Cummeragunja Walk Off in New South Wales. See, for example, Fiona Davis, *Australian Settler Colonialism and the Cummeragunja Aboriginal Station: Redrawing Boundaries* (Brighton: Sussex Academic Press, 2014).
7 See the examples quoted in Christobel Mattingly and Ken Hampton, *Survival in Our Own Land: 'Aboriginal' Experiences in 'South Australia' Since 1836* (Adelaide: Wakefield Press, 1988), 48, 52.
8 Katherine Ellinghaus, 'The Poisoned Chalice: Exemption Policies in Twentieth Century Australia and the Writing of "History,"' in *Black, White and Exempt: Aboriginal and Torres Strait Islander Lives Under Exemption*, eds. Lucinda Aberdeen and Jennifer Jones (Canberra: Aboriginal Studies Press, 2021), 24–41.
9 Alternative first-person accounts of exemption can be found in many biographies and works of history – see, in particular, Sally Morgan, *Wanamurraganya: The Story of Jack McPhee* (Fremantle: Fremantle Arts Centre Press, 1989), 125–128, 139; Marnie Kennedy, *Born a Half-Caste* (Canberra: Australian Institute of Aboriginal Studies, 1985); Ian Dudley, 'Growing Up Beige,' in *Growing up Aboriginal in Australia*, ed. Anita Heiss (Carlton: Black Inc., 2018), 59–62; Ann McGrath, *Illicit Love: Interracial Sex and Marriage in the United States and Australia* (Lincoln: University of Nebraska Press, 2015), 309–310; Thom Blake, *A Dumping Ground: A History of the Cherbourg Settlement* (St Lucia: University of Queensland Press, 2001), 136–137. On the general history of exemption, see *Black, White and Exempt: Aboriginal and Torres Strait Islander Lives under Exemption*, edited by Lucinda Aberdeen and Jennifer Jones (Canberra: Aboriginal Studies Press, 2021); Judi Wickes, 'A Study of the "Lived Experience" of Citizenship amongst Exempted Aboriginal People in Regional Queensland, with a Focus on the

South Burnett Region' (MA diss., University of the Sunshine Coast, 2010); Wickes and Lucinda Aberdeen, 'The Diaries of Daisy Smith: The Experience of Citizenship for an Exempted Family in Mid-Twentieth Century Queensland,' *Australian Journal of Politics and History* 63, no. 1 (2017), 62–77; Wickes and Marnee Shay, 'Aboriginal Identity in Education Settings: Privileging Our Stories as a Way of Deconstructing the Past and Re-Imagining the Future,' *Australian Educational Researcher* 44 (2017), 107–122. Wickes, '"Never Really Heard of It": The Certificate of Exemption and Lost Identity,' in *Indigenous Biography and Autobiography*, eds. Peter Read, Frances Peters-Little, and Anna Haebich (Canberra: Aboriginal Studies Press, 2008), 73–91; Katherine Ellinghaus, 'The Moment of Release: The Ideology of Protection and the Twentieth-Century Assimilation Policies of Exemption and Competency in New South Wales and Oklahoma,' *Pacific Historical Review* 87, no. 1 (Winter 2018): 128–148; and Ellinghaus and Wickes, 'A Moving Female Frontier: Aboriginal Exemption and Domestic Service in Queensland, 1897–1914,' *Australian Historical Studies* 51 (2020): 19–37.
10 'Column 8,' *Sydney Morning Herald*, Saturday 3 January 1948, 1.
11 Haebich, *Spinning the Dream*, 76. Historians have only briefly covered the topic of exemption and no one, to our knowledge, has explored its history using a gendered focus. See Chesterman and Galligan. *Citizens without Rights*, 55–56, 132–133, 141, 165–169; John Murphy, *Imagining the Fifties: Private Sentiment and Political Culture in Menzies' Australia* (Sydney: UNSW Press, 2000), 175–177; Goodall, *Invasion to Embassy*; Russell McGregor, 'Avoiding "Aborigines": Paul Hasluck and the Northern Territory *Welfare Ordinance, 1953*,' *Australian Journal of Politics and History* 51, no. 4 (2005): 513–529; McGregor, 'Nation and Assimilation: Continuity and Discontinuity in Aboriginal Affairs in the 1950s,' in *Modern Frontier: Aspects of the 1950s in Australia's Northern Territory*, eds. Julie T. Wells, Mickey Dewar, and Suzanne Parry (Darwin: Charles Darwin University Press, 2005), 17–31.
12 'For some Aborigines [sic] the coming of grog was much more significant than the less tangible arrival of citizenship. But then maybe grog *was* citizenship. And maybe grog was colonial rule. Perhaps it was in the interests of the state for Aborigines to remain under the rule of the grog.' Ann McGrath, '"Beneath the Skin": Australian Citizenship, Rights and Aboriginal Women,' *Journal of Australian Studies* 37 (June 1993), 110.
13 Julie Wells and Michael Christie, 'Namatjira and the Burden of Citizenship,' *Australian Historical Studies* 31, no. 114 (2000), 110–130.
14 Although in New South Wales, some women who were married to white men did apply for exemption in order to drink with their husbands in hotels. See Ellinghaus, 'The Moment of Release,' 142–143.
15 'Coming to Grips with Our Native Problem,' *The Mail* (Adelaide), 18 September 1948, 7.
16 On Queensland, see Wickes, 'Study of the "Lived Experience" of Citizenship.'
17 From Jack McGinness's speech to the All-Australian Trade Union Congress, held in Melbourne, 3–7 September 1951, reprinted in entirety in Joe McGinness, *Son of Alyandabu: My Fight for Aboriginal Rights* (St Lucia: University of Queensland Press, 1991), 61–64. For more on Northern Territory exemption and its impact on families, see Sue Stanton, 'The Australian Half-Caste Progressive Association: The Fight for Freedom and Rights in the Northern Territory,' *Journal of Northern Territory History* 4 (1993): 37–46.
18 See Aileen Moreton-Robinson, *Talkin' up to the White Woman: Aboriginal Women and Feminism* (St Lucia: University of Queensland Press, 2000); Haebich, *Spinning the Dream*; Goodall, *Invasion to Embassy*; Goodall, '"Assimilation Begins in the Home": The State and Aboriginal Women's Work as Mothers in New South Wales, 1900s to 1960s,' *Labour History* 69 (1995), 75–101; Victoria Haskins, '"A Better Chance"? Sexual Abuse and the Apprenticeship of Aboriginal Girls under the NSW Aborigines Protection Board,' *Aboriginal History* 28 (2004): 33–58.
19 Francesca Bartlett has shown how the ideology of domesticity aimed at middle-class white women dovetailed neatly with the emphasis on giving Aboriginal women

domestic skills. Francesca Bartlett, 'Clean, White Girls: Assimilation and Women's Work,'. In *Unmasking Whiteness: Race Relations and Reconciliation*, ed. Belinda McKay (Nathan: Queensland Studies Centre for Public Culture and Ideas, Griffith University, 1999), 52–67. Anna Cole has shown how white women played their part in the surveillance and control of Aboriginal people by training and employing Aboriginal women as domestic servants. Anna Cole, '"Would Have Known It by the Smell of It": Ella Hiscocks.' In *Common Ground: White Women in Aboriginal History*, eds. Anna Cole, Victoria Haskins, and Fiona Paisley (Canberra: Aboriginal Studies Press, 2005), 153–171. Victoria Haskins has shown how the placement of Aboriginal girls into white homes as domestic servants had a sinister undertone of sexual abuse. Haskins, '"A Better Chance"?'
20 Goodall, '"Assimilation Begins in the Home",' 83. However, Julia Martínez and Claire Lowrie point out that Aboriginal men also worked as domestic servants. Julia Martínez and Claire Lowrie, 'Colonial Constructions of Masculinity: Transforming Aboriginal Australian Men into "Houseboys",' *Gender and History* 21, no. 2 (August 2009), 305–323.
21 'Annual Report of the Aborigines Welfare Board, New South Wales, 1944,' *New South Wales Parliamentary Papers* 2 (1945–1946), 9–10; 'Report of the Aborigines Welfare Board, 1951,' *New South Wales Parliamentary Papers* 1 (1952–1953), 9; 'Annual Report of the Aborigines Welfare Board, New South Wales, 1945,' *New South Wales Parliamentary Papers* 2 (1945–1946), 6. For more on gender and exemption in New South Wales, see Ellinghaus, 'The Moment of Release.'
22 Goodall, '"Assimilation Begins in the Home",' 89.
23 'Shifting Camp,' *Queensland Times*, 13 November 1914, 4.
24 Wickes and Aberdeen, 'The Diaries of Daisy Smith,' 71–72.
25 Wickes and Aberdeen, 'The Diaries of Daisy Smith.'
26 This was a term used at the time for and by Aboriginal people.
27 Michel Foucault, *Discipline and Punish: The Birth of the Prison* (London: Penguin Books, 1977).
28 Janet Cleverley and John Mooney, *Taking Our Place: Aboriginal Education and the Story of the Koori Centre at the University of Sydney* (Sydney: Sydney University Press, 2010), 51.
29 Kella Robinson, 'Alice: Walking in Her Footsteps' (MA diss., Deakin University, 2014), 8.
30 Margaret Tucker, *If Everyone Cared: Autobiography of Margaret Tucker* (Sydney: Ure Smith, 1977).
31 Robinson, 'Alice,' 37, 73.
32 Wickes and Aberdeen, 'The Diaries of Daisy Smith.'
33 Wickes, '"Never Really Heard of It".'
34 Wickes, '"Never Really Heard of It".'

Bibliography

Primary

'Annual Report of the Aborigines Welfare Board, New South Wales, 1944.' *New South Wales Parliamentary Papers* 2 (1945–1946).
'Annual Report of the Aborigines Welfare Board, New South Wales, 1945.' *New South Wales Parliamentary Papers* 2 (1945–1946).
'Column 8.' *Sydney Morning Herald*, Saturday 3 January 1948, 1.
'Coming to Grips With Our Native Problem.' *The Mail* (Adelaide), 18 September 1948, 7.
Memo 2/7/56. NRS 11 Applications for Certificates of Exemption, Aborigines Welfare Board Records, State Records Office, New South Wales.
'Report of the Aborigines Welfare Board, 1951.' *New South Wales Parliamentary Papers* 1 (1952–1953).
'Shifting Camp.' *Queensland Times*, 13 November 1914.

Secondary

Aberdeen, Lucinda, Kella Robinson, and Judi Wickes. 'Playing the Game': A Comparative Case Study of Aboriginal Exemption in Queensland and New South Wales.' In *Black, White and Exempt: Aboriginal and Torres Strait Islander Lives under Exemption*, edited by Lucinda Aberdeen and Jennifer Jones, 62–84. Canberra: Aboriginal Studies Press, 2021.

AIATSIS. 'To Remove and Protect.' Accessed 25 January 2020. aiatsis.gov.au/collections/collections-online/digitised-collections/remove-and-protect.

Bartlett, Francesca. 'Clean, White Girls: Assimilation and Women's Work.' In *Unmasking Whiteness: Race Relations and Reconciliation*, edited by Belinda McKay, 52–67. Nathan: Queensland Studies Centre for Public Culture and Ideas, Griffith University, 1999.

Blake, Thom. *A Dumping Ground: A History of the Cherbourg Settlement*. St Lucia: University of Queensland Press, 2001.

Broome, Richard. *Aboriginal Victorians: A History since 1800*. St Leonards: Allen & Unwin, 2005.

Chesterman, John and Brian Galligan. *Citizens without Rights: Aborigines and Australian Citizenship*. Melbourne: Cambridge University Press, 1997.

Cleverley, Janet and John Mooney. *Taking Our Place: Aboriginal Education and the Story of the Koori Centre at the University of Sydney*. Sydney: Sydney University Press, 2010.

Cole, Anna. '"Would Have Known It by the Smell of It": Ella Hiscocks.' In *Common Ground: White Women in Aboriginal History*, edited by Anna Cole, Victoria Haskins, and Fiona Paisley, 153–171. Canberra: Aboriginal Studies Press, 2005.

Davis, Fiona. *Australian Settler Colonialism and the Cummeragunja Aboriginal Station: Redrawing Boundaries*. Brighton: Sussex Academic Press, 2014.

Dudley, Ian. 'Growing Up Beige.' In *Growing up Aboriginal in Australia*, edited by Anita Heiss, 59–62. Carlton: Black Inc., 2018.

Ellinghaus, Katherine. 'The Moment of Release: The Ideology of Protection and the Twentieth-Century Assimilation Policies of Exemption and Competency in New South Wales and Oklahoma.' *Pacific Historical Review* 87, no. 1 (Winter 2018): 128–148.

Ellinghaus, Katherine. 'The Poisoned Chalice: Exemption Policies in Twentieth Century Australia and the Writing of "History."' In *Black, White and Exempt: Aboriginal and Torres Strait Islander Lives under Exemption*, edited by Lucinda Aberdeen and Jennifer Jones, 24–41 (Canberra: Aboriginal Studies Press, 2021).

Ellinghaus, Katherine, and Judi Wickes. 'A Moving Female Frontier: Aboriginal Exemption and Domestic Service in Queensland, 1897–1914.' *Australian Historical Studies* 51 (2020): 19–37.

Foucault, Michel. *Discipline and Punish: The Birth of the Prison*. London: Penguin Books, 1977.

Goodall, Heather. '"Assimilation Begins in the Home": The State and Aboriginal Women's Work as Mothers in New South Wales, 1900s to 1960s.' *Labour History* 69 (1995): 75–101.

Goodall, Heather. *Invasion to Embassy: Land in Aboriginal Politics in New South Wales, 1770–1972*. St Leonards: Allen & Unwin, 1996.

Haebich, Anna. *For their Own Good: Aborigines and Government in the Southwest of Western Australia*. Nedlands: University of Western Australia Press, 1992.

Haebich, Anna. *Broken Circles: Fragmenting Indigenous Families, 1800–2000*. Fremantle: Fremantle Arts Centre Press, 2000.

Haebich, Anna. '"Imagining Assimilation".' *Australian Historical Studies* 33, no. 118 (2002): 61–70.

Haebich, Anna. *Spinning the Dream: Assimilation in Australia 1950–1970*. Fremantle: Fremantle Press, 2007.

Haskins, Victoria. '"A Better Chance"? Sexual Abuse and the Apprenticeship of Aboriginal Girls under the NSW Aborigines Protection Board.' *Aboriginal History* 28 (2004): 33–58.

Hercus, Luise Anna. *Wembawemba Dictionary.* Canberra: Australian Institute of Aboriginal and Torres Strait Island Studies, 1992.

Johnson, Darlene. 'Ab/Originality: Playing and Passing versus Assimilation.' *Olive Pink Society Bulletin* 5, no. 2 (1993): 19–23.

Kennedy, Marnie. *Born a Half-Caste.* Canberra: Australian Institute of Aboriginal Studies, 1985.

Kidd, Ros. *The Way We Civilise: Aboriginal Affairs – The Untold Story.* St Lucia: University of Queensland Press, 1997.

Martínez, Julia, and Claire Lowrie, 'Colonial Constructions of Masculinity: Transforming Aboriginal Australian Men into "Houseboys".' *Gender and History* 21, no. 2 (August 2009): 305–323.

Mattingly, Christobel, and Ken Hampton, *Survival in Our Own Land: 'Aboriginal' Experiences in 'South Australia' Since 1836.* Adelaide: Wakefield Press, 1988.

McGrath, Ann. '"Beneath the Skin": Australian Citizenship, Rights and Aboriginal Women.' *Journal of Australian Studies* 37 (June 1993): 99–114.

McGrath, Ann. *Illicit Love: Interracial Sex and Marriage in the United States and Australia.* Lincoln: University of Nebraska Press, 2015.

McGregor, Russell. 'Avoiding "Aborigines": Paul Hasluck and the Northern Territory Welfare Ordinance, 1953.' *Australian Journal of Politics and History* 51, no. 4 (2005): 513–529.

McGregor, Russell. 'Nation and Assimilation: Continuity and Discontinuity in Aboriginal Affairs in the 1950s.' In *Modern Frontier: Aspects of the 1950s in Australia's Northern Territory,* edited by Julie T. Wells, Mickey Dewar, and Suzanne Parry, 17–31. Darwin: Charles Darwin University Press, 2005.

McGregor, Russell. *Indifferent Inclusion: Aboriginal People and the Australian Nation.* Canberra: Aboriginal Studies Press, 2011.

McGinness, Joe. *Son of Alyandabu: My Fight for Aboriginal Rights.* St Lucia: University of Queensland Press, 1991.

Moreton-Robinson, Aileen. *Talkin' up to the White Woman: Aboriginal Women and Feminism.* St Lucia: University of Queensland Press, 2000.

Morgan, Sally. *Wanamurraganya: The Story of Jack McPhee.* Fremantle: Fremantle Arts Centre Press, 1989.

Murphy, John. *Imagining the Fifties: Private Sentiment and Political Culture in Menzies' Australia.* Sydney: UNSW Press, 2000.

Robinson, Kella. 'Alice: Walking in Her Footsteps.' MA diss., Deakin University, 2014.

Rowse, Tim. *White Flour, White Power: From Rations to Citizenship in Australia.* Cambridge: Cambridge University Press, 1998.

Rowse, Tim, ed. *Contesting Assimilation.* Perth: API Network, 2005.

Ryan, Lyndall. *The Aboriginal Tasmanians.* St Leonards: Allen & Unwin, 1996.

'Share Mungo Culture – Aboriginal Country.' http://www.visitmungo.com.au/aboriginal-country. Accessed 15 January 2020.

Silverstein, Ben. *Governing Natives: Indirect Rule and Settler Colonialism in Australia's North.* Manchester: Manchester University Press, 2018.

Stanton, Sue. 'The Australian Half-Caste Progressive Association: The Fight for Freedom and Rights in the Northern Territory.' *Journal of Northern Territory History* 4 (1993): 37–46.

Tucker, Margaret. *If Everyone Cared: Autobiography of Margaret Tucker.* Sydney: Ure Smith, 1977.

Wells, Julie, and Michael Christie. 'Namatjira and the Burden of Citizenship.' *Australian Historical Studies* 31, no. 114 (2000): 110–130.

Wickes, Judi. '"Never Really Heard of It": The Certificate of Exemption and Lost Identity.' In *Indigenous Biography and Autobiography,* edited by Peter Read, Frances Peters-Little, and Anna Haebich, 73–91. Canberra: Aboriginal Studies Press, 2008.

Wickes, Judi. 'A Study of the "Lived Experience" of Citizenship amongst Exempted Aboriginal People in Regional Queensland, with a Focus on the South Burnett Region.' MA diss., University of the Sunshine Coast, 2010.

Wickes, Judi, and Lucinda Aberdeen. 'The Diaries of Daisy Smith: The Experience of Citizenship for an Exempted Family in Mid-Twentieth Century Queensland.' *Australian Journal of Politics and History* 63, no. 1 (2017): 62–77.

Wickes, Judi, and Marnee Shay. 'Aboriginal Identity in Education Settings: Privileging Our Stories as a Way of Deconstructing the Past and Re-Imagining the Future.' *Australian Educational Researcher* 44 (2017): 107–122.

19
DAMAGE AND DISPOSSESSION
Indigenous people and nuclear weapons on Bikini Atoll and the Pitjantjatjara lands, 1946 to 1988

Heather Goodall

The nuclear bombs that were dropped on the civilians of Hiroshima and Nagasaki signalled the end of WW2 – and the end of old ways of seeing the world. Joseph Masco has written:

> Los Alamos scientists created much more than simply a new technology with the invention of a military atomic device in 1945: they engendered new forms of consciousness .... July 16, 1945, can only be narrated as a moment of historical rupture and transformation...[1]

But some things did not change, one of which was relations between major powers and Indigenous people. The newly invented bombs needed testing – and showing off – so all nations involved in the alliances of WW2 and 'blocs' of the emerging Cold War needed space. But it had to be space that was not in use by the current, dominant economy – land or waters that were designated as 'waste'. They could only be waters in the most remote oceanic zones or arid deserts with no agriculture or industrial development. The sites chosen for testing were, of course, never empty. They were places with few people or where residents had little political power – or both. In the 28-year period between the bombs over Japan and the Partial Test Ban in 1963, each of the sites chosen for 'tests' by the weapons-testing countries were the homes of Indigenous, often colonised, and always powerless peoples.[2]

The U.S. chose either the desert country of Native Americans or mid-Pacific sites, the homes of Micronesian or Polynesian peoples. The U.K. chose first its former colony Australia, and then the still-colonised mid-Pacific Kiritimati (Christmas) Island. The Soviet Union chose deserts and then Novaya Zemlya Island off the northern sub-Arctic coast, home of Nenets-speaking Indigenous reindeer herders. The French tests from 1960 affected mobile peoples in colonised Algeria, then the Islanders of colonised French Polynesia. The Chinese tested bombs on Uighur lands, while the Indian tests in the Thar Desert of western Rajasthan in 1974 affected mobile herders and impoverished sedentary pastoralists.

There is clearly much to be learnt from the experiences of all these Indigenous and disempowered peoples around the world as they faced nuclear testing. Yet, the effects of the nuclear testing itself has so dominated the consciousness of the world, just as Masco indicated, that attention has been diverted from the broader context of each of these groups. Because their country had been defined as 'wasteland', these groups had previously faced little direct imposition of colonial control. Not only did they have to cope with the testing programmes, but also the intense impacts of encroaching colonisation.

This chapter will address this broader context by briefly reviewing a number of case studies: two on the Bikini Atoll people of the Marshall Islands and two on the Pitjantjatjara in Australia. Drawing on these cases, the paper will raise some of the issues that are not usually identified in discussions of the impacts of nuclear testing on Indigenous people. It will close with the meeting between the Bikinians and the Pitjantjatjara in 1988.

It is important to recognise, however, before turning to these case studies, just how little the military and scientific establishments of any of the testing countries actually knew about the short- or long-term impacts of nuclear weapons. In 1945, it was believed that for most radioactive materials, the severity of the injury was related to the amount of radioactive material to which the person was exposed. This kind of effect is called 'non-stochastic' or non-random, which means that there is a predictable relationship between the level of exposure and the severity of injury, and that a threshold exposure could be defined below which no damage could be caused. For other radioactive materials, any exposure at all can have severe damaging effects (known as 'stochastic', or random). These effects are therefore *not* dose-related, which means that *no* exposure could be considered safe, so that *no* threshold could be set. Despite the years that had elapsed since Marie Curie had discovered radiation, and the injuries it was known to have caused, authorities believed at first that the main effect of nuclear weapons were non-stochastic effects related to the dose of radiation, so that a threshold could be set for maximum allowable exposure.

The first threshold standards were set in 1949 in a meeting between the U.S., the U.K., and Canada, then announced by the International Commission of Radiation Protection (ICRP) in 1951. This threshold was then revised downwards in 1954, 1957, and 1958. As the survivors of the bombs over Japan began to bear children, the damage to foetuses had become evident,[3] and as the survivors aged, the longer-term effects of the radiation to which they had been exposed became clear. Illnesses such as leukaemia and other cancers were 'stochastic' or random damage to human bodies, which could be caused by even very low doses of radiation. Threshold levels continued to be lowered until, in 1990, the ICRP recommended that no exposure at all should be allowed unless there was confirmed benefit to the individual. By 2007, there was, for the first time, recognition of the impact of any radiation exposure, not only on humans but also on non-human species.[4]

As this summary suggests, observing the illness patterns among Japanese survivors of the bombs as they aged was the most important source for the revisions of the exposure threshold. The actual mechanisms by which such damage occurred to living species was only revealed by studying the injuries to the lands and environments – and the Indigenous people themselves – who had to face the tests.[5]

Yet, there were few precautionary strategies in place for the nuclear testing that occurred during the 1940s and 1950s, driven as it was by military, political, and economic insecurities Certainly, the public relations approach in all the testing nations was to assert total confidence in the scientific knowledge of the time and to denigrate, and if possible suppress, any contradictory voices. An International Medical Commission visited Japan in May 1955, gathering results of recent research and surveying data on radiation damage and contamination after 1945 and on the presence of radiation across the Pacific after the March Bravo test. Reporting in *The Lancet*, Dr S. Sevitt, a member of the team, reiterated the Commission's preliminary report when he ended his accompanying letter:

> Doctors have to defend the public health [...] It is the duty of doctors all over the world to call for the prohibition of explosions which are a menace both to mankind today and to future generations.[6]

After discussions with the U.S. President Eisenhower, British Prime Minister Winston Churchill dismissed the Commission's evidence of severe health effects, both after the 1945 blasts and after the Bravo H-Bomb explosion, of which he said: 'some Japanese fishermen were slightly affected by the radioactivity generated by the second Bravo blast.'[7]

The Bikinians

By 1946, the Indigenous people of Bikini Atoll of the Marshall Islands had been colonised first by Spain and later Germany, then occupied by the Japanese (1942–1945) before being 'liberated' by the U.S. The conflict between the Japanese and American troops was worst on Kwajalein but affected all the other islands, although little is known about the impact on the Islanders. The U.S. assumed control of the islands for the remainder of the war, and the Marshalls eventually become a UN 'Strategic Trust Territory' administered by the U.S., a political position that was equivalent to colonisation.

Immediately after the Japanese surrender in August 1945, the U.S. began looking for a site for further testing of nuclear weapons, both to demonstrate its new weapon to world media and to test the impact of nuclear weapons on naval vessels. Bikini Atoll in the Marshall Islands was chosen not only because it was under the U.S. control, but because it was far from major shipping lines. It was believed, too, that oceanwater would dissipate any harmful products.[8] Equally important was that the population was small, easily transported, and it was believed that they could be convinced to leave. However, although the Bikinians had converted to Christianity, they continued to value traditional spiritual knowledge.[9] Central to this knowledge was their attachment to their atoll home, which supported them through lagoon fishing and the growing of coconuts and other crops. As Jukwa Jakeo, a Bikinian elder, explained it to the American Jack Niedenthal in 1987, using the language of monetary exchange introduced previously by missionaries so that Niedenthal could understand:

> I want now to speak about land and the reason we Marshallese treasure it so highly. The land we sit on now as we talk is like gold. ... If you were an owner of land you would be held up as a very important figure in our society. Without land you would be viewed as a person of no consequence.[10]

Jakeo was, of course, pointing out that the land was of far deeper significance than any monetary value:

> Islanders' traditional religious systems taught that the entire atoll environment was protected by the spirits of the ancestors and enchanted by spirits of the natural world.[11]

The Military Governor of the Marshall Islands asked the Bikinians in February 1946, using church networks and in language associated with the Bible, if they would move temporarily to another island 'for the good of mankind and to end all world wars'. The community considered the request carefully. Their troubled discussions resulted in an agreement of sorts to a temporary move, with their leader, King Juda, responding, according to his son, with: 'We will go believing that everything is in the hands of God.'[12] Jonathon Weisgall, the lawyer for the Bikinians in their all their subsequent cases against the U.S. government, was far more sceptical of this account of events. He argued that Juda had simply kept repeating 'everything is in the hands of God' until the Governor gave up and stopped asking.[13]

There appears to have been no review of the Bikinians' health status before they departed. Neither the people who recalled their departure,[14] nor the extensive photographic record of that departure, indicated any baseline recording of Bikinians' health. Consequently, any effects from the tests are difficult to assess.

The Bikinians were taken off their atoll in March 1946, shipped to Rongerik, an uninhabited island much smaller than their home, and left there with six weeks' supplies. They found that the plants on Rongerik did not fruit well and the fish in the lagoon were scarce. They were unable to secure enough food from traditional sources and their appeals to the U.S. to replenish their supplies produced only intermittent deliveries of airdropped food. In 1947, the whole area of Micronesia was designated a UN 'Strategic Trust Territory' to be administered by the U.S. which promised to 'protect the inhabitants'. It was the only such Trust Territory the UN created.

While the Bikinians were struggling with hunger on Rongerik, the U.S. Navy supervised the testing of two fission bombs off Bikini, each about the size of the bomb that had been exploded over Nagasaki. As these were intended to be demonstrations, there were many press reporters and politicians invited to witness the tests. To show how powerful the blast was, and to test its effect on naval vessels, 95 captured and U.S. navy ships had been assembled in order to be scuttled by the blasts. The first test, Able, was unimpressive, with the bomb exploding far above and away from the shipping, having little effect.

The effects of the second bomb, Baker, were totally unexpected. Detonated underwater, the explosion threw masses of irradiated seawater and solids, from the ocean floor and ship debris, into the atmosphere and across the lagoon, over the remaining ships and far more widely, over the surrounding ocean and islands.[15] Unprotected sailors on ships in the vicinity were photographed 'cleaning up' the radiation with scrubbing brushes, lye, and soap![16] On 11 August 1947, *Life* summarised the official report on the Baker test by stating that 'If all the ships at Bikini had been fully manned, the Baker Day bomb would have killed 35,000 crewmen. If such a bomb were dropped below New York's Battery in a stiff south wind, 2 million people would die.'[17]

David Bradley, a young surgeon, had been one of the scientific U.S. Atomic Energy Commission (AEC) team who were sent into the test area immediately. They found massive irradiation that sent their counters off the scale. He returned to San Francisco late in 1946, to find that public interest in Bikini had vanished. He realised then that 'the poisonous results of the tests were de-emphasised by the government and their implications largely ignored by the press'.[18] His widely publicised 1948 book *No Place to Hide* was intended to address that disinterest. Yet, the book received mixed reviews, and although it fuelled the anti-nuclear movement and was reissued in 1984, what public attention it did draw was to the test procedures, not to the displaced Bikinians.[19]

This was not to be the end of the story of radioactivity in Bikini Atoll. In July 1947, one year after the Baker explosion, a team of American Fisheries Society biologists were contracted by the U.S. government to re-survey Bikini Atoll to assess the level of residual radioactivity. They found little, until they used their Geiger counters on the hydroids, a life stage of the hydrozoans, a class of small aquatic predators related to jellyfish, which had attached themselves to underwater survey equipment. The radioactivity of the hydroids was about a thousand times that of the surrounding lagoon water, suggesting that the hydroids were concentrating what radioactive particles remained in circulation. There were more studies in later years, with more sophisticated equipment, and it became possible to identify that radioactivity was concentrating in the creatures' digestive systems. In 1972, when Bikinians attempted to return to their atoll, there were to be terrible demonstrations of this process.[20] Later work was done on Enewetak Atoll, near Bikini, where other U.S. tests were conducted: the U.S. AEC invited scientists to visit, saying it was 'a perfect aquatic laboratory'.[21]

But in 1947, the Bikinians were still starving on Rongerik. Their pleas for assistance were being ignored. After a series of reports from visiting American doctors expressing concern about their health and eventually a blistering media critique by former Secretary of the Interior Harold Ickes in his syndicated column, 'Man to

Man',[22] it still took months before the U.S. finally rescued the Bikinian population in March 1948. They found themselves dumped into tents on Kwajalein Atoll, next to the airstrip at the U.S. Air Force base. In June 1948, the Bikinians made the collective decision to choose Kili Island as a home and were sent there almost immediately.

Kilon Bauno explained this difficult choice to Jack Niedenthal in 1988:

> We lived a strange life on Kwajalein. From day to day we were frightened by all the airplanes that continuously landed very close to our homes. We were also frustrated by the small amount of space in which we were permitted to move around. We had to depend on the U.S. military for everything. We were always asking them to help us in one way or another. We were afraid of this alien environment and almost from the day we got there, we began thinking about another place to live.
>
> We talked about moving to many places like Wotho, Lae and Ujae Atolls. But we encountered the same types of problems with all of these islands. One major factor was that these islands already had people living on them and therefore we thought that we would have social conflicts with the inhabitants because they recognized the *iroij* [leader] of those atolls. We Bikinians did not. We were afraid that they wouldn't let us live by our own rules and so we began asking the Americans to find somewhere else for us. Then, Dr Mason asked us about Kili Island. We debated among ourselves about where we should go. Finally it came to a vote. We chose Kili by a large majority over Wotho and Ujae as the site of our third temporary home.
>
> They sent some Navy men along with some of us Bikinians to help set up our community there. I remember that time well because we were so tired of all this moving around, building new communities and then having to adjust to new places--always adjusting, adjusting, adjusting. Now, once again, we had to start thinking of how to move all of our people to this next island.[23]

Bauno's account is particularly important as it gives an insight into the psychological stress experienced by the Bikinians:

> It was terrible. We were so weary and exhausted, not only by the labour we were going through to get these places ready, but also by these thoughts in our minds: What was happening to Bikini? How long would we be in this new place?
>
> Sometimes we wouldn't eat for an entire day because of the combination of hard work and all the worry that we were experiencing. We were always asking ourselves, 'What are we doing here? What are we going to eat when we get our people to this new place? How will our lives be there?' Questions like this were a great burden for our leaders at that time.[24]

This decision, however, was only to lead to further problems. Kili Island was small with no inner lagoon, so the Bikinians' traditional fishing methods could not be used. The Bikinians had to fish on the open ocean, which was rough around the island, reducing their catch. Not enough coconuts or other crops could be grown either to support the Bikinians or for the copra trade. When the occasional shipment of U.S. aid supplies did come, the Navy vessels were often unable to dock and unload because of the rough seas. The Bikinians were short of food again, and the long years at Kili after 1948 were years of hunger and frustration.

The Pitjantjatjara: Wallatina

The Bikinians had faced terrifying warfare between America and Japan as well as the longer impact of European presence and Christian conversion. The pressures on the Pitjantjatjara in Australia in the decades before testing began were different but just as debilitating: a period of intensifying colonisation. These Western Desert people were traditionally mobile, travelling seasonally across wide areas of the Great Western Desert, navigating with the aid of *Tjukurpa* (or Law), the rich bodies of traditional knowledge encoding environmental information and water sources, along with complex oral narratives of creation and law. Relationships between people were mapped onto the landscape and fulfilled at ceremonial gatherings; a strong sense of identity with particular landscapes intensified as men and women grew to maturity.[25] At all levels, people and their country were entangled.

These ceremonial cycles continued into the mid-twentieth century, but missionaries were establishing strongholds in the east and west at an increasing pace, and mining companies were penetrating the arid lands, looking for uranium and other metals. At the same time, the presence of pastoral activity at the eastern edges of their country was drawing or forcing many Pitjantjatjara people to the cattle and sheep properties, rapidly interfering with their established social life and land management. But the most devastating catastrophes were the measles epidemics of 1948 and 1957.[26]

These viral epidemics struck a non-immune population. Prior to WW2, there had been no dense settler populations in inland Australia. Common viral illnesses like measles had not therefore reached the Aboriginal people in the Central Desert. Measles and similar viruses first entered the Aboriginal populations in these areas only once Alice Springs developed to have a substantial European population, including children.

The 1948 measles epidemic, in particular, took a terrible toll. This viral illness appears to have occurred in all the small scattered settlements of Aboriginal people across the area, including pastoral properties, but it was worst in the larger and more dense settlements like the Presbyterian Mission at Ernabella. People had been attracted by the missionary activities but there was no hygiene infrastructure. There is extensive missionary documentation of this epidemic, as well as the documentation of Dr Charles Duguid, a medical doctor and co-founder of the mission, who rushed up from Adelaide.[27] There was no other outside assistance for the sick, who suffered severe dysentery and respiratory infections as they were weakened by the measles virus. There being such intersecting outcomes for measles infection is a common pattern to this day in developing countries, although most Australians are unaware that experiences in developing countries are so different from their own.

The accounts of Aboriginal people are even more chilling. Perhaps a third of the population of the Mission died within a two-week period: no family was untouched. As the researchers for the Royal Commission into British Nuclear Testing in Australia discovered, the horrifying memories of the measles epidemic were burned into the minds of the Aboriginal people in the region. For some people, these were closed episodes of pain and grief in the past. For others, the memories were like continually troubling open wounds that refused to heal, because they felt that there had been no satisfactory explanation for the epidemic's particularly severe impact on their communities until they later learnt more about the developments for weapons testing, already underway from 1947.[28]

Such epidemics racking Pitjantjatjara communities must have compromised their health; yet, no reliable baseline health statistics were gathered before the detonations began. In fact, there appears to have been little information gathered at all prior to detonations beginning. The U.K. had been looking for opportunities to test their own weapon systems in order to restore their standing in the alliance with the U.S. They began in Australia: they built a Rocket Range for the firing of non-nuclear weapons at Woomera, South Australia in 1947, then began testing fission bombs in October 1952, with one explosion on the Monte Bello islands, just off the coast of Western Australia. There is simply no data on either the numbers of people who might have been in the path of the Monte Bello explosions, nor on their health status.

Next the British tested two bombs at Emu Junction, north of Woomera, in October 1953, then two more in haste on the Monte Bellos, in May and June 1956, to gather information for the concurrent British thermonuclear testing on Kiritimati Island in the mid-Pacific.

Unlike the first Monte Bello test, there was somewhat more planning for the next tests, code-named Totem 1 and Totem 2, held north of Woomera at Emu Junction in October 1953. A Patrol Officer was directed specifically to protect Aboriginal people: Walter MacDougall, who had been the manager of the sheep flock, kept on Ernabella Mission, but had left in 1947 to work at the Woomera Rocket Range. Aboriginal people therefore knew of his association with the testing and he presumably knew some Pitjantjatjara and related languages.

Despite being designated a 'Patrol Officer', MacDougall was given no vehicle, so he had to travel by train. A few weeks before the Totem tests, MacDougall had attempted to enumerate the population around the Emu Junction test site, travelling to Wallatina pastoral property and other camp sites, but he reported that there simply had not been enough time to do a complete job. There were no surveys on Aboriginal health despite knowledge of the widespread experiences of measles and other viral epidemics across the region in the recent past. It can be assumed that these had compromised the health of Aboriginal people at all the settlement areas, not just Ernabella.[29]

There was, however, substantial documentation created about the conditions of firing the Totem bombs. The meteorologists for the tests were alarmed by the weather conditions, advising in a report known as Report A32 that the wind would be blowing in the same direction through every height, which would act against dispersal of the explosion's radioactive plume and instead concentrate it into a narrow band. If wind direction was over one of the inhabited areas, such as Wallatina, there would be an unacceptably high radioactive contamination of such populated areas.[30]

The meteorological advice was ignored. The test had already been delayed eight days because of poor weather, including rain, and it seems the British military and scientific personnel feared that delay would make the U.K. appear indecisive. Totem 1 was fired in precisely the conditions warned against by the British meteorologists. Its yield was twice that expected and so the warnings issued by the meteorologists were doubly relevant. The persistence of concentrated radioactivity in the detonation plume was demonstrated by the effects on two of the tracking aircraft, which flew through the plume 10 hours after detonation, 400 miles from Emu. On their return to base, they were unexpectedly found to be 'heavily contaminated'.[31]

Yet with all the evidence that the Wallatina or surrounding populations may have been contaminated, no attempt was made to contact them or monitor their future health. There was not even a follow-up population survey: Native Patrol Officer Walter MacDougall did not pass through the area until September of the following year and then only on his way to Ernabella on other business. His failure to notice any problems there was the only British evidence that Totem 1 had not caused health problems. It is difficult to discount the argument that this neglect occurred because the majority of the population at risk was Aboriginal, more vulnerable to radiation because of their prior health and lifestyle but with little access to political power, despite their continued role in the ongoing pastoral operations of the area.[32]

The Yanykuntjatjara people at Wallatina did not forget. They spent many years trying to tell authorities what had happened to them. Yami Lester was one – a community leader by the 1970s, working at the Institute for Aboriginal Development (IAD) in Alice Springs, he spoke to many people in the emerging Aboriginal-controlled health service and legal service there. The investigations they triggered eventually led to the Royal Commission into British Nuclear Testing in Australia and many who had been Wallatina residents testified.[33] Yami later wrote about the events:

> I was thinking it might be a dust storm, but it was quiet .... just rolling and moving quietly .... This thing came over us – like a black smoke or a mist. The older people said they'd never seen anything like it before. Soon afterwards there was sickness in the camp. One of my uncles was pretty bad: he had sort of blisters all over his body and he never got better. There was no clinic at Wallatina. So they took him off to try to get help for him. But he died there, while they were waiting.[34]

Yami Lester's mother, Pingkai, testified that she remembered the low dark *puyu* to have deposited a moist, black substance on the leaves and ground, bringing a strong smoky smell that made her vomit. Like Yami, she recalled some people becoming sick and nauseated over the coming days while others developed sore eyes. Rumours of injury at Wallatina did reach MacDougall and his fellow Patrol Officer, Robert Macauley, in later years, but were never followed up.[35] The Royal Commission took evidence at Wallatina and many of the people who had experienced the *puyu* there gave evidence, as well as Aboriginal and non-Aboriginal witnesses from the Welbourn Hill pastoral property and Mintabie opal field who also remembered the low mist.

Ray Acaster was one of the meteorologists who was on duty at Emu Junction during the Totem tests. He was a co-author of Report A32, which had advised so strongly against firing under the meteorological conditions that day. He has since written about the events, and identified elements in Yanykuntjatjara memories that expand on the original Report A32. Acaster believed that, together, the memories and the Report fully explain what happened that day.[36] Report A32 had not identified any source of moisture in the fallout plume and had strongly emphasised the factor of uniform wind shear through all heights, which it argued would concentrate the radioactive fallout into a narrow cloud. Acaster pointed out in 2002, however, that all the Wallatina survivors recalled the *puyu* being broad and said that it deposited moist or sticky material on skin or on the ground that needed cleaning off. Acaster realised that the crucial factor was the persistence of high moisture content in the atmosphere, reminding readers that the test had been postponed because of rain. Furthermore, he argued that the fallout course through sandhills would have contributed some sideways dispersal to the cloud, ensuring that it was wider than the original Report A32 had predicted. Acaster has argued that the conditions at the time, confirmed by the memories of Aboriginal survivors, would indeed have created a moist, sticky, and highly radioactive cloud that moved low and wide in the directions suggested in A32. This meant that it would have enveloped not only Wallatina but Mintabie and Welbourn Hill, and it was Aboriginal and non-Aboriginal people from these places that gave evidence to the Royal Commission that they remembered seeing the dark low cloud rolling silently towards them.

The southern Pitjantjatjara

The southern Pitjantjatjara are the focus of this fourth brief review. The British began planning in 1954 to develop a permanent test ground to the west of Woomera, in an area they named Maralinga, supposedly meaning 'field of thunder' although the actual language from which the word was taken has never been confirmed. These were extremely arid lands, but the southern Pitjantjatjara were known to travel regularly from the more well-watered areas of the Musgrave Ranges in the north (where Ernabella was situated to the east), down across the desert lands on which Maralinga is situated, towards Ooldea (a community presided over by the missionary Daisy Bates), and the Great Australian Bight. There were ceremonial sites in this arid area that were of significance and needed to be visited.

Tests were conducted at Maralinga in 1956 (four bombs code-named Buffalo) and 1957 (three bombs called Antler). After the Buffalo tests, but before Antler, a small family group, the Milpuddies, had followed a traditional route from the north directly into the Maralinga test area and had camped in a Buffalo bomb crater. Range staff had no idea of their presence until the Milpuddies walked into a radiation monitoring area set up near the bomb sites. Edie Milpuddie, her husband, and two small children were met with panic by Range staff. They were hurriedly tested and found to be contaminated, although adequate records of those measurements were not kept. The family was then showered, their dogs were shot before their eyes, and they were hustled off to Yalata, a Lutheran mission set up in 1951.

Although other members of the family appeared to have suffered few immediate health effects, Edie Milpuddie's experience was different. She was pregnant at the time of her radiation exposure, a fact of which Weapons Research Establishment (WRE) was unaware because they did not attempt to gain effective or appropriate interpretation. Immediately after her arrival at Yalata, Edie went into labour, with her child stillborn. Edie and the Yalata women who assisted her in this labour are usually deeply reluctant to discuss 'woman's business' in public, but they spoke out at the Royal Commission in 1985 because they attribute the stillbirth to 'the poison' to which Edie had been exposed.

The sole concern of Australian and U.K. authorities was to cover up the Milpuddie's experience, as it was feared that such publicity would jeopardise the test programme given increasingly critical public attitudes in 1957. The staff who had witnessed the incident were threatened with 30 years jail under the Official Secrets Act should they ever reveal what had happened, and the family themselves were ignored once they had been dumped at Yalata. The priority was quite simply the tests rather than the safeguarding of Aboriginal health. There was no attempt at follow-up health monitoring.[37]

The effects on Aboriginal people were not limited to their physical health. All the Western Desert owners of the lands that were designated 'prohibited' around the new Maralinga site suffered significant cultural disruption as access was denied to them for traditional ceremonies and travel. The northern Pitjantjatjara recall that the Patrol Officer MacDougall attempted to compensate for his lack of surveillance staff by threatening the Pitjantjatjara away from their lands, terrifying them with mixed images drawn from what he knew of WW2 bombs, traditional culture and a limited understanding of radiation, suggesting evil spirits, death, and horrible disease if they should venture south. The psychological impact of these threats is impossible to estimate, but the social effect of isolating the northern Pitjantjatjara from those in the south, by breaking their established desert travel routes, has been real and persistent.[38]

The southern peoples also suffered both in health terms and culturally. After Ooldea Mission closed in 1952, Aboriginal people had remained living there as they always had, but the selection of nearby Maralinga as the test site in 1954 ensured their removal to Yalata. Many attempted to return to their own country to the north and east but were turned back by Patrol Officer MacDougall and forced to return to Yalata. Not satisfied that the desert Anangu would remain on the coast, MacDougall coerced a number of senior men to return to the area north of

Ooldea and Maralinga, to locate and remove all sacred ceremonial objects. MacDougall called this a 'clean up', which he believed would remove any motivation for Aboriginal people to return. He was wrong: ceremonial demands and the poor, unhappy conditions at Yalata led many Aboriginal people to trek northwards and MacDougall found he was frequently called on to turn back groups of Pitjantjatjara trying to regain their own country.[39]

In a further bizarre strategy, MacDougall influenced the adoption of a moving rationing system at Yalata, which he hoped would keep the Pitjantjatjara residents occupied. Food and water were supplied only at a sequence of depots placed around the reserve land. So the Pitjantjatjara were put on an endless treadmill, shuffled from one tank to the next around the boundary fences of their jail, in a parody of traditional life.[40] The cost of this cultural assault can be measured by the history of conflict, dissatisfaction, alcoholism, and petrol-sniffing at Yalata, as well as by the persistent Anangu demands, continued to the present, to be allowed to return to their country.

Even in his own terms, MacDougall could not do his job: he believed his patrols before the Totem tests at Emu Junction to have been barely adequate and he knew he had failed to survey fully the 'prohibited zone' before the Buffalo tests at Maralinga. An additional Patrol Officer, Robert Macauley, had been appointed for the Maralinga area, but even working together, the patrols succeeded only in a low intensity cover of an arc that went south, east, and north of the test sites. The area west of the 'prohibited zone' was not patrolled until the late 1950s, when MacDougall belatedly began to suspect what was confirmed in 1960: an extended family group of at least 15 Aboriginal people had been living continuously in the northwest of the zone throughout the testing. MacDougall protested bitterly at the lack of resources WRE gave the officers: his protests were dismissed contemptuously, and he was labelled 'subversive'. He was threatened with dismissal by the Australian government in 1956 for 'placing the affairs of a handful of natives above those of the British Commonwealth of Nations'.[41] Yet even MacDougall's view of the limited value of the patrols was optimistic: he continuously overestimated his own knowledge and so the ease with which Aboriginal people penetrated the prohibited zone from the north came as a total surprise to him.[42]

The Pitjantjatjara continued to demand the return of their lands, which became reality when 76,420 square kilometres of land surrounding the Maralinga and Emu test sites were granted to them permanently in the Maralinga Tjarutja Land Rights Act [South Australia] of 1984. The Pitjantjatjara selected a central campsite at Oak Valley, near Lake Dey Dey, northwest of Maralinga. Between 70 and 100 Aboriginal people began permanently living and foraging on these lands; the need to make the old Prohibited Zone safe once more for human occupation became all the more urgent. Yet the research around the Royal Commission demonstrated that the 'minor trials' in these areas were in fact often major explosions. Many led to the wide distribution of highly radioactive contaminants, such as plutonium and caesium-137, each with long half-lives, over vast distances, well outside the boundaries of the old 'Prohibited Zone'.[43]

Bikinians and their ill-fated return

The Bikinian community had lived unhappily on Kili for some years, but kept on asking when they could return to their home. The U.S., however, continued testing nuclear weapons, using Enewetak Atoll as well as other Marshall Islands locations, and then began using Bikini Atoll to test its new fusion bombs with two tests in 1952. In 1954, a third H-bomb was detonated, code-named Bravo.

Bravo was far more powerful than its American makers had expected, blowing apart much of the atoll's coral reef (inadvertently greatly advancing reef science!). Not only was it far larger than expected, it was dirtier. It produced far more radioactive debris than predicted, which fell as white ash across many of the islands of the Marshalls group, as well sending a plume of less visible radioactive particles far across the ocean. In the process, it irradiated the crew of the Japanese fishing boat, the *Daigo Fukuryū Maru* – known as the *Lucky Dragon Number 5* – which limped home with its crew already ill and one dying. The survivors remained in hospital for months.[44]

While there had been little attention paid in the past when it was Marshall Islanders facing irradiation, this injury to an international crew – even though they were humble fishermen – brought the major U.S. failure to predict the consequences of the explosion and ensure safety precautions to worldwide notice. While the Baker detonation at Bikini Atoll in 1946 and Totem 1 at Emu Junction in 1953 were each more destructive than expected, it was Bravo in March 1954 that woke the world to the risks of continuing nuclear testing.

Yet, in the Cold War climate, the Americans kept on testing at Bikini – although there was increasing global protest and mobilisation of opposition. The U.S.S.R. had exploded an H-bomb in a test in August 1953, a year before the U.S. began their H-bomb tests. The British decided that they too needed to have H-bomb capacity and began testing at Kiritimati (Christmas) Island in its colony of the Gilbert and Ellis Islands group in the central Pacific, later to become independent Kiribati. The first U.K. fusion test there, Grapple 1, was in May 1957 and drew on information from the 1956 Australian tests at Maralinga. Further Grapple tests occurred throughout the rest of 1957 and 1958.[45] Eventually, after a series of false starts, a Partial Test Ban Treaty was signed by the U.S., the U.S.S.R., and the U.K. in August 1963, which banned above-ground testing, although the British (and no doubt the others) continued 'minor trials'. These were based at Maralinga, and contributed major contaminants to the test sites for years afterwards.

In 1968, the Bikinians were told that they might be able to return to Bikini Atoll at some stage in the future once residual radiation had been assessed.[46] The surveys produced debatable results and, at the same time, the risks of radioactive exposure were increasingly recognised and allowable radiation limits continually revised downwards, as discussed earlier. Bikinians were deeply troubled by this indecision and were reluctant to return unless their safety could be assured. Their leaders travelled to Washington seeking reassurance but were not satisfied.⁴⁷ There were promises of an effective 'clean-up', re-building had proceeded, and the planting of the coconut trees was finally completed, but then in late 1972, just as the Bikinians were told it was all safe, the AEC announced that the coconut crabs on Bikini Island were still radioactive and could be eaten only in limited numbers.

The conflicting information on the radiological contamination of Bikini caused the Bikini Council to vote not to return to Bikini at the time previously scheduled by American officials but the Council did not try to dissuade those individuals or families who wished to return.⁴⁸ Three extended families did go back, along with workers from other Marshalls islands to help with continued building. By mid-1975, there were 139 people living on Bikini, while a series of scientific investigations added further concerns. Higher levels of radioactivity than expected were beginning to be detected and it appeared that some water sources were dangerously high in radioactivity. Late in 1975, the AEC, on review of the scientists' data, decided that all the local foods grown on Bikini Island, i.e. pandanus, breadfruit, and coconut crabs, were also too radioactive for human consumption. In October 1975, after these new, confusing, and terrifying reports, the Bikinians filed a lawsuit in the U.S. federal court demanding that a complete scientific survey of Bikini and the northern Marshalls be conducted. The lawsuit stated that the U.S. had used highly sophisticated and technical radiation detection equipment at Enewetak Atoll but had refused to employ it at Bikini. The Bikinians won this case, although the U.S. Departments of State, the Interior and Defence bickered for three years about who would pay to have the survey conducted.

While waiting for the radiological survey to be conducted, further discoveries of radiological dangers were made. In May 1977, the level of radioactive strontium-90 in the well water on Bikini Island was found to exceed the U.S. maximum allowed limits. A month later, a Department of Energy study stated that 'All living patterns involving Bikini Island exceed Federal [radiation] guidelines for thirty-year population doses.'⁴⁹ In April 1978, medical examinations performed by the U.S. physicians revealed radiation levels in many of the 139 people on Bikini to be well above the U.S. maximum permissible level. The very next month, the U.S. Interior Department officials described the increase in radioactive caesium-137 in the examined Bikinians as 'incredible'. It seems that, just like the tiny hydroids found by accident to be radioactive in 1947, the human Bikinians were bioaccumulating the atoll's residual radioactivity only in specific organs of their bodies.⁵⁰

The Interior Department then announced plans to move all the people from Bikini 'within 75 to 90 days', and so in September of 1978, Trust Territory officials arrived on Bikini to evacuate once again the people who were living on the atoll. An ironic footnote to the situation is that the long-awaited northern Marshalls radiological survey, forced by the 1975 lawsuit brought by the Bikinians against the U.S. government, finally began only after the people were again relocated from Bikini.⁵¹

Conclusions

All of these stories have been told in more detail elsewhere, but taken together they suggest some of the overall themes that need to be considered. First, the Indigenous peoples in the isolated, arid 'wastelands' or remote oceanic areas that were chosen as test sites were already likely to have compromised health because of the disease effects of recent colonisation and the impacts of warfare. The effects of any exposure to testing-induced radiation were likely to be even worse than if they were suffered by a more robust population.

Second, the definition of places such as the Western Desert in Australia as 'wasteland' and the oceans around Bikini Atoll as 'remote' and 'unused' were definitions that ignored their cultural significance to the Indigenous land and ocean owners. The failure to recognise such alternative cultural meanings not only led to irreparable damage of sites of significance and permanent destruction of lifestyles into the future, but also severely compromised any attempt to offer protection to people near the test site. In just one example, failure to recognise the importance of ceremony to the Pitjantjatjara, condemned to failure of all attempts to obstruct their movements into the irradiated test zones.

Third, there was severe ignorance about the effects of radiation damage as well as about the outcome of any nuclear explosion. Taking the long view of these decades of nuclear testing, it is clear that far more was learnt 30 or 40 years after the first bombs were exploded over Japan than had been known in 1945. The inability to predict accurately either blast power or radiation results of both fission and fusion explosions was demonstrated over and over again. 'Unanticipated' outcomes were far more common, either by overestimating predictions of bomb yields or, more catastrophically, by underestimating predictions of yields, than were accurate predictions. In each case, whether by displacement or by damage, it was invariably Indigenous and/or disempowered peoples who suffered the consequences.

Fourth, it was clear in the documentation of both the U.S. and the U.K. tests that there was only contempt and disinterest for the Indigenous peoples whose lands and waters were being damaged for the testing. The interests of the testing countries were in each case the overriding concern. British-born Australian Chief Scientist, Alan Butement, threatened to sack Patrol Officer Walter MacDougall when he expressed concerns about the inadequacy of protection for Aboriginal people in 1956, saying MacDougall was 'placing the affairs of a handful of natives above those of the British Commonwealth of Nations'.[52]

Fifth, each of the groups of people who were moved off their lands was tenacious in their sustained desire and demands to be returned to their homes. In the case of the Bikinians and the Pitjantjatjara, the two peoples whose stories have been told here, each remained committed in their demands to be allowed to return to their homes or, at the very least, to insist on the remediation of the damage that had been done. This commitment to their country, and their sustained and often courageous advocacy for its repair, lasted decades and indeed continues to this day.

Sixth, the nature of the damage they suffered in these tests has never adequately been recognised. This paper has already pointed out the situation of the people in each of the test areas discussed, who already had compromised health conditions before tests began, which made them even more vulnerable to the damage that blasts and radiation could do. The many campaigns to support the people displaced by the testing programmes have however concentrated on somatic (physical) damage. As the epidemiologists who gave evidence before the Australian Royal Commission into British Nuclear Testing made clear, with no baseline data and very little data collected after any of the tests among the irradiated or displaced populations, it would be difficult to identify damage. In addition, these populations were all relatively small, and epidemiology – particularly in cases of radiation damage – needs 'big data'. With small population figures, it is simply impossible to separate out the patterns of radiation damage from other forms of environmental damage.

Yet what each of these case study reviews indicate is the intense trauma and distress that each of these groups of people suffered. Whole communities of people were worried literally sick for decades about the risks to themselves, the risks to their homes, the risks to their futures. Kilon Buano's account of how exhausted and deeply distressed the Bikinian leaders were in the face of so much uncertainty and the demands to make such terrible decisions is deeply moving – and gives just a hint of the burden that so many people carried for many years. Just as heart-rending were the memories of some Aboriginal people at Ernabella, recorded during the Royal Commission research, about their years of worrying over the causes of the measles plague and their conviction that only the poison of warfare associated with the bomb tests could explain why it was only their people had died in such terrible numbers.[53] The burden of such sustained anxiety can only have added intolerably to the deep distress of displacement and the loss of a future.

None of this was seen by the many people all over the world who were horrified by the news of the Bravo test on 1 March 1954. This appalling detonation produced far more radioactive contaminants than had been expected.[54] All the newspaper reports covering the problems with the Bravo detonation addressed the radiation dangers posed for world populations and the dangers of such a weapon for world peace. Yet, the failure to predict the effects of the detonation was only really exposed because it caused an international incident by injuring crewmembers of another country's vessel – mobilising global concern and protest that Winston Churchill described as an 'intense sensation'.[55] It energised the Peace movements across the West and much of Asia, which continued to build strength and finally to exert real political power in many of the countries that had led the testing programme.[56] And yet, very few of the Peace activists of the 1950s and 1960s were aware of, or interested in, the Indigenous peoples like the Bikinians and the Pitjantjatjara. It was only after many years – and still more wearying journeys by the leaders of the Indigenous peoples themselves – that their stories began to be told.

The very isolation that made their lands and seas so attractive as nuclear test sites also made it harder for the people who carried the real burden of the tests to get their stories out into the world, but also to meet each other and to build a united front. As any of the narratives of these people's movements makes clear, spokespeople travelled endless miles across oceans or deserts – or both – to campaign for justice and to build support. Archie Barton was a spokesperson for the Maralinga Tjaraja community during the Royal Commission and, after the Land Rights Act had restored title, he became a tireless advocate for a serious clean-up of the continuing contamination of Aboriginal lands. It was in this role that he made the long journey to meet the Bikinians on Kili Island early in 1988. By this time, both communities had gained title of sorts over their homes, although Bikinians had been displaced a second time and the Pitjantjatjara, although now owning the title to Maralinga, had no effective access because, just like Bikini Atoll, the land was still contaminated. Barton invited the Bikinian leaders to come to Pitjantjatjara lands to meet the elders, who were the authorities on whose behalf the whole campaign had been waged.

The Bikinian leaders decided to take up the invitation and a group of them, led by elder Nathan Note, set out for the meeting, with Jack Niedenthal as assistant.[57] It took five days of air travel – via Adelaide and Ceduna – before the Bikinians arrived in Oak Valley (apparently thinking it was Maralinga itself) to meet the Pitjantjatjara community. With Niedenthal acting uncomfortably as an interpreter, and with a degree of confusion on all sides, the elders of both communities told each other their people's respective exodus stories and conferred about what strategies might be most helpful in applying pressure to achieve effective clean-ups. Niedenthal wrote:

> I studied the small circle that was a mix of islanders and aborigines as we sat around trying to figure out just what was up with all this. I thought about how this grouping personified the tragedies that can result when larger nations, in their unquenchable struggle to become even more powerful, show callous disregard toward a smaller country and the ancient human life that resides within its borders.[58]

Despite the challenges for the two groups, each of them has continued to travel and to campaign for justice. But the major change since 1988 has been the placement of satellites, which allows these small, remote, and embattled communities to have full use of the internet. Each of these communities now is networked into the various global Indigenous, anti-nuclear, and environmental movements, overcoming the deep disadvantage that they each faced when they had to travel for five days to reach each other. Yet for both groups, the problems of residual contamination continue to haunt their relationships with their homes and their futures.

Appendix

Date	Bombers	Location & type	Land (& sea) owners
30 June 1946	U.S.	Bikini Atoll, Marshall Islands. Fission.	Marshall Islanders affected by fallout. Bikinians displaced.
29 Aug 1949	U.S.S.R.	Semipalatinsk, Kazakhstan. Fission.	Mobile peoples on border between Kazakhstan and Russia.
27 Jan 1951	U.S.	Nevada Test Site, 65 miles north of Las Vegas Fission.	Lands of Shoshone and Southern Paiute peoples. All those downwind of the test site, particularly in Utah, experienced radioactive fallout effects. Native peoples (Shoshone, Southern Paiute, and others) living on their lands received 'substantial exposure' due to diets, e.g. eating small game, see Frohmberg et al., 'The assessment of radiation exposures'.
3 Oct 1952	U.K.	Monte Bello Islands, Australia. Fission.	Aboriginal people in mid-western Australia.
1 Nov 1952	U.S.	Bikini Atoll. First fusion explosion	Marshall Islanders. Bikinians remain displaced.
15–27 Oct 1953	U.K.	Emu Junction. Fission. Code named *Totem 1* and *Totem 2*. *Totem 1* fired against meteorological advice and far larger than expected.	*Pitjantjatjara-Yanykuntjatjara* people at Wallatina, and non-Aboriginal people at Mintabie and Welbourn Hill station saw fallout cloud and may have suffered effects.
1 Mar 1954	U.S.	Bikini Atoll, third ever fusion (H-bomb), code named *Bravo*. Far larger blast than expected. Wide surrounding region irradiated.	Marshall Islanders affected by fallout. The *Lucky Dragon*, a Japanese fishing boat, severely affected by fallout, one death, surviving crewmembers hospitalised for months.
July 1954	U.S.S.R.	Novaya Zemlya Island (a sub-Arctic island off north coast of Russia). First Soviet fusion test.	*Nenets* (Samoyed peoples), Indigenous mobile reindeer herders (similar lifestyle to *Sami* in Scandinavia).
16 May & 19 June 1956	U.K.	Monte Bello Islands. Fission.	Aboriginal people in WA.

Date	Bombers	Location & type	Land (& sea) owners
27 Sept–22 Oct 1956	U.K.	Maralinga. Fission.	*Pitjantjatjara* and others, central and southern South Australia.
15 & 31 May & 19 June 1957	U.K.	Gilbert & Ellice Island – Malden Island. First U.K. fusion bombs. Code named *Grapple*.	Kiribati Islanders.
14 Sept–9 Oct 1957	U.K.	Maralinga. Fission, *Antler* series. Three bombs.	*Pitjantjatjara* and others, central and southern South Australia, displaced.
8 Nov 1957	U.K.	Gilbert & Ellice Islands colony: Kiritimati (Christmas) Island. *Grapple X*. Fusion.	Kiribati Islanders.
28 Apr, 22 Aug 1958	U.K.	Gilbert & Ellice Islands colony: Kiritimati (Christmas) Island. *Grapple Y* and *Grapple Z*. Fusion.	Kiribati Islanders.
28 Apr–18 Aug 1958	U.S.	Enewetak Atoll, Marshall Islands and Johnston Atoll, north Pacific 35 bombs; multiple types.	Marshall Islanders. Johnston Atoll between Marshalls and Hawaii.

Notes

1 J. Masco, *Nuclear Borderlands: The Manhattan Project in Post-Cold War New Mexico* (Princeton, NJ and Oxford: Princeton University Press, 2006), 1.
2 See the Appendix, drawn from Nic Maclellan, *Grappling with the Bomb: Britain's Pacific H-Bomb Tests* (Canberra: ANU Press, 2017); R.H Clarke and J. Valentin, 'The History of ICRP and the Evolution of its Policies,' *Annals of the International Commission for Radiation Protection* 109 (2009): 75–110; E. Frohmberg et al., 'The Assessment of Radiation Exposures in Native American Communities from Nuclear Weapons Testing in Nevada,' *Risk Analysis* 20, no. 1 (2000): 101–111.
3 Only in 1954 did early results of genetic testing on foetuses by Japanese doctors begin to circulate among Western doctors. See the International Medical Commission preliminary report of their visit to Japan in 1955: International Medical Commission, 'Effects of Atomic and Hydrogen Bomb Explosions,' *The Lancet* 269, no. 6882 (1995): 187, 199–201.
4 William C. Inkret et al., 'A Brief History of Radiation Protection Standards,' *Los Alamos Science* 23 (1995): 116–123; Clarke and Valentin, 'The History of IRCP', 104.
5 Martin, Laura J., 'Proving Grounds: Ecological Fieldwork in the Pacific and the Materialization of Ecosystems,' *Environmental History* 23, no. 3 (2018): 567–592.
6 International Medical Commission, 'Effects,' 201.
7 'Hydrogen Bomb News Prompted Churchill's Washington Excursion,' *Canberra Times*, 14 July 1954, 1.

8. Martin, 'Proving Grounds,' 572.
9. Jack Niedenthal, *For the Good of Mankind: A History of the People of Bikini and their Islands* (Majuro, Marshall Islands: Bravo Publishers, 2013), 16–22. Jack Niedenthal was a Peace Corps volunteer who married a Bikinian, speaks fluent Marshallese, and lived for many years with the Bikini community on various islands. His book records numerous oral history accounts by Bikini community members, including a discussion about the widespread affiliation with Christianity and the continuing influence of traditional spirituality. Niedenthal is currently the Secretary of Health & Human Services for the Marshall Islands Government (appointed 2019) and the President of the Majuro Cooperative School (2003 to present).
10. Niedenthal, *For the Good of Mankind*, 86–87.
11. Many others have made this point explicitly; see, for example, M.X. Mitchell, 'Offshoring American Environmental Law: Land, Culture, and Marshall Islanders' Struggles for Self-Determination during the 1970s,' *Environmental History* 22, no. 2 (2017): 212.
12. Niedenthal, *For the Good of Mankind*, 1, 45. Rubon Juda recollecting his father, King Juda, in an interview with Niedenthal, December 1989.
13. Jonathon Weisgall, *Operation Crossroads: The Atomic Tests at Bikini Atoll* (Annapolis: Naval Institute Press, 1994), 113, 162; Stewart Firth, 'Review of *Operation Crossroads: The Atomic Tests at Bikini Atoll*, by Jonathan M. Weisgall,' *The Contemporary Pacific* (Fall 1995): 380–381.
14. Niedenthal, *For the Good of Mankind*.
15. Martin, 'Proving Grounds', 571; Kessai Note, 'Memories of Bikini Advocate and Marshall Is President (2000–2008),' interview by Ian Johnstone, *Radio New Zealand*, 5 August 2011, audio, 37:13, https://www.radionz.co.nz/international/programmes/new-flags-flying/audio/2495114/hon-kessai-note.
16. See photograph: 'Sailors wash down the highly contaminated deck of the captured German battleship USS Prinz Eugene (IX 300) after the Able test.' (NARA, Still Pictures Unit, Record Group 80-G, box 2228, folder 627483–627519), in 'Bikini A-Bomb Tests,' Briefing Book #555, ed. William Burr with Stav Geffner. National Security Archive, 22 July 2016. https://nsarchive.gwu.edu/briefing-book/environmental-diplomacy-nuclear-vault/2016-07-22/bikini-bomb-tests-july-1946.
17. Stafford L. Warren, 'Conclusions: Tests Proved Irresistible Spread of Radioactivity,' *Life*, 11 August 1947, 86, 88; David Bradley, *No Place to Hide* (Boston, MA: Little, Brown and Company, 1948), xii.
18. Bradley, *No Place to Hide*, 174–178; Alexander Hammond, 'Review of David Bradley, *No Place to Hide*,' *Bulletin of the Atomic Scientists*, 39, no. 9 (1983): 37–39.
19. Hammond, 'Review,' 39.
20. See discussion and references later in this chapter.
21. Martin, 'Proving Grounds,' 572–578.
22. Harold Ickes, 'Man to Man' column, *Honolulu Star*, 29 September 1947, quoted by Jack Niedenthal in 'A History of the People of Bikini following Nuclear Weapons Testing,' *Health Physics* 3, no. 1 (1997): 30. Ickes had been the U.S. Secretary of the Interior from 1933 until 1946, and wrote these as a syndicated column series, published by various newspapers and later in the *New Republic*. Typescripts of all the columns are held in the Syracuse University Archival Collection.
23. 'Life While Living in Tents on Kwajalein Atoll,' as described by Kilon Bauno to Jack Niedenthal in 1988 and 1990 (all in Marshallese). Kilon Bauno, who died in 1992, was the *iroij* [leader] of the Bikinians, and, earlier in his life, a councilman. This was his first-hand account of life on Kwajalein and the decisions that had to be made by the islanders, which included their transition to Kili Island. As cited in Niedenthal, *For the Good of Mankind*, 53–55.
24. Niedenthal, *For the Good of Mankind*, 54–55.
25. There is a substantial literature on the relationships between Western Desert peoples and their land, their *country*. See, for example, Fred R. Myers, *Pintupi Country, Pintupi Self* (Los Angeles: University of California Press, 1991).

26 For detailed discussions of these epidemics and Aboriginal memories, see H. Goodall, 'The Whole Truth and Nothing But ... Reflections of a Field Worker on the Intersections of Western Law, Aboriginal History and Community Memory,' *Journal of Australian Studies: Power, Knowledge and Aborigines* (special issue) 16, no. 35 (1992): 104–119; and H. Goodall, 'Colonialism and Catastrophe: Contested Remembrance of Measles and Bombs in a Pitjantjatjara Community,' in *Memory and History in Twentieth Century Australia*, ed. Paula Hamilton and Kate Darian-Smith (Melbourne: Oxford University Press, 1994), 55–76.

27 Charles Duguid, *Doctor and the Aborigines* (Adelaide: Rigby, 1972), 156–157; Melba Turner (sister-in-charge, Ernabella), 'First-hand Account of the 1948 Measles Epidemic,' Appendix 2, in *The People in Between: The Pitjantjatjara People of Ernabella*, ed. Winifred Hilliard (London: Hodder and Stoughton, 1968), 230–236.

28 Goodall, 'Colonialism and Catastrophe,' 55–76. As a researcher for the Aboriginal submission to this Royal Commission, and then living in Ernabella, I was involved in extensive oral history and archival historical research and analysis about the period from 1940 to 1975. My article 'Colonialism and Catastrophe' is an extended investigation of the way the 1948 measles episode has been remembered and interpreted among Pitjantjatjara communities.

29 Goodall, 'Colonialism and Catastrophe.'

30 Meteorological Report, A32, the meteorologists' report to the Weapons Range Controlling Authority detailing their concerns prior to the firing of Totem 1. The document was discovered by Counsel Assisting the Royal Commission into British Nuclear Tests in Australia [hereafter RCBNTA], and discussed extensively in their Report. *British Nuclear Tests in Australia*, vol. 1, 20 November 1985, 216.

31 RCBNTA, Report, vol. 1, 20 November 1985, 216.

32 Some years later, once the technology of the pastoral industry changed, with motorbikes and helicopters replacing Aboriginal stockmen on horseback, policies shifted to 'assimilation' and patrol officers 'encouraged' or forced Aboriginal people to move into larger settlements like Ernabella or towns like Alice Springs.

33 RCBNTA, Minutes of Evidence: Wallatina; Geoffrey Eames and Andrew Collett, 'Royal Commission into British Nuclear Tests in Australia: Final Submission by Counsel on Behalf of Aboriginal Organisations and Individuals', AIAS R85/56, Adelaide, 1985; Eames and Collett, 'Aboriginal Collation', statements of evidence presented to the Royal Commission, 14 volumes, 1985.

34 Yami Lester, *Yami: The Autobiography of Yami Lester* (Alice Springs: IAD Press, 1993). Quoted in Ray Acaster, 'Sherlock Holmes and the Grim Reaper of Wallatinna: Aboriginal Oral History Solves a Scientific Mystery,' *Oral History Association of Australia Journal* 24 (2002): 18, 21.

35 RCBNTA, Minutes of Evidence: Patrol Officer Long, vol 1: 174–194.

36 Acaster, 'Sherlock Holmes.'

37 RCBNTA, Report, vol. 1, 319–322.

38 See P. Toyne and D. Vachon, *Growing Up the Country: The Pitjantjatjara Struggle for Their Land* (Melbourne: McPhee Gribble, 1984), 33–51.

39 Eames and Collett, 'RCBNTA: Final Submission.'

40 Eames and Collett, 'RCBNTA: Final Submission,' 431–433.

41 Alan Butement, Chief Scientist, Australian Department of Supply, see Eames and Collett, 'RCBNTA: Final Submission,' 300; RCBNTA, Report, vol. 1, 309. Butement was British-born and educated and it is hard to believe that he was not expressing the interests of the British government here as well as those of the conservative Australian government of Robert Menzies.

42 Eames and Collett, 'RCBNTA: Final Submission,' 25–38, 63–86; RCBNTA, Report, vol. 1, 299–319.

43 RCBNTA, Report, vol. 2, 395–415, and Appendix G: Chronology, 8–11.

44 Oishi Matashichi, *The Day the Sun Rose in the West: Bikini, the Lucky Dragon and I* (Honolulu: University of Hawai'i Press, 2011), 26. For an account in the Japanese press,

see front page of *Yomiuri Shimbun*, 16 March 1954, with headlines 'Japanese Fishermen Encounter Bikini Nuclear Test'. The Australian teacher Lucy Woodcock visited Japan and reported to the NSW Peace Council, published in *Tribune*, 10 August 1955, after interviewing the survivors of the *Lucky Dragon* in hospital where they were 'quarantined'. See also the animated film directed by Keith Reimink, *Day of the Western Sunrise* (2018, animation, 75 minutes).
45 Maclellan, *Grappling with the Bomb*, 1–17.
46 Niedenthal, *For the Good of Mankind*, 7–12.
47 Niedenthal, *For the Good of Mankind*, 82–85.
48 Jack Niedenthal, 'A Short History of the People of Bikini Atoll,' accessed 18 August 2020, https://www.bikiniatoll.com/history.html.
49 Niedenthal, *For the Good of Mankind*, 10.
50 Niedenthal, *For the Good of Mankind*, 10; Martin, 'Proving Grounds,' 582.
51 Niedenthal, *For the Good of Mankind*, 12, 87–88.
52 Alan Butement, Chief Scientist, Australian Department of Supply, see Eames and Collett, 'RCBNTA: Final Submission,' 300; RCBNTA, Report, vol. 1, 309.
53 Goodall, 'Colonialism and Catastrophe.'
54 International Medical Commission, 'Effects,' 187, 199–201. The Commission pointed out that although the widespread contamination of crop-bearing land in Japan and the fish across the Pacific (from the coast of Japan south to PNG and Australia, and from Taiwan in the west to Hawaii in the east), the health impacts on the Marshall Islanders were far worse as they suffered 'the bloody diarrhoea, epilation and leucopenia of radiation disease'.
55 'Hydrogen Bomb News Prompted Churchill's Washington Excursion,' *Canberra Times*, 14 July 1954, 1. For an account in the Japanese press, see the front page of *Yomiuri Shimbun*, 16 March 1954, with headline 'Japanese Fishermen Encounter Bikini Nuclear Test'; also 'Death Ash', photograph and translation in Matashichi, *The Day the Sun Rose*, 26.
56 Lucy Woodcock's reports to NSW Peace Council, *Tribune*, 21 December 1954; 10 August 1955, after interviewing the survivors of the *Lucky Dragon* in Japan.
57 Niedenthal, *For the Good of Mankind*, 65–67.
58 Niedenthal, *For the Good of Mankind*, 67.

Bibliography

Acaster, Ray. 'Sherlock Holmes and the Grim Reaper of Wallatinna: Aboriginal Oral History Solves a Scientific Mystery.' *Oral History Association of Australia Journal* 24 (2002): 18–24.
Bradley, David. *No Place to Hide*. Boston, MA: Little, Brown and Company, 1948.
Clarke, R.H., and J. Valentin. 'The History of ICRP and the Evolution of its Policies.' *Annals of the International Commission for Radiation Protection* 109 (2009): 75–110.
Duguid, Charles. *Doctor and the Aborigines*. Adelaide: Rigby, 1972.
Firth, Stewart. 'Review of *Operation Crossroads: The Atomic Tests at Bikini Atoll*, by Jonathan M Weisgall.' *The Contemporary Pacific* (Fall 1995): 380–381.
Frohmberg E., R. Goble, V. Sanchez, and D. Quigley. 'The Assessment of Radiation Exposures in Native American Communities from Nuclear Weapons Testing in Nevada.' *Risk Analysis* 20, no. 1 (2000): 101–111.
Goodall, H. 'The Whole Truth and Nothing But … Reflections of a Field Worker on the Intersections of Western Law, Aboriginal History and Community Memory.' *Journal of Australian Studies: Power, Knowledge and Aborigines* (special issue) 16, no. 35 (1992): 104–119.
Goodall, H. 'Colonialism and Catastrophe: Contested Remembrance of Measles and Bombs in a Pitjantjatjara Community.' In *Memory and History in Twentieth Century Australia*,

edited by Paula Hamilton and Kate Darian-Smith, 55–76. Melbourne: Oxford University Press, 1994.
Hammond, Alexander. 'Review of David Bradley, *No Place to Hide*.' *Bulletin of the Atomic Scientists*, 39, no. 9 (1983): 37–39.
'Hydrogen Bomb News Prompted Churchill's Washington Excursion.' *Canberra Times*, 14 July 1954.
Inkret, William C., Charles B. Meinhold, and John C. Taschner. 'A Brief History of Radiation Protection Standards.' *Los Alamos Science* 23 (1995): 116–123.
International Medical Commission. 'Effects of Atomic and Hydrogen Bomb Explosions.' *The Lancet* 269, no. 6882 (1955): 187, 199–201.
Lester, Yami. *Yami: The Autobiography of Yami Lester*. Alice Springs: IAD Press, 1993.
Maclellan, Nic. *Grappling with the Bomb: Britain's Pacific H-Bomb Tests*. Canberra: ANU Press, 2017.
Martin, Laura J. 'Proving Grounds: Ecological Fieldwork in the Pacific and the Materialization of Ecosystems.' *Environmental History* 23, no. 3 (2018): 567–592.
Masco, J. *Nuclear Borderlands: The Manhattan Project in Post-Cold War New Mexico*. Princeton, NJ and Oxford: Princeton University Press, 2006.
Matashichi, Oishi. *The Day the Sun Rose in the West: Bikini, the Lucky Dragon and I*. Honolulu: University of Hawai'i Press, 2011.
Mitchell, M.X. 'Offshoring American Environmental Law: Land, Culture, and Marshall Islanders' Struggles for Self-Determination During the 1970s.' *Environmental History* 22, no. 2 (2017): 209–234.
Myers, Fred R. *Pintupi Country, Pintupi Self*. Los Angeles: University of California Press, 1991.
Niedenthal, Jack. 'A History of the People of Bikini following Nuclear Weapons Testing.' *Health Physics* 3, no. 1 (1997): 28–36.
Niedenthal, Jack. *For the Good of Mankind: A History of the People of Bikini and Their Islands*. Majuro, Marshall Islands: Bravo Publishers, 2013.
Niedenthal, Jack. 'A Short History of the People of Bikini Atoll.' Accessed 18 August 2020. https://www.bikiniatoll.com/history.html.
Note, Kessai. 'Memories of Bikini Advocate and Marshall Is President (2000–2008).' Interview by Ian Johnstone. *Radio New Zealand*, 5 August 2011. Audio, 37:13. https://www.radionz.co.nz/international/programmes/new-flags-flying/audio/2495114/hon-kessai-note.
Reimink, Keith, dir. *Day of the Western Sunrise*. 2018. Animation, 75 minutes.
Toyne, P., and D. Vachon. *Growing Up the Country: The Pitjantjatjara Struggle for Their Land*. Melbourne: McPhee Gribble, 1984.
Turner, Melba. 'First-hand Account of the 1948 Measles Epidemic.' Appendix 2. In *The People in Between: The Pitjantjatjara People of Ernabella*, edited by Winifred Hilliard, 230–236. London: Hodder and Stoughton, 1968.
Warren, Stafford L. 'Conclusions: Tests Proved Irresistible Spread of Radioactivity.' *Life*, 11 August 1947.
Weisgall, Jonathon. *Operation Crossroads: The Atomic Tests at Bikini Atoll*. Annapolis: Naval Institute Press, 1994.

Archival Sources

Eames, Geoffrey, and Andrew Collett. 'Aboriginal Collation', Statements of Evidence Presented to the Royal Commission, 14 volumes, 1985.
Eames, Geoffrey, and Andrew Collett. 'Royal Commission into British Nuclear Tests in Australia: Final Submission by Counsel on Behalf of Aboriginal Organisations and Individuals', AIAS R85/56, Adelaide, 1985.
Royal Commission into British Nuclear Tests in Australia (RCBNTA). *British Nuclear Tests in Australia*, 20 November 1985.

'Sailors Wash Down the Highly Contaminated Deck of the Captured German Battleship USS Prinz Eugene (IX 300) after the Able Test.' (NARA, Still Pictures Unit, Record Group 80-G, box 2228, folder 627483–627519). In 'Bikini A-Bomb Tests,' Briefing Book #555, edited by William Burr with Stav Geffner. National Security Archive, 22 July 2016. https://nsarchive.gwu.edu/briefing-book/environmental-diplomacy-nuclear-vault/2016-07-22/bikini-bomb-tests-july-1946.

20
THE BONES OF OUR MOTHER

Adivasi dispossession in an Indian state

Devleena Ghosh

> Leaving behind their homes,
> Their soil, and bales of straw
> Fleeing the roof over their heads, they often ask:
> O, city!
> Are you ever wrenched by the very roots
> In the name of so-called progress?[1]

The events related in this article happened in Kipling land. Mowgli, Baloo, Bagheera, and Sher Khan lived within these forests. Even Kipling, that Orientalist writer par excellence, recognised the ancient history and link to the land of the Adivasi Gond inhabitants of Chhattisgarh. 'So they sent for the head-man of the nearest tribe of wandering Gonds – little, wise, and very black hunters, living in the deep Jungle, whose fathers came of the oldest race in India – the aboriginal owners of the land.'[2] State control of these spaces, after Indian independence, continued the history of Adivasi marginalisation and dispossession, with the ongoing advocacy of scientific forestry, the intensive cultivation of commercial timber and other forest products, the mapping and extraction of forest resources, and a crackdown on shifting agriculture.

I met the villagers in their meeting hall to discuss their resistance to coal mining and their struggles to save their homes. In the distance, there was a crocodile of women walking towards the forests surrounding the village. They were boundary mapping, as required for claims that might be made under the complicated processes of the *Forest Rights Act*. Never before had the codification of their rights to land been so important. The *Forest Rights Act* confers many rights on Adivasis, but it also illuminates their changing relationship with the modern Indian state. Legal rights have to be written, on *pattas*, or ownership certificates. There must be material archives, not just those of memory or oral history.

The nexus between resource extraction and indigenous dispossession in the state of Chhattisgarh is complex and fraught. My research between 2014 and 2018 focussed on three villages in the district of Sarguja, two of which – Salhi and Ghatbarra – were particularly affected by the Parsa East Kete Basan (PEKB) mine and its extensions, and the third – Madanpur – was the site of protest movements against this expansion.

The stories I heard were ones of dispossession, displacement, and resistance. Chhattisgarh, a rapidly developing state in Central India, has one of the highest populations of indigenous forest dwellers – Scheduled Tribe, or Adivasi. They account for about 10% of Adivasis in India.[3] Chhattisgarh is also rich in mineral resources, ranking second in the nation for coal reserves and production, contributing over 20% to total national coal production. Many of these reserves are under pristine and dense contiguous tracts of forest that span over 40% of the state. The forests are home to perennial water sources, rare plants, and wildlife, including elephants and leopards, and contain resources essential to the livelihood of the Adivasis. These forests are now under major threat from coal mines, and the Adivasis there are part of an ongoing resistance to the loss of their land and livelihood. Several forest villages have been marked for new coal mines and their inhabitants have been protesting the compulsory acquisition of their villages and forest land, using both civic and legal remedies. In addition, the previous State and current Federal Governments have always been enthusiastically pro-development and pro-mining; the mining corporations are not only well-resourced but well-connected at all levels, government and bureaucratic. Those who oppose mining are labelled as Maoist by the police and subject to arrest and intimidation. Local people have had little recourse when dispossessed of their land or for the loss of their livelihoods. In spite of this, and to the increasing annoyance of the government and bureaucracy, there is a continuing strong resistance to land and forest alienation.

The narratives invoked by the Adivasis in their struggles against the mines were simple but powerful. They reiterated their rights to '*jal, jangal, jamin*' or 'water, land, forest'. This slogan was imbued with their fear of the loss of home, livelihood, and habitat. The forest, for them, was inscribed in their paddy and grazing land, marred by the pollution in the rivers and the air and the compromising of their religious rituals in which the forest was essential, the gods buried in the unquiet woods who emerged in terrible anger when their holy sites were damaged. A new generation of Adivasi poets, writers, and artists articulated this with poignant eloquence:

> We're here at the bazaar!
> What would you like to buy, the shopkeeper asked.
> Brother, a little rain, a handful of wet earth,
> A bottle of river, and that mountain preserved
> There, hanging on that wall, a piece of nature as well.
> And why is the rain so dear, pray tell?
> The shopkeeper said – This wetness is not of here!
> It comes from another sphere.
> Times are slack, have ordered just a sack.

Fumbling for money in the corner of my sari,
I untied the knot only to see
In place of a few folded rupees
The crumpled folds of my entire being.[4]

Background and history

The exploitation of natural resources, whether minerals or forests, was imperative to the European developmental discourses of the nineteenth century. These discourses formed a complex of the values and institutions of modernity that were assumed to be inevitable, universal, permanent, and Western, with an 'ineluctable destiny to transform the whole world into a replica of itself'.[5] Frederick Lugard's influential book on the 'dual mandate' for British colonial rule drew on the colonial experience of India and Africa to argue for the sacred trust of colonial officials who undertook the 'grave responsibility' of the imperial project. Colonial power was to ensure *inter alia* 'the institution of courts of justice, the supervision of native courts, the protection of the peasantry from oppression by their rulers, and the deposition of the latter when incorrigible, the reorganisation or imposition of taxation for revenue, the prohibition of slave-raiding or slave-dealing...'.[6] Such duties might involve 'the disposal in some cases of unused lands or minerals', for example, because

> the civilised nations have at last recognised that while on the one hand the abounding wealth of the tropical regions of the earth must be developed and used for the benefit of mankind, on the other hand an obligation rests on the controlling Power not only to safeguard the material rights of the natives, but to promote their moral and educational progress.[7]

The Crown alone should acquire rights in perpetuity in lands and minerals, acting as 'trustee for the natives on the one hand, and as custodian for the development of the country for the needs of civilised mankind on the other'.[8] The concept of modernity and industrial development hold particular relevance for colonised and decolonising spaces, playing a prominent role in empire, as signifying particular rational, empirical cultural practices essential to civilisation.

Such extractivism and progress were inextricably linked in the British colonial imagination. In the nineteenth century, railways were a major reason for deforestation in colonial India. Wood was used as fuel for engines and brick kilns and also for sleepers and carriages. In the early 1880s, an inspector-general of Indian forests estimated an annual railway demand of over 1,000,000 sleepers, each of which required one hardwood tree.[9] This increased the exploitation of India's forests and the displacement of forest-dwelling people. This story of forest depletion was repeated all across India.

The colonial forest department was created in 1864 to ensure a steady supply of timber for railway construction. The idea of protecting forests was not about conserving the ecological balance or protecting the environment but for the uninterrupted supply of firewood to the railways and for the protection of the commercial interest of English railway companies and the government of India. When the forests were declared as 'reserved' for government and commercial use only, the forest dwellers were forced to move out. This triggered serious clashes between people and colonial foresters as the former resisted state encroachment on their age-old customary rights to the use of forest resources for sustenance.[10] The *Indian Forest Act, 1878* was a chief instrument of subjugation as it legalised state control over forests. The Act was implemented through a well-established bureaucratic system of the Indian Forestry Service.[11] The colonial state took great care in creating records on the Adivasis, but the process consistently recorded them as backwards, thereby inaugurating the perception of the indigenes as uncivilised.[12]

Tribes and Adivasis are illegible in modern state archives, except as objects of counter-insurgency and/or policy. The colonial state upheld the Lockean principle of property: land, found given in nature and held in common, became property only through the investment of human labour. Locke's political thought was embodied in colonial India through the *Permanent Settlement* (1793) and the *Indian Forest Acts* (1865 and 1878). Tribes were defined as backwards as they did not use land purely as property and resource but simply inhabited it and sometimes sacralised it. They often claimed lands and forests on 'unverifiable' and 'irrational' grounds – they were the first settlers of such land and it was the abode of their gods and ancestral spirits.[13]

Colonial and modern attempts to 'pacify' tribes were primarily attempts to turn them into productive peasant communities. Colonial forest laws governed the lives and futures of Adivasis for well over 50 years after independence.[14] Post-independence, nation-building in India followed the same developmental agenda, emphasising coal mining and coal-based power generation, which became synonymous with the discourse of India's economic and social development. The amelioration of poverty in India's development narratives became inextricably linked to the availability of modern energy services.[15] Since much of the coal resource was based in forested lands, Adivasis became the unwitting barriers to its extraction.

Shiv Visvanathan recounts in his 2006 Verrier Elwin Lecture that the first Prime Minister of India, Jawaharlal Nehru, recognised that Adivasis were different from other citizens of the new India. He invited Adivasi leaders to Delhi for a conference at which Vallabhbhai Patel, a major figure of the independence struggle, insisted, 'Our preamble is non-negotiable. Our borders are non-negotiable.' In reply, Adivasi leader Jaipal Singh said,

> There is little you are offering us. The Constitution is yours. The borders are yours. The sovereignty is yours. The flag is yours. What is ours? What is it that is both Adivasi and Indian in the Constitution? What is the shared legacy, the common weave? You have defined rights, the isms, the industry, the science, let something be ours.

It was then that Nehru proposed that maybe Singh and other Adivasi leaders could define the Directive Principles of State Policy, the non-justiciable part of the Indian Constitution which, Nehru added, 'is a vision of the future'. Another Adivasi leader, Ram Dayal Munda, noted the irony, 'Your past as your future, our anthropology now as your science fiction.' Over the next two days, these Adivasis wrote or itemised the dreams of the future into the Directive Principles which became one of the most vibrant dialogues about the future of India.[16]

The rhetoric of modernity that equated colonial governance and technological transformation has power and resilience to this day. Modernity's authoritative narrative of developmentalism, its equation of progress with technology and growth, has continued into twenty-first-century India. The first Prime Minister of India, Jawaharlal Nehru's famous dictum about dams being the temples of modern India[17] has parallels in the statements made by current Indian leaders about the essential place that coal-fired power has in developmental goals and poverty reduction.[18] India has a massive development imperative. Nearly half of the children in India are malnourished,[19] 404 million people have no electricity, and over half the population lives in impermanent mud and thatch housing.[20] The average GNI per capita in India ($3,280 per year 2009 $ PPP) is about a third of the world average and a tenth of the OECD average.[21] Many policy-makers contend that India's economy needs to grow at 8%–10% per year for two to three decades to meet these human development deficits and provide essential public services such as infrastructure, education, and health and to create productive and adequately remunerated employment. Such growth, when combined with a burgeoning population and limited natural resources, is sure to make a significant impact on resources and the environment. Oskarsson points out, for example, that local, natural resource-based livelihoods tend to be lost when dominant interests move into marginal lands and the equity outcomes of land-hungry projects are meagre.[22] Recommendations by policy-makers regarding 'sustainable' growth, where the main concerns relate to quality of air and water, productivity of land, preservation of biodiversity, and ecological health,[23] are therefore often subsumed to the necessity of mining and forestry to support India's growth ambitions.

Chhattisgarh is thus at the nexus of debates about climate change, fossil fuel, energy security, development, and the crucial question of who bears the costs inherent in pursuing these goals. A member of a Panchayat (Village Council) said:

> Our whole village is dependent on the forest for everything. As you can clearly see, farming is not the main source of livelihood for us ... it's the forest that we rely upon ... there is not a day when we don't go to the forest to get something or else. It's a part of our everyday life.[24]

Forests, land acquisitions, and state regulation in India

For Adivasis, India's independence was just another stage in their ongoing struggle for rights and autonomy. The colonial practices of repression and discrimination remained even under an Indian administration independent of imperial rule. In fact, salient provisions of the colonial rule were 'unwittingly reworked and renewed' by the Constituent Assembly of India who created the Indian Constitution.[25] Jawaharlal Nehru contended that the colonial laws would only remain until there were better protections for the Adivasis: 'the tribal people should be protected in every possible way, and the existing laws – I do not know what those laws are, but certainly the existing laws should continue and may be, should be, added to when the time comes.'[26]

In 1950, when the Constitution of India was promulgated, the Fifth and Sixth Schedules introduced provisions that recognised 'Scheduled Tribes' and provided for 'scheduled areas' where Adivasi identity and Adivasi interests were to be protected. The Fifth Schedule areas are found in ten states, including Chhattisgarh, Jharkhand, and Orissa, while the Sixth Schedule applies to the North East of India. Among the chief concerns of the architects of the Constitution was the relationship between Adivasis and land. The Constitution gave the state the special responsibility to prevent land alienation that would result in Adivasis losing control over land in scheduled areas to the non-Adivasi. If any land was to leave Adivasi hands and move to a non-Adivasi, it could happen only with the assent of the Collector (in most places) who would have to ensure that the land alienation was not prompted by distress, fraud, or duress, and to assess what impact such land transfer would have in the scheduled area.[27]

In the early 1990s, this presumption of state protection was severely compromised when estimates of mass displacement due to projects that included dams, power companies, and mining emerged, suggesting that a shocking 40% of those displaced to make way for these projects were Adivasis.[28] This is in spite of the Supreme Court of India proclaiming in 2011, that the 'Scheduled Tribes' are the 'indigenous people of India' and that the Indian state needs to take steps 'to undo the historical injustice' done to them.[29] Decades of Adivasi struggle culminated in the enactment of two landmark pieces of legislation in 1996 and 2006 which transformed discourses around the ownership, governance, and management of forests in India. These Acts made some attempts to ameliorate the continuing injustices suffered by Adivasis and other forest-inhabiting communities when the forests were 'reserved' under colonial rule. One was the *Panchayat (Extension to Scheduled Areas) Act 1996* or *PESA*. This mandated consultation with Gram Sabhas (Village Assemblies) or Panchayats before land in constitutionally recognised Scheduled areas (the Fifth and Sixth Schedules of the Constitution) could be acquired for development projects or any activity involving acquisition/alienation of Adivasi land.

The other Act was the *Scheduled Tribes and Other Traditional Forest Dwellers (Recognition of Forest Rights) Act, 2006 (FRA)*.[30] Co-written by Adivasi activists, the Preamble to this Act spoke of remediation:

> forest rights on lands and their habitat were not adequately recognised in the consolidation of state forests during the colonial period as well as in independent India resulting in historical injustice to the forest-dwelling scheduled tribes and other traditional forest dwellers who are integral to the survival and sustainability of the forest ecosystem.

The Act recognised the 'historic injustice' done to the Adivasis and put in place a clear legal mechanism for recognition of rights both at an individual and community level for tribal and other traditional forest-dwelling communities, including forest workers.

This Act also vested secure community tenure on 'community forest resources' in Gram Sabhas. These include rights for pastoral or nomadic forest communities to seasonal resources and continuous access to and settlement in common forest land.[31] Adivasis have placed enormous hopes in these two Acts that are unlikely to be realised because the *FRA* does not confer absolute ownership of all forests. What emerges from both Acts is a partial and complicated bricolage of use rights, ownership, and management of forest land, depending on the nature and recognition of claims.

The nexus between Adivasi peoples and resource exploitation is inscribed into the jurisdictional landscape of central India. For more than a century, Adivasis had called for the creation of a majority Adivasi state, a 'Greater Jharkhand', in the region.[32] The central state responded by creating not one but three states: Chhattisgarh and Jharkhand in 2000, and Telangana in 2014. Adivasi people were divided across these three resource-rich states, ensuring that they would constitute no more than a third of the voting population in any of the three. The gerrymander was clearly designed to guarantee resource access to the region, and arguably has been very effective. A Chhattisgarh advocate, Sudiep Srivastava, who has prosecuted many mining and environment cases, ruminates:

> Why was this state created? There was no demand for it … There must have been a reason for it. Some said it was to give Adivasis more rights but all that has happened is they have much less rights now than before. Who benefited? Only those who want mines. You work it out for yourself.[33]

These *Acts* mean that most mining applications are contested both on the ground and legally and bureaucratically. These contestations create their own narratives of rights and responsibilities, of life worlds and livelihoods. These scripts are used by opposing actors; supporters of mines believe that the Adivasis have a responsibility to the nation, not just to themselves, and their livelihoods will be enhanced by the jobs that economic development brings. Adivasi counter-narratives are about marginalisation and oppression, by the colonial state, by religion, by the hyper-narratives of development and modernity. In their narratives, they are trying to articulate an alternate modernity that recognises the predicament of the siren song of development, that does not transmute the nature they inhabit into natural resources, their peoples into populations, and their lived knowledge into expertise. An elder of Salhi village said:

> We are growing rice and filling the godowns … All the profits that they earn on food, clothing, is due to the resources from our lands. They are fooling us and filling their coffers in the name of our development. The development is of outsiders and foreigners, we are getting destroyed.[34]

Dispossession and resistance

The victories for Adivasis in the battle against displacement and dispossession have been few. In Orissa in 2013, the Dongria Kondh, a particularly vulnerable Adivasi group, unanimously voted against a project by state government-owned Odisha

Mining Corporation (OMC) and Sterlite Industries (which is now Vedanta) to mine bauxite from the Niyamgiri hills. The villagers' decision followed a landmark Supreme Court verdict on 18 April 2013 that said that the forest clearance for the mining project, which had been withdrawn by the Environment Ministry in 2010, could be given only after the Gram Sabhas, or Village Councils, in the region consented.[35]

Another victory was in the state of Madhya Pradesh in the Mahan area. The Indigenous communities of Mahan forest succeeded in stopping a coal mine from going ahead, at least for now. The Ministry of Coal has given way to the Ministry of Environment, Forests and Climate Change and will not auction the Mahan coal block. This forest is one of the oldest and largest *sal* forests in Asia. Spread across 1,600 hectares, these dense forests are home to over 50,000 Indigenous people, some of the most ancient forest-dwelling people in India, and several endangered wildlife species.[36]

The issue of hydroelectric dams in North East India shows how local people produced alternative developmental scripts in response to Governmental agendas and the agendas of the hydroelectric companies. Manju Menon shows how there can be effective community building around environmental issues by building lines of solidarity that defy national or ethnic modes of identification. Such communities may be, as she says, unstable and contingent but they make visible spaces of political ecology that critics of 'neoliberal' capitalism and development can miss. She demonstrates how people can influence development planning decisions being made by governments by offering an in-depth narrative of the contestation of proposals for a series of large-scale hydroelectric dams in North East India by local subaltern and Indigenous peoples concerned about the downstream impacts of these dams on livelihood and environment across the local region. It demonstrates, in particular, how the local organisations were able to shift the discourses and outcomes of the public hearings as required under India's Environmental Impact Assessment legislation. The proposals for large-scale dams in the region were, as a result of local public pressure, largely deferred. This case demonstrates the potential leverage of such campaigns in shifting the agenda and debate around Indigenous rights and development in India.[37]

Nine years after the creation of Chhattisgarh, in early 2010, the issues over land, livelihood, and resources became so fraught that trade unions, community groups, and other progressive political parties formed an alliance called the Chhattisgarh Bachao Andolan (Save Chhattisgarh Movement). These protests drew inspiration from the special status that Adivasis had in the Indian Constitution – their autonomy and dignity, as set out in Article 21 and under Schedules V and VI, are often seen as the core of Adivasi rights as well as a test of the resilience of the Indian Constitution and its guarantees for the protection of minorities.

Most Adivasis in this region have three forms of livelihood intricately linked to the forests and water sources: subsistence agriculture, grazing animals, and access to forest produce, which they both use themselves and sell in local markets. According to a village elder in Salhi, they got all their funds and provisions from the forests: 'six months we survive with this (small cultivation) and six months from forests … Forests are our source of income. If these forests are gone, then we shall die.'[38]

Some activists in the area pointed out that some Adivasi traditional activity, such as hunting, is already completely banned in protected lands and national parks.[39] The forests also contain holy sites or *deyurs*, marked by groves of trees, which are essential to Adivasi religious and cultural practices:

> The Adivasi community worships ... trees and our deities and gods reside in forests ... There is a deity called Boodha Dev in the forest of Salhi village. He appeared in my dream ... there was also a pool where weapons were kept ... So we decided to go to the particular spot I had seen in the dream and worship the deity. Since then, the deity keeps appearing in my dreams and warns us about the future through different signs.[40]

In 2012, the Supreme Court of India revoked 214 mining licences that had been corruptly allocated. This happened at a time when the central government was looking to promulgate new coal mining laws through which several of these cancelled mining concessions could find new owners. An ordinance to this effect was soon passed, the consequences of which were immediate and punitive, turning Chhattisgarh's tribal farmlands and forests into potential private mines that, if they went ahead, would have a massive impact on forest areas. By September 2017, several of these coal concessions had been auctioned and were at different stages of approval, including applications for forest clearing, environmental approvals, and acquisition of village-owned land. In 2017, one Gram Sabha in Sarguja district was pressured to meet for the third time to decide on a mining project. They had refused to concede their land and forests to mining corporations on earlier occasions. The president of the Sarpanch Sangh (Association of Panchayat Heads) in this area was angry:

> The officials sent us a notice that in these villages they want the Gram Sabhas to give permission to acquire and mine our land. This includes land given to the Indigenous people for farming, forests, rivers, and lakes. Essentially it is a plan to displace us from our homes for coal.[41]

According to Sudha Bharadwaj, the Adivasis are now in a worse situation than in colonial times.[42] She explained that the colonial *Land Acquisition Act, 1894* (replaced in September 2013 by the *Right to Fair Compensation and Transparency in the Land Acquisition, Rehabilitation and Resettlement Act, 2013*) distinguished between acquisition for public and private purposes. In the latter case, there were stringent caveats against acquiring agricultural land. Whereas now, the presumption is that any application for acquisition by a company is for public purpose and can be dealt with under the current *Land Acquisition Act*. There are many examples of unsafe acquisition of lands by corporations where Adivasis have little recourse. The following examples were recounted by Bharadwaj who had advised or represented several plaintiffs in their grievances.[43]

In Choura village, the Adivasis protested when their lands were compulsorily acquired for mining by the South Eastern Coalfields Limited (SECL, a Public

Sector Mining Enterprise). The *PESA* was violated since the Village Council was not consulted before the acquisition. Instead, a forged Gram Sabha resolution was submitted to obtain clearances. About 5,000 Adivasis decided to march in protest to the Mines Offices on 26 December 2009 (the 13th anniversary of the day the *PESA* was notified). The SECL, which had already begun mining, sued the villagers for the loss of production on that day, filing a civil suit against six protestors for the recovery of Rs 360,000 with 9% interest.

In 2000, an Adivasi woman, Janki Sidar, found that two tracts of her land were fraudulently registered in the name of Monnet Steel. Another woman had been presented as her, and her land was registered in the name of a non-existent Adivasi with the co-operation of the revenue authorities. When Janki filed a fraud case, the City Superintendent of Police (who was later transferred to a hardship posting) investigated and, as a consequence, a manager of Monnet Steel and his collaborators were jailed. The case dragged on for 10 years despite repeated pleas by Janki for it to be dismissed. Eventually she won, but it was a Pyrrhic victory as by this time the land had been built on and was no longer suitable for farming. The lawyer for this Adivasi woman was jailed in 2018 under the *Unlawful Activities Prevention Act*.[44]

In 1968–1969, a scheme called the 'Singhdev Yojana' was initiated in Sarguja that entailed denotifying forest lands that had been occupied and cultivated by Adivasis for generations, converting them to revenue land. However, Adivasis never received land ownership documents for these areas and cannot apply for the documents under the *Forest Rights Act,* since the land is no longer forest land. In Gangapur, a village in this area, despite repeated resolutions of the Gram Sabha, police demolished the houses of a dozen Adivasi families, ostensibly at the behest of the Tribal Welfare Department.

Sometimes, the methods used by the proponents of land acquisition are truly Machiavellian. In 2010, the Gram Sabha of Premnagar, a village in this area, passed resolutions refusing land for a power plant on 14 occasions. The administration then decided that the village was not a village (or *gram*) but a town (or *nagar*) and set up a 'Nagar Panchayat' (Town Council), thus abolishing the Village Council and the rights of the Adivasis under the *FRA*.[45]

Khotkhorra is an impoverished village that displays the dark other of development. The villagers seem not to have understood their rights under the *PESA* and *FRA*. What followed was unfree migration and a form of covert coercion. They were first displaced by a dam; there was no rehabilitation so they informally occupied an area uphill from their original habitation. Within a couple of years, the water table failed. They now have to carry water from a seepage well located three to four kilometres away from their homes. Access to the village is via a sole steep dirt road. If the mines planned in the surrounding forests go ahead, that access will be removed and they will be uprooted again. The Khotkhorra villagers blame the disappearance of their water and the looming prospect of further dislocations on having to relocate their gods from their original homes. The gods are angry because they have been moved:

> There is one [place] in our old village in the neighbouring forest where we worship Mahadev. We believe that, like us, he is also dependent on the forest

> ... I can tell you that if the authorities try to force their way in the forest, they will not be spared by the deity.[46]

It is difficult to gain recognition under the *FRA*, which functions through the recognition of pre-existing rights. 'Claims' are submitted at the neighbourhood level in a Village Council. This is the grassroots interface at which Adivasis participate in the process of becoming complete citizens or subordinated subjects of the state. The rejection rate of claims is above 50% – at the end of September 2018, a total of 4,219,741 claims (individual and community claims) were filed and 1,889,835 titles or 17,848,733 acres of forest lands have been distributed. 1,934,345 claims, greater in number than the approved claims, were rejected by the government.[47] Evidence from the implementation of the *FRA* shows that, even when Adivasi land claims are recognised, the area they are granted is smaller than the area claimed. While the Act prescribes recognition of up to two hectares, Sarker points out that, on average at the national level, half an acre per successful claim was distributed.[48] The distribution of community claims is also abysmally low. It is possible that some individual claims may be rejected due to insufficient proof; the same explanation cannot be extended to community claims, as they are held in common by the entire Adivasi community for the purposes of fishing, grazing, and collection of forest produce. Archival or written documents may not be available, but community memory and oral history, as demonstrated in the examples above, are strong.

The reluctance of the Forest Department to relinquish rights over community forestlands emerges as a plausible explanation. While the 'participatory process' of claim submission calls on the Adivasi citizens to access the law, the subsequent stages of surveying and mapping the land claimed are monopolised by forest officials.[49] Thus, Adivasis have no knowledge of what transpires between claim submission and its acceptance or rejection by the higher-level committees and the basis on which final decisions are made. There is no transparency, and the decision-making process is monopolised by elite forest officials. The state also controls local livelihoods, as it is the sole purchaser of minor forest produce, on which Adivasis depend, even though the *FRA* proposes complete right of access to this produce for Adivasis.[50] These instances warn that the 'historic injustice' against Adivasis can only be corrected if the *FRA* is properly implemented.

When asked if the people in that area took the cash compensation and bought land elsewhere or moved to the city, the general consensus was that those who sold their land to the mining corporations would not thrive. A Panchayat member was passionate about this:

> I can tell you from my own experience that money alone does not bring prosperity to your life. The people of neighbouring village got *crores* (ten million) of rupees last year. A few managed to build houses and all but 75–80 per cent of the population is completely ruined. They have bought cars and there have been so many accidents since then ... so many widows ... So based on that, I feel that the coal mine would lead to our destruction rather than development ... We want the government to develop our region without pushing us out of our home.[51]

At two village meetings, I met three Adivasis who were intoxicated. Other people at the meeting said that they had money burning a hole in their pockets after selling land to the corporation:

> And look at them now. There is a saying here that if you sell your land you will be reborn as a jackal and we don't want that for us. These mining and other projects are an insult to our motherland and we don't want to participate in that. This land supports so many creatures and life forms and it is a mass murder and a crime.[52]

Those opposing the mines vehemently assert that they would utilise all of the rights available to Adivasis in the Constitution: working at the Gram Sabha level to withhold consent, applying for individual and community forest rights, contesting environmental and other violations before the National Green Tribunal, and taking cases of malfeasance and misappropriation to the various courts. In addition, there were civil society actions, protest meetings and demonstrations, and participation in Panchayat elections.

The tensions and disruption created by the threat of land alienation clearly brought the villagers together. Most of them were keen to emphasise their long-standing relationship to those particular lands and forests. To some extent, the *Forest Rights Act* codified the moral discourse of Adivasis' connection to the forests for the public and national audience of India; most of them have clear historical and familial memories of their ancestors' locations before the British Raj. The Sarpanch (head-man) of one village said:

> Our forefathers used to be kings, before British rule, when this was Gondwana kingdom, we were independent and kings in every village. Before the forest laws were implemented.[53]

This belonging articulated a form of kingship – 'our ancestors were kings' harnesses a concept familiar to them. It asserts a combination of responsibility for the domain of the community, a duty of care for the forests that sustain them and the various beings who live there, and a concern for handing these to the next generation. It expresses autonomy over land to which their relationship was never transactional or commodified. Like many other Indigenous peoples, they chart their links to the land and forest through the sacred, through the forests' plenitude in providing all that is necessary for living.

In modern India, Adivasis have been compelled to learn and articulate a new idiom of rights to carve out a space in the national imaginary. The modern nation-state that they inhabit is both rights-giver – through various instruments such as the *PESA*, *FRA*, and Schedules V and VI of the Constitution – and rights-taker – through the often coerced and sometimes illegal appropriation of their lands in the cause of modernity and development.

It is clear in the context of Chhattisgarh that the visions of development presented by the Government of India and mining corporations have not been realised for displaced Adivasis. Poverty has not been eradicated, livelihood opportunities have worsened, neither social safety nets nor growth infrastructure have been created. Consequently, there is no intrinsic loyalty to mining as a profession for displaced villagers who are virtually never given real jobs in the mines; villagers usually shun those who sell their land. There seems to be less and less common ground between these two points of view.

> Agents of mining corporations
> Knock on every village door.
> And no sooner is uttered a desperate sigh of hunger,
> Then disease, unemployment and helplessness,
> Are shoved down their throats
> Grains, medicines, utensils, and clothes.
> And the family carried away
> As labourers, for a pittance pay.[54]

Most villagers agreed with an articulate and engaging village elder in Salhi who used the phrase that I heard repeated often in the villages, '*yeh vikas nahin, vinas hai*' (this is not development but destruction). The villagers understood development as a contradictory and contested term and they were acutely aware of the differing priorities of the government, urban areas, and their own needs.

> They are fooling us and filling their coffers in the name of our development. The development is of outsiders and foreigners, we are getting destroyed ... Do these office-bearers in big cities produce rice or pulses that they eat? We feed them by ploughing these fields ... Don't they need to eat rice? He who is interested in digging coal will eat coal only. We don't want to eat coal.[55]

Rejection under the *FRA* provides a pretext for legally formalising the de-recognition of existing rights. In an echo of British law (using pre-independence legal precedents), in February 2019, the Supreme Court ruled that people were trespassing if they continued to access land claims rejected under the *FRA*. The case was brought by conservative Indian conservationist NGOs using the *FRA* to protect 'pristine' forests. The government, which has responsibility for implementing the *FRA*, failed to make a counter-submission, suggesting tacit approval. The court ruling and a later order enabled the legalised eviction of at least two million forest dwellers, close to half a million in Chhattisgarh. This would effectively clear the forests for mining.[56] Following widespread protests, the order was stayed on request from the central government, to allow the states to respond to allegations that the *FRA* process had been misapplied, opening up a new national field for contestation on *FRA* implementation. Already, the move is generating a major Adivasi upsurge and international outrage.

The mobilisation of local-level alliances in defence of Adivasi land and rights, and against the manipulation of the *FRA*, has had a major impact. Until 2018, the Bharatiya Janata Party had been in power in Chhattisgarh since its creation. In the November 2018 state elections, there was a 29% swing against the BJP in favour of the Congress Party, which, for the first time, stated that it would fully implement the *FRA* and *PESA*, including 'collective rights' for Gram Sabhas. The *FRA* became a 'core' commitment for Congress, which launched a series of large meetings in Adivasi constituencies, termed a 'Jungle Satyagraha', asserting Congress as the party that had instituted the *FRA*.

The Congress Party was voted in by a large turnout in 27 of the 29 Adivasi-dominated constituencies.[57] The election signalled a major backlash: the betrayal of the *FRA*, and the persistent mobilisations in defence of its principles, created a unifying dynamic, spilling over from the affected villages into state-level politicisation and creating opportunities for Congress and for the local campaigns.[58] In 2019, the campaigners we interviewed for this project were seeking to make good their electoral promises.[59]

As recently as November 2020, T.S. Singh Deo, the current senior minister in the Congress-dominated state government of Chhattisgarh, said that he was 'one hundred per cent, without any hesitation or doubt' opposed to the extension of coal mining, in the state. He added that such mining would also jeopardise the large Lemru elephant reserve proposed by the Chhattisgarh government and worsen human-elephant conflict in the vicinity of the mine.[60]

Through 2018 and into 2019, there was further spillover, as the Chhattisgarh actions were correlated with actions in neighbouring Jharkhand. There, Adivasi communities took forest rights into their own hands and, from 2016, had begun establishing large stone slabs, traditional Pathalgadi, inscribed with quotes from the *FRA*, *PESA*, and the Indian Constitution, to assert and mark out Adivasi lands and emphasise their status in the Indian Constitution. By inscribing the provisions of the Fifth Schedule, the Adivasis emphasised the fact that their legitimacy is inscribed in the Indian Constitution. They were asserting their autonomy from the imposition of state rule by literally setting in stone the authority of the Gram Sabha in the villages of the Scheduled Areas and restricting the entry of outsiders, including government officials and the police.[61] Adivasis in Jharkhand were highlighting this rupture with the state by a number of actions that demonstrated their struggle for autonomy. They established their own bank, and a school with a curriculum based on their own languages and cultures, organised a security force, and issued their own Tribal Identity Card through the Gram Sabha.[62] The movement was repressed by the military from 2018 with a wave of arrests statewide, creating a crisis of legitimacy for the Jharkhand state.[63]

Conclusion

Adivasis are finding it increasingly difficult to have their rights as Indigenous citizens upheld by the law as well as to make their way out of poverty. Nancy Fraser notes in her book *Justice Interruptus* that social and political struggles today have become confined to a fight for recognition rather than redistribution, an assertion of identity based on nationality, ethnicity, race, gender, sexuality, etc. The consequence is the obliteration of struggles for socioeconomic redistribution.[64] Adivasi activists, owing to their historical marginalisation and alienation from forestlands, have successfully demanded recognition from their postcolonial nation-state in the form of their rights to the forests in which they live. The *Panchayat (Extension to Scheduled Areas) Act* and the *Forest Rights Act*, with their admissions of historic injustices, mandating of Gram Sabha consultation before land acquisition, and restoration of individual and community forest rights, affirm the statutory recognition that Schedules V and VI of the Indian Constitution confer on Adivasis.[65] This recognition involved the revaluation of identities that have been denied legitimacy and desired status in both the colonial and modern nation-states.

However, this recognition has not been accompanied by redistributive justice. There has been no substantive redistribution of income, changes in labour relations, or transformation of economic structures. The material status of Adivasis has not been transformed through the surety and security of land titles they claim. The reality of *FRA* implementation in the context of the power of the mining lobby means that, in spite of this recognition, Adivasis are coerced into foregoing their rights in the face of illegal and unsafe land acquisition, complicity by state and other officials in non-compliance with environmental and other safeguards, and outright denial of compensation or rehabilitation to those affected. Overall, the contestations over forests through the *FRA* and *PESA* have shaped the subject-making of India's Indigenous peoples through a two-way process: claim-making by the Adivasis for forest rights and proscribing mining on their land, and the reduction of these demands by the state into a politics of development for the good of the nation. These contestations, nevertheless, have transformed the political theatre of forests – the state and the subaltern now actually 'see' each other, as obstacles, opposition, or oppressor. As Chemmencheri says, Adivasis now stand at the crossroads of democratic institutions, neoliberal economics, and welfare programmes, having to remake themselves as modern citizens with constitutional rights as well as negotiate the processes by which the state creates them as subjects.[66]

I returned to some of the villages in my field site after two years. At one, I saw two captured elephants who had rampaged through the area, because of the loss of their habitat. The villagers had attacked them with Molotov cocktails and the forest department had corralled them. The elephants were chained and rocking to and fro in distress; the villagers delegated to look after them were speaking soft comforting words while cooking a huge vat of treats with which to feed them. This scene encapsulated both the deep connections that Adivasis had to their forests and the tragedy that their dispossession caused to the whole ecosystem.

At another village, the dystopian paraphernalia of mining loomed over the landscape. There was coal dust on the fields, in the water, on the children who were running home from school. The complex forest ecosystem of the Adivasi life world that sustains humans, animals, insects, uncountable life forms, had vanished. Those were also sacred spaces, full of inspiration and terror; loss of those spaces is a loss of Adivasi spirit, personhood, and identity. Since nature is also an actor in the complex assemblage of eco-biological systems of this earth, the loss of Adivasi rights to the irresistible forces of resource extraction points to a bigger loss, that of the rights of the forests and of the life-systems they nurture.

An elder of the village put the case of his people poignantly:

> This land is our mother and we cannot dig up the bones of our mother. We will not flourish, rather we will face troubles and violence elsewhere. We have

grown here just as our ancestors and this land has given us everything from food, shelter, clean air, water, home, so considering all that this land is equivalent to our parents and God, and we cannot sell them. We are willing to face arrows and weapons with our children instead of being ashamed of having to sell our land and live like beggars or wanderers.[67]

Notes

1 Jacinta Kerketta, 'O, City!,' in *Angor* (Kolkata: Adivaani, 2016), 4.
2 Rudyard Kipling, 'Letting in the Jungle,' in *The Jungle Books*, ed. W.W. Robson (Oxford: Oxford University Press, 1998), 207.
3 Census of India, 2011, accessed 25 March 2019, http://www.censusindia.gov.in/2011census/population_enumeration.html.
4 Kerketta, 'The River, the Mountain and the Bazaar,' *Angor*, 48.
5 David Washbrook, 'From Comparative Sociology to Global History: Britain and India in the Pre-History of Modernity,' *Journal of the Economic and Social History of the Orient* 40, no. 4 (1997): 411.
6 Frederick Lugard, *The Dual Mandate in British Tropical Africa* (London: Frank Cass, 1922, 1965), 17–18.
7 Lugard, *Dual Mandate*, 17–18.
8 Lugard, *Dual Mandate*, 26.
9 Michael H. Fisher, *An Environmental History of India: From Earliest Times to the Twenty-First Century* (Cambridge: Cambridge University Press, 2019).
10 Madhav Guha and Ramachandra Gadgil, 'State Forestry And Social Conflict In British India,' *Past & Present* 123, no. 1 (May 1989): 141–177; Sanjukta Gupta, 'Accessing Nature: Agrarian Change, Forest Laws and their Impact on an Adivasi Economy in Colonial India,' *Conservation and Society* 7, no. 4 (2009): 227–238.
11 Benjamin Weil, 'Conservation, Exploitation, and Cultural Change in the Indian Forest Service, 1875–1927,' *Environmental History* 11, no. 2 (2006): 319–343.
12 Bhangya Bhukya, 'The Mapping of the Adivasi Social: Colonial Anthropology and Adivasis,' *Economic and Political Weekly* 43, no. 39 (27 September–3 October 2008): 103–109.
13 Bhukya, 'Mapping of the Adivasi Social'; Prathama Banerjee, 'Writing the Adivasi: Some Historiographical Notes,' *The Indian Economic and Social History Review* 53, no. 1 (2016): 141.
14 'Coal Mining in India: The Past,' 2015, accessed 25 November 2018, https://web.archive.org/web/20130831225354/http://www.coal.nic.in/abtcoal.htm.
15 'Coal Mining in India.'
16 'Walk with Me: Samvaad Adivasi Leadership Programme,' 2017, https://www.tatasteel.com/initiatives/samvaad/pdf/publications/TLP-2017-Walk%20With%20Me_new.pdf.
17 M.J. Akbar, 'India Today 35 Anniversary Issue's Essay on Jawahar Lal Nehru,' 15 December 2011, https://www.indiatoday.in/magazine/india-today-35th-anniversary/story/20111226-india-today-newsmaker-of-1950s-jawaharlal-nehru-750017-2011-12-15.
18 Tom Allard, 'Why Everything You Think about the Economy in 2015 Is Probably Wrong,' *The Sydney Morning Herald*, 16 January 2015, https://www.smh.com.au/business/the-economy/why-everything-you-think-about-the-economy-in-2015-is-probably-wrong-20150106-12iouc.html; Michael Edison Hayden, 'India Seeks to Balance Development with Need for Clean Energy,' *Los Angeles Times*, 15 December 2015, https://www.latimes.com/world/asia/la-fg-india-modi-climate-20151202-story.html; Avik Roy, 'No Renewables without Coal, Says Indian Energy Minister,' *Climate Home News*, 3 November 2015, http://www.climatechangenews.com/2015/11/30/no-renewables-without-coal-says-indian-energy-minister/; Avik Roy, 'Coal Mining Banned in India's Mahan Forest,' *Climate Home News*, 24 March 2015, https://www.climatechangenews.com/2015/03/24/coal-mining-banned-in-indias-mahan-forest/.

19 World Bank, 'Empowering Rural India – Expanding Electricity Access by Mobilizing Local Resources,' 2010, accessed 15 November 2015. https://openknowledge.worldbank.org/handle/10986/12532.
20 Girish Sant and Ashwin Gambhir, 'Energy Development and Climate Change,' in *Handbook of Climate Change and India: Development, Politics and Governance*, ed. Navroz K. Dubash (New York: Routledge, 2015), 291.
21 World Bank, 'World Development Indicators Database,' accessed 15 November 2015, https://data.worldbank.org/indicator/NY.GDP.PCAP.PP.CD.
22 Patrik Oskarsson, 'Marginalising People on Marginal Commons: The Political Ecology of Coal in Andhra Pradesh,' in *The Coal Nation: Histories, Ecologies and Politics of Coal in India*, ed. Kuntala Lahiri-Dutt (Surrey and Burlington: Ashgate, 2010), 200.
23 Kirit Parikh, 'Sustainable Development and Low Carbon Growth Strategy for India,' *Energy* 40 (2012): 31.
24 Ghatbarra, Panchayat member interview with author, 2016.
25 Uday Chandra, 'Liberalism and Its Other: The Politics of Primitivism in Colonial and Postcolonial Indian Law,' *Law Society Review* 47, no. 1 (2013): 135–168.
26 Constituent Assembly Debates, 30 April 1947 speech by Jawaharlal Nehru 31, available at http://cadindia.clpr.org.in/constitution_assembly_debates/volume/9/1947-04-30 (accessed 4 April 2018).
27 Usha Ramanathan, 'Where Do Adivasis Stand In Indian Law?' *Grist Media*, 27 February 2015, http://www.ielrc.org/content/n1504.pdf.
28 Ramanathan, 'Where Do Adivasis Stand.'
29 Kailas & Ors vs State of Maharashtra Tr.Taluka [2011] S.C.C. at para. 39.
30 Nesar Ahmad, 'Colonial Legislation in Postcolonial Times,' in *The Coal Nation: Histories, Ecologies and Politics of Coal in India*, ed. Kuntala Lahiri-Dutt (Surrey & Burlington: Ashgate, 2014), 258–260.
31 Ministry of Tribal Affairs, 'Forest Rights Act, 2006: Acts, Rules and Guidelines,' 2014, https://tribal.nic.in/FRA/data/FRARulesBook.pdf.
32 Stuart Corbridge, 'The Continuing Struggle for India's Jharkhand: Democracy, Decentralisation and the Politics of Names and Numbers,' *Commonwealth Comparative Politics* 40, no. 3 (2002): 55–71.
33 Sudiep Srivastava, interview with author, 2015.
34 Salhi, elder interview with author.
35 G. Seetharaman, 'The Story of One of the Biggest Land Conflicts: No Mine Now, But is it All Fine in Niyamgiri?' *The Economic Times*, 18 April 2018, http://www.ecoti.in/Sor9ZY.
36 Roy, 'No Renewables.'
37 Manju Menon, 'Making New Environmental Knowledges: EIAs and Public Hearings on Large Dams in Northeast India' (PhD diss., University of Technology Sydney, 2020).
38 Salhi interview.
39 Madanpur, village member interview with author, 2016.
40 Ghatbarra interview.
41 President, Sarpanch Sangh, interview with author, 2015.
42 Sudha Bharadwaj, interview with author, 2015.
43 Bharadwaj interview.
44 Chitrangada Choudhury, 'The Sudha Bharadwaj the Government Doesn't Want You to Know,' *Article 14*, 28 August 2020.
45 Aman Sethi, 'If Villagers Won't Go To Town, Town Will Come To Villagers,' *The Hindu*, 17 January 2011, http://www.thehindu.com/todays-paper/tp-national/if-villagers-wont-go-to-town-town-will-come-to-villagers/article1096339.ece.
46 Khotkorra, villager interview with author, 2016.
47 Ministry of Tribal Affairs, 'Monthly update on status implementation of the Scheduled Tribes and Other Traditional Forest Dweller (Recognition of Forest Rights) Act, 2006,' 15 November 2018, https://tribal.nic.in/FRA/data/MPRSep2018.pdf; see also

CFR-LA, *Promise and Performance: Ten Years of the Forest Rights Act in India* (New Delhi: Citizens' Report, Community Forest Rights–Learning and Advocacy, 2016).
48 Debnarayan Sarker, 'The Implementation of the Forest Rights Act in India: Critical Issues,' *Economic Affairs* 31, no. 2 (2011): 25–29.
49 Sudheesh R. Chemmencheri, 'Decentralisation, Participation and Boundaries of Transformation: Forest Rights Act, Wayanad, India,' *Commonwealth Journal of Local Governance* 12 (2013): 51–68.
50 Kumar Sambhav Shrivastava, 'New Rules to Make FRA Effective,' *Down to Earth*, 4 July 2015, www.downtoearth.org.in/news/new-rules-to-make-fra-effective-38706.
51 Ghatbarra and Salhi interviews.
52 Ghatbarra and Salhi interviews.
53 Salhi interview.
54 Kerketta, 'The Six Lane Freeway of Deceit,' *Angor*, 45.
55 Salhi interview.
56 Indira Basu, '"Govt Cares for Neither Tribals Nor Forests": Lawyer Ritwick Dutta,' *Bloomberg Quint*, 23 July 2019, www.bloombergquint.com/quint/supreme-court-tribal-forest-land-eviction-order-2019-general-elections.
57 Alison Saldanha, 'As India's Poor, Tribal Heartland Votes Today, Widespread Unrest over BJP Failure to Settle Land and Forest Claims,' *Sabrang*, 20 November 2018, https://sabrangindia.in/article/indias-poor-tribal-heartland-votes-today-widespread-unrest-over-bjp-failure-settle-land-and
58 Jacob Koshy, 'Aliens in Their Own Lands: When Chhattisgarh's Tribals Were Turned into Encroachers,' *The Hindu*, 6 April 2019, https://www.thehindu.com/news/national/encroachers-on-their-own-lands/article26749821.ece.
59 Mayank Aggarwal, 'The Hasdeo Arand Story: Is Coal Mining a Fait Accompli for the Pristine Forests?' *Mongabay*, 7 March 2019, https://india.mongabay.com/2019/03/the-hasdeo-arand-story-is-coal-mining-a-fait-accompli-for-the-pristine-forests/.
60 Adani Watch, 'Stoush over New Delhi's Move to Take over Hasdeo Forests for Adani Coal Mine,' 11 November 2020.
61 Anjana Singh, 'Many Faces of the Pathalgadi Movement in Jharkhand,' *Economic & Political Weekly* 54, no. 11 (2019): 29.
62 Marine Carrin, 'Jharkhand: Alternative Citizenship in an "Adivasi State",' in *The Modern Anthropology of India*, eds. Peter Berger and Frank Heidemann (London: Routledge, 2013), 106–120.
63 Santosh K. Kiro, 'The State's Violent Response to Tribal Discontent Is Fuelling the Pathalgadi Movement,' *The Wire*, 29 June 2018, https://thewire.in/rights/jharkhand-pathalgadi-movement-abduction-violence.
64 Nancy Fraser, *Justice Interruptus: Critical Reflections on the 'Postsocialist' Condition* (New York: Routledge, 1997).
65 Kundan Kumar and John M. Kerr, 'Democratic Assertions: The Making of India's Recognition of Forest Rights Act,' *Development and Change* 43, no. 3 (2012): 751–771.
66 Sudheesh R. Chemmencheri, 'State, Social Policy and Subaltern Citizens in Adivasi India,' *Citizenship Studies* 19, nos. 3–4 (2015): 436–449.
67 Salhi interview.

Bibliography

Adani Watch. 'Stoush over New Delhi's Move to Take over Hasdeo Forests for Adani Coal Mine.' 11 November 2020.

Aggarwal, Mayank. 'The Hasdeo Arand Story: Is Coal Mining a Fait Accompli for the Pristine Forests?' *Mongabay*, 7 March 2019. https://india.mongabay.com/2019/03/the-hasdeo-arand-story-is-coal-mining-a-fait-accompli-for-the-pristine-forests/.

Ahmad, Nesar. 'Colonial Legislation in Postcolonial Times.' In *The Coal Nation: Histories, Ecologies and Politics of Coal in India*, edited by Kuntala Lahiri-Dutt, 258–260. Surrey & Burlington: Ashgate, 2014.
Akbar, M.J. 'India Today 35 Anniversary Issue's Essay on Jawahar Lal Nehru.' 15 December 2011. https://www.indiatoday.in/magazine/india-today-35th-anniversary/story/20111226-india-today-newsmaker-of-1950s-jawaharlal-nehru-750017-2011-12-15.
Allard, Tom. 'Why Everything You Think about the Economy in 2015 Is Probably Wrong.' *The Sydney Morning Herald*, 16 January 2015. https://www.smh.com.au/business/the-economy/why-everything-you-think-about-the-economy-in-2015-is-probably-wrong-20150106-12iouc.html.
Banerjee, Prathama. 'Writing the Adivasi: Some Historiographical Notes.' *The Indian Economic and Social History Review* 53, no. 1 (2016): 131–153.
Basu, Indira. '"Govt Cares for Neither Tribals Nor Forests": Lawyer Ritwick Dutta.' *Bloomberg Quint*, 23 July 2019. www.bloombergquint.com/quint/supreme-court-tribal-forest-land-eviction-order-2019-general-elections.
Bhukya, Bhangya. 'The Mapping of the Adivasi Social: Colonial Anthropology and Adivasis.' *Economic and Political Weekly* 43, no. 39 (27 Sep–3 Oct 2008): 103–109.
Carrin, Marine. 'Jharkhand: Alternative Citizenship in an "Adivasi State".' In *The Modern Anthropology of India*, edited by Peter Berger and Frank Heidemann, 106–120. London: Routledge, 2013.
Census of India, 2011. Accessed 25 March 2019. http://www.censusindia.gov.in/2011census/population_enumeration.html.
CFR-LA. *Promise and Performance: Ten Years of the Forest Rights Act in India*. New Delhi: Citizens' Report, Community Forest Rights–Learning and Advocacy, 2016.
Chandra, Uday. 'Liberalism and Its Other: The Politics of Primitivism in Colonial and Postcolonial Indian Law.' *Law Society Review* 47, no. 1 (2013): 135–168.
Chemmencheri, Sudheesh R. 'Decentralisation, Participation and Boundaries of Transformation: Forest Rights Act, Wayanad, India.' *Commonwealth Journal of Local Governance* 12 (2013): 51–68.
Chemmencheri, Sudheesh R. 'State, Social Policy and Subaltern Citizens in Adivasi India.' *Citizenship Studies* 19, nos. 3–4 (2015): 436–449.
Choudhury, Chitrangada. 'The Sudha Bharadwaj the Government Doesn't Want You to Know.' *Article 14*, 28 August 2020.
'Coal Mining in India: The Past.' 2015. Accessed 25 November 2018. https://web.archive.org/web/20130831225354/http://www.coal.nic.in/abtcoal.htm
Corbridge, Stuart. 'The Continuing Struggle for India's Jharkhand: Democracy, Decentralisation and the Politics of Names and Numbers.' *Commonwealth Comparative Politics* 40, no. 3 (2002): 55–71.
Fisher, Michael H. *An Environmental History of India: From Earliest Times to the Twenty-First Century*. Cambridge: Cambridge University Press, 2019.
Fraser, Nancy. *Justice Interruptus: Critical Reflections on the 'Postsocialist' Condition*. New York: Routledge, 1997.
Guha, Madhav, and Ramachandra Gadgil. 'State Forestry And Social Conflict in British India.' *Past & Present* 123, no. 1 (May 1989): 141–177.
Gupta, Sanjukta. 'Accessing Nature: Agrarian Change, Forest Laws and their Impact on an Adivasi Economy in Colonial India.' *Conservation and Society* 7, no. 4 (2009): 227–238.
Hayden, Michael Edison. 'India Seeks to Balance Development with Need for Clean Energy.' *Los Angeles Times*, 15 December 2015. https://www.latimes.com/world/asia/la-fg-india-modi-climate-20151202-story.html.
Kerketta, Jacinta. *Angor*. Kolkata: Adivaani, 2016.
Kipling, Rudyard. 'Letting in the Jungle.' In *The Jungle Books*, edited by W.W. Robson, 183–211. Oxford: Oxford University Press, 1998.

Kiro, Santosh K. 'The State's Violent Response to Tribal Discontent Is Fuelling the Pathalgadi Movement.' *The Wire*, 29 June 2018. https://thewire.in/rights/jharkhand-pathalgadi-movement-abduction-violence.

Koshy, Jacob. 'Aliens in Their Own Lands: When Chhattisgarh's Tribals Were Turned into Encroachers.' *The Hindu*, 6 April 2019. https://www.thehindu.com/news/national/encroachers-on-their-own-lands/article26749821.ece.

Kumar, Kundan, and John M. Kerr. 'Democratic Assertions: The Making of India's Recognition of Forest Rights Act.' *Development and Change* 43, no. 3 (2012): 751–771.

Lugard, Frederick. *The Dual Mandate in British Tropical Africa.* London: Frank Cass, 1922, 1965.

Menon, Manju. 'Making New Environmental Knowledges: EIAs and Public Hearings on Large Dams in Northeast India.' PhD diss., University of Technology Sydney, 2020.

Ministry of Tribal Affairs. 'Forest Rights Act, 2006: Acts, Rules and Guidelines.' 2014. https://tribal.nic.in/FRA/data/FRARulesBook.pdf.

Ministry of Tribal Affairs. 'Monthly update on status implementation of the Scheduled Tribes and Other Traditional Forest Dweller (Recognition of Forest Rights) Act, 2006.' 15 November 2018. https://tribal.nic.in/FRA/data/MPRSep2018.pdf.

Oskarsson, P. 'Marginalising People on Marginal Commons: The Political Ecology of Coal in Andhra Pradesh.' In *The Coal Nation: Histories, Ecologies and Politics of Coal in India*, edited by Kuntala Lahiri-Dutt, 197–218. Surrey & Burlington: Ashgate, 2010.

Parikh, Kirit. 'Sustainable Development and Low Carbon Growth Strategy for India.' *Energy* 40 (2012): 31–38.

Ramanathan, Usha. 'Where Do Adivasis Stand In Indian Law?' *Grist Media*, 27 February 2015. http://www.ielrc.org/content/n1504.pdf.

Roy, Avik. 'Coal Mining Banned in India's Mahan Forest.' *Climate Home News*, 24 March 2015. https://www.climatechangenews.com/2015/03/24/coal-mining-banned-in-indias-mahan-forest/.

Roy, Avik. 'No Renewables Without Coal, Says Indian Energy Minister.' *Climate Home News*, 3 November 2015. http://www.climatechangenews.com/2015/11/30/no-renewables-without-coal-says-indian-energy-minister/.

Saldanha, Alison. 'As India's Poor, Tribal Heartland Votes Today, Widespread Unrest over BJP Failure to Settle Land and Forest Claims.' *Sabrang*, 20 November 2018. https://sabrangindia.in/article/indias-poor-tribal-heartland-votes-today-widespread-unrest-over-bjp-failure-settle-land-and.

Sant, Girish, and Ashwin Gambhir. 'Energy Development and Climate Change.' In *Handbook of Climate Change and India: Development, Politics and Governance*, edited by Navroz K. Dubash, 289–302. New York: Routledge, 2015.

Sarker, Debnarayan. 'The Implementation of the Forest Rights Act in India: Critical Issues.' *Economic Affairs* 31, no. 2 (2011): 25–29.

Seetharaman, G. 'The Story of One of the Biggest Land Conflicts: No Mine Now, But is it All Fine in Niyamgiri?' *The Economic Times*, 18 April 2018. http://www.ecoti.in/Sor9ZY.

Sethi, Aman. 'If Villagers Won't Go To Town, Town Will Come To Villagers.' *The Hindu*, 17 January 2011. http://www.thehindu.com/todays-paper/tp-national/if-villagers-wont-go-to-town-town-will-come-to-villagers/article1096339.ece.

Shrivastava, Kumar Sambhav. 'New Rules to Make FRA Effective.' *Down to Earth*, 4 July 2015. www.downtoearth.org.in/news/new-rules-to-make-fra-effective-38706.

Singh, Anjana. 'Many Faces of the Pathalgadi Movement in Jharkhand.' *Economic & Political Weekly* 54, no. 11 (2019): 28–33.

'Walk with Me: Samvaad Adivasi Leadership Programme.' 2017. https://www.tatasteel.com/initiatives/samvaad/pdf/publications/TLP-2017-Walk%20With%20Me_new.pdf.

Washbrook, David. 'From Comparative Sociology to Global History: Britain and India in the Pre-History of Modernity.' *Journal of the Economic and Social History of the Orient* 40, no. 4 (1997): 410–443.

Weil, Benjamin. 'Conservation, Exploitation, and Cultural Change in the Indian Forest Service, 1875–1927.' *Environmental History* 11, no. 2 (2006): 319–343.
World Bank. 'Empowering Rural India – Expanding Electricity Access by Mobilizing Local Resources.' 2010. Accessed 15 November 2015. https://openknowledge.worldbank.org/handle/10986/12532.
World Bank. 'World Development Indicators Database.' Accessed 15 November 2015. https://data.worldbank.org/indicator/NY.GDP.PCAP.PP.CD.

Interviews with author

Elder, Salhi, 2014, 2015, 2016.
Panchayat member, Ghatbarra, 2016.
President, Sarpanch Sangh, 2015.
Sudha Bharadwaj, 2015.
Sudiep Srivastava, 2015.
Village Member, Madanpur, 2016.
Villager, Khotkorra, 2016.

PART V

Memory, identities, and narratives

21
INDIGENOUS NARRATIVES, SEPARATIONS, DENIALS, AND MEMORIES
Moving beyond loss

Lynette Russell[1]

Introduction

Around the world, settler nations have begun to acknowledge traditional owners particularly when introducing a public event or activity.[2] This is an important gesture and one that frames all of my intellectual work. I write, and live, on the unceded lands of the Kulin people of Naarm, which is now known as Melbourne, in Victoria, Australia. For many Indigenous people, the acknowledgement of Country (or traditional owners) is unsatisfying, as it is often cursory, and all too frequently easily passed over. Conservative, and reactionary, media have described acknowledgements and welcomes as a 'racist mechanism of division'.[3] Perhaps for this very reason, I consider that to acknowledge those who have gone before us, and those who have endured, is integral to any work that takes place within 'Indigenous Studies'. Melbourne is a modern city, but beneath the kilometres of coaxial and broadband cables, tonnes of concrete, and mountains of steel, every footfall we take is on Aboriginal land. Where once there were dreaming tracks, today we have tram tracks, bike lanes, walking paths, and roads; beneath the buildings sits the land on which Aboriginal people have lived for tens of thousands of years, since time immemorial. Perhaps over 3,000 generations, mother to son, father to daughter, they (we) lived, thrived, survived. Born here, died here, were buried here, practised ceremonies here, hunted, fished, and gathered; they built their homes here. They told the stories of the night skies, the seasons, the changes over time, yearly events. They traded high-quality quarried stone across great distances, wove baskets and eel traps, and decorated magnificent possum skin cloaks with ochre designs that told the story of the owner's life. Cloaks that became a burial shroud. They saw drought, and floods; they practised fire-stick farming. They cared for and managed their landscape, ensuring they benefitted from its bounty. They watched the sea level rise and create Port Phillip Bay. They saw the Birrarung (Yarra River) flood and then retreat, where it once wound its way across the plain; it became the shipping channel. And through all of this – countless generations, thousands of stories – they maintained their connection to Country. A connection that has never been broken; it has indeed been tested at times, but never broken. It is all of those ancestors who went before that I acknowledge, who I respect and am guided by, and to whom I try to listen. And while acknowledgements like this might be determined tokenistic, as Gamilaraay author Luke Pearson notes: 'It is a TOKEN gesture. [And] It is meant to be a symbol of respect and understanding.'[4] This is what I ask the reader to note when I make an acknowledgement of Country.

Oral traditions are flexible, they are fluid, and they are adaptable. This does not mean that they are fiction, or made up, but they are iterative and palimpsestic. Family memoir and biography often draw on oral histories, but for many Indigenous families this must also be supplemented by archival research. A reconsideration of oral traditions, family histories, and Indigenous identity is timely. Here in Australia, the right-wing media and social media continue to take aim at the identity of Indigenous people, especially if they are fair-skinned or do not look identifiably Aboriginal. These attacks are not, however, only from non-Indigenous commentators, and some Indigenous voices can also be heard critiquing those who come to a late understanding of their heritage.[5] This is an experience Indigenous people from most settler colonies share.[6]

Indigenous identity is a post-colonial construct, in an Australian context, though translatable elsewhere; Sarah Maddison observes: 'Before colonisation, "Aboriginal" or "Indigenous" people did not exist in those terms, and there was no "Indigeneity" or "Aboriginality" in the sense that there is today.'[7] Jeffrey Sissons notes that:

> [t]he operation of oppressive authenticity has been integral to the foundation of all settler nations and it continues to haunt the formation and implementation of their cultural politics. Included in the excluded middles of many post-settler states today are millions of Indigenous people variously described as 'half-castes', 'mixed-blood', 'urbanized', non-traditional' and 'westernized' – usually the majority of their Indigenous citizens.[8]

'Oppressive authenticity' has had a profound impact on the lives and identities of many Indigenous individuals, families, and communities. In urban and territorialised communities, many people find that they are 'marginalised and dismissed as contaminated, impure and inauthentic'.[9]

Removals and separations

Against this backdrop, Aboriginal people have constantly told their stories both within and outside of their communities. As an expert on Aboriginal literacies, Penny Van Toorn writes:

> from as far back as 1796, Aboriginal people were recounting small segments of their lives in piece-meal, fragmentary, written forms in hundreds of handwritten letters, petitions, submissions to official inquiries and court testimonies.[10]

The non-Indigenous, settler-colonial nation was not, however, prepared to listen for over 150 years. It was as late as the 1970s before Australian Aboriginal people found that there was a non-Indigenous audience for their writings. This was when Indigenous narratives emerged, often sitting uncomfortably between the genres of memoir, history, biography, or fiction.[11] Literary theorist and scholar Kay Schaffer observes that these 'became a forum for indigenous people to speak in [sic] their own behalf, thus mediating 200 years of being spoken about' by non-Indigenous (supposed) experts such as ethnographers, linguists, anthropologists, historians, and government officials.[12] A key concern of these writings and narratives was the removal of children from their natal families, and their subsequent institutionalisation or (non-Indigenous) adoption.

In 1997, the statutory body the Australian Human Rights Commission (established in 1986) released the *Bringing Them Home* report.[13] The report documented the pervasiveness of forced child removals and effects on the Aboriginal children, their families, and communities. *Bringing Them Home* emphasised that Indigenous narratives of our history needed to be considered as a matter of urgent national concern. For the first time, non-Indigenous Australians could no longer claim to not know the history, effects, and consequences of the government's assimilationist policies towards Aboriginal children who were forcibly removed from their birth families between 1910 and 1970. As the report notes: 'In that time, not one Indigenous family has escaped the effects of forcible removal.'[14] Sadly, however, over two decades later, denialists – mostly conservative commentators – continue to claim that the removals have been exaggerated and those that did occur were for the child's 'own good'.

In the decade prior to the report, as Australia began to celebrate the bicentenary of European occupation, Aboriginal people organised political protests and began to assert that their stories must be heard. As the author and Aboriginal activist Ruby Langford Ginibi observed, audiences were hungry for 'authentic' Indigenous narratives, most notably represented in the phenomenal success of Sally Morgan's *My Place*, published in 1987,[15] which 'opened up the country', allowing Indigenous voices and experiences to be heard and acknowledged.[16]

Sally Morgan's *My Place* is a book that resonated with my own understandings of my family's history and its series of secrets. Deeply affected by, and implicated in, the colonial project, I began to research my family's Aboriginal story in 1996. At the time I was concerned not to over-claim either my Aboriginal identity or my sense of belonging. This was interpreted, largely by non-Indigenous commentators, as a fixed statement rather than an expression of a moment in time. Like many Indigenous people before me, the operationalising of oppressive authenticity was used against me.[17] Rather than seeing the reclamation of identity, or that loss is a quintessential Indigenous experience, my search and narrative were described by non-Aboriginal literary scholar, Jennifer Jones, as replicating it.

A Little Bird Told Me is the narrative I developed as I tried to understand the life of my Aboriginal great-grandmother Emily, and by extension her daughter, my grandmother Gladys.[18] I wrote the book for my father, for my children, but ultimately it was mostly for myself. I would argue that most indigenous memoir is similarly framed. Understanding the past is necessary in order to appreciate the present, particularly for those who choose to work in Indigenous studies and histories. I began the research as I wanted to know why Emily and Gladys had taken great care to keep a number of secrets and maintain mistruths through the generations. One of their secrets involved our family's Aboriginal heritage. Across the generations, we were purported to be 'Gypsies', and more latterly the descendants of a Polynesian princess.[19] Another secret, possibly even more 'shameful' in their eyes, was Emily's catastrophic mental breakdown and subsequent lengthy confinement. Emily was detained in several 'mental hospitals' under the Mental Hygiene Act 1933 (No. 4157), between Christmas 1925 and February 1941. She was for the most part an inmate at Caloola in Sunbury (Figure 21.2). After 16 years, she was released and declared 'relieved'. But her relationship with her daughter Gladys was irreparably broken. She had left when Gladys was a child and returned when she was a young mother, married with a son (my father) (Figure 21.1).

Figure 21.1 The cover of *A Little Bird Told Me: Family Secrets, Necessary Lies*, 2002

Before I began the research, I had always somewhat romantically thought of Emily's madness as more like that which Polonius comments on in *Hamlet*: 'Though this be madness, yet there is method in't.'[20] Or perhaps that of Emily Dickinson, in 'Much Madness Is Divinest Sense'.

> Much Madness is divinest Sense –
> To a discerning Eye –
> Much Sense – the starkest Madness –
> 'Tis the Majority
> In this, as all, prevail –
> Assent – and you are sane –
> Demur – you're straightway dangerous –
> And handled with a Chain –[21]

I had entertained the idea that she chose madness and insanity instead of buckling to the colonial system. None of these musings were correct, I now suspect. Emily heard voices and she responded to them. Perhaps she spoke to the spirits of her ancestors; the truth is that I cannot know with any certainty. Those around her, family and the medical fraternity, thought that this was a pathology. I have no way of knowing what she thought, as her medical records are largely silent of voice, apart from one or two comments over her 16-year period of incarceration. She was variously described as having auditory hallucinations, schizophrenia, mental breakdown, severe anxiety, psychosis, and mental collapse. At one point of her incarceration, she refused to speak, but rather she sang her replies. I will never forget the powerful jolt I experienced when I read the Doctor's notes that 'she sits and picks at the bars of her bird cage'. A bird cage was the vernacular term for a restraining device, commonly used in the early part of the twentieth century. It was, I was assured by the mental health archivist, much less gruesome than it sounds. As she was placed in the 'bird cage' and she answered in song, the title of the book became obvious (Figure 21.2).

Figure 21.2 The Caloola Psychiatric Asylum, where Emily was incarcerated for over 16 years
Source: Image from Wikicommons

Reception

A Little Bird Told Me sold reasonably well by Australian book industry standards. While Sally Morgan sold over 700,000 copies,[22] mine was a more modest number a little shy of 10,000. It was quickly placed on Higher School Certificate courses in New South Wales and Victoria, and most local libraries purchased copies. It was well reviewed, mostly positively, and the reception was incredibly pleasing. The period immediately after publication saw dozens of radio interview invitations, usually with the Australian Broadcasting Corporation's local and national radio stations. ABC television made it the focus of one of the 'postcards from history' short documentaries. Numerous Aboriginal people contacted me, often with more information on the family, and new connections were made. Some family members rejected the book outright and saw my outing myself as, I said in the book, having Aboriginal heritage, as an act of betrayal. In short, I lost some family members, but was rapidly welcomed into a much bigger family of Indigenous Victorians.

In almost all cases, in the first instance, those that reached out to me, who placed me and claimed me, were women. Later, some men came to include me, but it was first and foremost Aboriginal women who supported me. Aboriginal society, at least as it appears here in Victoria, and in my world, has always been heavily matriarchal. Kerrup-J'mara elder Aunty Iris Lovett-Gardner,[23] who figuratively and literally held my hand throughout the whole journey, guided me and became my mentor. She also played a crucial role in the post-publication period. Her wisdom and kindness became an important touchstone as I negotiated the ugly politics of internal-family and external racism. She was very amused when one relative asked about the book's royalties and who would get them. These were modest but not insubstantial for me as an early career researcher, precariously employed and uncertain what to do next. When one family member suggested that he should be entitled to half, as it was 'his story too', Aunty Iris saw the humour and told me that she'd never heard anything 'more Koori'[24]; she quipped, 'we share everything'. This would be, I suspect, a near-universal experience; success is expected to be shared even if failure is not.

Shortly after publication, I ran into the brilliant, luminous, Lisa Bellear, Aboriginal activist, poet, and photographer.[25] Lisa and I had attended the University of Melbourne together. We would often chat and she would entertain my young son, twirling him around and 'dancing' with him. In her usual fashion, she greeted me with warmth and humour, and congratulated me on the book. This was an acknowledgement that meant a great deal to me. Lisa went on to say that she saw Emily and Gladys' stories as part of the stolen generation, a different version of it, but nonetheless a sort of removed-family narrative. That characterisation, which I had not really considered before, was revealing. Over the next few years, I was able to use this as the lens to understand the intergenerational trauma I had observed but not comprehended. This is a trauma that for some families continues to the present, a trauma that, for the most part, I was able to leave behind by researching, writing, and acknowledging. I remain convinced that it is through the process of acknowledging and embracing the story of my history that I was able to control it.

It is not surprising to me at all that so many Indigenous women choose memoir or biography to tell their stories.[26]

When I published *A Little Bird Told Me*, I was careful not to unequivocally claim an Aboriginal identity. My reasons for doing this were complex. First, I was excruciatingly aware that recent declarations of Aboriginal identity were frequently met with assignations of 'Johnny-come-lately'. I had observed this both personally and remotely via the critique of Sally Morgan's *My Place*.[27] Over the last 30 years, my position has shifted; I am comfortable in acknowledging my heritage in myriad ways – it is flexible. Indeed, identity is context-specific and audience-dependant. A fundamental difference between my upbringing and that of my children was the direct result of the book. Where my childhood was shrouded in uncertainty and secrecy, theirs was not. They were always aware of their heritage, their powerful Aboriginal women ancestors. Their acceptance in the Aboriginal community is perhaps one of the most satisfying aspects of the entire journey. Knowing that the denial, the loss, the uncertainty is now in the past.

Women as secret keepers and story tellers

In all the research – the Public Records Office, the State Library, the Mental Health Archives, and the office of Births, Deaths, and Marriages – it was virtually always women who attended me. Meticulous and caring custodians of records and archives, only too willing to help disentangle the threads of a complicated story of which I initially knew just the barest of outlines. I felt, all the while, guided by the women in the story, Emily and Gladys, mentored by Aunty Iris, and tutored by archivists and librarians. It was this immersion into archives that led me to a later project in which we partnered with the Keeper of the Public Record Office, the State Library of Victoria, the Koorie Heritage Trust, and Monash University colleagues in archival science, to interview over 100 Indigenous Victorians about their experiences in accessing family records, and their needs to annotate, amend, and correct these where possible. Again this project was dominated by women archivists, researchers, scholars, and community members. The final report for this, the *Trust and Technology Project*, had a profound impact on the way archives and libraries interact with Indigenous community members.[28] The desire to correct records, once seen as a challenge, is now regarded as adding value to the records, demonstrating their relevance and contemporary utility. None of this would have been possible without *A Little Bird Told Me*.

With what I now think of as a sort of arrogance, partly the result of years of higher education and historical training, I thought I could learn all I needed to know from the archives alone. Though Aunty Iris was my guide and mentor, and she gently chided me that there was much to be gained by talking to people, I was initially reticent. Too much time had passed; no one would remember Emily, who had died in 1964. What I had not considered, however, was the universality of their story. As Lisa Bellear had commented, it was a 'sort of stolen generation story'. It was countless Aboriginal people, especially Elders, who pulled me aside and showed me that the experience of loss, dislocation, and dispossession is a quintessential Aboriginal story. One woman simply and succinctly said, 'we recognise this story, we recognise you'. So, I came to an understanding about the many family members who chose to reject me and the narrative: people with Aboriginal heritage can also be deeply affected and influenced by racism, and for them the knowledge of their Aboriginal ancestors was unwelcome. In choosing to reject me, they also rejected Emily and Gladys. However, it was far from a negative experience, as through the book I also gained family. A family connected by the fragmentation of the colonial experience, forged out of loss, and built on commonality. Overwhelmingly, I have been offered generosity. For every harsh critic, every act of lateral violence, such as denial or questioning and rejection of my Aboriginal identity, there has been ten times that in offerings of kindness, understanding, and acceptance. The power of this story has been with me these past decades and continues to shape how I interact with the world.

Family history as history

Family history is a vortex. It can be an endless search of official certificates, births, deaths, baptisms, and marriages. Ancestry websites, DNA tracing, and genealogical software proliferate, and family trees expand almost forest-like, with branches becoming choked and difficult to read, forever rewritten and reconfigured. Until I had undertaken the research, like many academic historians, I didn't really value family history; I would look for Emily and Gladys and I would tell their story and exit promptly. Of course, it is never that simple. Gladys, my grandmother, married Walter, whose family had worked on ships in the Bass Strait. They fished for lobsters, and in the off-season gathered mutton birds. Both he and his two brothers married Aboriginal women and the family connections stretch across the straits to Flinders Island and northern Tasmania. Their grandmother came from Boarhunt, just near Portsmouth, in Southern England. As Eric Richards notes, in the 1820s and 1830s, the debates on British poverty and colonisation led to the growth of free and assisted emigration to Australia.[29] This family was one of the hundreds of thousands of working-class poor who emigrated in the nineteenth century. And like many they merged with Aboriginal people, via 'heterosexual unions and intermarriage'.[30]

In 2019, I set out to visit Boarhunt and see where my English ancestors had lived. I pondered the life of a woman who travelled from southern England to Flinders Island, where she is now buried in Lady Barron Cemetery. On a gloriously sunny yet chilly Spring day I, and a family member, wandered the grounds of St Nicholas church and graveyard. Originally, this had been a Saxon church built of stone quarried from the Isle of Wight. I stopped and collected a flint pebble from the driveway; it rests on my desk as I write. We stood beneath the massive Yew tree that is on the national register of heritage trees, and noticed the ribbons new and old and very faded that had been tied to its boughs. This magnificent tree has been estimated to date from around CE 185, meaning that it was already 880 years old when the Saxon church was established here in the eleventh century. Generations of my ancestors would have seen it; hundreds are buried nearby. The tree has a large hollow in it. The church newsletter that I picked up noted:

> local legend has it that a family, in medieval times, sheltered within the hollow trunk throughout an entire winter. An alternative story suggests that the incumbent minister allowed a poor widow to shelter there during Victorian times.

On leaving, we drove along the romantically named Trampers Lane and located the seventeenth-century home named Russell Place. And it occurred to me that here, on the opposite side of the planet, other ancestors lived generation after generation in the same place. Until, one day, some left and, in time, connected to Emily and her ancestors, creating in me a lineage that spans the vast oceans. Against my better judgement, I know that the story of my great-great-grandmother from Boarhunt, her story of travel and relocation, is one I will eventually tell, not right now but at some point in the future. The irresistible pull of the vortex is ever-present.

For me, the doing of history is as important as the writing of it. When I wrote *A Little Bird Told Me*, I travelled to the asylums where Emily was constrained, and I visited the Country of her ancestors, and mine. I saw the small tin hut she was raised in, unexpectedly still standing, having operated as a post office into the 1930s. My father retraced our steps a few years back and visited the hut in Lillimur in western Victoria. Lillimur is thought to be derived from the word for wattle gum, in the Wergaia language of the Wotjobaluk people.[31] There is a sweet irony in this name as one of the few examples of 'cultural knowledge' my father has always held is that he would harvest and eat ripe wattle sap. Over the intervening decades, the hut had fallen over, probably in one of the strong windstorms the Wimmera is known for. I am thankful that it at least was there when I visited in the 1990s and I got to imagine what life might have been like for an Aboriginal girl and her family who grew up on the edge of the desert, long before she became a mental patient, before she became a subject of intrigue to me, and before she became a secret to be hidden. In a sense before she became white.

One of the challenges for me, as an academic historian writing a family history, or in the case of *A Little Bird Told Me* a biography and memoir, was the dismissive way many colleagues engaged with the narrative. It was my experience that many still want to keep capital H History separate from family history, and often even local histories are similarly dismissed. I understand this because I was guilty of it too. I gave an academic paper on my research at a biography symposium, much to the consternation of many assembled who were studying 'great men and women'. Several thought that Emily and Gladys were entitled to a life story but not a biography. I felt the sting of that intrusion into their space, and decided that I would not speak publicly about *A Little Bird Told Me*. But distance, time, experience, and perhaps confidence have made me reconsider. The Goenpul scholar Aileen Moreton-Robinson argued in *Talkin' Up to the White Woman* that she prefers 'life writings' for Aboriginal women's stories because of the collaborative and 'fundamentally social'

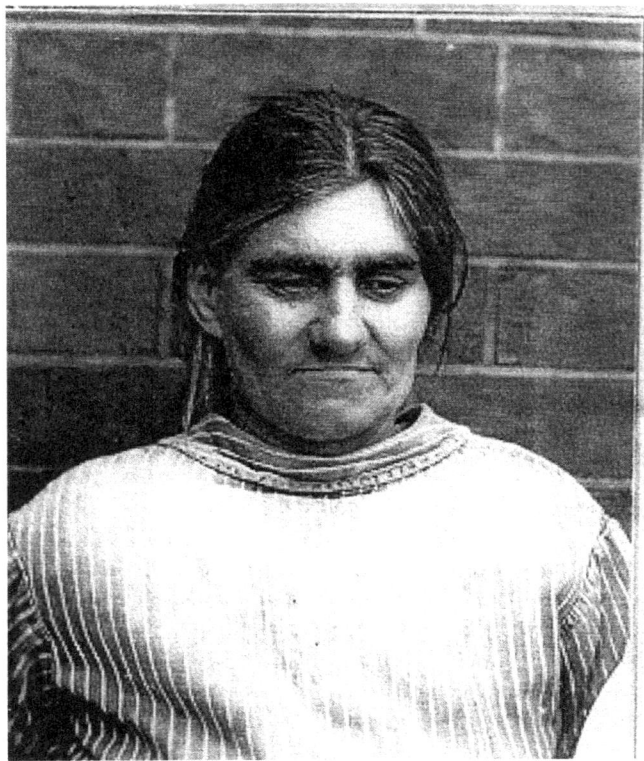

Figure 21.3 The author's great-grandmother Emily – patient photograph from circa 1920, wearing hospital issue pyjamas

aspects of the writers' life experiences.[32] By 'social', I take Moreton-Robinson to mean that the development of a life story is a joint if not group effort (Figure 21.3).

Having the opportunity to revisit *A Little Bird Told Me* has been an unexpected privilege – this has been a rare interlude, reflecting on previous work. The modern academy does not lend itself to slow research. We are constantly pressured to produce quality output and move on to the next project. The chance to reflect on prior work hardly ever eventuates. This process has allowed me to recalibrate the impact of the research and think deeply about the crucial role it has played in the way I do history. Writing *A Little Bird Told Me* grounded me, it showed me my connections to the past, and it allowed the development of new connections and the emergence of new and different types of engagement. While some family were critical and thought that the secrets should stay firmly hidden and in the past, I welcomed the chance to set to the record right. Every family historian, and indeed every biographer, will discover something that others want hidden. The question of whether some secrets should stay unexplored needs to be answered by the individual researcher. I went to great lengths to preserve the anonymity of family members, leaving out surnames where I could. However, for me at least, and in this context in particular, while the 'family secrets' were 'necessary lies', uncovering them and bringing them to light was equally necessary. What others saw as a betrayal I saw as an honouring.

Biographers make decisions, some big, some small; they layer interpretation, and create context. As a historian, I know that the stories we tell are always partial, and always subjective. Although we might try for objectivity, at best it is an illusion and worst it is a fraud. When I write Aboriginal history for the most part, I look for agency, and response. I want to see reaction; I want to find those moments in which Indigenous people exerted control, where they spoke back, where their actions had impact, where their voices were heard.

Notes

1 This paper derives from a lecture for the Royal Historical Society Victoria. An abbreviated version appeared in the Victorian History Journal. This contribution is a much more developed and expanded essay.
2 M. McKenna, 'Tokenism or Belated Recognition? Welcome to Country and the Emergence of Indigenous Protocol in Australia, 1991–2014,' *Journal of Australian Studies* 38, no. 4 (2014): 477–478; S. Blenkinsop and M. Fettes, 'Land, Language and Listening: The Transformations That Can Flow from Acknowledging Indigenous Land,' *Journal of Philosophy of Education* 54, no. 4 (2020), 1033–1046.
3 E. Kowal, 'Welcome to Country: Acknowledgment, Belonging and White Anti-Racism,' *Cultural Studies Review* 21, no. 2 (2015), 173–204.
4 Quoted in Kowal, 'Welcome to Country,' 191.
5 Gundijtmara activist and 'cultural healer' Dr Richard Frankland has identified lateral violence as endemic in Indigenous communities. He is not referring to episodes of physical violence per se but rather insidious attacks focussing on the identity and authenticity of community members especially those who are perceived as successful or imagined to be benefitting from their Aboriginality; see https://www.humanrights.gov.au/our-work/chapter-2-lateral-violence-aboriginal-and-torres-strait-islander-communities-social#fnB2. See also, B. Wingard, 'A Conversation with Lateral Violence,' *The International Journal of Narrative Therapy and Community Work* 1 (2010): 13–17. J. Huggins, 'Always Was Always Will Be,' *Australian Historical Studies* 25, no. 100 (1993): 459–464.
6 For Canadian examples, see J. Green, 'The Complexity of Indigenous Identity Formation and Politics in Canada,' *International Journal of Critical Indigenous Studies* 2, no. 2 (2009): 36–46; for Aotearoa, the United States of America, and other settler nations, see C. Allen, *Blood Narrative: Indigenous Identity in American Indian and Maori Literary and Activist Texts* (Durham, NC: Duke University Press, 2002).
7 S. Maddison, 'Indigenous Identity, "Authenticity" and the Structural Violence of Settler Colonialism,' *Identities* 20, no. 3 (2013): 289. See also, L. Russell, ed., *Colonial Frontiers: Indigenous-European Encounters in Settler Societies* (Manchester: Manchester University Press, 2001), 1–12; M. Kent, 'The Importance of Being Uros: Indigenous Identity Politics in the Genomic Age,' *Social Studies of Science* 43, no. 4 (2013): 534–556.
8 J. Sissons, *First Peoples: Indigenous Cultures and Their Futures* (London: Reaktion Books, 2005), 39.
9 M. Harris, M. Nakata, and B. Carlson, *The Politics of Identity: Emerging Indigeneity* (Sydney: UTS ePress, 2013), 2.
10 P. Van Toorn, 'Indigenous Australian Life Writing: Tactics and Transformations.' In *Telling Stories: Indigenous History and Memory in Australia and New Zealand*, ed. Bain Attwood and Fiona McGowan (St Leonards: Allen & Unwin, 2001), 1–2.

11 K. Schaffer, 'Stolen Generation Narratives in Local and Global Contexts,' *Antipodes* 16, no. 1 (June 2002): 5–10. See also, P. Van Toorn, 'Indigenous Texts and Narratives,' in *The Cambridge Companion to Australian Literature*, ed. Elizabeth Webby (Oakleigh: Cambridge University Press, 2000), 19–49; and G. Whitlock, 'Active Remembrance: Testimony, Memoir and the Work of Reconciliation,' in *Rethinking Settler Colonialism*, ed. Annie Coombes (Manchester: Manchester University Press, 2017), 25–43.
12 Schaffer, 'Stolen Generation Narratives,' 5.
13 National Inquiry into the Separation of Aboriginal and Torres Strait Islander Children from Their Families (Australia), *Bringing Them Home: Report of the National Inquiry into the Separation of Aboriginal and Torres Strait Islander Children from Their Families* (Sydney: Human Rights and Equal Opportunities Commission, 1997).
14 National Inquiry (Australia), *Bringing Them Home*, 37.
15 S. Morgan, *My Place* (Fremantle: Fremantle Arts Centre, 1987).
16 Quoted in Schaffer, 'Stolen Generation Narratives,' 6.
17 For example, see J. Jones, 'Indigenous Life Stories,' *Life Writing* 1, no. 2 (2004): 209–218.
18 L. Russell, *A Little Bird Told Me: Family Secrets, Necessary Lies* (St Leonards: Allen and Unwin, 2002).
19 The idea of descending from Polynesian royalty is not an uncommon trope among Indigenous people, particularly those affected by dispossession, dislocation, and family separations. I have heard several families cite the same story, where their ancestors had implied a Polynesian identity rather than an Aboriginal one. I am also aware of one family who on adopting an Aboriginal baby were assured that the child was in fact Māori. For an excellent exploration the idea of the Polynesian people as 'nearly white', see M.R. Arvin, *Possessing Polynesians: The Science of Settler Colonial Whiteness in Hawaii and Oceania* (Durham, NC: Duke University Press, 2019).
20 William Shakespeare, *Hamlet*, Act 2, Scene 2.
21 Emily Dickinson, 'Much Madness Is Divinest Sense,' 1862, https://www.edickinson.org/editions/2/image_sets/12170055.
22 Sales figures quoted in Schaffer, 'Stolen Generation Narratives,' 6.
23 The use of the term Aunty is, within Australian Indigenous culture, an honorific bestowed on elders and influential community members.
24 Koori is the term used to refer to Indigenous people in south-eastern Australia. Most people prefer to use their 'tribal' affiliation; however for many, this remains unknown.
25 For an excellent reading of Lisa's work and life, see A. Brewster, 'Brokering Cross-Racial Feminism: Reading Indigenous Australian Poet Lisa Bellear,' *Feminist Theory* 8, no. 2 (2007): 209–221.
26 This argument is supported by the scholarship of I. Dulfano, *Indigenous Feminist Narratives: I/We: Wo(men) of an(Other) Way* (Basingstoke: Palgrave Macmillan, 2015). See also M. McDonell, 'Locating the Text: Genre and Indigenous Australian Women's Life Writing,' *Life Writing* 2, no. 2 (2005): 71–90; J. Seran, 'Australian Aboriginal Memoir and Memory: A Stolen Generations Trauma Narrative,' *Humanities* 4 (2015): 661–675; G.T. Couser, *Memoir: An Introduction* (Oxford: Oxford University Press, 2011).
27 I am thinking here especially of the critique of Huggins, 'Always Was Always Will Be.' Many non-Indigenous people similarly criticised Morgan; however, they are of little concern to my position.
28 See S. McKemmish, L. Iacovino, L. Russell, and M. Castan, 'Editors' Introduction to Keeping Cultures Alive: Archives and Indigenous Human Rights,' *Archival Science: Special Issue: Keeping Cultures Alive: Archives and Indigenous Human Rights* 12, no. 2 (2012): 93–111; S. McKemmish, L. Iacovino, E. Ketelaar, M. Castan, and L. Russell, 'Resetting Relationships: Archives and Indigenous Human Rights in Australia,' *Archives & Manuscripts* 39, no. 1 (2011): 107–144.
29 E. Richards, 'How Did Poor People Emigrate from the British Isles to Australia in the Nineteenth Century?' *Journal of British Studies* 32, no. 3 (1993): 255.

30 For an outstanding analysis of the intermarriage between the Irish and Aboriginal people, see A. McGrath, 'Shamrock Aborigines: The Irish, the Aboriginal Australians and Their Children,' *Aboriginal History* 34 (2010): 56.
31 J. Reid, *Wergaia Community Grammar and Dictionary*, Melbourne Linguistics Program, Monash University, 2007.
32 A. Moreton-Robinson, *Talkin' Up to the White Woman: Indigenous Women and Feminism* (St Lucia: University of Queensland Press, 2000), 82.

Bibliography

Allen, C. *Blood Narrative: Indigenous Identity in American Indian and Maori Literary and Activist Texts*. Durham, NC: Duke University Press, 2002.

Arvin, M.R. *Possessing Polynesians: The Science of Settler Colonial Whiteness in Hawaii and Oceania*. Durham, NC: Duke University Press, 2019.

Blenkinsop, S., and M. Fettes. 'Land, Language and Listening: The Transformations That Can Flow from Acknowledging Indigenous Land.' *Journal of Philosophy of Education* 54 no. 4 (2020): 1033–1046.

Brewster, A. 'Brokering Cross-Racial Feminism: Reading Indigenous Australian Poet Lisa Bellear.' *Feminist Theory* 8, no. 2 (2007): 209–221.

Couser, G.T. *Memoir: An Introduction*. Oxford: Oxford University Press, 2011.

Dickinson, E. 'Much Madness Is Divinest Sense.' 1862. https://www.edickinson.org/editions/2/image_sets/12170055.

Dulfano, I. *Indigenous Feminist Narratives: I/We: Wo(men) of an(Other) Way*. Basingstoke: Palgrave Macmillan, 2015.

Green, J. 'The Complexity of Indigenous Identity Formation and Politics in Canada.' *International Journal of Critical Indigenous Studies* 2, no. 2 (2009): 36–46.

Harris, M., M. Nakata, and B. Carlson. *The Politics of Identity: Emerging Indigeneity*. Sydney: UTS ePress, 2013.

Huggins, J. 'Always Was Always Will Be.' *Australian Historical Studies* 25, no. 100 (1993): 459–464.

Jones, J. 'Indigenous Life Stories.' *Life Writing* 1, no. 2 (2004): 209–218.

Kent, M. 'The Importance of Being Uros: Indigenous Identity Politics in the Genomic Age.' *Social Studies of Science* 4, no. 4 (2013): 534–556.

Kowal, E. 'Welcome to Country: Acknowledgement, Belonging and White Anti-Racism.' *Cultural Studies Review* 21, no. 2 (2015): 173–204.

Maddison, S. 'Indigenous Identity, "Authenticity" and the Structural Violence of Settler Colonialism.' *Identities* 20, no. 3 (2013): 288–303.

McDonell, M. 'Locating the Text: Genre and Indigenous Australian Women's Life Writing.' *Life Writing* 2, no. 2 (2005): 71–90.

McGrath, A. 'Shamrock Aborigines: The Irish, the Aboriginal Australians and Their Children.' *Aboriginal History* 34 (2010): 55–84.

McKemmish, S., L. Iacovino, E. Ketelaar, M. Castan, and L. Russell. 'Resetting Relationships: Archives and Indigenous Human Rights in Australia.' *Archives & Manuscripts* 39, no. 1 (2011): 107–144.

McKemmish, S., L. Iacovino, L. Russell, and M. Castan. 'Editors' Introduction to Keeping Cultures Alive: Archives and Indigenous Human Rights.' *Archival Science: Special Issue: Keeping Cultures Alive: Archives and Indigenous Human Rights* 12, no. 2 (2012): 93–111.

McKenna, M. 'Tokenism or Belated Recognition? Welcome to Country and the Emergence of Indigenous Protocol in Australia, 1991–2014.' *Journal of Australian Studies* 38, no. 4 (2014): 477–8.

Moreton-Robinson, A. *Talkin' Up to the White Woman: Indigenous Women and Feminism*. St Lucia: University of Queensland Press, 2000.

Morgan, S. *My Place*. Fremantle: Fremantle Arts Centre, 1987.

National Inquiry into the Separation of Aboriginal and Torres Strait Islander Children from Their Families (Australia). *Bringing Them Home: Report of the National Inquiry into the Separation of Aboriginal and Torres Strait Islander Children from Their Families.* Sydney: Human Rights and Equal Opportunities Commission, 1997.

Reid, J. *Wergaia Community Grammar and Dictionary.* Melbourne Linguistics Program, Monash University, 2007.

Richards, E. 'How Did Poor People Emigrate from the British Isles to Australia in the Nineteenth Century?' *Journal of British Studies* 32, no. 3 (1993): 250–279.

Russell, L., ed. *Colonial Frontiers: Indigenous-European Encounters in Settler Societies.* Manchester: Manchester University Press, 2001.

Russell, L. *A Little Bird Told Me: Family Secrets, Necessary Lies.* St Leonards: Allen & Unwin, 2002.

Schaffer, K. 'Stolen Generation Narratives in Local and Global Contexts.' *Antipodes* 16, no. 1 (June 2002): 5–10.

Seran, J. 'Australian Aboriginal Memoir and Memory: A Stolen Generations Trauma Narrative.' *Humanities* 4 (2015): 661–675.

Shakespeare, William. *Hamlet.* Act 2, Scene 2.

Sissons, J. *First Peoples: Indigenous Cultures and Their Futures.* London: Reaktion Books, 2005.

Van Toorn, P. 'Indigenous Texts and Narratives.' In *The Cambridge Companion to Australian Literature*, edited by Elizabeth Webby, 19–49. Oakleigh: Cambridge University Press, 2000.

Van Toorn, P. 'Indigenous Australian Life Writing: Tactics and Transformations.' In *Telling Stories: Indigenous History and Memory in Australia and New Zealand*, edited by Bain Attwood and Fiona McGowan, 1–20. St Leonards: Allen & Unwin, 2001.

Whitlock, G. 'Active Remembrance: Testimony, Memoir and the Work of Reconciliation.' In *Rethinking Settler Colonialism*, edited by Annie Coombes, 25–43. Manchester: Manchester University Press, 2017.

Wingard, B. 'A Conversation with Lateral Violence.' *The International Journal of Narrative Therapy and Community Work* 1 (2010): 13–17.

22
REMEMBERING REMOVAL
Indigenous narratives of colonial collecting practices in the Gulf of Papua (Papua New Guinea)

Chris Urwin

Introduction

During the early colonial era, collectors from Australia, Europe, and North America descended on the Gulf of Papua (Papua New Guinea) in a rush to acquire 'primitive' artefacts for Western markets and institutions. The object hunters had a variety of intentions and approaches to acquiring artefacts from local Indigenous people. Field diaries, colonial records, and early ethnographic publications offer Western perspectives on the cross-cultural interactions that took place. In this essay, I explore contemporary Indigenous perspectives on the removal of material culture in the early 1900s. Narratives (oral and textual) told by the Kaivakovu and Larihairu village communities of Orokolo Bay in the Gulf of Papua describe a traumatic event: the extraction of a preserved ceremonial longhouse post (*ive*) at gunpoint by the anthropologist Francis Edgar Williams. I unpack these stories and relevant archival sources with reference to notions of remembering, trauma, and telescoping. For the inhabitants of Orokolo Bay, the silencing of materials of ancestral communal importance some 80–90 years ago has not caused forgetting. Rather, social memories of the now-absent *ive* and of violent acts of removal endure and inform Indigenous conceptions of museum institutions today.

Remembering difficult things: removal, trauma, and telescoping

Removals and their attendant societal effects (for example, inter-generational trauma) have long featured as a central theme in global Indigenous histories. In contexts such as Australia, Northern Europe, and North America, the term has predominantly been used to describe the removal of Indigenous people from their homelands by the colonial state[1]. These removals have taken many different forms. In Australia, Aboriginal children were removed from their families and communities from the early 1900s to the 1970s.² In Northern Europe, Sámi peoples were forcibly displaced from their reindeer-herding grounds in northern Sweden in the 1920s.³ Removals have been, and continue to be, subverted by those who are displaced. In spite of coercive removal events enacted by colonial states, in many instances, Indigenous community members retain or reconstruct connections to their ancestral homelands by visiting them, by imagining and remembering them, or by reclaiming them legally and thus physically from the state.⁴ Further, some sites of enforced relocation (e.g. missions, reservations, areas within Western city-scapes) have since become important historical, ancestral, and spiritual places for Indigenous community members.

Here, I examine a different form of removal: the extraction of cultural materials from Indigenous communities in Papua New Guinea's (PNG's) Gulf of Papua by colonial agents in the late 1800s and early 1900s. In this Indigenous context, people were not often removed from places, but colonial officials, traders, missionaries, and anthropologists took cultural materials from their social and ceremonial settings. As I explore in this essay, removals of 'things' share some commonalities with removals of people. Items of ancestral communal importance can be regarded as kin, and their loss from the landscape is felt deeply today. For example, key ancestral heirlooms (*taonga*) remind Maori people (of Aotearoa/New Zealand) of their genealogies and carry the 'spiritual essence' of the ancestors.⁵ Many *taonga* were removed from place or lost in the late nineteenth century at a time when the colonial state was attempting to dispossess Maori people of their lands. For Indigenous people in Australia, landscape features can be sacred reminders of ancestral actions and cosmological events.⁶ Even large landscape features have been 'salvaged' from Indigenous cultural landscapes, such as 92 blocks of stone with carved designs which were quarried from Gooreng Gooreng lands in the 1970s (and are today the subject of plans for repatriation).

The case study I present is from Orokolo Bay in the Gulf of Papua, where in 2015 I conducted archaeological and anthropological fieldwork. Oral tradition interviews with members of the villages of Kaivakovu and Larihairu are the primary material from which I examine how people currently understand and remember the removals of some 80–90 years prior. I explore how remembering endures despite physical erasure; how traumatic events are framed, known, and reconstructed across generations; and how narratives about the events frame how Orokolo Bay locals conceive of museums and collecting institutions today.

Central to my study are the ways in which personal and social memories are constituted. In recent years, memory researchers have emphasised the notion that memory is not an abstract store of information, but an engaged practice (sometimes called 'memory work').⁷ Broadly defined, the activities of memory are *remembering* (the perpetuation of and engagement with memories and knowledge) and *forgetting* (the temporary or permanent cessation of engagement with memories). Michael Lambek, for instance, describes memory as 'more intersubjective and dialogical than exclusively individual, more act (remembering) than object, and more ongoing engagement than passive absorption and 'playback'.⁸

Remembering takes place in relation to the surrounding social and physical world. 'Memory props' such as 'images, objects, oral histories, stories, folklore, myths, events and places' trigger recollections and remind people of their knowledge of the more distant past (events that happened before their lifetime).[9] Remembering is a process through which people reimagine the past to reflect how they presently view themselves, their communities, and the world.[10] In other words, imagining and remembering are 'co-constituents of perception'.[11] Through her memoirs, Annette Kuhn explores how 'memory shapes the stories we tell, in the present, about the past'.[12] Kuhn forensically traces how recollections of her childhood were imaginatively formed in relation to places, experiences (some of which were traumatic), photographs, and films. Based on her own reflexive autobiography, Kuhn concludes that 'events narrated or portrayed in memory texts often ... telescope or merge into one another in the telling, so that a single recounted memory fuses together a series of possibly discrete events'.[13] The 'memory texts' Kuhn refers to are memories that have been 'voiced' – they have been given narrative form through the activity of remembering.[14] While remembering may be 'preoccupied with the past', memories are given voice in the present; the purpose of remembering is not to establish chronology, but to construct meaning and identity.[15] Trauma has a deep impact on how remembering and forgetting play out. In some instances, traumatic events and their subsequent 'forgetting' are state-sanctioned.[16] Denis Byrne terms this the 'structures of forgetting', whereby the material evidences of traumatic events are erased to silence individual and social memories.[17] True silencing is seldom successful. Byrne sought to examine how Balinese people remembered a murderous military coup that took place in the mid-1960s, the physical evidence of which had mostly been erased. He found that people held 'buried' 'private memories' of the traumatic events, which they held in relation to 'things and landscapes'.[18] These emplaced reminders of past events are subtle, legible only to locals. Traumatic events can erode or transform individual and social memories by causing changes to local patterns of memorialisation and commemoration. Among the Haya in Tanzania, the deaths of many older community members due to the HIV/AIDS epidemic have brought about a 'loss of cultural memorials'.[19] The 'destruction and disappearance of ancient shrine trees' has led to a dramatic decline in engagement with and perpetuation of oral traditions.[20] These previous studies raise the question: how have removals of cultural materials from the Gulf of Papua changed the local landscape of remembering and forgetting?

Traces of trauma: the entanglement of collecting and colonial violence in the Papuan Gulf

The Gulf of Papua spans approximately 400 km of PNG's south coast, encompassing the great river deltas of Fly, Kikori, and Purari (Figure 22.1). This alluvial sand and swamp coastline is inhabited by many language groups, such as Eleman, Purari, Kiwai, Kerewo, and Bamu.[21] By the early 1900s, these groups had acquired global fame for their striking material culture and elaborate social and ceremonial lives. In the late 1800s and early 1900s, the Papuan Gulf language groups had aspects of material culture in common – carved boards depicting ancestor figures, shark-mouthed drums, and vast longhouse structures.[22] Their lives and material

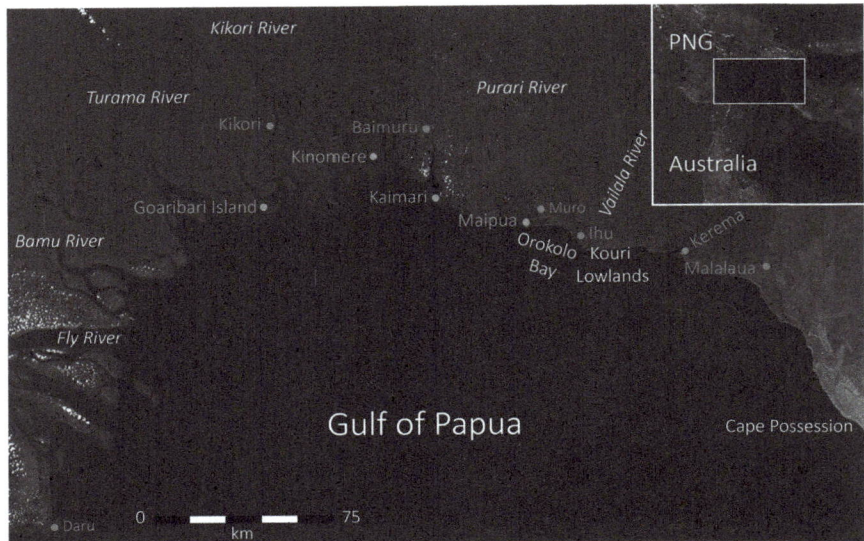

Figure 22.1 Key historical locations and current geographical regions in the Gulf of Papua. Names given are colonial-era village names (not necessarily modern nomenclature).

culture came to be known internationally through a number of channels: the activity of collectors, who brought visually spectacular items such as dance masks back to Western museums and private collections; the writings of anthropologists such as Francis Edgar Williams; and the widely popular photographs and public talks of 'adventurers' such as Frank Hurley.

Collectors descended on the Gulf of Papua even before the region was under formal colonial administration as part of the Territory of Papua from 1883 onwards.[23] The 'first major collector-trader of New Guinea ethnology', Andrew Goldie, travelled to the eastern Gulf of Papua in 1879, where he exchanged 'glass trade beads, tobacco, pieces of hoop-iron or iron hatchets' for locally produced objects.[24] In 1883, James Chalmers of the London Missionary Society (LMS) sailed to the region from Port Moresby – then the capital of the colony, now the capital city of the independent state of PNG – on an Indigenous Motu trading ship to evangelise the large coastal villages.[25] Chalmers gained some 'curios', but for 'neither love nor tomahawks' could he purchase ceremonial dance masks in Orokolo Bay.[26] Collections were also made by Theodore Francis Bevan in late 1886; his voyage of 'discovery' was sponsored by the shipping company Burns Philp and Co.[27] Émigré planters and traders such as S.G. MacDonell were prolific collectors. MacDonell lived in Orokolo Bay from 1911 to 1919, in which time he bought masks and ancestor boards from the Indigenous villagers. He sold these items to art dealers and museums – the Australian Museum and the Queensland Museum today hold around 400 of his acquisitions.[28] In 1912, MacDonell helped to facilitate the ethnological fieldwork of Alfred Buell Lewis of the Field Museum in Chicago.

Like Chalmers before him, Lewis found Papuan Gulf peoples unwilling to part with 'good planks and carved figures' such as bull-roarers and boards figured with totemic ancestors, which were valued for their use and meaning in ceremonies (as well as for their aesthetics).[29]

Violence and the removal of material culture were profoundly entangled during the early colonial era. In April 1901 – nearly two decades into his ministry in the Gulf of Papua – Chalmers entered a Kerewo longhouse (*dubu*) at Goaribari Island with a fellow missionary, nine Kiwai-speaking mission students, and a chief from Ipisia village.[30] All 12 outsiders were killed in the *dubu* and were ceremonially decapitated. Colonial retribution for the killings was swift.[31] Two retributive trips occurred, but I dwell here only on the first, which occurred on 1 May of the same year. A force of some 'six Europeans ... and thirty-six armed native constabulary' led by Lieutenant-Governor Sir George Le Hunte attacked the Kerewo villages, hoping to recover the remains of the two Europeans.[32] The force destroyed more than 100 'fighting canoes', burned longhouses to the ground (in one instance, the fire spread and destroyed the entire village), and killed 24 locals. The revenge party salvaged 'carved figures and weapons' from the longhouses prior to burning them, lest these be 'uselessly destroyed'. Colonial agents left behind 'embers, ashes and material ruin' while removing non-architectural cultural materials to prevent their destruction.[33]

In the latter months of 1922, the explorer and photographer Frank Hurley and Alan McCulloch of the Australian Museum would perpetuate this pattern of violence and theft. On 20 October, the unscrupulous collectors were visiting the village of Kaimari in the Purari River delta as part of Hurley's second visit to the region. The pair were joined by Williams, then the Assistant Government Anthropologist in Papua.[34] When 'the natives refused to sell or give' them bull-roarers, Hurley and McCulloch tried and failed to steal them from their keeping place in a longhouse. They later succeeded in pressing the Kaimari village elders to give them a selection of the bull-roarers.[35] Kaimari locals were aggrieved at the bullying tactics and complained to their administrators. The villagers believed that the collecting trip had been sanctioned by the colonial administration, due to the presence of the colonial agent Williams.[36] Williams was dismayed by Hurley and McCulloch's conduct. As a result, he would make only a modest collection of artefacts for the colonial administration during his tenure as Government Anthropologist in Papua (1928–1941).[37] The close relationship between colonial violence, collections, and collecting institutions in New Guinea is mirrored by near-contemporaneous events in Australia. Significant components of the Indigenous collections of the Queensland Museum were acquired in the 1910s by police, officials who only years prior had led regular and violent 'dispersals' of Aboriginal people.[38]

By the early 1900s, there was a small permanent population of colonists in the Gulf of Papua.[39] LMS and Roman Catholic missions had been established.[40] The Australian administration had set up strategic stations at Kerema, Baimuru, Kikori, and Daru, from which Regional Magistrates conducted exploratory trips with Australian patrols.[41] Over the coming decades, Indigenous cultural materials would continue to be distributed to the rest of the world through this network.

Towards the mid-1900s, the initial rush to mine artefacts from the Gulf of Papua slowed somewhat, and local craft industries and ceremonial landscapes transformed rapidly.[42] By the 1960s, items that Chalmers and Lewis had struggled to acquire only decades earlier were no longer being made for ceremonial use. The objects were instead being fashioned for the cash market.[43]

Totemic reminders to spiritual 'telephone system': posts and stories in Orokolo Bay

In Orokolo Bay, wooden posts can function as physical reminders of historical places and events. My research took place here alongside Orokolo-language-speakers (an Eleman language) in February and September–November 2015. On my second day in Orokolo Bay, locals introduced me and the research team to the legacy of two important posts. In meetings with the entire Kaivakovu and Larihairu village communities on 18 February 2015, villagers explained that the anthropologist Williams had forcibly taken a preserved longhouse post (*ive*) from their key ancestral village site, Popo. Robert Skelly, Henry Arifeae, and I were tasked with finding the post in the registers of European museums and ensuring its return.[44] Later the same day, we conducted preliminary cultural heritage surveys guided by village elders. Walking northwards from the coastal villages, Marepo Korela (Aripi clan, Larhairu village) stopped us only a few hundred metres north of the meeting place. In a small clearing, we saw what at first appeared to be a tree stump, but on closer inspection turned out to be a rotted post (see Figure 22.3). Marepo explained that the post – made of the tropical hardwood kwila (*Intsia bijuga*) – was called Hairita.

The first important post, the one apparently stolen by Williams, was one of the immense central posts of a longhouse (*eravo*). Like the Kerewo (and most Papuan Gulf language groups), the inhabitants of Orokolo Bay once built longhouses that were home to male community members and in which ceremonial objects were stored (see Figure 22.2). The social groups that lived in the *eravo* formed an important sub-village social unit called a *karigara* (*eravo*-community). Each *karigara* contained several clans (*bira'ipi*) of which one was the principal clan and namesake of the *eravo*. The clans, in turn, had totemic associations (*aualare*).[45] 'Dominating the whole [village] scene and redeeming it from the ordinary', each *eravo* measured some 18 metres high and 34 metres long.[46] They were raised 1.5 metres from the ground on numerous posts. Longhouse structures were regularly moved and rebuilt for two main reasons. First, their construction was scheduled according to cycles of a ceremony called *hevehe*. Hevehe cycles lasted 16–22 years.[47] Once a cycle had finished, longhouses were considered to be 'empty', lifeless and meaningless, awaiting removal and reconstruction upon the commencement of the next cycle.[48] Second, the *karigara* of Orokolo Bay were regularly moved southwards in order to keep pace with the rapidly growing shoreline. Each year, approximately three metres of sand builds up on the Orokolo Bay coast, in a pattern that has been ongoing for the past 2,700 years.[49]

Even though *eravo* were frequently removed and reconstructed, important past longhouse locations (e.g. a longhouse built by a legendary clan or totemic ancestor)

Figure 22.2 Ancestor boards (*hohao*) and figures in a longhouse (*eravo*) at Vailala, 1911
Source: Photo by A.B. Lewis, © The Field Museum, Image No. CSA37808

Figure 22.3 An *iki haveve* flagpole called 'Hairita' (now a degraded post), situated 170 m north of the current Larihairu village meeting place
Source: Photo by Robert Skelly

are given ongoing physical presence through commemorative posts and stones. Magic stones – known by locals to be animate spirits that move around by night – can be left to signify the past entrance of a longhouse.[50] Larihairu and Kaivakovu villagers told me that the stolen *ive* had been left in place by the ancestors to commemorate the longhouse site.[51] The post had been carved with the images of totemic ancestors. In this sense, the post, like the boards and masks collected by MacDonell, served a further mnemonic purpose: to evoke totemic stories and give presence to ancestral spirits. In the unpublished notes from his fieldwork in Orokolo Bay, Williams describes visiting an *eravo* called Hare Eravo, in which he saw a 'fine snake, almost 10 ft long in almost complete relief carved on *eravo* post'.[52] The *ive* also had two carved anthropomorphic totemic figures, which the *eravo*'s curator 'addresses ... before hunting'. The posts and stones are interactive spiritual agents.[53]

The second post that was explained to me, Hairita, was once a flagpole. Flagpoles were a central material aspect of a local social and spiritual movement called *iki haveve* that was active between 1919 and the early 1930s. Williams translated *iki haveve* as 'belly-don't-know' because participants reported a strange feeling in their stomachs.[54] By 1922, the movement was widespread among the Eleman language group. *Iki haveve* was a complex blend of Christian and local cultural beliefs about eschatology, spirits, exchange, and social relations.[55] Similar movements in the Pacific have been called 'cargo cults'.[56] Participants expected the spirits of their ancestors to return to them on a European steamship, carrying material riches for their kin. Leaders of the movement would stand at the bottom of the flagpoles to receive messages from their travelling ancestors, for whom feasts were prepared in anticipation of their arrival.[57] The movement caused significant disruption to existing ceremonies – in many villages the *hevehe* ceased and locals burned *eravo* and ceremonial masks. The colonial administration labelled the movement the 'Vailala Madness', and Williams blamed it for the 'wholesale destruction of native practice and tradition'.[58]

Orokolo Bay locals today see *iki haveve* as a period of spiritual change.[59] Paul Mahiro (Pakemara clan, Kaivakovu village) explained to me that during *iki haveve* people saw spiritual 'signs' of the advent of modernity.[60] Tyre marks appeared on the beach, and messages came through the flagpoles like 'telephone communication'. According to Kaiva Ipai (Pakemara clan, Kaivakovu village), 'civilisation was trying to come ... it's like God's divine intervention to give a message.'[61] One Indigenous interpretation of *iki haveve* is that it was precipitated by sorcerers who wished to rid neighbouring villages of their ceremonies and spiritually powerful objects.[62] One village group in Orokolo Bay (called 'Orokolo') did not take up *iki haveve*, meaning they were able to retain their ceremonies and *eravo* up until 1939.[63] Orokolo Bay locals express some synchronicity of ceremonial function between the purpose of the *eravo*'s *ive* and the flagpoles that featured in the *iki haveve* movement. In fact, a cult flagpole built in the Kaivakovu and Larihairu villages in the 1920s was given the name Ive Kera. Both types of wooden post are said to have been mediums of spiritual communication.

Remembering the traumatic removal of an *ive*

The Indigenous inhabitants of Orokolo Bay no longer see *iki haveve* as a destructive movement. Many villagers today assert that the LMS missionaries burned down the longhouses and removed the flagpoles.[64] Particular mention is made of the destructive actions of the missionary S.H. Dewdney, who was the LMS Reverend in Orokolo from 1935 to 1968.[65] Likewise, Williams is remembered as the thief who took away a commemorative post. Three days after first hearing about Williams and the *ive*, I sat down with members of the Kavapo family, who belong to the Iviki Kovoko Larihairu clan (Larihairu village). This encounter took place in the context of my PhD research – an archaeological and anthropological investigation of place-making in Orokolo Bay.[66] In providing me with oral traditional background to a particular excavation location, young members of the Kavapo family (in their late 20s) explained that their grandfather had been a young child in the 1930s when Williams took the post. He had been helping his family make gardens at an ancestral village site called Popo when they had dislodged a carved *ive* from the ground. The following day, the Government Anthropologist in Papua claimed the post from the Kavapos at gunpoint.

The same story was told in subtly different ways by several narrators during my stay in Orokolo Bay. On 18 October 2015, Malcolm Marepo (Aripi clan, Larihairu village) handed me a written document about his clan's history. The two-page document included the *ive* removal story, which Malcolm summarised as follows:

> During our grandparents time, our grandfather ... was digging the garden in Popo ... when he dug out the post of this building (*elavo*): the next day the white man name E.F. Williams [sic] came to our Larihairu village and took away the post with him. To this days [sic] now, this post is believed to be in museum in Europe (E/W Germany).

Malcolm and his family have a sense not only that the post is missing, but that it is in a foreign place. He gives the receiving museum's country (anachronistically) as East or West Germany, but others such as Amix Hulape (Pakemara clan, Kaivakovu village) told me that the post could be found in England.[67] On 27 October, Pastor Ivahae Ori and Houhii Iaupa (both of Pakemara clan, Kaivakovu village) gave a more detailed version of the story in an interview.[68] The pair explained that the *ive* had been part of an *eravo* built by the Larihairu and Kaivakovu 'tribes' at an ancestral village called Popo, now located c. 2.5 km inland of the Orokolo Bay coast. According to local genealogies, the village was occupied up until seven generations ago.[69] Like the Kavapos (but unlike Malcolm Marepo), the two narrators described a violent removal event: Williams demanded the post at gunpoint from their ancestor. Their ancestor had uncovered the post while digging to make gardens sometime in the 1920s or 1930s. Williams used local labour to excavate the post and package it for shipment. The shipment of the *ive* was organised by a Catholic priest working at the Orokolo village mission and schoolhouse. He sent the post to a distant museum on a ship called the 'Papuan Chief' owned by 'Burns Philp'.

While the timeframes of the stories fit Williams' activities, the narratives do not. The anthropologist's work in Orokolo Bay took place over the course of 21 months in 1923 and 1937. However, after his experiences with Hurley and McCulloch at Kaimari, Williams had become a strident critic of unethical collectors. He stated that although ethnological museums 'make a highly valuable contribution ... in some instances collecting has done serious, even irreparable, harm to the art or craft in its living state'.[70] The contents of Williams' well-documented collection, now housed at the Australian Museum and the South Australian Museum, do not include a carved *ive*, nor indeed any *eravo* post. In line with his concerns that collections of ceremonial items could cause harm to the ceremonies themselves, most of his contributions to Australian museums were 'everyday objects' such as 'shark tooth drills, bone and stingray spine needles and fishing equipment'.[71] He described collecting as the 'the handmaid of ethnology'.[72] For Williams, collected objects were only props with which to back up rigorous ethnographic research.[73]

The shipping company Burns Philp and Co. provides a fascinating link between several of the narratives explored in this essay. As regards the Orokolo Bay *ive*, a ship called the S.S. *Papuan Chief* was in regular operation across the Gulf of Papua in the late 1920s and through the 1930s.[74] However, it was not owned by Burns Philp and Co. as Ivahae and Houhii suggested to me in their interview, but by the Steamships Trading Company Limited. The *Papuan Chief* called in at Orokolo Bay approximately monthly. Ships owned by Burns Philp and Co. were certainly visiting Orokolo Bay in the same era. In the violent reprisal of 1901 at Goaribari Island, a Burns Philp and Co. steamer called *Parua* was chartered by the colonial government as a troop transport. In 1886, the junior partner of the company, Robert Philp, had arranged for Bevan to have free use of their steamer *Victory*. In return, Bevan named rivers in the Kikori River delta 'Philp' and 'Burns'.[75] Further, locals were encountering ships in the Gulf of Papua prior to the arrival of James Chalmers. On his first journey into the Papuan Gulf, Chalmers was told that a large ship had sailed past the coast near Orokolo Bay 'long, long ago'.[76] It is not hard to see how successive generations of inhabitants of the Papuan Gulf, through remembering, might meld the activities and intentions of these visitors and collectors across time and places. Removal events dispersed across several decades are threaded together by recognisable and persistent colonial networks.

A Western positivist reading of Kaivakovu and Larihairu village remembrances of Williams and of Dewdney might point out mnemonic 'inaccuracies' in the form of historical vagueness or narrative conflation. For example, Dewdney's tenure did not chronologically overlap with the *iki haveve* movement, nor with the majority of the *eravo* destructions. Rather, he was a long-standing missionary who arrived four years before one of the very last *eravo* structures was destroyed by members of Orokolo village. Chronological problems with the stories of erasure and removal are entirely consistent with the 'cultural constructions' and telescoping of time and events that occur in trauma narratives and in memories more generally.[77] *Ive* removal and *eravo* destruction stories reverberate with the real and traumatic experiences of inhabitants of the Gulf of Papua in the late 1800s and early 1900s. The stories have become important in perpetuating social memories of a several-decade-long period of rapid local and regional societal and ceremonial change. They are now vehicles for various themes and forms of remembrance for Kaivakovu and Larihairu villagers. By telling difficult stories and continuing to engage with the places they refer to, locals subvert the silencing of materials of ancestral communal importance. In this case, individual and social memories have been passed on as knowledge to second and third generations.[78] The loss of the ancestral longhouse post has not caused forgetting: it is now part of Orokolo Bay's story.

Removals, spiritual kin, and the museum

At this stage, it is worth returning to the concept of 'removal'. How can this term be rightly applied to the forcible excavation and exportation of a wooden post? Is it appropriate to use a term most commonly applied to the removal of Indigenous people from their homelands or families? Certainly, the longhouses and items of material culture housed therein were not like Western museums (i.e. stores of mostly inanimate artefacts or specimens). Williams records that the main items of material culture kept in an Orokolo Bay *eravo* were *apa-hevehe* (dance masks), *hohao* boards and bull-roarers. Tellingly, he described the *apa-hevehe* as the 'real inhabitants of the *eravo* ... they are more than mere masks; in fact it will be found that they have some highly complex spiritual implications'.[79] Likewise, *hohao* represented or housed 'the various spirits of the bush', which could be put in 'good humour' through 'fumigation ... re-painting ... offerings of food' (Figure 22.2).[80] The bull-roarers (smaller wooden boards) were believed to 'contain, or be animated by, spirits'.[81] The *ive*, which gave longhouses structure, were also part of Orokolo Bay's spiritscape. Under the floorboards of each *eravo* lived a grandmother spirit (*eravo-ve-uvari*). During the construction of a longhouse a specialist in building magic (*kariki haera*) would speak the *eravo-ve-uvari*'s name during the placing of the very first post. This *ive* was known as *loa hau* – the grandmother's shinbone.[82] The *eravo* was a populous place, alive with ancestral spirits.

The logical conclusion of these notions is that spiritual kin of Eleman-language-speaking and Papuan Gulf peoples were removed in the early late 1800s and early 1900s, and now reside in museums worldwide (especially in PNG and Australia). It is important to note that collections are 'the tangible outcomes of indigenous action' as well as of 'Western activities of classification and collecting'.[83] Certainly, Papuan Gulf peoples were tightly controlling outsider access to key ceremonial items when they interacted with Chalmers in 1883 and Lewis in 1912. However, for instances of forced or coerced removals, these power relations were highly imbalanced. Narratives about the dislocation of cultural materials imbued with spiritual presences play an important role in framing discussions and social knowledge of early relations between colonists and locals, along with notions of changing ceremonial practice and imaginings of far-flung museums as storehouses of Orokolo Bay's material past. As Joshua Bell found when working with I'ai people in the Purari River region, Papuan Gulf peoples hold 'disquiet ... about their dispersed heritage in national and foreign institutions'.[84] It is telling that during initial community meetings in February 2015, stories about thieving anthropologists surfaced quickly. In part, this was because the Kaivakovu and Larihairu villagers saw Henry, Robert, and I as cultural brokers, people who spoke the right languages and inhabited the right worlds in order to successfully find the *ive* in a foreign storeroom, communicate their demands with a museum institution, and negotiate its safe return. However, the story also functioned as a warning, a rebuke of former (and potentially current) patterns of cultural material extraction. Unwinding some of the systemic violence of colonial removals requires institutions and researchers to conduct long-term projects where knowledges generated through relationships are returned and communicated, and cultural materials are repatriated.

In terms of collections already made, here too institutions must invest in relationships with descendant communities. By being attentive to the remembrances of previous encounters, new stories about people and cultural materials can be co-produced, founded on mutual respect. Maintaining close relationships and dialogue between institutions and Indigenous communities will also help to resolve the status of the collections themselves. We might ask how museums are to adequately care for (or return) objects that were, and often still are, known by Indigenous peoples to be interactive embodiments of their ancestors? These questions can only be answered by the ancestors of the makers, and must be negotiated in the often emotional, difficult, yet immensely rewarding 'longue durée of collaboration'.[85]

Acknowledgements

A heartfelt thanks to hosts and friends from the Larihairu and Kaivakovu villages of Orokolo Bay. Thank you for sharing your homes, knowledge, and time with me. Henry Arifeae (Papua New Guinea National Museum and Art Gallery) was a tireless and genial colleague during fieldwork. Dr Brit Asmussen (Queensland Museum) assisted with collection records; Dr Asmussen and Prof. Lara Lamb (University of Southern Queensland) kindly read this essay and provided invaluable feedback. Thanks also to Dr Barry Craig for responding to my queries about the South Australian Museum collections back in 2015. I am grateful to Prof. Ann McGrath and Prof. Lynette Russell for the invitation to participate in this exciting volume and for their editorial feedback. Funding was provided by the ARC Centre of Excellence for Australian Biodiversity and Heritage and through Prof. Bruno David. I carried out the research under an Australian Government Research Training Program (Research Doctorate) at Monash Indigenous Studies Centre, Monash University.

Notes

1 See, for example: Claudie B. Haake, *The State, Removal and Indigenous Peoples in the United States and Mexico, 1620–2000* (New York: Routledge, 2007); Margaret D. Jacobs, *White Mother to a Dark Race: Settler Colonialism, Maternalism, and the Removal of Indigenous Children in the American West and Australia, 1880–1940* (Lincoln: University of Nebraska Press, 2009).
2 Robert Manne, 'The Stolen Generations,' in *The Best Australian Essays*, ed. Peter Craven (Melbourne: Bookman Press, 1998), 23–36.
3 Fae Korsmo, 'Swedish Policy and Saami Rights,' *The Northern Review* 11 (Winter 1993): 36–37.
4 Lynette Russell, 'Remembering Places Never Visited: Connections and Context in Imagined and Imaginary Landscapes,' *International Journal of Historical Archaeology* 16, no. 2 (June 2012): 401–417.
5 Paul Tapsell, 'The Flight of Parerautututu: An Investigation of Taonga from a Tribal Perspective,' *The Journal of the Polynesian Society* 106, no. 4 (1997), 332–333.
6 Brit Asmussen, Lester Michael Hill, Sean Ulm, and Chantal Knowles, 'Tangled Histories and Changing Contexts of the Burnett River Rock Engravings,' *Museum Worlds: Advances in Research* 4 (2016), 78–94.

7 See, for example: Edward S. Casey, *Remembering: A Phenomenological Study* (Bloomington: Indiana University Press, 1987); Edward S. Casey, 'Forgetting Remembered,' *Man and World* 25, no. 2 (1992): 281–311.
8 Michael Lambek, 'The Past Imperfect: Remembering as Moral Practice,' in *Tense Past: Cultural Essays in Trauma and Memory*, eds. Paul Antze and Michael Lambek (London: Routledge, 1996), 239; see also Laurence J. Kirmayer, 'Landscapes of Memory: Trauma, Narrative and Dissociation,' in Antze and Lambek, *Tense Past*, 176.
9 Siân Jones and Lynette Russell, 'Archaeology, Memory and Oral Tradition: An Introduction,' *International Journal of Historical Archaeology* 16, no. 2 (June 2012): 270.
10 Paul Connerton, *How Societies Remember* (Cambridge: Cambridge University Press, 1989), 28.
11 Quote from Edward S. Casey, 'Imagining and Remembering,' *The Review of Metaphysics* 31, no. 2 (1977): 205; see also: Kirmayer, 'Landscapes of Memory,' 174.
12 Annette Kuhn, *Family Secrets: Acts of Memory and Imagination* (London: Verso, 2002), 4.
13 Kuhn, *Family Secrets*, 162.
14 Kuhn, *Family Secrets*, 161.
15 Casey, *Remembering*, 181–182.
16 Casey, 'Forgetting Remembered'; Paul Connerton, 'Seven Types of Forgetting,' *Memory Studies* 1, no. 1 (2008): 59–71.
17 Denis Byrne, *Surface Collection: Archaeological Travels in Southeast Asia* (Lanham, MD: Altamira Press, 2007), 96.
18 Byrne, *Surface Collection*, 95.
19 Peter R. Schmidt, 'Social Memory and Trauma in Northwestern Tanzania,' *Journal of Social Archaeology* 10, no. 2 (2010): 269.
20 Schmidt, 'Social Memory and Trauma,' 274–275.
21 For a list of ethnographic sources for the Papuan Gulf, see Barry Craig, '"Scenes Hidden from Other Eyes" – Theodore Bevan's Collection from the Gulf of Papua in the South Australian Museum,' *The Artefact* 33 (2010): 30.
22 Robert Louis Welsch, 'Coaxing the Spirits to Dance,' in *Coaxing the Spirits to Dance: Art and Society in the Papuan Gulf of New Guinea*, eds. Robert Louis Welsch, Virginia-Lee Webb, and Sebastian Haraha (New York: Hood Museum of Art, 2008), 8–16.
23 In 1883, the Australian state of Queensland attempted to annex the Territory of Papua (now the southern half PNG) on behalf of Britain. In 1884, Britain agreed to make the territory a protectorate, before handing the administration of the colony to Australia in 1906.
24 Susan M. Davies, 'Andrew Goldie: His Ethnological Collecting and Collections,' *Memoirs of the Queensland Museum, Culture* 6 (2012): 135, 146.
25 James Chalmers, *Pioneer Life and Work in New Guinea* (London: The Religious Tract Society, 1895), 24–26. He was accompanied by Papuan and Cook Islander missionary colleagues.
26 Chalmers, *Pioneer Life*, 116.
27 Theodore Francis Bevan, *Toil, Travel and Discovery in British New Guinea* (London: Kegan Paul, 1890), 185; Craig, 'Scenes Hidden,' 30–48.
28 Brit Asmussen, collection summary provided to author, 12 March 2019; Robert Louis Welsch, *An American Anthropologist in Melanesia: A.B. Lewis and the Joseph N. Field South Pacific Expedition 1909–1913, Vol II: Who Was Who in Melanesia 1909–1913* (Honolulu: University of Hawai'i Press, 1998), 106–107.
29 Robert Louis Welsch, *An American Anthropologist … Vol I: Field Diaries* (Honolulu: University of Hawai'i Press, 1998), 475; Chalmers, *Pioneer Life*, 61.
30 British New Guinea, *Annual Report on British New Guinea from 1st July 1900 to 30th June 1901* (Brisbane: Government Printer, 1902), 25–35.

31 Dario Di Rosa, 'A Lesson in Violence: The Moral Dimensions of Two Punitive Expeditions in the Gulf of Papua, 1901 and 1904,' *Journal of Colonialism and Colonial History* 18, no. 1 (Spring 2017).
32 British New Guinea, *Annual Report*, 26–31.
33 Di Rosa, 'A Lesson in Violence.'
34 Williams was the Assistant Government Anthropologist from 1922 to 1928.
35 Field diary of Frank Hurley, 19–20 October 1922, in Robert Dixon and Christopher Lee, eds., *The Diaries of Frank Hurley 1912–1941* (London: Anthem Press, 2011), 201–202.
36 Michael W. Young and Julia Clark, *An Anthropologist in Papua: The Photography of F.E. Williams, 1922–29* (Honolulu: University of Hawai'i Press, 2001), 19.
37 Francis Edgar Williams, *The Collection of Curios and the Preservation of Native Culture* (Port Moresby: Government Printer, 1923); Ben Dibley, 'Assembling an Anthropological Actor: Anthropological Assemblage and Colonial Government in Papua,' *History and Anthropology* 25, no. 2 (2014): 273; Sylvia Schaffarczyk, 'A *Rara Avis*: F.E. Williams, the Government Anthropologist of Papua, and the Papuan Official Collection,' in *Hunting the Collectors: Pacific Collections in Australian Museums, Art Galleries and Archives*, eds. Susan Cochrane and Max Quanchi. (Cambridge: Cambridge Scholars, 2011), 192–214.
38 Gemmia Burden, 'From Dispossession to Display: Authenticity, Aboriginality and the Queensland Museum, c. 1862–1917' (PhD diss., The University of Queensland, 2017), 102–108.
39 In 1918, the European population of the 'Gulf Division' (part of the Gulf of Papua) consisted of 'one missionary, fourteen civil servants … nine traders, three planters, and four females – a total of 29' compared to an Indigenous population of around 25,000. G.H. Murray, 'Gulf Division,' in *Papua, Annual Report for the Year 1918–1919* (Melbourne: Government Printer, 1920), 23.
40 John Barker, '"Way Back in Papua": Representing Society and Change in the Publications of the London Missionary Society in New Guinea, 1871–1932,' *Pacific Studies* 19, no. 3 (1996): 110–111.
41 Penelope Hope, *Long Ago is Far Away: Accounts of the Early Exploration and Settlement of the Papuan Gulf Area* (Canberra: ANU Press, 1979), 43. Kerema is now the capital of PNG's Gulf Province.
42 Joshua A. Bell, 'Losing the Forest but Not the Stories in the Trees: Contemporary Understandings of F.E. Williams's 1922 Photographs of the Purari Delta,' *Journal of Pacific History* 41, no. 2 (2006): 195–196.
43 Ulli Beier and Albert Maori Kiki, *Hohao: The Uneasy Survival of an Art Form in the Papuan Gulf*, (Sydney: Thomas Nelson, 1970), 32; Sebastian Hahara, 'The Changing Meaning of Art in the Papuan Gulf: A View from the Papua New Guinea National Museum,' in Welsch, Webb and Haraha, *Coaxing the Spirits to Dance*, 46–51.
44 Robert Skelly is a researcher at Monash University; Henry Arifeae is the Cultural Coordinator at the National Museum and Art Gallery of PNG.
45 See Francis Edgar Williams, *Drama of Orokolo: The Social and Ceremonial Life of the Elema* (Oxford: Clarendon Press, 1940), 35–40 for discussions of kinship. *Aualare* (with the 'A' capitalised) is used today as a name for the Christian God.
46 Williams, *Drama of Orokolo*, 5.
47 Chris Urwin, 'Building and Remembering: Constructing Ancestral Place at Popo, Orokolo Bay, Papua New Guinea' (PhD diss., Monash University, 2019), Table 94.
48 Williams, *Drama of Orokolo*, 390.
49 Robert Skelly and Bruno David, *Hiri: Archaeology of Long-distance Maritime Trade Along the South Coast of Papua New Guinea* (Honolulu: University of Hawai'i Press, 2017), 474–475.
50 Skelly and David, *Hiri*, 399.
51 Urwin field diary, 20 Oct 2015.

52 Francis Edgar Williams, miscellaneous Orokolo notes, Dec 1931 (accession 447, box 2998, file number ML MSS 5/11, item 92: 69–71), National Archive of Papua New Guinea, Port Moresby.
53 Chris Urwin, 'Excavating and Interpreting Ancestral Action: Stories from the Subsurface of Orokolo Bay, Papua New Guinea,' *Journal of Social Archaeology* 19, no. 3 (2019): 279–306.
54 Francis Edgar Williams, 'The Vailala Madness,' in *Francis Edgar Williams: 'The Vailala Madness' and Other Essays*, ed. Erik Schwimmer (London: C. Hurst and Company, 1976), 332.
55 Kekeao, 'Vailala Madness,' *Oral History* 3, no. 7 (1973): 1–8; G.H. Murray, 'Appendix A: Reports by G.H. Murray, Acting Resident Magistrate, Gulf Division, re. the Vailala Madness,' in *The Vailala Madness and the Destruction of Native Ceremonies in the Gulf Division*, ed. F.E. Williams (Port Moresby: Edward George Baker, Government Printer, 1923), 66.
56 Glynn Cochrane, *Big Men and Cargo Cults* (Oxford: Oxford University Press, 1970); Kenelm Burridge, *New Heaven New Earth: A Study of Millenarian Activities* (New York: Schocken Books, 1969).
57 Williams, 'The Vailala Madness,' 348–349; Young and Clark, *An Anthropologist in Papua*, 17.
58 Williams, 'The Vailala Madness,' 332.
59 For accounts of the cult's continuation beyond the early 1900s, see Dawn Ryan, 'Christianity, Cargo Cults, and Politics among the Toaripi of Papua,' *Oceania* 40, no. 2 (1969): 99–118.
60 Urwin field diary, 27 Oct 2015.
61 Urwin field diary, 31 Oct 2015.
62 Albert Maori Kiki, *Kiki: Ten Thousand Years in a Lifetime* (Melbourne: F.W. Cheshire, 1968), 51. For an alternate Indigenous view, see Kekeao, 'Vailala Madness,' 1–8.
63 Kiki, *Kiki: Ten Thousand Years*, 30.
64 Urwin field diary, 27 Oct 2015.
65 Urwin field diary, 24 Sep 2015; 27 Oct 2015. For an account of their life and work in Orokolo Bay, see the memoirs of Stanley H. Dewdney's wife: Madie Dewdney, *Never the Last Straw: Memories of Orokolo* (Swaffham: Self Published, 1993).
66 Urwin, 'Building and Remembering.'
67 Urwin field diary, 20 Oct 2015.
68 Urwin field diary, 27 Oct 2015.
69 For a detailed study of the ethnography and archaeology of Popo, see Urwin, 'Building and Remembering.'
70 Francis Edgar Williams, 'Creed of a Government Anthropologist,' in Schwimmer, *Francis Edgar Williams*, 398.
71 Schaffarczyk, 'A *Rara Avis*,' 209.
72 Williams, 'Creed of a Government Anthropologist,' 398.
73 For a brief biography of Williams, see Erik Schwimmer, 'Introduction: F.E. Williams as Ancestor and Rain-maker,' in Schwimmer, *Francis Edgar Williams*, 11–38. Williams' private collection consisted of only 15 items; these were donated by his family to the South Australian Museum after his death in 1943. The size of his private collection is consistent with his stated reluctance to collect objects that were still being used or produced locally. Information on the collection was provided by Barry Craig (email correspondence, 2 March 2015).
74 Dewdney, *Never the Last Straw*, 24. The ship made 'regular round trips' from 'Port Moresby to Hisiu, Yule Island, Kukipi, Orokolo, Kikori, Daru and back': 'Shipping Services in the Pacific,' *The Pacific Islands Monthly*, 17 January 1931, 12.
75 Craig, 'Scenes Hidden,' 33.
76 James Chalmers, *Pioneering in New Guinea* (London: Religious Tract Society, 1887), 42–43.

77 Kirmayer, 'Landscapes of Memory,' 175; Siân Jones, '"Thrown Like Chaff in the Wind"': Excavation, Memory and the Negotiation of Loss in the Scottish Highlands,' *International Journal of Historical Archaeology* 16, no. 2 (2012): 346–366; Kuhn, *Family Secrets*, 162. For a detailed case study of traumatic events (measles outbreaks and nuclear tests in the 1940s–1950s), telescoping and memory among Pitjantjatjara (Indigenous Australian) people, see Heather Goodall, '"The Whole Truth and Nothing But …": Some Intersections of Western Law, Aboriginal History and Community Memory,' *Journal of Australian Studies* 16, no. 35 (1992): 104–119.

78 For deliberate inter-generational forgetting of violent encounters, see Pascale Bonnemère and Pierre Lemonnier, 'A Measure of Violence: Forty Years of "First Contact" among the Ankave-Anga (Papua New Guinea),' in *Oceanic Encounters: Exchange, Desire, Violence*, ed. Margaret Jolly, Serge Tcherkézoff, and Darrell Tryon (Canberra: ANU Press, 2009), 295–334.

79 Williams, *Drama of Orokolo*, 155; see also Francis Edgar Williams, 'Bull-roarers in the Papuan Gulf,' in Schwimmer, *Francis Edgar Williams*, 99.

80 Williams, *Drama of Orokolo*, 155–157.

81 Williams, *Drama of Orokolo*, 159.

82 Williams, *Drama of Orokolo*, 160.

83 Anne Clarke and Robin Torrence, 'Archaeology and the Collection: Tracing Material Relationships in Colonial Papua from 1875 to 1925,' *Journal of Australian Studies* 35, no. 4 (2011): 446.

84 Joshua A. Bell, 'The Veracity of Form: Transforming Knowledges and their Forms in the Purari Delta of Papua New Guinea,' in *Museum as Process: Translating Local and Global Knowledges*, ed. Raymond Silverman (London: Routledge, 2014), 111.

85 Joshua A. Bell, 'A Bundle of Relations: Collections, Collecting, and Communities,' *Annual Review of Anthropology* 46, no. 1 (2017): 253. In discussing the concept, Bell cites the notion of 'slow museology' developed by Silverman in *Museum as Process*, 12–14.

Bibliography

Antze, Paul, and Michael Lambek, eds. *Tense Past: Cultural Essays in Trauma and Memory.* New York: Routledge, 1996.

Asmussen, Brit, Lester Michael Hill, Sean Ulm, and Chantal Knowles. 'Tangled Histories and Changing Contexts of the Burnett River Rock Engravings.' *Museum Worlds: Advances in Research* 4 (2016): 78–94.

Barker, John. '"Way Back in Papua": Representing Society and Change in the Publications of the London Missionary Society in New Guinea, 1871–1932.' *Pacific Studies* 19, no. 3 (1996): 107–142.

Beier, Ulli, and Albert Maori Kiki. *Hohao: The Uneasy Survival of an Art Form in the Papuan Gulf.* Sydney: Thomas Nelson, 1970.

Bell, Joshua A. 'Losing the Forest but Not the Stories in the Trees: Contemporary Understandings of F.E. Williams's 1922 Photographs of the Purari Delta.' *Journal of Pacific History* 41, no. 2 (2006): 191–206.

Bell, Joshua A. 'The Veracity of Form: Transforming Knowledges and their Forms in the Purari Delta of Papua New Guinea.' In *Museum as Process: Translating Local and Global Knowledges*, edited by Raymond Silverman, 105–122. London: Routledge, 2014.

Bell, Joshua A. 'A Bundle of Relations: Collections, Collecting, and Communities.' *Annual Review of Anthropology* 46, no. 1 (2017): 241–259.

Bevan, Theodore Francis. *Toil, Travel and Discovery in British New Guinea.* London: Kegan Paul, 1890.

Burden, Gemmia. 'From Dispossession to Display: Authenticity, Aboriginality and the Queensland Museum, c. 1862–1917.' PhD diss., The University of Queensland, 2017.

Burridge, Kenelm. *New Heaven New Earth: A Study of Millenarian Activities.* New York: Schocken Books, 1969.
Bonnemère, Pascale, and Pierre Lemonnier. 'A Measure of Violence: Forty Years of "First Contact" among the Ankave-Anga (Papua New Guinea).' In *Oceanic Encounters: Exchange, Desire, Violence,* edited by Margaret Jolly, Serge Tcherkézoff, and Darrell Tryon, 295–334. Canberra: ANU Press, 2009.
Byrne, Denis. *Surface Collection: Archaeological Travels in Southeast Asia.* Lanham, MD: Altamira Press, 2007.
British New Guinea. *Annual Report on British New Guinea from 1st July 1900 to 30th June 1901.* Brisbane: Government Printer, 1902.
Casey, Edward S. *Remembering: A Phenomenological Study.* Bloomington: Indiana University Press, 1987.
Casey, Edward S. 'Forgetting Remembered.' *Man and World* 25, no. 2 (1992): 281–311.
Casey, Edward S. 'Imagining and Remembering.' *The Review of Metaphysics* 31, no. 2 (1977): 281–311.
Chalmers, James. *Pioneering in New Guinea.* London: The Religious Tract Society, 1887.
Chalmers, James. *Pioneer Life and Work in New Guinea.* London: The Religious Tract Society, 1895.
Clarke, Anne, and Robin Torrence. 'Archaeology and the Collection: Tracing Material Relationships in Colonial Papua from 1875 to 1925.' *Journal of Australian Studies* 35, no. 4 (2011): 433–448.
Cochrane, Glynn. *Big Men and Cargo Cults.* Oxford: Oxford University Press, 1970.
Connerton, Paul. *How Societies Remember.* Cambridge: Cambridge University Press, 1989.
Connerton, Paul. 'Seven Types of Forgetting.' *Memory Studies* 1, no. 1 (2008): 59–71.
Craig, Barry. '"Scenes Hidden from Other Eyes" – Theodore Bevan's Collection from the Gulf of Papua in the South Australian Museum.' *Artefact* 33 (2010): 30–48.
Davies, Susan M. 'Andrew Goldie: His Ethnological Collecting and Collections.' *Memoirs of the Queensland Museum, Culture* 6 (2012): 129–149.
Dewdney, Madie. *Never the Last Straw: Memories of Orokolo.* Swaffham: Self Published, 1993.
Di Rosa, Dario. 'A Lesson in Violence: The Moral Dimensions of Two Punitive Expeditions in the Gulf of Papua, 1901 and 1904.' *Journal of Colonialism and Colonial History* 18, no. 1 (Spring 2017).
Dibley, Ben. 'Assembling an Anthropological Actor: Anthropological Assemblage and Colonial Government in Papua.' *History and Anthropology* 25, no. 2 (2014): 263–279.
Dixon, Robert, and Christopher Lee, eds. *The Diaries of Frank Hurley 1912–1941.* London: Anthem Press, 2011.
Goodall, Heather. '"The Whole Truth and Nothing But ...": Some Intersections of Western Law, Aboriginal History and Community Memory,' *Journal of Australian Studies* 16, no. 35 (1992): 104–119.
Haake, Claudie B. *The State, Removal and Indigenous Peoples in the United States and Mexico, 1620–2000.* New York: Routledge, 2007.
Hahara, Sebastian. 'The Changing Meaning of Art in the Papuan Gulf: A View from the Papua New Guinea National Museum.' In *Coaxing the Spirits to Dance: Art and Society in the Papuan Gulf of New Guinea,* edited by Robert Louis Welsch, Virginia-Lee Webb, and Sebastian Haraha, 46–51. New York: Hood Museum of Art, 2008.
Hope, Penelope. *Long Ago is Far Away: Accounts of the Early Exploration and Settlement of the Papuan Gulf Area.* Canberra: ANU Press, 1979.
Jacobs, Margaret D. *White Mother to a Dark Race: Settler Colonialism, Maternalism, and the Removal of Indigenous Children in the American West and Australia, 1880–1940.* Lincoln: University of Nebraska Press, 2009.
Jones, Siân. '"Thrown Like Chaff in the Wind": Excavation, Memory and the Negotiation of Loss in the Scottish Highlands.' *International Journal of Historical Archaeology* 16, no. 2 (June 2012): 346–366.

Jones, Siân, and Lynette Russell. 'Archaeology, Memory and Oral Tradition: An Introduction.' *International Journal of Historical Archaeology* 16, no. 2 (June 2012): 267–283.
Kekeao, T.H. 'Vailala Madness.' *Oral History* 3, no. 7 (1973): 1–8.
Kiki, Albert Maori. *Kiki: Ten Thousand Years in a Lifetime*. Melbourne: F.W. Cheshire, 1968.
Kirmayer, Laurence J. 'Landscapes of Memory: Trauma, Narrative and Dissociation.' In *Tense Past: Cultural Essays in Trauma and Memory*, edited by Paul Antze and Michael Lambek, 173–198. New York: Routledge, 1996.
Korsmo, Fae. 'Swedish Policy and Saami Rights.' *The Northern Review* 11 (Winter 1993): 32–55.
Kuhn, Annette. *Family Secrets: Acts of Memory and Imagination*. London: Verso, 2002.
Lambek, Michael. 'The Past Imperfect: Remembering as Moral Practice.' In *Tense Past: Cultural Essays in Trauma and Memory*, edited by Paul Antze and Michael Lambek, 235–254. New York: Routledge, 1996.
Manne, Robert. 'The Stolen Generations.' In *The Best Australian Essays*, edited by Peter Craven, 23–36. Melbourne: Bookman Press, 1998.
Murray, G.H. 'Gulf Division.' In *Papua, Annual Report for the Year 1918–1919*, 23–25. Melbourne: Government Printer, 1920.
Murray, G.H. 'Appendix A: Reports by G.H. Murray, Acting Resident Magistrate, Gulf Division, re. the Vailala Madness.' In *The Vailala Madness and the Destruction of Native Ceremonies in the Gulf Division*, edited by F.E. Williams, 65–70. Port Moresby: Edward George Baker, Government Printer, 1923.
Russell, Lynette. 'Remembering Places Never Visited: Connections and Context in Imagined and Imaginary Landscapes.' *International Journal of Historical Archaeology* 16, no. 2 (June 2012): 401–417.
Ryan, Dawn. 'Christianity, Cargo Cults, and Politics among the Toaripi of Papua.' *Oceania* 40, no. 2 (1969): 99–118.
Schaffarczyk, Sylvia. 'A *Rara Avis*: F.E. Williams, the Government Anthropologist of Papua, and the Papuan Official Collection.' In *Hunting the Collectors: Pacific Collections in Australian Museums, Art Galleries and Archives*, edited by Susan Cochrane and Max Quanchi, 192–214. Cambridge: Cambridge Scholars, 2011.
Schmidt, Peter R. 'Social Memory and Trauma in Northwestern Tanzania.' *Journal of Social Archaeology* 10, no. 2 (2010): 255–279.
Schwimmer, Erik, ed. *Francis Edgar Williams: 'The Vailala Madness' and Other Essays*. London: C. Hurst and Company, 1976.
'Shipping Services in the Pacific.' *The Pacific Islands Monthly*, 17 January 1931.
Silverman, R.A., ed. *Museum as Process: Translating Local and Global Knowledges*. London: Routledge, 2015.
Skelly, Robert, and Bruno David. *Hiri: Archaeology of Long-distance Maritime Trade along the South Coast of Papua New Guinea*. Honolulu: University of Hawai'i Press, 2017.
Tapsell, Paul. 'The Flight of Parerautututu: An Investigation of Taonga from a Tribal Perspective.' *The Journal of the Polynesian Society* 106, no. 4 (1997): 323–374.
Urwin, Chris. 'Building and Remembering: Constructing Ancestral Place at Popo, Orokolo Bay, Papua New Guinea.' PhD diss., Monash University, 2019.
Urwin, Chris. 'Excavating and Interpreting Ancestral Action: Stories from the Subsurface of Orokolo Bay, Papua New Guinea.' *Journal of Social Archaeology* 19, no. 3 (2019): 279–306.
Welsch, Robert Louis. *An American Anthropologist in Melanesia: A.B. Lewis and the Joseph N. Field South Pacific Expedition 1909–1913, Vol I: Field Diaries*. Honolulu: University of Hawai'i Press, 1998.
Welsch, Robert Louis. *An American Anthropologist in Melanesia: A.B. Lewis and the Joseph N. Field South Pacific Expedition 1909–1913, Vol II: Who Was Who in Melanesia 1909–1913*. Honolulu: University of Hawai'i Press, 1998.

Welsch, Robert Louis. 'Coaxing the Spirits to Dance.' In *Coaxing the Spirits to Dance: Art and Society in the Papuan Gulf of New Guinea*, edited by Welsch, Robert Louis, Virginia-Lee Webb, and Sebastian Haraha, 1–45. New York: Hood Museum of Art, 2008.

Welsch, Robert Louis, Virginia-Lee Webb, and Sebastian Haraha, eds. *Coaxing the Spirits to Dance: Art and Society in the Papuan Gulf of New Guinea*. New York: Hood Museum of Art, 2008.

Williams, Francis Edgar. *The Collection of Curios and the Preservation of Native Culture*. Port Moresby: Government Printer, 1923.

Williams, Francis Edgar. *Drama of Orokolo: The Social and Ceremonial Life of the Elema*. Oxford: Clarendon Press, 1940.

Williams, Francis Edgar. 'Bull-roarers in the Papuan Gulf.' In *Francis Edgar Williams: 'The Vailala Madness' and Other Essays*, edited by Erik Schwimmer, 73–122. London: C. Hurst and Company, 1976.

Williams, Francis Edgar. 'Creed of a Government Anthropologist.' In *Francis Edgar Williams: 'The Vailala Madness' and Other Essays*, edited by Erik Schwimmer, 396–413. London: C. Hurst and Company, 1976.

Williams, Francis Edgar. 'The Vailala Madness.' In *Francis Edgar Williams: 'The Vailala Madness' and Other Essays*, edited by Erik Schwimmer, 331–359. London: C. Hurst and Company, 1976.

Williams, Francis Edgar. Unpublished Field Notes. National Archive of Papua New Guinea, Port Moresby, 1931.

Young, Michael W., and Julia Clark. *An Anthropologist in Papua: The Photography of F.E. Williams, 1922–29*. Honolulu: University of Hawai'i Press, 2001.

23
INDIGENOUS HISTORY AND IDENTITY IN THE CARIBBEAN

B.W. Higman

The islands of the Caribbean have a special place in global history.[1] While the first people to inhabit the region arrived relatively late – near the tail end of the spread of human beings out of Africa and around the world – the islands were the site of the earliest permanent European colonisation of the Americas and the initial focus of the great migration across the Atlantic. As a result, almost all of the peoples who lived in the Caribbean retained deep connections with older societies and cultures, the places they had left one or two or many more generations before. Thus, there was a referencing of mainland civilisations in everything from language to material culture and spirituality. Certainly, the islands were sites of creative activity, which contributed substantially to the development of island identities and loyalties, but this creativity has been seen as typically the product of synergies derived from the bringing together of concepts from outside, and blending them in a process of fusion, hybridity, or 'creolisation'. Within this framework, notions of indigeneity have taken on new meanings and the right of individuals to see themselves as indigenous is questioned, in the light of complex understandings of ancestry and identity.

Caribbean population history

Today, the islands of the Caribbean are populated by multilingual, multiethnic communities of people who can trace descent to Africa, India, Europe, China, and the Middle East, as well as the Americas. The proportions vary from place to place but, from a biological point of view, the islands have been the site of some of the world's most complex interactions between previously diverged human populations. Now, most of the islands are populated by native-born people, with only trickles of immigration contributing over the past century. Descendants of the original Indigenous peoples constitute a small minority, but their relative

Indigenous history and identity

displacement occurred at different times in different parts of the region. These contrasting patterns reflected both variations in the colonial experience and in the underlying geography of land and sea.

Looking at the map, the settlement of the Caribbean seems predetermined to follow a stepping-stone pattern, channelled naturally by the way the islands form an unbroken archipelago (Figure 23.1). Stretched out over 3,000 km, the islands are numerous but dramatically different in size. The largest islands – Cuba, Hispaniola, Jamaica, and Puerto Rico – are all found in the Greater Antilles, in the west, occupying almost 90% of the total land area, whereas the Lesser Antilles, in the east, are made up of many small islands. Today, in the Caribbean at large, there are about 1,600 named islands; almost all of them are inhabited, whereas the many unnamed islands are generally not. There have always been definite limits to the viability of life on very small islands.

Although recent archaeological and palaeoenvironmental research has pushed back understanding of the arrival of first peoples on the islands of the Caribbean, the beginning of this migration remains situated towards the end of the great movement out of Africa that began about 100,000 years ago. Most of this long period was occupied by movement across Asia, but once people reached the Bering Strait around 15,000 Before Present (BP), they then flowed quite rapidly south

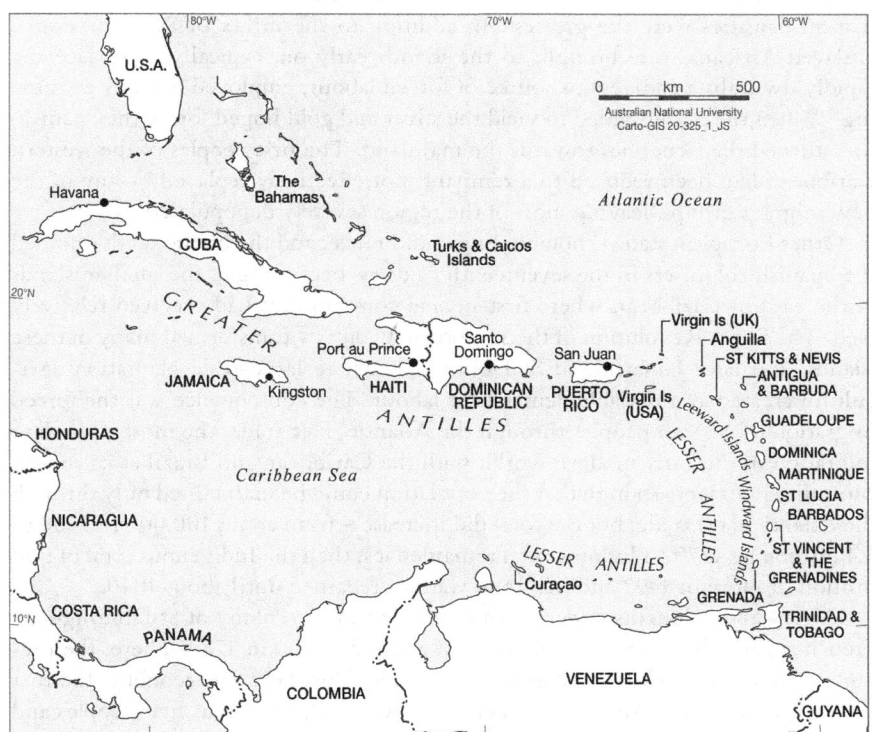

Figure 23.1 The modern Caribbean

through the mainland of the Americas. Still, the islands of the Caribbean long remained either unknown or unattractive because of their isolation and uncertain resources. Pioneer foragers began to enter the region around 7000 BP, followed by sedentary farming peoples who carried plants and technologies from the fertile tropical lands of the Amazon and the Orinoco that enabled efficient food production systems suited to the insular environments of the Caribbean.[2]

When Columbus arrived in 1492, all of the larger islands had significant populations, often settled in quite dense communities, drawing on the rich resources of land and sea. The numbers are disputed, but the most densely settled island – Hispaniola – probably had between one and two million people (some scholars say as many as eight million). The largest island – Cuba – had between 100,000 and 150,000, and Jamaica had less than 100,000. All told, at least two million people lived on the Caribbean islands, more than half of them in complex societies. Well adapted to the region's productive resources, the growth and stability of this Indigenous population was challenged only by occasional catastrophic natural events such as earthquakes, volcanic eruptions, and tsunamis.

Following the invasion by Europeans, the first peoples suffered rapid demographic collapse on the larger islands; in some parts of the eastern Caribbean, however, they remained a majority into the eighteenth century. The focus of early Spanish colonisation was particularly on Hispaniola, where the Indigenous population densities were the greatest. In addition to the influx of Spanish people, enslaved Africans were brought to the islands early on, typically to replace the rapidly dwindling Indigenous source of forced labour, employed initially in mining.[3] When the islands failed to yield the silver and gold hoped for by the Spanish, they turned their energies towards the mainland. The first peoples of the western Caribbean had been reduced to a remnant, not effectively replaced by any of the new migrant groups, leaving most of the region severely depopulated.

Other European states – notably England, France, and the Netherlands – joined the Spanish colonisers in the seventeenth century, beginning in the smaller islands of the eastern Caribbean where first-people communities had survived relatively well. The Sugar Revolution of the seventeenth century transformed many of these islands, and later Jamaica and St Domingue, where large-scale plantation agriculture created an insatiable demand for labour. The consequence was the forced migration of African peoples through the Atlantic slave trade, the most important migration in the early modern world, with the Caribbean and Brazil at its centre. Mortality rates were so high that the population could be maintained only through the Atlantic slave trade, but the total did increase – from about 100,000 in 1600 to 1.4 million by 1770.[4] This new total remained less than the Indigenous total of two million or more in 1492 and that total was not regained until about 1840.

Slavery and colonialism were torn down first in the colony of St Domingue, a French sugar colony with a population of about 500,000 in 1789. There, the revolutionaries took back the Indigenous name *Haiti* for their new republic, the first black republic in the Americas. Where they survived, rebellious first peoples and slaves were sometimes deported out of the islands. In-migration effectively ceased but the population flourished. Across the Americas, the Atlantic slave trade was gradually dismantled and slavery abolished, the final abolition in the region being that in Cuba in 1886. The inflow of African people ended. New peoples came from India and China, initially under indentures to work on sugar plantations, but these streams ended by 1920. By 1945, the population was 15 million and the Caribbean quickly came to be a region characterised by out-migration, mostly to North America and Europe.

Political independence did not necessarily break the old imperial links. Today, the Caribbean has a total population of 45 million and is home to 24 polities; of these, 13 are sovereign states, whereas the remainder remain associated with former colonial powers. The history of colonialism in the Caribbean is long, with only Haiti, the Dominican Republic, and Cuba attaining independence before 1900. Indigenous people lived within this colonial crucible for 500 years, a period in which they were rapidly outnumbered by migrant peoples from across the oceans. However, before 1492, over many millennia, the first peoples of the Caribbean had come exclusively from the surrounding American mainlands and shared a broadly common culture.

First peoples

The first steps into the region were cautious adventures, to islands immediately off the Caribbean coast of South America, places easily reached and offering familiar resources. Exploratory occupations began perhaps 7000 BP to Trinidad, an island only recently separated from the mainland and visible on a clear day. After this easy transit, the next step to the north was Grenada, some 140 km away and one of the longer between-island distances. Once this daunting space had eventually been conquered, people paddled their canoes less tentatively northwards from small island to small island, reaching as far as Martinique or perhaps Antigua by 5000 BP (Figure 23.2). This pattern of dispersal, characterised by an initial pulse, then a long pause, and then another pulse of rapid expansion, was similar to the model seen in the Pacific, though in the Pacific the distances were much greater between islands. The Pacific region also lacked the intervisibility that encouraged voyagers in the eastern Caribbean: the opportunity to stand at the highest point on an island – sometimes even at the shoreline – and be able to see one or more islands scattered across the surrounding waters.[5]

A separate entry into the Caribbean originated in Central and Middle America. Around 6000 BP, between the first pulse into Trinidad and the second towards the Leeward Islands, people crossed from Yucatan to the western end of Cuba, a distance of about 200 km. Like the colonisers from the south, these people were part of the preceramic Archaic Age – early to middle Holocene – and possessed a similar set of tools and knowledge, not yet producing ceramics and practising only an incipient variety of agriculture. Classic Maya civilisation would rise in this tropical lowland forest region but not until long after the initial move into the Caribbean. Following this first – experimental and possibly unintended – colonisation, other people quite quickly flowed along the coasts of the islands later known as the Greater Antilles, with the exception of Jamaica, establishing often ephemeral

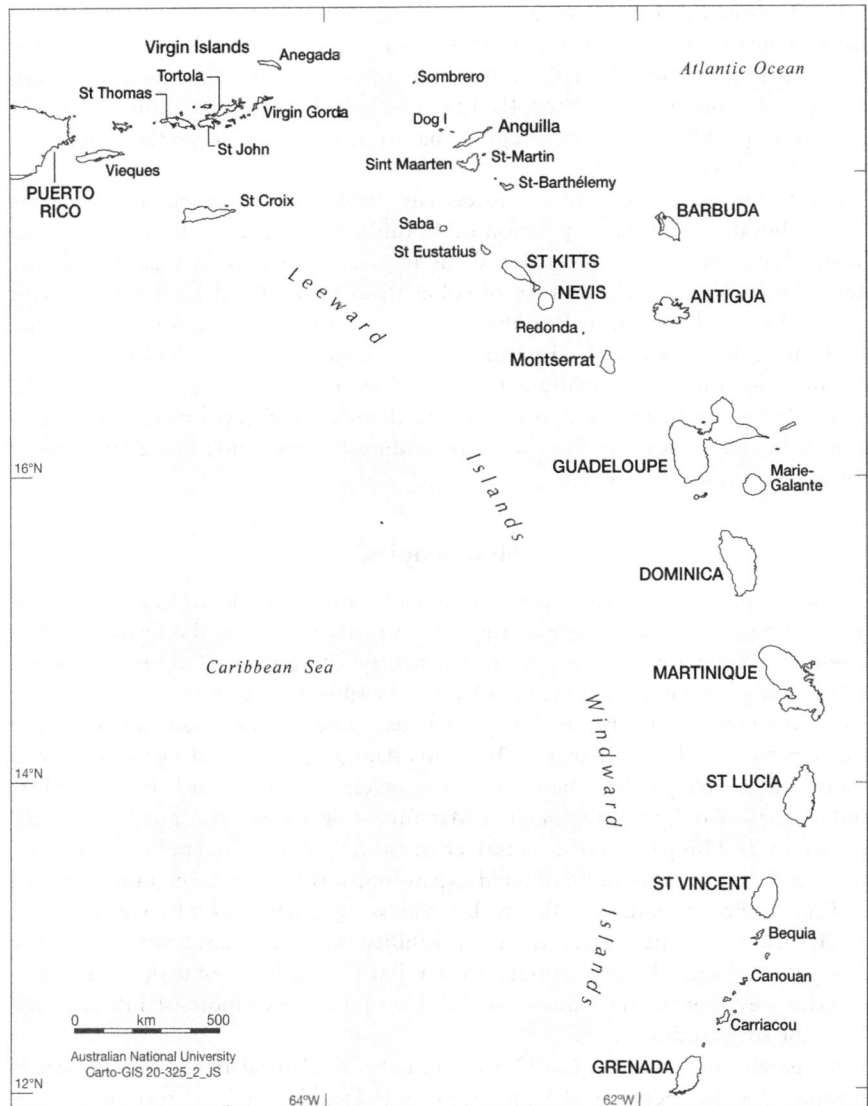

Figure 23.2 The Lesser Antilles

settlements in much the same way as occurred in the east Caribbean. By 5000 BP, these people had reached Puerto Rico and it is likely that members of the two arms of the migration movement first met in the Leeward Islands around this time. Certainly, these islands represented a zone of interaction for the next thousand years, but – aside from language – the two cultures had much in common and sharing was easy, with little competition for space.

In this early occupation of the Caribbean, some sites were no doubt opportunistic and quickly abandoned. Some of them are now under water, since the sea level is today 2–4 m higher. Along the way, the first entrants to the region left evidence of their modification of the ecosystems, including the use of fire to clear land for the planting of fruit trees brought from Yucatan – including the avocado and sapodilla – and an increase in the range of economically useful plants. Essentially, these activities represented the application of knowledge and lifeways learned on the mainland. Fire was also employed to facilitate the hunting of large land mammals, some of which quickly became extinct, forcing a considerable dependence on coastal marine resources. As elsewhere – in Indonesia and Oceania, for example – some of the islands were simply too small and lacking in resources to support permanent preagricultural colonisation.[6] Pioneer foragers were necessarily mobile, avoiding conflict and competition by seeking out fresh sites where food resources were plentiful and ripe for exploitative consumption.

The Archaic Age lasted for thousands of years. Not until about 2500 BP was there a second great wave of migration into the islands of the Caribbean, this time apparently coming exclusively from South America – a finding based on archaeology and linguistics and now supported by studies of ancient DNA derived from (often poorly preserved) skeletal remains unearthed in Cuba, the Dominican Republic, the Bahamas, and Guadeloupe.[7] This second wave brought with it an innovative package of cultural elements characterised as the Ceramic Age. In contrast to the stepping-stone model followed by the Archaic peoples, this new migration seems to have had multiple starting points along the southern coastline – mostly within the realm of modern Venezuela – the voyagers making brave long-distance journeys all the way to the Leeward Islands and Puerto Rico. These new peoples had distinctive pottery-making styles and these have been used by archaeologists to label their cultures – notably the Saladoid, so named because the pottery they made resembles that associated with Saladero in Venezuela – though the people themselves did not identify in this way. What they had in common was an enthusiasm for agriculture, a sedentary lifestyle, and a shared language base, Arawakan. Later, this term was generalised to mean the people rather than the language, in the form *Arawak*.

Early island identities

Archaic and Ceramic Age peoples appear to have lived in harmony, without competing for space and freely exchanging technologies. Most important for the emergence of complex societies was the technology associated with the processing of bitter cassava, a plant domesticated in Brazil around 4000 BP and brought to the Caribbean by Arawakan-speaking people. Once freed of its toxic cyanide and pressed and dried, cassava could be made into flat cakes with excellent preservation qualities, ideal for long-distance voyaging and as a resource in times of shortage. This enabled an economy based heavily on plants, which, in turn, encouraged the spread of settlement away from coastal zones and into the interiors of the larger islands of the Greater Antilles.[8] Larger, denser populations laid the foundation for complex societies and the emergence of social hierarchies.

Not all of the islands were occupied at the beginning of the Ceramic Age, and in some significant cases colonisation was long delayed. In particular, the many scattered islands of the Bahamas were not populated until about 700 CE. Today, many of these islands are dry and infertile. The environment was friendlier at the time of settlement but the dominance of the sea meant a much greater dependence on marine resources than developed in neighbouring Cuba. Harder to explain is the late colonisation of Jamaica, which is the third-largest of the Caribbean islands, after Cuba and Hispaniola, but was apparently unoccupied by human beings until about 600 CE. After an initial exploitative phase in which many of Jamaica's large defenceless birds, sloths, and rodents became extinct, the island quickly came to resemble the rest of the Greater Antilles, the first settlers bringing with them the ceramic and horticultural technologies developed on those large islands, particularly Hispaniola. This package included the so-called Ostionoid culture which flourished between about 600 and 1000 CE, defined by a style of pottery known descriptively in Jamaica as Redware.

Archaeologists term the period after 600 CE Late Ceramic, a period lasting until the arrival of Europeans. The complex societies that flourished in this period – most completely in Hispaniola and Puerto Rico – can be seen as responses to the growth of population density and the need to control resources (particularly water), giving rise to political and managerial hierarchies and chiefdoms. Cassava remained the major food source, which is a crop vulnerable to drought. Thus, the densest populations were in well-watered valleys, supporting a network of substantial settlements, with ceremonial plazas at the heart of chiefdoms. Ceremonial performances came to centre on a spirit world, connecting humankind with nature in a universal pact but without creating an institutional religion. These ideas were broadly shared. However, although the exchange of material goods certainly occurred, it was underdeveloped because land transport was confined to human bearers and oared vessels had a limited range. In spite of these constraints, the political/territorial power of the chiefdoms or *cacicazgos* increased impressively, notably in Hispaniola, which came to be dominated by just five such coalitions of settlements, the largest being known as Magua under the *cacique* Guarionex in 1492.[9]

Exactly how these peoples thought of themselves in terms of 'identity' is difficult to know, and whether they had a notion somehow equivalent to modern understandings of being 'indigenous' perhaps even harder. Those who came to empty islands must have seen themselves as pioneers, though wondering – especially on the larger islands – whether they might someday have to defend themselves from inhabitants not seen at their first landing place. As the centuries and millennia passed, the first of the first peoples were joined by more of their own kind, with shared appearance, language, and cultures. Blending took place and no doubt precedence gradually became lost in the mists of time, with little awareness of the 'founder effect' that determined the ways newcomers almost always had to accustom themselves to what had been put in place. As archaeologist Arie Boomert writes, in discussing the Indigenous archaeology of Trinidad and Tobago:

> ... ethnic identity, the expression of a feeling of belonging to a particular 'people' (nation), is a matter of self-ascription. In stateless societies such as those of

the pre-Columbian Caribbean, ethnic unity was expressed and reinforced by the use of a common name, by particular forms of body ornamentation and dress, and by adherence to an ideology involving recognition of a common origin, and sharing hostile feelings to and stereotyped images of other peoples.[10]

Inhabitants of the Caribbean most likely thought of themselves as belonging to particular islands or island groups. The common names the first peoples used for the islands are known, but few of these survive on the modern map; the most notable exceptions to this are found in the Greater Antilles – Cuba, Haiti, and Jamaica (*Xamayca*) (Figure 23.3). Names for population groupings are harder to find. Members of the complex societies of the Greater Antilles identified themselves to the first Europeans as *Taíno* but this was merely a word meaning 'noble' or 'good' and there is little to suggest that the people defined themselves as a Taínospeaking community. Local loyalties and allegiances were probably more important. However, *Taíno* has achieved considerable currency in the modern literature and is applied to societies in the entire northern sweep of islands from Cuba to the Leewards.

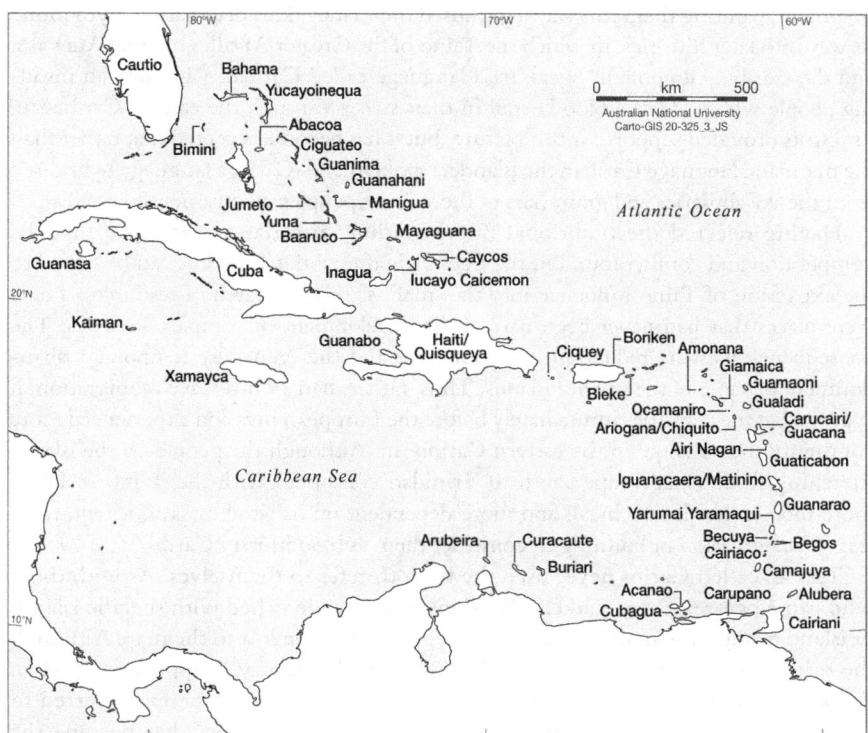

Figure 23.3 Taíno names for the Caribbean islands. Based on Jalil Sued-Badillo (ed.), *General History of the Caribbean, Volume I: Autochthonous Societies*

Source: Paris: UNESCO Publishing/London: Macmillan, 2003), Plate 8

Latecomers

It was in the Leeward Islands, on the eastern margin of Taíno culture, that a zone of competition and conflict first emerged. There it was that identities were forged in the context of what Boomert refers to as the sharing of 'hostile feelings to and stereotyped images of other peoples'. These stereotypes were constructed initially by contemporary peoples, reinterpreted by European invaders and colonists, and more recently revisited by scholars and modern politicians and activists.

Until recently, the roots of the conflict were found in a third wave of migration spreading northwards from the mainland of South America, replicating the pattern of earlier movements but this time encountering established societies, thus constituting a violent, invasive event. The people in this supposed migration have long been called Caribs (or Caribes or Caraïbes), though *Carib* is in fact a Taíno word meaning island or islander (particularly distant examples). Early Europeans used the term to create a dichotomy between the people Columbus labelled Indians (*indios*) and their opposite, *Caribs*. The Indians were painted as peace-loving settled communities living in harmony with the world, whereas the Caribs were vengeful cannibals. Europeans consistently regarded such savage traits as qualifying people for enslavement and harsh treatment; painting them this way legitimised their fate.[11] This originating myth found its way into later histories, in which the Taíno of the Greater Antilles became Arawaks, and the Caribs – supposedly speaking a language called Cariban – became an invading people who had left a bloody trail in their sweep through the eastern Caribbean. Linguists provided support for this picture, but it has become accepted that rather than the mainland language Cariban the islanders spoke Island-Carib, a language hybridised from the vocabularies and grammars of the various peoples who came into contact.

Having rejected the traditional interpretation, historians now argue that the competition and conflict found in the Leewards after about 1200 CE can be traced to the expansion of Taíno influence into the small islands, in search of resources. These were places that had never been part of the development of complex societies. The consequence was the reduction of populations and the (generally temporary) abandonment of some of the smaller islands. Thus, rather than a third wave of migration, it appears that the centuries immediately before the European invasion experienced more continuity than change in the eastern Caribbean. Although the people on the islands stretching from Guadeloupe south to Trinidad contrasted with the Taíno in being more mobile, less hierarchical, and more dependent on fish and cassava, it required a leap of imagination or cunning to construct them as bloodthirsty Caribs.

The so-called Caribs never used the term to refer to themselves. As with those who came before, it seems likely that they typically identified with specific islands or island groups, the names of which have generally been lost to the map. Although the term was first recorded only in the seventeenth century, it appears that when thinking of their belonging to a larger population group, the people referred to themselves as Kalinago or Kalipuna. In recent times, Kalinago has become the accepted term. However, it is perhaps an irony that in spite of these significant reinterpretations and renamings, *Carib* retains its visibility in the largest regional geographical term, namely the Caribbean Sea.

New peoples

Whatever the truth about conflict between Kalinago and Taíno – people with much in common – it was the arrival of Europeans that overturned the lives of the first peoples of the Caribbean. Certainly, Columbus began with a model of colonisation based on trade but he quickly abandoned this in favour of a system based on the forced labour of the Taínos – shipping some of them to Spain for sale – and the mining of high-value resources. Introduced horses, cattle, and pigs quickly became feral, trampling the people's gardens. The Spanish also brought influenza, dysentery, and other diseases, and they justified the slaughter of innocents.

Taíno resistance emerged swiftly in the face of this onslaught with its deadly demographic consequences. As early as 1495, they fought a pitched battle in the previously flourishing domain of Magua, but lost to the Spanish, following which Columbus imposed a harsh tribute on all the people of Hispaniola, to be paid three-monthly. Famine and disease, together with this imposition, led immediately to population loss. By 1514, there were only 26,000 Taínos still living in Hispaniola, the chiefdoms had collapsed, and the Spanish competed under the encomienda system to capture the labour of the remaining able-bodied.[12] Although the enslavement of Taínos was prohibited in 1530, the so-called Caribs could still be brought to the larger islands as slaves. Everywhere people did their best to avoid these hazards by finding secluded hideaways. Even in Hispaniola, in the early sixteenth century, Taínos together with (recently arrived) enslaved Africans sometimes managed to escape their masters and seek safety in mountain refuges, as *cimarrones* (Maroons). As was later to be the pattern elsewhere, the *cimarrones* carried out successful guerrilla warfare and accepted treaties with the Spanish which granted freedom along with loyalty to the crown.[13]

In the midst of all this conflict and strife, a genetic and cultural mixing occurred, between Taíno, Spanish, and African people, resulting in *mestizo* and *criollo*, the forging of new identities and new possibilities for the understanding of indigeneity. The process was not a simple trickle down but rather a complex interaction and integration, in which material artefacts and technologies overlapped and combined, particularly in households governed by Spanish men but ruled by Taíno women. In the early Spanish colonies, marriage between white men and Taíno women was sanctioned and indeed encouraged by church and state. Concubinage also flourished, and in consequence *mestizo* came to be associated with illegitimacy. By the eighteenth century, throughout the Caribbean, officials identified bewilderingly complex systems of ethnic classification, representing varieties of mixing, and formally determining the legal status of individuals and fixing their place in the social hierarchy.[14]

By the end of the sixteenth century, the Taíno population of Hispaniola was barely visible, just a few people continuing a traditional way of life. European habits and behaviours had come to dominate, yet almost always in combination with features surviving from Taíno and African cultures, as well as genetic heritage and the mixed offspring of all three. The slave societies created by the French, the Dutch, and the English in the seventeenth and eighteenth centuries shared elements of this model of colonisation but diverged significantly as a consequence of the dominance of the sugar plantation complex. Plantations used the labour of enslaved Taínos and Kalinago where they could find them, but the expansion of the system led to an almost exclusive dependence on enslaved Africans and the children of unions with white men. Although planters and plantation slaves ate many of the foods domesticated and cultivated by the first peoples, and incorporated some of their techniques into pottery-making, for example, a genetic link or recognition was rare.

By the end of the eighteenth century, peak population densities of the Taínos were once again achieved in Haiti, but the remnant Indigenous people were completely eclipsed by the plantation populations, dominated by Africans, together with smaller components of white and mixed or 'coloured' groups. People of African descent were distinguished as *criollo* or *creole* if born in the islands, as were whites, laying the foundations for future claims to indigeneity.

Survivors

The persistence of first-people cultures took varied forms and qualities. In demographic terms, the Kalinago of the eastern Caribbean survived more successfully than the Taínos of the Greater Antilles, in part because (except for sending raiding parties) the Spanish had less interest in the smaller islands and also because the scattered settlement pattern of the Kalinago offered some protection from epidemic disease. Thus, at the beginning of the seventeenth century, extensive regions in the Greater Antilles were depopulated and returning rapidly to rainforest, through which trampled large feral mammals introduced by the Spanish, while in the smaller islands of the eastern Caribbean, the Indigenous population maintained their numbers relatively well.

At the same time, the Kalinago proved more interested than the Taínos in adopting technologies from the Spanish, using iron axes to hack out large canoes and give them sails, thus gaining an advantage in their own style of trading and raiding. Kalinago societies were more male-dominated than Taíno ones, and they took prisoners from all the peoples of the region – old and new – particularly their women and children. A dialect quickly developed, and the mixing of genetic heritages established the basis for the 'Black Carib' communities of the seventeenth and eighteenth centuries.

The Sugar Revolution of the seventeenth century is generally agreed to have had its Caribbean origins in Barbados, followed by some of the Leeward Islands, as well as Martinique and Guadeloupe, before moving west towards the end of the century. Barbados was empty of people circa 1600, but the establishment of the English and French on the other islands brought them into armed conflict with the surviving Kalinago. In Guadeloupe, the war with the French continued until the 1640s when most of the Kalinago accepted refuge in Grand-Terre, the western part of Guadeloupe – where only 61 were counted in 1671 – or in neighbouring

Dominica.¹⁵ Guerrilla attacks continued, but the profitable management of the sugar and slavery complex demanded that a peaceful landscape and accommodation was achieved one way or another. By the end of the seventeenth century, 'Caribs' continued to defend their lands against colonisers in Grenada and Tobago, in the southern Caribbean, and continued relatively unmolested in St Vincent and Dominica where French imperial authority was weak.

Once securely established, the sugar plantation slavery complex had little place for Indigenous people. Thus, wherever their numbers remained significant, as in the eastern Caribbean, sugar was slow to become a dominant part of the colonial economy. An important point in the playing out of these themes came with the Treaty of Aix-la-Chapelle, negotiated in 1748, at the end of extended conflict between Spain, England, and France. The treaty declared Dominica, St Lucia, St Vincent, and Tobago 'neutral' islands, to be reserved forever for Carib people, generally recognised as a 'nation'. Any European settlement structures were to be removed. The objectives of this plan were not derived from a sudden desire to conserve Indigenous cultures, but rather reflect a wish to ensure the long-term security of existing colonial societies in the region. This form of political accommodation was observed earlier on a smaller scale, in the toleration of co-existing enclave communities and of separate Maroon groups co-opted to serve the ambitions of the colonisers. In the end, this arrangement was short-lived. At the end of the Seven Years War, in 1763, all of the neutral islands were allocated to European imperial states by the Treaty of Paris – which made no mention of the Indigenous people – thus clearing the way for sugar plantations and slavery. The last hope of the surviving Indigenous people to keep even a few islands free of plantations, so that they might continue some kind of independent cultural life, drifted away.¹⁶

Black Caribs and Garifuna

Last ditch battles with the invaders continued until the end of the eighteenth century. Notably, the Black Caribs of St Vincent fought bitter wars against the British, the first in the 1770s and the second in the 1790s. According to the most common origin story, these people were descended from Indigenous women who had borne children for African men whose slave ship had been wrecked on the close by island of Bequia in the late seventeenth century. British commentators claimed that the Black Caribs were really Africans masquerading as Natives, adopting a native national identity as well as individual Carib names.¹⁷ When the battle was finally lost, in 1797, some 4,000 were transported to the coast of Honduras. Their numbers were rapidly depleted, however, by disease and hunger, and the hostile malarial environment of coastal Central America, and the community's population was reduced by half before reaching its final destination. Such population loss rivalled the catastrophic collapse experienced in the first encounters of Indigenous peoples with European invaders.

The survivors of this harsh initiation proved resilient, in spite of the ecological challenges, and quickly established a successful population, numbering more than 200,000 today. They retained their separateness, becoming known as 'Garifuna'.

The Garifuna have long been of interest to medical science, particularly because of their demographic achievements, which some argue is explained by the selective mortality suffered in the first few years of the migration to Central America. This harsh process cut down all but the strongest of the children of Africans, those with inherited defences, notably genetic mutations that protected against malaria, though at the same time carried the persistent burden of sickle cell anaemia. It was this evolved relative immunity, it is claimed, that enabled the Garifuna to prosper in spite of the hostile disease environment of the coast.[18]

Modern studies of Garifuna genetic heritage range across a variety of disciplines and interests, stretching from forensics, to pathology, evolutionary science, and genealogy, as they do for most cultures. Answers are sought through the analysis of proteins found in blood, immunoglobins, and most recently DNA – particularly mitochondrial DNA, applied to the reconstruction of maternal ancestry, but also attempts to trace the paternal line through the Y chromosome. Beginning in the 1980s, data for immunoglobin markers were used to assess gene flows, comparing the Garifuna of Belize with the Black Caribs of St Vincent. These studies found that the Garifuna had a larger proportion of African genes (76%) than the Caribs (46%), whereas the Caribs had more 'Native American' genes than the Garifuna (38% and 20%, respectively). More recently, mitochondrial DNA studies suggest a greater contrast, making the Garifuna even more 'African'.[19]

These findings may seem to confirm the view of the British that the Black Caribs were really Africans masquerading as Indigenous people in hopes of securing land and freedom. However, the selective mortality in the earliest stages of relocation to Central America suggests that the original cohort deported from St Vincent may have had a significantly larger 'Native' component. Importantly, the case of the Garifuna raised controversial issues about the place of hybridity in Indigenous populations and cultures, and the desire to create new identities through embedding in older traditions. As Brooke Newman argues, the Black Caribs were 'phenotypically black but culturally and linguistically Carib'.[20]

To the distaste of the British colonisers, the Black Caribs advocated their rights through self-identification, and questioned the sovereignty claimed by George III while maintaining an allegiance to France. Their claims were not the product of a spontaneous land grab but rather were the outcome of gradual and organic community development, ethnic mixing, and cultural interchange and interaction. Elements of culture and genetics were blended to create a completely new identity, expressed in food traditions, dress, technologies, customs, and beliefs, which drew strongly on Indigenous heritage, as well as African and European sources.[21]

These qualities, and their blending, were carried forward to become part of the identity of the people of St Vincent when the island (associated with the string of smaller islands to the south known as the Grenadines) gained Independence from the United Kingdom in 1971. Later, in 2002, when the Government of St Vincent and the Grenadines decided to create National Heroes, the first to be declared was Chatoyer, Paramount Chief of the Caribs, who died in 1795. His elevation was regarded as recognition of his leading role as a resistance fighter and his struggle to regain sovereignty, which together qualified him to be considered 'the father of Independence'.[22] Official National Heroes have been declared in some other Caribbean territories, including warriors from among Maroons and freedom fighters, but Chatoyer is the only one with certain links to first peoples.

Contested claims

Until quite recently, it was broadly agreed that people with heritages derived from the First Peoples of the Caribbean were uncommon, the great majority of the original population having been wiped out by the end of the sixteenth century and replaced by enslaved Africans. Outside a few remnant enclaves, modern Caribbean people rarely claimed Indigenous identity. Fresh perspectives have, however, been provided by recent analysis of ancient human physical and genetic data (notably mitochondrial DNA), suggesting significant survivorship in some places. Often, these findings appear to confirm traditional claims. In Puerto Rico, for example, samples collected from people claiming a Taíno maternal ancestor proved to have a statistically higher frequency of 'Native American' mitochondrial DNA, suggesting a deep memory.[23]

Studies confined to acknowledged Indigenous communities naturally have stronger genetic links. A study of individuals from the First Peoples Community in Arima, Trinidad, and of 'Garifuna' living in St Vincent, found that 42% had maternal Indigenous ancestry, and a smaller percentage of males had paternal Indigenous heritage as shown by Y-chromosome variation.[24] Links also survived relatively strongly in *cimarrone* communities. In Jamaica in particular, Maroon groups initially established in rearguard action against the retreating Spanish at the English Conquest in 1655 long maintained their status as first peoples, however much mixed with African heritage. Archaeology has demonstrated that sometimes Maroon settlement sites developed where Taínos had earlier lived, in mountain refuges to escape the Spanish, and perhaps overlapping.[25] Oral histories (genealogies) combined with DNA testing confirm the presence of Taíno mitochondrial lineages in the present Maroon community.[26] These findings contribute to notions of identity and pride in a deep heritage. However, in contrast to the Black Caribs' claims to sovereignty and land rights grounded in identification as Indigenous, the Maroons of Jamaica never argued such a case for their ethnogenesis and needed only to point to the conditions of the treaties of the eighteenth century, won in hard battle, which provided for their (conditional) autonomy in governance, economy, and rights to territory.

The spread of DNA testing, together with the growth of community interest in ancestry facilitated by digital searching tools, has opened the door for new ways of claiming and understanding identity in the Caribbean and its diaspora. This evidence, added to existing techniques of oral and documentary history-writing, has complicated understandings of what is entailed in being 'indigenous' and expanded the varieties of 'identity' that can be claimed by individuals and communities. As well as the capacity to identify ancient Indigenous heritage, the many people whose multiple ancestries stretch back to the seventeenth and eighteenth centuries see their identities as primarily creole Caribbean, entitled to call themselves 'indigenous' should they so wish, and staking strong claims for such status.[27]

Negatively, the quantitative proportionality revealed by DNA testing, expressed as percentages of biogeographic ancestry, is sometimes viewed as a new variety of statistical objectification. It is too reminiscent of the hierarchical proportionalism applied during slavery to determine civil status. Early studies were costly and often derived from very small samples, casting doubt on the statistical robustness of the findings, but large populations are now prospected, and the commercial heritage-testing industry offers individuals precise percentages for a small price.[28] Positively, within the region, a spectrum of 'nativeness' has long existed, fusing the concept of indigeneity with a notion of neoendemism, representing the creation of a truly new 'creole' people – and whole beings, not parcels of genetic fragments.

Perhaps the first application of DNA studies to the tracing of ancestry in a Caribbean population was published in 1998, comparing Jamaica with a number of American states, and finding little evidence of indigenous contributions.[29] Many more studies have been undertaken over the past 20 years, using increasingly large samples drawn from living subjects. The results show relatively large proportions of indigenous contribution in the former Spanish colonies of Cuba, the Dominican Republic, and Puerto Rico, and less in the former French and English colonies of Haiti, Jamaica, Barbados, and the Bahamas, for example. Probably, these contrasts reflect differences in attitudes to miscegenation in the early colonial period. Further, the indigenous contribution rarely came through the paternal lineage, since it is understood that the fathers were most often European and the mothers Indigenous.[30]

The molecular evidence offered by DNA has opened up new ways of understanding identity formation and maintenance. In populations such as those of the Caribbean, where hybridity is routinely accepted as essential to national identity, this new evidence is readily embraced and easily incorporated into discourses of extinction and survival. A vital implication for the early colonial history of the islands is that the genetic evidence supports the interpretation that the genocide was not as complete or as rapid as traditionally argued, and that probably many people survived the initial onslaught of disease and slaughter by living in refuges, hidden in the mountainous north of Hispaniola, escaping the census-counters and thus making the population loss seem greater than it really was. Perhaps they remained hidden in this way for a very long time. However, this form of escape was not viable everywhere.

In the smaller islands of the eastern Caribbean, where Indigenous peoples survived more successfully through the first centuries of colonisation, their descendants sometimes found themselves pushed into remote niches, as in the Dominica Republic and St Vincent, regarded as marginal to the common process of creolisation, probably on the road to extinction or absorption.[31] Occasionally, they were allocated reserves, as in Dominica and Trinidad. In Guadeloupe, however, the last vestiges of the Kalinago, living at Pointe de la Grande Vigie, had disappeared by the end of the nineteenth century.[32]

The 'Carib Reserve' in Dominica was formally declared in 1903, by decree of the colonial government, an area of about 3,700 acres, with precise boundaries. Within this space, the Carib/Kalinago people were permitted to continue their custom of electing a chief (*ùbutu*), who was expected to maintain order. The peace was disturbed in 1930 by a police raid on the reserve, followed by arrests, shootings, the expulsion of the (Black, colonial) police by the Caribs, and in consequence the ending of the office of chief (not restored until 1952). An enquiry heard that the Caribs claimed (incorrectly) to have been signatories to the Treaty of Aix-la-Chapelle in 1748, using this as the basis for claims to sovereignty in their territory, and contended that they were not subject to taxation (which was partly true). The population of the Reserve in 1930 was roughly 500, a significant proportion of the people having mixed (African/Kalinago) ancestry. The census of 1946 counted only 40 'American Indians' in Dominica, most of the people being absorbed by the 'mixed' category. Outside observers declared them a 'fast disappearing' people, the last of the 'indigenous "Indians"' of the region. Ethnologists hurried to record language, legends, system of communal land tenure, and material culture, before it was too late.[33] It was a narrative played out across the globe.

Typically, little changed with political autonomy – varieties of 'independence' – and reinvention. Emphasis was often placed on absorption rather than multicultural co-existence. In the case of Cuba, the Revolution of 1959 was followed by an aggressive emphasis on the unity of the people, in a shared national identity or 'Cubanness' that ideally obliterated ethnic and social inequalities and differences. Much the same sentiment was found in the contemporary national motto of Jamaica, when it became independent in 1962 – 'out of many one people', depicted on the Coat of Arms in a scroll at the feet of a Taíno man and woman.

Advocacy of survival ideologies emerged and flourished within the context of a globalising world, with conscious connections to anti-colonial and anti-discrimination movements, such as Civil Rights and Black Power, and the struggle against Apartheid. In Cuba, the heavy emphasis on homogeneity, and the belief that Indigenous people had not survived on the island, was overturned only after the collapse of the Soviet Union and the coming of genetic testing. When Dominica gained independence from the United Kingdom in 1978, it passed a 'Carib Reserve Act' that reaffirmed its political status. The population of the Reserve grew in parallel to the larger population of the island, and the people and the landscape increasingly blended into the general island picture.

Within the Caribbean, movements towards regional association have given rise to transnational groups such as the Caribbean Organization of Indigenous Peoples and the United Confederation of Taíno People, in parallel to some of the broader Caribbean regional entities, gaining recognition from the United Nations and connecting to the global politics of rights and reparations. Underlying the discourse of survival is a rejection of the idea that hybridity and creolisation cancels out indigenous identification, but rather represents the resurgence of a hidden presence, now neatly revealed (or confirmed) by genetic testing.[34]

The resurgence takes many forms. In Dominica, where the Kalingo flourished in the census, the maintenance and revival of craft skills and performance served to support the internal economy, through sale to tourists, particularly at a model village – Kalinago Barana Auté – set up in 2006 as a stage for such enterprise. In Puerto Rico (Boriken) a movement emerged advocating the speaking of 'Taíno', a language without any active speakers and little documentation to enable reconstruction. Self-identifying 'Boricua' use language as an emblem of their indigeneity, though confronted by scepticism from many in the wider community.[35] Individuals in Boriken have taken on the mantle of *cacique*, seen as a resurfacing of hidden tradition rather than reinvention. On a larger stage, the growth of the internet as a medium has enabled the sharing of stories and cross-cultural experiences, but has simultaneously sheltered false or dubious claims of authorship and authenticity.[36]

In 2014, the newly formed Caribbean Reparations Commission gained approval from CARICOM (the Caribbean Community), for a plan to achieve justice for victims of slavery, racial apartheid, and, for the first time, 'native genocide'. These claims occurred in the context of wider Latin American demands for apologies for slavery and crimes against Indigenous peoples in the conquest, pointedly directed at the Roman Catholic Church and Spanish governments. The issue is tied up with land rights and the relative responsibilities of present and past (colonial) governments. In the colonial period, the appropriation of Indigenous lands seemed justified by the extinction discourse, but in the post-independence period – particularly in Dominica, St Vincent, and Trinidad and Tobago – demands and expectations are complicated by continuing violations of Indigenous rights.[37] Further claims to reparatory justice emerged where surviving Indigenous communities, having been pushed into marginal ecological zones, suffered by 'natural' disasters attributed to climate change.[38] More broadly, 'native' rights to compensation have always to confront the question, who exactly is 'indigenous'?

Changing understandings of indigeneity

Beyond the notion that indigeneity asserts precedence of settlement in a particular place, long-standing and intimate association with that place – both geophysical and spiritual – as well as a deep rootedness that underpins concepts of sovereignty, at least two new strands of thought have emerged in the contemporary Caribbean. One argues that 'new' peoples, having served their time as rooted inhabitants of a place and satisfied some further conditions, can come to rightfully see themselves as Indigenous. The second strand suggests that indigeneity is portable, a status that can rightfully be claimed by peoples forced to live in places other than their ancestral lands. In both of these models, connections with surviving first peoples appear to have only a marginal role.

Representative of the first new model, Shona N. Jackson has recently offered the concept of 'Creole indigeneity'. In her study of Guyana, published in 2012, she traces the ways in which the myth and reality of plantation experience enabled Creoles to become 'settlers and new natives'.[39] This widening of the space of settler colonialism allows the forced migrants of the Caribbean to be seen as settlers with the potential for belonging and nativist loyalties, and indeed in some of the islands — Jamaica, for example — those of the formerly enslaved population who chose to cultivate small holdings in mountainous frontiers were termed 'settlers' rather than a degraded 'peasantry' before the end of the nineteenth century. Further, Jackson sees 'that creolisation as a process of indigenisation — to the extent that it is based on difference and resistance — reflects a dialectic of being'.[40]

In Haiti, where the strength of the peasantry certainly justified its classification as a settler society, literary movements reacting to the American occupation (1915–1934) advocated black identity through *indigénisme*, an ideology that emphasised the African roots of the population and the ethnic uniqueness of the nation rather than connection with first peoples.[41] Haiti has received very few immigrants over the past 200 years, in dramatic contrast to the final years of French colonialism when tens of thousands of Africans were poured into the plantations; at the time of the Revolution, some two-thirds of the enslaved people in the colony were Africa-born. The last of the arrivals were swept up almost immediately in the midst of this chaos but very soon became citizens of a new nation and, as argued by Laurent Dubois, came to share 'a level of cultural, social, and economic autonomy that surpassed that of any other group of African birth or African descent in the Americas'.[42] They were out of Africa, not first people, but equally justified to think of themselves as the true children of their new land, legitimate indigenes. These were ideas that matched concepts of *indigenismo* and *criollismo* common in Latin American thought.

The portability model is perhaps best represented in Rastafarian thought. Emerging in Jamaica in the 1930s, the Rastafarian movement represented the dispossessed and those who prayed for repatriation to Africa. Rather than seeking return to the regions of West Africa where the ancestors of most Jamaicans had become enslaved, the objective was more symbolic, more spiritual, a desire to return to Ethiopia, the homeland of Haile Selassie — crowned Emperor of Ethiopia in 1930 and seen as divine. Some did achieve this goal but most somehow made a life in Jamaica, surviving the demands of daily life under colonialism and purported independence, yet always looking to Africa for spiritual sustenance.

In spite of seeking an ancestral homecoming far away, it came to be argued by about 2010 that the 'Rastafari nation' qualified under the UN conventions as legally defined as 'indigenous or tribal peoples'. Rights to lands they occupied should be respected, it was said, 'as a displaced indigenous African people'.[43] In addition to advocacy on the international political stage, these claims have also given rise to local enterprises, notably the Rastafari Indigenous Village, near the tourist town of Montego Bay, which was founded in 2008 by a group of artists, poets, and musicians (blending the reggae of the likes of Bob Marley with Nyabinghi African rhythms) known as the Initiating Circle of Nature. When set up as a tour company — led by a woman trained in heritage tourism and a local known as 'First Man' — some members of the local community lost interest, feeling that this incorporation drew them into the hated maw of capitalism and its executive arm, 'Babylon'.[44]

What is most striking about this project, beyond the morality of the market, is that the intellectual claims made to indigeneity rested on the 'ancient' cultural roots of Rastafari, making no apparent connection with Taíno first people, past or present. In this way, forced migrants generally might assert an original indigeneity, located perhaps in a faraway place they have never been to but from which their foreparents were taken, stripped of their relationship to their true homeland. Put together with the other new model, the idea that newcomers who became true 'settlers' might claim a creole indigeneity, these concepts contribute to a questioning of scholarly models of accommodation, absorption, acculturation, and, particularly, creolisation. Rather than attempting to find neat boxes in which to put each historical example – as in allocating all Caribbean societies to the creole category – it may be more useful to recognise that genetic and cultural blending was common throughout the early Atlantic World, simply playing out differently in different situations and times.[45] Accepting the virtues of an ontological framework structured along these lines, the Caribbean still claims a special place in history, including the history of indigeneity.

Acknowledgements

This essay was written in the School of History, Research School of Social Sciences, Australian National University, Canberra. The author thanks Laurence Brown, Alexandra Lord, and Ann McGrath for their support and encouragement.

Notes

1 The scope of this chapter is confined to the islands of the Caribbean (including Barbados and the Bahamas), with only occasional reference to the mainland/rimland.
2 Peter Bellwood, *First Migrants: Ancient Migration in Global Perspective* (Chichester: Wiley Blackwell, 2013); Peter E. Siegel et al., 'Paleoenvironmental Evidence for First Human Colonization of the Eastern Caribbean,' *Quaternary Science Reviews* 129 (2015): 275–295.
3 Corinne L. Hofman et al., 'Indigenous Caribbean Perspectives: Archaeologies and Legacies of the First Colonized Region in the New World,' *Antiquity* 92, no. 361 (2018): 200–216.
4 B.W. Higman, *A Concise History of the Caribbean* (Cambridge: Cambridge University Press, 2011), 130.
5 For more detailed accounts, see Samuel M. Wilson, *The Archaeology of the Caribbean* (Cambridge: Cambridge University Press, 2007); William F. Keegan and Corinne L. Hofman, *The Caribbean before Columbus* (Oxford: Oxford University Press, 2017); Higman, *Concise History*, 9–51.
6 Bellwood, *First Migrants*, 228.
7 Ricardo Lleonart et al., 'Analyses of DNA from Ancient Bones of a Pre-Columbian Cuban Woman and Child,' *Genetics and Molecular Biology* 22, no. 3 (1999): 285–289; C. Lalueza-Fox et al., 'MtDNA from Extinct Tainos and the Peopling of the Caribbean,' *Annals of Human Genetics* 65 (2001): 137–151; Hannes Schroeder et al., 'Origins and Genetic Legacies of the Caribbean Taino,' *PNAS* 115, no. 10 (2018): 2341–2346; F. Mendisco et al., 'Where are the Caribs? Ancient DNA from Ceramic Period Human Remains in the Lesser Antilles,' *Philosophical Transactions, Royal Society B* 370 (2014): 1–8.
8 Lee A. Newsom and Elizabeth S. Wing, *On Land and Sea: Native American Uses of Biological Resources in the West Indies* (Tuscaloosa: University of Alabama Press, 2004), 200–204.

9 Samuel M. Wilson, *Hispaniola: Caribbean Chiefdoms in the Age of Columbus* (Tuscaloosa: University of Alabama Press, 1990), 99–109.
10 Arie Boomert, *The Indigenous Peoples of Trinidad and Tobago: From the First Settlers until Today* (Leiden: Sidestone Press, 2016), 6.
11 Neil Whitehead, 'Carib Cannibalism: The Historical Evidence,' *Journal de la Société des Américanistes* 70 (1984): 69–87; William F. Keegan, 'Columbus Was a Cannibal,' in *The Lesser Antilles in the Age of European Expansion*, ed. Robert L. Paquette and Stanley L. Engerman (Gainesville: University of Florida Press, 1996), 17–32.
12 Kathleen Deagan and José María Cruxent, *Columbus's Outpost among the Taínos: Spain and America at La Isabela, 1493–1498* (New Haven, CT: Yale University Press, 2002), 61–62.
13 Deagan and Cruxent, *Columbus's Outpost* 209–210.
14 Deagan and Cruxent, *Columbus's Outpost*, 222–227.
15 Lucien-René Abenon, *La Guadeloupe de 1671 à 1759: Etude Politique, Economique et Sociale* (Paris: L'Harmattan, 1987), vol. 1, 31–32.
16 Gérard Lafleur, 'The Passing of a Nation: The Carib Indians of the Lesser Antilles,' in *Amerindians, Africans, Americans: Three Papers in Caribbean History*, eds. Gérard Lafleur, Susan Branson, and Grace Turner (Mona: Department of History, University of the West Indies, 1993), 3–20.
17 Brooke N. Newman, 'Identity Articulated: British Settlers, Black Caribs, and the Politics of Indigeneity on St Vincent, 1763–1797,' in *Native Diasporas: Indigenous Identities and Settler Colonialism in the Americas*, eds. Gregory D. Smithers and Brooke N. Newman (Lincoln: University of Nebraska Press, 2014), 122; Heather Freund, 'Who Should be Treated "With Every Degree of Humanity"? Debating Rights for Planters, Soldiers, and Caribs/Kalinago on St Vincent, 1763–1773,' *Atlantic Studies* 13, no. 1 (2016): 128.
18 Christine Phillips-Krawczak, 'Causes and Consequences of Migration to the Caribbean Islands and Central America: An Evolutionary Success Story,' in *Causes and Consequences of Human Migration*, eds. Michael H. Crawford and Benjamin C. Campbell (Cambridge: Cambridge University Press, 2012), 520–521; Lorena Madrigal, *Human Biology of Afro-Caribbean Populations* (Cambridge: Cambridge University Press, 2006), 108–115.
19 Phillips-Krawczak, 'Causes and Consequences,' 516–520; Edwin-Francisco Herrera-Paz, Mireya Matamoros, and Angel Carracedo, 'The Garifuna (Black Carib) People of the Atlantic Coasts of Honduras: Population Dynamics, Structure, and Phylogenetic Relations Inferred from Genetic Data, Migration Matrices, and Isonymy,' *American Journal of Human Biology* 22 (2010): 36–44.
20 Newman, 'Identity Articulated,' 111. See also, Michael Craton, 'The Black Caribs of St Vincent: A Reevaluation,' in *The Lesser Antilles in the Age of European Expansion*, eds. Robert L. Paquette and Stanley L. Engerman (Gainesville: University of Florida Press, 1996), 71–85; Peter Hulme, 'Black, Yellow, and White on St Vincent: Moreau de Jonnès's Carib Ethnography,' in *The Global Eighteenth Century*, ed. Felicity A. Nussbaum (Baltimore, MD: Johns Hopkins University Press, 2003), 182–194.
21 Nancie L. Gonzalez, *Sojourners of the Caribbean: Ethnogenesis and Ethnohistory of the Garifuna* (Urbana: University of Illinois Press, 1988), 127–129; Newman, 'Identity Articulated,' 132–133.
22 Adrian Fraser, *Chatoyer (Chatawae): National Hero of St Vincent and the Grenadines* (St Vincent: Galaxy Print Ltd., 2002), 29; Lafleur, 'Passing of a Nation,' 39.
23 J.C. Martinez-Cruzado et al., 'Mitochondrial DNA Analysis Reveals Substantial Native American Ancestry in Puerto Rico,' *Human Biology* 73, no. 4 (2001): 491.
24 Jada Benn Torres et al., 'Genetic Diversity in the Lesser Antilles and Its Implications for the Settlement of the Caribbean Basin,' *PLOS ONE* 10, no. 10 (2015): 1–27.
25 P. Allsworth-Jones, *Pre-Columbian Jamaica* (Tuscaloosa: University of Alabama Press, 2008), 25–26.

26 Nicole Madrilejo, Holden Lombard, and Jada Benn Torres, 'Origins of Marronage: Mitochondrial Lineages of Jamaica's Accompong Town Maroons,' *American Journal of Human Biology* 27 (2015): 432–437; Harcourt Fuller and Jada Benn Torres, 'Investigating the "Taíno" Ancestry of the Jamaican Maroons: A New Genetic (DNA), Historical, and Multidisciplinary Analysis and Case Study of the Accompong Town Maroons,' *Canadian Journal of Latin American and Caribbean Studies* 43, no. 1 (2018): 50–51.
27 Jada Benn Torres, 'Prospecting the Past: Genetic Perspectives on the Extinction and Survival of Indigenous Peoples of the Caribbean,' *New Genetics and Society* 33, no. 1 (2014): 21–41.
28 David Reich, *Who We Are and How We Got Here: Ancient DNA and the New Science of the Human Past* (Oxford: Oxford University Press, 2018), xvii–xviii.
29 Esteban J. Parra et al., 'Estimating African American Admixture Proportions by Use of Population-Specific Alleles,' *American Journal of Human Genetics* 63 (1998): 1839–1851.
30 See, for example, Areej Bukhari et al., 'Taino and African Maternal Lineage in the Greater Antilles,' *Gene* 637 (2017): 33–40; Martinez-Cruzado et al., 'Mitochondrial DNA,' 491–511; Isabel Mendizabal et al., 'Genetic Origin, Admixture, and Asymmetry in Maternal and Paternal Human Lineages in Cuba,' *BMC Evolutionary Biology* 8 (2008): article 213, 1–10; Tanya M. Simms et al., 'Paternal Lineages Signal Distinct Genetic Contributions from British Loyalists and Continental Africans Among Different Bahamian Islands,' *American Journal of Physical Anthropology* 146 (2011): 594–608; Tanya M. Simms et al., 'Y-STR Diversity and Sex-Based Gene Flow Among Caribbean Populations,' *Gene* 516 (2013): 82–92; Jamie L. Wilson et al., 'Forensic Analysis of mtDNA Haplotypes from Two Rural Communities in Haiti Reflects Their Population History,' *Journal of Forensic Sciences* 57, no. 6 (2012): 1457–1466.
31 Benn Torres, 'Prospecting the Past,' 24.
32 Lafleur, 'Passing of a Nation.'
33 *Conditions in the Carib Reserve, and the Disturbance of 19th September, 1930, Dominica: Report of a Commission Appointed by His Excellency the Governor of the Leeward Islands, July, 1931* (London: His Majesty's Stationery Office, 1932); Douglas Taylor, *The Caribs of Dominica* (Washington, DC: Smithsonian Institution, Bureau of American Ethnology, Anthropological Papers, no. 3, 1938); Lafleur, 'Passing of a Nation'; *West Indian Census 1946: General Report of the Census of Population 9th April, 1946* (Kingston: Government Printer, 1950), 16.
34 Roberto Borrero, 'Taíno Affirmation in the 21st Century: Proliferating Communities of Indigenous Consciousness Within and Out of the Caribbean,' in *Taino Legacies* (National Museum of the American Indian, Smithsonian Institution, 2013); Luciano Baracco, 'Globalization, Governance, and the Emergence of Indigenous Autonomy Movements in Latin America,' *Latin American Perspectives* 45, no. 6 (2018): 37–52; Benn Torres, 'Prospecting the Past,' 27–28.
35 Sherina Feliciano-Santos, 'How Do You Speak Taíno? Indigenous Activism and Linguistic Practices in Puerto Rico,' *Journal of Linguistic Anthropology* 27, no. 1 (2017): 4–21.
36 Maximilian C. Forte, ed., *Indigenous Resurgence in the Contemporary Caribbean: Amerindian Survival and Revival* (New York: Peter Lang, 2006).
37 Amy Strecker, 'Revival, Recognition, Restitution: Indigenous Rights in the Eastern Caribbean,' *International Journal of Cultural Property* 23 (2016): 167–190.
38 Rose-Ann J. Smith and Kevon Rhiney, 'Climate (In)justice, Vulnerability and Livelihoods in the Caribbean: The Case of the Indigenous Caribs in Northeastern St Vincent,' *Geoforum* 73 (2016): 22–31.
39 Shona N. Jackson, *Creole Indigeneity: Between Myth and Nation in the Caribbean* (Minneapolis: University of Minnesota Press, 2012), 34.
40 Jackson, *Creole Indigeneity*, 41.
41 Victoria Famin, 'Les Griots, entre Indigénisme et Négritude,' *Revue de Littérature Comparée* 364 (2017): 422–432.
42 Laurent Dubois, 'Complications,' *William and Mary Quarterly* 68, no. 2 (2011): 224–226.

43 Leonard P. Howell Foundation, 'Land and Human Rights of Rastafari as Indigenous Peoples,' blog post, 3 December 2013, lphfoundation.org/land-and-human-rights-of-rastafari-as-indigenous-peoples.
44 Jovan Scott Lewis, 'Rights, Indigeneity, and the Market of Rastafari,' *International Journal of Cultural Property* 24, no. 1 (2017): 57–77.
45 James Sidbury and Jorge Cañizares-Esguerra, 'Mapping Ethnogenesis in the Early Modern Atlantic,' *William and Mary Quarterly* 68, no. 2 (2011): 181–208.

Bibliography

Abenon, Lucien-René. *La Guadeloupe de 1671 à 1759: Etude Politique, Economique et Sociale*. Paris: L'Harmattan, 1987.
Allsworth-Jones, P. *Pre-Columbian Jamaica*. Tuscaloosa: University of Alabama Press, 2008.
Baracco, Luciano. 'Globalization, Governance, and the Emergence of Indigenous Autonomy Movements in Latin America.' *Latin American Perspectives* 45, no. 6 (2018): 37–52.
Bellwood, Peter. *First Migrants: Ancient Migration in Global Perspective*. Chichester: Wiley Blackwell, 2013.
Benn Torres, Jada. 'Prospecting the Past: Genetic Perspectives on the Extinction and Survival of Indigenous Peoples of the Caribbean.' *New Genetics and Society* 33, no. 1 (2014): 21–41.
Benn Torres, Jada, Miguel G. Vilar, Gabriel A. Torres, Jill B. Galeski, Ricardo Bharath Hernandez, Zoila E. Browne, Marlon Stevenson, Wendell Walters, Theodore G. Schurr, and The Genographic Consortium. 'Genetic Diversity in the Lesser Antilles and Its Implications for the Settlement of the Caribbean Basin.' *PLOS ONE* 10, no. 10 (2015): 1–27.
Boomert, Arie. *The Indigenous Peoples of Trinidad and Tobago: From the First Settlers until Today*. Leiden: Sidestone Press, 2016.
Borrero, Roberto. 'Taíno Affirmation in the 21st Century: Proliferating Communities of Indigenous Consciousness Within and Out of the Caribbean.' In *Taino Legacies*. National Museum of the American Indian, Smithsonian Institution, 2013. http://www.tainolegacies.com/170582894
Bukhari, Areej, Javier Rodriguez Luis, Miguel A. Alfonso-Sanchez, Ralph Garcia-Bertrand, and Rene J. Herrera. 'Taino and African Maternal Lineage in the Greater Antilles.' *Gene* 637 (2017): 33–40.
Conditions in the Carib Reserve, and the Disturbance of 19th September, 1930, Dominica: Report of a Commission Appointed by His Excellency the Governor of the Leeward Islands, July, 1931. London: His Majesty's Stationery Office, 1932.
Craton, Michael. 'The Black Caribs of St Vincent: A Reevaluation.' In *The Lesser Antilles in the Age of European Expansion*, edited by Robert L. Paquette and Stanley L. Engerman, 71–85. Gainesville: University of Florida Press, 1996.
Deagan, Kathleen, and José María Cruxent. *Columbus's Outpost among the Taínos: Spain and America at La Isabela, 1493–1498*. New Haven, CT: Yale University Press, 2002.
Dubois, Laurent. 'Complications.' *William and Mary Quarterly* 68, no. 2 (2011): 224–226.
Famin, Victoria. 'Les Griots, entre Indigénisme et Négritude.' *Revue de Littérature Comparée* 364 (2017): 422–432.
Feliciano-Santos, Sherina. 'How *Do You* Speak Taíno? Indigenous Activism and Linguistic Practices in Puerto Rico.' *Journal of Linguistic Anthropology* 27, no. 1 (2017): 4–21.
Forte, Maximilian C., ed. *Indigenous Resurgence in the Contemporary Caribbean: Amerindian Survival and Revival*. New York: Peter Lang, 2006.
Fraser, Adrian. *Chatoyer (Chatawae): National Hero of St Vincent and the Grenadines*. St Vincent: Galaxy Print Ltd., 2002.
Freund, Heather. 'Who Should be Treated "With Every Degree of Humanity"? Debating Rights for Planters, Soldiers, and Caribs/Kalinago on St Vincent, 1763–1773.' *Atlantic Studies* 13, no. 1 (2016): 125–143.

Fuller, Harcourt, and Jada Benn Torres. 'Investigating the "Taíno" Ancestry of the Jamaican Maroons: A New Genetic (DNA), Historical, and Multidisciplinary Analysis and Case Study of the Accompong Town Maroons.' *Canadian Journal of Latin American and Caribbean Studies* 43, no. 1 (2018): 47–78.

Gonzalez, Nancie L. *Sojourners of the Caribbean: Ethnogenesis and Ethnohistory of the Garifuna.* Urbana: University of Illinois Press, 1988.

Herrera-Paz, Edwin-Francisco, Mireya Matamoros, and Angel Carracedo. 'The Garifuna (Black Carib) People of the Atlantic Coasts of Honduras: Population Dynamics, Structure, and Phylogenetic Relations Inferred from Genetic Data, Migration Matrices, and Isonymy.' *American Journal of Human Biology* 22 (2010): 36–44.

Higman, B.W. *A Concise History of the Caribbean.* Cambridge: Cambridge University Press, 2011.

Hofman, Corinne L., Jorge Ulloa Hung, Eduardo Herrera Malatesta, Joseph Sony Jean, Till Sonnemann, and Menno Hoogland. 'Indigenous Caribbean Perspectives: Archaeologies and Legacies of the First Colonized Region in the New World.' *Antiquity* 92, no. 361 (2018): 200–216.

Hulme, Peter. 'Black, Yellow, and White on St Vincent: Moreau de Jonnès's Carib Ethnography.' In *The Global Eighteenth Century*, edited by Felicity A. Nussbaum, 182–194. Baltimore, MD: Johns Hopkins University Press, 2003.

Jackson, Shona N. *Creole Indigeneity: Between Myth and Nation in the Caribbean.* Minneapolis: University of Minnesota Press, 2012.

Keegan, William F. 'Columbus Was a Cannibal.' In *The Lesser Antilles in the Age of European Expansion*, edited by Robert L. Paquette and Stanley L. Engerman, 17–32. Gainesville: University of Florida Press, 1996.

Keegan, William F., and Corinne L. Hofman. *The Caribbean before Columbus.* Oxford: Oxford University Press, 2017.

Lafleur, Gérard. 'The Passing of a Nation: The Carib Indians of the Lesser Antilles.' In *Amerindians, Africans, Americans: Three Papers in Caribbean History*, edited by Gérard Lafleur, Susan Branson and Grace Turner, 3–20. Mona: Department of History, University of the West Indies, 1996.

Lalueza-Fox, C., F. Luna Calderón, F. Calafell, B. Morera, and J. Bertranpetit. 'MtDNA from Extinct Tainos and the Peopling of the Caribbean.' *Annals of Human Genetics* 65 (2001): 137–151.

Leonard P. Howell Foundation. 'Land and Human Rights of Rastafari as Indigenous Peoples.' Blog post, 3 December 2013. lphfoundation.org/land-and-human-rights-of-rastafari-as-indigenous-peoples.

Lewis, Jovan Scott. 'Rights, Indigeneity, and the Market of Rastafari.' *International Journal of Cultural Property* 24, no. 1 (2017): 57–77.

Lleonart, Ricardo, Eileen Riego, Roberto Rodriguez Suárez, Rafael Travieso Ruiz, and José de la Fuente. 'Analyses of DNA from Ancient Bones of a Pre-Columbian Cuban Woman and Child.' *Genetics and Molecular Biology* 22, no. 3 (1999): 285–289.

Madrigal, Lorena. *Human Biology of Afro-Caribbean Populations.* Cambridge: Cambridge University Press, 2006.

Madrilejo, Nicole, Holden Lombard, and Jada Benn Torres. 'Origins of Marronage: Mitochondrial Lineages of Jamaica's Accompong Town Maroons.' *American Journal of Human Biology* 27 (2015): 432–437.

Martinez-Cruzado, J.C., G. Toro-Labrador, V. Ho-Fung, M. Estevez-Montero, A. Lobaina-Manzanet, D.A. Padovani-Claudio, H. Sanchez-Cruz, et al. 'Mitochondrial DNA Analysis Reveals Substantial Native American Ancestry in Puerto Rico.' *Human Biology* 73, no. 4 (2001): 491–511.

Mendisco, F., M.H. Pemonge, E. Leblay, T. Romon, G. Richard, P. Courtaud, and M.F. Deguilloux. 'Where are the Caribs? Ancient DNA from Ceramic Period Human Remains in the Lesser Antilles.' *Philosophical Transactions, Royal Society B* 370 (2014): 1–8.

Mendizabal, Isabel, Karla Sandoval, Gemma Berniell-Lee, Francesc Calafell, Antonio Salas, Antonio Martínez-Fuentes, and David Comas. 'Genetic Origin, Admixture, and Asymmetry in Maternal and Paternal Human Lineages in Cuba.' *BMC Evolutionary Biology* 8 (2008): article 213, 1–10.

Newman, Brooke N. 'Identity Articulated: British Settlers, Black Caribs, and the Politics of Indigeneity on St Vincent, 1763–1797.' In *Native Diasporas: Indigenous Identities and Settler Colonialism in the Americas*, edited by Gregory D. Smithers and Brooke N. Newman, 109–150. Lincoln: University of Nebraska Press, 2014.

Newsom, Lee A., and Elizabeth S. Wing, *On Land and Sea: Native American Uses of Biological Resources in the West Indies*. Tuscaloosa: University of Alabama Press, 2004.

Parra, Esteban J., Amy Marcini, Joshua Akey, Jeremy Martinson, Mark A. Batzer, Richard Cooper, Terrence Forrester, et al. 'Estimating African American Admixture Proportions by Use of Population-Specific Alleles.' *American Journal of Human Genetics* 63 (1998): 1839–1851.

Phillips-Krawczak, Christine. 'Causes and Consequences of Migration to the Caribbean Islands and Central America: An Evolutionary Success Story.' In *Causes and Consequences of Human Migration*, edited by Michael H. Crawford and Benjamin C. Campbell, 512–524. Cambridge: Cambridge University Press, 2012.

Reich, David. *Who We Are and How We Got Here: Ancient DNA and the New Science of the Human Past*. Oxford: Oxford University Press, 2018.

Schroeder, Hannes, Martin Sikora, Shyam Gopalakrishnan, Lara M. Cassidy, Pierpaolo Maisano Delser, Marcela Sandoval Velasco, Joshua G. Schraiber, et al. 'Origins and Genetic Legacies of the Caribbean Taino.' *PNAS* 115, no. 10 (2018): 2341–2346.

Sidbury, James, and Jorge Cañizares-Esguerra. 'Mapping Ethnogenesis in the Early Modern Atlantic.' *William and Mary Quarterly* 68, no. 2 (2011): 181–208.

Siegel, Peter E., John G. Jones, Deborah M. Pearsall, Nicholas P. Dunning, Pat Farrell, Neil A. Duncan, Jason H. Curtis, et al. 'Paleoenvironmental Evidence for First Human Colonization of the Eastern Caribbean.' *Quaternary Science Reviews* 129 (2015): 275–295.

Simms, Tanya M., Emanuel Martinez, Kristian J. Herrera, Marisil R. Wright, Omar A. Perez, Michelle Hernandez, Evelyn C. Ramirez, et al. 'Paternal Lineages Signal Distinct Genetic Contributions from British Loyalists and Continental Africans among Different Bahamian Islands.' *American Journal of Physical Anthropology* 146 (2011): 594–608.

Simms, Tanya M., Marisil R. Wright, Emanuel Martinez, Maria Reguerio, Quinn McCartny, and Rene J. Herrera. 'Y-STR Diversity and Sex-Based Gene Flow Among Caribbean Populations.' *Gene* 516 (2013): 82–92.

Smith, Rose-Ann J., and Kevon Rhiney. 'Climate (In)justice, Vulnerability and Livelihoods in the Caribbean: The Case of the Indigenous Caribs in Northeastern St Vincent.' *Geoforum* 73 (2016): 22–31.

Strecker, Amy. 'Revival, Recognition, Restitution: Indigenous Rights in the Eastern Caribbean.' *International Journal of Cultural Property* 23 (2016): 167–190.

Taylor, Douglas. *The Caribs of Dominica*. Washington, DC: Smithsonian Institution, Bureau of American Ethnology, Anthropological Papers, no. 3, 1938.

West Indian Census 1946: General Report of the Census of Population 9th April, 1946. Kingston: Government Printer, 1950.

Whitehead, Neil. 'Carib Cannibalism: The Historical Evidence.' *Journal de la Société des Américanistes* 70 (1984): 69–87.

Wilson, Jamie L., Vertus Saint-Louis, Jensen O. Auguste, and Bruce A. Jackson, 'Forensic Analysis of mtDNA Haplotypes from Two Rural Communities in Haiti Reflects Their Population History.' *Journal of Forensic Sciences* 57, no. 6 (2012): 1457–1466.

Wilson, Samuel M. *Hispaniola: Caribbean Chiefdoms in the Age of Columbus*. Tuscaloosa: University of Alabama Press, 1990.

Wilson, Samuel M. *The Archaeology of the Caribbean*. Cambridge: Cambridge University Press, 2007.

24
SUBTTSASA BIEHTSEVUOMÁTJISTEMA
Recalling the memories and stories from our little pine forest

May-Britt Öhman Tuoeha Rim

Mid-1970s. I am around ten years old and on one of my recurrent weeklong summer visits to my maternal grandparents, 20 kilometres east of Jokkmokk, by the little Lule River. I don't know the three boys my own age in what is now a small village – although only a decade earlier it was full of kids – so not having anyone to play with and to keep busy I get to go rod fishing in the river.[1] It doesn't take long until my fishing lure is stuck in the bottom of the river, like so many times before. It has happened so often that I have developed a way to think around it; I am not stuck, but instead I imagine that I have the whole world on my fishing rod. However, my philosophical illusion does not help in the long run. I grow up thinking that I am incapable of ever catching a fish. What I don't realise, until I am an adult, returning to the river to study the consequences of hydropower exploitation, is the reason for this, that the river had been regulated, the dam was finished the year after my birth, and what is catching the fishing lure every time are the dead tree roots left from the inundation.

A story recalling the very same stretch of the river around 70 years earlier, told by Lars Johan Andersson in 1932, a relative and neighbour of my grandfather Sten Nilsson:

> I was spearfishing in the calm waters in the year 1906, it was the beginning of the spearfishing season, around the 12th of August. First, I caught a 20 kilo salmon; then I found another big fish. The first stab I made to the second fish hit over its back, but the salmon was so big that the spear could not enter beneath its spine. Johan Stenman was rowing, and as he turned the boat I tried to push the salmon along the bottom of the river towards the land; I did this as much as the forces of both myself and the salmon allowed for. As we arrived to shallow water I climbed out of the boat, put my right hand into the salmon's gill, and managed with great effort to lift it onto the boat. The salmon

immediately fought loose from the spear, and, as it was about to escape out of the boat, Johan hit the fish directly on the head with a log. It was the biggest salmon I've ever seen. It weighed 33 kilos, and that considering that it must have lost weight since it had come all the way from the sea.[2]

The salmon fishing adventure from early 1900s and my own from 1970s are but two of several stories from my stretch of the river, from our pine forested area by the little Lule River, or in Lule Sámi, Unna Julevädno. My maternal grandfather's family has lived here since time immemorial. We survived, lived, prospered, here on ancestral lands, water, and forests. And we actually still do, despite the destructive regulation of the river, which made Jokkmokk blossom for only a couple of decades, providing ten per cent of the electricity produced within Sweden, half of all hydropower produced, while next to no money is returned to the region.

Subttsasa Biehtsevuomátjistema means 'Stories from Our Little Pine Forest', in Lule Sámi, a Sámi language from the region of the Lule River Valley, on the Swedish side of Sábme, and the language of my maternal grandfather's family. I never learned this language, nor about our traditional knowledges. Nor did I learn Meänkieli – from Tornedalen (the Torne River Valley) – which was my maternal grandmother's first language. While earlier Sámi people were part of the elite – an important group for Nordic kings and lords, paying taxes in furs and fish – since the sixteenth century and the establishment of the nation states of Fenno-Scandinavia, the Sámi people have been ethnically cleansed, deported to reservations, and forced into assimilation, through different more or less violent means.[3] These experiences are shared with Indigenous peoples around the world. It was and is an ongoing genocide and an epistemicide[4] – the destruction of local and traditional knowledge and languages, along with the destruction of forests, lands, and waters. While it is important to point out that this epistemicide is still ongoing, and to fight it, I find it equally important to spend time on reclaiming our history, knowledge, and ways to learn and teach, as a way of living, learning, and resting.

Hence, in this chapter, I recall glimpses of the history of a specific stretch of the Lule River. Foreign and outsider researchers have studied this area since at least the seventeenth century – with the Sámi considered exotic people, to 'discover' and tell stories about – for different purposes, a major one being control and colonisation. The area has also been of importance for control by the Swedish state church, in close collaboration with the Swedish state, from kings to democratically elected governments. Thus, researchers have come here to study both the people and the landscape.[5] Work has also been done by locals, both academics and authors, who are not in academia. I can hardly claim to be writing a completely unwritten history. My contribution as a historian is rather that of documenting a family history, using certain sources no one else has access to and thereby providing an insider perspective, and also turning the gaze, voicing Sámi perspectives, and drawing on a growing tradition of Indigenous historical methodologies. I am telling the important story of my own family, and thereby Forest Sámi history as experienced by us.

What is interesting is, first of all, that while there is so much studied here, by outsiders, so many books and dissertations written, in several languages, how come I didn't learn about my family history, and our Forest Sámi heritage, until the age of 42? Why did we never talk about being Sámi? Why did my mother fiercely deny being Sámi when I asked her in the mid-1990s? In school and at university, like all the other students, I learned the history of Sweden, but never about Sámi history, and Sámi–Swedish relationships. This is to a large extent still the case.[6] It is an imposed amnesia, part of a colonial epistemicide, which needs to be challenged. The knowledge production in academia, and thereby the knowledge taught within the education system should be updated to include Indigenous – Sámi – history.

Second, what I find urgent, important, and interesting is to write my family history, within the frame of colonial history, with an insider perspective and a critical Indigenous perspective that challenges this shame of being Sámi that haunted my mother and so many others. It is also a recurrent theme in almost all work on Sámi history, all these definitions on who are Sámi and who are not. Why is this so important? And why shouldn't we be proud of our Sámi heritage?

My family belong to the Forest Sámi, those that live in the forested area, and when we had reindeer, we did not withdraw to the mountain area in the summertime but instead lived in the border areas, making a living from many different trades. There is an idea that the only Sámi occupation was reindeer herding, but at this point it is time to challenge this idea. This has actually never been the case. Sámi have maintained a diverse economy, with herding, small-scale farming with farm animals, hunting, fishing, iron works, tar production, and handicrafts, for consumption and use but also for trade. The focus only on reindeer herding is a state-imposed activity of the colonial state starting from the late nineteenth century, which has caused the Sámi culture severe damage and subjected it to extensive vulnerability.[7]

As the Forest Sámi would not adapt to this way of life, the Swedish state did not want Forest Sámi interfering with territories that were to be colonised for agriculture, forestry, and industrialisation. Since the late nineteenth century, policies, legislation, and actions have been undertaken to erase Forest Sámi culture and to assimilate the Forest Sámi into Swedishness.[8] Understanding how and why Forest Sámi were, and still are, erased in policies, practices, and history writing forms a major part of my work. This also turns an eye to how the depiction of the nomadic, reindeer herding Mountain Sámi became the 'real Sámi' stereotype. Further, while Mountain Sámi people were supported for their perceived purity, at the same time, they were and are subject to explicit racism and discrimination. In other words, there has existed very outspoken divide and conquer colonial politics.

I thereby join in the Indigenous scholarship on writing our own history, from our own perspectives, including emotions and affect, as an important contribution and decolonising healing practice, and also as part of historical methodology that needs to be given part of mainstream history scholarship.[9] Diné historian Jennifer Nez Denetdale states:

> ... writing our own history means that as Native scholars we are obligated to expose the colonial structures that shape our lives as Native people and

to become critically conscious of how we have taken American truths about Native people as our realities, thereby accepting our marginal positions in American society.[10]

In doing this, I draw on my own work, made over a decade, in which I have had numerous interviews and conversations, funded by different research projects. Geographically, my focus has been on the Lule River Valley. For this chapter, I am concentrating mainly on one particular place, 20 kilometres downstream of the city of Jokkmokk, a Forest Sámi area, where my mother was born and in the region where my family have been living probably as far back as the last ice age, 10,000 years ago. I see this chapter as part of an ongoing investigation; there is certainly more work to be done, any historian reading this should be aware that I have not gone through all studies that exist, there is a lot available. However, I find it important to publish my findings and insights along the way. This place, and this river, connects with the city of Luleju – Luleå – by the mouth of the river, downstream about 160 kilometres. My mother moved to Luleå to attend secondary school, and stayed there for the rest of her life. Luleå is where I grew up, and Luleå is 'the town' for those living in Jokkmokk. And people in Luleå would – and still do – come inland for trade and fishing.[11]

The chapter builds on historical methodologies and egohistoire[12] elements. I refer to photos in the family album, the house and landscape and waterscape as an archive, conversations and interviews I have had with family members and neighbours in the area as well as my own memories, preliminary archaeological investigations, and genealogy studies of my family. I have been coming to this stretch of the Lule river, named Skällarim, since I was born and still spend a lot of time here. Part of this chapter was written while being in this place, living in the very house that my grandfather (then aged 30) and grandmother (then aged 24) built in 1937, with the support of my grandfather's brother, and for which my grandmother's father came from Tornedalen to help out. I recover stories that have been silenced, as the area has been subject to fierce industrial colonisation with hydropower, militarisation, and forestry.

Sábme – the original territory of Fennoscandia

There are written records of Sámi as distinct people, separate from the Nordic, as early as the first century CE. In 98 CE, the Roman historian Tacitus mentions two northern peoples, the suiones, the Swedes, and the fenni, the Sámi.[13] Sábme, the territories of the Sámi, are vast areas that actually encompass most of the Fennoscandian Peninsula – thus the area of today's nation states of Norway, Sweden, Finland, and the northeast part of Russia. Sábme (or Sápmi in North Sámi, or Saepmie in South Sámi) is an intercultural melting pot of different cultures, which have had documented exchange for many centuries, and also exchange with Sweden's capital, Stockholm, and with the primary site for the church and university, Uppsala. Sábme has been inhabited by the Sámi people for as long as any human can remember; as the Sámi author Johan Turi states: 'maybe we were actually always here'.[14] We have different languages than the nation states; ten different major Sámi languages exist, but also smaller varieties. In the region that I refer to in this chapter, mainly Lule Sámi and North Sámi are spoken today. Lule Sámi is the original Sámi language here, while North Sámi came with those that were forced to move with their reindeer herds after the ending of the union with Norway in 1905.[15]

The links with Finland, and thus the Finnish language, are part of the local history too. The region in question is close to Finland, and until 1809, Finland was part of Sweden. The river Torne then became the border, but the cultural exchange has never ceased. The distance from Luleå to the border to Finland is – on land, and following the route of today – about 130 kilometres, a short distance today as well as earlier. The Swedish language was introduced early, through trade exchanges, but it is hard to tell when precisely the entire population in the two-river area knew Swedish. It is known though that the work by the state church to have good Christian subjects in the area was of major importance.

Until early in the sixteenth century, Sámi people were openly a part of the elite, and Swedish regional chiefs – kings – would be proud to claim Sámi heritage. The Sámi were part of a global trade, with trade exchanges East–West and North–South.[16] Sámi were members of local courts in the northern regions well into the eighteenth century. Sámi were also trained at Uppsala University since the seventeenth century and were sent out to work as vicars.[17] In the seventeenth century, several academic scholars as well as political decision-makers depicted the Sámi as Others – other than Swedish – and as exotic and strange people. However, these depictions should be considered as myths created for different purposes, mainly for territorial claims. It was a useful strategy to depict Sámi as less knowledgeable and needing to be educated by the church and state, or as too strong and thus to be tamed and the land to be governed by those in power.[18]

Like most other families, my family has experiences of this exchange. My family tree, made by my mother, shows an ancestor immigrating from Pyhäjoki, Finland, to Jokkmokk in the seventeenth century.[19] My maternal grandmother, Ellen Nilsson (born Tuohea), came to Skällarim from Hietaniemi parish in Tornedalen (the Torne River Valley), a border to Finland since the lost Napoleonic war with Russia in 1809. According to family story, she moved to Skällarim – in this little Lule River area 20 kilometres downstream of Jokkmokk – to work as a maid, and married my grandfather Sten. Among her ancestors, I find seventeenth-century immigrants, including a coal master from Namur, present-day Belgium, and a coppersmith master from Aachen in what is now Germany. They came to work at the Kengis copper and iron works, in Tornedalen.[20] Ellen's maternal language was Meänkieli, a language close to Finnish. Her sister, Julia, also came here, and married Sten's brother Viktor. They set up their homes within 150 metres of each other, on inherited lands that had earlier been the so-called Lap Tax Lands. My mother told me – I cannot recall precisely when, but probably in the 1990s when we visited Skällarim together once – that the sisters would talk in their maternal language, but they never taught it to their children. Instead they kept it as a language to be able to talk without their children understanding, which made my mother and her sister very angry when they were young. In the photo album there are photos from their trips to visit the home of Ellen in Tornedalen, including a trip in the 1950s to Luppio-Lövdalen.

The Lule River – Julevädno and the Forest Sámi in the two-river country

The name of the Lule River derives from *lulasj*, a Lule Sámi word meaning eastwards or towards the forest region. The name 'Lulu', referring to a place by the coast, today known as the city Luleå, is documented in written sources from the fourteenth century.[21] The Lule River has its origins in the mountain areas of the current borders between Norway and Sweden. For many centuries, it was a central highway and an important economic link between the two seas, and between eastern and western societies.[22]

The Lule River is actually not one but two rivers: the Great Lule or North River, Stuor Julevädno, and the Little Lule or South River, Unna Julevädno. They converge at Vuollerim, 20 kilometres downstream of Skällarim, before continuing towards Luleå by the Baltic Sea coast. It is around this confluence that the Forest Sámi of the Jokkmokk area have thrived over the millennia.

Forest Sámi reindeer herding has, through state intervention, legislation, and discrimination, been severely reduced. Today, there are two Forest Sámi reindeer herding villages (*samebyar*) in the Lule River Valley around Jokkmokk, Udtja, and Slakka, and a third has grazing lands further downstream along the river, from Boden to the archipelago.[23] These three were earlier part of what was a major Forest Sámi region – Sjokksjokk (Sjocksjock).[24]

Starting from 1910, and throughout the twentieth century, the state-owned power company converted the Lule River from a free-flowing river into an energy-producing factory. It is now a staircase of 16 regulation reservoirs with attached power plants, a total installed capacity of 4,350 MW, and an annual output of almost 14 TWh. The system produces more than ten per cent of the totality of Swedish-produced electricity.[25] Or, as the state-owned power company Vattenfall boasts in an online report from 2008, the Lule River is 'producing enough electricity to bring light to the whole of Sweden, 24 hours a day, 365 days per year'.[26] The regulation of the stretch by my maternal grandfather's lands was finalised the year after my birth, in 1967, with the Letsi dam and reservoir.

What stories have been already told, and how and by whom were they told?

The two-river country that is my maternal grandfather's family homeland has been investigated extensively. There are voids yet to fill, but as I set out doing my own academic scholarly research, doing the literature search in preparation for this chapter, I find myself overwhelmed by the amount of scholarly and other literature available on Jokkmokk. I did learn over the course of the last decade as I started doing research on my own home river that there is a lot of work written on Sámi territories, but the amount of literature on Jokkmokk, and even the small village of Skällarim, makes my head spin. I am overwhelmed as I can't really understand how I could not have read about it all, having grown up here, having been at school for so long, even becoming a PhD in history of technology. There is so much work available! Studies have been conducted by both outsiders and locals to the area since at least the seventeenth century, for many different reasons such as scientific exploration – curiosity, economy – taxation, mining, forestry, hydropower, and racial biology.[27] A comparison with studies based on Stockholm, the capital, would certainly be interesting. Whose is the gaze? For whom are the studies made, and how are they made? And how come all of this is still not taught in schools and at universities as part of Swedish and Sámi–Swedish relationship history?

It is obvious, however, that the region is of major interest to power-holders further south. From the establishment of the Swedish nation state in the sixteenth century, it was of importance to gain control over the northern areas.[28]

In 1932, J.G. Ullenius – himself born in 1868 in Jokkmokk, and raised there – conducted interviews in the Forest Sámi villages during August and September, on behalf of Norrbotten County Local Heritage Association.[29] Based on these interviews along with his own observations, earlier and later, his descriptions of the history of and contemporary life in Skällarim are probably the most detailed existing of this place.[30] The Norrbotten County Local Heritage Association was part of the national Swedish Local Heritage Federation which was started in 1916.[31]

Furthermore, there is a 1968 academic thesis within the discipline of geography, produced and defended at Uppsala University, that deals with Jokkmokk. The field work was developed over three decades by Filip Hultblad (1907–1970), tracing the people and their livelihoods, in the thesis title described as changing from (reindeer) nomadism to agrarian settler life. Hultblad describes his relationship to the place as his home area (*hembygd* in Swedish) in the very first sentence of the thesis preface.[32] Is he himself Sámi? He does not mention his own background, and to know I would probably need to go through his family genealogy. Another academic scholar from the region (born in Porjus) working on Sámi history, with a PhD from Uppsala University in 1962,[33] is Phebe Fjellström (1924–2007), who later on became professor of Ethnology at Umeå University.[34] Also her husband, Karl-Erik, a medical doctor born in Jokkmokk, had family background in this region and is a descendant of a well-known Sámi vicar, Pehr Fjellström, who developed Sámi–Swedish dictionaries and translations to Sámi of the Bible in the eighteenth century.[35] Phebe Fjellström has produced major articles on Sámi history, with specific focus on handicraft. It is unclear if she is of Sámi descent. What is of importance is that the closest university for them both was Uppsala University (first established in 1477), the centre of knowledge production in Sweden for many centuries. From Jokkmokk to Uppsala the distance is about 1,000 kilometres. Umeå University, where Fjellström later became a professor, became the fifth university and the most northern, about 400 kilometres from Jokkmokk, when it was established in 1965. Umeå University was followed by Luleå University of Technology, initially focusing on engineering sciences, established during the 1970s, 170 kilometres from Jokkmokk.

Two authors, the siblings Yngve and Lilian Ryd, who are also from the Jokkmokk area (Vuollerim, 20 kilometres downstream of Skällarim), have made major contributions in ethnological descriptions — oral history on practices and knowledges in the Jokkmokk region.[36] What strikes me, going through the authors and scholars, is the 'non-Sámi' etiquette. None of the above-mentioned authors stand out as Sámi, while it is highly probable that they all have Sámi heritage. I myself did not know about my family's Sámi heritage until the age of 42, and I have — with support from several persons within the Sámi community — made a major effort to reclaim this Sámi identity, to remember our Sámi history.[37]

It is still not beneficial to one's career to claim a Sámi identity, but instead one may be — or is — considered to be the problem. While today in Sweden there are a handful of Sámi with PhDs, a few more PhD students and one professor who is open with his Sámi identity, being Sámi and highly educated within the colonial education system is considered somewhat contradictory. To become a scholar — or a vicar or a medical doctor — those that are from Sámi families have since long been devoid of their Sámi identity. Historical Sámi intellectuals and scholars — such as the well-known priest and founder of the religious Lutheran revival movement Laestadianism, Lars Levi Laestadius (1800–1869) — may be described as having Sámi heritage, but not as being Sámi, even by Sámi authors.[38]

I know from my own conversations that there are active professors and scholars who are Sámi, but who do not openly talk about their Sámi heritage.[39] This calls for deeper discussion on what Sámi identity is in relationship to knowledge production. The colonial Swedification policies from the nineteenth century, within which Sámi were depicted as primitive and to be kept as primitive, and the so-called 'Lap should be Lap' policies from early 1900s, along with racial biology studies of Sámi, all play a major role.[40] When I write my family story, how do I write to make it 'Sámi', or from 'a Sámi perspective'? Who defines what is a Sámi perspective? When I write our family story, what markers are necessary to turn this story into a Sámi history? The Forest Sámi livelihood was strongly impacted and regulated by the Swedish state regulations.[41] Is resisting being referred to as Swedish even useful today? Why bother fighting for a Sámi identity, and, if doing so, what does this Sámi identity imply?

Skällarim prehistories

My family have lived here for millennia. How long is of course difficult to be certain about, as the historical records in which I can trace my ancestors by their names end around the 1600s. There are also traces in the landscape dating back at least 6,000 years, probably longer, and it is highly likely that there is a continuity, not a shift of population. The landscape bears witness, but its history remains open to further study. Upstream of Skällarim, about 10 kilometres, at Nelkerim, where my grandfather's mother was born and grew up, extensive studies have been done and records made by a local archaeologist, Ulf Westfal (1950–2012).[42] Downstream of Skällarim, 20 kilometres, at Vuollerim, extensive archaeological investigations have been made, proving presence dating back 6,000 years, and a museum called

Vuollerim 6,000 years was established in 1990.[43] Due to lack of funding, the museum has had to close down recently.

At Skällarim (also spelled Skällerim, Själlarim, or Sjellarim), there has so far not been any extensive investigations, but together with archaeologist Gunilla Larsson, we have made a pilot inventory, which documents preliminary traces estimated to be around 4,000–6,000 years old.[44] Furthermore, while there seems to be no actual investigation, a pilot inventory was made by the county museum in August 1966 just before the inundation for the Letsi reservoir. It started with a letter from a local inhabitant, Rudolf Nyström, to the museum, telling about an old knife he had found by the river in his childhood in the early 1900s. There is an exchange of letters that tells of the investigation and that it is indeed a stone-age knife, from a settlement by the river. They found more at the 1966 inventory: a single-edged bent green slate knife, quartzite scrapers, and parts from an arrowhead or spearhead. The site seemed to have been missed when there were studies done in 1959, to secure findings before the dam construction. The site had also been already noted by Ullenius in 1934, as a similar slate knife had been sent in to the Norrbotten county museum the year prior.[45] However, no more studies were done, and the dam construction went on and the site was inundated.[46] Today, checking to see if the findings were reported, I cannot find any traces of it in Fornsök, the Swedish National Heritage Board's online database for archaeological sites and monuments.[47] As the finds were reported, it seems odd. Maybe it was too controversial, maybe it would have slowed down the dam construction. It still remains for the study to be continued. The prehistory of Sámi culture is in general not well investigated, and studies today are generally only done when there's an industrial exploitation planned.[48]

Skällarim – the Lap Tax Land and settlement

Skällarim is described by both Ullenius and Hultblad as a so-called Lap Tax Land.[49] This was a policy with earliest documented historical evidence from the sixteenth century, as described by Korpijaakko.[50] There were the so-called Sámi ('Lapp') villages, which covered a vast area of land, and can be compared with municipalities, rather than villages. Within these Sámi villages, each family would have control over and use a defined area, like in the case of Skällarim. Documented sources have defined these as hereditary or tax lands. The common term used today is Lap Tax Land, or 'Lappskatteland' in Swedish. According to Ullenius, in 1785 Skällarim was owned by Pål Persson Rim, born 1758. It was a big area, 20 square kilometres, of which 20 kilometres was along the salmon-rich river.[51] Ullenius pointed out the borders of the tax land on a map. However, the crown policies provided certain privileges if a settlement was opened, such as a 15-year tax exemption and also not having to do military service. Hence, such settlements were established within several Lap Tax Lands.

The Skällarim Lap Tax Land was used for reindeer herding, but also fishing, hunting game, and probably many other trades. Ullenius states that tar was burned for selling by several Forest Sámi and settlers, and while he had no evidence that this was the case in Skällarim, he thought that would have been common here as well.⁵² It was here that my grandfather's grandmother Sigrid Elsa Larsdotter Rim (1835–1919), and her husband Nils Jakobsson, settled.⁵³ Sigrid, or Sigmora as she was called within the family, was born in Slakka, north of the river and about 7 kilometres from Skällarim.⁵⁴ In 1860 she married Nils Jakobsson (1829–1882), from Kuouka, located about 12 kilometres north of Skällarim, crossing two rivers.⁵⁵ They set up a so-called 'settlement' in Skällarim and lived initially in a traditional *goatje*. They bought their settlement from an older relative within the extended Rim family. It came with privileges but also with several conditions – they would have to prove they could cultivate and live off the land like farmers. Ullenius describes, based on interviews for the Norrbotten County Local Heritage Association of 1932, how they built a small cabin, with a kitchen and a living room, while living in the *goatje*:

> They [Ullenius writes 'he', but he was not alone so I write 'they'] also built a stable and a barn for storing hay. They cultivated barley and potato as soon as they had opened up and fertilized land. I have seen several trial cultivation lands, that is stated to be by Nils Jakobsson [and his wife]. These were attempts to find locations where they could succeed with the cultivation of barley and potato without being damaged by frost. They also built a little water mill by the Årrejaur creek.⁵⁶

There are still today remains of the old buildings at the site, and a couple of timber storage houses. In one of the storage houses, I found a spinning wheel and a loom – traces of Sigmora and her daughter-in-law's housework, making their clothes.⁵⁷ There is a photo of the house with the family members in front of it probably around early 1930s, and a fly-over photo probably from the 1950s.⁵⁸ It was a big house by then. Family tradition has it that it was too big for Sigmora and Nils' unmarried eldest grandson Alfred, who could not afford to keep it all heated. He would only use a small part of it. He eventually tore it down, having planned to build a more modern house, but this never happened before he passed away in the 1950s.

The house, garden, and barn as archives, and the shoe band mystery

Following tradition, the house and settlement – which had been turned into a *hemman* (estate) – was given by Sigmora and Nils' son to his oldest son, Alfred, who was born in 1891.⁵⁹ His two brothers, my grandfather Sten born 1906, and Viktor born 1908, were able to buy their own small lots within the bigger area in the 1930s when they had met their respective wives, the sisters Ellen and Julia, being ready to marry and settle down a couple of hundred metres away. So my mother's parental home was built in 1937, by my grandfather and his brothers, with the support of his father-in-law, and of course supported by my grandmother and her sister. I have been told that it is a so-called 'Per Albin' house, meaning that there was support made available through the Swedish government led by prime minister Per Albin Hansson in the 1930s, loans that were not too difficult to get and not too hard to pay back.[60] It is a house with a kitchen and a living room and two rooms upstairs – which were not standard but allowed for when there were means available. There is a small potato-field. The lot measures about 4 hectares, or 40,000 square metres. There is a bog and there are trees, mainly pine trees. I can see from the 1950s fly-over photo, which hangs in one of the upstairs rooms, that back then, there were fewer trees. I assume they used many of them to build the house. There are the remains of a small sawmill by the barn, where they could turn the trees into appropriate planks. Viktor was a well-known building manager in Jokkmokk,[61] so he probably managed both the constructions. There are documents in the house showing that Viktor and Julia's house was built first, then Sten and Ellen's. There's an outhouse, toilet, with its own door as part of the barn, and an outside wash-boiler, to do the laundry. I am told that the house was not built with a toilet inside, but one was installed later.[62]

I have been coming to this house ever since I was born – there is a photo of me there when I was very little, at most a month or two – and I have spent most of my life coming here without thinking of it as an archive. To me, it was my grandparent's home, and when they passed, my uncle's home until he passed in 2009. From 2008, when I started doing research on the Lule River hydropower exploitation, I started coming back more regularly, and now I consider this place as one of three homes. During this decade, I have had the opportunity to go through the house and the barn as well as the outside, looking at it as an archive, for my own personal curiosity but also as a historian. There are tools – fishnets and skis, snowmobiles, building tools, a sauna, and furniture – that tell a story of the way of life. There are several photos and photo albums and also records, books, and even a few handwritten letters. I still haven't been able to go through everything, yet.

Another part of it is the understanding, or interpretation, of the things that I, and my partner, find. Most items that we find, I have to ask around to understand what it is, how it got there, and to see how it can be interpreted in different ways today. For instance, in 2009 we found a Lule Sámi shoe band in a small storage room within the barn. I made a record of this in my research diary, so I know the exact date: 12 August 2009. When found by my partner, who had made himself busy looking through the barn while I was away doing something else, it was completely black from dirt. Through asking around – starting out the very next day with Ájtte at the Swedish Mountain and Sami Museum in Jokkmokk, followed by staff at the Sámi Duodji (the Sámi Handicraft Foundation) – I learned that it is a Lule Sámi shoe band for a man, probably around a century old. These are used to tie around the ankles of hide boots (shoes). Two elderly Sámi interviewees, a married couple, who I visited to ask about the consequences of the hydropower regulations, said that this one was a band braided using no reed – in Lule Sámi *vuoddaga* – and exceptionally well made.[63]

The shoe band is braided with dark red, green, pink, and yellow. These shoe bands are worn with specific Sámi beak shoes, for winter usage the shoes were and are made of reindeer fur, for summer reindeer hide. There are still people alive who remember using these shoes filled with hay as insulation. Today the shoes are used with socks. The beak has a practical usage; it locks the shoe into a ski binding.

Another part of this shoe band story is to find out how it got there, who made it, who wore it? I cannot know for sure, but there are items in the barn and house that came from the older house, Nils and Sigmora's, and Sigmora was the last so-called 'real Sámi' of our family. By 'real Sámi', I refer to the oral tradition within the family that was revealed to me by my uncle in 2008. Sigmora was considered to be 'real' as she owned reindeer, or at least had the right to own reindeer.[64] As I delved into the Swedish state register, I found that she was also registered as Sámi (the Swedish word used was 'Lapp', which is considered derogatory by many Sámi) in the censuses from 1870 to 1910.[65] The whole issue about who is a 'real Sámi', and who is not, is hard to escape when looking into my family history. It forms an inherent part of Swedish colonial history.

While the Sámi had for a long time been targeted and referred to as different people for various purposes, from the nineteenth century, racial categorisation turned into a scientific methodology to distinguish the Sámi as a race different from the Swedish. Alongside this was an ambition to make the Sámi population as small as possible and kept under control – hence, only those who were nomadic reindeer herders were referred to as real Sámi. Meanwhile, those who were settlers – in Swedish *nybyggare* – were, by a number of means and forces, assimilated into being Swedish. The *nybyggare* were created by a Swedish state institutionalised policy starting from the seventeenth century with the Lappland Acts (Lappmarksplakaten). The purpose was to populate the northern regions, to colonise, to secure the territory from the competing power of Russia. The idea was to introduce cultivation, farming practices, and to avoid interference with Sámi who paid for their tax lands. This northern region was, and is, rich in game and fish – the reindeer herding being an important source of food – but cultivation was, and still is, very difficult due to the cold Arctic climate with long winters and short summers. As this area was a harsh place to make a living as a farmer, there were several privileges tied to become a settler, such as the previously mentioned tax and military service exemptions. The condition for a settlement was to cultivate land and hold farm animals.[66]

Reading Lilian Ryd's ethnographic interviews with women *nybyggare* it turns out that the use of Sámi shoes was widespread.[67] Hence, though the shoes are commonly referred to as Sámi shoes, almost everyone wore them. What does that mean? Well, we do know that most *nybyggare* were of Sámi heritage, and becoming settlers was something that happened with the strong encouragement of – and was in fact enforced by – the Swedish crown/state. So, what does this do to the category of being Sámi or Swedish? And, another just as important question, why this obsession with defining who was and is 'real Sámi', who is mixed, who is Swedish?

To return to the shoe band mystery, maybe it was Sigmora who had braided it, for her husband or her son – her only surviving child – or one of the grandsons. I can only guess, though due to the timing I think it might have been the firstborn grandson, Alfred. I have done some searching to find the estate inventory made after her death, but so far without success.[68] In those days, most things owned by the deceased – including clothes – would be catalogued.

I carry this shoe band with me ever since we found it, in my backpack together with my computer.

Swedification, assimilation, and the Sámi language in Skällarim

As he visits them in 1932, Ullenius claims that the Forest Sámi villagers in Skällarim have been completely Swedified.[69] I wrestle with that idea, Swedification. In what way were the Forest Sámi Swedified? What does it mean, to become Swedified? The main marker for being Sámi in Sweden today is being a reindeer herder. I can't know for sure if Sigmora herself ever owned reindeer, but her sister did, as I can see from her estate inventory, and they most likely had exchanges. Anyway, the owning of reindeer as a marker for being 'real Sámi' is a definition made by the Swedish state and racial biologists (from the start of the twentieth century at least up to the 1950s), wanting to define a pure breed Sámi, and assimilate the Others into Swedishness and being obedient Swedish citizens. The Swedish State Institute for Racial Biology operated from 1922 until 1958, when the institute was closed and the research section merged with the Institute of Medical Genetics at Uppsala University. Its collection of documentation and more than 12,000 photographs, used to categorise humans according to phenotype, were later transferred to the Uppsala University archive.[70] Legislation intended to divide people into Sámi – reindeer herders – and Swedish – landowners, farmers – started in the late 1800s, with the beginning of reindeer herding legislation. A major blow to Forest Sámi happened in 1928 with the reindeer grazing act of that year – paragraph 3:3 stipulated that wherever Forest Sámi reindeer herding was a problem for Mountain Sámi reindeer herding or for farmers, the Forest Sámi would have to step back.[71]

What else is there? Another important aspect of Sámi culture is language. So I set out to find the traces of Sámi language here. It is harder than I expected. That my grandmother Ellen spoke Meänkieli as her first language was never a family secret. But when I have tried to find out if my maternal grandfather spoke Sámi, this has been a lot harder. I am still not sure. Within the family, the answer I have gotten – when first asking in the late 1990s and early 2000s, and again later on as a part of research interviewing older family members – is that he did not speak Sámi at all, only a local dialect called Lulebondska. As he was born in 1906, in the time when many people still spoke Lule Sámi in Jokkmokk, I found it odd that he would not understand or speak the language.

While exchange probably happened long before this, there is historical evidence pointing at languages intermixing with the Christian mission, which was known to be coming to northern Sámi regions from the eleventh century. A Sámi woman, Margareta, came to the Swedish royal court in around 1388 to ask for support with bringing Christianity to her people. But we don't know where she came from, nor what happened. In any case, we do know that she was able to communicate with Swedish queens and priests.[72] Starting from the 1600s, the teaching of Christianity would have been in both Sámi and Swedish. Textbooks were translated to Sámi and dictionaries published, and there were Sámi vicars, educated with the aim of promoting Christianity and exercising crown/state influence. Teaching for Sámi children had started in Piteå in 1619, with the vicar – son of a tradesperson, a *birkarl* – experienced from the exchange with the Sámi. In 1632, a school for Sámi children was established in Lycksele.[73] In the early seventeenth century, the Swedish state increased its interest in the northern territories – as did foreign trade – with the discovery of silver ore in Nasafjell and copper in Svappavaara, and the opening of the copper and iron works in Kengis, to which some of my ancestors immigrated.[74] There was also a growing interest in securing fishery in the Arctic Ocean. In Jokkmokk, we know that several Sámi were early on well trained in Swedish. My own ancestor, Nicolaus Lundius (ca 1640–1726), along with several other Sámi men, went to school and also on to Uppsala University, where in 1675 he provided ethnographic studies of Sámi to a work by Schefferus, which became internationally renowned and translated into several languages. He later returned to Jokkmokk.[75]

Sigmora would have spoken and read both Sámi and Swedish. Her Sámi language skills I have no documented traces of, so far. But as the Sámi language was common language here, it would have been odd if she did not know it. Regarding her Swedish skills I find more traces. In the house I found *Luther's Small Catechism* in Swedish, with Sigmora's name on the inside. She uses her Swedish name, after having remarried after the death her first husband in 1882: Sigrid Johansson. In her psalm book, I find a letter from her grandson, Alfred, dated 31 September 1905. He is, at the age of 14, called in to military service in Boden (130 kilometres downstream by today's car road, near the coast) during the massive military mobilisation as Norway demands, and receives, its freedom from the union with Sweden. He writes to her in perfect Swedish, thanking her for a letter he has received from her.[76] As the Swedification push was strong, it might be the case that she did not teach them Sámi. However, the Sámi language may have survived at least two more generations after Sigmora's, in my family and among the others in Skällarim. A neighbour born in 1935 remembers that the Mountain Sámi would come and stay over in her home, and when this happened the visitors would speak Sámi and communicate with her parents. This took place every year until the late 1940s at least.[77] I also asked in a local Facebook group, for people with roots and living in Jokkmokk. I posted a photo from a photo album in the house. The photo is from the (Lutheran Church) Confirmation in Jokkmokk in 1921, which all children had to go through as a rite of passage by the age of 14. My grandfather Sten is in the photo, together with another boy from Skällarim, Anders Andersson.[78] In the photo, around 70 children are standing outside the new church in Jokkmokk, the boys in dark suits, the girls in white dresses, no one is wearing Sámi traditional dress. With the photo, I asked the Facebook group if they knew how come so many Jokkmokk children, of which many must have been Sámi, were wearing this clothing, and also if they might have spoken Sámi. One woman responded that for sure the Anderssons in Skällarim did not speak Sámi (*lapska*); she herself grew up in the village and would have known. She said:

> My father and his brothers were proud of their Sámi heritage and would have spoken [Sámi] if they could, but my grandmother was from Dorotea and knew

no Sámi, so that might be the reason that they did not speak Sámi. But my father taught me the [Swedish] national hymn in Sámi.[79]

But soon after, she was contradicted by a niece:

> My grandfather, Fritiof Andersson (brother of Anders), spoke and understood Sámi. Reindeer herders often stayed overnight with him and my grandmother. My mother told me that the Sámi would sleep in the kitchen and dry the shoe hay by the oven. My grandfather knew how to stop bleeding, it was something one did not speak about openly. Many got help from him and when he did this he spoke Sámi. This knowledge ended with him. He taught my mother the Swedish national anthem in Sámi, and she still knows it by heart, at the age of 80.[80]

So, apparently, the Sámi language lived on some time. But it seems it was hidden, and also not transferred to the later generations, like to my mother who was born in 1941. Probably it was different in different families, even if they were close. It certainly calls for further investigation. Maybe there is a reason why I received the answer that my own grandfather did not speak Sámi.

The inherited land and the Forest Sámi family becoming Swedish

My maternal grandfather's family is, like all the other families in Skällarim, of the Sjokksjokk Forest Sámi village with the family name 'Rim'.[81] The name is directly connected to the river in this area, its topography, behaviour, and the salmon richness here. *Riebme* is the Lule Sámi word for a specific type of calm water (*sel* in Swedish), that typified this stretch of the river before the hydropower regulation[82] – a short stretch of calm water between two rapids.[83] Lule Sámi language researcher Olavi Korhonen and Jokkmokk writer Hans Anderson explain:

> In those contexts that 'riebme' was used, the term pointed at the place in the river where the water suddenly (!) flowed more rapidly and where the salmon, because of this, would stay to rest, for instance behind a stone, before its continued rush upstream. It was also the place where the spearfisher knew he (she) could have the chance to find it.[84]

Ullenius gives a similar explanation, and also recounts how he himself has been spearfishing in these waters.[85] The rapids and also settlements along this stretch are all named with 'rim': Nelkerim, Kuotjerim, Tårarim, Skällarim, Padjerim, Vuollerim. The *riebme* is caused by a terraced rock formation, described by geologists,[86] and the calm waters provided excellent salmon fishing, as described in the story at the beginning of this chapter and by a villager who remembers life before the hydropower regulation.[87] According to Korhonen and Anderson, the first part of my family village's name, 'Skälla-' (Själla-), is related to a place of rite or sacrifice.[88] This might be referring to a place on a small island in the river, related to the fishery. The island was inundated due to the hydropower regulation.

Hence the family name Rim is directly linked to the waters and fishery, the salmon richness, that made this place a good place to live. The last person in my family who had the name Rim officially registered was my maternal grandfather's paternal grandmother, described above, Sigrid Elsa Larsdotter Rim – Sigmora. It is interesting to think about all the labour she and her husband put into trying to do as ordered by the state, to achieve successful agricultural cultivation here, where the freezing season starts from September and lasts into June. Meanwhile, the river was full of salmon, the lakes full of other fish, there was game in the forest, and they would have access to reindeer meet. Ullenius states that it was rather late, by mid-nineteenth century, that seed cultivation started.[89] Hence, it seems that to be able to keep their estate they had to do as ordered by the Swedish state and live the state-enforced livelihood – as per the norm from the southern areas – as farmers.

They somehow did achieve what was expected. When the final strike of Swedish state colonisation in regard to territory struck Jokkmokk, with Sámi land being taken over within the so-called '*avvittringen*' – meaning 'apportionment of the land between the crown on the one hand and the individual villagers on the other'[90] – they had already managed to turn their plot into a *hemman*, a cultivated estate productive enough to be fully taxed, and thus they were allowed to keep it.[91] They also gained a portion of forestland that was turned into a common (*allmänning*), to be shared with all other landowners in Jokkmokk.[92] I have, together with others in the family, inherited this share of the common forest, and with that also rights to hunt and fish in certain areas. Meanwhile, Sigmora's sister Stina and her husband Johan, who were reindeer herders, were not as fortunate. They had opened a small settlement across the river on the Sámi tax land owned by Sigmora and Stina's father in 1873.[93] When the *avvittring* inspection came, their settlement was cancelled. It took them five years to be able to establish it as a lease for land instead.[94] Owning and cultivating land according to state policies was part of the Swedification – assimilation – process. There seem to have been hard times to keep reindeer, due to the Swedificaton policies and also tough winters where many Forest Sámi in this area lost a lot of reindeer to starvation. The pressure to focus on agriculture rather than reindeer herding came from the state, but by the early twentieth century there was also severe competition with nomadic Mountain Sámi, who complained about Forest Sámi reindeer herding and wanted it gone. This state-provoked conflict between Mountain Sámi and Forest Sámi was noted by Ullenius in the 1930s.[95]

Concluding stories

There are certainly many more stories from this 'little pine forest' to be told. As noted, there are already a lot written. The interesting thing to discuss is how come these stories, this history, are forgotten? Why is the documentation not transferred and taught in schools, at universities? Is it because it is unimportant? I argue the complete opposite. There has been an imposed amnesia with a political aim. As we forget the livelihood that was a self-sufficient way of life – living from nature, hunting, fishing, herding reindeer, collecting vegetables, and most importantly, depending on good relations between those that do different trades – this becomes a way of introducing and enforcing a control from elsewhere.

The hydropower regulation of the Lule River that stopped the salmon from coming here from the sea had a major negative impact on the possibility of living a good life without having a lot of money. Becoming Swedish, the Swedification project, was a undertaking of colonial control, within which giving up a Sámi identity is also a process of giving up self-sufficiency and becoming dependent on the Swedish state, for money, and thereby for food and survival.

The coordinated resistance against these plans has been forgotten. In the 1950s, my grandfather, his brother, and all other estate-owners as well as reindeer herders in the Sirges Mountain Sámi village and residents from the Serri (Slakka) Forest Sámi village came together and protested. I found the evidence in a box – a complaint put together by a lawyer and submitted to the Water Court.[96] As we now know, they lost the case. Today, in Jokkmokk, there is a similar situation, with people from reindeer herding communities, landowners, and individuals struggling against an iron mine that they argue will destroy their livelihood and chance at a good life.

In a region where life can be really hard if one does not have access to the resources from nature, good relations were so important for being able to live together. But the Swedification project had serious impacts on the relationships, and also livelihoods, of people in this region. The obsession of defining who is a nomad, who is a settler – the former being a 'Lapp' and the latter a 'Swede' – also included a racial biology project defining which people were 'in' and which were 'out', just as occurred later on in Nazi Germany, and is certainly still at play with more or less open conflicts. Relationships between reindeer herding Forest Sámi and the Mountain Sámi are another aspect that emerges as a source of conflict. People living in Jokkmokk, in the villages, deserve to know where these conflicts came from, and how state interference has both caused them and cheered them on.

Remembering is indeed a political project, one that now needs to be taken seriously. Our own memories and stories are the start.

Notes

1 Urban Andersson, born the same year as I, who lived in the village until 2005, tells me that at the time there were three boys the same age. As I only went for shorter visits, and probably due to being a girl, I didn't get to know them. Personal communication 26 October 2020.
2 J.G. Ullenius, ['Research Notes Concerning Forest Sámi Areas along Both Sides of the Little Lule River Downstream of Jokkmokk 1932'] 'Undersökningsanteckningar rörande skogslappsområden å Lilla Luleälvs båda sidor nedom Jokkmokk 1932,' Norrbotten Museum Archive, Box F:92, Luleå, Sweden. Transcribed by Agneta Silversparf, 2011. Translated from Swedish by May-Britt Öhman.
3 Cf Inger Zachrisson, 'Encounters in Border Country: Saami and Scandinavian Peoples in Central Scandinavia,' in *Finno-Ugric People in the Nordic Countries: Roots 5*, ed. Birger Winsa (Övertorneå: Academia Tornedaliensis – Meän akateemi, 2005), 40–45; Else Mundal, 'The Relationship between Sami and Nordic Peoples Expressed in Terms of Family Associations,' *Journal of Northern Studies* no. 2 (2009): 25–37.

4 Cf Ramón Grosfoguel, 'The Structure of Knowledge in Westernized Universities: Epistemic Racism/Sexism and the Four Genocides/Epistemicides of the Long 16th Century,' *Human Architecture: Journal of the Sociology of Self-Knowledge* 11, no. 1 (2013): article 8.
5 There are many studies in different languages. For overviews (in English) of studies of Sámi and some of the purposes of these, see, for instance, Greggor Mattson, 'Nation-State Science: Lappology and Sweden's Ethnoracial Purity,' *Comparative Studies in Society and History* 56, no. 2 (2014): 320–350; Carl-Gösta Ojala, 'Sámi Prehistories: The Politics of Archaeology and Identity in Northernmost Europe' (PhD diss., Uppsala University, 2009); Krister Stoor, 'Carl Linnæus from a Sámi Point of View,' *TijdSchrift voor Skandinavistiek* 29, no. 1–2 (2008): 77–84; Veli-Pekka Lehtola, 'Our Histories in the Photographs of the Others: Sámi Approaches to Visual Materials in Archives,' *Journal of Aesthetics & Culture* 10, no. 4 (2018).
6 Cf Anna Lydia Svalastog, 'On Teachers' Education in Sweden, School Curriculums, and the Sámi People,' in *Re: Mindings: Co-Constituting Indigenous, Academic, Artistic Knowledges*, eds. Johan Gärdebo, May-Britt Öhman, and Hiroshi Maruyama (Uppsala: Uppsala University, Hugo Valentin Centre, 2014), 153–171.
7 Cf Patrik Lantto and Ulf Mörkenstam, 'Sami Rights and Sami Challenges,' *Scandinavian Journal of History* 33, no. 1 (2008): 26–51; Bertil Marklund, 'Det milsvida skogsfolket: skogssamernas samhälle i omvandling 1650–1800' (PhD diss., Umeå University, 2015); Gudrun Norstedt, 'A Land of One's Own: Sami Resource Use in Sweden's Boreal Landscape Under Autonomous Governance' (PhD diss., Umeå University, 2018); Gudrun Norstedt and Lars Östlund, 'Fish or Reindeer?: The Relation between Subsistence Patterns and Settlement Patterns among the Forest Sami,' *Arctic Anthropology* 53, no. 1 (2016): 22–36.
8 Cf Marklund, 'Det milsvida skogsfolket.'
9 Cf among many others, Dian Million, 'Felt Theory: An Indigenous Feminist Approach to Affect and History,' *Wicazo Sa Review* 24, no. 2 (2009): 53–76; Jennifer Nez Denetdale, *Reclaiming Diné History: The Legacies of Navajo Chief Manuelito and Juanita* (Tucson: University of Arizona Press, 2007); Frances Wyld and Bronwyn L. Fredericks, 'Earth Song as Storywork: Reclaiming Indigenous Knowledges,' *Journal of Australian Indigenous Issues* 18, no. 2 (2015): 2–12; K. Tsianina Lomawaima, 'Domesticity in the Federal Indian Schools: The Power of Authority over Mind and Body,' *American Ethnologist* 20, no. 2 (May 1993): 227–240.
10 Denetdale, *Reclaiming Diné History*, 160.
11 Cf Ingela Bergman and Per H. Ramqvist, 'Farmer Fishermen: Interior Lake Fishing among Coastal Communities in Northern Sweden AD 1200–1600,' *Acta Borealia* 34, no. 2 (2017): 134–158.
12 May-Britt Öhman and Frances Wyld, 'From Hi-Story to History in the Lands of Fire and Ice: Embodiment as Indigenous in a Colonised Hemisphere,' in *Ngapartji Ngapartji: In Turn, in Turn: Ego-Histoire, Europe and Indigenous Australia*, eds. Vanessa Castejon, Anna Cole, Oliver Haag, and Karen Hughes (Canberra: ANU Press, 2014); Pierre Nora, 'Between Memory and History: Les Lieux de Mémoire,' *Representations* Special Issue: Memory and Counter-Memory, no. 26 (Spring 1989): 7–24.
13 Cf Inger Zachrisson, 'Vittnesbörd om pälshandel?: ett arkeologiskt perspektiv på romerska bronsmynt funna i norra Sverige,' *Fornvännen* 105, no. 3 (2010): 187–202; Tacitus, *Tacitus' Germania*, trans. Vilhelm Lundström (Göteborg: Elander, 1912) [ca 98 CE].
14 Johan Turi (1910), *An Account of the Sámi: A Translation of Muitalus Sámiid Birra*, ed. Mikael Svonni, trans. Thomas Andrew DuBois (Chicago, IL: Nordic Studies Press, 2011), 161.
15 Cf Patrik Lantto, 'Borders, Citizenship and Change: The Case of the Sami People, 1751–2008,' *Citizenship Studies* 14, no. 5 (2010): 543–556; Patrik Lantto, 'The Consequences of State Intervention: Forced Relocations and Sámi Rights in Sweden, 1919–2012,' *Journal of Ethnology and Folkloristics* 8, no. 2 (2014): 53–73.

16 Cf Zachrisson, 'Encounters in Border Country'; Mundal, 'Relationship between Sami and Nordic Peoples.'
17 Filip Hultblad, 'Övergång från nomadism till agrar bosättning i Jokkmokks socken' ['Transition from nomadism to farming in the parish of Jokkmokk'] (PhD diss., Uppsala University, 1968), 72ff.
18 Cf Mattson, 'Nation-State Science'; Sverker Sörlin, 'Guldet från Norden: norrlandsvisioner från Olaus Magnus till Johan Galtung,' in *Älvdal i norr: människor och resurser i Luledalen 1300–1800*, eds. Sune Åkerman and Kjell Lundholm (Umeå: Umeå University, 1990), 82–147 (translated title: 'The Gold from Scandinavia: Visions of Norrland from Olaus Magnus to Johan Galtung'); Lehtola, 'Our Histories.'
19 His name was Grels Mattsson. Genealogy of my maternal grandfather's family, by Else-May Öhman and Alf Nilsson, undated (copy in the author's archive).
20 They were Petter Servio (1600–1662) and Baltzar Thun (1611–1676). My Torne River Valley family tree is well documented by several genealogists, among others Darrin Lythgoe, 'Pedigree Chart for Hjalmar Anton Maurits TUOHEA, born 1886,' my maternal grandmother's father, accessed 4 January 2020, www.singletonfamily.org/pedigree.php?personID=I40347&tree=1.
21 Nationalencyklopedin Online, s.v. 'Luleå,' accessed 19 July 2020, www.ne.se.ezproxy.its.uu.se/uppslagsverk/encyklopedi/lång/luleå; Anders Kintel, 'Julevsáme-dárro báhkogirjje - Norsk-lulesamisk Ordbok' (Tromsö: Giellatekno UiT and Sámediggi-Sametinget, 2012), gtweb.uit.no/webdict/ak/smj2nob/index.html.
22 Cf Phebe Fjellström, 'Humanekologiskt system i Lule älvdal – fjällbygd, skogsbygd, kustbygd,' in *Att leva vid älven – Åtta forskare om människor och resurser i Lule älvdal*, eds. Erik Bylund and Evert Baudou (Bjästa, Cewe-förl., 1996), 79–110; Bergman and Ramqvist, 'Farmer Fishermen.'
23 Website of the Sámi Parliament on Swedish side on reindeer herding and interactive maps over the Sámi reindeer herding areas, Sametinget, 'Rennäringens markanvändning,' accessed 6 January 2020, www.sametinget.se/8382.
24 Cf Marklund, 'Det milsvida skogsfolket.'
25 Electricity production in Sweden in 2020 is about 80% based on equal parts of hydropower and nuclear power, with the nuclear power functioning as a stable base and the hydropower being used to regulate, corresponding to the different needs over the seasons, the weeks and the 24 hours. Over the last decade, wind power has increased to about 10%. 'Elektricitet i Sverige,' Statistics Sweden (SCB), last modified 30 August 2020, www.scb.se/hitta-statistik/sverige-i-siffror/miljo/elektricitet-i-sverige. On the history of the regulation of the Lule River, see Staffan Hansson, 'Porjus: En vision för industriell utveckling i Övre Norrland' (PhD diss., Tekniska högskolan i Luleå, 1994), 272; Tore Nilsson, *Fyra gånger Suorva: en tillbakablick på regleringsarbetena i Suorva* (Stockholm: Statens vattenfallsverk, 1972), 10.
26 Translated from Swedish by May-Britt Öhman from the web brochure by Vattenfall, 'En resa längs Lule älv' ['A journey along the Lule River'], published in 2008, accessed 1 September 2010 (copy in the author's archive), 2.
27 Stoor, 'Carl Linnæus.'
28 Cf Sörlin, 'Guldet från Norden.'
29 Ullenius, 'Research Notes Concerning Forest Sámi.'
30 J.G. Ullenius, 'Laxljustring i rödlövsreka,' *Norrbotten: Norrbottens läns hembygdsförenings tidskrift* (1934), 112–127; J.G. Ullenius, 'Något om skogslapparnas bovallar,' *Norrbotten: Norrbottens läns hembygdsförenings tidskrift*, 1937, 107–126; Ullenius, 'Research Notes Concerning Forest Sámi'; J.G. Ullenius, ['Research Notes for the Nordic Museum in Stockholm by the former teacher J.G. Ullenius born 1868'] 'Anteckningar för Nordiska Museet i Stockholm av f d seminarieläraren J.G. Ullenius, född 1868,' 1935, unpublished research notes, Norrbotten Museum Archive, F:92, Transcribed by Agneta Silversparf, 2002 (copy in the author's archive).

31 Cf Kjell Nilsson and Göran Furuland, eds., *Eldsjälar: hundra år med hembygdsrörelsen: jubileumsbok till Sveriges hembygdsförbund: Hembygdens år 2016* (Stockholm: Sveriges hembygdsförbund, 2016).
32 Hultblad, 'Övergång från nomadism,' 5.
33 Phebe Fjellström, 'Lapskt silver: studier över en föremålsgrupp och dess ställning inom lapskt kulturliv' (PhD diss., Uppsala University, 1962).
34 Katarina Ek-Nilsson, 'Phebe Maria Fjellström,' Svenskt kvinnobiografiskt lexikon, accessed 9 January 2019, www.skbl.se/sv/artikel/PhebeFjellstrom.
35 While there is no easily available biographical data of Karl-Erik Fjellström, he appears in records on Phebe Fjellström and his family appears in an archive (donated by his wife) at Umeå University library. I have traced his family to the Sorsele, Arvidsjaur, and Jokkmokk area, where the men are recorded as medical doctors and vicars. The family is described in several published records: Kerstin Öhström, 'Phebe Fjellström,' in *Vem är hon: kvinnor i Sverige: biografisk uppslagsbok*, eds. Kerstin Öhrström and Sigrid Andersson (Stockholm: Norstedt, 1988), 144; Curt Carlsson, 'Ansedel Fjellström, Alberg Helmer Alexander 1889–1977,' 2018, accessed 11 January 2019, www.nenca.se/gw-slakttrad/004/00/061.htm; Hans Laestadius, 'Ansedel Fjellström, Carl-Johan 1783–1853,' accessed 11 January 2019, www.laestadiusfriends.se/LMV-sv/SlaktLs-sv/0001/2110.htm; Sten Henrysson and Carl-Henry Johansson, *Prästerna och livet i lappmarken* (Umeå: Forskningsarkivet, Umeå universitet, 1990); Tuuli Forsgren, *Samisk kyrko- och undervisningslitteratur i Sverige 1619–1850* (Umeå: Forskningsarkivet, Umeå universitet, 1988).
36 For instance, Yngve Ryd with a huge production from 1980 to 2017 (the last book was published posthumously). Yngve Ryd, ed., *Timmerskogen: skogsarbetare från Jokkmokk berättar* (Luleå: Skrivarförl./Norrbottens bildningsförb., 1980). Lilian Ryd has an extensive production, among others Lilian Ryd, *Kvinnor i väglöst land: nybyggarkvinnors liv och arbete* (Stockholm: Arena, 1995).
37 Cf May-Britt Öhman, 'Being May-Britt Öhman: Or, Reflections on My Own Colonized Mind Regarding Hydropower Constructions in Sápmi,' in *Travelling Thoughtfulness: Feminist Technoscience Stories*, eds. Pirjo Elovaara, Johanna Sefyrin, May-Britt Öhman, and Christina Björkman (Umeå: Umeå University, 2010), 269–292; May-Britt Öhman, 'TechnoVisions of a Sámi Cyborg: Re-claiming Sámi Body-, Land- and Waterscapes after a Century of Colonial Exploitations in Sápmi,' in *Ill-Disciplined Gender: Nature/Culture and Transgressive Encounters*, eds. Jacob Bull and Margaretha Fahlgren (Cham: Springer International Publishing, 2016), 63–98.
38 See, for instance, 'Lars Levi Laestadius och samerna,' Samiskt informationscentrum, accessed 11 January 2019, www.samer.se/laestadianismen.
39 Cf Öhman, 'TechnoVisions,' 68.
40 Cf Lehtola, 'Our Histories.'
41 Cf Marklund, 'Det milsvida skogsfolket.'
42 Ulf Westfal, *Rapport över arkeologiska inventeringar och undersökningar av utvalda områden inom skogslandet längs Lule älvdal* (Umeå: Umeå University, Institutionen för arkeologi, 1983).
43 David Loeffler, 'Vuollerim: Six Thousand and Fifteen Years Ago,' *Current Swedish Archaeology* 7 (1999): 103f.
44 Investigations 18 September 2014, by archaeologist Dr Gunilla Larsson and Dr May-Britt Öhman. Cf Gunilla Larsson, *Gállokjaure: Lämningar efter ett samiskt kulturlandskap. Rapport över arkeologisk utredning. Rapport 2012:1 Uppdaterad 2015* (Rimbo: Revita Archaeology and History, 2015).
45 Ullenius, 'Laxljustring i rödlövsreka,' 113.
46 'Copy of Letter to the Swedish National Heritage Board,' Dnr 489/66, dated 24 October 1966; 'Copy of Letter to Rudolf Nyström,' Dnr 489/66, dated 6 October 1966; 'Copy of Letter from Landsantikvarie Birgitta Hjolman,' 24 October 1966 (copies in the author's archive).

47 Search at Fornsök for Skällarim/Lenatorp area, last accessed 22 January 2019, www.fmis.raa.se/cocoon/fornsok/search.html.
48 Cf Gunilla Larsson, 'Protecting Our Memory from Being Blasted Away: Archaeological Supradisciplinary Research Retracing Sámi History in Gállok/Kallak,' in *Re: Mindings: Co-Constituting Indigenous, Academic, Artistic Knowledges*, eds. Johan Gärdebo, May-Britt Öhman, and Hiroshi Maruyama (Uppsala: Uppsala University, Hugo Valentin Centre, 2014), 41–53.
49 Hultblad, 'Övergång från nomadism,' 311; Ullenius, 'Research Notes Concerning Forest Sámi.'
50 Kaisa Korpijaakko-Labba, 'The History of Rights to Resources in Swedish and Finnish Lappland,' in *Law and the Management of Divisible and Non-Excludable Renewable Resources*, eds. Erling Berge, Derek Ott, and Nils Chr. Stenseth (Aas: The Agricultural University of Norway, 1994), 255–264, 258.
51 Ullenius, 'Research Notes Concerning Forest Sámi.'
52 Ullenius, 'Research Notes Concerning Forest Sámi.'
53 Hultblad, 'Övergång från nomadism,' 312; Ullenius, 'Research Notes Concerning Forest Sámi.'
54 My mother told me in the 1980s she was called Sigmora, which in direct translation means 'Sigmother', thus a short for the name 'Sigrid' and 'mother' together. In Ullenius, 'Research Notes Concerning Forest Sámi', 14, she is referred to as 'Skällarim-Sigg'.
55 Agneta Silversparf, 'Ättlingar till Silfversparre-Rim,' *Silbonah Sámesijdda – Medlemsnytt* 13, April 2009.
56 Ullenius, 'Research Notes Concerning Forest Sámi,' 14.
57 Cf Larsson, *Gállokjaure*; Personal visit to the timber huts in July 2011.
58 A neighbour, Anny Harnesk, stated in a personal interview January 2019 that the photo was taken in the 1950s. Every house had the possibility to acquire similar fly-over photos, and her family house has one too.
59 Alfred Nilsson as the owner is mentioned in Ullenius, 'Research Notes Concerning Forest Sámi', and it is also what I have been told by family members.
60 See for comparison the article by Hanna Pahlén, 'Småbrukarliv på 30-talet: Per Albin-torp och egen ko,' in *Hård var striden: arbetarminnen från Bräckebygden. D. 2, 1920–1950*, eds. Lo Rindberg and Mats Rolén (Bräcke: Fören. Bräcke arbetarehistoria, 1984).
61 According to Anna-Maria Spik, personal interview 2010, who stated that Viktor was in charge of building their house in central Jokkmokk, in Gielas – 'Lappstaden'.
62 Personal interview Anny Harnesk, January 2019.
63 Author's research diary entry 17 September 2009.
64 Author's research diary entry 22 July 2008.
65 The censuses every tenth year from 1870 to 1910 are available on the website of the National Archive, Riksarkivet, accessed 18 January 2019, sok.riksarkivet.se/folkrakningar.
66 Cf Hultblad, 'Övergång från nomadism,' 436–439; Bengt Hjalmar Andersson, *Ett bidrag till historien om byn Satter/Järämä i Lule lappmark* (Umeå: Forskningsarkivet, Umeå University, 1992).
67 Ryd, *Kvinnor i väglöst land*.
68 I was kindly assisted by archivist Niklas Wiberg at the National Archive, Regional State Archives in Härnösand, who looked through the minutes of the estate inventory of 1–2 September 1919, Jokkmokks tingslags häradsrätts arkiv, volym A II:19. Email from Niklas Wiberg to author, 14 January 2019.
69 Ullenius, 'Research Notes Concerning Forest Sámi.'
70 Cf Lantto, 'Consequences of State Intervention'; Ulrika Kjellman, 'A Whiter Shade of Pale: Visuality and Race in the Work of the Swedish State Institute for Race Biology,' *Scandinavian Journal of History* 38, no. 2 (2013): 180–201; Lehtola, 'Our Histories.'
71 'Lag om de svenska lapparnas rätt till renbete i Sverige,' SFS *Svensk författningssamling* 1928, no. 309, 852.

72 Bo Lundmark, 'Medeltida vittnesbörd om samerna och den katolska kyrkan,' in *De historiska relationerna mellan Svenska kyrkan och samerna: en vetenskaplig antologi Bd 1*, eds. Daniel Lindmark and Olle Sundström, 221–240 (Skellefteå: Artos & Norma, 2016).
73 Forsgren, *Samisk kyrko- och undervisningslitteratur*; Sölve Anderzén, 'Kyrkans undervisning i Lappmarken under 1800-talet,' in *De historiska relationerna mellan Svenska kyrkan och samerna: en vetenskaplig antologi Bd 1*, eds. Daniel Lindmark and Olle Sundström (Skellefteå: Artos & Norma, 2016), 371–402.
74 Cf Jonas M. Nordin and Carl-Gösta Ojala, 'Copper Worlds: A Historical Archaeology of Abraham and Jakob Momma-Reenstierna and Their Industrial Enterprise in the Torne River Valley, c. 1650–1680,' *Acta Borealia* 34 no. 2 (2017): 103–133.
75 Gösta Ganetz, 'Släktutredning', unpublished genealogy document, 1999 (copy in the author's archive); genealogy of my mother's family, by Else-May Öhman and Alf Nilsson, undated (copy in the author's archive); Nicolai Lundi Lappi (Nicolaus Lundius), 'Descriptio Lapponiae,' 1675, handwritten original at the National Library of Sweden, manuscripts, volume D68b (copy in the author's archive).
76 Letter from 'No. 239 Nilsson,' Boden, 31 September 1905 (in the author's personal archive).
77 Personal conversation with Anny Harnesk, 2018.
78 Family photo album with written information to several photos (copy in the author's archive).
79 Facebook comment, last accessed 19 January 2019.
80 Facebook comment by Mona Lindberg, last accessed 19 January 2019.
81 Cf Ullenius, 'Research Notes Concerning Forest Sámi.'
82 Information from interviewee who wished to be anonymous, 2015.
83 Lule Sámi online dictionary of the Sámi Parliament, accessed 13 January 2019, ordbok. sametinget.se.
84 Olavi Korhonen and Hans Anderson, *Samiska ortnamn vid vägar och färdleder i Lule lappmark* (Jokkmokk: Förlag Hans Anderson, 2010), 113.
85 Ullenius, 'Research Notes Concerning Forest Sámi.'
86 Cf Axel Hamberg, *Öfversikt af Lule älfs geologi* (Stockholm: Sveriges geologiska undersökning, 1906).
87 Personal interview with Anny Harnesk (born in 1935), January 2019; Ullenius, 'Research Notes Concerning Forest Sámi.'
88 Korhonen and Anderson, *Samiska ortnamn*, 113, 127.
89 Ullenius, 'Research Notes Concerning Forest Sámi.'
90 'Avvittringen' was a transfer of land from private ownership to the crown/state, and had started further south – as early as 1683 – as the Swedish crown/state wanted access to territory for mining. Avvittringen was carried out in the Jokkmokk area between 1875 and 1890. Cf Hultblad, 'Övergång från nomadism,' 439; Nils Häggström, 'Norrland's Direct Foreign Trade 1850–1914' (PhD diss., Umeå University, 1971).
91 For any reader who wishes to follow up, I have not gone through archives to see how they managed this, there must be documents available.
92 Cf Hultblad, 'Övergång från nomadism,' 439. See also the website of Jokkmokk Allmänning (last accessed 22 January 2019), www.allmanningen.se.
93 Ullenius, 'Research Notes Concerning Forest Sámi,' 29.
94 Ullenius, 'Research Notes Concerning Forest Sámi,' 29.
95 Cf Agneta Silversparf, 'Norrbottens Kuriren March 23, 1906,' *Silbonah Sámesijdda – Medlemsnytt* 28, December 2012; Ullenius, 'Research Notes Concerning Forest Sámi,' 24ff.
96 Copy of complaint to the Water Court – Övre Norrbygdens Vattendomstol, case no. Ans.D. 20/1959, dated 1 October 1959 (copy in the author's archive).

Bibliography

Allmänning, Jokkmokk. Accessed 22 January 2019. www.allmanningen.se.
Andersson, Bengt Hjalmar. *Ett bidrag till historien om byn Satter/Järämä i Lule lappmark.* Umeå: Forskningsarkivet, Umeå University, 1992.
Anderzén, Sölve. 'Kyrkans undervisning i Lappmarken under 1800-talet.' In *De historiska relationerna mellan Svenska kyrkan och samerna: en vetenskaplig antologi Bd 1*, edited by Daniel Lindmark and Olle Sundström, 371–402. Skellefteå: Artos & Norma, 2016.
Bergman, Ingela, and Per H. Ramqvist. 'Farmer Fishermen: Interior Lake Fishing among Coastal Communities in Northern Sweden AD 1200–1600.' *Acta Borealia* 34, no. 2 (2017): 134–158.
Carlsson, Curt. 'Ansedel Fjellström, Alberg Helmer Alexander 1889–1977.' 2018. Accessed 11 January 2019. www.nenca.se/gw-slakttrad/004/00/061.htm.
Denetdale, Jennifer Nez. *Reclaiming Diné History: The Legacies of Navajo Chief Manuelito and Juanita.* Tucson: University of Arizona Press, 2007.
Ek-Nilsson, Katarina. 'Phebe Maria Fjellström.' Svenskt kvinnobiografiskt lexikon. 2018. Accessed 9 January 2019. www.skbl.se/sv/artikel/PhebeFjellstrom.
Fjellström, Phebe. 'Lapskt silver: studier över en föremålsgrupp och dess ställning inom lapskt kulturliv.' PhD diss., Uppsala University, 1962.
Fjellström, Phebe. 'Humanekologiskt system i Lule älvdal – fjällbygd, skogsbygd, kustbygd.' In *Att leva vid älven – Åtta forskare om människor och resurser i Lule älvdal*, edited by Erik Bylund and Evert Baudou, 79–110. Bjästa: Cewe-förl., 1996.
Fornsök. The Swedish National Heritage Board's database for archaeological sites, search in Skällarim/Lenatorp area. Accessed 22 January 2019. www.fmis.raa.se/cocoon/fornsok/search.html.
Forsgren, Tuuli. *Samisk kyrko- och undervisningslitteratur i Sverige 1619–1850.* Umeå: Forskningsarkivet, Umeå universitet, 1988.
Ganetz, Gösta. 'Släktutredning.' Unpublished genealogy document, 1999. Copy in the author's archive.
Grosfoguel, Ramón. 'The Structure of Knowledge in Westernized Universities: Epistemic Racism/Sexism and the Four Genocides/Epistemicides of the Long 16th Century.' *Human Architecture: Journal of the Sociology of Self-Knowledge* 11, no. 1 (2013): article 8.
Häggström, Nils. 'Norrland's Direct Foreign Trade 1850–1914.' PhD diss., Umeå University, 1971.
Hamberg, Axel. *Öfversikt af Lule älfs geologi.* Stockholm: Sveriges geologiska undersökning, 1906.
Hansson, Staffan. 'Porjus: En vision för industriell utveckling i Övre Norrland.' PhD diss., Tekniska högskolan i Luleå, 1994.
Henrysson, Sten, and Carl-Henry Johansson. *Prästerna och livet i lappmarken.* Umeå: Forskningsarkivet, Umeå universitet, 1990.
Hultblad, Filip. 'Övergång från nomadism till agrar bosättning i Jokkmokks socken.' ['Transition from nomadism to farming in the parish of Jokkmokk']. PhD diss., Uppsala University, 1968.
Kintel, Anders. 'Julevsáme-dárro báhkogirjje – Norsk-lulesamisk Ordbok.' Tromsö: Giellatekno UiT and Sámediggi-Sametinget, 2012. gtweb.uit.no/webdict/ak/smj2nob/index.html.
Kjellman, Ulrika. 'A Whiter Shade of Pale: Visuality and Race in the Work of the Swedish State Institute for Race Biology.' *Scandinavian Journal of History* 38, no. 2 (2013): 180–201.
Korhonen, Olavi, and Hans Anderson. *Samiska ortnamn vid vägar och färdleder i Lule lappmark.* Jokkmokk: Förlag Hans Anderson, 2010.
Korpijaakko-Labba, Kaisa. 'The History of Rights to Resources in Swedish and Finnish Lappland.' In *Law and the Management of Divisible and Non-Excludable Renewable Resources*, edited by Erlinge Berge, Derek Ott, and Nils Chr. Stenseth, 255–264. Aas: The Agricultural University of Norway, 1994.

Laestadius, Hans. 'Ansedel Fjellström, Carl-Johan 1783–1853.' Accessed 11 January 2019. www.laestadiusfriends.se/LMV-sv/SlaktLs-sv/0001/2110.htm
Lantto, Patrik. 'Borders, Citizenship and Change: The Case of the Sami People, 1751–2008.' *Citizenship Studies* 14, no. 5 (2010): 543–556.
Lantto, Patrik. 'The Consequences of State Intervention: Forced Relocations and Sámi Rights in Sweden, 1919–2012.' *The Journal of Ethnology and Folkloristics* 8, no. 2 (2014): 53–73.
Lantto, Patrik, and Ulf Mörkenstam. 'Sami Rights and Sami Challenges.' *Scandinavian Journal of History* 33, no. 1 (2008): 26–51.
Larsson, Gunilla. 'Protecting Our Memory from Being Blasted Away: Archaeological Supradisciplinary Research Retracing Sámi History in Gállok/Kallak.' In *Re: Mindings: Co-Constituting Indigenous, Academic, Artistic Knowledges*, edited by Johan Gärdebo, May-Britt Öhman, and Hiroshi Maruyama, 41–53. Uppsala: Uppsala University, Hugo Valentin Centre, 2014.
Larsson, Gunilla. *Gállokjaure: Lämningar efter ett samiskt kulturlandskap. Rapport över arkeologisk utredning. Rapport 2012:1 Uppdaterad 2015.* Rimbo: Revita Archaeology and History, 2015.
Lehtola, Veli-Pekka. 'Our Histories in the Photographs of the Others: Sámi Approaches to Visual Materials in Archives.' *Journal of Aesthetics & Culture* 10, no. 4 (2018): 1510647.
Loeffler, David. 'Vuollerim: Six Thousand and Fifteen Years Ago.' *Current Swedish Archaeology* 7 (1999): 89–106.
Lomawaima, K. Tsianina. 'Domesticity in the Federal Indian Schools: The Power of Authority over Mind and Body.' *American Ethnologist* 20, no. 2 (May 1993): 227–240.
Lundi Lappi, Nicolai (Nicolaus Lundius). 'Descriptio Lapponiae.' 1675. Handwritten original at the National Library of Sweden. Manuscripts, volume D68b. Copy in the author's archive.
Lundmark, Bo. 'Medeltida vittnesbörd om samerna och den katolska kyrkan.' In *De historiska relationerna mellan Svenska kyrkan och samerna: en vetenskaplig antologi Bd 1*, edited by Daniel Lindmark and Olle Sundström, 221–240. Skellefteå: Artos & Norma, 2016.
Lythgoe, Darrin. 'Pedigree Chart for Hjalmar Anton Maurits TUOHEA, born 1886.' Accessed 4 January 2020. www.singletonfamily.org/pedigree.php?personID=I40347&tree=1.
Marklund, Bertil. 'Det milsvida skogsfolket: skogssamernas samhälle i omvandling 1650–1800.' PhD diss., Umeå University, 2015.
Mattson, Greggor. 'Nation-State Science: Lappology and Sweden's Ethnoracial Purity.' *Comparative Studies in Society and History* 56, no. 2 (2014): 320–350.
Million, Dian. 'Felt Theory: An Indigenous Feminist Approach to Affect and History.' *Wicazo Sa Review* 24, no. 2 (2009): 53–76.
Mundal, Else. 'The Relationship between Sami and Nordic Peoples Expressed in Terms of Family Associations.' *Journal of Northern Studies* no. 2 (2009): 25–37.
Nationalencyklopedin Online, s.v. 'Luleå.' Accessed 19 July 2020. www.ne.se.ezproxy.its.uu.se/uppslagsverk/encyklopedi/lång/luleå.
Nilsson, Kjell, and Göran Furuland, eds. *Eldsjälar: hundra år med hembygdsrörelsen: jubileumsbok till Sveriges hembygdsförbund: Hembygdens år 2016.* Stockholm: Sveriges hembygdsförbund, 2016.
Nilsson, Tore. *Fyra gånger Suorva: en tillbakablick på regleringsarbetena i Suorva.* Stockholm: Statens vattenfallsverk, 1972.
Nora, Pierre. 'Between Memory and History: Les Lieux de Mémoire.' *Representations* Special Issue: Memory and Counter-Memory, no. 26 (Spring 1989): 7–24.
Nordin, Jonas M., and Carl-Gösta Ojala. 'Copper Worlds: A Historical Archaeology of Abraham and Jakob Momma-Reenstierna and Their Industrial Enterprise in the Torne River Valley, c. 1650–1680.' *Acta Borealia* 34, no. 2 (2017): 103–133.
Norstedt, Gudrun. 'A Land of One's Own: Sami Resource Use in Sweden's Boreal Landscape Under Autonomous Governance.' PhD diss., Umeå University, 2018.

Norstedt, Gudrun, and Lars Östlund. 'Fish or Reindeer? The Relation between Subsistence Patterns and Settlement Patterns among the Forest Sami,' *Arctic Anthropology* 53, no. 1 (2016): 22–36.
Öhman, Else-May, and Alf Nilsson. Släktutredning. Unpublished Genealogy Document, Undated. Copy in the Author's Archive.
Öhman, May-Britt. 'Being May-Britt Öhman: Or, Reflections on My Own Colonized Mind Regarding Hydropower Constructions in Sápmi.' In *Travelling Thoughtfulness: Feminist Technoscience Stories*, edited by Pirjo Elovaara, Johanna Sefyrin, May-Britt Öhman, and Christina Björkman, 269–292.Umeå: Umeå University, 2010.
Öhman, May-Britt. 'TechnoVisions of a Sámi Cyborg: Re-claiming Sámi Body-, Land- and Waterscapes after a Century of Colonial Exploitations in Sápmi.' In *Ill-Disciplined Gender: Nature/Culture and Transgressive Encounters*, edited by Jacob Bull and Margaretha Fahlgren, 63–98. Cham: Springer International Publishing, 2016.
Öhman, May-Britt, and Frances Wyld. 'From Hi-Story to History in the Lands of Fire and Ice: Embodiment as Indigenous in a Colonised Hemisphere.' In *Ngapartji Ngapartji: In Turn, in Turn: Ego-Histoire, Europe and Indigenous Australia*, edited by Vanessa Castejon, Anna Cole, Oliver Haag, and Karen Hughes. Canberra: ANU Press, 2014.
Öhström, Kerstin. 'Phebe Fjellström.' In *Vem är hon: kvinnor i Sverige: biografisk uppslagsbok*, edited by Kerstin Öhrström and Sigrid Andersson. Stockholm: Norstedt, 1988.
Ojala, Carl-Gösta. 'Sámi Prehistories: The Politics of Archaeology and Identity in Northernmost Europe.' PhD diss., Uppsala University, 2009.
Pahlén, Hanna. 'Småbrukarliv på 30-talet: Per Albin-torp och egen ko.' In *Hård var striden: arbetarminnen från Bräckebygden. D. 2, 1920–1950*, edited by Lo Rindberg and Mats Rolén. Bräcke: Fören. Bräcke arbetarehistoria, 1995.
Riksarkivet. Website. Accessed 18 January 2019. sok.riksarkivet.se/folkrakningar.
Ryd, Lilian. *Kvinnor i väglöst land: nybyggarkvinnors liv och arbete*. Stockholm: Arena, 1995.
Ryd, Yngve, ed. *Timmerskogen: skogsarbetare från Jokkmokk berättar*. Luleå: Skrivarförl./Norrbottens bildningsförbund, 1980.
Sametinget. Lule Sámi online dictionary of the Sámi Parliament. Accessed 13 January 2019. ordbok.sametinget.se.
Sametinget. 'Rennäringens markanvändning.' Website of the Sámi Parliament on Swedish side on reindeer herding and interactive maps over the Sámi reindeer herding areas. Accessed 6 January 2020. www.sametinget.se/8382.
Samiskt informationscentrum. 'Lars Levi Laestadius och samerna.' Accessed 11 January 2019. www.samer.se/laestadianismen.
SFS *Svensk författningssamling* (The Swedish Code of Statutes) 1928, no. 309. Lag om de svenska lapparnas rätt till renbete i Sverige.
Silversparf, Agneta. 'Ättlingar till Silfversparre-Rim.' *Silbonah Sámesijdda – Medlemsnytt* 13, April 2009.
Silversparf, Agneta. 'Norrbottens Kuriren March 23, 1906.' *Silbonah Sámesijdda – Medlemsnytt* 28, December 2012.
Sörlin, Sverker. 'Guldet från Norden: norrlandsvisioner från Olaus Magnus till Johan Galtung.' In *Älvdal i norr: människor och resurser i Luledalen 1300–1800*, edited by Sune Åkerman and Kjell Lundholm, 82–147 (Umeå: Umeå University, 1990).
Statistics Sweden (SCB). 'Elektricitet i Sverige.' Accessed 1 May 2020. www.scb.se/hitta-statistik/sverige-i-siffror/miljo/elektricitet-i-sverige.
Stoor, Krister. 'Carl Linnæus from a Sámi Point of View.' *TijdSchrift voor Skandinavistiek* 29, no. 1–2 (2008): 77–84.
Svalastog, Anna Lydia. 'On Teachers' Education in Sweden, School Curriculums, and the Sámi People.' In *Re: Mindings: Co-Constituting Indigenous, Academic, Artistic Knowledges*, edited by Johan Gärdebo, May-Britt Öhman, and Hiroshi Maruyama, 153–171. Uppsala: Uppsala University, Hugo Valentin Centre, 2014.

Swedish National Heritage Board archive, Antikvarisk-topografiska arkivet: Letter to the Swedish National Heritage Board, Dnr 489/66, Oct. 24, 1966; Letter to Rudolf Nyström Dnr 489/66, Oct. 6, 1966. from Landsantikvarie Birgitta Hjolman, October 24, 1966.

Tacitus, *Tacitus' Germania*, trans. Vilhelm Lundström. (Göteborg: Elander, 1912) [ca 98 CE] https://regina.kb.se/F/?func=find-b&request=003990092&find_code=SYS&local_base=KBS01

Turi, Johan. 1910. *An Account of the Sámi: A Translation of Muitalus Sámiid Birra*. Edited by Mikael Svonni. Translated by Thomas Andrew DuBois. Chicago, IL: Nordic Studies Press, 2011.

Ullenius, J.G. ['Research Notes Concerning Forest Sámi Areas along Both Sides of the Little Lule River Downstream of Jokkmokk 1932'] 'Undersökningsanteckningar rörande skogslappsområden å Lilla Luleälvs båda sidor nedom Jokkmokk 1932.' Norrbottens Museum Archive, F:92. Luleå, Sweden. Unpublished research notes. Transcribed by Agneta Silversparf, 2011. Copy in the author's archive.

Ullenius, J.G. 'Laxljustring i rödlövsreka.' *Norrbotten: Norrbottens läns hembygdsförenings tidskrift* (1934): 112–127.

Ullenius, J.G. ['Research Notes for the Nordic Museum in Stockholm by the Former Teacher J.G. Ullenius born 1868'] 'Anteckningar för Nordiska Museet i Stockholm av f d seminareläraren J.G. Ullenius, född 1868.' 1935. Unpublished research notes, Norrbotten Museum Archive, F:92, Transcribed by Agneta Silversparf in 2002. Copy in the author's archive.

Ullenius, J.G. 'Något om skogslapparnas bovallar.' *Norrbotten: Norrbottens läns hembygdsförenings tidskrift* (1937): 107–126.

Vattenfall. 'En resa längs Lule Älv.' Published 2008. Accessed 1 September 2010. Copy in the author's archive.

Westfal, Ulf. *Rapport över arkeologiska inventeringar och undersökningar av utvalda områden inom skogslandet längs Lule älvdal*. Umeå: Umeå University, 1983.

Wyld, Frances, and Bronwyn L. Fredericks, 'Earth Song as Storywork: Reclaiming Indigenous Knowledges.' *Journal of Australian Indigenous Issues* 18, no. 2 (2015): 2–12.

Zachrisson, Inger. 'Encounters in Border Country: Saami and Scandinavian Peoples in Central Scandinavia.' In *Finno-Ugric People in the Nordic Countries: Roots 5*, edited by Birger Winsa, 40–45. Övertorneå: Academia Tornedaliensis – Meän akateemi, 2005.

Zachrisson, Inger. 'Vittnesbörd om pälshandel?: ett arkeologiskt perspektiv på romerska bronsmynt funna i norra Sverige.' *Fornvännen* 105, no. 3 (2010): 187–202.

25
ASSISTING INDIGENOUS RESISTANCE THROUGH SECULARISM
Legal limits to Christianisation in Canada (1867–1939)

Claude Gélinas

The Canadian government's policy towards Indigenous peoples,[1] particularly during the first 70 years after the Confederation of 1867, was mainly based on objectives of territorial dispossession and assimilation, which included, in the latter case, a moral transformation through conversion to Christianity. However, federal laws, and the Indian Act[2] in particular, were curiously restrained when it came to Christianisation, whereas other assimilation measures such as education, the imposition of an election system, and the promotion of economic individualism were explicitly addressed. Should we conclude that political leaders attributed less importance to the religious dimension in their efforts to culturally transform Indigenous peoples? Or instead that the belief in the ineluctable progress of Christianity made all coercive measures appear unnecessary, especially since a large number of Indigenous individuals seemed to have already abandoned their 'paganism' by the time the Indian Act was adopted?[3] Such explanations tend to be inconsistent with the well-known and documented efforts by Indian Affairs – the administrative branch of the government charged with the implementation of Indigenous policy – up until the 1930's to separate Indigenous peoples from their traditional religious systems, whether through the support provided to missionaries or by the deterrence measures taken by its own officers. The idea put forward here is that an analysis of the wording, evolution, and application of the formal provisions of the Indian Act, which has often been the basis of studies about Canada's Indigenous policy, may be insufficient to fully grasp the government's intentions. Regarding Christianisation, for instance, the Indian Act in no way reflected the real objectives of the government, since the broader normative framework for the management of religious pluralism in Canada at the time, which had the characteristics common to a secular regime, apparently restricted the government's legislative capacity on this matter.

Although at the moment of its foundation in 1867 the Canadian state did not explicitly affirm its secular status, the constitutive principles that usually underlie a secular regime – the separation of political and religious powers, state neutrality, freedom of conscience and religion, and the moral equality of persons and cults – had been in effect since the British colonial era.[4] While since 1791 it was prohibited for any cleric, Protestant or Catholic, to be elected as a deputy, the Act of Union of 1840 stipulated that the colonial government could not adopt 'any Bill or Bills [...] containing any Provisions which shall in any Matter relate to or affect the Enjoyment or Exercise of any Form or Mode of Religious Worship, or shall impose or create any Penalties, Burdens, Disabilities, or Disqualifications in respect of the same'.[5] The 1854 Act repealing the last legal provisions in relation to the government-administered Anglican clergy reserves also stated that 'it is desirable to remove all semblance of a union between Church and the State'.[6] As for freedom of religion and the moral equality of cults, which were gradually extended to include different denominations from 1763 onwards, the general principles were stated in 1851:

> Whereas the recognition of legal equality among all Religious Denominations is an admitted principle of Colonial Legislation; And whereas in the state and condition of this Province, to which such a principle is peculiarly applicable, it is desirable that the same should receive the sanction of direct Legislative Authority, recognizing and declaring the same as a fundamental principle of our civil policy : [...] the free exercise and an enjoyment of Religious Profession and Worship, without discrimination or preference, so as the same be not made an excuse for acts of licentiousness, or a justification of practices inconsistent with the peace and safety of the Province, is by the constitution and laws of this Province allowed to all Her Majesty's subjects within the same.[7]

In the absence of any explicit reference to religion, with the exception of a provision concerning the protection of schools for Catholic and Protestant minorities (section 93), the new Constitutional Act of 1867 was implicitly based on the principles of neutrality and separation of Church and State, while article 129 on previous laws maintained in force the provisions already mentioned concerning freedom of religion and non-discrimination.[8] All this did not mean that the state gave up the exercise of a moral authority imbued with Christian values on which the nation had to be founded,[9] or that the Protestant and Catholic churches, in the wake of their hegemonic aspirations, have been devoid of influence on political power, simply that the acceptance of religious pluralism to preserve order and social peace, in its most pragmatic dimension, seemed able to provide the best results when articulated around such constitutive principles. However, the Canadian government seems to have ignored these principles as part of its Indigenous policy, working closely with religious orders to promote the adoption of Christianity and forcing the abandonment of traditional belief systems deemed ideologically inferior or contested as legitimate religions. These practices also departed from a more general attitude of tolerance towards cultural and religious diversities in the country, as long as it did not endanger morality and public order.

Nevertheless, by studying the legislation as well as the Indian Affairs' administrative correspondence, it seems reasonable to conclude that the government sought to implement its policy of assimilation in accordance with the constitutive principles that directed legislation around freedom of religion generally. Not only officials and civil servants were concerned with carrying out their actions in accordance with these principles, but members of Parliament and influential political figures were opposed to the restriction of freedoms upon Indigenous peoples or were at least sensitive to their situation.[10] As the Secretary of Indian Affairs explained to one of his officers concerned about the frequency of traditional dances in a community for which he was responsible in Manitoba: 'As regards amending the Indian Act to make it stricter in forbidding dances, it is not easy to get such legislation through Parliament. Many members in both Houses think Indians should have the same right to hold dances as white people have who sometimes dress in rather odd costumes.'[11] Thus, at least some elected representatives and higher officials of Indian Affairs seemed aware and concerned that certain governmental initiatives were not necessarily in keeping with the spirit of the larger normative framework regarding religious rights in the country. Consequently, by being in some way an obstacle to itself, the Canadian state contributed not only to limit the scope of Indian Affairs' partnership with missionaries, but the capacity of its officials to directly and effectively undermine the traditional religious beliefs and practices of Indigenous peoples.

At the same time, advocacy for non-interference and tolerance towards Indigenous customs and religion also came from other sectors of society. While missionaries seem to have been overwhelmingly hostile to traditional beliefs and practices, at least one of them, John McDougall, publicly opposed the criminalisation of rituals, referring precisely to the right to religious freedom.[12] Like other anthropologists, Edward Sapir, then in charge of the Anthropological Division of the Geological Survey of Canada, was opposed to the criminalisation of Indigenous rituals, stating in particular, 'I have always failed to understand why we pride ourselves so much on tolerance in dealing with European foreigners, and so conspicuously fail to apply this same tolerance in dealing with our own aborigines. To my mind the abolition of the potlatch is no more praise-worthy an act than would be a law forbidding the Catholics to hold wakes or Jews to refrain from working on Saturdays.'[13] In 1931, Agent William Halliday, a staunch opponent of the potlatch, explained that

> the [Indian] Act itself is not a popular one with the white people, even with the judges, who all take a very sympathetic view of the Indians' view point [concerning the ban on potlatch], and think that it is more or less like the eighteenth amendment to the American Constitution, that interferes with the liberties of a great many people.[14]

This broad context ensured that in matters of religion, a space was maintained between the political power and the Indigenous peoples, in which the latter were able to organise resistances and preserve significant dimensions of their culture and spirituality. This lasted up until the aftermath of the Second World, when Indigenous peoples went on to benefit from a socio-political context gradually more favourable to the recognition and promotion of their cultural and religious particularisms. Thus, the aim of this paper is both to trace the outline of this space of resistance and to underline the need to consider the involuntary assistance coming from the colonial regime itself when analysing and understanding the success Indigenous peoples in Canada have met in preserving parts of their cultural heritage amidst assimilation pressures.

Partnership with religious orders

For a long time, the Canadian government remained convinced that the adoption of Christianity by Indigenous peoples was a necessary condition for their successful amalgamation into civil society. Prime Minister John A. MacDonald explained in 1883 that 'a secular education is a good thing among white men but among Indians the first object is to make them better men, and, if possible, good Christian men by applying proper moral restraints'.[15] Indian Affairs officials shared this view, including the influential Duncan Campbell Scott, for whom the civilisation of Indigenous peoples had to include the 'substitution of Christian ideals of conduct and morals for aboriginal conceptions of both'.[16] As late as 1936, agent Charles Todd, based on the Northwest Coast, expressed his personal position as follows: 'We are today living in a Christian world and the laws of our land are for the uplifting of humanity, not to suppress a minority people but to assist them....'[17] Such opinions seemed even more legitimate as traditional Indigenous religious beliefs and practices were often characterised as forms of paganism and superstitions, as reflected in these brief passages about the Sun Dance and the medicine men included in the 1896 Indian Affairs annual report:

> ... the department's policy has been in the direction of suppressing it [Sun Dance] and, step by step, it has been robbed of its most revolting ceremonies. [...] So long as it remained a prominent performance, so long did it keep burning those superstitions which it was sought to eradicate. The abandoning of this dance evidences in no small degree the civilising influences brought upon the Indian, and the great change in his feelings and modes of thought. [...] The 'medicine men,' the guiders of thought and action and the inspirers of fear in all but the very boldest, had to be fought.[18]

To succeed in Christianising its wards, the government relied first and foremost on a close partnership with religious congregations, the basis of which had been established well before 1867, notably through joint projects of residential and industrial schools.[19] Indian Affairs tried to facilitate the missionaries' endeavours by allowing them to stay on reserve and, among other things, continuing to financially support their educational activities in which religion was both part of the curriculum and extracurricular content.[20] In return, clerics provided administrative support by acting as counsellors and informants to public servants, and in some cases as

Figure 25.1 Mi'kmaq girls in sewing class at the Roman Catholic-run Shubenacadie Indian Residential School in Shubenacadie (ca. 1929)
Source: Library and Archives Canada, RG10, R216

paid agents,[21] while providing services such as summary health care and relief distribution to remote and unserved Indigenous populations. Nevertheless, despite a certain ideological kinship and a convergence of interests, this collaboration did not mean that the state confused its power with that of the religious orders, or that it renounced any degree of autonomy to them (Figure 25.1).

On the one hand, this collaboration found very little normative echo. In addition to the immunity granted to missionaries to distribute alcohol to Indigenous people for medical purposes,[22] the Indian Act stated only that they could be required to provide, as of the mid-1880s, a sworn letter of support for Indigenous individuals wishing to be emancipated, which meant renouncing their Indian and band member status in exchange for Canadian citizenship.[23] Such provisions were related to the logistical support provided to Indian Affairs by the missionaries, and not directly to their evangelistic work, as if the government wanted to avoid being legally associated with any proselytising activities. In addition, since the Indian Act provided that only 'Indians and those intermarried with Indians' could settle and reside on reserves, except by revocable permission from the authorities,[24] the presence of missionaries on reserves remained a prerogative of Indian Affairs, who evaluated each application to establish a ministry on merit,[25] although only two refusals were reported. One involved a group of Shakers forced out of a reserve, as they were accused of having a bad influence over their local coreligionists who were neglecting their economic responsibilities.[26] The other related to Pentecostal pastors who were denied access to a reserve for a few years as their presence was creating strife among the Indigenous population, although they could still preach to their worshipers from a nearby village.[27]

On the other hand, religious congregations have repeatedly tried to influence the government to adopt legal provisions to further facilitate their work as agents of Christianisation, whether it was to put an end to the recognition of customary marriages,[28] or to reinforce or even relax certain coercive measures regarding Indigenous cultural practices.[29] However, such attempts have rarely translated into concrete action on the part of the government. Some contemporaries, such as anthropologist Marius Barbeau, have attributed to missionary efforts the adoption of legal provisions aimed at banning traditional rituals.[30] But it remains to be seen that the representations of missionaries were influential to that extent, as economic, social, and health considerations with immediate costly consequences for the state seemed equally if not more worrying from the government's perspective.[31] At the same time, civil servants were reluctant to grant privileges to religious congregations or to evade rules of procedure in their favour. When clerics approached Indian Affairs authorities to circumvent unfavourable decisions by a band council, to reduce the cost of renting land for the mission, or to prevent the establishment of a rival congregation, there was usually little consideration given to such grievances, even when the petitioners were pressing through deputies, senators, or even the minister responsible for Indian Affairs. Missionaries acting as agents for the Indian Affairs also failed to receive special considerations from the Department, as when asking for funds to pay for the construction of a church.[32]

In addition, the responsibility to protect Indigenous peoples' interests and the will to maintain order on reserves frequently led Indian Affairs officials to oppose the wishes of missionaries, even when dealing with issues related to traditional beliefs. For example, when a bishop wanted to move Indigenous burials from an old cemetery in 1879, the initial response of Deputy Superintendent Vankoughnet was to recall that 'in consequence of the superstition with which the Indians generally regard their dead and their unwillingness to allow any interference with the places where they are buried, it was not considered advisable to bring such matters before the Indians for consideration'.[33] Such distancing from clerical authorities was also reflected in the provisions of the Indian Act affecting land ownership on reserves. Indian Affairs has always resisted the will of religious orders to gain full ownership of lands on which places of worship were erected within the boundaries of reserves, or to access the funds available to Indian bands; from the Indian Affairs' perspective, such public money could not be used to finance religious congregations directly.[34]

Finally, Indian Affairs officials strictly avoided interfering in the internal affairs of religious orders. As Secretary McLean summed it up in 1898:

> the rule of the Department regarding Church work on Indian Reserves is, that any denomination desiring to erect a church upon a reserve for mission purposes may do so, provided the Indians give their consent; but the Department assumes no responsibility whatever, and the prejudices of the Indians, if any, must be overcome by the denomination desiring to erect the church. [...] So far as strife between religious bodies for supremacy is concerned, the policy of the Department is not to interfere, although it may sometimes advise.[35]

Meanwhile, in response to Indigenous communities' complaints about their missionaries, whether related to personal conflicts or disputes over the ownership of movable and immovable property of the missions, or to missionaries denouncing the actions of rival congregations or wishing to have them expel from a reserve, officials systematically maintained that these matters fell within the jurisdiction of the ecclesiastical authorities. So, when Indigenous individuals from Kettle Point Reserve protested to the Indian Affairs about the closing of the United Church in 1936, the position of the Deputy Superintendent General was that '[the decision] was one of mutual arrangement as between the authorities [of the church]. The Indian members and adherents of the United Church should make their protest to the church authorities not to this Department'.[36] In addition, Indian Affairs officials refused to have their officers collect Indigenous followers' financial contributions to their churches or intervene to enforce order during liturgical ceremonies.[37]

Overall, the close partnership between the government and religious orders, judged in many ways profitable by both sides, seemed nevertheless in keeping with the principle of separation of powers from a normative standpoint. This contributed to anchor relations between both parties in a negotiation dynamic subject to the challenge of conciliating divergent visions and goals at times, including in matters of Indigenous cultural transformation where missionaries were not all convinced of the usefulness of complete assimilation.[38] Moreover, the apparent desire of the government not to explicitly instrument the Indian Act to support proselytising efforts contributed to limit the political and legal support missionaries received from the state. For the government itself, this translated into a less systematic influence on congregational postures and actions, which occasionally led Indian Affairs officials to deplore certain missionary behaviours which seemed rather harmful towards the wider aims of its Indigenous policy. Reacting to a publication by Reverend John Antle in favour of relaxing the legal provisions against the potlatch, Duncan Campbell Scott summarised the consensual rather than normative nature of Indian Affairs' relationship with missionaries as follows: 'If he expects the support of the Department for his activities, I think he should be loyal to the Department and to its policy, even if he should be opposed to it.'[39]

Legal limits

The Indian Act did not contain provisions explicitly designed to impose a religious orientation on Indigenous peoples, nor to eradicate their traditional religious beliefs and practices, including the influence of 'medicine men'. The adoption of Christianity itself has never been a legally established criterion for granting emancipation.[40] However, one obvious exception to this approach is the prohibition of certain rituals by the end of the nineteenth century. In 1884, the Indian Act was amended to make any person, Indigenous or non-Indigenous, who engaged in, assisted in the organisation of, or encouraged the participation of Indigenous individuals in the 'festival known as "Potlach" or in the Indian dance known as the "Tamanawas"' subject to imprisonment.[41] These rituals certainly had a spiritual dimension from the perspective of the Northwest Coast Indigenous peoples mainly affected by this prohibition. However, it was not the spiritual aspect that primarily troubled the authorities, but rather the corporal mutilations and the 'giving-away' or redistribution of goods that could take place in the wake of the ceremonies. The authorities' specific concerns with the ceremony were to be clarified in a reformulation of the article of law in 1895, which at the same time broadened the scope of the prohibition to other rituals with spiritual connotations, more specifically certain dances practised in the Prairie Provinces:

> Every Indian or other person who engages in, or assists in celebrating or encourages either directly or indirectly another to celebrate, any Indian festival, dance or other ceremony of which the giving away or paying or giving back of money, goods or articles of any sort forms part, or is a feature, whether such gift of money, goods or articles takes place before, at, or after the celebration of the same, and every Indian or other person who engages or assists in any celebration or dance of which the wounding or mutilation of the dead or living body of any human being or animal forms a part or is a feature, is guilty of an indictable offence and liable to imprisonment for a term not exceeding six months.[42]

While the proscription of mutilations was primarily driven by moral considerations and a concern for the damaging portrayal of Western Canada, at a time when the government was looking to attract settlers in the region,[43] the redistributive component appeared to be inconsistent with the notion of private property and risk impoverishing Indigenous peoples, likely to result in additional costs for reliefs. As such, in its legal endeavours the government appeared mostly guided by non-religious considerations, though it was certainly hoped that such prohibitive measures would also undermine the rituals' spiritual components (Figures 25.2 and 25.3).

Figure 25.2 Raising the centre pole, sun dance tent, 1899
Source: Library and Archives Canada/PA-028889

Figure 25.3 Potlatch, 1907
Source: Library and Archives Canada/PA-74038

Other provisions of the Indian Act were not necessarily compatible with an overriding concern on the government's part to promote Christianity among Indigenous peoples. For instance, emancipated individuals were not required to adopt a Christian name,[44] and 'any Indian or aboriginal native or native of mixed blood [...] destitute of the knowledge of God, and of any fixed and clear belief in religion or in a future state of rewards and punishments' had nevertheless the right to take an oath.[45] The law also aimed to protect heritage components such as petroglyphs, pictographs, grave houses, and totem poles found on reserves, essentially in British Columbia, which could still carry a spiritual charge for Indigenous peoples.[46] At the same time, as long as marriages and deaths were legally registered, Indian Affairs did not formally object to the traditional ceremonies and rituals associated with them, providing that corporal mutilations and 'giving-away' were absent and adequate sanitary conditions put in place.[47] On occasions, the right to practise such traditional rituals seems to have been promised to Indigenous peoples, whether by missionaries or by state officials, in order to expedite the signature of treaties.[48]

Despite a lack of explicit utterances linking a reluctance to address religion in the Indian Act with respect for principles of state neutrality, religious freedom, and equality, there is little doubt that this concern hovered above government actions. From the beginning, Indigenous leaders openly demanded respect and protection for their freedom of religion in response to governmental and missionary interference, qualifying, for instance, the prohibitions on rituals as 'an example of intolerance'[49] and 'a great innovation upon their liberty'.[50] Appeals to lawyers to defend these same rights and the multiplication of petitions raising the inequality of treatment between Indigenous and non-Indigenous religious ceremonies and practices, regularly reminded state officials of such concerns.[51] Some officers of Indian Affairs recognised that Indigenous peoples had rights and that they were being discriminated against in this way. Hence the message repeated by senior authorities within the Department to act cautiously in the application of the law tends to indicate that the latter were aware that provisions relating to the prohibition of rituals were perhaps problematic on a legal basis, and could eventually be declared illegal.[52] As Deputy Superintendent General Hayter Reed put it in 1895: 'the ability to retain the law depends on the exercise of discretion.'[53]

Combined with public opinion mentioned earlier, this overall context renders unconvincing the idea that a belief in the inevitable disappearance of traditional beliefs and practices alone prompted the Canadian government to ignore religion in its drafting of the Indian Act. On the contrary, records show that high-level officials within Indian Affairs were motivated to increase coercive measures to support Christianisation against these apparently tenacious customs. Rather, the government probably stayed away from the legislative option to avoid normalising breaches of the governing principles that otherwise supported the state management of religious diversity in the country. Such an interpretation was reiterated in the discussions surrounding a proposed amendment to the Indian Act in 1895, in which it was proposed to add a ban on grass-dance, though it was carefully stated that the latter was 'not regarded as a religious dance, and there should be less difficulty in abolishing its practice if made punishable as proposed'.[54] Two years later, Commissioner Forget summed up what would be Indian Affairs' usual position towards legally prohibited dances:

> you may inform the Chiefs that while the Department can in no way countenance the celebration of this rite [Sun Dance] and therefore cannot give assistance in any form towards it, there will on account of its religious nature in their eyes and of the representations which have been made, be no interference therewith on this occasion, provided they will give you a positive assurance:
>
> 1. That, as proposed by themselves, the gathering into one camp will only be for five days.
> 2. That no compulsion will be used with regard to those who are not desirous of joining in.
> 3. That there will be no making of braves or any form of torture whatever.
> 4. That there will be no giving away of property.
> 5. That they will not interfere with the workers before, during, or after the dance.
> 6. That the children will not be taken away from School.
> 7. And that they will engage to fill the existing Schools to their full capacity.[55]

For the government, attacking the religious dimension head-on appeared an undesirable option.

'We do not want to lose our religion'[56]

This apparent restraint on the legislator's part has impacted government policies of assimilation. From the first half of the nineteenth century, it was established that, outside specific provisions of the Indian Act, Indigenous peoples enjoyed in principle the same rights as other Canadians.[57] Thus, in the absence of restrictive religious provisions, Indigenous peoples enjoyed the same freedom of religion and the same protection against all forms of discrimination – again, in principle. Hence in all likelihood the hesitation by the officials to hinder the religious dimensions of otherwise proscribed rituals. While prohibitions and other conditions placed on such practices undermined the Indigenous peoples' capacity to freely express their cultural requirements, the legal context also helped to keep open interstices of freedom through which the latter could manage to articulate a cultural and spiritual resistance. Traces of this appear, for example, in several police reports produced in the 1920s:

> The indians [sic] are very keen on having this [Sun Dance] and I am afraid in spite of the fact that I have told them not to hold it [they] will do so in some off corner of the Reserve. They inform me this is a religious ceremony, fasting and a secret rite with a pipe, this is no mutilation of the body or the giving away or paying back money goods or articles of any sort, to prove their statement any police officer can be present and see that the law is not violated in any shape or form…[58]
>
> The dances which took place at the above mentioned Indian Reserves [Long Lake and Frog Lake] are in the nature of a religious ceremony, and I am informed by [Indian agent] Mr Turner that they are sometimes termed 'Horse dances', as horses are used in procession at the dance. None of the objectionable features specified in the Indian Act are in evidence at these dances, so the Indian Agent is satisfied to discourage them rather than to forbid them.[59]

In the absence of proscriptive legal provisions specifically targeting traditional religious components, civil servants and law enforcement officials were powerless to repress customs deemed reprehensible that did not fall under other legal dispositions, such as those targeting polygamy,[60] or marriages contracted under threat, including under duress by conjurors.[61] In 1939, when faced with a case of witchcraft aimed at curing a young girl, a government official could again only take notice of the limits imposed by the operative legal framework:

> As the matter stands it is not clear to me what action might be taken as a remedy. Section 445 of the Criminal Code does not appear to apply to this case, so far as I can tell from the above report. Further investigation might disclose sufficient evidence of an infraction of the Provincial Medical Act if sufficient evidence could be obtained of such a case as the payment of money etc. […] Or some offence might be disclosed in regard to Sections 241 to 244 of the Criminal Code, I do not find anything in the Indian Act to apply to this case.[62]

These limits resulted in frustrations within Indian Affairs. As late as 1934, Assistant Commissioner Perry wrote that:

> as long as the Indian potlatch and its suppression are left to the mercy of the varied interpretation of the existing provisions of Section 140 [of the Indian

Act], we shall never be able to deal effectively with this vexed question; and the Indians will continue to defy the law and retard the desired advancement.[63]

In conjunction with public servants' desire to avoid Indigenous peoples' discontent and uprisings, to refrain from adding further precariousness to the latter's socio-economic status, or to avoid being ultimately dismissed in court, such limitations contributed to restricting the charge against religious traditional beliefs and practices to the realm of persuasion and passive tolerance,[64] excluding occasional coercive bursts attributable to a few zealous high officials. Efforts were made to discourage Indigenous peoples to resort to their traditional religious habits, to restrict the scope of the latter, and to replace them with Christian rituals. Overall, Indian Affairs were more preoccupied with negotiating the conditions of practice of such customs than with pressing for their eradication, hoping that they would gradually disappear by themselves.

In the late 1930s, officials noted that there were still traditional rituals taking place, that legal prohibitions were unsuitable, and that missionaries had helped counter them to a greater extent than the Indian Act. Discouragement prevailed to the point that the government dropped the idea of further amending the law to facilitate repressive work from its civil servants. Allowing the practice of the potlatch in moderation was even discussed among Indian Affairs authorities, who now preferred to avoid prosecution for fear of nurturing among Indigenous peoples the idea that the legal framework was favourable to them. Legal prohibitions were finally abolished in 1951, in the wake of the last major revision of the Indian Act. Growing international concern for the protection of minority rights and the public criticism of the way the government handled its responsibilities towards Indigenous peoples forced a certain relaxation of the guardianship system.[65] This preceded the adoption of the national policy of multiculturalism by 1971, according to which not only cultural freedom was to be protected, but cultural pluralism was to become the very essence of the Canadian identity, including its Indigenous component.

Conclusion

Canada's colonial policy regarding Indigenous peoples certainly had an impact on the latter's traditional religious systems. Reserve confinement cut cultural and spiritual ties to the land, mandatory education of Indigenous youth distanced children from their community's cosmology, and the use of biomedicine was disruptive to customary healing practices. Meanwhile, state support for missionary work allowed the Christianisation project to make significant progress, not always contrary to the will of Indigenous peoples themselves. Nevertheless, government officials were not able to go as far as they hoped in their plan to eradicate 'paganism', since one of the main tools at their disposal, the law, was subject to constraints arising from a wider normative framework in connection with the management of religious diversity. The government and its Department of Indian Affairs were to act in keeping with the State's obligation of neutrality and the expected respect towards principles of religious freedom and non-discrimination. This restricted their coercive power and reinforced the need to rely mostly on the work of religious congregations. However, in a context where a distance between political and religious powers was expected, the government was not in the position to fully control the missionaries' actions. From a historiographical standpoint, this should be a reminder that the Indian Act is only one part of a wider normative context that contributed to frame the Canadian government's Indigenous policy. On some levels, this law may even appear contrary to the political will, while revealing apparent inconsistencies between the authorities' official message and their actions, especially in connection with Christianisation. Why was such a goal not reflected in the law? Why only partially prohibit customs that the government wanted to see disappear in their entirety? And why did Indian Affairs officials often oppose the wishes of missionaries when both parties seemed to share a common intent? Such questions start to draw plausible responses when one embraces a more decentralised perspective at the normative level.

However, Indigenous peoples' own capacity to withstand the politics of Christianisation and assimilation has long been recognised and documented. Resorting to secrecy, concealing traditional beliefs and practices under the guise of Christian behaviour, or adapting their customs to the legal framework are among their better-known strategies. What has been overlooked is the way the Canadian state itself, paradoxically, provided them with support by subjecting the federal government to the primacy of the law and the underlying principles regarding the management of religious diversity in Canada. In other words, the Indigenous peoples' cultural and religious resistance cannot be fully understood solely from the latter's own perspective and dynamics. It must take into consideration the state's framework and actions as well as public opinion which, voluntarily or not, came to benefit their cause. The same way newcomers' polities and actions in the colonial era must be understood by considering the influence exercised by Indigenous peoples. While the perspective proposed here certainly deserves a more comprehensive treatment, it would be interesting to apply a similar kind of analysis in other colonial contexts, not only to put the Canadian experience in perspective but to bring out other ways by which secular-like regimes may have influenced Indigenous policies and Indigenous peoples' cultural and spiritual resistance.

Notes

1 In this text, the term 'Indigenous' refers to the individuals and communities (usually designated as Indians at the time) to whom the federal government, during the period under review, asserted responsibility under section 91(24) of the Constitution Act of 1867 and the Indian Act, to the exclusion of Inuit and Métis who would later be recognised as Indigenous (Aboriginal) peoples by the Constitution Act of 1982 (clause 35(2)).

2 The Indian Act was adopted in 1876 as a consolidation of previous laws applying to Indigenous peoples. It was mostly concerned with the management of Indian status, reserve land, band funds (several Indian bands had cash capital, usually from the sale of reserve lands or from the granting of permits for the exploitation of natural resources located on reserves), and the assimilation of the latter into the larger Canadian society. Not pertaining to Inuit and Métis people, the Indian Act has been amended several

times since. John Leslie and Ron Maguire eds., *The Historical Development of the Indian Act* (Canada: Indian and Northern Affairs, 1978).
3   For a portrait of current research on this topic, see Tolly Bradford and Chelsea Horton eds., *Mixed Blessings: Indigenous Encounters with Christianity in Canada* (Vancouver: UBC Press, 2016).
4   José Woehrling and Rosalie Jukier, 'Religion and the Secular State in Canada,' in *Religion and the Secular State – National Reports*, eds. Javier Martinez Torrón and W. Cole Durham, Jr (Provo, Utah: The International Center for Law and Religion Studies, Brigham Young University, 2010), 183–212; Micheline Milot, *Laïcité dans le Nouveau Monde* (Turnhout: Brepols Publishers, 2002), 44–80.
5   Statutes of Great Britain 1840, c. 35, art. XLII.
6   Statutes of Canada (S.C.) 1854, c. 2, art. 3. These reserves were tracts of land made available for the support of 'Protestant clergy' (Constitutional Act of 1791).
7   S.C. 1851, c. 175, art. 1.
8   Margaret H. Ogilvie, *Religious Institutions and the Law in Canada* (Toronto, ON: Irwin Law, 2010), 97.
9   Carolyn Strange and Tina Loo, *Making Good: Law and Moral Regulation in Canada, 1867–1939* (Toronto, ON: University of Toronto Press, 1997).
10 Library and Archives Canada (LAC), 'Vowell to Deputy Superintendent General, June 8th 1897,' General Correspondence Regarding Laws to Curtail the Practice of Potlatch Among the Indians of British Columbia (Newspaper Clippings) 1883–1899, volume 3628, file 6244-1, reel C-10110.
11 LAC, 'Secretary to Logan, February 14th 1912,' Manitoba & Northwest Territories – Correspondence Regarding Indian Dances More Particularly the Sun Dance 1909–1915, RG10, volume 3826, file 60511-3, reel C-10144.
12 J.R. Miller, *Reflections on Native-Newcomer Relations: Selected Essays* (Toronto, ON: University of Toronto Press, 2004), 206–207; Brian Titley, *A Narrow Vision: Duncan Campbell Scott and the Administration of Indian Affairs in Canada* (Vancouver: UBC Press, 1986), 170–171; Katherine Pettipas, *Severing the Ties that Bind: Government Repression of Indigenous Religious Ceremonies on the Prairies* (Winnipeg: University of Manitoba Press, 1994), 141–142.
13 LAC, 'Sapir to Scott, February 11th 1915,' General Correspondence Regarding Steps to Curtail Potlatch Among the Indians of British Columbia 1914–1919, RG10, volume 3629, file 6244-3, reel C-10110. See also Douglas Cole and Ira Chaikin, *An Iron Hand Upon the People: The Law Against the Potlatch on the Northwest Coast* (Vancouver and Toronto, ON: Douglas & McIntyre, 1990), 177. The term 'potlatch' usually refers to the ceremonial distribution of property and gifts in relation to social status among Indigenous communities of the Northwest Pacific Coast.
14 LAC, 'Halliday to Ditchburn, February 12th 1931,' Indian Commissioner for British Columbia – Law Enforcement – Kwawkewlth Agency – Correspondence re Potlatch (including police reports) 1929–1939, RG10, C-11-2, volume 11297, reel T-16110.
15 Cited in Miller, *Reflections*, 195.
16 Duncan Campbell Scott, 'Indian Affairs, 1867–1912' in *Canada and Its Provinces: A History of the Canadian People and Their Institutions*, ed. A. Shortt and A.G. Doughty (Toronto, ON: Publisher's Association of Canada, 1913), 616.
17 LAC, 'Todd to Secretary, April 16th 1936,' General Correspondence Regarding Potlatch and Sun Dance 1922–1958, RG10, volume 8481, file 1/24-3, reel C-13815.
18 Dominion of Canada, *Annual Report of the Department of Indian Affairs of the Year Ended 30th June 1896* (Ottawa: S.E. Dawson, 1897), xxxii. The Sun Dance was a religious ceremony among Indigenous peoples of Western Canada, which at times included acts of self-mutilation. The term 'medicine men' usually referred to traditional healers or individuals recognised as spiritual leaders among these populations.
19 John Leslie, 'The Bagot Commission: Developing a Corporate Memory for the Indian Department,' *Historical Papers* 171 (1982): 50; John Webster Grant, *Moon of Wintertime*:

Missionaries and the Indians of Canada in Encounter since 1534 (Toronto, ON: University of Toronto Press, 1984), 81–95.

20 Dominion of Canada, Annual Report of the Department of Indian Affairs for the Year Ended 30th June 1894 (Ottawa: S.E. Dawson, 1895), 246–242.
21 Dominion of Canada, *Annual Report 1896*, 457–459; James Douglas Leighton, 'The Development of Federal Indian Policy in Canada, 1840–1890' (PhD diss., Western University, 1975), 366, 425.
22 S.C. 1868, c. 42, art. 12.
23 S.C. 1884, c. 27, art. 16.
24 S.C. 1868, c. 42, art. 17–18.
25 The basic administrative principles regarding the presence of missionaries on reserves in Western Canada have been proposed in LAC, 'Memorandum de Dennis, July 12th 1875,' Correspondence Regarding Land for Use of Church of England Missions in the Northwest Territories 1876, RG10, volume 3627, file 6170, reel C-10110, in which it was proposed that 'it would be better, as applications may be made for establishing missions, to deal with each application as it may come up, as a special case'.
26 LAC, Manitowapah Agency – Fairford Reserve – Apostolic Faith Church – Reports of Trespassing by 'Shakers' and the Bad Influence of This Group on Indians, 1913–1928, BAC, RG10, volume 6610, file 4127-11SH, reel C-8016.
27 LAC, Alnwick Agency – Alnwick Indian Reserve Pentecostal Church – Controversy Over Holding Services in Private Homes, 1936–1946, BAC, RG10, volume 6607, file 4025-2P, reel C-8015.
28 LAC, 'Petition to Walkem, September 25th 1879,' Correspondence Regarding the Potlatch and an Indian Confederation in British Columbia (Newspaper Clippings) 1878–1879, RG10, volume 3669, file 10661, reel C-10117; 'Schofield to Perry, December 20th 1935,' Indian Commissioner for British Columbia, Correspondence re Potlatch. The Indian Act, which covered almost every facet of Indigenous life in Canada, contained no specific provisions related to marriage.
29 LAC, 'Halliday to Ditchburn, February 12th 1931'; 'Perry to Secretary, August 8th 1933'; 'Newnhan to Perry, August 17th 1933'; 'Mackay to Todd, June 14th 1937,' Indian Commissioner for British Columbia, Correspondence re Potlatch; 'Antle to Minister of Interior, June 8th 1931,' General Correspondence Regarding Steps to Curtail Potlatch Among the Indians of British Columbia (Newspaper Clippings) 1925–1934, RG10, volume 3631, file 6244-5, reel C-10110.
30 LAC, 'The Potlatch Among the B.C. Indians and Section 149 of the Indian Act [Marius Barbeau], 1921 [p. 44],' Correspondence, Reports, Publications, Newspaper Clippings and Photographs on the Preservation of the Totem Poles in British Columbia 1931–1938, RG10, volume 4088, file 507787-2C, reel C-10186.
31 Cole, *An Iron Hand*, 14–24; Pettipas, *Severing the Ties*, 98–105.
32 LAC, Richmond County Agency – Chapel Island Reserve – Repairs to Indian Chapel Island, 1890–1923, BAC, volume 6608, file 4050-3, reel C-8015.
33 LAC, 'Memo from Vankoughnet, May 7th 1879,' Application by Bishop Racine of Chicoutimi to Have the Remains of Indians Removed from the Cemetery, RG-10, volume 2086, file 13,105, reel C-11154.
34 Claude Gélinas and Caroline Desruisseaux, 'Les Affaires indiennes et les lieux de culte chrétiens sur les réserves, 1875–1940,' *Bulletin d'histoire politique* 27 (2019): 100–101.
35 LAC, 'Memo from McLean, May 2nd 1898,' Assiniboine Agency – Assiniboine Reserve – Presbyterian Church – Complaint Against Establishment of a Roman Catholic Mission and Dispute as to Whether Land Occupied by Presbyterian Mission Belongs to Church or to Indians (Map) 1898–1932, RG10, volume 6609, file 4114-7P, reel C-8015.
36 LAC, 'Deputy Superintendent General to Pardee, Gurd, Fuller & Taylor, June 29th 1936,' Sarnia Agency – Kettle Point Reserve – Church Repairs to United (Previously Methodist) Church and Controversy over Ownership, 1923–1945, BAC, RG10, volume 6607, file 4029-2M, reel C-8015.

37 LAC, 'McLean to McIver, March 6th 1903,' Cape Croker Agency – Correspondence Regarding the Roman Catholic Church and Repairs to be Made to It, 1908–1924, RG10, volume 7565, file 4008, reel C-11548; 'McLean to Ashquabe, September 22nd 1926,' Georgina Island Agency – Application by the Band Council for Money to Enable Them to Build a New Church and Maintenance of it Afterwards, 1878–1927, RG10, volume 2073, file 10,786, reel C-11150.
38 See, for instance, Miller, *Reflections*, 193–213.
39 LAC, 'Scott to Ditchburn, December 1st 1931'; see also 'Monthly Report of Newnham, April 1933'; 'Perry to Secretary, December 3rd 1934,' General Correspondence Regarding Steps to Curtail Potlatch Among the Indians of British Columbia (Newspaper Clippings) 1925–1934, RG10, volume 3631, file 6244-5, reel C-10110.
40 S.C. 1857, c. XXVI, art. III; 1876, c. 18, art. 86. Between 1876 and 1927, however, the Indian Act provided that an Indigenous individual in Eastern Canada – and by proclamation of the Governor-General an Indigenous individual in Western Canada – 'who may enter Holy Orders or who may be licensed by any denomination of Christians as a Minister of the Gospel, shall *ipso facto* become and be enfranchised under this Act': S.C. 1876, c. 18, art. 86(1), 94; 1880, c. 28, art. 99(1), 107; R.S.C. 1886, c. 43, art. 82, 86.
41 S.C. 1884, c. 27, art. 3.
42 S.C. 1895, c. 35, art. 6.
43 Guillaume Teasdale, 'La politique autochtone du gouvernement canadien dans l'Ouest à la fin du XIXe siècle : une analyse de l'interdiction de la Danse du Soleil' (MA diss., Université de Sherbrooke, 2005), 114–148.
44 S.C. 1920, c. 50, art. 3.
45 S.C. 1874, c. 21, art. 3.
46 S.C. 1927, c. 32, art. 4; R.S.C. 1927, c. 98, art. 181. Otherwise, the Criminal Code rendered punishable by fine or imprisonment 'Every one who steals, or unlawfully injures or removes any image, bones, article or thing deposited in or near any Indian grave': *Criminal Code* 1892, c. 29, art. 352.
47 LAC, 'MacKay to Secretary, March 10th 1937'; 'Todd to Secretary, February 18th 1937,' Indian Commissioner for British Columbia, Correspondence re Potlatch.
48 J.R. Miller, *Skyscrapers Hide the Heavens: A History of Indian-White Relations in Canada*. Revised Edition (Toronto, ON: University of Toronto Press, 1994), 204; Miller, *Reflections*, 207.
49 LAC, 'West Coast Indians to Government of Canada, December 4th 1914,' General Correspondence Regarding Steps to Curtail Potlatch Among the Indians of British Columbia 1914–1919, RG10, volume 3629, file 6244-3, reel C-10110.
50 LAC, 'Powell to Superintendent General, May 22nd 1885,' General Correspondence Regarding Laws to Curtail the Practice of Potlatch Among the Indians of British Columbia (Newspaper Clippings) 1883–1899, volume 3628, file 6244-1, reel C-10110; Constance Backhouse, *Color-Coded: A Legal History of Racism in Canada, 1900–1950* (Toronto, ON: University of Toronto Press, Osgoode Society for Canadian Legal History, 1999), 68.
51 See, for instance, Keith D. Smith, *Strange Visitors: Documents in Indigenous-Settler Relations in Canada from 1876* (Toronto, ON: University of Toronto Press, 2015), 105–107; Titley, *A Narrow Vision*, 177–178; Cole, *An Iron Hand*, 46–47; Miller, *Skyscrapers*, 218; Pettipas, *Severing the Ties*, 116–117, 128–135, 168–172.
52 LAC, 'The Potlatch Among the B.C. Indians and Section 149 of the Indian Act [Marius Barbeau], 1921 [p. 15],' Correspondence, Reports, Publications, Newspaper Clippings and Photographs on the Preservation of the Totem Poles in British Columbia 1931–1938, RG10, volume 4088, file 507787-2C, reel C-10186.
53 LAC, 'The Potlatch Among the B.C. Indians and Section 149 of the Indian Act [Marius Barbeau], 1921 [p. 44],' Correspondence, Reports, Publications, Newspaper Clippings and Photographs on the Preservation of the Totem Poles in British Columbia 1931–1938, RG10, volume 4088, file 507787-2C, reel C-10186.

54 LAC, 'Clink to the Assistant Indian Commissioner, January 24th 1895,' General Correspondence Regarding Laws to Curtail the Practice of Potlatch Among the Indians of British Columbia (Newspaper Clippings) 1883–1899, RG10, volume 3628, file 6244-1, reel C-10110.
55 LAC, 'Forget to Indian Agent, June 3rd 1897,' Manitoba & Northwest Territories – Correspondence Regarding Indian Dances More Particularly the Sun Dance 1889–1903, RG10, volume 3825, file 60511-1, reel C-10144.
56 LAC, 'Chief Cross Child to Scott, July 13th 1931,' Manitoba & Northwest Territories – Correspondence Regarding Indian Dances More Particularly the Sun Dance 1922–1933, RG10, volume 3827, file 60511-4B, reel C-10145.
57 Sydney L. Harring, '"The Liberal Treatment of Indians": Native People in Nineteenth Century Ontario Law,' *Saskatchewan Law Review*, 56 (1992): 315–317.
58 LAC, 'Crime Report re Little Pine Reserve Indians ... Alleged Sun Dance, July 6th 1928,' Manitoba & Northwest Territories – Correspondence Regarding Indian Dances More Particularly the Sun Dance 1922–1933, RG10, volume 3827, file 60511-4B, reel C-10145.
59 LAC, 'Report re Patrol to Long Lake and Frog Lake Indian Reserves to Attend Sundance, July 17th 1924,' Manitoba & Northwest Territories – Correspondence Regarding Indian Dances More Particularly the Sun Dance 1922–1933, RG10, volume 3827, file 60511-4B, reel C-10145.
60 See R. v. Bear's Shin Bone 1899, 3 C.C.C. 329 (N.W.T.C.A.).
61 LAC, 'Johnston to Deputy Minister of Justice, July 7th 1918'; 'Edwards to Assistant Deputy Minister, July 13th 1918,' Correspondence Regarding the Annulment of the Marriage of Ada Severight & Kahpoese, A Conjuror 1916–1920, RG10, volume 4083, file 492617, reel C-10205.
62 LAC, 'King to Officer Commanding, September 22th 1922,' British Columbia – Problems With Medicine Men 1891–1922, RG10, volume 3863, file 84021, reel C-10152.
63 LAC, 'Perry to Secretary, December 3rd 1934,' General Correspondence Regarding Steps to Curtail Potlatch Among the Indians of British Columbia (Newspaper Clippings) 1925–1934, RG10, volume 3631, file 6244-5, reel C-10110.
64 LAC, 'McLean to Forget, April 15th 1898,' Manitoba & Northwest Territories – Correspondence Regarding Indian Dances More Particularly the Sun Dance 1889–1903, RG10, volume 3825, file 60511-1, reel C-10144.
65 John F. Leslie, 'Assimilation, Integration or Termination? The Development of Canadian Indian Policy, 1943–1963' (PhD diss., Carleton University, 1999).

Bibliography

Backhouse, Constance. *Color-Coded: A Legal History of Racism in Canada, 1900–1950*. Toronto, ON: University of Toronto Press, Osgoode Society for Canadian Legal History, 1999.

Bradford, Tolly, and Chelsea Horton, eds. *Mixed Blessings: Indigenous Encounters with Christianity in Canada*. Vancouver: UBC Press, 2016.

Cole, Douglas, and Ira Chaikin. *An Iron Hand upon the People: The Law Against the Potlatch on the Northwest Coast*. Vancouver and Toronto, ON: Douglas & McIntyre, 1990.

Dominion of Canada. *Annual Report of the Department of Indian Affairs for the Year Ended 30th June 1894*. Ottawa: S.E. Dawson, 1895.

Dominion of Canada, *Annual Report of the Department of Indian Affairs of the Year Ended 30th June 1896*. Ottawa: S.E. Dawson, 1897.

Gélinas, Claude, and Caroline Desruisseaux. 'Les Affaires indiennes et les lieux de culte chrétiens sur les réserves, 1875–1940.' *Bulletin d'histoire politique* 27 (2019): 87–118.

Grant, John Webster. *Moon of Wintertime: Missionaries and the Indians of Canada in Encounter since 1534*. Toronto, ON: University of Toronto Press, 1984.

Harring, Sydney L. '"The Liberal Treatment of Indians": Native People in Nineteenth Century Ontario Law.' *Saskatchewan Law Review* 56 (1992): 298–371.
Leighton, James Douglas. 'The Development of Federal Indian Policy in Canada, 1840–1890.' PhD diss., Western University, 1975.
Leslie, John F. 'The Bagot Commission: Developing a Corporate Memory for the Indian Department.' *Historical Papers* 171 (1982): 31–52.
Leslie, John F. 'Assimilation, Integration or Termination? The Development of Canadian Indian Policy, 1943–1963.' PhD diss., Carleton University, Canada, 1999.
Leslie, John F., and Ron Maguire, eds. *The Historical Development of the Indian Act*. Canada: Indian and Northern Affairs, 1978.
Miller, J.R. *Skyscrapers Hide the Heavens: A History of Indian-White Relations in Canada*. Toronto, ON: University of Toronto Press, 1994.
Miller, J.R. *Reflections on Native-Newcomer Relations: Selected Essays*. Toronto, ON: University of Toronto Press, 2004.
Milot, Micheline. *Laïcité dans le Nouveau Monde*. Turnhout: Brepols Publishers, 2002.
Ogilvie, Margaret H. *Religious Institutions and the Law in Canada*. Toronto, ON: Irwin Law, 2010.
Pettipas, Katherine. *Severing the Ties that Bind: Government Repression of Indigenous Religious Ceremonies on the Prairies*. Winnipeg: University of Manitoba Press, 1994.
Scott, Duncan Campbell. 'Indian Affairs, 1867–1912.' In *Canada and Its Provinces: A History of the Canadian People and Their Institutions*, edited by A. Shortt and A.G. Doughty, 593–626. Toronto, ON: Publisher's Association of Canada, 1913.
Smith, Keith D. *Strange Visitors: Documents in Indigenous-Settler Relations in Canada from 1876*. Toronto, ON: University of Toronto Press, 2015.
Strange, Carolyn, and Tina Loo. *Making Good: Law and Moral Regulation in Canada, 1867–1939*. Toronto, ON: University of Toronto Press, 1997.
Teasdale, Guillaume. 'La politique autochtone du gouvernement canadien dans l'Ouest à la fin du XIXe siècle: une analyse de l'interdiction de la Danse du Soleil.' MA diss., Université de Sherbrooke, 2005.
Titley, Brian. *A Narrow Vision: Duncan Campbell Scott and the Administration of Indian Affairs in Canada*. Vancouver: UBC Press, 1986.
Woehrling, José, and Rosalie Jukier. 'Religion and the Secular State in Canada.' In *Religion and the Secular State – National Reports*, edited by Javier Martinez Torrón and W. Cole Durham, Jr, 183–212. Provo: The International Center for Law and Religion Studies, Brigham Young University, 2010.

Library and Archives Canada (LAC)

Alnwick Agency – Alnwick Indian Reserve Pentecostal Church – Controversy Over Holding Services in Private Homes, 1936–1946, BAC, RG10, volume 6607, file 4025-2P, reel C-8015.
Application by Bishop Racine of Chicoutimi to Have the Remains of Indians Removed from the Cemetery, RG-10, volume 2086, file 13,105, reel C-11154.
Assiniboine Agency – Assiniboine Reserve – Presbyterian Church – Complaint Against Establishment of a Roman Catholic Mission and Dispute as to Whether Land Occupied by Presbyterian Mission Belongs to Church or to Indians (Map) 1898–1932, RG10, volume 6609, file 4114-7P, reel C-8015.
British Columbia – Problems With Medicine Men 1891–1922, RG10, volume 3863, file 84021, reel C-10152.
Cape Croker Agency – Correspondence Regarding the Roman Catholic Church and Repairs to be Made to It, 1908–1924, RG10, volume 7565, file 4008, reel C-11548.
Correspondence Regarding Land for Use of Church of England Missions in the Northwest Territories 1876, RG10, volume 3627, file 6170, reel C-10110.
Correspondence Regarding the Annulment of the Marriage of Ada Severight & Kahpoese, A Conjuror 1916–1920, RG10, volume 4083, file 492617, reel C-10205.

Correspondence Regarding the Potlatch and an Indian Confederation in British Columbia (Newspaper Clippings) 1878–1879, RG10, volume 3669, file 10661, reel C-10117.

Correspondence, Reports, Publications, Newspaper Clippings and Photographs on the Preservation of the Totem Poles in British Columbia 1931–1938, RG10, volume 4088, file 507787-2C, reel C-10186.

General Correspondence Regarding Laws to Curtail the Practice of Potlatch Among the Indians of British Columbia (Newspaper Clippings) 1883–1899, volume 3628, file 6244-1, reel C-10110.

General Correspondence Regarding Potlatch and Sun Dance 1922–1958, RG10, volume 8481, file 1/24-3, reel C-13815.

General Correspondence Regarding Steps to Curtail Potlatch Among the Indians of British Columbia 1914–1919, RG10, volume 3629, file 6244-3, reel C-10110.

General Correspondence Regarding Steps to Curtail Potlatch among the Indians of British Columbia (Newspaper Clippings) 1925–1934, RG10, volume 3631, file 6244-5, reel C-10110.

Georgina Island Agency – Application by the Band Council for Money to Enable Them to Build a New Church and Maintenance of it Afterwards, 1878–1927, RG10, volume 2073, file 10,786, reel C-11150.

Indian Commissioner for British Columbia – Law Enforcement – Kwawkewlth Agency – Correspondence re Potlatch (including police reports) 1929–1939, RG10, C-11–2, volume 11297, reel T-16110.

Manitoba & Northwest Territories – Correspondence Regarding Indian Dances More Particularly the Sun Dance 1889–1903, RG10, volume 3825, file 60511-1, reel C-10144.

Manitoba & Northwest Territories – Correspondence Regarding Indian Dances More Particularly the Sun Dance 1909–1915, RG10, volume 3826, file 60511-3, reel C-10144.

Manitoba & Northwest Territories – Correspondence Regarding Indian Dances More Particularly the Sun Dance 1922–1933, RG10, volume 3827, file 60511-4B, reel C-10145.

Manitowapah Agency – Fairford Reserve – Apostolic Faith Church – Reports of Trespassing by 'Shakers' and the Bad Influence of This Group on Indians, 1913–1928, BAC, RG10, volume 6610, file 4127-11SH, reel C-8016.

Richmond County Agency – Chapel Island Reserve – Repairs to Indian Chapel Island, 1890–1923, BAC, volume 6608, file 4050-3, reel C-8015.

Sarnia Agency – Kettle Point Reserve – Church Repairs to United (Previously Methodist) Church and Controversy over Ownership, 1923–1945, BAC, RG10, volume 6607, file 4029-2M, reel C-8015.

PART VI

Pathways towards future Indigenous histories

26
TRANSMISSION'S END?
Cataclysm and chronology in Indigenous oral tradition

Chris Ballard

A persistent problem at the interface of Indigenous oral tradition and academic history is the question of chronology, widely seen as critical to the commensurability of these two broad ways of communicating about the past. Allied to but in some respects distinct from the question of precise chronology is that of the longevity of communal memory, as expressed through oral tradition. Claims from the emergent field of geomythology that oral traditions accurately encode experiences of cataclysmic events such as sea level rise or volcanic eruptions that date to hundreds or thousands of years in the past have been met with disbelief on the part of some professional historians and archaeologists, such as David Henige and Roland Mason, who argue for a general limit of about 150 years for accurate oral transmission of memories of events, prior to their initial documentation on paper.[1] This chapter seeks to chart a middle ground between these two positions, by addressing issues of content and context in oral tradition, focusing on the ways in which formal narratives are embedded within culturally specific forms of historical consciousness, and reconsidering the contribution of oral tradition to questions of chronology and temporal depth.

Two case studies from the Pacific, both relating to volcanic eruptions, provide access to some of the mechanisms that enable long-term transmission by societies with profoundly different historicities, or regimes of historical consciousness.[2] The first relates to a fifteenth-century eruption in central Vanuatu, charting both the causes and consequences of the destruction of the island of Kuwae and the subsequent resettlement of its remnants. The second focuses on living traditions among Huli speakers and their neighbours in central New Guinea, which describe a process of cosmological elaboration following the ashfall from a distant mid-seventeenth-century eruption. Both traditions date well prior to Henige's chronological limit, and both have been recorded almost continuously since first contact with outsiders. Instead of testing these traditions for their accuracy, viewed uniquely from the perspectives of a universalising chronology and historicity, we need first to appreciate them on their own terms and understand what it is that their narrators seek to communicate, and the temporal logics or historicities under which they operate. Only then can we turn to questions of chronology and commensurability, and model some of the ways in which oral traditions might be brought into collaboration with disciplines such as geology and archaeology in the production of hybrid histories of the deep past.

Geomythology and historical scepticism

Preceded by a long history of speculation and attempted correlation between mythological traditions and geological events, the field of geomythology has been given its recent shape by Dorothy Vitaliano's 1973 monograph, *Legends of the Earth: Their Geologic Origins*.[3] Broadly defined as 'the study of etiological oral traditions created by pre-scientific cultures to explain – in poetic metaphor and mythological imagery – geological phenomena such as volcanoes, earthquakes, floods, fossils, and other natural features of the landscape', geomythology presents as a diffuse field, dominated by natural scientists rather than oral historians.[4] Geomythology's central goal, which is to match myths or oral traditions to particular geological events, places questions of chronology at the forefront of enquiry, but the process of that enquiry has been marked more by enthusiasm for pushing the temporal limits of oral traditional recall than by methodological development.[5] Some of the more ambitious claims made by geomythologists include those for Australian Aboriginal memories: of megafauna, generally considered to have been extinct for at least the last 10,000–15,000 years; of the process of sea level rise at the end of the last glacial maximum which ended about 7,000 years ago; and of the 9,000-year-old volcanic formation of maar lakes.[6] A recent review of these claims by geographer Patrick Nunn argues on this basis for an 'edge of memory' for Indigenous oral traditions that extends back 10,000 years before the present, leaving open the possibility of even earlier memories.[7]

David Henige, historian and historiographer, former editor of *History in Africa* and long-standing sceptic regarding the chronological value of oral traditions, has summarised his criticisms of the use of oral traditions in the reconstruction of cataclysmic events in the deep past.[8] In large part, his objections reprise positions that he has adhered to throughout his career, but his particular target in this paper is the proliferation of claims that 'myth qua oral tradition can preserve details of geological events that occurred as long as 40,000 years ago, perhaps even longer'.[9] In Henige's view,

> at best, only very recent earthquakes, volcanic eruptions, and tsunamis have been remembered and at worst none at all have … claiming geological origins for some myths is absolutely plausible, but going on to attribute them to specific datable instances early in a very long chain can only be considered even more implausible.[10]

Henige's argument focuses on three related problems of accuracy in the use of oral traditions: failure to interpret correctly the original content of oral tradition; the fallibility of individual human memory; and the challenges of transmission in oral cultures.

Henige's critique of much of the writing on oral tradition and cataclysm focuses on what he identifies as 'unrestrained belief in the content of oral tradition', and in particular the uncritical equation of oral traditions of cataclysms with specific events dated through earth sciences or archaeology.[11] Henige's objections on matters of content are organised around two broad questions: the first queries whether those documenting and interpreting the oral traditions have correctly identified a specific cataclysmic event; the second addresses the capacity for accurate oral transmission of the content of these events over long periods.

Why should certain cataclysms be memorialised in oral tradition, but not others? D. Wayne Moodie, A.J.W. Catchpole, and Kerry Abel confidently assign oral memories of an eruption of the White River volcano in Alaska to events in either 20 CE or 720 CE, but Henige observes that more than 250 volcanic eruptions have been recorded in Alaska during the past two centuries alone, with the implication that there may be as many as 3,000 other candidate eruptions since the eighth century that would need to be ruled out of contention: 'if what appears to be an eruption is mentioned in a tradition, how can we determine which one is involved? Would it be the largest, the most recent, the most proximate spatially?'[12]

Limited critical attention to sources does appear common to much of the geomythological literature, which is often dependent on transcripts and translations of uncertain quality and unspecified origin. Henige demands to know why oral traditions should be 'exempt … from the same kinds of testing that we routinely apply to written sources'.[13] If use of a tradition depends on documented versions, when was that tradition first documented, from whom and by whom, and in what language(s)? What was the scope for 'feedback', or the incorporation of elements from other, usually literate, traditions, such as the Biblical Flood?[14] How might other sources of distortion, such as the lengthening or telescoping of genealogies, or continuous political manipulation of traditions, have influenced the content finally received in documentary form? And how have the successive influences of textualism, colonialism, and Christianity further contributed to what Henige refers to as the 'contamination' of oral traditions?[15]

Along with archaeologist Roland Mason, Henige largely discounts the role in oral transmission of communal memory, focusing instead on the scope for fallibility of individual human memory, and thus of all oral traditions over time: 'The problem is two-fold: the limitations of memory generally in the human species, and whether the memories of those persons delegated to transmit oral data were repeatedly and invariably up to that task.'[16] External aids to memory, or mnemonics, are also dismissed for their 'potential … for immediate and unbridled departure from the Ur-Text'.[17]

Geomythology is often particularly poor at demonstrating or modelling likely modes and means of transmission of oral traditions relating to deep past events. Proponents who advocate that original eyewitnesses of cataclysmic events 'shot these little time capsules of knowledge down the pipeline to listeners of the future' and that 'properly encoded information has passed unscathed through the oral pipeline for one to ten thousand years or more', or that the 'texts of oral traditions were preserved intact and inherited by each subsequent generation' simply elide consideration of critical issues around transmission.[18] But his insistence that the measure of historical value is the 'intactness' of a tradition permits Henige to arrive at a conclusion that is equally unsupported by detailed consideration of either the nature of transmission or vernacular understandings of accuracy in Indigenous communities: 'claims that oral societies recollect unusual and cataclysmic events are perfectly in harmony with what we might expect, but claims that they have remembered specific centuries-old occasions accurately simply lack inherent plausibility.'[19] In stark contrast to the 10,000-year 'edge of memory' proposed by Nunn, Henige suggests that 'four or five generations seems a generous maximum period to withstand all the exigencies noted above', equating to about 150 years.[20] Elsewhere, Henige is less grudging, if still narrow in his definition of accuracy, insisting that his 'targets are not oral traditions per se, but claims about their ability to retain word-perfectness over long periods – say 300 years or more'.[21]

How might a middle path be charted between enthusiastic geomythologists and sceptical historians? The argument I pursue here is that neither position adequately addresses the dynamic, lived experience of oral traditions in Indigenous societies, their enmeshment within other forms of knowledge, and the impetus behind their transmission. Both extremes mistake oral traditions for texts, even prior to their documentation: Nunn writes of Australian Dreaming stories as 'books', gathered together within a 'Dreaming Library'[22]; Henige describes his 'Ur-traditions' as '*original* texts'.[23] Both also invest considerable significance in the initial moment of documentation or transcription of an oral tradition – 'unquestionably the epiphanic moment in any oral tradition's life' – sometimes to the exclusion of further engagement with descendants in source communities.[24] But oral traditions are neither conceived, nor transmitted, nor received by audiences as texts; they exist only in performance and in the act of transmission.[25] Transcribed as texts, they are shorn of much of the contextual knowledge and referents that endow them with meaning – the temporal and material settings, the narrators, and the prescience of an audience largely familiar with the narrative, as well as all of the quotidian mnemonics ingrained within landscapes, names, and practices that sustain communal knowledge of the past in Indigenous communities.[26]

Henige chides the geomythologists for their assumption that 'pristine' oral traditions can survive 'intact' or 'unscathed', 'that such traditions were learned and transmitted word-perfectly time and again',[27] but he then effectively adopts a notion of word-perfect transmission as the standard against which oral traditions are to be judged (and found wanting) as accurate historical sources. Henige treats his 'Ur-traditions' or 'original texts' as pristine, and their transmission over time as an entropic process of degeneration further compounded by the 'contaminating' influence or 'foreign pollution' of external contact.[28] Transmission, under these terms, is a history of 'wear and tear' of an original eyewitness testimony, from which what remains is rescued only through the initial act of documentation.[29]

His conception of the steady erosion of the original content as a consequence of multiple acts of communication from one individual to another in a 'direct line of transmission' ignores the work done by communities as a whole in sustaining memories of the past, even where the formal enunciation of narratives is reserved to particular individuals.[30] Henige's verdict on the accuracy of oral transmission and the value of oral traditions as historical sources is bleak: 'By transmission's end, the content can become so bowdlerized that such otherwise tell-tale signs as archaisms and anachronisms will have lost their analytical potency.'[31]

Neither geomythological enthusiasm nor historical scepticism supplies us with the means to understand and confidently integrate Indigenous oral traditions and geological or archaeological accounts of the past. Both approaches adopt a narrow understanding of oral traditions as texts, which more or less accurately record deep-time events and transmit these memories to the point of first documentation. Both approaches share an obsession with chronology and antiquity, as though oral traditions either stand or fall on their capacity to be mined for chronological correlates or, worse still, chronological depth. Both approaches depend heavily on appeals to 'plausibility' as the basis of method.[32] Missing from either approach are many of the broader contexts of social practice and cultural memory – the culturally specific historicities – within which particular narratives are embedded and from which they draw meaning. Before turning to the two case studies, which explore some of the ways in which these contexts might enrich our ability to use oral traditions in understanding and calibrating deep-time events, I briefly consider the particular properties of volcanic eruptions and ashfalls, and the ways in which they are recalled under the conditions of different cultural forms of historical consciousness.

Volcanic eruptions in oral tradition

In certain crucial respects, volcanic eruptions feature differently in oral traditions from most other natural hazards or cataclysms. Volcanoes are fixed features of landscapes but their eruptions vary considerably in frequency from constant activity to events that are unique within the period of human occupation. No two eruptive events are identical, even at the same site, and their effects can range from the local (lava and pyroclastic flows, volcanic gas, debris avalanches, etc.), through the regional (ashfalls, tsunamis, associated earthquakes), to the global (temporary changes in global climatic conditions). Importantly, substantial material traces of volcanic activity are registered in landscapes, archaeological deposits, tree rings, and cores (terrestrial, deep sea, and ice), both locally and, on occasion, globally.[33] These materials can often be dated, more or less precisely, and even tracked to source. The scope for correlation of oral traditions with this scientific evidence for eruptions is thus considerable, and the temptation to do so is correspondingly compelling.

Oral traditions tend to acknowledge eruptions as singular events, but range from accounts of direct experience at source to the more distant effects of ashfall or changes in climate, which are seldom linked in local understandings to volcanic activity.[34] Most eruption traditions feature certain elements in common: accounts of the impact on local communities, property, and landscapes; analogies and metaphors that make sense of the event within the context of local cosmologies and systems of belief; and an attribution of moral agency, whether to human or divine actors.[35] Transformation of the landscape is central to the transmission of these traditions, both because it serves as a mnemonic of the event and because subsequent claims to land often draw on memories of the event and its consequences. Volcanic events are also registered in the names of people and places, and tied to the survival or production of specific items of material culture, and in this way are not captured solely in the 'texts' of oral traditions.[36] Where traditions of eruption are consistently maintained, they are often linked to the idea of potential recurrence, and can thus contain injunctions about precursor signals as well as measures for mitigation, including details of house construction or morally appropriate behaviour.[37]

But the interpretation of volcanoes in oral traditions is not without problems, many of them familiar from Henige's broader critique of geomythology. The extreme stress of experiencing an eruption can produce striking inconsistencies even in eyewitness accounts, compounded by the struggle to generate meaning from the event and its consequences, including the assignment of cause or blame.[38] Interpreting and understanding a received eruption tradition presents another level of challenge, for two broad sets of reasons. The first addresses the question of identification, ensuring that an eruption or ashfall in a tradition can clearly and unambiguously be assigned to a specific volcanic source and a particular event of known date, and can be distinguished from other phenomena, such as earthquakes, landslides, eclipses, or dust veils.[39] The second revolves around the culturally specific form in which an account is transmitted, with the effects of an eruption or ashfall often understood by analogy and expressed through metaphor, requiring a grasp of the poetics particular to the language of communication, and a profound sense of cultural and environmental context.[40]

These challenges have not deterred attempts to identify volcanic activity in oral traditions from every habitable continent and to link these traditions to specific eruptions of known date.[41] Note that in many regions, such as East and Southeast Asia and Europe, long histories of documentation have tended to supersede and displace oral traditions of eruption that might otherwise have persisted. Only where Indigenous or local communities have remained more or less in situ and maintained oral traditions is there localised continuity of recall, as among Ayta communities of interior Luzon, Philippines, whose traditions of eruption at Mt Pinatubo were documented before the mountain was recognised by geologists as a volcano, and well prior to the major and unexpected eruption of 1991.[42]

In the Americas, key sites on which attention has focused include: the Mt Churchill volcano on the Upper White River, for which eruptions in 20 CE and 720 CE are said to feature in Athabascan accounts[43]; Mt Mazama or Crater Lake in Oregon, where Klamath traditions are linked to a known eruption dated to 5700 BCE;[44] and Sunset Crater in Arizona, where a sequence of activity ending in the mid-thirteenth century appears to be reflected in lengthy Hopi narratives.[45] Adolph Bandelier's precocious study of volcanoes in South American oral traditions, as these were related to Spanish writers in the sixteenth century, inspired a major review by W. Bruce Masse and Michael J. Masse, drawing on a collection of

4259 documented myths, matched against 203 volcanoes with known Holocene activity.[46] Masse and Masse also consider a variety of catastrophes, including flood, intense cold, and fire, but particular attention is paid to stories of sky fall or darkness (which the authors note may refer to hail, smoke, intense rain or tornado debris, in addition to volcanic ashfall). While some of these traditions credibly recall eruptions and ashfall, they are of indeterminate age and there are simply too many candidate volcanoes and eruptions, too few of which are adequately dated, to be certain of correspondence with particular traditions.

Australia is unusual in that the last significant volcanic activity, associated with the Newer Volcanics Province in Victoria, dates to more than 5,000 years before the present, though this falls well within the long period of 65,000 years or more of continuous occupation, often within the same locality, by Aboriginal people.[47] Within a context where claims are made for memories of sea level rise from over 7,000 years before the present, the idea that Aboriginal traditions have preserved the experience of mid-Holocene volcanic eruptions may not appear exceptional.[48] The oral traditions are inevitably fragmentary and many were documented a century or more before the present, but the possibility that some memory has been preserved of volcanic activity over such long periods of time is intriguing.[49]

Traditions of volcanic activity in the Pacific are usefully summarised by Katharine Cashman and Shane Cronin, with numerous claims made for the recall of eruptions and associated ashfall from at least as early as the seventeenth century and possibly earlier.[50] The near-constant low-level activity of volcanoes in Hawai'i has generated a large body of mythology and oral tradition that attributes the activity to the goddess Pele, but that also provides details, documented from as early as the 1820s, for specific eruptive and lava flow events, including a ca. 1800 CE eruption of Hualalai and the fifteenth-century eruption sequence at Kīlauea.[51] The role of volcanic eruptions and other forms of subterranean activity is similarly elaborate in Māori cosmology, with individual volcanic peaks associated with divinities (*atua*), and in particular with the lizard-like divinity Rūaumoko.[52] Most divinities are linked genealogically to living Māori populations, and all volcanic activity is thus situated within understandings of inter-generational reciprocity, and located within family histories.[53] Oral traditions describing specific volcanic eruptions and their effects are harder to distinguish. The major pre-European eruption in Aotearoa/New Zealand during the period of human occupation, that of Mt Tarawera in 1314 CE (± 12 years), produced the widely distributed Kaharoa tephra but has left no obvious imprint in oral tradition.[54] Likewise, any memory of the ca. 1400 CE eruption of Rangitoto Island has not survived in oral tradition.[55]

Oral traditions of eruptions from Tonga, Samoa, and Fiji share a number of elements that reflect their common cultural sphere of interaction, and are characterised by mythologies that attribute eruptions to conflict among divinities and attempts to steal volcanic peaks.[56] While certain place names imply a memory of volcanic activity, and it may be possible to link particular narrative details to geological processes of caldera formation or ashfall, there is no substantial corpus of living tradition presently available that would allow for a more confident attribution of specific stories to firmly dated events.[57] For example, what appear to be credible accounts of ashfall around Nabukelevu volcano in Kadavu, Fiji, may refer to one or more eruptions 'between 220–400 AD and 1630–1680 AD'.[58]

The Island Melanesian chain from the Bismarck Archipelago to Vanuatu is in large part a product of volcanic activity, which continues into the present. In a context of frequent eruption, the tendency is for oral traditions to focus on more recent events of the past few centuries. The communities of Savo, Solomon Islands, describe two distinct eruptive periods: the more recent one corresponding closely to an eruption during the 1830s–1840s, which was soon documented by the first Europeans to settle in the area, but the earlier event likely dating either to the eruption witnessed by Spanish explorer Mendaña in 1568 CE or to a possible subsequent event dated tentatively to 1630–1670 CE.[59] On Ambae Island, Vanuatu, which has a long but poorly described eruptive history, communities retain an intimate familiarity with both the signs of impending activity and transformation of the landscape by past events, extending back to at least the eighteenth century.[60] Lastly, the oral traditions of Tolai people of the Rabaul area in New Britain, Papua New Guinea, describe numerous eruptions from multiple named vents, along with associated tectonic events, and weave these into genealogies and claims to land.[61] The contested nature of Tolai land rights produces highly complex histories of overlapping claims, to which sequences of particular volcanic events, dated from volcanological evidence to as early as the 1790s, are recruited to establish precedence.

A number of general observations can be made on the basis of this brief review of the global literature on oral traditions and volcanic eruptions. In most cases, the available oral traditions – or at least those drawn upon – are highly fragmentary and potentially ambiguous, particularly when the sources consist solely or largely of early documentation. The most compelling cases draw instead on living traditions, which introduce the possibility of working with and between both documented and living sources, and with multiple versions. Attention to the ways in which these traditions are embedded within other forms of proof (as these are locally understood), and continue to be deployed in contemporary social process (such as genealogy or land disputes), produces a much richer understanding of the event itself and the nature of its transmission in oral tradition. Finally, those cases that bring to bear expertise in both volcanology and oral tradition tend to be more convincing, reflecting their ability to delimit credible candidate events, interpret local contexts for oral traditions, and express caution about claims in either domain. The two cases on which I now focus illustrate something of the potential for insight when most or all of these conditions are met.

'Everything was gone': the eruption of Kuwae

The volcanic destruction of the former island of Kuwae, in what are now the Shepherd Islands of central Vanuatu, has been dated at source by archaeologists and volcanologists to the middle of the fifteenth century.[62] All of the available evidence points to an eruption on a massive scale, which tore apart the island of Kuwae, leaving a large submarine crater between the remnant islands of Epi and Tongoa (Figure 26.1). Global lines of corroboration from ice cores, tree rings, and

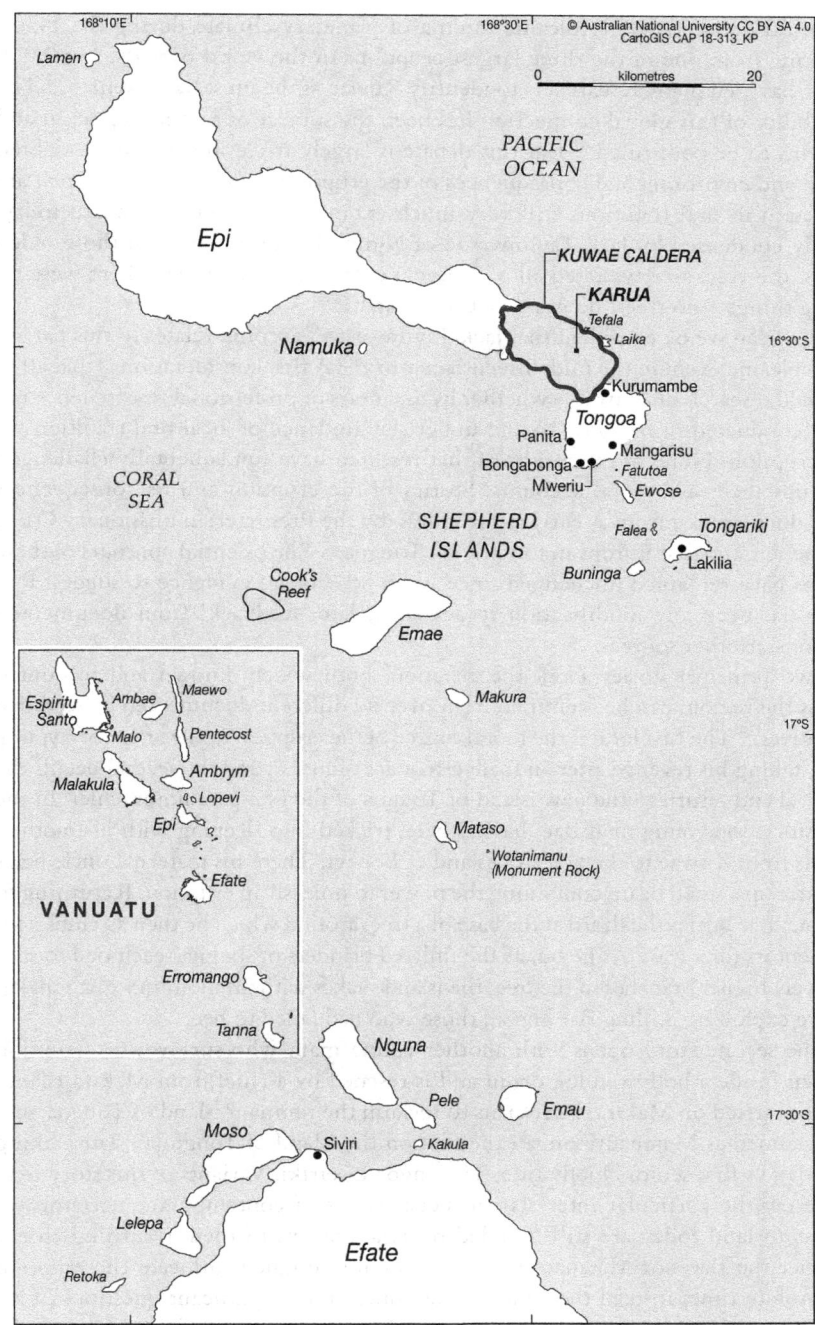

Figure 26.1 Location of the Kuwae Caldera, Central Vanuatu
Source: CartoGIS, ANU.

historical documents for volcanic forcing of planetary climate during the 1450s, resulting from one of the three largest eruptions in the world over the last 2,000 years, have led many researchers to identify Kuwae as the most likely source.[63] The possibility of this global connection has been the subject of recent scepticism and remains to be confirmed.[64] But this debate is largely irrelevant to the undoubted social and environmental consequences of the eruption on a local scale, which are addressed in oral traditions still very much extant across central Vanuatu today, starkly condensed by Jack Tavimwasoe of Nguna Island in 1967: 'In those olden times, the volcano devastated all of Tongoa; everything was gone. There were no living things – no trees, no grass, but only earth.'[65]

How can we be confident that Jack Tavimwasoe's account relates to this particular volcanic event in the mid-fifteenth century?[66] A first consideration is that all of the field research on Kuwae – whether by amateurs or professional researchers – has been conducted in response to and under the guidance of local oral traditions of the eruption. None of the results of that research have fundamentally challenged the substance of the oral accounts. Stories of the eruption and its consequences were documented from as early as the 1880s, by the Presbyterian missionary Oscar Michelsen, the first European to settle on Tongoa.[67] The essential contours of these stories have remained unchanged since, with little or no evidence to suggest that there has been any modification to accommodate 'feedback' from documented versions or other sources.

Two principal stories about the eruption, both widely known and recounted across the region, can be identified from over 50 different documented or recorded narratives.[68] The first locates the moral source of the eruption in the anger of a young man, taking his revenge after an inadvertent act of incest, and the second details the survival and return to the new island of Tongoa of the first paramount chief. In the first story, the young man Bae, having been tricked into sleeping with his mother, travels from Kuwae to the volcanic island of Lopevi. There his maternal uncle helps him to trap a small lizard containing the power to unleash an eruption. Returning to Kuwae, Bae buries the lizard at the base of a tree, around which he then assembles his tormentors for a feast. As he bursts the inflated bladders of six pigs, each tied to successively higher branches in the tree, the island shakes with premonitory earthquakes before exploding, killing Bae and all those who had failed to flee.

The second story opens with another young man, who survives the eruption hidden inside a hollowed log drum and is rescued by a chief from Makira Island. Once married on Makira, he returns to reclaim the remnant island of Tongoa, and is acclaimed as Matanauretonga ('the first on the island of Tong[o]a'), later taking the island's first senior chiefly title, Ti Tongoa Liseiriki. Variants of this story tend to betray the particular interests and perspectives of contemporary narrators, as claims to land today are still founded on relationships to these returning chiefs. Neither the Bae nor Matanauretonga stories are designed to locate the eruption in absolute time; instead they address the much more significant questions of attributing moral cause and identifying priority in claims to titles and land in the post-eruptive settlement of Tongoa – fixing the eruption and its consequences in social time.

There are various grounds for confidence that these two stories, along with many other less formal or less widespread accounts of Kuwae, relate to an event in the mid-fifteenth century. The stories are not contradicted in their broad outlines by other local narratives, and the event of the eruption is located within and confirmed by multiple chiefly histories that extend back to periods well prior to the eruption.[69] The stories accurately describe a massive event that separated the islands of Epi and Tongoa, a cataclysm not known to outsiders until it was essentially confirmed by volcanologists in the 1980s.[70] The stories also detail the staggered recolonisation of Tongoa after the eruption, first by survivors from the nearby Shepherd Islands to the less damaged southern portion of the island, and later from distant Efate to the northern side; this accounts for the curious linguistic division today in the culturally homogenous population, between southern villages on Tongoa speaking the Namakura language of the Shepherd Islands (possibly also the language spoken before on eastern Kuwae), and northern villages where the language is Nakanamanga, adopted from their temporary hosts in north Efate.[71] Crucially, there has been no other local eruption of significant magnitude during the roughly 3,000-year period of human occupation of central Vanuatu, eliminating the possibility of confusion with other events.[72]

These histories are also powerfully contextualised within the local landscape, which is saturated with mnemonics that call to mind the eruption. Chiefly, burials marked by headstones, including the graves of those who first returned to Tongoa, and sacred sites containing individual stone markers for each holder of a senior chiefly title, are some of the locally accepted forms of proof for the chiefly histories. The grave identified as that of Matanauretonga or Ti Tongoa Liseiriki, the first chief to return to Tongoa, was excavated by archaeologist José Garanger, working together with the contemporary holder of the title; their findings confirmed the details of oral traditions of the burial, which was dated to 1475+/−85 CE.[73] Seacliff exposures of the pre-eruptive landscape continue to yield fragments of human bone, pottery, and other artefacts, and early visitors to Tongoa were shown the different layers of this stratigraphic sequence, which were well understood locally and even named.[74] Perhaps most strikingly, the volcano regularly reminds Tongoans of its presence, both through the active fumaroles of Natorotoro, perched above the crater rim on the northwestern tip of Tongoa, and less frequently through the eruption of the submarine volcano of Karua and the occasional surfacing of an island cone above the waters between Tongoa and Epi.[75]

Just as important as these various forms of proof is the continuing significance of the Kuwae stories to daily life in Tongoa and the other Shepherd Islands, which serves to account for their ongoing transmission and universal recognition in Shepherd Islands communities. Writing of the history of the senior chiefly title of Purau village on Tongoa, ethnographer Susanna Kelly concludes that:

> The principle factor in this common history [of all the titles on Tongoa] is the resettlement of Tongoa approximately twenty generations ago, following the Kuwae explosion ... The chiefs' passage between the islands, the canoes they travelled in, the men accompanying them and the location they came ashore

on Tongoa, all structure the chiefly relationships on Tongoa in the present. The narratives also depict the original distribution of land on Tongoa and in addition frame explanations of land tenure on the island today.[76]

Few major disputes over land in Tongoa, such as those that touch on major boundaries between villages, fail to refer to the events of Kuwae and its aftermath, and specifically to the sequence of recolonisation of Tongoa by chiefs and other refugees returning from islands to the south.[77]

Attempts to generate an absolute date for the Kuwae eruption have been a project for outsiders, rather than for Shepherd Islanders, and confusions over chronology have been largely an artefact of this external will to chronologise. Outsider accounts of the oral traditions of Kuwae invariably attempt to estimate the antiquity of the eruption, based on the numbers of generations reported since the event. The earliest estimates, all made during the 1880s and 1890s, and most of them likely to have the missionary Michelsen as their intermediate source, ranged from 'upwards of eight generations'[78] to 'twelve generations ago'.[79] Michelsen himself produced a spread of estimates, even within the same document: 'about 350 years ago'; 'ten generations now past – or about 300 years'[80]; and, writing 40 years later, 'some four hundred years ago'.[81] Visiting Tongoa in 1960, administrator Bernard Hébert documented local estimates of 'fifteen generations' since the eruption, allowing him to calculate a date for the event of 1585, based on an average of 25 years for a 'generation'; more detailed interviews with three chiefs on the histories of their individual titles produced dates of 1634, 1653, and 1654.[82] Generational depths for Kuwae reported by geologists during the 1960s were even more divergent: '15 generations'[83] and 'nine generations'.[84] More recently, historian David Luders, working closely with individual chiefly families, has reconstructed four histories in rather more detail, including one that 'spanned 48 generations, of which 26 were said to precede the Kuwae explosion and 22 to follow it'.[85]

In the case of Tongoan oral history, generational depth may give a very broad impression of antiquity – these are not recent events, but neither are they at the outer limits for claims of distinctly human ancestral activity, which include names, voyaging itineraries, and involvement in wars well prior to the eruption. Quite evidently, Tongoan chiefly histories and genealogies cannot supply us independently with absolute dates, and even estimates based on average generational length need to be treated with a high degree of caution. Only senior chiefly genealogies extend back as far as Kuwae, and these are not strictly genealogies of paternity, but lists of holders of particular chiefly titles. While there is a preference for passing titles from fathers to eldest sons, the actual path of title succession is considerably more convoluted, as demonstrated in Chihiro Shirakawa's detailed case analysis of title transmission on Tongoa, in which accidents, intrigue, 'regencies', and the personal failings of title claimants feature regularly in a substantial proportion of chiefly histories.[86]

Quite simply, a concern for absolute dates is not a feature of Tongoan oral tradition, which focuses instead on questions of priority, sequence, and seniority among chiefs, and claims to record these matters with some accuracy for long periods of time. Who came first to this land? What was the sequence of landings on different islands? Who conducted the ceremony of investiture for a particular chiefly title? The eruption of Kuwae is the single most important event in any of these histories of sequence, and many of the larger land disputes on Tongoa today are attempts to resolve matters thrown into disarray by this event and its aftermath. An eruption on the scale of Kuwae, and without the confusion of multiple events, lends itself well to collaboration between oral history and the sciences of archaeology and volcanology, which can generate precise dates and measures of scale for the event, but for the wealth of content and context that might help us to resolve questions around the nature of Kuwae society and its response to the eruption, the process of recolonisation, or the current distribution of languages in the Shepherd Islands, we are dependent on local oral traditions.

'The time of darkness': oral traditions of the ashfall from Long Island

The second case study describes the effects of an eruption on Long Island, off the north coast of New Guinea, during the latter half of the seventeenth century. The ashfall from this eruption was experienced by a large number of different and widely separated language groups in the mainland interior of Papua New Guinea, most of which would have had no direct knowledge of volcanoes. Stories about a fall of sand from the sky, accompanied by a period of darkness across one or more full days, were first documented along the north coast of the Papua New Guinea mainland from the 1920s, and then in the highland interior from the early 1930s, as outsiders began to make contact with the large central valley populations. The oral historical enquiries of volcanologist Russell J. Blong have established the 'time of darkness' associated with the Long Island eruption as one of the best known and most widely cited instances of correlation between oral tradition and volcanic eruption – or perhaps any form of cataclysm.[87]

Blong's discovery and dating of the Long Island eruption developed in the context of the archaeological excavations led by Jack Golson of the Kuk Swamp early agricultural site in the highland interior, where traces of the Long Island ashfall were identified as 'Tibito Tephra'.[88] At Kuk and elsewhere in the highlands, Tibito is found as a distinctive layer of greyish olive green sandy tephra, and as the uppermost or youngest visible tephra across the region – with the exception of an anomalous find at a single location of a possibly younger tephra, Tibito is the only volcanic ash during the last 1,200 years over an area of more than 100,000 square kilometres.[89] Chemical characterisation, along with the correlation of dates for Tibito Tephra and the sequence of eruptions at Long Island, allowed Blong to propose a seventeenth-century eruption of Long Island as the source of Tibito – an eruption rather smaller than Kuwae, but still one of the ten largest of the past thousand years. Further work on dating has constrained the most likely age of the eruption to 1665–1668 CE, certainly pre-dating Dampier's observations in 1700 on the island and its distinctive modern – and thus post-eruptive – profile, and probably correlated with the global temperature anomalies of 1666–1667.[90]

Blong's own encounters in the New Guinea highlands with oral traditions of the 'time of darkness', which he associated with Tibito as the last known ashfall across the region, inspired him to conduct a sweeping survey, supplementing his interviews and review of the historical literature with a questionnaire sent to researchers, missionaries, and others working across the northern half of Papua New Guinea.[91] A substantial number of respondents to Blong's questionnaire noted that they had not heard these stories until prompted to enquire about them, despite often long periods of residence in particular communities. Although, as with the Kuwae stories on Tongoa, the time of darkness stories in Papua New Guinea described a unique event, the latter were seldom implicated in daily life and only rarely retold.

Blong's survey yielded reports from over 40 locations in 26 different language groups, closely matching the distribution of the Long Island tephra (Figure 26.2).[92] Not surprisingly, the almost uniform term used to refer to this event across the different language groups is the 'time of darkness'. But, while the reports of the physical character and effects of the ashfall are recognisably similar, the manner in which they are positioned in local histories of migration or cosmologies argues strongly for their status as historical memories of an event experienced at multiple locations, rather than a single narrative diffused over a wide region and locally modified. Stories of the time of darkness had been documented first in many societies of this interior region in the 1930s, often by the earliest visitors, including mining prospectors, colonial administrators, and missionaries – 'this legend occurs all over New Guinea', claimed mission authors Georg Vicedom and Herbert Tischner by the 1940s.[93] Further confirmation came during the 1950s and 1960s as the first generation of researchers fanned out across interior Papua New Guinea, some of whom assigned the event to just a few generations earlier, or the 1880s, and

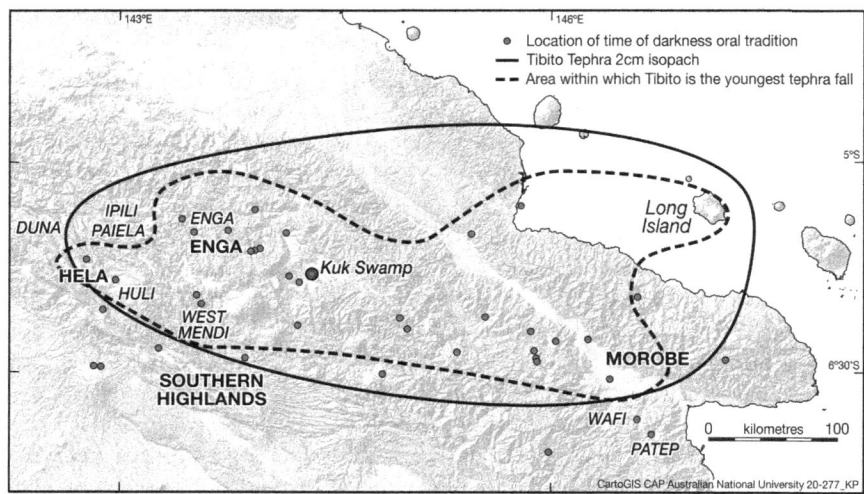

Figure 26.2 Distribution of Tibito Tephra and Oral Traditions of the Time of Darkness
Source: CartoGIS, ANU, after Blong, and Kurbatov, 'Steps and Missteps'

speculated that it might be 'Krakatoa's echo'.[94] None of those documenting these traditions detected any hint of feedback from Biblical or other recently introduced traditions, with some noting that the stories were explicitly rejected as pagan heritage by recent converts.[95]

Some of Blong's cases clearly referred either to hail storms at higher altitudes or more recent eclipses, but the vast majority shared enough elements to be considered as referring to the same event: one or more days of total darkness, sand falling from the sky, covering and sometimes damaging houses and gardens, and then often a bloom of soil fertility and plant growth in the ensuing months. Many highland communities know of and can still find thin layers of this sand in the walls of their ditches, and of five samples picked out in this way and collected by Blong, four were clearly (and the fifth likely) assigned to Tibito Tephra.[96]

Blong's attempts to make sense of this diversity of traditions struggled with sources of highly variable quality and detail, often documented by interviewers with long histories of residence among particular communities, but not necessarily experienced at eliciting oral histories. He found 'few meaningful spatial patterns' in terms of details such as the duration of darkness, size of sand particles or accompanying physical effects, and any correlation among these details was rendered largely meaningless in the absence of adequate cultural contextualisation for the questionnaire responses.[97] In part, this indicates the complexity of working with multiple sources and perspectives on an event, rather than the certainty of a single authoritative and uncontested fragment.[98] Nevertheless, Blong found that:

> ... the legends, viewed as a whole, provide a largely accurate version of the likely effects of a fall of up to 100 mm of ash. While the duration of the darkness or the thickness of the ashfall is commonly exaggerated, and the length of time elapsed since the tephra fall occurred is seriously underestimated, most details are plausible, indeed likely.[99]

Additional traditions of a time of darkness have been recorded since Blong's survey, which was completed in 1979, principally from two areas: the first lies at the eastern end of Blong's range, in Morobe Province, and the second at the south-western end, in Enga, Hela, and Southern Highlands provinces. In both areas, the additional materials confirm and expand on Blong's findings. In Morobe Province a series of stories have been documented that conform with each other in describing an earthquake, followed by days turned dark by sand falling from the sky, before the light returned from the east; these stories come from Patep and six separate communities in the Wafi area.[100] While ancestors alive at the time of this ashfall are often identified by name, the genealogies that link them to living individuals appear highly truncated, with crude estimates based on an average generational length of 25 years placing the event in the first half of the nineteenth century. More significant and perhaps more accurate are the settlement 'genealogies' or sequence histories that are traced back to (and often beyond) the settlement at which ancestors were living when the ash fell. Stories about the ashfall in this region are thus retold not in their own right but as notable events tied to particular locales in histories of ancestral migration, as in this extract from a lengthy migration history:

> While they were at Elmun, sand [Tok Pisin: *waitsan*] fell from the sky. At this time, Nguagov and his father [also called] Nguagov were alive, as were Mumpie, Hengemun, Kapiembanga, Mungilin and Kavindatuk. The sky went dark, the clouds thundered and sand fell from the sky.[101]

The additional material from Enga, Hela, and Southern Highland provinces is intriguing, as these are among the most distant and most westerly locations from Long Island to have experienced the ashfall, and yet they have the most elaborate traditions of the original event, as well as the strongest belief in the need to prepare for its possible recurrence. Blong had already noted the detail in traditions from the region, but we can now say much more about the way that these stories were embedded in local historicities and cosmologies, which must already have been present in something approaching their modern form at the time of the ashfall.[102] More detailed accounts of time of darkness traditions have been described since Blong's collection for most of the language groups of this region, including the Duna,[103] Paiela,[104] Ipili,[105] Enga,[106] West Mendi,[107] and Huli (see below). The cosmologies of each of these groups invoke the spectre of an end-time modelled on, or perhaps modified by, the historical experience of the Long Island ashfall, and their oral traditions of the original event thus encode practices to ensure survival or even active management of a future event.[108]

Positioned at the centre of this region are Huli speakers of the Tari Basin and adjacent valleys, and their oral traditions about the time of darkness are probably the most elaborate and the most deeply embedded in local cosmology.[109] Huli knowledge of what they refer to as *mbingi* (*mbi* darkness + *angi* time) was communicated as a category of formal knowledge or *mana*, and thus a code for future conduct, rather than a tale (*bi te*), a clan genealogy (*malu*), or even a historical narrative (*tene te*) about the origins of an event or social connection.[110] This knowledge was held by designated and widely identified 'holders of the knowledge of *mbingi*' (*mbingi manayi*), a role conventionally transmitted from eldest child to eldest child, often but not exclusively hereditary clan leaders. The narratives recorded by individual knowledge-holders betray occasional differences in detail, but vary little in the broad substance of their message. There is also little variance over time since their first documentation in 1953 by an administration officer, shortly after the establishment of the first government post in the area in 1952.[111]

In Huli oral traditions, clouds gather on the northern and eastern horizons and, before long, the sky darkens to pitch black and then breaks, falling as sand (*mu*), soil (*dindi*), or sky stuff (*da pindu*) that covers gardens and blocks rivers, but slides off the sloping roofs of houses.[112] On the first day of darkness, singletons are the only people allowed to venture out of the houses in search of food, on the second day those with just one sibling can go out, and so on with successively larger sibling sets emerging for as long as the darkness persists. While potentially dangerous during the period of darkness, the broken sky reintroduces fertility to the land and people, and humans, pigs, and crops all experience exceptional growth.

Huli continue to understand *mbingi* as a historical event or series of events, extending from the past into the future, with the archetypal occurrence being the fall of sandy soil from the sky. Ancestors in genealogies and specific features of the landscape such as individual trees are identified as having been present at the time of *mbingi*. The thin gritty layer of olive green sand (*mbi mu*, or darkness sand) is picked out by Huli in the walls of their ditches, and was formerly extracted and used to remove facial hair.[113]

The most striking feature of Huli traditions of *mbingi* is their insistence on its inevitable recurrence. While the original or archetypal event is invariably identified with the ashfall, *mbingi* is understood as the consequence of cosmic imbalance, and any global perturbation, whether manifest as earthquake, flood, eclipse, or mudflow can be set within the frame of *mbingi*.[114] A logic of entropy pervades Huli cosmology, according to which all things – people and their behaviour, the land and its fertility, crops and domestic animals – decline inexorably over time. Elements of this deep-seated logic are likely to have been in place prior to the Long Island ashfall but, allied to fear about the event itself and subsequent observations on the flush of soil fertility after the eruption, *mbingi* has become incorporated within an epochal historicity. As such, the knowledge of *mbingi* is oriented as much to the future as it is to the past: 'The myth of *mbingi* is more than an account of its last occurrence. It also comprises the lore to guide people in their preparations for and survival from the next *mbingi*.'[115] Any portents interpreted as signs of an impending recurrence of *mbingi* are the subject of discussion about appropriate responses, and as recently as the 1990s, fears about the disturbance to the land of gold-mining operations led people to build distinctive *mbingi* houses, raised on stilts (to protect from flood) and with hardwood rafters (to ward off the fall of sand).[116]

Despite the remarkable focus on maintaining memories of the event among groups such as the Huli and their neighbours, attempts to reconcile scientific dates with estimates based on the oral traditions and local genealogies have been notably unsuccessful. Blong has written at length on the lack of consilience between dates for the Long Island ashfall derived from genealogical estimates on the one hand and scientific methods on the other.[117] Almost all of the estimates based on oral traditions and genealogies fall during the nineteenth century, and yet we know that there was no significant volcanic eruption and ashfall anywhere in this region during this period.[118] If we are certain that the majority of these stories refer to the Long Island eruption of 1665–1668 CE, then the evidence for an almost universal telescoping of genealogies is a salutary reminder of the limitations of dating based solely on oral tradition.

How are we to account for this lack of consilience in chronologies for the Long Island ashfall? The simple answer is that most oral traditions are neither formulated nor transmitted to communicate a sense of absolute chronology, in communities for which such a scale holds little value or meaning. Interviews that set out to determine an absolute date for an event such as the Long Island ashfall thus confront the narrators of oral traditions with an impossible challenge. Discussions with Huli holders of *mbingi* knowledge have provided genealogical depths for the time of darkness ranging from 11 generations before the present, to more detailed reconstructions of precise family genealogies for four different individuals said to have been alive during *mbingi*, which generated estimates for the event ranging between 1770 and 1853 CE.[119] As Polly Wiessner and Akii Tumu noted of their attempts to integrate accounts of the time of darkness within their very fine reconstructions of Enga clan histories, by asking directly about genealogical depth,

> We received similar answers upon first questioning, but when we asked whether it occurred around the same time as better-known events in these generations – major wars or migrations – informants immediately retracted their statements and said that it had occurred much earlier, sometime in the founding generations.[120]

Oral historian Rod Lacey has also discussed the difficulty of reconciling Enga genealogies with a scientific chronology for the Long Island eruption, and writes of 'floating genealogical blocks' that linked segmentary groups across multiple scales without necessarily retaining all the individual ancestors between those blocks.[121] Clearly, oral traditions of the time of darkness in Papua New Guinea place emphasis on questions of sequence and priority, rather than absolute chronology.

This insight helps us to understand why certain events in the deep past are communicated in such detail, and remain so salient for particular communities. In the case of both the Shepherd Islanders of Vanuatu and the Huli of Papua New Guinea we find communities in which precedence, or the prestige of priority, continues to play a particularly important role in contemporary life and in the resolution of disputes. The eruption of Kuwae and the ashfall from Long Island provide the temporal hooks around which communal histories are organised and sequences calibrated. When Henige asks, 'What gives us reason to expect the past to be so important in oral societies that remembering it accurately would consume so disproportionate a share of the available intellectual capital?' the answer is that these pasts still determine the distribution today of land and resources, the essential bases for successful social and cultural reproduction.[122] What could be more important?

Content, chronology, and context

So how might Indigenous oral traditions be engaged in tackling questions of chronology and temporal depth? Henige's central charge, which is that most claims for the recall of deep-time events in what he calls 'oral societies' do not lend themselves to rigorous testing, deserves to be heard and addressed.[123] But the real problem with his critique is that he uses the limitations of vernacular chronologies (viewed from a scientific perspective) to discredit the content of oral traditions more broadly. As the two case studies of Kuwae and the time of darkness demonstrate, there is enormous value and potential for the historical disciplines – including archaeology, linguistics, and genetics – in closer and more careful consideration of the content of oral traditions.[124] The principal challenge for this approach to

Indigenous pasts lies in generating more rigorous methodologies for the integration of these widely disparate lines of evidence that respect their very different strengths and limitations.

That oral traditions are capable of providing a wealth of content about events in the deep past – certainly deeper than the limits of 150 years or even 300 years proposed by Henige and other sceptical historians – appears undeniable. Our knowledge of the physical form of the cataclysms of the Kuwae eruption and the time of darkness ashfall is considerably enhanced by the oral traditions available for both events, but more significant still is the opening that these traditions provide to an understanding of the social and cultural consequences of these cataclysms. Oral traditions both encode and structure social relations and priority, temporal sequence and process. Whether these traditions are accurate or not in their recall of the original events, they have been accepted by their narrators and acted upon as historical truth, influencing or structuring subsequent concrete action, such as land disputes and regional rituals. Oral traditions both become and beget historical fact, and need to be understood in their own right and on their own terms.

What oral traditions cannot do, independent of other lines of evidence, is provide absolute chronologies for the events they describe. Yet, oral traditions can and do provide a sense of series or sequence at a much finer grain than any scientific reconstruction. The processes of flight from Kuwae during the eruption, the sequence of the linguistic recolonisation of Tongoa, or the impact of the Long Island ashfall on Huli ritual elaboration are all detailed in oral traditions to a degree that is simply inaccessible through documentary or archaeological methods alone. The articulation in hybrid histories of scientific dates and oral tradition is enormously productive, on both sides. Oral traditions that relate to the Kuwae and Long Island eruptions establish and confirm processes of continuous oral transmission of approximately 570 and 360 years, respectively. In combination, Tibito Tephra and the time of darkness stories provide 'a chronological marker across a very large area and the only one that predates the arrival of Europeans in the region'.[125] Likewise, the Kuwae eruption emerges as a temporal hinge or horizon that articulates narratives and reconstructions of historical process on local, regional, and possibly global scales.

Mason's proposition that the 'after-the-fact demonstration of oral tradition's reliability in particular instances is not an argument for its a priori acceptance in others' may be true, but so too is its obverse, which is that the more dubious instances of recruitment of oral traditions by certain geomythologists to make claims about absolute dates need not invalidate the historical value of all oral traditions.[126] A focus on the first instance of a tradition's transcription – 'transmission's end' – as a watershed moment in its historical reliability is misplaced, as richer and more nuanced variants of oral traditions such as Kuwae have been recorded more than a century after their initial documentation.[127] These are, in many cases, living traditions, and contemporary descendant communities often have much more to say and to add in terms of context to the narrow 'text' of a tradition. There is no pure, original or uncontaminated expression of an oral tradition, no pristine moment captured in its 'text'. As with all other forms of history, oral traditions are always hybrid constructions, drawing on and incorporating observations and elements from different eyewitnesses, different historical moments, different narrative genres, and even different communities.

There is no end in sight for the transmission of either Kuwae or time of darkness narratives. If anything, there is much more still to be done to re-contextualise traditions now received as texts, re-positioning them within the broader sweep and practice of local historicities, and appreciating them as examples of particular vernacular genres with their own histories of positionality and contestation, and their own codes of truth.[128] At the core of this process or method is a focus on understanding transmission: the relationship between individual and communal or collective memory; the precise modes and lines of communication; the multiple and intersecting genres of utterance; their embeddedness within broader forms of knowledge and practice; and the ways in which transmission interweaves and binds together human communities and their material and immaterial landscapes.

Acknowledgements

This chapter draws on research conducted for the 'Kuwae 1452 AD' project, which is supported by the Australian Government through the Australian Research Council's Discovery Projects funding scheme (project DP200102320). I am grateful to Russell Blong for sharing his ideas and materials, and to Stuart Bedford, Dario Di Rosa, Laura Rademaker, and the editors for their suggestions for improvements to the text. Karina Pelling of the ANU's CartoGIS unit kindly produced both figures.

Notes

1 David Henige, 'Impossible to Disprove Yet Impossible to Believe: The Unforgiving Epistemology of Deep-Time Oral Tradition,' *History in Africa* 36 (2009): 127–234; Ronald J. Mason, *Inconstant Companions: Archaeology and North American Indian Oral Traditions* (Tuscaloosa: University of Alabama Press, 2006).

2 Charles Stewart, 'Historicity and Anthropology,' *Annual Review of Anthropology* 45 (2016): 79–94; Chris Ballard, 'Oceanic Historicities,' *The Contemporary Pacific* 26 no. 1 (2014): 96–124.

3 Dorothy B. Vitaliano, *Legends of the Earth: Their Geologic Origins* (Bloomington: Indiana University Press, 1973); see also Vitaliano, 'Geomythology: Geological Origins of Myths and Legends,' in *Myth and Geology*, eds. Luigi Piccardi and W. Bruce Masse (Geological Society of London Special Publications 273, no. 1; London: Geological Society, 2007), 1–7.

4 Adrienne Mayor, 'Geomythology,' in *Encyclopedia of Geology*, eds. Richard C. Selley, L. Robin M. Cocks, and Ian R. Plimer (Oxford: Elsevier, 2005), 96.

5 The most substantial collection of geomythological studies is Luigi Piccardi and W. Bruce Masse, eds., *Myth and Geology* (Geological Society of London Special Publications 273, no. 1; London: Geological Society, 2007).

6 Patrick Nunn and Nicholas Reid, 'Aboriginal Memories of Inundation of the Australian Coast Dating from More than 7000 Years Ago,' *Australian Geographer* 47, no. 1 (2016): 11–47; Patrick Nunn, *The Edge of Memory: Ancient Stories, Oral Tradition*

and the Post-Glacial World (London: Bloomsbury Sigma, 2018); Patrick Nunn, Loredana Lancini, Leigh Franks, Rita Compatangelo-Soussignan, and Adrian McCallum, 'Maar Stories: How Oral Traditions Aid Understanding of Maar Volcanism and Associated Phenomena during Preliterate Times,' *Annals of the American Association of Geographers* 109, no. 5 (2019): 1618–1631.
7. Nunn, *The Edge of Memory*.
8. Henige, 'Impossible to Disprove'; Michel R. Doortmont, 'Making History in Africa: David Henige and the Quest for Method in African History,' *History in Africa* 38 (2011): 7–20.
9. Henige, 'Impossible to Disprove,' 207. For earlier statements of his broader position on oral tradition see Henige, *The Chronology of Oral Tradition: Quest for a Chimera* (Oxford: Clarendon Press, 1974); Henige, '"Day Was of Sudden Turned into Night"': On the Use of Eclipses for Dating Oral History,' *Comparative Studies in Society and History* 18, no. 4 (1976): 476–501; Henige, *Historical Evidence and Argument* (Madison: University of Wisconsin Press, 2005).
10. Henige, 'Impossible to Disprove,' 223.
11. Henige, 'Impossible to Disprove,' 132.
12. D. Wayne Moodie, A.J.W. Catchpole, and Kerry Abel, 'Northern Athapaskan Oral Traditions and the White River Volcano,' *Ethnohistory* 39, no. 2 (1992): 148–171; Henige, 'Impossible to Disprove,' 218.
13. Henige, 'Impossible to Disprove,' 129.
14. At times, Henige can be read as implying, with an enthusiasm equal to that of the geomythologists, that almost all oral traditions of floods are somehow derivative of contact with the Christian Bible (Henige, 'Impossible to Disprove,' 161–162, 172, 209–210, 217); a Klamath flood myth thus 'reeks of biblical feedback' (Henige, 'Impossible to Disprove,' 167).
15. Henige, 'Impossible to Disprove,' 138.
16. Henige, 'Impossible to Disprove,' 182.
17. Henige, 'Impossible to Disprove,' 187.
18. Elizabeth Weyland Barber and Paul T. Barber, *When They Severed Earth from Sky: How the Human Mind Shapes Myth* (Princeton, NJ: Princeton University Press, 2004), 3, 9; Andrew R.C. Martindale and Susan Marsden, 'Defining the Middle Period (3500 BP to 1500 BP) in Tsimshian History through a Comparison of Archaeological and Oral Records,' *BC Studies* 138–139 (2003): 17; both sources are singled out for attention by Henige ('Impossible to Disprove,' 192, 193).
19. Henige, 'Impossible to Disprove,' 201.
20. Nunn, *The Edge of Memory*; Henige, 'Impossible to Disprove,' 232. A similar estimate has been proposed by A. Irving Hallowell, writing in 1937: 'One hundred and fifty years is the outside limit of any genuine historic past' (Mason, *Inconstant Companions*, 120).
21. Henige, 'Impossible to Disprove,' 133. Henige is at pains to ensure that his critique is not construed as a blanket dismissal of deep-time memories: 'Some of the instances mentioned here – and particularly that of Mt Mazama – remain provocative and intriguing' (Henige, 'Impossible to Disprove,' 230).
22. Nunn, *The Edge of Memory*, 51.
23. Henige, 'Impossible to Disprove,' 153, emphasis in original.
24. Henige, 'Impossible to Disprove,' 148.
25. Ballard, 'Oceanic Historicities.'
26. Henige's fellow sceptic, Mason, is alert to these contexts: 'The "text" is only partly the medium. In translating orality to literacy, that compound component of seeing, hearing, feeling, and participating in a social event is inescapably forfeited' (*Inconstant Companions*, 100).
27. Henige, *Historical Evidence*, 85; on 'intactness', see Henige, 'Impossible to Disprove,' 128, footnote 7.

28 Henige, 'Impossible to Disprove,' 175, 231; the metaphor of pollution is drawn approvingly from Rhys Richards.
29 Henige, 'Impossible to Disprove,' 147–148, 172, 174. In its most succinct form, this theory of content degeneration is expressed as 'transmission = use = change' (Henige, 'Survival of the Fittest? Darwinian Evolution and the Transmission of Information,' *History in Africa* 30 (2003): 174). Mason argues along similar lines: 'The longer a story's preliterate genealogy, the greater the inherent likelihood of mutations great and small and with them the degeneration of whatever historical fidelity may once have existed' (*Inconstant Companions*, 89).
30 Henige, 'Impossible to Disprove,' 198. Space precludes a more substantial discussion of the relationship between individual and communal transmission, but even the most specialised of history-keeping roles depends upon both communal memory and communal acknowledgement of accuracy; see Henige, 'Impossible to Disprove,' 151, footnote 87.
31 Henige, 'Impossible to Disprove,' 155. One of the reviewers of his published doctoral dissertation comments that 'we might reasonably have expected rather more discussion of the extent to which "oral tradition" can in fact be proved a reliable guide to chronology' (A.D. Roberts, 'Review of David P. Henige, *The Chronology of Oral Tradition*,' *Bulletin of the School of Oriental and African Studies* 38, no. 3 (1995): 693).
32 Henige advocates the application of 'overall plausibility' as a reasonable strategy, with historians presumably positioned as arbiters of the plausible ('Impossible to Disprove,' 155); see also Henige, 'The Implausibility of Plausibility/The Plausibility of Implausibility,' *Historical Reflections/Réflexions Historiques* 30, no. 2 (2004): 311–335. Nunn is similarly reliant on appeals to plausibility (*The Edge of Memory*, 71, 73, 130, 141).
33 Felix Riede, 'Doing Palaeo-Social Volcanology: Developing a Framework for Systematically Investigating the Impacts of Past Volcanic Eruptions on Human Societies using Archaeological Datasets,' *Quaternary International* 499 (2019): 266–277.
34 Barber and Barber, *When They Severed Earth*, 88; Gordon C. Jacoby, Karen W. Workman, and Rosanne D. D'Arrigo, 'Laki Eruption of 1783, Tree Rings, and Disaster for Northwest Alaska Inuit,' *Quaternary Science Reviews* 18 (1999): 1365–1371.
35 Katharine V. Cashman and Shane J. Cronin, 'Welcoming a Monster to the World: Myths, Oral Tradition, and Modern Societal Response to Volcanic Disasters,' *Journal of Volcanology and Geothermal Research* 176 (2008): 417.
36 Shane J. Cronin and Katharine V. Cashman, 'Volcanic Oral Traditions in Hazard Assessment and Mitigation,' in *Living under the Shadow: Cultural Impacts of Volcanic Eruptions*, eds. John Grattan and Robin Torrence (Walnut Creek: Left Coast Press, 2007), 196.
37 Cronin and Cashman, 'Volcanic Oral Traditions,' 180.
38 Cashman and Cronin, 'Welcoming a Monster,' 410; Cronin and Cashman identify a further ten forms of potential modification of the primary experience of an eruption in the process of its communication, Cronin and Cashman, 'Volcanic Oral Traditions,' 177.
39 Ronald W. Davis, 'Volcanic Dust in the Atmosphere and the Interpretation of African Eclipse Traditions,' *History in Africa* 4 (1977): 40.
40 Cashman and Cronin, 'Welcoming a Monster,' 417.
41 Vitaliano lists many of the classic cases of oral traditions of eruption that continue to be cited: from Hawai'i and Aotearoa/New Zealand, Iceland, the Cascadia region of the northwestern United States, Japan, Java in Indonesia, the Democratic Republic of the Congo (Zaire), Greece, and Italy (*Legends of the Earth*, chapter 6).
42 Jean-Christophe Gaillard et al., 'Planning for the Future: A Multidisciplinary Approach to Reconstructing the Buag Episode of Mt Pinatubo Philippines,' in *Living under the Shadow: Cultural Impacts of Volcanic Eruptions*, eds. John Grattan and Robin Torrence (Walnut Creek: Left Coast Press, 2007), 225–252; Kelvin S. Rodolfo and Jess V. Umbal, 'A Prehistoric Lahar-Dammed Lake and Eruption of Mount Pinatubo

Described in a Philippine Aborigine Legend,' *Journal of Volcanology and Geothermal Research* 176 (2008): 432–437.
43 Moodie, Catchpole, and Abel, 'Northern Athapaskan Oral Traditions'; Phyllis A. Fast, 'The Volcano in Athabascan Oral Narratives,' *Alaska Journal of Anthropology* 6, no. 1 & 2 (2008): 131–139.
44 Rick Budhwa, 'Correlations between Catastrophic Paleoenvironmental Events and Native Oral Traditions of the Pacific Northwest,' MA diss., Department of Archaeology, Simon Fraser University, 2002.
45 Ekkehart Malotki with Michael Lomatuway'ma, *Earth Fire: A Hopi Legend of the Sunset Crater Eruption* (Flagstaff: Northland Press, 1987).
46 Adolph F. Bandelier, 'Traditions of Precolumbian Earthquakes and Volcanic Eruptions in Western South America,' *American Anthropologist* 8, no. 1 (1906): 47–81; W. Bruce Masse and Michael J. Masse, 'Myth and Catastrophic Reality: Using Myth to Identify Cosmic Impacts and Massive Plinian Eruptions in Holocene South America,' in *Myth and Geology*, eds. Piccardi and Masse, 177–202.
47 Jozua Van Otterloo, Raymond A.F. Cas, and Malcolm J. Sheard, 'Eruption Processes and Deposit Characteristics at the Monogenetic Mt Gambier Volcanic Complex, SE Australia: Implications for Alternating Magmatic and Phreatomagmatic Activity,' *Bulletin of Volcanology* 75, no. 8 (2013): 737.
48 Nunn and Reid, 'Aboriginal Memories of Inundation'; Nunn, *The Edge of Memory*; Amy L. Roberts, Adrian Mollenmans, Lester-Irabinna Rigney, and Geoff Bailey, 'Marine Transgression, Aboriginal Narratives and the Creation of Yorke Peninsula/Guuranda, South Australia,' *The Journal of Island and Coastal Archaeology* 15, no. 3 (2020): 305–332.
49 Nunn, *The Edge of Memory*, 169; Nunn et al., 'Maar Stories.'
50 Cronin and Cashman, 'Volcanic Oral Traditions.'
51 Cronin and Cashman, 'Volcanic Oral Traditions,' 192; Donald A. Swanson, 'Hawaiian Oral Tradition Describes 400 Years of Volcanic Activity at Kilauea,' *Journal of Volcanology and Geothermal Research* 176 (2008): 427–431.
52 Elsdon Best, 'The Polynesian Method of Generating Fire: With Some Account of the Mythical Origin of Fire, and of its Employment in Ritual Ceremonies as Observed among the Maori Folk of New Zealand,' *Journal of the Polynesian Society* 33, no. 2 (1924): 95.
53 Cashman and Cronin, 'Welcoming a Monster,' 415; H. Gabrielsen et al., 'Reflections from an Indigenous Community on Volcanic Event Management, Communications and Resilience,' *Advances in Volcanology* 2018 (2018): 463–479.
54 D.J. Lowe, R.M. Newnham and J.D. McCraw, 'Volcanism and Early Maori Society in New Zealand,' in *Natural Disasters and Cultural Change*, eds. Robin Torrence and John Grattan (London and New York: Routledge, 2002), 126–161; David J. Lowe and Adrian Pittari, 'An Ashy Septingentenarian: The Kaharoa Tephra Turns 700 (with Notes on its Volcanological, Archaeological, and Historical Importance),' *Geoscience Society of New Zealand Newsletter* 13 (2014): 35–46.
55 Lowe, Newnham and McCraw, 'Volcanism and Early Maori Society,' 150.
56 Paul W. Taylor, 'Myths, Legends and Volcanic Activity: An Example from Northern Tonga,' *Journal of the Polynesian Society* 104, no. 3 (1995): 327–329; Károly Németh and Shane J. Cronin, 'Volcanic Structures and Oral Traditions of Volcanism of Western Samoa (SW Pacific) and Their Implications for Hazard Education,' *Journal of Volcanology and Geothermal Research* 186 (2009): 223–237.
57 S.J. Cronin and V.E. Neall, 'Impacts of Volcanism on Pre-European Inhabitants of Taveuni, Fiji,' *Bulletin of Volcanology* 62 (2000): 199–213.
58 Shane J. Cronin, Marie A. Ferland, and James P. Terry, 'Nabukelevu Volcano (Mt Washington), Kadavu: A Source of Hitherto Unknown Volcanic Hazard in Fiji,' *Journal of Volcanology and Geothermal Research* 13, no. 3–4 (2004): 371–396.

59 M.G. Petterson et al., 'The Eruptive History and Volcanic Hazards of Savo, Solomon Islands,' *Bulletin of Volcanology* 65 (2003): 165–181.
60 Shane J. Cronin et al., 'Participatory Methods of Incorporating Scientific with Traditional Knowledge for Volcanic Hazard Management on Ambae Island, Vanuatu,' *Bulletin of Volcanology* 66, no. 7 (2004): 659.
61 R. Wally Johnson, *Fire Mountains of the Islands* (Canberra: ANU Press, 2013); Peter Sack, 'The Emergence and Settlement of Matupit Island: Vulcanological Evidence, Oral Tradition and "Objective" History in Papua New Guinea,' *Bikmaus* 7, no. 1 (1987): 1–14.
62 José Garanger, *Archéologie des Nouvelles-Hébrides: Contribution à la connaissance des îles du Centre* (Paris: ORSTOM, 1972); Claude Robin, Michel Monzier, and Jean-Philippe Eissen, 'Eruption of the Mid-Fifteenth Century Kuwae Caldera (Vanuatu) by an Initial Hydroclastic and Subsequent Ignimbritic Eruption,' *Bulletin of Volcanology* 56 (1994): 170–183.
63 Chaochao Gao et al., 'The 1452 or 1453 A.D. Kuwae Eruption Signal Derived from Multiple Ice Core Records: Greatest Volcanic Sulphate Event of the Past 700 Years,' *Journal of Geophysical Research* 111 (2006): D12107; C.T. Plummer et al., 'An Independently Dated 2000-yr Record from Law Dome, East Antarctica, Including a New Perspective on the Dating of the 1450s CE Eruption of Kuwae, Vanuatu,' *Climate of the Past* 8 (2012): 1929–1940.
64 Matthew Toohey and Michael Sigl, 'Volcanic Stratospheric Sulfur Injections and Aerosol Optical Depth from 500 BCE to 1900 CE,' *Earth System Science Data* 9 no. 2 (2017): 809–831; Zaria Gorvett, 'The Massive Volcano that Scientists Can't Find,' *BBC*, 3 July 2017. http://www.bbc.com/future/story/20170630-the-massive-volcano-that-scientists-cant-find.
65 Albert J. Schütz, *Nguna Texts: A Collection of Traditional and Modern Narratives from the Central New Hebrides* (Honolulu: University of Hawai'i Press, 1969), 194.
66 Kuwae is singled out by Henige as another instance of dubious chronologising, but his key source on local oral traditions is a brief field report by a student archaeologist working on Epi Island, the western remnant of Kuwae (Henige, 'Impossible to Disprove,' 221); Andrew Hoffman, 'Looking to Epi: Further Consequences of the Kuwae Eruption, Central Vanuatu, AD 1452,' *Bulletin of the Indo-Pacific Prehistory Association* 26 (2007): 62–71. While Henige refers to some early amateur work on genealogical reckoning, he appears unaware of almost 70 years of subsequent work by professional anthropologists, linguists, and archaeologists and volcanologists (summarised in Chris Ballard, 'The Lizard in the Volcano: Narratives of the Kuwae Eruption,' *The Contemporary Pacific* 32, no. 1 (2020): 98–123.
67 Oscar Michelsen, *Cannibals Won for Christ: A Story of Missionary Perils and Triumphs in Tongoa, New Hebrides* (London: Morgan & Scott, 1893), 13–16.
68 Ballard, 'Lizard in the Volcano.'
69 Jean Guiart, 'Le dossier rassemblé,' in *Système des titres électifs ou héréditaires dans les Nouvelles-Hébrides centrales d'Efate aux îles Shepherd*, Jean-Jacques Espirat, Jean Guiart, Marie-Salomé Lagrange, and Monique Renaud (Paris: Institut d'ethnologie, Musée de l'Homme, 1973), 47–365; Jean Guiart, *Cultures on the Edge: Caught Unwittingly between the White Man's Concepts of Polynesia Opposed to Melanesia, From Efate to Epi, Central Vanuatu* (Pape'ete: Te Pito o te Fenua, 2014); David Luders, 'Legend and History: Did the Vanuatu-Tonga Kava Trade Cease in A.D. 1447?,' *Journal of the Polynesian Society* 105, no. 3 (1996): 287–310.
70 Robin, Monzier, and Eissen, 'Eruption of the Mid-Fifteenth Century Kuwae Caldera.'
71 Ross Clark, 'Linguistic Consequences of the Kuwae Eruption,' in *Oceanic Culture History: Essays in Honour of Roger Green*, eds. Janet Davidson, Geoffrey Irwin, Foss Leach, Andrew Pawley, and Dorothy Brown (Dunedin North: New Zealand Journal of Archaeology, 1996), 275–285.
72 Shane Cronin, pers. comm., 2020.

73 Garanger, *Archéologie des Nouvelles-Hébrides*, 94.
74 Bernard Hébert, 'Contribution à l'étude archéologique de l'île Efate et des îles avoisinantes,' *Études Mélanésiennes* 18–20 (1963–1965): 71–98.
75 Jean-Philippe Eissen, Claude Blot, and Rémy Louat, *Chronologie de l'activité volcanique historique de l'arc insulaire des Nouvelles-Hébrides de 1595 à 1991* (Noumea: ORSTOM, 1991), 43–46.
76 Susanna Katharine Kelly, 'Unwrapping Mats: People, Land and Material Culture in Tongoa, Central Vanuatu' (PhD diss., University College London, 1999), 141.
77 Ethnographer Maëlle Calandra witnessed a land court case on Tongoa over five days in 2013 at which those in dispute marshalled their arguments almost entirely around the disposition of land claims and boundaries immediately before and after the eruption (Maëlle Calandra, pers. comm., 2020).
78 George Adam Smith, *The Life of Henry Drummond* (London: Hodder & Stoughton, 1899), 378.
79 H. Boyle Townshend Somerville, *The Chart-Makers* (Edinburgh: William Blackwood & Sons, 1928), 138.
80 Michelsen, *Cannibals Won for Christ*, 13, 16.
81 Oscar Michelsen, *Misi* (London and Edinburgh: Marshall, Morgan & Scott, 1934), 232.
82 Hébert, 'Contribution à l'étude archéologique.'
83 A.J. Warden, 'Shepherds,' in *Annual Report of the Geological Survey for the Year 1964*, Geological Survey, New Hebrides Anglo-French Condominium (London: HMSO, 1966), 8.
84 C.E.F. Williams and A.J. Warden, *Progress Report of the Geological Survey for the Period 1959–1962* (New Hebrides: British Service, 1964).
85 Luders, 'Legend and History,' 294.
86 Chihiro Shirakawa, 'The Titular System of Tongoa, Vanuatu' (in Japanese, with English summary), *Kokuritsu Minzokugaku Hakubutsukan kenkyū hōkoku* (*Bulletin of the National Museum of Ethnology*) 23, no. 2 (1998): 267–319.
87 Russell J. Blong, *The Time of Darkness: Local Legends and Volcanic Reality in Papua New Guinea* (Canberra and Seattle: ANU Press and University of Washington Press, 1982). It is curious to find this case passed over by Henige in his otherwise thorough review of the literature; Henige, 'Impossible to Disprove.'
88 Blong, 'Tibito Tephra, *Taim Tudak* and the Impact of Thin Tephra Falls,' in *Ten Thousand Years of Cultivation at Kuk Swamp in the Highlands of Papua New Guinea*, eds. Jack Golson, Tim Denham, Philip Hughes, Pamela Swadling, and John Muke (Canberra: ANU Press, 2017), 133–143.
89 Blong, *The Time of Darkness*, 90–91.
90 Blong and Andrei V. Kurbatov, 'Steps and Missteps on the Path to a 1665–1668 CE Date for the VEI 6 Eruption of Long Island, Papua New Guinea,' *Journal of Volcanology and Geothermal Research* 395 (2020); Blong, 'Tibito Tephra'; Blong, John Kemp, and Keping Chen, 'Dating the Last Major Eruption of Long Island, Papua New Guinea: The Evidence from Dampier's 1700 Voyage on the Roebuck,' *Terrae Incognitae* 48, no. 2 (2016): 139–159.
91 The interviews and survey responses have been published and the original materials deposited in an archive; Blong, ed., 'Time of Darkness Legends from Papua New Guinea,' *Oral History* 7, no. 10 (1979); Blong, 'Time of Darkness Legends from Papua New Guinea: Questionnaire Returns, Correspondence and Reports,' PMB MS 1329 (Canberra: Pacific Manuscripts Bureau, 1977–1982).
92 Blong, *The Time of Darkness*, 66.
93 Blong, 'Time of Darkness Legends,' 76.
94 Blong, *The Time of Darkness*, 69.
95 Blong, 'Time of Darkness Legends,' 111.
96 Blong, *The Time of Darkness*, 94.
97 Blong, *The Time of Darkness*, 134.

98 A single source for an event, as Jan Vansina has observed, can be neither challenged nor tested. Vansina, 'Memory and Oral Tradition,' in *The African Past Speaks: Essays on Oral Tradition and History*, ed. J.C. Miller (Folkestone: Dawson, 1980), 262–279.
99 Blong, 'Tibito Tephra,' 143.
100 K. Adams and L. Lauck, 'Patep,' in *From the Mouths of Ancestors*, ed. K.A. McElhanon (Ukarumpa: Summer Institute of Linguistics, 1982), 163–172; Chris Ballard, 'The Hahiv: Further Social Mapping Studies at Golpu (Wafi) Prospect,' report for CRA Minerals (PNG) Pty Ltd (Boroko: Unisearch, 1992); Chris Ballard with Biama Kanasa, 'Golpu (Wafi) Prospect Social Mapping Study,' report for CRA Minerals (PNG) Pty Ltd (Boroko: Unisearch, 1992).
101 Kitumbing Nganiatuk, in Ballard with Kanasa, 'Golpu (Wafi) Prospect,' 42.
102 Blong, *The Time of Darkness*, 130–132.
103 Gabriele Stürzenhofecker, *Times Enmeshed: Gender, Space, and History among the Duna of Papua New Guinea* (Stanford, CA: Stanford University Press, 1998), 66–68; Nicole Haley, 'Ipakana Yakaiya: Mapping Landscapes, Mapping Lives, Contemporary Land Politics among the Duna' (PhD diss., Australian National University, 2002), 166.
104 Aletta Biersack, 'Prisoners of Time: Millenarian Praxis in a Melanesian Valley,' in *Clio in Oceania: Toward a Historical Anthropology*, ed. Aletta Biersack (Washington DC: Smithsonian Institution Press, 1991), 264–265.
105 Jerry K. Jacka, *Alchemy in the Rain Forest: Politics, Ecology, and Resilience in a New Guinea Mining Area* (Durham, NC: Duke University Press, 2015), 263–266.
106 Polly Wiessner and Akii Tumu, *Historical Vines: Enga Networks of Exchange, Ritual, and Warfare in Papua New Guinea* (Washington DC: Smithsonian Institution Press, 1998), 70–71; Hans Reithofer, *The Python Spirit and the Cross: Becoming Christian in a Highland Community of Papua New Guinea* (Berlin: Lit Verlag, 2006), 56–58.
107 Paul Sillitoe, *A Place against Time: Land and Environment in the Papua New Guinea Highlands* (Amsterdam: Harwood Academic, 1996), 131–134.
108 Aletta Biersack, 'Introduction: The Huli, Duna, and Ipili Peoples Yesterday and Today,' in *Papuan Borderlands: Huli, Duna, and Ipili Perspectives on the Papua New Guinea Highlands*, ed. Aletta Biersack (Ann Arbor: University of Michigan, 1995), 20–23.
109 Bryant J. Allen and Andrew W. Wood, 'Legendary Volcanic Eruptions and the Huli, Papua New Guinea,' *Journal of the Polynesian Society* 89, no. 3 (1980): 341–347; Stephen J. Frankel, *The Huli Response to Illness* (Cambridge: Cambridge University Press, 1986), 17–18; R.M. Glasse, 'Time Belong Mbingi: Religious Syncretism and the Pacification of the Huli,' in *Papuan Borderlands: Huli, Duna, and Ipili Perspectives on the Papua New Guinea Highlands*, ed. Aletta Biersack (Ann Arbor: University of Michigan, 1995), 57–86; Chris Ballard, 'The Sun by Night: Huli Moral Topography and Myths of a Time of Darkness,' in *Fluid Ontologies: Myth, Ritual and Philosophy in the Highlands of Papua New Guinea*, eds. Laurence R. Goldman and Chris Ballard (Westport, CT and London: Bergin & Garvey, 1998), 67–85.
110 On Huli speech genres, see Laurence R. Goldman, *Talk Never Dies: The Language of Huli Disputes* (London and New York: Tavistock Publications, 1983), 62–63.
111 C.E.T. Terrell, 'Lake Kutubu Patrol Report No. 3 of 1953/54,' National Archives of Papua New Guinea, Port Moresby.
112 An example of a complete *mbingi* narrative is provided in Ballard, 'The Sun by Night.'
113 Identification of the historical event with remnants of Tibito Tephra was also common among Engans (Roderic Lacey, 'Temps Perdu et Temps Vécu: Cross-Cultural Nuances in the Experience of Time among the Enga,' *Pacific Studies* 13, no. (1990): 99).
114 Allen and Wood, 'Legendary Volcanic Eruptions'; for similar Duna beliefs see Haley, 'Ipakana Yakaiya,' 166.
115 Frankel, *Huli Response to Illness*, 17
116 Chris Ballard, 'The Death of a Great Land: Ritual, History, and Subsistence Revolution in the Southern Highlands of Papua New Guinea' (PhD diss., Australian National University, 1995), 127–128.

117 Blong, 'Time of Darkness Legends'; Blong, *The Time of Darkness*; Blong et al., 'Significance and Timing of the Mid-17th-Century Eruption of Long Island, Papua New Guinea,' *The Holocene* 28, no. 4 (2017): 529–544.
118 Blong et al., 'Significance and Timing,' fig. 5.
119 Frankel, *Huli Response to Illness*, 18; Ballard, 'Death of a Great Land,' appendix B10.
120 Wiessner and Tumu, *Historical Vines*, 71
121 Lacey, 'Temps Perdu et Temps Vécu,' 98
122 Henige, 'Implausibility of Plausibility,' 329.
123 Mike Smith, for instance, takes up Henige's challenge in his re-reading of claims for Australian *kardimarkara* narratives, proposing a framework for the textual analysis of Indigenous historical narratives; M.A. Smith, 'The Historiography of *Kardimarkara*: Reading a Desert Tradition as Cultural Memory of the Remote Past,' *Journal of Social Archaeology* 19, no. 1 (2019): 47–66.
124 A striking perspective on this potential is offered by archaeologist Patrick Kirch, 'Voices on the Wind, Traces in the Earth: Integrating Oral Narrative and Archaeology in Polynesian History,' *Journal of the Polynesian Society* 127, no. 3 (2018): 275–306.
125 Blong, 'Tibito Tephra,' 143.
126 Mason, *Inconstant Companions*, 249.
127 Ballard, 'Lizard in the Volcano,' 104.
128 With reference to Terence Turner's original formulation of the project of contextualisation of Kayapó histories: Turner, 'History, Myth, and Social Consciousness among the Kayapó of Central Brazil,' in *Rethinking Myth and History: Indigenous South American Perspectives on the Past*, ed. J.D. Hill (Urbana: University of Illinois Press, 1988), 195–213.

Bibliography

Adams, K., and L. Lauck. 'Patep.' In *From the Mouths of Ancestors*, edited by K.A. McElhanon, 163–172. Ukarumpa: Summer Institute of Linguistics, 1982.

Allen, Bryant J., and Andrew W. Wood. 'Legendary Volcanic Eruptions and the Huli, Papua New Guinea.' *Journal of the Polynesian Society* 89, no. 3 (1980): 341–347.

Ballard, Chris. 'The Hahiv: Further Social Mapping Studies at Golpu (Wafi) Prospect.' Report for CRA Minerals (PNG) Pty Ltd. Boroko: Unisearch, 1992.

Ballard, Chris. 'The Death of a Great Land: Ritual, History, and Subsistence Revolution in the Southern Highlands of Papua New Guinea.' PhD diss., Australian National University, 1995.

Ballard, Chris. 'The Sun by Night: Huli Moral Topography and Myths of a Time of Darkness.' In *Fluid Ontologies: Myth, Ritual and Philosophy in the Highlands of Papua New Guinea*, edited by Laurence R. Goldman and Chris Ballard, 67–85. Westport and London: Bergin & Garvey, 1998.

Ballard, Chris. 'Oceanic Historicities.' *The Contemporary Pacific* 26 no. 1 (2014): 96–124.

Ballard, Chris. 'The Lizard in the Volcano: Narratives of the Kuwae Eruption.' *The Contemporary Pacific* 32, no. 1 (2020): 98–123.

Ballard, Chris, with Biama Kanasa. 'Golpu (Wafi) Prospect Social Mapping Study.' Report for CRA Minerals (PNG) Pty Ltd. Boroko: Unisearch, 1992.

Bandelier, Adolph F. 'Traditions of Precolumbian Earthquakes and Volcanic Eruptions in Western South America.' *American Anthropologist* 8, no. 1 (1906): 47–81.

Barber, Elizabeth Weyland, and Paul T. Barber. *When They Severed Earth from Sky: How the Human Mind Shapes Myth*. Princeton: Princeton University Press, 2004.

Best, Elsdon. 'The Polynesian Method of Generating Fire: With Some Account of the Mythical Origin of Fire, and of its Employment in Ritual Ceremonies as Observed among the Maori Folk of New Zealand.' *Journal of the Polynesian Society* 33, no. 2 (1924): 87–102.

Biersack, Aletta. 'Prisoners of Time: Millenarian Praxis in a Melanesian Valley.' In *Clio in Oceania: Toward a Historical Anthropology*, ed. Aletta Biersack, 231–295. Washington DC: Smithsonian Institution Press, 1991.

Biersack, Aletta. 'Introduction: The Huli, Duna, and Ipili Peoples Yesterday and Today.' In *Papuan Borderlands: Huli, Duna, and Ipili Perspectives on the Papua New Guinea Highlands*, ed. Aletta Biersack, 1–54. Ann Arbor: University of Michigan Press, 1995.

Blong, Russell J., ed. 'Time of Darkness Legends from Papua New Guinea.' *Oral History* 7, no. 10 (1979): 1–135.

Blong, Russell J. 'Time of Darkness Legends from Papua New Guinea: Questionnaire Returns, Correspondence and Reports.' PMB MS 1329. Canberra: Pacific Manuscripts Bureau, 1977–1982.

Blong, Russell J. *The Time of Darkness: Local Legends and Volcanic Reality in Papua New Guinea*. Canberra and Seattle: ANU Press and University of Washington Press, 1982.

Blong, Russell J. 'Tibito Tephra, *Taim Tudak* and the Impact of Thin Tephra Falls.' In *Ten Thousand Years of Cultivation at Kuk Swamp in the Highlands of Papua New Guinea*, edited by Jack Golson, Tim Denham, Philip Hughes, Pamela Swadling, and John Muke, 133–143. Canberra: ANU Press, 2017.

Blong, Russell J., Stewart Fallon, Rachel Wood, Chris McKee, Keping Chen, Christina Magill, and Peter Barter. 'Significance and Timing of the Mid-17th-Century Eruption of Long Island, Papua New Guinea.' *The Holocene* 28, no. 4 (2017): 529–544.

Blong, Russell J., John Kemp, and Keping Chen. 'Dating the Last Major Eruption of Long Island, Papua New Guinea: The Evidence from Dampier's 1700 Voyage on the *Roebuck*.' *Terrae Incognitae* 48, no. 2 (2016): 139–159.

Blong, Russell J., and Andrei V. Kurbatov. 'Steps and Missteps on the Path to a 1665–1668 CE Date for the VEI 6 Eruption of Long Island, Papua New Guinea.' *Journal of Volcanology and Geothermal Research* 395 (2020).

Budhwa, Rick. 'Correlations between Catastrophic Paleoenvironmental Events and Native Oral Traditions of the Pacific Northwest.' MA diss., Department of Archaeology, Simon Fraser University, 2002.

Cashman, Katharine V., and Shane J. Cronin. 'Welcoming a Monster to the World: Myths, Oral Tradition, and Modern Societal Response to Volcanic Disasters.' *Journal of Volcanology and Geothermal Research* 176 (2008): 407–418.

Clark, Ross. 'Linguistic Consequences of the Kuwae Eruption.' In *Oceanic Culture History: Essays in Honour of Roger Green*, edited by Janet Davidson, Geoffrey Irwin, Foss Leach, Andrew Pawley, and Dorothy Brown, 275–285. Dunedin North: New Zealand Journal of Archaeology, 1996.

Cronin, Shane J., Marie A. Ferland, and James P. Terry. 'Nabukelevu Volcano (Mt Washington), Kadavu: A Source of Hitherto Unknown Volcanic Hazard in Fiji.' *Journal of Volcanology and Geothermal Research* 13, no. 3–4 (2004): 371–396.

Cronin, Shane J., David R. Gaylord, Douglas Charley, Brent V. Alloway, Sandrine Wallez, and Job W. Esau. 'Participatory Methods of Incorporating Scientific with Traditional Knowledge for Volcanic Hazard Management on Ambae Island, Vanuatu.' *Bulletin of Volcanology* 66, no. 7 (2004): 652–668.

Cronin, Shane J., and Katharine V. Cashman. 'Volcanic Oral Traditions in Hazard Assessment and Mitigation.' In *Living under the Shadow: Cultural Impacts of Volcanic Eruptions*, edited by John Grattan and Robin Torrence, 165–176. Walnut Creek: Left Coast Press, 2007.

Cronin, Shane J., and V.E. Neall. 'Impacts of Volcanism on Pre-European Inhabitants of Taveuni, Fiji.' *Bulletin of Volcanology* 62 (2000): 199–213.

Davis, Ronald W. 'Volcanic Dust in the Atmosphere and the Interpretation of African Eclipse Traditions.' *History in Africa* 4 (1977): 31–41.

Doortmont, Michel R. 'Making History in Africa: David Henige and the Quest for Method in African History.' *History in Africa* 38 (2011): 7–20.

Eissen, Jean-Philippe, Claude Blot, and Rémy Louat. *Chronologie de l'activité volcanique historique de l'arc insulaire des Nouvelles-Hébrides de 1595 à 1991*. Noumea: ORSTOM, 1991.

Fast, Phyllis A. 'The Volcano in Athabascan Oral Narratives.' *Alaska Journal of Anthropology* 6, no. 1 & 2 (2008): 131–139.
Frankel, Stephen J. *The Huli Response to Illness.* Cambridge: Cambridge University Press, 1986.
Gabrielsen, H., J. Procter, H. Rainforth, T. Black, G. Harmsworth, and N. Pardo. 'Reflections from an Indigenous Community on Volcanic Event Management, Communications and Resilience.' *Advances in Volcanology* 2018 (2018): 463–479.
Gaillard, Jean-Christophe, F.G. Delfin, Eusebio Z. Dizon, Victor J. Paz, Emmanuel G. Ramos, Cristina T. Remotigue, Kelvin S. Rodolfo, F. Siringan, J.L.A. Soria, and Jesse V. Umbal. 'Planning for the Future: A Multidisciplinary Approach to Reconstructing the Buag Episode of Mt Pinatubo Philippines.' In *Living under the Shadow: Cultural Impacts of Volcanic Eruptions*, edited by John Grattan and Robin Torrence, 225–252. Walnut Creek: Left Coast Press, 2007.
Gao, Chaochao, Alan Robock, Stephen Self, Jeffrey B. Witter, J.P. Steffenson, Henrik Brink Clausen, Marie-Louise Siggaard-Andersen, Sigfus Johnsen, Paul A. Mayewski, and Caspar Ammann. 'The 1452 or 1453 A.D. Kuwae Eruption Signal Derived from Multiple Ice Core Records: Greatest Volcanic Sulphate Event of the Past 700 Years.' *Journal of Geophysical Research* 111 (2006): D12107.
Garanger, José. *Archéologie des Nouvelles-Hébrides: Contribution à la connaissance des îles du Centre.* Paris: ORSTOM, 1972.
Glasse, R.M. 'Time Belong *Mbingi*: Religious Syncretism and the Pacification of the Huli.' In Biersack, *Papuan Borderlands*, 57–86.
Goldman, Laurence R. *Talk Never Dies: The Language of Huli Disputes.* London and New York: Tavistock Publications, 1983.
Gorvett, Zaria. 'The Massive Volcano that Scientists Can't Find.' *BBC*, 3 July 2017. http://www.bbc.com/future/story/20170630-the-massive-volcano-that-scientists-cant-find.
Guiart, Jean. 'Le dossier rassemblé.' In *Système des titres électifs ou héréditaires dans les Nouvelles-Hébrides centrales d'Efate aux îles Shepherd*, edited by Jean-Jacques Espirat, Jean Guiart, Marie-Salomé Lagrange, and Monique Renaud, 47–365. Paris: Institut d'ethnologie, Musée de l'Homme, 1973.
Guiart, Jean. *Cultures on the Edge: Caught Unwittingly between the White Man's Concepts of Polynesia Opposed to Melanesia, From Efate to Epi, Central Vanuatu.* Pape'ete: Te Pito o te Fenua, 2013.
Haley, Nicole. 'Ipakana Yakaiya: Mapping Landscapes, Mapping Lives, Contemporary Land Politics among the Duna.' PhD diss., Australian National University, 2002.
Hébert, Bernard. 'Contribution à l'étude archéologique de l'île Efate et des îles avoisinantes.' *Études Mélanésiennes* 18–20 (1963–1965): 71–98.
Henige, David. *The Chronology of Oral Tradition: Quest for a Chimera.* Oxford: Clarendon Press, 1974.
Henige, David. '"Day Was of Sudden Turned into Night": On the Use of Eclipses for Dating Oral History.' *Comparative Studies in Society and History* 18, no. 4 (1976): 476–501.
Henige, David. 'Survival of the Fittest? Darwinian Evolution and the Transmission of Information.' *History in Africa* 30 (2003): 161–181.
Henige, David. 'The Implausibility of Plausibility/The Plausibility of Implausibility.' *Historical Reflections/Réflexions Historiques* 30, no. 2 (2004): 311–335.
Henige, David. *Historical Evidence and Argument.* Madison: University of Wisconsin Press, 2005.
Henige, David. 'Impossible to Disprove Yet Impossible to Believe: The Unforgiving Epistemology of Deep-Time Oral Tradition.' *History in Africa* 36 (2009): 127–234.
Hoffman, Andrew. 'Looking to Epi: Further Consequences of the Kuwae Eruption, Central Vanuatu, AD 1452.' *Bulletin of the Indo-Pacific Prehistory Association* 26 (2007): 62–71.
Jacka, Jerry K. *Alchemy in the Rain Forest: Politics, Ecology, and Resilience in a New Guinea Mining Area.* Durham: Duke University Press, 2015.
Jacoby, Gordon C., Karen W. Workman, and Rosanne D. D'Arrigo. 'Laki Eruption of 1783, Tree Rings, and Disaster for Northwest Alaska Inuit.' *Quaternary Science Reviews* 18 (1999): 1365–1371.

Johnson, R. Wally. *Fire Mountains of the Islands.* Canberra: ANU Press, 2013.
Kelly, Susanna Katharine. 'Unwrapping Mats: People, Land and Material Culture in Tongoa, Central Vanuatu.' PhD diss., University College London, 1999.
Kirch, Patrick Vinton. 'Voices on the Wind, Traces in the Earth: Integrating Oral Narrative and Archaeology in Polynesian History.' *Journal of the Polynesian Society* 127, no. 3 (2018): 275–306.
Lacey, Roderic. 'Temps Perdu et Temps Vécu: Cross-Cultural Nuances in the Experience of Time among the Enga.' *Pacific Studies* 13, no. (1990): 77–102.
Lowe, David J., R.M. Newnham and J.D. McCraw, 'Volcanism and Early Maori Society in New Zealand.' In *Natural Disasters and Cultural Change*, edited by Robin Torrence and John Grattan, 126–161. London and New York: Routledge, 2002.
Lowe, David J., and Adrian Pittari. 'An Ashy Septingentenarian: The Kaharoa Tephra Turns 700 (with Notes on its Volcanological, Archaeological, and Historical Importance).' *Geoscience Society of New Zealand Newsletter* 13 (2014): 1–14.
Luders, David. 'Legend and History: Did the Vanuatu–Tonga Kava Trade Cease in A.D. 1447?' *Journal of the Polynesian Society* 105, no. 3 (1996): 287–310.
Malotki, Ekkehart, with Michael Lomatuway'ma. *Earth Fire: A Hopi Legend of the Sunset Crater Eruption.* Flagstaff: Northland Press, 1987.
Martindale, Andrew R.C., and Susan Marsden. 'Defining the Middle Period (3500 BP to 1500 BP) in Tsimshian History through a Comparison of Archaeological and Oral Records.' *BC Studies* 138–139 (2003): 13–50.
Mason, Ronald J. *Inconstant Companions: Archaeology and North American Indian Oral Traditions.* Tuscaloosa: University of Alabama Press, 2006.
Masse, W. Bruce, and Michael J. Masse. 'Myth and Catastrophic Reality: Using Myth to Identify Cosmic Impacts and Massive Plinian Eruptions in Holocene South America.' In Piccardi and Masse, *Myth and Geology*, 177–202.
Mayor, Adrienne. 'Geomythology.' In *Encyclopedia of Geology*, edited by Richard C. Selley, L. Robin M. Cocks, and Ian R. Plimer, 96–100. Oxford: Elsevier, 2005.
Michelsen, Oscar. *Cannibals Won for Christ: A Story of Missionary Perils and Triumphs in Tongoa, New Hebrides.* London: Morgan & Scott, 1893.
Michelsen, Oscar. *Misi.* London and Edinburgh: Marshall, Morgan & Scott, 1934.
Moodie, D. Wayne, A.J.W. Catchpole, and Kerry Abel. 'Northern Athapaskan Oral Traditions and the White River Volcano.' *Ethnohistory* 39, no. 2 (1992): 148–171.
Németh, Károly, and Shane J. Cronin. 'Volcanic Structures and Oral Traditions of Volcanism of Western Samoa (SW Pacific) and Their Implications for Hazard Education.' *Journal of Volcanology and Geothermal Research* 186 (2009): 223–237.
Nunn, Patrick. *The Edge of Memory: Ancient Stories, Oral Tradition and the Post-Glacial World.* London: Bloomsbury Sigma, 2018.
Nunn, Patrick, Loredana Lancini, Leigh Franks, Rita Compatangelo-Soussignan, and Adrian McCallum. 'Maar Stories: How Oral Traditions Aid Understanding of Maar Volcanism and Associated Phenomena during Preliterate Times.' *Annals of the American Association of Geographers* 109, no. 5 (2019): 1618–1631.
Nunn, Patrick, and Nicholas Reid. 'Aboriginal Memories of Inundation of the Australian Coast Dating from More than 7000 Years Ago.' *Australian Geographer* 47, no. 1 (2016): 11–47.
Petterson, M.G., S.J. Cronin, P.W. Taylor, D. Tolia, A. Papabatu, T. Toba, and C. Qopoto. 'The Eruptive History and Volcanic Hazards of Savo, Solomon Islands.' *Bulletin of Volcanology* 65 (2003): 165–181.
Piccardi, Luigi, and W. Bruce Masse, eds. *Myth and Geology.* Geological Society of London Special Publications 273, no. 1. London: Geological Society, 2007.
Plummer, C.T., M.A.J. Curran, T.D. van Ommen, S.O. Rasmussen, A.D. Moy, T.R. Vace, H.B. Clausen, B.M. Vinther, and P.A. Mayewesi. 'An Independently Dated 2000-yr Record from Law Dome, East Antarctica, Including a New Perspective on the Dating of the 1450s CE Eruption of Kuwae, Vanuatu.' *Climate of the Past* 8 (2012): 1929–1940.

Reithofer, Hans. *The Python Spirit and the Cross: Becoming Christian in a Highland Community of Papua New Guinea*. Berlin: Lit Verlag, 2006.
Riede, Felix. 'Doing Palaeo-Social Volcanology: Developing a Framework for Systematically Investigating the Impacts of Past Volcanic Eruptions on Human Societies using Archaeological Datasets.' *Quaternary International* 499 (2019): 266–277.
Roberts, A.D. 'Review of David P. Henige, *The Chronology of Oral Tradition*.' *Bulletin of the School of Oriental and African Studies* 38, no. 3 (1995): 692–693.
Roberts, Amy L., Adrian Mollenmans, Lester-Irabinna Rigney, and Geoff Bailey. 'Marine Transgression, Aboriginal Narratives and the Creation of Yorke Peninsula/Guuranda, South Australia.' *The Journal of Island and Coastal Archaeology* 15, no. 3 (2020): 305–332.
Robin, Claude, Michel Monzier, and Jean-Philippe Eissen. 'Eruption of the Mid-Fifteenth Century Kuwae Caldera (Vanuatu) by an Initial Hydroclastic and Subsequent Ignimbritic Eruption.' *Bulletin of Volcanology* 56 (1994): 170–183.
Rodolfo, Kelvin S., and Jess V. Umbal. 'A Prehistoric Lahar-Dammed Lake and Eruption of Mount Pinatubo Described in a Philippine Aborigine Legend.' *Journal of Volcanology and Geothermal Research* 176 (2008): 432–437.
Sack, Peter. 'The Emergence and Settlement of Matupit Island: Vulcanological Evidence, Oral Tradition and "Objective" History in Papua New Guinea.' *Bikmaus* 7, no. 1 (1987): 1–14.
Schütz, Albert J. *Nguna Texts: A Collection of Traditional and Modern Narratives from the Central New Hebrides*. Honolulu: University of Hawaiʻi Press, 1969.
Shirakawa, Chihiro. 'The Titular System of Tongoa, Vanuatu' (in Japanese, with English summary). *Kokuritsu Minzokugaku Hakubutsukan kenkyū hōkoku (Bulletin of the National Museum of Ethnology)* 23, no. 2 (1998): 267–319.
Sillitoe, Paul. *A Place against Time: Land and Environment in the Papua New Guinea Highlands*. Amsterdam: Harwood Academic, 1996.
Smith, George Adam. *The Life of Henry Drummond*. London: Hodder & Stoughton, 1899.
Smith, M.A. 'The Historiography of *Kardimarkara*: Reading a Desert Tradition as Cultural Memory of the Remote Past.' *Journal of Social Archaeology* 19, no. 1 (2019): 47–66.
Somerville, H. Boyle Townshend. *The Chart-Makers*. Edinburgh: William Blackwood & Sons, 1928.
Stewart, Charles. 'Historicity and Anthropology.' *Annual Review of Anthropology* 45 (2016): 79–94.
Stürzenhofecker, Gabriele. *Times Enmeshed: Gender, Space, and History among the Duna of Papua New Guinea*. Stanford: Stanford University Press, 1998.
Swanson, Donald A. 'Hawaiian Oral Tradition Describes 400 Years of Volcanic Activity at Kilauea.' *Journal of Volcanology and Geothermal Research* 176 (2008): 427–431.
Taylor, Paul W. 'Myths, Legends and Volcanic Activity: An Example from Northern Tonga.' *Journal of the Polynesian Society* 104, no. 3 (1995): 323–346.
Terrell, C.E.T. 'Lake Kutubu Patrol Report No. 3 of 1953/54.' National Archives of Papua New Guinea, Port Moresby.
Toohey, Matthew, and Michael Sigl. 'Volcanic Stratospheric Sulfur Injections and Aerosol Optical Depth from 500 BCE to 1900 CE.' *Earth System Science Data* 9, no. 2 (2017): 809–831.
Turner, Terence. 'History, Myth, and Social Consciousness among the Kayapó of Central Brazil.' In *Rethinking Myth and History: Indigenous South American Perspectives on the Past*, edited by J.D. Hill, 195–213. Urbana: University of Illinois Press, 1988.
Van Otterloo, Jozua, Raymond A.F. Cas, and Malcolm J. Sheard. 'Eruption Processes and Deposit Characteristics at the Monogenetic Mt Gambier Volcanic Complex, SE Australia: Implications for Alternating Magmatic and Phreatomagmatic Activity.' *Bulletin of Volcanology* 75, no. 8 (2013): 737.
Vansina, Jan. 'Memory and Oral Tradition.' *The African Past Speaks: Essays on Oral Tradition and History*, edited by J.C. Miller, 262–279. Folkestone: Dawson, 1980.

Vitaliano, Dorothy B. *Legends of the Earth: Their Geologic Origins.* Bloomington: Indiana University Press, 1973.

Vitaliano, Dorothy B. 'Geomythology: Geological Origins of Myths and Legends.' In *Myth and Geology*, edited by Luigi Piccardi and W. Bruce Masse, 1–7. Geological Society of London Special Publications 273, no. 1. London: Geological Society, 2007.

Warden, A.J. 'Shepherds.' In *Annual Report of the Geological Survey for the Year 1964*, Geological Survey, New Hebrides Anglo-French Condominium, 8–9. London: HMSO, 1966.

Wiessner, Polly, and Akii Tumu. *Historical Vines: Enga Networks of Exchange, Ritual, and Warfare in Papua New Guinea.* Washington DC: Smithsonian Institution Press, 1998.

Williams, C.E.F. and A.J. Warden. *Progress Report of the Geological Survey for the Period 1959–1962.* New Hebrides: British Service, 1964.

27
ARCHAEOLOGY, HYBRID KNOWLEDGE, AND COMMUNITY ENGAGEMENT IN AFRICA
Thoughts on decolonising practice

Paul Lane

Introduction

The number and frequency of calls and proposals for decolonising the practice, teaching, and presentation of archaeology in Africa have grown steadily over the last few decades.[1] Such concerns have even prompted some scholars to argue that the 'practice of archaeology in Africa has failed communities within which archaeologists work'.[2] Moreover, as calls to decolonise the field have intensified, there has been a shift in focus on how such decolonisation might be approached to enable genuine transformation of disciplinary practices. In the 1980s and 1990s, reviews concerning the future of archaeology on the continent, and especially in sub-Saharan Africa, stressed the urgency of training more African archaeologists.[3] Embedding and strengthening secondary and tertiary education in archaeology,[4] and increasing public understanding of the discipline were similarly emphasised.[5] A third set of concerns centred on developing effective responses to mitigating intensifying threats to archaeological resources from development[6] and combating the upsurge in the looting of archaeological sites.[7] Regular calls for greater commitment on the part of the international donor community to facilitating and funding such efforts helped reinforce these positions.[8]

The influence of inherent biases derived from archaeology's colonial origins and frameworks[9] – which emphasised external drivers of change and innovation, denying or at least disregarding African agency, and tribalised identities[10] – was also recognised, as was their continuing influence on archaeological practice and knowledge production.[11] However, there were few, if any, calls for the dismantling of the archaeological project itself. Instead, *the localisation of archaeological practice* through increasing the numbers of African students and scholars trained in

DOI: 10.4324/9781315181929-33

archaeology was regarded, by and large, to be the best strategy for redressing the issues. The critiques of 'Western' archaeology by the Nigerian archaeologist Bassey Andah perhaps came closest to framing an alternative approach, especially in proposing greater attention be given to African Indigenous environmental knowledge in archaeological interpretations of ancient settlement and subsistence practices.[12] Yet, despite an overt emphasis on the need to engage more explicitly with African modes of thought and Indigenous knowledge (IK), his proposal for a new 'behavioural archaeology' still relied heavily on many of the conventions of processualist environmental and economic archaeologies.

Other archaeologists likewise emphasised the need to expose the biased and often racist dimensions of colonial thinking and to replace these with alternative methodologies and theories drawn from the repertoires of processual and post-processual archaeologies. Thus, for instance, in their stringent and ground-breaking critique of older explanations of the origins of urbanism in the West African Sahel, Roderick McIntosh and Susan Keech McIntosh drew extensively on the value of systematic regional survey grounded in an explicit sampling strategy, carefully controlled excavation of deeply stratified tell sites, and a rigorous programme of radiocarbon dating, backed by theoretical insights drawn from settlement archaeology.[13] Used together, these generated an incontestable body of empirical evidence to support arguments for early, indigenous origins of political complexity and urbanism, challenging older colonial models of external stimulus and innovation.[14] Pioneering research on pre-Aksumite urbanism by Rodolfo Fattovich similarly employed a suite of conventional archaeological approaches to demonstrate its indigenous genesis,[15] overturning long held ideas concerning the foreign origins of complex society and ancient states in the Horn of Africa.[16] The critique by Martin Hall of the colonialist assumptions about tribal identities, especially those promulgated under Apartheid,[17] that had shaped interpretations of southern Africa's Iron Age ceramic typologies, provides another example from this era. Drawing on a combination of Marxist anthropology and emerging historical research on regional social dynamics in the eighteenth and nineteenth centuries, Hall was also influenced by New Archaeology's critique[18] of older concepts of archaeological cultures as articulated by Gordon Childe.[19] Similarly, pioneering work by the likes of Mark Horton and Felix Chami on dismantling earlier models of the foreign, especially 'Arab' or 'Persian', origins of Swahili stone towns along the East African seaboard all emphasised the radical potential of archaeological methods and approaches,[20] coupled with evidence drawn from recent historical linguistic research,[21] as the means to critique these earlier hypotheses and provide the necessary empirical evidence of the African genesis of the Swahili. In other words, as the discipline 'came of age' on the continent,[22] the archaeological method (albeit one modified through close integration of other evidential sources, especially oral history) was something to be celebrated as a means to 'remake African history'[23] despite its colonial roots and continuing 'European encumbrances'.[24] As the Egyptian-born archaeologist Fekri Hassan reflected at the end of the century:

> Our fascination and preoccupation with the past as human beings remain a basic foundation for archaeology as a young scholarly discipline. It is to this

fundamental and elemental concept of archaeology that we must return in re-examining the scope and goals of African archaeology in particular and archaeology as a discipline in general.[25]

Two decades on, most of those who practise archaeology on the continent and engage in research about its varied pasts would probably concur with such a sentiment. They would likely also endorse the view that archaeology remains a powerful tool for decolonising historical narratives about the nature of those pasts, whether these are those found in older scholarly literature or ones that continue to circulate within the public sphere and are recycled periodically by Western politicians, such as by the former French President Nicolas Sarkozy in his now-infamous speech at the University of Dakar in 2007.[26] Yet, it is also evident that there is increasing unease among some African archaeologists concerning aspects of current archaeological practice on the continent and the epistemology and ontological frames of reference that undergird archaeological practice and heritage work more generally.[27] As Shadreck Chirikure, Janet Deacon, and Webber Ndoro observed recently, '[i]f there is anything post-colonial Africa has been slow to learn, it is the fact that success in today's world depends on domesticating ... international solutions *and internationalizing local values* to create best practice informed by multiple worlds.'[28] Sentiments such as these are shared by many other African scholars, and have found expressions in various ways, among them proposals for renewed efforts at engaging with local communities and incorporating their 'traditional' knowledge and values into heritage management systems, and adopting knowledge co-production as a means of redressing the hegemonic dominance and unequal power structures of conventional archaeology. The importance of effecting such changes in approach has also been underscored more generally by Paul Silitoe:

> If people constitute and verify knowledge in different ways to that current in development agencies, how can their IK [Indigenous Knowledge] assist in development? It suggests that their participation under current arrangements is unlikely to result in their understandings significantly informing interventions.[29]

Decolonising archaeology

This intellectual unease with archaeology's underlying premises and *modus operandi* is by no means unique to those who engage in archaeological knowledge production about the African continent, and bears comparison with trends and debates elsewhere relating to the emergence and development of Indigenous archaeology as a distinct disciplinary field.[30] Indeed, as François Richard has astutely observed, the necessary response to utterances such as those made by President Sarkozy is not simply to declaim something along the lines of "Hey! Africa also has a history ...", however important it is to reiterate this,[31] but to pose the far more salient and challenging questions being asked in a rather similar manner in other contexts of former European colonial overrule. Namely, what 'kinds of histories of Africa ... have been written, [what] ... kinds of historical imaginations ... have [they] permitted, and ... [what] kinds of alternatives ... are possible'?[32]

In a wide-ranging review of several of these issues and how they might shape the future of archaeology on the continent, the distinguished Zimbabwean archaeologist Innocent Pikirayi has identified a number of core challenges.[33] Pikirayi is someone who lived through the end of White minority rule in his country and entered archaeology at a time of optimism and economic growth in Zimbabwe, during the first two decades of independence, when there was increased national and international investment in the training of a new generation of archaeologists and a corresponding upsurge in its public profile within the country. More recently, he has been the head of a department of archaeology and anthropology at the University of Pretoria during a period of significant transformation in South African higher education and student protests over the perceived slow pace of change. Given such lived experience, Pikirayi's observations and concerns merit careful consideration. Key among these is his suggestion that 'universalising approaches to archaeology in Africa are bound to fail',[34] which he attributes in part to the fact that, across the continent, archaeology syllabi at university level and national research agendas continue to follow:

> ... the model set by British, North American and, to some extent, mainland European universities. The academic curriculum remains weak in terms of decolonising the discipline, and it is largely unable to challenge the dominant theoretical and even philosophical positions, which have prevailed since the rapid development of archaeology as a discipline in the twentieth century.[35]

Albeit mindful of the levels of poverty on the continent that lead to a questioning of the morality of directing scarce financial resources towards archaeology, and of the continuing political and security challenges that can limit opportunities for new field research, Pikirayi proposed a process of change as a way forward to resolving these deficiencies:

1. 'the diversification of archaeological theory post-1990 [necessitates] that theory in African archaeology be informed by locally-based epistemologies and worldviews';
2. 'as African archaeology is about the writing of the past of Africa, scholars must attach importance to memory because it is an integral part of African history-making';
3. 'while acknowledging the divide between heritage management and mainstream academic archaeology, the latter must communicate relevance to non-professionals to ensure its survival as a discipline'.[36]

These sentiments can be distilled into three core concepts: 'Indigenous Knowledge', 'Historical Memory', and 'Making the Past Relevant to Today'. All three are closely connected with each other, as Pikirayi's article makes clear, and all three have been the focus of research and debate with reference to Africa in recent decades. However, each also requires some unpacking and clarification, as explored below.

Indigenous knowledge and hybrid archaeologies

Research on the epistemologies and ontologies of non-Western societies has been a mainstay of anthropology since its inception[37] and in subsequent theorisation concerning these systems of thought.[38] The equal valorisation of these different philosophies of knowledge remains a guiding principle of contemporary anthropology.[39] Yet, the wider salience of IK as having applied relevance (Pikirayi's third requirement) only began to attract broad academic interest in the 1980s and early 1990s, initially within the context of development studies,[40] although there were certainly earlier efforts.[41] The primary drivers behind this rise in interest came from growing dissatisfaction with the lack of success of the many interventions in 'less developed countries', aimed at stimulating economic growth; reducing poverty; improving agricultural productivity, public health, and socio-economic equity; and redressing environmental degradation.[42] Other contributory factors, such as the promotion of development interventions centred on the adoption and dissemination of Intermediate Technologies, and early manifestations of the Green Movement[43] alongside reactions to the consequences of industrial scale pollution in the West,[44] also weakened the authority of Western expertise.

As is well documented, the recurrent 'failure' of large-scale development projects began during the colonial era, such as the ill-fated Groundnut Scheme in Tanganyika (now Tanzania),[45] and the equally problematic programme of large-scale irrigation implemented under the auspices of the Office du Niger in central French Soudan (now Mali).[46] However, many large-scale projects initiated after independence, such as those linked to major dam construction and irrigation schemes, have similarly often failed to provide the promised social and economic development that regional and national governments hoped to achieve.[47] Moreover, critical assessment of the environmental narratives that frequently underpinned development interventions in sub-Saharan Africa, such as those concerning the drivers of severe soil erosion[48] and deforestation,[49] has also highlighted many of the erroneous assumptions underpinning these and their colonial origins, prompting reappraisal of how best to ensure equitable and sustainable development on the continent. Within this context, IK, and especially its subset Traditional Ecological Knowledge (TEK), has increasingly been positioned in contrast to Western scientific knowledge and the accompanying technical and bureaucratic approaches to the uses and implementation of such knowledge for social and economic development, encouraging widespread calls for the promotion of 'local' indigenous solutions and models of development.[50]

Notwithstanding the merits of such arguments, as Daryl Stump has cogently argued, there has been a tendency to treat 'ethnoscience', IK and TEK, in a largely ahistorical manner resulting in reification and essentialisation of such knowledge systems, while at the same time IK/TEK systems have often been perceived as impermeable to external influence and change.[51] As Stump notes, just as older conceptions of African land use practices as being inherently environmentally destructive relied on very limited (if any) empirical evidence to support such claims, it is also misleading to claim, in the absence of relevant historical data, that Indigenous land use systems are necessarily and inherently 'sustainable'.[52] In other words, a fundamental role that archaeology (in its guise as a Western scientific, post-Enlightenment discipline) can play, alongside other cognate fields such as palaeoecology, environmental history, and historical ecology, is to provide the empirical evidence against which to assess claims concerning either the sustainability or unsustainability of Indigenous practices[53] and more precise temporal measures of their duration.[54] Recent cross-disciplinary comparative study of the origins and subsequent histories of intensive agricultural systems at Engaruka, northern Tanzania,[55] and Konso, southern Ethiopia,[56] and elsewhere on the continent[57] have sought to do precisely that, resulting in, among other outputs, valuable policy guidelines for landscape managers.[58]

Studies such as these align well with Pikirayi's call for archaeology to demonstrate its relevance to addressing contemporary challenges. However, as also explored in some detail by Stump,[59] the tendency to treat IK systems as timeless, or at the very least failure to consider how these knowledge systems may have evolved, has broader implications that resonate more directly with Pikirayi's view that African archaeology needs to 'be informed by locally-based epistemologies and worldviews'.[60] To accomplish this, at least three impediments to change need to be addressed. The first, as already hinted at, is to recognise that IK systems, like any other knowledge system, evolve over time based on combinations of learning from experience, borrowing (or instruction) from others, and experimentation. Far from being static and unchanging – although as in any cultural context there may well be resistance to change from certain quarters or vested interests – all forms of 'traditional knowledge' on the African continent (as elsewhere) are temporally specific and are also often hybrid constructs. Consequently, labelling a set of practices or beliefs as 'traditional' and contrasting these with Western knowledge, without further qualification, effectively denies the historical agency of those who produced such knowledge. In view of the considerable contributions that archaeologists working on the African continent have made over the last 70 years or so to reinsert African historical agency into global, regional, and local narratives of the past, it is especially ironic that these efforts are now at risk of being undermined by uncritical use and promotion of notions of 'tradition' by archaeologists and heritage managers in their calls for decolonisation of the discipline.

The second impediment that needs to be addressed requires dismantling some of the assumptions that underpin conventional distinctions between the so-called 'Western' forms of historical knowledge production, of which the discipline of archaeology forms a part, and 'local', 'indigenous', and/or 'traditional' forms of history- and heritage-making. This is not to suggest that these share a similar epistemological and ontological basis; there are real differences, and these need to be recognised, examined, and even celebrated. However, despite the best intentions to do otherwise, this contrast commonly creates a structural imbalance between Western and non-Western historical constructs, with the latter being seen to have only local, contextually specific relevance or significance. As Paul Sillitoe has noted more generally, while promoting the role of IK is certainly a welcome and long overdue 'attempt to give local voices and practices more prominence in development contexts', it will never 'be a straightforward endeavour if people differ in their ideas about what constitutes knowledge (leaving aside for a moment the issues of political power)'.[61] Put another way, while efforts at community and Indigenous archaeology on the continent maintain this kind of structural imbalance between differing knowledge systems, there will be little opportunity for any genuine hybridisation of Western archaeological concepts or practices, and thus genuine decolonisation of the discipline. To be clear, while acknowledging the important points made by Stephen Silliman[62] in his robust critique of some recent archaeological applications, the concept of hybridity as used by Homi Bhabha offers a powerful alternative to essentialist concepts of identity, belonging, and tradition, requiring not just recognition and negotiation of difference, *but also affinity*.[63]

In this regard, a particularly key misconception that needs to be abandoned is the notion that archaeology, i.e. the use of material traces to construct historical narratives, is a Western construct. Although woefully under-researched, there is sufficient evidence to suggest that this is, instead, possibly a human universal[64] albeit finding expression and application in a less formalised manner than the disciplinary practice that is now closely associated with Western concepts of modernity,[65] or even those associated with other academic traditions.[66] Lack of recognition that all societies use material traces in the construction of their pasts and as memory devices (Pikirayi's second criterion needing recognition) forecloses on the possibility of identifying affinities between what are otherwise ostensibly different ways of knowing the past, and consequentially limits engagement between different knowledge stakeholders to a focus on *conflicting* interpretations of the past and resolution of these.

The third impediment to change, namely the unequal knowledge and power structures inherent to current forms of knowledge production about Africa's past, has received much greater attention from scholars and heritage managers in recent decades, and many recent examples of community archaeology are premised on achieving such goals.[67] A key shift in approach, as also seen elsewhere, has been a move away from treating community collaborators just as 'informants' to recognition that they are 'knowledge holders' and, increasingly, 'knowledge co-producers', with a corresponding emphasis on establishing collaborative partnerships that allow the 'voices' of different knowledge stakeholders to be heard equally and given equal recognition.

Welcome though these changes may be, as noted over a decade ago, the creation of equitable partnerships has not always been accomplished successfully.[68] Even where progress has been made towards the normalisation of less 'governmental' approaches, such as those that have long characterised the management of Great Zimbabwe,[69] there remain markedly few examples of community archaeology in sub-Saharan Africa that have sought to generate, as Pikirayi's first step for decolonising the discipline asserts, novel theoretical constructs 'informed by locally-based epistemologies and worldviews'.[70] Thus, while archaeological and heritage management projects may well be more inclusive and supportive of Indigenous perspectives about archaeological sites, monuments, landscapes, and other heritage places, these are still treated by and large as epistemically distinct from archaeological concepts. Put another way, effective decolonisation of the discipline requires much more than promoting multivocality and power sharing, important though these are, and must include the 'internationalization of local values'.[71] Without such 'internationalization', the epistemic culture of scientific archaeology will remain largely unchanged. To illustrate this further, the following section summarises a recent effort to accomplish this, with reference to an ongoing collaborative and multidisciplinary study with Samburu agro-pastoralists in northern Kenya and the theoretical insights that emanated from scholarly engagement with the Indigenous concept of *'ntoror'*.

Discovering *ntoror*

The Samburu landscape idiom of *ntoror* emerged within the context of a collaborative three-field (archaeology, cultural anthropology, and physical anthropology) research project on the date and uses of a series of stone cairns on a hillside known locally as Naakedi, located a few kilometres northwest of the modern village of Baawa, Samburu District, northern Kenya.[72] The excavation (Figure 27.1) was undertaken at the invitation of some members of the local community, following deliberate disturbance of some of the cairns by a member (or members) of the community for reasons that remain unclear.[73] In the event, these acts of disturbance exposed the remains of several well-preserved inhumation burials, prompting local speculation as to their origin. Formal archaeological excavation was seen by some members of the community as a way to answer this question, although others, especially community elders, had reservations about inviting such scrutiny. The collaborative project that eventually unfolded sought, in part, to understand how local sensibilities and historical narratives about the cairns and the individuals they contained were altered as a consequence of archaeological and anthropological investigation.

Figure 27.1 Lucas Lekimargo, James Lekaleosi and Charles Hilton excavating Cairn 1, Naakedi cairnfield, July 2008

Source: Photo: Paul Lane

Among Samburu, the term *ntoror* is used to refer to any 'open space that attracts conflict because of the sweet pastures and water points it offers in an environment that is simultaneously generative and destructive'.[74] As discussed elsewhere, the concept was brought to the attention of the project's cultural anthropologist by her long-time research associate and interlocutor, the late Musa Letua, who was also a member of the Baawa project and the wider Baawa community. It is a distinctly Indigenous idea, that for contemporary Samburu 'evokes the transitory status of any community that both coheres and settles in place', and its meaning encapsulates 'the emotional force of being collective survivors of "*mutai*" – disaster, broadly understood'.[75] *Ntoror*, as conceived by Samburu, had not previously been a focus of academic enquiry, although Maasai (with whom Samburu are linguistically aligned) use the name *Entorror* to refer to their entire northern territorial range prior to expropriation of this land in 1911 under a now contested treaty with the colonial government of the Kenya Protectorate.[76] As a toponym, *Entorror* certainly evokes many of the same notions (and emotions) as *ntoror*, most notably remembrance of its 'sweetness ... compared to the bitterness'[77] of the Southern Reserve (*Ngatet*) where the Maasai sections evicted after 1911 were relocated, and also the memory of the loss of access to the Laikipia landscape.[78] Yet, as a concept for thinking about how a society negotiates cultural continuities and change arising as a consequence of interaction between two or more communities, it would appear that for Samburu *ntoror* has additional resonances of a more existential nature. These, in particular, inform their own sense of 'being' Samburu as deriving in part from histories of contestation over 'sweet' places.

It is perhaps also telling that academic awareness of the idea of *ntoror* emerged within the context of a research project that deliberately sought to explore contrasting understandings of certain material traces of the past, and that juxtaposed different Western disciplinary practices and ways of thinking about material evidence (which in themselves did not always align with one another)[79] alongside those of local Samburu collaborators, participants, and observers. In the act of constituting the stone cairns on the Naakedi hillside as a locus of collective scholarly endeavour, both the literal and metaphorical spaces of the excavation were instantiated as places of ambivalence, with the cairns ultimately acquiring properties of *ntoror* – simultaneously metaphorically a 'sweet' place attracting new forms of financial and cultural capital, yet also a 'site' of contestation played out in different ways between the multiple actors both present at the excavations and elsewhere – that they had not seemingly possessed beforehand. As Musa Letua pointed out, 'when two or more communities meet in [the] sweet spaces' that manifest as *ntoror*, 'one often powerfully overtakes the other'.[80] In this specific case, as a direct consequence of our interventions, archaeological and anthropological readings of the human and material assemblages have added additional layers of meaning to those that originally constituted the Naakedi cairnfield for local Samburu, which must now be heard and if necessary contested. Likewise, the human remains that had lain dormant within the cairns are now entangled in a much wider network of social, political, and economic relations that include Western-trained archaeologists, anthropologists, and geneticists, state actors from the National Museums of Kenya, and members of local government, as debate over the future of these remains, once their study has been completed, continues. At the same time, the performance of archaeological excavation has enabled the very concept of *ntoror* (which otherwise may have remained a latent and unacknowledged Indigenous concept familiar only to Samburu and perhaps other speakers of Maa languages), both within our own research project and in terms of its potential to serve as a generic term for a specific form of social interaction. It is intriguing, then, that our Samburu interlocutors were readily able to accommodate the disturbances, both literal and metaphorical, introduced by the archaeological project as just another instance of 'development' that, like other examples of *maendeleo* (to use the Swahili term) introduces both opportunities and new challenges.[81]

What is especially striking about *ntoror* as a concept, and would allow its wider theoretical application to other contexts around the globe and concerning other times, are its resonances with contemporary ideas about archaeology and assemblage,[82] and about the affective power of things as they refer, and apply, to landscapes.[83] Perhaps the closest comparison that can be drawn is to Anna Lowenhaupt Tsing's conceptualisation of landscapes as multi-species and multi-entity 'gatherings in the making',[84] properties she also attributes to 'moots', drawing inspiration from the word's eleventh-century origins as a word for 'a meeting, an assembly of people, *esp.* one for judicial or legislative purposes. Also: *a place where a meeting is held*',[85] rather than the more specialised and narrower legal usage of the term that now dominates. For Tsing, following Kenneth Olwig's observation[86] concerning the etymological connections between land, 'customary law, the institutions embodying the law, and the people enfranchised to participating in the making and administration of law' in Germanic languages, moots are 'landscape assemblages' wherein 'many living beings – and non-vital things' are drawn together through processes of negotiation and the search for affinity.[87] Here, it is also worth recalling that the English word 'thing', originally meaning a meeting (or moot), derives from the Danish institution of the *ting* (*Ding* in German).

Moots are neither static nor predetermined. Instead, the different multi-species and non-vital participants in a moot decline or flourish only in relation to 'the effects of the world-making projects initiated and maintained' by the other elements.[88] Aspects of our research project share many of the characteristics Tsing attributes to moots. The excavation of the cairns at Naakedi in 2006 and 2008, like other archaeological projects, comprised particular assemblages of vital human and non-human things that, moot-like, became entangled in debates over their meaning, significance, and historical roots. Likewise, our Samburu interlocutors' categorisation of the human burials these excavations exposed as material expressions of a past *ntoror* signifying both disaster and survival brought to the fore previously latent signs of older gatherings and contestations. In a similar vein, the re-emergence of the cairnfield as a place once again exhibiting generic, but far from identical, properties of *ntoror* was a consequence of the world-making projects of different actors and agents that coalesced to form, and were given shape by, the archaeological excavations. At this level of comparison, the concepts of 'moot' and '*ntoror*' can be treated as broadly equivalent, and perhaps even interchangeable.

However, what the Samburu concept adds is a distinctive perspective on 'sweet' places, and how it is that spaces possessed of desirable properties and resources simultaneously attract harmony and discord, creating tensions between different agents, and from which all involved emerge transformed through the processes of assemblage and entanglement. Tradition may still adhere and even take precedence in such places, but such tradition has itself been transformed and in a sense remains, much like landscapes themselves, in a state of becoming.

Conclusion

The processes and strategies for decolonising academic disciplines vary widely. In her ground-breaking and highly acclaimed manifesto for Indigenous research, the Māori scholar Linda Tuhiwai Smith, for example, proposed 25 distinct strategies, from claiming rights and celebrating survival to reframing narratives, protecting intangible heritage, and sharing knowledge.[89] The emphasis placed on the significance and merit of a particular strategy for decolonising knowledge will also vary, inevitably, on the specific vantage point of those engaged in the process of un-disciplining the disciplines, predicating against any move towards more prescriptive approaches. This diversity is certainly evident within African archaeology, although as argued here the majority of efforts to date have been directed towards redressing current power imbalances, and especially the differential power of archaeologists and heritage agencies over interpretation and representation of the past relative to those of the local communities residing in those areas that become the focus of archaeological and heritage management concern.[90] Recognition of such power imbalances and the erasure of Indigenous histories of place and belonging that arise,[91] has prompted researchers working on the African continent, and elsewhere, to create the intellectual space for generating, celebrating, and listening to alternative histories[92] and to challenge the dominance of governmental approaches to heritage management.[93] More holistic approaches to the attribution of value to heritage sites – and the development of management approaches that can accommodate the different ways tangible heritage is understood – have also been proposed as a way to reduce recurrent tensions and to promote cultural healing,[94] while also recognising some of the challenges associated with promoting multivocality in particular settings.[95]

Alongside such strategies, as argued here, attention also needs to be given to identifying affinities between disciplinary archaeology and the knowledge systems and memory-making practices of the African communities with whom archaeologists and heritage professionals work, mindful of the fact that neither are static entities but also of the long legacy of historical erasure of Indigenous perspectives on the past. Recognising that people construct and verify knowledge, whether about the present or the past, in different ways, is obviously the first step, and the 'ontological turn' within archaeology and other social sciences in recent decades has done much to advance this as a guiding principle for research. Yet, if we persist in holding these contrasting knowledge systems in tension, constantly invoking a Western/Indigenous, scientific/traditional binary that forever situates Indigenous/

traditional, knowledge within 'local' rather than 'global' space, we risk perpetuating the same contestations over knowledge claims and the authority to make these that we seek to resolve. Instead, as practices shift towards genuine knowledge co-production, an element of unlearning of Western epistemic belief in the universal character of generalisations[96] would seem to be called for, alongside greater acknowledgement of fluidity and contextual contingency. At the same time, researchers need to work harder at identifying the shared affinities between contrasting means of history-making and the processes of assemblage that constitute and reconstitute that knowledge, and at incorporating these into existing interpretative frameworks.

Acknowledgements

I would like to thank the editors Ann McGrath and Lynette Russell for their kind invitation to contribute to this volume, and, with David Haworth, for their endless patience while I dithered, prevaricated, and delayed producing anything half-decent. Thanks are also due to Hannah Cartmel for her excellent copy-editing. I would also like to thank Federica Sulas, Daryl Stump, and Bilinda Straight for their insightful comments on an earlier draft of the paper; Holly Marriott Webb for alerting me to Anna Tsing's discussion of moots; and our Samburu research collaborators and interlocutors for their insights into 'sweet' and 'bitter' landscapes of knowledge production. The research undertaken at Baawa has been funded thus far by the British Institute in Eastern Africa and the British Academy and both are warmly thanked for their support, as well as the Office of the President, Government of Kenya and the National Museums of Kenya, for research permits and archaeological excavation licences, respectively. An earlier version of this paper was presented at the ASAPA2019 Conference, Kimberley, South Africa in July 2019, and I am grateful to the organisers and especially David Morris for their invitation, hospitality, and the financial support provided. Any errors and misinterpretations are solely my responsibility.

Notes

1 For example, Bassey Andah, 'European Encumbrances to the Development of Relevant Theory in African Archaeology,' in *Theory in Archaeology: A World Perspective*, ed. Peter Ucko (Abingdon: Routledge, 1995), 116–128; Nick Shepherd, 'Heading South, Looking North: Why We Need a Post-Colonial Archaeology,' *Archaeological Dialogues* 9, no. 2 (2002): 74–82; Sven Ouzman, 'Silencing and Sharing Southern African Indigenous and Embedded Knowledge,' in *Indigenous Archaeologies: Decolonizing Theory and Practice*, eds. Claire Smith and H. Martin Wobst (Abingdon: Routledge, 2005), 208–225; George Abungu, 'Practising Archaeology in Eastern and Southern Africa,' in *A Future for Archaeology*, eds. Robert Layton, Stephen Shennan, and Peter Stone (London: University College London Press, 2006), 143–155; Ndukuyakhe Ndlovu, 'Decolonizing the Mind-Set: South African Archaeology in a Postcolonial, Post-Apartheid Era,' in *Postcolonial Archaeologies in Africa*, ed. Peter Schmidt (Santa Fe: School of American Research Press, 2009), 177–192; Peter Schmidt, 'What is Postcolonial About Archaeologies in Africa?' in *Postcolonial Archaeologies in Africa*, ed. Peter Schmidt (Santa Fe: School of American Research Press, 2009), 1–20; Paul Lane, 'Possibilities for a Postcolonial

Archaeology in Sub-Saharan Africa: Indigenous and Usable Pasts,' *World Archaeology* 43, no. 1 (2011): 7–25; Innocent Pikirayi, 'The Future of Archaeology in Africa,' *Antiquity* 89, no. 345 (2015): 531–541; Munyaradzi Manyanga and Shadreck Chirikure, 'Archives, Objects, Places and Landscapes: The Multidisciplinary and Decolonising Imperative,' in *Archives, Objects, Places and Landscapes: Multidisciplinary Approaches to Decolonised Zimbabwean Pasts*, eds. Munyaradzi Manyanga and Shadreck Chirikure (Bemenda: Langaa Research & Publishing CIG, 2017), 1–11.

2. Innocent Pikirayi and Peter Schmidt, 'Introduction: Community Archaeology and Heritage in Africa – Decolonizing Practice,' in *Community Archaeology and Heritage in Africa*, eds. Peter Schmidt and Innocent Pikirayi (Abingdon: Routledge, 2016), 19.

3. For example, Merrick Posnansky, 'African Archaeology Comes of Age,' *World Archaeology* 13, no. 3 (1982): 345–358; Nwana Nzewunwa, 'Nigeria,' in *Approaches to the Archaeological Heritage*, ed. Henry Cleere (Cambridge: Cambridge University Press, 1984), 101–108; Gabebah Abrahams, 'A Review of the South African Cultural Heritage Legislation, 1987,' in *Archaeological Heritage Management in the Modern World*, ed. Henry Cleere (London: Unwin Hyman, 1989), 207–218; Francis Musonda, 'African Archaeology: Looking Forward,' *African Archaeological Review* 8, no. 1 (1990): 3–22; Mohamed Sahnouni, 'Changing Paradigms: A Call for Training' (part of 'The Future of African Archaeology'), *African Archaeological Review* 13, no. 1 (1996): 27–28; see also John Alexander, 'Saving the African Heritage is a Global Priority: How Can a New Subdiscipline of Rescue Archaeology Aid It?' *African Archaeological Review* 28, no. 1 (2011): 93–96, for a later reiteration of this point.

4. Gilbert Pwiti, 'Archaeology, Prehistory and Education in Zimbabwe,' in *The Presented Past: Heritage, Museums and Education*, eds. Peter Stone and Brian Molyneaux (Abingdon: Routledge, 1994), 338–347; Simuyu Wandibba, 'Archaeology and Education in Kenya, the Present and the Future,' in *The Presented Past: Heritage, Museums and Education*, eds. Peter Stone and Brian Molyneux (London: Unwin Hyman, 1994), 349–358; Alinah Segobye, 'Political Instabilities and Education' (part of 'The Future of African Archaeology'), *African Archaeological Review* 13, no. 1 (1996): 29–34.

5. For example, Bertram Mapunda, 'The Role of Archaeology in Development: The Case of Tanzania,' *Transafrican Journal of History* 20 (1991): 19–34; Andrew Hall and Cynthia Kros, 'New Premises for Public History in South Africa,' *The Public Historian* 16, no. 2 (1994): 15–32; Patrice Jeppson, '"Leveling the Playing Field" in the Contested Territory of the South African Past: A "Public" Versus a "People's" Form of Historical Archaeology Outreach,' *Historical Archaeology* 31, no. 3 (1997): 65–82.

6. For example, Thurstan Shaw, 'African Archaeology: Looking Back and Looking Forward,' *African Archaeological Review* 7, no. 1 (1989): 3–31; Chapurukha Kusimba, 'Kenya's Destruction of the Swahili Cultural Heritage,' in *Plundering Africa's Past*, eds. Peter Schmidt and Roderick McIntosh (Bloomington: Indiana University Press, 1996), 201–224; Audax Mabulla, 'Tanzania's Endangered Heritage: A Call for a Protection Program,' *African Archaeological Review* 13, no. 3 (1996): 197–214; Gilbert Pwiti, 'Taking African Cultural Heritage Management into the Twenty-First Century: Zimbabwe's Masterplan for Cultural Heritage Management,' *African Archaeological Review* 14, no. 2 (1997): 81–83.

7. Roderick McIntosh, 'Resolved: To Act for Africa's Historical and Cultural Patrimony,' *African Arts* 24, no. 1 (1991): 18–22; Samuel Sidibe, 'The Pillage of Archaeological Sites in Mali,' *African Arts* 28, no. 4 (1995): 52–55; Peter Schmidt and Roderick McIntosh, eds. *Plundering Africa's Past* (Bloomington: Indiana University Press, 1996).

8. John Alexander, 'A Suggested Training Scheme for Archaeological Resource Managers in Tropical Countries,' in *Archaeological Heritage Management in the Modern World*, ed. Henry Cleere (London: Unwin Hyman, 1989), 280–284; Susan Keech McIntosh, 'Archaeological Heritage Management and Site Inventory Systems in Africa,' *Journal of Field Archaeology* 20, no. 4 (1993): 500–504; Fekri Hassan, 'African Archaeology: The Call of the Future,' *African Affairs* 98, no. 392 (1999): 393–406.

9 Bruce Trigger, 'Alternative Archaeologies: Nationalist, Colonialist, Imperialist,' *Man* N.S. (1984): 355–370; Bruce Trigger, 'Paradigms in Sudan Archaeology,' *International Journal of African Historical Studies* 27, no. 2 (1994): 323–345; Shaw, 'African Archaeology,' 3–31; Peter Robertshaw, ed., *A History of African Archaeology* (London: James Currey, 1990).

10 For example, Martin Hall, 'The Burden of Tribalism: The Social Context of Southern African Iron Age Studies,' *American Antiquity* 49, no. 3 (1984): 455–467.

11 Jean-Aimé Rakotoarisoa, 'The Burden of an Encumbered Inheritance Upon the Study of the Past of Madagascar,' in *Conflict in the Archaeology of Living Traditions*, ed. Robert Layton (London: Unwin Hyman, 1989), 82–87.

12 Bassey Andah, 'Prologue to Cultural Resource Management: An African Dimension,' *West African Archaeological Review* 20 (1991): 2–8; Andah, 'European Encumbrances,' 116–128.

13 Roderick McIntosh and Susan Keech McIntosh, 'The Inland Niger Delta Before the Empire of Mali: Evidence from Jenne-Jeno,' *Journal of African History* 22, no. 1 (1981): 1–22; Susan Keech McIntosh and Roderick McIntosh, 'The Early City in West Africa: Towards an Understanding,' *African Archaeological Review* 2, no. 1 (1984): 73–98.

14 Roderick McIntosh, *Ancient Middle Niger: Urbanism and the Self-Organizing Landscape* (Cambridge: Cambridge University Press, 2005).

15 Rodolfo Fattovich, 'Pre-Aksumite Civilization of Ethiopia: A Provisional Review,' *Proceedings of the Seminar for Arabian Studies* 7 (1977): 73–78; Rodolfo Fattovich, 'Remarks on the Pre-Aksumite Period in Northern Ethiopia,' *Journal of Ethiopian Studies* 23 (1990): 1–33.

16 Rodolfo Fattovich, 'The Development of Ancient States in the Northern Horn of Africa, c. 3000 BC–AD 1000: An Archaeological Outline,' *Journal of World Prehistory* 23, no. 3 (2010): 145–175.

17 Martin Hall, 'Tribes, Traditions and Numbers: The American Model in Southern African Iron Age Ceramic Studies,' *South African Archaeological Bulletin* 38, no. 138 (1983): 51–57; Hall, 'Burden of Tribalism,' 455–467.

18 David Clarke, *Analytical Archaeology* (London: Methuen, 1968).

19 Gordon Childe, 'Races, Peoples and Cultures in Prehistoric Europe,' *History* 18, no. 71 (1933): 193–203; Gordon Childe, *Piecing Together the Past: The Interpretation of Archaeological Data* (London: Routledge and Keegan Paul, 1956).

20 Mark Horton, 'Early Muslim Trading Settlements on the East African Coast: New Evidence from Shanga,' *The Antiquaries Journal* 67, no. 2 (1987): 290–323; Mark Horton, *Shanga: The Archaeology of a Muslim Trading Community on the Coast of East Africa* (London: British Institute in Eastern Africa, 1996); Felix Chami, *The Tanzanian Coast in the First Millennium AD: An Archaeology of the Iron-Working, Farming Communities* (Uppsala: Uppsala University, Societas Archaeologica Upsaliensis, Studies in African Archaeology Vol. 7, 1994).

21 Derek Nurse and Thomas Spear, *The Swahili: Reconstructing the History and Language of an African Society, 800–1500* (Philadelphia: University of Pennsylvania Press, 1985).

22 Posnansky, 'African Archaeology,' 345–358.

23 Peter Schmidt, 'Using Archaeology to Remake African History,' in *Making Alternative Histories: The Practice of Archaeology and History in Non-Western Settings*, eds. Peter Schmidt and Thomas Patterson (Santa Fe: School of American Research Press, 1995): 118–147.

24 Andah, 'European Encumbrances,' 116–128.

25 Hassan, 'African Archaeology,' 398.

26 Gordon Cumming, 'Nicolas Sarkozy's Africa Policy: Change, Continuity or Confusion?' *French Politics* 11, no. 1 (2013): 24–47.

27 For example, Francis Musonda, 'Decolonising the Broken Hill Skull: Cultural Loss and a Pathway to Zambian Archaeological Sovereignty,' *African Archaeological Review* 30, no. 2 (2013): 195–220; Peter Schmidt and Innocent Pikirayi, eds., *Community Archaeology*

and Heritage in Africa: Decolonizing Practice (Abingdon: Routledge, 2016); Manyanga and Chirikure, 'Archives,' 1–11; George Abungu, 'Museums: Geopolitics, Decolonisation, Globalisation and Migration,' *Museum International* 71, no. 1–2 (2019): 62–67.

28 Shadreck Chirikure, Webber Ndoro, and Janette Deacon, 'Approaches and Trends in African Heritage Management and Conservation,' in *Managing Heritage in Africa: Who Cares?*, eds. Webber Ndoro, Shadreck Chirikure, and Janette Deacon (Abingdon: Routledge, 2018), 2, emphasis added.

29 Paul Sillitoe, 'Trust in Development: Some Implications of Knowing in Indigenous Knowledge,' *Journal of the Royal Anthropological Institute* 16, no. 1 (2010): 24.

30 For example, Joe Watkins, *Indigenous Archaeology: American Indian Values and Scientific Practice* (Walnut Creek, CA: Altamira Press, 2000); Claire Smith and Martin Wobst, eds., *Indigenous Archaeologies: Decolonizing Theory and Practice* (Abingdon: Routledge, 2004); Ian McNiven and Lynette Russell, *Appropriated Pasts: Indigenous Peoples and the Colonial Culture of Archaeology* (Lanham, MD: AltaMira Press, 2005); Sonya Atalay, 'Indigenous Archaeology as Decolonizing Practice,' *American Indian Quarterly* 30 (2006): 280–310; George Nicholas, ed., *Being and Becoming Indigenous Archaeologists* (Abingdon: Routledge, 2010); Cristóbal Gnecco and Patricia Ayala, eds., *Indigenous Peoples and Archaeology in Latin America* (Walnut Creek, CA: Left Coast Press, 2011).

31 See Scott MacEachern, 'Time on the Timeless Continent: History and Archaeological Chronologies in the Southern Lake Chad Basin,' in *Big Histories, Human Lives: Tackling Problems of Scale in Archaeology*, eds. Timothy Pauketat and John Robb (Santa Fe: School for Advanced Research Press, 2013), 123–144.

32 François Richard, 'Recharting Atlantic Encounters: Object Trajectories and Histories of Value in the Siin (Senegal) and Senegambia,' *Archaeological Dialogues* 17, no. 1 (2010): 2.

33 Pikirayi, 'Future of Archaeology in Africa,' 531–541.

34 Pikirayi, 'Future of Archaeology in Africa,' 532.

35 Pikirayi, 'Future of Archaeology in Africa,' 531.

36 Pikirayi, 'Future of Archaeology in Africa,' 532.

37 Lucien Levy-Bruhl, *Les Fonctions Mentales dans les Sociétés Inférieurs* (Paris: Alcan & Réunies, 1910); Bronislaw Mallinowski, *Coral Gardens and Their Magic* (London: Routledge and Keegan Paul, 1935).

38 Claude Lévi-Strauss, *The Savage Mind* (Chicago, IL: Chicago University Press, 1966); Robin Horton, 'African Traditional Thought and Western Science. Part I: From Tradition to Science,' *Africa* 37 (1967): 50–71; Jack Goody, *The Domestication of the Savage Mind* (Cambridge: Cambridge University Press, 1977); Bruno Latour, *We Have Never Been Modern* (Cambridge, MA: Harvard University Press, 1993).

39 Michel-Rolph Trouillot, *Global Transformations: Anthropology and the Modern World* (Basingstoke: Palgrave Macmillan, 2003).

40 David Brokensha, Dennis M. Warren, and Oswald Werner, eds., *Indigenous Knowledge Systems and Development* (Washington, DC: University Press of America, 1980); Arun Agrawal, 'Dismantling the Divide Between Indigenous and Scientific Knowledge,' *Development and Change* 26, no. 3 (1995): 413–439; Paul Sillitoe, 'The Development of Indigenous Knowledge: A New Applied Anthropology,' *Current Anthropology* 39, no. 2 (1998): 223–252.

41 For example, Polly Hill, 'A Plea for Indigenous Economics: The West African Example,' *Economic Development and Cultural Change* 15, no. 1 (1966): 10–20; Christopher Hallpike, *The Konso of Ethiopia: A Study of the Values of a Cushitic People* (Oxford: Clarendon Press, 1972).

42 Paul Richards, *Indigenous Agricultural Revolution: Ecology and Food Production in West Africa* (London: Hutchinson, 1985); World Commission on Environment and Development (WCED), *Our Common Future, From One Earth to One World*, edited by V. Hauff (Oxford: Oxford University Press, on behalf of the WCED, 1987).

43 For example, Ernst Schumaker, *Small Is Beautiful: A Study of Economics As If People Mattered* (London: Blond & Briggs, 1973).

44 Rachel Carson, *Silent Spring* (Boston, MA: Houghton Mifflin, 1962).
45 Jan Hogendorn and K.M. Scott, 'The East African Groundnut Scheme: Lessons of a Large-Scale Agricultural Failure,' *African Economic History* 10 (1981): 81–115; Matteo Rizzo, 'What Was Left of the Groundnut Scheme? Development Disaster and Labour Market in Southern Tanganyika 1946–1952,' *Journal of Agrarian Change* 6, no. 2 (2006): 205–238.
46 Emil Schreyger, *L'Office du Niger au Mali de 1932 à 1982: La Problématique d'une Grande Entreprise Agricole dans la Zone du Sahel* (Wiesbaden: Steiner, 1984); Monica Van Beusekom, 'Colonisation Indigene: French Rural Development Ideology at the Office du Niger, 1920–1940,' *International Journal of African Historical Studies* (1997): 299–323.
47 For example, Elizabeth Colson, *The Social Consequences of Resettlement: The Impact of the Kariba Resettlement upon the Gwembe Tonga* (Kariba Studies IV) (Manchester: Manchester University Press, 1971); Tony Barnett, *The Gezira Scheme: An Illusion of Development* (London: Cass, 1977); William Adams and Francine Hughes, 'The Environmental Effects of Dam Construction in Tropical Africa: Impacts and Planning Procedures,' *Geoforum* 17, no. 3–4 (1986): 403–410.
48 Katherine Showers, *Imperial Gullies: Soil Erosion and Conservation in Lesotho* (Athens: Ohio University Press, 2005); Paul Lane, 'Environmental Narratives and the History of Soil Erosion in Kondoa District, Tanzania: An Archaeological Perspective,' *International Journal of African Historical Studies* 42, no. 3 (2009): 457–483.
49 James Fairhead and Melissa Leach, *Misreading the African Landscape: Society and Ecology in a Forest-Savanna Mosaic* (Cambridge: Cambridge University Press, 1996); James McCann, 'The Plow and the Forest: Narratives of Deforestation in Ethiopia, 1840–1992,' *Environmental History* 2, no. 2 (1997): 138–159; Christian Kull, 'Deforestation, Erosion, and Fire: Degradation Myths in the Environmental History of Madagascar,' *Environment and History* 6, no. 4 (2000): 423–450.
50 Julian Inglis, ed., *Traditional Ecological Knowledge: Concepts and Cases* (Ottawa: International Program on Traditional Ecological Knowledge & International Development Research Centre, 1993); Dennis Warren, 'Indigenous Knowledge, Biodiversity Conservation and Development,' in *Sustainable Development in Third World Countries: Applied and Theoretical Perspectives*, ed. Valentine James (Westport, CT: Praeger Publishers, 1996), 81–88; Louise Grenier, *Working with Indigenous Knowledge: A Guide for Researchers* (Ottawa: International Development Research Centre (Canada), 1998).
51 Daryl Stump, '"Ancient and Backward or Long-Lived and Sustainable?" The Role of the Past in Debates Concerning Rural Livelihoods and Resource Conservation in Eastern Africa,' *World Development* 38, no. 9 (2010): 1251–1262; Daryl Stump, 'On Applied Archaeology, Indigenous Knowledge, and the Usable Past,' *Current Anthropology* 54, no. 3 (2013): 268–298.
52 Stump, '"Ancient and Backward",' 1258.
53 Matthew Davies, 'Some Thoughts on a "Useable" African Archaeology: Settlement, Population and Intensive Farming Among the Pokot of Northwest Kenya,' *African Archaeological Review* 29, no. 4 (2012): 319–353; Robert Marchant and Paul Lane, 'Past Perspectives for the Future: Foundations for Sustainable Development in East Africa,' *Journal of Archaeological Science* 51 (2014): 12–21.
54 Paul Lane, 'Just How Long Does "Long-Term" Have to Be? Matters of Temporal Scale as Impediments to Interdisciplinary Understanding in Historical Ecology,' in *The Oxford Handbook of Historical Ecology and Applied Archaeology*, eds. Christian Isendahl and Daryl Stump (Oxford: Oxford University Press, 2019), 49–71; Daryl Stump, 'Digging for Indigenous Knowledge: "Reverse Engineering" and Stratigraphic Sequencing as a Potential Archaeological Contribution to Sustainability Assessments,' in *The Oxford Handbook of Historical Ecology and Applied Archaeology*, eds. Christian Isendahl and Daryl Stump (Oxford: Oxford University Press, 2019), 137–155.
55 Carol Lang and Daryl Stump, 'Geoarchaeological Evidence for the Construction, Irrigation, Cultivation, and Resilience of 15th–18th Century AD Terraced Landscape at Engaruka, Tanzania,' *Quaternary Research* 88, no. 3 (2017): 382–399.

56 Cruz Ferro-Vázquez, Carol Lang, Joeri Kaal, and Daryl Stump, 'When Is a Terrace Not a Terrace? The Importance of Understanding Landscape Evolution in Studies of Terraced Agriculture,' *Journal of Environmental Management* 202 (2017): 500–513.
57 Matthew Davies, 'Economic Specialisation, Resource Variability, and the Origins of Intensive Agriculture in Eastern Africa,' *Rural Landscapes: Society, Environment, History* 2, no. 1 (2015): 1–18; Amanda Logan, '"Why Can't People Feed Themselves?": Archaeology as Alternative Archive of Food Security in Banda, Ghana,' *American Anthropologist* 118, no. 3 (2016): 508–524; Kristina Douglass et al., 'Toward a Just and Inclusive Environmental Archaeology of Southwest Madagascar,' *Journal of Social Archaeology* 19, no. 3 (2019): 307–332.
58 Daryl Stump and Susie Richer, 'Terraces Are Good, But Sometimes Sediment Traps Are Better,' (York: University of York, Archaeology of Agricultural Resilience in Eastern Africa Project, Policy Brief 1, November 2017).
59 Stump, 'On Applied Archaeology,' 268–298.
60 Pikirayi, 'Future of Archaeology in Africa,' 532.
61 Sillitoe, 'Trust in Development,' 15.
62 Stephen Silliman, 'A Requiem for Hybridity? The Problem with Frankensteins, Purées, and Mules,' *Journal of Social Archaeology* 15, no. 3 (2015): 277–298.
63 Homi Bhabha, *The Location of Culture* (Abingdon: Routledge, 1994).
64 Paul Lane, 'The Material Culture of Memory,' in *The Qualities of Time: Anthropological Approaches*, eds. Wendy James and David Mills (Oxford: Berg, 2005), 19–34; Paul Lane, 'Envisioning a Different Notion of "Indigenous Archaeology" from the Perspective of Sub-Saharan Africa,' in *Archaeologies of 'Us' and 'Them': The Ethics and Politics of Indigeneity in Archaeology and Heritage*, eds. Charlotta Hillerdal, Anna Karlström and Carl-Gösta Öjala (Abingdon: Routledge, 2017), 113–126.
65 Julian Thomas, *Archaeology and Modernity* (Abingdon: Routledge, 2004).
66 Richard Rudolph, 'Preliminary Notes on Sung Archaeology,' *Journal of Asian Studies* 22, no. 2 (1963): 169–177; Bruce Trigger, *A History of Archaeological Thought* (Cambridge: Cambridge University Press, 1989).
67 For example, Sada Mire, 'Preserving Knowledge, Not Objects: A Somali Perspective for Heritage Management and Archaeological Research,' *African Archaeological Review* 24, no. 3–4 (2007): 49–71; Albino Jopela, 'Traditional Custodianship: A Useful Framework for Heritage Management in Southern Africa?,' *Conservation and Management of Archaeological Sites* 13, no. 2–3 (2011): 103–122; Peter Schmidt, 'Community Heritage Work in Africa: Village-Based Preservation and Development,' *Conservation Science in Cultural Heritage* 14, no. 2 (2014): 133–150; Chapurukha Kusimba, 'Community Archaeology and Heritage in Coastal and Western Kenya,' *Journal of Community Archaeology & Heritage* 4, no. 3 (2017): 218–228; Nthabiseng Mokoena, 'Community Involvement and Heritage Management in Rural South Africa,' *Journal of Community Archaeology & Heritage* 4, no. 3 (2017): 189–202.
68 Shadreck Chirikure and Gilbert Pwiti, 'Community Involvement in Archaeology and Cultural Heritage Management: An Assessment from Case Studies in Southern Africa and Elsewhere,' *Current Anthropology* 49, no. 3 (2008): 467–485; Shadreck Chirikure et al., 'Unfulfilled Promises? Heritage Management and Community Participation at Some of Africa's Cultural Heritage Sites,' *International Journal of Heritage Studies* 16, no. 1–2 (2010): 30–44.
69 Webber Ndoro, *Your Monument Our Shrine: The Preservation of Great Zimbabwe* (Uppsala: Uppsala University Studies in African Archaeology Vol. 19, 2001); Joost Fontein, *The Silence of Great Zimbabwe: Contested Landscapes and the Power of Heritage* (London: UCL Press, 2006).
70 Pikirayi, 'Future of Archaeology in Africa,' 532.
71 Chirikure et al., 'Approaches and Trends,' 2.
72 Paul Lane, Bilinda Straight, and Charles Hilton, 'Excavations at Baawa, Samburu District, Kenya: Preliminary Report on the 2006 Season,' *Nyame Akuma* 68 (2007): 34–46.

73 Bilinda Straight et al., '"It Was *Maendeleo* That Removed Them": Disturbing Burials and Reciprocal Knowledge Production in a Context of Collaborative Archaeology,' *Journal of the Royal Anthropological Institute* 21, no. 2 (2015): 391–418.
74 Bilinda Straight et al., '"Dust People": Samburu Perspectives on Disaster, Identity, and Landscape,' *Journal of Eastern African Studies* 10, no. 1 (2016): 169.
75 Straight, et al., '"Dust People",' 169.
76 Lotte Hughes, *Moving the Maasai: A Colonial Misadventure* (Basingstoke: Palgrave Macmillan, 2006), x.
77 Here, the contrast between 'sweet' and 'bitter' evokes common distinctions between different types of grass found in the semi-arid rangelands of eastern Africa and thus signals the presence of higher or lower quality grazing conditions for livestock and other positive ecological properties, such as a low prevalence of livestock diseases and other hazards; also embedded within such categorisation are notions of the different qualities of life offered by inhabitation of 'sweet' or 'bitter' places.
78 Hughes, *Moving the Maasai*, 105.
79 See Straight et al., '"It Was *Maendeleo*",' 391–418.
80 Straight et al., '"Dust People",' 169.
81 Straight et al., '"It Was *Maendeleo*",' 391–418.
82 Yanis Hamilakis and Andrew Jones, 'Archaeology and Assemblage,' *Cambridge Archaeological Journal* 27, no. 1 (2017): 77–84.
83 Ben Anderson, 'Becoming and Being Hopeful: Towards a Theory of Affect,' *Environment and Planning D: Society and Space* 24, no. 5 (2006): 733–752; Joost Fontein, 'Graves, Ruins, and Belonging: Towards an Anthropology of Proximity,' *Journal of the Royal Anthropological Institute* 17, no. 4 (2011): 706–727.
84 Anna Tsing, 'The Buck, the Bull, and the Dream of the Stag: Some Unexpected Weeds of the Anthropocene,' *Suomen Antropologi: Journal of the Finnish Anthropological Society* 42, no. 1 (2017): 9.
85 *Oxford English Dictionary Online*, https://www-oed-com.ezp.lib.cam.ac.uk/view/Entry/122011?rskey=vdwHL0&result=1#eid, my emphasis. Accessed 17 August 2020.
86 Kenneth Olwig, 'Recovering the Substantive Nature of Landscape,' *Annals of the Association of American Geographers* 86, no. 4 (1996): 633.
87 Tsing, 'The Buck, the Bull,' 7.
88 Tsing, 'The Buck, the Bull,' 7.
89 Linda Tuhiwai Smith, *Decolonizing Methodologies: Research and Indigenous People* (London: Zed Books, 1999), 142–162.
90 Webber Ndoro, Shadreck Chirikure, and Janette Deacon, *Managing Heritage in Africa: Who Cares?* (Abingdon: Routledge, 2018).
91 Timothy Clack and Marcus Brittain, 'Place-Making, Participative Archaeologies and Mursi Megaliths: Some Implications for Aspects of Pre- and Proto-History in the Horn of Africa,' *Journal of Eastern African Studies* 5, no. 1 (2011): 85–107; Timothy Clack, Marcus Brittain, and David Turton, 'Oral Histories and the Impact of Archaeological Fieldwork in Contact Encounters: Meeting Socrates on the Omo,' *Journal of the Royal Anthropological Institute* 23, no. 4 (2017): 669–689; Anneli Ekblom, Michel Notelid, and Rebecca Witter, 'Negotiating Identity and Heritage Through Authorised Vernacular History, Limpopo National Park,' *Journal of Social Archaeology* 17, no. 1 (2017): 49–68.
92 Peter Schmidt and Thomas Patterson, eds., *Making Alternative Histories: The Practice of Archaeology and History in Non-Western Settings* (Santa Fe: School of American Research Press, 1995).
93 Ndoro, *Your Monument*; Fontein, *Silence of Great Zimbabwe*; Lynn Meskell, *The Nature of Heritage: The New South Africa* (Oxford: Wiley-Blackwell, 2011); Albino Jopela and Per Ditlef Fredriksen, 'Public Archaeology, Knowledge Meetings and Heritage Ethics in Southern Africa: An Approach from Mozambique,' *World Archaeology* 47, no. 2 (2015): 261–284.

94 Paul Basu, 'Confronting the Past? Negotiating a Heritage of Conflict in Sierra Leone,' *Journal of Material Culture* 13, no. 2 (2008): 233–247; Michael Rowlands, 'Civilization, Violence and Heritage Healing in Liberia,' *Journal of Material Culture* 13, no. 2 (2008): 135–152; John Giblin, 'Decolonial Challenges and Post-Genocide Archaeological Politics in Rwanda,' *Public Archaeology* 11, no. 3 (2012): 123–143; Mélanie Duval et al., 'Towards a Holistic Approach to Heritage Values: A Multidisciplinary and Cosmopolitan Approach,' *International Journal of Heritage Studies* 25, no. 12 (2019): 1279–1301.

95 John Giblin, 'Post-Conflict Heritage: Symbolic Healing and Cultural Renewal,' *International Journal of Heritage Studies* 20, no. 5 (2014): 500–518; David Morris, 'Wildebeest Kuil Rock Art Centre, South Africa: Controversy and Renown, Successes, and Shortcomings,' *Public Archaeology* 13, no. 1–3 (2014): 187–199; Shanade Barnabas, 'Heritage-Making and the Dilemma of Multivocality in South Africa: A Case of Wildebeest Kuil,' *International Journal of Heritage Studies* 22, no. 9 (2016): 690–701.

96 Helen Verran, *Science and an African Logic* (Chicago, IL: University of Chicago Press, 2001).

Bibliography

Abrahams, Gabebah. 'A Review of the South African Cultural Heritage Legislation, 1987.' In *Archaeological Heritage Management in the Modern World*, edited by Henry Cleere, 207–218. London: Unwin Hyman, 1989.

Abungu, George H. Okello. 'Practising Archaeology in Eastern and Southern Africa.' In *A Future for Archaeology*, edited by Robert Layton, Stephen Shennan, and Peter Stone, 143–155. London: University College London Press, 2006.

Abungu, George H. Okello. 'Museums: Geopolitics, Decolonisation, Globalisation and Migration.' *Museum International* 71, no. 1–2 (2019): 62–71.

Adams, William M., and Francine M.R. Hughes. 'The Environmental Effects of Dam Construction in Tropical Africa: Impacts and Planning Procedures.' *Geoforum* 17, no. 3–4 (1986): 403–410.

Agrawal, Arun. 'Dismantling the Divide Between Indigenous and Scientific Knowledge.' *Development and Change* 26, no. 3 (1995): 413–439.

Alexander, John. 'A Suggested Training Scheme for Archaeological Resource Managers in Tropical Countries.' In *Archaeological Heritage Management in the Modern World*, edited by Henry Cleere, 280–284. London: Unwin Hyman, 1989.

Alexander, John. 'Saving the African Heritage is a Global Priority: How Can a New Subdiscipline of Rescue Archaeology Aid It?' *African Archaeological Review* 28, no. 1 (2011): 93–96.

Andah, Bassey W. 'Prologue to Cultural Resource Management: An African Dimension.' *West African Archaeological Review* 20 (1991): 2–8.

Andah, Bassey W. 'European Encumbrances to the Development of Relevant Theory in African Archaeology.' In *Theory in Archaeology: A World Perspective*, edited by Peter Ucko, 116–128. Abingdon: Routledge, 1995.

Anderson, Ben. 'Becoming and Being Hopeful: Towards a Theory of Affect.' *Environment and Planning D: Society and Space* 24, no. 5 (2006): 733–752.

Atalay, Sonya. 'Indigenous Archaeology as Decolonizing Practice.' *American Indian Quarterly* 30 (2006): 280–310.

Barnabas, Shanade Bianca. 'Heritage-Making and the Dilemma of Multivocality in South Africa: a Case of Wildebeest Kuil.' *International Journal of Heritage Studies* 22, no. 9 (2016): 690–701.

Barnett, Tony. *The Gezira Scheme: An Illusion of Development*. London: Cass, 1977.

Basu, Paul. 'Confronting the Past? Negotiating a Heritage of Conflict in Sierra Leone.' *Journal of Material Culture* 13, no. 2 (2008): 233–247.

Berkes, Fikret, and Mina Kislalioglu Berkes. 'Ecological Complexity, Fuzzy Logic, and Holism in Indigenous Knowledge.' *Futures* 41, no. 1 (2009): 6–12.
Bhabha, Homi. *The Location of Culture*. Abingdon: Routledge, 1994.
Brokensha, David, Dennis M. Warren, and Oswald Werner, eds. *Indigenous Knowledge Systems and Development*. Washington, DC: University Press of America, 1980.
Carson, Rachel. *Silent Spring*. Boston, MA: Houghton Mifflin, 1962.
Challis, Sam. 'Collections, Collecting and Collectives: Gathering Heritage Data with Communities in the Mountains of Matatiele and Lesotho, Southern Africa.' *African Archaeological Review* 35, no.2 (2018): 257–268.
Chami, Felix. *The Tanzanian Coast in the First Millennium AD: An Archaeology of the Iron-Working, Farming Communities*. Uppsala: Uppsala University, Societas Archaeological Upsaliensis, Studies in African Archaeology Vol. 7, 1994.
Childe, V. Gordon. 'Races, Peoples and Cultures in Prehistoric Europe.' *History* 18, no. 71 (1933): 193–203.
Childe, V. Gordon. *Piecing Together the Past: The Interpretation of Archaeological Data*. London: Routledge and Keegan Paul, 1956.
Chirikure, Shadreck, Munyaradzi Manyanga, Webber Ndoro, and Gilbert Pwiti. 'Unfulfilled Promises? Heritage Management and Community Participation at Some of Africa's Cultural Heritage Sites.' *International Journal of Heritage Studies* 16, no. 1–2 (2010): 30–44.
Chirikure, Shadreck, Webber Ndoro, and Janette Deacon. 'Approaches and Trends in African Heritage Management and Conservation.' In *Managing Heritage in Africa: Who Cares?*, edited by Webber Ndoro, Shadreck Chirikure, and Janette Deacon, 1–21. Abingdon: Routledge, 2018.
Chirikure, Shadreck, and Gilbert Pwiti, 'Community Involvement in Archaeology and cultural Heritage Management: An Assessment from Case Studies in Southern Africa and Elsewhere.' *Current Anthropology* 49, no. 3 (2008): 467–485.
Clack, Timothy, and Marcus Brittain. 'Place-Making, Participative Archaeologies and Mursi Megaliths: Some Implications for Aspects of Pre- and Proto-History in the Horn of Africa.' *Journal of Eastern African Studies* 5, no. 1 (2011): 85–107.
Clack, Timothy, Marcus Brittain, and David Turton. 'Oral Histories and the Impact of Archaeological Fieldwork in Contact Encounters: Meeting Socrates on the Omo.' *Journal of the Royal Anthropological Institute* 23, no. 4 (2017): 669–689.
Clarke, David L. *Analytical Archaeology*. London: Methuen, 1968.
Colson, Elizabeth. *The Social Consequences of Resettlement: The Impact of the Kariba Resettlement upon the Gwembe Tonga* (Kariba Studies IV). Manchester: Manchester University Press, 1971.
Cumming, Gordon D. 'Nicolas Sarkozy's Africa Policy: Change, Continuity or Confusion?' *French Politics* 11, no. 1 (2013): 24–47.
Davies, Matthew I.J. 'Some Thoughts on a "Useable" African Archaeology: Settlement, Population and Intensive Farming Among the Pokot of Northwest Kenya.' *African Archaeological Review* 29, no. 4 (2012): 319–353.
Davies, Matthew I.J. 'Economic Specialisation, Resource Variability, and the Origins of Intensive Agriculture in Eastern Africa.' *Rural Landscapes: Society, Environment, History* 2, no. 1 (2015): 1–18.
Douglass, Kristina, Eréndira Quintana Morales, George Manahira, Felicia Fenomanana, Roger Samba, Francois Lahiniriko, Zafy Maharesy Chrisostome, et al. 'Toward a Just and Inclusive Environmental Archaeology of Southwest Madagascar.' *Journal of Social Archaeology* 19, no. 3 (2019): 307–332.
Duval, Mélanie, Benjamin Smith, Stéphane Hœrlé, Lucie Bovet, Nokukhanya Khumalo, and Lwazi Bhengu. 'Towards a Holistic Approach to Heritage Values: A Multidisciplinary and Cosmopolitan Approach.' *International Journal of Heritage Studies* 25, no. 12 (2019): 1279–1301.

Effros, Bonnie. 'Indigenous Voices at the Margins: Nuancing the History of French Colonial Archaeology in Nineteenth-Century Algeria.' In *Unmasking Ideology in Imperial and Colonial Archaeology: Vocabulary, Symbols, and Legacy*, edited by Bonnie Effros and Goulong Lai, 201–266. Los Angeles: University of California, Cotsen Institute of Archaeology Press.

Ekblom, Anneli, Michel Notelid, and Rebecca Witter. 'Negotiating Identity and Heritage Through Authorised Vernacular History, Limpopo National Park.' *Journal of Social Archaeology* 17, no. 1 (2017): 49–68.

Engmann, Rachel A.A. 'Autoarchaeology at Christiansborg Castle (Ghana): Decolonizing Knowledge, Pedagogy, and Practice.' *Journal of Community Archaeology & Heritage* 6, no. 3 (2019): 204–219.

Fairhead, James, and Melissa Leach. *Misreading the African Landscape: Society and Ecology in a Forest-Savanna Mosaic*. Cambridge: Cambridge University Press, 1996.

Fattovich, Rodolfo. 'Pre-Aksumite Civilization of Ethiopia: A Provisional Review.' *Proceedings of the Seminar for Arabian Studies* 7 (1977): 73–78.

Fattovich, Rodolfo. 'Remarks on the Pre-Aksumite Period in Northern Ethiopia.' *Journal of Ethiopian Studies* 23 (1990): 1–33.

Fattovich, Rodolfo. 'The Development of Ancient States in the Northern Horn of Africa, c. 3000 BC–AD 1000: An Archaeological Outline.' *Journal of World Prehistory* 23, no. 3 (2010): 145–175.

Ferro-Vázquez, Cruz, Carol Lang, Joeri Kaal, and Daryl Stump. 'When Is a Terrace Not a Terrace? The Importance of Understanding Landscape Evolution in Studies of Terraced Agriculture.' *Journal of Environmental Management* 202 (2017): 500–513.

Fontein, Joost. *The Silence of Great Zimbabwe: Contested Landscapes and the Power of Heritage*. London: UCL Press, 2006.

Fontein, Joost. 'Graves, Ruins, and Belonging: Towards an Anthropology of Proximity.' *Journal of the Royal Anthropological Institute* 17, no. 4 (2011): 706–727.

Giblin, John D. 'Decolonial Challenges and Post-Genocide Archaeological Politics in Rwanda.' *Public Archaeology* 11, no. 3 (2012): 123–143.

Giblin, John D. 'Post-Conflict Heritage: Symbolic Healing and Cultural Renewal.' *International Journal of Heritage Studies* 20, no. 5 (2014): 500–518.

Gnecco, Cristóbal, and Patricia Ayala, eds. *Indigenous Peoples and Archaeology in Latin America*. Walnut Creek, CA: Left Coast Press, 2011.

Goody, Jack. *The Domestication of the Savage Mind*. Cambridge: Cambridge University Press, 1977.

Grenier, Louise. *Working with Indigenous Knowledge: A Guide for Researchers*. Ottawa: International Development Research Centre (Canada), 1998.

Hall, Andrew, and Cynthia Kros. 'New Premises for Public History in South Africa.' *The Public Historian* 16, no. 2 (1994): 15–32.

Hall, Martin. 'Tribes, Traditions and Numbers: The American Model in Southern African Iron Age Ceramic Studies.' *South African Archaeological Bulletin* 38, no. 138 (1983): 51–57.

Hall, Martin. 'The Burden of Tribalism: The Social Context of Southern African Iron Age Studies.' *American Antiquity* 49, no. 3 (1984): 455–467.

Hallpike, Christopher R. *The Konso of Ethiopia: A Study of the Values of a Cushitic People*. Oxford: Clarendon Press, 1972.

Hamilakis, Yannis, and Andrew Meirion Jones. 'Archaeology and Assemblage.' *Cambridge Archaeological Journal* 27, no. 1 (2017): 77–84.

Hassan, Fekri A. 'African Archaeology: The Call of the Future.' *African Affairs* 98, no. 392 (1999): 393–406.

Hill, Polly. 'A Plea for Indigenous Economics: The West African Example.' *Economic Development and Cultural Change* 15, no. 1 (1966): 10–20.

Hogendorn, Jan S., and K.M. Scott. 'The East African Groundnut Scheme: Lessons of a Large-Scale Agricultural Failure.' *African Economic History* 10 (1981): 81–115.

Horton, Mark C. 'Early Muslim Trading Settlements on the East African Coast: New Evidence from Shanga.' *The Antiquaries Journal* 67, no. 2 (1987): 290–323.
Horton, Mark C. *Shanga: The Archaeology of a Muslim Trading Community on the Coast of East Africa*. London: British Institute in Eastern Africa, 1996.
Horton, Robin. 'African Traditional Thought and Western Science. Part I: From Tradition to Science.' *Africa* 37 (1967): 50–71.
Houde, Nicolas. 'The Six Faces of Traditional Ecological Knowledge: Challenges and Opportunities for Canadian Co-Management Arrangements.' *Ecology and Society* 12, no. 2 (2007): http://www.ecologyandsociety.org/vol12/iss2/art34/
Hughes, Lotte. *Moving the Maasai: A Colonial Misadventure*. Basingstoke: Palgrave Macmillan, 2006.
Inglis, Julian T., ed. *Traditional Ecological Knowledge: Concepts and Cases*. Ottawa: International Program on Traditional Ecological Knowledge & International Development Research Centre, 1993.
Jeppson, Patrice L. '"Leveling the Playing Field" in the Contested Territory of the South African Past: A "Public" Versus a "People's" Form of Historical Archaeology Outreach.' *Historical Archaeology* 31, no. 3 (1997): 65–82.
Jopela, Albino P. de J. 'Traditional Custodianship: A Useful Framework for Heritage Management in Southern Africa?' *Conservation and Management of Archaeological Sites* 13, no. 2–3 (2011): 103–122.
Jopela, Albino P. de J., and Per Ditlef Fredriksen. 'Public Archaeology, Knowledge Meetings and Heritage Ethics in Southern Africa: An Approach from Mozambique.' *World Archaeology* 47, no. 2 (2015): 261–284.
Kull, Christian A. 'Deforestation, Erosion, and Fire: Degradation Myths in the Environmental History of Madagascar.' *Environment and History* 6, no. 4 (2000): 423–450.
Kusimba, Chapurukha M. 'Kenya's Destruction of the Swahili Cultural Heritage.' In *Plundering Africa's Past*, edited by Peter R. Schmidt and Roderick J. McIntosh, 201–224. Bloomington: Indiana University Press, 1996.
Kusimba, Chapurukha M. 'Community Archaeology and Heritage in Coastal and Western Kenya.' *Journal of Community Archaeology & Heritage* 4, no. 3 (2017): 218–228.
Lane, Paul J. 'The Material Culture of Memory.' In *The Qualities of Time: Anthropological Approaches*, edited by Wendy James and David Mills, 19–34. Oxford: Berg, 2005.
Lane, Paul J. 'Environmental Narratives and the History of Soil Erosion in Kondoa District, Tanzania: An Archaeological Perspective.' *International Journal of African Historical Studies* 42, no. 3 (2009): 457–483.
Lane, Paul J. 'Possibilities for a Postcolonial Archaeology in Sub-Saharan Africa: Indigenous and Usable Pasts.' *World Archaeology* 43, no. 1 (2011): 7–25.
Lane, Paul J. 'Envisioning a Different Notion of "Indigenous Archaeology" from the Perspective of Sub-Saharan Africa.' In *Archaeologies of 'Us' and 'Them': The Ethics and Politics of Indigeneity in Archaeology and Heritage*, edited by Charlotta Hillerdal, Anna Karlström, and Carl-Gösta Öjala, 113–126. Abingdon: Routledge, 2017.
Lane, Paul J. 'Just How Long Does "Long-Term" Have to Be? Matters of Temporal Scale as Impediments to Interdisciplinary Understanding in Historical Ecology.' In *The Oxford Handbook of Historical Ecology and Applied Archaeology*, edited by Christian Isendahl and Daryl Stump, 49–71. Oxford: Oxford University Press, 2019.
Lane, Paul J., Bilinda Straight, and Charles Hilton. 'Excavations at Baawa, Samburu District, Kenya: Preliminary Report on the 2006 Season.' *Nyame Akuma* 68 (2007): 34–46.
Lang, Carol, and Daryl Stump. 'Geoarchaeological Evidence for the Construction, Irrigation, Cultivation, and Resilience of 15th–18th Century AD Terraced Landscape at Engaruka, Tanzania.' *Quaternary Research* 88, no. 3 (2017): 382–399.
Latour, Bruno. *We Have Never Been Modern*. Cambridge, MA: Harvard University Press, 1993.
Lévi-Strauss, Claude. *The Savage Mind*. Chicago, IL: Chicago University Press, 1966.

Levy-Bruhl, Lucien. *Les Fonctions Mentales dans les Sociétés Inférieurs.* Paris: Alcan & Réunies, 1910.
Logan, Amanda L. '"Why Can't People Feed Themselves?'": Archaeology as Alternative Archive of Food Security in Banda, Ghana.' *American Anthropologist* 118, no. 3 (2016): 508–524.
Mabulla, Audax Z.P. 'Tanzania's Endangered Heritage: A Call for a Protection Program.' *African Archaeological Review* 13, no. 3 (1996): 197–214.
MacEachern, Scott. 'Time on the Timeless Continent: History and Archaeological Chronologies in the Southern Lake Chad Basin.' In *Big Histories, Human Lives: Tackling Problems of Scale in Archaeology*, edited by Timothy R. Pauketat and John Robb, 123–144. Santa Fe: School for Advanced Research Press, 2013.
Mallinowski, Bronislaw. *Coral Gardens and Their Magic.* London: Routledge and Keegan Paul, 1935.
Manyanga, Munyaradzi, and Shadreck Chirikure. 'Archives, Objects, Places and Landscapes: the Multidisciplinary and Decolonising Imperative.' In *Archives, Objects, Places and Landscapes: Multidisciplinary Approaches to Decolonised Zimbabwean Pasts*, edited by Munyaradzi Manyanga and Shadreck Chirikure, 1–11. Bemenda: Langaa Research & Publishing CIG, 2017.
Mapunda, Bertram B.B. 'The Role of Archaeology in Development: The Case of Tanzania.' *Transafrican Journal of History* 20 (1991): 19–34.
Marchant, Robert, and Paul Lane. 'Past Perspectives for the Future: Foundations for Sustainable Development in East Africa.' *Journal of Archaeological Science* 51 (2014): 12–21.
McCann, James C. 'The Plow and the Forest: Narratives of Deforestation in Ethiopia, 1840–1992.' *Environmental History* 2, no. 2 (1997): 138–159.
McIntosh, Roderick J. 'Resolved: To Act for Africa's Historical and Cultural Patrimony.' *African Arts* 24, no. 1 (1991): 18–22.
McIntosh, Roderick J. *Ancient Middle Niger: Urbanism and the Self-Organizing Landscape.* Cambridge: Cambridge University Press, 2005.
McIntosh, Roderick J., and Susan Keech McIntosh. 'The Inland Niger Delta Before the Empire of Mali: Evidence from Jenne-Jeno.' *Journal of African History* 22, no. 1 (1981): 1–22.
McIntosh, Susan Keech. 'Archaeological Heritage Management and Site Inventory Systems in Africa.' *Journal of Field Archaeology* 20, no. 4 (1993): 500–504.
McIntosh, Susan Keech, and Roderick J. McIntosh. 'The Early City in West Africa: Towards an Understanding.' *African Archaeological Review* 2, no. 1 (1984): 73–98.
McNiven, Ian J., and Lynette Russell. *Appropriated Pasts: Indigenous Peoples and the Colonial Culture of Archaeology.* Lanham, MD: AltaMira Press, 2005.
Meskell, Lynn. *The Nature of Heritage: The New South Africa.* Oxford: Wiley-Blackwell, 2011.
Mire, Sada. 'Preserving Knowledge, Not Objects: A Somali Perspective for Heritage Management and Archaeological Research.' *African Archaeological Review* 24, no. 3–4 (2007): 49–71.
Mokoena, Nthabiseng. 'Community Involvement and Heritage Management in Rural South Africa.' *Journal of Community Archaeology & Heritage* 4, no. 3 (2017): 189–202.
Morris, David. 'Wildebeest Kuil Rock Art Centre, South Africa: Controversy and Renown, Successes, and Shortcomings.' *Public Archaeology* 13, no. 1–3 (2014): 187–199.
Musonda, Francis B. 'African Archaeology: Looking Forward.' *African Archaeological Review* 8, no. 1 (1990): 3–22.
Musonda, Francis B. 'Decolonising the Broken Hill Skull: Cultural Loss and a Pathway to Zambian Archaeological Sovereignty.' *African Archaeological Review* 30, no. 2 (2013): 195–220.
Näser, Claudia, and Gemma Tully. 'Dialogues in the Making: Collaborative Archaeology in Sudan.' *Journal of Community Archaeology & Heritage* 6, no. 3 (2019): 155–171.

Ndlovu, Ndukuyakhe. 'Decolonizing the Mind-Set: South African Archaeology in a Post-colonial, Post-Apartheid Era.' In *Postcolonial Archaeologies in Africa*, edited by Peter R. Schmidt, 177–192. Santa Fe: School of American Research Press, 2009.

Ndoro, Webber. *Your Monument, Our Shrine: The Preservation of Great Zimbabwe*. Uppsala: Uppsala University, Societas Archaeologica Upsaliensis, Studies in African Archaeology Vol. 19, 2001.

Ndoro, Webber, Shadreck Chirikure, and Janette Deacon, eds. *Managing Heritage in Africa: Who Cares?* Abingdon: Routledge, 2018.

Nicholas, George, ed. *Being and Becoming Indigenous Archaeologists*. Abingdon: Routledge, 2010.

Nurse, Derek, and Thomas Spear. *The Swahili: Reconstructing the History and Language of an African Society, 800–1500*. Philadelphia: University of Pennsylvania Press, 1985.

Nzewunwa, S. Nwana. 'Nigeria.' In *Approaches to the Archaeological Heritage*, edited by Henry Cleere, 101–108. Cambridge: Cambridge University Press, 1984.

Olwig, Kenneth R. 'Recovering the Substantive Nature of Landscape.' *Annals of the Association of American Geographers* 86, no. 4 (1996): 630–653.

Ouzman, Sven. 'Silencing and Sharing Southern African Indigenous and Embedded Knowledge.' In *Indigenous Archaeologies: Decolonizing Theory and Practice*, edited by Claire Smith and H. Martin Wobst, 208–225. Abingdon: Routledge, 2005.

Pikirayi, Innocent. 'The Future of Archaeology in Africa.' *Antiquity* 89, no. 345 (2015): 531–541.

Pikirayi, Innocent, and Peter R. Schmidt. 'Introduction: Community Archaeology and Heritage in Africa – Decolonizing Practice.' In *Community Archaeology and Heritage in Africa*, edited by Peter R. Schmidt and Innocent Pikirayi, 15–34. Abingdon: Routledge, 2016.

Posnansky, Merrick. 'African Archaeology Comes of Age.' *World Archaeology* 13, no. 3 (1982): 345–358.

Prabhu, Anjali. *Hybridity: Limits, Transformations, Prospects*. SUNY Press, 2007.

Pwiti, Gilbert. 'Archaeology, Prehistory and Education in Zimbabwe.' In *The Presented Past: Heritage, Museums and Education*, edited by Peter G. Stone and Brian L. Molyneaux, 338–347. Abingdon: Routledge, 1994.

Pwiti, Gilbert. 'Let the Ancestors Rest in Peace? New Challenges for Cultural Heritage Management in Zimbabwe.' *Conservation and Management of Archaeological Sites* 1, no. 3 (1996): 151–160.

Pwiti, Gilbert. 'Taking African Cultural Heritage Management Into the Twenty-First Century: Zimbabwe's Masterplan for Cultural Heritage Management.' *African Archaeological Review* 14, no. 2 (1997): 81–83.

Rakotoarisoa, Jean-Aimé. 'The Burden of an Encumbered Inheritance Upon the Study of the Past of Madagascar.' In *Conflict in the Archaeology of Living Traditions*, edited by Robert Layton, 82–87. London: Unwin Hyman, 1989.

Richard, François G. 'Recharting Atlantic Encounters: Object Trajectories and Histories of Value in the Siin (Senegal) and Senegambia.' *Archaeological Dialogues* 17, no. 1 (2010): 1–27.

Richards, Paul. *Indigenous Agricultural Revolution: Ecology and Food Production in West Africa*. London: Hutchinson, 1985.

Rizzo, Matteo. 'What Was Left of the Groundnut Scheme? Development Disaster and Labour Market in Southern Tanganyika 1946–1952.' *Journal of Agrarian Change* 6, no. 2 (2006): 205–238.

Robertshaw, Peter, ed. *A History of African Archaeology*. London: James Currey, 1990.

Rowlands, Michael. 'Civilization, Violence and Heritage Healing in Liberia.' *Journal of Material Culture* 13, no. 2 (2008): 135–152.

Rudolph, Richard C. 'Preliminary Notes on Sung Archaeology.' *Journal of Asian Studies* 22, no. 2 (1963): 169–177.

Sahnouni, Mohamed. 'Changing Paradigms: A Call for Training.' (Part of 'The Future of African Archaeology.') *African Archaeological Review* 13, no. 1 (1996): 27–28.
Schmidt, Peter R. 'Using Archaeology to Remake African History.' In *Making Alternative Histories: The Practice of Archaeology and History in Non-Western Settings*, edited by Peter R. Schmidt and Thomas C. Patterson, 118–147. Santa Fe: School of American Research Press, 1995.
Schmidt, Peter R. 'What is Postcolonial About Archaeologies in Africa?' In *Postcolonial Archaeologies in Africa*, edited by Peter R. Schmidt, 1–20. Santa Fe: School of American Research Press, 2009.
Schmidt, Peter R. 'Community Heritage Work in Africa: Village-Based Preservation and Development.' *Conservation Science in Cultural Heritage* 14, no. 2 (2014): 133–150.
Schmidt, Peter R. 'Peter Ucko Memorial Lecture. Decolonizing Archaeological Practice: Gazing into the Past to Transform the Future.' *Archaeologies* 13, no. 3 (2017): 392–411.
Schmidt, Peter R., and Kathryn W. Arthur. 'Community-Based Approaches to African History.' In *Oxford Research Encyclopaedia of African History*, edited by Thomas Spear. 20 December 2018. https://oxfordre.com/africanhistory/view/10.1093/acrefore/9780190277734.001.0001/acrefore-9780190277734-e-617.
Schmidt, Peter R., and Roderick J. McIntosh, eds. *Plundering Africa's Past*. Bloomington: Indiana University Press, 1996.
Schmidt, Peter R., and Thomas C. Patterson, eds. *Making Alternative Histories: The Practice of Archaeology and History in Non-Western Settings*. Santa Fe: School of American Research Press, 1995.
Schmidt, Peter R., and Innocent Pikirayi, eds. *Community Archaeology and Heritage in Africa: Decolonizing Practice*. Abingdon: Routledge, 2016.
Schreyger, Emil. *L'Office du Niger au Mali de 1932 à 1982: La Problématique d'une Grande Entreprise Agricole dans la Zone du Sahel*. Wiesbaden: Steiner, 1984.
Schumaker, Ernst F. *Small Is Beautiful: A Study of Economics As If People Mattered*. London: Blond & Briggs, 1973.
Segobye, Alinah Kelo. 'Political Instabilities and Education.' (Part of 'The Future of African Archaeology.') *African Archaeological Review* 13, no. 1 (1996): 29–34.
Shaw, Thurstan. 'African Archaeology: Looking Back and Looking Forward.' *African Archaeological Review* 7, no. 1 (1989): 3–31.
Shepherd, Nick. 'Heading South, Looking North: Why We Need a Post-Colonial Archaeology.' *Archaeological Dialogues* 9, no. 2 (2002): 74–82.
Showers, Katherine. *Imperial Gullies: Soil Erosion and Conservation in Lesotho*. Athens: Ohio University Press, 2005.
Sidibe, Samuel. 'The Pillage of Archaeological Sites in Mali.' *African Arts* 28, no. 4 (1995): 52–55.
Silliman, Stephen W. 'A Requiem for Hybridity? The Problem with Frankensteins, Purées, and Mules.' *Journal of Social Archaeology* 15, no. 3 (2015): 277–298.
Sillitoe, Paul. 'The Development of Indigenous Knowledge: A New Applied Anthropology.' *Current Anthropology* 39, no. 2 (1998): 223–252.
Sillitoe, Paul. 'Trust in Development: Some Implications of Knowing in Indigenous Knowledge.' *Journal of the Royal Anthropological Institute* 16, no. 1 (2010): 12–30.
Simakole, Brutus Mulilo, Trisia Angela Farrelly, and John Holland. 'Provisions for Community Participation in Heritage Management: Case of the Zambezi Source National Monument, Zambia.' *International Journal of Heritage Studies* 25, no. 3 (2019): 225–238.
Smith, Claire, and H. Martin Wobst, eds. *Indigenous Archaeologies: Decolonizing Theory and Practice*. Abingdon: Routledge, 2004.
Smith, Linda Tuhiwai. *Decolonizing Methodologies: Research and Indigenous People*. London: Zed Books, 1999.
Stahl, Ann B. 'Africa in the World:(Re)centering African History Through Archaeology.' *Journal of Anthropological Research* 70, no. 1 (2014): 5–33.

Straight, Bilinda, Paul Lane, Charles Hilton, and Musa Letua. '"It Was *Maendeleo* That Removed Them": Disturbing Burials and Reciprocal Knowledge Production in a Context of Collaborative Archaeology.' *Journal of the Royal Anthropological Institute* 21, no. 2 (2015): 391–418.

Straight, Bilinda, Paul Lane, Charles Hilton, and Musa Letua. '"Dust People": Samburu Perspectives on Disaster, Identity, and Landscape.' *Journal of Eastern African Studies* 10, no. 1 (2016): 168–188.

Stump, Daryl. '"Ancient and Backward or Long-Lived and Sustainable?" The Role of the Past in Debates Concerning Rural Livelihoods and Resource Conservation in Eastern Africa.' *World Development* 38, no. 9 (2010): 1251–1262.

Stump, Daryl, 'On Applied Archaeology, Indigenous Knowledge, and the Usable Past.' *Current Anthropology* 54, no. 3 (2013): 268–298.

Stump, Daryl. 'Digging for Indigenous Knowledge: "Reverse Engineering" and Stratigraphic Sequencing as a Potential Archaeological Contribution to Sustainability Assessments.' In *The Oxford Handbook of Historical Ecology and Applied Archaeology*, edited by Christian Isendahl and Daryl Stump, 137–155. Oxford: Oxford University Press, 2019.

Stump, Daryl, and Susie Richer. 'Terraces are Good, But Sometimes Sediment Traps Are Better.' York: University of York, Archaeology of Agricultural Resilience in Eastern Africa Project, Policy Brief 1, November 2017.

Sowunmi, M. Adebisi. 'Beyond Academic Archaeology in Africa: The Human Dimension.' *African Archaeological Review* 15, no. 3 (1998): 163–172.

Thomas, Julian. *Archaeology and Modernity*. Abingdon: Routledge, 2004.

Trigger, Bruce G. 'Alternative Archaeologies: Nationalist, Colonialist, Imperialist.' *Man* N.S. (1984): 355–370.

Trigger, Bruce G. *A History of Archaeological Thought*. Cambridge: Cambridge University Press, 1989.

Trigger, Bruce G. 'Paradigms in Sudan Archaeology.' *International Journal of African Historical Studies* 27, no. 2 (1994): 323–45.

Trouillot, Michel-Rolph. *Global Transformations: Anthropology and the Modern World*. Basingstoke: Palgrave Macmillan, 2003.

Tsing, Anna L. 'The Buck, the Bull, and the Dream of the Stag: Some Unexpected Weeds of the Anthropocene.' *Suomen Antropologi: Journal of the Finnish Anthropological Society* 42, no. 1 (2017): 3–21.

Van Beusekom, Monica M. 'Colonisation Indigene: French Rural Development Ideology at the Office du Niger, 1920–1940.' *International Journal of African Historical Studies* (1997): 299–323.

Verran, Helen. *Science and an African Logic*. Chicago, IL: University of Chicago Press, 2001.

Wandibba, Simuyu. 'Archaeology and Education in Kenya, the Present and the Future.' In *The Presented Past: Heritage, Museums and Education*, edited by Peter G. Stone and Brian L. Molyneux, 349–358. London: Unwin Hyman, 1994.

Warren, Dennis M. 'Indigenous Knowledge, Biodiversity Conservation and Development.' In *Sustainable Development in Third World Countries: Applied and Theoretical Perspectives*, edited by Valentine Udoh James, 81–88. Westport, CT: Praeger Publishers, 1996.

Watkins, Joe. *Indigenous Archaeology: American Indian Values and Scientific Practice*. Walnut Creek, CA: Altamira Press, 2000.

World Commission on Environment and Development (WCED). *Our Common Future, From One Earth to One World*, edited by V. Hauff. Oxford: Oxford University Press, on behalf of the WCED, 1987.

28
INDIGENOUS PHOTOGRAPHY AS SUBJECT AND METHOD FOR GLOBAL HISTORY

Oliver Haag

Laughter filled the grand auditorium at London's King's College during my presentation on Nazi idealisation of Indigenous peoples. I showed a photograph of an Indigenous woman from the Keta Lagoon area (modern-day Ghana) that appeared in a National Socialist book entitled *Menschenschönheit* (human beauty). The photo portrays a young woman, indicating slight motion, while at the same time exuding a static, almost Hellenic, stoicism (see Figure 28.1). It was not the image that elicited laughter, but the caption that I read a few moments later: 'how wonderful the curve of the breasts, as though wrought from bronze'.[1] *Menschenschönheit* contains dozens of photographs of Indigenous people from across the world as well as Europeans, all presented in a similar fashion. Portrayed as archetypes of their respective races, only 'full-blooded' sitters gained entry to the book. None was of Jewish, Romany, or settler origin. Approximately 43% of the images are of males and 57% are of females, while younger people, irrespective of their race and gender, are shown wearing less clothing, with some shown naked. Gender seemed to have played a significant role insofar that most of the images did not portray men and women together, perhaps trying to avoid an overly sexualised connotation.

This strict separation by gender suggests a homoerotic interpretation of male figures in particular, since males were rather shown in groups and in bodily activity. Yet, the contextual arrangement of the images was certainly far from any idea of racial, gendered, or sexual liberation. The photos were used to foreground seemingly healthy and idealised bodies free of any blemish and following a 'natural', seemingly healthy, gender regime. Human beauty followed concepts of idealised strength and ideas of natural order (muscular male bodies and immaculate bodies of female grace). None of the portrayed bodies seem to permit readings that cross the boundaries of gender and race, or meddle with heterosexuality, with no man being shown in effeminate and no woman in masculine pose. Beautiful humans, the book suggests, could only be found in their innate countries, thus being

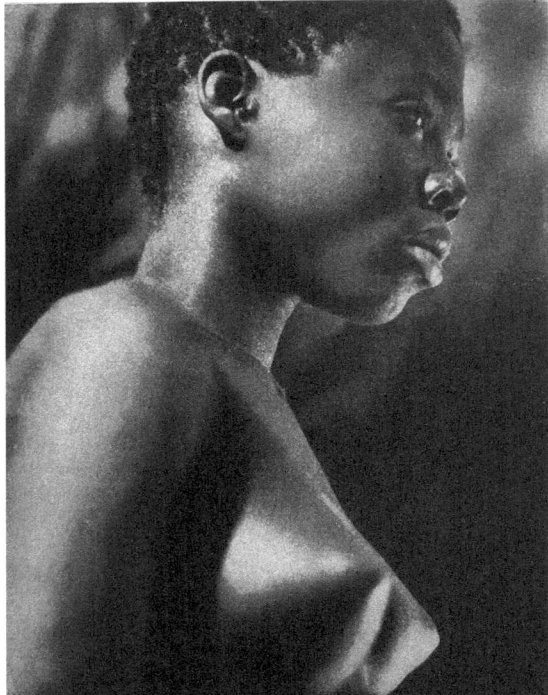

Figure 28.1 Woman from the Keta Lagoon (Gold Coast), in Fischer, Menschenschönheit, 50

quintessentially indigenous. Such an idea plays out idealised German Indigeneity as the relation between 'traditional' people and their blood-based ancestral land. This form of beauty attached to a racially denoted land is mentioned implicitly in the text:

> Certainly many a face seems strange to us… but the figures are appealing: the men are well-built, powerful yet smooth in their musculature, and the women often have an animal-like grace. One can tell that these creatures are well-created in their place and completely adapted to nature; the instinctive aversion towards these races is only justified if they cross our circles or, even more so, if their cultures are imposed on us as models.[2]

The statement that Indigenous people were 'well-created *in their place*' bears out the importance attached to a calcified primordiality that infused German narratives of race in the first half of the twentieth century: different racial subjects were idealised as long as they remained within their racially confined lands ('if they cross our circles') and as long as different cultures were kept separate ('as long as their cultures are not imposed on us').

I was approached in the break after my presentation, as delegates were interested in the seeming obscurity of Nazi idealisation of Blackness. How could the Nazis, known for their annihilation of 'alien' races, have exhibited any sense of admiration? As outlined below, this idealisation stabilised the logics of imperial rule and did not unravel the hierarchic dogma of race. What seems noteworthy for the present study was the audience reactions to the photo that appeared to be trapped in the context of its accompanying text: it is deeply sexist and racist, opined one person. Another said that it was horrible to use Indigenous people as pawns for evil ends; yet, another said that it was exactly what the current Neo-Nazis did, that is, using Indigenous people as a means to deter immigration, while keeping them in subjugated state of primitivism. I encountered very similar responses at other talks and when engaging students with the source material.

Yet is the Keta Lagoon woman, whose name and life went unmentioned in the publication, just a product of sexism and racism? While the critique of Nazism seems quite appropriate, I feel at unease to dismiss Indigenous photography as a pure instrument of imperial representation. This contribution focuses on what I call moments of agency in a setting that is certainly dominated, yet not completely paralysed by imperialism. In looking at photography, I do not try to retrace the history of individual people. It is not the objective of my current research to repatriate particular photos. Instead, I try to make an intervention in German history by introducing Indigenous photos less as historical sources than as sovereign histories to probe a more nuanced story of the dissemination of Indigenous photography in global environments. Indigenous photography can help unearth the complexities of racial narratives and tell astoundingly richer stories than simple textual criticism could provide.

German colonialism and the construction of Indigeneity

German colonialism was characterised by a relatively short period of actual rule, starting in 1884 and ending quite abruptly with the loss of its colonies after the end of the First World War (1918/19). The German colonial empire included territories in the Pacific (German New Guinea, parts of Micronesia and Samoa) as well as sub-Saharan Africa (German East Africa, Cameroon, and Togo, as well as major parts of contemporary Namibia). With the establishing of the German colonies, publications increased on these colonies. In a partly annotated bibliography, I counted more than 4,200 publications on Indigenous people published in German writing issued during National Socialist rule.[3] For the preceding period (1884–1933), the number of publications is likely to have exceeded 20,000 items. The Indigenous nations most reported on were sub-Saharan Africa (50%), Melanesia, and Papua New Guinea, but also those outside the former German colonies, especially those of North America and Australia. German ideas of Indigenous people in this period followed a transnational path of primitivism that placed different Indigenous nations in hierarchy to each other, with Aboriginal Australians and the Twa and Mbuti people (Rwanda/Ituri Rainforest) being placed on the lowest scale of human evolution.[4] German publications in this phase can be categorised according to Gustav Jahoda's concepts of primitivism-as-animalism and primitivism-as-childlikeness that organised imperial constructions of Indigeneity – the former, briefly put, portrayed Indigenous people as needing to be 'civilised', while the latter denotes already 'civilised' subjects that reflected the success of colonial 'education'.[5] Using the concept of 'colonial fantasies', Susanne Zantop shows that German imperial aspirations continued on after the actual reign of colonialism.[6] This applied in particular to the period when Germany tried to regain its former colonies after 1918. As Lora Wildenthal emphasises, the loss of the German colonies went hand in hand with campaigns to regain the former colonies, many of which entailed castigation of British cruelties.[7]

While the mutual reproach of colonial cruelties was an inherent practice of European colonialism, as Christina Twomey has shown,[8] this practice led to an increase in idealisation of Indigenous people who were re-cast as Germany's most loyal friends. A photo in a 1940 propaganda text, for example, shows an Indigenous person, probably from Papua New Guinea, holding a swastika flag and captioned 'in the German South Pacific the faith in Germany is still alive' (see Figure 28.2).[9] Idealisation also applied to formerly highly negatively stereotyped Indigenous nations, especially Aboriginal Australians and the Twa and Mbuti peoples. As I have shown elsewhere, German idealisation of Aboriginal Australians increased perceptibly after the loss of the colonies, with Aboriginal people re-envisioned not as the least developed human group but as strong, intelligent, and of ancient Aryan stock.[10]

For example, decade-old images of what was apparently the last Tasmanian woman re-appeared in German publications to decry British policies of annihilation (see Figure 28.3). While older texts explained the so-called vanishing of the Tasmanians as a natural consequence of historical progress, writing in the later period re-interpreted the Tasmanians as a once proud race.[11] The photo of the supposed last Tasmanian, however, remained the same and was used to bolster both arguments. In Grühl's 1930 journalistic text, the naming of the sitter ('Woman from Tasmania') exhibits a profound lack of individuality, reflecting the very nature of colonial discourse that tended to homogenise and depersonalise Indigenous people. The sitters' biographic data was rarely revealed; yet surprisingly in this case, both the date of death (1876) and a name were mentioned – an almost unique occurrence, marred by the fact that the information was incorrect. The 1930 text mentions the last Tasmanian woman as having died in 1876, designated as Truganini, whereas the person photographed was Wapperty who died in 1867.[12] This careless practice was different to an earlier text (1899) that showed the same photo but that referred to it with the right name; yet in contrast to the 1930 piece, the earlier text was much more derogatory and far from idealising, in that it explained Tasmanians as the least developed among human races.[13] The more idealising article, in turn, did not show any concern for Indigenous knowledge and individuality. The practice of idealisation, as this example demonstrates, did not truly care for Indigenous individuality but rather reflect Germany's changing political discourses.

Moreover, idealising constructions of Indigeneity were contingent upon a perceived state of traditionalism. Efforts of dissimilation, as Pascale Grosse contends, became a German counter-strategy to the assimilation of Indigenous peoples, perceived as a threat to German supremacy.[14] German colonialism initially tried to

Figure 28.2 Man from German South Pacific, probably PNG, in Reichskolonialbund, Deutscher Kolonialkalender, n.p

assimilate Indigenous people, even before the onset of formal colonialism; German missionaries in particular advocated religious conversion, European clothing, and formal education for Indigenous people. Towards the turn of the nineteenth century, thinking on assimilation changed, and efforts of dissimilation increased: not as a formal policy as such, as colonial rule was too short for many polices to be fully implemented, but as a massive output of writing (in propaganda but also in

Figure 28.3 Woman from Tasmania, in Grühl, 1930, 392

popular culture) that criticised assimilation, Europeanisation, and missionaries. These were aimed at reversing the effects of European assimilation, especially the growth in literacy levels and economic influence among Indigenous peoples, which were feared to threaten colonial rule. Equipped with European education and wealth, Indigenous peoples were increasingly suspected to be questioning their state of subjugation, leading to not only Indigenous unrest within the colonies but also a potential Indigenous invasion and destruction of Europe. Concepts of traditionalism became a defining element of such discourses of dissimilation that sought to combat not only miscegenation, but all forms of cultural assimilation and Europeanisation. Colonial propaganda and popular culture increasingly stressed the needs for 'protection' of untouched and 'authentic' tribal Indigenous groups. At a textual level, Indigenous peoples were idealised as long as they were considered racially pure and free from any European influence. European forms of clothing and urban settings – particularly top hats, trousers, and modern cities – were condemned and led to extremely stigmatising descriptions. German imperial discourses on Indigenous peoples thus came to evince the paradox of extreme stigmatisation and physical persecution on the one hand, and on the other, moments of exalted idealisation. Take this decidedly National Socialist text on Aboriginal Australians, for example:

> These were not *Australneger* (Australian Negroes) but *Australarier* (Australian Aryans), or rather female Aryans, since it was women and very beautiful women at that ... [They] were not half-blooded but authentic full-blooded Aranda and Loritja. They had a unique and lovely charm.[15]

Indigenous people were not conceded any room for change or adaptation. Not only miscegenation but any form of cross-cultural exchange and embracing of modernisation were strictly criticised. Modernisation came to be seen as the abhorrent opposite to the much-idealised state of nature. Put succinctly, German idealisation of Indigenous people in this period constituted an inherently asymmetrical venture in which Indigenous people could only establish ideal Indigeneity through recourse to traditionalism, and could equally lose their Indigeneity by becoming 'too' modern.

Indigenous photography as documents of agency

With most publications having included photographs to substantiate the written text, German discourse produced an outpouring of visual material. The photographs reflected to some extent the trajectory of assimilation and dissimilation. In the late nineteenth century, visual material tended to show sitters in European dress, seated on chairs in outdoor area, particularly gardens. School children in neat uniforms were a frequent motif in missionary writing, and white Europeans also featured in the photos. During the dissimilationist phase and especially as National Socialism gained traction, idealising photos shifted dramatically towards showing few to no urban scenes but rather wilderness and untouched nature. Indigenous people appeared wearing little clothing or only traditional dress and were no longer shown with Europeans. Images of nuclear families, sitters with pets, couples, or people showing affection did not occur. Photographs in this era also tended to present younger and physically attractive people, usually with neat haircuts and a cultivated appearance. Yet in contrast to the paintings that dominated the visual material on Indigenous people in the 1870s and 1880s, and that portrayed Indigenous peoples according to the tropes of animalist primitivism, the photos did not explicitly illustrate the textual differences between outright stigmatisation and idealisation. Indigenous people castigated for having been assimilated appeared in the same bodily pose as those framed by idealising narratives, that is, sitters were not shown any weaker, less groomed, or in any way less attractive. The only recognisable codes that indicated a specific value judgement were an urban background and the wearing of European clothes. The photos, in other words, did not fully correspond to the texts in which they were embedded: the nexus between photo and text only became recognisable in discourse.

Moreover, the names and specific origins of the sitters were not acknowledged. This rather careless practice suggests that Indigenous owners of the photographs did not fully control the contexts of production, and particularly not the political use of the photos. Most German writers took their own photos; Austrian anthropologist Hugo Adolf Bernatzik, for example, was an immensely prolific author in the 1930s and 1940s who did not merely publish for academic audiences but whose pictorials and travelogues were principally aimed at a broader readership interested in the colonies. His photographs of Indigenous people from Germany's former African and Pacific colonies were re-used in subsequent publications, with the original sources often but not always acknowledged. Bernatzik's image material was often re-used without payment and German copyright law – especially under the strict censorship of Nazism – easily allowed free re-use of material for national benefits.[16] Colonial propaganda material in particular simply used older photographic sources without any acknowledgement. None of the publications refer to any economic compensation to the Indigenous sitters who were *de jure* never considered co-owners of their images. Only few publications mention – in passing – the exchange of goods or gifts, and especially symbolic compensation. For example, in her travel memoir Bernatzik's wife, Emmy, praised the Kasanga and Balanta people (Guinea Bissau, Senegal, and Gambia) as strong and proud, endangered by European assimilation; convinced of the rising power of Hitlerite Germany, the author follows, sitters would have been eager to be photographed so that the world might know about the danger of letting traditions fade.[17] The compensation of being photographed was, in this case, explained as residing in the mutual benefit for racial survival afforded by Hitler's ostensible wisdom and courtesy. The motive for publishing Indigenous photos was indeed often explained as complying with apparent Indigenous demands to inform the world about the vanishing of their traditions.

Drawing on Susan Sontag's critique of photographs as part of an aesthetic consumerism, Jae Emerling suggests that photographs justified colonialism and propelled the construction of race.[18] The aesthetic conventions of German Indigenous photography certainly helped blur the power imbalance inherent in colonial projects. They made racial segregation appear just and were used to normalise the power imbalances of imperialism, and peacefulness was indeed one of the major tropes that German colonial propaganda tried to convey. Yet, I argue, it was the usage of the photos in certain contexts, rather than the particular photos per se, that seem to be the real problem, for while Indigenous sitters could not influence the hijacking of the photos, they were not merely passive objects. Instead, Indigenous sitters still exhibit profound agency in being read differently – that is, not necessarily as ruled colonial victims but as active agents with persisting yet varying impact upon audiences. As this contribution shows, audiences tend to take notice of the individuality of the Indigenous sitters once the photos become freed from their colonial contexts.

As Christraud Geary and Adamou Ndam Njoya argue, while German photography did serve colonial propaganda, it was never simply a one-sided instrument of power.[19] Photos became hugely popular emblems of modernity among Indigenous inhabitants of central African colonies. Speaking of a mutual co-authoring of images, Geary explains that the elites used photos to reclaim their local rule.[20] The photos showed sitters in European clothing but equally in anti-modern and traditional pose: 'African photographic subjects began to present themselves to the cameras of the Westerners in ways they wanted to be seen and assumed agency in the photographic encounter.'[21]

Although not frequent in the nineteenth and early twentieth centuries, Indigenous people also stood behind the camera. In a meticulous biographical study of Ijo photographer Jonathan Adogogo Green (1873–1905), Lisa Aronson documents how Indigenous photographers appropriated the colonial camera and how also images of semi-nudity played a crucial role in Green's oeuvre.[22] Not intended as objects of eroticism but as portrayals of young, uninitiated women, Green's photos attracted massive interest in Europe and, remarkably, contained images highly similar to the one opening this chapter (Figure 28.1): women shown with bare breasts, wearing traditional necklaces and ornaments, usually not looking right into the camera. Similar agency in production also occurred in other regions. In the Australian context, for example, Jane Lydon retraces in an astute study of Aboriginal photography the often-enthusiastic participation of Aboriginal sitters who managed to influence the production of their photographs.[23] These moments of agency in the stages of production invite us to reconsider ideas of passivity, as deployed in Thomas Theye's collection on German colonial photographs; while Theye's book can be considered the first systematic study of German colonial photography, it oversimplifies colonial power relations and suggests that Indigenous photos had been merely instrumentalised in German colonial discourse.[24]

Notwithstanding Indigenous agency, images in circulation followed complex mechanisms of reception and could indeed be used for political ends and be consumed for different reasons, including joy, adventurism, and the fulfilment of sexual pleasures. Individual photos could fulfil various purposes in reception, as an example from Australia testifies: Helen Pringle shows in a study of Walter Roth's ethnographic research how late nineteenth-century photos of nudity and sexual intercourse, initially used to reject a theory that introcision was performed to prevent procreation, became subject of a fiercely debated scandal over promiscuity and exploitation in colonial contexts.[25] Ann McGrath retraces this scandal and explains its origin in the clashes between the state protection of, and the private demands for, Aboriginal labour in Queensland: white frontiersmen tried to sack Roth, who in his position as Protector of Aborigines tried to curb the exploitation of Indigenous labour; Roth's ethnographic photos of Indigenous nudity and sexual intercourse became the central argument in this debate.[26] Having first been published in an ethnographic journal, then re-publicised to wide public debate, some of Roth's photos were eventually freely re-published in a thoroughly pornographic collection in 1935. Entitled *Venus Oceanica*, the newly established context of the images was indeed of a highly sexualised and pornographic nature, aimed at an elite male readership.[27]

Venus Oceanica contains a few images similar to those distributed in Germany – that is, photos of (semi-)nudity – with the distinction that German publications did not show photos of sexually explicit content, with even couples having rarely been shown. As with Fascist idealisation of human bodies more generally, some Indigenous photos could be (re-)interpreted as erotic, or at times homoerotic. In contrast to *Venus Oceanica*, however, acts of sexual intercourse or descriptions of sexual organs did not appear in German texts. German captions and contexts were explicitly non-sexual and often tried to preclude any sexual fantasy in stressing miscegenation as illicit and as *Rassenschande* (lit. race disgrace). The degree of exploitation of Indigenous photos thus seemed to have depended on the context in which they re-appeared, with the same photo often appearing in highly different contexts. Importantly, McGrath's re-tracing of the circulation of Roth's photos also contains a story of production, suggesting that the sitters, a couple, had been clearly amused at Roth's request to perform the pose of intercourse.[28] Thus, while the dissemination of photos could follow different purposes, often rendering Indigenous sitters the subjects of exploitation, the photos per se seem to be equally complex, telling dynamic stories of agency and reaction: how can the reaction of the Indigenous couple in suppressing their laughter be interpreted? Did they consider the anthropologist's demand ridiculous? Was is stupid, immoral, exploitative, or welcome to them? Can the laughter be interpreted as a form of resistance? An irony, sarcasm perhaps, or mere amusement? Whatever their reaction, the story shows that even highly scandalous images can offer traces of Indigenous agency that exhibit different narratives from those in reception.

Indigenous agency in the history of photography can also be discerned at a contemporary level of re-claiming photos that once were stored in colonial archives. For instance, Laura Peers and Alison Brown describe the dynamic reception of repatriated ethnographic photos among the Kainai community in Alberta, where relatives identified histories of community and local culture and thus liberated their ancestors from the dominating narrative of assimilation.[29] In Australia, colonial photographs have enormous significance for Indigenous descendants and communities. Brenda Croft stresses the gulf of power relations between the largely anonymous sitters and the usually well-documented biographies of their white photographers; the re-naming and repatriation of orphan photos, the author follows, thus counts among the prerogatives of engaging with historic Indigenous photography.[30] Alongside re-naming, there seem to be innovative analytical approaches being taken by Indigenous viewers. As Jane Lydon emphasises, photographs are not necessarily treated as representations of past events but in some instances as 'the powers of the ancestors, embedded within social relationships with both the living and the dead'.[31] Indigenous artists have come to decontextualise colonial images and equip them with tales of empowerment, a method of image-reading that Andrew Brook and Jessica Neath describe as decolonising.[32] In a nutshell, Indigenous photos are not read as documents confined to a past era, as mere resources. They have relevant meaning for contemporary social relations and history, suggesting that historic photography may also be engaged methodologically through decolonising performance. Roslyn and Axel Poignant assert that the meanings of photos for members of the Maningrida community exceed isolated instances of past events, or captured moments in a sequence of social interaction, functioning instead as narrative and history in its own right: 'Structured remembering and telling are more than a recollection of past events – they are events in themselves; they are performances. And interpretation of performances is done by audiences.'[33]

I wish to take up the concepts of decolonising performance and, reified through storytelling, implement them as Indigenous methodologies of reading colonial photography. Joanna Scherer, for one, ponders over the possibilities of processing photos as primary anthropological data. The author suggests that a holistic understanding of photos could only be achieved with a thorough quantification of thousands of similar photos and through analysis of the context of production, intention of the photographer, the subject of the photo, and the viewers' interpretations.[34] This is not wrong. But I still consider this methodology limited, for to be truly holistic, Indigenous methods should not be mentioned in passing but actively implemented, not merely to explain the 'Indigenous' but also to explain the 'centre'. In other words, what I propose here is an employment of Indigenous readings to explain German history.

Towards an Indigenous methodology of German history

A few years back, my mother kindly agreed to pick up an interlibrary loan. The book, a pictorial of South-West Africa, contained photos printed on thick high gloss paper that made the tome heavy. The material felt more like real photographic paper than the pages of a book, firm and a bit grainy. Before handing over the book to me, my mother scrolled through the pages and was amazed to see what she described as beautiful photos. She stopped at the portrayal of a Herero woman (Figure 28.4) who, she reckoned, was about to say something. The photo affected her: this was a humorous and witty woman that had lived through hard times, my mother suggested. While she did not look at the date of the publication, she was aware of the book being 'old'. She then pointed to the portrait of my grandmother above the kitchen table where we were seated (Figure 28.5). 'It's eerie, but they both look at the same direction.'

In my ego-histoire, I have expanded part of my family history, especially my grandmother's Romany heritage that she had concealed for most of her life.[35] My mother was often angry with my grandmother's strategy of assimilating to Austrian social norms. A housewife, she kept her house and garden cleaner than necessary, washed, mowed, and kept everything pretty, so that neighbours would not have any chance to say something bad. She acquired the Styrian dialect so quickly that nobody would have ever assumed she came from Jimbolia, Romania rather than Straßgang, Graz. She was perfectly adapted. Perhaps too adapted, as my mother indicated the tension between necessary survival during the Nazi regime and later convenience. My mother's eyes went back to the Herero woman and to my mother she, too, appeared adapted. The dress made her look different from the other Herero people portrayed in the book. 'But she's resilient', this is so clear.

The photo of the Herero woman spurred family stories. John Berger conceives of photos as stories, provided that readers consider them meaningful and thus

Figure 28.4 Herero woman, in Steinhoff, Deutsche Heimat, n.p

confer on the photos a past as much as a future. Photos quote from experience, Berger argues, but only if they are established as active narratives into which listeners can enter.[36] This narrative ended abruptly. A few pages behind the Herero woman's portrait, my mother stopped at a page with a group of Herero women shown in front of a swastika. 'What the hell ...' My mother put on her reading glasses, looked at the publication date and read through the pages.

The book was penned in 1939 by Ilse Steinhoff, a stern National Socialist.[37] The text is a propaganda argument for regaining the former German colonies, and portrays the Herero as a ruling people (*Herrschervolk*) whose appearance emanated dignity; while the Herero uprising is briefly mentioned, the subsequent genocide (1904–1908) remains unnoticed. Instead, the Herero uprising is vindicated as a heroic battle instigated by the instinct of racial survival. Having been pacified, the Herero are eventually described as Germany's most loyal comrades. Although vexed by the triumphant undertone of racial idealisation, my mother kept the

Figure 28.5 The author's grandmother, early 1940s

pervious nodes of narrative (gender, adaptation, charisma) and related them to the newly established context. Both the Herero woman and my grandmother survived this racist regime, she eventually uttered, and they don't seem crushed. 'Our grannie wasn't perhaps ideal, but who's ideal in in an unideal world?' Intending to proceed with family reminiscences, I interrupted my mother and reminded her that she had just forgiven her mother – for the first time.

What my mother did, quite unconsciously, was what Tina Campt dubs a practice of 'listening' to photography. Elizabeth Edwards suggests deeming photographs not merely visual devices, but also social objects that establish meaning from multi-sensory physical engagement, which, in turn, can trigger the narration of history.[38] Drawing on Edwards' theory, Campt proposes to listen to, rather than merely look at, Black colonial photographs.[39] The author understands such listening to take place not at an audible level, but at a felt level of lower frequencies. Photos can touch audiences, both literally and affectively, in connecting viewers to what the author calls the event of the photo. The nexus between the viewing of the image and its affects through the haptic and the sonic results in a feeling of the image beyond what is merely visible. The acoustic resonances of colonial photography, the author concludes, meant a tension emanating from the photographed bodies that spoke less of a past event but of Black futurity.[40] Indeed, my mother actually touched the image, the spotted paper it was printed on. She became affected, established a nexus familiar to her and perceived the woman in motion, as if saying something. Yet when the photo's context became dominating, she fell into silence. She stopped reading the photo as such but continued to read it through the text in which it was embedded. It took her a while to deconstruct – or should I say *decolonise* – its colonial context.

In a study on images of the African diaspora in Europe, Tina Campt suggests that a haptic and sonic reading of photographs can be achieved through an intermittent silencing of the biographic details in order to understand the meanings of the past: 'rather than using photographs as documents or evidence of the past in the sense of an illustration, confirmation, or supplement to historical facts or information we already know, what if we thought of the image instead as itself *an enactment* of that past?'[41] The Indigenous photos in German publications register primarily at the level of colonialism. I suggest implementing Campt's theoretic proposal of interim decontextualisation to the register of colonialism. What if we, for one moment, sideline the colonial contexts in which the photos appear?

The reason for this intervention lies in the discrepancy between the audience's reactions in London and my mother's reaction. While the former could not engage the photo as a historical document in itself, but were immediately confronted with its imperial framing, my mother approached the photo in the reverse order. The results of how the images were read suggest a striking difference: a view of victimhood on the one side, a view of agency on the other.

I eventually replicated the experiment in two different classrooms.[42] The first group read the texts in which Figures 28.1–28.4 appeared (shown and numbered accordingly in the present chapter). The second group of students were handed photocopies of the same images without reading the texts first. After half an hour of discussing the photos without text, I invited students to read the full texts, as Group 1 did from the outset. I tried to free the photos from their original context only to place them back into it later. To be clear, it is not my intention to obliterate the photographic contexts completely. As Jane Lydon warns, decontextualising colonial photographs can entail a consolidation of their original colonial meanings, that is, Indigenous sitters can be potentially reduced to their bodies (nudity) and a historic status of colonial servitude. Decontextualisation can, in other words, reproduce images of neo-primitivism.[43] Yet, colonial contexts can also pose too much of a distraction. As Anna Haebich and Corinna Erckenbrecht theorise, colonial photographs have multiple meanings, ranging from historic to those imparted by contemporary audiences, thus rendering meanings stratified and the photo perforce a vehicle with which, in Elizabeth Edwards' terms, to 'decontexualise time and space'.[44]

Although Group 1 had access to the contexts in which the photos were embedded, both clusters were given no additional information and were asked to generate a discussion about their impressions of the texts and photos, respectively. I recorded the discussion, identified major threads of arguments and analysed them according to frequency and intensity. Students in the first group were generally surprised to learn about German idealisation of Indigenous people. There was agreement that the texts were racist. Idealisation was explained as being part of the illogical, arbitrary, and contradictory nature of racism; a few respondents believed that racial idealisation was a means of (colonial) rule. The main focus of the discussion rested on the written texts, with the photos given significantly less weight. As Table 28.1 shows in fuller detail, the most frequently discussed themes in this group were racism, followed by the political use of the photos for colonial ends, sexism, and that the photos trivialised colonial crimes. Respondents thought some photos (Figures 28.1 and 28.4) to foreground physical beauty, which was interpreted as reducing Indigenous women to their bodies and negating their intellectual capacity. The foregrounding of beauty was deciphered as a sexist venture that also led to a euphemising of colonial rule. Said one student: 'the beautiful naked

Table 28.1 Most frequently discussed threads

	Group 1	Group 2
Figure 28.1	Racism; Sexism (female nudity); Exploitative intention (reduction to physical beauty); Euphemises colonialism through idyllic portrayal; Misleading autonomy	Self-confidence; Female independence; Counter-acting sexism; A woman, not a girl; Eludes passive consumption
Figure 28.2	Racism; Politically instrumentalised; Sitter degraded to a Nazi puppet; Euphemising colonialism; Treats sitter as a child	Teasing the Nazis; Evokes irony and amusement; Agency against racism; Shows absurdity of racial ideology; Desire to know more about the sitter
Figure 28.3	Racism; Degrading portrayal as careworn and less human; Sexist because no clear gender applicable; Arrogance because of dying race dogma; Evokes pity	Strict person; Must have gone through hard times; A leader; Female independence; Desire to know more about the sitter
Figure 28.4	Racism; Sexist (adult described as girl); Inferior colonial status (sitter in pose of a domestic); Euphemising colonialism through idyllic portrayal (smiling pose); Abused for political ends	Self-confidence; Well-groomed and welcoming; Female independence; A woman in motion; Values her traditions

breasts are, in truth, signs of exploitation.' Regarded as a servant, the image of the Herero woman (Figure 28.4) was equally seen as exploitative in reflecting the hierarchy of colonial work. Students also read the photo purported to be Truganini's (Figure 28.3) through the prisms of racism and sexism. Because of her short haircut Truganini was perceived as exhibiting an ambiguous gender status that reflected racist dogmas of gender deviance. 'They let her appear as kind of masculine to underline racial inferiority', opined one student. Truganini's appearance as such was seen as evoking pity. Exploitation was also the frame through which Figure 28.2 was interpreted; assuming that the sitter had been coerced to hold the swastika flag, he was regarded as a puppet of the Nazi regime.

The interpretations made in Group 2 stood in stark contrast to those of seeing Indigenous photos as racist and sexist devices of German colonialism. Having virtually touched each of the photos, students agreed to consider them 'old'. The interpretation in Figure 28.2 was handed out later in order to keep the contextual influence low. Interestingly, this image was not pigeonholed as colonial. Smirking, respondents thought the photo funky because it teased the Nazis: 'this guy is really brilliant! The Nazis would have hated him for disgracing their hallowed flag on such a crooked flagpole being made of palm tree, not German oak ... and held by a Black guy.' Nobody assumed it was a Nazi colonial journal in which the photo appeared; instead it was interpreted as a conscious parody of Nazism. In contrast to Group 1, there was strong desire to know more about this particular sitter. Gender also played a significant role. While two female students brought up the possibility of sexism in the portrayal of semi-nudity in Figure 28.1, they were not sure if the sitter might not have deliberately chosen the very pose. Agreement existed in seeing the sitter in Figure 28.1 as confident and independent. Her pose was eventually interpreted as a rebuttal of sexism. Physical beauty was not mentioned in this context, but rather an arcane aura that reminded one student of actress Grace Jones who, he explained, was 'sort of yet not really a Bond girl'. 'Yes', replied a female student, 'she's definitely not a girl ... nothing easy to consume, I'd say'. The Herero woman was, in a similar vein, seen as self-aware yet older, without any nexus being established to (colonial) servitude. Her garment was regarded as old-fashioned, while the teeth, it was stressed, indicated a meticulous dental care. 'She'd be a real joy for any dentist,' said one participant in amusement. The group then ruminated as to whether the sitter might have been wealthy or a public figure. Respondents also discussed the sitter's movement, which was considered a sign of modernity. In her motion, she exerted an impression of (gendered) independence and was expected to have been more than 'just a husband's wife', as one student suggested.

The motion captured in the photo, in this case, functioned like an enactment: the sitter was indeed literally moving, while at the same time moving her audiences. The interpretation of Truganini's photo deviated from those of the other photos, for it was anger, hardship, and sternness that were seen in her portrayal. Her photo was indeed different from the bulk of images that appeared during the period of the 1930s, not only because it originated in the 1880s but also because it showed an elderly woman. The group agreed that the sitter must have gone through suffering and hard times. 'She makes me a bit afraid,' said one student, 'as she seems really strict'. She looks 'adamant' and thereby reminded another student of Ruth Bader Ginsburg, justice of the Supreme Court of the United States. Truganini's unpretentious garment resembled, in her opinion, a judicial robe and her stiff, almost accusatory look evoked a parallel to the liberal U.S. justice. 'She looks frozen, full of anger. Perhaps she was a leader, a justice, or a simple mother, irrelevant, but someone who tried to bring justice to this world. She's like someone who doesn't mince her words.' The group agreed Truganini's photo to be the most touching because it engendered an unsettling feeling. One felt intimidated, 'as if I'd done something wrong when looking into her eyes'. Another said, 'she looks frightening, yes, but also like someone with a deep personality, someone you'd like to ultimately meet.' The group concurred in wishing to know more about Truganini's life.

The group plunged into silence upon reading the short texts in which the photos appeared. Attentively they read and I could sense disbelief, eyes widening and a slightly doubtful 'oookay' being uttered. Someone broke the silence and said, 'I don't think we were completely on the wrong track.' Truganini's appearance was still seen as emanating anger and being accusatory. 'If I'd been declared extinct and then to see my photo being used a hundred years later for such rubbish, I'd be super angry,' was one of the reactions. Truganini's stern look seemed all the more apt in the now disclosed context. The group agreed that the context and use of the photo was degrading, yet its sitter was not degraded. This re-interpretation also applied to Figure 28.2: students pondered over the question as to whether the sitter deliberately chose to be portrayed with the swastika flag because he might have thought to forge alliances, might not have been aware of its meaning or might have even sympathised with the former German colonialists. None, however, explained the person behind the camera as an uncritical or childlike puppet of the Nazis, as Group 1 did. Neither did the re-interpretation of Figures 28.1 and 28.4 follow the assessments of sexism and racism discernible in Group 1. Here, too, it was the written text that was considered degrading and racist but not the photos per se. 'I do not think they [the Nazis] got to the photos, to the people in them,' said one student. Asked to elaborate her argument, the respondent said that the texts claimed to possess the sitters as commodities of colonialism but that the photos actually told different stories. Ultimately, Group 2 concluded that all four photos told stories of colonial dispossession and de-racialisation.

Such stories are certainly individual and complex. For all their individuality, the experiment of a decontextualised reading nonetheless allows us to observe major trends between both groups. A perceptible difference is the reading of Indigenous photos as responses to versus mere subordination to colonial dominance. Group 1 tended to treat Indigenous people as victims of German colonialism because the weight of the texts predetermined the reading of the photos. Unconsciously, readers in this group treated the individual photos as textual devices in line with the intention of the publications, that is, to substantiate the written words and suggest conformity among colonial subjects. While the texts were criticised for their colonial ambitions, the photos were equally treated as devices of the very colonial ambitions, thus leading to a conflation of the written text with the photo, as if both constituted an inseparable entity. Group 2, by contrast, saw more individuality and less racialisation in the photos. Photos came to be interpreted through familiar cultural codes, and decontextualised story telling came closer to the individual complexity of the photos than did mere textual analysis. Indeed, Group 2 did not see the photos as static types and textual embellishments but found them to be in motion, alive in their own right, and saw them through categories other than race, especially gender, resilience, and agency. This group engaged Indigenous photos as nodes of storytelling, which led not only to the acknowledgement of Indigenous agencies but also to consideration of how much such agencies matter to German history.

The Nazis would have hated the scene of a Black man holding their flag, as one student opined. But in this case they obviously instigated it – or at least did not object to the very scene. Why? Was it merely colonial propaganda? The decontextualised reading suggests audiences came to consider Indigenous sitters as unconquered, to neither belong to the written text in which they appeared nor to the German imagery of idealised Indigeneity. There is a paradox between the written texts and their photos: while the former did adapt to changing colonial discourses, the latter remained in presentation relatively stable yet flexible in reading. Photos could be hijacked by ideology but could not be possessed, for in their very nature of allowing fresh engagement they are literally vulnerable to change. In their vulnerability lies their futurity. At the same time, their vulnerability also has its history. Photos were not only *used* in the past, but they were equally consumed, enjoyed, hence *read* by past audiences. Although this is a future story to tell, let me suggest a hypothesis. Were there, perhaps, deeper readings of a Black Indigenous man holding the swastika flag? Readings that exceeded mere propaganda? Could this photo have affected past audiences as beautiful, strong, natural, or sovereign? German narratives of race drew heavily on ideas of *Ursprünglichkeit* (lit. nativeness) and autochthony. The role of Indigenous history is much underestimated in modern German history. Indigenous photos literally dominated racial narratives in Germany and partly complemented, partly thwarted racial narratives of German Indigeneity. Engaging with Indigenous history seems to be a fruitful method of increasing understanding of how historical narratives of race worked in Germany, and to what extent concepts of Indigeneity influenced the formation of race. In other words, Indigenous photography – both by and about Indigenous people – tells Indigenous history but can also help explain German and global history of race. It is time to make Indigenous history an intrinsic part of global history.

Notes

1. Hans Fischer, *Menschenschönheit: Gestalt und Antlitz des Menschen in Leben und Kunst* (Berlin: Der Büchermarkt, 1935), 50. (All translations from German are the author's.)
2. Fischer, *Menschenschönheit*, 42.
3. Oliver Haag, 'Idealised Race: The Function of Idealised Indigeneity in German Imperialist Discourses. Analytical Part' (PhD diss., University of Edinburgh, 2004), 219.
4. Oliver Haag, 'Idealized Australian Aboriginality in German Narratives of Race,' in *The Persistence of Race. Change and Continuity in Germany from the Wilhelmine Empire to National Socialism*, eds. Oliver Haag and Lara Day (New York: Berghahn, 2017), 233.

5 Gustav Jahoda, *Images of Savages: Ancient Roots of Modern Prejudice in Western Culture* (London: Routledge, 1999), 131–139.
6 Susanne Zantop, *Colonial Fantasies: Conquest, Family, and Nation in Pre-Colonial Germany, 1770–1870* (Durham, NC: Duke University Press, 1997), 6–8.
7 Lora Wildenthal, *German Women for Empire, 1884–1945* (Durham, NC: Duke University Press, 2001), 173.
8 Christina Twomey, 'The Incorruptible Kodak: Photography, Human Rights and the Congo Campaign,' in *The Violence of the Image. Photography and International Conflict*, eds. Liam Kennedy and Caitlin Patrick (London and New York: I.B. Tauris, 2014), 11, 17.
9 Reichskolonialbund, *Deutscher Kolonialkalender* (Minden: Wilhelm-Köhler-Verlag, 1940), n.p.
10 Haag, 'Idealized Australian Aboriginality,' 230–257.
11 Max Grühl, 'Die letzten Tasmanier,' *Atlantis* 2 (1930): 392–393.
12 In this chapter, I maintain the name Truganini for Figure 28.3, since this is the person the original text describes as such.
13 A. Vierkandt, 'Die Eingeborenen Tasmaniens,' *Globus* 76 (1899): 290.
14 Pascal Grosse, *Kolonialismus, Eugenik und bürgerliche Gesellschaft in Deutschland 1850–1918* (Frankfurt: Campus, 2000), 26–29.
15 Colin Ross, *Der unvollendete Kontinent* (Leipzig: Brockhaus, 1940), 249–250.
16 Jan-Pieter Barbian, *Literaturpolitik im 'Dritten Reich': Institutionen, Kompetenzen, Betätigungsfelder* (Frankfurt am Main: Buchhändler-Vereinigung, 1993), 206–208.
17 Emmy Bernatzik, *Afrikafahrt: Eine Frau bei den Negern Westafrikas* (Vienna: Schroll, 1941), 6, 130–147.
18 Jae Emerling, *Photography: History and Theory* (London: Routledge, 2012), 136–142.
19 Christraud Geary and Adamou Ndam Njoya, *Mandu Yenu: Bilder aus Bamum, einem westafrikanischen Königreich, 1902–1915* (Trickster: Munich, 1985), 29, 169.
20 Christeaud Geary, *In and Out of Focus: Images from Central Africa, 1885–1960* (London: Wilson, 2002), 52, 83–85, 97.
21 Geary, *In and Out of Focus*, 20.
22 Lisa Aronson, 'Image Maker Jonathan Adagogo Green and His Practice,' in *African Photographer J.A. Green: Reimagining the Indigenous and the Colonial*, eds. Martha Anderson and Lisa Aronson (Bloomington: Indiana University Press, 2017), 93, 117.
23 Jane Lydon, *Eye Contact: Photographing Indigenous Australians* (Durham, NC: Duke University Press: 2005), 2–5, 30, 64.
24 Thomas Theye, ed., *Der geraubte Schatten: Die Photographie als ethnographisches Dokument* (Munich: Münchner Stadtmuseum, 1989), 46–48.
25 Helen Pringle, 'Walter Roth and Ethno-Pornography,' in *The Roth Family, Anthropology & Colonial Administration*, eds. Russell McDougall and Iain Davidson (London and New York: Routledge, 2016), 225–230.
26 Ann McGrath, 'Naked Shame: Nation, Science and Indigenous Knowledge in Waler Roth's Interventions into Frontier Sexualities,' in *The Roth Family, Anthropology & Colonial Administration*, eds. Russell McDougall and Iain Davidson (London and New York: Routledge, 2016), 195–203.
27 Ronald Burton, *Venus Oceanica: The Sexual Life of South Sea Natives* (New York: The Oceanica Research Press, 1935).
28 McGrath, 'Naked Shame', 194.
29 Laura Peers and Alison K. Brown, '"Just by Bringing These Photographs …": On the Other Meanings of Anthropological Images,' in *Photography, Anthropology and History: Expanding the Frame*, eds. Christopher Morton and Elizabeth Edwards (Surrey: Ashgate, 2009), 265–276.
30 Brenda Croft, 'Laying Ghosts to Rest,' in *Colonialist Photography: Imag(in)ing Race and Place*, eds. Eleanor Hight and Gary Sampson (London: Routledge, 2002), 21, 28.
31 Jane Lydon, 'Introduction: The Photographic Encounter,' in *Calling the Shots: Aboriginal Photographies*, ed. Jane Lydon (Canberra: Aboriginal Studies Press, 2014), 9.

32 Andrew Brook and Jessica Neath, 'Encounters with Legacy Images: Decolonising and Re-imagining Photographic Evidence from the Colonial Archive,' *History of Photography* 42, no. 3 (2018): 223, 238.
33 Roslyn Poignant and Axel Poignant, *Encounter at Nagalarramba* (Canberra: National Library of Australia, 1996), 16.
34 Joanna Scherer, 'The Photographic Document: Photographs as Primary Data in Anthropological Enquiry,' in *Anthropology and Photography, 1860–1920*, ed. Elizabeth Edwards (New Haven, CT and London: Yale University Press, 1992), 32–35.
35 Oliver Haag, 'Becoming Privileged in Australia: Romany Europe, Indigenous Australia and the Transformation of Race,' *Ngapartji Ngapartji Reciprocal Engagement: Ego-Histoire, Europe and Indigenous Australia*, eds. Anna Cole et al. (Canberra: ANU Press 2014), 125–139.
36 John Berger and Jean Mohr, *Another Way of Telling: Writers and Readers* (London: Publishing Cooperative Society, 1982), 279–286.
37 Ilse Steinhoff, *Deutsche Heimat in Afrika: Ein Bildbuch aus unseren Kolonien* (Berlin: Limpert, 1939), n.p.
38 Elizabeth Edwards, 'Photographs and the Sound of History,' *Visual Anthropology Review* 21, no. 1–2 (2006): 27–46.
39 Tina Campt, *Listening to Images* (Durham, NC: Duke University Press, 2017), 9, 55, 100.
40 Campt, *Listening to Images*, 57–59.
41 Tina Campt, *Image Matters: Archive, Photography, and the African Diaspora in Europe* (Durham, NC: Duke University Press, 2012), 7.
42 Group 1 consisted of 12 students of which 8 were female; Group 2 comprised 13 students, with 7 being female.
43 Lydon, *Eye Contact*, 241.
44 Corinna Erckenbrecht and Anna Haebich, 'Aboriginal People in Chains,' in *Visualising Australia: Images, Icons, Imaginations*, eds. Renate Brosch and Kylie Crane (Trier: Wissenschaftlicher Verlag, 2014), 39; Elizabeth Edwards, 'Introduction,' in *Anthropology and Photography, 1860–1920*, ed. Elizabeth Edwards (New Haven, CT and London: Yale University Press, 1992), 7.

Bibliography

Aronson, Lisa. 'Image Maker Jonathan Adagogo Green and His Practice.' In *African Photographer J.A. Green: Reimagining the Indigenous and the Colonial*, edited by Martha Anderson and Lisa Aronson, 85–118. Bloomington: Indiana University Press, 2017.
Barbian, Jan-Pieter. *Literaturpolitik im 'Dritten Reich': Institutionen, Kompetenzen, Betätigungsfelder*. Frankfurt am Main: Buchhändler-Vereinigung, 1993.
Berger, John, and Jean Mohr. *Another Way of Telling: Writers and Readers*. London: Publishing Cooperative Society, 1982.
Bernatzik, Emmy. *Afrikafahrt: Eine Frau bei den Negern Westafrikas*. Vienna: Schroll, 1941.
Brook, Andrew, and Jessica Neath. 'Encounters with Legacy Images: Decolonising and Re-imagining Photographic Evidence from the Colonial Archive.' *History of Photography* 42, no. 3 (2018): 217–238.
Burton, Ronald. *Venus Oceanica: The Sexual Life of South Sea Natives*. New York: The Oceanica Research Press, 1935.
Campt, Tina. *Image Matters: Archive, Photography, and the African Diaspora in Europe*. Durham, NC: Duke University Press, 2012.
Campt, Tina. *Listening to Images*. Durham, NC: Duke University Press, 2017.
Croft, Brenda. 'Laying Ghosts to Rest.' In *Colonialist Photography. Imag(in)ing Race and Place*, edited by Eleanor Hight and Gary Sampson, 20–30. London: Routledge, 2002.
Edwards, Elizabeth. 'Introduction.' In *Anthropology and Photography, 1860–1920*, edited by Elizabeth Edwards, 3–17. New Haven, CT and London: Yale University Press, 1992.

Edwards, Elizabeth. 'Photographs and the Sound of History.' *Visual Anthropology Review* 21, no. 1–2 (2006): 27–46.
Emerling, Jae. *Photography: History and Theory*. London: Routledge, 2012.
Erckenbrecht, Corinna, and Anna Haebich. 'Aboriginal People in Chains.' In *Visualising Australia: Images, Icons, Imaginations*, edited by Renate Brosch and Kylie Crane, 39–59. Trier: Wissenschaftlicher Verlag, 2014.
Fischer, Hans. *Menschenschönheit: Gestalt und Antlitz des Menschen in Leben und Kunst*. Berlin: Der Büchermarkt, 1935.
Geary, Christraud. *In and Out of Focus: Images from Central Africa, 1885–1960*. London: Wilson, 2002.
Geary, Christraud, and Adamou Ndam Njoya. *Mandu Yenu: Bilder aus Bamum, einem westafrikanischen Königreich, 1902–1915*. Trickster: Munich, 1985.
Grosse, Pascal. *Kolonialismus, Eugenik und bürgerliche Gesellschaft in Deutschland 1850–1918*. Frankfurt: Campus, 2000.
Grühl, Max. 'Die letzten Tasmanier.' *Atlantis* 2 (1930): 392–393.
Haag, Oliver. 'Idealised Race: The Function of Idealised Indigeneity in German Imperialist Discourses. Analytical Part.' PhD diss., University of Edinburgh, 2014.
Haag, Oliver. 'Becoming Privileged in Australia: Romany Europe, Indigenous Australia and the Transformation of Race.' In *Ngapartji Ngapartji Reciprocal Engagement: Ego-Histoire, Europe and Indigenous Australia*, edited by Anna Cole et al., 125–139. Canberra: ANU Press, 2014.
Haag, Oliver. 'Idealized Australian Aboriginality in German Narratives of Race.' In *The Persistence of Race. Change and Continuity in Germany from the Wilhelmine Empire to National Socialism*, edited by Oliver Haag and Lara Day, 230–257. Berghahn: New York, 2017.
Jahoda, Gustav. *Images of Savages: Ancient Roots of Modern Prejudice in Western Culture*. London: Routledge, 1999.
Lydon, Jane. *Eye Contact: Photographing Indigenous Australians*. Durham, NC: Duke University Press, 2005.
Lydon, Jane. 'Introduction: The Photographic Encounter.' In *Calling the Shots: Aboriginal Photographies*, edited by Jane Lydon, 1–18. Canberra: Aboriginal Studies Press, 2014.
McGrath, Ann. 'Naked Shame: Nation, Science and Indigenous Knowledge in Walter Roth's Interventions into Frontier Sexualities.' In *The Roth Family, Anthropology & Colonial Administration*, edited by Russell McDougall and Iain Davidson, 193–208. London and New York: Routledge, 2016.
Peers, Laura, and Alison K. Brown. '"Just by Bringing These Photographs ...": On the Other Meanings of Anthropological Images.' In *Photography, Anthropology and History: Expanding the Frame*, edited by Christopher Morton and Elizabeth Edwards, 265–280. Surrey: Ashgate, 2009.
Poignant, Roslyn, and Axel Poignant. *Encounter at Nagalarramba*. Canberra: National Library of Australia, 1996.
Pringle, Helen. 'Walter Roth and Ethno-Pornography.' In *The Roth Family, Anthropology & Colonial Administration*, edited by Russell McDougall and Iain Davidson, 221–231. London and New York: Routledge, 2016.
Reichskolonialbund. *Deutscher Kolonialkalender*. Minden: Wilhelm-Köhler-Verlag, 1940.
Ross, Colin. *Der unvollendete Kontinent*. Leipzig: Brockhaus, 1940.
Scherer, Joanna. 'The Photographic Document: Photographs as Primary Data in Anthropological Enquiry.' In *Anthropology and Photography, 1860–1920*, edited by Elizabeth Edwards, 32–41. New Haven, CT and London: Yale University Press, 1992.
Steinhoff, Ilse. *Deutsche Heimat in Afrika: Ein Bildbuch aus unseren Kolonien*. Berlin: Limpert, 1939.
Theye, Thomas, ed. *Der geraubte Schatten. Die Photographie als ethnographisches Dokument*. Munich: Münchner Stadtmuseum, 1989.
Twomey, Christina. 'The Incorruptible Kodak: Photography, Human Rights and the Congo Campaign.' In *The Violence of the Image. Photography and International Conflict*,

edited by Liam Kennedy and Caitlin Patrick, 9–33. London and New York: I.B. Tauris, 2014.
Vierkandt, A. 'Die Eingeborenen Tasmaniens.' *Globus* 76 (1899): 289–292.
Wildenthal, Lora. *German Women for Empire, 1884–1945*. Durham, NC: Duke University Press, 2001.
Zantop, Susanne. *Colonial Fantasies: Conquest, Family, and Nation in Pre-Colonial Germany, 1770–1870*. Durham, NC: Duke University Press, 1997.

29
AFRICAN LITERATURE AS INDIGENOUS HISTORY IN SOUTH AFRICA'S 'DECOLONISE THE CURRICULUM' MOVEMENT

Ashleigh Harris[1]

In 2015, South African university and college students galvanised by the recent successes of the country-wide #RhodesMustFall movement, which demanded the removal of a statue of Cecil John Rhodes at the University of Cape Town (UCT), turned their attention to more concrete economic concerns. That year, fee hikes across the university sector made an already outlandishly expensive higher education impossible for most South Africans to afford. The result was #FeesMustFall, a movement that resulted in major disruptions at university campuses across the country and led to hundreds of student arrests. The images that circulated on social media and in the press of clashes between police and students were traumatically reminiscent of clashes between protesters and the police during apartheid. The presence of police on campuses provoked even more violent protests and acts of vandalism. Two of the most symbolically loaded and controversial acts of vandalism during this time involved the burning of university-owned art and books. In 2015, 75 works of art, owned by UCT, were set alight and destroyed by student protesters and, in 2016, protesters on the University of KwaZulu Natal's Howard Campus set light to the Law Library, which resulted in the destruction of thousands of books. Both acts of arson were roundly condemned in the media as evidence of an anti-democratic and anti-intellectualist trend in the #RhodesMustFall and #FeesMustFall movements, now commonly referred to as the fallist movements. Many commentators felt that these students were attacking the wrong symbols – vandalism to the statue of Cecil John Rhodes at the UCT was broadly understood and accepted, but the destruction of art and books hit a nerve across society. Yet, if we look beyond the irate and bifurcated rhetoric of the students on the one side and their numerous detractors on the other, it is obvious that the objects were very precisely chosen metaphors for the symbolic and economic capital these students felt universities were excluding them from.

Books, more specifically, are objects of ambivalence in South Africa. On the one hand, they are clearly objects of exclusion: more often than not, books are written in colonial languages, they are reminiscent of the colonial imposition of a written culture on an oral one, they represent an inaccessibly costly education, and more immediately, they are too expensive for the majority of South Africans, unless bought second hand or copied illegally.[2] On the other hand, books also symbolise the ideals of a free and open education, an education that can raise one out of poverty and that can give a learner access to the global market economy. As such, books in South Africa are often revered to the point that they appear metonymically tied to the ultimate 'good book', the Bible. This ambivalence about the object of the book gets to the heart of the dilemma faced by students demanding the decolonisation of the curriculum in South Africa: if academic and economic success is still governed by neo-colonial structures, epistemes, and languages, then calls for decolonisation will, ultimately, only lead to further exclusion. This ambivalence can be traced in the eventual dissipation of the fallist movement, as more extreme student calls lost the support of a mass student body.

In this chapter, I argue for the use of Indigenous history, literature, and oral forms in decolonising the literary and language curricula in South Africa. I focus, specifically, on literary studies, not only because I myself am a literary scholar, but because South African Indigenous history, which is one of many oral forms, has been valuably theorised by Isabel Hofmeyr as being literary in form. Writing about oral history, Hofmeyr points out that 'most small-scale societies do not have a special word for historical narration. Instead, it is often included under a more general word meaning "affairs" or "happenings" while in other instances it falls under the broader heading "story"'.[3] In the context of Hofmeyr's study, the Northern Sesotho word used for oral history is '*nonwane,* meaning "narrative", "tale" or "story"'.[4] I follow Hofmeyr's lead here, and see South African literary traditions as deeply entangled in, and inseparable from, Indigenous history.

Moreover, the inevitable loss of pre-colonial oral archives in, and through, the annihilating impulse of the colonial encounter, with its emphasis on the written word, means that these forms can mainly be traced in the resilience of oral forms that are, today, largely literary in form. To paraphrase Hofmeyr, it is not only literary scholars that need historians, but historians who need literary scholars, in this context, too.[5] I put forward here a set of interventions that are intended to address student alienation from a colonial education, while also tethering that curriculum to their rights and desires to participate in the world. These four interventions are multilingualism, multimodality, intertextuality, and interdisciplinarity.

* * *

Aryan Kaganof's film *Opening Stellenbosch: From Assimilation to Occupation* includes a video clip of an unnamed student who stands up in his class at the University of Stellenbosch and pronounces, 'I can't breathe in this lecture because my education is colonised.' Other students join in and chant the phrase 'I can't breathe'. This is a powerful trans-Atlantic recitation of Eric Garner's dying words that became a mobilising slogan in the #BlackLivesMatter campaign in the United States. In the South African context, the phrase was appropriated to describe black students' experience of a claustrophobic curriculum, symbolically complicit with the racist, physical violence of the chokehold that killed Eric Garner.

How, one might ask, is this situation possible 27 years after the end of apartheid? Can it really be the case that the curriculum remains so engrained in colonial epistemes? To investigate this question in terms of the literary curriculum, I examined all the literary texts prescribed on the South African Department of Basic Education's 2015 national curriculum for upper secondary school, in all 11 official languages.[6] I also looked at the literary curricula, across all official languages, from all 18 institutions of higher education that offer humanities and language degrees.[7]

A lot has, indeed, changed since apartheid. The Department of Basic Education has made good on its promises of implementing curricula in all 11 national languages throughout primary and secondary education, and the literary content of these curricula seem to equal those of English and Afrikaans in scope, variety of genre, and complexity.[8] The one notable difference is that folklore is taught in all languages excepting English and Afrikaans. This appears to be the only attempt to include Indigenous and oral forms in the otherwise book-based curriculum, and even these are prescribed in the form of printed book anthologies. Another point worth noting is that, while more African writers are now represented on the English curriculum than in the past, the curriculum still contains one Shakespeare play per year. There is little evidence from this document of attempts to work across languages, or multilingually.

Literary studies at university level is still largely the domain of English departments. That said, one can trace a real commitment to change, on the whole, across English literary curricula, as well as to the growth of African language literature at universities across the country. While African language departments clearly require further development (not all universities teach African language programmes, and those that do tend to focus on only a few languages), it is at least possible to study all nine Indigenous languages at university level somewhere in South Africa.[9] Almost all English literature departments include a wide range of anglophone African, African diaspora, and postcolonial content. The University of the Witwatersrand's African Literature department has been committed to this positionality since its inauguration in 1983. More recently, and perhaps in the aftermath of #RhodesMustFall, UCT offers an impressively South African and African-oriented English literature curriculum, including undergraduate modules that are multimodal, interdisciplinary, and distinctly embedded in African perspectives.[10] The multimodal and cross-genre elements of the texts taught across this curriculum can also be traced in other innovative courses, such as Deborah Seddon's 'Spoken Word: from South Africa to South Carolina', taught at Rhodes University, which reveals a solid commitment to rethinking the curriculum in similar ways to the ones I propose below. Some of most exciting developments of all include the PhD in Comparative Literature offered at the University of Stellenbosch – enabling students to study across Afrikaans, English, Northern Sesotho, Sesotho, isiXhosa, and isiZulu – and the University of Limpopo's 'Contemporary

English Languages and Multilingual Studies' undergraduate programme, where the study of English is accompanied by the compulsory study of an Indigenous South African language.

So, with real changes afoot – even at some of the most criticised universities of the fallist movements – what is it, in at least the literary curriculum, that continues to make students feel suffocated by this education? I believe that the answer to this question is primarily about language, a question at the heart of Ngũgĩ wa Thiong'o's *Decolonising the Mind: The Politics of Language in African Literature*. Here, Ngũgĩ analyses two historical moments of challenge to the literary curriculum in Kenya – moments that significantly overlap with fallist calls to decolonise the curriculum. The first was catalysed by a now-famous 1968 polemic by Ngũgĩ, Henry Owuor-Anyumba, and Taban Lo Liyong, entitled 'On the Abolition of the English Department'. The three teachers of literature called for a Department of African Literatures and Languages to replace the English department at the University of Nairobi.[11] The manifesto calls for key curriculum and pedagogical changes that reorientate literary study so that 'Kenya, East Africa, and then Africa' are placed 'in the centre' and that all 'other things are to be considered in their relevance to our situation, and their contribution towards understanding ourselves'.[12] In practice, this involves a multilingual approach, as well as a multimodal one, in which oral tradition is given proper place in the curriculum. Indeed, the oral tradition will require, the authors add, a 'multi-disciplinary outlook' since the social, political, and historical functions of this rich tradition are so varied.[13] The curriculum, as imagined by Ngũgĩ, Owuor-Anyumba, and Liyong, would not read African literatures in isolation, but would offer a comparative approach in which world literatures would also be read, but 'only for their relevance to the East African perspective'.[14]

While this intervention led to much debate and to significant changes in the curriculum at the University of Nairobi, there was still much left to discuss in 1974 at a conference, held at Nairobi School, entitled 'The Teaching of African Literature in Kenyan Schools'.[15] This conference also highlighted the importance of global connection, and many insisted on the importance of Kenyan children being 'exposed to world literature and the democratic tradition in world literature'.[16] Yet, the debate as to the value of the English language operating as a pan-African and diasporic *lingua franca* remained unresolved. The consequence is something that we can see even in the current South African literary curriculum: while there is a great deal more content by African writers across the English curriculum, there is comparatively little focus on African language literature. Ngũgĩ bemoans this dominance of what he calls 'Afro-European literature',[17] and admits, somewhat defeatedly, that at the time of writing *Decolonising the Mind* in 1986, 'English [was] still the linguistic medium of the debate; and of the temporary solutions of the 1968–1969 and 1974 conferences'.[18] For Ngũgĩ, language was the core issue in the process of decolonisation and I argue here that it remains the key aspect of why higher education in South Africa has failed to meet the needs of the majority of South African students.

Multilingualism

The continued (and seemingly unstoppable) rise of English as the *lingua franca* of the global economy and of academic capital means that the messier, more complex histories through which the written word and the English language entered the South African context and perpetuated the ideologies of apartheid and colonialism are often conveniently swept aside in students' and their parents' desire for a language that will enable access to the global economy. As such, university English departments across South Africa still attract large student numbers, while African languages and literatures are comparatively under-subscribed – a curious situation in the time of rising student frustration with a neo-colonial education. The result is fewer qualified teachers of Indigenous languages in the primary and secondary school system, which, in turn, means students of university-going age having greater academic literacy in English or Afrikaans than in their home languages, a fact that is reconfirmed by university instructions being dominantly in these two languages across the country.

It is interesting to observe that, despite this situation, the question of Indigenous languages was not a significant aspect of the fallist movements.[19] As Leketi Makalela notes, 'the Fees Must Fall movement present[ed] a continuation of an age-old struggle with more focus on the negative effects of corporate African universities, with issues around culture and language not explicitly stated.'[20] In Kaganof's film *Opening Stellenbosch*, the student who takes the brave step to declare to his teacher that he cannot breathe because his education is colonised is later interviewed in the film and asked specifically about the Stellenbosch students' demand that all classes be taught in English.[21] The student, looking a little embarrassed when the interviewer points out that English, like Afrikaans, is a colonial language, states: 'It's part of a long agenda' and admits that 'we should not be speaking English, [that is] obviously the end goal'.[22] But the lack of an overtly stated politics about the dominance of the English language during the fallist movement reveals students' ambivalence about the language.

As Makalela also notes, the obvious starting point for an investigation into language politics is, once again, Ngũgĩ's *Decolonising the Mind*, in which he argues that colonialism's 'destruction [and] deliberate undervaluing of a people's culture [...] and the conscious elevation of the language of the coloniser' has resulted in a long-lived situation in which there is 'often not the slightest relationship between the child's written world [...] and the world of his immediate environment in the family and community'.[23] Despite the fact that the work of Frantz Fanon became central to the consciousness-raising and mobilising processes of the fallist movements, the first chapter of *Black Skin, White Masks,* which focuses on language has, as far as I have been able to ascertain, not been significantly engaged across fallist literature and debates. This is striking, because in that chapter Fanon takes on a key problem regarding double-consciousness and language, arguing that what he sees as the 'inferiority complex' of the colonised 'is particularly intensified among the most educated'.[24] This, for Fanon, is because this education has occurred in a foreign, and colonial, language, thus forcing the colonised to adopt 'a language different from that of the group into which he was born'.[25] The observation goes to the core of the call for a decolonised curriculum.

Following the lead of numerous South African linguists and theorists of multi-languaging,[26] I see the disjuncture between Indigenous languages and the linguistic medium of university study as the most fundamental legacy of colonialism in South African education. Following Ngũgĩ, it is clear that this disjuncture creates not only the psychological schism that Fanon theorises, but also radically separates classrooms and communities. In *Decolonising the Mind*, Ngũgĩ writes about the danger of knowledge that mystifies rather than demystifies.[27] For him, mystifying knowledge is written, produced in isolation, in languages and registers that are inaccessible to the peasantry. Demystified knowledge production, however, is cooperative, shared, and multilingual. The only way of demystifying knowledge in South Africa is to open it beyond the two colonial languages that currently dominate its production.

But this is no easy task. In a country where there are 11 official languages, it is no surprise that English and Afrikaans, for reasons of logistics, retained their hold of the education system. Moreover, how does one balance students' need for academic languages that engage with Indigenous cultural, historical, and community spaces and their simultaneous desire to participate in global markets and cultural flows, which require them to know English? These balances have been hard to achieve. The most exciting work on pedagogy in South Africa creating ways forward for this problem is on trans- and multi-languaging. Makalela coins the phrase 'ubuntu trans-languaging' to elaborate this process.[28] He writes that 'ubuntu trans-languaging or its variant, multi-languaging, in particular, has shown that African multilingualism is a reflection of a cultural competence where no one language is complete without the other, and it has invariably associated monolingualism with colonialism'.[29]

This is strikingly similar to Ngũgĩ's call for 'unity in multi-lingual diversity'[30] *across* Africa. The idea of trans-languaging could, argues Ngũgĩ, become a site for pan-African connection that no longer relies on the mediation of colonial languages. For Ngũgĩ, this would require work in translation across African languages (he even goes so far as to say, 'I see this kind of communication between African languages as forming the real foundation of a genuinely African novel').[31] To return to the South African context, literary critic Michael Green has made a similar observation when he argues that 'a major requirement of non-exclusionary South Africanness must [...] be a radical act – or rather a series of radical acts – of translation.'[32]

When it comes to literary curricula, the idea of trans-languaging might seem too complex to achieve immediately, since building language competence in monolingual faculty would take time. But the reality is that the majority of South Africans do speak multiple South African languages. Moreover, during the time it would take to build up language competence where needed, a process that should begin with compulsory education in at least one Indigenous language at primary and high school, co-teaching could be implemented immediately. This would also change classroom dynamics, allowing for a more dialogic structure to knowledge production.

The language of learning materials in all disciplines is, of course, also a problem. While textbooks and learning materials dominate publishing in African languages, even these materials are vastly surpassed by learning materials in English and Afrikaans. This remains a problem across the continent. According to a survey from 2000 conducted by the Association for Development and Education in Africa and the African Publishers Network, the entire African continent stands for less than 3% of global book production.[33] Furthermore, two areas that are most vulnerable in African-based publishing are Indigenous languages and the literary arts.[34] In the absence of a sustainable buying market, NGO support has kept various initiatives afloat. However, scholars and publishers point to the unsustainability of this funding[35] and the ethical compromises it can often impose.[36]

For the literary curriculum, the comparative approach that I am recommending might be seen as an investment in the future of multilingual publishing since it develops multilingual skills and skills for translation. But existing initiatives already point the way towards new models of literary publishing beyond the book. One impressive example is African Storybook,[37] an online NGO initiative that provides a platform for readers to produce and translate African children's stories. All the content on the site is free and open for translation, editing, or revision for older or younger audiences. At the time of writing this paper, the site boasts 1,102 storybooks, with a staggering 5,683 translations in 179 African languages. Other online self-publishing initiatives include FunDza[38] and *WritePublishRead*,[39] the latter being, as Hans Zell explains,

> the brainchild of publisher Via Afrika, working in association with the African Languages Association of South Africa. It aims to give hitherto unpublished local writers of indigenous language fiction the chance to be published digitally in their home language by way of a self-publisher starter kit, thus enabling anyone to read these texts if they access to a mobile phone or any other digital device.[40]

These free and easily accessible multilingual sites have immense potential for the classroom. Following the pedagogical methods of writing-across-the-curriculum and writing-to-learn, one might implement a translation-across-the-curriculum, or translating-to-learn, model where students do translation work as part of their learning process. This could also have longer-term positive effects on the infrastructures of the translation industry, which would, in turn, increase interest in the formal study of Indigenous languages.

Multimodality

The potential of online translation leads us back to the problems surrounding the object of the book that this chapter began with. Because of the annihilating impulse of colonialism and apartheid, Indigenous archives – all of which were oral before colonial and missionary orthographies of Indigenous languages intervened – are not always easily recuperable. The rapid shift in social relations and the interception of colonial education, the English language, Christianity, and literacy, all facilitated (and sped up) the fragmentation and diminishment of oral practices. Even more devastating to the practices of oral narrative, as Hofmeyr proves in *'We Spend Our Years as a Tale That is Told'*, are the series of forced migrations and relocations that various polities underwent in the late nineteenth and early twentieth centuries. These led to a rearrangement of social life from 'cluster-style settlements into grid-plan villages' that had serious consequences for public oral practices, which 'struggled to reconstitute themselves in the new layout'.[41]

Yet, as Hofmeyr points out, even if oral literature was fundamentally changed by the colonial encounter, it proved to be resilient as a cultural form precisely because it is inherently plastic and mutable: 'Oral literature', she writes, 'is always changing, and during the nineteenth and twentieth centuries oral forms in South Africa have altered drastically. Any serious study of oral tradition is obliged to take cognizance of such transformation'.[42] We needn't see this only as evidence of ephemerality or of a lost archive. Russell Kaschula, for example, writes of the 'resilience' of the Xhosa tradition of praise poetry.[43] He notes how panegyric praise poems in both isiXhosa and isiZulu (*izibongo*) continue to play an important role in contemporary South African social practices. Thus, we need to change our methodological practices to address historical change in and through texts if we are to recuperate Indigenous forms into the current curricula. We may not have a substantial oral archive of historical literature, but we do have a living Indigenous oral literature, the traces of which remain in contemporary oral forms. To read these contemporary forms as Indigenous history requires a significant methodological shift away from the critical repertoires based on book production, distribution, and consumption – methods that are the standard fare of literary studies, from new criticism to distant reading. As I have already argued above, the first methodological shift is towards comparativism and away from monolingualism. But more than this, this approach must be multimodal to enable a serious inclusion of oral forms.

This does not imply the end of the book in the decolonised curriculum. On the contrary, the multimodal approach justifies its continued inclusion. As Hofmeyr points out, 'the interaction of orality and literacy cannot be imagined as a straight, evolutionary line in which the written eventually triumphs over the spoken'; the 'two areas', she asserts, 'can never be neatly separated'.[44] Hofmeyr's case-study considers a historical event that written English history refers to as 'The Siege of Makapansgat', but which in Sesotho oral narrative has been called *taba ya legolo la Gwasa* (the 'Story of the Cave of Gwasa').[45] Hofmeyr's analysis of the various accounts, oral and written, of this historical event reveals 'that a neat distinction between chiefly/oral and settler/written is not possible'.[46] By turning attention not only to how oral narrative and history is transformed in its encounter with the written text and the English and Afrikaans languages, but to how European languages and cultures become 'oralised' in this context is a methodological intervention that should be brought to bear on the pedagogical processes of decolonising the curriculum. The starting point for this work is to invert the binary of ephemeral oral text and archived written text that continues to dominate pedagogical approaches to literature. That is, oral forms are assumed to be ephemeral where print is seen as enduring, which perpetuates a further high/low culture bias against orality and for the written word.

Through the interventions of Indigenous history and new materialisms/book history, we know that neither of these positions is correct: oral narrative, as Kaschula points out, is remarkably resilient in ways that keep it relevant in the contemporary moment, and books and print are ever-changing technologies, which, in the digital age, are becoming precarious forms. We might even go so far as to say that the published book is an unsustainable form in the South African context, where book costs are far too high for most South Africans. Indeed, across the sub-Saharan African region the book is diminishing in relevance as non-commercial and multilingual literary forms and socialities are becoming dominant, many of which are oral –such as spoken word poetry, storytelling, and theatre – or digital. Many of these literary forms also operate multimodally: spoken word poems often appear transcribed for publication in print, many storytelling or slam poetry events reappear on YouTube for broader consumption, and so forth.[47] To read these literary forms as ephemeral would be to miss a major opportunity since they offer traces of deep Indigenous literary practice even as they speak the experience of (often young) South Africans in today's world. Moreover, these forms often involve communities in their making: spoken word and storytelling content develops through performance and audience feedback, and as such the development of the text is public, not confined to the commercial process of written composition to published book.

Ngũgĩ makes a relevant observation about his work at the Kamĩrĩĩthũ Community Education and Culture Centre, where he was involved in the creation of community-workshopped plays. Here, he extends his idea of mystifying and de-mystifying knowledge by elaborating these terms through a discussion of literary form.[48] The plays produced at the centre were created and practised in public view, in what he calls the 'empty space', with the input of the community.[49] Because the language of these plays was Gĩkũyũ, there was, writes Ngũgĩ, 'no barrier between the content of [the audience's] history and the linguistic medium of [the play's] expression'.[50] Moreover, because they were created, practised, and performed in full view, with the participation of the community, there was nothing obscure about how the literary work came into being. It was an expression of community. The same can be said of current oral literary forms popular in South Africa. This is very unlike the novel, which is written (and often read) in isolation, in Africa most likely in a language foreign to the reader, which places this form at a remove from (particularly rural) communities.

Given, as observed above by Makalela, that the fallist movements did not overtly politicise the inclusion of Indigenous languages in their education, it is interesting that across all campuses, protest included one of South Africa's richest oral traditions: protest and struggle songs. To perform these songs, one needs not only to know the languages in which they are sung, but to have learned them, orally, from a community of elders who would have sung them during apartheid. While many speeches and most negotiations took place in English during the fallist movement, it is important that these songs, in the vernaculars, emerged in the site of demonstration, a site performatively outside the institutional control of the university. Aryan Kaganof's two films about the fallist movement, *Opening Stellenbosch* and *Decolon I sing Wits*, capture how fundamental these songs are to today's students. In *Opening Stellenbosch*, a student sings *Senzeni na?*, a lament that emerged in the 1950s that was commonly sung at funerals of those killed by apartheid violence.[51] In Kaganof's film, the singer is standing next to an installation of white crosses, which have the names of some of the people killed in the Marikana massacre of 2012, where striking miners were killed by South African Security Force gunfire. The Marikana killings were a traumatic return of a recognisable, violent South African past, and the fact that students saw it as symbolically linked to their own struggle, and performed the oral forms of mourning and bearing witness in that acknowledgement, brings these songs very palpably into the present. The songs become a historical bridge, articulated in Indigenous language and form, between the struggle against apartheid and the continued struggles young people are facing in the aftermath of that violent system.

Later in *Opening Stellenbosch*, one of South Africa's most accomplished poets, Lesego Rampolokeng, recites a poem about the 'cannibalistic horrors' of colonialism over images of Marikana.[52] Again, the literary is an important site of bearing witness, but it is presented here as part-poem, part-song, a multimodality that covers expressions as relevant to student's present contexts as they are to their cultural histories.[53]

In *Decolonising the Mind*, Ngũgĩ reflects on his and his fellow teachers' call for the abolition of the English department back in 1968: 'Our boldest call was for the placing, within the national perspective, of oral literature (orature) at the centre of the syllabus.'[54] This reorientation of form did not write out print forms altogether. Indeed, Ngũgĩ still feels that the novel can convey a properly African literary tradition, so long as we invest in more than what he calls 'Afro-European literature',[55] that being a literature 'produced in European languages [which has been] given the identity of African literature as if there had never been literature in African languages'.[56] In an anecdote that makes his point, he writes about how his writings in Gĩkũyũ became read out among families and in bars across Kenya,[57] pointing, once more, to the ways the novel form might need to operate multimodally if it is to have relevance across African contexts, particularly rural ones. For Ngũgĩ, Owuor-Anyumba, and Liyong:

> The study of the Oral Tradition would therefore supplement (not replace) courses in Modern African Literature. By discovering and proclaiming loyalty to indigenous values, the new literature would on the one hand be set in the stream of history to which it belongs and so be better appreciated; and on the other be better able to embrace and assimilate other thoughts without losing its roots.[58]

Just as ubuntu trans-languaging is a necessity for the decolonised curriculum, I wonder what an ubuntu approach to literary form might look like. This would involve necessarily thinking through the complex ways in which written and oral forms, to mould Makalela's linguistic concept to the literary, are 'not complete without the other',[59] an idea that adds a slightly new dimension to Hofmeyr's insistence that literary and oral traditions 'can never be neatly separated'.[60] To see print and oral forms as mutually constitutive of one another, or as Deborah Seddon puts it, '[b]ringing orature into the literary curriculum alongside other works of literature', could be radically transformative.[61] This further evokes a multimodal body of work that Liz Gunner describes as 'a three-way dialectic between print, performance, and the more self-contained orality of the older culture'.[62]

Such multimodal approaches could contribute to a more substantially integrated history of African printed literatures, including the novel. Mũkoma wa Ngũgĩ's recent book *The Rise of the African Novel*, follows Ngũgĩ wa Thiong'o's insistence that the work of literary critics of African writing today is to establish a multilingual, and multimodal, approach to the rise of the novel form in and for Africa. He begins his book by citing the rich array of African language novels that emerged in the early to mid-1900s in South Africa, among them Thomas Mofolo's *Moeti oa Bochabela* (1907) and *Chaka* (1925); R.R.R. Dhlomo's *UNomalanga kaNdengezi* (1934); A.C Jordan's *Ingqumbo yeminyanya* (1940); and Samuel Mqhayi's *Ityala Lamawele* (1912).[63] Deborah Seddon and Jeff Opland have focused on Mqhayi's production and place in the South African canon, noting that his 'publication record is immense: as well as poems in newspapers he published four volumes of poetry, an autobiography, translations, essays, allegories, essays and a novel'.[64] Mqhayi was also an *imbongi* of such note that Nelson Mandela referred to him as 'the poet laureate of the Xhosa people'[65] and, as Seddon notes, described 'in detail the impact of witnessing Mqhayi perform his *izibongo*'.[66] Illustrating how these different modes influenced and overlapped with one another, Seddon, following Opland, notes that '[t]wo of Mqhayi's *izibongo* were recorded in a studio in 1934 but it was in reaching readers in print, as *imbongi* for the whole nation, that Mqhayi made his lasting impact'.[67] As Opland elaborates, as 'the first Xhosa *imbongi* to write his *izibongo* for publication in Western media [Mqhayi] erected a bridge that succeeding poets tread'.[68]

This account suggests that Mqhayi's novel should not be read outside of the context of this multimodal production and that his poetry requires analyses in both its oral and written forms. More broadly, despite the fact that most of these works were translated into English relatively early, the South African canon as taught in schools remains largely based on texts written in English, rather than translated into English. Note, for example, that Sol Plaatje's *Mhudi* (1930), the first novel written in English by a black South African, is included in the 2015 national curricula for upper secondary school English (grade 10). Yet, Plaatje's *Sechuana Proverbs* (1916), a translation of 732 Setswana proverbs, published as a corrective to the loss of Indigenous languages as a result of the onslaught of colonialism,[69] is a document that remains in a library archive at the University of the Witwatersrand, rather than a text incorporated into the curriculum as a major source of literary comparativism.[70]

Intertextuality

A further potential when it comes to literary comparativism is the possibility of including world literatures, but addressing their relevance to African or South African perspectives and forms. One germane example is Plaatje's translations of William Shakespeare, which have been discussed extensively by Deborah Seddon.[71] Seddon points out that 'Plaatje's translations were a reactivation of the oral elements of Shakespeare, a registering of Shakespeare's relationship with an oral tradition that was long absent from English assessments of the play-texts in the early twentieth century.'[72] Even more than this reactivation of the orality of the plays, Plaatje used his translations of Shakespeare to reactivate Setswana proverbs. Seddon, again, informs us:

> Throughout the text of *Diphosho-phosho* [the Setswana translation of *The Comedy of Errors*], Plaatje employs Setswana proverbs; where appropriate, he translates Shakespeare's language into such indigenous idiomatic forms. Replete with his creative deployment of Setswana idiom, his translation thus both preserves and 'performs' the orature of his own language.[73]

The potential that this example provides for a multilingual, multimodal, interdisciplinary, and intertextual classroom is unbelievably rich. As might be, for example, a reading of *Antigone* alongside Athol Fugard, Winston Ntshona, and John Kani's *The Island*,[74] or a material reading of the Robben Island Shakespeare[75] – a copy of the complete works of Shakespeare owned by Robben Island prisoner Solly Venkatrathnam, who got his fellow prisoners to sign their names besides their favourite passages from Shakespeare. We could also, for example, introduce in our teaching of Shakespeare (recall, after all, the continued cultural capital of his works as evidenced by the basic education curriculum in English) the fact that Robert Sobukwe, founder of the Pan-Africanist Congress, had, as David Schalkwyk informs us, begun a translation of *Macbeth* into isiZulu shortly before his imprisonment on Robben Island.[76] The translation is, to the best of my knowledge, lost, but the mere fact of one of the key figures in the anti-apartheid movement being invested in such a work of translation becomes fertile ground for a discussion of both the play itself and the possibilities for its translation (Welcome Msomi's production *uMabatha* in 1970 is just one such production that relocates Shakespeare's text into the time and context of King Shaka). Another productive intertext might then be Thomas Mofolo's *Chaka* (published in Sesotho in 1925 and translated into English in 1931), which could prompt an interdisciplinary as much as a translingual approach to the literary text. In short, the methods required to reorient world literature to the South African context are historical, comparative, multilingual, multimodal, and intertextual.

Conclusion

> In order to set our institutions firmly on the path of future knowledges, we need to reinvent *a classroom without walls* in which we are all *co-learners*.
> Achille Mbembe – 'Decolonizing Knowledge and the Question of the Archive'

When it comes to the content of the decolonised literary curriculum it seems that we have numerous paths to follow, and the scholarship upon which we can base this work is diverse and multi-disciplinary. But what about the pedagogical methods of curriculum construction? As a white Southern African, with English as my mother-tongue, I do not put these reflections forward as a template for how to fix the problem of colonial education in South Africa. Rather, I offer them as a rumination on what white failure to listen, learn, understand, and communicate has done to the education system in South Africa. If I were to offer a curriculum to South African students, based on *my* selection of literary texts, no matter how anti-colonial I presumed them to be, I would only reiterate the problem. I believe that the pedagogies and curricula of the future decolonised universities (the world over), must, rather, be collaboratively constituted. Much like Ngũgĩ's 'empty space' of the community theatre, the classroom should be a clearing in which everyone can participate in the creation of knowledge. To do this, I, as a teacher, need to open myself to things I do not know, and accept the contributions that might unsettle my own repertoires of knowledge, especially when those repertoires carry the history of colonial power and language in them. This would be a collaborative, multilingual, and interdisciplinary pedagogy that would begin from the local and, even as it extends to the global, would always be rooted in the material, political, formal, and aesthetic contexts of the students involved.

While the book object will remain an important technology of this decolonisation of knowledge, and while the English language will no doubt retain its hold on global academia, I believe that both can be displaced and decentred in the interests of a radically new approach to knowledge production. We might call this an ubuntu pedagogy in which there is no knowledge complete without a student who participates in its creation. If we address our knowledge production to this ethical principle, then the burning of books will no longer be a symbol of anti-intellectualism so much as the emptying of the space from which we can participate in new forms of knowledge production.

Notes

1 I gratefully acknowledge the support of the Swedish Research Council (2016-01144) for their support for this research, which forms a part of the project 'African Street Literature and the Futures of Literary Form'.
2 Ashleigh Harris, 'Hot Reads, Pirate Copies, and the Unsustainability of the Book in Africa's Literary Future,' *Postcolonial Text* 14, no. 2 (2019): 1–15.
3 Isabel Hofmeyr, *'We Spend Our Years as a Tale That is Told': Oral Historical Narrative in a South African Chiefdom* (Johannesburg: Wits University Press, 1993), 4.
4 Hofmeyr, 'We Spend Our Years,' 9.
5 Hofmeyr, 'We Spend Our Years,' 8.
6 These are Afrikaans, English, isiNdebele, Sepedi, Sesotho, SiSwati, Xitsonga, Setswana, Tshivenda, isiXhosa, and isiZulu.
7 These are the University of Cape Town, the University of Fort Hare, the University of the Free State, the University of Johannesburg, the University of KwaZulu-Natal, the University of Limpopo, Nelson Mandela University, North-West University, the

University of Pretoria, Rhodes University, Sefako Makgatho University, the University of South Africa, the University of Stellenbosch, the University of Venda, Walter Sisulu University, the University of the Western Cape, the University of the Witwatersrand, and the University of Zululand.

8   English, Tshivenda, and Sepedi include six novels in the three years of upper secondary school, whereas isiXhosa has four, and all the others (including Afrikaans) teach three. Poetry is the most consistent genre – between two and three anthologies are taught across these three years in all languages. Drama is a little more erratic (between two and five texts), but is covered by all languages other than Setswana (based on the Government of the Republic of South Africa, National Catalogue of Literature 2015).

9   These are often geographically motivated, for example, Fort Hare University teaches isiXhosa; University of Kwa-Zulu Natal teaches isiZulu; North-West University teaches Setswana and Sesotho; University of Venda teaches SiSwati, Tshivenda, Xitsonga, Northern Sotho, and isiNdebele; and the University of Zululand offers a comprehensive education in isiZulu, SeSotho, and SiSwati.

10 On the undergraduate level, these include courses such as 'Image, Voice, Word', 'Cultures of Empire, Resistance and Postcoloniality', 'Literature and the Work of Memory', 'Movements, Manifestos and Modernities', and at the Honours level, a course on 'Small Magazines and Black Print Cultures'.

11 Ngũgĩ wa Thiong'o, Taban Lo Liyong, and Henry Owuor-Anyumba (1968), 'On the Abolition of the English Department,' in *The Norton Anthology of Theory and Criticism*, ed. Vincent B. Leitch, 2nd ed. (New York: W.W. Norton & Company, 2010), 1997.

12 wa Thiong'o et al., 'Abolition of the English Department,' 1996.

13 wa Thiong'o et al., 'Abolition of the English Department,' 1998.

14 wa Thiong'o et al., 'Abolition of the English Department,' 1998.

15 Ngũgĩ wa Thiong'o, *Decolonising the Mind: The Politics of Language in African Literature* (London: James Curry, 1986), 96.

16 wa Thiong'o, *Decolonising the Mind*, 98.

17 wa Thiong'o, *Decolonising the Mind*, 26–27.

18 wa Thiong'o, *Decolonising the Mind*, 106.

19 More recent commentators have taken the matter up in substantial depth. See Mago W. Mndwane, 'A Critique of Africanised Curricula in Higher Education: Possibilities for the African Renaissance,' in *Decolonising Knowledge for Africa's Renewal: Examining African Perspectives and Philosophies*, ed. Vuyisile Msila (Randburg: K.R. Publishing, 2017), 201–222; and Berrington X.S. Ntombela, '"The Double-Edged Sword": African Languages Under Siege,' in *Decolonising Knowledge for Africa's Renewal: Examining African Perspectives and Philosophies*, ed. Vuyisile Msila (Randburg: K.R. Publishing, 2017), 161–179.

20 Leketi Makalela, '"Our Academics Are Intellectually Colonised": Multi-Languaging and Fees Must Fall,' *Southern African Linguistics and Applied Language Studies* 36, no. 1 (2018): 2.

21 Aryan Kaganof, dir., *Opening Stellenbosch: From Assimilation to Occupation* (2016), Johannesburg, South Africa, African Noise Foundation, video, 1:37. The University of Stellenbosch was, until OS, an Afrikaans medium university.

22 Kaganof, *Opening Stellenbosch*, 1:37–38.

23 wa Thiong'o, *Decolonising the Mind*, 16–17.

24 Frantz Fanon, *Black Skin, White Masks,* trans. Charles Lam Markmann (London: Pluto Press, 2008), 14.

25 Fanon, *Black Skin*, 14.

26 See Neville Alexander, Theo Du Plessis, Mbulungeni Madiba, and the extensive work of Leketi Makalela.

27 wa Thiong'o, *Decolonising the Mind*, 56–57.

28 Makalela elaborates this idea as such: 'In order to move away from "linguistic tribes" of the past, teaching African languages can be aligned with the African cultural and

epistemological conception of being, ubuntu, which propagates a communal orientation and continuum of social, linguistic and cultural resources and denotes the interconnectedness of all human existence [...] "I am because you are; you are because we are".' (Leketi Makalela, 'Moving Out of Linguistic Boxes: The Effects of Translanguaging for Multilingual Classrooms,' *Language and Education* 29, no. 3 (2015): 214.)

29 Makalela, 'Our Academics,' 2.
30 wa Thiong'o, *Decolonising the Mind*, 30.
31 wa Thiong'o, *Decolonising the Mind*, 84. Perhaps a better educational infrastructure for translation and linguistic exchange across African languages without the need for mediation by colonial languages is becoming a reality. The South African School Curriculum will offer kiSwahili from 2020.
32 Michael Green, 'Translating the Nation: Phaswane Mpe and the Fiction of Post Apartheid,' *Scrutiny2* 10, no. 1 (2005): 5; cited in Deborah Seddon, 'Written Out, Writing In: Orature in the South African Literary Canon Author(s),' *English in Africa* 35, no. 1 (May 2008): 145.
33 The survey is summarised in Walter Bgoya and Mary Jay, 'Publishing in Africa from Independence to the Present Day,' *Research in African Literatures* 44, no. 2 (2013): 22.
34 See Bgoya and Jay, 'Publishing in Africa'; Mary Jay, 'African Books Collective: A History of 23 Years Trading,' *Logos* 23, no. 4 (2012): 21–29; Harris, 'Hot Reads'; and Irene Staunton, 'Publishing for Pleasure in Zimbabwe: The Experience of Weaver Press,' *Wasafiri* 31, no. 4 (2016): 49–54.
35 Jay, 'African Books Collective,' 26–27.
36 See Sarah Brouillette, 'The African Literary Hustle,' *Blind Field Journal: A Journal of Cultural Inquiry* (August 2017), accessed 2 July 2018, blindfieldjournal.com/2017/08/14/on-the-african-literary-hustle/; Katherine Haines, 'Literary Networks and the Making of 21st Century African Literature in English: Kwani Trust, Farafina, Cassava Republic Press and the Production of Cultural Memory' (PhD diss., University of Sussex, 2016); and Doreen Strauhs, *African Literary NGOs: Power, Politics, and Participation* (London: Palgrave Macmillan, 2013).
37 See africanstorybook.org.
38 See www.fundza.co.za.
39 See viaafrika.com/writepublishread.
40 Hans Zell, 'Publishing in African Languages: A Review of the Literature,' Read African Books, 2018, accessed 18 December 2019, https://www.readafricanbooks.com/opinion/publishing-in-african-languages/.
41 Hofmeyr, 'We Spend Our Years,' 11.
42 Hofmeyr, 'We Spend Our Years,' 2.
43 Russell Kaschula, *The Bones of the Ancestors are Shaking: Xhosa Oral Poetry in Context* (Landsdowne: Juta & Co, 2002), 227
44 Hofmeyr, 'We Spend Our Years,' 12.
45 Hofmeyr, 'We Spend Our Years,' 14.
46 Hofmeyr, 'We Spend Our Years,' 14.
47 For a substantial investigation of these forms, see my research project with Nicklas Hållén, 'African Street Literatures and the Future of Literary Form,' based at Uppsala University, Sweden.
48 wa Thiong'o, *Decolonising the Mind*, 56–57.
49 wa Thiong'o, *Decolonising the Mind*, 34–62.
50 wa Thiong'o, *Decolonising the Mind*, 45.
51 The song, sung in either isiZulu or isiXhosa, translates as 'What have we done?' Kaganof, *Opening Stellenbosch,* 08:00.
52 Kaganof, *Opening Stellenbosch*, 43:00.
53 Mxolisi Nyezwa makes an important intervention into the significance of music in a decolonising methodology in 'Duende in Maskanda Music,' in *Decolonising Knowledge for Africa's Renewal: Examining African Perspectives and Philosophies*, ed. Vuyisile Msila (Randburg: K.R. Publishing, 2017), 237–255.

54 wa Thiong'o, *Decolonising the Mind*, 94.
55 wa Thiong'o, *Decolonising the Mind*, 26–27.
56 wa Thiong'o, *Decolonising the Mind*, 22.
57 wa Thiong'o, *Decolonising the Mind*, 83.
58 wa Thiong'o et al., 'Abolition of the English Department,' 1998.
59 Makalela, 'Our Academics,' 2.
60 Hofmeyr, *'We Spend Our Years,'* 12.
61 Seddon, 'Written Out,' 145.
62 Liz Gunner, 'Orality and Literacy: Dialogue and Silence,' in *Discourse and its Disguises: The Interpretation of African Oral Texts*, eds. Karin Barber and P. De Moraes Farias (Birmingham: Birmingham University Press, 1989), 55; cited in Seddon, 'Written Out,' 145.
63 Mũkoma wa Ngũgĩ, *The Rise of the African Novel: Politics of Language, Identity and Ownership* (Ann Arbor: University of Michigan Press, 2018), 4.
64 Jeff Opland, *Xhosa Oral Poetry: Aspects of a Black South African Tradition* (Johannesburg: Ravan Press, 1983), 93–94; cited in Seddon, 'Written Out,' 137.
65 Nelson Mandela, *Long Walk to Freedom* (London: Abacus, 1995), 47–50, 302; cited in Seddon, 'Written Out,' 137
66 Seddon, 'Written Out,' 137.
67 Seddon, 'Written Out,' 137, paraphrasing Opland, *Xhosa Oral Poetry*, 91.
68 Opland, *Xhosa Oral Poetry*, 95.
69 Seddon, 'Written Out,' 137.
70 Jane Starfield, 'The Lore and the Proverbs: Sol Plaatje as Historian,' paper presented to the African Studies Seminar (University of the Witwatersrand, 26 August 1991), n.p.; cited in Seddon, 'Written Out,' 137. Even more devastating is the tale that Seddon outlines of Plaatje's hopes to raise funds through the sale of his English novel, *Mhudi*, for a major archive of Setswana folktales and orature. This never came into being, and as Seddon points out, '[we now] only have his letters as evidence for the significant body of Setswana orature he had collected to disseminate in print'. Seddon, 'Written Out,' 138.
71 Deborah Seddon, 'The Colonial Encounter and *The Comedy of Errors*: Solomon Plaatje's *Diphoshophosho*,' in *The Shakespeare International Yearbook: Volume 9*, eds. Graham Bradshaw and Tom Bishop (London: Routledge, 2016), 66–86; and 'Shakespeare's Orality: Solomon Plaatje's Setswana Translations,' *English Studies in Africa* 47, no. 2 (2004): 77–95.
72 Seddon, 'Shakespeare's Orality,' 82.
73 Seddon, 'Shakespeare's Orality,' 90.
74 Ashleigh Harris, '"The Island Is Not a Story in Itself": Apartheid's World Literature,' *Safundi* 19, no. 3 (2018): 321–337.
75 See David Schalkwyk, *Hamlet's Dreams: The Robben Island Shakespeare* (London: The Arden Shakespeare, Bloomsbury, 2013).
76 Schalkwyk, *Hamlet's Dreams*, 12.

Bibliography

Alexander, Neville. *Language Policy and National Unity in South Africa/Azania*. Cape Town: Buchu Books, 1989.

Bgoya, Walter, and Mary Jay. 'Publishing in Africa from Independence to the Present Day.' *Research in African Literatures* 44, no. 2 (2013): 17–34.

Brouillette, Sarah. 'The African Literary Hustle.' *Blind Field Journal: A Journal of Cultural Inquiry* (August 2017). Accessed 2 July 2018. blindfieldjournal.com/2017/08/14/on-the-african-literary-hustle/.

Du Plessis, Theo. 'From Monolingual to Bilingual Higher Education: the Repositioning of Historically Afrikaans-Medium Universities in South Africa.' *Language Policy* 5 (2009): 87–113.

Fanon, Frantz. *Black Skin, White Masks*. Translated by Charles Lam Markmann (1967). London: Pluto Press, 2008.
Government of the Republic of South Africa. 'National Catalogue, Grades 10–12 FET Literature Catalogue.' Department of Basic Education, 2015. Accessed 2 April 2019. https://www.education.gov.za/Portals/0/Documents/Publications/2015%20 LTSM%20Catalogue%20Grades%2010%20-%2012%20FET%20Literature. pdf?ver=2015-06-11-151951-493.
Green, Michael. 'Translating the Nation: Phaswane Mpe and the Fiction of Post Apartheid.' *Scrutiny2* 10, no. 1 (2005): 3–16.
Gunner, Liz. 'Orality and Literacy: Dialogue and Silence.' In *Discourse and its Disguises: The Interpretation of African Oral Texts*, edited by Karin Barber and P. De Moraes Farias, 49–56. Birmingham: Birmingham University Press, 1989.
Haines, Katherine. 'Literary Networks and the Making of 21st Century African Literature in English: Kwani Trust, Farafina, Cassava Republic Press and the Production of Cultural Memory.' PhD diss., University of Sussex, 2016.
Harris, Ashleigh. '"The Island is Not a Story in Itself": Apartheid's World Literature.' *Safundi* 19, no. 3 (2018): 321–337.
Harris, Ashleigh. 'Hot Reads, Pirate Copies, and the Unsustainability of the Book in Africa's Literary Future.' *Postcolonial Text* 14, no. 2 (2019): 1–15.
Hofmeyr, Isabel. *'We Spend Our Years as a Tale That Is Told': Oral Historical Narrative in a South African Chiefdom*. Johannesburg: Wits University Press, 1993.
Jay, Mary. 'African Books Collective: A History of 23 Years Trading.' *Logos* 23, no. 4 (2012): 21–29.
Kaganof, Aryan, dir. *Opening Stellenbosch: From Assimilation to Occupation*. 2016. Johannesburg, South Africa. African Noise Foundation. Video, 104:20, https://vimeo.com/173585724.
Kaschula, Russell H. *The Bones of the Ancestors are Shaking: Xhosa Oral Poetry in Context*. Landsdowne: Juta & Co, 2002.
Madiba, Mbulungeni. 'Promoting Concept Literacy through Multilingual Glossaries: A Translanguaging Approach.' In *Multilingual Teaching and Learning in Higher Education in South Africa*, edited by C. Van der Walt and L. Hibbert, 68–87. Clevedon: Multilingual Matters, 2014.
Makalela, Leketi. 'We Speak Eleven Tongues: Reconstructing Multilingualism in South Africa.' In *Languages of Instruction for African Emancipation: Focus on Postcolonial Contexts and Considerations*, edited by B. Brock-Utne and R. Hopson, 147–174. Cape Town and Dar es Salaam: CAsAs and Mkuki na Nyota, 2005.
Makalela, Leketi. 'Teaching Indigenous African Languages to Speakers of Other African Languages: the Effects of Translanguaging for Multilingual Development.' In *Multilingual Teaching and Learning in Higher Education in South Africa*, edited by C. Van der Walt and L. Hibbert, 88–104. Clevedon: Multilingual Matters, 2014.
Makalela, Leketi. 'Moving Out of Linguistic Boxes: The Effects of Translanguaging for Multilingual Classrooms.' *Language and Education* 29, no. 3 (2015): 200–217.
Makalela, Leketi. 'Bilingualism in South Africa: Reconnecting with Ubuntu Translanguaging.' In *Bilingual and Multilingual Education*, edited by O. García, A. Lin, and S. May, 297–309. New York: Springer International Publishing, 2017.
Makalela, Leketi. *From Cloning African Children to Translanguaging: Language, Literacy and Multilingual Return in sub-Saharan Africa*. Dar es Salaam: Mkuki na Nyota, 2018.
Makalela, Leketi. '"Our Academics Are Intellectually Colonised": Multi-Languaging and Fees Must Fall.' *Southern African Linguistics and Applied Language Studies* 36, no. 1 (2018): 1–11.
Mandela, Nelson. *Long Walk to Freedom*. London: Abacus, 1995.
Mbembe, Achille. 'Decolonizing Knowledge and the Question of the Archive.' Wits Institute of Social and Economic Research, 2015. Accessed 2 April 2019. https://wiser. wits.ac.za/system/files/Achille%20Mbembe%20-%20Decolonizing%20Knowledge%20 and%20the%20Question%20of%20the%20Archive.pdf

Mndwane, Mago W. 'A Critique of Africanised Curricula in Higher Education: Possibilities for the African Renaissance.' In *Decolonising Knowledge for Africa's Renewal: Examining African Perspectives and Philosophies*, edited by Vuyisile Msila, 201–222. Randburg: K.R. Publishing, 2017.

wa Ngũgĩ, Mũkoma. *The Rise of the African Novel: Politics of Language, Identity and Ownership*. Ann Arbor: University of Michigan Press, 2018.

Ntombela, Berrington X.S. '"The Double-Edged Sword": African Languages Under Siege.' In *Decolonising Knowledge for Africa's Renewal: Examining African Perspectives and Philosophies*, edited by Vuyisile Msila, 161–179. Randburg: K.R. Publishing, 2017.

Nyezwa, Mxolisi. 'Duende in Maskanda Music.' In *Decolonising Knowledge for Africa's Renewal: Examining African Perspectives and Philosophies*, edited by Vuyisile Msila, 237–255. Randburg: K.R. Publishing, 2017.

Opland, Jeff. *Xhosa Oral Poetry: Aspects of a Black South African Tradition*. Johannesburg: Ravan Press, 1983.

Seddon, Deborah. 'Shakespeare's Orality: Solomon Plaatje's Setswana Translations.' *English Studies in Africa* 47, no. 2 (2004): 77–95.

Seddon, Deborah. 'Written Out, Writing in: Orature in the South African Literary Canon Author(s).' *English in Africa* 35, no. 1 (May 2008): 133–150.

Seddon, Deborah. 'The Colonial Encounter and *The Comedy of Errors*: Solomon Plaatje's *Diphoshophosho*.' In *The Shakespeare International Yearbook: Volume 9*, edited by Graham Bradshaw and Tom Bishop, 66–86. London: Routledge, 2016.

Schalkwyk, David. *Hamlet's Dreams: The Robben Island Shakespeare*. London: The Arden Shakespeare, Bloomsbury, 2013.

Starfield, Jane. 'The Lore and the Proverbs: Sol Plaatje as Historian.' Paper presented to the African Studies Seminar, University of the Witwatersrand, 26 August 1991.

Staunton, Irene. 'Publishing for Pleasure in Zimbabwe: The Experience of Weaver Press.' *Wasafiri* 31, no. 4 (2016): 49–54.

Strauhs, Doreen. *African Literary NGOs: Power, Politics, and Participation*. London: Palgrave Macmillan, 2013.

wa Thiong'o, Ngũgĩ. *Decolonising the Mind: The Politics of Language in African Literature*. London: James Curry, 1986.

wa Thiong'o, Ngũgĩ, Taban Lo Liyong, and Henry Owuor-Anyumba (1968). 'On the Abolition of the English Department.' In *The Norton Anthology of Theory and Criticism* (second edition), edited by Vincent B. Leitch, 1995–2000. New York: W.W. Norton & Company, 2010.

Timeslive. '831 arrests mar 2016 Fees Must Fall protests.' *Dispatch Live Online*. Accessed 16 December 2019. https://www.dispatchlive.co.za/news/2016-10-29-831-arrests-mar-2016-fees-must-fall-protests/

Zell, Hans. 'Publishing in African Languages: A Review of the Literature.' Read African Books. 2018. Accessed 18 December 2019. https://www.readafricanbooks.com/opinion/publishing-in-african-languages/.

30
HAPTIC HISTORY IN SOUTHEAST ASIA – ARCHIVING THE PAST IN BODIES AND LANDSCAPES

Emilie Wellfelt[1]

In a dark corner under the thatched roof of the main lineage house Fet Lakatuil, the culture of history can be studied. There, in the Indonesian village of Bampalola, stand the heirlooms that make history tangible and the lives of past generations present. Every item is a reminder of past people, events, victories, and defeats. Sunlight that filters through chinks in the walls reveals the objects covered with dust and cobwebs, together with small offerings in the form of cooked rice and clove-scented *kretek* cigarettes.

Twice a year, the most important heirlooms are cleared of the dust and displayed on the veranda of Fet Lakatuil, and a feast is held with food, rituals, storytelling, singing, and dances, to celebrate the first harvest of rice and maize. It is during these events that the young learn about village history. According to tradition, ancestors many generations ago left Bampalola, the origin village of all humans, and settled in other parts of the world. Hence, foreigners arriving in Bampalola are perceived as distant relatives, and by extension Indigenous history encompasses a global community of humans (Figure 30.1).

The harvest feast when the stories are recounted begins in the morning and continues through the day. As the sun sets, a *lego-lego*, an all-night circle dance accompanied by singing and drumming, commences. At dawn, the rhythm of the drumbeats intensifies and the dancing goes into a crescendo, creating a whirl of dust that envelopes the dance place in the centre of the village. By the time the dust has settled, everybody has gone home.

In *The Writing of History*, Michel de Certeau discussed history as an academic practice entangled with colonialism: while Western colonial powers were writing their own histories, they were also un-writing embodied traditions of Indigenous peoples that they wanted to control.[2] It is embodied history, and how this relates to ideals of history as text, that is the main focus in this chapter.

Figure 30.1 The past and the present meet in the dark corner where heirlooms are kept in the lineage house Fet Lakatuil. Through offerings and prayers, the living contact the ancestors and ask for support in the present

Source: Photo Emilie Wellfelt

De Certeau's observations invite questions about power and the properties and endurance of Indigenous knowledge practices. To clarify, the term 'indigenous' as it is used here does not refer exclusively to a legal rights context; instead, the concept is attributed with a social and geographical meaning that loosely translates into self-defined Indigenous communities attached to places through historical bonds.[3] My argumentation arises from long-term research with members of Indigenous oral cultures in eastern Indonesia, areas that are commonly regarded as peripheries of the state. These communities share the historical experience of being subject to European colonial rule, and of the post-independence Indonesian state. The pressure for Indigenous oral societies to change – to become modern – is characteristic of both the late colonial period and the post-independence era.

Through a series of political events, a window for formulation of local history opened after 2002 when the district level in the nationwide administrative system of Indonesia began to gain a new level of importance: in 1998, the centralistic and authoritarian New Order regime under President Soeharto was forced to step down under the pressure of the economic crisis that hit Asia. In the wake followed democratisation, and far-reaching decentralisation reforms. Economic resources and political control were redistributed from Jakarta to the district capitals – in the case of Alor, to the town Kalabahi.[4] A side effect of this shift was a new interest in history at the district level. This was evident in Alor, where true cravings for history concerned with events in Alor rather than existing Java-centred narratives of Indonesian historiography surfaced. This urge for history engaged people ranging from the political and administrative elite (with resources to hire historians and other writers to work for them), to customary keepers of historical traditions in distant villages (without resources to hire anyone). In this period of momentum, a variety of history practices interacted and initially there was a widely shared idea that the aim was to formulate history in textual form. However, experiences in the years to follow proved that not all knowledge can be written.

The impact of the written is evident both in the sources that historians within academic practice draw from, and in the written narratives that they produce. The historical period conventionally refers to the period when there are written sources. This becomes an issue when you work with communities without a writing tradition. A less obvious problem with the emphasis on written sources is that the importance given to textual content tends to be paired with an underestimation of materiality.[5] In Alor, where literacy only began to be introduced among the local elites in the early twentieth century, the few existing historical documents (primarily of Dutch colonial origin) are treated as precious historical objects, similar to other heirlooms.[6] The actual text is often less important than the intimacy with power that the document represents.[7]

Communities without written historical sources have long been perceived as 'people without history'.[8] This idea of people deprived of history has been challenged through the emergence of academic fields researching oral traditions and oral history. At least since the 1960s, oral history has been associated with emancipation and empowerment, questioning inequalities based on race and class.[9] Parallel to this, an extensive discussion developed around orality as opposed to literacy.[10] One drawback from that discussion was a lasting impression that 'oral' and 'written' are exclusive categories, resulting in a simplistic dichotomy of history as either oral or written. Meanwhile, a key point in this chapter is that history goes beyond the oral and written, and beyond aural and visual senses.

The main focus here is not history as an academic practice; instead, the interest lies in vernacular history as a complex lived sensory experience, drawing on cases from Indigenous groups where bodies, well-known environments (landscape, village, etc.), and objects together constitute interconnected archives.[11] The combination of corporeal experience and space resonates with research in social sciences and humanities on haptic senses, where the Finnish architect Juhani Pallasmaa's work *The Eyes of the Skin: Architecture and the Senses* has become a standard work.[12] 'Haptic' refers to tactile sense, and Pallasmaa states that '[t]ouch is the sensory mode which integrates our experiences of the world and of ourselves,' and goes on to state that '[m]y body is truly the navel of my world, not in the sense of the viewing point of the central perspective, but as the very locus of reference, memory, imagination and integration.'[13] All senses, including vision, are in Pallasmaa's understanding extensions of the sense of touch.

This accords with uses of history in Indigenous communities in Asia and beyond, where history as a vernacular practice is oriented towards the senses and the surrounding environment. The past comprises stories plotted in a familiar landscape, and it is experienced through the body and its senses. History is in this case not written, nor oral. It is an experiential totality, which I argue demands a new concept to grasp, with a suggested haptic history approach. The concept is developed further after a brief introduction of the geographical setting in which it was formulated.

Setting and methods: a landscape evoking haptic senses

I build my case on research in the Indonesian archipelago, concentrating mainly on Alor, an island just north of Timor. Alor is about 100 kilometres in the east-west orientation, and 80 kilometres deep in the north-south orientation. The island is characterised by ethnolinguistic diversity; some 15–20 languages are spoken among a population that in 2010 had reached 165,000.[14] During a series of fieldwork visits in the years 2009–2012, I documented Indigenous histories across the island. Analysing the resulting corpus, I found narratological connections that formed four clusters of peoples with shared historical pasts, sometimes as friends, sometimes foes. These narratological spaces, which I chose to call historyscapes, were surprisingly independent of administrative divisions on existing maps.[15]

Alor is a mountainous island, mostly consisting of a rugged landscape cut through by ravines and riverbeds. The topography is important in that it highlights the senses. Steep hillsides provide many opportunities for a person traversing it on foot to bodily experience the landscape in a manner different from traversing flat terrain.[16] The island is small enough for the traveller to be always in walking distance from the coast, but large enough to have divisions between inland and coastal livelihoods. The historyscapes, and many oral traditions, underline differences between inland groups that rely on farming, hunting, and foraging and coastal groups that find their subsistence from the sea and from crafts such as weaving, pottery, and salt production. There still is an island-wide taboo against weaving in the mountains and textiles are only produced in coastal settlements. A pragmatic explanation to the taboo is that during periods of drought, people in the arid coastal areas needed to have goods to offer bartering partners in the more fertile interior.[17] In the past, there were ample possibilities and pressing reasons to travel between coast and inland, carrying barter goods.[18]

The ethnolinguistic diversity is paired with variations in social organisation, which also play out in uses of history. For example, in the East Alor historyscape, the Kula-speaking population living in the interior deal with historical knowledge according to their clan structure: a clan consists of several lineages owning their own stories. Also when these stories have become public knowledge, only the appropriate person (usually the most senior male) in the lineage is allowed to recount it. The model, where knowledge and power are divided between lineages, underlines interdependence. To obtain clan history, all lineages need to contribute their specific piece of knowledge, demonstrating that power among the Kula is based on cooperation. Meanwhile, in the coastal Wersing-speaking areas, knowledge is centralised: history, especially secret knowledge, is to a large extent in the hands of the former raja's family.[19] Both structures share an emphasis on secret properties of history, which is in line with observations that the Australian researcher Lynne Kelly made in her study of memory, knowledge, and power in a wide range of oral societies across the world and through time. Kelly argues that in oral cultures, keeping certain things secret is a way to ensure that critical knowledge remains intact over long time periods. She argues that a common denominator in oral societies is the existence of a dichotomy between public and restricted knowledge, and that the relations between general and secret knowledge are enshrined in traditional law.[20]

Indigenous historiography in Alor relies on orality as mnemonic strategy for remembering 'messages from the ancestors' in songs and poems that are remembered by rote. Orality is also crucial in situations where history is narrated in less fixed ways. At such occasions, relevant episodes are selected from a larder filled with stories that the knowledgeable have access to. Despite the central role of orality in Alor historiography, I argue that referring to Indigenous history in Alor as oral history or oral traditions is a simplification. As is the case in Kodi, west Sumba – another Indonesian context – where the anthropologist Janet Hoskins worked:

> Local knowledge of the past is organized not only in narrative, but also in the visual and tactile traces left by past events: heirloom objects, features of the landscape, the special relationship established with a particular animal or location.[21]

Some of these features are universal, intuitive ways of relating to the past – it is vernacular history that can relate to any human context. However, the past is also particular: uses of history depend on the ontologies where they appear. In Alor as in many other parts of Asia, the presence of ancestors as active agents creates a special kind of continuity between past, present, and future. The geographical setting and the familiarity with landscape are two other features that have implications for haptic history.

In his work in Maluku, the anthropologist Timo Kaartinen explains that while his intent was to document Indigenous history in the village of Banda Eli in Kei, Maluku, logistical problems in getting there led him to work first with urbanised Indigenous groups from the Banda community. After making it to Banda Eli, Kaartinen realised that history 'at a distance' was very different from history 'inside'. He notes:

> What from the village perspective appears as a contested plurality of ancestral groups and their territorial and hierarchical claims is condensed into a singular point of origin from the outside perspective of 'travellers'.[22]

Dispersed multi-vocal history relies not only on spatial and haptic memories, but also on being 'inside' the landscape and the social contexts where it is inscribed. At a distance, the voices merge and other meanings of origins and past are made. This distance can also be created through the practice of writing. A body-landscape, however, can hold many simultaneous, sometimes competing or contradictory narratives without this necessarily being conflicting, as each narrative has its geographical location.

Haptic history in multidisciplinary context

Haptic history is about learning by moving in, experiencing and internalising such landscapes invested with memories and stories. Externalising and internalising can also be discussed in terms of knowledge and knowing, where knowledge can be externalised, put on a piece of paper, but knowing is inside.[23] To know requires a mind, and in the haptic way of knowing also a body. In place-oriented oral and haptic history, the landscape is a repository of memory. It is the 'piece of paper'. By moving in the landscape, experiencing it and hearing the stories, knowledge can be imprinted back into new generations knowing their past.

Space and memory are the focus of interest in a wide range of research disciplines, from neuroscience to anthropology, human geography, oral history, and architecture. Research on the neural processes behind spatial memory, or 'the storage and retrieval of information within the brain that is needed both to plan a route to a desired location and to remember where an object is located or where an event occurred' was awarded a Nobel Prize in Medicine in 2014.[24] Neuroscience is one way of understanding the fundamental importance of spatiality to human experience, and in this context, it is interesting to see how the sense of time has proven to be an indistinct property in the human brain. Moving to social sciences and humanities, geographer Jon Anderson suggests making 'talking whilst walking' through 'co-ingredient environments for recollection' a method for qualitative research.[25]

An important point is that in Indigenous oral societies 'talking whilst walking' is not a one-way process. There is a listening whilst walking and learning to read the landscape and the stories inscribed in it. This learning is often repeated, and recollected while moving through the landscape embedded with meaning. This historical knowledge gives sense to place, while disconnectedness and lack of historical knowledge does the opposite, as can be illustrated by the way Dutch official van Galen described the geography of Alor in a report from 1946:

> The entire island is extraordinarily heavily accidental in form. A certain systematic-ness in the appearance of the mountains cannot be denied, but the ridges, summits and ravines with mostly quite steep sides lie helter-skelter through each other, and the whole thing gives a very confused impression.[26]

For the people who live in and know this landscape, it is impregnated with familiarity that conveys anything but confusion. The holistic way of knowing based on spatial perception together with movement and bodily senses such as sound, touch, balance, and memory of previous experiences can be summarised as haptic knowledge.[27] There are distinct differences between the colonial understandings of place in Indonesia and the local modes of perceiving it. Kaartinen has argued that the key for understanding the forms of society and consciousness of the past that he dealt with in his study of the Banda Eli community in the Kei Islands was a 'mode of social existence based on relations between places, rather than territorial unity'.[28] In an archipelago that in the east mainly consists of small islands, both land and water are the connecting media, and considerable efforts are made to uphold relations over generations.[29] Often the historical landscape is better understood as trails or routes with significant places, peoples, or events, somehow connecting to each other, than as realms.[30] In the Alor case, the idea of large territories ruled by a raja was a late colonial (late 1800s, early 1900s) construction that has caused much disruption and conflict with consequences into the present.

Haptic history handling contradictions and inconsistencies

Máire O'Neill, who specialises in vernacular architecture and human behaviour, has stated that '[p]eople gain environmental understanding from tangible physical experience, from coming in contact with natural and built elements, and from moving through spaces, as well as from seeing objects in space.'[31] Haptic history combines this environmental understanding with narratives about the past. The spatial, material, and corporeal properties of Indigenous history is the basis for a dispersed history-mode in which a wealth of stories can coexist despite being contradictory, because they are 'archived' in different locations in space and memory and hence tend to be activated separately. In this haptic setting, history is located in space rather than along a timeline.

One expression of this is found in the concept of topogeny, which anthropologist James J. Fox coined when describing how recitation of ordered sequences of place names, as is commonly done in the Austronesian world, is a way of condensing the memory of travels or migrations by seminal ancestors. While a genealogy commemorates generations translatable to a timeline, a topogeny condenses the spatial aspect of the past lived by these ancestors. Fox rightly states that a topogeny is a 'projected externalization of memories that can be lived as well as thought about'.[32] Instead of a timeline, we have a trail of places that reflect chronology but not elapsed time. Topogeny is a mnemonic device in which memory is externalised into the landscape. A point that I want to make here is that the landscape with its narratives is also internalised.[33]

The East Alor historyscape

As already discussed, a common theme in Island Southeast Asian history is inland-coast relations, where inland peoples rely on land, while coastal groups depend on the sea for subsistence.[34] In my documentation of Indigenous histories in Alor, all historyscapes that emerged from analysis of the corpus included both coastal and inland groups. The most elaborate historyscape was East Alor.

In a condensed version, the oral traditions in the area tell us that the Kula speakers originated from East Timor and arrived in Alor in ancient times, forcing submission or causing extinction of the existing population. They established themselves as the keepers of the lands (Indonesian: *tuan tanah*) and founded villages in the interior, in the vicinity of Padang Panjang, an area suitable for hunting and foraging, and for farming. At a later time, the Wersing speakers arrived over sea, from the west.[35] They were received by the Kula speakers in a place that was named Kanimang, which means 'we are good', commemorating the good intention of the newcomers. An exchange relationship was set up, in which the Wersing speakers should make earthenware pots, salt, and chalk, to be bartered with tubers and maize from the Kula speakers. The agreement is materialised in two heirloom objects, a paddle acting as a reminder of the people arriving over sea, and a clay pot to commemorate the introduction of locally produced pottery.[36] The paddle and the pot are examples of items that Hoskins calls 'history objects':

They are used didactically, as 'evidence' of the past and a reminder of what has been lost, giving a permanent, external form to contingent events and preserving the memory of a promise, a covenant, or an alliance.[37]

At one point, a war broke out between the two groups, also involving other subgroups in the region. This was a devastating conflict. After years of recurring outbursts of violence, it ended with a peace agreement, sealed by a blood oath sworn in Kaipera on the east coast, at a dance place marked by piled stones (*mesbah*). The Kaipera oath means that any open dispute between Kula and Wersing will cause immense consequences in this and coming generations. People are very cautious not to provoke conflicts between the Kula and the Wersing.[38]

To avoid such conflicts the two groups have created the *mudileng-ilingleng* institution. *Mudileng-ilingleng* translates as 'man of fur-man of [fish] scales', fur referring to the prey that inland peoples hunt, scales to the fish caught on the coast. Two men hold these hereditary positions, one among the Kula and one among the Wersing. Their task is to mediate between the groups.[39] The *mudileng-ilingleng* institution protects and animates the peace oath sworn by ancestors in the past. People of the East Alor historyscape manage to balance competition and complementarity through the Kaipera oath.

Historyscapes, narratology, and haptic practices

Society in the present is regulated by telling about the past, and it is a common perception in Alor that history can only be shared in specific circumstances. This varies between groups. In some places the apprentice sits behind the person who shares history; this cuts out the visual part of listening and enhances focus on listening, on the aural sense. In other places, certain especially sensitive and important knowledge is taught by inflicting pain. The current head of a leading clan learnt about a secret part of his clan genealogy when he was a young man. To make sure he would never forget the lesson, he was made to swallow burning coal. However, the predominant mass of knowledge is conveyed in colloquial situations, walking to the fields, foraging or going to meeting points with bartering partners.

'Historyscapes' refers both to narrative spaces and to the methodology that I developed in my research. As a method, 'historyscapes' draws on the literary theory of narratology and focuses on one narratological layer, the story level. The narratological geographies represented in each historyscape were based on extensive documentation, where a large corpus of oral traditions across the islands were recorded, transcribed, and analysed together with other Indigenous sources such as the already-mentioned history objects. A puzzling fact was that the connected spaces that grew out of my documentation refused to fit with existing maps, historical or contemporary.

It was only in 2012, towards the end of the collecting stage, that I fully realised that the haptic experiences derived from collecting oral traditions across Alor were one important key to understanding the narrative geographies of the region. I had many times been taken to historically significant places and walked trails that were part of historical narratives together with local experts, custodians of history,

Haptic history in Southeast Asia

because as they explained to me, some stories can only be told in situ. Maybe I had been too intent on listening and recording the stories to realise that an important part of the lesson was the haptic experience; the stories really needed to be told 'where they happened'? The East Alor historyscape became intelligible to me in this new way in 2012 when I walked a casual but challenging path from the inland plain where the Kula-speaking community are centred to the south coast inhabited by the Wersing speakers of Pureman village – without a narrator.

On 26 October 2012, Yosafat Modena, a Kula-speaking man in his 30s, accompanied me along the ancient trail that mostly follows ridges from north to south. Yosafat was a young man, not more knowledgeable of history than anyone else, but very familiar with the path. After arriving in Pureman I asked Yosafat to describe the route we had taken. His description, which is discussed below, contained the following information (Figure 30.2):

> Beginning in Kaipera[40] we hiked up the slopes of Buntalan Mountain to the rest place Peibasa[41] and after a break continued to the dry riverbed Kunggung[42] where people on customary (*adat*) missions stop to beat their gongs. From Kunggung we hiked up Nei Duka Mountain to Lake Apengmang and further up to an opening in the eucalyptus where the views open towards Timor Island in the south. This is the old barter place called Kimang.
>
> From Kimang the trail follows mountain ridges down to the coast. The first rest place is Wuigomu, and then the trail continues to Tukumang, which is a place where people go to dig for wild turmeric. The trail descends to Klasimang and further down to Ayageyemeng. Formerly, this was the place to go and ask for rain in times of drought. Up a mountainside is the former

Figure 30.2 Yosafat Modena on the trail from Kaipera to Pureman village. Here, walkers see the ocean and on clear days, Timor Island is visible at a distance. Along this stretch of the walk, the place names are in the coastal language Wersing; closer to Kaipera, places are named using the inland language Kula

Source: Photo Emilie Wellfelt

village site of the Mopani clan, which is called Peibakang or pig manger.[43] The origin village of the Mopani stood on rocky ground, with formations shaped as troughs for feeding the pigs. From Peibakang the trail descends to the rest place Kinebakang Kila,[44] descends to Latarang Mená, down to Wokata, continues to Lolang and finally reaches Pureman.

One telling detail in Yosafat's account is that he presented place names north of the barter site in Kula language, while place names below Kimang were in Wersing language, indicating which group is dominant in the respective area. The resting places along the way give the trail a rhythm between effort and rest, which is part of the haptic experience. The specific place for beating gongs literally resonates with aural memories, its distance from villages on the plain allows people who are about to receive guests some time to prepare.

Ayageyemeng, the place to call for rains, is ritually important in an area with yearly droughts. Although no longer in use, it is fresh in memory – Eastern Alor is a Christian part of the island. The new religion was introduced during the twentieth century, but ritual life relating to local religion was widely upheld until the mid-century and many traditions are still strong.[45] The abandoned Mopani clan origin village is important to the descendants – now mostly living in more recent settlements in the Padang Panjang plain – but also to others as the village site manifests historical claims, situating the Mopani both socially and geographically. The main features that Yosafat pointed out to me in the abandoned village were some strangely shaped stones, and a stone pile, a *mesbah*, that is a significant feature of Alor culture. The *mesbah* stands in the centre of a dance place where people gather for all-night dances called *lego-lego*. The *mesbah* used to be the place to display skulls in former times when head hunting was part of warfare.[46]

All-night sessions, the *lego-lego* dances that take place around *mesbah* across the island are part of the uses of history in Alor: they involve the chanting of songs in a set order. Certain songs are historically significant as they retell stories of the ancestors. In some instances, the songs are in languages of other groups, illustrating through language the migration of ancestors.[47]

From an economic perspective, the most important site is Kimang, the rendezvous-point for barter between peoples living in two ecological niches with different subsistence strategies. It is the site where inland people used to bring their yields from the fertile plain where they live from farming, gathering, and hunting, while inhabitants from the arid coastal settlements below brought their products, including dried fish, salt, chalk made of corals used for chewing betel, pottery, and textiles. Kimang is one of many such exchange points between inland and coast that can be found in Alor. In this case, it is further from the coast than from the plain, and the walk from the coast is considerably more difficult than the distance between the plain and Kimang. Possibly this reflects an intergroup hierarchy (Figure 30.3).

Until 1997, weekly markets were held in Kimang. It is still a place for informal barter, but changes in infrastructure have altered the status of Kimang from an essential to an almost obsolete site. A road connects the fertile Padang Panjang

Haptic history in Southeast Asia

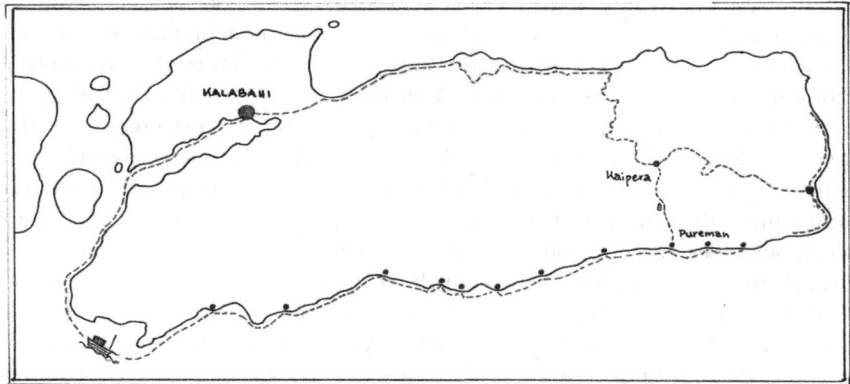

Figure 30.3 The trail between Kaipera and Pureman was used for barter between coastal and inland groups. Today, an asphalt road connecting east and west Alor passes Kaipera, and boats that cater for villages and markets along the south coast makes stops in Pureman, rendering the old barter trail obsolete. The district capital Kalabahi, established by the Dutch in the early twentieth century, is the dominant hub in modern Alor

Source: Lennart Hildingsson

plain where Kaipera and other Kula villages are situated with the district capital Kalabahi. Meanwhile, boats run by ethnic Chinese traders from Kalabahi cater for the villages along south coast Alor on market days. The meeting point for people from Kaipera and Pureman is the district capital Kalabahi rather than a glade on a mountainside, hours of strenuous walk from home.

Along the old barter, a wealth of haptic history is contained, but only as long as there are people like Yosafat Modena who can walk it in a manner that means they know every step, and custodians of history who know the stories that are contained in this path.

Uses of history, ontology, and time metaphors

In his model for 'uses of history', the Swedish historian Peter Aronsson distinguishes between the concepts 'culture of history', 'uses of history', and 'historical consciousness'.[48] The 'culture of history' is the paraphernalia of the past, 'uses of history' refers to processes where (parts of) the culture of history is activated, while 'historical consciousness' refers to views of the past-present-future that steer the use of history.[49] Aronsson combines the three concepts with the historical categories 'space of experiences' and 'horizon of expectations', where knowledge (false or true) of the past is formative for assumptions about the future. And vice versa, hopes and fears about the future influence how memory, and that which is forgotten, is formed in the spaces of experience. Aronsson argues that the 'uses of history take place in the dynamic process that links the spaces of experience and horizon of expectations in a specific situation.'[50]

This basic theoretical model for uses of history is useful, but not flawless. Representation of time is one major ontological issue. The model represents time as a box with three separate compartments: past, present, and future. This time metaphor is not universal. In the Australian Aboriginal context, we find Dreaming, described by the late Japanese historian Minoru Hokari as place-oriented stories that are active throughout history and take place 'everywhere' and 'everywhen'.[51] The Jicarilla Apache/Hispanic philosopher V.F. Cordova has argued that the western compartmentalisation of past, present, and future gives time a thing-like nature which generates normative ideas about linear progress, fantasies about travelling through time, and religious conviction about the end of time. Cordova proposes another understanding of time, one that she attributes to Native Americans. In this model, time is perceived as a ball where layers of present are slowly added to a continuously expanding past; the world is not moving ahead from past via present to future, but is constantly being created through actions in the present.[52] A related metaphor proposed by the historian Gunlög Fur, also working in the American Indian context, is time as sedimentation. She compares the professional historian's work to archaeology, digging through time layers. Fur argues that seeing time as sedimentation opens up an approach where place is the owner of history, '... instead of, or at least alongside, people'.[53] However, place needs interpretation, or else it will be silent.

In the Southeast Asian context, divisions between past, present, and future are blurred by the presence of ancestors. The ancestors meddle with the present and take an active part in shaping the future. When people are convinced that ancestors are agents in their spaces of experience, and that ancestors need to be appeased in order for the living to have success in their endeavours, the past becomes an active agent in both present and future.

Ritualised haptic history and animistic ontologies

While the walk from Padang Panjang to Pureman was a colloquial haptic lesson, Alor also presents ample possibilities to study more formalised and ritualised haptic history, as in the village Bampalola that was introduced in the very beginning of this chapter. Bampalola is situated on a hilltop with breath-taking views over land and sea. It is an origin village of the Adang-speaking community in Alor. In local discourse, it is the origin village of all humans. According to a Bampalola foundation myth, a dragon escorted the first man from the underworld to the surface of the earth, while the first woman descended from the upper world. They united and had descendants that multiplied and populated Alor and the lands beyond. As generations passed, some lost contact with their origin. In colonial times, when the Dutch settled in Alor, they were seen as relatives returning home to their ancestors. Today when a trickle of tourists make it to the village, they are perceived as members of one of the Bampalola clans with a lineage house in the origin village.[54] Through this manoeuvre, literally all humans are turned into members of one Indigenous group.

People originating from Bampalola come to Fet Lakatuil where the lord of the land, the *raja tanah*, resides. He is the most senior male descendant of a founding ancestor, more than 70 generations ago, and in his role as the *raja tanah* he is a living link to the past and to the ancestors. It is to the *raja tanah* that the villagers turn when they need support in their undertakings. Through the *raja tanah* the ancestors are asked to assure success in life challenges such as school exams, finding a job, becoming pregnant. It is in the heirloom corner that the *raja tanah* conveys these requests and it is the offerings that make the ancestors listen; while perishable they serve as communicators across the time-space continuum. Meanwhile, the heirloom objects have lasting materiality that bridges human life spans, as does the unbroken line of descent to the *raja tanah*, and the ancestors who are always aware of what goes on with the living.[55]

The offerings point to entanglements between the culture of history and the culture of religion: revisiting the concept 'animism', the Swedish anthropologist Kaj Århem states that sacrifice is 'the central religious act in Southeast Asian societies'.[56] It is also an act that can qualify as being part of the culture of history in Southeast Asia.

In the example from Bampalola village, the prime time for using history occurs biannually during the harvest feasts called *ala baloi* (rice harvest) and *bate baloi* (maize harvest). The village has five named houses, each associated with a clan. While most families occupy other less imposing houses in the old village site or the nearby new Bampalola village, everybody belongs to a clan based in one of these houses. During the *baloi*, all five houses are involved in ritual exchanges and enactments. At the opening of a *baloi* feast, heirloom bronze drums called *moko* are moved from their secluded storage and displayed on the veranda of Fet Lakatuil as reminders of the prestige and status of Bampalola.

Ultimately, the *baloi* is a celebration of a mythological ancestor, a young girl called Luintang who saved the people when struck by famine following a disaster that spoiled all seeds. In accordance with instructions from ancestors speaking to her in a dream, Luintang consented to be killed by her own family. Her body was cut into small pieces which were spread in the fields where they sprouted. It is said that all crops that are cultivated in Alor grew out of the flesh of Luintang, and the *baloi* is held to commemorate her unselfish sacrifice.[57] The *baloi* is also the time for adults to discuss historical events and for the young to hear and learn about the past. The rituals performed are enactments and a form of walking through the village while haptically experiencing it. The *baloi* entails carrying food stuff to Bampalola, cooking, reading the signs from the ancestors, eating, drinking, smoking, chewing betel, talking, performing the rituals, and then dancing *lego-lego*, drumming and chanting from sunset to sunrise. The village and its history is mapped out, and internalised. Similar history seasons, annual times for performing and remembering haptic history, can be found in other parts of Alor. However, these practices are increasingly being replaced with Christian and Muslim calendars and feasts.

In Southeast Asia, animism is an integrated part of life, even in societies dominated by world religions, or better expressed: transcultural religions. While Islam, Christianity, Buddhism, Hinduism, and Chinese cosmologies are majority religions in regions of Southeast Asia, these ideologies coexist with systems of animist relationships.[58] Indonesia as a whole has a vast majority of Muslims, but in areas where conversion happened during the colonial period many came to embrace Christianity. Alor has a Christian majority with small pockets of Muslims in or near the coasts. Regardless of religious affiliation, most people share the same ontological worlds that in some respects concur with the following description of animism: 'In the animist cosmos, animals and plants, beings and things, may all appear as intentional subjects and persons, capable of will, intention and agency.'[59]

If people do not believe ancestors have agency in the present, some uses of history in places like Bampalola may seem pointless, or be misunderstood as purely symbolic, which they are not.[60] The ancestors are a real force in Bampalola ontology. The lord of the land (*raja tanah*) connects the living with the past, or with layers closer to the core in Cordova's metaphor, or deeper layers in Fur's sedimentation model. Through his special contact with the ancestors – actors from the past who by involvement in the present have power to shape the future – he is the guarantor of historical truthfulness. The personification of the historical repository together with its oral form opens a fluidity in narration and interpretation that is lost when history and its sources have a written form. In the Bampalola case, narration of history is arranged in a manner where the *raja tanah* sits silent, while his spokespersons, men who are appointed based on kinship and individual competence, are his voice.[61] The presence of the *raja tanah*, and by extension the ancestors, warrants the accuracy of the narrative as performed. The oral form provides flexibility to speak as fits the occasion; through reformulation, the repository of the past stays alive and relevant.

History, written or oral, will always be the result of a selection of facts and events, but in the Bampalola case the *raja tanah* is assumed to know and personify knowledge of the 'full story' while his spokespersons give voice to chosen pieces of information, suitable for the occasion. History is not perceived as changing; on the contrary the stability and uniformity of history is imperative. While the exact rules deciding who has authority vary in different parts of Alor, there is a general agreement that only the right persons may speak, and what they utter must be true – or they will die. This conviction is set in a 'space of experiences' where unexpected or irregular death tends to be interpreted as a result of breaches against the rules of the ancestors. Speaking history is restricted by danger and fear.

Is there a future for haptic history?

It would not be viable for academic historians to claim that they experience history through their bodies, use the landscape as their mnemonic archive, and do source criticism by reading the signs from the ancestors as seen in the intestines of a sacrificed rooster. These actions, however, would make perfect sense in Alor. But there is an interesting gradual change: the humanities and social sciences have had their literary turn, material turn, spatial turn, and more recently a sensory turn. Writing is still the dominant practice of academic history, but the historian engaged in writing practices is at least potentially becoming sensitised to the role of orality, place, and space, and of the haptic experiences of historical actors, and experimental archaeology is important and accepted scientifically.

In a western vernacular strain, we find historical re-enactments where the actors dress up and perform, often re-enacting battles, somehow feeling they follow in the footsteps of the original participants. The combination of walking while visiting a heritage site attributed with historical meaning, real or fictive, has a great attraction for humans. In the twenty-first century, it is paired with mass tourism. Some choose to walk along famous pilgrimage trails, feeling an urge to reach Santiago de Compostela in Spain, though not always with the religious fervour of devout pilgrims. Others travel to places they have read about in a novel or seen in a movie. In Stockholm they can walk to the 7-Eleven where Lisbeth Salander bought a Billy's Pan Pizza, a carton of cigarettes, a few pies, and some ready-made gratins as described on page 179 in the Swedish version of *The Girl with the Dragon Tattoo*. This can be done both as an actual activity or virtually via the keyboard.[62] There is a long continuity to the tourist-pilgrimage practice; already in the fourth century (probably earlier) it was fashionable for Christians to travel to Jerusalem. At a specific place along the trail they got the first glimpse of Jerusalem; this was a place to cry. In the city, they visited the important places, and were pleased to buy a souvenir – a popular one was a piece of salt allegedly deriving from the wife of Lot who according to the Bible turned into a pillar of salt, a pillar that, deeming from the amount of medieval souvenirs she turned into, was huge.

It is not entirely surprising that attention has been drawn to the haptic senses by architects, as architects actively design the environments that people are meant to move in and hence become intimately knowledgeable about. The book mentioned earlier, *The Eyes of the Skin* by the Finnish architect Pallasmaa, is a reaction to and a critique of architecture that only caters for the eye.[63] This creates environments, haptic landscapes, that are expressions of what philosopher David Michael Levin refers to as ocularcentrism and the hegemony of vision.[64]

In our time, there is clearly a longing for the haptic experience of a historical past – whether considered factual or fictional – that characterises Indigenous history in oral cultures. Meanwhile, Indigenous groups in oral cultures, here exemplified by Alor, want to have books about their history (not the colonial history or the nationalist version of history, but history drawing on their own experiences). The question is whether it is possible to make the practices of haptic and academic history meet, and if this would be desirable.

In the post-Soeharto era of decentralisation when I conducted the research presented here, several attempts to write history were made in Alor. Apart from a few volumes commissioned by the district government, there was limited success. The main reason was that when stories that had been plotted into specific places in the landscape, or had been exclusive knowledge to a certain group, were extracted and written up, conflicting versions and understandings surfaced – much to the surprise of those involved in the process. Where there had seemed to be accordance, an unexpected number of subjects turned out to be historical minefields. The enthusiasm, or naivety, that marked the urge to write local history was dampened, but not stifled.

Possibly the problem could be resolved through digital presentations of history, where narratives are released from the two-dimensional limitations of paper technology and plotted in a manner similar to the dispersed landscape repository. This would still involve a reduction of the embodied knowledge of haptic history, but would answer to a demand for documentation of threatened knowledge. Urbanisation and modernisation accelerate in Alor as elsewhere in the world, and those living in town are getting worried that nobody, or literally speaking 'no Body', will know the landscape and the stories of the past.

Notes

1 I wish to thank the people I have collaborated with in Indonesia, especially in Alor where so many have shared so much with me. This chapter draws on research conducted in the period 2009–2016 when I worked at the Linnaeus University in Sweden. The chapter was written while working at Stockholm University and is a development of ideas first presented at the EuroSEAS conference in Oxford in 2017. I am grateful to my colleagues at both universities and participants at the conference session for valuable input. I am especially indebted to Doctor Ida Ohlson Al Fakir and Professor Kurt Villads Jensen at Stockholm University and Lisa Palmer, associate professor at the University of Melbourne for reading and commenting on early versions of the text. The editors of this volume, Professors Ann McGrath and Lynette Russell, provided very constructive comments and suggestions. I have a permanent debt to Doctor Fiona Kerlogue, Research Associate at SOAS, for her invaluable input. Finally, I want to mention Joseph C. Miller, Professor Emeritus at the University of Virginia, who in his kind and encouraging manner provided comments when I was trying out some of the ideas presented in this chapter. Sadly Joe Miller passed away in March 2019. He is greatly missed.
2 Michel de Certeau, *The Writing of History*, trans. Tom Conley (New York: Columbia University Press, 1988).
3 While there are similarities with a concept like 'local history', I find it misleading to speak of 'local' as the peoples I have worked with in Indonesia perceive history more as a trail of migrating ancestors and networks of historically grounded alliances. People might be local, but their history is not.
4 For an overview of political developments in this period, see Henk Schulte Nordholt and Gerry van Klinken, eds., *Renegotiating Local Boundaries: Local Politics in Post-Suharto Indonesia* (Leiden: KITLV Press, 2007).
5 A special case to illustrate the materiality in text are inscriptions in protective amulets and talismans in the Islamic world.
6 Jack Goody has argued that oral cultures in Africa and Southeast Asia have been under Islamic literate influence, which needs to be taken into account also when studying oral societies. Jack Goody, *The Interface between the Written and the Oral* (Cambridge: Cambridge University Press, 1987), 5. In Alor, this is definitely the case in coastal areas, less so in the interiors. There is no evidence of Indigenous writing practices in Alor.
7 Old documents are sometimes used as historical proof in eastern Indonesia, for instance, to support land claims. However, it is significant how documents are treated in a strategic manner – the idea of an archive accessible to all seems very far off. Similar uses of documents as objects are discussed in Franz and Keebet von Benda-Beckmann, 'Texts in Context: Historical Documents as Political Commodity in Islamic Ambon,' in *Texts from the Islands: Oral and Written Traditions of Indonesia and the Malay World*, edited by Wolfgang Marschall (Berne: University of Berne, Institute of Ethnology, 1994), 223–243. For a discussion of the transformative power of writing, see William Cummings, *Making Blood White: Historical Transformations in Early Makassar* (Honolulu: University of Hawai'i Press, 2002).
8 The false assumption that large parts of the world somehow lack history is a persistent trope. The work by anthropologist Eric Wolf, *Europe and the Peoples without History*, was

an influential work questioning this Eurocentric perspective. Eric R. Wolf, *Europe and the People without History* (Berkeley: University of California Press, 1982).
9 Oral traditions as sources to for history is a field that has strong associations to historical research in Africa, where methodological approaches to oral tradition were developed by scholars such as Jan Vansina and Ruth Finnegan. See Jan Vansina, *Oral Tradition: A Study in Historical Methodology* (New Brunswick and London: Aldine Transaction, 2006 [first published 1961]); Jan Vansina, *Oral Tradition as History* (Oxford: James Currey, 1997 [1985]); Ruth Finnegan, *Oral Traditions and the Verbal Arts: A Guide to Research Practices* (London and New York: Routledge, 1992). For an introduction to oral history, and the emancipatory implications of this research field, see Robert Perks and Alistair Thomson, eds., *The Oral History Reader* (London and New York: Routledge 2006). *Silencing the Past* is an excellent work, set in Haiti, highlighting the issue of what history gets told. Michel-Rolph Trouillot, *Silencing the Past: Power and the Production of History* (Boston, MA: Beacon Press, 1995).
10 An igniting spark to the discussion was Walter J. Ong, *Orality and Literacy: The Technologizing of the Word* (London: Methuen, 1982).
11 I have chosen to use the term 'vernacular' history here, not referring to the practice among medievalists to oppose Latin to vernacular, but to underline that I am referring to universal human approaches to history that goes beyond the 'local' or the 'indigenous'. In doing so, I am following the suggestion of Joseph C. Miller. Email correspondence 20 February 2019.
12 Juhani Pallasmaa, *The Eyes of the Skin: Architecture and the Senses* (London: Wiley, 2005).
13 Pallasmaa, *Eyes of the Skin*, 12.
14 BPS Kabupaten Alor/Statistical office of Alor, *Alor Dalam Angka/Alor In Figures 2011, Katalog BPS: 1403.5307* (Kalabahi: BPS Kabupaten Alor/Statistical office of Alor, 2011), 57, Table 4.1.1 'Population, Area, and Population Density 2010'. The population figure refers to Alor Island; other parts of the district are excluded.
15 Emilie Wellfelt, 'Historyscapes in Alor: Approaching Indigenous Histories in Eastern Indonesia' (PhD diss., Linnaeus University, 2016).
16 All landscapes have their specific properties. Walking through a flat landscape is also a haptic experience, but it is different from climbing a mountain. Alor is part of an archipelago, and in some areas paddling a canoe and experiencing the island from the sea is an important way of sensing the landscape.
17 The period towards the end of the dry season is commonly known as the 'hunger season'. In such dire times, barter is essential, especially to the coastal groups who exchange craft products for foodstuff with inland farmers. This pattern is also found in other islands, such as Sumba. See Danielle C. Geirnaert-Martin, *The Woven Land of Laboya: Socio-Cosmic Ideas and Values in West Sumba, Eastern Indonesia* (Leiden: Centre of Non-Western Studies, Leiden University, 1992).
18 These coast-inland relations have parallels with lowland (wet rice farming) cultures and upland groups in mainland southeast Asia. For further discussions on this subject, see Tania Murray Li, ed., *Transforming the Indonesian Uplands: Marginality, Power and Production* (London and New York: Routledge, 2004).
19 Wellfelt, 'Historyscapes in Alor.'
20 Lynne Kelly, *Knowledge and Power in Prehistoric Societies: Orality, Memory and the Transmission of Culture* (New York: Cambridge University Press, 2015), xvii, 14–35.
21 Janet Hoskins, *The Play of Time: Kodi Perspectives on Calendars, History and Exchange* (Berkeley and Los Angeles: California University Press 1997), 118.
22 Timo Kaartinen, *Songs of Travel, Stories of Place: Poetics of Absence in an Eastern Indonesian Society* (Helsinki: Academia Scientiarum Fennica, 2010), 54.
23 The difference between knowledge and knowing is a point that I have adapted from discussions with Joseph C. Miller. He also emphasised the social aspect of knowledge in oral societies; history is based on agreements about how things happened. Email correspondence 25 September 2017.

24 James A. Bisby and Neil Burgess, 'Spatial memory,' Encyclopaedia Britannica, accessed 3 November 2020, www.britannica.com/science/spatial-memory.
25 Jon Anderson, 'Talking Whilst Walking: A Geographical Archaeology of Knowledge,' *Area* 36, no. 3 (2004): 255.
26 Hans Hägerdal, 'Van Galen's Memorandum on the Alor Islands in 1946: An Annotated Translation with an Introduction. Part 1,' *HumaNetten* 25 (2010): 36.
27 Máire Eithne O'Neill, 'Corporeal Experience: A Haptic Way of Knowing,' *Journal of Architectural Education* 55, no. 1 (2001): 4.
28 Kaartinen, *Songs of Travel*, 47.
29 This seems especially crucial in Maluku where considerable efforts are made to visit historically connected villages and distant relatives. Maybe this is due to experiences of conflict enhancing the need to have a network of peoples and places that can offer a safe haven in troubled times.
30 In her work in Baucau, East Timor, Lisa Palmer has traced a similar feeling, knowing and telling of history in relation to water and watercourses. Lisa Palmer, *Water Politics and Spiritual Ecology: Custom, Environmental Governance and Development* (Abingdon/New York: Routledge, 2015).
31 O'Neill, 'Corporeal Experience,' 4.
32 James J. Fox, 'Genealogy and Topogeny: Towards an Ethnography of Rotinese Ritual Place Names,' in *The Poetic Power of Place: Comparative Perspective on Austronesian Ideas of Locality*, ed. James J. Fox (Canberra: ANU Press, 2006), 8. Topogenies can be found in many parts of the world, including northern Sweden.
33 There is a large body of research on landscape and memory. For comparative materials on landscape and history in a North American context, an important contribution is Peter Nabokov, *A Forest of Time: American Indian Ways of History* (New York: Cambridge University Press, 2009); For interesting insights into African contexts, see Sandra E. Greene, *Sacred Sites and the Colonial Encounter: A History of Meaning and Memory in Ghana* (Bloomington: Indiana University Press, 2002); and Gérard Chouin, 'Archaeological Perspectives on Sacred Groves in Ghana,' in *African Sacred Groves: Ecological Dynamics and Social Change*, eds. Michael J. Sheridan and Celia Nyamweru (Oxford: James Currey, 2008), 178–194. A comparative selection of cases from different places and times is found in Kelly, *Knowledge and Power*.
34 For an account on how people with different interests and subsistence understand the same landscape, see Jan Bender Shetler, *Imagining Serengeti: A History of Landscape Memory in Tanzania from the Earliest Times to the Present* (Athens: Ohio University Press, 2007).
35 In one version, they came from Majapahit, a famous kingdom in Java, in another version from Munaseli, a locally famous kingdom in Pantar. Wellfelt, 'Historyscapes in Alor,' 78.
36 Wellfelt, 'Historyscapes in Alor,' 81.
37 Hoskins, *Play of Time*, 119. In many ways, this echoes the kind of collections you find in national museums, or in Sweden in the Royal Armoury (Livrustkammaren).
38 The groups are usually referred to using the names of the respective leading clan, Talpi for Kula and Taruama for Wersing.
39 Wellfelt, 'Historyscapes in Alor,' 81.
40 There are two places called Kaipera; this is the inland village, not the coastal site where the Kaipera oath was sworn.
41 Kula: *pei* – pig, *basa* – trap.
42 Kula: *kung* – gong, *gung* – sound.
43 Wersing: *pai* – pig, *bakang* – manger.
44 Wersing: *kine* – knife, *bakang* – sheath, *kila* – wood that is almost cut through.
45 In many narrations of Indigenous history in eastern Indonesia, the Second World War is a milestone; old ways ceased at the time of the war.

46 The last reported cases of headhunting in Alor date from the Second World War. For headhunting in the wider region, see Janet Hoskins, ed., *Headhunting and the Social Imagination in Southeast Asia* (Stanford, CA: Stanford University Press, 1996).
47 Emilie Wellfelt and Antoinette Schapper, 'Enriching the Archival Picture: The Use of Local Sources in Assessing the Nature and Impact of Historical Contact,' paper presented at the Eighth Convention of Asia Scholars (ICAS 8), Macao, 24–27 June 2013; Antoinette Schapper and Emilie Wellfelt, 'Reconstructing Contact between Alor and Timor: Evidence from Language and Beyond,' *NUSA: Linguistic Studies of Languages in and around Indonesia* 64 (2018): 95–116.
48 Aronsson's model draws on the work of Bernard Eric Jensen, Reinhart Koselleck, and Raphael Samuel.
49 Peter Aronsson, *Historiebruk: Att Använda det Förflutna* (Lund: Studentlitteratur, 2004); Peter Aronsson, 'The Old Cultural Regionalism – and the New,' in *An Agenda for Regional History*, eds. Bill Lancaster, Diana Newton, and Natasha Vall (Newcastle: Northumbria University Press 2007), 263.
50 Aronsson, 'The Old Cultural Regionalism,' 263–264.
51 Minoru Hokari, *Gurindji Journey: A Japanese Historian in the Outback* (Sydney: University of New South Wales Press 2011), 94. Hokari worked with the Gurindji, an Indigenous group in northern Australia. The concept of 'everywhen' was introduced by the anthropologist William Edward Hanley Stanner in his essay 'The Dreaming,' first published in 1956. See W.E.H. Stanner, *The Dreaming and Other Essays* (Carlton: Black Inc. Agenda, 2011).
52 V.F. Cordova, *How It Is: The Native American Philosophy of V.F. Cordova*, eds. Kathleen Dean Moore, Kurt Peters, Ted Jojola, and Amber Lacy (Tucson: University of Arizona Press, 2007), 118; Wellfelt, 'Historyscapes in Alor,' 17–18.
53 Gunlög Fur, 'Concurrences as Methodology for Discerning Concurrent Histories,' in *Concurrent Imaginaries, Postcolonial Worlds: Towards Revised History*, eds. Diana Brydon, Peter Forsgren, and Gunlög Fur (Leiden and Boston, MA: Brill, 2017), 48.
54 Emilie Wellfelt, 'Heritage in Alor: Sustaining Local Identity in a Globalized World,' in *Sites, Bodies and Stories: Imagining Indonesian History*, eds. Susan Legêne, Bambang Purwanto, and Henk Schulte Nordholt (Singapore: National University of Singapore Press), 67–88.
55 Wellfelt, 'Heritage in Alor.'
56 Kaj Århem, 'Southeast Asian Animism in Context,' in *Animism in Southeast Asia*, eds. Kaj Århem and Guido Sprenger (New York: Routledge, 2016), 28.
57 Wellfelt, 'Heritage in Alor,' 75.
58 Guido Sprenger, 'Dimensions of Animism in Southeast Asia,' in *Animism in Southeast Asia*, eds. Kaj Århem and Guido Sprenger (New York: Routledge, 2016), 37.
59 Århem, 'Southeast Asian Animism,' 17.
60 A parallel can be found in the old dispute of transubstantiation in Christianity, where the Roman Catholic Church teaches that the bread and wine offered in communion is the actual body and blood of Jesus, while other Churches have a symbolic interpretation of the communion.
61 This is an expression of a dual system found in parts or eastern Indonesia where the ruler 'sits' while his counterpart acts. For parallels in West Timor, see Tom Therik, *Wehali: The Female Land: Traditions of a Timorese Ritual Centre* (Canberra: Pandanus Books, in association with the Department of Anthropology, Research School of Pacific and Asian Studies, Australian National University, 2004).
62 'Reseguide Stockholm: Stadsvandring på nätet,' website with detailed instructions in Swedish for 'Walks in the footsteps of Stieg Larsson,' accessed 12 January 2020, https://redviking.se/guidestockholm/?page_id=15.
63 Pallasmaa, *Eyes of the Skin*.
64 David Michael Levin, ed., *Modernity and the Hegemony of Vision* (Berkeley and Los Angeles: University of California Press, 1993), 1.

Bibliography

Anderson, Jon. 'Talking Whilst Walking: A Geographical Archaeology of Knowledge.' *Area* 36, no. 3 (2004): 254–261.

Århem, Kaj. 'Southeast Asian Animism in Context.' In *Animism in Southeast Asia*, edited by Kaj Århem and Guido Sprenger, 17–36. New York: Routledge, 2016.

Aronsson, Peter. *Historiebruk: Att Använda det Förflutna*. Lund: Studentlitteratur, 2004.

Aronsson, Peter. 'The Old Cultural Regionalism – and the New.' In *An Agenda for Regional History*, edited by Bill Lancaster, Diana Newton, and Natasha Vall, 251–270. Newcastle: Northumbria University Press 2007.

Bisby, James A., and Neil Burgess. 'Spatial memory.' Encyclopaedia Britannica. Accessed 3 November 2020. www.britannica.com/science/spatial-memory.

BPS Kabupaten Alor/Statistical office of Alor. *Alor Dalam Angka/Alor In Figures 2011, Katalog BPS: 1403.5307*. Kalabahi: BPS Kabupaten Alor/Statistical office of Alor 2011.

Chouin, Gérard. 'Archaeological Perspectives on Sacred Groves in Ghana.' In *African Sacred Groves: Ecological Dynamics and Social Change*, edited by Michael J. Sheridan and Celia Nyamweru, 178–194. Oxford: James Currey, 2008.

Cordova, V.F. *How It Is: The Native American Philosophy of V.F. Cordova*, edited by Kathleen Dean Moore, Kurt Peters, Ted Jojola, and Amber Lacy. Tucson: University of Arizona Press, 2007.

Cummings, William. *Making Blood White: Historical Transformations in Early Modern Makassar*. Honolulu: University of Hawai'i Press, 2002.

de Certeau, Michel. *The Writing of History*. Translated by Tom Conley. New York: Columbia University Press, 1988.

Finnegan, Ruth. *Oral Traditions and the Verbal Arts: A Guide to Research Practices*. London and New York: Routledge, 1992.

Fox, James J. 'Genealogy and Topogeny: Towards an Ethnography of Rotinese Ritual Place Names.' In *The Poetic Power of Place: Comparative Perspective on Austronesian Ideas of Locality*, edited by James J. Fox. Canberra: ANU Press, 2006.

Fur, Gunlög. 'Concurrences as Methodology for Discerning Concurrent Histories.' In *Concurrent Imaginaries, Postcolonial Worlds: Toward Revised History*, edited by Diana Brydon, Peter Forsgren, and Gunlög Fur, 33–57. Leiden and Boston, MA: Brill, 2017.

Geirnaert-Martin, Danielle C. *The Woven Land of Laboya: Socio-Cosmic Ideas and Values in West Sumba, Eastern Indonesia*. Leiden: Centre of Non-Western Studies, Leiden University, 1992.

Goody, Jack. *The Interface between the Written and the Oral*. Cambridge: Cambridge University Press, 1987.

Greene, Sandra E. *Sacred Sites and the Colonial Encounter: A History of Meaning and Memory in Ghana*. Bloomington: Indiana University Press, 2002.

Hägerdal, Hans. 'Van Galen's Memorandum on the Alor Islands in 1946: An Annotated Translation with an Introduction. Part 1.' *HumaNetten* 25 (2010): 14–44

Hoskins, Janet, ed. *Headhunting and the Social Imagination in Southeast Asia*. Stanford, CA: Stanford University Press, 1996.

Hoskins, Janet. *The Play of Time: Kodi Perspectives on Calendars, History and Exchange*. Berkeley and Los Angeles: California University Press, 1997.

Hokari, Minoru. *Gurindji Journey: A Japanese Historian in the Outback*. Sydney: University of New South Wales Press 2011.

Kaartinen, Timo. *Songs of Travel, Stories of Place: Poetics of Absence in an Eastern Indonesian Society*. Helsinki: Academia Scientiarum Fennica, 2010.

Kelly, Lynne. *Knowledge and Power in Prehistoric Societies: Orality, Memory, and the Transmission of Culture*. New York: Cambridge University Press, 2015.

Levin, David Michael, ed. *Modernity and the Hegemony of Vision*. Berkeley and Los Angeles: University of California Press, 1993.

Li, Tania Murray, ed. *Transforming the Indonesian Uplands: Marginality, Power and Production.* London and New York: Routledge, 2004.
Nabokov, Peter. *A Forest of Time: American Indian Ways of History.* New York: Cambridge University Press, 2009.
Nordholt, Henk Schulte, and Gerry van Klinken, eds. *Renegotiating Local Boundaries: Local Politics in Post-Suharto Indonesia.* Leiden: KITLV Press, 2007.
O'Neill, Máire Eithne. 'Corporeal Experience: A Haptic Way of Knowing.' *Journal of Architectural Education* 55, no. 1 (2001): 3–12.
Ong, Walter J. *Orality and Literacy: The Technologizing of the Word.* London: Methuen, 1982.
Pallasmaa, Juhani. *The Eyes of the Skin: Architecture and the Senses.* London: Wiley, 2005.
Palmer, Lisa. *Water Politics and Spiritual Ecology: Custom, Environmental Governance and Development.* Abingdon and New York: Routledge, 2015.
Perks, Robert, and Alistair Thomson, eds. *The Oral History Reader.* London and New York: Routledge, 2006.
Reseguide Stockholm. 'Stadsvandring på nätet.' Website with detailed instructions in Swedish for 'Walks in the footsteps of Stieg Larsson.' Accessed 12 January 2020. https://redviking.se/guidestockholm/?page_id=15.
Schapper, Antoinette, and Emilie Wellfelt. 'Reconstructing Contact between Alor and Timor: Evidence from Language and Beyond.' *NUSA: Linguistic Studies of Languages in and around Indonesia* 64 (2018): 95–116.
Shetler, Jan Bender. *Imagining Serengeti: A History of Landscape Memory in Tanzania from the Earliest Times to the Present.* Athens: Ohio University Press, 2007.
Sprenger, Guido. 'Dimensions of Animism in Southeast Asia.' In *Animism in Southeast Asia,* edited by Kaj Århem and Guido Sprenger, 37–52. New York: Routledge, 2016.
Stanner, W.E.H. *The Dreaming and Other Essays.* Collingwood: Black Inc. Agenda, 2011.
Therik, Tom. *Wehali: The Female Land: Traditions of a Timorese Ritual Centre.* Canberra: Pandanus Books, in association with the Department of Anthropology, Research School of Pacific and Asian Studies, Australian National University, 2004.
Trouillot, Michel-Rolph. *Silencing the Past: Power and the Production of History.* Boston, MA: Beacon Press, 1995.
Vansina, Jan. *Oral Tradition as History.* Oxford: James Currey, 1997.
Vansina, Jan. *Oral Tradition: A Study in Historical Methodology,* New Brunswick and London: Aldine Transaction, 2006.
von Benda-Beckmann, Franz, and Keebet von Benda-Beckmann. 'Texts in Context: Historical Documents as Political Commodity in Islamic Ambon.' In *Texts from the Islands: Oral and Written Traditions of Indonesia and the Malay World,* edited by Wolfgang Marschall, 223–243. Berne: University of Berne, Institute of Ethnology, 1994.
Wellfelt, Emilie. 'Heritage in Alor: Sustaining Local Identity in a Globalized World.' In *Sites, Bodies and Stories: Imagining Indonesian History,* edited by Susan Legêne, Bambang Purwanto, and Henk Schulte Nordholt, 67–88. Singapore: National University of Singapore Press, 2015.
Wellfelt, Emilie. 'Historyscapes in Alor: Approaching Indigenous Histories in Eastern Indonesia.' PhD diss., Linnaeus University, 2016.
Wellfelt, Emilie, and Antoinette Schapper. 'Enriching the Archival Picture: The Use of Local Sources in Assessing the Nature and Impact of Historical Contact.' Paper presented at the Eighth Convention of Asia Scholars (ICAS 8), Macao, 24–27 June 2013.
Wolf, Eric R. *Europe and the People without History.* Berkeley: University of California Press, 1982.

31
THE USES OF HISTORY IN GREENLAND

Claire McLisky and Kirstine Eiby Møller[1]

For the Kalaallit of Greenland, as for many Indigenous peoples, the uses of 'history' are diverse and complicated. How Greenlandic history is understood, by Indigenous Greenlanders and by others, impacts the lives of Greenlanders every day: in their self-understanding and the construction of individual and collective identities, in how they formulate policy domestically and engage with the world outside, and in the futures that they envision for themselves. Yet since the Dano-Norwegian colonisation of Greenland in 1721, most written histories of Greenland and its people have been produced by outsiders. The past 30 years have thus seen several calls for the right of Kalaallit to write their own histories, and the publication of a handful of important volumes written by Greenlanders, for Greenlanders.[2] However many commentators remain concerned that most of Greenland's 56,000 inhabitants still only have access to outside accounts of the history of their people and their country. Indeed, the first two recommendations of the Greenlandic Reconciliation Commission (2014–2017) were that Greenlandic history should be re-written 'as seen through our eyes', and that a national 'Knowledge Centre for History and Reconciliation' should be established.[3]

While it is true that formal written and academic histories of Greenland in the eighteenth, nineteenth, and twentieth centuries were dominated by European (particularly Danish) perspectives, a closer look at Greenlandic literature and cultural productions reveals a parallel tradition of Greenlanders representing themselves and their histories in a variety of fora: through storytelling and song in pre-colonial times; and in literature, art, photography, and popular music in the centuries since. During this period, Greenlanders have represented the histories of their people and their interactions with those from other cultures in a range of ways, which are marked but not defined by the colonial relationship with Denmark. In this chapter, we investigate Greenlandic uses of history from the pre-colonial period to the current day. In a series of short case studies, we consider both the distinctiveness of Greenlandic engagements with history over time and their global resonances. While Greenland is currently in a process of re-negotiating its relationship with the past, subversive and emancipatory uses of history have been a longstanding feature of Greenlandic cultural and literary production, and continue to thrive in current-day Kalaallit Nunaat.

Eighteenth-century representations: foundational European histories of Greenland, and Greenlanders writing back to power

Before 1721, Greenlanders, like other Indigenous peoples, relied primarily on oral transmission to preserve and develop their histories. Greenlandic storytellers were 'capable of managing an extensive amount of material and giving historical accounts that stretched over multiple generations and a large geographical area'.[4] Indeed, according to the Greenlandic historian H.C. Petersen, 'some of the Eskimos' traditional stories go back more than 10,000 years' to the time of the woolly mammoth – far longer, as Petersen notes, 'than the actual Eskimos' history'.[5] Ordered according to different logics than European histories, Greenlandic oral histories incorporated sophisticated representations of spatial orientation and landscape[6] and distinguished between *unikkaat*, 'stories of events that happened in recent times', and *unikkaartuat* which 'refer to the very distant past, when animals were able to transform in to humans'.[7] In line with this intricate understanding of different kinds of history, Greenlanders in pre-colonial times told stories, or histories, for a multitude of reasons: to recount genealogies or establish relations with other groups[8]; to understand changes in environmental conditions and the effect this might have on hunting and human subsistence[9]; to make sense of current events or relationships; and for entertainment – to 'make the winter seem shorter'.[10]

The first European observers to come into sustained contact with the Kalaallit did not recognise this rich tradition of historical engagement. Despite living amongst the Kalaallit and experiencing their oral history traditions, eighteenth-century observers such as the founding Lutheran missionary Hans Egede and the Moravian historian David Cranz instead understood Greenlandic culture as part of a 'primitive' past that was already in the process of being replaced by Christianity and civilisation.[11] Later in the eighteenth century, a new generation of commentators such as Poul Egede (son of Hans) and Henrik Glahn drew on a more sympathetic Rousseauian discourse on 'noble savagery' to produce texts that displayed more knowledge of, and sympathy for, Greenlandic culture and norms.[12] However, these were still written from a European perspective, their focus on celebrating and protecting Greenlandic culture sitting alongside their Christianising and modernising work.[13]

During this period, Greenlanders were rapidly learning to read and write in their own language, a product of both the Dano-Norwegian mission's decision to work in the vernacular and Greenlanders' hunger for knowledge.[14] Yet despite burgeoning literacy, and evidence that some Greenlanders learned Danish in the process,[15] very few Greenlandic written sources survive from this time. In this section, we consider two of the best-known surviving eighteenth-century sources.

Both were published by missionaries, with a significant delay between composition and publication, and as such their provenance is uncertain. Both texts represent the Lutheran mission and Dano-Norwegian colonialism in a largely positive light, which suggests that they may have been either written or heavily edited by the missionaries who published them. However, both texts also contain explicit and implicit criticisms of Dano-Norwegian colonialism, indicating that they might reflect contemporary critical Greenlandic perspectives, and they are therefore useful to consider as precursors to the subsequent self-representations explored later in this chapter.

The first of these two sources is a song purportedly written by Pápa (baptismal name Frederik Christian) and Peder, two of the first Greenlandic converts to Christianity, who both had close relationships with the Egede family. Composed on the occasion of the Danish Crown Prince's birthday in 1729, the song was published in Hans Egede's 1741 work *Description of Greenland* in both Danish and Greenlandic.[16] Written in the style of a traditional Kalaallit drum dance, with recurring call-and-response chorus, the song also employs conventions from the Danish genre of 'lejlighedssang' or birthday tribute song, leading several historians to comment on its cross-cultural characteristics.[17] While, as Søren Thuesen points out, we cannot know whether the song was commissioned by Hans Egede, or to what extent he influenced or edited its content,[18] recent research by Flemming Nielsen shows that despite the long gap between composition and publication, it was almost certainly in circulation amongst Greenlanders soon after being written.[19]

The song's initial stated intention is to 'make (the King's son) famous', to 'praise him', and to 'rejoice' that 'he shall be our King'. Yet, it also looks to the future with a wary eye. 'Be thou (like your father the King)', who 'sent priests to us to teach us about God/so shall we love thee and cherish thee and be thy servants'. The implication here is that if Christian VI is not like his father, Greenlandic love, service and devotion will not be forthcoming.

In the next stanza, the Danish version of the song continues: 'Everything we own/You will have all of it/When Greenland has got knowledge'. The Greenlandic version, however, reads: 'What we hunt/You may have some of/When Greenland has got knowledge'.[20] The two versions' divergent promise is rooted in fundamentally different notions of property ownership. While the Danish version represents Pápa and Peder's offer to the Prince as being that of a wholesale transfer of property from the Greenlanders to the Dano-Norwegian crown, the Greenlandic version suggests a notion of collective ownership or custodianship more consonant with traditional (and contemporary) Greenlandic ideas about property, and indeed global Indigenous understandings of human relationships with land more generally.[21]

This was not the first or the last time in European colonial history that an important ceremonial document published in an Indigenous and a European language would have distinctly different meanings. For example, in 1840 in Aoteroa (New Zealand), the English and Maori versions of the Treaty of Waitangi were transcribed by the British with significantly different wordings which mirror the Greenlandic example above. While the English version of the Treaty gave the

British Queen 'all the rights and powers of sovereignty' over the land, the Maori version gave her 'kawanatanga' or 'governance'.[22] In the case of Egede's mistranslation of Pápa and Peder's song, the purpose (and even the pursposefulness) of the discrepancies between the two versions is unclear. Were they an honest mistake (a possibility given Egede's uneven skills in the Greenlandic language)? Or were they an attempt to convince his Dano-Norwegian supporters (not least the Crown Prince, who had by the time of publication become the King) that Greenlanders accepted the expropriation of their lands and their property when in fact they did not? Interestingly, even in its Danish translation, the stanza can still be read as an assertion of the continuation of Greenlandic relationships to land: despite the presence of Dano-Norwegian missionaries and colonists, Greenland's land and resources still belong to Greenlanders, and they will only be given to, or shared with, the Danish Crown once Greenlanders are provided with 'knowledge'. Though the authors probably used the term 'knowledge' here in the Christian sense of a knowledge of God, they did not explicitly define the word, and may also have intended to refer to more secular knowledge. Thus, while the song frames the brief history of Dano-Norwegian colonialism and the Royal mission up to 1729 in a positive light, its support for the continuation of the colonial project is contingent on continued Royal patronage for Greenlanders' education. If this condition is met, then the Danish King will be richly rewarded; if it is not, the invitation to share in Greenland's wealth might well be retracted.

Forty-seven years later, Hans Egede's son Poul published another text ostensibly written by a Greenlander. This was a letter that Pavia (baptised Poul Grønlænder after Poul Egede himself) had written to him in 1756. At the time of writing the two men had known each other for many years and Pavia was the Royal Mission's most prominent Greenlandic catechist. Pavia had come to live with the Egede family in 1729, when he was nine years old, and was baptised in 1731. After Hans and Poul Egede's departures from Greenland in 1735 and 1740 respectively, he became one of the Lutheran mission's staunchest allies. Pavia kept the father and son informed of developments in a series of letters written in Greenlandic, one of which Poul Egede published in his 1788 *Accounts of Greenland*. Unfortunately, the Greenlandic version of this letter has not survived; all we have left is the Danish translation published by Egede.[23]

In the translation of the letter, Pavia presents Europeans in conflicting lights: while he expresses his support for the Danish Royal mission and its missionaries, he also evinces horror at European greed, bloodthirstiness, lack of empathy and immoral behaviour. Like Pápa and Peder, Pavia represents Greenland and the sea surrounding it as belonging to Greenlanders, though he writes that 'we gladly wish for others to take from this great stock as much as they please'.[24] In this narrative, the history of Greenlandic contact with Europeans, and even Danish colonialism, has made Greenlanders wary in their dealings with them; while Pavia is still eager to learn from the missionaries and to teach his countrymen about their God, he is uncertain about the sinful behaviour of the Europeans and hopes to understand more about how this behaviour developed so that he and his people can avoid the same fate.

Indeed, Pavia writes:

> You have probably heard more than once, of what my countrymen thought about you and yours, that you were raised to gentleness in our land, and when they see a pious man amongst you, they will gladly say, that he is like a human or a Greenlander.[25]

This notion of the Greenlander character as synonymous with piety, virtue, and even humanity itself, calls to mind the work of Ann Fienup-Riordan, whose work on the Yup'ik people of Western Alaska details how they describe themselves as 'real people', and the Europeans as the 'children of the thunder'.[26] 'Real people', in the Yup'ik view, are people who understand their relationship to the spirits, animals, plants, and objects around them as one of collaborative reciprocity; what is important is not the individual but the collective.[27] Europeans could only become 'real people' after many years of commitment to the Yup'ik community. Similarly, in Pavia's letter, the Europeans that can be described as 'human beings' are those who have proved their 'good behaviour', not just on Christian but also on Greenlandic terms.

The Greenlandic concept of 'good behaviour' resonates with the concept of 'right behaviour', which according to Australian historian Richard Broome was an important value for the Aboriginal people of the nineteenth-century southeast Australian reserve Coranderrk, and a concept that they drew on in descriptions of some of the Europeans who worked amongst them.[28] In his letter, then, Pavia presents the history of Europeans in Greenland as a transition from depravity to grace as Europeans learn 'good behaviour' from the Greenlanders and become 'like humans' or 'Greenlanders'; this transition is by no means complete. Alongside this history sits another narrative, of the Christianisation of Greenlanders, although the outcomes of this process are also not yet clear at the time of writing. Whatever the future might hold, Greenlanders still maintain their traditional relationships with their land and resources and are happy to share these boons with pious and well-behaved Europeans. Europeans who do not conform to Greenlandic standards of good behaviour are a source of fear for some (such as Kaua, one Greenlander of whom Pavia wrote, who 'dared not become a Christian for fear he should come to be like the wicked sailors').[29] However, despite considerable misgivings about the effects of European colonialism, Pavia remains loyal to Poul Egede and the mission.

The question of whether Pavia actually wrote this letter, or whether it was fabricated or significantly reworked by Poul Egede before publication is difficult to resolve. As early as 1983, Christian Berthelsen observed that without the original Greenlandic letter, we could not know how Pavia expressed his ideas; the Danish translation was, rather, 'Poul Egede's interpretation'.[30] In 2001, Michael Harbsmeier went further, arguing that the letter belonged to a genre of eighteenth-century literature in which European authors allowed non-Europeans to give critical accounts of European conditions, a literary device through which they were able to both bypass censorship and claim weight for their observations by giving the impression they were made by impartial observers.³¹ Indeed, he contended, the natural history aspects and critical religious context and the form of 'Poul Grønlænder's letter' made it very unlikely that its author was anyone other than Poul Egede. However, unlike most other contemporary accounts of non-European views of Europe, the 'precisely described conditions of origin' and the 'linguistically- and ethnographically-delineated verbatim reproductions of the utterances of foreign pagan voices' of Poul Egede's version of Pavia's letter made it appear 'extraordinarily realistic'.³² The observations that Egede attributed in the letter to Pavia undoubtedly stemmed from Egede's many conversations with Greenlanders both in Greenland and in Denmark, and there was 'no doubt that Poul Egede himself, his contemporary readers, and almost all subsequent generations of eskimologists and historians were firmly convinced that these were the authentic words of authentic Greenlanders'.³³

Building on Harbsmeier's work, Inge Kleivan pointed out in 2009 that even the strong evidence of Egede's involvement in shaping the Danish version of the letter should not lead us to exclude the possibility that the letter published in 1788 was based on a real letter he received from Pavia in 1756. For Kleivan, 'whether the whole letter or only a large part of it was designed by Poul Egede in his namesake's name, he has nevertheless taken his point of departure from the thoughts of Greenlanders, as they have been expressed in various observations and comments'.³⁴

Whatever its provenance, Pavia's letter – like Pápa and Peder's song – stands in marked contrast to the body of eighteenth-century European work on Greenland. In both these texts, Greenlanders are represented as writing from a position of strength, confidence, and sovereignty and Greenlandic ideas of property ownership – of land, of sea, of possessions – are contrasted with contemporary European ones. Far from seeing their relationship to property as a mark of inferiority or savagery, these Greenlandic writers frame their people's approach to property as more generous, more peaceful, and ultimately more conducive to 'civilised' behaviour than the European approach. The historical encounter between Greenlanders and Europeans is represented as a story of 'good behaviour' between the Greenlanders and the Dano-Norwegian Crown; amicable relations that will hopefully lay the foundation for positive relations in the future. However, for Pavia this future is not inevitable; indeed, his letter points to the dangers that may lie ahead if the Crown or its representatives do not continue to behave as 'humans' or 'Greenlanders'.

Nineteenth-century developments: Aron of Kangeq and the depictions of personal history – everyday life as a means of history telling

By the beginning of the nineteenth century Greenlandic trade, administered by the Royal Greenlandic Company, had expanded considerably, and Greenlanders were exposed to greater European influences with both positive and negative effects on their culture and demographics. In particular, a growing reliance on European foods and epidemics of smallpox presented challenges for the Greenlandic population, with changing social norms threatening traditional practices and creating new opportunities.³⁵ The period of conflict between England and Denmark (1807–1814) during the Napoleonic Wars was particularly difficult for Greenlanders, as Danish supplies were cut off and trade and mission employees were forced to return to Denmark. At the end of the war the dual Dano-Norwegian kingdom was broken up, leaving Greenland in the hands of a severely impoverished Denmark, and Greenlanders began a new phase in their status as colonised peoples.

During this period, European representations of Greenland proliferated, with several new translations of earlier works as well as new accounts of the country's natural and human history.³⁶ In 1861, Greenland's first national newspaper gave Greenlanders a forum in which to represent their own lives and histories. Founded by Heinrich Rink (at the time the Danish governor of the Southern District of Greenland), the newspaper was part of the Danish colonial administration's restoration programme designed to increase Greenlandic participation in civil society and 'enhance Greenlandic self-respect'.³⁷ The newspaper's first two editors, Rasmus Berthelsen (1861–1873) and Lars 'Aqqaluk' Møller (1873–1922), were both Greenlanders and were responsible for writing and soliciting articles on 'topics of socio-political enlightenment as well as those simply meant for reader entertainment'.³⁸ While the newspaper published news from around the world and within Greenland, its most important function was to give Greenlanders a forum to represent their own lives and histories, drawing on a pre-existing discourse of ethno-national identity to discuss, debate, and recreate ideas and stories about Greenlandic identity and belonging.³⁹

To voice these histories, Heinrich Rink sent out the first call for oral histories, drawings, and maps to Greenlanders in 1858, resulting in the publication *Kaládlit ássilialiait* (1860) where the drawings were reproduced.⁴⁰ Aron of Kangeq,⁴¹ a catechist belonging to the Moravian Mission, was one of the first to react to the call and is to this day considered the founder of Greenlandic art.⁴² Aron was first and foremost a hunter, the harvesting of animals being the primary source of sustenance for Inuit at the time. However, Aron suffered from tuberculosis and during his relapses he documented oral histories both in writing and in drawing.⁴³ His depictions read like a graphic novel, with the oral histories accompanied by images of the immutable Greenlandic landscape with only the humans' attire communicating whether the history is set in the past or in present memory (*oqaluttuaq/unikkaartuat* or *oqalualaarut/unikkaat* as discussed above).⁴⁴ The oral histories and myths are a window into the customs, values, and behavioural patterns regarded by (pre-Christian) Inuit as essential for the structure of society. Through his artworks, Aron translates the art of oral storytelling into an image, full of movement yet entirely still.⁴⁵

One work with particular resonance is Aron's portrait of Qasapi, the pre-Christian Greenlander who in a south Greenlandic version of *Oqaluttuaq Uunngortumik* [The Story about Uunngortoq] is said to have killed Uunngortoq, the supreme chief of the Norsemen (see Figure 31.1).⁴⁶ According to the story, which was provided to Aron by Rink for illustration, conflict between the two groups begins after a Greenlander kills a Norseman collecting mussels on the shore.⁴⁷ Sometime later, a large group of Norsemen arrive at the Greenlanders' house and surround it, massacring all its inhabitants except Qasapi and his younger brother. As they are

The uses of history in Greenland

Figure 31.1 Woodcut by Aron of Kangeq showing Qasapi standing over the fallen Uunngortoq
Source: Greenland National Museum and Archives

making their escape, Qasapi's younger brother slips and falls, and the Norse chief Uunngortoq kills him, hacking off his arm with an axe and saying: 'I wonder, Qasapi, whether you will ever forget your little brother, as long as you live?' Using his skills as a hunter of seals and men, and enlisting magical help from the southern Inuit, Qasapi pursues Uunngortoq and eventually corners him, despite the Norseman's own considerable powers of sorcery. Having fatally wounded Uunngortoq using his bow and arrow, Qasapi hacks off the Norseman's arm and holds it up to show his already unconscious quarry, repeating Uunngortoq's own words about his brother back to him.

Aron illustrated this climactic and somewhat brutal moment using woodcut and the resulting black-and-white print of Qasapi standing above the fallen Uunngortoq, brandishing the chief's severed right arm, is a stark and powerful image. Despite his violent death, the Norse chief lies peacefully on the ice, his left hand resting on his stomach with his fingers gently curled. The folds of his tunic are beautifully rendered, echoing the contour lines of the ice, mountains and sky above, and his face and body are bathed in light that seems to emanate from the sky and sea. Qasapi, meanwhile, is clothed in a dark sealskin anorak, his back turned to the fjord. He wears an expression that combines happiness and sorrow, relief at vengeance achieved, but also weariness and a sense of loss evident in his stooped stance and rounded shoulders. The benign facial expressions of the two men belie the extreme violence of the story and suggest a more complicated relationship than merely that of mortal enemies.

One way of interpreting the meaning of this story and Aron's illustration of it is offered by Kirsten Thisted, who has suggested that stories such as *Oqaluttuaq Uunngortumik* were not understood or intended by Greenlanders as accurate depictions of the meeting between the Kalaallit and the Norse (which at the time was thought to have resulted in the extermination of the latter group).[48] Rather, nineteenth-century Greenlanders told these stories in order to work through their own experiences of domination by, and coexistence with, the Dano-Norwegians who had arrived in the eighteenth century, and who this time had come to stay. For Thisted, 150 years of close contact between Scandinavians and Greenlanders had already, by the mid-nineteenth century, led to a situation where the Norsemen were 'symbolic of both strangers and of the strangers within'.[49] While the Norsemen symbolised 'successful cultural encounters and peaceful coexistence', they also represented 'the division caused by this encounter, a division which in Greenlandic terms is based on the persistent asymmetrical power relation, which remained basically unaltered far beyond the end of colonial times'.[50]

Aron, a hunter whose father was a catechist and who himself worked as a catechist assistant, storyteller, and illustrator, was himself representative of this ambivalence. He was, according to Thisted, 'simply not in a position to sympathise with one group at the expense of another, but rather [felt] he must adopt the kind of binocular view of the conflict that gives a tragic perspective to the rupture between the two peoples'.[51] And yet, while this 'multicultural' perspective is certainly evident in Aron's portrait of Qasapi and Uunngortoq, the image is multivalent enough to allow other readings, and has since become an iconic symbol of Greenlandic agency, solidarity, and uncompromising instinct for survival. As Thisted writes:

> The extermination of the Norsemen provides a setting in Greenlandic history for exactly the kind of archetypal event upon which many nations build the myth of their birth. The murder of the Norsemen is the one inescapable, mythological incident in which the Greenlanders stood together for the first time and stepped forward as a people. In Greenlandic culture, the myth endures regardless of how much doubt archeology has cast on it.[52]

While Aron's intent was not necessarily related to nation-building, his application of sublime artistry and perspectival ambivalence to this crucial (real or imagined) historical moment in Greenlandic-European history made the production of this image a significant moment for Greenlandic representations of the past. Combining both historical and mythological elements, 'traditional' nineteenth-century stories such as *Oqaluttuaq Uunngortumik*, and Aron's illustrations of them, made sense of the present by reworking and reshaping Greenlanders' understandings of the past.

Mathias Storch, Augo Lynge, and the development of Greenlandic literature in the first half of the twentieth century

In the first half of the twentieth century, Greenlanders' perspectives on their own history continued to gain visibility, although Europeans still wrote the scholarly and popular histories of the country.⁵³ In 1913, a second newspaper *Avangnamiok* ('The North Greenlander') was founded and soon the first two Greenlandic novels – Mathias Storch's *A Greenlander's Dream* (1915) and Augo Lynge's *300 Years After* (1931) – were published. Both (at least partially) set in the future, these works did not explicitly deal with Greenland's past, but the utopian futures that they imagined were implicitly contrasted with the problems associated with the colonial period in which the authors were writing (Figure 31.2).

In Storch's novel, the protagonist is Pavia, a 'settlement boy' who we follow from childhood to young adulthood through his growing awareness of the problems facing Greenlandic society. These include divisive class distinctions introduced by the colonial administration; insufficient prioritisation of, and funding for, the education of Greenlandic youth; traditional customs such as arranged marriages; the sham democracy of the Guardian Councils (*forstanderskaber* – the first Greenlandic self-governing bodies); lack of vision and commitment on the part of Danish colonial administrators and priests; waning Greenlandic interest in continuing the harsh traditional hunting lifestyle; and the poverty these problems created for Greenlanders, especially those living in remote settlements. Early on in

Figure 31.2   Mathias Storch
Source: John Møller/Greenland National Museum and Archives

the novel, Pavia converses with a visionary elder called Simon, who tells him that he will one day become a worker amongst his countrymen, and that 'the worker will have his day' (Figures 31.3 and 31.4).[54]

Pavia resolves to follow Simon's advice, and events in the years following this interaction confirm in his mind that education is the only solution to the problems facing his people. Accepting the local priest's offer for him to train as a catechist, Pavia begins his training at the seminary, but during his time there loses confidence after hearing 'so many conflicting opinions between his countrymen'.[55] By the close of the novel, Pavia is suffering an existential crisis and loses consciousness only to

Figure 31.3 A Guardian Council in the Godthåb (now Nuuk) region
Source: John Møller/Greenland National Museum and Archives

Figure 31.4 An agreement is signed by a Guardian Council in Nuuk, 1903
Source: John Møller/Greenland National Museum and Archives

awake in a utopian future, which he soon learns is the year 2105. In this new, independent Greenland fishing, coal mining and whaling have replaced traditional economic activities, and Greenlanders vote for their own politicians and control their own foreign policy. Pavia encounters the elder Simon, who tells him that the development of his people is due to the expansion of their knowledge, both sacred and secular. Simon thus urges Pavia to 'work now to make this happen'.[56] For Storch, education and modernisation needed to sit alongside continued reverence for God if the problems faced by Greenland in the early twentieth century were to be solved. And – crucially – the educative project needed to be led by Greenlanders.[57]

A similar message can be found in the 1931 work *300 Years After*,[58] written by Augo Lynge (Figure 31.5). Set in 2021, 300 years after Hans Egede's arrival in Greenland, this novel uses the device of a crime plot to focus on the social and economic development that is projected to have occurred between 1931 and 2021. In this vision of the future, Greenlanders have embraced both fishing and agriculture, and now enjoy complete equality with the Danes who live amongst them. Greenland is not independent but rather a self-governing Danish territory integrated with the wider world, 'where a mixed Danish-Greenlandic population administers its region which is on a par with Denmark'.[59] Yet if Lynge, unlike Storch, saw the future of the two nations as together rather than separate, his book was similarly premised on an indirect criticism of early twentieth-century conditions of inequality between Greenlanders and Danes and the lack of economic development pursued by the colonial administration.[60] Indeed, Storch and Lynge's advocacy for fishing, farming, and agriculture as potential routes to Greenlandic prosperity can be seen as a direct challenge to the nineteenth-century Danish colonial policy of privileging traditional hunting practices to the detriment of economic development.[61]

Despite their primary concern being to imagine a utopian future rather than to critique the past, these two authors drew on specific interpretations of Greenland's colonial history to highlight the issues faced by Greenlandic society in the early twentieth century. While they saw some of the changes that had come with colonisation (including conversion to Christianity and exposure to modern ideas) as useful to future adaptation and success, in general they represented Danish colonial rule as repressive and backward-looking. In this sense, Storch and Lynge were using history to support their arguments for social and economic changes. Both authors went on to become public figures – in 1927 Storch became the first Greenlandic Vice-Provost of Greenland, and in 1938 Lynge became one of the first Greenlanders elected to the Danish Parliament – and both men contributed to public discourse during the Second World War and the post-war years, a period during which Greenland's status, its political scene, and the ways in which its history was represented were to change dramatically.

1970s political and cultural awakening: Sume and the uses of history in Greenlandic rock music

From 1782 until the German occupation of Denmark in 1940, Greenland was a closed country. Foreigners could only travel there with permission from the Danish

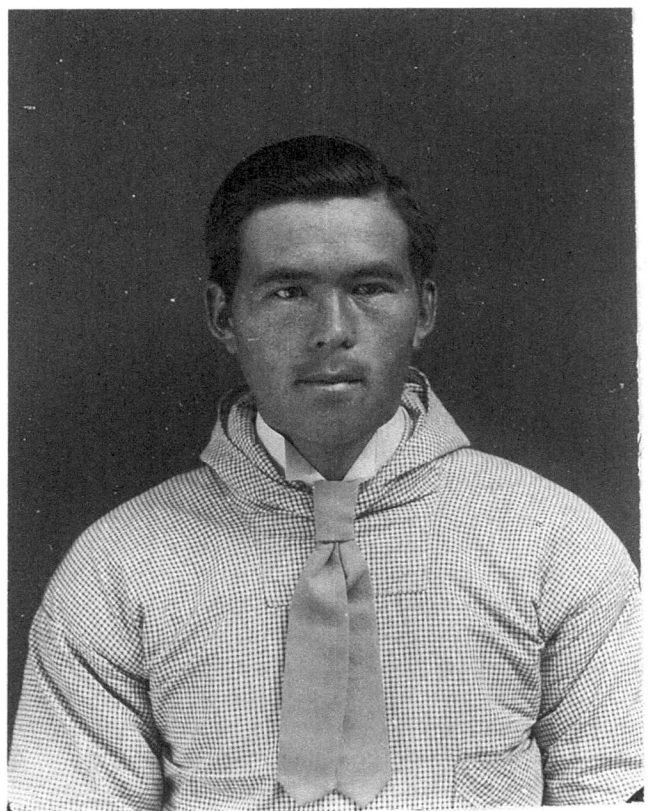

Figure 31.5 Augustinus 'Augo' Telef Nis Lynge
Source: John Møller/Greenland National Museum and Archives

state, and exceptionally few Greenlanders were allowed to travel to Denmark, and only for educational visits.[62] During the Second World War, the German occupation of Denmark forced Greenland to seek support and protection from the U.S., and the two countries agreed that in exchange for cryolite and the usage of Greenlandic soil for American military installations, the U.S. would provide supplies and other necessities. Due to the newly established and successful cod fishery, Greenlanders found themselves with money to spend and, for the first time in Greenlandic history, multiple options for what to spend their money on. Where the Danes had controlled everything from Copenhagen and by default censored how Greenland perceived the world, the Americans had no such interests, and during this period Greenlanders were exposed to a greater variety of media, literature, and consumer products.

When the Second World War ended, pressure from the newly formed United Nations led the former European colonial powers to phase out their respective colonies. Denmark, which had already sold the Danish West Indies (now the Virgin

Islands) to the U.S. in 1917, transitioned into a commonwealth with Greenland and the Faroe Islands in 1954. The phasing out of Greenland's colonial status resulted in two decrees, G-50 and G-60, designed to modernise and centralise Greenland. This modernisation was also known as the Danification of Greenland; the goal was to make the Greenlanders good Danish citizens.[63] The Danish-led government jettisoned its previous focus on Greenlandic language and lifestyle for a prioritisation of Danish language and cultural norms, which had an enormous impact on Greenlanders' ability to practise their culture.[64] By the 1970s, the Greenlandic elite youth, who had studied in Denmark and become politically aware, began to counter the Danification with a Greenlandification.

The 1970s thus marked a return to the 'traditional'. In pre-colonial times and during the colonial era, *aasiviit* (summer camps) were an important social activity for Kalaallit communities. Here, social, economic, and cultural ties were strengthened, and disagreements settled. Inuit from all over Greenland would travel for months to gather at one of the known *aasivik* (summer camp) sites.[65] In the 1970s, this form of social gathering was revitalised,[66] and the Aasivik Movements arranged *aasiviit* from 1976 to 1996, centred around cultural, spiritual, and political engagement.[67] At the forefront of the political tides of Greenland at this time were the rock band Sume.[68,69] Sume played a significant role in raising political awareness in Greenland through their popular rock songs and by being the first to sing Greenlandic lyrics. The lyrics dealt mainly with contemporary society but also incorporated oral histories and reflections on colonial history. Their first album, *Sumut*,[70] demanded a political and cultural awakening from the Greenlandic population. The album cover was a visual representation of this demand: the cover was a reproduction of Aron of Kangeq's woodcut of Qasapi, made 100 years earlier. For a new audience of rock music fans, the image of Qasapi standing over the slain Norse chief represented strength, defiance, and perhaps even the inevitability of Greenlandic independence: if the Kalaallit had forced Northern European settlers out of Greenland once before, then they could do it again.

The 1974 song 'Inuit Nunaat' from their second album of the same name, was especially a call to action. In three short verses Sume summed up the history of Greenland and sketched out their wish for the future, an independent Inuit Nunaat consisting of all the Inuit homelands across the Arctic. Firstly, the band described the Inuit people's arrival in Kalaallit Nunaat and their sustainable way of life ('We lived off the rich nature/And gathered our strengths there'). The mercenary motivations of the Europeans, who 'imposed their way of life' and 'preached holy scriptures', was also referred to: 'Their crowned heads/Commanded them to govern our land/Take the riches[71]/And sell them over our heads'. Finally, the band addressed their own political representatives, who had been 'lulled to sleep' by participation in representative councils which did not give them full power or autonomy. The time for action, Sume argued, was now: 'As a people we will rise/ What our ancestors possessed/Must befall our descendants/It is the lands of Inuit/ They must govern them as one/It must remain in their hands'.[72]

Sume succeeded in 'Greenlandifying' their music by performing a sense of place through the use of *kalaallisut*[73] and by including verses from the pre-colonial drum songs (on the first album). On one track, 'Kalaaliuvunga',[74] from the introduction to their third album, Egon Sikivat drummed on a *qilaat* (traditional frame drum) and sang a drum song. This was the first use of traditional culture in modern Greenlandic music. With their political lyrics and modern rock sound, Sume paved the road for later musicians. Much like the oral histories of the past, music became a way for people to reflect on historical narratives and express contemporary societal criticism. 'Inuit Nunaat', for example, criticised not only the behaviour of Europeans ('the ones with different eyes') during the colonial era, but also the Greenlanders 'who we have voted into the councils' who were represented as complicit with stagnation and oppression.

Sume's calls for self-governance were inspired by, and, in turn, inspired, a movement of young Greenlanders who called for a cultural revival in the form of 'a more Greenlandic Greenland' and came to wield significant influence on the country's political development.[75] Such calls were coeval with Indigenous movements for traditional revitalisation and self-determination; for example, the Sámi ČSV movement in Norway which 'became a rallying call for the Sámi people'.[76] For the Kalaallit, as for the Sámi, such agitation led in time to legislative change: in 1975, a Greenlandic-Danish home rule commission was established, and in 1979 the Home Rule law was enacted, giving Greenland its own parliament (*Inatsisartut*) and a government (*Naalakkersuisut*). While Home Rule gave Greenland responsibility for most domestic policy, matters such as justice affairs (including police, criminal procedures, and the courts of law), defence and national security, financial sectors and monetary system, civil rights law, and foreign affairs were all still under Danish jurisdiction.[77] Furthermore, a large majority of the administrators and public service employees (teachers, police, medical staff, etc.) continued to be Danish, with different wages and conditions for Danish and Greenlandic employees. In addition, academic and popular histories of Greenland continued to be written solely by outsiders.[78] Thus while the advent of Home Rule marked a significant shift in Greenland's governance, relationships between the different groups in Greenlandic society remained strained and often ambiguous.

Art, history, and ethno-aesthetics: Pia Arke at the turn of the twenty-first century

It was in this context of increasing political autonomy but also cultural and social uncertainty that the work of visual artist Pia Arke began to gain prominence. Like most Kalaallit,[79] Arke had a mixed Inuit-European background. The very fact of her existence, then, unsettled the idea of Greenlandic history as a single strand, monolithic and teleological. Using history as a component of her artwork, Arke sought to show that there was more than one colonial history of Greenland,[80] more than one point of departure and more than one way of understanding the course of history. While her work has since been (perhaps mis)interpreted as an 'affected anthropology',[81] it can also be read as a different method of using and disseminating history – by taking it and making it personal.[82]

Arke used herself as a product, a 'mongrel',[83] of one of Greenland's colonial histories, deploying this term to create a 'third space' for her identity, 'a position that would be neither Greenlandic nor Danish'.[84] Through her mixed heritage she created and challenged art in colonial, postcolonial, and decolonial frameworks.[85] Within Arke's body of work, the 2003 *Stories from Scoresbysund* is most easily recognised as a history as art project, and perhaps autoethnographic work, taking the form of a book of narratives and photography.[86] Although all of Arke's work is centred on postcoloniality, identity, and (self-)representation, she presents the colonial decision to relocate the East Greenlanders to Scoresbysund[87] in 1925 not just as an historical fact but as multiple personal narratives of a historic event. The infinitely large becomes the infinitely small in her engagement with the photographic records and witnesses' memories, resulting in minuscule biographies of the inhabitants, both Greenlanders and Danes, of Ittoqqortoormiit. By insisting on using the colonial name Scoresbysund, Arke firmly places the work as colonial history rather than Indigenous history, though the two are interlinked.

Through her essays and other literary compositions, Arke contextualised her work and unraveled entangled colonial, cultural, and national histories, foregrounding the lack of collective colonial memory in Denmark. In her 1995 essay *Ethno-Aesthetics*, Arke defines ethno-aesthetics as 'a description of the West seen from the outside, from the point of view of the "other", from a point of view such as mine, the Greenlander's'.[88] By using an ethno-aesthetic framework instead of engaging in postcolonial studies, Arke changes how the images are viewed and dismantles the binary structure of the West and the 'Other', 'traditional' and 'contemporary'. The focus is not on ethnic non-Westerners, but on how Westerners have reproduced images of themselves in their imaginings of the 'Other'. Here and in other works, Arke explores problematic representations of Inuit. Her 1997 work *Arctic Hysteria*,[89] for example, repositions a montage of naked Greenlandic women instructed to pose in front of the camera, interspersing them with Western expeditioners in their almost excessive amount of skin clothing. The photographs of more or less naked Inuit women were from the private collections of the Arctic explorers. By juxtaposing the 'Other' women with the Western men, Arke strips and exposes the male fantasies. She positions the images without moral condemnation, but lets the spectator interpret for themselves.[90] The ethnographical object becomes the lens through which we see the photographer, and thus the view becomes ethno-aesthetic (Figure 31.6).

Another way in which Arke's work challenged dominant approaches to Kalaallit history was how she problematised contemporary understandings of Greenlandic art as 'traditional'. In the second chapter of *Ethno-Aesthetics*, 'Eskimo Art', Arke discusses how ethno-aesthetics implicitly permeate Bodil Kaalund's book *Grønlands Kunst* [The Art of Greenland] (1990).[91] Kaalund approaches the subject of Greenlandic art from an art-history, linguistic-history, and theoretical angle, but Arke points out that linguistically this is problematic, since there exists no original word for art in Kalaallisut. The artificially created Kalaallisut word for art, *eqqumiitsuliorneq*, can mean either something odd and peculiar or something artificial. However when Kaalund discusses the term she leaves out this second

Figure 31.6 Pia Arke, early collage sketch from c. 1996–97 for the photo montage *Arctic Hysteria* alias *Arctic Hysteria IV* (1997). The original collage has since been lost (Søren Arke)

meaning, thus limiting her definition of art to objects that are 'natural'. This definition is borne out in the book's contents, which avoid any discussion of Greenlandic abstract art and instead present a catalogue of archaeological artefacts, hunting tools, handicrafts, utensils, clothing, and accessories.[92] By her choice of objects, Kaalund thus proclaims that Greenlandic art is natural, authentic, and purposeful. A Greenlander is then automatically an artist, because everything a Greenlander makes is artfully made; art is an integral part of any Inuit product.[93] Somehow, in the Inuit world, everything and nothing becomes art. For Arke, if the objects in Kaalund's book alone represented Greenland's art, then most modern Greenlandic artists would not be able to call themselves 'artists' or even perhaps 'Greenlandic', because most modern Greenlandic artists no longer produce exclusively 'natural' or 'purposeful' artworks. This discussion sparked a still-ongoing debate: what is Greenlandic art? Who can be categorised as a Greenlandic artist?

The arguments Kaalund presents when deciphering *eqqumiitsuliorneq* lean towards a Western understanding of the concept of art. Yet the objects she presents as Greenland's art does not fit the mould of Western art. Instead, the ethnographica[94] confirm Kaalund's view as that of a Westerner. Kaalund's construction of Greenlandic art as 'traditional', and Arke's critique of her thesis, resonate with a broader European inability to see Greenlanders (or Indigenous peoples more generally) as 'modern', creating a repressive notion of authenticity which imagines them as fixed in history, without access to contemporary forms of meaning-making and self-expression.[95] In the Greenlandic context, Søren Rud has described how nineteenth-century definitions of the authentic Greenlander as a hunter and kayakker meant that post-contact, hybrid Greenlandic activities and identities were classified as inauthentic and therefore un-Greenlandic.[96] In the early twentieth century, as we have seen, Mathias Storch and Augo Lynge critiqued this romanticised association of Greenlandicness with hunting and kayakking, instead emphasising the potential of modern industries and the role of Western-educated Greenlanders in building their country's future. Eighty years later, Arke took discussions of Greenlandic history beyond the monolithic and the teleological, instead focusing on the micro-level, the feminine, and the 'mongrel'. This focus on the personal, hybrid, and pluralistic nature of Greenlandic histories was ground-breaking at the time, and – as we shall see in the next section – continues to be a major influence on Kalaallit artists today.

The uses of history in contemporary Greenland: literature, music, and oral histories

With the passing of the Self-Government Act (SGA) in June 2009, Greenland was granted the right to eventual full independence from Denmark. The Naalakkersuisut (parliament) of Greenland is now responsible for most governmental portfolios – notably mineral exploration – although the State constitution, citizenship, the supreme court, security and foreign affairs, and currency and monetary politics all remain under Danish control. With its 'main focus on modern nation-building within the framework of Western institutionalisation', the SGA has been described as 'a unique means of implementing indigenous self-government', and an 'inspiration for other Indigenous peoples, especially other Inuit in the Arctic'.[97] One result of the SGA has been to accelerate the economic development of mineral extraction. Revenue from mining is a key prerequisite for the country's independence. Yet while the SGA gave Greenland both the means of obtaining and the legal right to full independence from Denmark, Greenlanders themselves have a wide variety of views on whether this will be possible, or even desirable, in the future.

Uncertainty about the future necessarily affects how Greenlanders represent their pasts, and young Greenlandic artists, musicians, and writers today tend to emphasise the intersectionality of their identities; rather than identifying primarily as Greenlanders, Danes, or even 'mongrels'. One such figure is Pivinnguaq Mørch, whose writing career began in 2013 when he became one of the ten winners of the Allatta![98] writing competition. His literary work is centred around social realism and explores existential themes related to everyday life and the coming of age in contemporary Greenland. Mørch narrates the inner history and lives of regular people. He presents their hardships and successes in a no-nonsense manner. Through contrasts, he uses the minutiae of daily lives to critique the shortcomings of the Greenlandic government and elite in the failed caretaking of the Greenlandic people. In his poem 'Nunap inua' (Carnal Man), Mørch paints an image of the dangers of progress for its own sake.[99] The Greenlandic people are embodied by the carnal man, who is easily hurt by knives. The poem is a critique of the government and some of the seemingly impulsive decisions it has made over the years in the name of progress, with the second stanza referencing past and projected future foreign mining activity: 'Many a surgeon sheaths the crust of the land/coveting every bit of it/in the name of progress/and makes their profit.'[100] In the quest for progress and profit, the land and the people suffer, but the fault is their own because they voted for the politicians in power: 'In a state repeatedly stabbed by a knife/ it hurts severely/And when my heart was hurt I realise/that it acquiesced.' Mørch paints contemporary Greenlandic society in a rather stark light, where ambition trumps charity.

Another young Greenlandic writer, Niviaq Korneliussen, rose to prominence in the Greenlandic literary scene with the publication of her 2014 novel, *Homo. Sapienne*, which was published in English in 2018 under the title *Crimson*.[101] The novel is based on the lives of five young queer Greenlanders, and is narrated by each, in turn. While Korneliussen's narrative is based in the present and does not refer directly to historical events, her characters' backstories and the ways they understand their lives are based on particular understandings of the country's history.

When Inuk, who has left Greenland after a failed affair with a married politician, reflects on his home country, all he can see is decay and corruption and he is 'ashamed of being a Greenlander'.[102] Yet, exiled in Denmark, he realises that he will never fit in there either: 'I can't act like the Danes. I'm unable to imitate them. I can't share Danish values. I don't respect them.'[103] Part of Inuk's frustration with Greenland is 'that Greenlanders are so full of anger', and yet he reveals that he is himself sick with anger: anger that he looks like a Greenlander; anger that he is not a Dane; anger at everyone else's anger.[104] This anger, then, is at least in part an historical anger, informed by centuries of inequality between Danes and Greenlanders and their legacy for Greenlanders today (Figure 31.7).

Later, having processed his own emotion, Inuk writes to his friend Arnaq, who earlier in the novel caused his departure from Greenland by making public the news of his affair. Here, Inuk writes that Arnaq has a 'history' of her own, which she uses to justify her often immoral behaviour to herself and others:

> I know your history. I know you're struggling with problems in your life. I know who you are. I know that my parents weren't alcoholics even though they grew up under Danish rule. I know that my parents weren't neglected as children. I know that I wasn't neglected the way you were. What you've experienced is awful; I'm aware of that. Your struggle is tough; I can well understand. But let me tell you this: you're responsible for your own actions. Believe me when I say I've been to hell and back, but I don't blame others when the fault is mine… Stop feeling so sorry for yourself because there's no reason that you should be pitied. Enough of this postcolonial shit.[105]

Critics have interpreted this, and other passages in the book, as indicative of Korneliussen's view that Greenlanders need to take responsibility for the problems in their society rather than blaming them on the colonial past. While sympathetic to Arnaq's suffering and the history (both personal and national) that has caused it, Inuk challenges Arnaq to overcome the 'postcolonial' narrative that, as he sees it, traps her in a constant cycle of victimhood.[106] Yet Inuk's is not the only voice

Figure 31.7 The cover of Niviaq Korneliussen's *HOMO sapienne*
Source: Milik Publishing, 2014

in Korneliussen's novel; other characters Arnaq, Fia, Sara, and Ivik all have their own take on the impact of Greenland's colonial history on their lives. By telling a complex, multi-layered story which includes contrasting and sometime conflicting perspectives on Greenland's history, *Crimson* reprises Arke's focus on hybrid, pluralistic Greenlandic identities for a millennial, global audience. Here, differing interpretations of Greenlandic history mediate the relationship between present and past, Greenland and Denmark, self and other, though history is not seen to be the only factor at play, nor does re-framing history alone hold all the solutions.

A similar theme runs through the work of the young Greenlandic rapper Tarrak (Josef Tarrak Petrussen), whose song 'Tupilak' was released on his Facebook page in August 2016 and has since been viewed 135,400 times there and 49,000 times on YouTube.[107] In 'Tupilak', Tarrak directly links the discrimination with which *qallunaat* (Danes) currently treat Greenlanders to the country's colonial history. Standing at the foot of the colonial-era statue of Hans Egede (a contested monument which has long been a target for protest and graffiti), Tarrak recounts how he has been targeted with racial slurs; how Greenlanders are discriminated against if they don't speak Danish, yet foreigners who don't speak Kalaallisut 'flow right in' to Greenlandic society and jobs; and refers to the tragic case of a homeless Greenlandic man who was denied treatment at a hospital in Copenhagen in 2014. The *qallunaat*, Tarrak charges, is nothing but a *tupilak* – an avenging spirit created 'by holding onto bad thoughts and energies, which grow and distort you, so that you become one with your own hate'.[108] Yet while *qallunaat* behave reprehensibly, 'looking down on us from up there', Tarrak does not 'put all the blame on [them]'.[109] Greenlanders need to snap out of apathy and 'WAKE UP/TALK BACK/BE MAD/ MAKE YOURSELF/BE INDEPENDENT'; until they do, Tarrak quips, 'I'm gonna say we are tupilak.' Here, as Kirsten Thisted has observed, Tarrak is 'neither going after Danes nor Greenlanders, but rather the unhealthy relations in which they are stuck'.[110]

In the video for 'Tupilak', Tarrak wears a 'Pray for Pac' cap, a sartorial choice that links him to the North American rapper Tupac, the oppression of African American peoples and to global hip hop culture (often associated with globally minoritised groups, including Indigenous groups)[111] more generally. However, Tarrak never loses sight of the local context that is the subject of his song, a context that for him is defined by the vastly different opportunities available to Danes and Greenlanders in contemporary Greenland. While Tarrak aims for a future in which both groups can overcome the 'cursed' history of vengeance and counter-vengeance, his song suggests, in Thisted's words, that 'the border between Greenlandic and Danish seems to still be constitutive of Greenlandic identity'.[112]

In a more recent song, 'Qimiinnarl'[113] ('Meaningless Suicide'), uploaded to Youtube in June 2019, Tarrak delves deeper into Greenland's social problems, linking alcoholism, depression, and suicide to several internal factors: bullying – both on and offline; a history of social and family dysfunction in urban Greenland; political corruption; tall poppy syndrome; and the prioritisation of 'the elite' over the 'weak ones'.[114] Yet if Greenlanders are primarily to blame for the problems they face today, these problems have their roots in the history of colonisation – for example, in the second verse, he sings, 'They are shutting off the lights, and we need the light/ And the ones they're working for are the new Qullissat' [a Danish coal mine near Ilulissat which the Danish authorities closed in 1972, forcing Greenlandic workers to relocate to other settlements]. For Tarrak, then, Greenland's current social problems are inextricably linked to the country's history: its colonisation and cultural and political domination by Denmark; the persistent gap between Danish-speaking Greenlandic elites and non-Danish-speaking Greenlanders; and the inferiority complex of Greenlanders who fail to stand up for themselves and their people.

In his music, Tarrak uses history to draw links between contemporary issues in Greenland and its past, including images of historical monuments and important institutions such as the G-50 concrete apartment buildings and the Inatsisartut, Greenland's parliament. It also references to historical events such as the closure of the mine at Qullissat and the music of Sume ('let's give SUME a comeback'), in order to show how history lives on in Greenland today. Like Korneliussen, he idenitifies apathy, self-pity, and despair as some of the major obstacles preventing the Kalaallit from breaking the chains of history and achieving independence (both personal and national) and equality. However, Tarrak also acknowledges that these emotions also have their root in centuries of colonial subjugation, a continuing factor which plays out in all sectors of society, including but not limited to health, education, and politics.

In different ways, and for different audiences, these three young Greenlandic artists use history to explore the relationship between personal and collective agency and larger social forces: colonisation, political corruption, inequality, poverty, addiction, and hopelessness. Tarrak and Mørch emphasise historical injustice more than Korneliussen, for whom personal responsibility is central to addressing contemporary Kalaallit social problems. But by engaging with, criticising, and ultimately writing their own stories about Greenland's past all three use history to unsettle comfortable orthodoxies and to imagine new futures for their people.

Conclusion

Seventeen years ago the Danish scholar Kirsten Thisted argued that 'the power to represent Greenland and the Greenlanders abroad still to a very large degree rests with the Danes'.[115] However, despite unequal power dynamics, Greenlanders have always been able to represent themselves and their history, and have done so in ways that are creative, subversive, and often profoundly affecting. Over the almost 300 years since the Dano-Norwegian colonisation of Greenland, Greenlanders' experiences, perspectives, and opportunities to represent themselves and their histories have, of course, changed enormously. However, persistent themes run through the works surveyed in this chapter: how to live with colonial and/or decolonising power dynamics; how to cope with uncertainty about the future; the struggle to maintain or revive Kalaallit language and culture while take advantage of the opportunities of engagement with new cultures; the stark contrast between Greenlandic and European relationships to land and nature; tension between different models of economic development; the social problems caused by colonisation and continuing inequality; the hybrid and dynamic nature of Greenlandic culture; and the difficulties that accompany knowing or acknowledging, representing, and ultimately transcending personal and collective pasts.

By seeking to understand their lives and those of their countrypeople through reflecting upon and retelling their histories, Greenlandic artists, writers, and musicians have created a rich body of work that tells the history of Greenland in more detailed, nuanced, and provocative ways than the conventional 'canon' of academic and popular histories of Greenland. However, Greenlanders who sought to represent their own pasts were never 'just' writing against a European tradition of representation; rather, they were making significant interventions in national discussions around identity, economics, and politics. As Greenlandic histories written by and for Greenlanders become more widespread, this body of local knowledge will continue to be transformed by new forms and ways of telling histories, and Greenlanders themselves will hopefully be recognised in the role they have always played as producers of, rather than merely subjects of, Greenlandic histories.

Notes

1. The authors would like to thank the editors of this volume, along with Søren Thuesen and Benjamin Silverstein for their helpful comments on earlier drafts of this chapter. Any remaining errors are entirely our own.
2. See, for example, H.C. Petersen, *Grønlændernes historie før 1925* [Greenlanders' History before 1925] (Nuuk: Atuakkiorfik, 1991); Tupaarnaq Rosing Olsen, *I Skyggen af Kajakkerne* [In the Shadow of the Kajaks] (Nuuk: Atuakkiorfik, 2005).
3. Saamaatta, *Vi forstår fortiden, vi tager ansvar for nutiden, vi arbejder sammen for en bedre fremtid : Betænkning udgivet af Grønlands Forsoningskommission* [We understand the past, we take responsibility for the future, we work together for a better future: Report issued by the Greenlandic Reconciliation Commission] (Nuuk: Toptryk, December 2017), 45.
4. Inge Kleivan, 'Historie og historier i Grønland' [History and (Hi)stories in Greenland], in *Klaus Khan Baba: en etnografisk kaleidoskopi tilegnet Klaus Ferdinand den 19. April 1991*, ed. S. Dybbroe (Aarhus: Aarhus Universitetsforlag, 1991), 235–236.
5. Petersen, *Grønlændernes Historie*, 14.
6. Yvon Csonka, 'Changing Inuit Historicities in West Greenland and Nunavut,' *History and Anthropology* 16, no. 3 (2005): 324–325.
7. Frederic Laugrand, 'Mythology of the Inuit,' in *Encyclopedia of the Arctic* 2, ed. M. Nuttall (New York: Routledge, 2005), 551–552. Note that these two terms are now more commonly referred to as *oqalualaarut* and *oqaluttuaq* in most of west Greenland, while the above terms are still used in the south.
8. Kleivan, 'Historie og historier,' 236.
9. Csonka, 'Changing Inuit Historicities,' 326.
10. Kirsten Thisted, 'On Narrative Expectations: Greenlandic Oral Traditions about the Cultural Encounter between Inuit and Norsemen,' *Scandinavian Studies* 73, no. 3 (2001): 277.
11. Hans Egede was the instigator of both the Lutheran mission to, and the Dano-Norwegian colonisation of, Greenland in 1721. His 1741 work *Den Gamle Grønlands nye Perlustration* was at the time the most comprehensive account of Greenland's natural history ever undertaken. It was translated into English and Dutch in 1745 and 1746, respectively. For the English translation, see Egede, *A Description of Greenland* (London: C. Hitch, 1745). David Cranz was a member of the Moravian Brethren who travelled to Greenland for the purpose of researching and writing a history of the Moravian mission, founded in 1733. His two-volume *Historie von Grönland* became highly influential throughout Europe after its initial publication in German, and within a few short years was translated into English, Swedish, and Dutch. See Cranz, *The History of Greenland: Containing a Description of the Country and its Inhabitants* (London: Brethren's Society for the Propagation, 1767). For an analysis of this text's reception in Greenland and Denmark, see Claire McLisky, 'Cranz Revisited: *Greenland* in Greenland,' in *David Cranz's 1765 'Historie von Grönland': Context, Reception and Resonance*, eds. Felicity Jensz and Christina Petterson (University Park: Penn State University Press, forthcoming).
12. See, for example, Henric Glahn, *Anmærkninger over de tre første bøger af Hr. David Crantzes Historie om Grønland* [Remarks on the First Three Books of Mr David Cranz's History of Greenland], 1771, re-published in *Glahns Anmærkninger: 1700-tallets Grønlændere, Et nærbillede*, ed. Mads Lidegaard (Copenhagen: Det Grønlandske Selskab, 1991); Poul Egede, *Efterretninger om Grønland* [Intelligence on Greenland] (Copenhagen: 1788).
13. Jan Andersen, *Poul Hansen Egede: En Grønlandsforsker i 1700-tallet* [Poul Hansen Egede: A Greenland Researcher in the Eighteenth Century] (Aalborg: Aalborg Universitetsforlag, 2007).
14. Christian Berthelsen, 'Greenlandic Literature: Its Traditions, Changes and Trends,' *Arctic Anthropology* 23, nos. 1/2 (1986): 340.

15 See, for example, Hans Egede's claim that Pápa could 'talk, write and sing from our Danish books'. Søren Thuesen, Hans Christian Gulløv, Inge Seiding, and Peter A. Toft, 'Erfaringer, ekspansion og konsolidering 1721–82' [Experiences, Expansion and Consolidation 1721–82], in *Grønland: den Arktiske Koloni*, ed. Hans Christian Gulløv (Copenhagen: Gads Forlag, 2017), 63.
16 Egede, *A Description of Greenland*, 151, 155–159. The song is also reprinted in Christian Berthelsen, *Grønlandsk Litteratur: en kommenteret antologi* (Copenhagen: Centrum, 1983), 28–30.
17 See Søren Thuesen, 'Grønlænderne og det Danske Kongehus – Magt, Ceremonier og Følelser' [Greenlanders and the Danish Royal Family – Power, Ceremony and Emotion], in *Grønlændernes syn på Danmark: Historiske, Kulturelle og Sproglige Perspektiver*, eds. Ole Høiris and Ole Marquardt (Aarhus: Aarhus Universitetsforlag, 2019), 236–238; Flemming A.J. Nielsen, 'Hyldest til Christian VI – Begyndelsen til en Grønlandsk Litteratur,' in *Grønlandsk Kultur- og Samfundsforskning 2015–2017*, eds. Birgit Kleist Pedersen, Flemming A. J. Nielsen, Karen Langgård, Kennet Pedersen, and Jette Rygaard (Ilisimatusarfik: Forlaget Atuagkat, 2017), 50–51.
18 Thuesen, 'Grønlænderne,' 238.
19 Nielsen, 'Hyldest,' 50.
20 Thuesen (2019) and Thuesen et al. (2017) note the discrepancy between the two versions but do not comment on its significance. See Thuesen, 'Grønlænderne,' 238; Thuesen et al., 'Erfaringer,' 62.
21 Rie Odgaard and Agnete Weis Bentzon, 'The Interplay Between Collective Rights and Obligations and Individual Rights,' *The European Journal of Development Research* 10, no. 2 (1998): 105–116. Some argue that collectivism is a characteristic of Indigenous approaches to property ownership across the globe. See, for example, Julian Brave NoiseCat, 'Slaying the Carbon-Consuming Colonial Hydra: Indigenous Contributions to Climate Action,' *Development* 59 (2016): 199.
22 Claudia Orange, *The Treaty of Waitangi* (Wellington: Bridget Williams Books, 2015), 31.
23 Poul Grønlænder's letter, published in Poul Egede, *Efterretninger om Grønland*, 230–236. Translation by Kirstine Eiby Møller.
24 Poul Grønlænder's letter, in Egede, *Efterretninger om Grønland*, 232.
25 Poul Grønlænder's letter, in Egede, *Efterretninger om Grønland*, 233.
26 Ann Fienup-Riordan, 'The Real People and the Children of Thunder,' in *Eskimo Essays: Yup'ik Lives and How We See Them*, ed. Ann Fienup-Riordan (New Brunswick: Rutgers University Press, 1991), 71–93.
27 Fienup-Riordan, 'The Real People,' 72.
28 Richard Broome, '"There Were Vegetables Every Year Mr Green Was Here": Right Behaviour and the Struggle for Autonomy at Coranderrk Aboriginal Reserve,' *History Australia* 3, no. 2 (2006): 43.1–43.16. In the Australian context, ongoing work explores this concept of 'right', or 'lawful' behaviour and its implications for how we understand lawful relations between Europeans and Indigenous peoples, both in the past and today. See, for example, Julie Evans, 'The Ethos of the Historian: The Minutes of Evidence Project, and Lives Lived with Law on the Ground,' *Law Text Culture* 20 (2016): 136–163.
29 Poul Grønlænder's letter, in Egede, *Efterretninger om Grønland*, 233.
30 Berthelsen, *Grønlandsk Litteratur*, 31.
31 In works such as these, European writers co-opted Indigenous peoples' voices in order to draw attention to the loss of virtues amongst urban modern Europeans, who they perceived to have strayed from godliness. Works in this genre included Charles-Louis de Secondat Montequieu's *Persian Letters* (1721) and Gian-Paolo Maranas' *Letters from a Turkish Spy* (1682). See Michael Harbsmeier, *Stimmen aus dem äussersten Norden. Wie die Grönländer Europa für sich entdeckten* (Stuttgart: Jan Thorbecke Verlag, 2001), 69–78.

32 Harbsmeier, *Stimmen*, 72. This 'realism of empathy', Harbsmeier argues, is 'an exception in the European context that is characteristic of the Danish apprach in Greenland'.
33 Harbsmeier, *Stimmen*, 73.
34 Inge Kleivan, 'Poul Egede,' in *Grønland. En refleksiv udfordring*, ed. Ole Høiris (Århus: Aarhus Universitetsforlag, 2009), 122.
35 Petersen, *Grønlændernes historie*, 31.
36 See, for example, Hans Egede, *Description of Greenland* (London: T. & J. Allman, 1818); Religious Tract and Book Society for Ireland, *Greenland Missions: With Biographical Sketches of Some of the Principal Converts* (Dublin: Thomas I. White, 1831); Wilhelm August Graah, *Narrative of an Expedition to the East Coast of Greenland, Sent by Order of the King of Denmark, in Search of the Lost Colonies, Under the Command of Captain W.A. Graah*, trans. G. Gordon McDougall (London: John W. Parker, 1837); Fridjtof Nansen, *The First Crossing of Greenland* (Longmans, Green & Company, 1890).
37 Karen Langgård, 'An Examination of Greenlandic Awareness of Ethnicity and National Self-consciousness through Texts Produced by Greenlanders 1860s–1920s,' *Etudes/Inuit/Studies* 22, no. 1 (1998): 85.
38 Langgård, 'An Examination,' 86.
39 Karen Langgård, 'Greenlandic Attitudes towards Norwegians and Danes from Nansen's Icecap Crossing to the 1933 World Court Verdict in The Hague,' *Etudes/Inuit/Studies* 38, no. 1/2 (2014): 53–71. See also Langgård, 'An Examination,' 104.
40 Kirsten Thisted, *Således skriver jeg, Aron*, [Thus Write I, Aron] (Nuuk: Atuakkiorfik, 1999), 20; Eigil Knuth, 'Aron fra Kangeq' [Aron of Kangeq], in *Nationalmuseets Arbejdsmark 1960* (Copenhagen: National Museum, 1960), 49.
41 Thisted, *Således*. Aron from Kangeq published a total of 56 oral histories with 350 artworks depicting the histories.
42 Thisted, *Således*, 7.
43 Thisted, *Således*, 70; Knuth, 'Aron,' 52.
44 See Knuth, 'Aron,' 56; Birgitte Sonne, 'Genuine Humans and "Others": Criteria of "Otherness" at the Beginning of Colonization in Greenland,' in *Cultural and Social Research in Greenland 95/96. Essays in Honour of Robert Petersen*, ed. Birgitte Jacobsen (Nuuk: Atuakkiorfik, 1996), 244.
45 Knuth, 'Aron,' 56.
46 The Norsemen lived on the southwest coast of Greenland for approximately 400 years from the tenth century, but their settlements began to decline in the fourteenth century due to climatic change which made trade with Europe, and survival in colder conditions, difficult. As Kirsten Thisted has observed, nineteenth-century Greenlandic stories such as Aron's do not represent factual accounts of their meetings with the Norse but are rather complicated cultural texts which reflect both European and Greenlandic 'narrative expectations'. See Thisted, 'On Narrative Expectations.'
47 This story had been recounted to Peter Nissen, a priest in Julianehåb (1853–1862) by a Greenlander named Jonathan, who was also known as Saamik. The version told here is simplified for brevity; for a fuller version, see Thisted, 'On Narrative Expectations,' 269–271.
48 While the exact causes of the failure of the Norse settlement are still uncertain, new archaeological research suggests that changing climate combined with a drop in the price of ivory (now believed to be the Norsemen's main motivation for settling Greenland and their primary source of income) led to emigration and a slowly dwindling population rather than extermination through conflict with the Inuit. See Eli Kintisch, 'The Lost Norse,' *Science* 354, no. 6313 (11 November 2016): 696–701.
49 Thisted, 'On Narrative Expectations,' 293. Thisted's point here resonates with later work by Sara Ahmed on stories about strangers and the complicated work that they do in 'multicultural' societies. See Ahmed, *Strange Encounters: Embodied Others in Post-Coloniality* (Routledge, 2013).
50 Thisted, 'On Narrative Expectations,' 293.

51 Thisted, 'On Narrative Expectations,' 292.
52 Thisted, 'On Narrative Expectations,' 293.
53 See, for example, H. Rink, *Tales and Traditions of the Eskimo* (Edinburgh and London: W. Blackwood and Sons, 1875); W. Thalbitzer, *The Ammassalik Eskimo: Contributions to the Ethnology of the East Greenland Natives* (Meddelelser om Grønland series, vols. 39 and 40; Copenhagen: Printed by B. Luno, 1914).
54 Mathias Storch, *Singnagtugaq: A Greenlander's Dream* (1915), trans. Torben Hutchings (Copenhagen: International Polar Institute Press, 2016), 39–40.
55 Storch, *Singnagtugaq*, 97.
56 Storch, *Singnagtugaq*, 120.
57 As Thisted observes, 'the novel illustrates the connection between the development of the individual (through religion, education and the emergence of national consciousness), and the development of society as a whole.' Thisted, 'Grönländische Literatur' [Greenlandic Literature], in *Skandinavische Literaturgeschichte*, ed. I.J. Glauser, 2nd ed. (Stuttgart: Verlag J.B. Metzler, 2016), 508–527.
58 Translated into Danish in 1989.
59 Langgård, 'An Examination,' 102.
60 Søren Rud, 'Grønland til Debat, 1909–1935' [Greenland in Debate, 1909–1935], in *Grønland: Den Arktiske Koloni*, 274.
61 For description and analysis of these policies, see Søren Rud, *Colonialism in Greenland* (London: Palgrave Macmillan, 2017), 33–54.
62 Ole Marquardt, Inge Seiding, Niels Frandsen and Søren Thuesen, 'Koloniale Strategier i en Ny Samfundsorden 1845–1904' [Colonial Strategies in a New Social Order 1845–1904], in *Grønland: Den Arktiske Koloni*, 174–176.
63 Lill Rastad Bjørst, *En anden verden: Fordomme og stereotype om Grønland og Arktis* [A Different World: Prejudice and Stereotypes on Greenland and the Arctic] (Copenhagen: Forlaget BIOS, 2008), 23–24.
64 Karen Langgård, 'Literature, Greenlandic,' in *Encyclopedia of the Arctic*, 1185.
65 Sermermiut near Ilulissat, Taseralik near Sisimiut, Kangeq near Nuuk, Uunartoq near Nanortalik, and Aluk in the southeast corner of Greenland.
66 The summer camps of the 1970s–1990s also focused on revitalising pre-colonial intangible cultural elements, such as *qilaatersorneq* (drum dancing and singing), *uaajeerneq* (mask dancing), and *qajaq* (kayak) building and paddling. For more on this, see Hjalmar Dahl, *Aasivik – Inuit isumasioqatigiiffiat* [Summercamps – Places of Inuit Counsels] (Nuuk: Atuakkiorfik 2005), 75–77.
67 Dahl, *Aasivik*, 9.
68 Literal translation of Sume: Where?
69 For the seminal importance of Sume in the political and social history of Greenland, the documentary *Sume – the Sound of a Revolution* by Inuk Silis Høegh (2014) is highly recommended.
70 Literal translation: Where to?
71 By riches, the band did not mean monetary wealth but the natural resources of the land.
72 Translation by Kirstine Eiby Møller.
73 The Greenlandic language.
74 Literal translation: I am a Greenlander.
75 Jens Heinrich, 'For a Greenlandic Independence,' in *Being Indigenous: Perspectives on Activism, Culture, Language and Identity*, ed. Neyooxet Greymorning (Abingdon: Routledge, 2018), chapter 9.
76 Ivar Bjørklund, *Sápmi: Becoming a Nation: The Emergence of a Sami National Community* (Tromsø: Tromsø University Museum, 2000), 29.
77 'Politics in Greenland,' Naalakkersuisut [Government of Greenland], https://naalakkersuisut.gl/en/About-government-of-greenland/About-Greenland/Politics-in-Greenland.

78 The most comprehensive history of Greenland to be published during this period was the Danish historian Finn Gad's three-volume *The History of Greenland* (its three volumes published in 1967, 1969 and 1976, with English translations in 1970, 1971 [London: C. Hurst] and 1983 [Copenhagen: Nyt Nordisk Forlag]). For a brief survey of Greenlandic historiography from 1946–2000 see Harry Haue, 'Greenland – History Teaching in a Former Danish Colony,' *Yearbook of the International Society for History Didactics* 25 (2014): 101–114.
79 More than 80% of Greenlanders today come from a mixed Inuit-European heritage. See Ida Moltke et al., 'Uncovering the Genetic History of the Present-Day Greenlandic Population,' *American Journal of Human Genetics* 96, no. 1 (2015): 54–69.
80 Classical Danish and Greenlandic colonial history presents West Greenland as colonised in 1721, East Greenland in 1895, and Northern Greenland in 1910.
81 'Affected anthropology' is a term coined specifically to describe Pia Arke's work. It is used to explain how she engaged with her subjects 'from below' through her mixed background. See Kuratorisk Aktion, *Tupilakosaurus – an Incomplete(able) Survey of Pia Arke's Artistic Work and Research* (Copenhagen: Pia Arke Society, 2012), 93–98.
82 Pia Arke, *Scoresbysundhistorier: Fotografier, Kolonisering og Kortlægning* [Stories from Scoresbysund – Photographs, Colonisation and Mapping] (Valby: Borgen, 2003), 11.
83 Stefan Jonsson, 'Förbundna i tystnad. Pia Arke utforskar banden mellan Grönland och Danmark' [Connected in Silence. Pia Arke Explores the Relationship between Greenland and Denmark], *Dagens Nyheter*, 18 March 1995. https://www.dn.se/arkiv/kultur/forbundna-i-tystnad-pia-arke-utforskar-banden-mellan-gronland-och-danmark/
84 Kirsten Thisted, 'De-framing the Indigenous Body. Ethnography, Landscape and Cultural Belonging in the Art of Pia Arke,' *Nordlit* 16, no. 1 (May 2012): 282.
85 Other works by Arke that circle the themes of colonial history, time, memories, identity, and myths in and about Greenland include *Telegrafi, Nature Morte, Tupilakosaurus, and Legend I–V*.
86 Pia Arke, *Scoresbysundhistorier*. For the English-Greenlandic-Danish version, see *Stories from Scoresbysund, Photographs, Colonisation and Mapping* (Copenhagen: Pia Arke Selskabet, 2010).
87 The Danish name of present-day Ittoqqortoormiit.
88 Pia Arke, *Etnoæstetik* (Århus: Ark, 1995), 12.
89 Also known as *Arctic Hysteria IV*.
90 Kirsten Thisted in Kuratorisk Aktion, *Tupilakosaurus*, 287.
91 Arke, *Etnoæstetik*, chapter 2.
92 Bodil Kaalund, *Grønlands Kunst* (Copenhagen: Gyldendal, 1990).
93 Arke, *Etnoæstetik*, 16.
94 An ethnographica is a collection of ethnographic objects, and represents a colonial legacy of representation through objects. Every former colonial power owns vast ethnographical collections, often to be viewed in their national museums.
95 For an extended definition and discussion of the concept of 'repressive authenticity', see Patrick Wolfe, 'Nation and MiscegeNation: Discursive Continuity in the Post-Mabo Era,' *Social Analysis: The International Journal of Social and Cultural Practice* 36 (1994): 110–118.
96 Søren Rud, 'Erobringen af Grønland: Opdagelsesrejser, Etnologi og Forstanderskab i Attenhundredetallet' [The Conquest of Greenland: Expeditions, Anthropology and Colonial Management in the Nineteenth Century], *Historisk tidsskrift* (2006): 498.
97 Rauna Kuokkanen, '"To See What State We Are In": First Years of the Greenland Self-Government Act and the Pursuit of Inuit Sovereignty,' *Ethnopolitics* 16, no. 2 (2017): 193.
98 Literal translation: Let's write! The competition is the result of a collaboration between NAPA (The Nordic Institute in Greenland), Milik Publishing, Nunatta

Atuagaateqarfia (the National Library of Greenland) and Kalaallit Atuakkiortut. For more information see https://napa.gl/en/projects/Allatta.
99 A more direct translation of the poem's title would be 'The Inhabitants'. From Pivinnguaq Mørch, *Arpaatit qaqortut* (Nuuk: Milik publishing, 2005). English translation by Nuka Møller, available at http://transpoesie.eu/poems/826.
100 There have been a total of 15 mines in Greenland, of which two are still active. See Poul Johansen et al., *Minedrift og miljø i Grønland* (Roskilde: Danmarks Miljøundersøgelser, 2001).
101 Niviaq Korneliussen, *Crimson* (London: Virago, 2018).
102 Korneliussen, *Crimson*, 103.
103 Korneliussen, *Crimson*, 103.
104 Korneliussen, *Crimson*, 110.
105 Korneliussen, *Crimson*, 106.
106 See, for example, Tina Maria Winther, 'I Grønland Holder man Kæft' [In Greenland You Keep Quiet], *Politiken*, 23 November 2014, 8; Jean-Francois Villeneuve, 'Enough of This Postcolonial Sh#%,' *Eye on the Arctic*, 1 December 2017, https://www.rcinet.ca/eye-on-the-arctic/2017/12/01/enough-of-this-postcolonial-sh-an-interview-with-greenlandic-author-niviaq-korneliussen/.
107 Josef Tarrak Petrussen, 'Tupilak,' video, 3:41, https://www.facebook.com/JosefTarrakpetrussen/videos/627194077458236. This is an impressive number of watches and sharings given that there are only 56,000 inhabitants in Greenland.
108 Kirsten Thisted, 'Der er en Tupilak i Rummet' [There's a Tupilak in the Room], *Baggrund*, 19 February 2017, https://baggrund.com/2017/02/19/der-er-en-tupilak-rummet/.
109 Petrussen, 'Tupilak.'
110 Thisted, 'Tupilak.'
111 Tony Mitchell, 'Doin' Damage in My Native Language: The Use of "Resistance Vernaculars" in Hip Hop in France, Italy, and Aotearoa/New Zealand,' *Popular Music & Society* 24, no. 3 (2000): 41–54; Chiara Minestrelli, *Australian Indigenous Hip Hop: The Politics of Culture, Identity, and Spirituality* (Abingdon: Routledge, 2016); Crystal McKinnon, 'Indigenous Music as a Space of Resistance,' in *Making Settler Colonial Space: Perspectives on Race, Place and Identity*, eds. Tracey Banivanua Mar and Penelope Edmonds (London: Palgrave Macmillan, 2010), 264.
112 Thisted, 'Tupilak.'
113 Within a month, it had already been watched 26,000 times, recieved 1,284 likes and shared 575 times on Facebook.
114 Josef Tarrak Petrussen, 'Qimiinnarl,' 21 June 2019, video, 5:12, https://www.youtube.com/watch?v=Cs_9E7diAp8.
115 Kirsten Thisted, 'The Power to Represent: Intertextuality and Discourse in Miss Smilla's Sense of Snow,' in *Narrating the Arctic: A Cultural History of Nordic Scientific Practice*, eds. Michael Bravo and Sverker Sörlin (Canton: Science and History Publications, 2002), 312.

Bibliography

Ahmed, Sara. *Strange Encounters: Embodied Others in Post-Coloniality*. New York: Routledge, 2013.
Andersen, Jan. *Poul Hansen Egede: En Grønlandsforsker i 1700-tallet* [Poul Hansen Egede: A Greenland Researcher in the Eighteenth Century]. Aalborg: Aalborg Universitetsforlag, 2007.
Arke, Pia. *Etnoæstetik*. Århus: Ark, 1995.
Arke, Pia. *Scoresbysundhistorier: Fotografier, Kolonisering og Kortlægning* [Stories from Scoresbysund – Photographs, Colonisation and Mapping]. Valby: Borgen, 2003.

Arke, Pia. *Stories from Scoresbysund, Photographs, Colonisation and Mapping*. Copenhagen: Pia Arke Selskabet, 2010.
Berthelsen, Christian. *Grønlandsk Litteratur: en kommenteret antologi*. Copenhagen: Centrum, 1983.
Berthelsen, Christian. 'Greenlandic Literature: Its Traditions, Changes and Trends.' *Arctic Anthropology* 23, nos. 1/2 (1986): 339–345.
Bjørklund, Ivar. *Sápmi: Becoming a Nation: The Emergence of a Sami National Community*, 29. Tromsø: Tromsø University Museum, 2000.
Bjørst, Lill Rastad. *En anden verden: Fordomme og Stereotype om Grønland og Arktis* [A Different World: Prejudice and Stereotypes on Greenland and the Arctic]. Copenhagen: Forlaget BIOS, 2008.
Broome, Richard. '"There Were Vegetables Every Year Mr Green Was Here": Right Behaviour and the Struggle for Autonomy at Coranderrk Aboriginal Reserve.' *History Australia* 3, no. 2 (2006): 43.1–43.16.
Cranz, David. *The History of Greenland: Containing a Description of the Country and its Inhabitants*. London: Brethren's Society for the Propagation, 1767.
Csonka, Yvon. 'Changing Inuit Historicities in West Greenland and Nunavut.' *History and Anthropology* 16, no. 3 (2005): 321–334.
Dahl, Hjalmar. *Aasivik – Inuit isumasioqatigiiffiat* [Summercamps – Places of Inuit Counsels]. Nuuk: Atuakkiorfik, 2005.
Egede, Hans. *A Description of Greenland*. London: C. Hitch, 1745.
Egede, Hans. *Description of Greenland*. London: T. & J. Allman, 1818.
Egede, Poul. *Efterretninger om Grønland* [Intelligence on Greenland]. Copenhagen: 1788.
Evans, Julie. 'The Ethos of the Historian: The Minutes of Evidence Project, and Lives Lived with Law on the Ground.' *Law Text Culture* 20 (2016): 136–163.
Fienup-Riordan, Ann. *Eskimo Essays: Yup'ik Lives and How We See Them*. New Brunswick: Rutgers University Press, 1991.
Gad, Finn. *The History of Greenland Volume I*. London: C. Hurst, 1970.
Gad, Finn. *The History of Greenland Volume II*. London: C. Hurst, 1971.
Gad, Finn. *The History of Greenland Volume III*. Copenhagen: Nyt Nordisk Forlag, 1983.
Glahn, Henric. *Anmærkninger over de tre første bøger af Hr. David Crantzes Historie om Grønland* [Remarks on the First Three Books of Mr David Cranz's History of Greenland], 1771, re-published in *Glahns Anmærkninger: 1700-tallets Grønlændere, Et nærbillede*, edited by Mads Lidegaard. Copenhagen: Det Grønlandske Selskab, 1991.
Graah, Wilhelm August. *Narrative of an Expedition to the East Coast of Greenland, Sent by Order of the King of Denmark, in Search of the Lost Colonies, Under the Command of Captain W.A. Graah*. Translated by G. Gordon McDougall. London: John W. Parker, 1837.
Harbsmeier, Michael. *Stimmen aus dem äussersten Norden. Wie die Grönländer Europa für sich entdeckten*. Stuttgart: Jan Thorbecke Verlag, 2001.
Haue, Harry. 'Greenland – History Teaching in a Former Danish Colony.' *Yearbook of the International Society for History Didactics* 25 (2014): 101–114.
Heinrich, Jens. 'For a Greenlandic Independence.' In *Being Indigenous: Perspectives on Activism, Culture, Language and Identity*, edited by Neyooxet Greymorning, chapter 9. Abingdon: Routledge, 2018.
Johansen, Poul, Gert Asmund, Christian M. Glahder, Peter Aastrup, and Karsten Secher. *Minedrift og miljø i Grønland*. Roskilde: Danmarks Miljøundersøgelser, 2001.
Jonsson, Stefan. 'Förbundna i tystnad. Pia Arke utforskar banden mellem Grönland och Danmark' [Connected in Silence. Pia Arke Explores the Relationship between Greenland and Denmark]. *Dagens Nyheter*, 18 March 1995.
Kaalund, Bodil. *Grønlands Kunst*. Copenhagen: Gyldendal, 1990.
Kintisch, Eli. 'The Lost Norse.' *Science* 354, no. 6313 (11 November 2016): 696–701.
Kleivan, Inge. 'Historie og Historier i Grønland' [History and (Hi)stories in Greenland]. In *Klaus Khan Baba: en etnografisk kaleidoskopi tilegnet Klaus Ferdinand den 19. April 1991*, edited by S. Dybbroe, 234–248. Aarhus: Aarhus Universitetsforlag, 1991.

Knuth, Eigil. 'Aron fra Kangeq' [Aron of Kangeq]. In *Nationalmuseets Arbejdsmark 1960*, edited by Harald Andersen, 45–64. Copenhagen: National Museum, 1960.

Korneliussen, Niviaq. *Crimson*. London: Virago, 2018.

Kuokkanen, Rauna. '"To See What State We Are In": First Years of the Greenland Self-Government Act and the Pursuit of Inuit Sovereignty.' *Ethnopolitics* 16, no. 2 (2017): 179–195.

Kuratorisk Aktion. *Tupilakosaurus – an Incomplete(able) Survey of Pia Arke's Artistic Work and Research*. Copenhagen: Pia Arke Society, 2012.

Langgård, Karen. 'An Examination of Greenlandic Awareness of Ethnicity and National Self-consciousness through Texts Produced by Greenlanders 1860s–1920s.' *Etudes/Inuit/Studies* 22, no. 1 (1998): 83–107.

Langgård, Karen. 'Literature, Greenlandic.' In *Encyclopedia of the Arctic* 2, edited by M. Nuttall, 1184–1186. New York: Routledge, 2005.

Laugrand, Frederic. 'Mythology of the Inuit.' In *Encyclopedia of the Arctic* 2, edited by M. Nuttall, 551–552. New York: Routledge, 2005.

Langgård, Karen. 'Greenlandic Attitudes towards Norwegians and Danes from Nansen's Icecap Crossing to the 1933 World Court Verdict in The Hague.' *Etudes/Inuit/Studies* 38, no. 1/2 (2014): 53–71.

Marquardt, Ole, Inge Seiding, Niels Frandsen, and Søren Thuesen. 'Koloniale strategier i en ny samfundsorden 1845–1904' [Colonial Strategies in a New Social Order 1845–1904]. In *Grønland: den Arktiske Koloni*, edited by Hans Christian Gulløv, 170–235. Copenhagen: Gads Forlag, 2017.

McKinnon, Crystal. 'Indigenous Music as a Space of Resistance.' In *Making Settler Colonial Space: Perspectives on Race, Place and Identity*, edited by Tracey Banivanua Mar and Penelope Edmonds, 255–272. London: Palgrave Macmillan, 2010.

McLisky, Claire. 'Cranz Revisited: *Greenland* in Greenland.' In *Legacies of David Cranz's 'Historie von Grönland'* (1765), edited by Felicity Jensz and Christina Petterson, 263–288. London: Palgrave MacMillan, 2021.

Minestrelli, Chiara. *Australian Indigenous Hip Hop: The Politics of Culture, Identity, and Spirituality*. Abingdon: Routledge, 2016.

Mitchell, Tony. 'Doin' Damage in My Native Language: The Use of "Resistance Vernaculars" in Hip Hop in France, Italy, and Aotearoa/New Zealand.' *Popular Music & Society* 24, no. 3 (2000): 41–54.

Moltke, Ida, Matteo Fumagalli, Thorfinn S. Korneliussen, Jacob E. Crawford, Peter Bjærregaard, Marit E. Jørgensen, Niels Grarup, et al. 'Uncovering the Genetic History of the Present-Day Greenlandic Population.' *American Journal of Human Genetics* 96, no. 1 (2015): 54–69.

Mørch, Pivinnguaq. *Arpaatit qaqortut*. Translated by Nuka Møller. Nuuk: Milik Publishing, 2005. http://transpoesie.eu/poems/826.

Naalakkersuisut [Government of Greenland]. 'Politics in Greenland.' https://naalakkersuisut.gl/en/About-government-of-greenland/About-Greenland/Politics-in-Greenland.

Nansen, Fridjtof. *The First Crossing of Greenland*. London: Longmans, Green & Company, 1890.

Nielsen, Flemming A.J. 'Hyldest til Christian VI – Begyndelsen til en Grønlandsk Litteratur.' In *Grønlandsk Kultur- og Samfundsforskning 2015–2017*, edited by Birgit Kleist Pedersen, Flemming A. J. Nielsen, Karen Langgård, Kennet Pedersen & Jette Rygaard, 50–51. Ilisimatusarfik: Forlaget Atuagkat, 2017.

NoiseCat, Julian Brave. 'Slaying the Carbon-Consuming Colonial Hydra: Indigenous Contributions to Climate Action.' *Development* 59 (2016): 199–204.

Odgaard, Rie, and Agnete Weis Bentzon. 'The Interplay between Collective Rights and Obligations and Individual Rights.' *The European Journal of Development Research* 10, no. 2 (1998): 105–116.

Orange, Claudia. *The Treaty of Waitangi*. Wellington: Bridget Williams Books, 2015.

Petersen, Hans Christian. *Grønlændernes Historie før 1925* [Greenlanders' History before 1925]. Nuuk: Atuakkiorfik, 1991.

Religious Tract and Book Society for Ireland. *Greenland Missions: With Biographical Sketches of Some of the Principal Converts*. Dublin: Thomas I. White, 1831.

Rink, Heinrich. *Tales and Traditions of the Eskimo*. Edinburgh and London: W. Blackwood and Sons, 1875.

Rosing Olsen, Tupaarnaq. *I Skyggen af Kajakkerne* [In the Shadow of the Kajaks]. Nuuk: Atuakkiorfik, 2005.

Rud, Søren. 'Erobringen af Grønland: Opdagelsesrejser, Etnologi og Forstanderskab i Attenhundredetallet' [The Conquest of Greenland: Expeditions, Anthropology and Colonial Management in the Nineteenth Century]. *Historisk tidsskrift* (2006): 488–520.

Rud, Søren. *Colonialism in Greenland*. London: Palgrave Macmillan, 2017.

Rud, Søren. 'Grønland til Debat, 1909–1935' [Greenland in Debate]. In *Grønland: den Arktiske Koloni*, edited by Hans Christian Gulløv, 236–279. Copenhagen: Gads Forlag, 2017.

Saamaatta. *Vi forstår fortiden, vi tager ansvar for nutiden, vi arbejder sammen for en bedre fremtid: Betænkning udgivet af Grønlands Forsoningskommission* [We understand the past, we take responsibility for the future, we work together for a better future: Report issued by the Greenlandic Reconciliation Commission]. Nuuk: Toptryk, December 2017.

Sonne, Birgitte. 'Genuine Humans and "Others": Criteria of "Otherness" at the Beginning of Colonization in Greenland.' In *Cultural and Social Research in Greenland 95/96. Essays in Honour of Robert Petersen*, edited by Birgitte Jacobsen, 241–252. Nuuk: Atuakkiorfik, 1996.

Storch, Mathias. *Singnagtugaq: A Greenlander's Dream* (1915). Translated by Torben Hutchings. Copenhagen: International Polar Institute Press, 2016.

Tarrak Petrussen, Josef. 'Tupilak.' 29 August 2016. Video, 3:41. https://www.facebook.com/JosefTarrakpetrussen/videos/627194077458236/.

Tarrak Petrussen, Josef. 'Qimiinnarl.' 21 June 2019. Video, 5:12. https://www.youtube.com/watch?v=Cs_9E7diAp8.

Thalbitzer, William. *The Ammassalik Eskimo: Contributions to the Ethnology of the East Greenland Natives*. Meddelelser om Grønland series, vols. 39 and 40. Copenhagen: Printed by B. Luno, 1914.

Thisted, Kirsten. 'De-framing the Indigenous Body: Ethnography, Landscape and Cultural Belonging in the Art of Pia Arke.' *Nordlit* 16, no. 1 (May 2012): 282.

Thisted, Kirsten. *Således Skriver Jeg, Aron* [Thus Write I, Aron]. Nuuk: Atuakkiorfik, 1999.

Thisted, Kirsten. 'On Narrative Expectations: Greenlandic Oral Traditions about the Cultural Encounter between Inuit and Norsemen.' *Scandinavian Studies* 73, no. 3 (2001): 253–296.

Thisted, Kirsten. 'The Power to Represent: Intertextuality and Discourse in Miss Smilla's Sense of Snow.' In *Narrating the Arctic: A Cultural History of Nordic Scientific Practice*, edited by Michael Bravo and Sverker Sörlin, 311–342. Canton: Science and History Publications, 2002.

Thisted, Kirsten. 'Grönländische Literatur' [Greenlandic Literature]. In *Skandinavische Literaturgeschichte*, edited by I.J. Glauser, 2nd ed., 508–527. Stuttgart: Verlag J.B. Metzler, 2016.

Thisted, Kirsten. 'Der er en Tupilak i Rummet' [There's a Tupilak in the Room]. *Baggrund*, 19 February 2017. https://baggrund.com/2017/02/19/der-er-en-tupilak-rummet/.

Thuesen, Søren, Hans Christian Gulløv, Inge Seiding, and Peter A. Toft. 'Erfaringer, Ekspansion og Konsolidering 1721–82' [Experiences, Expansion and Consolidation 1721–82]. In *Grønland: den Arktiske Koloni*, edited by Hans Christian Gulløv, 44–107. Copenhagen: Gads Forlag, 2017.

Thuesen, Søren. 'Grønlænderne og det Danske Kongehus – Magt, Ceremonier og Følelser' [Greenlanders and the Danish Royal Family – Power, Ceremony and Emotion]. In *Grønlændernes syn på Danmark: historiske, kulturelle og sproglige perspektiver*, edited by Ole Høiris and Ole Marquardt, 219–268. Aarhus: Aarhus Universitetsforlag, 2019.

Villeneuve, Jean-Francois. 'Enough of This Postcolonial Sh#%.' *Eye on the Arctic*, 1 December 2017. https://www.rcinet.ca/eye-on-the-arctic/2017/12/01/enough-of-this-postcolonial-sh-an-interview-with-greenlandic-author-niviaq-korneliussen/.
Winther, Tina Maria. 'I Grønland Holder man Kæft' [In Greenland You Keep Quiet]. *Politiken*, 23 November 2014.
Wolfe, Patrick. 'Nation and MiscegeNation: Discursive Continuity in the Post-Mabo Era.' *Social Analysis: The International Journal of Social and Cultural Practice* 36 (1994): 93–152.

32
YURAKI – AN AUSTRALIAN ABORIGINAL PERSPECTIVE ON DEEP HISTORY

John Maynard

This chapter will focus on history, memory, and stories from an Australian Aboriginal perspective. In the context of Deep Time or Big History, it is important to understand that history on the Australian continent did not begin in 1788. Aboriginal people of the continent had a strong sense of recording and noting their history, including significant events and heroes and heroines of the past, through history remembering. This long memory was achieved through repetition and the retelling of important events as well as artistic depiction. While I will analyse history with a 65,000-year clock in mind, it is of equal importance to consider the construction of history, particularly across the twentieth and twenty-first centuries. How do we remember? Why is it important? History can provide Indigenous people the means to challenge the paralysis of the perennial victim paradigm and inspire future generations with their proud past. The Aboriginal history of the Australian continent is one of coexistence, appreciation, and respect for the environment, encompassing all within – in essence a partnership with nature. As part of that understanding, I will discuss two significant collaborative partnerships Aboriginal people forged: one was with the dingo and the other with the dolphin.

Dreaming of the past

In 1879, J.D. Woods delivered his eulogy of the future for Aboriginal people in Australia. And sadly, his viewpoint remains embedded in the misguided concept of Australian history:

> Without a history, they have no past; without a religion, they have no hope; without the habits of forethought and providence, they can have no future. Their doom is sealed, and all that the civilized man can do ... is to take care that the closing hour shall not be hurried on by want, caused by culpable neglect on his part.[1]

In the twenty-first century, this startling statement should be held up as laughable, if it were not for the continued ignorance of many in Australia today. Indigenous people like myself remain classified by many in the wider population as people without history or religion, and consigned to the very back blocks of the Stone Age of development. These misinformed sentiments have been expressed not just by sections of the right-wing media but even by a former Prime Minister of the Country. Tony Abbott remarked that 'it's hard to think that back in 1788 it was nothing but bush'[2] – 'bush' being another word for wilderness – and followed that up by declaring that 'what happened on the 26th of January 1788 was on balance, for everyone – Aboriginal people included – a good thing because it brought Western civilisation to this country, it brought Australia into the modern world'.[3] John Howard was adamant during his time as Prime Minister that 'Australians of the current generation should not be required to accept blame for past policies over which they had no control'.[4] Sociologist Charles Rowley sums up the onset of this mindset of Australian historical amnesia:

> White folklore has been powerful in the development of the 'white Australia' mythology and attitudes. It has excluded the Aboriginal tragedy from many historical works, and poisoned many a school history text. It has softened the story of Aboriginal 'disappearance' with fantasies which make the brutalities almost respectable.[5]

The irony of these comments, historically and even today, is that Aboriginal Australia is scientifically recognised as carrying the longest cultural memory known to humankind. The recent dating of the Madjedbebe site in Arnhem Land has seen the date of Aboriginal occupation of the continent pushed back to a staggering 65,000 years. We as Aboriginal people knew what history was and its importance. In his extensive language recording between 1821 and 1842, Reverend Lancelot E. Threlkeld – the missionary to Aboriginal people on the shores of Lake Macquarie – noted that the local Aboriginal people had the word *yuraki* for long ago, since, and past. The Gathang-speaking Worimi of the Port Stephens region likewise had the word *dangay* for formerly or long time ago. Clearly, these are Aboriginal words defining an understanding of a long past or history. As Bruno David explains: 'Like all things cultural, the Dreaming must have a history; it must have arisen out of human practice some time in the past.'[6]

The significance of Aboriginal spiritual connection to Country and deep time history is very difficult to comprehend for the majority within Western understanding. That spiritual connection is one attached to the long historical memory of the land and ancestors. Ronald and Catherine Berndt delivered a wonderful appraisal from many decades of close working relationships, stating that the 'land is the most enduring and tangible expression in [the Aboriginal people's] scheme of things. It is their major resource. Their relationship with it has an intimacy and familiarity that is unsurpassed by any other ... even the relationship between parent and child or brother and sister'.[7] T.G.H. Strehlow also commented on this all-powerful Aboriginal connection to Country: 'He sees, recorded in the surrounding landscape, the ancient stories of their lives and the deeds of the immortal beings whom he reveres.'[8]

Charles Mountford was acutely aware 'of the deep personal affection the Aborigines feel for their country. Everything they see about them is reminiscent of the creation stories of their origins and is proof of their authenticity'.[9]

A.P. Elkin and W.E.H. Stanner, two revered anthropologists of the past, significantly drew reference to the connection of Aboriginal people in the present to their founding historical moment in time. Elkin felt that the Aboriginal ceremonial initiation rites 'intended to maintain and renew the life of natural species, appeared in some sense to recapitulate some features or aspects of the founding drama'.[10] Stanner also witnessed this long connection to the past:

> In following the Dreaming, the black-fellow 'lives' this philosophy ... the black-fellow holds his philosophy in mythology attained as the social product of an indefinitely ancient past, and proceeds to live it out in life, in part through a ritual and an expressive art, and in part through non-sacred social customs.[11]

We as Aboriginal people had our historians thousands of years before the Greeks, Egyptians, and Romans, and our people also celebrated great heroes and heroines and recorded great events, including earthquakes, great floods, fires, erupting volcanoes, ice ages, and dramatically rising and falling sea levels. Our historians, like the Greeks, told history through storytelling, performance, and art. Our people made connections with not just the landscape but everything within it. Some of these connections were a partnership of benefit forged across thousands of years. I will analyse two such long-term Aboriginal connections, namely with the dingo and the dolphin.

The dingo

One of the most significant human introductions to the Australian continent was that of the Aboriginal dog, the dingo. In his 1881 publication, James Dawson stated that the dingo, among all animals, 'deservedly holds the first place in the estimation of the [A]borigines'.[12] The dingo was not native to the Australian continent but was brought by a later arrival of people somewhere between 3,000 and 4,000 years ago.[13] The dingo was introduced to the northern part of the continent and rapidly spread to all areas except Tasmania[14] – the absence of the dingo in Tasmania indicates confirmation that its arrival was after the rising sea levels cut through Bass Strait some 11,000–12,000 years ago. John Mulvaney advises that there is no evidence of dingoes being on the continent during the Pleistocene Period.[15] There have been a number of significant archaeological dingo discoveries, including a dating of 3,000 years at Fromm's Landing in South Australia. Another site in South Australia, at the Mount Burr Rock shelter, originally provided evidence of the presence of dingoes between 7,000 and 8,000 years ago, but this discovery was found to have been earlier disturbed and the dating was discounted. Further dingo skeletal remains have been discovered in the Madura Cave on the Nullarbor Plain in Western Australia and dated at close to 3,500 years. The presence of the dingo has been discounted as impacting in any significant way upon the megafauna of the continent because of the dogs' late arrival, but they may have played a role in the destruction of some smaller species across the continent.[16]

The dingo was very useful to Aboriginal people and can be classified as a domesticated animal. Its arrival 'enabled a great increase in hunting efficiency, whether for large kangaroos or smaller animals',[17] and it has been described as indispensable to Aboriginal hunters.[18] Aboriginal camp dogs, unlike wild dogs, 'rarely hunted by themselves, and when they did go hunting it was always under the direction of men'.[19] The dogs hunted as a pack and were very clever at distracting the roos, such as in this example:

> ... they kept beyond its reach and worried it from opposite sides. This sealed the fate of the 'old man', since it was unable to run, move or jump; the moment it attempted to do so, the dogs fastened their teeth in its flanks and pulled it down.
>
> The end came quickly. One of the hunters ran up and gave the animal a sharp blow between the ears with his *nulla-nulla* and stretched it lifeless on the ground.[20]

Dawson gave a glowing estimation of the hunting abilities and reliability of the dogs when on the hunt with their owners:

> They were also trained to hunt, which was their principal use. They were active and skilful in killing kangaroos, and seldom got cut with the powerful hind toes of these animals. When they killed one they yelped to let their master know where they were. Some well-trained dogs would even come home and lead their owners to dead game.[21]

In some areas, women also hunted and were noted as not missing the opportunity of bringing down bigger game with the assistance of their dogs.[22]

Dingoes were useful domesticated animals in more ways than just for hunting. In dry areas, dingoes were known to dig and indicate the presence of water to their owners. And in cold weather, the dogs provided additional warmth to snuggle up to:

> ... elderly people and children slept clasping one dog in their arms, with their back and feet against others for warmth. Women when not carrying children, often 'wore' a dog draped across their lower back, with its head and tail in the crook of their arms, in order to keep their kidneys warm.[23]

This close, comforting connection at night has been recognised with the Martu of the Western Desert, and not just for warmth:

> Dingoes are significant to the Martu. People slept close to them to keep themselves warm on cold winter nights and protect them from evil spirits. Dingoes can also sense the presence of strangers, 'featherfeet' and revenge expeditions.[24]

This recognition of the dingo as a reliable guard dog for the community was clearly widespread across the continent, since Dawson was making his account in the southeast, far from the Western Desert:

> The dingoes were trained to guard the *wuurns*, which they did by growling and snarling. Dingoes never bark ... In watching they were vigilant and fierce. They would let fly at the throat of visitors; and strangers had often to take refuge from them by climbing into a tree.[25]

Convict artist Joseph Lycett in his time at Coal Town (Newcastle) captured many beautiful artworks of Aboriginal cultural life and the dingo is prominently featured in many images. The dog is portrayed as a happy part of the group and can be seen in night images laying by the fire or close to their owners.[26] According to Ashley Montagu, the Bloomfield River Aboriginal people of far northern Queensland had an idea of 'wau-wu', or a state of being that includes one's will and thought. The incorporation of the dingo into Aboriginal spiritual life and story is clearly recognised in this region, as dingoes:

> ... are reckoned upon having thinking powers, etc., or wau-wu, and bear a sort of relationship to their masters, who will often speak to them as their mother, son, brother, etc., in addition to mentioning them by their proper names, these being conferred upon them according to the districts whence they have been obtained, or to the various tracts of country occupied by their owners.[27]

From the time of their arrival, dingoes proved themselves an indispensable asset to their Aboriginal owners and have been commemorated through Aboriginal rock art and carvings and included into significant creation stories. An Aboriginal senior man with the Yarralin community of the Northern Territory's remote Victoria River Valley, Tim Yilngayarri, was described as 'an owner of country rich with Dingo Dreamings; he is a "dog man" *par excellence*, with an intimate concern for, and understanding of, dingoes and dogs'.[28] Clearly, the importance of the dingo and stories connected with the Yarralin are long ones. It was related that 'in Dreaming, only the dingo (wild dog, *Canis familiiaris dingo*) walked then as he does now. He was shaped like a dog, he behaved like a dog, and dingo and human were one'.[29] The significance of the dingo in Yarralin stories simply states that it was the dingo 'who made people human in the first place'.[30]

The dogs were prized parts of the Aboriginal camp and life and, in most cases, were regarded more as pets than just assistants in hunting – they were loved, revered, and cared for with affection. There are reflections of strong bonds between Aboriginal people and their dingoes. Anthropologist Herbert Basedow was adamant that the animals were kept only for the love their owners lavished upon them. The dogs were assumed to be spoiled and ruined beyond belief, 'on account of the unreasonable amount of petting and pampering, received at the hands of their masters'.[31] When a dog took sick or had been injured, the concerned owners ensured that 'it is nursed like a sick child; it is placed by the fireside, upon the best rug available, and covered with other rags, the natives themselves going without any cover. One might occasionally find a gin going so far as to even suckle a pup at her breast'.[32]

The impact of European arrival after 1788 may have had a severely detrimental effect on the formerly close relationship between Aboriginal people and the dingo in many areas. Norman Tindale stated that in some remote areas, the dog was seen 'as a kind of last hope meal for people facing abject starvation'.[33] In southern Australia, 'the wild dingo can be speared [and] it is killed for food and special attention is given to hunting for the lairs in which the fat puppies, whelped once a year, are being suckled'.[34] Henry Reynolds and Rani Kerin have written of the dingo bounty hunters, or 'doggers', who were picking up rewards for the numbers of dingo scalps they turned in. Kerin revealed that in the far north of South Australia, these 'doggers' were in fact cheating and acquiring the dingo scalps 'from local Aboriginal people in exchange for rations'.[35] In fact, the greatest numbers of scalps turned in were through trading with Aboriginal people:

> ... whose minute knowledge of the habits of the dogs, and particularly of their seasonal movements and breeding places, enable[d] them to get results quite beyond the reach of a white man ... whereas 'a white man will labouriously secure two or three [scalps] in a week, the tribe comes in with twenty slung across its shoulders'.[36]

But in most instances, this was not a fair trade. Aboriginal groups were gaining small rations of flour, sugar, tea, and tobacco in the exchange, while the doggers were picking up seven shillings and sixpence per scalp from the government.

While this was a sad downturn in a relationship that had endured for thousands of years, in some areas, the connection between Aboriginal people and their dogs continued on as before. John J. Moloney, who lived at the time in Menangle, New South Wales, recalled the late nineteenth-century visits to his family's property of many travelling Aboriginal groups. One regular visitor over many years provided 'a very vivid remembrance'. He recalled her as '"Black Nellie," a full-blood [A]boriginal women who made periodical visits to Menangle accompanied by several dogs of various breeds'.[37] These long connections and attachment continue through to today. Over 20 years ago, I interviewed Steve Blunden, then CEO of the Durri Aboriginal Medical Service (AMS) in Kempsey, and he related a 1997 incident that impacted on both the local dogs and people. The AMS was facing a major worm infestation within the community, particularly with the children. It was discovered that the problem was emanating from the large numbers of dogs kept in the community. The local Council solution was to send in dog catchers, and all the dogs were picked up and were to be put down. This caused a major upset, and Steve told me, 'the people were crying, "please don't let them kill the dogs"'. They loved their dogs'.[38] A compromise was reached and all the dogs were immunised and then returned to their owners.

The dolphin

There are countless traditional stories relating to whales, sharks, and dolphins and their importance and connection to people. In today's world, there are numerous accounts of dolphin and human interaction and collaboration, and some of these involve dolphins protecting and saving human lives from shark attack. Dolphin pods at Monkey Mia in Western Australia and Tin Can Bay in Queensland are noted for their interactions with humans. Partnerships between dolphins and Aboriginal people are long-standing and forged across a deep period of time. Two years before her passing, Oodgeroo Noonuccal (Kath Walker) told a story common to many Aboriginal clans on the east coast of Australia:

> In an early time, the Dreamtime, when the land was still young an old man stood on a beach watching out to sea. He watched a pod of dolphins as they played and hunted for fish, observing that they seemed to want for nothing while his own people could not find enough food. His thoughts were interrupted by a dolphin spirit, who rose out of the water and spoke to the elder, asking him what troubled him. The old man explained that his people were going hungry. The dolphin man listened and then offered to help, but told the old man that in return he must first agree to take only what was needed, nothing more. The people were starving, so the elder agreed. The dolphin man told the old man to go to the cliffs and watch, and when he saw the dolphin splashing and jumping to tell his people to go down to the shallows to fish. There would be plenty for all, but if they took more than they needed, the dolphins could never help him again. The man went to his people and instructed them, and when they fished they were careful to take only what they needed. They ate well that night, and the next day the elder returned to the beach. He walked out into the water and the dolphin man came to him. The dolphin man was pleased that the people had listened, and told the elder that now his people would have plenty of fish.[39]

Dennis Foley relates a story of similar powerful connections within the bays and coves of Collaroy on the northern beaches of present-day Sydney. A long time ago, a great Aboriginal Gatlay fisherman made lasting connections with the shark people and dolphin clans of the coast. He became friends with both the sharks and dolphins and was often seen talking to both in the shallows. The man never married and with age his hair turned white. He only came back to his own people at night with large provisions of fish for all. The day arrived when he did not return and his people heard a distressing crying noise coming from the sea. They went down and found his body floating in the shallows. He had died of old age while undertaking his favourite past-time, fishing. The dolphins were nudging and pushing his body back to the shoreline, and the noise was them crying with distress at having lost a long-time close friend. The people carried the man's body back to camp and he was wrapped in a possum cloak and placed within the branches of a high tree. The cries of the dolphins continued unabated and their upset was clear to the people.

So the people decided to construct a funeral canoe and place the man back with his only family, the dolphins:

> The fisherman was placed in the canoe, wrapped tightly in many possum-skin rugs, his white hair garnished with sweet fruits of the forest and his body wrapped in bark, painted with ochre and washed in oil. He was smoked and his loved ones bade him farewell. They placed him in the canoe and pushed him away from the shore with the receding tide ... To the clan's amazement the dolphins surrounded the canoe and with gently nudged pushed him far out to sea. As the night's shadows settled on the water, the canoe vanished over the horizon and so left our land. The dolphins also left the waters for many cycles of the moon. When the wattle next bloomed, the children came running back to the camp of the elders; 'the dolphins, the dolphins are back', they yelled in unison. When the clan came to the beach, there were the dolphins with a large school of mullet cornered in the bay and there was the white headed dolphin, splashing as if telling the other dolphins what to do, and the people realized this was the old man. From that day in a certain place now called the Collaroy Basin, the members of this clan have spoken to the dolphins and they have helped them to fish, and the white-headed dolphin can still be seen with the pod.[40]

There is a great dolphin story remembered by our Māori brothers and sisters that concerns the story of Tuhirangi, the dolphin who guided Kupe, a Māori voyager, across the ocean to Aotearoa (New Zealand). Tuhirangi then guided Kupe and his group safely through the outer Marlborough Sounds to the west coast of the South Island. The Europeans have adopted this story and Tuhirangi the dolphin appears on the inter-island ferry logo. Māori legends also tell of a dolphin who guided their canoes between Pelorus Sound and French Pass. Later, the canoes were replaced by sailing ships and then steamers. The guiding dolphin known as Pelorus Jack continued to pilot the boats in their navigation through these dangerous waters. The Māori called him Kaikaiwaro, which translates as 'god of the ocean'. It was reported that Māori lore cited him as 275 years old in 1914.[41] Another account concerning Pelorus Jack stated that he was a constant companion and guide to ships sailing from the Cook Islands between 1888 and 1912. The dolphin would respond to the noise of ships both day and night and soon be seen riding the bow waves:

> One regular traveller recalled: 'When he was late for the steamer that we were boarding, we would hear the passengers say, "Here he comes!" and I would look up and see Pelorus Jack approaching at a racing speed with great leaps and bounds out of the water, often ending close by with a mighty splash. This delighted the passengers.'[42]

It was reported that someone once fired a shot at Jack from a steamship. So great was the public outrage that the government ensured that he was the 'only fish in the world protected by an Act of Parliament'.[43]

Tales of the protective nature of dolphins and their assistance have been recorded in Australia as well. The late Patricia Davis-Hurst recorded a wonderful story looking back to when she was ten years old during the early 1940s. Davis-Hurst recalled that a number of Aboriginal families were at Saltwater Beach near Taree. The men were all fishing and the kids were swimming in the surf. Suddenly, her father came running down the beach, screaming for everyone to get out of the water. From his vantage point while fishing, he had spotted a large shark heading towards the kids, and Davis-Hurst talked about that frightening moment:

> Then we saw a huge shark coming towards us. A lot of the older boys were swimming further out. All of a sudden, a pod of dolphins came straight at them as if to hunt them out of the water. Mum swam out to help the boys get back to shore. After everyone was out, Mum was left standing waist deep in water when a dolphin came up and gently pushed her towards the shore. The dolphins then turned and chased the shark off.[44]

During the 1950s on the North Coast of New South Wales, two very respected elders – Kumbaingari man Lambert Whaddy and Daingatti man Harry Kelly – told a story of how 'Aborigines Caught Their Fish'. The men stated that

> dolphins used to drive the mullet in close to shore. Two groups of Aboriginal hunters went out into the water four to five hundred yards apart. Each hunter carried two stones, which they tapped together. These were special stones found in the hills – "Sonates" or singing stones. The dolphins would hear the call and bring in the mullet to be speared and then the Aboriginal hunters would reward their dolphin hunting companions with their share of the catch.[45]

A similar cooperative partnership was recorded in 1856 in Moreton Bay, Queensland, when a Mr Fairholme noted: 'It seems from time immemorial a sort of understanding has existed between the blacks and the porpoises for their mutual advantage, and the former pretend to know all the porpoises about the spot, and even have names for them.'[46] This account went on to say that when Aboriginal men sighted a large shoal of mullet, they would run down to the water:

> ... and with their spears make a peculiar splashing in the water. Whether the porpoises really understand this as a signal, or think it is the fish, it is difficult to determine, but the result is always the same; they at once come in towards the shore, driving the mullet before them. As they near the edge, a number of blacks with spears and hand-nets quickly divide to right and left, and dash into the water. The porpoises being outside the shoal, numbers of fish are secured before they can break away. In the scene of apparent confusion that takes place, the blacks and porpoises are seen splashing about close to each other. So fearless are the latter, that strangers, who have expressed doubts as to their tameness, have often been shown that they will take fish from the end of a spear, when held to them ... I cannot doubt that the understanding is real,

and that the natives know these porpoises ... The oldest men of the tribe say that the same kind of fishing has always been carried on as long as they can remember.[47]

When the H.M.S. *Rattlesnake* was anchored off Moreton Island in 1847, one John MacGillivray was fascinated by what he referred to as a new species of porpoise. He was prevented from killing and acquiring one for study because 'the natives believed the most direful consequences would ensue from the destruction of one, and I considered the advantages resulting to science from the addition of a new species ... would not have justified me in outraging their strongly expressed superstitious feelings on the subject'.[48] Tom Petrie's reminiscences in 1887 recalled that, in the same region, one 'old porpoise was well known and spoken of fondly' and the blacks regarded him as 'the big fellow of the tribe of porpoises. I have seen this creature take fish from a spear, and the white men working on the island told me that they often saw him knocking about with the blacks'.[49] Another reference to this same porpoise by Henry Stuart Russell in 1888 stated that the porpoise was 'as tame – with those blacks – as a pussy cat'.[50]

There were similar memories from the Yuin people on the South Coast of New South Wales, and their connection and working relationship was with not just dolphins but also killer whales. After a visit to Shoalhaven in 1836, James Backhouse recalled his conversation with early settler Alexander Berry, stating that the 'blacks' believe in reincarnation and coming back as another life form. Berry said that

> he had wounded a porpoise, which some blacks, who were with him in the boat, tried to dissuade him from firing at. On landing, the men told the women what had been done, at which they made great lamentation; and he learned from them that they regarded the porpoises as having been the ancient chiefs of the neighbourhood, who, when they had died, had changed into these animals; and who, they said, drove fish on shore for them, sometimes whales, when they were very hungry![51]

In a similar fashion, the killer whales would pursue humpback whales into the bay at Eden, where Aboriginal hunters awaited their arrival and killed them if they beached themselves in attempts to escape the killer whales. The Aboriginal hunters shared their bounty with their co-hunters. This remarkable relationship was instrumental in the whaling industry being established at Eden in the nineteenth century. Unquestionably, our people had established a unique relationship with their environment and all within. The marine mammal/Aboriginal partnership of shared cooperation was a very long and important one.

Conclusion

I have sought here to project the importance of history and discussed the neglect of an Aboriginal place in Australian national history. The relationships between Aboriginal people and the dingo and dolphin reveal the productive collaborative partnerships forged between Aboriginal people, animals, and their environment. These stories help us understand the magnitude of deep time history and the importance of working with nature and the environment. History for us is embedded within the landscape and our connection to both Country and other life forms is a central part of our cultural belief. In the twenty-first century, we have reached a critical point in global history and memory. Rising sea levels, catastrophic storms, and global warming are markers of dire warnings for the future. As a reminder, upon witnessing destruction in his Country and environment with trees killed by bulldozers, Aboriginal elder Daly Pulkara could not contain his anger. 'We'll run out of history,' he said, because '*kartiya* [Europeans] fuck the law up and [they're] knocking all the power out of this country'.[52] Since 1788, over 65,000 years of history and connection to this continent has been draining from Country. It is our role to ensure that does not happen and that the reservoir of deep knowledge and wisdom is maintained for the benefit of mankind.

Notes

1 J.D. Woods, *The Native Tribes of South Australia* (Adelaide: E.S. Wigg & Son, 1879), xxxviii.
2 'Remarks at Infrastructure Breakfast with Prime Minister Cameron, Sydney,' PM Transcripts, 14 November 2014, https://pmtranscripts.pmc.gov.au/release/transcript-2395.
3 'First Fleet "Good" for Indigenous Australians, Tony Abbott Says,' *Sydney Morning Herald*, 22 January 2018, https://www.smh.com.au/politics/federal/first-fleet-good-for-indigenous-australians-tony-abbott-says-20180122-h0lyzc.html.
4 J. Howard, *Lazarus Rising: A Personal and Political History* (Sydney: Harper Collins Publishers, 2010), 277.
5 C.D. Rowley, *A Matter of Justice* (Canberra: Australian National University Press, 1978), 5.
6 B. David, *Landscapes, Rock Art and the Dreaming: An Archaeology of Preunderstanding* (London: Leicester University Press, 2002), 1; as quoted in B. Griffiths, *Deep Time Dreaming: Uncovering Ancient Australia* (Melbourne: Black Inc., 2018), 195.
7 R.M. Berndt and C.H. Berndt, *Man, Land and Myth in North Australia: The Gunwinggu People* (Sydney: Ure Smith, 1970), 1.
8 T.G.H. Strehlow, *Aranda Traditions* (Melbourne: Melbourne University Press, 1947), 30.
9 C. Mountford, *Nomads of the Australian Desert* (Sydney: Rigby, 1976), 54.
10 M. Charlesworth et al., *Religion in Aboriginal Australia* (St Lucia: University of Queensland Press, 1986), 147.
11 W.E.H. Stanner, *White Man Got No Dreaming: Essays 1938–1973* (Canberra: Australian National University Press, 1979), 29–30.
12 J. Dawson, *Australian Aborigines: The Languages and Customs of Several Tribes of Aborigines in the Western District of Victoria, Australia* (Melbourne: George Robertson, 1881), 89.
13 P. Clarke, *Where the Ancestor Walked* (Sydney: Allen & Unwin, 2003), 13.
14 T. Flannery, *The Future Eaters: An Ecological History of the Australasian Lands and People* (Sydney: Reed New Holland, 1994), 275; S. Cane, *First Footprints: The Epic Story of the First Australians* (Sydney: Allen & Unwin, 2013), 213.
15 J. Mulvaney, *The Prehistory of Australia* (London: Thames & Hudson, 1969), 65.
16 Clarke, *Where the Ancestor Walked*, 13.
17 N. Butlin, *Economics and the Dreamtime* (Cambridge: Cambridge University Press, 1993), 92.
18 R.M. Berndt and C.H. Berndt, *The World of the First Australians: Aboriginal Traditional Life* (Sydney: Rigby, 1985), 115.
19 Berndt, *World of the First Australians*, 148.

20 W. Robertson, *'Brin-ga's' Coo-ee Talks* (Sydney: Angus & Robertson, 1928), 73.
21 Dawson, *Australian Aborigines*, 89.
22 Berndt, *World of the First Australians*, 119; Mountford, *Nomads of the Australian Desert*, 48.
23 N. Tindale, *Aboriginal Tribes of Australia* (Berkeley: University of California Press, 1974), 109.
24 S. Davenport, P. Johnson, and Yuwali, *Cleared Out: First Contact in the Western Desert* (Canberra: Aboriginal Studies Press, 2005), 71.
25 Dawson, *Australian Aborigines*, 89.
26 J. Maynard, *True Light and Shade: An Aboriginal Perspective of Joseph Lycett's Art* (Canberra: National Library of Australia, 2014), 99.
27 A. Montagu, *Coming into Being Among the Australian Aborigines* (London: Routledge & Keegan Paul, 1974), 144.
28 D. Rose, *Dingo Makes Us Human: Life and Land in Australian Aboriginal Culture* (Cambridge: Cambridge University Press, 2000), 29.
29 Rose, *Dingo Makes Us Human*, 47.
30 Rose, *Dingo Makes Us Human*, 177.
31 H. Basedow, *The Australian Aboriginal* (Adelaide: F.W. Preece & Sons, 1925), 118.
32 Basedow, *Australian Aboriginal*, 118–119.
33 Tindale, *Aboriginal Tribes of Australia*, 109.
34 Tindale, *Aboriginal Tribes of Australia*, 109.
35 R. Kerin, 'Dogging for a Living,' in *Frontier, Race, Nation: Henry Reynolds and Australian History*, eds. B. Attwood and T. Griffiths (Melbourne: Australian Scholarly Publishing, 2009), 137.
36 Kerin, 'Dogging for a Living,' 142.
37 J.J. Moloney, *Early Menangle* (Newcastle: The Australasian Society of Patriots, Dally Branch, 1929).
38 Conversation John Maynard with Steve Blunden, Kempsey Aboriginal Medical Services, 1997.
39 J. Ogden, *Saltwater People of the Fatal Shore: Sydney's Southern Beaches* (Sydney: Cyclops Press, 2012), 53.
40 J. Ogden, *Saltwater People of the Broken Bays: Sydney's Northern Beaches* (Sydney: Cyclops Press, 2011), 52–53.
41 'Famous Dolphin Pilot of French Pass No Longer Meets Passing Ships,' *Nowra Leader*, 25 October 1935, 1. http://nla.gov.au/nla.news-page23699675.
42 C. Moore, 'Wellington to Picton with Interislander,' accessed 27 July 2020, wanderlusters.com/crossing-the-cook-strait.
43 'A Fish Protected by an Act of Parliament,' *Dubbo Dispatch and Wellington Independent*, 24 July 1909, 8. http://nla.gov.au/nla.news-page24871302.
44 P. Davis-Hurst, *Sunrise Station* (Taree: SunBird Publications, 1996), 161.
45 Coffs Harbour Historical Society Notes. Third drawer in middle section, settlement 2, file name: Aborigines.
46 Mr Fairholme, 'The Blacks of Moreton Bay and the Porpoises,' *Annals and Magazine of Natural History* 19 (1857): 498; this and the following porpoise stories are also summarised in 'Curious Allies: Blacks and Porpoises, Co-operation in Fishcatching,' *The Queenslander* (Brisbane), 17 April 1926, 11. http://nla.gov.au/nla.news-page2392810.
47 Fairholme, 'The Blacks of Moreton Bay and the Porpoises,' 498.
48 J. MacGillivray, *Narrative of the Voyage of H.M.S. Rattlesnake* (London: T. & W. Boone, 1852), 48.
49 C.C. Petrie, *Tom Petrie's Reminiscences of Early Queensland* (Brisbane: Watson, Ferguson & co., 1904), 70.
50 H.S. Russell, *The Genesis of Queensland* (Sydney: Turner & Henderson, 1888), 290.
51 J. Backhouse, *A Narrative of a Visit to the Australian Colonies* (London: Hamilton Adams and Company, 1843), 431.
52 Rose, *Dingo Makes Us Human*, 234.

Bibliography

Abbott, Tony. 'Remarks at Infrastructure Breakfast with Prime Minister Cameron, Sydney,' PM Transcripts, 14 November 2014, https://pmtranscripts.pmc.gov.au/release/transcript-2395.
Backhouse, J. *A Narrative of a Visit to the Australian Colonies*. London: Hamilton Adams and Company, 1843.
Basedow, H. *The Australian Aboriginal*. Adelaide: F.W. Preece & Sons, 1925.
Berndt, R.M., and C.H. Berndt. *Man, Land and Myth in North Australia: The Gunwinggu People*. Sydney: Ure Smith, 1970.
Berndt, R.M., and C.H. Berndt. *The World of the First Australians: Aboriginal Traditional Life*. Sydney: Rigby, 1985.
Butlin, N. *Economics and the Dreamtime*. Cambridge: Cambridge University Press, 1993.
Cane, S. *First Footprints: The Epic Story of the First Australians*. Sydney: Allen & Unwin, 2013.
Charlesworth, M., H. Morphy, D. Bell, and K. Maddock. *Religion in Aboriginal Australia*. St Lucia: University of Queensland Press, 1986.
Clarke, P. *Where the Ancestor Walked*. Sydney: Allen & Unwin, 2003.
Davenport, S., P. Johnson, and Yuwali. *Cleared Out: First Contact in the Western Desert*. Canberra: Aboriginal Studies Press, 2005.
David, B. *Landscapes, Rock Art and the Dreaming: An Archaeology of Preunderstanding*. London: Leicester University Press, 2002.
Davis-Hurst, P. *Sunrise Station*. Taree: SunBird Publications, 1996.
Dawson, J. *Australian Aborigines: The Languages and Customs of Several Tribes of Aborigines in the Western District of Victoria, Australia*. Melbourne: George Robertson, 1881.
Fairholme, Mr. 'The Blacks of Moreton Bay and the Porpoises.' *Annals and Magazine of Natural History* 19 (1857): 497–498.
Flannery, T. *The Future Eaters: An Ecological History of the Australasian Lands and People*. Sydney: Reed New Holland, 1994.
Griffiths, B. *Deep Time Dreaming: Uncovering Ancient Australia*. Melbourne: Black Inc., 2018.
Howard, J. *Lazarus Rising: A Personal and Political History*. Sydney: Harper Collins Publishers, 2010.
Kerin, R. 'Dogging for a Living.' In *Frontier, Race, Nation: Henry Reynolds and Australian History*, edited by B. Attwood and T. Griffiths, 136–156. Melbourne: Australian Scholarly Publishing, 2009.
MacGillivray, J. *Narrative of the Voyage of H.M.S. Rattlesnake*. London: T. & W. Boone, 1852.
Maynard, J. *True Light and Shade: An Aboriginal Perspective of Joseph Lycett's Art*. Canberra: National Library of Australia, 2014.
Moloney, J.J. *Early Menangle*. Newcastle: The Australasian Society of Patriots, Dally Branch, 1929.
Montagu, A. *Coming into Being Among the Australian Aborigines*. London: Routledge & Keegan Paul, 1974.
Moore, C. 'Wellington to Picton with Interislander.' Accessed 27 July 2020. wanderlusters.com/crossing-the-cook-strait.
Mountford, C. *Nomads of the Australian Desert*. Sydney: Rigby, 1976.
Mulvaney, J. *The Prehistory of Australia*. London: Thames & Hudson, 1969.
Ogden, J. *Saltwater People of the Broken Bays: Sydney's Northern Beaches*. Sydney: Cyclops Press, 2011.
Ogden, J. *Saltwater People of the Fatal Shore: Sydney's Southern Beaches*. Sydney: Cyclops Press, 2012.
Petrie, C.C. *Tom Petrie's Reminiscences of Early Queensland*. Brisbane: Watson, Ferguson & co., 1904.
Robertson, W. *'Brin-ga's' Coo-ee Talks*. Sydney: Angus & Robertson, 1928.
Rose, D. *Dingo Makes Us Human: Life and Land in Australian Aboriginal Culture*. Cambridge: Cambridge University Press, 2000.

Rowley, C.D. *A Matter of Justice*. Canberra: Australian National University Press, 1978.
Russell, H.S. *The Genesis of Queensland*. Sydney: Turner & Henderson, 1888.
Tindale, N. *Aboriginal Tribes of Australia*. Berkeley: University of California Press, 1974.
Stanner, W.E.H. *White Man Got No Dreaming: Essays 1938–1973*. Canberra: Australian National University Press, 1979.
Strehlow, T.G.H. *Aranda Traditions*. Melbourne: Melbourne University Press, 1947.
Woods, J.D. *The Native Tribes of South Australia*. Adelaide: E.S. Wigg & Son, 1879.

Newspapers

'A Fish Protected by an Act of Parliament,' *Dubbo Dispatch and Wellington Independent*, 24 July 1909. http://nla.gov.au/nla.news-page24871302.
'Curious Allies: Blacks and Porpoises, Co-operation in Fishcatching.' *The Queenslander* (Brisbane), 17 April 1926. http://nla.gov.au/nla.news-page2392810.
'Famous Dolphin Pilot of French Pass No Longer Meets Passing Ships.' *Nowra Leader*, 25 October 1935. http://nla.gov.au/nla.news-page23699675.
'First Fleet "Good" for Indigenous Australians, Tony Abbott Says,' *Sydney Morning Herald*, 22 January 2018. https://www.smh.com.au/politics/federal/first-fleet-good-for-indigenous-australians-tony-abbott-says-20180122-h0lyzc.html.

Archives

Coffs Harbour Historical Society Notes – Third drawer in middle section. Settlement 2. File name: Aborigines.

33
DEEP HISTORY'S DIGITAL FOOTPRINTS

Ann McGrath[1]

Dinosaurs and arrival narratives

On a sandy rock on a beach in Broome, Western Australia, I placed my foot in a dinosaur footprint. I then took a foot-selfie, a picture on my iPhone, posting it on Facebook and Twitter, adding the name of our latest research project, Rediscovering the Deep Human Past.[2] We had to hurry as the tide was about to cover up this section of the beach, as it did on a daily basis. Each of my actions was automatically encoded with markings of modern – or perhaps post-modern time: the hour, date, month, and the year, 2018, as accurately as the precision of the atomic clock allowed. My location was GIS place-tagged as Riddell Beach, in an area with the Indigenous name of Minyirr. After an interregnum of a hundred years or so of English names, the Yawuru names are making their return. Via my phone camera and social media, this image, this captured millisecond of time, raced off to the digital devices of a small community of people around the world (Figures 33.1–33.3).

First imprinted circa 130,000,000 before the present, the dinosaur whose footprint I photographed lived in the era classified in Western science as the Cretaceous period, a late stage of the Mesozoic. The foot, with three prominent toes in an elongated triangle, was over five times as big as my own. Dramatic actions in the earth's tectonic plates created this accidental archive in a densely forested ancient river delta. Part of the big story of massed lands not yet divided by today's vast oceans, the carving up of continents is the stuff of big time, and took place long before human time. Near this footprint, on the flat rocks skirting the Indian Ocean, are the tracks of 20 other dinosaur species – some with large bird-like feet, and others hoof-like. A Sauropod footprint found nearby is 1.7 metres in size and reputedly the largest found in the world.[3] It resembles the shape of a giant human foot.

Deep history's digital footprints

Figure 33.1 Human foot in dinosaur footprint, Minyirr region, August 2018. Photo by author

Figure 33.2 Yuwuru man Bart Pigram pointing out dinosaur footprints, Minyirr region, August 2018. Photo by author

Figure 33.3 Riddell Beach, Minyirr: a beachscape of dinosaur tracks. Photo by author.

The Yawuru Indigenous owners of the Broome area share narrative traditions associated with the arrival of their superhuman ancestors. They locate a particular spot where they first stepped onto the earth. It is akin to a creation site – a genesis. These are not 'oral histories' in the biographical timeframes in which we usually think of them. They are epic narratives, the deep-time memory traditions of ancient biospheres circulating over innumerable generations and across the continent. Described as songlines or song cycles, they are a form of multimedia in every sense of the word, for they incorporate song, music, dance, body paint, and rock art, and share precise knowledge of landscape features and plant life as it changed over time.[4]

Around the world, Indigenous conceptualisations are not limited to modernity's European-focused time-zones. A popular adage, much quoted by historians, was that a good historian 'should don a sturdy pair of boots'[5] and actually go to the sites where historical events had taken place. Presumably, this was a plea that historians get away from their reliance upon text-based archives, that they take in the landscape in which events took place in a multi-sensory way – that they breathe the air, observe the environment – we might imagine, the angles of hills and mountains, the smells of sea, the colours of the grass. Researchers of Indigenous history, however, cannot simply observe what they might see in 2021 or 2022. Think of an example of any place in the world, bar Antarctica and some other exceptions, and it will be the Indigenous people who are likely to have the ancient stories, and possibly a deep-time knowledge of those places, their ecologies, the role they played in people's survival, the major events that took place there, and their associated stories. Theirs is often a detailed and embodied knowledge, both personalised and collective. It goes beyond that, too, for their insights traverse deep time, and transmit memories of their ancestors seeing those landscapes changing – lakes drying, oceans rising, volcanoes erupting. Colonialism's disruptive forces and the changes wrought by modernity mean that much of that knowledge is now lost, and these landscapes have forever changed, overlain with towns, cities, dams, farms, mines, and other developments. Yet, many Indigenous people do retain or have retrieved the oral accounts of events that took place in epochs so long ago – 10,000, 20,000 years past. These are chunks of human time, what I call the epochs of 'deep history', that are not yet encompassed within the timeframes of history writing. They are not post-modern, modern, medieval, early modern, or ancient; they predate all these periodisations and conceptualisations.

Interpreting and explaining the deep past, as in the ancient narratives of the fossilised dinosaur footprints, interconnected the 250 or so Indigenous language groups and nations across the landscape and to the islands beyond. With humans residing on this southern continent for 60,000 years or more, Australian Indigenous history and history-tellings jump beyond the Anthropocene and the Holocene to enter the Pleistocene.[6] Other Indigenous people around the globe have been on their lands for 1,000 years – for 2,000 or 8,000, or tens of thousands of years. They may not consider the Western calendar of dates particularly important, but certainly it has been a key tool for the narrating of written, scholarly history. For Indigenous peoples, their history in particular landscapes predates modernity. As discussed in this volume's introduction, Western ideas about the static character and unsophisticated status of Indigenous people precluded them from fitting into the idea of 'ancient civilisations' and into the prevailing accounts of 'ancient history'. Only recently, in fact, have historians been using the term 'civilisation' for Indigenous societies.

Over the past decade, leading historians have made important calls to expand their discipline beyond the eras of modernity and pre-modernity.[7] But they did not do so with the case of Indigenous peoples in mind. In this volume, we see value in the term 'deep history', for it suggests the expansive time period over which Indigenous people prospered around the globe. The term has been popularised in the works of Andrew Shryock and Daniel Smail, particularly in *Deep History: The Architecture of Past and Present* and in their rejection of the 'Pre' in 'Prehistory'. David Armitage, Jo Guldi, and David Christian have each called for historians to expand their temporal reach, to look at the foundations that made humans what they are today. Despite critiques that expanding history's timeframes may detract from its strengths, we agree with this call to expand history's relatively shallow reach.[8] Shryock and Smail propose that historians collaborate with scientists in order to draw upon new and relevant insights and they model this most eloquently in their publications. We also appreciate David Christian's call to consider history as starting with the Big Bang.[9] But these discussions have lacked a cross-cultural emphasis, and have not sought to reflect upon how such an approach might open up fresh ways of narrating the past. Arguably, Indigenous storytelling or Indigenous historicity already does some of this – it takes us back to creation; it incorporates and embeds ecological knowledge in local landscapes. It is not troubled by delimiting timeframes or hard chronologies. So, in order to undertake a truly global history, how might we shift the old modes of Western history-telling?

As argued in the Introduction to this Companion, for Indigenous history, a long perspective, a deep history perspective, is even more important. In order to take account of *global* Indigenous history – or at least Indigenous history globally – it is more important again. After all, Indigenous history has been excluded from history itself; it has been relegated to the 'Pre' of 'prehistory' and consequently Indigenous pasts have become the province of scholars of culture, of material artefacts and dating. Archaeologists have specialised in the study of 'prehistoric' Indigenous cultures, and their research is revealing vital information about them.[10] Our argument here, however, is that while Indigenous pasts may be a subject of science, their history remains excluded from the mainstream in two ways. First, it has been ignored or sidelined in histories covering the past several hundred years for instrumental reasons – because mainstream histories were being used to justify the building of imperial and colonial nations that were premised upon Indigenous dispossession; history writing, too, so often served to justify the pre-eminence of white invaders, to deny Indigenous sovereignty and their place in the past and future. But there is another reason too, which is that the wide expanses of Indigenous pasts – the thousands and tens of thousands of years of their residence and survival in landscapes and waterscapes around the globe – did not fit into current historical periodisations. They did not necessarily fit into 'ancient civilisations' as previously defined, or into the modern story. Without written texts, human history that took place so long ago is considered impossible to write. But we must find ways to undertake such research, so that we can acknowledge and recognise Indigenous pasts and Indigenous achievements. Working with Indigenous knowledge holders will be vital, and learning to work fruitfully with archaeologists will be another important strategy. In order to do so, new techniques and approaches are urgently required.

Digital strategies have the power to tell stories through digitally mapping landscapes of historical significance, through presenting those same landscapes via visual and audio-visual means on websites, television, and film, and through digital animation, using 3D and other effects. Many Indigenous people are being trained as experts in digital humanities and are forming international networks accordingly. Indigenous people in far-flung places are meeting up via Skype, Zoom, and other technologies. Workshops and courses are being held online, which enables them to be truly international events from the get-go.

Digital innovations

A great deal of innovation is taking place in the Indigenous digital space, both in Australia and internationally. Several sites have educational objectives and are aimed at the general public, while others are designed for internal community purposes. A pioneering development in the field, Ara Irititja: the Anangu Community Archive,[11] was developed by a major Central Australian community of the Western Desert region. The site's aim was to document and create an archive of community stories and heritage, to be used within the community itself. Password-protected with most of its content locked to external users, this strategy allowed for the integrity of secret-sacred knowledge to be accessed by appropriate persons according to Anangu protocols. A free platform designed for international use, Mukurtu

CMS, was developed out of Washington State University as a 'mobile, and open source platform built with Indigenous communities to manage and share digital cultural heritage'.[12]

Indigenous digital mapping projects constitute fresh ways of envisaging landscapes and sharing deep histories of connection. These offer an important corrective to the maps of European navigators and explorers that dominated the history books of settler-coloniser nations such as the United States and Australia.[13] One development of this kind is the Welcome to Country application. Location-linked, it enables users to learn the name and language of the Aboriginal group upon whose traditional lands they are visiting, and to receive a welcome greeting from an elder.[14] Another, SahulTime, is a site that shows the changing coastlines of the Australian continent in an interactive time-sequence, including when it was joined to current-day New Guinea.[15] Although a visualisation of geography alone, it is highly informative, for it was Indigenous people who were the primary occupants during the times of the changing coastlines of the Holocene and Pleistocene.

Many new Indigenous sites have mapping components. This fits with the historical practices of many Indigenous people, which emphasise place as a site and essential component of storytelling, as well as operating as an archive of history. Mapping approaches also articulate and assert their long associations and sovereignty over never-ceded tracts of land. One example of this is LandMark, a global platform of Indigenous and community lands, which helps Indigenous communities stake their claims to land on their own terms.[16] In Canada, a site called Native Land enables communities to share their digital cultural heritage.[17] Another important site – Return, Reconcile, Renew – focuses on repatriation of ancestral remains, with a strong digital component, including interviews with Indigenous custodians about the process and its impact.[18]

A high-impact Massacre Map project has been carefully documenting massacre sites around Australia.[19] It allows for community input and has strong research principles underpinning it and has also been taken up by a complementary platform hosted by the *Guardian* newspaper, entitled 'The Killing Times'.[20] A database of photographic and textual materials documenting the activities of the Queensland Native Mounted Police reveals the militaristic nature of a supposedly benign colonisation and also includes a mapping component.[21] The Digital Daisy Bates digitised a text-based linguistic archive by a non-Indigenous ethnographer, linking information to an interactive map, which enables easy access to key words in Indigenous languages and their English translations.[22] A sophisticated Aotearoa site, Kā Huru Manu, uses high-resolution satellite mapping, with a selection of other Basemap options, to document Māori place names for the South Island of New Zealand.[23]

Indigenous-centred virtual reality projects around the world are collated in the ever-evolving digital map of the FourthVR project.[24] In another animation project drawing upon virtual reality – Wunungu Awara: Animating Indigenous Knowledges – the creators explain:

> The loss of a language is a lot more than just the loss of words. It is also the loss of identity, spirituality, cultural knowledge and values. Using the latest 3D

animation technology Indigenous stories and languages come to life – records the past, preserves the present, and protects Indigenous languages and knowledge into the future.[25]

Other exciting projects include a Virtual Songlines site,[26] the Hunter Living Histories Deep Time Project,[27] and various virtual reality video games, including one devised in the Torres Straits, northern Queensland.[28]

★ ★ ★

Before turning to the content of some of the digital sites, we developed for the Deepening Histories of Place (DHoP) project, I will discuss some of the pertinent themes that emerged out of a previous interdisciplinary project that explored Indigenous history deep time – a project called Lake Mungo: Australia's Ancient Past. This research was concerned with expanding the narrow time scale of Australian history, which is generally confined to the era of British colonisation since 1788, and sometimes back to 1770 when James Cook and party arrived at Botany Bay in the *Endeavour* ship. Another priority was to take Indigenous modes of historical practice into account.[29] We wanted to tackle themes of temporality, scale, continuity, and change. We would not be abandoning our historical training or techniques. Rather, we hoped to broaden them. Our projects would not only engage with Indigenous narrative practices; they would also experiment with appropriate methods of research and delivery. As well as contributing to a more inclusive national narrative, we hoped that such research would create valuable repositories of knowledge about the deep past.[30] Collaborating closely with Indigenous knowledge custodians, the outcomes would give primacy to their framings of the past. With each telling, each platform and mode of telling, and each audience response, we hoped that historical knowledge and the discipline itself might shift, even if ever so slightly.

The speed of data being propelled around the world today might appear in stark contrast to Indigenous modes of circulating history. Stories and songs were transmitted through trade and exchange networks on foot; they are inscribed in rock art, and on exchange message sticks, shields, and other equipment. Were they 'histories' at all? They have often been referred to as myths, dreamings, and, more recently, songlines. We are still searching for the right terms. The Yaruwu term *buru* means place and time together. *Muju-muju* and *Yulberu* indicate 'a long time ago'.[31] *Tjukurrpa,* an Arrente word from Central Australia, encompasses the law of everything – humans, land, nature, philosophy, dreaming, history. Stories are the backbone, the knowledge set, for Indigenous Law. Orientation, space, and place are important, and in the case of the Gurindji and other peoples of the Northern Territory, the morality of historical characters is congruent with their travels being the 'right way' or East to West direction, following the sun's daily journey. Wik people of North Queensland talk about the future being behind the person speaking, and the past in front of them – the logic is that, unlike the future, the past can be seen, 'known'.[32]

'Dreaming' or 'dreamtime' traditions have been likened to an 'everywhen', an 'eternal now', and as collapsing time. In a kind of multi-layered past, present, and future, the deep past is always present and acting on the future.[33] The notion of a kind of temporal flatness, a landscape of historical continuity and endless reconnection, is in keeping with classical Indigenous notions of temporality. Indigenous people's experiences of place could be at once time-shallow and transcendent. Some of this is due to the ruptures of colonialism, which caused many Indigenous Australians to become disconnected from their traditional 'Country' or custodial lands. Clans and language groups have intermixed with each other, and with Europeans, Asians, and Pacific Islanders.[34] Dispossession, massacres, removal to reserves, missionary impact, and government-enforced acculturation that included banning their languages and cultural practices severed people from crucial platforms of historical transmission. Forcible child removal was followed by compulsory Western education that included 'Australian history lessons' about navigators and explorers who 'discovered' Australia. Their 'landings' came with dates and names like 1770/Captain Cook and assertions of 'first arrivals' in 1788 – powerful British/European narratives that expunged the long, long histories of Indigenous firsts.

As discussed in the Introduction, like other Indigenous people, Australian Aboriginal people today are diverse, living different urban, regional, and remote lifeways and practising different cultural mores. They always were culturally diverse, speaking 250 different languages, with various associated dialects, contrasting ritual practices, stories, protocols, mark-making or art traditions, and law. Contemporary people engage with multiple concepts of time and history, varying in worldviews, residence, cultural traditions, linguistic, landscape, and other knowledge, and in the degree of shared community with other Australian citizens. They are, however, all part of a modern/post-modern world and of the Australian nation. What distinguishes them from other Australians, however, is a shared historical identity, with a landed sovereignty that British-Australian colonialism attempted to extinguish. To address cultural loss, many Indigenous people around Australia are investing a great deal of energy reconnecting with their cherished heritages, and then teaching this to the next generation and to wider audiences in order to ensure that it is transmitted to the future. Our projects have aimed to foster and support such enterprises.

Historical footprints – times slow or fast?

Ancient prints, bones, and other material manifestations of the deep past pierce the meniscus of the present day. Human intervention allows these 'irruptions' of the deep past or the 'irruptions of the dreaming' to mediate between the past and present.[35]

For a historian interested in escaping modernity's shallow timeframe to expand the scale of history, it is exciting to encounter tangible material evidence of times so long ago, and to reflect upon how that might be integrated in history-telling. If we define 'history' as the formal historical scholarship typical of the academy,[36] the past 60,000 years of Aboriginal occupation in Australia arguably stand outside the historical imagination. Such a span of time is not necessarily beyond the imagination of Aboriginal people, however, who assert that they have 'always been here' – in Australia. Consequently, they can be sceptical of research that focuses on arrival dates and migrations. Their connectedness over so many epochs, among other factors, also leads many Indigenous Australians to reject the 'out of Africa' theory.

At the same time, many Indigenous stories reveal an abiding interest in the creation of landscape, of the earth, stars, moon, and sky, and their enduring presence in that wider universe. A Mutthi Mutthi custodian of the Willandra Lakes/Mungo region told me: 'We were here even before those stars left the ground.'[37] The Emu constellation in the Milky Way is a shared story around Australia, as are star stories about the Seven Sisters and those of the Rainbow Serpent, of Eaglehawk and Crow. Some raise interpretative mysteries, while others are backed by scientific insights about reefs and islands forming, lands being swallowed by sea, ecologies changing, and volcanoes erupting – the kinds of stories discussed in Christopher Ballard's chapter in special relation to New Guinea and Pacific islands.[38]

Proponents of 'big history' have espoused a progressive narrative of increasing complexity – mirroring the biosphere, where the argument is difficult to argue against, but they extend this to social evolution.[39] This potentially reinforces some of the 'grand narratives' where the Enlightenment becomes the turning point and Aboriginal people occupy a 'timeless', historyless past. Despite numerous critiques, popular archaeological timelines still place Aboriginal Australians in the 'stone age', which equates to the bottom of the ladder. Yet, Australian Aboriginal culture had complex social organisation, with continuous development of sophisticated artistic and knowledge traditions and technologies. What is more, they used ingenious, effective techniques to disseminate information about key resources and crucial historical stories.

Sparked by the unique human history on the Australian continent, our community-collaborative projects aimed to deepen public knowledge of Australian landscapes beyond the prevailing national narratives, which defined them as places awaiting colonising 'firsts'. Seeking information and stories from Indigenous informants, the projects sought to assert that Indigenous Australia had prior, longer histories – ones in which Indigenous Australians might apply their expert interpretative knowledge.

For example, in 2003, a human trackway in the form of a series of 700 human footprints, dating back probably 18,000–20,000 years, became exposed across a drying lakebed. The footprints have been photographed and digitised, with digital printing enabling 3D casts to be made. Located in the Willandra Lakes World Heritage area, they were imprinted in clay when the lakes were full of water during the Pleistocene. Today, they are on eroding dry lands surrounded by dramatic, shifting dune-scapes.[40]

When Pintupi desert men from Central Australia were invited south to interpret the tracks, their trained eyes and skills enabled observations of family groups going on a kangaroo hunt, a spear being thrown at a kangaroo and missing. They helped people imagine an action scene from deep time, of mobile individuals in that same place around 20,000 years ago.[41] With all the human elements we treasure: family groups – children gambolling around, adults moving more purposefully – hunting, having a picnic, and caring for each other – with one man moving speedily with only one leg and a stick as aid. Depending on the evidence available, digital platforms lend themselves to exploring the moments of history evidenced in such a kangaroo hunt.

Indigenous people carried their stories, embedding them in the landscapes of their long journeys – often thousands of kilometres and by foot. It does seem 'a slow narrative', especially its means of embodied transmission. In a different kind of knowing, people's skin – their soles and their toes – physically connected with a storied ground. From limited enduring evidence, we assume that change was more incremental and slower back then, but how can we know that it was? It is a fantasy of modernity to imagine that past times were necessarily slow in every way. We know that these people invented fishing and cooking technologies, they created new art styles and burial rituals, they exchanged goods, traded, and developed insights from wide networks of clans and distant nations. The very tall adults of the trackway were moving extremely fast, probably faster than our best Olympic runners. We should also stop assuming that their lives were necessarily 'simpler'. Our modern eyes could readily miss both the complexity and the speed of change.

Digital history – or just history?

Each of our collaborative history projects has experimented with digital techniques. The Willandra Lakes project resulted in a documentary feature film, *Message from Mungo*, and our Australian Research Council Linkage project, Deepening Histories of Place: Landscapes of National and International Significance, was self-consciously digital from the outset.[42] It attempted to address the seemingly straightforward research question: How do we reframe Australian history so that it takes in deep histories? We selected significant landscapes of national and international heritage, such as National Parks and World Heritage. We hoped that digital techniques would be more user-friendly, reaching wider audiences than a scholarly book or article, and possibly more congruent with Indigenous modes of storytelling. Open access sites can reach wider audiences, and certainly wider ones than most scholarly publications. Their capacity for showcasing visual imagery, in both still and moving footage, could potentially create platforms to facilitate Indigenous narratives of connection to place. Digital strategies might then address a key problem for Australian history – as a platform for direct storytelling, they might provide a method for escaping Australian history's delimiting timeframe, stuck in post-Enlightenment 'modernity' (Figure 33.4).

As Indigenous Australians do not see their long history as beyond the human imagination, many Australian Aboriginal people trace a close connection and a sense of cultural continuity with very ancient people. What is more, as demonstrated by Indigenous speakers in the co-directed film *Message from Mungo*, they see no temporal obstacle in proclaiming close kinship with ancestors who lived 40,000 years ago – such as Lady Mungo and Mungo Man. They speak of familiar lives lived as if only yesterday.[43] Indigenous people's implicit sense of the *longue durée* means that they do not see a vast temporal scale as any obstacle whatsoever.

Ann McGrath

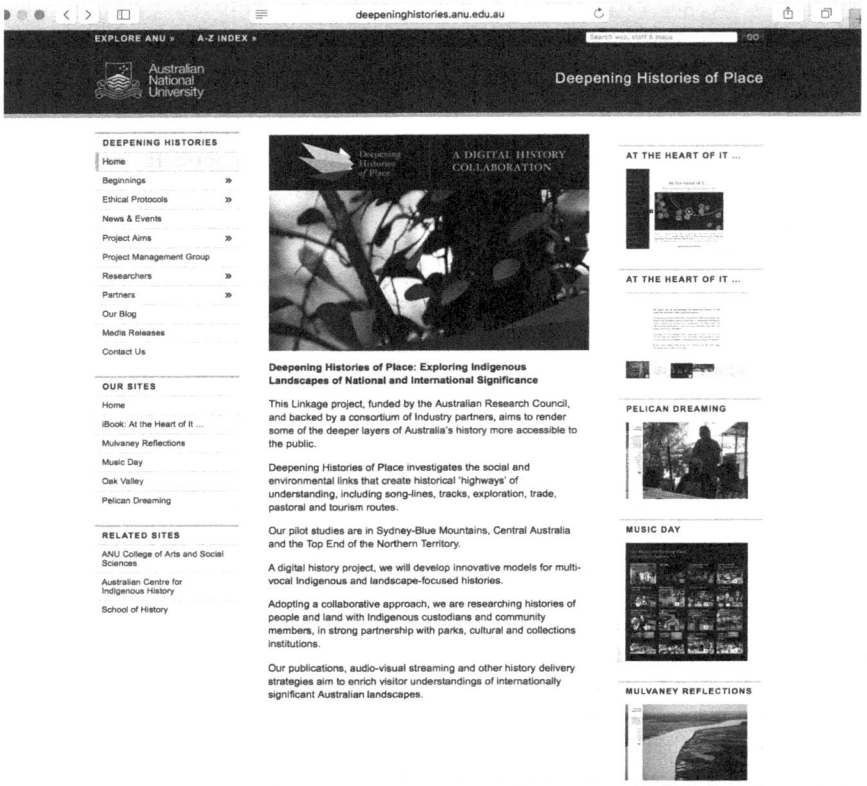

Figure 33.4 The home page of Deepening Histories, www.deepeninghistories.anu.edu.au, 12 September 2018

Overall, digital strategies seemed to offer a promising way of addressing Indigenous perspectives on deep time. Poor access to Western education, especially in remote regions, meant that many Indigenous Australians have varying literacy skills; however, several communities we worked with were already adept at engaging in custom-made family history platforms.[44] Decisions around formats took place after extensive consultations with participating individuals, with each project bringing different media solutions into play.

Producing a series of short videos and stills for web platforms with a multivocal approach would allow us to showcase various perspectives in first-person accounts from Aboriginal Australians. These would be gathered and presented in places of significance to their personal or ancestral history. Our team of Indigenous and non-Indigenous researchers wanted to broaden audio-only 'oral history' practices, which are often quickly transcribed and used in text form and therefore lack gesture, expression, and most significantly, the place context.

In much Indigenous thinking, the landscape itself tells history. It is the proof, the evidence of ancient stories. Consequently, our researchers used videography in relevant locations. Returning to 'Country' and telling embedded stories in and 'on Country' (their traditional ancestral lands) is vital. Affective relationships with current-day landscapes constitute a spiritual, deep-time-connected sense of association. Even if someone has never been there previously, it is believed their spirits and custodial spirit-protectors know that they are present and they anticipate a response. Practising these memory traditions is believed to animate the spirits of the land, which, in turn, protects people and communities.

Indigenous knowledge is empowering and contested. Stories have long been transmitted in complex song cycles and by other means, and there can be many versions of one larger story. We had to be cautious about earlier presumptions that there would be a singular authorised storyteller or one 'authentic version'. Authority was crucial, but that, too, could be contested, challenges often exaggerated by colonising disruptions and later migrations.

I had originally hoped that we might develop accessible products that could be used on a tablet device or a smart phone so that people could travel in their cars through 'deep time landscapes'. At DHoP's starting point in 2010, there was uncertainty about future technologies and concerns about accessibility for remote Indigenous communities. Smart phones did not have their current market share, capacity, or features. The recently introduced tablet devices seemed to offer a promising direction, but we were uncertain about their future uptake. We took care not to be brand-specific. We were concerned that without good internet access for travellers on the road, material could not be downloaded readily. Eventually we decided that our various digital products would be hosted on a website with side tabs and sub-sites; we would develop these free of the restrictions of the University's standardised internal webpages.

Our digital developer for the DHoP project, Jason Ensor, has a Doctorate in digital history and was active in international digital humanities networks. Jason convinced us that the research must drive the technology processes and products. Our team of researchers, including senior historians, representatives from state and federal parks, the National Film and Sound Archive and three PhD students, worked collaboratively with Indigenous representatives and liaison officers in Sydney, the Blue Mountains, Central Australia, and in the far north of the Northern Territory. Through digital recordings, Indigenous history participants became presenters and directors; they could speak directly to the audience and have significant control in developing how the stories would be told.

We created a data asset management system that was intended to work as the team's 'research commons' for uploading multimedia research materials. In collaboration with leading IP expert Terri Janke,[45] we developed built-in intellectual property protocols for protecting the copyright of Indigenous knowledge in digital media. We devised a suite of templates for participant consent to allow for various online and multimedia uses beyond the more commonly used sets of oral history permissions.[46]

Building upon this system, our diverse range of digital products reflected synergies and strategies decided upon between the researchers and communities. Julia Torpey, an Eora woman whose mother was a child of the stolen generations, developed various interpretative products. Her first project was organising a one-day musical event where Indigenous people of the Sydney region explored their connections to the land and its history. The performers – including relative newcomers to Eora lands – presented an eclectic selection of songs and slide presentations in many different musical genres from hip hop and jazz to classical, and an Eora song of Bennelong, transcribed in the 1790s. The event was held at the iconic Sydney Conservatorium of Music, and Julia then developed a quality audio recording, 'Our Music, Performing Place, Listening to Sydney', which can be streamed for playing on a smart phone, tablet device, or via the website.[47] Performers were proud of having a permanent record of the day, which was the first devoted to Indigenous performance at the Conservatorium (Figures 33.5 and 33.6).

Julia, assisted by Karen Maber and Peter Read, also conducted research with Aboriginal people in the Blue Mountains World Heritage area. They produced an attractively designed ebook (downloadable via iTunes) entitled *At the Heart of It*, featuring 15 edited interviews, which can be read on either a tablet device or an iPhone.[48] They included place-based stories across Darug and Gundungurra Lands, highlighting 'emotional and affective links'. Although Julia presented people's stories on their own terms,

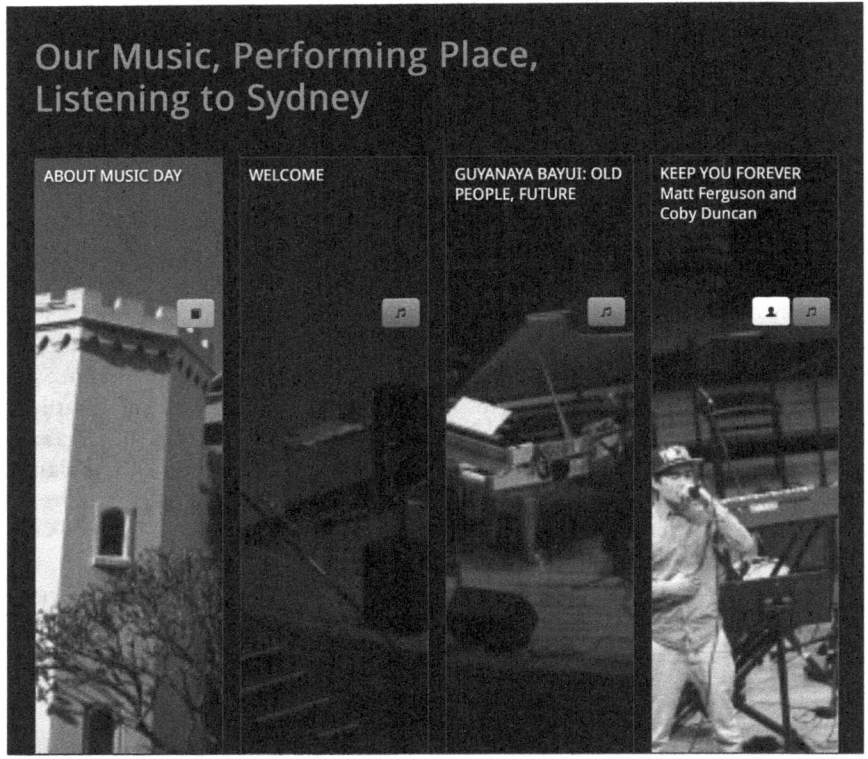

Figure 33.5 The home page of 'Our Music, Performing Place, Listening to Sydney', www.deepeninghistories.anu.edu.au/sites/music-day, 12 September 2018

Deep history's digital footprints

Figure 33.6 Julia Torpey filming the Blue Mountains cultural festival, 2011. Photo by author

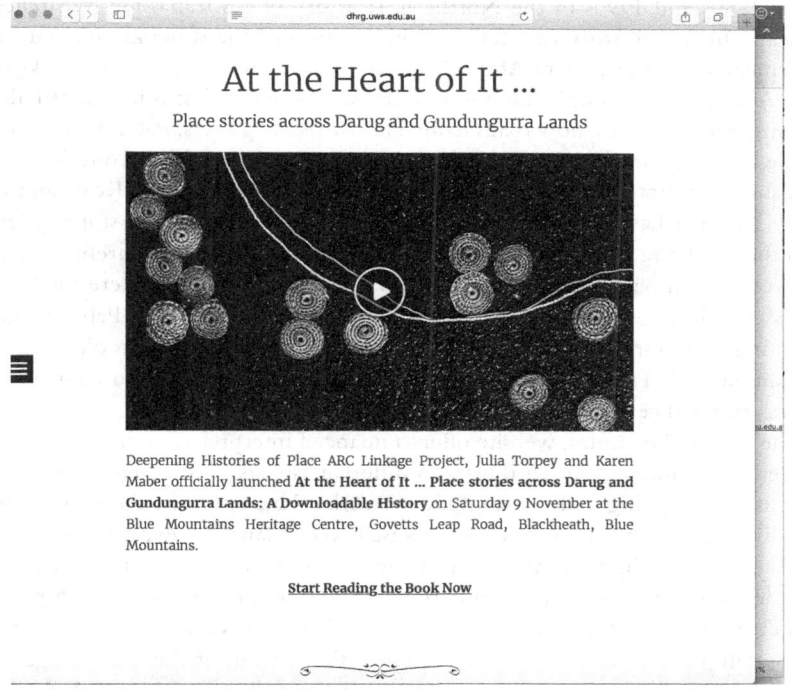

Figure 33.7 Page from *At the Heart of It... Place Stories Across Darug and Gundungurra Lands: A Downloadable History*, dhrg.uws.edu.au/at-the-heart-of-it, 12 September 2018

she became aware that some narratives were dynamic reinventions of identity, a politics of memory she considered more appropriate to critique in her Doctoral thesis rather than on a publicly accessible website (Figure 33.7).[49]

Other web products offered the potential to conserve and potentially repatriate related historical knowledge held in existing historical archives or in private collections. Consequently, eminent prehistorian John Mulvaney approached our project because he was concerned about the preservation of a series of 800 slides relating to Aboriginal heritage sites, including rock art, that he had taken in Arnhem Land from the late 1960s. Mary-Anne Jebb agreed to work with him and digitise them. 'Mulvaney Reflections' became a digital archive with thematic navigation tabs, complemented by a long interview, uploaded prior to Mulvaney's death. It provides 'an overview of Arnhem Land that takes us through two billion years of time from geological beginnings to the places of enormous creativity of Aboriginal people from around 40,000 years ago'. Digitisation offers a form of conservation for such an archive, a life's work that might otherwise be lost to the public or kept in a relatively inaccessible storage facility. Our project thus created new archives, preserved some old ones, and also provided interpretations and historical analysis.[50]

Another Doctoral student with the project, Rob Paton, an experienced archaeologist, created a website project that revisited fieldwork that he had conducted in the 1980s and 1990s in the Northern Territory of Australia. He researched a 'Pelican Dreaming' story that follows 'the creation of the stone knives and their movement along the ancient Aboriginal trade routes and exchange networks that cross Australia's Top End'. Some follow tracks of song cycles; others travel along the same routes that are now roads named for British explorers. Paton worked with people who explained exchange cycles or *winnun* (Law) stretching from the inland township of Elliott, north to the Arafura Sea, then west to Port Keats and east to the Arnhem Land Coast. His earlier archaeological research on stone quarries with the Mudbura and Jingili people questioned why they had so carefully manufactured certain objects but later destroyed them, unused. These were the Leilira long stone blades – associated with the distinctive long beak of the Pelican and its dreamings. He started to suspect that the Leilira tradition was not as old as he had first anticipated. Through various dating techniques, he was able to confirm that the practice had certainly endured for over a thousand years.[51]

The Pelican Dreaming website offers a nuanced interpretation of historical and archaeological imagery and it illustrates different aspects of the *winnun* trade cycle story. It uses mapping to illustrate trade networks. Thematic tabs allow for navigation, linking to historic images and concise text-explanatory explanations. Paton included links to digitised historical movie/video footage of the storytellers, and uploaded a new video of his consultations, including the consent sign-off process with current-day Indigenous knowledge custodians. This record showed that the appropriate people were present to authorise the sharing of this knowledge, and they also needed to ensure it was not of a sacred secret character unsuitable for public dissemination. Videoing such negotiations offers a particularly good fit when working with people not necessarily comfortable with the legal jargon of intellectual property forms (Figures 33.8 and 33.9).

Paton found that the Pelican Dreaming story played a dynamic role for the community in the 1980s, which had become dysfunctional following a terrible tragedy where several people died. Elders purposefully realigned the story and its

Figure 33.8 The home page of Pelican Dreaming, www.deepeninghistories.anu.edu.au/sites/pelican-dreaming, 12 September 2018

ritual exchanges and journey points in order to 'heal history'. Hence, these were powerful stories with many functions; in this case, the vital one of enabling the community to regain its wellbeing.[52]

Lastly, the team developed a website with the le Rossignol family of Oak Valley, who live on the red soils of the desert lands of Central Australia. They run a tourist business and an olive farm. Their website features four edited videos that have an additional purpose of helping promote their cultural tourism venture. Sharing autobiographical and transgenerational family stories, the le Rossignols explain the significance of key sites in the landscape. They discuss rock art, an array of edible native plants, a stone quarry, and in situ artefacts such as cutting tools and grinding stones. Their land contains a Precambrian fossil site with an array of creatures from the deep past that long precede the dinosaur age. Using the ancient quarry to demonstrate how to identify and manufacture stone tools, the last video provides a lesson by Paton and Indigenous archaeologist and traditional owner Sam Wickman on interpreting the local archaeological evidence (Figure 33.10).[53]

Our new Laureate research project, entitled *Rediscovering the Deep Human Past: Global Networks, Future Opportunities*, will include a big data survey that will feed into an interactive map. We hope to develop a digital 'Ancient Memory Atlas'

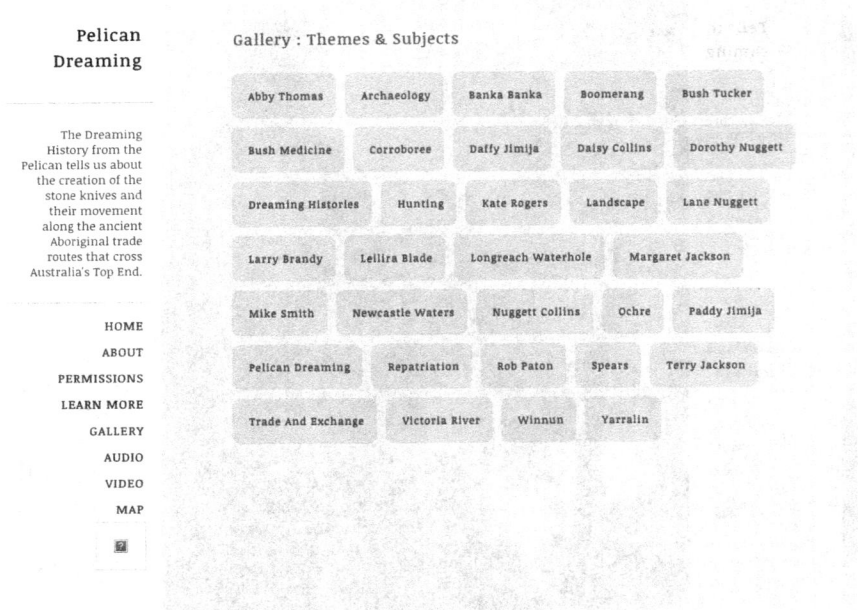

Figure 33.9 Gallery tabs on the Pelican Dreaming site, www.deepeninghistories.anu.edu.au/sites/pelican-dreaming/index.php?action=gallery, 12 September 2018

suited both to larger scale presentation in museum spaces and to smaller scale interactive platforms. Indigenous Australians have called for a truth-telling about all aspects of their history,[54] and their deep past narratives will play a crucial role in the future for asserting past and present sovereignty. We aim to retrieve recorded deep history stories in existing archival collections, then run repatriation and interpretative workshops around these materials with interested Indigenous communities, including the Yawuru of Broome. Where possible, Indigenous tellings of the deep human past will be accompanied by relevant scientific research. Many of our findings will be showcased on websites or in larger digital formats and, with this in mind, we are establishing partnerships with Indigenous communities, key libraries, and museums.

Long histories

Although this final chapter has focused particularly on the southern hemisphere continent of Australia, it constitutes a plea to extend history's time-zones globally, so that they include the full expanse of world history. Indeed, we do not believe that there is any such thing as 'global history', 'big history', or 'deep history' that does not make substantial efforts to integrate the human epochs in which Indigenous people had domain over their lands. To do so, academic historians should consider the distinctive modes of Indigenous historical practice, and how these,

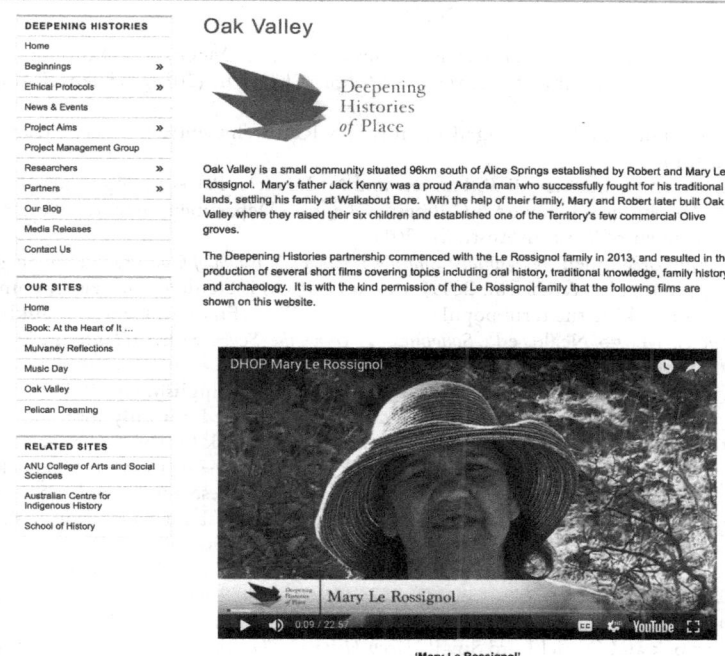

Figure 33.10 Oak Valley website, Mary le Rossignol's story, www.deepeninghistories.anu.edu.au/oak-valley, 12 September 2018

too, can enliven the discipline. If we wish to expand the scale of history beyond the temporal constraints of Western modernity, we will need to explore new modes of historical practice. It goes without saying that such research must be undertaken in collaboration with Indigenous knowledge custodians, in arrangements that respect their goals, their project design input, their intellectual property, and their protocols for best practice.

Digital platforms showcasing Indigenous people's modes of historical practice may offer some clues as to how 'history time' might be expanded. Digital strategies have so much scope to provide a useful way to research and publish narratives that deploy direct and multivocal storytelling and that offer wide public access. Via the digital space and scale of the internet, Indigenous storytelling can be researched locally and presented internationally. Such tellings will broaden the history discipline, for Indigenous knowledge practices are already challenging conventional ontologies around history. They enable us to rethink periodisation, temporalities, emotion, embodiment, the multi-sensory nature of experience, deep associations of place – and indeed, the very time of history, including the *longue durée*. Long before the invention of the atomic clock, there were other methods of thinking about and capturing places in time – ones that will implicitly challenge and inform how academic historians might imagine the deep past and its enduring ancestral connections with the people, the landscapes and waterscapes of the present and future.

Notes

1. This is an expanded version of a chapter published as A. McGrath, 'Die digitalen Fußspuren der Tiefengeschichte,' *Archiv für Mediengeschichte* 18 (2018): Tiefenzeit und Mikrozeit.
2. The Twitter handle has since changed and it is now Research Centre for Deep History @redeephistory.
3. R.T. McCrea, M.G. Lockley, P.W. Haines, and N. Draper, 'Palaeontology Survey of the Broome Sandstone – Browse LNG Precinct Report,' Department of State Development, Government of Western Australia, 2011.
4. Gay'Wu Group of Women, *Songspirals: Sharing Women's Wisdom of Country through Songlines* (Crows Nest: Allen & Unwin, 2019); Bruce Chatwin is credited with either coining the term or making the term popular in The Songlines (Franklin Center: Franklin Library, 1987); Margo Neale, ed., *Songlines: Tracking the Seven Sisters* (Canberra: National Museum of Australia Press, 2017).
5. Historian W.K. Hancock wrote: 'A great historian and great Englishman, R.H. Tawney, said on a famous occasion that historians of land-use need not only more documents but stronger boots. By this he meant that they must look for their evidence not only in archives and libraries but also in paddocks and fields.' – from W.K. Hancock, *Perspective in History* (Canberra: Dept. of Economic History, Research School of Social Sciences, Australian National University, 1982). Some debate about whether it was in fact Tawney; historian Manning Clark frequently used the quote too.
6. Ann McGrath and Mary Anne Jebb, eds., *Long History, Deep Time: Deepening Histories of Place* (Canberra: ANU Press, 2015), 241–252; *Message from Mungo*, film produced and directed by Andrew Pike and Ann McGrath (Canberra: Ronin Films, 2014), 70 mins.
7. Andrew Shryock and Daniel Lord Smail, *Deep History: The Architecture of Past and Present* (Berkeley: University of California Press, 2011); Daniel Lord Smail and Andrew Shryock, 'History and the "Pre",' *The American Historical Review* 118, no. 3 (2013): 709–757; Jo Guldi and David Armitage, *The History Manifesto* (Cambridge: Cambridge University Press, 2014).
8. S. Aslanian, J. Chaplin, K. Mann, and A. McGrath, 'AHR Conversation – How Size Matters: The Question of Scale in History,' *The American Historical Review* 118, no. 5 (2013): 1431–1472.
9. David Christian, *Maps of Time: An Introduction to Big History* (Berkeley: University of California Press, 2004).
10. Smail and Shryock, 'History and the "Pre".'
11. Ara Irititja: the Anangu Community Archive, accessed 15 December 2020, https://ai.ara-irititja.com/welcome.
12. Mukurtu CMS, accessed 15 December 2020, https://mukurtu.org/.
13. Ann McGrath, 'Monumental Discovery Narratives and Deep History,' *Humanities Australia* 11 (2020): 69–80.
14. 'Welcome to Country,' Weerianna Street Media, 2013. https://apps.apple.com/au/app/welcome-to-country/id1005047597. The Welcome to Country application was not comprehensive, and it does not appear to have been updated or expanded for some years.
15. SahulTime, accessed 15 December 2020, http://sahultime.monash.edu.au.
16. LandMark, accessed 15 December 2020, http://www.landmarkmap.org/; see also, Karen Emslie, 'This Alternative to Google Maps Aims to Protect Indigenous Land,' *OneZero*, 14 June 2019, https://onezero.medium.com/this-alternative-to-google-maps-aims-to-protect-indigenous-land-62e2e414eb04.
17. Native Land, accessed 15 December 2020, https://native-land.ca/.
18. Return, Reconcile, Renew, accessed 15 December 2020, https://returnreconcilerenew.info.

19 'Colonial Frontier Massacres, Australia (Date Range: 1780 to 1930),' Centre For 21st Century Humanities, accessed 15 December 2020, https://c21ch.newcastle.edu.au/colonialmassacres/map.php.
20 Nick Evershed and Andy Ball, 'The Killing Times,' *The Guardian*, 18 November 2019, https://www.theguardian.com/australia-news/ng-interactive/2019/mar/04/massacre-map-australia-the-killing-times-frontier-wars.
21 The Queensland Native Mounted Police Research Database, accessed 15 December 2020, https://frontierconflict.org.
22 Digital Daisy Bates, accessed 15 December 2020, http://bates.org.au.
23 'Ngāi Tahu Atlas,' Kā Huru Manu, accessed 15 December 2020, https://www.kahurumanu.co.nz/atlas.
24 Fourth VR, accessed 15 December 2020, https://fourthvr.com/.
25 Wunungu Awara: Animating Indigenous Knowledges, accessed 15 December 2020, https://www.monash.edu/arts/monash-indigenous-studies/wunungu-awara.
26 Virtual Songlines, Bilbie Virtual Labs, accessed 15 December 2020, https://www.virtualsonglines.org/
27 'Deep Time Project,' Hunter Living Histories, University of Newcastle, 17 November 2017, https://hunterlivinghistories.com/2017/11/17/deep-time-project/.
28 In terms of maps, apart from the Massacre Map (and the Guardian's Killing Times), there is the NZ project Kā Huru Manu. There are a number of other virtual reality, augmented reality, and game-based initiatives too, some of which are already mentioned in this chapter, including the Hunter Living Histories Deep Time Project; Virtual Songlines; SahulTime; Wunungu Awara; and Torres Strait Virtual Reality (http://ojs.decolonising.digital/index.php/decolonising_digital/article/view/TSVR).
29 Alison Bashford, 'The Anthropocene is Modern History: Reflections on Climate and Australian Deep Time,' *Australian Historical Studies* 44, no. 3 (2013): 341–349.
30 Neale, *Songlines*; B. Glowczewski, 'The Meaning of "One" in Broome, Western Australia: From Yawuru Tribe to Rubibi Corporation,' *Aboriginal History* 22 (1998): 203–222; for a review of terminology see Philip Jones, 'Beyond Songlines,' *Australian Book Review* 394 (September 2017).
31 Digital Daisy Bates.
32 Minoru Hokari, *Gurindji Journey: A Japanese Historian in the Outback* (Sydney: University of New South Wales Press, 2011; Honolulu: University of Hawai'i Press, 2011); Rafael E. Núñez and Eve Sweetser, 'With the Future Behind Them: Convergent Evidence From Aymara Language and Gesture in the Crosslinguistic Comparison of Spatial Construals of Time,' *Cognitive Science* 30, no. 3 (2006): 401–450.
33 W.E.H. Stanner, *The Dreaming and Other Essays* (Collingwood: Black Inc., 2011); D. James, 'Tjukurrpa Time,' in McGrath and Jebb, *Long History, Deep Time*, 33–45.
34 Ann McGrath, *Illicit Love: Interracial Sex and Marriage in the United States and Australia* (Lincoln: University of Nebraska Press, 2015); Regina Ganter, *Mixed Relations: Asian-Aboriginal Contact in North Australia* (Perth: UWA Publishing, 2006).
35 Karen Hughes, 'Arnhem Land to Adelaide,' in McGrath and Jebb, *Long History, Deep Time*, 83–100.
36 Understandably, archaeologists warn that the scarcity of evidence makes it difficult, if not impossible, to draw conclusions about the people of such distant times.
37 Personal communication; for relevant interviews see *Message from Mungo*.
38 See also, Duane W. Hamacher, 'Meteoritics and Cosmology Among the Aboriginal Cultures of Central Australia,' *Journal of Cosmology* 13 (2011): 3743–3753; Patrick D. Nunn and Nicholas J. Reid, 'Aboriginal Memories of Inundation of the Australian Coast Dating from More than 7000 Years Ago,' *Australian Geographer* 47, no. 1 (2016): 11–47.
39 Christian, *Maps of Time*.

40 Ann McGrath and Malcolm Allbrook, 'Collaborative Histories of the Willandra Lakes,' in McGrath and Jebb, *Long History, Deep Time*, 241–252.
41 Steve Webb, Matthew L. Cupper and Richard Robins, 'Pleistocene Human Footprints from the Willandra Lakes, Southeastern Australia,' *Journal of Human Evolution* 50 (2006): 405–413.
42 Deepening Histories of Place: Landscapes of National and International Significance, The Australian National University and Sydney University (2011–2013), http://www.deepeninghistories.anu.edu.au/.
43 *Message from Mungo*.
44 Such as Ara Irititja: the Anangu Community Archive.
45 Terri Janke, *Indigenous Cultural Protocols and the Arts* (Sydney: Terri Janke & Company Pty Ltd, 2016), 60–65.
46 'Clearance Forms,' Deepening Histories, accessed 15 December 2020, http://www.deepeninghistories.anu.edu.au/documents/.
47 'Our Music, Performing Place, Listening to Sydney,' Deepening Histories, accessed 15 December 2020, http://www.deepeninghistories.anu.edu.au/sites/music-day/.
48 Julia Torpey, *At the Heart of It … Place Stories Across Darug and Gundungurra Lands: A Downloadable History* (Apple Books, 2014), https://books.apple.com/au/book/at-the-heart-of-it/id849121205, https://dhrg.uws.edu.au/at-the-heart-of-it/.
49 Julia Torpey, 'Re-Imagining Identities: Aboriginal People Living on Darug and Gundungurra Lands' (PhD diss., Australian National University, 2018).
50 'Mulvaney Reflections,' Deepening Histories, accessed 15 December 2020, http://www.deepeninghistories.anu.edu.au/sites/mulvaney-reflections/.
51 'Pelican Dreaming,' Deepening Histories, accessed 15 December 2020, http://www.deepeninghistories.anu.edu.au/sites/pelican-dreaming/.
52 Rob Paton, 'The Mutability of Time and Space as a Means of Healing History in an Australian Aboriginal Community,' in McGrath and Jebb, *Long History, Deep Time*, 67–82.
53 'Oak Valley,' Deepening Histories, accessed 15 December 2020, http://www.deepeninghistories.anu.edu.au/oak-valley/.

Bibliography

Aslanian, S., J. Chaplin, K. Mann, and A. McGrath. 'AHR Conversation – How Size Matters: The Question of Scale in History.' *The American Historical Review* 118, no. 5 (2013): 1431–1472.
Bashford, Alison. 'The Anthropocene is Modern History: Reflections on Climate and Australian Deep Time.' *Australian Historical Studies* 44, no. 3 (2013): 341–349.
Chatwin, Bruce. *The Songlines*. Franklin Center: Franklin Library, 1987.
Christian, David. *Maps of Time: An Introduction to Big History*. Berkeley: University of California Press, 2004.
Emslie, Karen. 'This Alternative to Google Maps Aims to Protect Indigenous Land.' *OneZero*, 14 June 2019. https://onezero.medium.com/this-alternative-to-google-maps-aims-to-protect-indigenous-land-62e2e414eb04.
Evershed, Nick, and Andy Ball. 'The Killing Times.' *The Guardian*, 18 November 2019. https://www.theguardian.com/australia-news/ng-interactive/2019/mar/04/massacre-map-australia-the-killing-times-frontier-wars.
Ganter, Regina. *Mixed Relations: Asian-Aboriginal Contact in North Australia*. Perth: UWA Publishing, 2006.
Gay'Wu Group of Women. *Songspirals: Sharing Women's Wisdom of Country through Songlines*. Crows Nest: Allen & Unwin, 2019.
Glowczewski, B. 'The Meaning of "One" in Broome, Western Australia: From Yawuru Tribe to Rubibi Corporation.' *Aboriginal History* 22 (1998): 203–222.

Guldi, Jo, and David Armitage. *The History Manifesto*. Cambridge: Cambridge University Press, 2014.

Hamacher, Duane W. 'Meteoritics and Cosmology Among the Aboriginal Cultures of Central Australia.' *Journal of Cosmology* 13 (2011): 3743–3753.

Hancock, W.K. *Perspective in History*. Canberra: Dept. of Economic History, Research School of Social Sciences, Australian National University, 1982.

Hokari, Minoru. *Gurindji Journey: A Japanese Historian in the Outback*. Sydney: University of New South Wales Press, 2011; Honolulu: University of Hawai'i Press, 2011.

Hughes, Karen. 'Arnhem Land to Adelaide.' In *Long History, Deep Time: Deepening Histories of Place*, edited by Ann McGrath and Mary Anne Jebb, 83–100. Canberra: ANU Press, 2015.

James, D. 'Tjukurrpa Time.' In *Long History, Deep Time: Deepening Histories of Place*, edited by Ann McGrath and Mary Anne Jebb, 33–45. Canberra: ANU Press, 2015.

Janke, Terri. *Indigenous Cultural Protocols and the Arts*. Sydney: Terri Janke & Company Pty Ltd, 2016.

Jones, Philip. 'Beyond Songlines.' *Australian Book Review* 394 (September 2017).

McCrea, R.T., M.G. Lockley, P.W. Haines, and N. Draper. 'Palaeontology Survey of the Broome Sandstone – Browse LNG Precinct Report.' Department of State Development, Government of Western Australia, 2011.

McGrath, Ann. *Illicit Love: Interracial Sex and Marriage in the United States and Australia*. Lincoln: University of Nebraska Press, 2015.

McGrath, Ann. 'Monumental Discovery Narratives and Deep History.' *Humanities Australia* 11 (2020): 69–80.

McGrath, Ann, and Mary Anne Jebb, eds. *Long History, Deep Time*: Deepening Histories of Place. Canberra: ANU Press, 2015.

McGrath, Ann, and Malcolm Allbrook. 'Collaborative Histories of the Willandra Lakes.' In *Long History, Deep Time: Deepening Histories of Place*, edited by Ann McGrath and Mary Anne Jebb, 241–252. Canberra: ANU Press, 2015.

Message from Mungo. Film produced and directed by Andrew Pike and Ann McGrath. Canberra: Ronin Films, 2014. 70 mins.

Neale, Margo, ed. *Songlines: Tracking the Seven Sisters*. Canberra: National Museum of Australia Press, 2017.

Núñez, Rafael E., and Eve Sweetser. 'With the Future Behind Them: Convergent Evidence From Aymara Language and Gesture in the Crosslinguistic Comparison of Spatial Construals of Time.' *Cognitive Science* 30, no. 3 (2006): 401–450.

Nunn, Patrick D., and Nicholas J. Reid. 'Aboriginal Memories of Inundation of the Australian Coast Dating from More than 7000 Years Ago.' *Australian Geographer* 47, no. 1 (2016): 11–47.

Paton, Rob. 'The Mutability of Time and Space as a Means of Healing History in an Australian Aboriginal Community.' In McGrath and Jebb, *Long History, Deep Time*, 67–82.

Shryock, Andrew, and Daniel Lord Smail. *Deep History: The Architecture of Past and Present*. Berkeley: University of California Press, 2011.

Smail, Daniel Lord, and Andrew Shryock. 'History and the "Pre".' *The American Historical Review* 118, no. 3 (2013): 709–757.

Stanner, W.E.H. *The Dreaming and Other Essays*. Collingwood: Black Inc., 2011.

Torpey, Julia. *At the Heart of It… Place Stories Across Darug and Gundungurra Lands: A Downloadable History*. Apple Books, 2014. https://books.apple.com/au/book/at-the-heart-of-it/id849121205.

Torpey, Julia. 'Re-Imagining Identities: Aboriginal People Living on Darug and Gundungurra Lands.' PhD diss., Australian National University, 2018.

Webb, Steve, Matthew L. Cupper, and Richard Robins. 'Pleistocene Human Footprints from the Willandra Lakes, Southeastern Australia.' *Journal of Human Evolution* 50 (2006): 405–413.

Websites and Apps

Animating Indigenous Knowledges. https://www.monash.edu/arts/monash-indigenous-studies/wunungu-awara.

Ara Irititja: the Anangu Community Archive. https://ai.ara-irititja.com/welcome.

Centre for 21st Century Humanities. https://c21ch.newcastle.edu.au/colonialmassacres/map.php.

Deepening Histories of Place: Landscapes of National and International Significance. The Australian National University and Sydney University (2011–2013). http://www.deepeninghistories.anu.edu.au/.

Digital Daisy Bates, http://bates.org.au.

Fourth VR. https://fourthvr.com/.

From the Heart. https://fromtheheart.com.au/.

Hunter Living Histories, University of Newcastle. https://hunterlivinghistories.com/2017/11/17/deep-time-project/.

Kā Huru Manu. https://www.kahurumanu.co.nz/atlas.

LandMark. http://www.landmarkmap.org/.

Mukurtu CMS. https://mukurtu.org/.

Native Land. https://native-land.ca/.

The Queensland Native Mounted Police Research Database. https://frontierconflict.org.

Return, Reconcile, Renew. https://returnreconcilerenew.info.

SahulTime. http://sahultime.monash.edu.au.

Torres Strait Virtual Reality. http://ojs.decolonising.digital/index.php/decolonising_digital/article/view/TSVR.

Virtual Songlines, Bilbie Virtual Labs, https://www.virtualsonglines.org/.

'Welcome to Country.' Weerianna Street Media, 2013. https://apps.apple.com/au/app/welcome-to-country/id1005047597.

INDEX

Aberdeen, L. 401
Aboriginal Societies and the Common Law (McHugh) 262
Aboriginals Restriction and the Sale of Opium Act 1897 403
academic history 10, 15, 47, 571, 682–683
accelerator mass spectrometry (AMS) **196**, 202, 203, 727
Adam, R. 247
Adivasi dispossession, Indian state: Adivasi Gond inhabitants of Chhattisgarh 443; background and history 445–447; Bharatiya Janata Party 455; Chhattisgarh Bachao Andolan (Save Chhattisgarh Movement) 450; coal mining laws 451; colonial governance and technological transformation 447; complex forest ecosystem 457; concept of modernity and industrial development 445; context of Chhattisgarh 454–455; Directive Principles of State Policy 446; dispossession and resistance 449–456; extractivism and progress 445; *Forest Rights Act* 443, 452–457; forests and water sources 450; forests, land acquisitions, and state regulation 447–449; 'historic injustice' 448–449; history of Adivasi marginalisation 443; hyper-narratives of development and modernity 449; idea of protecting forests 445–446; Indian Constitution 447–448; Indian Forestry Service 446; issue of hydroelectric dams 450; legal rights 443; Lockean principle of property 446; mining corporations 453–454; Ministry of Coal 450; National Green Tribunal 454; Odisha Mining Corporation (OMC) 449–450; pacify tribes 446; 'participatory process' 453; *PESA* 448, 452–453, 456; poets, writers, and artists 444–445; proponents of land acquisition 452; religious and cultural practices 451; and resource exploitation 449; resource extraction and Indigenous dispossession 444; 'scheduled areas' 448; 'Singhdev Yojana' 452; South Eastern Coalfields Limited (SECL) 451–452; story of forest depletion 445; threat from coal mines 444; troubles and violence 457–458

adoption: Indigenous people by United Nations (UN) 6; of Intermediate Technologies 607; of moving rationing system, Pitjantjatjara 430

Africa: biological evidence 143; colonial origins and frameworks 603; continental migrations and mobilities 9; critiques of 'Western' archaeology 604; decolonising archaeology 603, 605–606; discovering *ntoror* 610–613; gorillas and chimpanzees in 116; Indigenous knowledge and hybrid archaeologies 603, 607–610; inhabitation of 'sweet' or 'bitter' places 620n77; internationalizing local values 605; levels of poverty 606; localisation of archaeological practice 603–604; national research agendas 606; origins

Index

of urbanism 604; premises and *modus operandi* 605; 'remake African history' 604; secondary and tertiary education 603; settlement archaeology 604
African literature: 'Afro-European literature' 654; #BlackLivesMatter campaign 653; books, in South Africa 652; decolonised literary curriculum 663; Department of Basic Education 653; English literary curricula 653; #FeesMustFall movements 651; FunDza and *WritePublishRead* 657; intertextuality 662; Kenya, literary curriculum in 654; language of learning materials 657; literary studies 652, 653; loss of pre-colonial oral archives 652–653; multilingualism 655–657; multimodality 657–661; #RhodesMustFall movement 651, 653; University of Nairobi 654
Age of Trauma: 'Beyond the Pleasure Principle' 349; 'Indian Problem' 350; 'peace neurosis' 349
Ainu, Japan 9
Alfred, T. 367
Aliansi Masyarakat Adat Nusantara (AMAN) 102
Altman, J. 122
Amazon 16, 241, 368–369
America 18; Indigenous peoples 103
American Civil War 350, 353
American Historical Association 58
American Indians 6
ancestors: archaeological sites 168–179; ceremonies of reclaiming, re-telling, and respect 165–168; creation histories 184–187; Iroquois and Mohawks 165; oral traditions 183–184; rock art 180–183; Western Hemisphere 165–166
Andersen, C. 260
Andersen, H. C. 287
Anderson, H. 538
Anderson, J. 674
Anglo World 113, 114
Anthropocene 49
Anti-Slavery and Aborigines Protection Society (ASAPS) 114
Anti-Slavery Society in London 115
Antle, J. M. 556
Aotearoa, New Zealand: British-Māori alliance 231–232; British naval vessel *Ferret* 231; missionaries 232–233; Māori voyagers 230–233; nineteenth-century voyaging 231; political rivalries 232; role of European weaponry 233–234

Apocalypticism 36
Aquinas, T. 370
archaeological evidence: archaic or pre-modern behaviours 147; artefacts and technologies 147; cognitive or behavioural complexity 147; in East Asia and Australasia 146–148; environmental modelling 147; movement of modern humans 146; Upper Palaeolithic or Late Stone Age lithics 146
archaeological sites: American 179; Bering Land Bridge theory 168–169; Clovis horizon 168; Clovis People 168; Eastern Hemisphere **178–179**; evidence of human experiences 170; genetic studies of Hominin 170; Kimmswick, Missouri 170; La Sena, southwest Nebraska 170; locations of 171; material evidence 169; Monte Verde, Chile 169, 170; North America **172–175**; in North America 170; oral traditions, rock art, and petroglyphs 169; Pleistocene *171, **172–179***; Pleistocene-age artefact 170; South America **176–178**; Western Hemisphere 171
Arhem, K. 681
Arisi, B. M. 366, 368, 372
Armitage, D. 739
Arne, T. 244
Aron of Kangeq 695–698, *697*
Aronson, L. 637
Aronsson, P. 679
Asia: colonial Asia, defining indigeneity in 95–100; destruction of first-people communities 87; doctrines of Asian nationalism 87; in early modern and colonial eras 91–95; First peoples 87–95; legal recognition and modern Indigenous movement 101–102; societies from sixteenth century 86–87
assimilation: Australian exemption policies 402; European 632–634; government policies of 559–560, 562; Indigenous photography 635; native agents 69; Skällarim 536, 539
Atlantic slave system 327, *328*
Atwater, C. 386
Australasia: archaeological evidence 146–148; fossil and genetic evidence 144–146; human origins 141–144; Indigenous peoples 103; Out-of-Africa II 144–148
Australia: Australian settler rule 119; cases of abuse and murder 122;

Index

Commonwealth of Australia 119; future of environmental history 122; history of safari 114; Indigenous peoples of 111, 112; indirect rule 113; NAIDOC Week 8; preservation of 'wild animal' life 114–115; proximity of 'primitive peoples' 114; 'settler-colonial extractivism' 122; 'settler revolution' 113; state and federal governments 8; transnational histories 114
Australian Aboriginal people 5; advanced of 'primitive native people' 120; gathering way of life 150; human evolution 119; hunting 118, 150; injustices of 113; link between animal and human life 115; mobilisation of 'the Aborigines of Australia' in 1913 114; preservation of primitive race 121; 'sentiment' of humanitarians 116; sufferings 114; tribes or Nations 6
Australian Human Rights Commission 469
Austroasiatic languages 90
authentic cultures 13
authentic native 13
autonomous modernism 42
Axtell, J. 346, 356

Baartman, S. 286
Bachelard, G. 33
Backhouse, J. 731
Ballantyne, T. 304, 313
Ballara, A. 233
Bandelier, A. F. 576
Bangkok dynasty 91
Banivanua Mar, T. 70
Barbados: American Independence, 1783 330–331; importation of New England Indians 330; Indian slavery in 329–331; 'Negroes and other slaves' 330–331; seventeenth-century 329–330
Barkley, F. 228
Bartlett, F. 402
Basedow, H. 726
Beddoe, J. 291
behavioural modernity 149
Behind the Trail of Broken Treaties (Deloria) 269–270
Belich, J. 113
Bellear, L. 63, 472, 473
Bell, J. A. 491
Benjamin, W. 347, 348, 349, 357
Benton, L. 326
Bering agreement, 1892 117
Bernatzik, H. A. 636

Berry, A. 232, 731
Berthelsen, C. 694, 696
Betasamosake, L. 260
Biblical text 37
Bikinians 420; Baker, effects of second bomb 423; Enewetak Atoll 431; fission bombs 422–423; H-bomb tests 431; health status 422; and ill-fated return 431–432; Japanese and American troops 421; *Lucky Dragon Number 5* 431; in Marshall Islands 421–422; monetary value 422; in Oak Valley 435; Partial Test Ban Treaty 431; psychological stress 424; radiological contamination 432; 'remote' and 'unused' 433; story of radioactivity 423; traditional fishing methods 424–425; UN 'Strategic Trust Territory' 422; U.S. Air Force base 424; U.S. Atomic Energy Commission (AEC) team 423
biological evolution 139, 148
Birch, T. 63
blackbirding, history of 14
Black Caribs: 'the father of Independence' 513; and Garifuna 511–512; genetic heritage 512; as Natives 511, 512; self-identification 512
Blackhawk, M. 268
#BlackLivesMatter campaign 653
Bligh, W. 226
Blondin, C. 289
Blong, R. J. 583, 584, 585, 586, 590
Blumenbach, J.F. 286
Bolshevik revolution, 1917 98
Bolton, H. E. 61
Bonaparte, R. 290
Bonyhady, T. 118
Boomert, A. 506, 508
Borrows, J. 271
Boswell, J. 245
Bradley, D. 423
Brakstad, H. L. 287
Brant, J. 245, 246, 250
Brennan, C. 114
Britain's Caribbean colonies 326
British Burma 95
British Commonwealth 114
British India 95
British justice 118, 122
British rule 370
Broca, P. 290
Brooks, L. 15
Broome, R. 61, 694, 736, 738, 752
Browne, R. 333

Index

Brown, R. 285
Brown, R. D. 357
Bruce, G. 232
Bruce, M. W. 576
Buckland, F. T. 286
Buddhism 87
Burton, A. 116
Byrd, J. 66
Byrne, D. 483
Byzantine Empire 39

Campbell, J. F. 291
Canada 120, 183, 241, 245; B.C. Treaty Commission 264; colonial policy 561; *Constitution Act, 1982* 263, 264; First Nations' rights 265; Indian Act 267; Indigenous people lands, poverty 4–5; Indigenous policy 550; Indigenous treaty-making 263; International Commission of Radiation Protection 420; Iroquois Confederacy 242; modern treaty-making 264, 268; religious diversity 562; religious pluralism management 550; Royal Proclamation of 1763 271; Treaty of Niagara of 1764 271
carbon dating 13
Caribbean: archaeological and palaeoenvironmental research 501–502; Archaic Age 505; 'Black Carib' communities 510; Black Caribs and Garifuna 511–513; 'Carib Reserve Act' 515; 'Carib Reserve' in Dominica 515; Caribs (or Caribes or Caraibes) 508; CARICOM (the Caribbean Community) 516; in Central and Middle America 503; Ceramic Age 505–506; ceremonial performances 506; changing understandings of indigeneity 516–518; Classic Maya civilisation 503; concepts of *indigenismo* and *criollismo* 517; contested claims 513–516; 'Creole indigeneity' 516; early island identities 505–507; early occupation of 505; First peoples 503–505; 'founder effect' 506; guerrilla attacks 511; in Haiti 517; inhabitants of 507; latecomers 508; Lesser Antilles *504*; migration movement 504; modern Caribbean 501, *501*; molecular evidence 514; 'Native American' mitochondrial DNA 513; new peoples 509–510; oral histories 513; Ostionoid culture 506; political independence 503; population history 500–503; 'Rastafari nation' 517–518; Seven Years War 511; slavery and colonialism 502–503; Spanish people 502; spread of DNA testing 513–514; Sugar Revolution 502, 510; survivors 510–511; Taino names for 507, *507*; Treaty of Aix-la-Chapelle 515; varieties of 'independence' and reinvention 515; Y-chromosome variation 513
Carlson, K. 249
Carroll, E. 118
case for continuity, Kimberley *see* Kimberley rock art, Australia
Casement, R. 115
Cashman, K. V. 577
Catawba 386
Catchpole, A. J.W 573
Catlin, G. 117
Caucasians 117
Chaka (Mofolo) 661
Chakrabarty, D. 17, 152, 241, 282
Chalmers, J. 484, 485, 486, 490, 491
Chami, F. 604
Chang, D. 227, 228
Changing Ones (Roscoe) 367
Chappell, D. 222
Cherokee Nation 17
Cherokees 386
China: Manchu rulers 91; pre-Mongol and Mongol invasions 95; Yunnan and Guizhou 94
Chinese Communist Party 98–99
Chinese empires 88; principle of *tianxia* 90; 'raw' or 'cooked' barbarians 90
Chinese settlers 93
Chirikure, S. 605
Christian, D. 739
Christianity 118; and culture 119
Churchill, Winston (Prime Minister) 244, 421, 434
Civil War 350, 353
Clarke, M. 325, 332
Coalition for Indigenous People's Rights and Ancestral Domains (CIPRAD) 102
coercive labour 14
Cole, A. 402
colonial Asia: 'aboriginal' status 96; Asian nationalist movements 97; 1917 Bolshevik revolution 98; defining indigeneity in 95–100; direct and indirect rule 95; dominant nationalist movements 99; Gondi, Indigenous

people of Central India 97, *98*; Indian Constitution 99–100; Indigenous man of Negros Island 96, *97*; nature of 'primitive man' 96; nineteenth-century colonialism 95; 'Proto-Malays' and 'Deutero-Malays' 95; 'scheduled tribes' 97; Sinhala people 95

colonial encounter 20; Age of Trauma 349–350; anecdotal and archival, relationship between 353; awareness of trauma 347–348; colonial- Indigenous relational experiences 346; corrupt traders and Indian agents 350; debates 347; Discovery of the New World 346; experience of trauma 352; generations of stories 350–353; genetic archives 356–358; Great Sioux Uprising 353; hauntings 353–356; 'hermeneutics of the other' 347; historical consciousness 345–346; historical inequities and injustices 346; imperialism and colonialism 345; 'legitimate' history 352–353; post-traumatic stress disorder (PTSD) 347; settler-colonial societies 354; stories 348–349; traumatic inheritance 345; 'traumatic repetition' 352; violence of colonial history 346

colonial translators: Christian doctrine 310; 'holy scripture' 308; Joseph Brant 309, *310*; Massachusett Bible, 1663 308, *309*, 310; missionaries 309–311; Zulu word 310

Comaroff, J. 305
'Conference on African Wild Life' 115
Confucianism 87
Connelly, J. 279
1989 Convention 102
Cook, J. 224, 247
Cook, K. 227, 234
Cooper, W. 118, 120, 315
Cordova, V.F. 680
Corntassel, J. 266, 367
Coulthard, G. S. 67, 261, 268
Cranz, D. 691
creation histories 184–187; Anishnaabe creation history 185; creation of earth and people's place 186–187; Dine oral history 185; Geezhigo-Quae (Sky-Woman) 185–186; 'Indian' stories 185; North and South America 184–185
Cronin. S. J. 577
Cusicanqui, S. R. 373
Cuvier, G. 285

Dancing on Our Turtle's Back (Simpson) 260
Darwin: concept of evolution 46; evolutionary thinking 148
Darwin, C. 292
Darwinism 46
Dat läh mijen situd: En vädjan till svenska nationen från samefolket (Lindholm) 294
David, B. 723
Dawson, J. 724, 725, 726
Deacon, J. 605
de Certeau, M. 345, 346, 347, 669, 670
Declaration on the Rights of Indigenous Peoples (UNDRIP) 6, 7
decolonisation: 'decolonising the academy' 15; of imperial institutions 15
Decolonising the Mind: The Politics of Language in African Literature (Thiong'o) 654, 655, 656
Decolonizing Methodologies (Smith) 242
De Deckker, P. 205
Deep History 11
deep history's digital footprints: digital history 745–752; digital innovations 740–743; Dinosaurs and arrival narratives 736–740; historical footprints 743–745; long histories 752–753
Deep History: The Architecture of Past and Present (Shryock and Smail) 739
Deloria, P. J. 14
Deloria, V. Jr. 167, 168, 261, 269, 346, 371
Denetdale, J. N. 526
Denoon, D. 66
Der Bund (Swiss progressive newspaper) 120
Description of Greenland (Egede) 692
de Surville, J.F.M. 230
Dewdney, S.H. 488, 490
Diagnostic and Statistical Manual of Mental Disorders (DSM-5) 349
Dickinson, E. 471
digital history 745–752, *746, 748, 749, 751, 752*
digital innovations, Greenland: Anangu Community Archive 740; Deepening Histories of Place (DHoP) project 742; 'dreaming' or 'dreamtime' traditions 743; FourthVR project 741; Hunter Living Histories Deep Time Project 742; LandMark 741; Massacre Map project 741; *Muju-muju* and *Yulberu* 742; Mukurtu CMS 740–741; Native Land 741; Return, Reconcile, Renew 741; SahulTime 741; Welcome to Country application 741

Index

dingo 724–727
Dinosaurs: ancient civilisations and history 739; digital strategies 740; European-focused time-zones 738; footprints 736, 737; global Indigenous history 740; oral histories 738; periodisations and conceptualisations 739; Riddell Beach 736, *738*
dispossession: of Aboriginal and Torres Strait Islander people 399–400; Adivasi (*see* Adivasi dispossession, Indian state); 'big data' 434; Bikinians 420, 421–425, 431–432; civilians of Hiroshima and Nagasaki 419; documentation of U.S. and U.K. tests 433; effects of radiation damage 433, 434; and frontier violence 72n18; genetic testing 437n3; Indigenous 15; Indigenous and disempowered peoples 420; 'intense sensation' 434; intense trauma and distress 434; land 67; major powers and Indigenous people, relations between 419; Micronesian or Polynesian peoples 419–420; narratives of people's movements 435; nature of damage 434; 'non-stochastic' or non-random 420; nuclear testing 421; nuclear weapons, impacts of 420; Pitjantjatjara 420, 425–430; and resistance 449–456; 'stochastic,' or random 420; survivors of bombs 420–421; 'wastelands' or remote oceanic areas 433; Western Desert in Australia 433
'dissociative archaeology' 208
dolphin 728–731
Double Ghosts (Chappell) 222
dreaming of past 722–724
The Dual Mandate in British Tropical Africa (Lugard) 113
Duckworth, W.L.H. 280
Duguid, C. 425
Dungan Revolt (1862–1877) 94
Durri Aboriginal Medical Service (AMS) 727
Dutch sovereignty 92
Dwarris, F. 326, 327, 331, 332, 333, 334, 335, 336, 337, 338

early modern and colonial eras, Asia 91–95; colonial plantation sector 94; geopolitical enclosure movement 92; imperial armies 91–92; imperial centres 91; Miao in Chinese province 94; in pre-modern times 92; rise of frontier economy 93; risk of Russian settlement 93; scale of violence 94; trade and communication 93; transformation 91; Treaty of Nerchinsk 92
East Asia: Out-of-Africa II: the archaeological evidence in 146–148; Out-of-Africa II: the fossil and genetic evidence in 144–146
Echo-Hawk, R. C. 183
'economic man' 149
Edmonds, P. 65
Edwards, E. 641, 642
Edward VII. 248, 249
Egede, H. 691, 692, 709
Egede, P. 691, 693, 694, 695
1800 (after), European history: access to written sources 44; astronomical clock time 46; 'discovery of the social' 47; documents and testimony 44; historical writing 44; metaphor of 'source' 45; 'modernisation' and 'development' 45; rise of the novel 45; social history, emergence of 47
Eisenhower, Dwight D. (President) 421
Elbourne, E. 312
Elder, C. 183
Eliot, J. 308
Elkin, A.P. 724
Ellinghaus, K. 67, 68
Elwin, V. 446
Emerling, J. 636
'the Empire' 38
Erckenbrecht, C. 642
Errington, J. 305
Eschricht, D. 281
Étoile 10
Etowaucum 242
Europe 18; arrivals 13; Christian scholarship 40; colonial expansion 86; discoverers 11; expansionism 4; focussed histories 17; Travellers or Romani of 8
European Aborigines: collection of photographs, Sami 290–291; exhibitions of Sami people 287–290; nineteenth-century ethnographic exhibitions 290; and non-European Aborigines 291–292; Scottish 'pygmy theory' 291; three-stage chronological development model 291
European enlightenment 11
European history: 1500–1800 39–43; Before 1500 35–39; After 1800 44–49; cultural practices 33; historiography 33–34; 'knowledge of the past' 34; opposition of history and (social, collective) 'memory 34; political

ideologies 33; regimes of historicity 34–35; writing-based cultures of history 35
evolution, theory of 46
'exemplary center' 103n6
extinction, tragic narratives of 123n10
The Eyes of the Skin: Architecture and the Senses (Pallasmaa) 671

Fanon, F. 655, 656
Farini, G. A. 287
Farrar, F. W. 292
Fattovich, R. 604
#FeesMustFall movements 651
feet dancing 22
Fenton, W. N. 356
Ferguson, A. 281
Fernandes, E. R. 366, 368, 372
Fienup-Riordan, A. 694
1500 (before), European history: annals and chronicles 37; culture of commemoration 38; cycles of eternal repetition 36; emergence of political theology of monarchy 38; Herodotus and Thucydides 35; *historia magistra vitae* 35; 'in eternity' 38; inscriptions (technique of writing in stone) 36; philological criticism of textual traditions 37; 'realms,' or 'empires' 38; Roman Cicero 35; tradition of Hebrew Scripture and Greek New Testament 36
1500–1800, European history: antiquarianism 40; authenticity 40; chronological order of world time 40; classicism 40–41; concept of 'civilisation' 41; critique of political power 42; culture of learning 39; 'Donation of Constantine' 39; emergence of nation-building movements 43; 'formula of amnesia' 42–43; French Revolution of 1789 42; historical writing 39; notion of equality 41; notion of natural 'nobility' 41; notion of the sublime 40; peace treaties 42; 'polygenesis' of humans 41; religious learning 40; 'savagery' of the 'savages' 41; 'theory of history' 43
First peoples in Asia: in early modern and colonial eras 91–95; and expansion of pre-modern empires 87–90
First World Conservation Conference 19, 111
First World War 47, 113
Fisher, L. D. 330
Fixico, D. L. 18

Fjellstrom, P. 530
Foley, D. 728
Foley, G. 63
Ford, L. 66, 326
fossil and genetic evidence: 'Deep Skull,' Niah Cave 145; discovery of *Homo floresiensis* 145; in East Asia and Australasia 144–146; *Homo erectus* populations 145; *Homo luzonensis* 145–146; *Homo sapiens* groups 144–145, 146
Foucault, M. 404
Fox, J. J. 675
Franklin D. Roosevelt (President) 115
Franklin, J. 286
Freud, S. 349, 352
Frobisher, M. 246
FULRO (United Front for the Liberation of Oppressed Races) 99
Fur, G. 680

Garanger, J. 581
Garson, J.G. 290, 291
Gayanashagowa (Great Law of Peace) 242
Gay, J. 243
Geary, C. 636, 637
gender and diaspora in Australian policies relating to Aboriginal and Torres Strait Islander people 399–401, 412n1, 413n6; Alice and Alma Kelly 408, *408*; Anglo-Australian citizens 410; cultural heritage 410–411; education 404–405; exemption certificates 400; half-life of exemption 409–411; Lucinda Aberdeen 409–411; impact of assimilation policies 402; *Invalid and Old-age Pension Act 1908* (Commonwealth) 401; journeys of women in my family 403–409; Judi Wickes 403–405; Kella Robinson 406–409; Kelly's fear of child removal 408–409; Moonahcullah Mission *406*, 406–407, 409; Murrin Bridge Aboriginal Mission 409; policies of exemption 399–403; power women, Daisy Smith and Nancy Mittabong 405, *405*; 'protectionist legislation' 399; Queensland system of exemption 411; threat of child removals 407–408; Wemba-Wemba nation 406, *406*
genetic archives: *Angelus Novus* 357–358, *358*; hypothalamic-pituitary-adrenal (HPA) axis 356; intergenerational trauma 356; 'trauma tracking' 357; upstreaming, traumatic histories 356–357

Index

genocidal frontier: British Australia 112; in northern Australia 112; 'problem' of settler colonialism 112

geomythology: Australian Aboriginal memories 572; Biblical Flood 573; definition 572; 'direct line of transmission' 575; and historical scepticism 572–575; social practice and cultural memory 575; transcripts and translations 573; 'Ur-traditions' as *'original* texts' 574

German colonialism 645; colonial cruelties 632; concept of 'colonial fantasies' 632; concepts of traditionalism 634; and construction of Indigeneity 631–635; decade-old images 632; European assimilation 632–634; idealising constructions of Indigeneity 632–633; Indigenous person, Papua New Guinea 632, *633*, 645; modernisation 635; National Socialist 635; National Socialist rule 631; primitivism-as-animalism 631; primitivism-as-childlikeness 631; transnational path of primitivism 631; vanishing of Tasmanians 632; woman from Tasmania 632, *634*

Gilmour, R. 308
Ginibi, R. L. 469
Glahn, H. 691
global expansionism 2
Global Indigenous History 15
'globalization of the settler-colonial ethos' 76n56
Golson, J. 583
Gomme, G. L. 291
Gondi, Indigenous people of Central India 97, *98*
Goodall, H. 118, 400, 402
Gordon, C. V. 604
Gould, S. J. 291
Government of India Act, 1935 97
Graham, J. 335
Grant, K. 115
Gray, T. 247
green imperialism 121
Green, J. A. 637
Greenland: Aron of Kangeq 695–698; art, history, and ethno-aesthetics 704–707; Augo Lynge 698–701, *702*; development of 698–701, *702*; eighteenth-century representations 691–695; foundational European histories 691–695; Greenlanders writing 691–695; Guardian Council 700; literature, music, and oral histories 707–711; Mathias Storch 698–701, *699*; nineteenth-century developments 695–698; Niviaq Korneliussen's *HOMO sapienne 709*; Pia Arke 706; 1970s political and cultural awakening 701–704; Sume and Greenlandic rock music 701–704; uses of history in 707–711

Green, M. 656
Green, R. D. 347
Group Boundary Formation (GBF) Theory 197–199; cultural practices 197; with fissioning and increasing heterogeneity in rock art 197, *198*; as product of environmental gradient and isolation 197, *198*; socially transmitted behaviours 199
Grove, R. 114
Guldi, J. 739
Gunner, L. 661

Haddon, A. C. 291
Haebich, A. 642
Halliday, W. 552
Hamalainen, P. 62
Han Chinese culture 98
Hansson, Per Albin (Prime Minister) 534
Hanuman 88
Harbsmeier, M. 694
Harriot, T. 246
Harvey, S. P. 316
Haskins, V. 402
Hassan, F. A. 604
hauntings: American Indian historical trauma (AIHT) 354; 'Chivington's Colorado Territorial Constabulary' 355; definition of 354–355; historical trauma 353–354; mythologies 355; post-traumatic slave syndrome (PTSS) 354; 1864 Sand Creek Massacre 355; settler-colonial histories 355; 'trauma mastery' 354
Havai'i diaspora, voyagers from: Aotearoa 230–234; biography 222, 223; Bougainville's *Étoile* 221; effects of European intrusion 222; *Étoile* 221; island of Tahiti 221; Mokupuni o Hawai'i 227–230; political motivation 223; Polynesian 222; 'second diaspora' 222; second great Pacific diasporic movement 222; travellers, categories 222; Tōtaiete mā 223–227; Wallis' *Dolphin* 221, 224
Hebert, B. 582

Index

Hebraist scholarship, emergence of 39
Hegel, G.W.F. 45, 282
Henige, D. 571, 572, 573, 574, 588, 589
Herodotus 35
heterogeneity 194, *198*, 202, 207
Hika, H. 223, 233
Hildebrand, E. 280
Hiroshima and Nagasaki, civilians of 419
historia nullius, state of 12
historical footprints, Greenland 743–745
historical narratives 11–12, 37, 152, 345, 586, 605, 609, 610, 646, 676, 704
historical time 11, 40, 51n24
historical writing: and antiquarianism 41–42; historical justice 48; innovative 47; inscriptions (technique of writing in stone) 36; interview-based oral history 48; introduction of moveable letter types 39; language of 47; methodological innovation 48; modern, history of 43; pervasive genealogies 38–39; prominence of 'memory' 38; research-driven 43; self-interrogation of 43; source-based 44–45; variety of genres 37
historicisation 34, 42, 45–47
'historicism,' concept of 47
historicity 10, 18, 34, 36–40, 42–43, 45–47
historiography 14, 21, 33, 47, 57–58, 61, 65, 241, 353, 670, 673
History in Africa (Henige) 572
History of America (Robertson) 282
history of historical writing *see* historiography
history's outsiders 11, 19
Hogarth, W. 244
Hokari, M. 18, 680
Holocene 23, 183, 194, **196**, 196–197, 202, 207–210, 503, 577
Homeric epics 37
Homo erectus 141–142
homogeneity 194, 199, 515
Homo sapiens 148–149; origin of 139
Horton, M. C. 604
Hoskins, J. 673, 675
'hostile natives' 13
Howard, John (Prime Minister) 723
Hoxie, F. 65
Hultblad, F. 530, 532
human evolution: archaeological and ethnographic museums 151–152; biological explanations 151; Denisovans 146; DNA sequencing 146; generation of scientific narratives 150; human existence 152; impact of molecular genetic research 146; and Indigenous histories 150–152; and individual human growth 150; teleological narrative 151
humanitarianism 111, 121
human origins: African modern 141–144; archaic populations 140–141; Asian and Australasian evidence 141–144; Denisovans 143; development of archaeology 139; Great Ape species 141; hominin presence in Asia 144; *Homo sapiens*, origin of 139, 141, 143; Indigenous-histories perspective 140; 'Mitochondrial Eve' 142; 'modern' 140, 148–150; molecular genetic studies 144; notions of chronopolitics and political ontology 141; Out-of-Africa II 144–148; processual/post-processual debates 140
human zoos 10
Hunter, J. 284
hunting: Australian Aboriginal people 118, 150; culture, conservation as 126n35; wildlife 115
Huxley, T. H. 286
hybrid knowledge 21

Ibsen, H. 287
imperialism 2, 4, 21
India: Adivasi ('original inhabitants') 99–100 (*see also* Adivasi dispossession, Indian state); Aryans 95; British colonial administration 94–95; Chola forces 92; civilisations, *mleccha* ('incomprehensible') 88; 1957 Convention 101; 'criminal tribes' 94; Indian-Pioneer Papers (IPP) project 379; invasions by Muslim peoples 95; Mughal empire 91; Odisha (Orissa) 100, *100*; political disorder 94; Ramayana epic 88; scheduled district system 97; 'scheduled tribes' 99; tribes, map of 381, *382*
Indian Act 550, 562n2
Indian Forest Acts (Locke) 446
Indian Removal Act 383
Indians in Unexpected Places (Deloria) 14
Indian slavery: in Barbados 329–331; hereditary Native slavery 329; in Honduras 327; and *partus sequitur ventrem* 327–329; Slave Trade Act in March 1807 329; unlawful enslavement 327
Indigenous activism, Asia 101
Indigenous and Tribal Populations Convention 101, 102
Indigenous city *see* London, Indigenous engagement

Index

Indigenous history tellings 1; academic field of 14; *Cherokee Phoenix* 306; Christianity and Māori language 311; co-translators as authors 308–311; defined 16; European missionaries 303–304; familial, community, and national levels 1–2; 'global approach' 18; Indigenous experience 16; Indigenous modes of historical practice 16; interpreters and mediators 303–304; legends 17; missionary translation projects 305; native missionaries 311–312; Old Testament 312–313; people's linguistic and cultural autonomy 316; practitioners of 18; primacy of language 302; processes of settler-colonisation 316–317; reducing language to writing 305–308; Sequoyah *307*; settler-colonialism 312; traditions of history telling 18; translation of language 303; Treaty of Waitangi 312; *whare wanaga* (secret law) 312; writing cultures 313–316

Indigenous identities 5; 'blood quantum' or racial ideas 8; discrimination policies 8; substitute identities 8; suppressing identities 8

Indigenous knowledge (IK): Green Movement 607; history- and heritage-making 608; and hybrid archaeologies 603, 607–610; ill-fated Groundnut Scheme in Tanzania 607; intensive agricultural systems 608; Intermediate Technologies, adoption and dissemination of 607; 'internationalization of local values' 610; management of Great Zimbabwe 609; Traditional Ecological Knowledge (TEK) 607; unequal knowledge and power structures 609; Western construct 609; Western knowledge 608–609

Indigenous languages: performative practices 10

Indigenous legends: anthropological portrayals of 21

Indigenous material culture 13; stone tools and durable artefacts 13

Indigenous narratives: Aboriginal or Indigenous people 468–469; biographers 477; *Bringing Them Home* report 469; Caloola Psychiatric Asylum *471*; connection to Country 468; 'cultural knowledge' 475; family history as history 474–477; 'heterosexual unions and intermarriage' 474; intergenerational trauma 472–473; internal-family and external racism 472; *A Little Bird Told Me* 469–470, *470, 472, 473, 475, 476*; Mental Hygiene Act 1933 470; oppressive authenticity 468; oral traditions 468; Polynesian royalty 478n19; 'racist mechanism of division' 467; reception 472–473; removals and separations 468–471; Saxon church 474–475; *Talkin' Up to the White Woman* 475–476; *Trust and Technology Project* 473; women as secret keepers and story tellers 473–474; writings and narratives 469

Indigenous Nations 2, 15; cultural transformation and renewal 2

Indigenous people: academic scholarship 10; adoption by United Nations (UN) 6; arrival of outsider populations 3; in Asia (*see* Asia); biblical images of 117; cohesion and autonomy 3; cultures and economies 2–3; definition 5, 7, 23n2; European 'discoverer' 12; European populations and forces 3, 4; global history 1; global travellers 5; group descriptors 5–6; historical experiences 2; historical imaginations 22; Indigenous Tribe or Nation 6; individual rights 6–7; New World histories 11; nineteenth-century Europe 11; pancontinental descriptors 6; pattern of triumphalism and denialism 12; performative practices 10; political complexity and diversity 7; removal of 12; scholarly trends 12–13; scholarship 9; self-identification 2; societies 11; sustainable future 1; violent patterns 3; Western-style gender roles 3–4

Indigenous People's Rights Act 102

Indigenous rights 6, 12, 96, 101–102, 113, 120, 264–265, 267–268, 270, 274, 450, 516

Indigenous rituals 22, 552

Indonesia: Indigenous peoples in 102

Indus and Ganges in northern India 88

Indus Valley civilisation 87

Information Exchange Theory (IET) 196, 199

Ingqumbo yeminyanya (Jordan) 661

inscriptions: of monumental kind 36; technique of writing in stone 36

International Commission of Radiation Protection (ICRP) 420–421

International Labour Organisation (ILO) 7, 101; Indigenous and Tribal Peoples Convention 7

Index

International Work Group for Indigenous Affairs (IWGIA) 101–102
Inuit of Alaska 9
Invalid and Old-age Pension Act 1908 (Commonwealth) 401
The Invention of Culture (Wagner) 149
Ityala Lamawele (Mqhayi) 661
ive, traumatic removal 488–490; Burns Philp and Co 490; *iki haveve* movement 490; Larihairu and Kaivakovu 'tribes' 489, 491; LMS missionaries 488–489; Orokolo Bay 489–490

Jackson, Andrew (President) 381, 383
Jackson, S. N. 516
Jahoda, G. 631
Japan: Indigenous Emishi people in 89; Japanese archipelago 87; Tokugawa military authorities 91
Jefferson, Thomas (President) 381, 382
Joachim of Fiore 38
Johnson, E. P. 245, 251
Johnson, W. 68
Johnston, A. 308
Johnston, B. H. 185
Jones, J. 469
Jordan, M. D. 369
Justice Interruptus (Fraser) 456

Kaartinen, T. 673, 674
Kames, Henry Home, Lord. 281, 282
Karnell, V. 293
Karuka, M. 67
Kaschula, R. H. 658, 659
Kauanui, J. K. 67, 69, 372
Keane, A.H. 280, 288, 290, 291, 292, 293
Kelley, R. 260
Kelly, S. K. 581
Kimberley rock art, Australia: Aboriginal settlement and aggregation behaviours 202; AustArch database 208; chronological analysis 208–209; 'continuous occupation' 195; cupule and rock marking style phase 204, *204*; data sets 196–197; dating techniques 202–203; 'dissociative archaeology' 208; 'Dynamic Figures' of Arnhem Land 205, 210; 'Elegant Action Figures' style phases 205–206, 210; First Australians' material cultures 199; Group Boundary Formation (GBF) Theory 197–199, 210; Gwion Gwion figures 205–206, *206*; Hooked Stick' Figures of Arnhem Land 207; human behaviour, changing landscapes, and climate 196; human occupation and activity 195, **196**; iconographic or 'stylistic' analysis 196; Information Exchange Theory (IET) 196, 199, 210; irregular infill animal style phase 204, *205*; landscape, people, and rock art over the last 50,000 years 195–197; macro-style phases 199, *200, 201*; major art traditions 201, *201*; map of 195, *195*; in mid–late Holocene 208; Painted Hand style phases 207; pigment style phase (IIA) 201–202; possible age ranges for 201–203; proliferation events 203; proposed age ranges 203–207; static polychrome style phase 206–207, *207*, 210; style phases 199–201; theoretical approach 197–199; Wandjina style phases 202, 207, *208*, 210

kingdom of Anuradhapura in Ceylon 92
King George III 226, 512
King George IV. 230, 231, 233
King George VI 315
King Kamehameha III 230
Kinoshita, A. 181
Kirshenblatt-Gimblett, B. 288
Klaatsch, H. 115, 116, 119, 122
Kleivan, I. 695
Konbaung dynasty 91, 92
Konishi, S. 66, 67
Korean peninsula 87
Korneliussen, N. 708, 710, 711
Kovach, M. 183
Kuhn, A. 483
Kuwae, eruption of: case of Tongoan oral history 582; confusion of multiple events 583; generational depths 582; location of 578, *579*; mid-fifteenth century 580–581; moral source of 580; recolonisation of Tongoa 581; Shepherd Islands communities 581–582; volcanic destruction 578

LaCapra, D. 352
Lacey, R. 588
Land Acquisition Act, 1894 451
Land Rights 101, 265, 430, 435, 513, 516, 578
land, settlers and: Aboriginal historical experiences of violence 59; antagonism and violence and 61; Australian collectivism 59; availability of 'free land' 59; 'borderlands' concept 61–62; components of American nationhood and exceptionalism 58; 'composite nationality' 59; emergence of morality discourse 61; emergence of 'nomad

tribe' of men 59; history of fur trade 60; 'history war' 62; 'kinetic empire' 62; nomad tribe 60; notion of 'Indian side to the story' 60
Last Glacial Maximum (LGM) 194, 195, 196, **196**
Law on the Territories of Traditional Nature Use, 2001 102
League of Nations 113, 119–120
Lectures on the Philosophy of World History (1822–1828) (Hegel) 282
legal rights: *pattas*, or ownership certificates 443
Legends of the Earth: Their Geologic Origins (Vitaliano) 572
Lepore, J. 347
Levin, D. M. 683
Levi-Strauss, C. 49
Lewis, A. B. 484, 485, 486, 491
Limerick, P. N. 60, 64, 355
Lincoln, Abraham (President) 350
Lindholm, V. 294
Livingstone, D. 286
Livy 35
Locke, J. 371, 446
London, Indigenous engagement: Bedford Street 244; Canada House 246; Charing Cross 246; colonial history 241–242; Covent Garden via King Street 243–244; Craven Street 247; exhibition, British material about 288; 'Four Kings' 242–243, 245, 250–251; Great George Street 248; identity of foreigners 250; London exhibition of 1885 at Alexandra Palace 287; National Gallery, Trafalgar Square 245; Northumberland Avenue 247; observers, documentation 244–245; Oxford Street 251; S7aplek 248–249; spaces of Indigenous history and colonial encounter 250; St James's Park 247–248; St Martin's Lane 245; Trafalgar Square 245; troupe of 1885 287–289; urban violence 243; Villiers Street 246–247; Westminster Hall 249–250
Lorde, A. 260
Lowery, M. M. 384
Lubbock, J. 281, 286, 292
Luders, D. 582
Lugard, F. 445
Lule River: Great Lule or North River, Stuor Julevadno 529; hydropower regulation of 540; Little Lule or South River, Unna Julevadno 529
Lundius, N. 537

Lydon, J. 642
Lyell, C. 286

MacDonald, John A. (Prime Minister) 553
MacDonell, S.G. 484, 488
MacDougall, W. 426, 427, 428, 429, 430, 433
MacKenzie, J. M. 122, 250
MacRitchie, D. 291
Maddison, S. 468
Maddock, H. 326, 327, 331, 332, 333, 334, 335, 336, 337
Makalela, L. 655, 656, 659, 661
Malaya/Malaysia: Malayan Emergency (1948–60) 99; 'Malay' population 99
Maltz, W. 352
Mandela, N. 661
Maralinga, Central Australia: British atomic testing 16
Marsden, S. 312
Marxist: 'historical materialism' 46
Masai, Kenya 7–8
Masco, J. 419, 420
Mason, R. J. 571, 573
Masse, M. J. 576
masyarakat adat 102
Matsuda, M. 311
Mawani, R. 116
McBride, Sir Peter 118
McDougall, J. 552
McGinness, J. 402
McGrath, A. 61, 637, 638
McIntosh, R. J. 604
McIntosh, S. K. 604
McKinnon, C. 69
McNiven, I. J. 208
Meares, J. 228
Medak-Saltzman, D. 288
memory, identities, and narratives 20
Métis 5, 251, 260, 562n1, 562n2
Mihesuah, D. A. 346
Milky Way 21
Million, D. 350
Ming dynasty 91
Mirazon Lahr, M. 197
modernity: historical 'march of progress' 14
modern treaty-making, Canada: B.C. Treaty Commission 263, 264; *Constitution Act, 1982* 263–264; First Nations engagement 264; history of 263; role of Indigenous protocols and ceremony 264; Sami peoples 264–265; *sui generis* 265; use of language of extinguishment of Indigenous rights

264–265; 'whole of government approach' 264
Moeti oa Bochabela (Mofolo) 661
Mokupuni o Hawai'i 227–230; British trading vessel *Imperial Eagle* 228; British trading vessel *Nootka* 228–229; Kahiki 227; *kapu* system 229; reign of Kamehameha III, 230; relationship with Britain 229–230; voyagers of second-diaspora era 227–229
Molbech, C. 281
Moloney, J.J. 727
Mongol forces 92
Montagnards 96
Montelius, O. 280
Moodie, D. W. 573
Moor, F.R. 315
Morch, P. 707, 708, 711
Moreton-Robinson, A. 267, 475, 476
Māori, New Zealand 5; people of Aotearoa 21; personal identity 6
Mortensen, D. 294
'mountain tribes' 102
Mountford, C. 724
Movius, H. L. 142
multimodality: 'cannibalistic horrors' of colonialism 660; colonial and missionary orthographies 657; fallist movements 659–660; *Opening Stellenbosch* and *Decolon I sing Wits* 660; oral literature 658; oral narrative 659; public oral practices 658; *taba ya legolo la Gwasa* (the 'Story of the Cave of Gwasa') 658; ubuntu trans-languaging 660–661; Xhosa tradition of *ukubonga* 658
Mulvaney, D. J. 724, 750
Munda, R. D. 447
Murdoch, W. 13
Musket Wars 233
My Place (Morgan) 469

Nabokov, P. 17
Nakata, M. 304
Namatjira, A. 401
Nansen, F. 288
National Aboriginal and Islander Day of Celebration (NAIDOC) 412
National Aboriginal and Islanders Day Observance Committee (NAIDOC) celebrations 8
National Day of Aboriginal and Islander Celebration, 2018 404
Nationalism (Tagore) 115

native agents: assimilation and enact community 69; 'attenuated agency' 68; Barkindji social structure 69; 'categories of nineteenth-century liberalism' 68; economic and political organization 66; Hawaiian sovereignty movements 69–70; Indigenous elimination 67; kind of soliloquy 68; land dispossession 67; listening and reading 68; Mohawk Nationals 69; natural freedom of white men 68; self-determining individualism 69; spatiality and temporality 67; structuralism of settler colonialism 66–68, 70; 'the universality of a liberal notion of selfhood' 68
Native American Indian Nations 275n32, 275n33
Native Americans 6
Native Title Act 150
naturalistic materialism 149
Ndoro, W. 605
'Negritos' 96
Negros Island, Indigenous man of 96, 97
Nehru, Jawaharlal (Prime Minister) 97, 99, 446, 447
Nepal 102
Nesuton, J. 308
Newman, B. N. 512
New Testament Book of Revelations 38
'New Worlds' 187, 370
New Zealand: Māori rights 266; Treaty of Waitangi, 1840 266
Niedenthal, J. 422, 424, 435
Nielsen, F. A. J. 692
Nilsson, J. E. 294
Nilsson, S. 280, 281, 282, 283, 284, 285, 286, 287, 292, 294
Njoya, A. N. 636
No Place to Hide (Bradley) 423
North America: Dakota pipeline development 16; Iroquois and Mohawks 165; members of Indigenous Nations 8
North American Indian treaty history: ability of 'rights talk' 260; archetypal American literature 259–260; case for re-examination of 259–264; Chi-Naaknigewin Constitution of the Anishinabek Nation 261; contemporary activists and thinkers 260; cross-cultural relationships 261; historical scholarship 262; Indigenous-authored futures 260; international law and state sovereignty 261–262; 1855 Lame Bull Treaty 262; 'measured separatism' 262; 'overlapping

Index

consensus' 261; re-examination of treaties 262; Treaty Alliance Against Tar Sands Expansion 263; 1868 Treaty of Fort Laramie 262; tribe-specific studies 261; U.S.-Indian treaties 261
Northern Territory Times 116
Nourishing Terrains (Rose) 122
ntoror, Africa: archaeological projects 612; communities engagement 613–614; concept of 'moot' 612; excavation 610, *610*, 612; 'landscape assemblages' 612; survivors of *"mutai"* disaster 611; Western disciplinary practices 611
nuclear weapons, impacts of 420
Nunn, P. D. 17, 572, 574

Oak Valley website *753*
O'Brien, C. 284
O'Brien, J. M. 15
Occom, S. 244, 245
Oceania 18
O'Malley, V. 233
O'Neill, M. E. 675
Onioheriago 242
Opening Stellenbosch: From Assimilation to Occupation (Kaganof) 652, 655
Opland, J. 661
optically stimulated luminescence (OSL) **196**, 202
oral traditions 183–184; Anishinabek 183; of ashfall from long island 583–588; of cataclysms 573–574; challenges of transmission 573–574; chemical characterisation 583; chronology and temporal depth 571; Cree language 184; diversity of traditions 585; of eruptions from Tonga, Samoa, and Fiji 577–578; eruption traditions 575–576; events in the deep past 588; failure to interpret original content 573; fallibility of individual human memory 573; first-hand observations 183; historical information 183; historic environmental events 184; Holocene activity 577; in Huli oral traditions 586–587; Huli ritual elaboration 589; and intergenerational memories 184; interpretation of volcanoes 576; knowledge of *mbingi* 586–588; language groups 586; memories of event 587; Māori cosmology 577; and myths 184; narrators of 587–588; Newer Volcanics Province 577; pristine 574; in reconstruction of cataclysmic events 572; settlement 'genealogies' or sequence histories 585–586; during 1830s–1840s 578; 'texts' of 576; 'Tibito Tephra' 583; 'time of darkness' 584, *584*, 585; of Tolai people 578; verbal first-hand memories 183; of volcanic activity in Pacific 577; volcanic eruptions in 571, 575–578; volcanology and 578

Orang Rimba ('jungle people') 90
Orientals 42
OSL *209*
The Other Side of the Frontier (Reynolds) 59
Out-of-Africa I 139
Out-of-Africa II: archaeological evidence in East Asia and Australasia 146–148; fossil and genetic evidence in East Asia and Australasia 144–146
Owre, Z. 287
Owuor-Anyumba, H. 654, 660
Pakistan 101; 1957 Convention 101
palaeoanthropology 139
Palaeoclimate and Palaeoenvironment 194
Palaeolithic archaeology 139
Pallasmaa, J. 671, 683
Palmer, E. L. 18, 379, 380, 383
Panchayat (Extension to Scheduled Areas) Act 1996 or *PESA* 448, 452–453, 456
Panthay Rebellion (1856–1873) 94
Papua New Guinea 5, 17, 18, 20, 481–496, 578, 583, 584, 588, 595n87, 595n90–91, 596n106–109, 596n111, 596n116, 597n117, 631, 632; European hunters 93
Parsa East Kete Basan (PEKB) 444
Partial Test Ban Treaty 431
partus sequitur ventrem 328
Pascoe, P. 61, 62
Patel, Vallabhbhai (Prime Minister) 446
pathways towards future Indigenous histories 20–21
Pearson, L. 468
Pember, M. A. 356
Penn, W. 242
Permanent Settlement (Locke) 446
Petersen, H.C. 691
Peterson, D. R. 308
Petrie, T. 731
petroglyphs *see* rock art
Philosophical Investigations (Wittgenstein) 270
photography, Indigenous: aesthetic consumerism 636; animalist primitivism 635; assimilation and dissimilation 635; author's grandmother, early 1940s 639, 641, *641*; biographical study of Ijo photographer Green 637; Black

futurity 642; censorship of Nazism 636; concepts of decolonising performance 639; contexts of production 636; decontextualisation 642; dissimilationist phase 635; as documents of agency 635–639; German colonialism 631–635; German Indigeneity 630; of Herero woman 639–641, *640*, 644; history of photography 638; individual complexity 646; 'listening' to photography 641; mechanisms of reception 637; *Menschenschönheit* (human beauty) 629; Nazi idealisation of Blackness 630–631, 644, 646; person from Papua New Guinea 632, *633*; racism 643, **643**; separation by gender 629; towards an Indigenous methodology of German history 639–646; *Venus Oceanica* 637–638; woman from Keta Lagoon 629, *630*, 631, 644–645; woman from Tasmania 632, *634*

physics or natural philosophy 43

pictographs *see* rock art

Piggott, E. 325, 326, 332

Pioneer Epic (Milner) 354

Pitjantjatjara 420; adoption of moving rationing system 430; British Nuclear Testing 426; British thermonuclear testing 426; ceremonial cycles 425; effects on Aboriginal people 429; missionary activities 425–426; Monte Bello explosions 426; Ooldea Mission 429–430; 'prohibited zone' 430; Report A32 428; southern Pitjantjatjara 428–430; Totem bombs 426–427; viral epidemics 425; Wallatina 425–428; Weapons Research Establishment (WRE) 429; weapon systems 426; Western Desert people 425; WW2 bombs 429; Yanykuntjatjara people 427

Pitjantjatjara people 16

Pleistocene 170, *171*, **172–179**, 194

Polly Indian (case study): in 1822 326; aftermath of great hurricane of 1780 325; between 1786 and 1789 325–326; Atlantic slave system 327, *328*; Britain's Caribbean colonies 326; commissioners' verdict 337–338; determining 'Indian' identity 335–337; enslaved Indians in Honduras 327; enslavement and freedom in Tobago 333–335, *334*; epilogue 338–339; Indian slavery and partus sequitur ventrem 327–329; Indian slavery in Barbados 329–331; native maternal ancestry 331–333; unlawful enslavement of Indians 327, 332

Pope Alexander VI 371

Pope Urban II 371

prehistoric colonialism: artefacts in British Museum 284, *284*; cranial measurements of skulls 283–284; degraded race 283; depiction of Sami as dwarf race 286; development theory of human history 286; economic stages 281; eighteenth-century stadial writing 282; emergence of 'developed' European societies 282; human crania in Museum national d'histoire naturelle *285*; humanity 281–282; Irish Giant Charles O'Brien, skeleton of 284–285; as natural and engine of progress 282–283; *Skandinaviska Nordens Urinvånare* 281, 283; in *Skandinavisk Fauna* 281; Stone, Bronze, and Iron Ages 280–281, 286–287; three-age system and concept of prehistory 283

pre-modern empires, Asia: barbarian 88; *Comprehensive Institutions* 88; 'exemplary centres' 89; experience of peoples 87–88; location of Indigenous peoples 90, *91*; mechanism of imperial expansion 89; process of cultural transmission 89–90; slave trade 89; subsidies 89; technologies of warfare and communication 88–89

The Primitive Inhabitants of Scandinavia (Nilsson) 283–284

Printer, J. 308

progressivism 112, 121

Prophetism 36

protectionism 111

purchas, w. 249

Purdy, B. A. 170

Purga Mission 403, 404

Pyrrhonism 43

Qing dynasty 91, 97–98

Qin Shi Huang 90

'race' categories 5

Radiocarbon *209*

Rainders, E. 305

Raleigh, W. 246

Rampolokeng, L. 660

Rasmussen, K. 288

Red Stick War 382

Regnard, J.-F. 286

reimagining home: Cherokee kinship 388–389; Christian notions of 'wilderness' spaces 387; colonial narratives 386; Compact of Georgia 381–382; diaspora 381; frontier violence 391n12; *Ge-no'sqwa*, or the Stone Giant 384; Great Depression 379; Great Spirit 386; Hitchiti and Alabama peoples 386; Indian-Pioneer Papers (IPP) project 379; Indian Territory 382, 387; Indian tribes, map of 381, *382*; influence of Christianity in Native communities 388; kinship community 380; kinship networks 384; memories 380–381; Miami Mission 379; Native Americans 380–383; nineteenth-century Native people 389; oral traditions 384; origin narratives 385–386; personal narratives 379–380; 1906 Portrait of Potawatimis 388, *388*; 'The Powerful Boy' 385; settler colonialism 379, 381; storytelling traditions 383, 387; tribal leaders 383

religious learning 40

religious stock-farmers 118

removals: Australian Museum 485; cargo cults 488; ceremonial objects 486, *487*; coercive removal events 482; cultural materials 492; entanglement of collecting and colonial violence, Papuan Gulf 483–486; extraction of cultural materials 482; *Hevehe* cycles 486; historical locations and current geographical regions, Gulf of Papua 483, *484*; *iki haveve* 488; of Indigenous people 481; *ive,* traumatic removal 488–490; *karigara* of Orokolo Bay 486; Larihairu and Kaivakovu villagers 487–488; London Missionary Society (LMS) 484; Magic stones 487; memory props 482–483; 'memory texts' 483; memory work 482; oral tradition 482; Orokolo Bay *eravo*, material culture 491; Papua New Guinea's (PNG's) Gulf of Papua 482; posts and stories in Orokolo Bay 486–488; Roman Catholic missions 485–486; spiritual kin and museum 491–492; 'structures of forgetting' 483; Totemic reminders to spiritual 'telephone system' 486–488; traces of trauma, Papuan Gulf 483–486; trauma and telescoping 481–483; violence and removal of material culture 485

Renberg, E. L. 294

Retzius, A. 283

Reynolds, H. 58, 59, 60, 61, 727

Rhodes, Cecil John (Prime Minister) 651

#RhodesMustFall movement 651, 653

Richard, F. G. 605

Richards, E. 474

Richter, D. K. 62

Rifkin, M. 372

Rink, H. 696

Rio Tinto 16

Robertson, W. 281, 282

Robinson, K. 401

Roche, G. 290

rock art 194; Coast Salish rock art 180; Lake Winnemucca petroglyphs, Nevada *181,* 181–182; Nine Mile Canyon, Utah 182, *182*; North or South America 182–183; Pedra Furada rock art, Brazil *180,* 180–181; Writing-on-Stone Provincial Park, or Aisinai'pi 181

Rose, D. B. 64, 122

Ross, J. 17, 202, 203, 383

Roth, W. 116, 119, 122, 637

Rowley, C.D. 59, 723

Rowley-Conwy, P. 281

Rowse, T. 66

Russell, H.S. 731

Russell, L., 59, 68, 112, 475

Russian Association of Indigenous Peoples of the North 102

Russian Federation 102

Ryd, L. 531, 535

Ryd, Y. 531

Sábme, original territory of Fennoscandia 527–529; exotic and strange people 528; family stories 528; Finnish language 528; Lule Sami and North Sami 528; territories of Sami 527

Sagayenkwaraton 242

Sahul 5

Sallust 35

Salmond, A. 224

Sámi indigeneity: 'Aborigines of Europe' 287–291; archaeological model of development 293; collection of photographs 290–291; colonial histories 280; colonising Indigenous people 292–294; concepts of time 292–294; European and non-European Aborigines 291–292; Europe's Aboriginal race 279; exhibitions of 287–290; Forest Sami 526–527, 529; human exhibitions 280; identity 531; Lule Sami and North Sami 528; modern treaty-making,

Canada 264–265; and narratives 294; performances of foreign peoples 279–280; prehistoric colonialism 280–287; rhetoric of primitivism and extinction 293; Sami ('Lapp') villages 532; Scandinavia 5; territories of 527; wilderness tourism 293
Sami Parliament 6, 266
Sampson, J. 305
Sanneh, L. 308, 310
Sapir, E. 552
Saranillio, D. 63, 472, 473
Sarasin, P. 111–122
Sarkozy, Nicolas (President) 605
Savage, J. 231
Schaffer, K. 469
Schalkwyk, D. 662
Scheduled Tribe *see* Adivasi dispossession, Indian state
Scheduled Tribes and Other Traditional Forest Dwellers (Recognition of Forest Rights) Act, 2006 (FRA) 448
scholarship: academic 10; Christian 40; Hebraist 39; historical 15, 262, 743; on imperial contexts of conservation 111; on settler colonialism 57–58; textual 37
Scott, D. C. 553, 556
Scottish enlightenment 46
Scott, J. C. 90
Scott, W. 45
scripture 36
Second Indo-China War 99
Second World War 48, 86, 404
secularism, Indigenous resistance: assimilation, government policies of 559–560, 562; British colonial era 551; Canadian citizenship 554; Christianisation 550, 556, 558, 559, 562; Christian rituals 561; Constitutional Act of 1867 551; cultural and spiritual resistance 560; government and religious orders, partnership between 556; guardianship system 561; Indian Affairs 553–555, 560–561; Indian Affairs' administrative correspondence 552; individuals and communities 562n1; legal limits 556–559; Mi'kmaq girls 554, *554*; non-interference and tolerance 552; operative legal framework 560; partnership with religious orders 553–556; personal conflicts or disputes 556; political power and Indigenous peoples 552–553; Potlatch 557, *558*; Prairie Provinces 557; prohibition of rituals 559; proscription of mutilations 557; religious ceremonies and practices 558–559; religious congregations 555; religious orders, internal affairs of 555; sun dance tent 557, *557*; use of biomedicine 561
Seddon, D. 653, 661, 662
Self-Government Act (SGA) 707
Sellards, E.H. 170
settler colonialism 6; increasing urban population 56; Indigenous juridical experience 57; newly settled population 56; (non-Indigenous) people and land, relationship between 56–57; scholarship on settler colonialism 57–58; settler-coloniser nations 13; space of 'frontier' 57; violence and conquest 58
sex and doctrine of discovery: Christian faith 371–372; colonial chronicles 371; heteronormativity 372; notion of *terra nullius* 371; ongoing violence 373; process of 'heterohomemaking' 372; sexual colonisation 372
sexual removals: Amazon Indigenous languages 368–369; Christian doctrine of discovery 373; *chuqui chinchay* 367; 'civilised' and 'savage' bodies 370; codification of sodomy 370; colonial violence 365–366; epistemological translation 366; gender and sexuality 367; gender roles 368; Hawai'ians and Zapotecs 365; *ikouetas* 367; Indigenous experiences 366; Indigenous genders and sexualities 365; logic of sexual colonisation 366; multiplicity of peoples 366–367; queer practices 369; regulating sex: crimes against nature 369–370; same-sex practices 368; sex and doctrine of discovery 371–373; sexual and gender diversity 367–369; social fabrics 369; understandings of gender 368
Shakespeare, W. 653, 662
Shirakawa, C. 582
Shoemaker, N. 65
Shohat, E. 114
Shryock, A. 11, 739
'Siberian wolves' 116
Siddhartha Gautama 87
Silitoe, P. 605
Simmons, J. 388
Simpson, L. B. 372
Singh Deo, T.S. 456
Singh, J. 446
Sissons, J. 468

Skällarim: assimilation 536, 539; Christian mission 536–537; Lap Tax Land 532–533; prehistories 531–532; Sámi language 536–538; Sami ('Lapp') villages 532; settlement 533; Swedification 536, 540
Skelly, R. 486
slavery: Atlantic slave system 327, *328*; and colonialism 502–503; European 41; horrors of 14; Indian (*see* Indian slavery); 'Negroes and other slaves' 330–331; post-traumatic slave syndrome (PTSS) 354; slave trade, Asia 89
Sleeper-Smith, S. 15
Slotkin, R. 347
Smail, D. L. 11, 739
Smith, A. 281
Smith, H. N. 347
Smith, L.T. 242, 251, 613
social engineering 47, 294
Society for the Preservation of Fauna in the Empire 115
Soeharto (President) 670
South Africa: books in 652; Khoi and San peoples 96
SouthEast Asia: academic practice 671; community of humans 669, *670*; East Alor historyscape 675–676; future for haptic history 682–684; haptic history handling contradictions and inconsistencies 675; haptic history in multidisciplinary context 673–674; haptic practices 676–679; historyscapes 676–679; Kaipera and Pureman 678–679, *679*; landscape evoking haptic senses 672–673; *Mudileng-ilingleng* 676; narratology 676–679; nationwide administrative system 670; ritualised haptic history and animistic ontologies 680–682; uses of history, ontology, and time metaphors 679–680; written narratives 671; Yosafat Modena 677, *677*
South Eastern Coalfields Limited (SECL) 451–452
Soviet nationality policy, complexities of 106n49
Spence, T. 309
Spivak, G. C. 57
'spontaneous transmigrants' 101
Stanner, W.E.H. 59, 724
Stapp, D. 184
Steeves, P.F. 165
Stenberg, K. 294
Stevens, M. J. 313

Stoler, A. L. 353, 354
'Stone Age' men *see* the Veddas
storytelling 18; Stories of the Seven Sisters 22–23; tradition of *subttsasa biehtsevuomátjistema* 19; women as story tellers 473–474
Strange Multiplicity (Tully) 270
Strehlow, C. 309
Strehlow, T.G.H. 723
Stremlau, R. 388, 389
Stuart-Glennie, J. S. 291
Stump, D. 607
Subttsasa Biehtsevuomátjistema: 1968 academic thesis 530; '*avvittringen*' 539; consequences of hydropower exploitation 524; ethnological descriptions 531; Forest Sami 526–527; Forest Sámi family becoming Swedish 538–539; garden and barn as archives 534; genocide and epistemicide 525; historical methodologies and egohistoire 527; house and settlement 533; inherited land 538–539; from Jokkmokk to Uppsala 530; 'Lap should be Lap' policies 531; Lule River hydropower exploitation 534; Lule River, Julevädno and Forest Sámi 529; Norrbotten County Local Heritage Association 530; 'Per Albin' house 533–534; racial categorisation 535; Sábme, original territory of Fennoscandia 527–529; Sami identity 531; Sami perspectives 525–526; Sami–Swedish relationship 530; scientific exploration 530; shoe band mystery 534–535; Skällarim prehistories (*see* Skällarim); Swedish *nybyggare* 535; two-river country 529–531
Suetonius 35
Swift, J. 243

Tacitus 35, 527
Tagore, R. 115
Taiping Rebellion of 1850–1864 94
Taiwan: Dutch trading settlement 93; Japanese colony of 95
TallBear, K. 366
Tangut Empire (Xi Xia) 92
Taylor, E. B. 286
Tejonihokarawa, H. 242, 243, 244
teleology 43
textual scholarship 37
Thailand: 'mountain tribes' 102
theoretical frontiers: to aborigines, settlers and land 58–62; Australian frontier

violence 63; 'imperialist nostalgia' 63; 'logic of elimination' 63, 74n39; marginalisation and segmentation 63; native agents 66–70; 'primary paradigm' of settler colonisation 63–64; return of 63–66; settler and native, relation between 64; as settler colonial condition 56–58
thermoluminescence (TL) dates 209
This Is Not a Peace Pipe (Turner) 260
Thisted, K. 698, 710, 711
Thomsen, C. J. 280
Thornhill, D. 325, 326, 332
Thucydides 35
Tischner, H. 584
Tobago: enslavement and freedom in 333–335
Todd, C. 553
Tomasson, T. 294
Tout, D. 122
Traditional Communities Alliance of the Archipelago 102
transmission: chronology and commensurability 572; chronology, and context 588–590; content of oral traditions 588; eruption of Kuwae 578–583; geomythology and historical scepticism 572–575; individual and communal or collective memory 590; oral traditions of the ashfall from long island 583–588; 'transmission's end' 589; volcanic eruptions in oral tradition 575–578
Trask, Haunani-Kay. 57, 63
'traumatic neurosis' 349
treatied space: *Aboriginal Title* 267; American Indian peoples 268–269; 2010 Census 267; disharmony 267–268; evidence of intercultural relationship 271–272; historic treaties 268; illusion of Indigenous inclusion 266; importance of inter-generational or 'longue durée' thinking 269–271; limitations of 'rights talk' 266–268; modern treaty-making 264–266; Penn's Treaty with the Indians, 1775 271–272, *272*; re-examination of North American Indian treaty history 259–264; settler-colonial nations 267
Treaty of Nerchinsk 92
tribes 86; definition 446
Tromholt, S. 292
Trouillot, M. -R. 352
Truett, S. 62

truth-telling 14, 349, 752
Tōtaiete mā 223–227; *Águila* 225–226; Bora Boran 'Oro worshippers 223; *Endeavour* voyage 224; European voyagers 226–227; 'incorrigible blockheads' 224; local fighting among Tahitians 225; motivations for voyaging 224–225; Pomare dynasty 227; Raiatean 'Oro-worshipping elite 223; Tahitians 'Oro worshippers 223, 225
Tully, J. 270, 271
Tumu, A. 588
Turi, J. 527
Turner, D. 260
Turner, F. J. 12, 56, 57, 58, 59, 60, 61, 62
Tylor, E. B. 291

Ullenius, J.G. 530, 532, 533, 536, 538, 539
Unaipon, D. 17
UN Declaration on the Rights of Indigenous Peoples 122, 267
Under the Rays of the Aurora Borealis (Tromholt) 292
'undiscovered lands' 13
UNDRIP 6–7, 15, 267
United Kingdom (UK): Irish and Welsh of 8
United Nations (UN): Indigenous people, adoption by 6; International Labour Organisation (ILO) 7
United Nations Declaration on the Rights of Indigenous Peoples, 2007 102, 266
United States (US): tribal status 8; U.S. colony of the Philippines 95
Universal Declaration on Human Rights 267
Unlawful Activities Prevention Act 452
UNomalanga kaNdengezi (Dhlomo) 661
uranium-series 202
U.S.-Dakota War (or 'Great Sioux Uprising') 350, 353

Valla, V. 39
Van Buren, Martin (President) 381
van Kirk, S. 60
Van Toorn, P. 315, 468
the Veddas 115
Vicedom, G. F. 584
victimisation 22
Vietnam: Nguyen lords 91; Vietnam War 349
violence: Indigenous people 3; internecine violence 14; rape and sexual assault 4

Visvanathan, S. 446
Vitaliano, D. B. 572

Wallis, S. 221
wa Thiong'o, N. 654, 656, 659, 660, 661
Wawn, A. 291
Waziyatawin 350, 351, 352, 353, 357
Weisgall, J. 422
Western Hemisphere: archaeological record of 166, 188; Eurocentric conjecture 167; human and mammalian evolution 167; Indigenous oral traditions 168; knowledge production of Indigenous histories 166; language families 166; violence of erasure of Indigenous 168
Western ontology or cosmology 149
White, R. 60
Wickes, J. 401
Wiessner, P. 588
Wildenthal, L. 632
wildlife hunting 115
Williams, F. E. 481, 484, 485, 486, 488, 489, 490

Wilson, D. 281
Wolfe, P. 57, 63, 64, 66, 67, 68
Woods, J. D. 722
Woollacott, A. 59
world conservation 111–122
Worsaae, J. J. A. 280
Wren, C. 245
writing cultures: literacy and civilisation 315; missionary education 315–316; 'Māori modernity' 314; 'syncretic literacy practices' 313; in te reo Māori 314
The Writing of History (de Certeau) 669
Wroth, L. C. 259, 272
WWII: outbreak of 141

Young, R. 289
Young, W. 333
Yuraki, Australian aboriginal perspective: dingo 724–727; dolphin 728–731; dreaming of past 722–724

Zantop, S. 632
Zell, H. 657

9781138743106